STREET ATLAS
Surrey

Dorking, Epsom, Guildford, Leatherhead, Reigate, Woking

First published in 1996 by

Philip's, a division of
Octopus Publishing Group Ltd
2-4 Heron Quays, London E14 4JP

Fourth colour edition 2007
First impression 2007
SURDA

ISBN-10   0-540-09051-4 (hardback)
ISBN-13   978-0-540-09051-8 (hardback)

ISBN-10   0-540-09049-2 (spiral)
ISBN-13   978-0-540-09049-5 (spiral)

© Philip's 2007

Ordnance Survey®

Data for the speed cameras provided by PocketGPSWorld.com Ltd.

Ordnance Survey and the OS Symbol are registered trademarks of Ordnance Survey, the national mapping agency of Great Britain.

Printed by Toppan, China

Contents

II **List of mobile speed cameras**

III **Key to map symbols**

IV **Key to map pages**

VI **Route planning**

VIII **Administrative and Postcode boundaries**

1 **Street maps** at 3½ inches to 1 mile

219 **Street maps of centres of Dorking, Epsom, Guildford, Kingston upon Thames, Leatherhead, and Woking** at 7 inches to 1 mile

222 **Index** of towns, villages, streets, hospitals, industrial estates, railway stations, schools, shopping centres, universities and places of interest

Digital Data

The exceptionally high-quality mapping found in this atlas is available as digital data in TIFF format, which is easily convertible to other bitmapped (raster) image formats.

The index is also available in digital form as a standard database table. It contains all the details found in the printed index together with the National Grid reference for the map square in which each entry is named.

For further information and to discuss your requirements, please contact james.mann@philips-maps.co.uk

Mobile speed cameras

The vast majority of speed cameras used on Britain's roads are operated by safety camera partnerships. These comprise local authorities, the police, Her Majesty's Court Service (HMCS) and the Highways Agency.

This table lists the sites where each safety camera partnership may enforce speed limits through the use of mobile cameras or detectors. 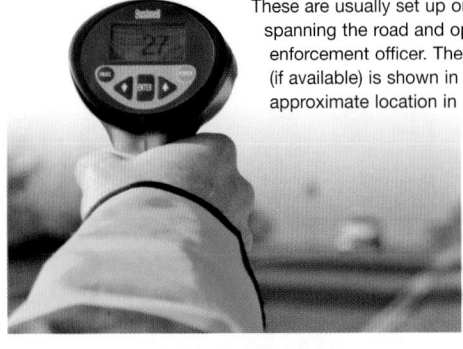 These are usually set up on the roadside or a bridge spanning the road and operated by a police or civilian enforcement officer. The speed limit at each site (if available) is shown in red type, followed by the approximate location in black type.

A3
50/70 Grayshott to Cobham

A23
40 Salfords, Brighton Rd

A24
50 Mickleham

A25
30/60/70 Westcott to West Clandon

A30
40 Staines

A31
60 Hogs Back (Central and Eastern sections)

A217
40 Lower Kingswood to Banstead

A242
30 Reigate to Merstham

A243
30 Hook

A246
30 Guildford

A248
30 Chilworth

A307
30 Esher

A308
50 Staines

A320
30/40 Guildford to Staines

A3016
30 Hale

A3100
40 Guildford to Godalming

B367
30 Ripley

B375
30 Chertsey

B380
30 Mayford

B385
30 Woodham

B386
30 Windlesham

B389
40 Virginia Water

B2030
30 Caterham to Old Coulsdon

B2031
30 Caterham to Chaldon

B2126
30 Holmbury St Mary

B2127
30 Ewhurst

B2130
30 Godalming

B3411
30 Ash Vale

Unclassified
30 Effingham, Effingham Common Rd

30 Epsom, Longdown Lane South

30 Frith Hill, Charterhouse Rd

30 Hurtmore, Hurtmore Rd

30 Leigh, Apners Rd

30 Lightwater, Macdonald Rd

30 Staines, Kingston Rd

	Motorway with junction number
	Primary route – dual/single carriageway
	A road – dual/single carriageway
	B road – dual/single carriageway
	Minor road – dual/single carriageway
	Other minor road – dual/single carriageway
	Road under construction
	Tunnel, covered road
	Speed cameras - single, multiple
	Rural track, private road or narrow road in urban area
	Gate or obstruction to traffic (restrictions may not apply at all times or to all vehicles)
	Path, bridleway, byway open to all traffic, road used as a public path
	Pedestrianised area
DY7	**Postcode boundaries**
	County and unitary authority boundaries
	Railway, tunnel, railway under construction
	Tramway, tramway under construction
	Miniature railway
Walsall	**Railway station**
	Private railway station
	London Underground station
	Tram stop, tram stop under construction
	Bus, coach station

	Ambulance station		
	Coastguard station		
	Fire station		
	Police station		
	Accident and Emergency entrance to hospital		
H	**Hospital**		
	Place of worship		
i	**Information Centre** (open all year)		
	Shopping Centre		
P P&R	**Parking, Park and Ride**		
PO	**Post Office**		
	Camping site, caravan site		
	Golf course, picnic site		
Prim Sch	**Important buildings, schools, colleges, universities and hospitals**		
	Built up area		
	Woods		
River Medway	**Water name**		
	River, weir, stream		
	Canal, lock, tunnel		
	Water		
	Tidal water		
Church	**Non-Roman antiquity**		
ROMAN FORT	**Roman antiquity**		
87	**Adjoining page indicators and overlap bands** The colour of the arrow and the band indicates the scale of the adjoining or overlapping page (see scales below)		
237			

Enlarged mapping only

	Railway or bus station building
	Place of interest
	Parkland

Acad	**Academy**	Inst	**Institute**	Recn Gd	**Recreation Ground**
Allot Gdns	**Allotments**	Ct	**Law Court**		
Cemy	**Cemetery**	L Ctr	**Leisure Centre**	Resr	**Reservoir**
C Ctr	**Civic Centre**	LC	**Level Crossing**	Ret Pk	**Retail Park**
CH	**Club House**	Liby	**Library**	Sch	**School**
Coll	**College**	Mkt	**Market**	Sh Ctr	**Shopping Centre**
Crem	**Crematorium**	Meml	**Memorial**	TH	**Town Hall/House**
Ent	**Enterprise**	Mon	**Monument**	Trad Est	**Trading Estate**
Ex H	**Exhibition Hall**	Mus	**Museum**	Univ	**University**
Ind Est	**Industrial Estate**	Obsy	**Observatory**	W Twr	**Water Tower**
IRB Sta	**Inshore Rescue Boat Station**	Pal	**Royal Palace**	Wks	**Works**
		PH	**Public House**	YH	**Youth Hostel**

■ The small numbers around the edges of the maps identify the 1 kilometre National Grid lines

■ The dark grey border on the inside edge of some pages indicates that the mapping does not continue onto the adjacent page

The scale of the maps on the pages numbered in blue is 5.52 cm to 1 km • 3½ inches to 1 mile • 1: 18103	0 ¼ ½ ¾ 1 mile
	0 250 m 500 m 750 m 1 kilometre

The scale of the maps on pages numbered in red is 11.04 cm to 1 km • 7 inches to 1 mile • 1: 9051	0 220 yards 440 yards 660 yards ½ mile
	0 125 m 250 m 375 m ½ kilometre

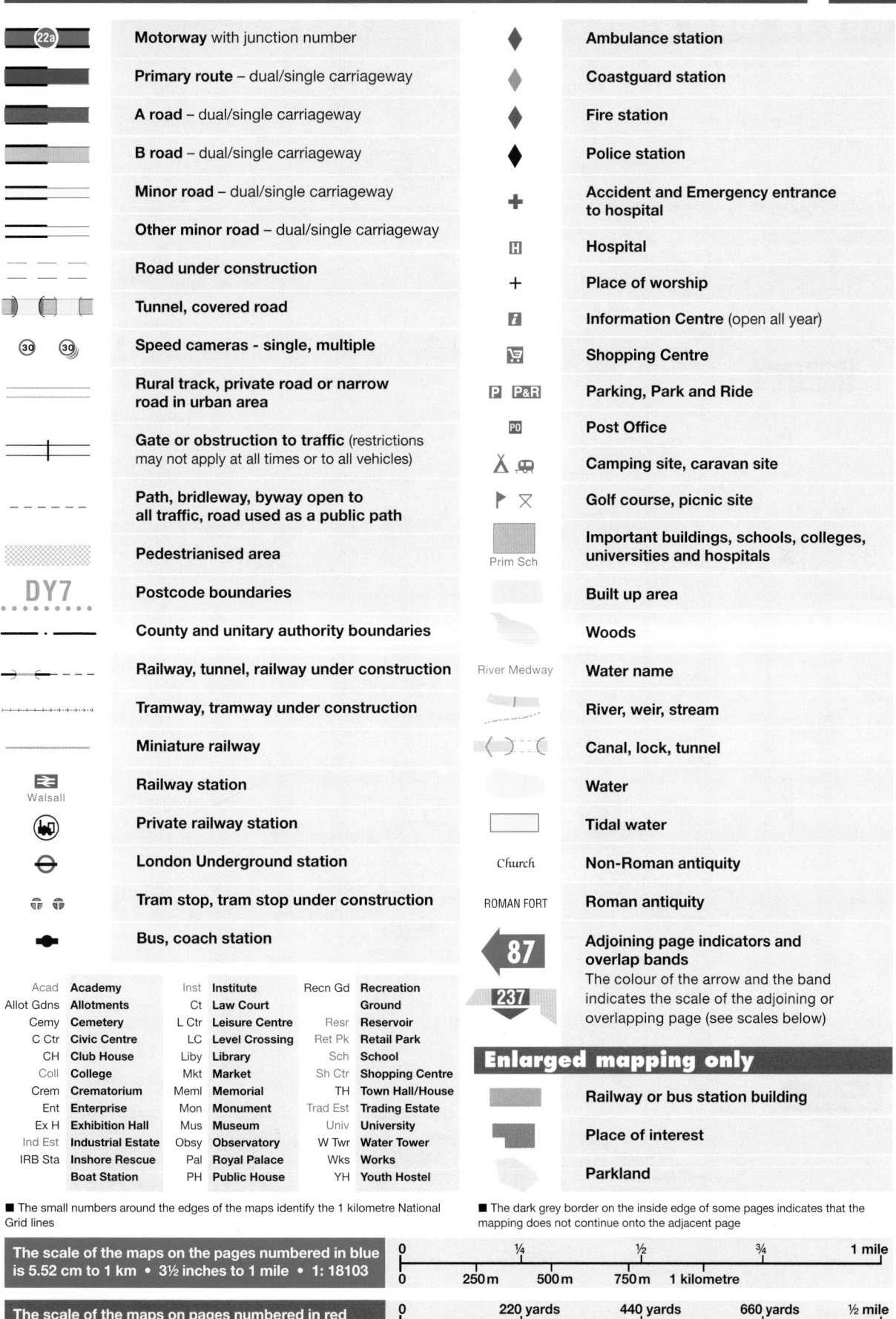

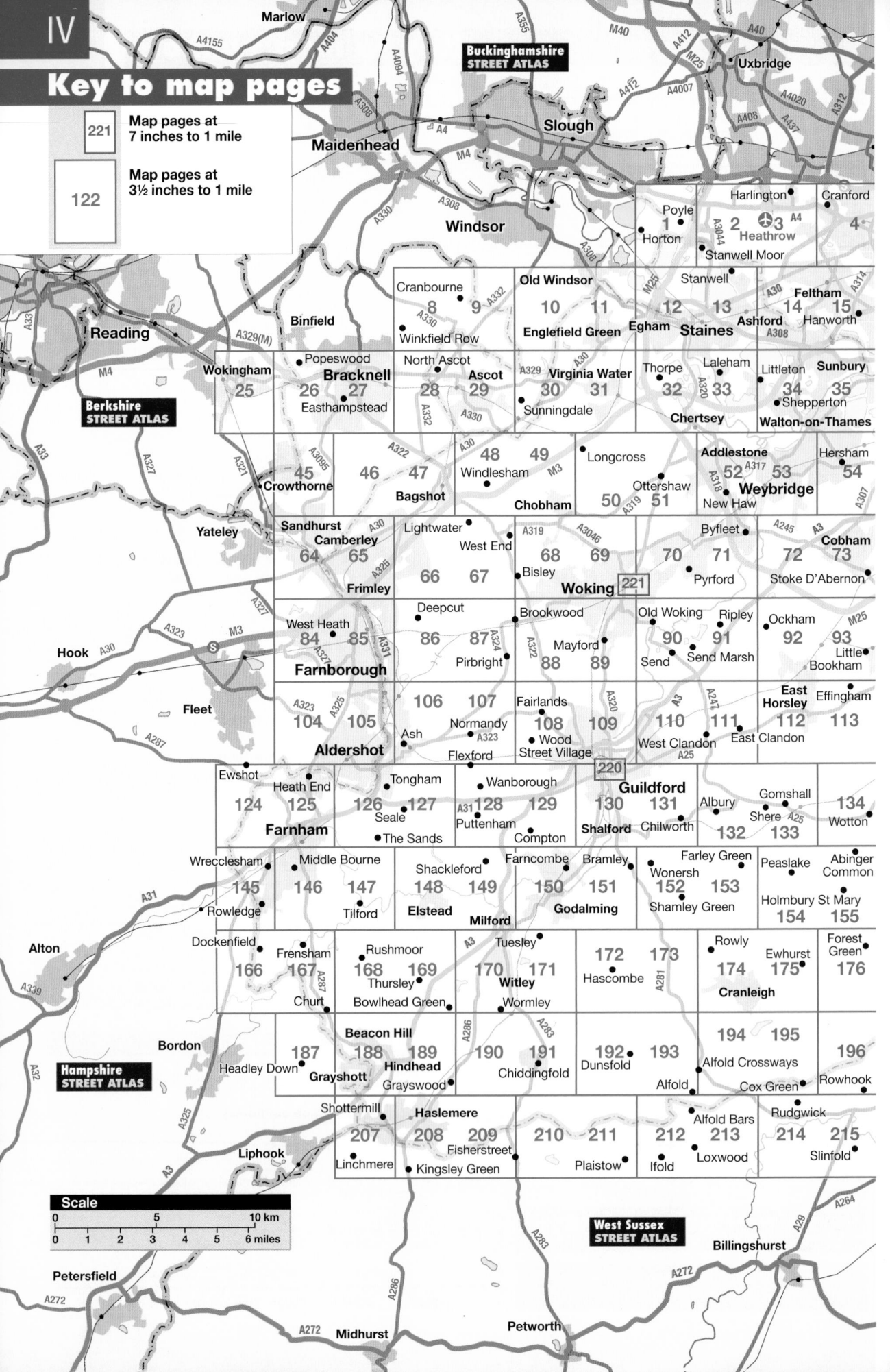

IV
Key to map pages
221
Map pages at 7 inches to 1 mile
122
Map pages at 3½ inches to 1 mile
Marlow
A4155
A404
A4094
A355
M40
A412
M25
A40
Uxbridge
Buckinghamshire STREET ATLAS
A308
A4
A412
A4007
A4020
A312
A408
A437
Slough
Maidenhead
M4
A308
A330
Windsor
A308
Harlington
Cranford
Poyle
1
Horton
A3044
2
3
Heathrow
A4
4
Stanwell Moor
Cranbourne
8
9
A332
A330
Winkfield Row
Old Windsor
10
11
Englefield Green
M25
Stanwell
12
13
Egham
Staines
A30
Feltham
14
15
A314
Ashford
Hanworth
A308
Reading
A33
A329(M)
Binfield
M4
Wokingham
25
Popeswood
Bracknell
26
27
Easthampstead
North Ascot
28
Ascot
29
A332
A330
A329
A30
Virginia Water
30
31
Sunningdale
Thorpe
32
Laleham
A320
33
Chertsey
Littleton
Sunbury
34
35
Shepperton
Walton-on-Thames
Berkshire STREET ATLAS
A33
A327
A321
A3095
45
Crowthorne
46
A322
47
Bagshot
A30
48
49
Windlesham
M3
Chobham
Longcross
Ottershaw
50
A319
51
Addlestone
A317
52
53
A318
Weybridge
New Haw
Hersham
54
A307
Yateley
Sandhurst
Camberley
A30
64
65
A325
Frimley
Lightwater
West End
66
67
A319
A3046
68
69
Bisley
Woking
221
Byfleet
70
71
Pyrford
A245
A3
Cobham
72
73
Stoke D'Abernon
A327
Hook
A30
A323
M3
West Heath
84
85
A327
A331
Farnborough
Deepcut
86
87
A324
Pirbright
Brookwood
A322
88
Mayford
89
Old Woking
Ripley
90
91
Send
Send Marsh
Ockham
92
M25
93
Little Bookham
Fleet
A287
A323
A325
104
105
Aldershot
106
107
Ash
Normandy
A323
Flexford
Fairlands
108
Wood Street Village
A320
109
A3
110
A247
111
West Clandon
East Clandon
A25
East Horsley
112
Effingham
113
Ewshot
Heath End
124
125
Farnham
Tongham
126
127
Seale
The Sands
Wanborough
A31
128
129
Puttenham
Compton
220
Guildford
130
131
Shalford
Chilworth
Albury
Gomshall
Shere
A25
132
133
134
Wotton
Wrecclesham
145
Rowledge
A31
Middle Bourne
146
147
Tilford
Shackleford
148
149
Elstead
Milford
Farncombe
150
Bramley
151
Godalming
Farley Green
Wonersh
152
153
Shamley Green
Peaslake
Abinger Common
Holmbury St Mary
154
155
Alton
A339
Dockenfield
166
Frensham
167
A287
Churt
Rushmoor
168
169
Thursley
Bowlhead Green
A3
Tuesley
170
171
Witley
Wormley
172
173
Hascombe
A281
Rowly
174
Ewhurst
175
Cranleigh
Forest Green
176
Bordon
A32
Hampshire STREET ATLAS
Headley Down
187
Beacon Hill
188
189
Grayshott
Hindhead
Grayswood
A286
190
A283
191
Chiddingfold
192
Dunsfold
193
194
195
Alfold Crossways
Alfold
Cox Green
196
Rowhook
Shottermill
207
Linchmere
Haslemere
208
209
Fisherstreet
Kingsley Green
210
211
Plaistow
212
Ifold
Alfold Bars
213
Loxwood
Rudgwick
214
215
Slinfold
A325
Liphook
A3
Scale
0
5
10 km
0
1
2
3
4
5
6 miles
West Sussex STREET ATLAS
A283
A264
A29
Billingshurst
A272
Petersfield
A272
A286
A272
Midhurst
Petworth

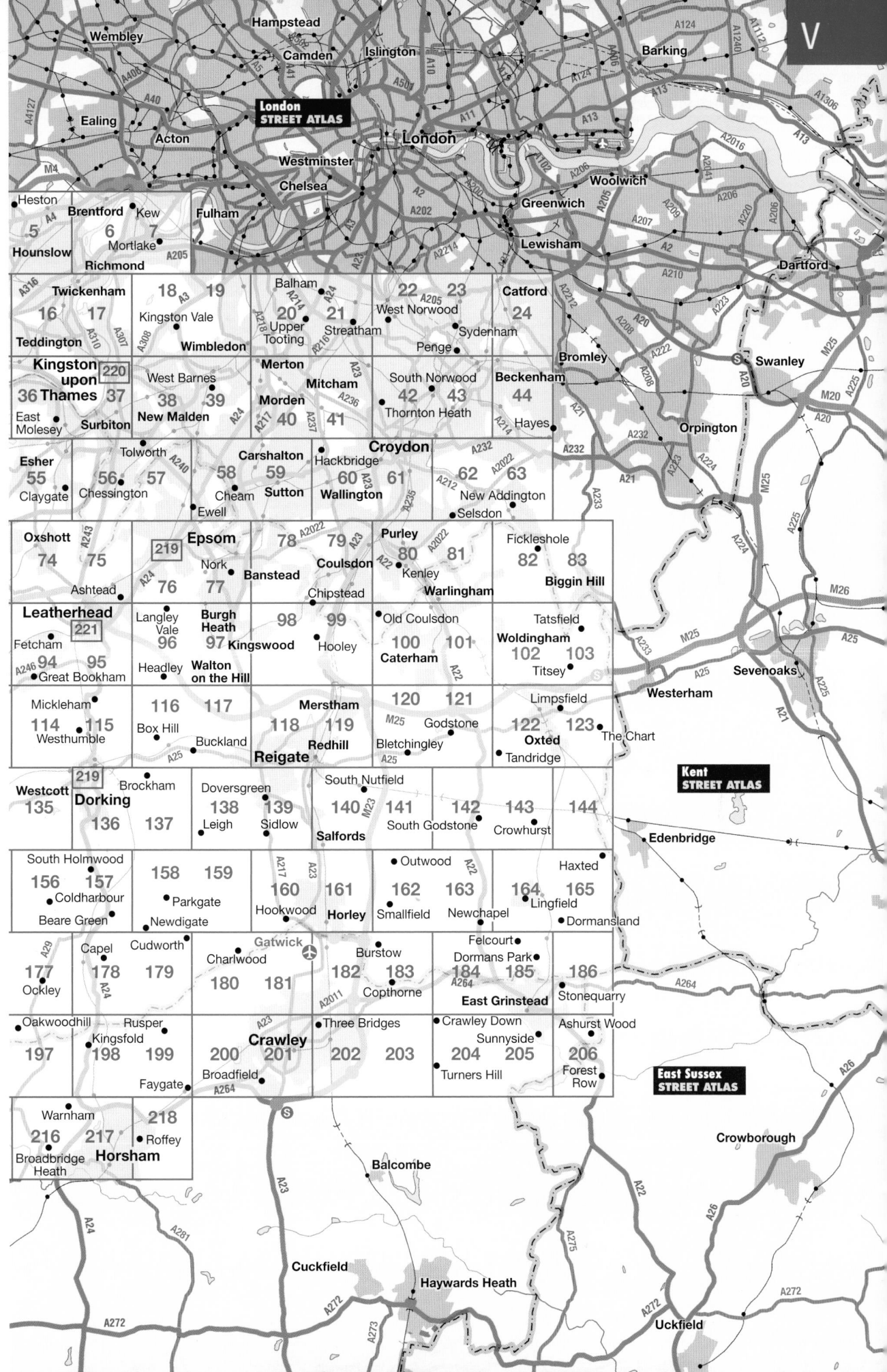
London STREET ATLAS
Kent STREET ATLAS
East Sussex STREET ATLAS
Hampstead
Wembley
Camden
Islington
Barking
Ealing
Acton
London
Westminster
Chelsea
Fulham
Woolwich
Greenwich
Lewisham
Dartford
Heston
Brentford
Kew
Hounslow
Mortlake
Richmond
Twickenham
Teddington
Kingston Vale
Wimbledon
Balham
Upper Tooting
Streatham
West Norwood
Sydenham
Penge
Catford
Bromley
Swanley
Kingston upon Thames
East Molesey
Surbiton
West Barnes
New Malden
Merton
Mitcham
Morden
South Norwood
Thornton Heath
Beckenham
Hayes
Orpington
Esher
Claygate
Tolworth
Chessington
Carshalton
Cheam
Ewell
Sutton
Croydon
Hackbridge
Wallington
New Addington
Selsdon
Oxshott
Ashtead
Epsom
Nork
Banstead
Coulsdon
Chipstead
Purley
Kenley
Warlingham
Fickleshole
Biggin Hill
Leatherhead
Fetcham
Great Bookham
Langley Vale
Headley
Burgh Heath
Kingswood
Walton on the Hill
Hooley
Old Coulsdon
Caterham
Tatsfield
Woldingham
Titsey
Westerham
Sevenoaks
Mickleham
Westhumble
Box Hill
Buckland
Reigate
Merstham
Redhill
Godstone
Bletchingley
Limpsfield
Oxted
Tandridge
The Chart
Westcott
Dorking
Brockham
Doversgreen
Leigh
Sidlow
South Nutfield
Salfords
South Godstone
Crowhurst
Edenbridge
South Holmwood
Coldharbour
Beare Green
Parkgate
Newdigate
Hookwood
Horley
Outwood
Smallfield
Newchapel
Haxted
Lingfield
Dormansland
Capel
Cudworth
Ockley
Charlwood
Gatwick
Burstow
Copthorne
Felcourt
Dormans Park
East Grinstead
Stonequarry
Oakwoodhill
Rusper
Kingsfold
Faygate
Crawley
Broadfield
Three Bridges
Crawley Down
Sunnyside
Turners Hill
Ashurst Wood
Forest Row
Warnham
Roffey
Broadbridge Heath
Horsham
Balcombe
Crowborough
Cuckfield
Haywards Heath
Uckfield
5 6 7 16 17 18 19 20 21 22 23 24 36 37 38 39 40 41 42 43 44 55 56 57 58 59 60 61 62 63 74 75 76 77 78 79 80 81 82 83 94 95 96 97 98 99 100 101 102 103 114 115 116 117 118 119 120 121 122 123 135 136 137 138 139 140 141 142 143 144 156 157 158 159 160 161 162 163 164 165 177 178 179 180 181 182 183 184 185 186 197 198 199 200 201 202 203 204 205 206 216 217 218 219 220 221
M25
M26
M20
M23
A23
A24
A22
A21
A25
A26
A264
A272

Route planning

Scale

| 0 | | 5 | | 10 km |

| 0 | 1 | 2 | 3 | 4 | 5 miles |

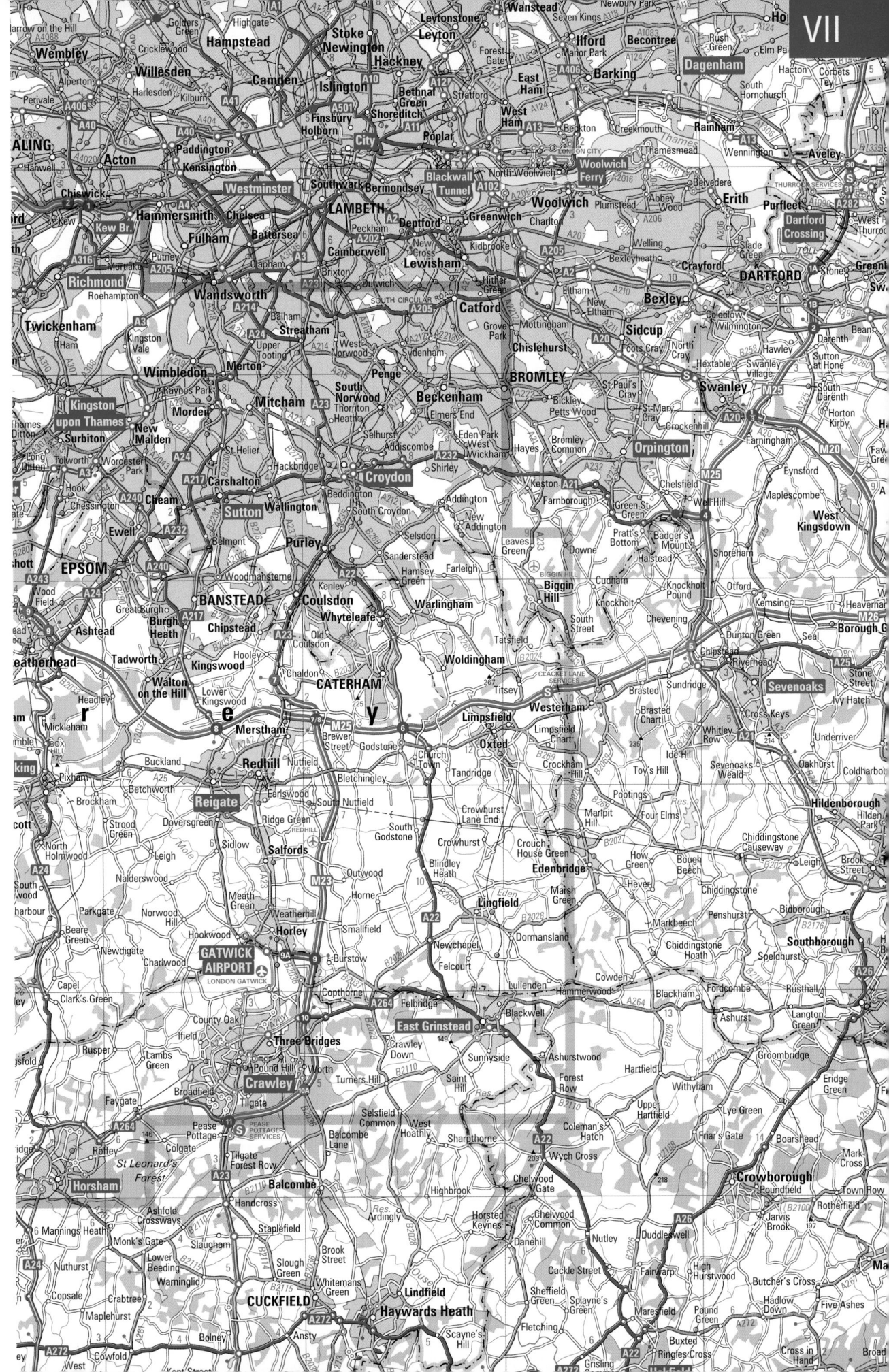

VII
Wembley
Hampstead
Stoke Newington
Hackney
Leytonstone
Leyton
Wanstead
Ilford
Becontree
Dagenham
Willesden
Camden
Islington
Barking
East Ham
West Ham
Bethnal Green
Shoreditch
Finsbury
Holborn
City
Poplar
Beckton
Creekmouth
Rainham
Thames
Thamesmead
Wennington
Aveley
EALING
Acton
Paddington
Kensington
Westminster
Southwark
Bermondsey
Blackwall Tunnel
North Woolwich
LONDON CITY
Woolwich Ferry
Belvedere
Erith
Purfleet
THURROCK SERVICES
Dartford Crossing
Chiswick
Kew
Kew Br.
Hammersmith
Chelsea
Fulham
Battersea
LAMBETH
Deptford
Greenwich
Charlton
Woolwich
Plumstead
Abbey Wood
Peckham
Camberwell
New Cross
Lewisham
Kidbrooke
Welling
Bexleyheath
Crayford
DARTFORD
Slade Green
Stone
Richmond
Mortlake
Putney
Clapham
Brixton
Dulwich
Hither Green
Eltham
Bexley
Roehampton
Wandsworth
SOUTH CIRCULAR ROAD
Catford
New Eltham
Sidcup
Wilmington
Twickenham
Balham
Streatham
Grove Park
Mottingham
Chislehurst
Foots Cray
North Cray
Hextable
Swanley Village
Hawley
Darenth
Sutton at Hone
Bean
Ham
Kingston Vale
Upper Tooting
West Norwood
Sydenham
Wimbledon
Merton
Penge
BROMLEY
St Paul's Cray
Swanley
South Darenth
Raynes Park
Mitcham
South Norwood
Beckenham
Bickley
Petts Wood
St Mary Cray
Horton Kirby
Kingston upon Thames
Morden
Thornton Heath
Elmers End
Crockenhill
Farningham
Thames Ditton
New Malden
Selhurst
Eden Park
West Wickham
Hayes
Bromley Common
Orpington
Surbiton
St Helier
Addiscombe
Long Ditton
Tolworth
Worcester Park
Hackbridge
Croydon
Shirley
Chelsfield
Eynsford
Carshalton
Keston
Farnborough
Hook
Cheam
Beddington
Addington
Green St Green
Well Hill
Maplescombe
Chessington
Sutton
Wallington
South Croydon
New Addington
Pratt's Bottom
Badger's Mount
West Kingsdown
Ewell
Belmont
Selsdon
Leaves Green
Downe
Purley
Sanderstead
Halstead
Shoreham
EPSOM
Hamsey Green
Farleigh
BIGGIN HILL
Woodmansterne
Kenley
Biggin Hill
Cudham
Knockholt Pound
Otford
Wood Field
BANSTEAD
Coulsdon
Knockholt
Kemsing
Great Burgh
Whyteleafe
Warlingham
Ashtead
Burgh Heath
Chipstead
Old Coulsdon
South Street
Chevening
Dunton Green
Seal
Borough Green
Tatsfield
Leatherhead
Tadworth
Hooley
Woldingham
Chipstead
Riverhead
Kingswood
Chaldon
CATERHAM
CLACKET LANE SERVICES
Brasted
Sundridge
Sevenoaks
Stone Street
Walton on the Hill
Lower Kingswood
Titsey
Westerham
Ivy Hatch
Headley
Brasted Chart
Mickleham
Merstham
Limpsfield
Cross Keys
Brewer Street
Godstone
Oxted
Limpsfield Chart
Whitley Row
Underriver
Box Hill
Buckland
Nutfield
Church Town
Crockham Hill
Ide Hill
Redhill
Tandridge
Toy's Hill
Sevenoaks Weald
Oakhurst
Pixham
Betchworth
Bletchingley
Coldharbour
Brockham
Reigate
Earlswood
South Nutfield
Crowhurst Lane End
Pootings
Hildenborough
Strood Green
Doversgreen
Ridge Green
REDHILL
South Godstone
Marlpit Hill
Four Elms
Hildenborough
North Holmwood
Sidlow
Leigh
Salfords
Crowhurst
Crouch House Green
Edenbridge
Chiddingstone Causeway
How Green
Bough Beech
Leigh
Brook Street
Mole
Blindley Heath
Outwood
South Holmwood
Nalderswood
Horne
Lingfield
Hever
Marsh Green
Chiddingstone
Capel
Parkgate
Norwood Hill
Meath Green
Weatherhill
Penshurst
Bidborough
Eden
Beare Green
Hookwood
Horley
Smallfield
Dormansland
Markbeech
Southborough
Newdigate
Charlwood
GATWICK AIRPORT
LONDON GATWICK
Newchapel
Chiddingstone Hoath
Speldhurst
Burstow
Felcourt
Clark's Green
Copthorne
Felbridge
Lullenden
Hammerwood
Cowden
Blackham
Fordcombe
Rusthall
Ashurst
Langton Green
County Oak
East Grinstead
Blackwell
Ifield
Rusper
Three Bridges
Crawley Down
Sunnyside
Ashurstwood
Groombridge
Lambs Green
Pound Hill
Worth
Turners Hill
Saint Hill
Forest Row
Hartfield
Withyham
Eridge Green
Crawley
Broadfield
Faygate
Tilgate
Selsfield Common
West Hoathly
Upper Hartfield
Lye Green
Pease Pottage
PEASE POTTAGE SERVICES
Coleman's Hatch
Roffey
Colgate
Balcombe Lane
Sharpthorne
Friar's Gate
Boarshead
Mark Cross
St Leonard's Forest
Tilgate Forest Row
Wych Cross
Horsham
Balcombe
Chelwood Gate
Highbrook
Crowborough
Poundfield
Town Row
Handcross
Ashfold Crossways
Ardingly
Horsted Keynes
Chelwood Common
Rotherfield
Jarvis Brook
Mannings Heath
Monk's Gate
Slaugham
Staplefield
Danehill
Nutley
Duddleswell
Lower Beeding
Nuthurst
Slough Green
Brook Street
Cackle Street
Fairwarp
High Hurstwood
Warninglid
Copsale
Crabtree
Whitemans Green
Lindfield
Sheffield Green
Splayne's Green
Butcher's Cross
Hadlow Down
Five Ashes
Maplehurst
CUCKFIELD
Haywards Heath
Fletching
Maresfield
Pound Green
Bolney
Ansty
Scayne's Hill
Buxted
Ringles Cross
Cross in Hand
Cowfold
West
Grisling

Major administrative and Postcode boundaries

County and unitary authority boundaries
District boundaries
Postcode boundaries
Area covered by this atlas

Scale

10 miles

15 km

1 Hammersmith and Fulham
2 Royal Borough of Kensington and Chelsea
3 City of Westminster
4 City of London
5 Richmond upon Thames
6 Kingston upon Thames

SURREY

Bucks · Slough · Windsor and Maidenhead · Hillingdon · Ealing · Hounslow · Spelthorne · Runnymede · Surrey Heath · Bracknell Forest · Wokingham · Hampshire · Elmbridge · Mole Valley · Waverley · Guildford · Epsom and Ewell · Sutton · Merton · Wandsworth · Lambeth · Southwark · Tower Hamlets · Newham · Greenwich · Bexley · Bromley · Croydon · Reigate and Banstead · Tandridge · Kent · East Sussex · West Sussex

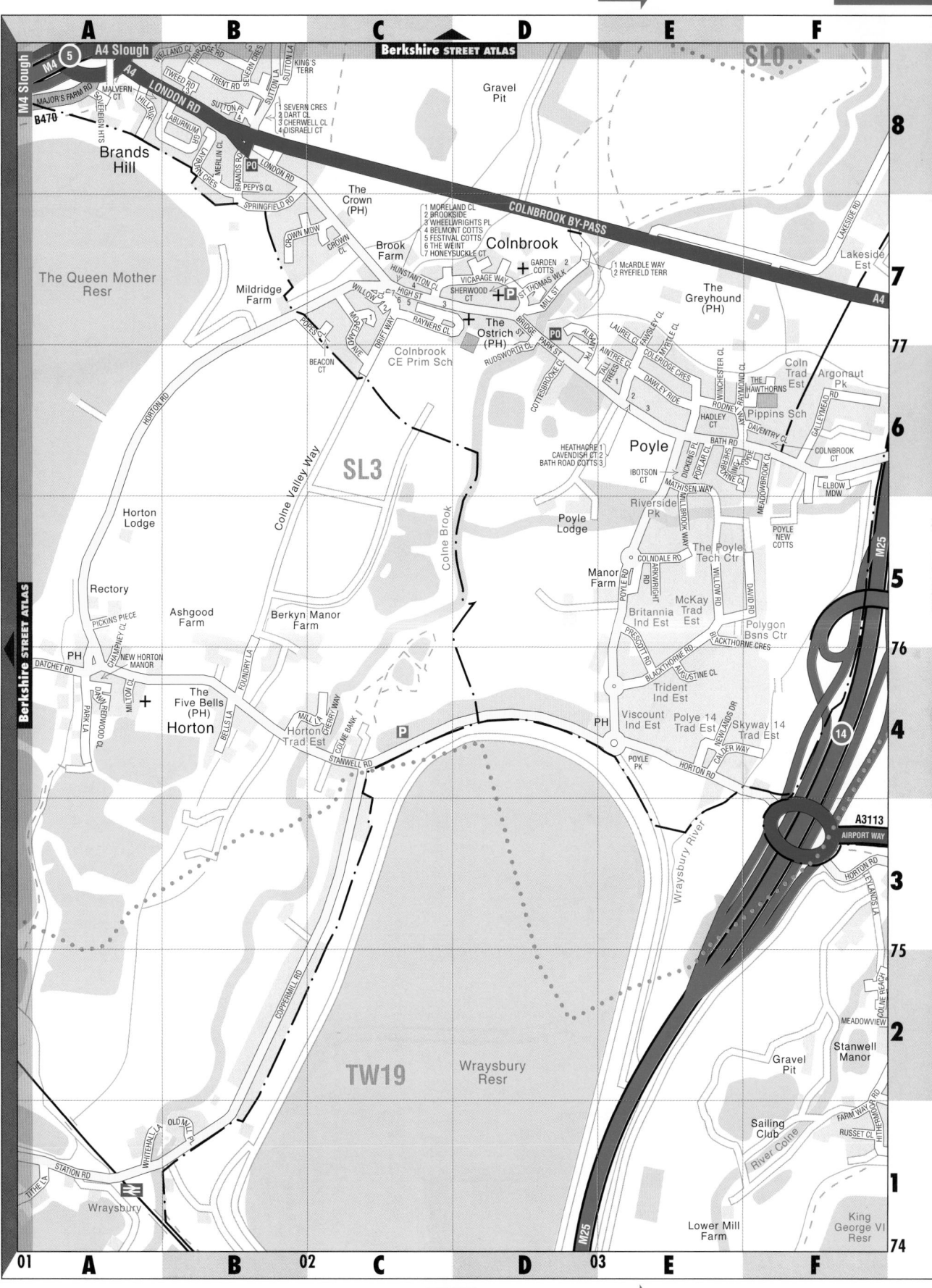

Berkshire STREET ATLAS

A B C D E F

SLO

A4 Slough
M4 Slough
M4
A4
B470
MAJOR'S FARM RD
SOVEREIGN HTS
MALVERN CT
HILLSIDE
LABURNUM
MERLIN CL
LATBROOK CRES
SPRINGFIELD RD
CROWN MDW
CROWN CL

Brands Hill
LONDON RD

WELLAND CL
TWEED RD
TRENT RD
SUTTON PL
SUTTON LA
KING'S TERR
SEVERN CRES

1 SEVERN CRES
2 DART CL
3 CHERWELL CL
4 DISRAELI CT

BRANDS RD
PEPYS CL
LONDON RD
PO

Mildridge Farm

The Crown (PH)

Brook Farm

1 MORELAND CL
2 BROOKSIDE
3 WHEELWRIGHTS PL
4 BELMONT COTTS
5 FESTIVAL COTTS
6 THE WEINT
7 HONEYSUCKLE CT

COLNBROOK BY-PASS

Gravel Pit

Colnbrook

Garden Cotts
VICARAGE WAY
ST THOMAS WALK
SHERWOOD CT
HUNSTANTON CL
WILLOW CL
HIGH ST
DRIFT WAY
RAYNERS CL

1 McARDLE WAY
2 RYEFIELD TERR

The Greyhound (PH)

Lakeside Est
LAKESIDE RD
A4

The Queen Mother Resr

PAPERS LA
BEACON CT
MORE LA
CAVE AVE

The Ostrich (PH)

Colnbrook CE Prim Sch

BRIDGE ST
PARK ST
RUDSWORTH CL
ALBA
W LANE
ARTHUR CL
AINTREE CL
TRESS RD
TALL TREES
LAUREL CL
COLERIDGE CRES
PAISLEY CL
MYRTLE CL
RAYMOND CL
WINCHESTER CL
DAWLEY RIDE

Coln Trad Est
Argonaut Pk

THE HAWTHORNS
GALLEYMEAD RD

COTTESBROOKE CL

HADLEY CT
RODNEY
DAVENTRY CL
BATH RD

Pippins Sch
Colnbrook CT
ELBOW MDW

Poyle

HEATHACRE
CAVENDISH CT
BATH ROAD COTTS

BATH RD

POYLE NEW COTTS

IBOTSON CT
MATHISEN WAY
DICKENS PL
POPLAR CL
PAYNE CL
MEADOWBROOK CL

Riverside Pk

HORTON RD

Colne Valley Way

SL3

Colne Brook

Poyle Lodge

The Poyle Tech Ctr

Horton Lodge

Manor Farm

COLNDALE RD
POYLE RD
ARKWRIGHT
WILLOW RD
DAVID RD
MILLBROOK WAY

McKay Trad Est

Britannia Ind Est

Polygon Bsns Ctr

Rectory

PICKINS PIECE

Ashgood Farm

Berkyn Manor Farm

PRESCOTT RD
BLACKTHORNE RD
AUGUSTINE CL
BLACKTHORNE CRES

Trident Ind Est

M25

PH
NEW HORTON MANOR
CHANNEY CL
DATCHET RD

MILTON CL
REDWOOD CL
PARK LA
DAVY CL

The Five Bells (PH)
Horton

FOUNDRY LA
BELLS LA
CHERRY WAY
MILL
COLNE BANK

Horton Trad Est

STANWELL RD

Viscount Ind Est
Polye 14 Trad Est
Skyway 14 Trad Est

NEWLANDS DR
CALDER WAY

PH
POYLE PK
HORTON RD

14

A3113
AIRPORT WAY

COPPERMILL RD

P

Wraysbury River

75

MEADOWVIEW
COLNE BEACH

Gravel Pit
Stanwell Manor

FARM WAY
HITHERMOOR RD
HORTON RD
LEYLANDS LA

TW19

Wraysbury Resr

Sailing Club
RUSSET CL
River Colne

WHITEHALL LA
OLD MILL LA
STATION RD
TITHE LA

Wraysbury

M25

Lower Mill Farm

King George VI Resr

8
77
6
5
76
4
75
2
1
74

01 A B 02 C D 03 E F

Berkshire STREET ATLAS

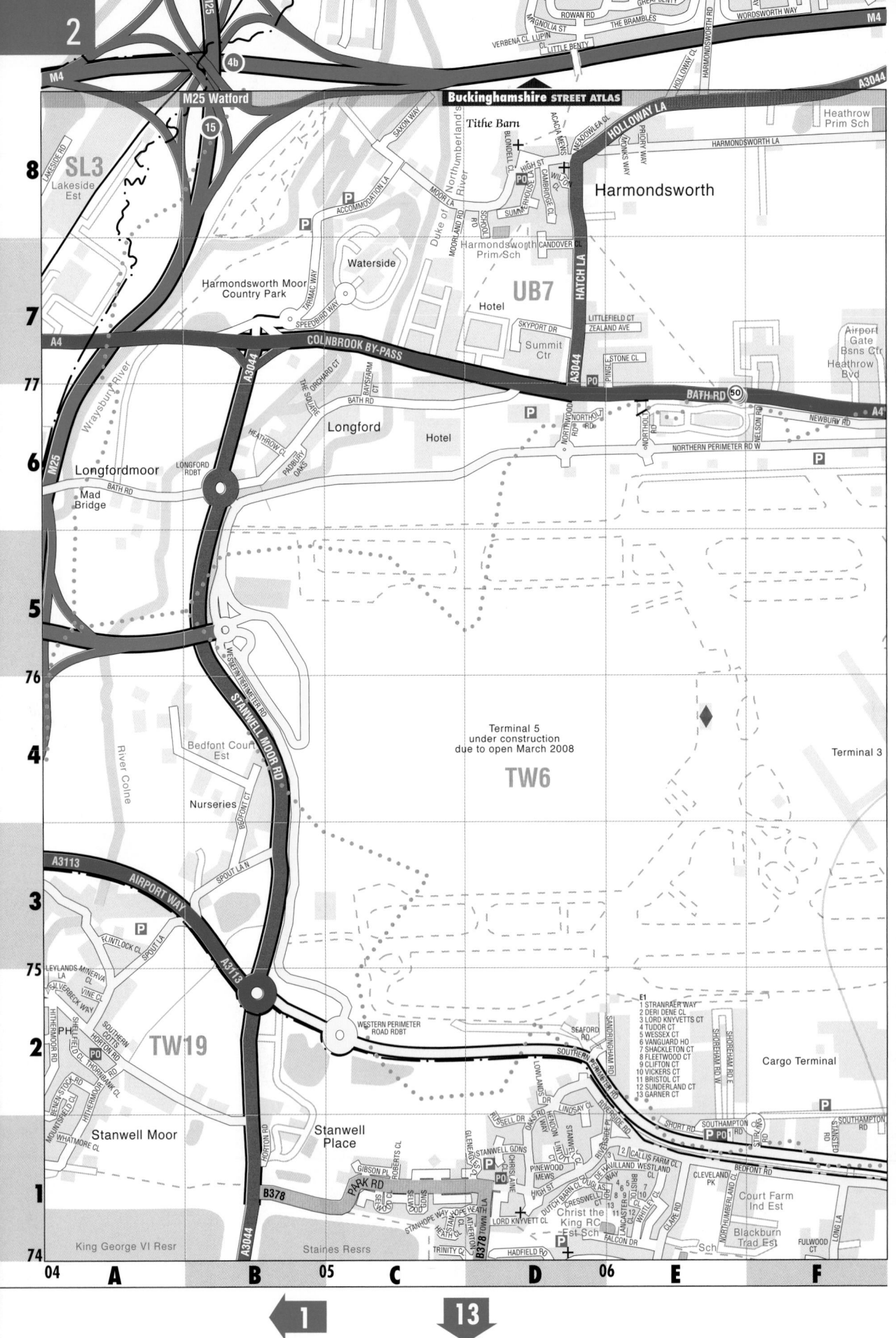
Buckinghamshire STREET ATLAS
M25 Watford
Harmondsworth
Harmondsworth Moor Country Park
Waterside
Tithe Barn
Harmondsworth Prim Sch
UB7
SL3
Lakeside Est
Hotel
Summit Ctr
Airport Gate Bsns Ctr
Heathrow Bvd
Heathrow Prim Sch
COLNBROOK BY-PASS
BATH RD
Longford
Longfordmoor
Mad Bridge
LONGFORD RDBT
HOLLOWAY LA
HATCH LA
NORTHERN PERIMETER RD W
Terminal 5 under construction due to open March 2008
TW6
Terminal 3
Bedfont Court Est
Nurseries
River Colne
Wraysbury River
STANWELL MOOR RD
AIRPORT WAY
TW19
Stanwell Moor
Stanwell Place
WESTERN PERIMETER ROAD RDBT
SOUTHERN PERIMETER RD
Cargo Terminal
E1
1 STRANRAER WAY
2 DERI DENE CL
3 LORD KNYVETTS CT
4 TUDOR CT
5 WESSEX CT
6 VANGUARD HO
7 SHACKLETON CT
8 FLEETWOOD CT
9 CLIFTON CT
10 VICKERS CT
11 BRISTOL CT
12 SUNDERLAND CT
13 GARNER CT
Christ the King RC Est Sch
Court Farm Ind Est
Blackburn Trad Est
King George VI Resr
Staines Resrs
PARK RD
BEDFONT RD
04 A B 05 C D 06 E F
8 7 77 6 5 76 4 3 75 2 1 74

1
13

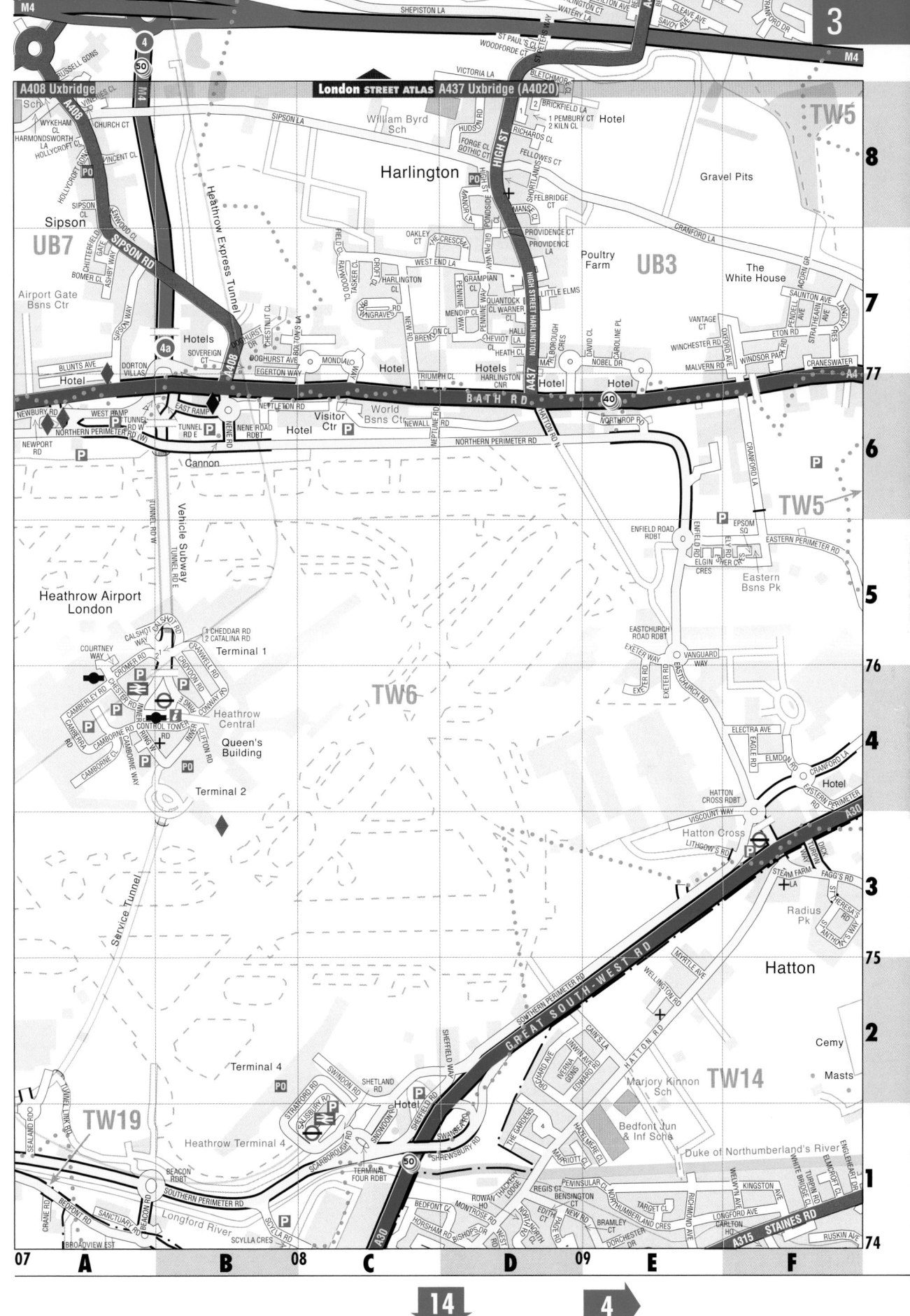
A408 Uxbridge
London STREET ATLAS A437 Uxbridge (A4020)
M4
SHEPISTON LA
VINE CL
RUSSELL GDNS
VINERIES CL
WYKEHAM CL
HARMONDSWORTH LA
HOLLYCROFT CL
HOLLYCROFT GDNS
CHURCH CT
VINCENT CL
SIPSON CL
SIPSON RD
Sipson
UB7
CHITTERFIELD GATE
ASHBY WAY
BOMER CL
LENWOOD CL
Airport Gate Bsns Ctr
SIPSON WAY
BLUNTS AVE
Hotel
DORTON VILLAS
Hotels
SOVEREIGN CT
DOGHURST DR
DOGHURST AVE
EGERTON WAY
CHESTNUT CL
BOLTON'S LA
MONDIAL WAY
Heathrow Express Tunnel
SIPSON LA
William Byrd Sch
Harlington
HIGH ST
HUDSON RD
FORGE CL
GOTHIC CT
MANOR LA
PONDSIDE CL
FIELD CL
RAYWOOD CL
TASKER CL
CROFT CL
OAKLEY CT
THE CRESCENT
WEST END LA
HARLINGTON CL
BROWNINGRAVE RD
NEW RD
BRENDON CL
GRAMPIAN CL
PENNINE WAY
MENDIP CL
QUANTOCK CL
WARNER CL
CHEVIOT CL
HALL LA
HEATH CL
GILPIN WAY
HARLINGTON CNR
Hotels
TRIUMPH CL
VICTORIA LA
BLETCHMORE CL
BRICKFIELD LA
1 PEMBURY CT
2 KILN CL
Hotel
RICHARDS CL
FELLOWES CT
SHORTLANDS
FELBRIDGE CT
MANSE CL
PROVIDENCE CT
PROVIDENCE LA
LITTLE ELMS
HIGH STREET HARLINGTON
A437
Poultry Farm
UB3
Gravel Pits
CRANFORD LA
The White House
ST PAUL'S CL
WOODFORDE CT
ST PETERS WAY
ARLINGTON CT
CARLTON AVE
WATERY LA
BEDWELL
CROYDE AVE
CLEAVE AVE
SAVOY AVE
CRANFORD DR
TW5
SAUNTON AVE
ACORN GR
PENDELL AVE
STRATHEARN AVE
LANGLEY CRES
VANTAGE CT
ETON RD
WINCHESTER RD
OXFORD AVE
WINDSOR PARK RD
MALVERN RD
CRANESWATER
FELBOROUGH CRES
DAVID CL
CAROLINE PL
NOBEL DR
Hotel
A4
BATH RD
NEWBURY RD
WEST RAMP
TUNNEL RD W
NORTHERN PERIMETER RD (W)
NEWPORT RD
TUNNEL RD E
EAST RAMP
NENE RD
NENE ROAD RDBT
NETTLETON RD
Visitor Ctr
Hotel
World Bsns Ctr
NEWALL RD
NEPTUNE RD
NORTHERN PERIMETER RD
HATTON RD N
NORTHROP RD
Cannon
CRANFORD LA
TW5
Vehicle Subway
TUNNEL RD W
TUNNEL RD E
ENFIELD ROAD RDBT
ENFIELD RD
ELGIN CRES
FISHER CL
ELY RD
EPSOM SQ
EASTERN PERIMETER RD
Eastern Bsns Pk
Heathrow Airport London
CALSHOT WAY
CALSHOT RD
1 CHEDDAR RD
2 CATALINA RD
Terminal 1
COURTNEY WAY
CROMER RD
CRANWELL RD
CROYDON RD
CONWAY RD
CHESTER RD
CAMBERLEY RD
CAMBERRA RD
CAMBORNE RD
CAMBORNE CL
CAMBORNE WAY
INNER RING W
INNER RING E
CONTROL TOWER RD
CLIFTON RD
Heathrow Central
Queen's Building
Terminal 2
TW6
EASTCHURCH ROAD RDBT
EXETER WAY
EXETER RD
VANGUARD WAY
EASTCHURCH RD
ELECTRA AVE
EAGLE RD
ELMDON RD
CRANFORD LA
Hotel
HATTON CROSS RDBT
VISCOUNT WAY
Hatton Cross
LITHGOW'S RD
EASTERN PERIMETER RD
A30
STEAM FARM LA
TURPIN WAY
DICK
FAGG'S RD
ST THERESA'S RD
ST ANTHONY'S WAY
Radius Pk
Hatton
Service Tunnel
SOUTHERN PERIMETER RD
GREAT SOUTH-WEST RD
MYRTLE AVE
WELLINGTON RD
HATTON RD
CAIN'S LA
UNWIN AVE
EDWARD RD
IVERNA GDNS
ORCHARD AVE
Marjory Kinnon Sch
TW14
Bedfont Jun & Inf Schs
Cemy
Masts
Terminal 4
SHEFFIELD WAY
SHETLAND RD
SWINDON RD
STRATFORD RD
SALISBURY RD
SNOWDON RD
SHEFFIELD RD
SWANSEA RD
SHREWSBURY RD
SCARBOROUGH RD
Hotel
THE GARDENS
HAZELMERE CL
MARRIOTT CL
Duke of Northumberland's River
TW19
TUNNEL LINK RD
SEALAND RD
Heathrow Terminal 4
BEACON RDBT
TERMINAL FOUR RDBT
SOUTHERN PERIMETER RD
Longford River
SCYLLA RD
SCYLLA CRES
CRANE RD
BEDFONT RD
SANCTUARY RD
BEACON RD
BROADVIEW EST
A30
BEDFONT CL
HORSHAM RD
BISHOPS DR
MONTROSE RD
ROWAN HO
THICKEY LODGE
WEST RD
NORTH RD
NORTH CT
EDITH CT
PAGE RD
REGIS CT
PENINSULAR CL
BENSINGTON CT
NEW RD
NORTHUMBERLAND CRES
BRAMLEY CT
DORCHESTER DR
TARGET CL
RICHMOND AVE
WELWYN AVE
KINGSTON AVE
LONGFORD AVE
CARLTON HO
WHITE BRIDGE CL
TURPIN RD
ELMCROFT CL
ENGLEHEART DR
STAINES RD
A315
RUSKIN AVE
8
7
77
6
5
76
4
3
75
2
1
74
07
A
B
08
C
D
09
E
F

14
4

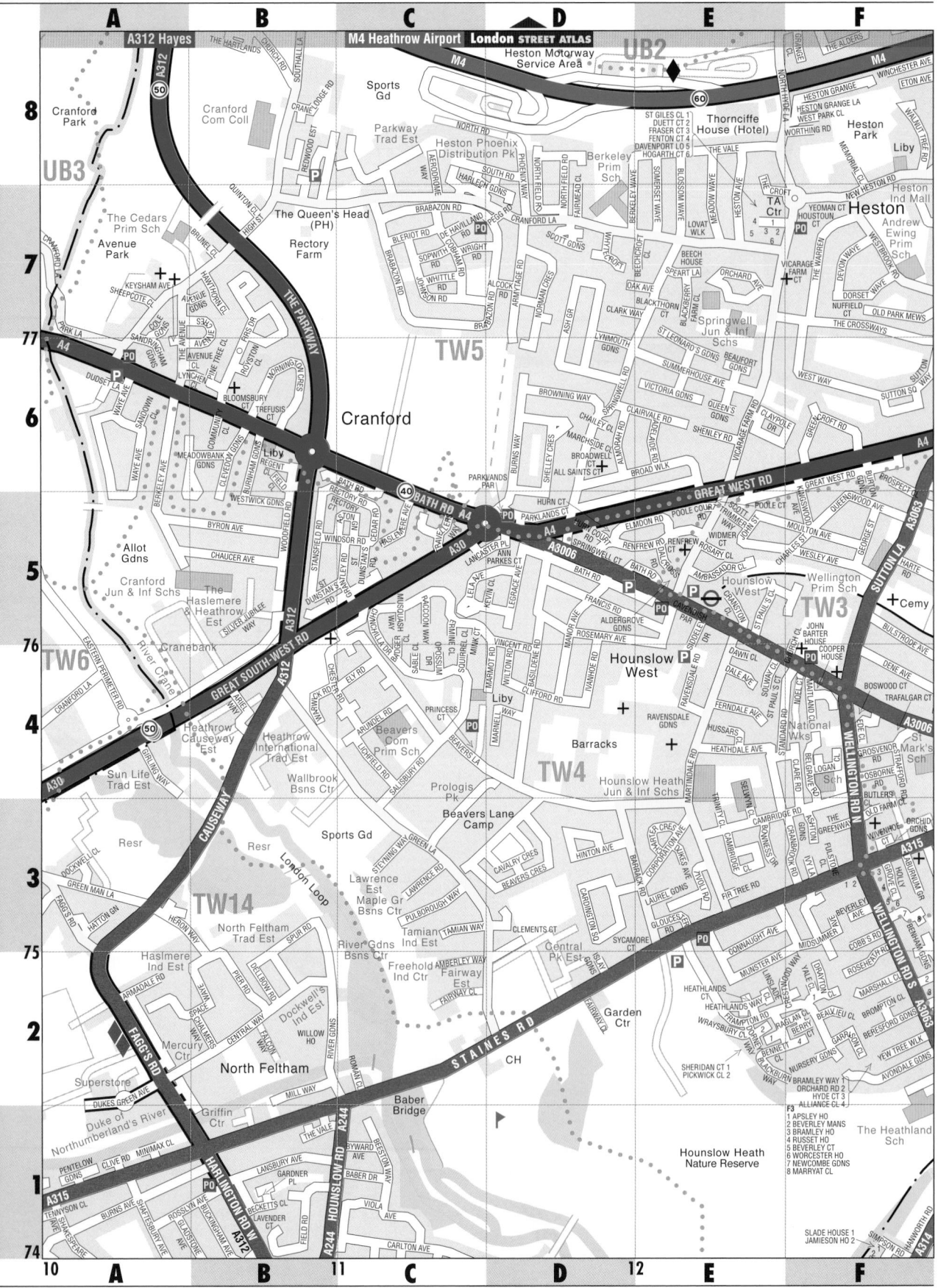

6

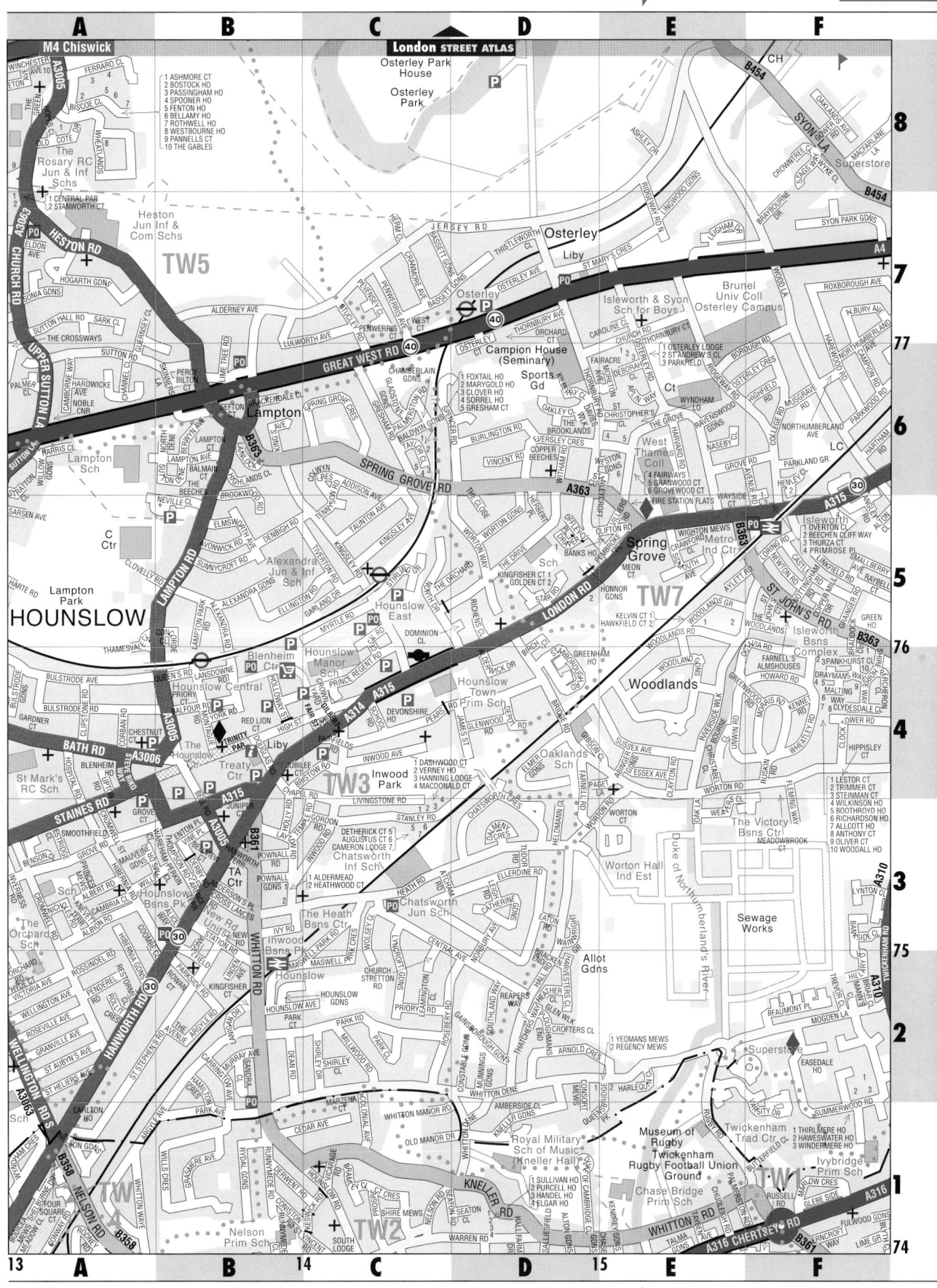
A
B
C
D
E
F
M4 Chiswick
London STREET ATLAS
Osterley Park House
Osterley Park
8
7
77
6
5
76
4
3
75
2
1
74
13
14
15
The Rosary RC Jun & Inf Schs
Heston Jun Inf & Com Schs
TW5
HESTON RD
CHURCH RD
UPPER SUTTON LA
GREAT WEST RD
Lampton
Lampton Sch
LAMPTON RD
Lampton Park
HOUNSLOW
Osterley
Liby
Brunel Univ Coll Osterley Campus
Isleworth & Syon Sch for Boys
Campion House (Seminary)
Sports Gd
West Thames Coll
SPRING GROVE RD
Spring Grove
TW7
LONDON RD
Hounslow East
Alexandra Jun & Inf Sch
Blenheim Ctr
Hounslow Manor Sch
Hounslow Central
Hounslow Town Prim Sch
Woodlands
Isleworth
Isleworth Bsns Complex
Oaklands Sch
Inwood Park
TW3
BATH RD
STAINES RD
St Mark's RC Sch
Treaty Ctr
Liby
Chatsworth Inf Sch
Chatsworth Jun Sch
Worton Hall Ind Est
Duke of Northumberland's River
Sewage Works
The Victory Bsns Ctr
Allot Gdns
Hounslow
WHITTON RD
HANWORTH RD
Superstore
Museum of Rugby
Twickenham Rugby Football Union Ground
Royal Military Sch of Music (Kneller Hall)
Chase Bridge Prim Sch
Twickenham Trad Ctr
Ivybridge Prim Sch
KNELLER RD
WHITTON RD
TW2
TW1
TW4
Nelson Prim Sch
NELSON RD
WELLINGTON RD S
A316 CHERTSEY RD
A3005
A3063
A315
A314
A363
A4
A310
B454
B363
B361
B358
A3006

16

6

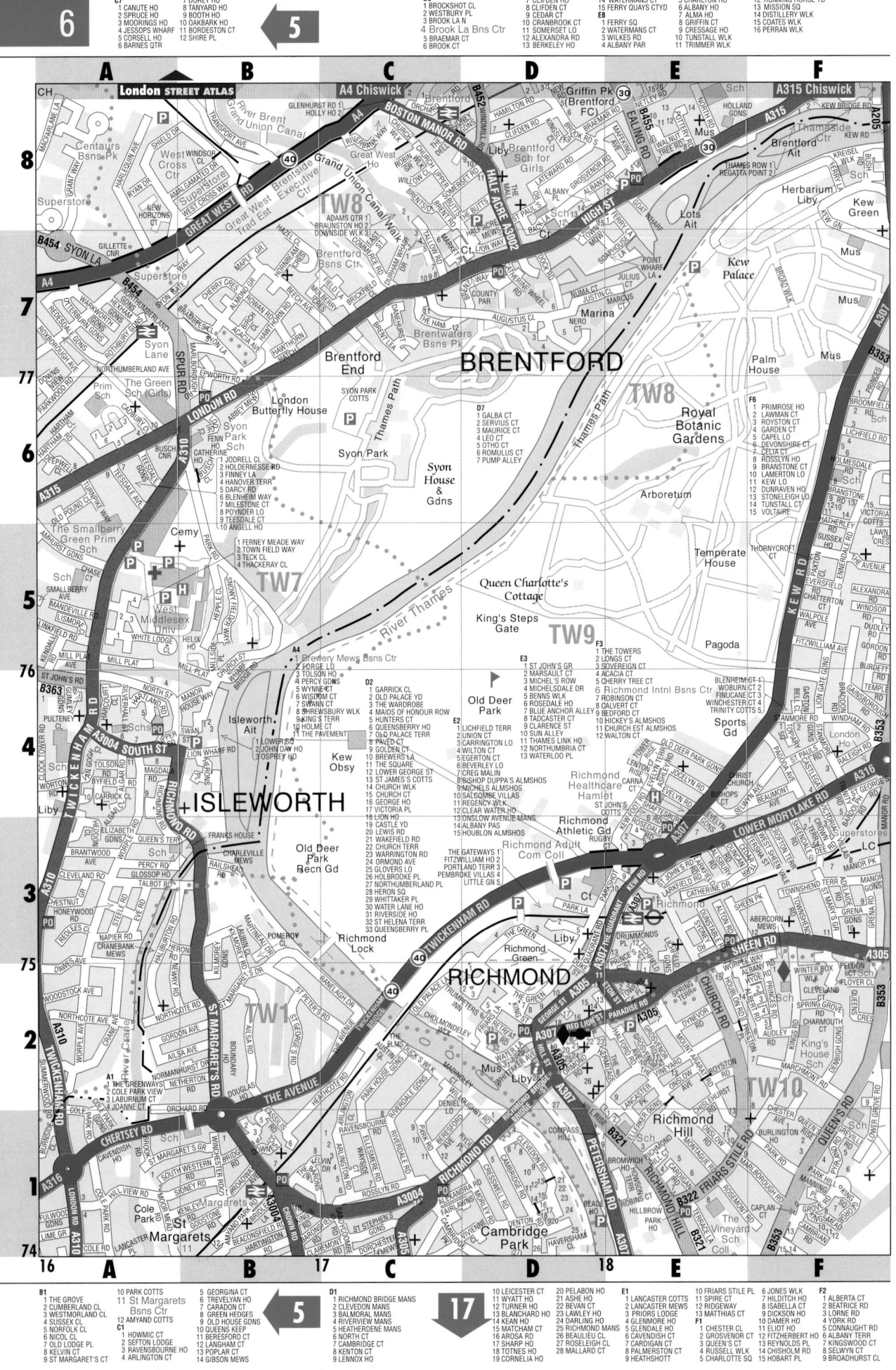
C7
1 CANUTE HO
2 SPRUCE HO
3 MOORINGS HO
4 JESSOPS WHARF
5 CORSELL HO
6 BARNES QTR
7 DOREY HO
8 TANYARD HO
9 BOOTH HO
10 OAKBARK HO
11 BORDESTON CT
12 SHIRE PL
5
D8
1 BROCKSHOT CL
2 WESTBURY PL
3 BROOK LA N
4 Brook La Bns Ctr
5 BRAEMAR CT
6 BROOK CT
7 CLIFDEN HO
8 CLIFDEN CT
9 CEDAR CT
10 CRANBROOK CT
11 SOMERSET LO
12 ALEXANDRA RD
13 BERKELEY HO
14 WATERMANS CT
15 FERRY QUAYS CTYD
E8
1 FERRY SQ
2 WATERMANS CT
3 WILKES RD
4 ALBANY PAR
5 CHARLTON HO
6 ALBANY HO
7 ALMA HO
8 GRIFFIN CT
9 CRESSAGE HO
10 TUNSTALL WLK
11 TRIMMER WLK
12 RUNNING HORSE YD
13 MISSION SQ
14 DISTILLERY WLK
15 COATES WLK
16 PERRAN WLK
A B C D E F
London STREET ATLAS
A4 Chiswick
A315 Chiswick
8
7
77
6
5
76
4
3
75
2
1
74
16 17 18
BRENTFORD
TW8
Brentford End
Syon Park
Syon House & Gdns
London Butterfly House
Griffin Pk (Brentford FC)
Lots Ait
Brentford Ait
Kew Palace
Kew Green
Herbarium Liby
Palm House
Royal Botanic Gardens
Arboretum
Temperate House
Pagoda
Queen Charlotte's Cottage
King's Steps Gate
TW9
River Thames
Thames Path
TW7
ISLEWORTH
Isleworth Ait
West Middlesex Univ
Kew Obsy
Old Deer Park
Old Deer Park Recn Gd
Richmond Lock
Richmond Athletic Gd
Richmond Healthcare Hamlet
Richmond Adult Com Coll
RICHMOND
Richmond Green
Richmond Hill
TW1
TW10
Cambridge Park
Cole Park
St Margarets
King's House Sch
The Vineyard Sch
Sports Gd
London Ho
BOSTON MANOR RD
GREAT WEST RD
LONDON RD
TWICKENHAM RD
SOUTH ST
RICHMOND RD
ST MARGARET'S RD
CHERTSEY RD
THE AVENUE
TWICKENHAM RD
KEW RD
LOWER MORTLAKE RD
SHEEN RD
PETERSHAM RD
HIGH ST
HALF ACRE
EALING RD
SYON LA
D7
1 GALBA CT
2 SERVIUS CT
3 MAURICE CT
4 LEO CT
5 OTHO CT
6 ROMULUS CT
7 PUMP ALLEY
F6
1 PRIMROSE HO
2 LAWMAN CT
3 ROYSTON CT
4 GARDEN CT
5 CAPEL LO
6 DEVONSHIRE CT
7 CELIA CT
8 ROSSLYN HO
9 BRANSTONE CT
10 LAMERTON LO
11 KEW LO
12 DUNRAVEN HO
13 STONELEIGH LO
14 TUNSTALL CT
15 VOLTAIRE
A4
1 Brewery Mews Bsns Ctr
2 FORGE LO
3 TOLSON HO
4 PERCY GDNS
5 WYNNE CT
6 WISDOM CT
7 SWANN CT
8 SHREWSBURY WLK
9 KING'S TERR
10 HOLME CT
11 THE PAVEMENT
D2
1 GARRICK CL
2 OLD PALACE YD
3 THE WARDROBE
4 MAIDS OF HONOUR ROW
5 HUNTERS CT
6 QUEENSBERRY HO
7 OLD PALACE TERR
8 PAVED CT
9 GOLDEN CT
10 BREWERS LA
11 THE SQUARE
12 LOWER GEORGE ST
13 ST JAMES'S COTTS
14 CHURCH WLK
15 CHURCH CT
16 GEORGE HO
17 VICTORIA PL
18 LION HO
19 CASTLE YD
20 LEWIS RD
21 WAKEFIELD RD
22 CHURCH TERR
23 WARRINGTON RD
24 ORMOND AVE
25 GLOVERS LO
26 HOLBROOKE PL
27 NORTHUMBERLAND PL
28 HERON SQ
29 WHITTAKER PL
30 WATER LANE HO
31 RIVERSIDE HO
32 ST HELENA TERR
33 QUEENSBERRY PL
E2
1 LICHFIELD TERR
2 UNION CT
3 CARRINGTON LO
4 WILTON CT
5 EGERTON CT
6 BEVERLEY LO
7 CREG MALIN
8 BISHOP DUPPA'S ALMSHOS
9 MICHELS ALMSHOS
10 SALCOMBE VILLAS
11 REGENCY WLK
12 CLEAR WATER HO
13 ONSLOW AVENUE MANS
14 ALBANY PAS
15 HOULBON ALMSHOS
E3
1 ST JOHN'S GR
2 MARSAULT CT
3 MICHEL'S ROW
4 MICHELSDALE DR
5 BENNS WLK
6 ROSEDALE HO
7 BLUE ANCHOR ALLEY
8 TADCASTER CT
9 CLARENCE ST
10 SUN ALLEY
11 THAMES LINK HO
12 NORTHUMBRIA CT
13 WATERLOO PL
F3
1 THE TOWERS
2 LONGS CT
3 SOVEREIGN CT
4 ACACIA CT
5 CHERRY TREE CT
6 Richmond Intnl Bsns Ctr
7 ROBINSON CT
8 CALVERT CT
9 BEDFORD CT
10 HICKEY'S ALMSHOS
11 CHURCH EST ALMSHOS
12 WALTON CT
A1
1 THE GREENWAYS
2 COLE PARK VIEW
3 LABURNUM CT
4 JOANNE CT
B1
1 THE GROVE
2 CUMBERLAND CL
3 WESTMORLAND CL
4 SUSSEX CL
5 NORFOLK CL
6 NICOL CL
7 OLD LODGE PL
8 KELVIN CT
9 ST MARGARET'S CT
10 PARK COTTS
11 St Margarets Bsns Ctr
12 AMYAND COTTS
C1
1 HOWMIC CT
2 SEFTON LODGE
3 RAVENSBOURNE HO
4 ARLINGTON CT
5 GEORGINA CT
6 TREVELYAN HO
7 CARADON CT
8 GREEN HEDGES
9 OLD HOUSE GDNS
10 QUEENS KEEP
11 BERESFORD CT
12 LANGHAM CT
13 POPLAR CT
14 GIBSON MEWS
5
D1
1 RICHMOND BRIDGE MANS
2 CLEVEDON MANS
3 BALMORAL MANS
4 RIVERVIEW MANS
5 HEATHERDENE MANS
6 NORTH CT
7 CAMBRIDGE CT
8 KENTON CT
9 LENNOX HO
17
10 LEICESTER CT
11 WYATT HO
12 TURNER HO
13 BLANCHARD HO
14 KEAN HO
15 MATCHAM CT
16 AROSA RD
17 SHARP HO
18 THORNE HO
19 CORNELIA HO
20 PELABON HO
21 ASHE HO
22 BEVAN CT
23 LAWLEY HO
24 DARLING HO
25 RICHMOND MANS
26 BEAULIEU CL
27 ROSELEIGH CL
28 MALLARD CT
E1
1 LANCASTER COTTS
2 LANCASTER MEWS
3 PRIORS LODGE
4 GLENMORE HO
5 GLENDALE HO
6 CAVENDISH CT
7 CARDIGAN CT
8 PALMERSTON CT
9 HEATHSHOTT
10 FRIARS STILE PL
11 SPIRE CT
12 RIDGEWAY
13 MATTHIAS CT
F1
1 CHESTER CL
2 GROSVENOR CT
3 QUEEN'S CT
4 RUSSELL WLK
5 CHARLOTTE SQ
6 JONES WLK
7 HILDITCH HO
8 ISABELLA CT
9 DICKSON HO
10 DAMER HO
11 ELIOT HO
12 FITZHERBERT HO
13 REYNOLDS PL
14 CHISHOLM RD
15 HOBART PL
F2
1 ALBERTA CT
2 BEATRICE RD
3 LORNE RD
4 YORK RD
5 CONNAUGHT RD
6 ALBANY TERR
7 KINGSWOOD CT
8 SELWYN CT
9 BROADHURST CL

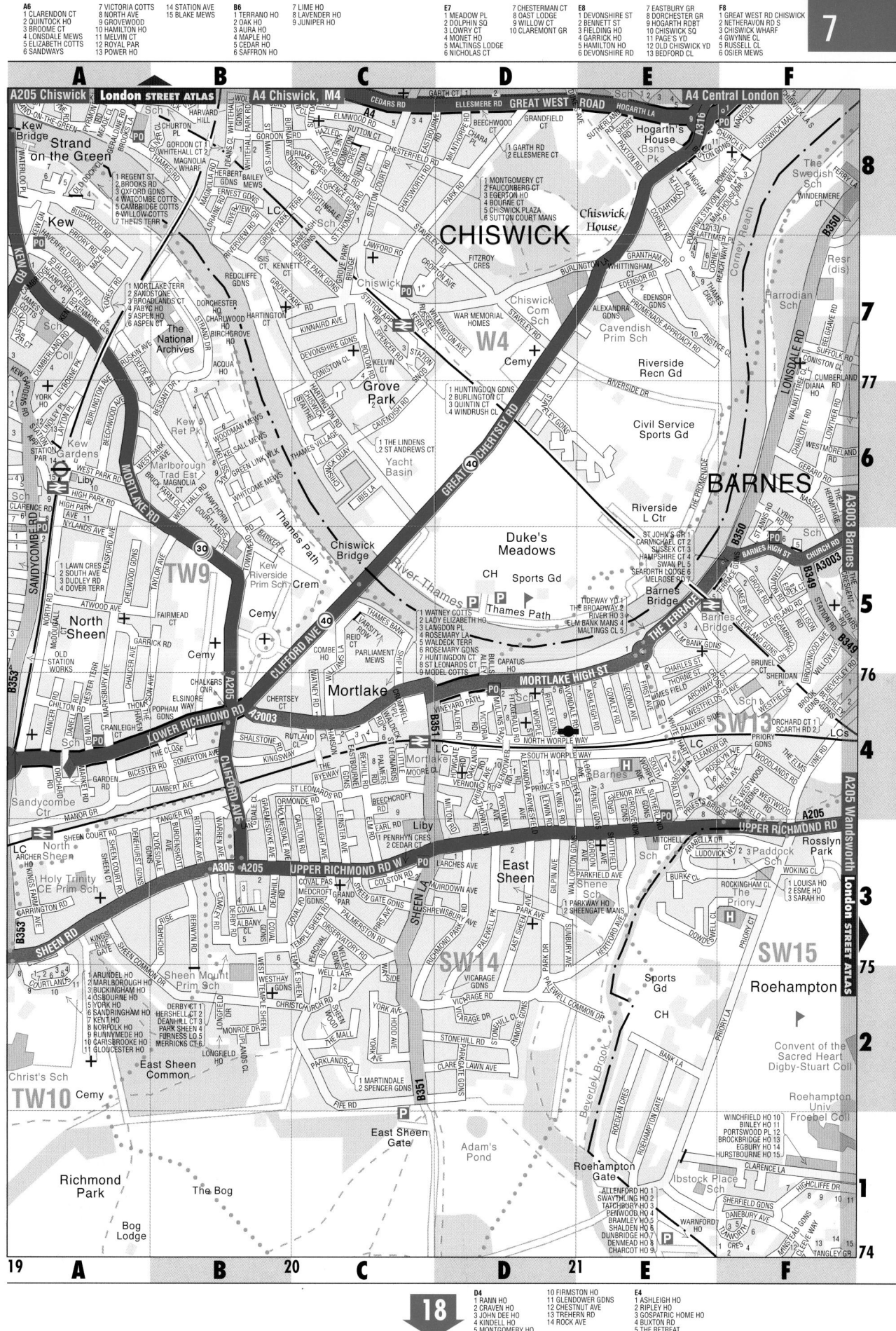

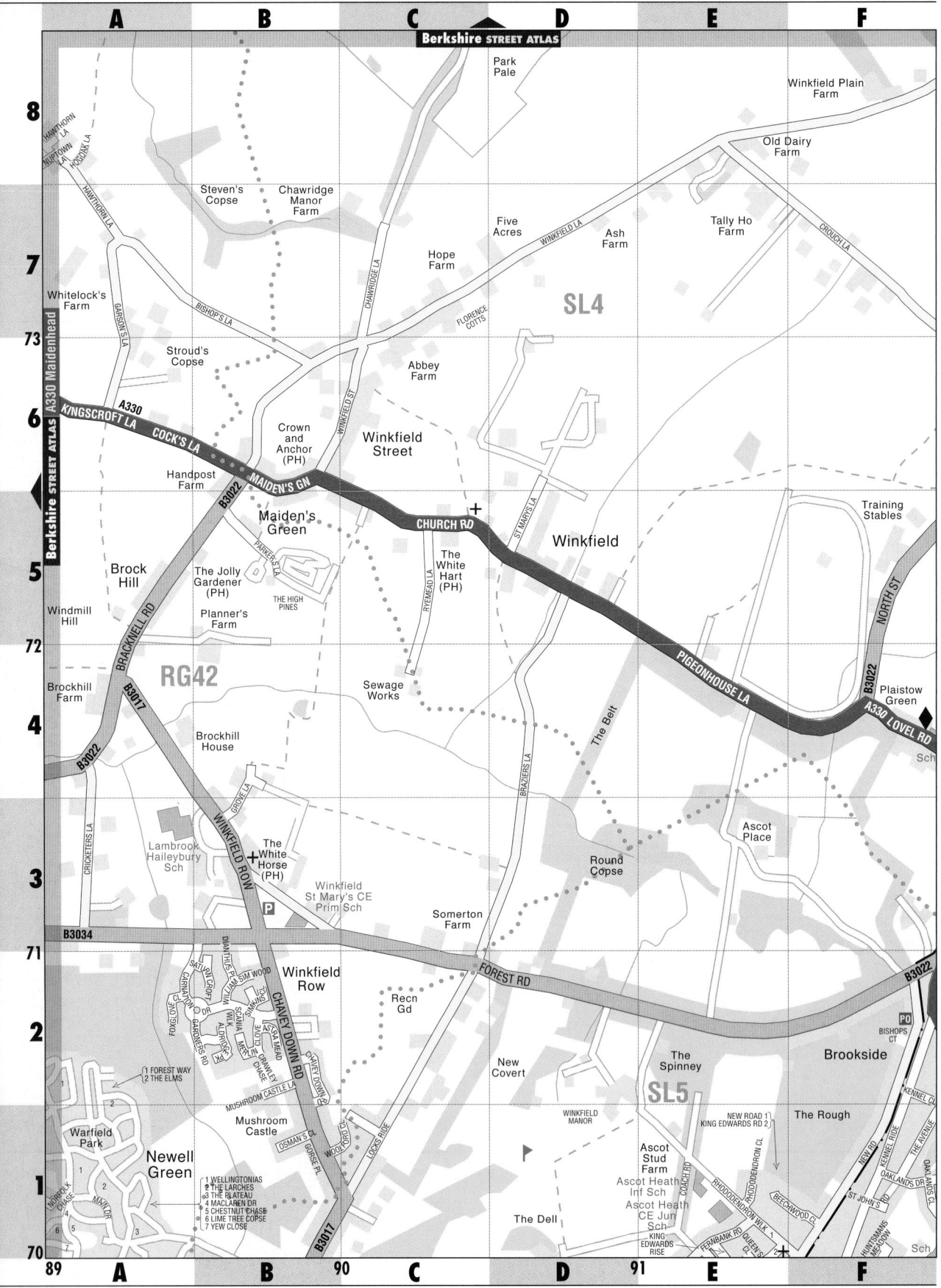

Berkshire STREET ATLAS
A330 Maidenhead
Park Pale
Winkfield Plain Farm
Old Dairy Farm
Steven's Copse
Chawridge Manor Farm
Five Acres
Ash Farm
Tally Ho Farm
Hope Farm
Whitelock's Farm
SL4
Stroud's Copse
Abbey Farm
Crown and Anchor (PH)
Winkfield Street
Handpost Farm
Maiden's Green
Winkfield
Training Stables
Brock Hill
The Jolly Gardener (PH)
The White Hart (PH)
Windmill Hill
Planner's Farm
THE HIGH PINES
RG42
Brockhill Farm
Sewage Works
Plaistow Green
Brockhill House
Lambrook Haileybury Sch
The White Horse (PH)
Winkfield St Mary's CE Prim Sch
Ascot Place
Round Copse
Somerton Farm
Winkfield Row
Recn Gd
New Covert
The Spinney
Brookside
SL5
Mushroom Castle
Warfield Park
Newell Green
WINKFIELD MANOR
Ascot Stud Farm
Ascot Heath Inf Sch
Ascot Heath CE Jun Sch
The Dell
The Rough
Sch
KINGSCROFT LA
COCK'S LA
MAIDEN'S GN
CHURCH RD
PIGEONHOUSE LA
A330 LOVEL RD
NORTH ST
B3022
B3017
B3034
FOREST RD
BRACKNELL RD
WINKFIELD ROW
CHAVEY DOWN RD
BRAZIERS LA
The Belt
WINKFIELD LA
CROUCH LA
BISHOP'S LA
GARSON'S LA
HAWTHORN LA
NUPTOWN LA
HOGOAK LA
CHAWRIDGE LA
WINKFIELD ST
FLORENCE COTTS
ST MARY'S LA
RYEMEAD LA
PARKER'S LA
GROVE LA
CRICKETERS LA
LOCKS RIDE
WOOLFORD CL
OSMAN'S CL
GORSE PL
MUSHROOM CASTLE LA
1 FOREST WAY
2 THE ELMS
1 WELLINGTONIAS
2 THE LARCHES
3 THE PLATEAU
4 MACLAREN DR
5 CHESTNUT CHASE
6 LIME TREE COPSE
7 YEW CLOSE
NEW ROAD 1
KING EDWARDS RD 2
RHODODENDRON CL
RHODODENDRON WLK
BEECHWOOD CL
COACH RD
FERNBANK RD
QUEEN'S CL
KING EDWARDS RISE
BISHOPS CT
KENNEL CL
KENNEL RIDE
NEW RD
THE AVENUE
OAKLANDS DR
OAKLANDS CL
ST JOHN'S RD
HUNTSMANS MEADOW
NORFOLK CHASE
MAYLOR
A B C D E F
8 7 6 5 4 3 2 1
73 72 71 70
89 90 91

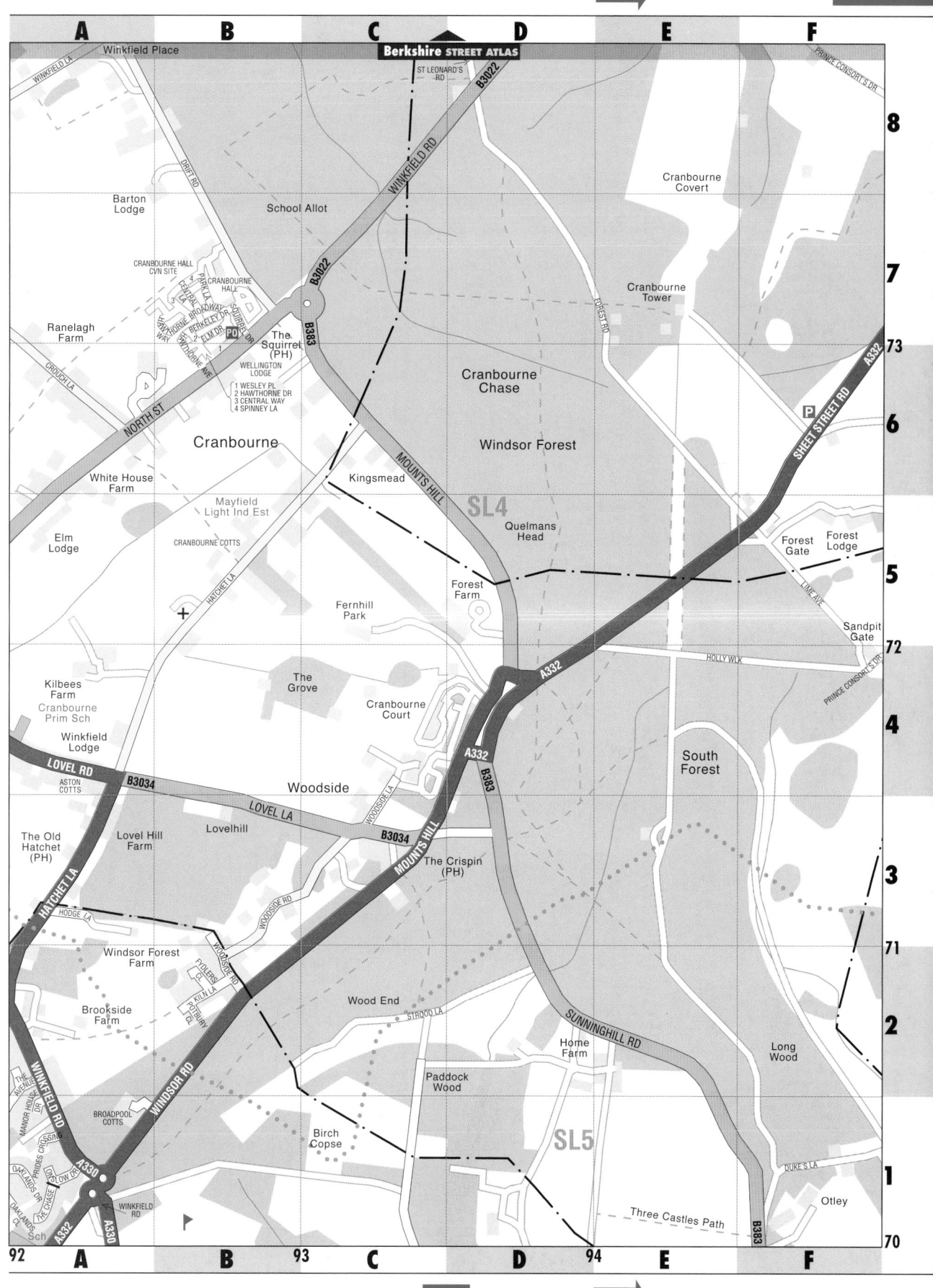
Berkshire STREET ATLAS
A
B
C
D
E
F
Winkfield Place
WINKFIELD LA
ST LEONARD'S RD
B3022
PRINCE CONSORT'S DR
DRIFT RD
WINKFIELD RD
Barton Lodge
School Allot
Cranbourne Covert
CRANBOURNE HALL CVN SITE
CRANBOURNE HALL
PARK LA
CENTRAL WAY
BROADWAY
BERKELEY DR
SQUIRES DR
ELM DR
HAWTHORNE WAY
HAWTHORNE AVE
Ranelagh Farm
The Squirrel (PH)
B383
FOREST RD
Cranbourne Tower
WELLINGTON LODGE
1 WESLEY PL
2 HAWTHORNE DR
3 CENTRAL WAY
4 SPINNEY LA
CROUCH LA
Cranbourne Chase
A332
NORTH ST
Cranbourne
Windsor Forest
SHEET STREET RD
White House Farm
Kingsmead
MOUNTS HILL
Mayfield Light Ind Est
SL4
Quelmans Head
Forest Gate
Forest Lodge
Elm Lodge
CRANBOURNE COTTS
HATCHET LA
Forest Farm
LIME AVE
Fernhill Park
Sandpit Gate
HOLLY WLK
The Grove
Kilbees Farm
Cranbourne Prim Sch
Cranbourne Court
PRINCE CONSORT'S DR
Winkfield Lodge
South Forest
LOVEL RD
ASTON COTTS
B3034
Woodside
LOVEL LA
WOODSIDE LA
The Old Hatchet (PH)
Lovel Hill Farm
Lovelhill
The Crispin (PH)
HATCHET LA
HODGE LA
WOODSIDE RD
Windsor Forest Farm
FYDLERS CL
KILN LA
POTBURY CL
Wood End
STROOD LA
Brookside Farm
SUNNINGHILL RD
Home Farm
Long Wood
Paddock Wood
THE AVENUE
MANOR HOUSE DR
WINKFIELD RD
WINDSOR RD
BROADPOOL COTTS
Birch Copse
SL5
PRIDES CROSSING
OAKLANDS DR
OAKLANDS CL
THE CHASE
ONSLOW DR
A330
DUKE'S LA
WINKFIELD RD
Otley
Three Castles Path
Sch
8
7
73
6
5
72
4
3
71
2
1
70
92
93
94

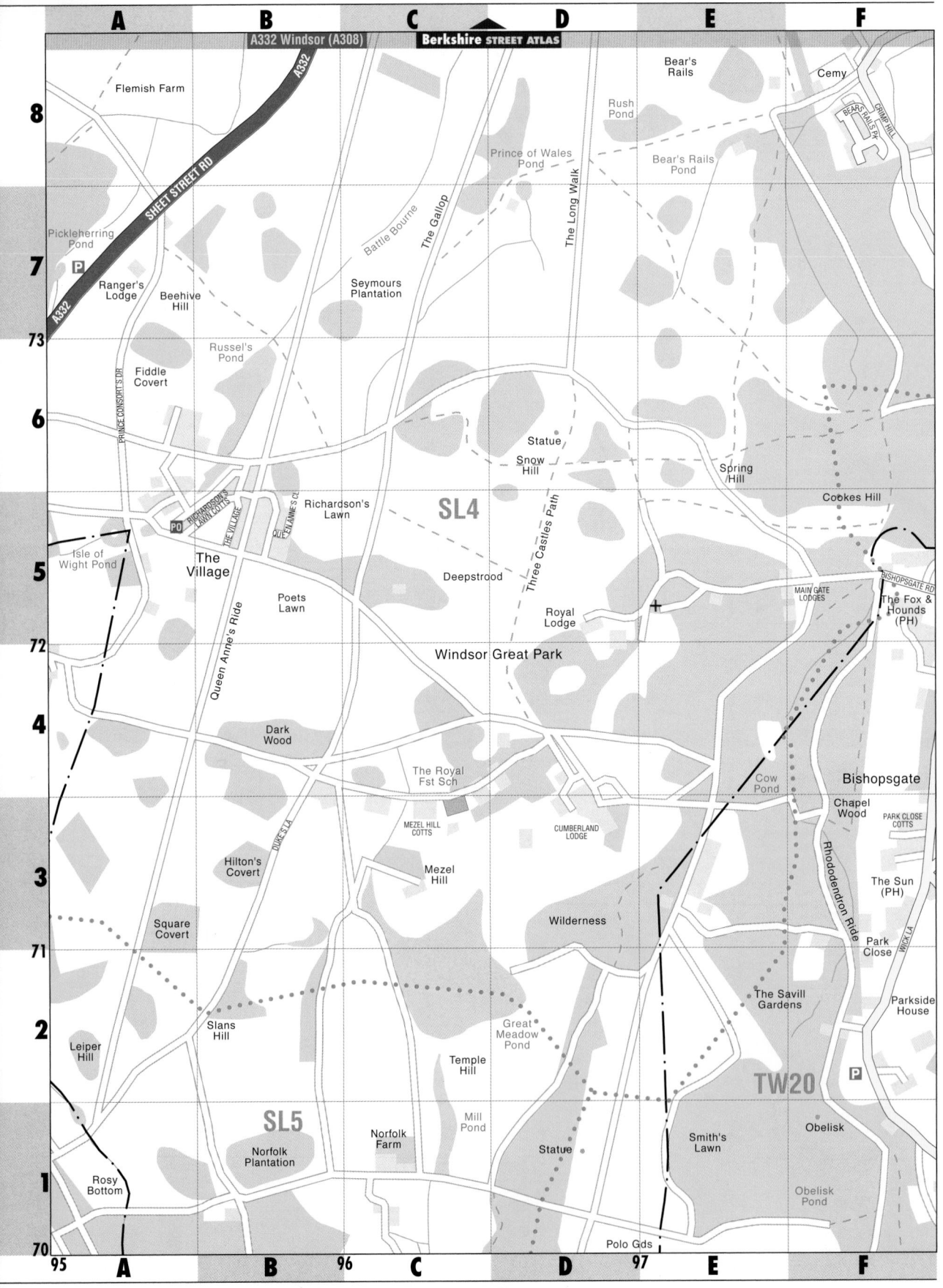

Berkshire STREET ATLAS

A332 Windsor (A308)

SHEET STREET RD

A332

Flemish Farm

Pickleherring Pond

P

Ranger's Lodge

Beehive Hill

Russel's Pond

PRINCE CONSORT'S DR

Fiddle Covert

Battle Bourne

The Gallop

Seymours Plantation

Prince of Wales Pond

The Long Walk

Rush Pond

Bear's Rails

Bear's Rails Pond

Cemy

BEAR'S RAILS PK

CRIMP HILL

Statue

Snow Hill

Spring Hill

Cookes Hill

RICHARDSON'S LAWN COTTS

THE VILLAGE

QUEEN ANNE'S CL

PO

Richardson's Lawn

SL4

Three Castles Path

MAIN GATE LODGES

BISHOPSGATE RD

Isle of Wight Pond

The Village

Poets Lawn

Deepstrood

Royal Lodge

The Fox & Hounds (PH)

Queen Anne's Ride

Windsor Great Park

Dark Wood

DUKE'S LA

The Royal Fst Sch

MEZEL HILL COTTS

Mezel Hill

Cumberland Lodge

CUMBERLAND LODGE

Wilderness

Cow Pond

Bishopsgate

Chapel Wood

PARK CLOSE COTTS

Rhododendron Ride

The Sun (PH)

Park Close

WICK LA

Hilton's Covert

Square Covert

Slans Hill

Leiper Hill

Temple Hill

Great Meadow Pond

The Savill Gardens

Parkside House

TW20

P

Rosy Bottom

SL5

Norfolk Plantation

Norfolk Farm

Mill Pond

Statue

Smith's Lawn

Obelisk

Obelisk Pond

Polo Gds

12

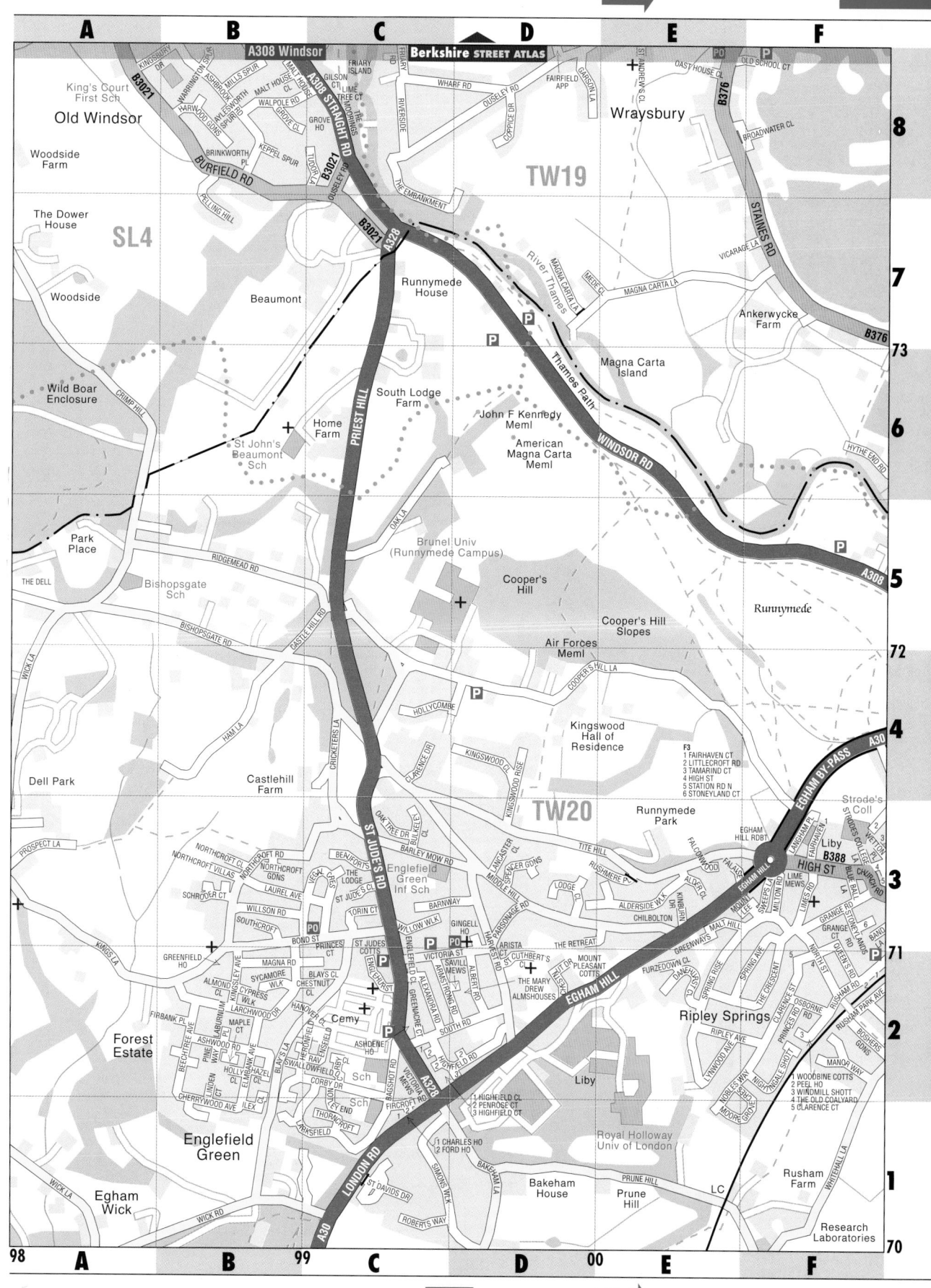

A
B
C
D
E
F
A308 Windsor
Berkshire STREET ATLAS
King's Court First Sch
Old Windsor
Woodside Farm
The Dower House
SL4
Woodside
Beaumont
Wild Boar Enclosure
St John's Beaumont Sch
Home Farm
Runnymede House
South Lodge Farm
John F Kennedy Meml
American Magna Carta Meml
Wraysbury
TW19
River Thames
Thames Path
Magna Carta Island
Ankerwycke Farm
WINDSOR RD
STAINES RD
PRIEST HILL
Park Place
Bishopsgate Sch
Brunel Univ (Runnymede Campus)
Cooper's Hill
Cooper's Hill Slopes
Air Forces Meml
Runnymede
Kingswood Hall of Residence
Dell Park
Castlehill Farm
TW20
Runnymede Park
Strode's Coll
EGHAM BY-PASS
HIGH ST
Liby
Englefield Green Inf Sch
ST JUDE'S RD
EGHAM HILL
Forest Estate
Cemy
Sch
Ripley Springs
Royal Holloway Univ of London
Englefield Green
Egham Wick
Bakeham House
Prune Hill
Rusham Farm
Research Laboratories
LONDON RD
F3
1 FAIRHAVEN CT
2 LITTLECROFT RD
3 TAMARIND CT
4 HIGH ST
5 STATION RD N
6 STONEYLAND CT
1 WOODBINE COTTS
2 PEEL HO
3 WINDMILL SHOTT
4 THE OLD COALYARD
5 CLARENCE CT
1 HIGHFIELD CL
2 PENROSE CT
3 HIGHFIELD CT
1 CHARLES HO
2 FORD HO
8
7
73
6
5
72
4
3
71
2
1
70
98
99
00

31

12

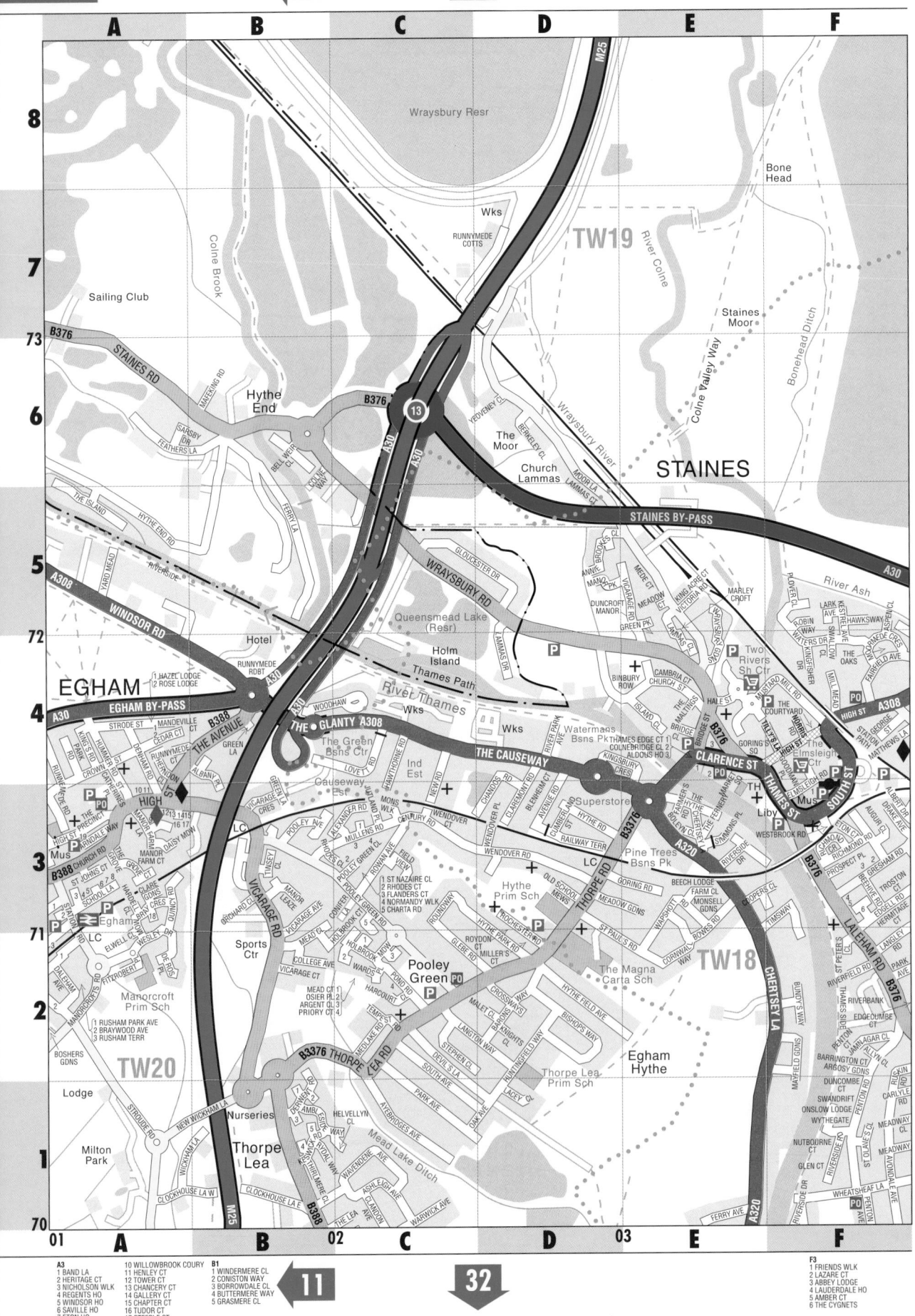

← 11

32

A3
1 BAND LA
2 HERITAGE CT
3 NICHOLSON WLK
4 REGENTS HO
5 WINDSOR HO
6 SAVILLE HO
7 ETON HO
8 ASCOT HO
9 MANOR FARM
10 WILLOWBROOK COURY
11 HENLEY CT
12 TOWER CT
13 CHANCERY CT
14 GALLERY CT
15 CHAPTER CT
16 TUDOR CT
17 STEEPLE CT
18 CADDY CL
19 TUDOR CT

B1
1 WINDERMERE CL
2 CONISTON WAY
3 BORROWDALE WAY
4 BUTTERMERE WAY
5 GRASMERE CL

F3
1 FRIENDS WLK
2 LAZARE CT
3 ABBEY LODGE
4 LAUDERDALE HO
5 AMBER CT
6 THE CYGNETS

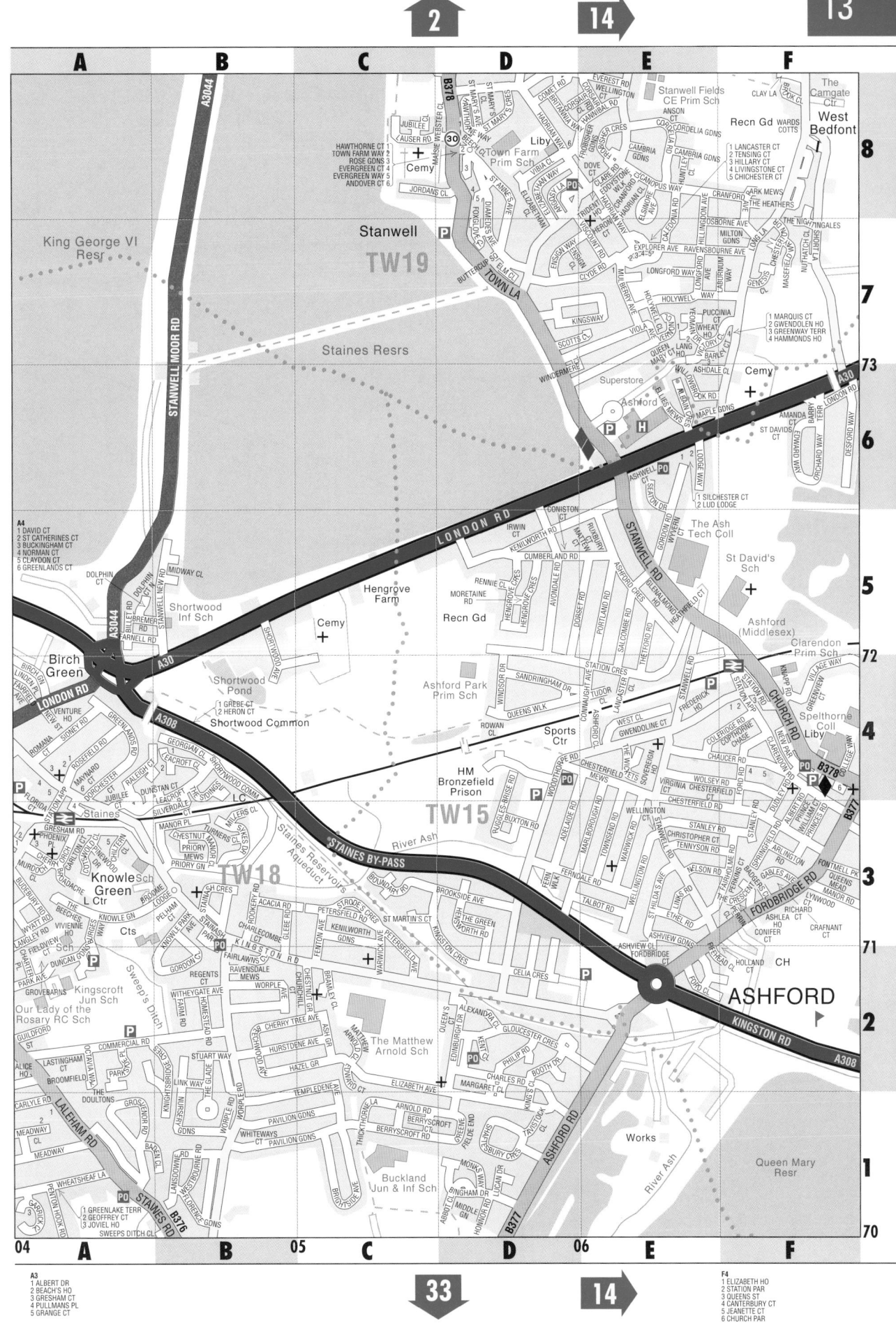

A3
1 ALBERT DR
2 BEACH'S HO
3 GRESHAM CT
4 PULLMANS PL
5 GRANGE CT

F4
1 ELIZABETH HO
2 STATION PAR
3 QUEENS ST
4 CANTERBURY CT
5 JEANETTE CT
6 CHURCH PAR

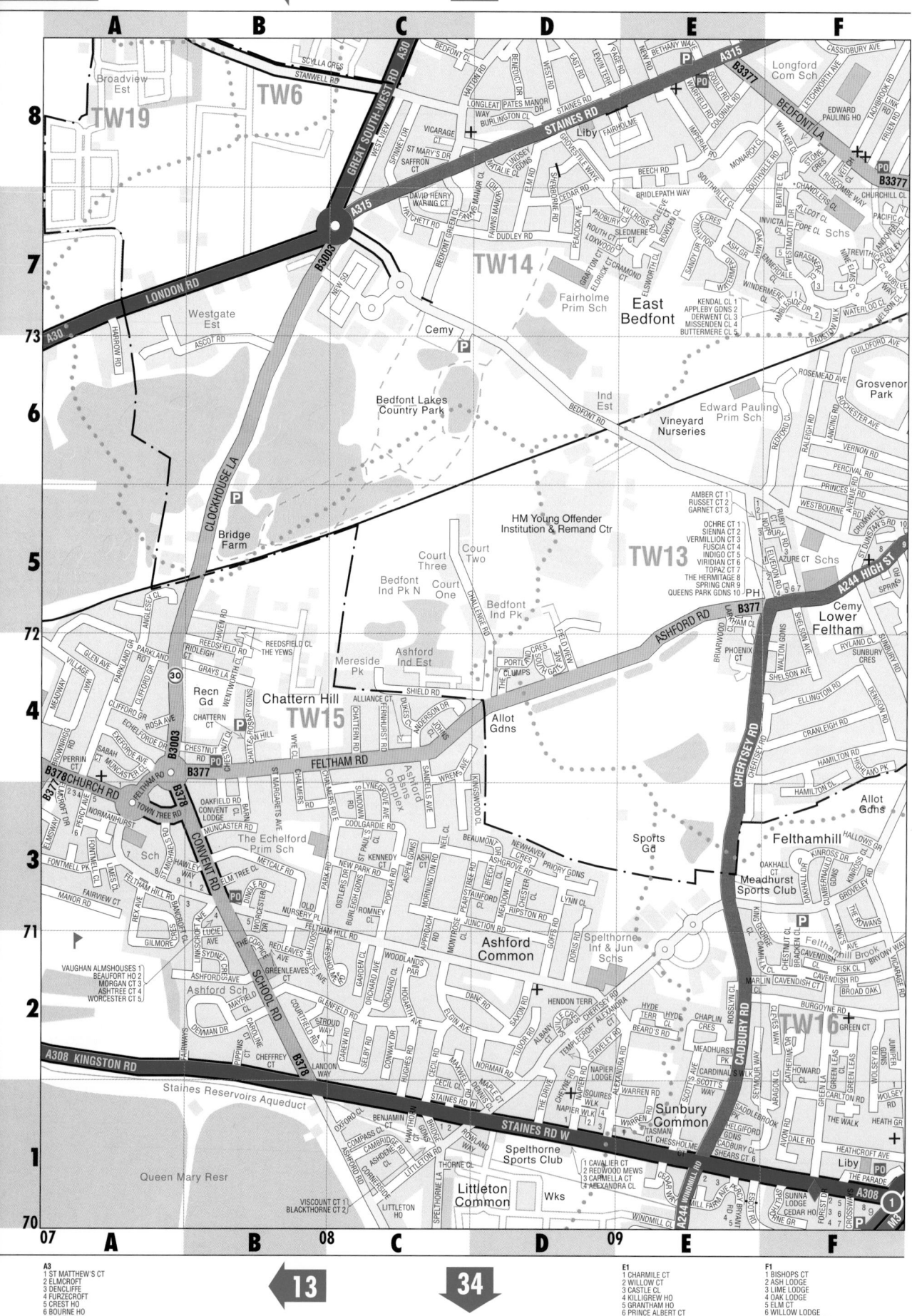

A3
1 ST MATTHEW'S CT
2 ELMCROFT
3 DENCLIFFE
4 FURZECROFT
5 CREST HO
6 BOURNE HO
7 THE ELMS
8 ROXETH CT
9 ROWLAND HILL ALMSHOUSES

E1
1 CHARMILE CT
2 WILLOW CT
3 CASTLE CL
4 KILLIGREW HO
5 GRANTHAM HO
6 PRINCE ALBERT CT

F1
1 BISHOPS CT
2 ASH LODGE
3 LIME LODGE
4 OAK LODGE
5 ELM CT
6 WILLOW LODGE
7 SYCAMORE LODGE
8 PRISCILLA HO
9 Sunbury Cross Ctr

4
16

F5
1 WHITELEY CT
2 BEL LA
3 BUTTS COTTS

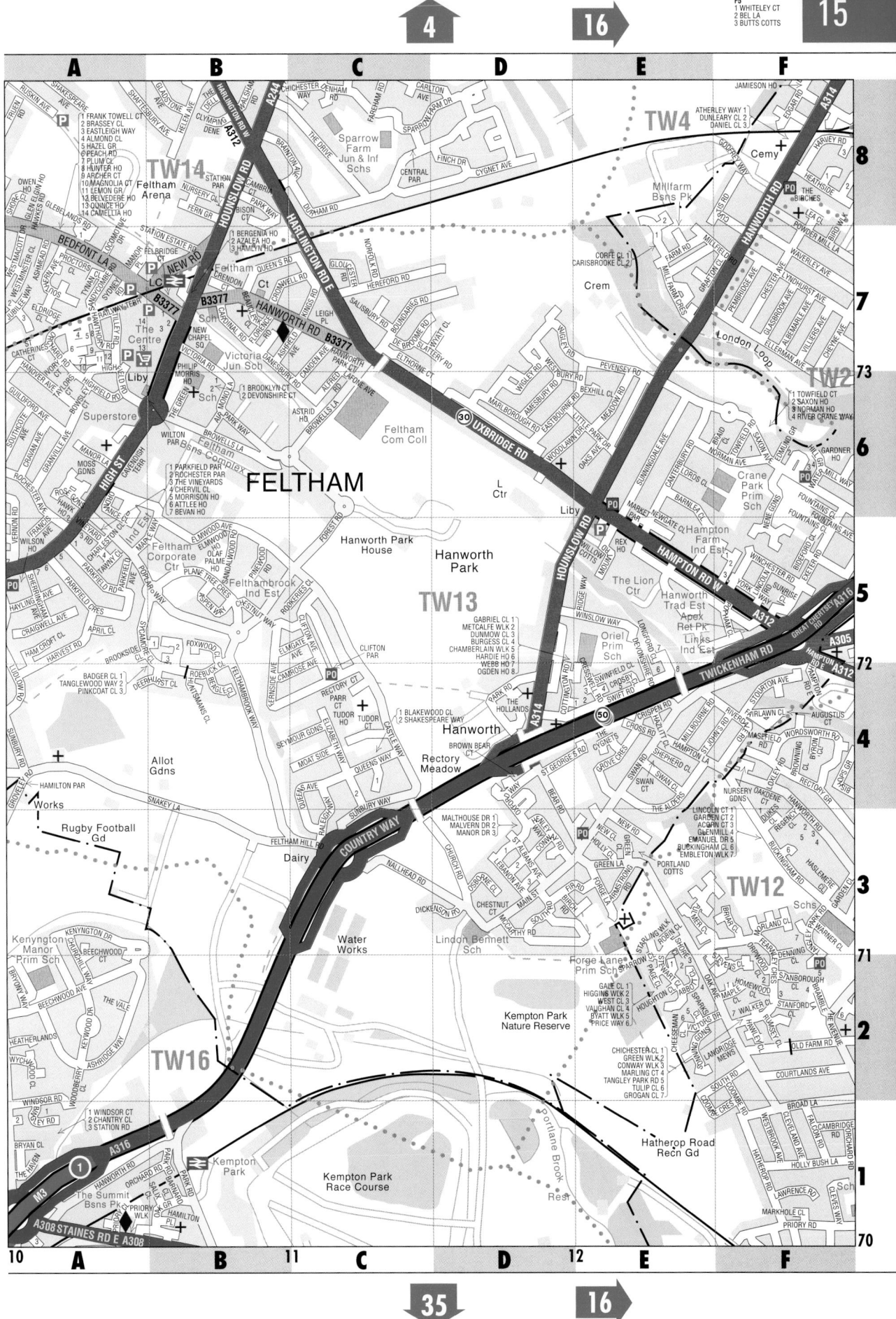

35
16

15
5

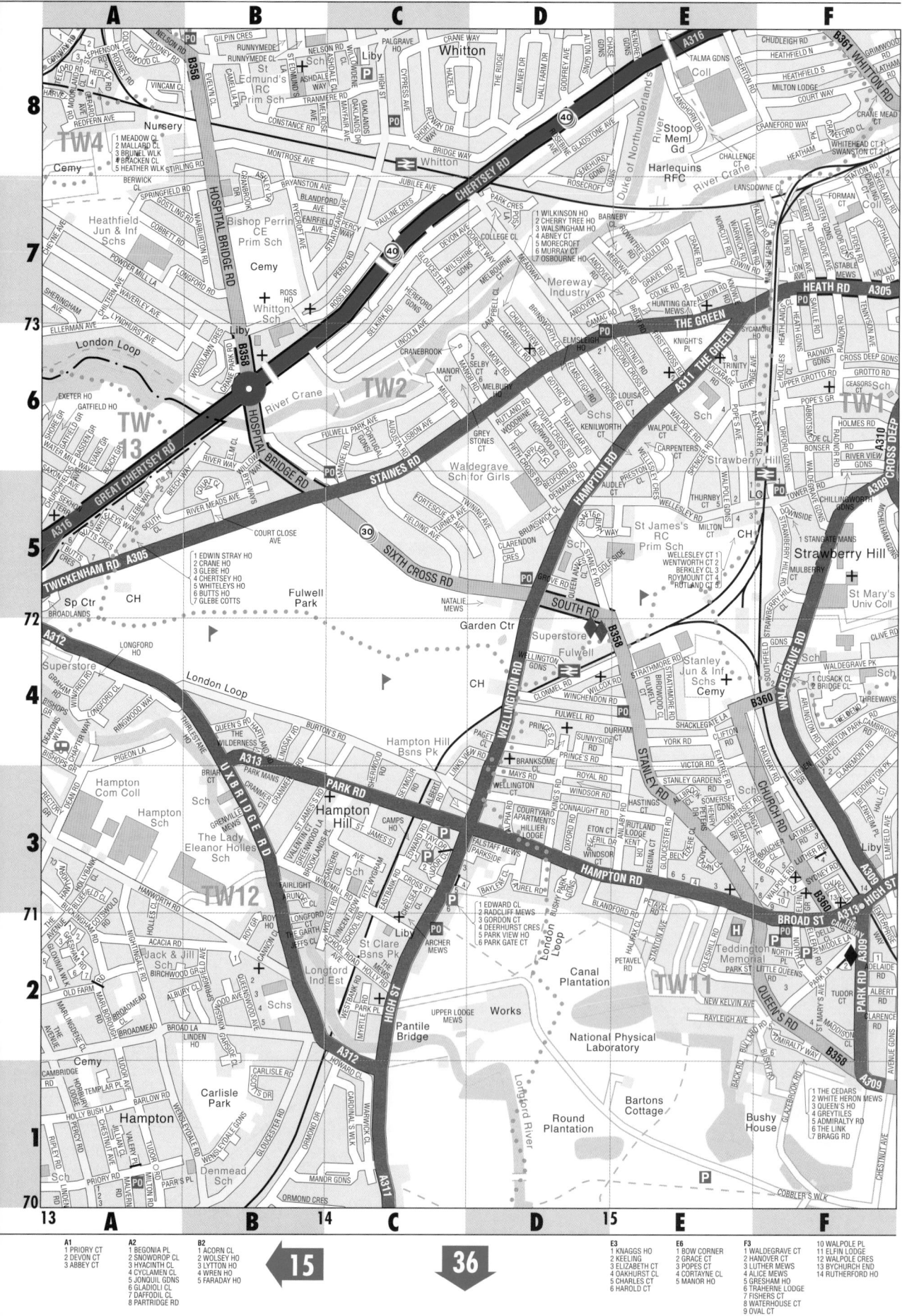

A1
1 PRIORY CT
2 DEVON CT
3 ABBEY CT

A2
1 BEGONIA PL
2 SNOWDROP CL
3 HYACINTH CL
4 CYCLAMEN CL
5 JONQUIL GDNS
6 GLADIOLI CL
7 DAFFODIL CL
8 PARTRIDGE RD

B2
1 ACORN CL
2 WOLSEY HO
3 LYTTON HO
4 WREN HO
5 FARADAY HO

15
36

E3
1 KNAGGS HO
2 KEELING
3 ELIZABETH CT
4 OAKHURST CL
5 CHARLES CT
6 HAROLD CT

E6
1 BOW CORNER
2 GRACE CT
3 POPES CT
4 CORTAYNE CL
5 MANOR HO

F3
1 WALDEGRAVE CT
2 HANOVER CT
3 LUTHER MEWS
4 ALICE MEWS
5 GRESHAM HO
6 TRAHERNE LODGE
7 FISHERS CT
8 WATERHOUSE CT
9 OVAL CT
10 WALPOLE PL
11 ELFIN LODGE
12 WALPOLE CRES
13 BYCHURCH END
14 RUTHERFORD HO

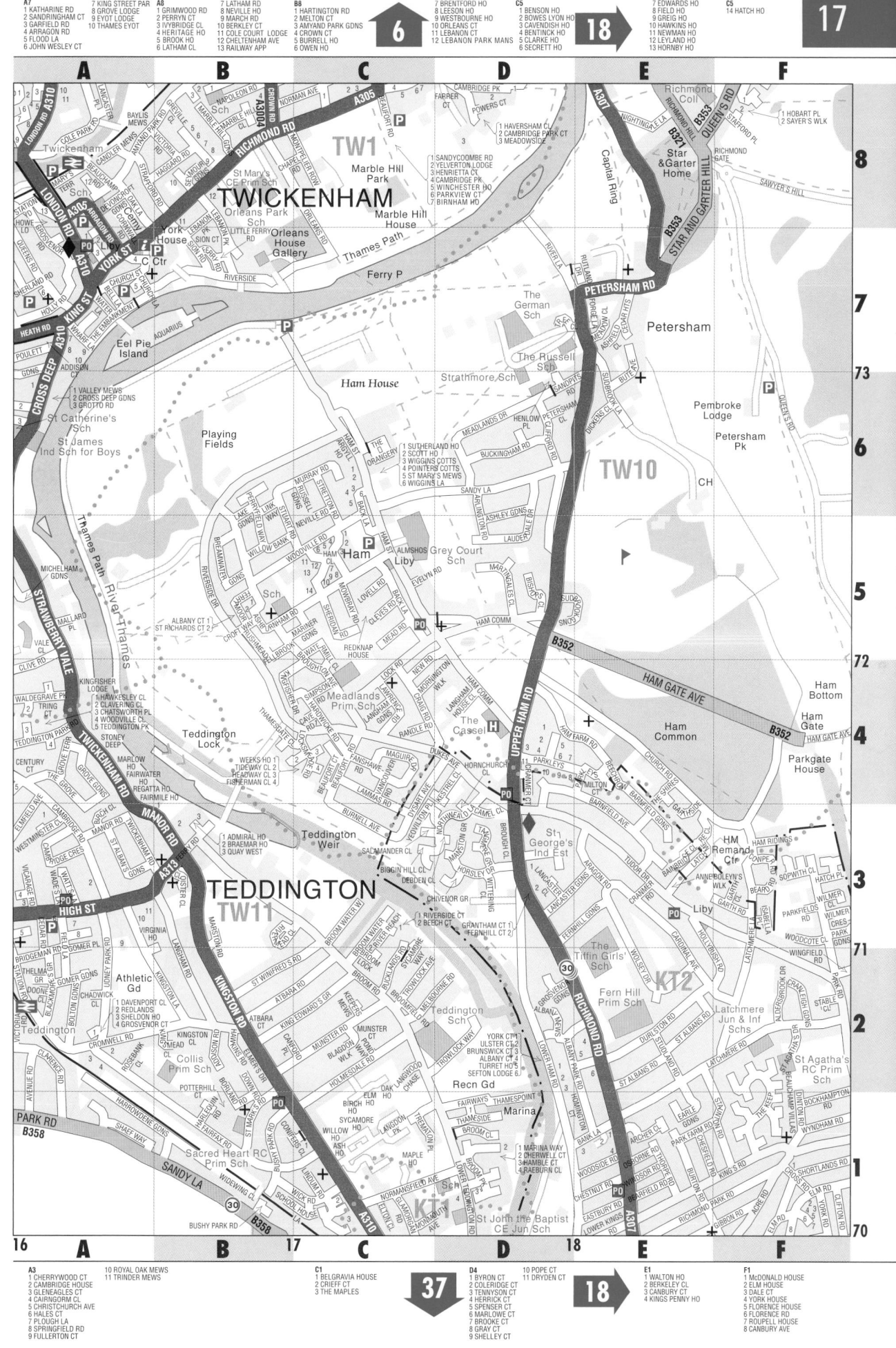
A7
1 KATHARINE RD
2 SANDRINGHAM CT
3 GARFIELD RD
4 ARRAGON RD
5 FLOOD LA
6 JOHN WESLEY CT
7 KING STREET PAR
8 GROVE LODGE
9 EYOT LODGE
10 THAMES EYOT
A8
1 GRIMWOOD RD
2 PERRYN CT
3 IVYBRIDGE CL
4 HERITAGE HO
5 BROOK HO
6 LATHAM CL
7 LATHAM RD
8 NEVILLE HO
9 MARCH RD
10 BERKLEY CT
11 COLE COURT LODGE
12 CHELTENHAM AVE
13 RAILWAY APP
B8
1 HARTINGTON RD
2 MELTON CT
3 AMYAND PARK GDNS
4 CROWN CT
5 BURRELL HO
6 OWEN HO
6
7 BRENTFORD HO
8 LEESON HO
9 WESTBOURNE HO
10 ORLEANS CT
11 LEBANON CT
12 LEBANON PARK MANS
C5
1 BENSON HO
2 BOWES LYON HO
3 CAVENDISH HO
4 BENTINCK HO
5 CLARKE HO
6 SECRETT HO
18
7 EDWARDS HO
8 FIELD HO
9 GREIG HO
10 HAWKINS HO
11 NEWMAN HO
12 LEYLAND HO
13 HORNBY HO
C5
14 HATCH HO
17
A
B
C
D
E
F
8
7
73
6
5
72
4
3
71
2
1
70
16
17
18
TWICKENHAM
TW1
Marble Hill Park
Marble Hill House
Orleans House Gallery
Eel Pie Island
Ham House
Petersham
TW10
Ham
Ham Common
TEDDINGTON
TW11
Teddington Lock
Teddington Weir
KT1
KT2
RICHMOND RD
UPPER HAM RD
KINGSTON RD
STRAWBERRY VALE
HAM GATE AVE
PETERSHAM RD
STAR AND GARTER HILL
A3
1 CHERRYWOOD CT
2 CAMBRIDGE HOUSE
3 GLENEAGLES CT
4 CAIRNGORM CL
5 CHRISTCHURCH AVE
6 HALES CT
7 PLOUGH LA
8 SPRINGFIELD RD
9 FULLERTON CT
10 ROYAL OAK MEWS
11 TRINDER MEWS
C1
1 BELGRAVIA HOUSE
2 CRIEFF CT
3 THE MAPLES
37
D4
1 BYRON CT
2 COLERIDGE CT
3 TENNYSON CT
4 HERRICK CT
5 SPENSER CT
6 MARLOWE CT
7 BROOKE CT
8 GRAY CT
9 SHELLEY CT
10 POPE CT
11 DRYDEN CT
18
E1
1 WALTON HO
2 BERKELEY CL
3 CANBURY CT
4 KINGS PENNY HO
F1
1 McDONALD HOUSE
2 ELM HOUSE
3 DALE CT
4 YORK HOUSE
5 FLORENCE HOUSE
6 FLORENCE RD
7 ROUPELL HOUSE
8 CANBURY AVE

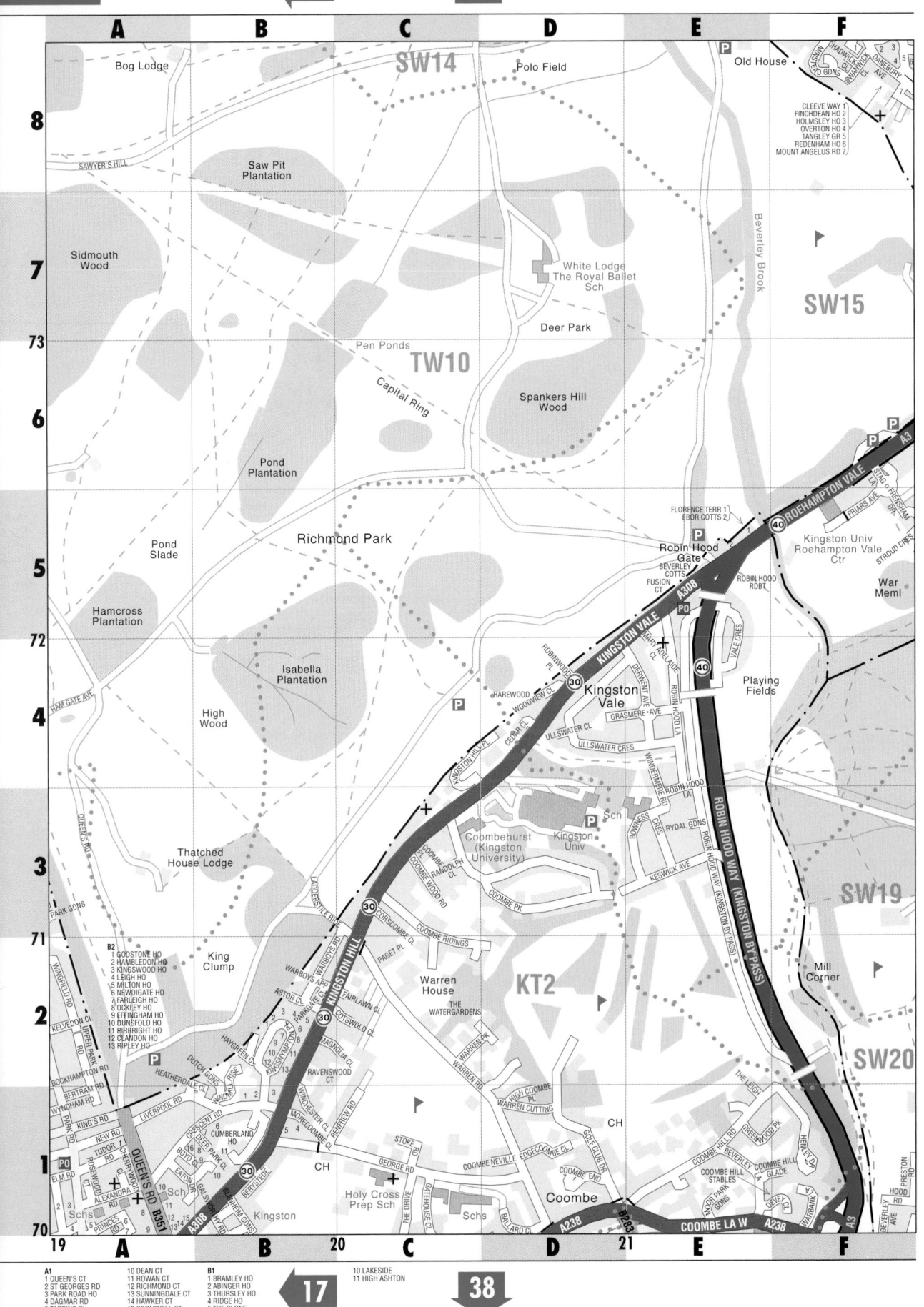

A **B** **C** **D** **E** **F**

8
7
73
6
5
72
4
3
71
2
1
70

Bog Lodge

SW14

Polo Field

Old House

CLEEVE WAY 1
FINCHDEAN HO 2
HOLMSLEY HO 3
OVERTON HO 4
TANGLEY GR 5
REDENHAM HO 6
MOUNT ANGELUS RD 7

SAWYER'S HILL

Saw Pit
Plantation

White Lodge
The Royal Ballet
Sch

Beverley Brook

Sidmouth
Wood

Deer Park

SW15

Pen Ponds

TW10

Capital Ring

Spankers Hill
Wood

Pond
Plantation

Richmond Park

ROEHAMPTON VALE

A3

40

Kingston Univ
Roehampton Vale
Ctr

FLORENCE TERR 1
EBDR COTTS 2

Pond
Slade

Robin Hood
Gate

War
Meml

Hamcross
Plantation

BEVERLEY
COTTS

FUSION
CT

A308

Robin Hood
RDBT

HAM GATE AVE

Isabella
Plantation

KINGSTON VALE

HAREWOOD

Kingston
Vale

Playing
Fields

High
Wood

P

30

WOODVIEW CL

CEDAR CL

ULLSWATER CL

ULLSWATER CRES

GRASMERE AVE

WINDERMERE CRES

ROBIN HOOD LA

40

VALE CRES

SW19

Thatched
House Lodge

QUEEN'S RD

PARK GDNS

30

Coombehurst
(Kingston
University)

Kingston
Univ

Sch

ROBIN HOOD WAY (KINGSTON BYPASS)

Mill
Corner

B2
1 GODSTONE HO
2 HAMBLEDON HO
3 KINGSWOOD HO
4 LEIGH HO
5 MILTON HO
6 NEWDIGATE HO
7 FARLEIGH HO
8 OCKLEY HO
9 EFFINGHAM HO
10 DUNSFOLD HO
11 RIPBRIGHT HO
12 CLANDON HO
13 RIPLEY HO

King
Clump

WARBOYS APP

WARBOYS RD

ASTOR CL

KINGSTON HILL

FAIRLAWN CL

COTSWOLD CL

CORSCOMBE CL

PAGET PL

COOMBE RIDINGS

Warren
House

THE
WATERGARDENS

KT2

WINGFIELD RD

KELVEDON CL

UPPER PARK

P

HAYGREEN CL

30

HEATHERDALE CL

DUTCH GDNS

MAGNOLIA CL

RAVENSWOOD
CT

WARREN PK

WARREN RD

SW20

BOCKHAMPTON RD

BERTRAM RD

WYNDHAM RD

PARK RD

LIVERPOOL RD

CRESCENT RD

CLIFF PARK CL

BOYD CL

WINCHESTER CL

MORECOOMBE CL

RENFREW RD

HIGH COOMBE
PL

WARREN CUTTING

CH

THE LEIGH

KING'S RD

NEW RD

TUDOR
DR

ROSEWOOD

CHERRYWOOD

GALSWORTHY RD

CUMBERLAND
HO

STOKE RD

GEORGE RD

THE DRIVE

COOMBE NEVILLE

EDGECOMBE CL

COOMBE END

COOMBE HILL RD

BEVERLEY

SHEENWOOD PK

COOMBE HILL
GLADE

P

ELM RD

ALEXANDRA

PRINCES RD

QUEEN'S RD

B351

A308

30

BERRYLANDS

Kingston

CH

Holy Cross
Prep Sch

Schs

GATEHOUSE CL

BALLARD RD

Coombe

A238

B283

GOLF CLUB DR

CH

MAJOR PK
GDNS

COOMBE HILL
STABLES

HENLEY'S

COOMBE LA W

A238

A3

Schs

Schs

A1
1 QUEEN'S CT
2 ST GEORGES RD
3 PARK ROAD HO
4 DAGMAR RD
5 TAPPING CL
6 ARTHUR RD
7 BOROUGH RD
8 BELVEDERE CT
9 BRAYWICK CT

10 DEAN CT
11 ROWAN CT
12 RICHMOND CT
13 SUNNINGDALE CT
14 HAWKER CT
15 CROMWELL CT
16 KINGS CT

B1
1 BRAMLEY HO
2 ABINGER HO
3 THURSLEY HO
4 RIDGE HO
5 THE CLONE
6 MOUNT CT
7 HILLSIDE CT
8 HILL CT
9 ROYAL CT

10 LAKESIDE
11 HIGH ASHTON

A8
1 WOODCOTT HO
2 LYNDHURST HO
3 WHEATLEY HO
4 NEPEAN ST
5 ALLBROOK HO
6 BORDON WLK
7 CHILCOMBE HO
8 VICARAGE CT
9 SHAWFORD CT
10 EASTLEIGH WLK
11 KINGS CT
12 SOMBORNE HO

20

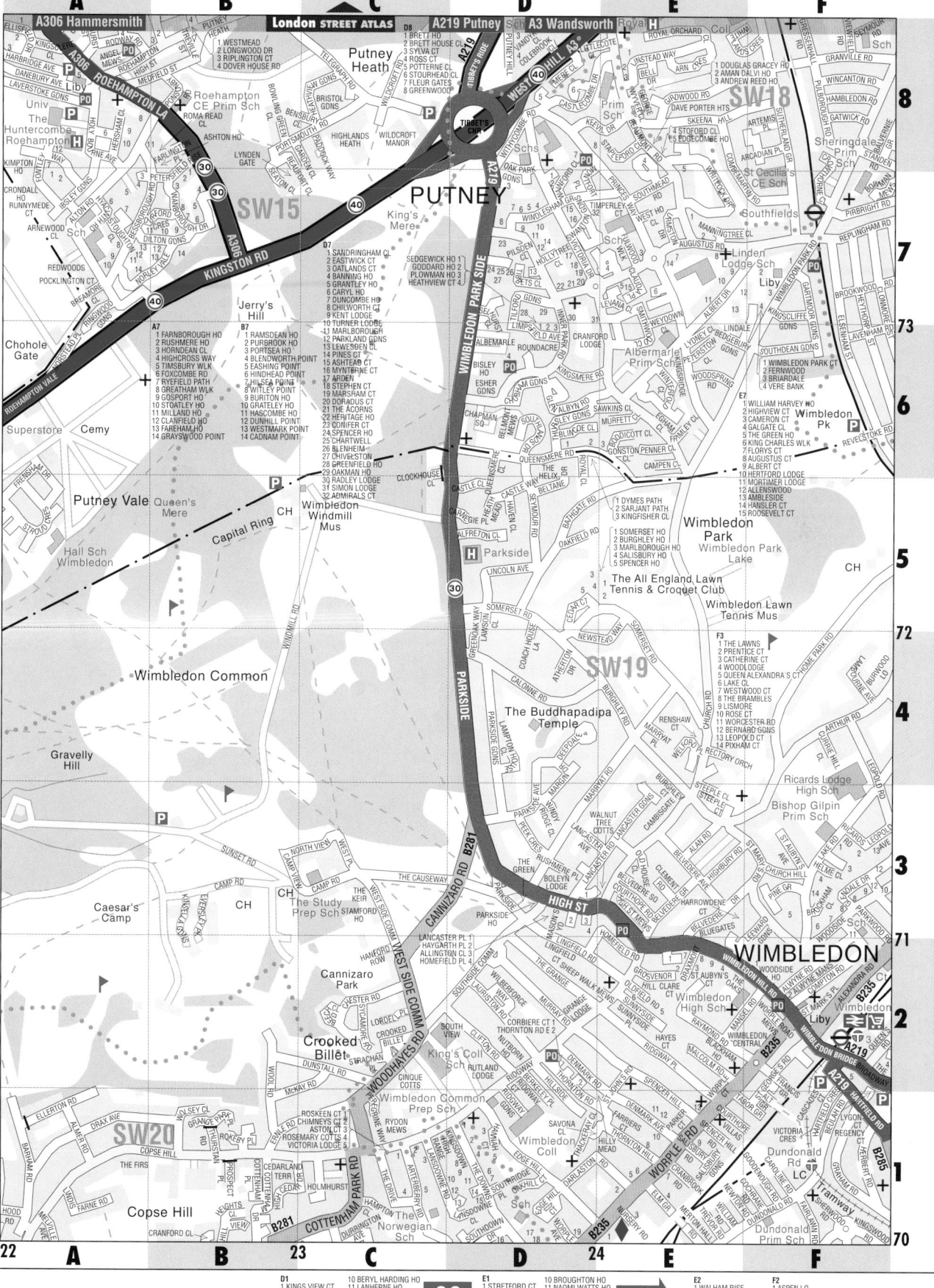

22 A B 23 C D 24 E F 70

D1
1 KINGS VIEW CT
2 WIMBLEDON CL
3 TINA CT
4 RATHBONE HO
5 BEAUMONT CT
6 GORDON CT
7 PRINCESS CT
8 UPTON CT
9 MARIAN LODGE
10 BERYL HARDING HO
11 LANHERNE HO
12 THE TERRACES
13 CUMBERLAND CL
14 THAXTED PL
15 PARKFIELD
16 CLAREMONT LODGE
17 DOWNS CT
18 RAVENSCAR LODGE
19 HAVERLEY

39

E1
1 STRETFORD CT
2 BRUNSWICK CT
3 PAVILION CT
4 LOUIE BLACK HO
5 WARWICK HO
6 ERICA HO
7 ADYAR CT
8 THORNTON LO
9 ASH CT
10 BROUGHTON HO
11 NAOMI WATTS HO
12 WELLESLEY HO
13 MAYFAIR CT

20

E2
1 WALHAM RISE
2 GROSVENOR CT
3 SOVEREIGN HO
4 HOLLY LODGE
5 FLORENCE CT
6 LINDEN COTTS
7 EMERSON CT
8 HILL CT
9 POWELL HO

F2
1 ASPEN LO
2 GLADEBURY CT
3 Centre Court Sh Ctr
4 BROADWAY CT
5 BROADWAY PL

19

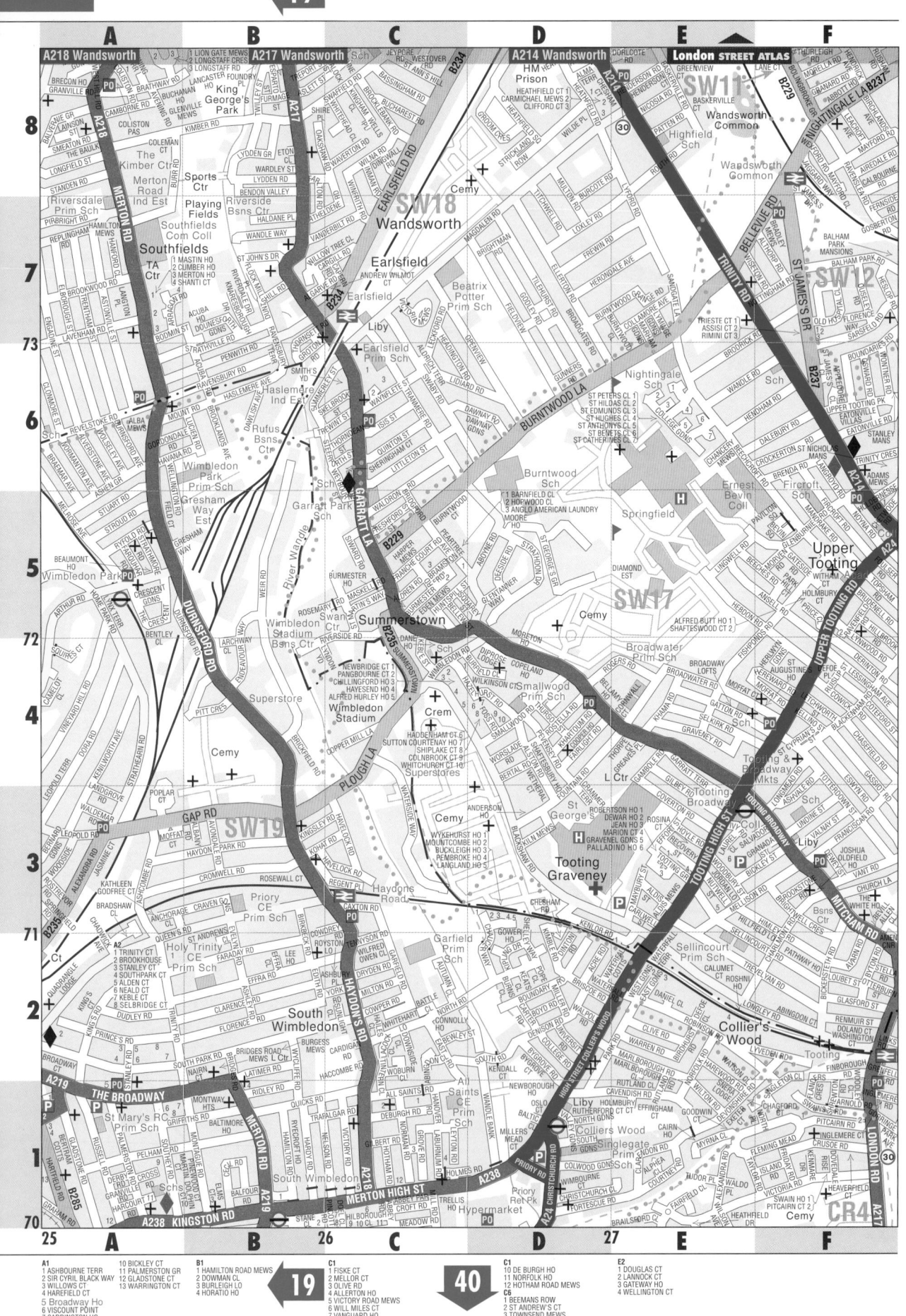

A1
1 ASHBOURNE TERR
2 SIR CYRIL BLACK WAY
3 WILLOWS CT
4 HAREFIELD CT
5 Broadway Ho
6 VISCOUNT POINT
7 CARRINGTON HO
8 CLOISTERS HO
9 DOWNING HO
10 BICKLEY CT
11 PALMERSTON GR
12 GLADSTONE CT
13 WARRINGTON CT

B1
1 HAMILTON ROAD MEWS
2 DOWMAN CL
3 BURLEIGH LO
4 HORATIO HO

C1
1 FISKE CT
2 MELLOR CT
3 OLIVE RD
4 ALLERTON HO
5 VICTORY ROAD MEWS
6 WILL MILES CT
7 VANGUARD HO
8 MYCHELL HO
9 MERTON PL
10 DE BURGH HO
11 NORFOLK HO
12 HOTHAM ROAD MEWS

C6
1 BEEMANS ROW
2 ST ANDREW'S CT
3 TOWNSEND MEWS

E2
1 DOUGLAS CT
2 LANNOCK CT
3 GATEWAY HO
4 WELLINGTON CT

19
40

22 →

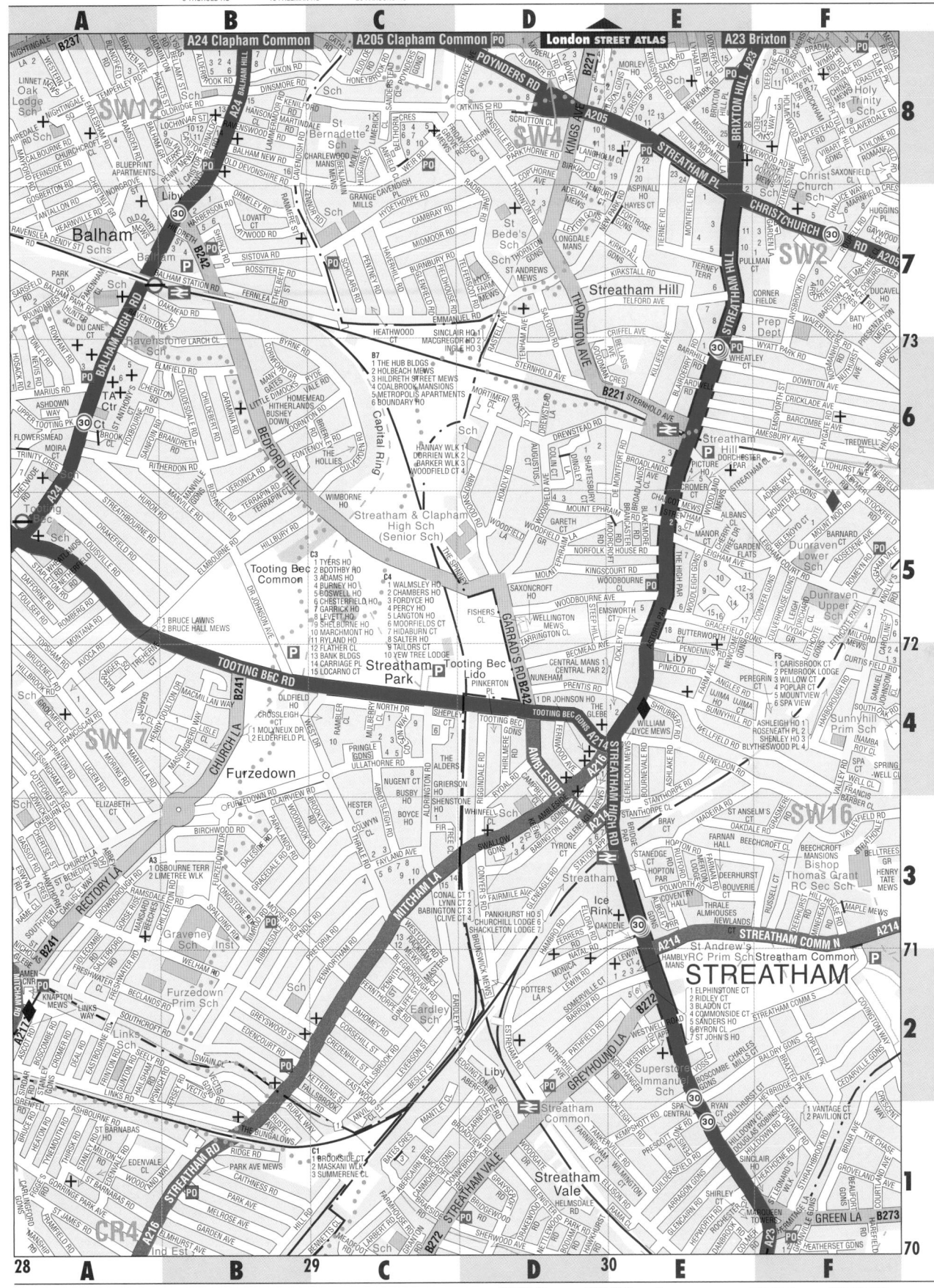

London Street Atlas

41

A3
1 BELLTREES GR
2 COLYTON LA
3 ASH CT
4 ALDER CT
5 BEECH CT
6 ACACIA CT

7 BLACKTHORN CT
8 CYPRESS CT
9 HAWTHORN CT
10 HAZEL HO
11 SYCAMORE CT
12 MAPLE CT
13 LABURNAM CT

14 FERN LODGE
A4
1 JAMES BOSWELL
2 ST ALBANS CT
3 SUFFOLK CT
4 ROCKHAMPTON CL
5 DELPHIAN CT

A7
1 VALENS HO
2 LOVEDAY HO
3 STRODE HO
4 ETHELWORTH CT
5 HARBIN HO
6 BROOKS HO

8 GODOLPHIN HO
9 SHEPPARD HO
10 MCCORMICK HO
11 TAYLOR HO
12 SAUNDERS HO
13 DERRICK HO

14 WILLIAMS HO
15 BALDWIN HO
16 JEMMA CL
17 CHURSTON CL
18 NEIL WATES CRES
19 BURNELL HO
20 PORTLAND HO

A8
1 ELLACOMBE HO
2 DEARMER HO
3 BRERETON HO
4 HOLDSWORTH HO
5 CHERRY CL
6 GREENLEAF CL

7 LANGTHORNE LODGE
8 CHARLES HALLER ST
9 BROCKWELL PARK ROW
10 LONGFORD WLK
11 CHANDLERS WAY
12 UPGROVE MANOR WAY
13 ROPERS WLK

14 TEBBS HO
15 BELL HO
16 WORTHINGTON HO
17 COURIER HO
18 MACKIE HO
19 HAMERS HO
20 KELYWAY HO

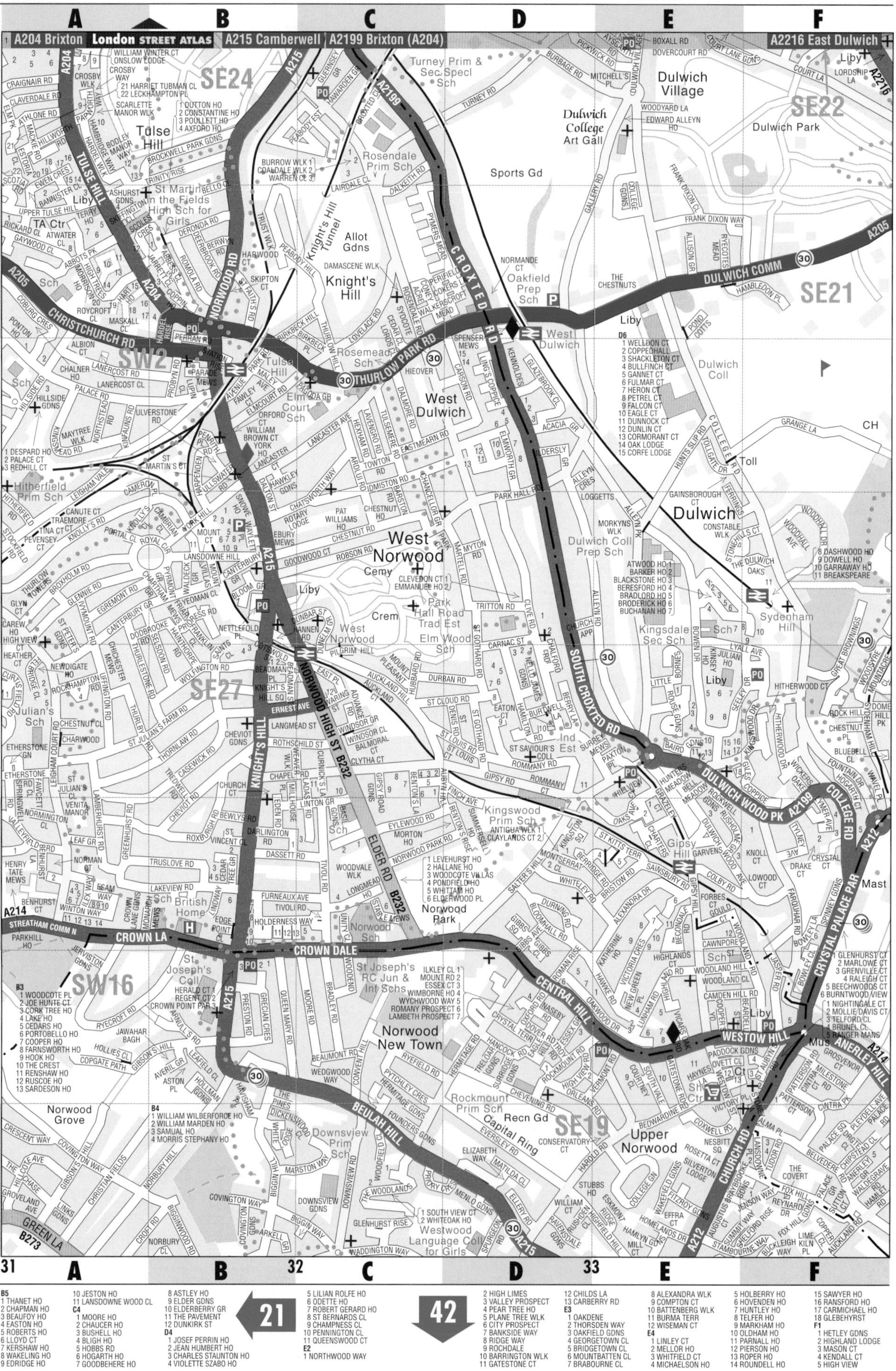

A204 Brixton London STREET ATLAS A215 Camberwell A2199 Brixton (A204)   A2216 East Dulwich

B5
1 THANET HO
2 CHAPMAN HO
3 BEAUFOY HO
4 EASTON HO
5 ROBERTS HO
6 LLOYD CT
7 KERSHAW HO
8 EDGSON HO
9 EDRIDGE HO

10 JESTON HO
11 LANSDOWNE WOOD CL
C4
1 MOORE HO
2 CHAUCER HO
3 BUSHELL CT
4 BLIGH HO
5 HOBBS RD
6 HOGARTH HO
7 GOODBEHERE HO

8 ASTLEY HO
9 ELDER GDNS
10 ELDERBERRY GR
11 THE PAVEMENT
12 DUNKIRK ST
D4
1 JOSEF PERRIN HO
2 JEAN HUMBERT HO
3 CHARLES STAUNTON HO
4 VIOLETTE SZABO HO

5 LILIAN ROLFE HO
6 ODETTE HO
7 ROBERT GERARD HO
8 ST BERNARDS CT
9 CHAMPNESS CL
10 PENNINGTON CL
11 QUEENSWOOD CL
E2
1 NORTHWOOD WAY

2 HIGH LIMES
3 VALLEY PROSPECT
4 PEAR TREE HO
5 PLANE TREE WLK
6 CITY PROSPECT
7 BANKSIDE WAY
8 RIDGE WAY
9 ROCHDALE
10 BARRINGTON WLK
11 GATESTONE CT

12 CHILDS LA
13 CARBERRY RD
E3
1 OAKDENE
2 THORSDEN WAY
3 GEORGETOWN CL
4 BRIDGETOWN CL
5 MOUNTBATTEN CL
6 BRABOURNE CL

8 ALEXANDRA WLK
9 COMPTON CT
10 BATTENBERG WLK
11 BURMA TERR
12 WISEMAN CT
E4
1 LINLEY CT
2 MELLOR HO
3 WHITFIELD CT
4 MICHAELSON HO

5 HOLBERRY HO
6 HOVENDEN HO
7 HUNTLEY HO
8 TELFER HO
9 MARKHAM HO
10 CHOLDERS WAY
11 PARNALL HO
12 PIERSON HO
13 ROPER HO
14 ROUNDELL HO

15 SAWYER HO
16 RANSFORD HO
17 CARMICHAEL HO
18 GLEBEHYRTON
F1
1 HETLEY GDNS
2 HIGHLAND LODGE
3 MASON CT
4 KENDALL CT
5 HIGH VIEW

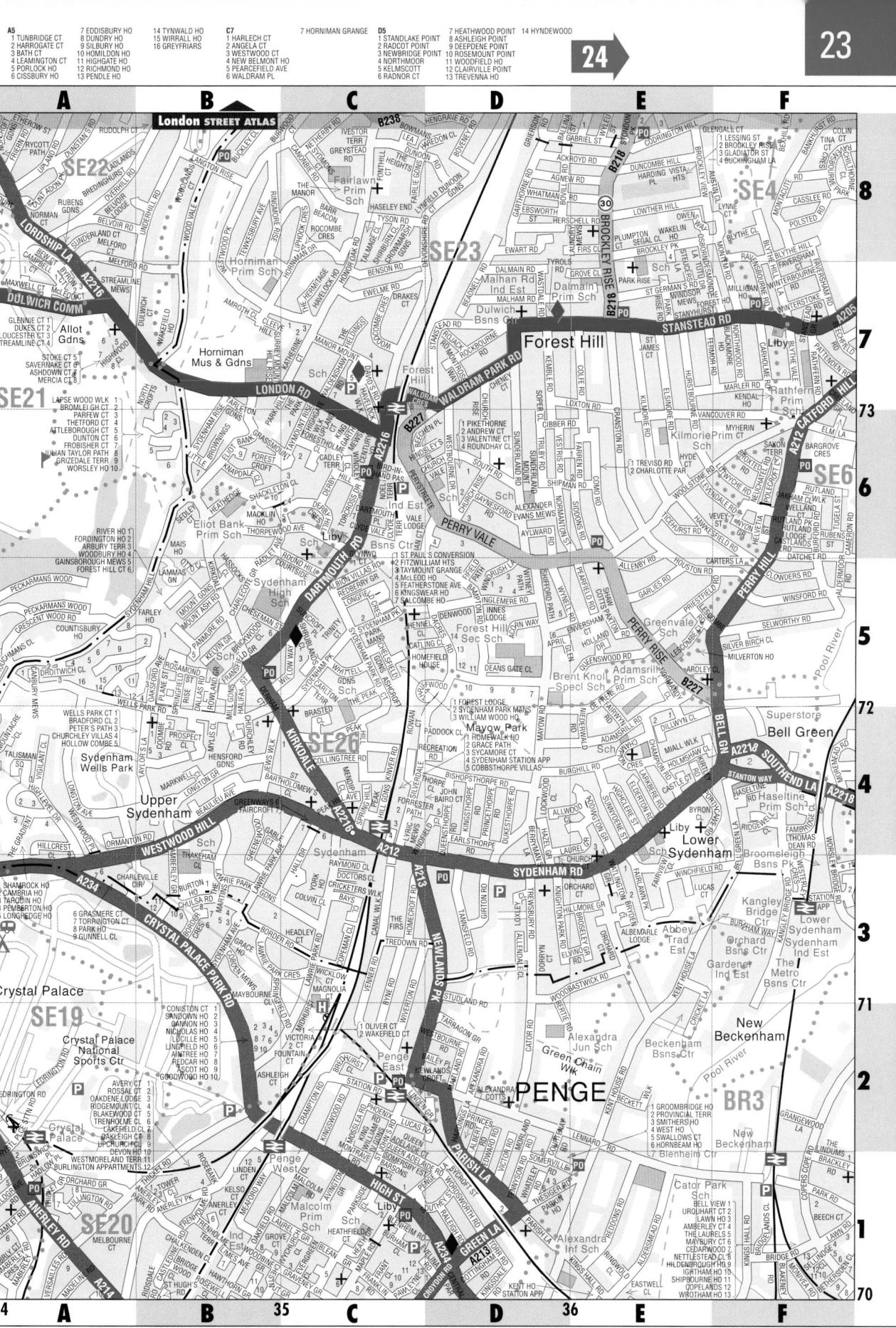

A5
1 TUNBRIDGE CT
2 HARROGATE CT
3 BATH CT
4 LEAMINGTON CT
5 PORLOCK HO
6 CISSBURY HO

7 EDDISBURY HO
8 DUNDRY HO
9 SILBURY HO
10 HOMILDON HO
11 HIGHGATE HO
12 RICHMOND HO
13 PENDLE HO

14 TYNWALD HO
15 WIRRALL HO
16 GREYFRIARS

C7
1 HARLECH CT
2 ANGELA CT
3 WESTWOOD CT
4 NEW BELMONT HO
5 PEARCEFIELD AVE
6 WALDRAM PL

7 HORNIMAN GRANGE

D5
1 STANDLAKE POINT
2 RADCOT POINT
3 NEWBRIDGE POINT
4 NORTHMOOR
5 KELMSCOTT
6 RADNOR CT

7 HEATHWOOD POINT
8 ASHLEIGH POINT
9 DEEPDENE POINT
10 ROSEMOUNT POINT
11 WOODFIELD HO
12 CLAIRVILLE POINT
13 TREVENNA

14 HYNDEWOOD

24 →

23

A1
1 HANOVER CT
2 BRUNSWICK CT
3 ANERLEY VALE
4 NEW CHURCH CT
5 MILLER HO
6 REGENCY CT
7 BARGROVE CL
8 BEAVER CL
9 BROOKLYN

10 OWEN WLK
B3
1 RAGWORT CT
2 THE FIRS
3 WINGHAM HO
4 SEATH HO
5 RIPLEY HO
6 LATHWOOD HO
7 HURST HO
8 GEORGE HO

9 BROWNE HO
10 BEACON HO
11 BAILEY HO
12 AGATE HO

C1
1 WATERMEN'S SQ
2 ST JOHN'S COTTS
3 SUSSEX TERR
4 MIDDLESEX CT
5 GLADSTONE MEWS
6 BETHESDA CT
7 UPTON CT
8 OSPRINGE CT
9 GOUDHURST HO

10 WALMER HO
11 STRODD HO
12 GREATSTONE HO
13 JOHN BAIRD HO

← 43

24 →

E3
1 FAIRLAWN CT
2 WATLINGTON COTTS
E4
1 PAXTON CT
2 KENTON CT
3 GROVE CT
4 SHIRLEY LODGE

F3
1 MEADOWVIEW RD
2 MONTANA GDNS

F4
1 ST MICHAELS CT
2 STANTON SQ
3 CORBETT CT
4 RIVERSIDE

24 ←23

B8
1 SILVERMERE RD
2 BROOKDALE RD
3 SCROOBY ST

D8
1 HOSPITAL WAY
2 HEATHER CL
3 HILLCREST CT
4 ATHLONE CT

E8
1 BEAUMONT TERR
2 LITTLEBOURNE
3 VERDANT CT

F8
1 KIMBOLTON CL
2 ANNE COMPTON MEWS
3 KENDALL HO

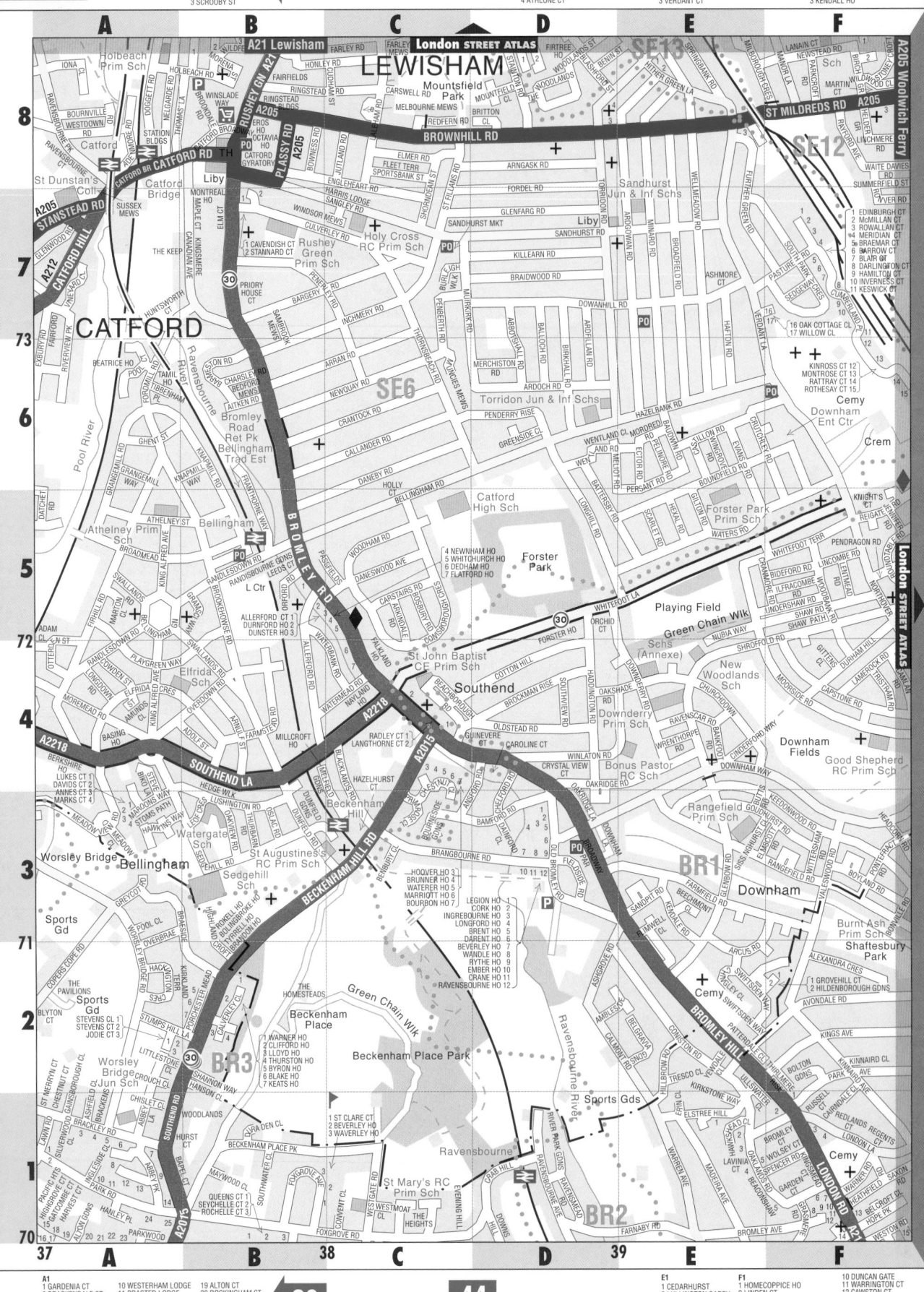

A1
1 GARDENIA CT
2 BRACKENDALE CT
3 DANIEL CT
4 MOLINER CT
5 CHARTWELL LODGE
6 RANDMORE CT
7 DOVER HO
8 LUCERNE CT
9 MALLING HO
10 WESTERHAM LODGE
11 BRASTED LODGE
12 MILTON HO
13 BRADSOLE HO
14 SANDGATE HO
15 ADELAIDE CT
16 NETTLESTEAD CL
17 COPERS COPE RD
18 WARREN CT
19 ALTON CT
20 ROCKINGHAM CT
21 CAMELLIA CT
22 SINCLAIR CT
23 REGENTS CT
24 MINSHULL PL
25 SOUTH PARK CT

E1
1 CEDARHURST
2 LULLINGTON GARTH
3 PINEWOOD
4 ST ANDREWS CT
5 PALISADE CT

F1
1 HOMECOPPICE HO
2 LINDEN CT
3 IVY HATCH CT
4 THE CAVENDISH APARTMENTS
5 INGLEWOOD CT
6 LEICESTER CT
7 MARLBOROUGH CT
8 MAVERY CT
9 GLEN CT
10 DUNCAN GATE
11 WARRINGTON CT
12 CAWSTON CT
13 PAMELA CT
14 HIGHLAND RD
15 MOORELAND CT

←23 44

26

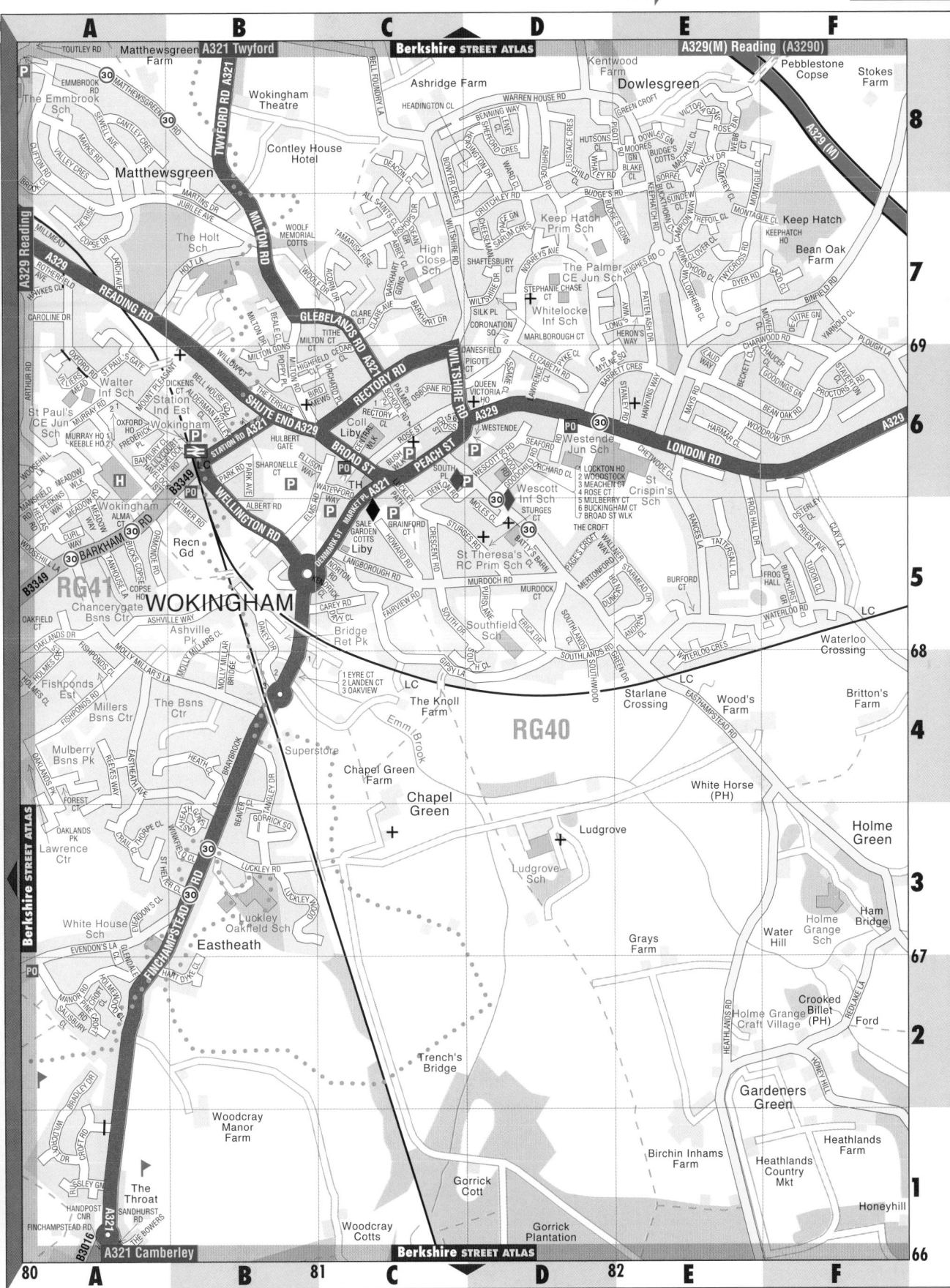

A
B
C
D
E
F
Berkshire STREET ATLAS
A321 Twyford
A329(M) Reading (A3290)
A329 Reading
A321 Camberley
Matthewsgreen Farm
Matthewsgreen
The Emmbrook Sch
Wokingham Theatre
Contley House Hotel
Ashridge Farm
Kentwood Farm
Dowlesgreen
Pebblestone Copse
Stokes Farm
Keep Hatch
Keep Hatch Prim Sch
Bean Oak Farm
The Holt Sch
High Close Sch
The Palmer CE Jun Sch
Whitelocke Inf Sch
Walter Inf Sch
St Paul's CE Jun Sch
Station Ind Est
Wokingham
Coll Liby
Westende Jun Sch
Wescott Inf Sch
St Crispin's Sch
St Theresa's RC Prim Sch
Recn Gd
WOKINGHAM
RG41
RG40
Chancerygate Bsns Ctr
Ashville Pk
Bridge Ret Pk
Southfield Sch
Waterloo Crossing
Starlane Crossing
Wood's Farm
Britton's Farm
Fishponds Est
Millers Bsns Ctr
The Bsns Ctr
Mulberry Bsns Pk
Superstore
The Knoll Farm
Chapel Green Farm
Chapel Green
Ludgrove
Ludgrove Sch
White Horse (PH)
Holme Green
Lawrence Ctr
Luckley Oakfield Sch
Eastheath
White House Sch
Grays Farm
Water Hill
Holme Grange Sch
Ham Bridge
Holme Grange Craft Village
Crooked Billet (PH)
Ford
Trench's Bridge
Gardeners Green
Woodcray Manor Farm
Birchin Inhams Farm
Heathlands Farm
Heathlands Country Mkt
The Throat
Gorrick Cott
Honeyhill
Woodcray Cotts
Gorrick Plantation
READING RD
MILTON RD
TWYFORD RD
GLEBELANDS RD
RECTORY RD
WILTSHIRE RD
SHUTE END
BROAD ST
PEACH ST
LONDON RD
WELLINGTON RD
BARKHAM RD
FINCHAMPSTEAD RD
DENMARK ST
MARKET PL
1 EYRE CT
2 LANDEN CT
3 OAKVIEW
1 LOCKTON HO
2 WOODSTOCK
3 MEACHEN CT
4 ROSE CT
5 MULBERRY CT
6 BUCKINGHAM CT
7 BROAD ST WLK
80
81
82
66
67
68
69
1
2
3
4
5
6
7
8

26

25

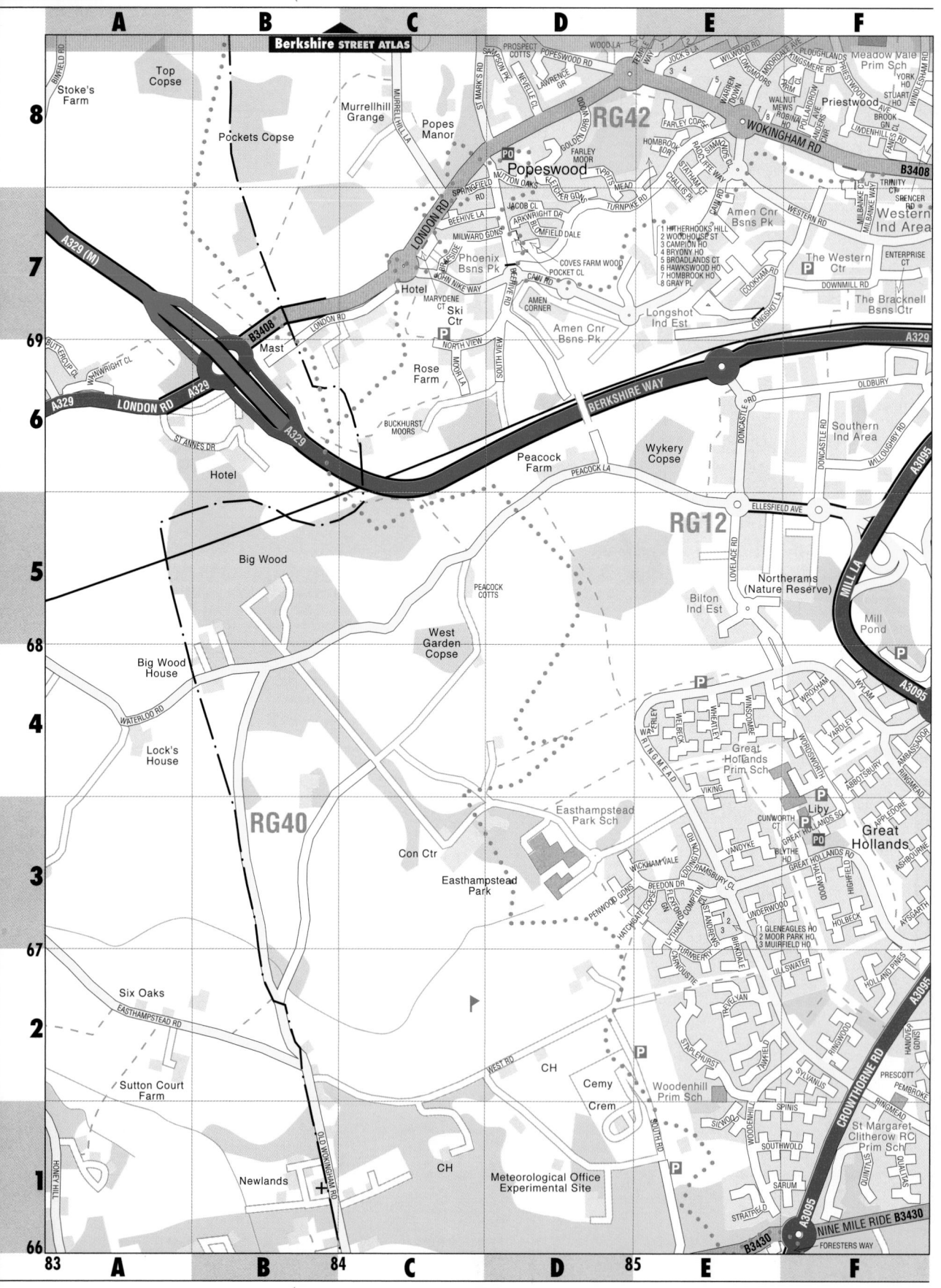
Berkshire STREET ATLAS
A
B
C
D
E
F
8
7
69
6
5
68
4
3
67
2
1
66
83
84
85
Stoke's Farm
Top Copse
Pockets Copse
Murrellhill Grange
Popes Manor
Popeswood
RG42
Priestwood
Meadow Vale Prim Sch
Western Ind Area
Amen Cnr Bsns Pk
The Western Ctr
The Bracknell Bsns Ctr
Phoenix Bsns Pk
Hotel
Ski Ctr
Longshot Ind Est
Amen Cnr Bsns Pk
Mast
Rose Farm
A329 (M)
A329
B3408
LONDON RD
BERKSHIRE WAY
WOKINGHAM RD
WESTERN RD
DOWNMILL RD
PEACOCK LA
ELLESFIELD AVE
Southern Ind Area
Wykery Copse
Peacock Farm
RG12
Big Wood
Northerams (Nature Reserve)
Bilton Ind Est
Mill Pond
MILL LA
A3095
West Garden Copse
Big Wood House
WATERLOO RD
Lock's House
Great Hollands Prim Sch
Liby
Great Hollands
Easthampstead Park Sch
RG40
Con Ctr
Easthampstead Park
Six Oaks
EASTHAMPSTEAD RD
WEST RD
CH
Cemy
Crem
Woodenhill Prim Sch
Sutton Court Farm
CROWTHORNE RD
St Margaret Clitherow RC Prim Sch
Newlands
OLD WOKINGHAM RD
Meteorological Office Experimental Site
NINE MILE RIDE B3430
B3430
FORESTERS WAY
SOUTH RD
HONEY HILL
1 HITHERHOOKS HILL
2 WOODHOUSE ST
3 CAMPION HO
4 BRYONY HO
5 BROADLANDS CT
6 HAWKSWOOD HO
7 HOMBROOK HO
8 GRAY PL
1 GLENEAGLES HO
2 MOOR PARK HO
3 MUIRFIELD HO

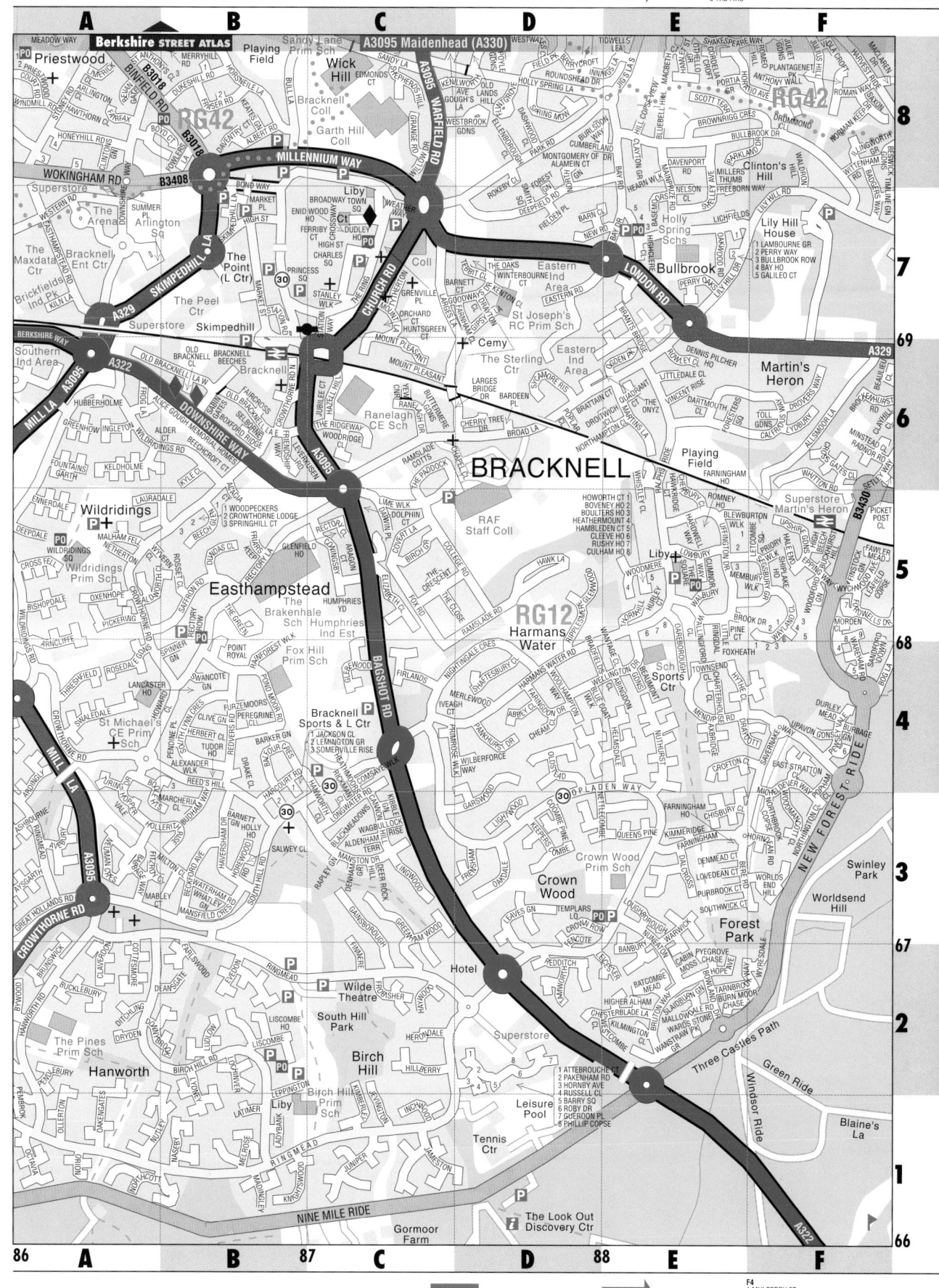

A8
1 PRIESTWOOD SQ
2 SALTIRE GDNS
3 WINDLEBROOK GN
4 APPLETREE PL
5 PORTMAN CL

B8
1 BIRCHETTS CL
2 ASHRIDGE CL
3 GORDON CLIFFORD CT

28

F5
1 THE WILLOWS
2 CEDARS
3 MAPEL CT
4 GREENWOOD
5 LARCHWOOD
6 THE FIRS
7 CHARLBURY CL
8 HOLTON HEATH
9 BLOXWORTH CL

27

F4
1 MULBERRY CT
2 ROWAN
3 LINDEN
4 LYTCHET MINSTER CL
5 STOKEFORD CL
6 FROXFIELD DOWN

27
8

F8
1 HANOVER PK
2 GATCOMBE CRES

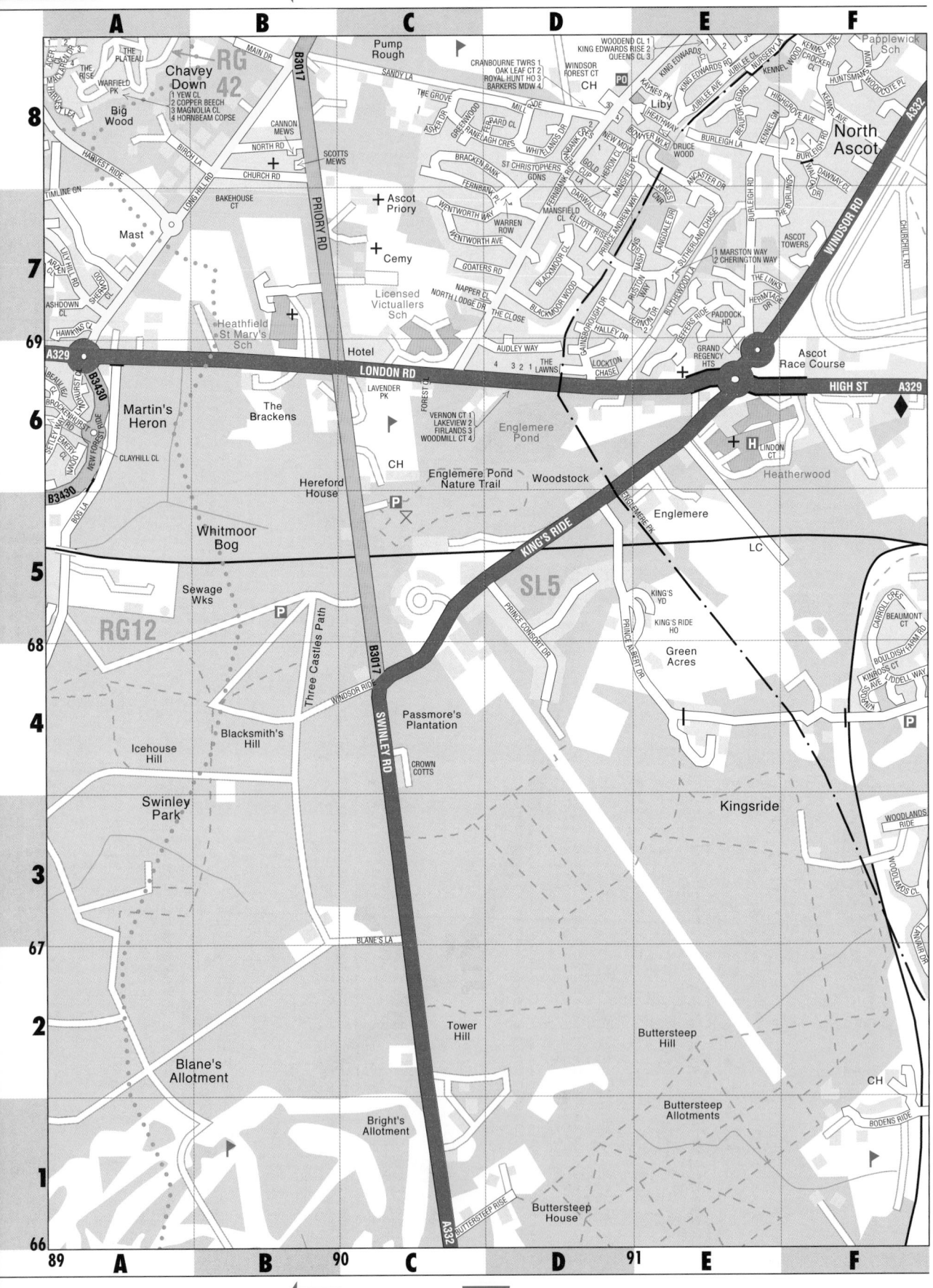

27
47

9
30

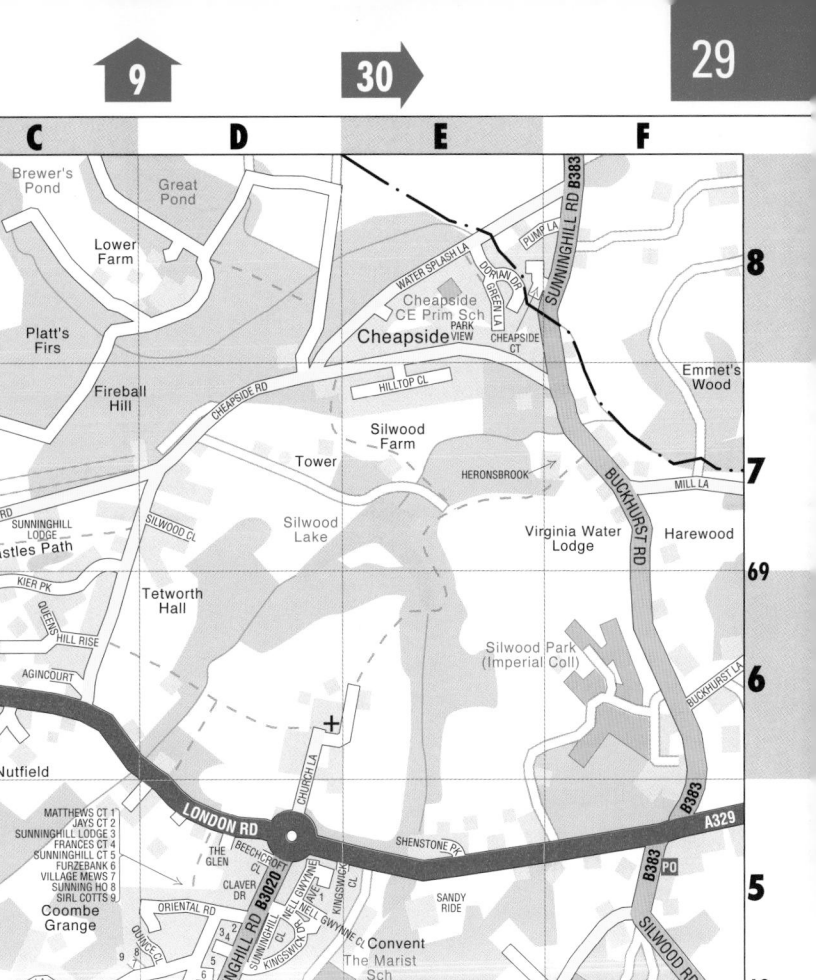
A
B
C
D
E
F
Papplewick Sch
WINDSOR RD A332
A330
Resr
Old Waterfield
Ascot Heath
Ascot Farm
Brewer's Pond
Great Pond
Lower Farm
Platt's Firs
Fireball Hill
WINKFIELD RD
CH
Royal Ascot Golf Club
NEW MILE RD
SUNNINGHILL LODGE
Three Castles Path
CHEAPSIDE RD
WATER SPLASH LA
Cheapside CE Prim Sch
Cheapside
PARK VIEW
CHEAPSIDE CT
HILLTOP CL
SUNNINGHILL RD B383
PUMP LA
Emmet's Wood
Silwood Farm
Tower
HERONSBROOK
BUCKHURST RD
MILL LA
Silwood Lake
SILWOOD CL
Virginia Water Lodge
Harewood
Tetworth Hall
KIER PK
QUEENS HILL RISE
AGINCOURT
Silwood Park (Imperial Coll)
BUCKHURST LA
Ascot
QUEEN'S PL
COURSE RD
PO
HIGH ST
Liby
STEEPLE POINT
CARBERY LA
HERMITAGE PAR
CATHERINE HO 1
ALEXANDRA HO 2
QUEENSHILL LODGE
WELLSWOOD
WELLS LA
ASCOT WOOD
St George's Sch
Nutfield
LONDON RD
CHURCH LA
STATION HILL
Hotel
1 SUNNYBANK
2 STANMORE CL
ST GEORGE'S LA
MATTHEWS CT 1
JAYS CT 2
SUNNINGHILL LODGE 3
FRANCES CT 4
SUNNINGHILL CT 5
FURZEBANK 6
VILLAGE MEWS 7
SUNNING HO 8
SIRL COTTS 9
THE GLEN
BEECHCROFT CL
CLAVER DR
SHENSTONE PK
A329
B383
SANDY RIDE
Coombe Grange
ORIENTAL RD
QUINCE CL
NELL GWYNNE AVE
NELL GWYNNE CL
KINGSWICK DR
KINGSWICK CL
Convent
The Marist Sch
SILWOOD RD
RINGWOOD CL
LYNDHURST RD
PORCHESTER
BOULDISH FARM RD
FENNEL CL
ALL SOULS RD
CHURCH RD
OLIVER RD
SPRING GDNS
CROMWELL RD
LIDDELL WAY
Swinley Prim Sch
VICTORIA RD
ROYAL VICTORIA GDNS
VICARAGE GDNS
FRANCIS CHICHESTER CL
CROWN HILL CT
ELIZABETH GDNS
THE DOWER HO
LOWER VILLAGE RD
EXCHANGE RD
FARM CL
HILLSIDE
UPPER VILLAGE RD
SCHOOL RD
THE TERRACE
BOWDEN RD
VILLAGE CT
TRUSS HILL RD
SUNNINGHILL RD B3020
Sch
HIGHCLERE
SL5
Sunningdale Park (National Sch of Government)
South Ascot
CARDWELL CRES
LYTHAM CT 1
BIRKDALE CT 2
ST ANDREWS CT 3
TROON CT 4
Sunninghill
NORTON PK
HIGH ST
QUEEN'S RD
1 BROOME LODGE
2 CASTLEMAN HO
KING'S RD
TENBY DR
PEMBROKE CL
PEMBROKE MEWS
PINEHURST
BEHARRELL HO 1
LYNWOOD FLATS 2
HEATHFIELD AVE
LARCH AVE
THE SPINNEY
GLADE HO
FOXHAVEN CT
BRIDGE RD
CHARTERS LA
CHARTERS CL
FOX COVERT CL
ARMITAGE CT
ST MARY'S HILL
THE GLADE
WOODEND DR
WHYNSTONES RD
RAVENSDALE RD
THE POPLARS
WOODLANDS RIDE
HURSTWOOD
GREYFRIARS DR
BROCKENHURST RD
FRIARY RD
MURRAY CT
CAVENDISH MEADS
HIGHFIELDS
PARK CRES
PARK DR
WAINSCOT
MORLEY CT
CORIANDER CT
The Rise
LYNWOOD CRES
RISE RD
OAKDENE
CHARNWOOD
BEECH HILL RD
GALTON RD
DRY ARCH RD
St Francis Prim RC Sch
MONKS WLK
MONKS DR
MONKS CL
HOLMES CL
HANCOCKS MOUNT
WYLDEWOOD
JERSEY PL
LLANVAIR CL
HORSE GATE RIDE
ST MARY'S RD
Hotel
REGENTS WLK
Heathermount, The Learning Ctr
Sunningdale Sch
CHARTERS RD
St Mary's Sch
King's Beeches
BAGSHOT RD
DEVENISH RD
Charters Sch
HILLHAMPTON
WOODBY DR
LLANVAIR DR
CORONATION RD
BROADLANDS DR
CHARTERS WAY 1
CLAREWAYS 2
SILVERWOOD GRANGE 3
BALLENCRIEFF RD
BEARSDEN CT
FIR TREE CL
THE COVERT
Broadlands
FIREBALL HILL
SUNNING AVE
PINECOTE DR
HAMILTON DR
LADY MARGARET RD
GRANT WLK
CHANCTONBURY DR
BODENS RIDE
FIELD HOUSE CL
MERIDIAN CT
Broadlands Farm
DEVENISH LA
GREENWAYS DR
LADYWOOD GRANGE
HILLSIDE PK
CROSS RD
Hurst Lodge Sch
Old Windsor Bog
Scotswood
KNOLE WOOD
ELM PK
LONDON RD
A30
B3020
EARLEYDENE
GU20
8
7
69
6
5
68
4
3
67
2
1
66
92
93
94

48
30

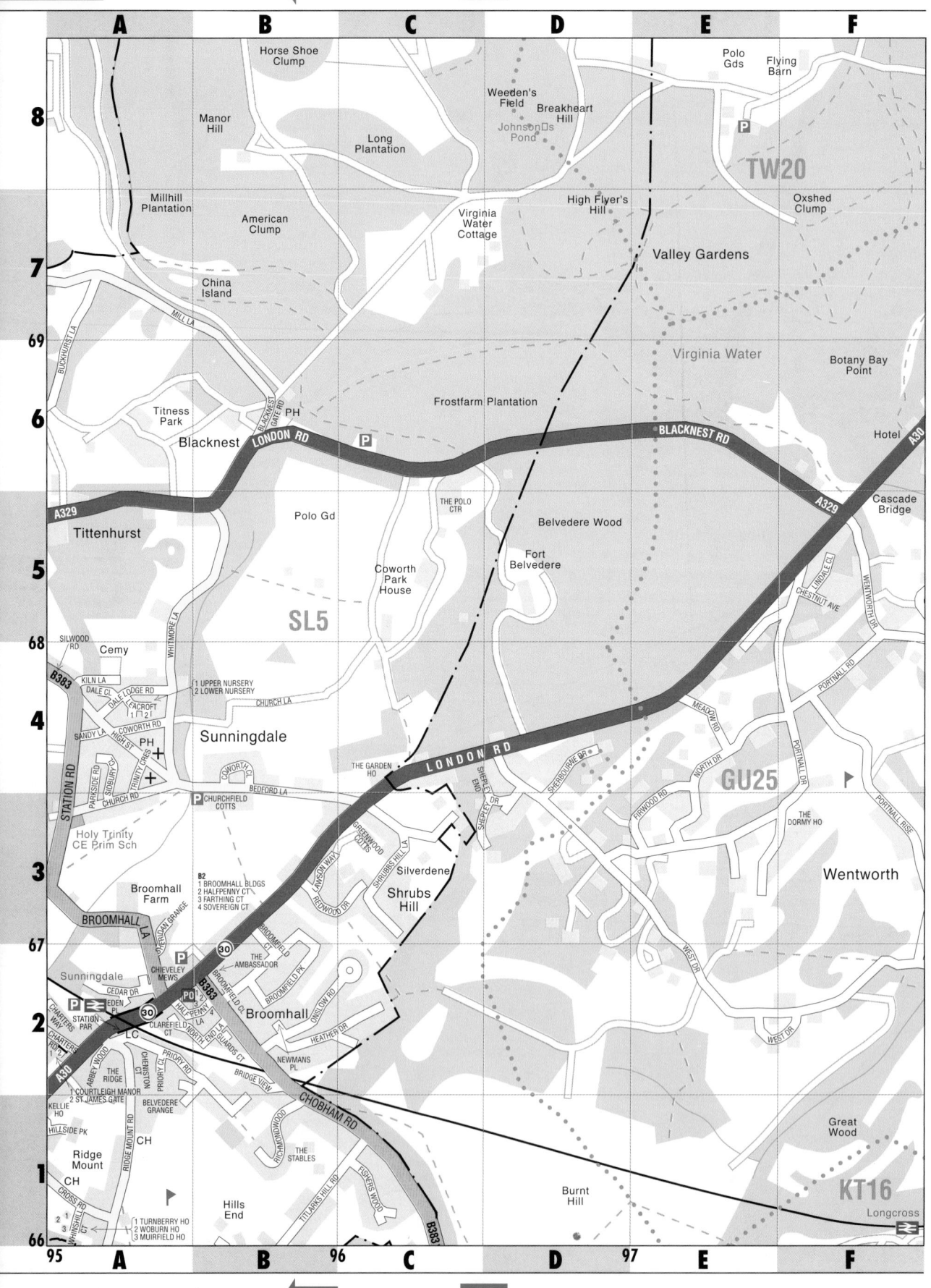
29
10
A
B
C
D
E
F
Horse Shoe Clump
Polo Gds
Flying Barn
Manor Hill
Weeden's Field
Breakheart Hill
Long Plantation
TW20
Millhill Plantation
American Clump
Virginia Water Cottage
High Flyer's Hill
Oxshed Clump
Valley Gardens
China Island
MILL LA
BUCKHURST LA
Virginia Water
Botany Bay Point
Frostfarm Plantation
Titness Park
PH
Blacknest
LONDON RD
BLACKNEST RD
Hotel
A30
A329
Tittenhurst
Polo Gd
THE POLO CTR
Belvedere Wood
Cascade Bridge
Fort Belvedere
Coworth Park House
SL5
CHESTNUT AVE
WENTWORTH DR
LINDALE CL
SILWOOD RD
Cemy
WHITMORE LA
PORTNALL RD
B383
KILN LA
DALE CL
DALE LODGE RD
1 UPPER NURSERY
2 LOWER NURSERY
CHURCH LA
MEADOW RD
COWORTH RD
SANDY LA
HIGH ST
Sunningdale
GU25
THE GARDEN HO
NORTH DR
PORTNALL DR
STATION RD
PARKSIDE RD
SIDBURY CL
TRINITY CRES
CHURCH RD
COWORTH CL
BEDFORD LA
CHURCHFIELD COTTS
SHERBOURNE DR
SHEPLEY END
SHEPLEY DR
FIRWOOD RD
PORTNALL RISE
THE DORMY HO
Holy Trinity CE Prim Sch
GREENWOOD COTTS
Silverdene
Shrubs Hill
SHRUBBS HILL LA
LAWSON WAY
REDWOOD DR
Wentworth
Broomhall Farm
B2
1 BROOMHALL BLDGS
2 HALFPENNY CT
3 FARTHING CT
4 SOVEREIGN CT
BROOMHALL LA
SHERIDAN GRANGE
BROOMFIELD CT
THE AMBASSADOR
BROOMFIELD PK
WEST DR
CHIEVELEY MEWS
CEDAR DR
EDEN PL
STATION PAR
CHARTERS WAY
BROOMFIELD CL
Broomhall
ONSLOW RD
HEATHER DR
CLAREFIELD CT
HALFPENNY LA
NORTH END LA
GUARDS CT
LC
CHARTERS RD
ABBEY WOOD
THE RIDGE
CHENISTON CT
PRIORY CL
PRIORY RD
NEWMANS PL
BRIDGE VIEW
CHOBHAM RD
1 COURTLEIGH MANOR
2 ST JAMES GATE
KELLIE HO
BELVEDERE GRANGE
HILLSIDE PK
RICHMONDWOOD
CH
THE STABLES
Great Wood
Ridge Mount
RIDGE MOUNT RD
TITLARKS HILL RD
FISHERS WOOD
CROSS RD
WHINSHILL CT
1 TURNBERRY HO
2 WOBURN HO
3 MUIRFIELD HO
Hills End
Burnt Hill
KT16
Longcross
8
7
69
6
5
68
4
3
67
2
1
66
95
96
97
29
49

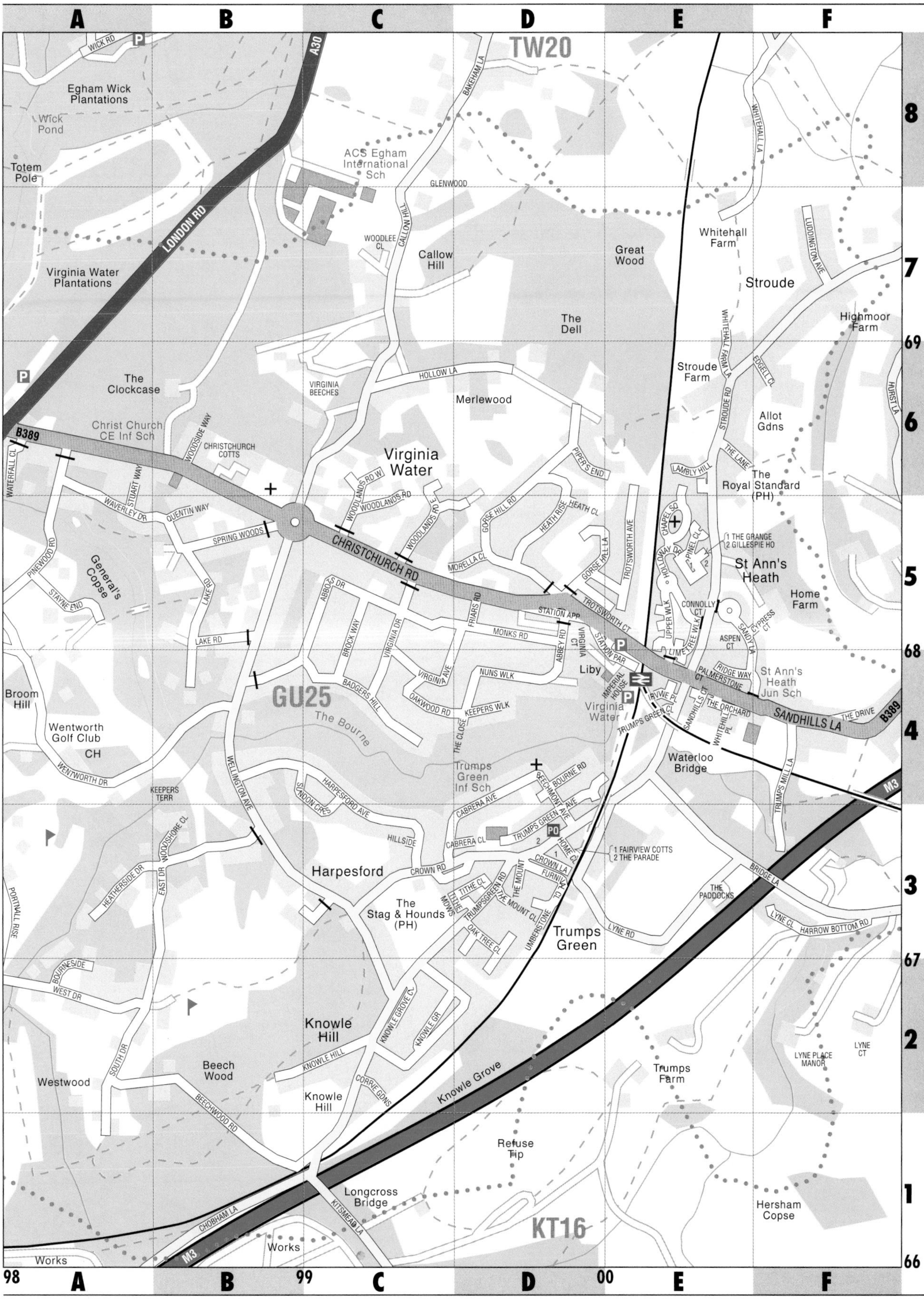

11
32

A B C D E F
TW20
Egham Wick Plantations
Wick Pond
Totem Pole
Virginia Water Plantations
ACS Egham International Sch
Callow Hill
Great Wood
Whitehall Farm
Stroude
Highmoor Farm
The Dell
Stroude Farm
The Clockcase
Merlewood
Allot Gdns
Christ Church CE Inf Sch
Virginia Water
The Royal Standard (PH)
St Ann's Heath
Home Farm
General's Copse
Liby
Virginia Water
St Ann's Heath Jun Sch
Broom Hill
Wentworth Golf Club
CH
GU25
The Bourne
Trumps Green Inf Sch
Waterloo Bridge
Harpesford
The Stag & Hounds (PH)
Trumps Green
Knowle Hill
Beech Wood
Westwood
Knowle Grove
Trumps Farm
Lyne Place Manor
Lyne Ct
Refuse Tip
Longcross Bridge
Hersham Copse
KT16
Works
Works
LONDON RD
A30
B389
M3
CHRISTCHURCH RD
SANDHILLS LA
1 THE GRANGE
2 GILLESPIE HO
1 FAIRVIEW COTTS
2 THE PARADE
8 7 69 6 5 68 4 3 67 2 1 66
98 99 00

50
32

31
12

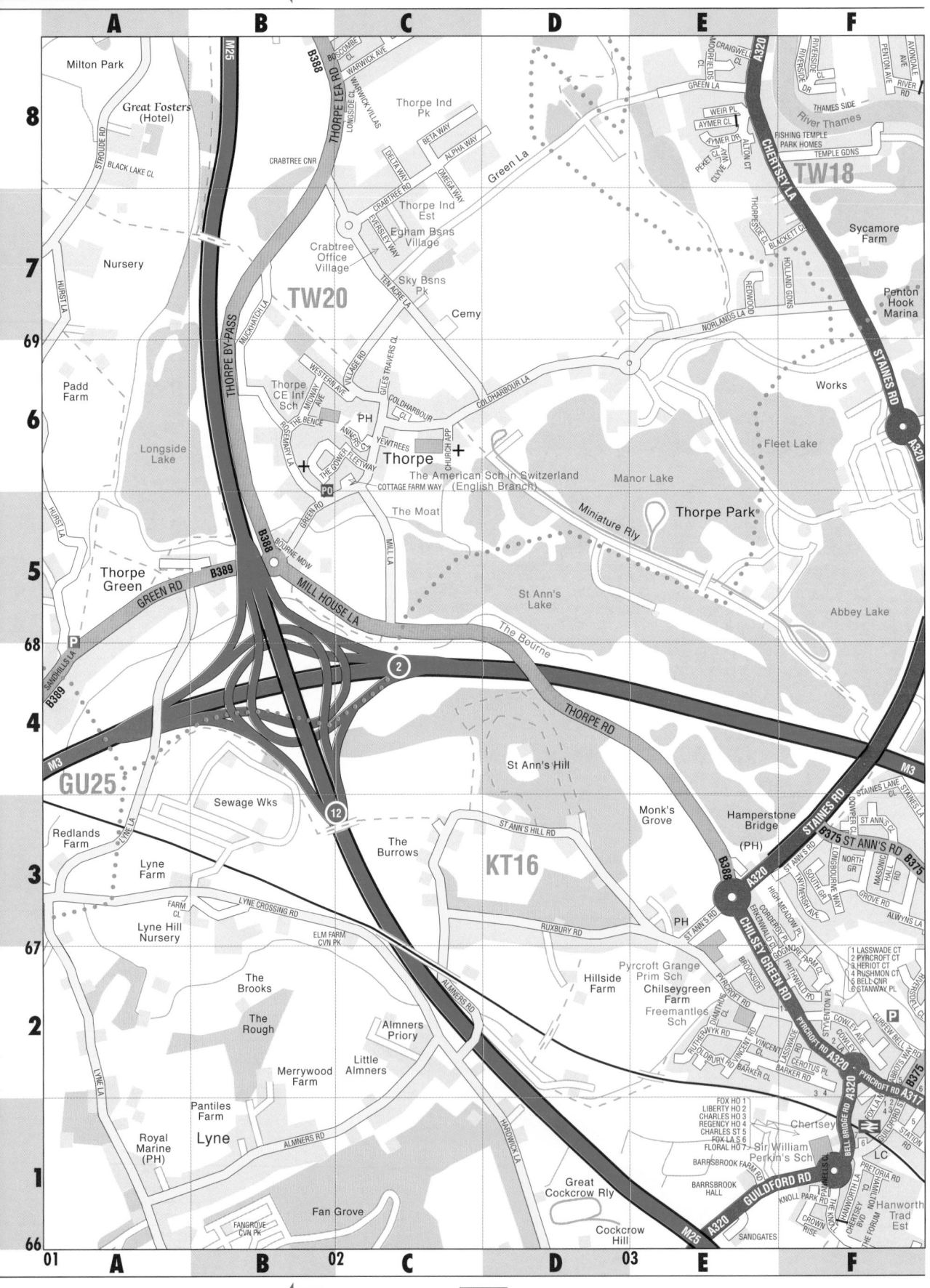
A
B
C
D
E
F
8
7
69
6
5
68
4
3
67
2
1
66
01
02
03
Milton Park
Great Fosters
(Hotel)
STROUDE RD
BLACK LAKE CL
M25
B388
THORPE LEA RD
BOSCOMBE CL
WARWICK AVE
LONGSIDE CL
WARWICK VILLAS
Thorpe Ind
Pk
BETA WAY
ALPHA WAY
DELTA WAY
OMEGA WAY
CRABTREE CNR
CRABTREE RD
Thorpe Ind
Est
Green La
EVERSLEY WAY
Egham Bsns
Village
Crabtree
Office
Village
TEN ACRE LA
Sky Bsns
Pk
Cemy
TW20
Nursery
HURST LA
MUCKHATCH LA
THORPE BY-PASS
GILES TRAVERS CL
VILLAGE RD
WESTERN AVE
Thorpe
CE Inf
Sch
MIDWAY AVE
THE BENCE
PH
COLDHARBOUR CL
COLDHARBOUR LA
ROSEMARY LA
ANNERS CL
YEWTREES
CHURCH APP
THE GOWER
FLEETWAY
Thorpe
The American Sch in Switzerland
(English Branch)
COTTAGE FARM WAY
PO
Padd
Farm
Longside
Lake
The Moat
GREEN RD
MILL LA
B388
BOURNE MDW
MILL HOUSE LA
Thorpe
Green
B389
GREEN RD
SANDHILLS LA
B389
P
St Ann's
Lake
The Bourne
2
THORPE RD
M3
GU25
St Ann's Hill
Sewage Wks
12
Redlands
Farm
LYNE LA
Lyne
Farm
The
Burrows
ST ANN'S HILL RD
KT16
Monk's
Grove
FARM CL
LYNE CROSSING RD
Lyne Hill
Nursery
ELM FARM
CVN PK
RUXBURY RD
PH
ST ANN'S RD
The
Brooks
The
Rough
ALMNERS RD
Almners
Priory
Merrywood
Farm
Little
Almners
Hillside
Farm
Pyrcroft Grange
Prim Sch
Chilseygreen
Farm
Freemantles
Sch
Pantiles
Farm
Royal
Marine
(PH)
Lyne
ALMNERS RD
HARDWICK LA
Fan Grove
FANGROVE
CVN PK
Great
Cockcrow Rly
Cockcrow
Hill
M25
CRAIGWELL CL
MOORFIELDS CL
GREEN LA
A320
RIVERSIDE CL
RIVERSIDE DR
PENTON AVE
AVONDALE AVE
RIVER RD
THAMES SIDE
River Thames
WEIR PL
AYMER CL
AYMER DR
PEKET CL
CLYVE WAY
ALTON CT
FISHING TEMPLE
PARK HOMES
TEMPLE GDNS
CHERTSEY LA
TW18
THORPESIDE CL
BLACKETT CL
Sycamore
Farm
HOLLAND GDNS
REDWOOD
NORLANDS LA
Penton
Hook
Marina
STAINES RD
Works
A320
Fleet Lake
Manor Lake
Miniature Rly
Thorpe Park
Abbey Lake
M3
STAINES RD
STAINES LANE CL
STAINES LA
COWPER CL
ST ANN'S CL
Hamperstone
Bridge
(PH)
B375
ST ANN'S RD
B375
NORTH GR
SOUTH GR
TWYNERSH AVE
LONGBOURNE WAY
MASONIC HALL RD
GROVE RD
ALWYNS LA
B388
A320
HIGH MEADOW PL
CORDERBY PL
ERKENWALD CL
GOGMORE FARM CL
FRITHWALD RD
CHILSEY GREEN RD
STYVENTON PL
1 LASSWADE CT
2 PYRCROFT CT
3 HERIOT CT
4 RUSHMON CT
5 BELL CNR
6 STANWAY PL
P
BROOKSIDE
PYRCROFT RD
DIANTHUS CL
COWLEY LA
COWLEY AVE
CURFEW BELL RD
ABBOTS WAY
RUTHERWYK RD
VINCENT RD
VINCENT CL
LASSWADE RD
CEROTUS PL
BARKER RD
OLDBURY RD
BARKER CL
PYRCROFT RD
A320
PYRCROFT RD
A317
B375
FOX HO 1
LIBERTY HO 2
CHARLES HO 3
REGENCY HO 4
CHARLES ST 5
FOX LA S 6
FLORAL HO 7
Chertsey
Sir William
Perkin's Sch
BELL BRIDGE RD
GUILDFORD ST
STATION RD
BARRSBROOK FARM RD
BARRSBROOK
HALL
LC
PRETORIA RD
GUILDFORD RD
A320
PANNELLS CL
KNOLL PARK RD
HANWORTH LA
HAMILTON CL
CHERTSEY BVD
THE KNOLL
THE FORUM
CROWN RISE
SANDGATES
Hanworth
Trad
Est

31
51

13
34

A
B
C
D
E
F
8
7
69
6
5
68
4
3
67
2
1
66
04
05
06
TW15
TW18
TW17
KT16
KT15
KT13
Greenfield Nurseries
Gravel Pit
Queen Mary Resr
Nursery
Manor Farm
Laleham CE Prim Sch
Penton Hook Island
Penton Hook
Penton Hook Marina
Penton Park Est
Laleham
Recn Gd
Laleham Park
Laleham Burway
Resr
Laleham Nurseries
Shepperton Studios
Sailing Club
Abbey Mead
Abbey Chase
Abbey Chase Farm
CHERTSEY
Abbeyfields
Riverscroft
Chertsey Bridge
Dumsey Eyot
Mead Farm
Marina
Chertsey Meads
Dockett Eddy
Fordwater Trad Est
Stepgates Com Sch
St Anne's RC Prim Sch
The Sainsbury Ctr
Mus
L Ctr
Liby
TA Ctr
TH
PH
CH
PO
Sweep's Ditch
River Thames
Thames Path
Burway Ditch
Abbey River
River Ash
STAINES RD
ASHFORD RD
THE BROADWAY
SHEPPERTON RD
LALEHAM RD
CHERTSEY RD
CHERTSEY BRIDGE RD
BRIDGE RD
LONDON ST
WINDSOR ST
GUILDFORD ST
HERIOT RD
EASTWORTH RD
WEIR RD
FORDWATER RD
LITTLETON LA
DOCKETT EDDY LA
SHEEPWALK
THAMES SIDE
MIXNAMS LA
B376
B377
B375
B387
A317
M3
A3
1 ONSLOW MEWS
2 WINDSOR PL
3 ALWYNS CL
4 ALWYNS LA
5 WILLATS CL
6 DEAN CT
7 SPIRES CT
A2
1 FOUNDRY MEWS
2 WHITE HART ROW
3 BURWOOD PAR
4 BEOMONDS ROW
5 BEOMONDS
6 GALSWORTHY RD
7 CHERTSEY WLK
ASTLEHAM RD 1
ASTLEHAM WAY 2
1 ISIS HO
2 KEEL

52
34

33
14

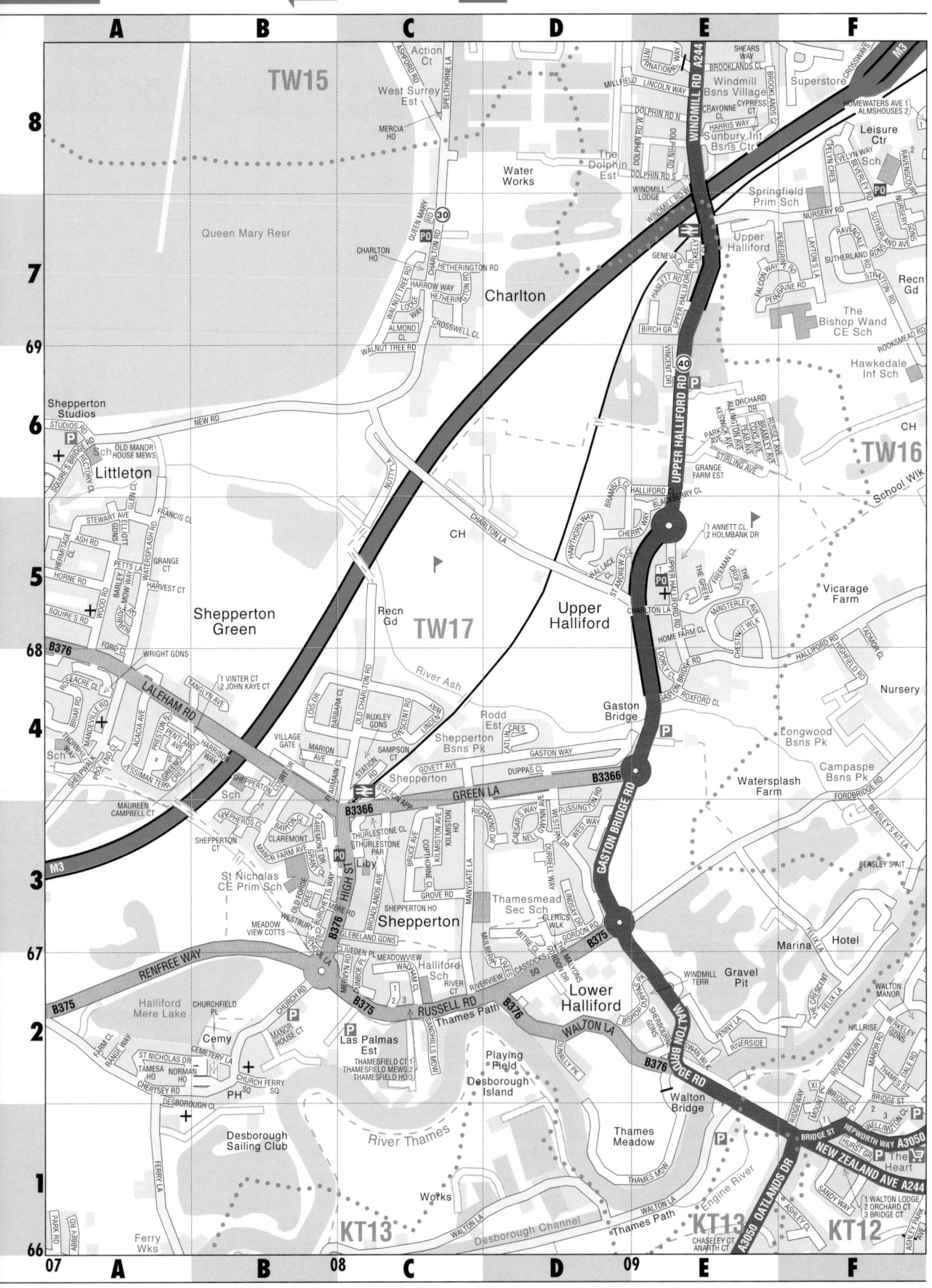
A
B
C
D
E
F
8
7
69
6
5
68
4
3
67
2
1
66
07
08
09
TW15
Queen Mary Resr
Action Ct
West Surrey Est
MERCIA HO
ASHFORD RD
SPELTHORNE LA
Water Works
The Dolphin Est
Windmill Bsns Village
Sunbury Int Bsns Ctr
Superstore
Leisure Ctr
Springfield Prim Sch
Upper Halliford
The Bishop Wand CE Sch
Recn Gd
Hawkedale Inf Sch
Charlton
CHARLTON HO
HETHERINGTON RD
HARROW WAY
CROSSWELL CL
WALNUT TREE RD
Shepperton Studios
Littleton
NEW RD
CH
TW16
School Wlk
Shepperton Green
Recn Gd
TW17
Upper Halliford
CHARLTON LA
UPPER HALLIFORD RD
WINDMILL RD A244
Vicarage Farm
Nursery
River Ash
Rodd Est
Shepperton Bsns Pk
Gaston Bridge
Longwood Bsns Pk
Campaspe Bsns Pk
Watersplash Farm
LALEHAM RD
B376
B3366
GREEN LA
GASTON WAY
GASTON BRIDGE RD
Shepperton
HIGH ST
Liby
St Nicholas CE Prim Sch
Thamesmead Sec Sch
Shepperton
M3
B375
RENFREE WAY
RUSSELL RD
Halliford Sch
Lower Halliford
WALTON LA
WALTON BRIDGE RD
Marina
Hotel
Gravel Pit
Halliford Mere Lake
Cemy
Las Palmas Est
Thames Path
Playing Field
Desborough Island
Walton Bridge
Thames Meadow
Desborough Sailing Club
River Thames
Works
Ferry Wks
Desborough Channel
Engine River
KT13
KT13
KT12
A3050 OATLANDS DR
NEW ZEALAND AVE A244
BRIDGE ST
HEPWORTH WAY A3050
The Heart

33
53

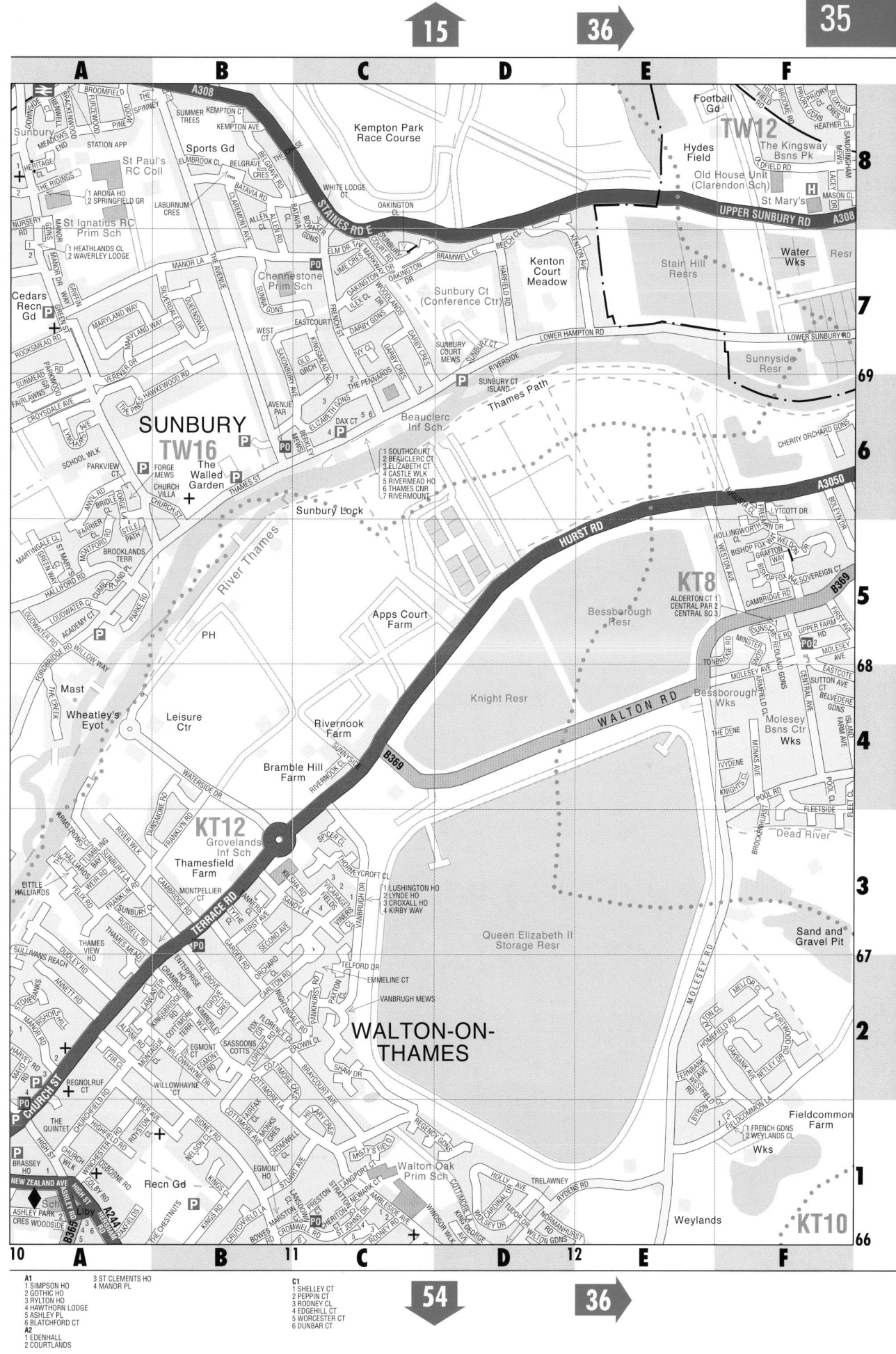

SUNBURY
TW16

TW12

KT8

KT12

WALTON-ON-THAMES

KT10

1 SOUTHCOURT
2 BEAUCLERC CT
3 ELIZABETH CT
4 CASTLE WLK
5 RIVERMEAD HO
6 THAMES CNR
7 RIVERMOUNT

1 LUSHINGTON HO
2 LYNDE HO
3 CROXALL HO
4 KIRBY WAY

1 FRENCH GDNS
2 WEYLANDS CL

A1
1 SIMPSON HO   3 ST CLEMENTS HO
2 GOTHIC HO   4 MANOR PL
3 RYLTON HO
4 HAWTHORN LODGE   C1
5 ASHLEY PL   1 SHELLEY CT
6 BLATCHFORD CT   2 PEPPIN CT
                      3 RODNEY CL
A2   4 EDGEHILL CT
1 EDENHALL   5 WORCESTER CT
2 COURTLANDS   6 DUNBAR CT

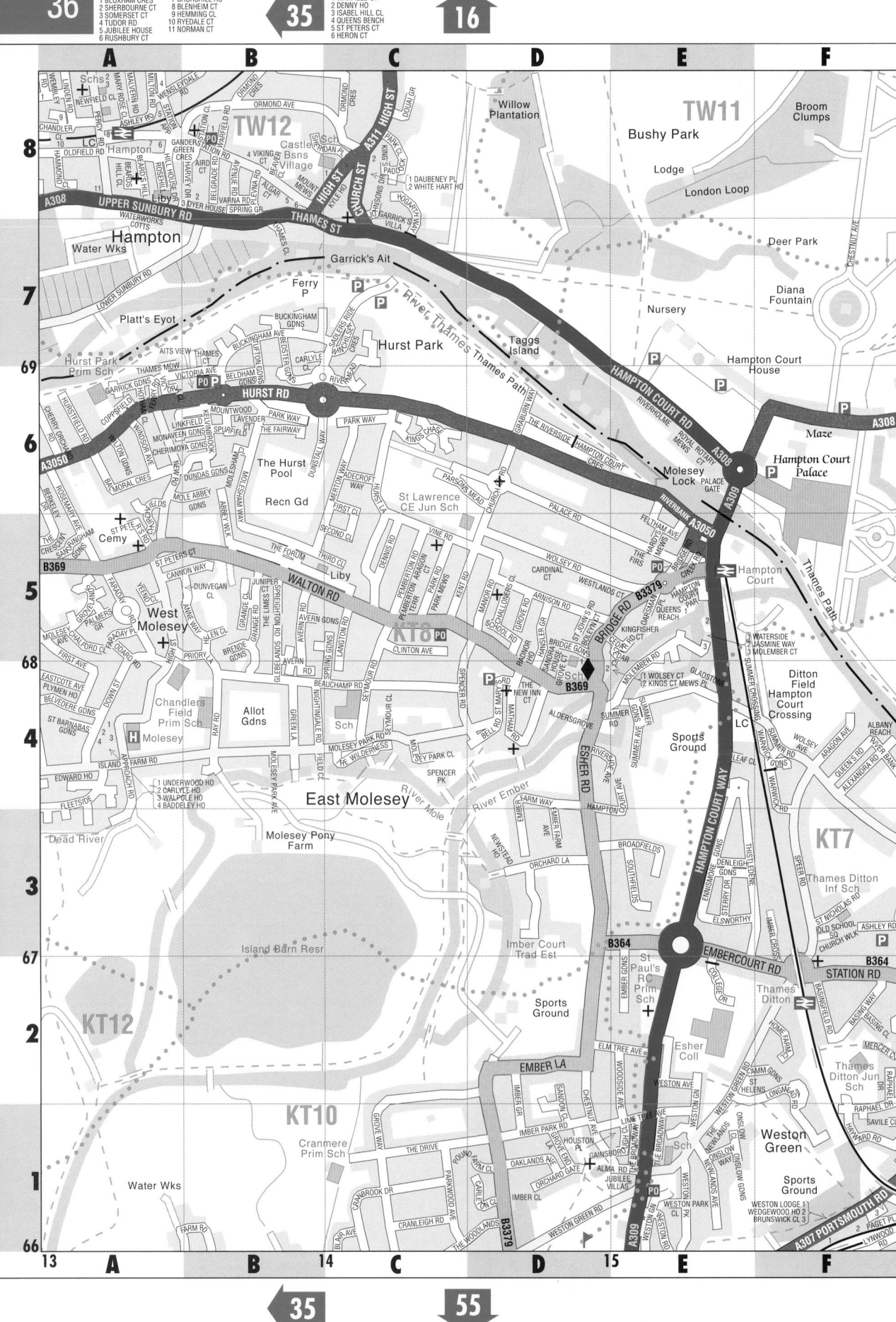

36

A8
1 BLOXHAM CRES
2 SHERBOURNE CT
3 SOMERSET CT
4 TUDOR RD
5 JUBILEE HOUSE
6 RUSHBURY CT
7 CHURCHILL HO
8 BLENHEIM CT
9 HEMMING CL
10 RYEDALE CT
11 NORMAN CT

B8
1 WARFIELD CT
2 DENNY HO
3 ISABEL HILL CL
4 QUEENS BENCH
5 ST PETERS CT
6 HERON CT

35

16

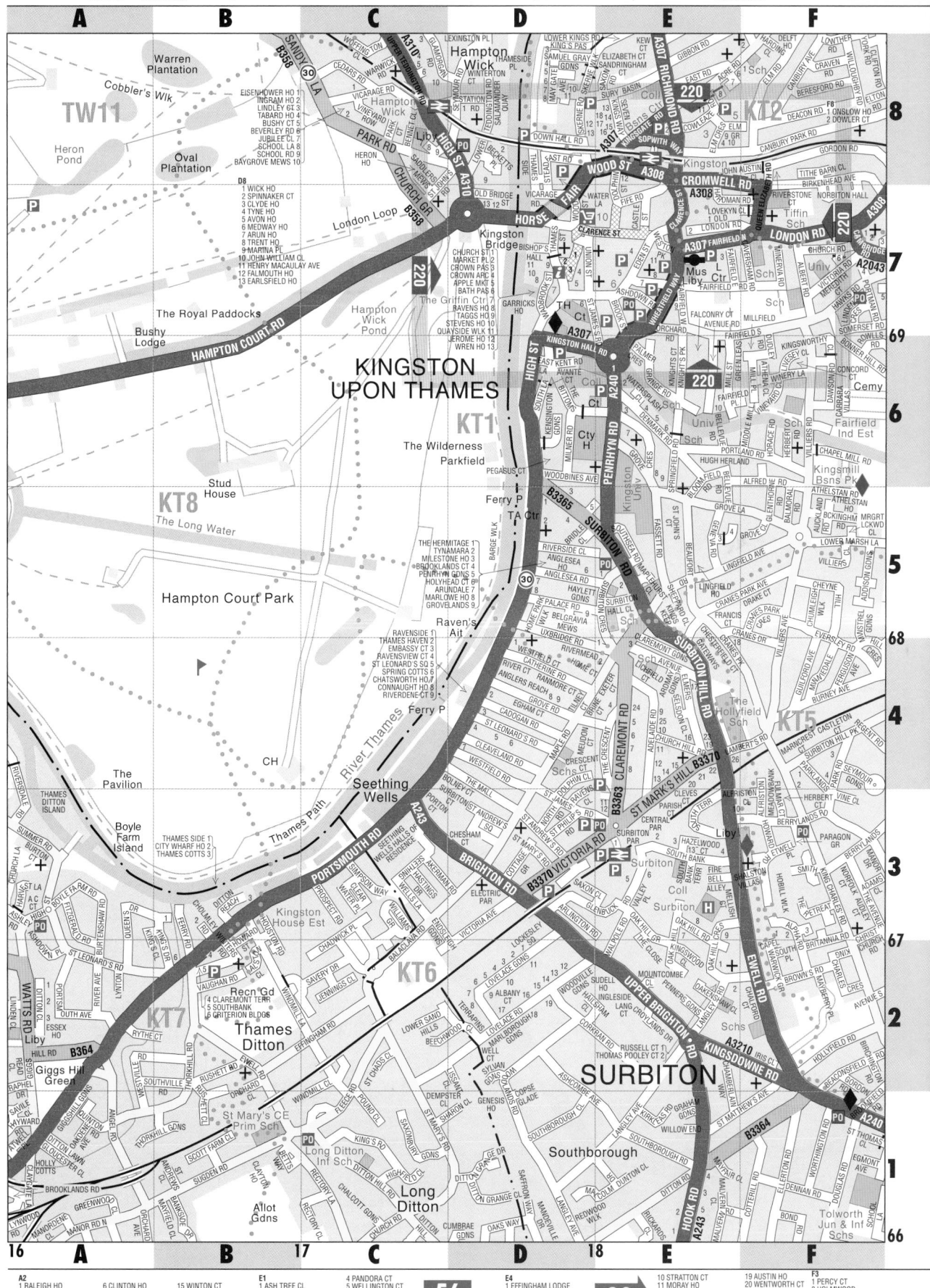

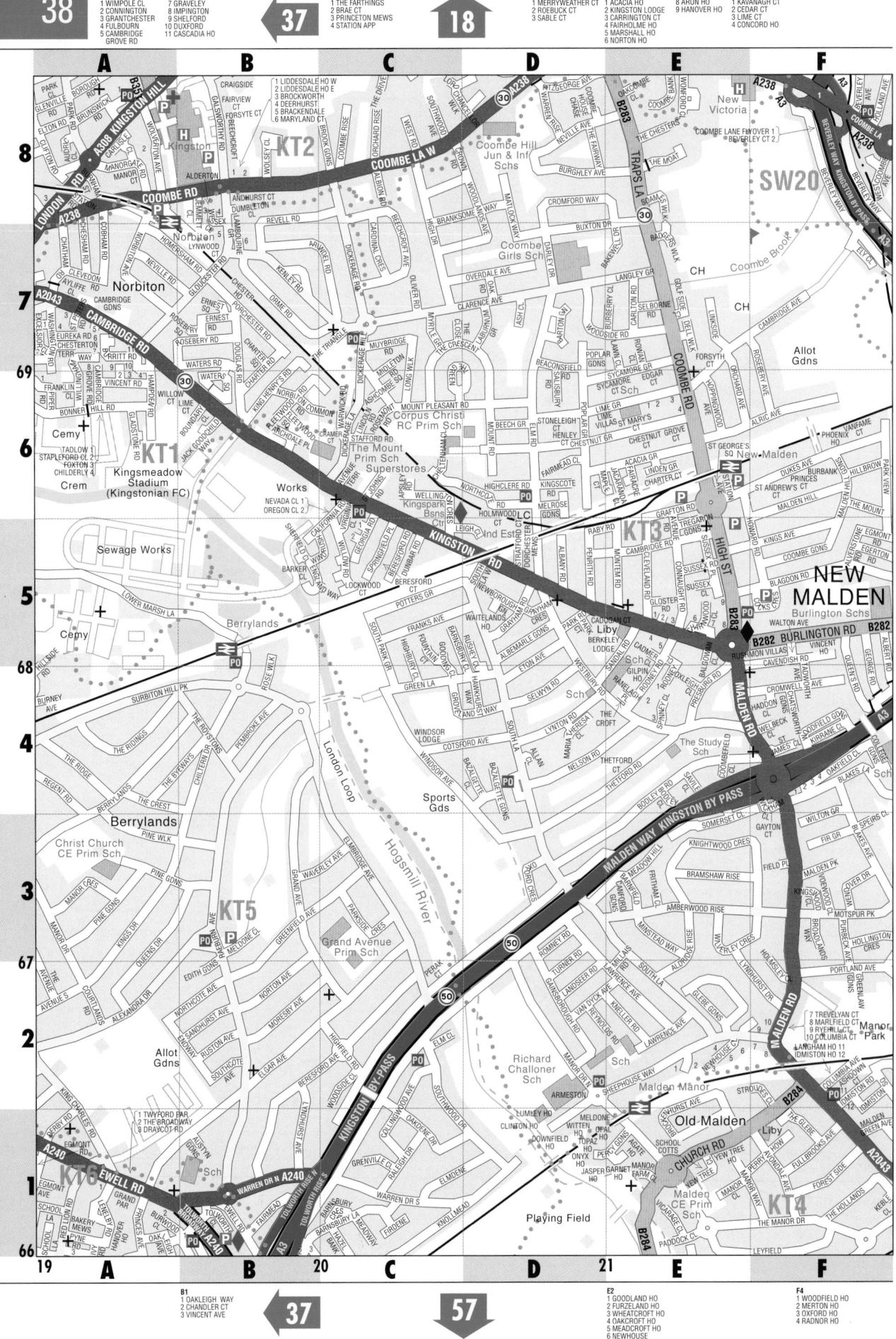

19
40

D8
1 RYDAL CT
2 SAVONA CT
3 SWINBURN CT
4 LANTERN CT
5 RANMORE CT
6 DUNSTER CT
7 KINNEAR CT
8 CRESCENT HO
9 BEAUFORT HO
10 GREENER CT

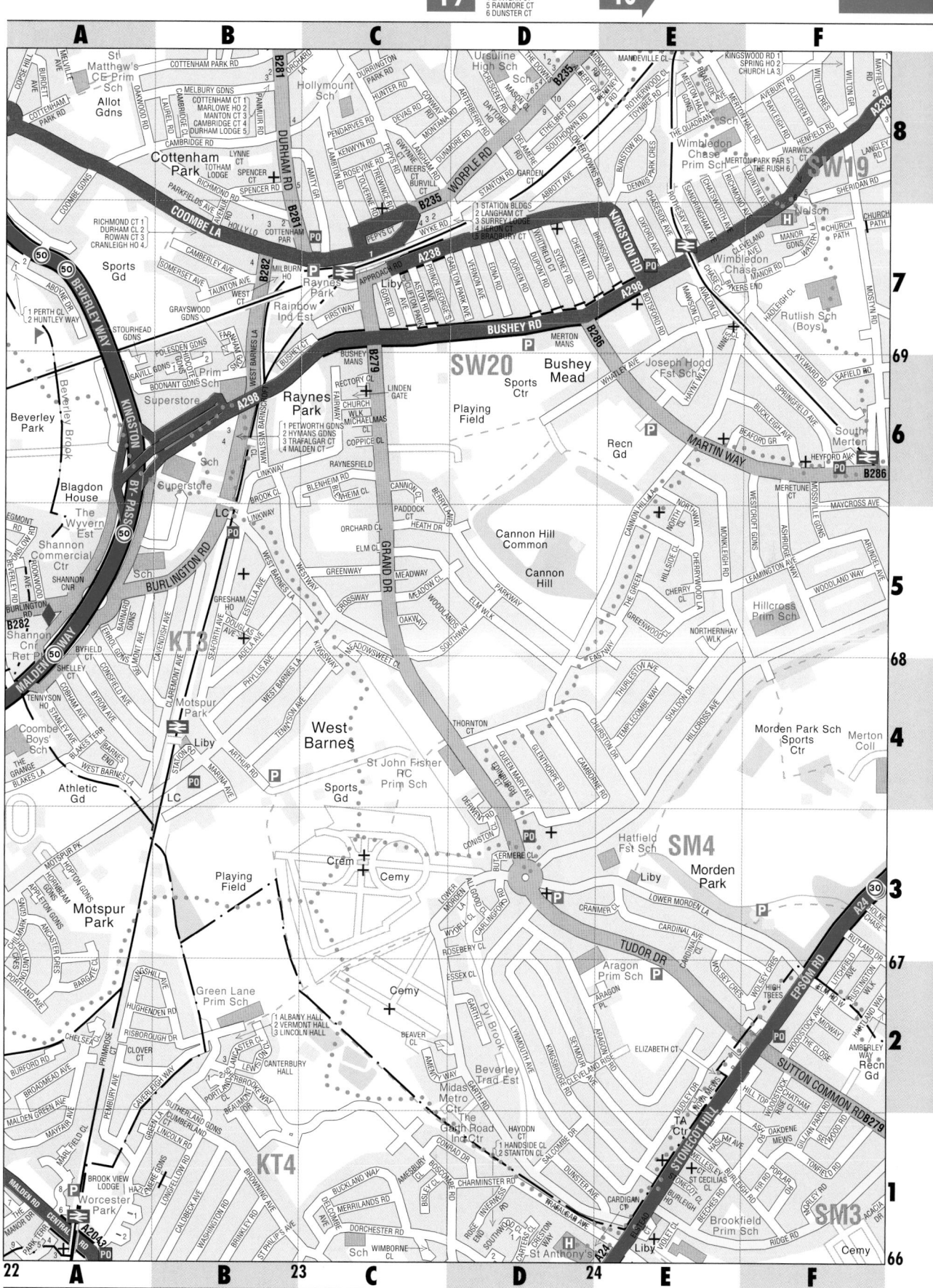

A1
1 BROOKSIDE CRES
2 BEVERLEY GDNS
3 PURDEY CT
4 THE AVENUE
5 BRIARWOOD CT
6 STATION APP
7 DOWNFIELD
8 LOWER GREEN GDNS
9 ORCHARD CT

58
40

B8
1 Gilbert Cl
2 Becket Cl
3 Priory Cl
4 Hudson Ct
5 Ryder Ho
6 Eleanor Ho

7 Ramsey Ho
8 Colborne Ct
9 Falcon Ho
10 Spur Ho

39

C8
1 Tanner Ho
2 May Ct
3 Marsh Ct
4 Lovell Ho

20

D8
1 Yarborough Rd
2 Vista Ho
3 Prospect Ho
4 Independence Ho
5 Nonsuch Ho
6 Baron Ho

7 Thorburn Way
8 Landseer Cl
9 Stubbs Way

E8
1 Wells Ct
2 Hartley Ho
3 Heron Ho

D4
1 Merlin Ct
2 Linnet Ct
3 Linford Ct
4 Searle Ct
5 Gunnell Ct
6 Tyrrell Sq

F6
1 Fair Green Ct
2 Regal Ct
3 Esher Mews
4 Queen Anne's Gdns
5 Lewes Ct
6 Sibford Ct

F7
1 Chart Ho
2 Gladstone Ho
3 Fountain Ho
4 Sirthorp Rd
5 Armfield Cotts
6 Sir Arthur Bliss Ct

7 Deseret Ho
8 Standor Ho
9 Langdale Par
10 Clarendon Gr
11 Newman Terr

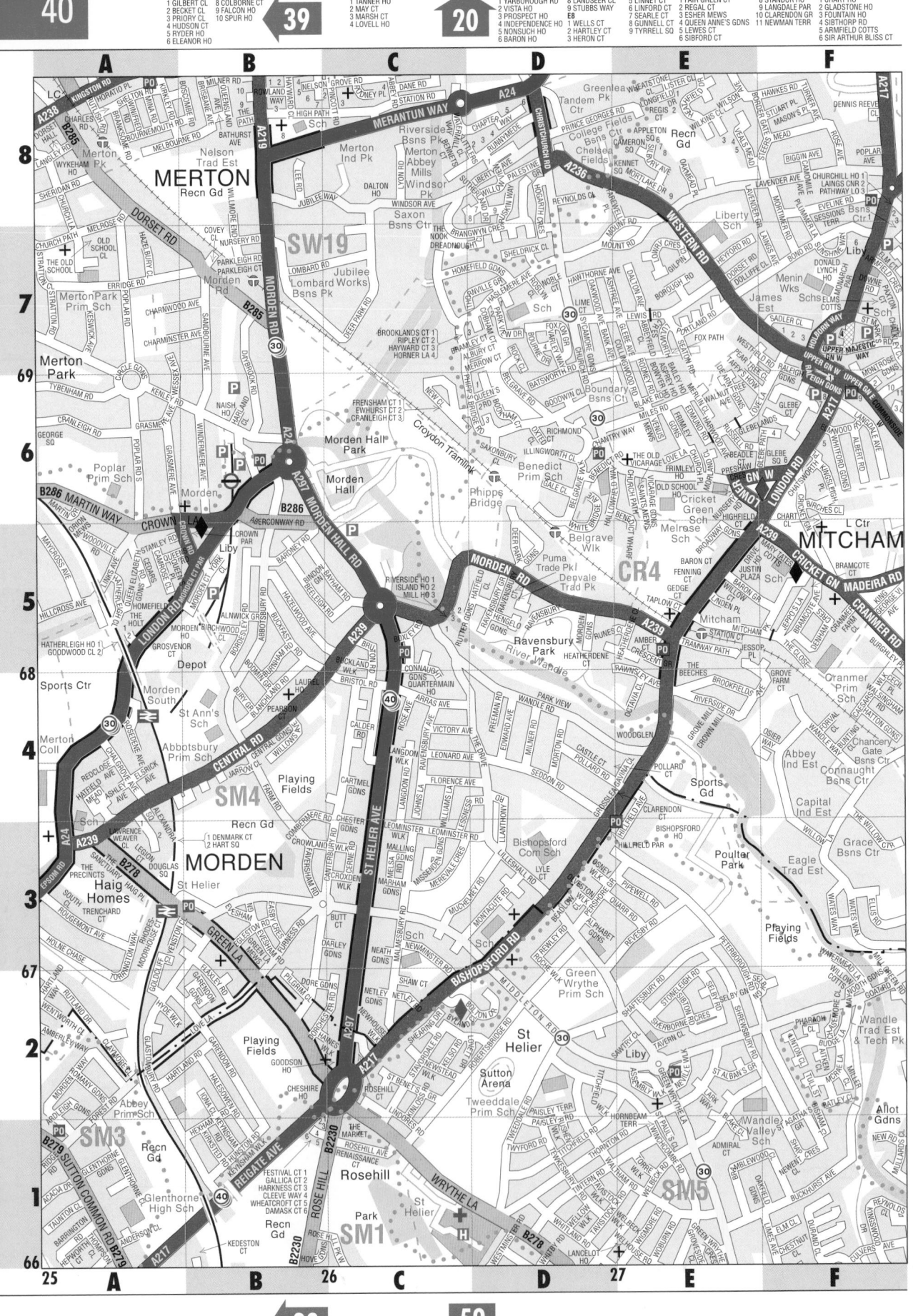

21
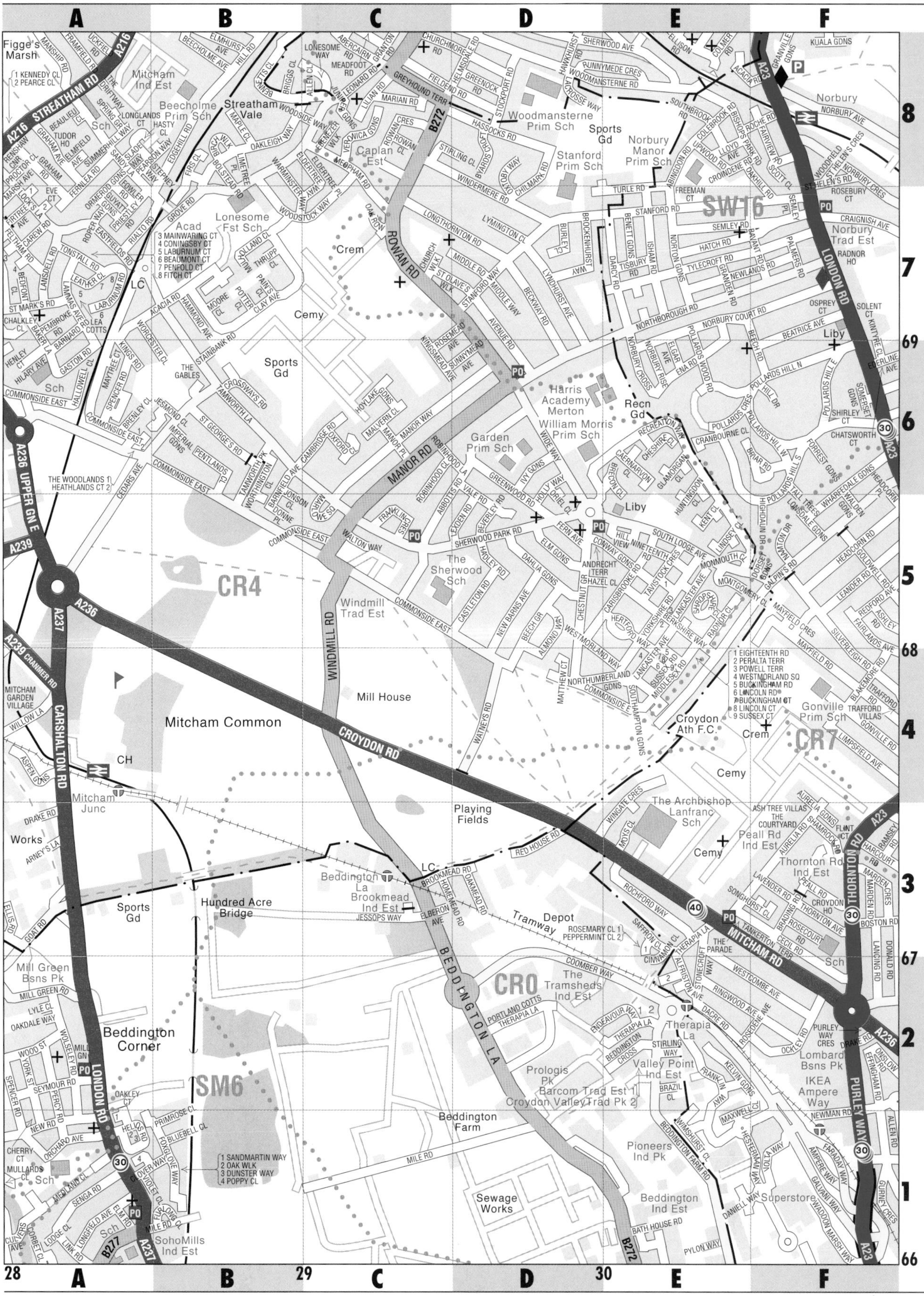
42

A B C D E F

8
Figge's Marsh
1 KENNEDY CL
2 PEARCE CL
A216 STREATHAM RD
Mitcham Ind Est
Beecholme Prim Sch
Streatham Vale
ELMHURST AVE
BEECHOLME AVE
HILL RD
LONESOME WAY
ABERCAIRN RD
MEADFOOT RD
GRANTON RD
CHURCHMORE RD
HELMSDALE RD
GREENOCK RD
FIELDEND RD
GREYHOUND TERR
MARIAN RD
LILIAN RD
LEONARD RD
B272
Woodmansterne Prim Sch
HASSOCKS RD
STOCKPORT RD
SHERWOOD AVE
RUNNYMEDE CRES
WOODMANSTERNE RD
LACROSSE WAY
HAWKHURST RD
Sports Gd
Norbury Manor Prim Sch
SOUTHBROOK RD
COLEBROOK RD
ELLISON RD
COLMER RD
ACACIA RD
GRANVILLE GDNS
KUALA GDNS
Norbury
NORBURY AVE
LONGLANDS CT
HASTY CL
WOODSIDE WAY
OAKLEIGH WAY
EDGEHILL RD
Caplan Est
Stanford Prim Sch
STIRLING CL
WINDERMERE RD
CHILMARK RD
ABINGDON RD
UPWOOD RD
CROINDENE RD
FAIRVIEW RD
ROCHE RD
OAKHILL RD
SCOTT CL
ST HELEN'S RD
ROSEBURY CT
TURLE RD
FREEMAN CT
SW16

7
Acad
Lonesome Fst Sch
3 MAINWARING CT
4 CONINGSBY CT
5 LABURNUM CT
6 BEAUMONT CT
7 PENFOLD CT
8 FITCH CT
GROVE RD
EASTFIELDS RD
TONSALL RD
CAREW RD
Crem
ROWAN RD
LONGTHORNTON RD
LYMINGTON CL
MIDDLE RD
CHURCH WALK
ST OLAVE'S WALK
STANFORD WAY
MIDDLE WAY
BECKWAY RD
LYNDHURST AVE
BURLEY CL
BROCKENHURST WAY
DARCY RD
BENETT GDNS
TISBURY RD
ISHAM RD
NORTON GDNS
STANFORD RD
SEMLEY RD
HATCH RD
TYLECROFT RD
GRANDEN RD
NEWLANDS RD
PALMERS RD
CRAIGNISH AVE
Norbury Trad Est
RADNOR HO
LONDON RD
MOORE CL
POTTER CL
PAIN'S CL
CLAY AVE
THRUPP CL
ACACIA RD
HAMMOND AVE
LC
Cemy
AVENUE RD
NORTHBOROUGH RD
NORBURY COURT RD
OSPREY CT
SOLENT CT
KINTYRE CL
ST MARK'S RD
CHALKLEY CL
PEMBROKE AVE
BARNARD RD
LABURNUM RD
LEA COTTS

69
HENLEY CT
HILARY AVE
GASTON RD
Sch
KINGS RD
MAYTREE CT
SPENCER RD
STAINBANK RD
THE GABLES
Sports Gd
ROSEMEAD AVE
KINGSMEAD AVE
SUNNYMEAD AVE
NORBURY CROSS
NORBURY RISE
ELGAR AVE
ENA RD
POLLARDS WOOD RD
BEATRICE AVE
BEECH RD
POLLARDS HILL N
POLLARDS HILL E
Liby
EDGELINE

6
COMMONSIDE EAST
HALLOWELL CL
BRENLEY CL
JESMOND CL
IMPERIAL GDNS
PENTLANDS CL
ST GEORGE'S RD
TAMWORTH LA
CROSSWAYS RD
HOYLAKE GDNS
MALVERN CL
OXFORD CL
CAMBRIDGE RD
MANOR WAY
MANOR PL
Harris Academy Merton
William Morris Prim Sch
Garden Prim Sch
WIDE WAY
Recn Gd
RECREATION WAY
CHESHIRE CL
CRANBOURNE CL
POLLARDS CRES
POLLARDS HILL W
HILL DR
SOMERSET GDNS
SHIRLEY CT
CHATSWORTH CL
FORREST GDNS
A23
30
THE WOODLANDS 1
HEATHLANDS CT 2
A236 UPPER GN E
COMMONSIDE EAST
TAMWORTH PK
WORTHINGTON CL
BARNFIELD AVE
JONSON CL
DONNE PL
MANOR RD
ROBINHOOD LA
ROBINHOOD CL
IVY GDNS
HOLLY WAY
GREENWOOD RD
CARNARVON
GLAMORGAN CL
BRECON CL
HUNTINGDON CL
KENT CL
Liby
BRIAR RD
POLLARDS HILLS
HIGHDAUN DR
TALL TREES
LONSDALE GDNS
WHARFEDALE GDNS
WALDEN GDNS
HEADCORN PL

5
CEDARS AVE
A239
FRANKLIN CRES
ABBOTTS RD
VALE RD
LEYDEN RD
BEVERLEY RD
SHERWOOD PARK RD
ELM GDNS
FERN AVE
HILL VIEW
CONWAY GDNS
NINETEENTH RD
SOUTH LODGE AVE
MONMOUTH CL
LINDSEY CL
DORSET GDNS
NAMTON DR
GALPIN'S RD
HEADCORN RD
GOLDWELL RD
COMMONSIDE EAST
WALTON WAY
CR4
The Sherwood Sch
HADLEY RD
DAHLIA GDNS
ANDRECHT TERR
HAZEL CL
CARISBROOKE RD
TAVISTOCK CRES
MONTGOMERY CL
LEANDER RD
REDFORD AVE
ASHLEY RD
A236
A237
Windmill Trad Est
WINDMILL RD
CASTLETON RD
NEW BARNS AVE
BEECH GR
ALMOND WAY
CHESTNUT GR
WESTMORLAND WAY
HERTFORD WAY
YORKSHIRE RD
LANCASTER AVE
SHROPSHIRE CL
BERKSHIRE WAY
RADNOR CL
MAYFIELD CRES
MAYFIELD RD
SILVERLEIGH RD
FAIRLANDS AVE

68
A239 CRANMER RD
MITCHAM GARDEN VILLAGE
WILLOW LA
CARSHALTON RD
Mill House
MATHEW CT
NORTHUMBERLAND GDNS
COMMONSIDE E
SOUTHAMPTON GDNS
SUSSEX RD
MIDDLESEX RD
1 EIGHTEENTH RD
2 PERALTA TERR
3 POWELL TERR
4 WESTMORLAND SQ
5 BUCKINGHAM RD
6 LINCOLN RD
7 BUCKINGHAM CT
8 LINCOLN CT
9 SUSSEX CT
BLAKEMORE RD
TRAFFORD RD
Gonville Prim Sch
TRAFFORD VILLAS
GONVILLE RD

4
Mitcham Common
CROYDON RD
WATNEYS RD
Croydon Ath F.C.
Crem
CR7
LIMPSFIELD AVE
CH
ASPEN GDNS
Mitcham Junc
Cemy
Playing Fields
WINGATE CRES
MOYS CL
The Archbishop Lanfranc Sch
ASH TREE VILLAS
THE COURTYARD
AURELIA GDNS
SHAMROCK RD
AURELIA RD
Peall Rd Ind Est
Cemy
FLINT CL
A23
THORNTON RD
RAMSEY
HARCOURT RD
DRAKE RD
Works
ARNEY'S LA
RED HOUSE RD

3
LC
Beddington La
Brookmead Ind Est
BROOKMEAD RD
HOMEMEAD RD
OAKMEAD RD
JESSOPS WAY
ELBERON AVE
Sports Gd
Hundred Acre Bridge
ELLIS RD
GOAT RD
Tramway
Depot
ROSEMARY CL 1
PEPPERMINT CL 2
ROCHFORD WAY
SAFFRON CL
CINNAMON CL
THERAPIA LA
40
MITCHAM RD
THE PARADE
STONECROFT WAY
Thornton Rd Ind Est
LAVENDER RD
PEALL RD
SONGHURST CL
BRADING RD
THORNTON AVE
CROYDON HO
ROSECOURT RD
TANKERTON TERR
CECIL RD
Sch
MARDEN CRES
MARDEN RD
BOSTON RD
DONALD RD
LANGING RD

67
Mill Green Bsns Pk
MILL GREEN RD
LYLE CL
OAKDALE WAY
BEDDINGTON LA
CR0
The Tramsheds Ind Est
COOMBER WAY
PORTLAND COTTS
THERAPIA LA
ENDEAVOUR WAY
ALFRISTON AVE
WESTCOMBE AVE
RINGWOOD AVE
DACRE RD
ROSEDENE AVE
Therapia La
STIRLING WAY
BEDDINGTON CROSS
THERAPIA LA

2
Beddington Corner
WOOD ST
YORK ST
WOLSELEY RD
MILL GN
LONDON RD
SPENCER RD
SEYMOUR RD
PERCY RD
Prologis Pk
Barcom Trad Est 1
Croydon Valley Trad Pk 2
Valley Point Ind Est
BRAZIL CL
FRANKLIN WAY
KELVIN GDNS
OCKLEY RD
PURLEY WAY CRES
Lombard Bsns Pk
IKEA Ampere Way
DRAKE RD
ONSLOW RD
EFFINGHAM RD
A236
SM6
OAKLEY CT
PRIMROSE CL
BLUEBELL CL
FOXGLOVE WAY
HELIOS RD
NEW RD
ORCHARD AVE
CHERRY CT
MULLARDS CL
Sch
Beddington Farm
WIMSHURST CL
BEDDINGTON FARM RD
MAXWELL CL
HESTERMAN WAY
VOLTA WAY
NEWMAN RD
ALLEN RD
AMPERE WAY
FARADAY WAY
PURLEY WAY
Pioneers Ind Pk
MILE RD
1 SANDMARTIN WAY
2 OAK WLK
3 DUNSTER WAY
4 POPPY CL
30

1
MEDLAND CL
SENGA RD
CLOVER WAY
VIOLET CL
FURLONG CL
MILE RD
Sewage Works
Beddington Ind Est
DANIELL WAY
Superstore
GALVANI WAY
WADDON MARSH WAY
GURNEY CRES
LONGFIELD AVE
ELM RD
LODGE CL
LINK RD
CORBET CL
CULVERS AVE
B277
A237
SohoMills Ind Est
BATH HOUSE RD
PYLON WAY
B272
A23

66
28 A B 29 C D 30 E F

60
42

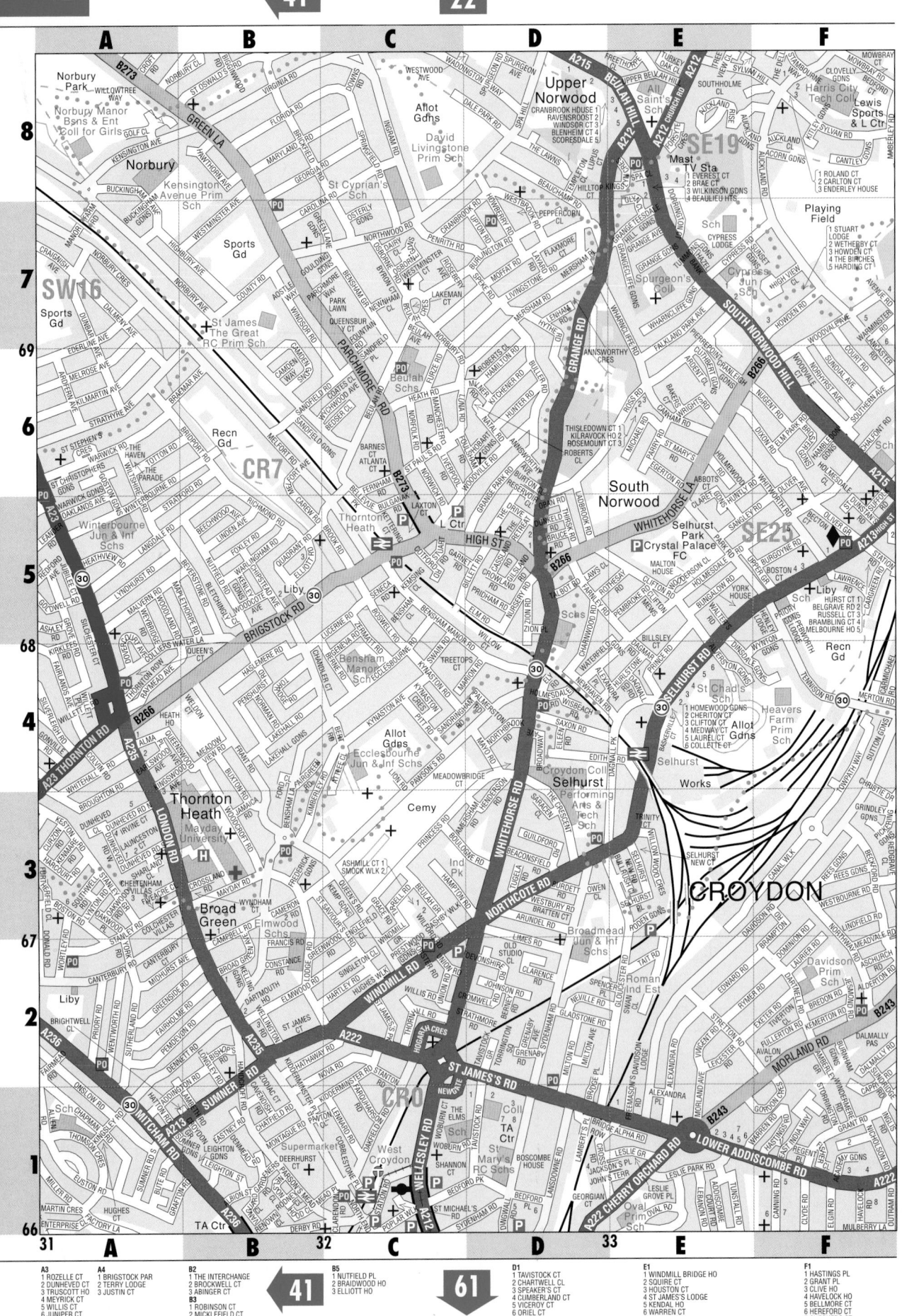

A3
1 ROZELLE CT
2 DUNHEVED CT
3 TRUSCOTT HO
4 MEYRICK CT
5 WILLIS CT
6 JUNIPER CT

A4
1 BRIGSTOCK PAR
2 TERRY LODGE
3 JUSTIN CT

B2
1 THE INTERCHANGE
2 BROCKWELL CT
3 ABINGER CT
B3
1 ROBINSON CT
2 MICKLEFIELD CT

B5
1 NUTFIELD PL
2 BRAIDWOOD HO
3 ELLIOTT HO

D1
1 TAVISTOCK CT
2 CHARTWELL CL
3 SPEAKER'S CT
4 CUMBERLAND CT
5 VICEROY CT
6 ORIEL CT
7 SOLA CT
8 GAMMA CT

E1
1 WINDMILL BRIDGE HO
2 SQUIRE CT
3 HOUSTON CT
4 ST JAMES'S LODGE
5 KENDAL HO
6 WARREN CT
7 KENDAL CT

F1
1 HASTINGS PL
2 GRANT PL
3 CLIVE HO
4 HAVELOCK HO
5 BELLMORE CT
6 HEREFORD CT
7 CHEQUERS CT
8 HAVELOCK HALL

23
44

B8
1 ST HUGH'S RD
2 DORSET HO
3 COLLINGWOOD CL
4 CHARTWELL WAY
5 ESSEX TOWER
6 APPLETREE CL
7 DITTON PL
8 KELVIN CT
9 READMAN CT
10 GLEN CT
11 KINGSBRIDGE HO
12 CARLTON CT
13 BENHURST CT
14 CAROLE HO
15 DOVER HO
16 BETTSWOOD CT

F7
1 RECTORY CT
2 MOLVIC CT
3 FIRBANK

F8
1 ASHTON CT
2 COOMBE CT
3 FONTAINE CT
4 RICHFIELD CT
5 LATHKILL CT
6 ELSA CT

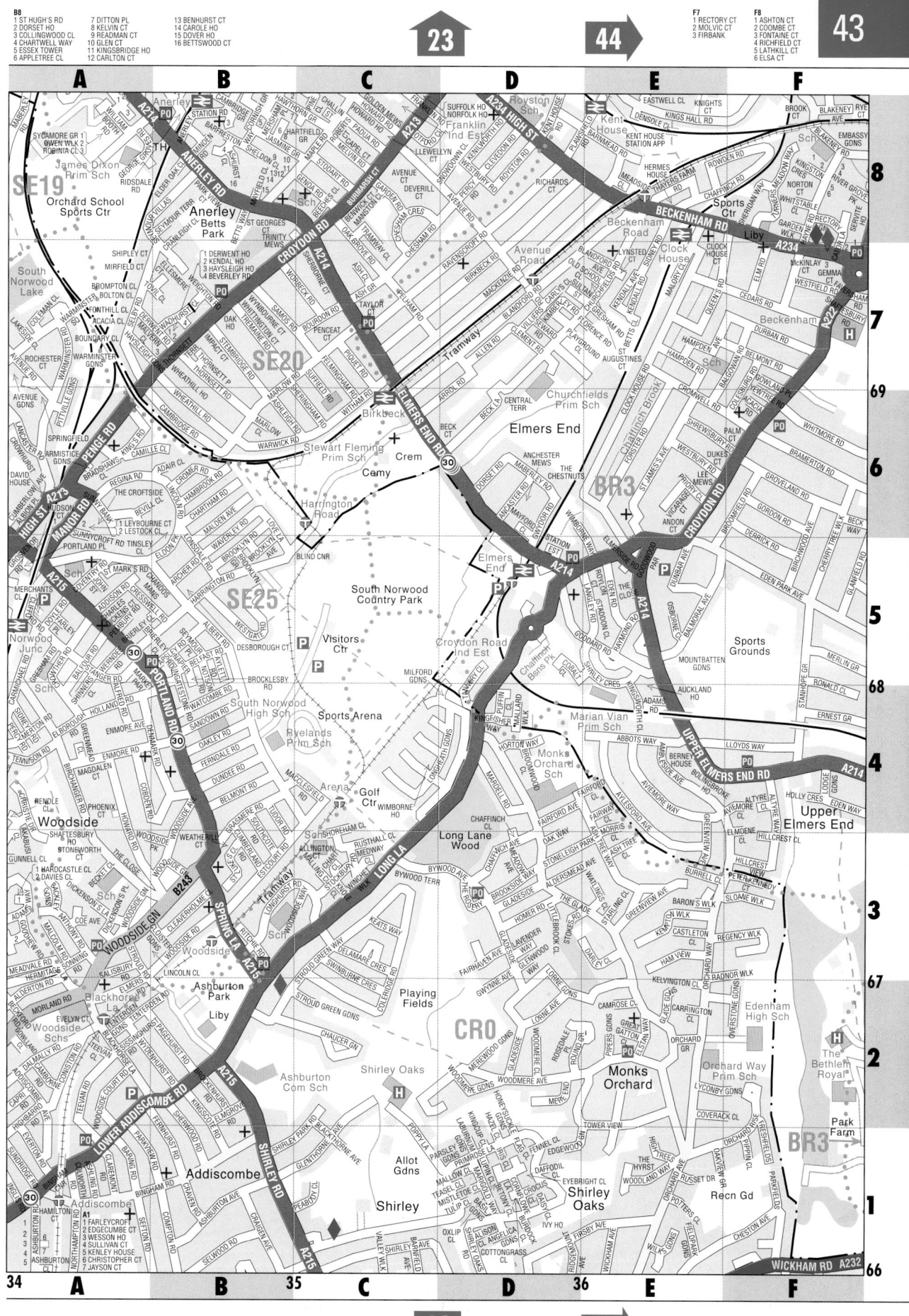

43

24

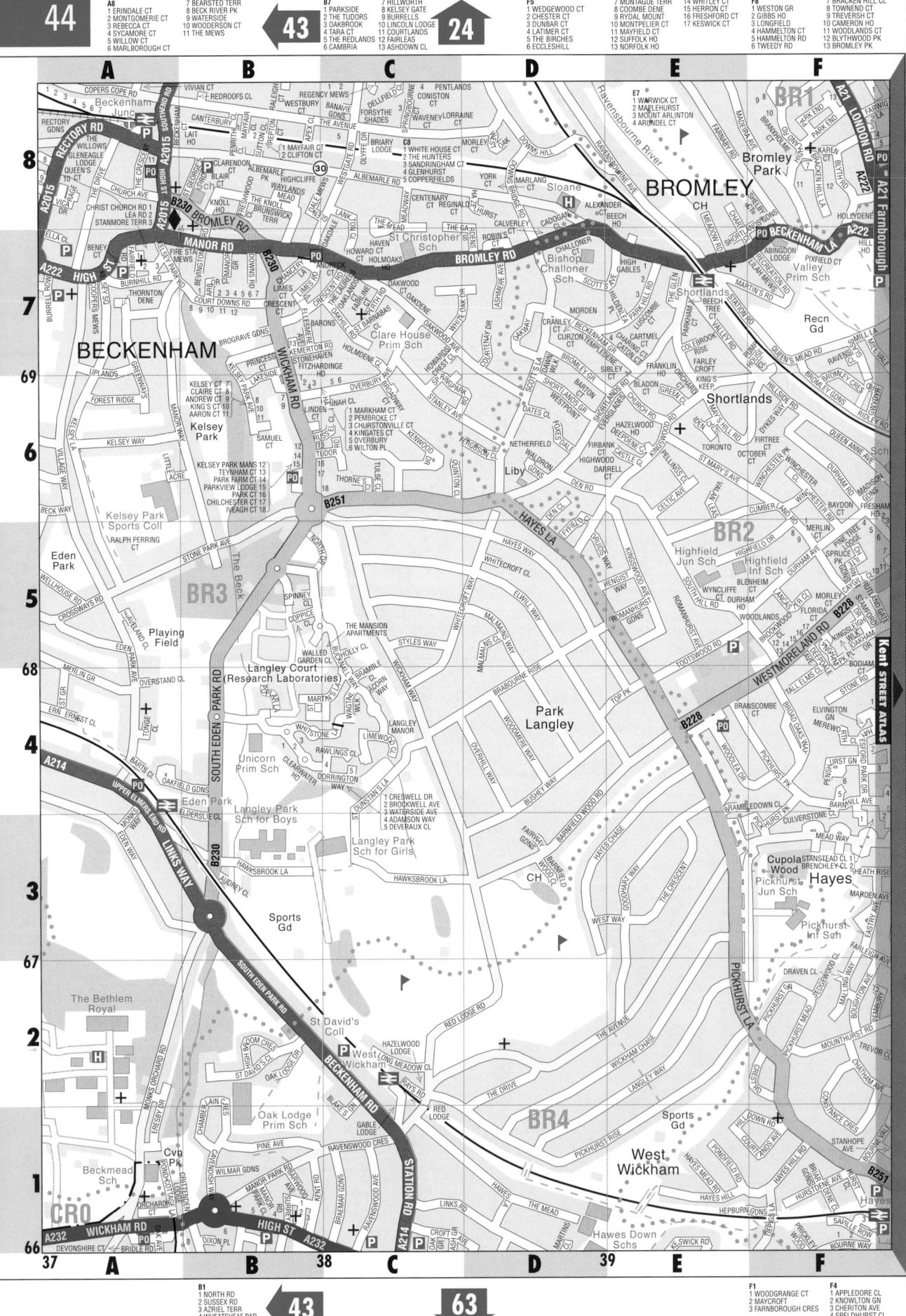

43

63

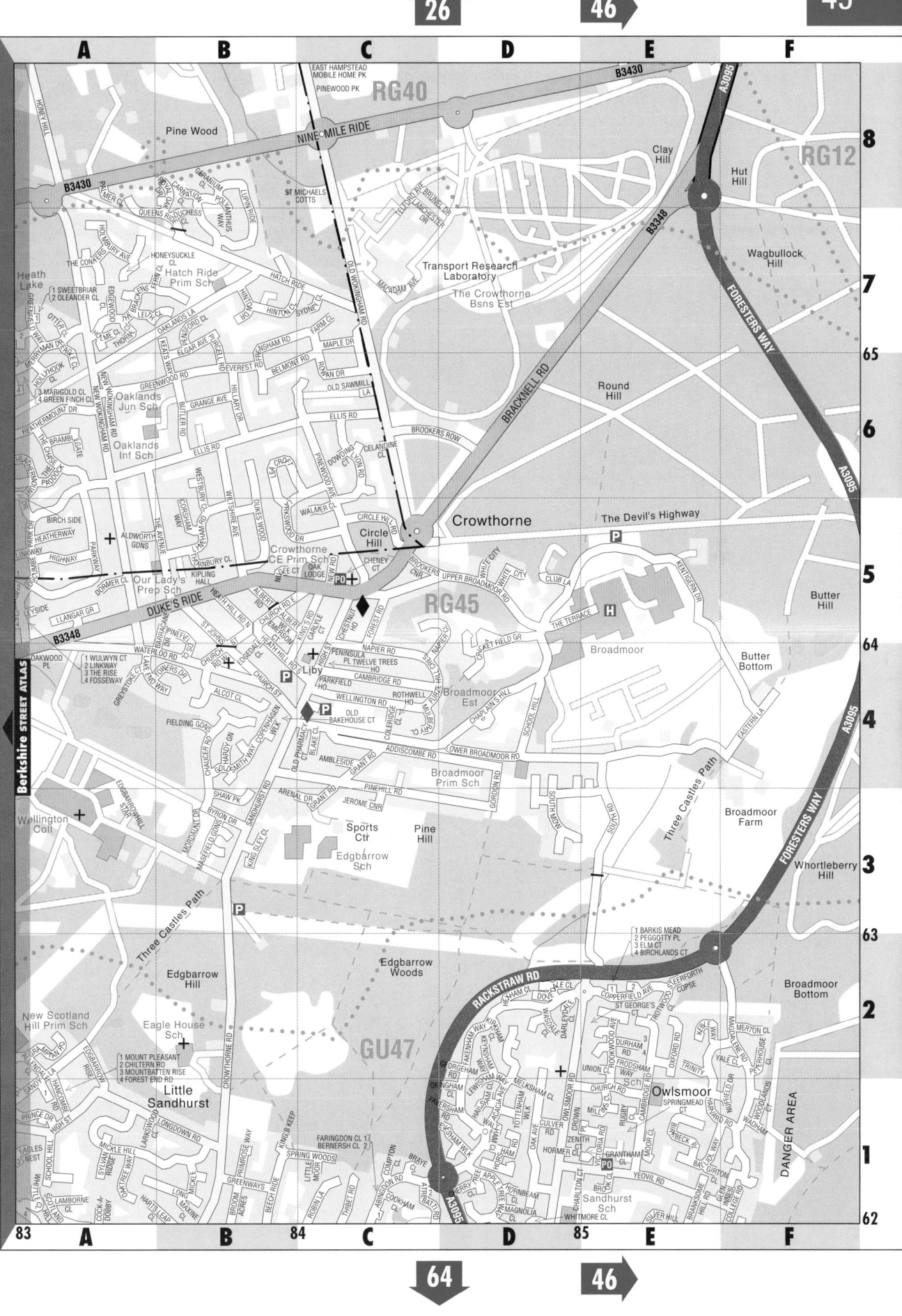

Berkshire STREET ATLAS

RG40
RG12
RG45
GU47

East Hampstead Mobile Home Pk
Pinewood Pk
Pine Wood
NINE MILE RIDE
B3430
St Michaels Cotts

Clay Hill
Hut Hill
Wagbullock Hill

Heath Lake
Hatch Ride Prim Sch
Transport Research Laboratory
The Crowthorne Bsns Est
Round Hill

FORESTERS WAY
BRACKNELL RD
B3348

Oaklands Jun Sch
Oaklands Inf Sch

Crowthorne
The Devil's Highway
Butter Hill

Circle Hill
Crowthorne CE Prim Sch
Our Lady's Prep Sch
Broadmoor
Butter Bottom

DUKE'S RIDE
B3348

Liby
Twelve Trees Ho
Broadmoor Est
Three Castles Path
Broadmoor Farm

Old Bakehouse Ct
Broadmoor Prim Sch
Whortleberry Hill

Wellington Coll
Sports Ctr
Pine Hill
Edgbarrow Sch

Three Castles Path
Edgbarrow Hill
Edgbarrow Woods
RACKSTRAW RD
Broadmoor Bottom

New Scotland Hill Prim Sch
Eagle House Sch
Owlsmoor
Springmead Ct
DANGER AREA

Little Sandhurst
Sandhurst Sch

FORESTERS WAY
A3095

1 SWEETBRIAR
2 OLEANDER CL

1 MARIGOLD CL
4 GREEN FINCH CL

1 WULWYN CT
2 LINKWAY
3 THE RISE
4 FOSSEWAY

1 MOUNT PLEASANT
2 CHILTERN RD
3 MOUNTBATTEN RISE
4 FOREST END RD

1 BARKIS MEAD
2 PEGGOTTY PL
3 ELM CT
4 BIRCHLANDS CT

FARINGDON CL 1
BERNERSH CL 2

45
27

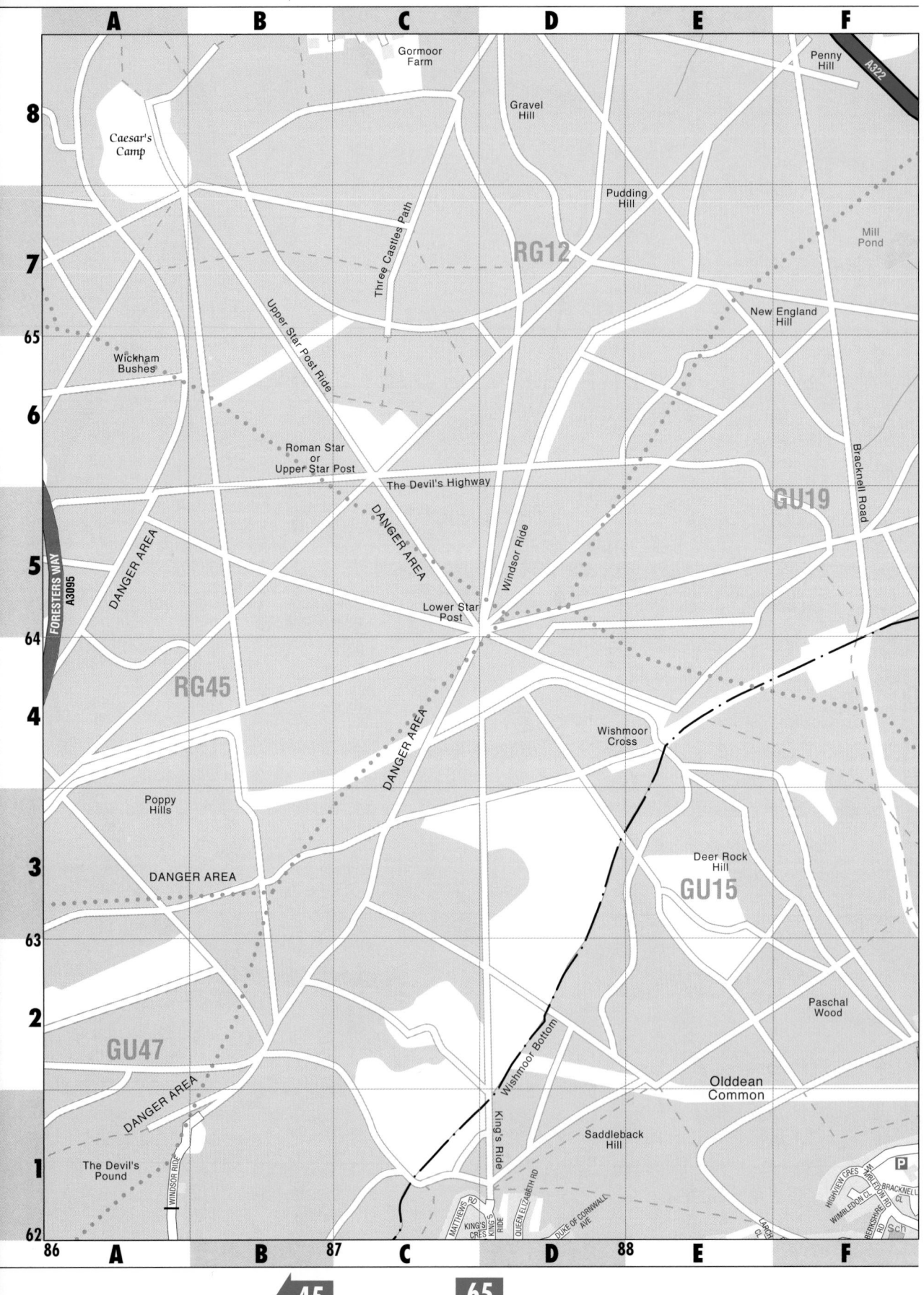
Gormoor Farm
Penny Hill
A322
Gravel Hill
Caesar's Camp
Pudding Hill
RG12
Three Castles Path
Mill Pond
New England Hill
Upper Star Post Ride
Wickham Bushes
Roman Star or Upper Star Post
The Devil's Highway
Bracknell Road
GU19
DANGER AREA
Windsor Ride
FORESTERS WAY
A3095
Lower Star Post
RG45
Wishmoor Cross
Poppy Hills
Deer Rock Hill
GU15
Paschal Wood
GU47
Wishmoor Bottom
Olddean Common
King's Ride
Saddleback Hill
The Devil's Pound
WINDSOR RIDE
MATTHEWS RD
KING'S CRES
KING'S RIDE
QUEEN ELIZABETH RD
DUKE OF CORNWALL AVE
LARCH CL
HIGHVIEW CRES
WIMBLEDON CL
WIMBLEDON RD
BRACKNELL CL
BERKSHIRE RD
Sch
P
A B C D E F
8 7 65 6 5 64 4 3 63 2 1 62
86 87 88

45
65

28
48

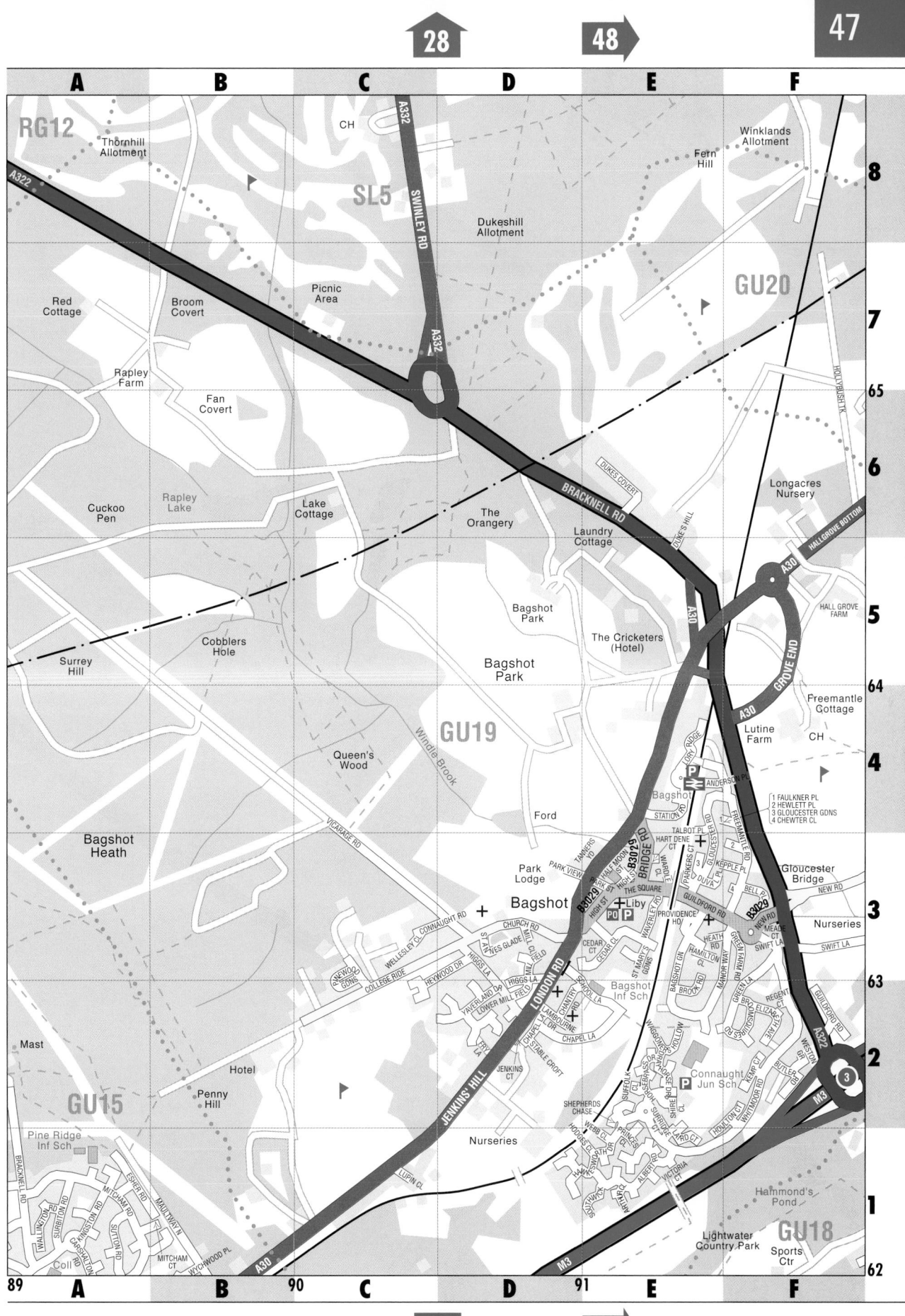
RG12
Thornhill Allotment
CH
SL5
SWINLEY RD
A332
A322
Dukeshill Allotment
Fern Hill
Winklands Allotment
GU20
Red Cottage
Broom Covert
Picnic Area
Rapley Farm
Fan Covert
Cuckoo Pen
Rapley Lake
Lake Cottage
The Orangery
BRACKNELL RD
DUKES COVERT
DUKE'S HILL
Laundry Cottage
Longacres Nursery
HALLGROVE BOTTOM
HOLLYBUSH LA
A30
HALL GROVE FARM
Surrey Hill
Cobblers Hole
Bagshot Park
The Cricketers (Hotel)
GROVE END
Freemantle Cottage
Lutine Farm
GU19
Windle Brook
Queen's Wood
Bagshot Heath
VICARAGE RD
Ford
Bagshot
STATION RD
ANDERSON PL
1 FAULKNER PL
2 HEWLETT PL
3 GLOUCESTER GDNS
4 CHEWTER CL
Park Lodge
Bagshot
B3029
BRIDGE RD
HIGH ST
THE SQUARE
GUILDFORD RD
Liby
PO
Gloucester Bridge
NEW RD
Nurseries
SWIFT LA
CONNAUGHT RD
CHURCH RD
WELLESLEY CL
COLLEGE RIDE
HEYWOOD DR
HIGGS LA
LONDON RD
Bagshot Inf Sch
Mast
Hotel
Penny Hill
JENKINS' HILL
Connaught Jun Sch
GU15
Pine Ridge Inf Sch
Nurseries
LUPIN CL
Hammond's Pond
GU18
Lightwater Country Park
Sports Ctr
M3
A322
3
BRACKNELL RD
WALLINGTON RD
SURBITON RD
KINGSTON RD
CARSHALTON RD
MITCHAM RD
SUTTON RD
ESHER RD
MAULTWAY N
MITCHAM CT
WYCHWOOD PL
Coll

66
48

Earlywood
SL5
Windsor Manor
King's Hill
Windlesham Hall
Windlemere
Windlesham Hall Farm
Windlesham Moor
Merrywood
Lennoxwood
LONDON RD
SUNNINGHILL RD
BAGSHOT RD
The Windmill (PH)
Erl Wood Manor
Ribs Down
Nursery
Allerton Hill
The Brickmakers Arms (PH)
Ribsden Hall
Camus
Hatton Hill
Windlesham Village Inf Sch
SCHOOL RD
Woodcote House Sch
GU20
Mast
CHERTSEY RD
KENNEL LA
Hall Grove Sch
Recn Gd
UPDOWN HILL
Windlesham
Heathpark Wood
NEW RD
The Half Moon (PH)
Birch Hall
Oak Wood
WOODLANDS LA
Ashleigh Farm
Windlesham Park
GU19
Caravan Site
Twelve Oaks
South Farm
Windlesham Arboretum
Old House Farm
Windle Brook
Scutley La
GU24
Halebourne Copse
Lee Lane Farm
Broadway Green Farm
Manor Farm Wood
Rectory Farm
Cemy
Sch
GU18
Sewage Works
Lightwater
Hale Bourne

30
50

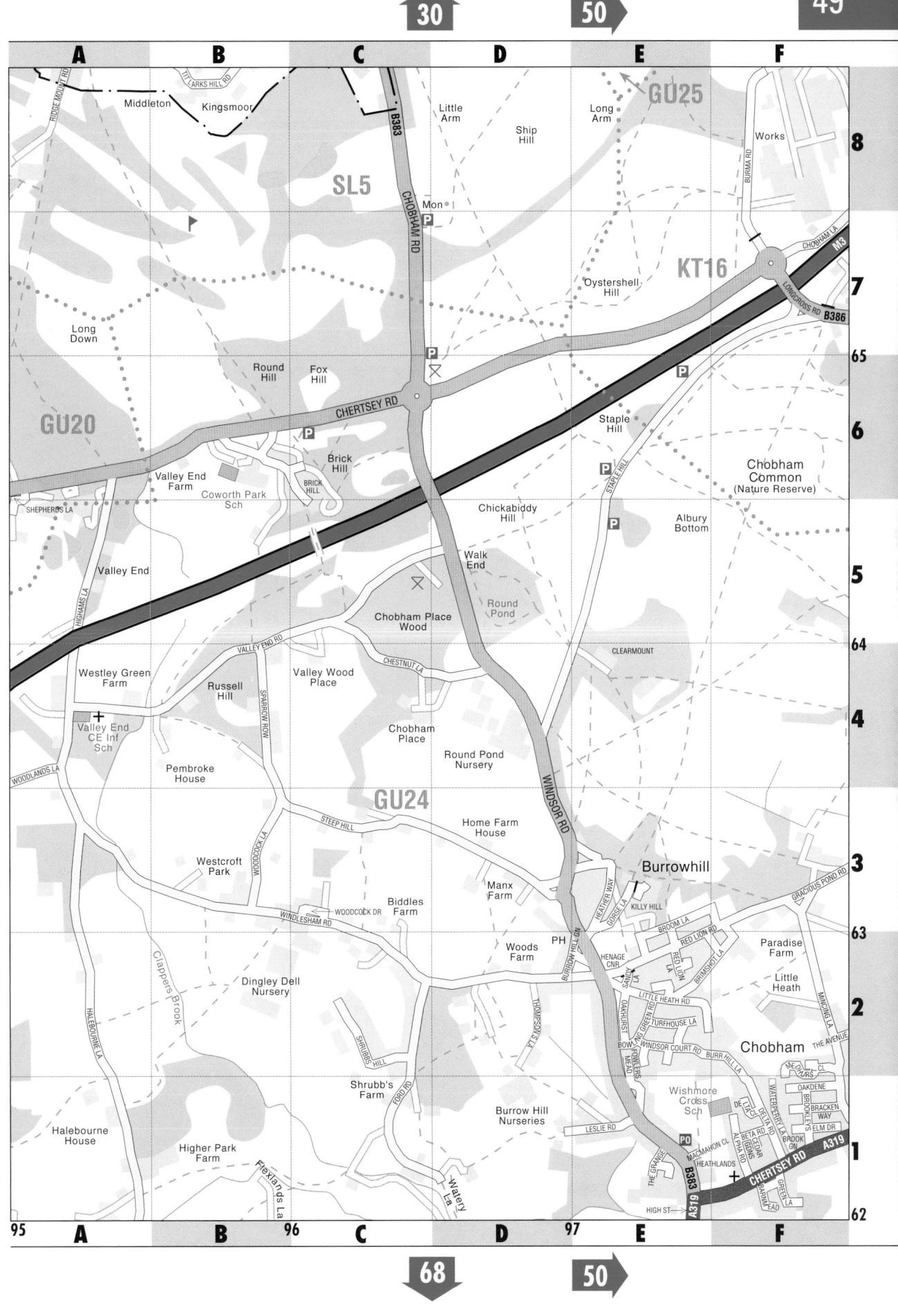
A
B
C
D
E
F
8
7
65
6
5
64
4
3
63
2
1
62
95
96
97
Middleton
Kingsmoor
LARKS HILL RD
RIDGE MOUNT RD
B383
Little Arm
Ship Hill
Long Arm
GU25
Works
BURMA RD
SL5
CHOBHAM RD
Mon
KT16
CHOBHAM LA
M3
Oystershell Hill
LONGCROSS RD
B386
Long Down
Round Hill
Fox Hill
CHERTSEY RD
GU20
Staple Hill
Brick Hill
Chobham Common
(Nature Reserve)
Valley End Farm
Coworth Park Sch
BRICK HILL
STAPLE HILL
SHEPHERDS LA
Chickabiddy Hill
Albury Bottom
Walk End
Valley End
Round Pond
HIGHAMS LA
Chobham Place Wood
VALLEY END RD
CLEARMOUNT
CHESTNUT LA
Westley Green Farm
Russell Hill
Valley Wood Place
SPARROW ROW
Valley End CE Inf Sch
Chobham Place
Round Pond Nursery
WOODLANDS LA
Pembroke House
GU24
WINDSOR RD
STEEP HILL
Home Farm House
Westcroft Park
WOODCOCK LA
Burrowhill
GRACIOUS POND RD
Manx Farm
HEATHER WAY
KILLY HILL
GORSE LA
Biddles Farm
WOODCOCK DR
WINDLESHAM RD
BROOM LA
RED LION RD
PH
Woods Farm
Paradise Farm
BURROW HILL GN
HENAGE CNR
RED LION LA
BRIMSHOT LA
SANDY LA
Dingley Dell Nursery
Clappers Brook
Little Heath
LITTLE HEATH RD
THOMPSON'S LA
BOWLING GREEN RD
OAKHURST
TURFHOUSE LA
MINCING LA
HALEBOURNE LA
SHRUBBS HILL
WINDSOR COURT RD
BURR HILL LA
Chobham
THE AVENUE
BOWLING GREEN MEAD
FOWLERS
MEDHURST CL
OAKDENE
Shrubb's Farm
FORD RD
Wishmore Cross Sch
WATERPERRY LA
DELTA RD
BROOKLEYS
BRACKEN WAY
ELM DR
Burrow Hill Nurseries
LESLIE RD
BETA RD
CEDAR GDNS
BROOK GN
Halebourne House
ALPHA RD
PO
MACMAHON CL
A319
Higher Park Farm
THE GRANGE
HEATHLANDS
CHERTSEY RD
Flexlands La
Watery La
BARNMEAD
GREEN LA
HIGH ST
B383
A319

68
50

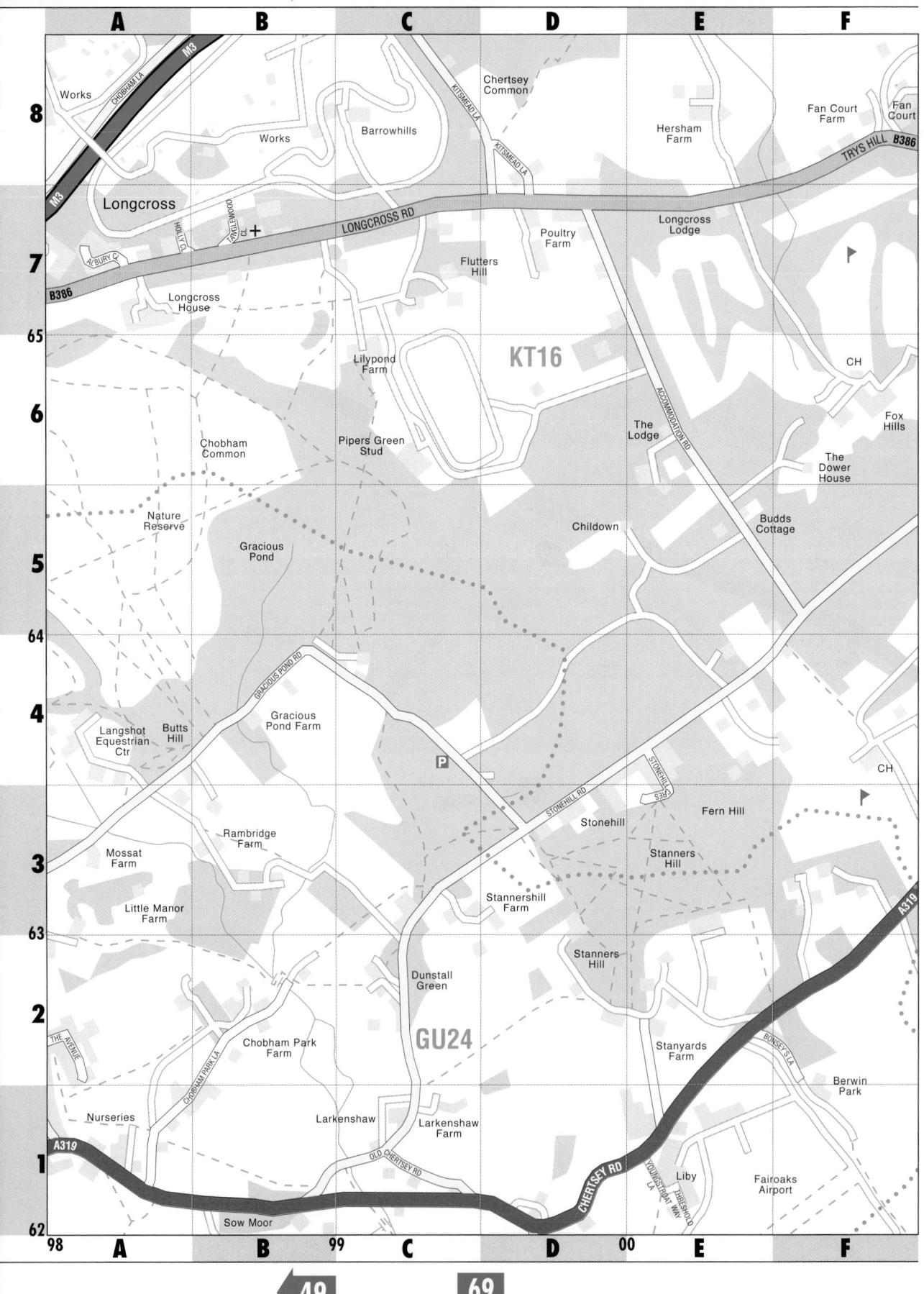

A B C D E F

8 Works Works Barrowhills Chertsey Common Hersham Farm Fan Court Farm Fan Court

Longcross Longcross Lodge

7 LONGCROSS RD Poultry Farm TRYS HILL B386

Longcross House Flutters Hill

65 KT16

Lilypond Farm

6 Chobham Common Pipers Green Stud The Lodge Fox Hills The Dower House

Nature Reserve Childown Budds Cottage

5 Gracious Pond

64

Gracious Pond Farm CH

4 Langshot Equestrian Ctr Butts Hill

STONEHILL RD Stonehill Fern Hill

3 Mossat Farm Rambridge Farm Stannershill Farm Stanners Hill

Little Manor Farm

63 Stanners Hill

2 Dunstall Green GU24 Stanyards Farm Berwin Park

Chobham Park Farm

Nurseries Larkenshaw Larkenshaw Farm Liby Fairoaks Airport

1 A319 OLD CHERTSEY RD CHERTSEY RD A319

62 Sow Moor

98 A B 99 C D 00 E F

32
52

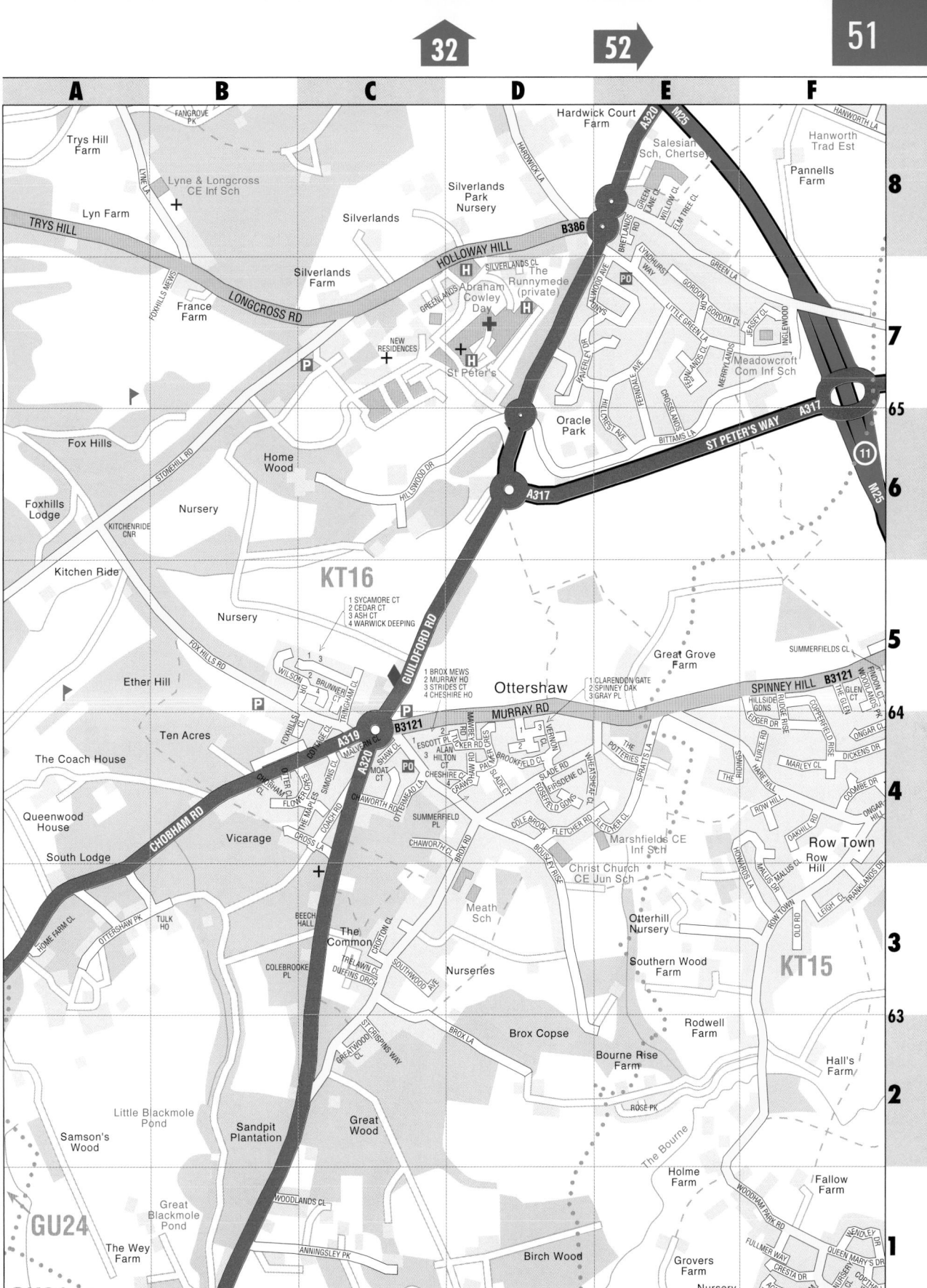
Hardwick Court Farm
Trys Hill Farm
Lyne & Longcross CE Inf Sch
Salesian Sch, Chertsey
Hanworth Trad Est
Pannells Farm
Silverlands Park Nursery
Lyn Farm
Silverlands
TRYS HILL
HOLLOWAY HILL
LONGCROSS RD
Silverlands Farm
France Farm
Abraham Cowley Day
The Runnymede (private)
St Peter's
NEW RESIDENCES
Meadowcroft Com Inf Sch
ST PETER'S WAY
Oracle Park
Fox Hills
Home Wood
Foxhills Lodge
Nursery
Kitchen Ride
KT16
GUILDFORD RD
Great Grove Farm
Ether Hill
Ottershaw
SPINNEY HILL
MURRAY RD
Ten Acres
The Coach House
CHOBHAM RD
Queenwood House
Vicarage
South Lodge
Marshfields CE Inf Sch
Christ Church CE Jun Sch
Row Town
Row Hill
Meath Sch
Otterhill Nursery
The Common
Southern Wood Farm
KT15
Nurseries
Brox Copse
Rodwell Farm
Bourne Rise Farm
Hall's Farm
Little Blackmole Pond
Samson's Wood
Sandpit Plantation
Great Wood
The Bourne
Holme Farm
Fallow Farm
GU24
Great Blackmole Pond
The Wey Farm
Birch Wood
Grovers Farm
Nursery
GU21
Anningsley Park

70
52

51
33

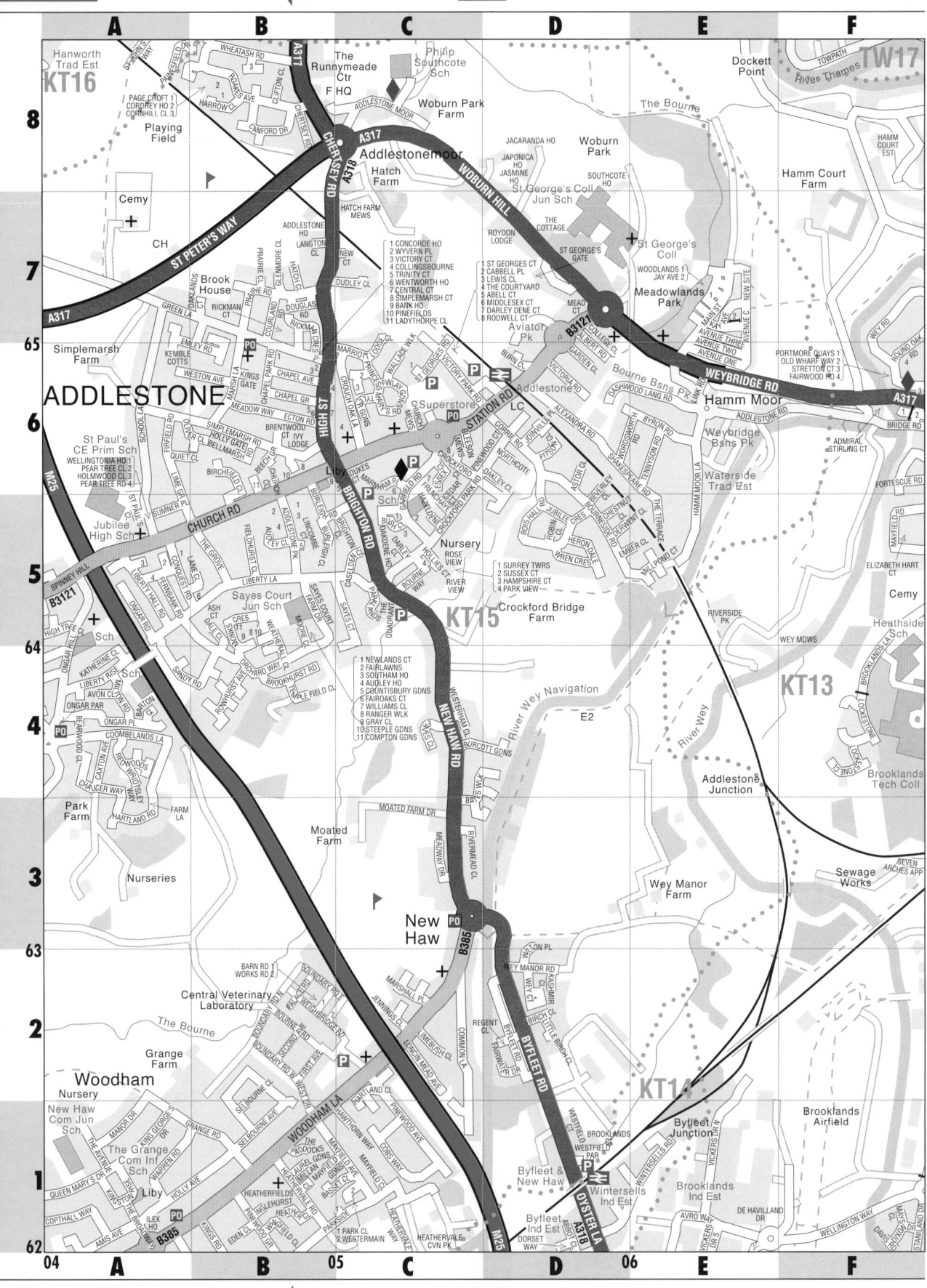
A
B
C
D
E
F
8
7
65
6
5
64
4
3
63
2
1
62
04
05
06
Hanworth Trad Est
KT16
TW17
Dockett Point
River Thames
TOWPATH
The Runnymeade Ctr
F HQ
Philip Southcote Sch
Woburn Park Farm
The Bourne
Playing Field
Addlestonemoor
Hatch Farm
Woburn Park
Hamm Court Farm
HAMM COURT EST
Cemy
CH
St George's Coll Jun Sch
St George's Coll
ST PETER'S WAY
A317
A318
CHERTSEY RD
WOBURN HILL
WEYBRIDGE RD
Brook House
Meadowlands Park
Simplemarsh Farm
ADDLESTONE
Aviator Pk
Addlestone
Superstore
STATION RD
LC
Bourne Bsns Pk
Hamm Moor
Weybridge Bsns Pk
Waterside Trad Est
HIGH ST
BRIGHTON RD
CHURCH RD
St Paul's CE Prim Sch
Jubilee High Sch
Liby
Sch
Nursery
B3121
M25
SPINNEY HILL
Sayes Court Jun Sch
KT15
Crockford Bridge Farm
Cemy
Heathside Sch
KT13
River Wey Navigation
River Wey
E2
Addlestone Junction
Brooklands Tech Coll
NEW HAW RD
Park Farm
Moated Farm
Nurseries
Wey Manor Farm
Sewage Works
New Haw
B385
Central Veterinary Laboratory
The Bourne
Grange Farm
Woodham
Nursery
New Haw Com Jun Sch
The Grange Com Inf Sch
WOODHAM LA
BYFLEET RD
KT14
Byfleet Junction
Brooklands Airfield
Byfleet & New Haw
Wintersells Ind Est
Brooklands Ind Est
Byfleet Ind Est
OYSTER LA
HEATHERVALE CVN PK
1 CONCORDE HO
2 WYVERN PL
3 VICTORY CT
4 COLLINGSBOURNE
5 TRINITY CT
6 WENTWORTH HO
7 CENTRAL CT
8 SIMPLEMARSH CT
9 BANK HO
10 PINEFIELDS
11 LADYTHORPE CL
1 ST GEORGES CT
2 CABBELL PL
3 LEWIS CL
4 THE COURTYARD
5 ABELL CT
6 MIDDLESEX CT
7 DARLEY DENE CT
8 RODWELL CT
1 SURREY TWRS
2 SUSSEX CT
3 HAMPSHIRE CT
4 PARK VIEW
1 NEWLANDS CT
2 FAIRLAWNS
3 SOUTHAM HO
4 AUDLEY HO
5 COUNTISBURY GDNS
6 FAIROAKS CT
7 WILLIAMS CL
8 RANGER WLK
9 GRAY CL
10 STEEPLE GDNS
11 COMPTON GDNS
PAGE CROFT 1
CORDREY HO 2
CORNHILL CL 3
WELLINGTONIA HO 1
PEAR TREE CL 2
HOLMWOOD CL 3
PEAR TREE RD 4
PORTMORE QUAYS 1
OLD WHARF WAY 2
STRETTON CT 3
FAIRWOOD HO 4
BARN RD 1
WORKS RD 2
1 PARK CL
2 WESTERMAIN

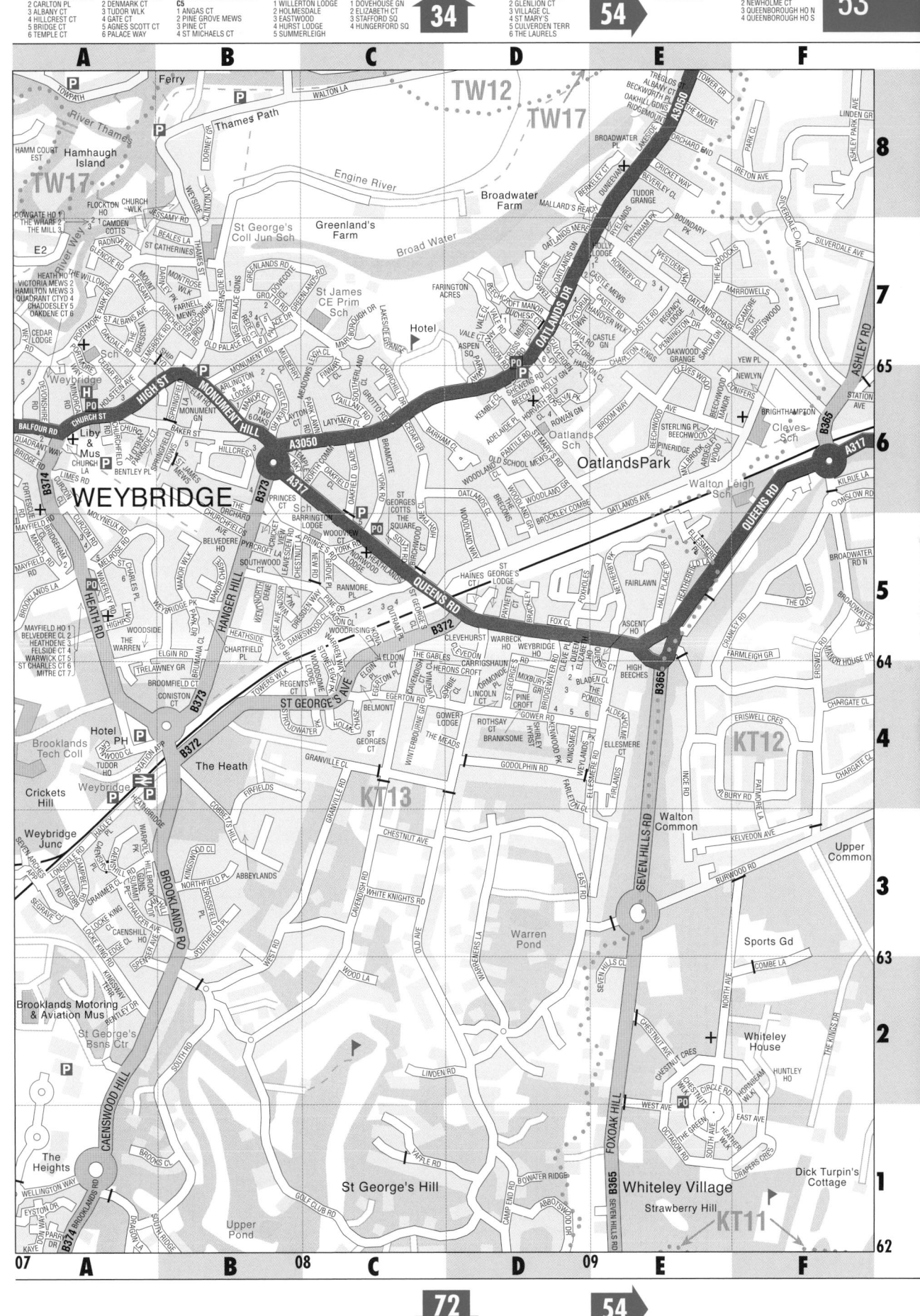

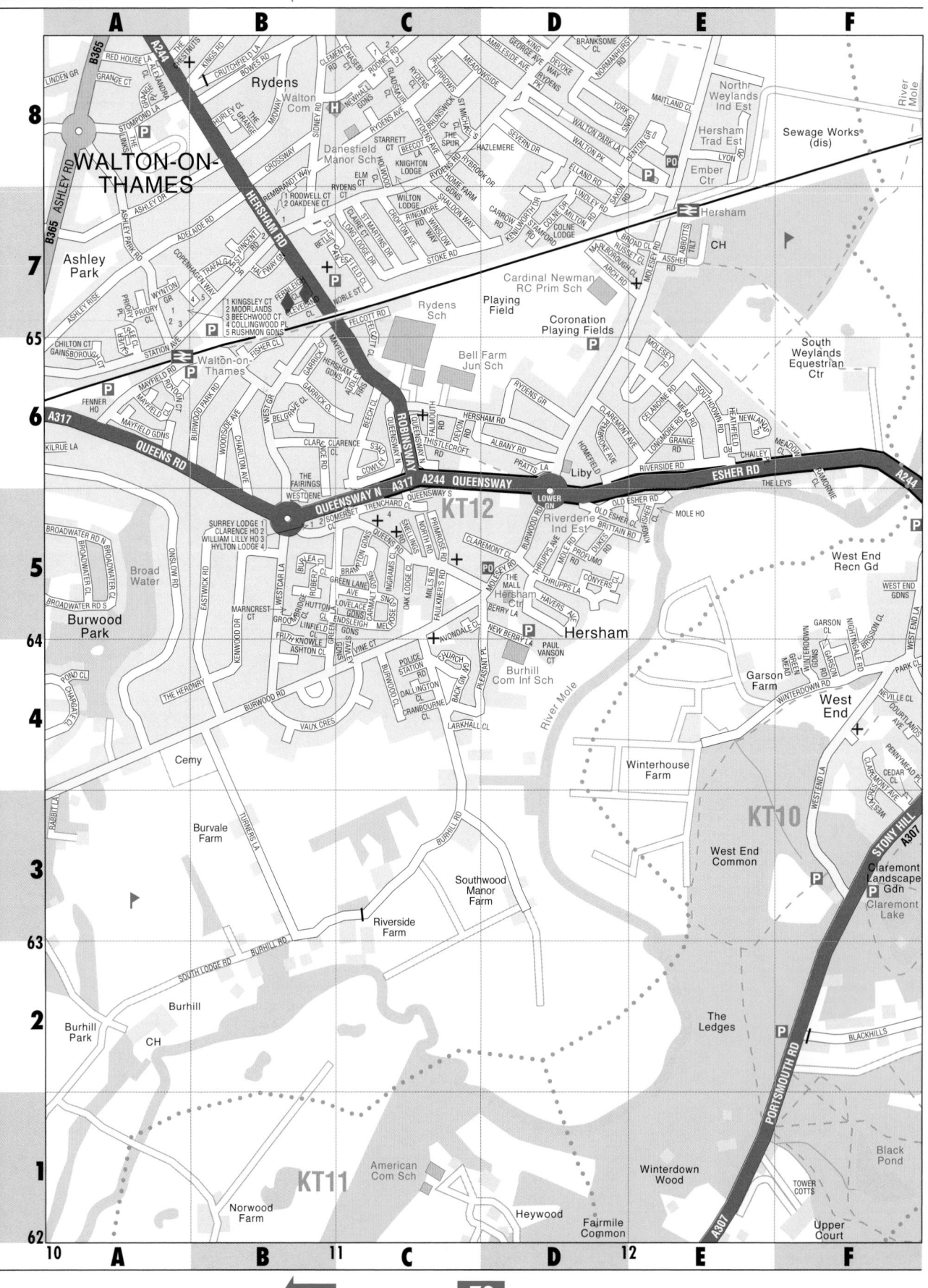

36
56

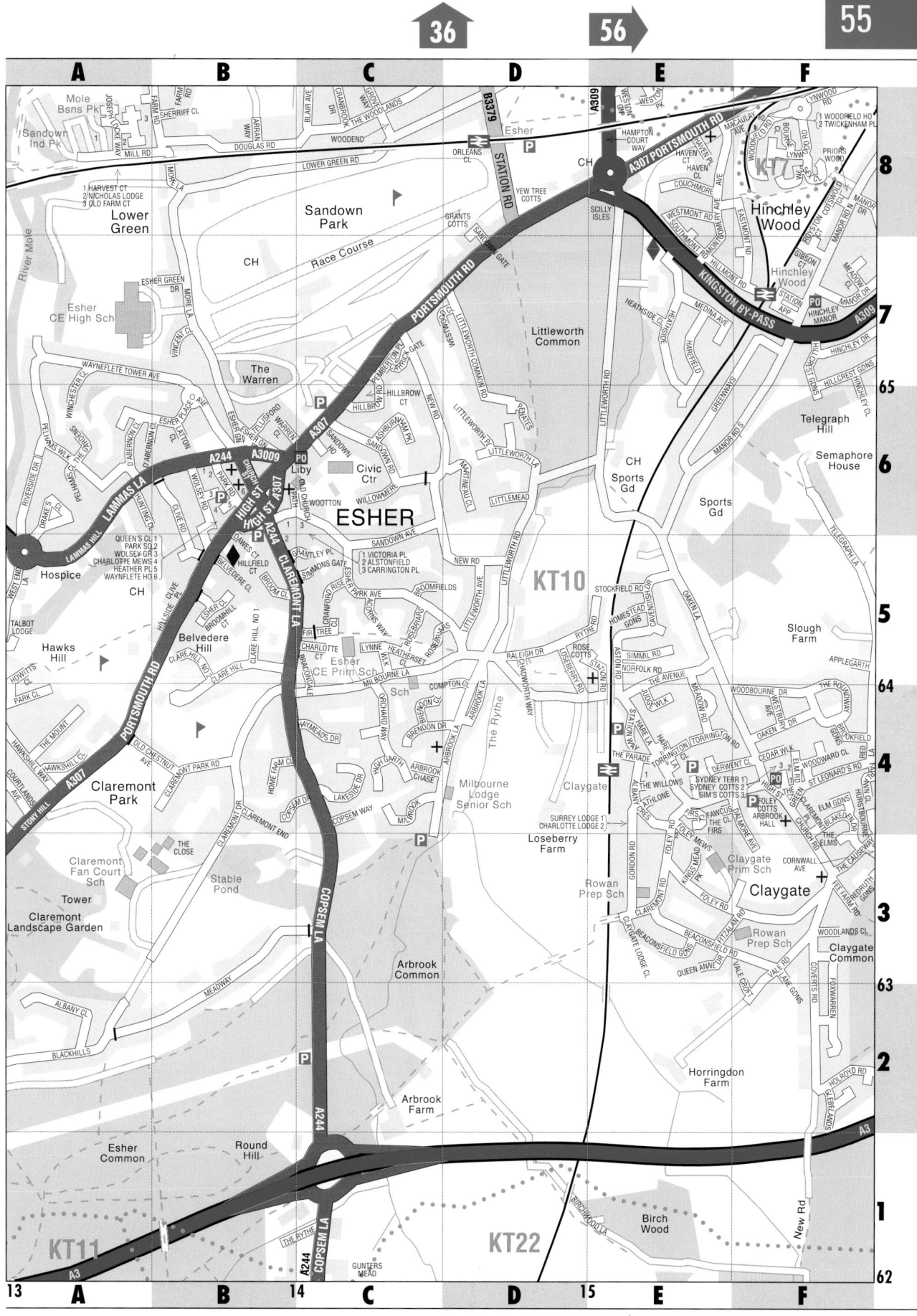
ESHER
Esher
Sandown Park
Race Course
Lower Green
Esher CE High Sch
The Warren
Civic Ctr
Littleworth Common
Hinchley Wood
Telegraph Hill
Semaphore House
Sports Gd
Hospice
Hawks Hill
Belvedere Hill
Claremont Park
Claremont Fan Court Sch
Claremont Landscape Garden
Stable Pond
Arbrook Common
Arbrook Farm
Esher Common
Round Hill
Milbourne Lodge Senior Sch
Loseberry Farm
Claygate
Claygate Prim Sch
Rowan Prep Sch
Claygate Common
Horringdon Farm
Slough Farm
Birch Wood
KT10
KT11
KT22
KT7
PORTSMOUTH RD
KINGSTON BY-PASS
COPSEM LA
CLAREMONT LA
LITTLEWORTH RD
STATION RD
A307
A244
A309
A3
B3379

74
56

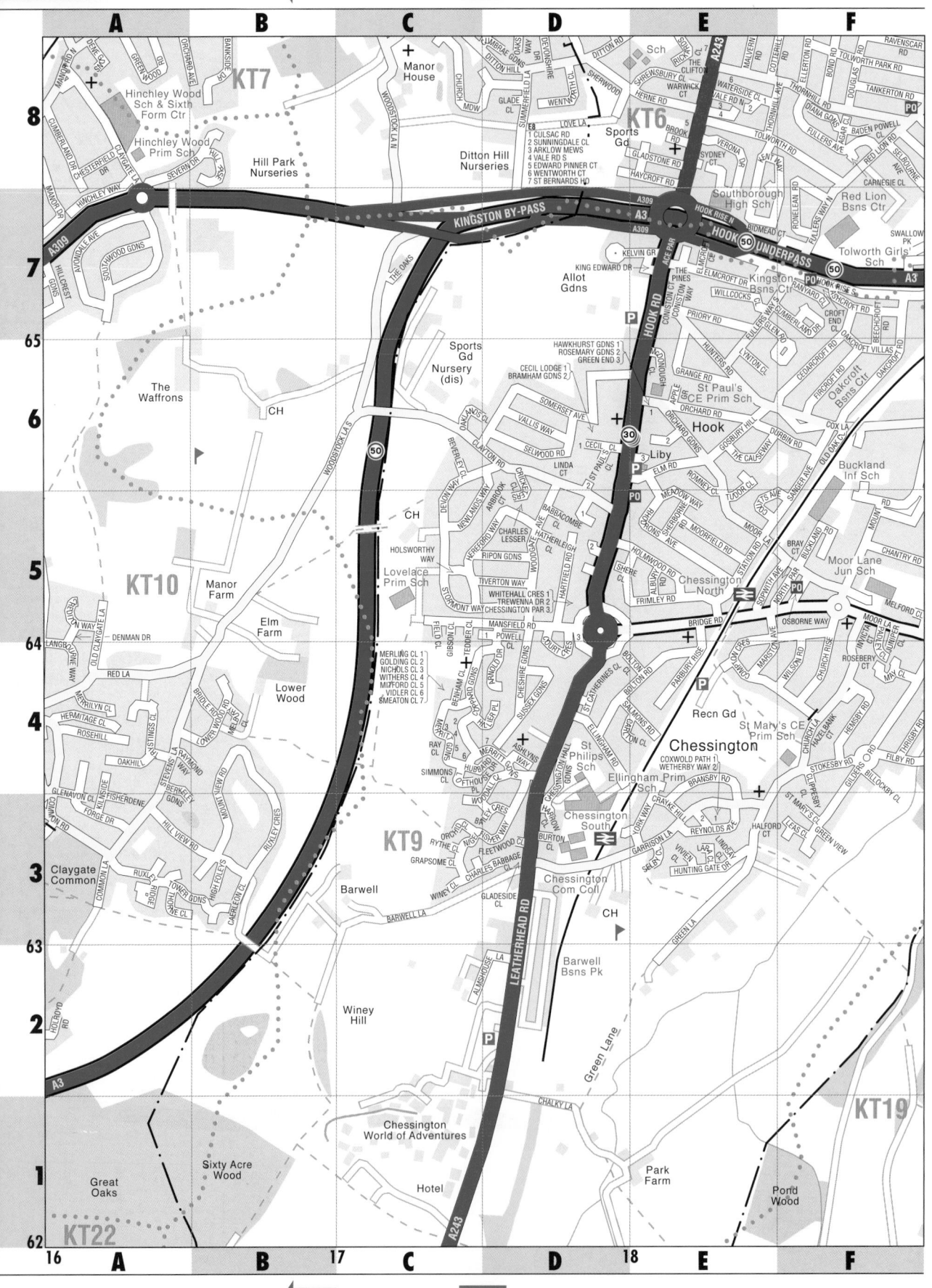
KT7
KT6
KT10
KT9
KT19
KT22
Hinchley Wood Sch & Sixth Form Ctr
Hinchley Wood Prim Sch
Hill Park Nurseries
Manor House
Ditton Hill Nurseries
Sports Gd
KINGSTON BY-PASS
HOOK UNDERPASS
Southborough High Sch
Red Lion Bsns Ctr
Tolworth Girls' Sch
Allot Gdns
Kingston Bsns Ctr
Sports Gd
Nursery (dis)
The Waffrons
St Paul's CE Prim Sch
Hook
Oakcroft Bsns Ctr
Buckland Inf Sch
Lovelace Prim Sch
Manor Farm
Elm Farm
Chessington North
Moor Lane Jun Sch
Lower Wood
Recn Gd
St Mary's CE Prim Sch
Chessington
St Philips Sch
Ellingham Prim Sch
Chessington South
Claygate Common
Barwell
Chessington Com Coll
Barwell Bsns Pk
Winey Hill
Green Lane
Chessington World of Adventures
Hotel
Park Farm
Pond Wood
Great Oaks
Sixty Acre Wood
LEATHERHEAD RD
HOOK RD
E8
1 CULSAC RD
2 SUNNINGDALE CL
3 ARKLOW MEWS
4 VALE RD S
5 EDWARD PINNER CT
6 WENTWORTH CT
7 ST BERNARDS HO
HAWKHURST GDNS 1
ROSEMARY GDNS 2
GREEN END 3
CECIL LODGE 1
BRAMHAM GDNS 2
WHITEHALL CRES 1
TREWENNA DR 2
CHESSINGTON PAR 3
MERLING CL 1
GOLDING CL 2
NICHOLS CL 3
WITHERS CL 4
MITFORD CL 5
VIDLER CL 6
SMEATON CL 7
COXWOLD PATH 1
WETHERBY WAY 2

38
58

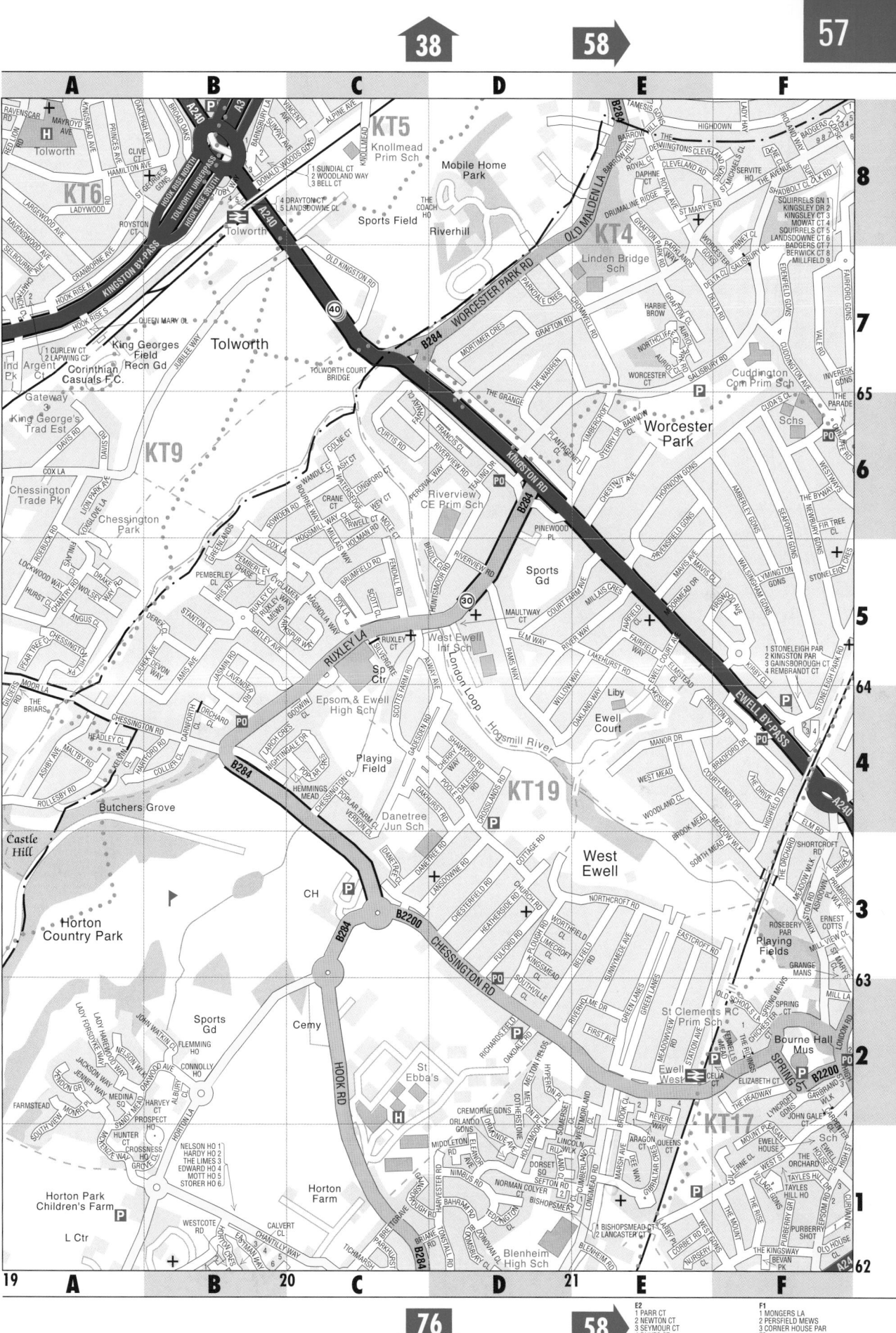

76
58

E2
1 PARR CT
2 NEWTON CT
3 SEYMOUR CT
4 DUKES CT

F1
1 MONGERS LA
2 PERSFIELD MEWS
3 CORNER HOUSE PAR

F2
1 LAVENDER LODGE
2 AUSTYNS PL
3 MARKET PAR
4 EWELL GROVE CT

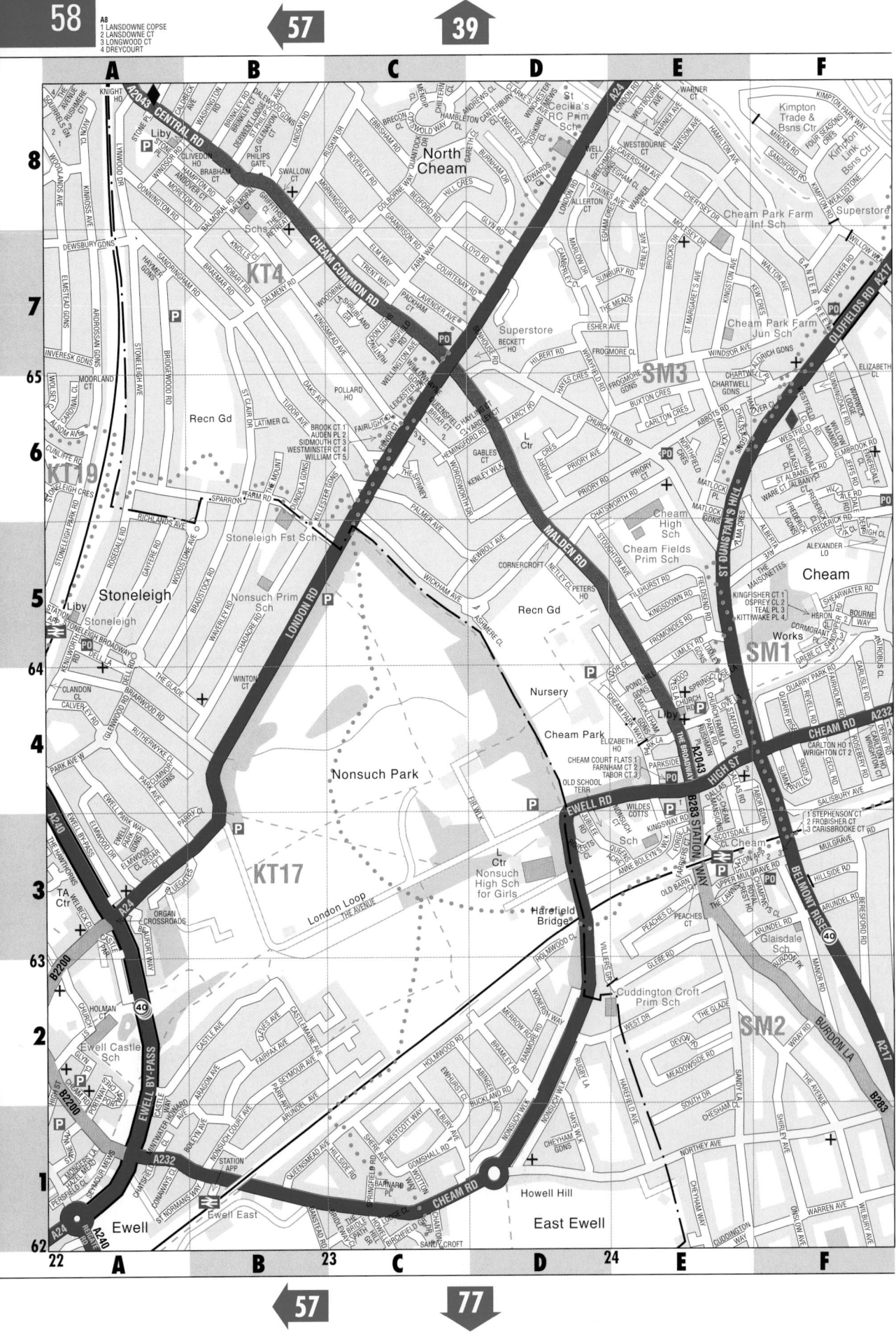
A B C D E F
8
7
65
6
5
64
4
3
63
2
1
62
22 23 24
North Cheam
St Cecilia's RC Prim Sch
Kimpton Trade & Bsns Ctr
Kimpton Link Bsns Ctr
Superstore
Cheam Park Farm Inf Sch
Cheam Park Farm Jun Sch
KT4
SM3
KT19
SM1
SM2
KT17
CENTRAL RD
CHEAM COMMON RD
LONDON RD
MALDEN RD
ST DUNSTAN'S HILL
OLDFIELDS RD
CHEAM RD
HIGH ST
EWELL RD
STATION WAY
BELMONT RISE
EWELL BY-PASS
BURDON LA
Recn Gd
Stoneleigh Fst Sch
Stoneleigh
Liby
Nonsuch Prim Sch
Cheam High Sch
Cheam Fields Prim Sch
Cheam
Works
Nursery
Cheam Park
Nonsuch Park
London Loop
Nonsuch High Sch for Girls
Harefield Bridge
Glaisdale Sch
Cuddington Croft Prim Sch
Ewell Castle Sch
Ewell East
Howell Hill
East Ewell
Ewell
A24
A217
A232
A240
A2043
B2200
B283
B279

B5
1 CORNELIAN COTTS
2 WALPOLE CT
3 FARMSTEAD CT
4 DERBY HO
5 SALISBURY HO
6 CHATHAM HO

B6
1 LORAINE HO
2 HARCOURT LODGE
3 CONISTON CT
4 ALCESTER CT
5 FRIARS CT
6 CAMPBELL HO
7 BRODIE HO
8 LESLEY CT
9 BIRCH CT
10 AIRBORNE HO

59
41

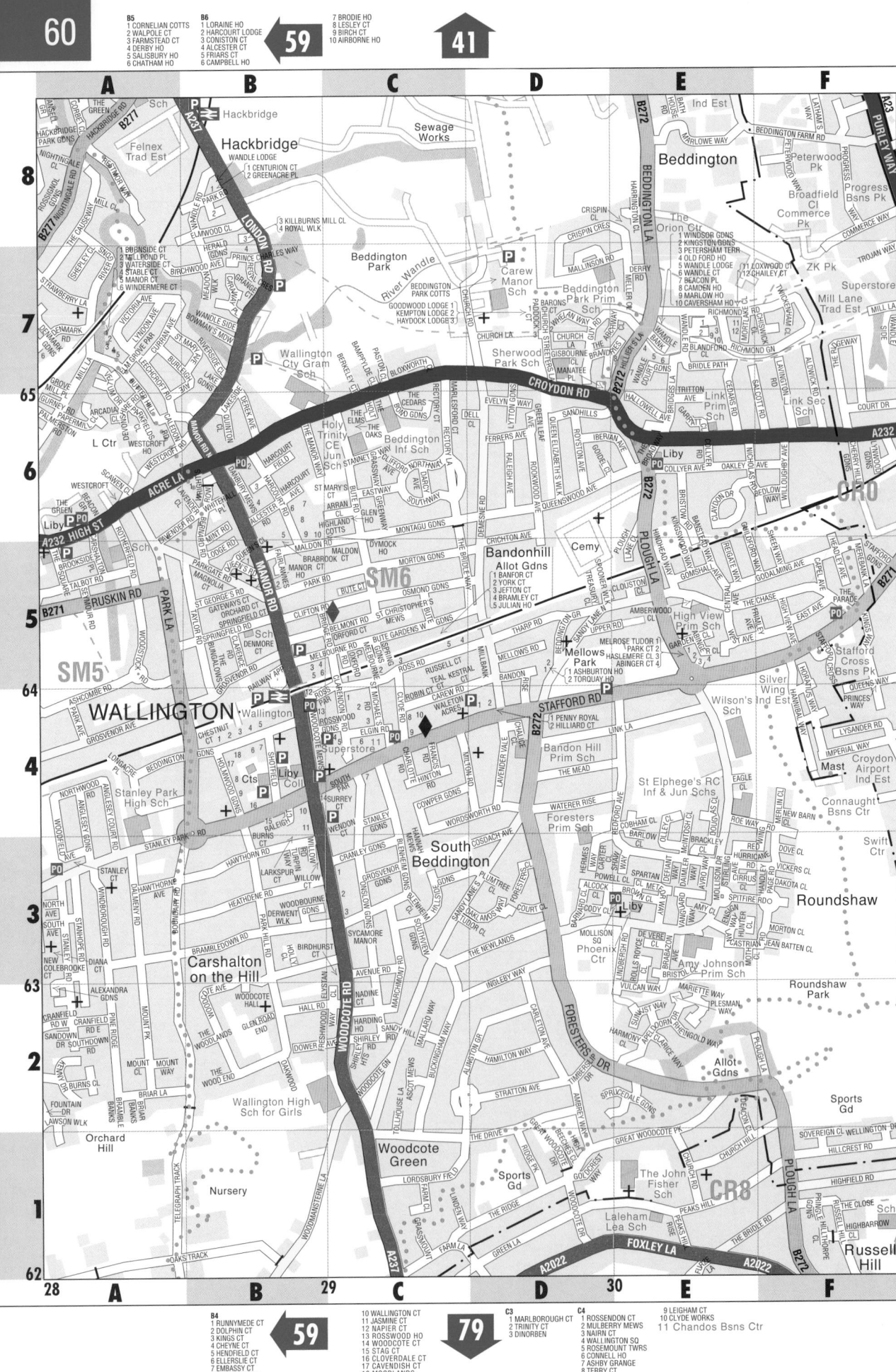

B4
1 RUNNYMEDE CT
2 DOLPHIN CT
3 KINGS CT
4 CHEYNE CT
5 HENDFIELD CT
6 ELLERSLIE CT
7 EMBASSY CT
8 CHANDLER CT
9 HAMBLEDON CT
10 WALLINGTON CT
11 JASMINE CT
12 NAPIER CT
13 ROSSWOOD HO
14 WOODCOTE CT
15 STAG CT
16 CLOVERDALE CT
17 CAVENDISH CT
18 MOORLANDS

C3
1 MARLBOROUGH CT
2 TRINITY CT
3 DINORBEN

C4
1 ROSSENDON CT
2 MULBERRY MEWS
3 NAIRN CT
4 WALLINGTON SQ
5 ROSEMOUNT TWRS
6 CONNELL HO
7 ASHBY GRANGE
8 TERRY CT
9 LEIGHAM CT
10 CLYDE WORKS
11 Chandos Bsns Ctr

59
79

C5
1 Trent Ct
2 Sherwood Ct
3 Archers Ct
4 Keepers Ct
5 Lincoln Ct
6 The Mount
7 Fairhaven Ct
8 Brockham Ct
9 Chelwood Ct
10 Morey Ct
11 Landau Ct
12 Dene Ct
13 Walton Ct
14 Sovereign Ct
15 Sharon Ct
16 Park Ct

C6
1 West Street Pl
2 Maple Ct
3 St Andrew's Ct
4 Albury Ct
5 Chestnut Ct
6 Elgin Ct

C7
1 Chanderie Ct
2 Waterworks Yd
3 Katherine Ct
4 Fellmongers Yd
5 The Arcade

C7 (right column)
7 Beechfield Ct
8 Barham Ct
9 Whitstable Pl
10 Thanet Ho

C8
1 Otterbourne Rd
2 Charrington Rd
3 Tamworth Pl
4 Priddy's Yd
5 HOSPITAL OF THE HOLY TRINITY
(ALMSHOUSES)

◄ 42

D8
1 Wellesley Court Rd
2 Norfolk Ho
3 Station App
4 Suffolk Ho
5 Essex Ho
6 Cherry Orchard Gdns

62 ►

7 Harrington Ct
8 Skyview Appartments
9 Emerald Ho

61

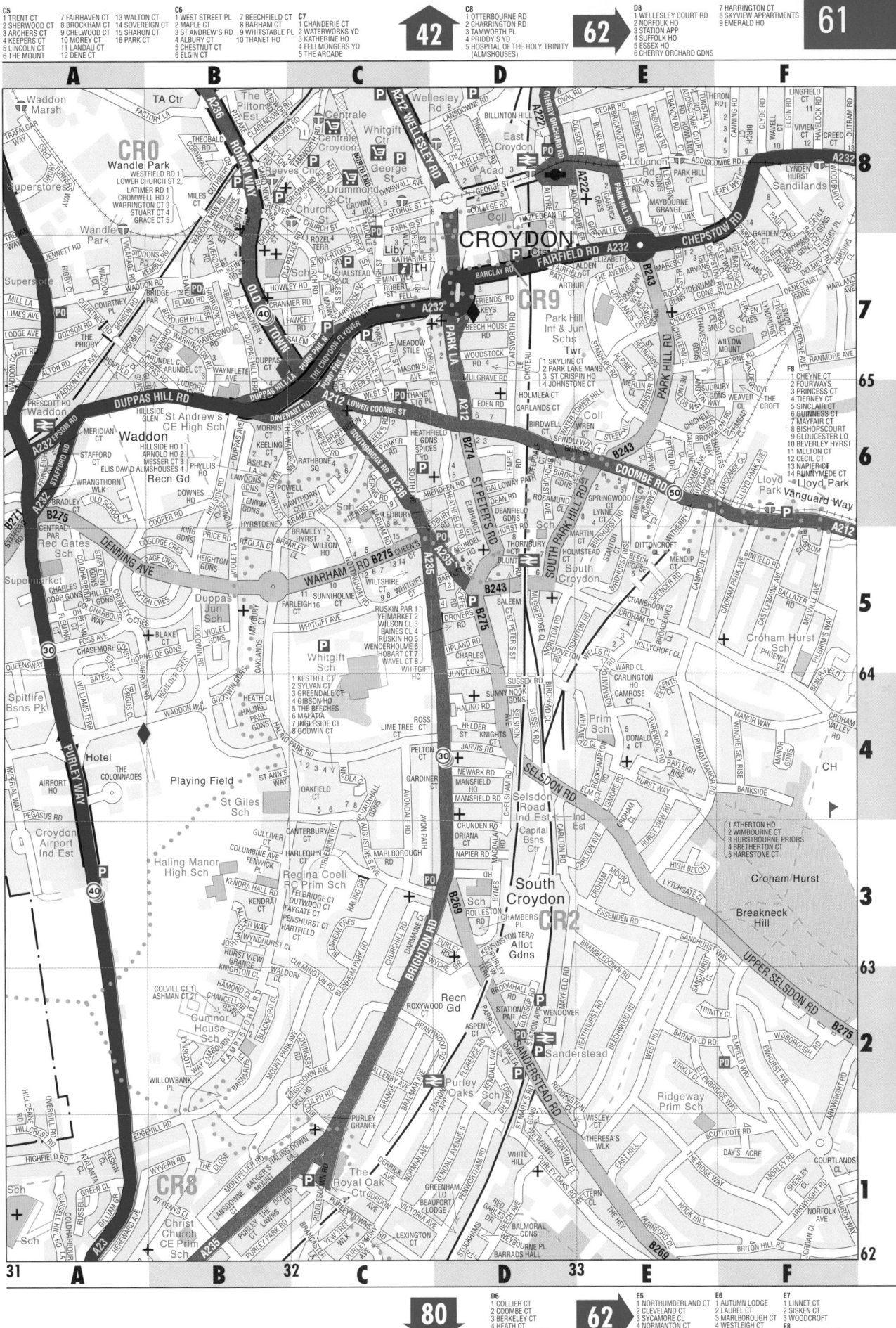

◄ 80

62 ►

D6
1 Collier Ct
2 Coombe Ct
3 Berkeley Ct
4 Heath Ct
5 Chesterton Ho
6 Lindsay Ct
7 Lancing Ho

E5
1 Northumberland Ct
2 Cleveland Ct
3 Sycamore Cl
4 Normanton Ct
5 Stoneleigh Ct
6 Holembury Ct

E6
1 Autumn Lodge
2 Laurel Ct
3 Marlborough Ct
4 Westleigh Ct
5 Lynford Ct
6 Edwards Ct
7 Sheridan Ct
8 Cambrian Ct

E7
1 Linnet Ct
2 Sisken Ct
3 Woodcroft

E8
1 Park Hill Mans
2 St Nicholas Ho

61
43

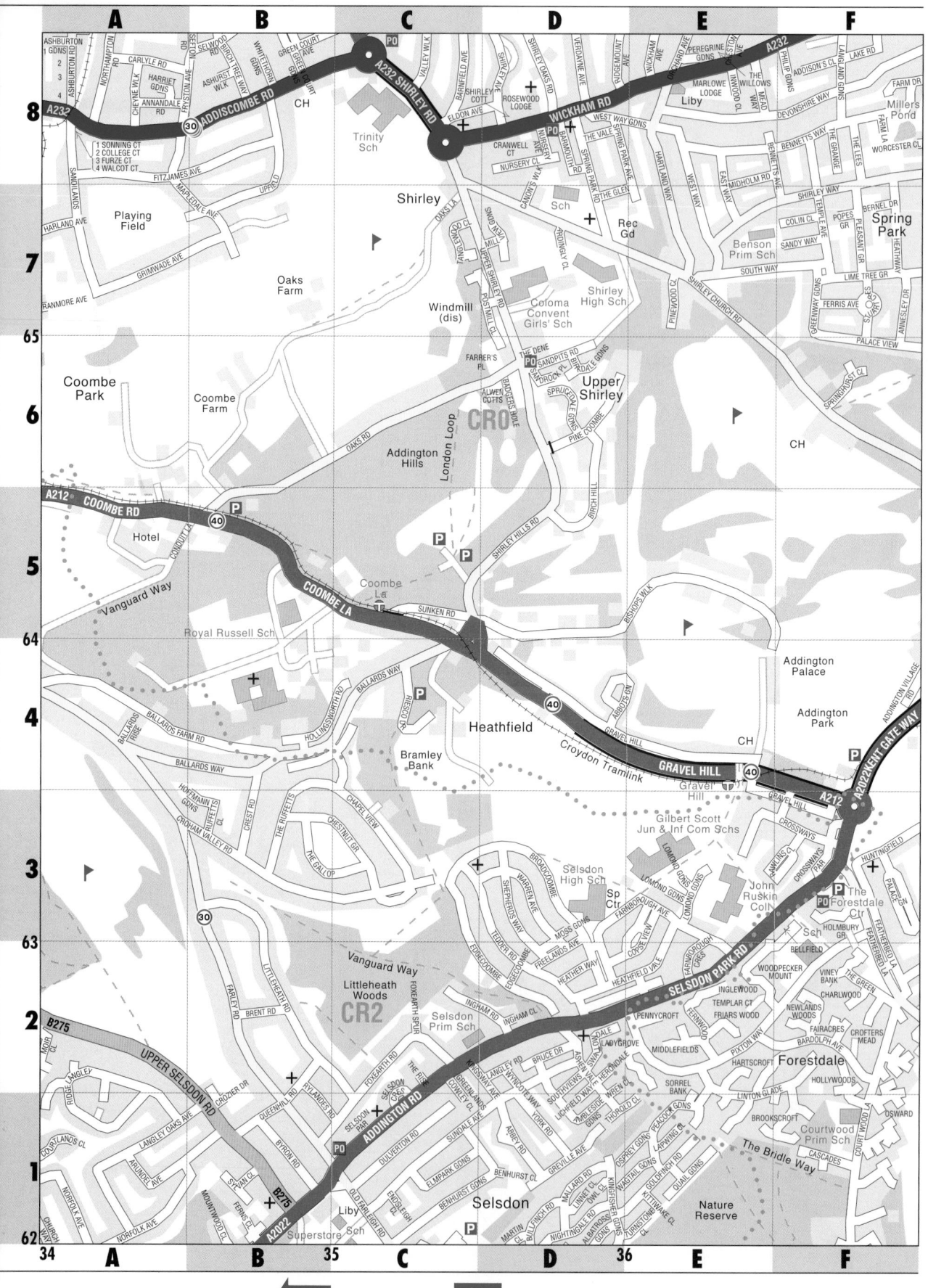
A
B
C
D
E
F
8
7
65
6
5
64
4
3
63
2
1
62
34
35
36
A232
ADDISCOMBE RD
A232 SHIRLEY RD
WICKHAM RD
ASHBURTON GDNS
ASHBURTON RD
NORTHAMPTON RD
CARLYLE RD
CHEYNE WLK
HARRIET GDNS
ANNANDALE RD
FRYSTON AVE
SEFTON RD
SELWOOD RD
ASHURST WLK
BIRCH TREE WAY
WHITETHORN GDNS
GREEN COURT AVE
GREEN COURT GDNS
CH
1 SONNING CT
2 COLLEGE CT
3 FURZE CT
4 WALCOT CT
FITZJAMES AVE
MAPLEDALE AVE
UPFIELD
SANDILANDS
HARLAND AVE
Playing Field
GRIMWADE AVE
RANMORE AVE
Trinity Sch
Shirley
OAKS LA
Oaks Farm
Windmill (dis)
VALLEY WLK
BARNFIELD AVE
SHIRLEY AVE
SHIRLEY COTT
ELDON AVE
ROSEWOOD LODGE
SHIRLEY OAKS RD
VERDAYNE AVE
RIDGEMOUNT AVE
WICKHAM AVE
ORCHARD AVE
PEREGRINE GDNS
INWOOD CL
THE WILLOWS
MEAD WAY
MARLOWE LODGE
Liby
PHILIP GDNS
ADDISON'S CL
LANGLAND GDNS
LAKE RD
FARM DR
Millers Pond
DEVONSHIRE WAY
FARM LA
WORCESTER CL
BENNETTS WAY
THE GRANGE
THE LEES
BENNETTS AVE
CRANWELL CT
NURSERY AVE
NURSERY CL
BARMOUTH RD
THE VALE
SPRING PARK AVE
SPRING PARK RD
WEST WAY GDNS
THE GLEN
CANON'S WLK
Sch
Rec Gd
HARTLAND WAY
WEST WAY
EAST WAY
MIDHOLM RD
SHIRLEY WAY
TEMPLE AVE
POPES GR
BERNEL DR
COLIN CL
SANDY WAY
Spring Park
HEATHWAY
PLEASANT GR
Benson Prim Sch
SOUTH WAY
LIME TREE GR
GREENWAY GDNS
FERRIS AVE
ST JOHN'S RD
ANNESLEY DR
PALACE VIEW
SHIRLEY CHURCH RD
PINEWOOD CL
TANGLEWOOD CL
UPPER SHIRLEY RD
POSTMILL CL
Coloma Convent Girls' Sch
Shirley High Sch
ARDINGLY CL
FARRER'S PL
THE DENE
SANDPITS RD
ALWEN COTTS
BADGERS HOLE
Upper Shirley
SPRUCEDALE GDNS
PINE COOMBE
SPRINGHURST CL
Coombe Park
Coombe Farm
OAKS RD
Addington Hills
London Loop
CR0
BIRCH HILL
SHIRLEY HILLS RD
A212
COOMBE RD
Hotel
CONDUIT LA
Vanguard Way
COOMBE LA
Coombe La
SUNKEN RD
BISHOPS WLK
Royal Russell Sch
Addington Palace
Addington Park
ADDINGTON VILLAGE RD
A2022 KENT GATE WAY
BALLARDS WAY
HOLLINGSWORTH RD
RIESCO DR
Heathfield
ABBOTS GN
GRAVEL HILL
Croydon Tramlink
CH
BALLARDS RISE
BALLARDS FARM RD
Bramley Bank
Graveł Hill
Gilbert Scott Jun & Inf Com Schs
HOFFMANN GDNS
RUFFETTS CL
CROHAM VALLEY RD
CREST RD
THE RUFFETTS
CHAPEL VIEW
CHESTNUT GR
THE GALLOP
BROADCOOMBE
WARREN AVE
SHEPHERDS WAY
Selsdon High Sch
Sp Ctr
LOMOND GDNS
John Ruskin Coll
CROSSWAYS
HAWKINS CL
CROSSWAYS PAR
HUNTINGFIELD
PALACE GN
The Forestdale Ctr
Sch
HOLMBURY GR
FEATHERBED LA
BELLFIELD
MOSS GDNS
FARNBOROUGH AVE
COPSE VIEW
FARNBOROUGH CRES
HEATHFIELD VALE
TEDDER RD
EDGECOOMBE
FREELANDS AVE
HEATHER WAY
SELSDON PARK RD
WOODPECKER MOUNT
VINEY BANK
THE GREEN
INGLEWOOD
TEMPLAR CT
CHARLWOOD
FRIARS WOOD
NEWLANDS WOODS
FAIRACRES
CROFTERS MEAD
BARDOLPH AVE
Forestdale
HOLLYWOODS
Vanguard Way
Littleheath Woods
CR2
LITTLEHEATH RD
FOXEARTH SPUR
FARLEY RD
BRENT RD
INGHAM RD
INGHAM CL
Selsdon Prim Sch
PENNYCROFT
FERNWOOD
LADYGROVE
MIDDLEFIELDS
PIXTON WAY
HARTSCROFT
SORREL BANK
LINTON GLADE
BROOKSCROFT
OSWARD
Courtwood Prim Sch
COURT WOOD LA
CASCADES
The Bridle Way
B275
UPPER SELSDON RD
MOIR CL
RIDGELANGLEY
CROZIER DR
QUEENHILL RD
RYLANDES RD
FOXEARTH RD
SELSDON CRES
SELSDON PAR
THE RISE
ADDINGTON RD
KINGSWAY AVE
GREENLANDS
COWLEY CL
LANGLEY RD
WYNCOTE WAY
BRUCE DR
YORK RD
ABBEY RD
LANGLEY OAKS AVE
COURTLANDS CL
ARUNDEL AVE
BYRON RD
DULVERTON RD
SUNDALE AVE
ELMPARK GDNS
BENHURST GDNS
BENHURST CL
GREVILLE AVE
SOUTHVIEWS
LICHFIELD WAY
AMBLESIDE GDNS
THOROLD CL
WREN CL
PEACOCK GDNS
LAPWING CL
OSPREY GDNS
WAGTAIL GDNS
GOLDFINCH RD
QUAIL GDNS
KINGFISHER GDNS
KITTIWAKE CL
TURNSTONE CL
Nature Reserve
Selsdon
MALLARD RD
LINNET CL
OWL CL
BULLFINCH RD
NIGHTINGALE RD
ALBATROSS GDNS
MARTIN CL
SYLVAN CL
MOUNTWOOD CL
FERNS CL
NORFOLK AVE
CHURCH WAY
A2022
OLD FARLEIGH RD
ENDSLEIGH CL
Liby
Superstore
Sch
PO
P
30
40

61
81

44

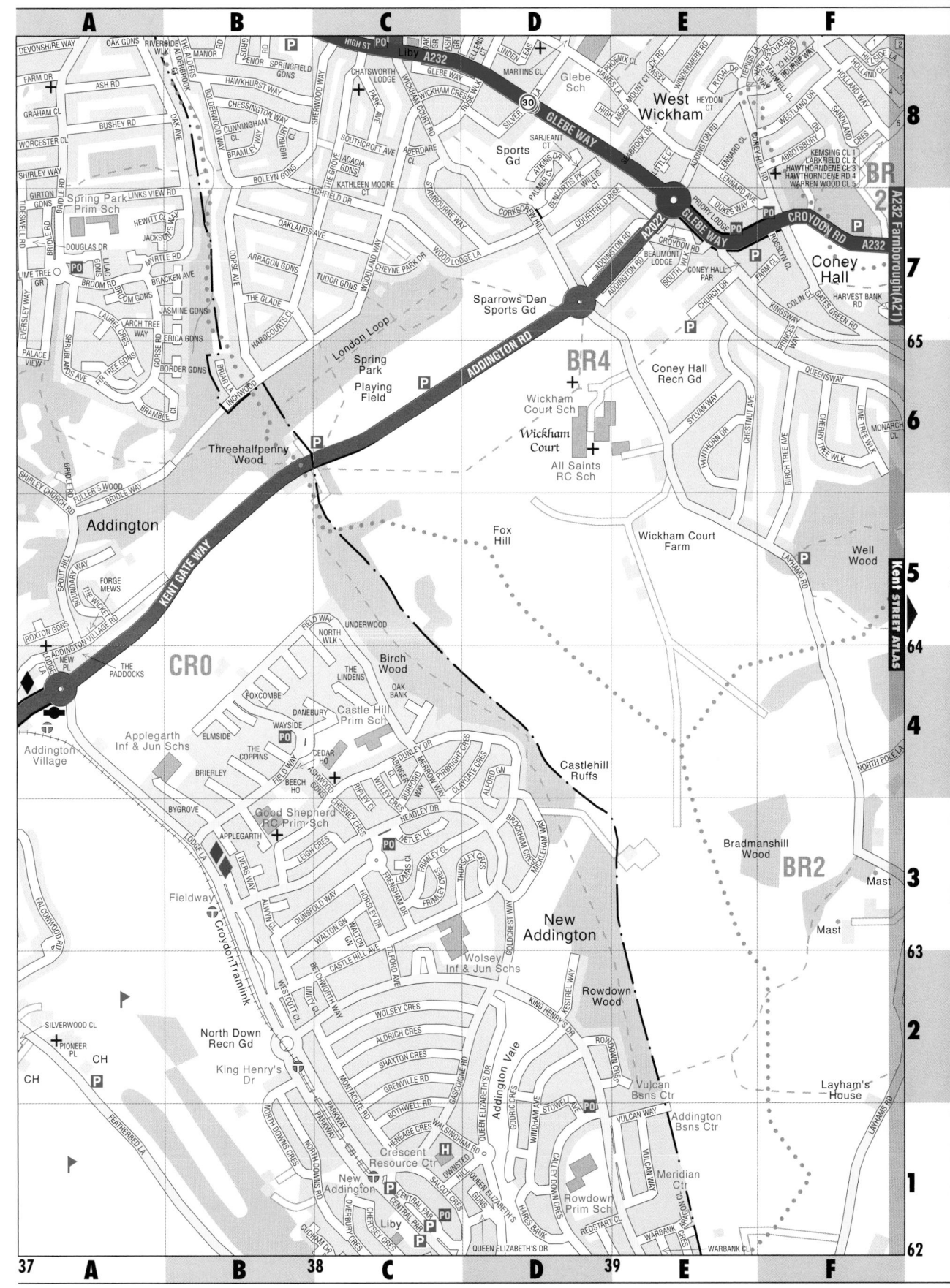
A
B
C
D
E
F
8
7
6
5
4
3
2
1
65
64
63
62
37
38
39
HIGH ST
A232
GLEBE WAY
West Wickham
Glebe Sch
Sports Gd
CROYDON RD
Coney Hall
A232 Farnborough (A21)
Sparrows Den Sports Gd
ADDINGTON RD
A2022
BR4
Coney Hall Recn Gd
Wickham Court Sch
Wickham Court
All Saints RC Sch
Spring Park Prim Sch
Spring Park Playing Field
London Loop
Threehalfpenny Wood
Addington
KENT GATE WAY
Fox Hill
Wickham Court Farm
Well Wood
LAYHAMS RD
Kent STREET ATLAS
CR0
Birch Wood
Castle Hill Prim Sch
Applegarth Inf & Jun Schs
Addington Village
Castlehill Ruffs
Good Shepherd RC Prim Sch
Bradmanshill Wood
BR2
Mast
Fieldway
Croydon Tramlink
New Addington
Wolsey Inf & Jun Schs
Rowdown Wood
North Down Recn Gd
King Henry's Dr
Addington Vale
Vulcan Bsns Ctr
Addington Bsns Ctr
Layham's House
Crescent Resource Ctr
Meridian Ctr
Rowdown Prim Sch
FEATHERBED LA
Liby

82

D8
1 MULBERRY CL
2 MAY CL
3 SHRIVENHAM CL
4 CENTURION CL
5 CHAFFINCH CL
6 TARBAT CT

7 ROCKFIELD WAY
8 BALINTORE CT

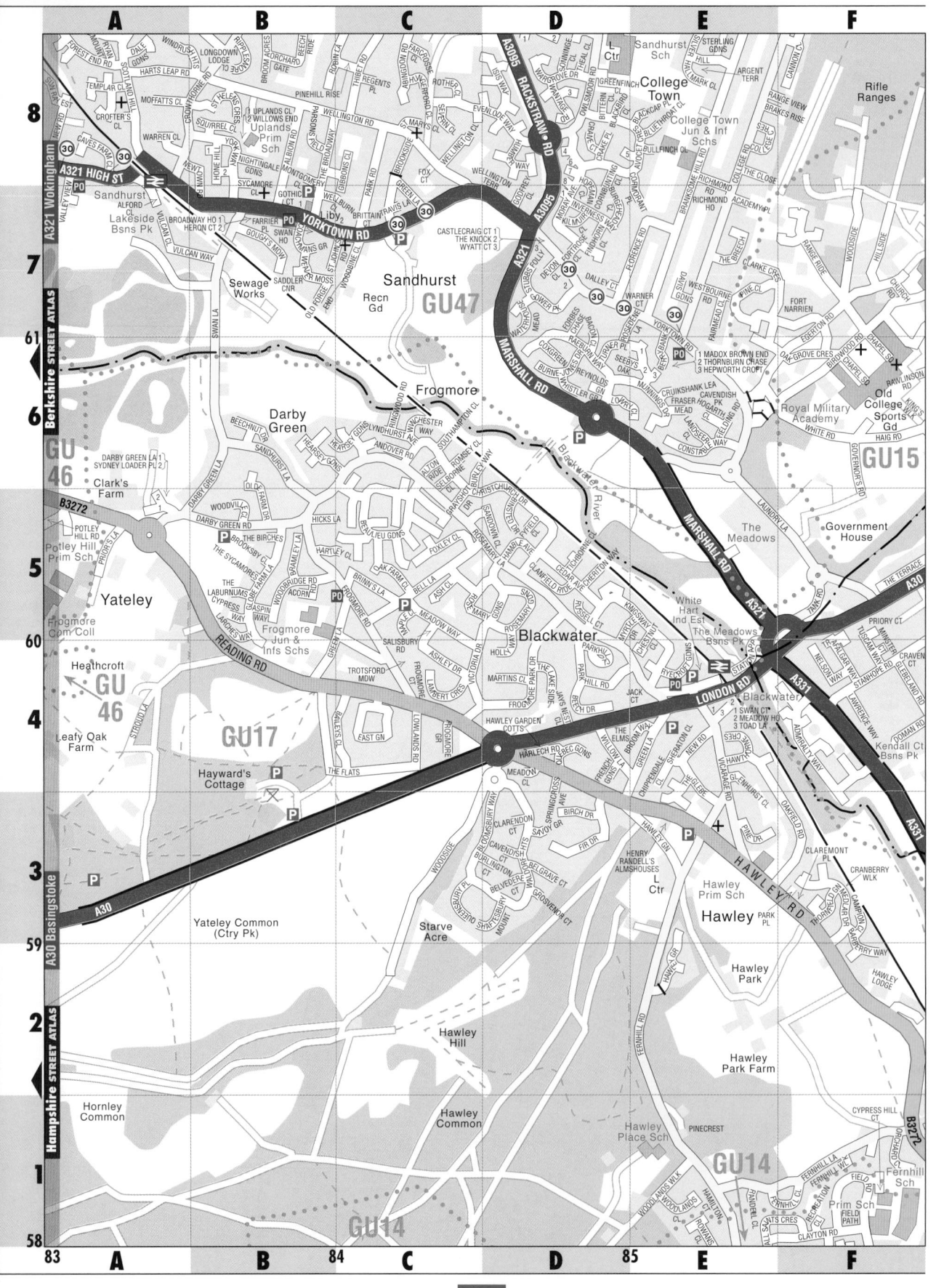

A B C D E F

8 7 61 6 5 60 4 3 59 2 1 58

Royal Military Acad
Wishton
Barossa Common
Playing Field
Alanbrooke Hall
Lorraine Sch
Liby
KURNOOL MORTAR CROSS ROADS
QUEEN VICTORIA CROSS ROADS
GU15
Upper Lake
Lower Lake
TA Ctr
Arena L Ctr
CAMBERLEY
Mus
Liby
TH
Sch
Camberley
Ct
LC
Camberley Inf Sch
Lyndhurst Sch
Crawley Hill
Crawley Ridge Inf &Jun Schs
Tekels Park
Bsns Ctr
Stanhope Gate
York Town Ind Est
York Town
Compton Place Bsns Ctr
Watchmoor Pk
Sewage Works
Watchmoor Trade Ctr
Sampson Bsns Pk
Bridge Wks
St Georges Ind Est
Playing Field
Helix Bsns Pk
Hoskins Place Ind Est
Recn Gd
Superstore
Watchetts Jun Sch
Kings International Coll
Bristow Inf Sch
Cove Brook
Blackwater River
GU17
GU14
Park Farm Ind Est
Lyon Way Ind Est
Albany Park Ind Est
Frimley Park
Sch
FRIMLEY
Tomlin's Pond
Schs
Lakeside Prim Sch
GU16
Sch

EVEREST RD, KINGS CRES, MATTHEWS RD, OVERLORD CL, GOODWOOD CL, WINDSOR RIDE, EGERTON RD, DAWNAY RD, CAPPER RD, BIRDWOOD RD, JACOB RD, SLIM RD, GREEN LANE CL, STAFF COLLEGE RD, ALLENBY RD, ROBERTS RD, THE TERRACE, PLANTATION ROW, OSNABURGH HILL, LONDON RD, A30, KING'S RIDE, MOUNTBATTEN MEWS, WOODLARK GLADE, WHITEHILL, FOSSEWOOD DR, COLLEGE CL, COLLEGE RIDE, OLD GREEN LA, WYCHWOOD, OLD DEAN RD, UPLAND RD, LAWRENCE LODGE, BAROSSA RD, BLUEBELL MEWS, WETHERBY HOUSE, CROMWELL RD, YORK PL, YORK RD, HARTFORD RISE, BATH RD, THE BOWLINGS, DIAMOND RIDGE, DIAMOND HILL, WOODBRIDGE MANOR, MINSTER CT, NUTFIELD CT, THE MANOR HOUSE, PORTESBERY HILL, GEORGIAN CL, BURBURY WOODS, CLAREWOOD DR, MACNAGHTEN WOODS, GRASMERE, KNIGHTSBRIDGE RD, AMBERWOOD DR, DAWN CT, THE PINES, LINDEN CT, MIDDLETON RD, GAINSBOROUGH CL, CARLINWARK DR, CROSBY HILL DR, CORNWALL CL, DEVONSHIRE DR, ACADEMY CL, LARCH CL, BIRCH CL, SADDLEBACK RD, WISHMOOR RD, WISHMOOR CL, STAR POST RD, ROWAN CL, HORSESHOE CL, HAMPSHIRE RD, BERKSHIRE RD, KINGSTON RD, DEAN PARADE, DORSET CT, PASCHAL RD, UPPER COLLEGE RIDE, HIGHLAND RD, POPPYHILLS RD, WICKHAM RD, RAPLEY CL, TURF HILL RD, CORDWALLES CRES, DEANSIDE, DEER ROCK RD, PRINCE OF WALES WLK, BIETIGHEIM WAY, CAMBRIDGE WLK, GRACE REYNOLDS WLK, WILLINGTON CL, DEREK HORN CT, ACADEMY GATE, DORCHESTER CT, ST MICHAEL'S PL, APPLEY DR, APPLEY CT, CHARLES ST, UPPER CHARLES ST, LOWER CHARLES ST, GRAND AVE, OBELISK WAY, SPRINGWELL WAY, TOWN SQ, ST MARY'S RD, CAMBRIDGE SQ, PRINCESS WAY, PEMBROKE BROADWAY, KNOLL RD, HIGH ST, ST GEORGE'S RD, VALROY CL, MARKHAM CT, LYNNSIDE PL, LANCASTER DR, PORTESBERY RD, BARN CL, UPPER PARK RD, EARLSWOOD, HALL CL, MARLBOROUGH RISE, ASHWELL AVE, FENTON LODGE, SANDY LA, WAYSWOOD, TUDOR HALL, FRIMLEY HALL DR, LIME AVE, COPSE END, CRAWLEY DR, CRAWLEY RIDGE, CRAWLEY WOOD CL, CRAWLEY HILL, BRANKSOME PARK RD, BRANKSOME CL, CHURCH HILL, BELLEVUE RD, BELTON RD, GRANGE RD, REDCREST GDNS, CONNAUGHT RD, ALISON DR, STOCKWOOD RISE, CLAREMONT AVE, WAVERLEY DR, GROVE RD, WALKER'S RIDGE, YEOMANS WAY, DEEP WELL DR, SHERBOURNE RISE, CASTLE CL, CASTLE RD, FERNIEHURST, WAVERLEY CT, TIDES END CT, PETWORTH CT, A325, M3, HOPE FOUNTAIN, GOLF DR, GRESHAM CT, MERRYWOOD PK, BADGERS COPSE, TEKELS WAY, CADOGAN CT, SCARLET OAKS, RALEIGH WAY, GLENSWOOD, LE MARCHANT RD, WILMOT WAY, TICHBOURNE CL, CONNOP WAY, CAMPBELL PL, LONGMEADOW, FAIRFIELD DR, OLD PASTURE RD, WARREN RISE, MULGRAVE RD, EVERGREEN RD, HAWTHORN RD, COACH HOUSE CL, HEATHER MEAD CT, HEATHER MEAD, B311, CHOBHAM RD, FARM RD, THE MALLARDS, DELL GR, MEADWAY, BROADWAY WLK, STIRLING CL, LANARK CL, LAUDER CL, HOLLY HEDGE RD, WILDERNESS RD, NAIRN CL, BICKNELL RD, MONTROSE CL, GORSE RD, PORTSMOUTH RD, BRACKENDALE CL, OVERDALE RISE, BAYFIELD AVE, HOLLY HEDGE CL, ABBEY CT, QUEENS KEEP, UPPER GORDON RD, WEST RD, ELMHURST CT, HEATHCOTE RD, FIRLANDS AVE, MIDDLE GORDON RD, COURT GDNS, DENNISTOUN CL, HEATHWAY CL, HEATHWAY, CHAUCER GR, BUCKINGHAM CT, HEATH RISE, LONGFORD CL, TEKELS AVE, TEKELS CT, SOUTHWELL PARK RD, FOXDOWN CL, FRANCE HILL DR, FIRWOOD DR, FIRWOOD CT, PARK ST, SOUTHERN RD, BENNETT CL, GORDON RD, SHELLEY CT, GARFIELD RD, KINGS APARTMENTS, FAIRMEAD CT, CARLIN PL, KINGSCLEAR PK, LAUREL CL, ORIEL HILL, PINE MOUNT RD, GLEN DELL, BRACKENDALE RD, HEATHERDALE RD, WAYS END, BEECH AVE, RUDD HALL RISE, PARK AVE, NORWICH AVE, PINE AVE, KINGSLEY AVE, UPPER VERRAN RD, THE PAVILIONS END, RUSSET GDNS, VERRAN RD, WATCHETTS LAKE CL, WATCHETTS DR, PARKWAY, LINKWAY, ST CATHERINES WOOD, SADDLEWOOD, GORDON CRES, PARKSTONE DR, CHILLINGHAM WAY, BIRCHFIELDS, GORDON AVE, BELMONT RD, BELMONT MEWS, BUCKINGHAM, WATCHETTS RD, DARWIN CT, ABBETTS LA, GODDARDS LA, MURRELLS LA, BLENHEIM PL, SQUIRES CT, WORCESTER CT, HANBURY WAY, BRISTOW RD, FARRELL CL, WELLER DR, APRIL CL, JAMES WAY, JAMES RD, WESTFIELD RD, CRABTREE RD, BRAMLEY RD, ORCHARD WAY, ORCHARD CT, RIVERMEAD RD, LEA RD, BAIN AVE, GREENLANDS RD, MAYFIELD RD, NEWLANDS RD, WOOD RD, ALSACE WLK, OLD POND CL, ALBANY CT, ALBANY PK, LYON WAY, STATION RD, FRIMLEY HIGH ST, FRIMLEY RD, B3411, A331, GILBERT RD, GREENBANK WAY, HIGH BEECHES, BADGERWOOD DR, BLYTHWOOD DR, SANDOWN DR, GREENLEAS, DENTON WAY, FALCON CT, CHANTRY CT, MERLIN CT, THE CLOISTERS, CHURCH RD, APEX DR, GROVE CROSS RD, PARTRIDGE CL, THE GROVE, GROVEFIELDS AVE, FRIMLEY GROVE GDNS, WILLOW CT, PARSONAGE WAY, KIRKBY CT, FIELD LA, STONEHOUSE RISE, MIDDLEMOOR RD, ANSELL RD, STURDEE CL, BRET HARTE RD, LAKEMEAD DR, HANOVER CL, FRIMLEY SQ, MARTINS CL, SYCAMORE DR, SYCAMORE CT, LATHAM AVE, OAKWAY, YEW TREE WLK, STAMFORD AVE, BROUGHTON MEWS, TINTAGEL DR, BUCKINGHAM WAY, CORE GDNS, STONELEIGH CT, BELVOIR CL, KILMARTIN GDNS, ST CATHERINES RD, TIVERTON WAY, CONWAY CL, MELVILLE AVE, ARMITAGE DR, HERMITAGE CL, ALPHINGTON AVE, TOMLINS AVE, HAWKSWOOD AVE, CROFT WAY, FELBRIDGE CL, KENTON CL, WATCHMOOR RD, RIVERSIDE WAY, WILTON RD, KROONER RD, BRIDGE RD, DORCAS CT, BRIDGE END, OAKLEY RD, BURFORD RD, BROOK RD, QUEENS RD, SINHURST RD, MOORLANDS RD, SOUTHWAY, SURREY AVE, AVENUE SUCY, VALE RD, WENTWORTH PL, DOMAN RD, EATON RD, BERNARD CT, BUTTERFIELD, DONNINGTON CL, WHINS DR, WHINS CL, FOREST HILLS, ROBIN'S BOW, SEATON RD, CAMBRIAN CL, THE AVENUE, CRONDALL CT, RIDGEWAY CL, WOODLANDS RD, WOODWAY, HOLLYFIELDS CL, CRAWFORD GDNS, MONTAGUE CL, HATFIELD CT, HEATHERLEY RD, HEATHERLEY CL, HARCOURT RD, CHAPEL ST, ST MICHAELS RD, WEY CL, OAKFIELDS, ALEXANDRA AVE, EDWARD AVE, SULLINGS RD, VICTORIA AVE, QUEEN MARY AVE, BRACEBRIDGE, STANHOPE RD, HAWLEY RD, HAWLEY LA, B3272, CHAPEL LA, MOORSIDE CL, BROOKSIDE PK, BAYFORD CL, ASHBURY DR, CLAYDON GDNS

86 A B 87 C D 88 E F

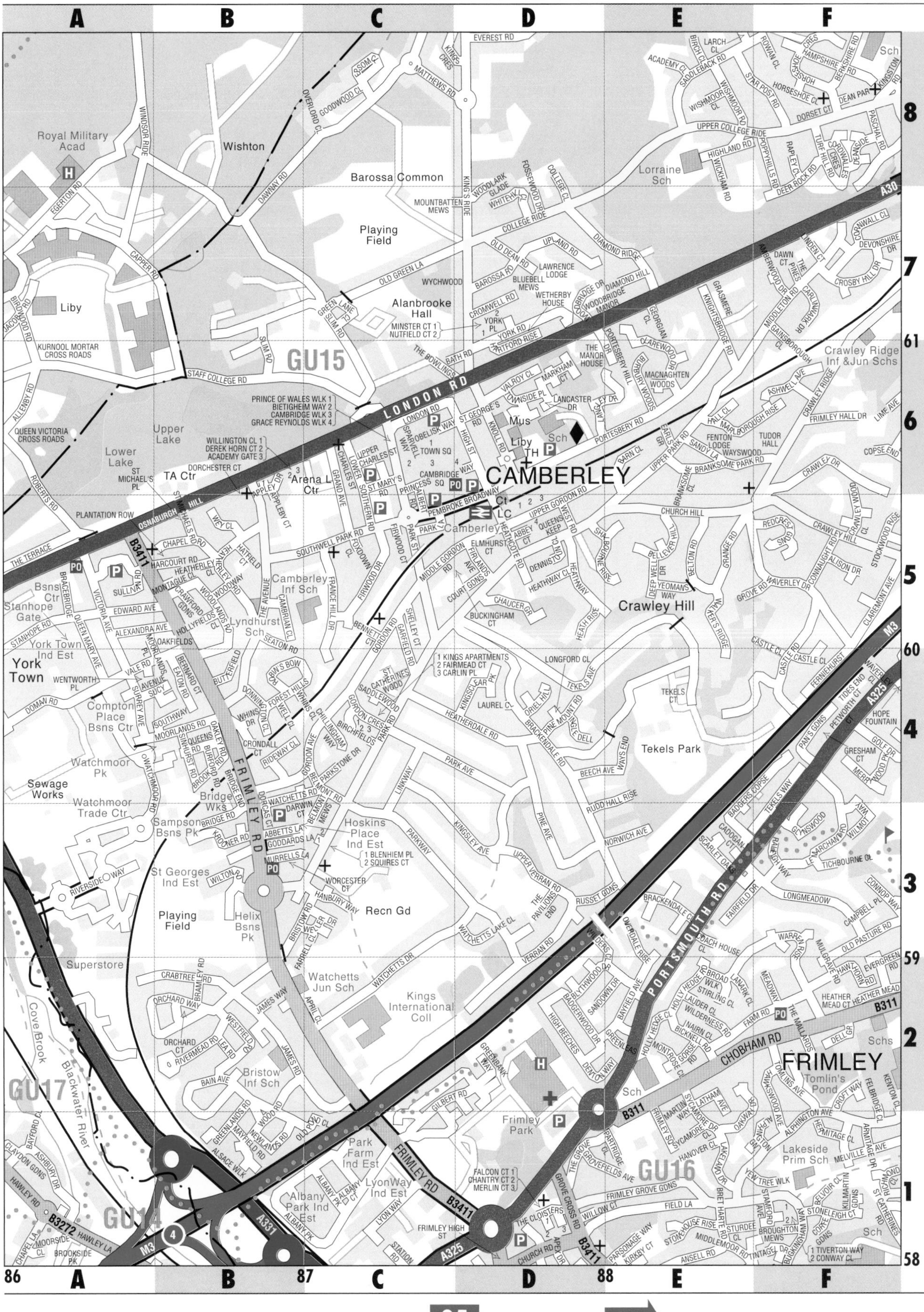

65
47

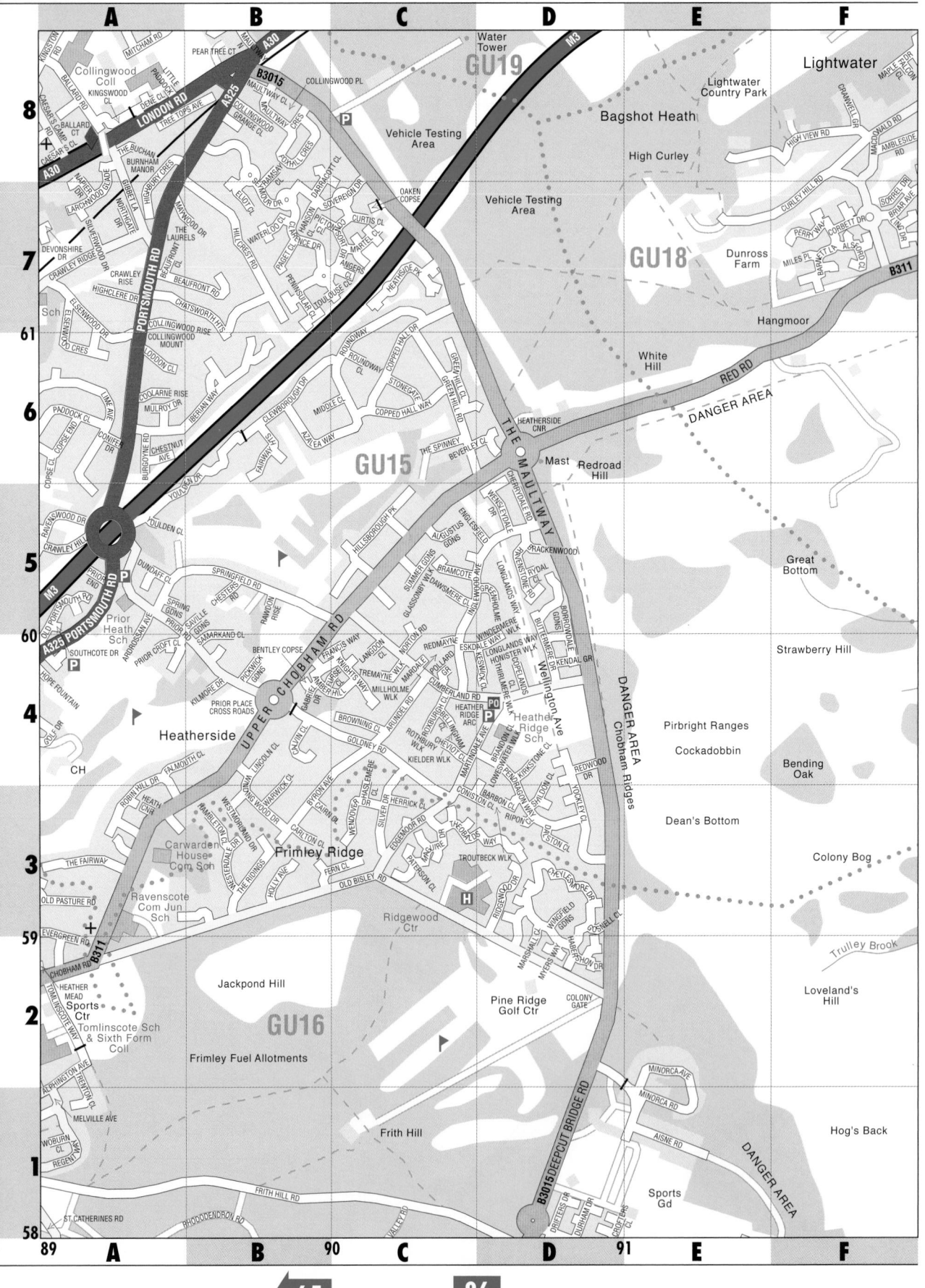
A
B
C
D
E
F
8
7
61
6
5
60
4
3
59
2
1
58
89
90
91
Water Tower
GU19
M3
A30
LONDON RD
A325
B3015
PEAR TREE CT
MAULTWAY
COLLINGWOOD PL
Collingwood Coll
KINGSWOOD CL
MITCHAM RD
KINGSTON RD
BALLARD RD
LITTLE PADDOCK
DENE CL
TREE TOPS AVE
BALLARD CT
CAESAR'S CAMP RD
CAESAR'S CL
THE BUCHAN
BURNHAM MANOR
NAPIER DR
LARCHWOOD GLADE
GIBBET LA
NORTHGATE DR
HIGHBURY CRES
SILVERWOOD DR
DEVONSHIRE DR
CRAWLEY RIDGE
CRAWLEY RISE
HIGHCLERE DR
Sch
ELSENWOOD DR
ELSENWOOD CRES
MAULTWAY CL
MAULTWAY CRES
COLLINGWOOD GRANGE CL
FOXHILL CRES
RAMSAY CL
SEYMOUR DR
ELIOT CL
DARRACOTT CL
SOVEREIGN DR
OAKEN COPSE
CURTIS CL
HANSON CL
PICTON CL
WATERLOO CL
PAGET CL
CLARENCE DR
MARTEL CL
ANGERS CL
HILLCREST RD
PENINSULAR CL
TOULOUSE CL
HEATHSIDE PK
MAYWOOD DR
THE LAURELS
BEAUFRONT CL
BEAUFRONT RD
CHATSWORTH HTS
PORTSMOUTH RD
COLLINGWOOD RISE
COLLINGWOOD MOUNT
LODDON CL
COOLARNE RISE
MULROY DR
IBERIAN WAY
LIME AVE
PADDOCK CL
COPSE END
COPSE CL
CONIFER DR
BURGOYNE RD
CHESTNUT AVE
Vehicle Testing Area
P
ROUNDWAY
ROUNDWAY CL
COPPED HALL DR
STONEGATE
COPPED HALL WAY
MIDDLE CL
CLEWBOROUGH DR
AZALEA WAY
FAIRWAY HTS
GREEN HILL CL
GREEN HILL RD
THE SPINNEY
BEVERLEY CL
GU15
HEATHERSIDE CNR
THE MAULTWAY
Mast
Redroad Hill
Bagshot Heath
High Curley
Lightwater
Lightwater Country Park
MAPLE DR
FALCON DR
CRANWELL GR
HIGH VIEW RD
MACDONALD RD
AMBLESIDE RD
CURLEY HILL RD
SORREL DR
BRIAR AVE
KING DR
PERRY WAY
CORBETT DR
ALSFORD CL
BARTLETT LA
MILES PL
GU18
Dunross Farm
B311
Hangmoor
White Hill
RED RD
DANGER AREA
YOULDEN DR
YOULDEN CL
RAVENSWOOD DR
CRAWLEY HILL
PRIOR END
OLD PORTSMOUTH RD
A325 PORTSMOUTH RD
DUNDAFF CL
SPRINGFIELD RD
CHESTERS RD
SPRING GDNS
SAVILLE GDNS
PRIOR RD
RAWDON RISE
SAMARKAND CL
Prior Heath Sch
ARDROSSAN AVE
PRIOR CROFT CL
SOUTHCOTE DR
HOPE FOUNTAIN
GOLF DR
CH
KILMORE DR
PICKWICK GDNS
BENTLEY COPSE
PRIOR PLACE CROSS ROADS
Heatherside
UPPER CHOBHAM RD
HILLSBOROUGH PK
WENSLEYDALE DR
CHERRYDALE RD
ENGLESFIELD
AUGUSTUS GDNS
SUMMER GDNS
BRAMCOTE
DAWSMERE CL
GLASSONBY WLK
RACKENWOOD
RAVENSTONE RD
RYDAL CL
LONGLANDS WAY
INGLEWOOD AVE
GREENHOLME
WINDERMERE WLK
BORROWDALE GDNS
BUTTERMERE DR
KENDAL GR
ESKDALE WAY
LONGLANDS WAY
HONISTER WLK
KESWICK CL
THIRLMERE WLK
COPELANDS CL
NORTON RD
REDMAYNE
FRANCIS WAY
LANGDON CL
KNIGHTS WAY
TREMAYNE WLK
MARDALE
POLLARD GR
MILLHOLME WLK
CUMBERLAND RD
GABRIEL DR
AMBER HILL
ARUNDEL RD
BROWNING CL
HEATHER RIDGE ARC
PO
Heather Ridge Sch
Wellington Ave
ROXBURGH CL
BELLINGHAM CL
ROTHBURY WLK
CHEVIOT CL
KIELDER WLK
MARTINDALE AVE
BRANDON CL
LOWESWATER WLK
KIRKSTONE CL
REDWOOD DR
CALVIN CL
LINCOLN CL
GOLDNEY RD
FALMOUTH CL
ROBIN HILL DR
HEATH CNR
WARWICK CL
WINDING WOOD DR
HAMBLETON CL
WESTMORLAND DR
BYRON AVE
CAIRN CL
WENDOVER DR
HASLEMERE CL
SILVER DR
HERRICK CL
CONISTON CL
BARBON CL
PENDRAGON WAY
SHILDON CL
YOCKLEY CL
RIPON CL
DAISTON CL
Carwarden House Com Sch
CARLTON CL
Frimley Ridge
EDGEMOOR RD
MAGUIRE DR
THEOBALDS WAY
PATERSON CL
TROUTBECK WLK
THE FAIRWAY
WESTERDALE DR
THE RIDINGS
HOLLY AVE
FERN CL
OLD BISLEY RD
H
RIDGEWOOD DR
CHEYLESMORE DR
WINGFIELD GDNS
GOSNELL CL
MARSHALL CL
MYERS WAY
HABERSHON DR
OLD PASTURE RD
Ravenscote Com Jun Sch
Ridgewood Ctr
EVERGREEN RD
CHOBHAM RD
B311
HEATHER MEAD
Sports Ctr
TOMLINSCOTE WAY
Tomlinscote Sch & Sixth Form Coll
Jackpond Hill
GU16
Frimley Fuel Allotments
Pine Ridge Golf Ctr
COLONY GATE
DANGER AREA
Chobham Ridges
Pirbright Ranges
Cockadobbin
Strawberry Hill
Great Bottom
Bending Oak
Dean's Bottom
Colony Bog
Trulley Brook
Loveland's Hill
Hog's Back
ALPHINGTON AVE
TRENTON CL
MELVILLE AVE
WOBURN CL
REGENT WAY
Frith Hill
FRITH HILL RD
ST CATHERINES RD
RHODODENDRON RD
VALLEY RD
B3015 DEEPCUT BRIDGE RD
DRIFTERS DR
DURHAM DR
CROFTERS CL
MINORCA AVE
MINORCA RD
AISNE RD
Sports Gd

65
86

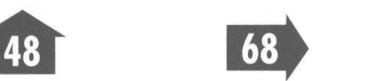

Grid columns: A B C D E F

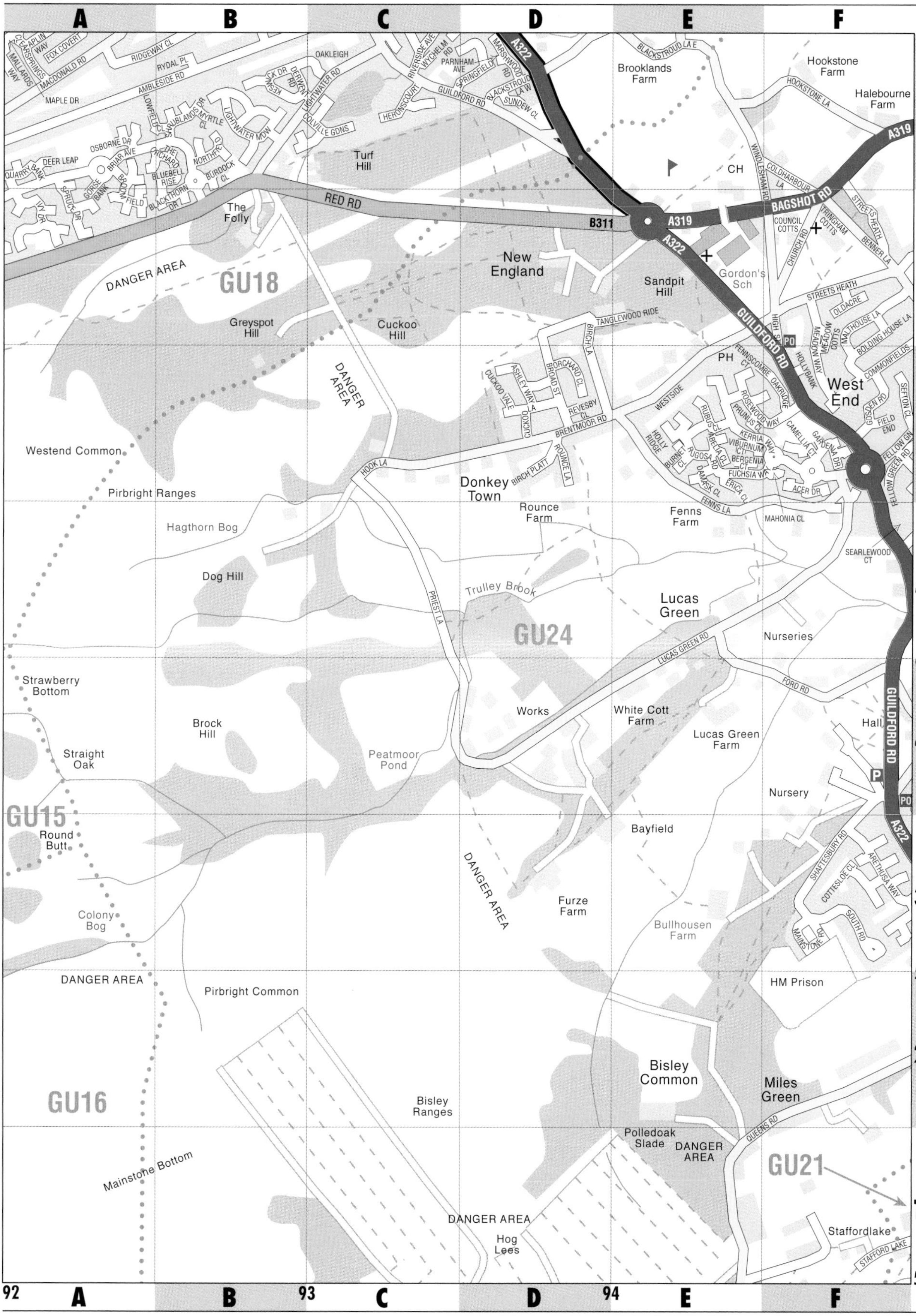

Grid rows: 8 7 61 6 5 60 4 59 3 2 1 58

Place and feature names:

CHAPLIN MALLERIONS WAY, CASEMAKERS WAY, FOX COVERT, MACDONALD RD, MAPLE DR, RIDGEWAY CL, RYDAL PL, OAKLEIGH, LIGHTWATER RD, RIVERSIDE AVE, WYCHELM, PARNHAM AVE, SPRINGFIELD, MARSHWOOD, GUILDFORD RD, HEATHERLEY RD, BLACKSTROUD, SUNDEW CL, BLACKSTROUD LA E, Brooklands Farm, Hookstone Farm, Halebourne Farm

AMBLESIDE RD, LOWFIELD, SUBLANDS CL, MYRTLE CL, KS DR, DEVON CL, CEDAR DR, OAKLEIGH, COLVILLE GDNS, HEROMDCOURT

OSBORNE DR, DEER LEAP, QUARRY BANK, GORSE BANK, SPRUCE DR, IVY DR, BROOM ACRE, BLUEBELL RISE, THE CHASE, BLACKTHORN CROFT, NORTHEY, BURDOCK CL, The Folly, RED RD, Turf Hill, CH, HOOKSTONE LA

A322, A319, BAGSHOT RD, Council Cotts, STREETS HEATH, FRINGHAM CL, BENNER LA, WINKLESHAM RD, COLDHARBOUR LA, CHURCH LA

DANGER AREA, GU18, New England, Sandpit Hill, B311, A319, A322, GUILDFORD RD, Gordon's Sch, PH, PO, A319

Greyspot Hill, Cuckoo Hill, DANGER AREA, TANGLEWOOD RIDE, BIRCH LA, HIGH ST, PENNISCOMBE CT, CAMBRIDGE, West End, STREETS HEATH, MALTHOUSE LA, OLDACRE, BOLDING HOUSE LA, COMMONFIELDS

Westend Common, HOOK LA, BORCHARD CL, BROAD ST, CUCKOO DALE, ASHLEY WAY, CUCKOO LA, REVESBY CL, BRENTMOOR RD, BIRCH PLATT, ROUNCE LA, WESTSIDE, ROSEWOOD WAY, ROSEWOOD CT, HOLLY RIDGE, RUBUS, BURNE CL, VIBURNUM, KERRIA, CAMELLIA CT, GARDEN LA, FIELD END, SEFTON CL, GOSEN RD

Pirbright Ranges, Donkey Town, Rounce Farm, RUGOSA CL, DAMASK CL, BERGENIA, FUCHSIA WAY, ACER DR, ERICA CL, FENNS LA, Fenns Farm, MAHONIA CL, FELLOW GREEN RD

Hagthorn Bog, Dog Hill, PRIEST LA, Trulley Brook, GU24, Lucas Green, Nurseries, SEARLEWOOD CT, GUILDFORD RD

Strawberry Bottom, Brock Hill, Peatmoor Pond, Works, LUCAS GREEN RD, White Cott Farm, Lucas Green Farm, FORD RD, Hall, A322, PO, P

Straight Oak, GU15, Round Butt, DANGER AREA, Bayfield, Nursery, SHAFTESBURY RD, COTTES OF CL, ARETHUSA WAY, MAINSTONE CL, SOUTH RD

Colony Bog, Furze Farm, Bullhousen Farm, HM Prison

DANGER AREA, Pirbright Common, Bisley Common, Bisley Ranges, Polledoak Slade, DANGER AREA, Miles Green, QUEENS RD, GU21

GU16, Mainstone Bottom, Hog Lees, DANGER AREA, Staffordlake, STAFFORD LAKE

92 93 94

67
49

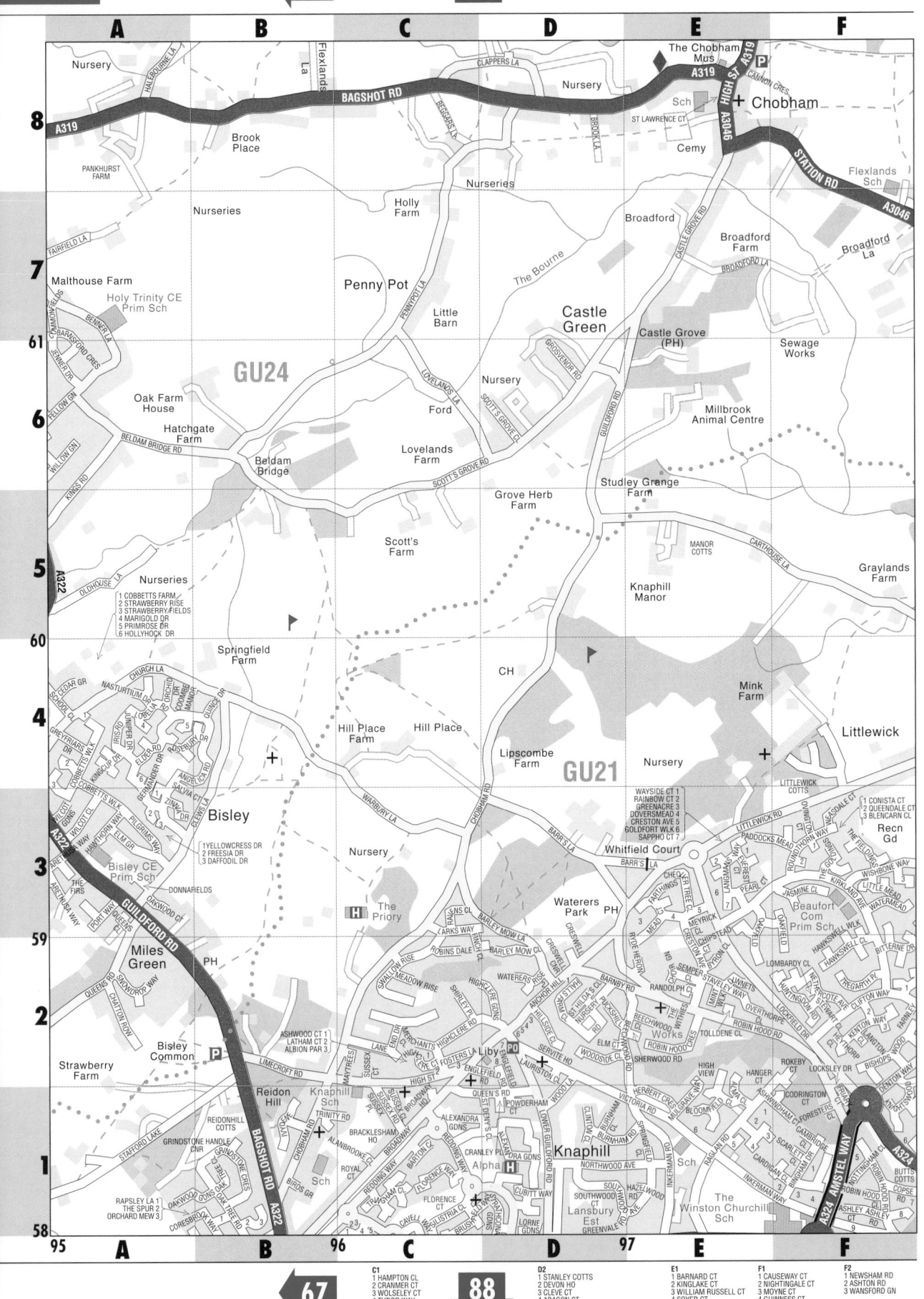

C1
1 HAMPTON CL
2 CRANMER CT
3 WOLSELEY CT
4 TUDOR WAY
5 BOLEYN CT

D2
1 STANLEY COTTS
2 DEVON HO
3 CLEVE CT
4 ARAGON CT
5 KNAP CT
6 TUDOR CT
7 ANCHOR CRES
8 KINGS GATE

E1
1 BARNARD CT
2 KINGLAKE CT
3 WILLIAM RUSSELL CT
4 SOYER CT
5 ROBERTSON CT
6 WELLINGTON TERR

F1
1 CAUSEWAY CT
2 NIGHTINGALE CT
3 MOYNE CT
4 GUINNESS CT
5 NOTTINGHAM CT
6 CRANFIELD CT
7 ST JOHNS WATERSIDE
8 CAPSTANS WHARF
9 BARRACK PATH

F2
1 NEWSHAM RD
2 ASHTON RD
3 WANSFORD GN

67
88

50
70

A B C D E F

Emmett's Mill
Nursery
Fairoaks Airport
Mill Bourne
Willow Farm
GU24
Sunfield Farm
Nursery
Highfield
The Bourne
Scotchers Farm
Bonseys Cottages
Milford Green
Mimbridge
Wapshott Farm
White Lodge Farm
Cox Hill
Coxhill Green
Mim Bridge
Heather Farm
Border Farm
Horsell Common
Deep Pool Farm
Garden Ctr
The Woking Nuffield
Wesbury Farm
GU21
Woking High Sch
Parley Brook Farm
Horsell Birch
Horsell CE Jun Sch
Horsell
St Andrew's Sch
Goldsworth Park Trad Est
Horsell Village Sch
Sythwood Prim Sch
Goldsworth Park
Goldsworth Park Ctr
Basingstoke Canal
WOKING
Woking Com
GU22

BOUNDARY RD 1
BOARD SCHOOL RD 2
THE VILLAS 3
GLOSTER CT 4
BRAMWELL PL 5
BRIDGEWATER PL 6
KENNET CT 7
STRATFORD CT 8
ASHTON CT 9
REGENTS CT 10

1 KETTLEWELL DR
2 HEATHLANDS CL

1 THURLTON CT
2 BROOMHALL END
3 GRAYLANDS

TOLVADDON 1
HURLFORD 2
TRENANCE 3

WHOPSHOTT CL 1
WHOPSHOTT DR 2

SLOCOCK HILL 1
HARELANDS LA 2

1 VANTAGE CT
2 THE OLD DAIRY
3 BEAUFORT MEWS

98 A B 99 C D 00 E F

A1
1 HALLEY'S CT
2 WENDRON CL
3 HELFORD WLK
4 BUTTS COTTS
5 LOWTHORPE
6 GOLDSWORTH ORCH
7 WOODLANDS CT
8 ROSLYN CT
9 WINDERMERE CT

B1
1 SELBY WLK
2 WATERSIDE WAY
3 HELMSDALE
4 ALLOWAY CL
5 MILCOMBE CL

E1
1 CONSORT CT
2 MONTGOMERY RD
3 THE HOLLANDS
4 LAMPETER HO
5 CHARTWELL
6 EVERLANDS CL
7 HOMEBEECH HO
8 HOMEWORTH
9 CARMEL CL
10 THORSDEN CT
11 PARK GATE CT
12 ELMCROFT
13 HILLMOUNT
14 SOUTHVIEW CT
15 HILL VIEW CT
16 WOODLANDS
17 PARK HTS

E2
1 The Peacocks Sh Ctr
2 The Victoria Ent Ctr
3 Wolsley Pl Sh Ctr
4 THE METRO

89

F1
1 MOUNTSIDE PL
2 ST ANDREWS GATE
3 BEECHVALE
4 PARK PL
5 WESTVIEW
6 HIGHDENE
7 MEADSIDE
8 PINEHURST
9 QUEENS CT

70

F1
10 FIRCROFT CT
11 RADSTONE CT
12 WILDBANK CT
13 BELL CT
14 THE ORCHARDS
15 OCKENDEN CL
16 ABINGDON CT

F2
1 GROSVENOR PL
2 CENTRAL BLGS
3 CHOBHAM RD
4 ADDISON RD
5 CHRISTCHURCH WAY
6 TOWN SQ
7 WOLSEY WLK
8 MERCIA WLK
9 CHURCH PATH
10 ALBION HO
11 CHAPEL ST
12 EASTGATE
13 CENTRIUM
14 THE EXCHANGE
15 SOMERSET HO
16 HOLLY LODGE
17 COPPER BEECH HO
18 OAK HO

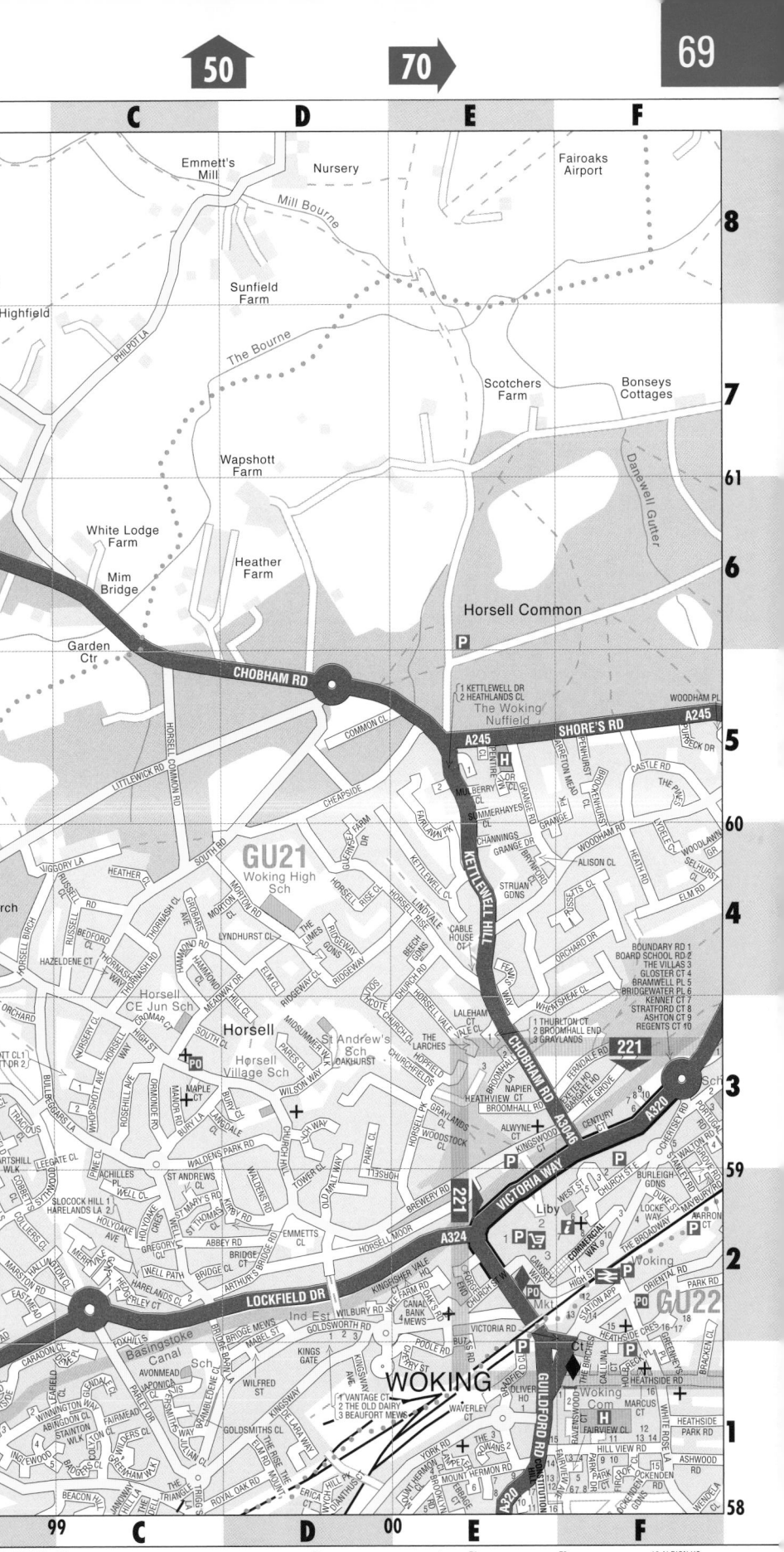

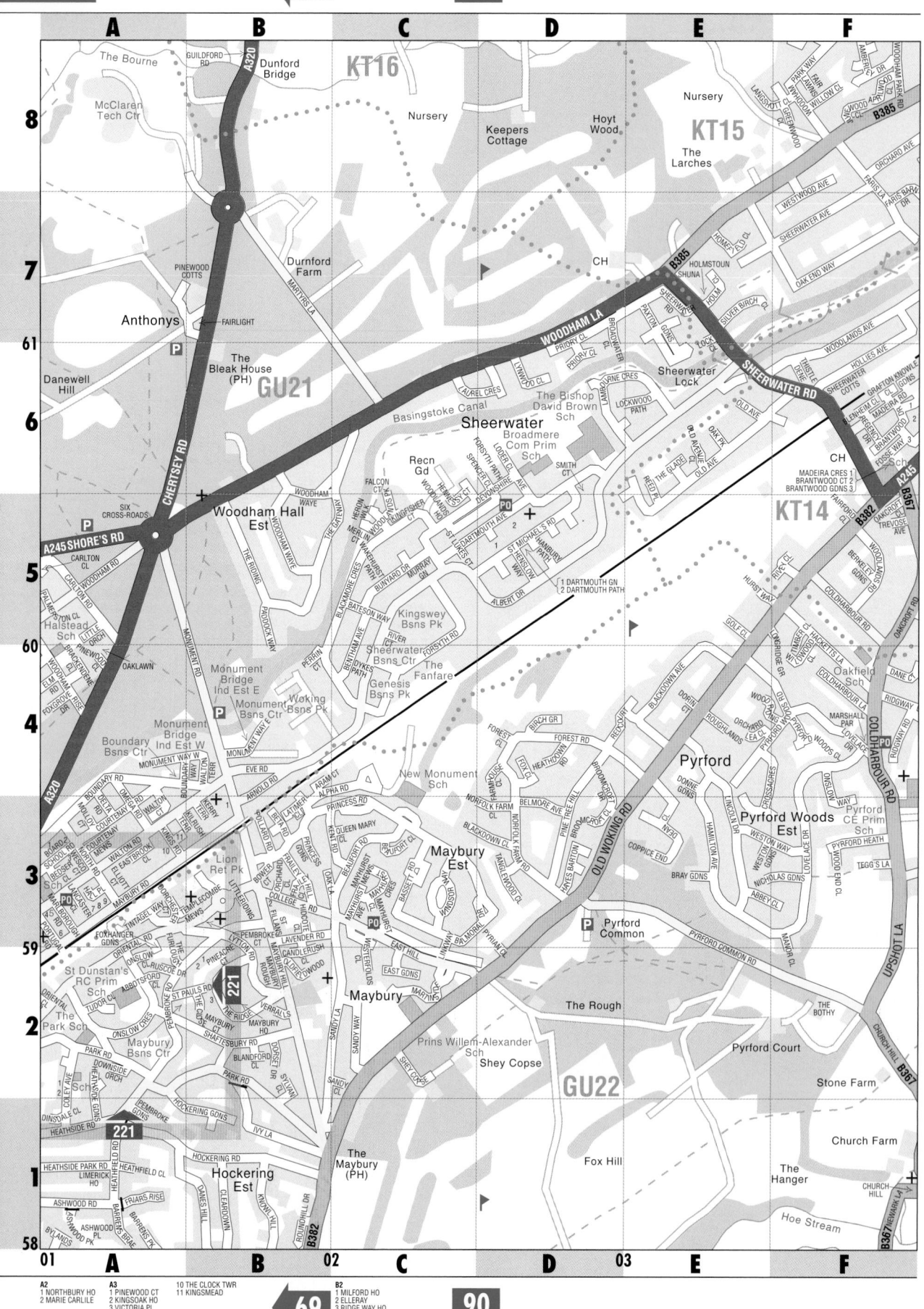

A2
1 NORTHBURY HO
2 MARIE CARLILE

A3
1 PINEWOOD CT
2 KINGSOAK HO
3 VICTORIA PL
4 HANNAH CT
5 Stadium House Bsns Ctr
6 JARMAN CT
7 ROSEWOOD CT
8 PALACE CT
9 THE LIMES
10 THE CLOCK TWR
11 KINGSMEAD

B2
1 MILFORD HO
2 ELLERAY
3 RIDGE WAY HO

B3
1 HUMBERSTONE CT
2 PETWORTH CT

A6
1 BRANTWOOD CL
2 BRANTWOOD GDNS
3 FLEETWOOD CT
4 ORCHARD DENE
5 LAVENDER PARK RD
6 LYNDALE CT
7 ROSEMOUNT HO
8 WOODLANDS HO
A7
1 MILL CLEAVE
2 PARKSIDE HO

52
72

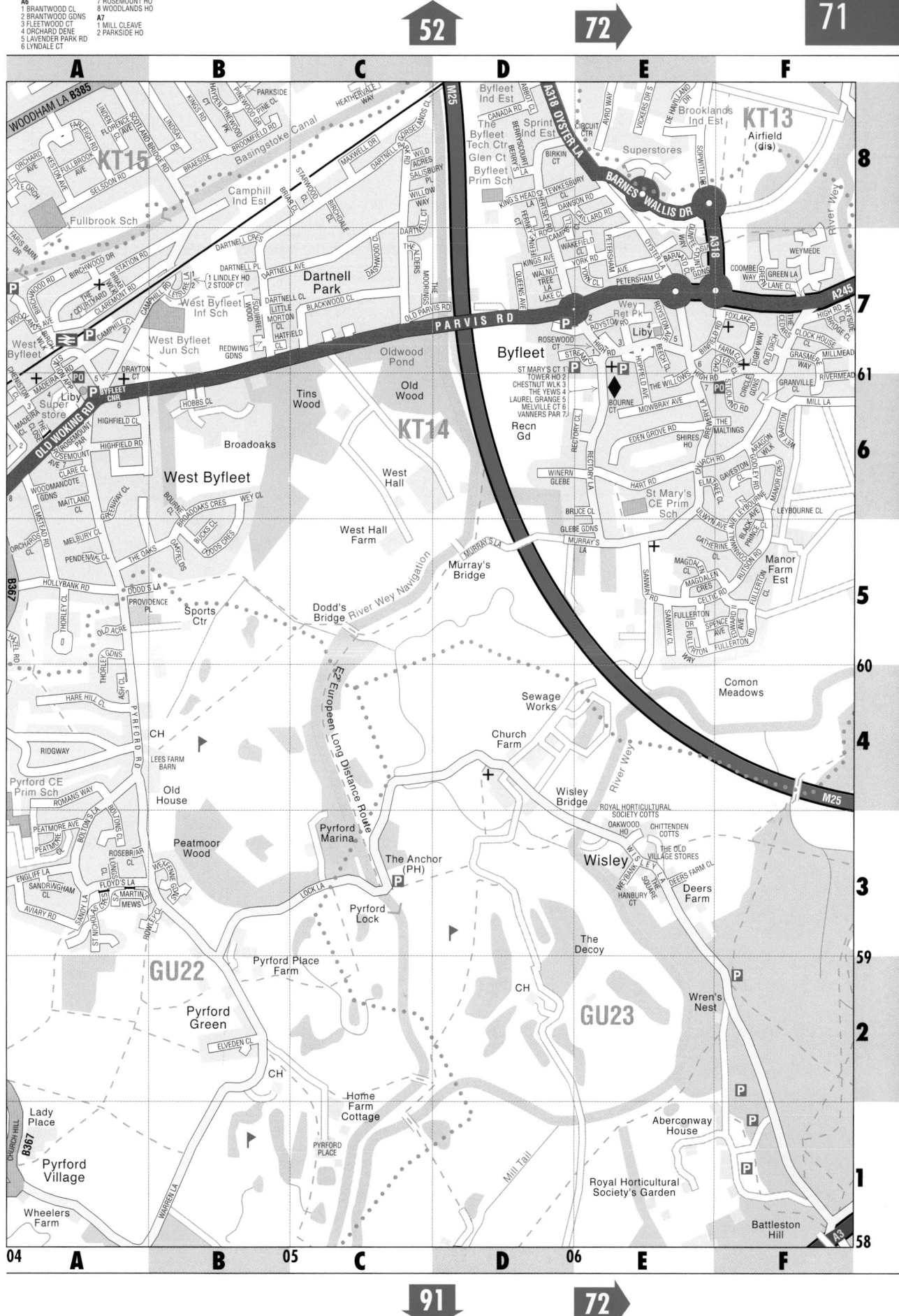

91
72

71
53

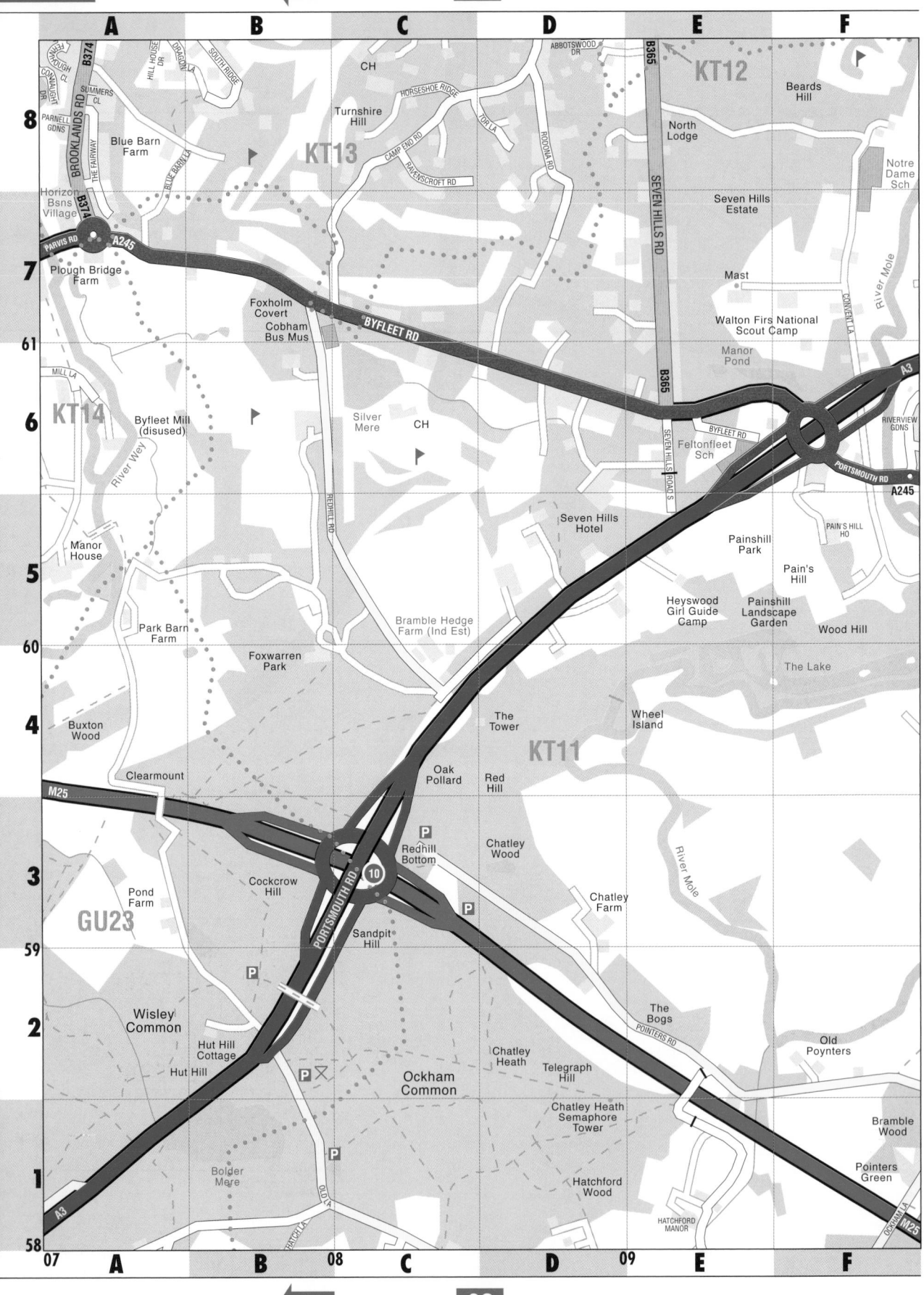
A
B
C
D
E
F
KT12
KT13
KT14
KT11
GU23
Beards Hill
North Lodge
Notre Dame Sch
Seven Hills Estate
Mast
Walton Firs National Scout Camp
Manor Pond
Turnshire Hill
Blue Barn Farm
Horizon Bsns Village
Plough Bridge Farm
Foxholm Covert
Cobham Bus Mus
BYFLEET RD
SEVEN HILLS RD
Byfleet Mill (disused)
Silver Mere
Feltonfleet Sch
Seven Hills Hotel
Painshill Park
Pain's Hill
Manor House
Park Barn Farm
Bramble Hedge Farm (Ind Est)
Heyswood Girl Guide Camp
Painshill Landscape Garden
Wood Hill
Foxwarren Park
The Lake
Buxton Wood
The Tower
Wheel Island
Clearmount
Oak Pollard
Red Hill
M25
Redhill Bottom
Chatley Wood
Cockcrow Hill
PORTSMOUTH RD
Pond Farm
Chatley Farm
River Mole
Sandpit Hill
Wisley Common
The Bogs
Hut Hill Cottage
Hut Hill
Chatley Heath
Telegraph Hill
Old Poynters
Ockham Common
Chatley Heath Semaphore Tower
Bramble Wood
Bolder Mere
Hatchford Wood
Pointers Green
A3
A245
B365
B374
07
08
09
58
59
60
61

71
92

54
74

A B C D E F

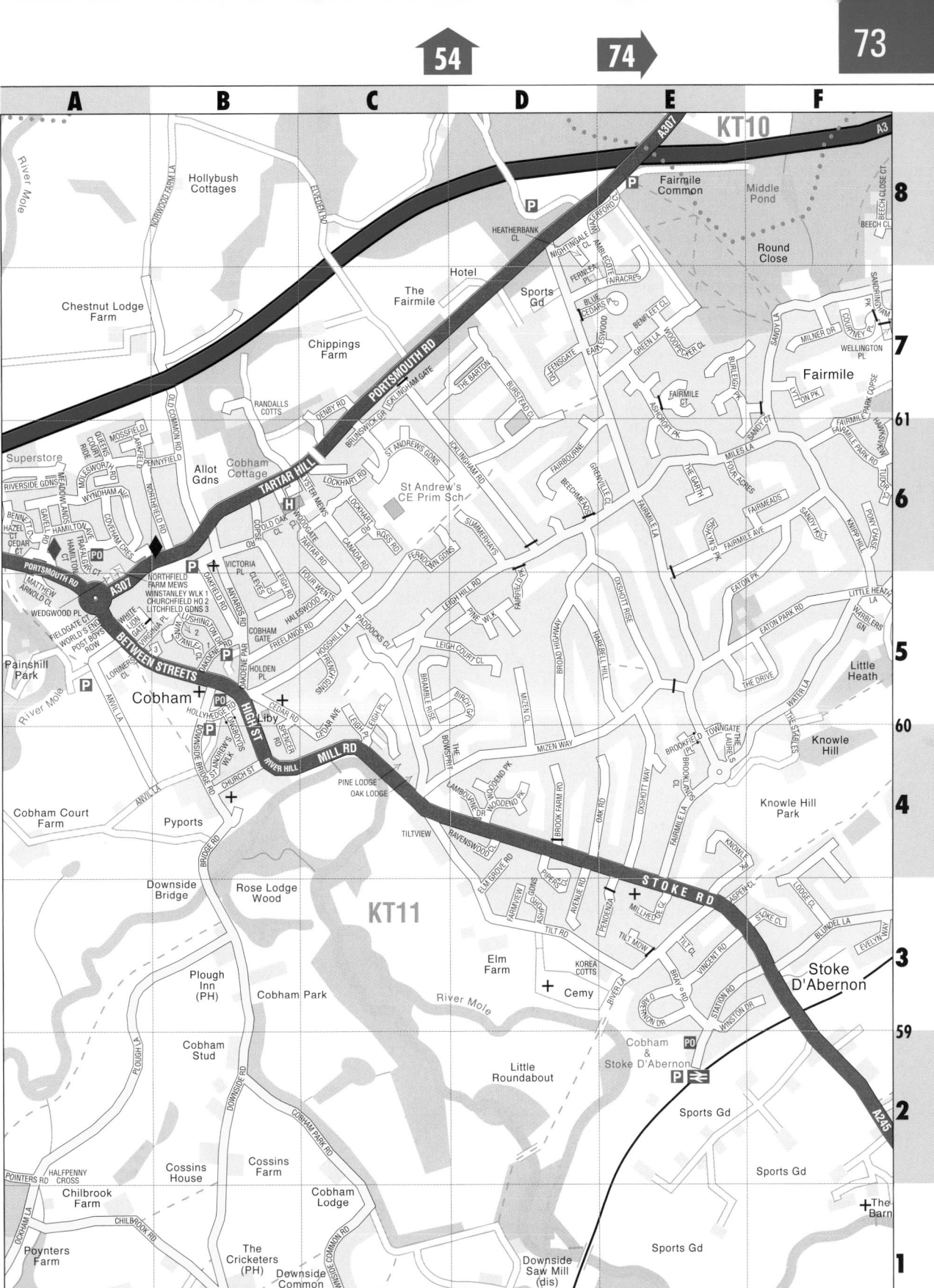

8 7 61 6 5 60 4 3 59 2 1 58

10 A B 11 C D 12 E F

93
74

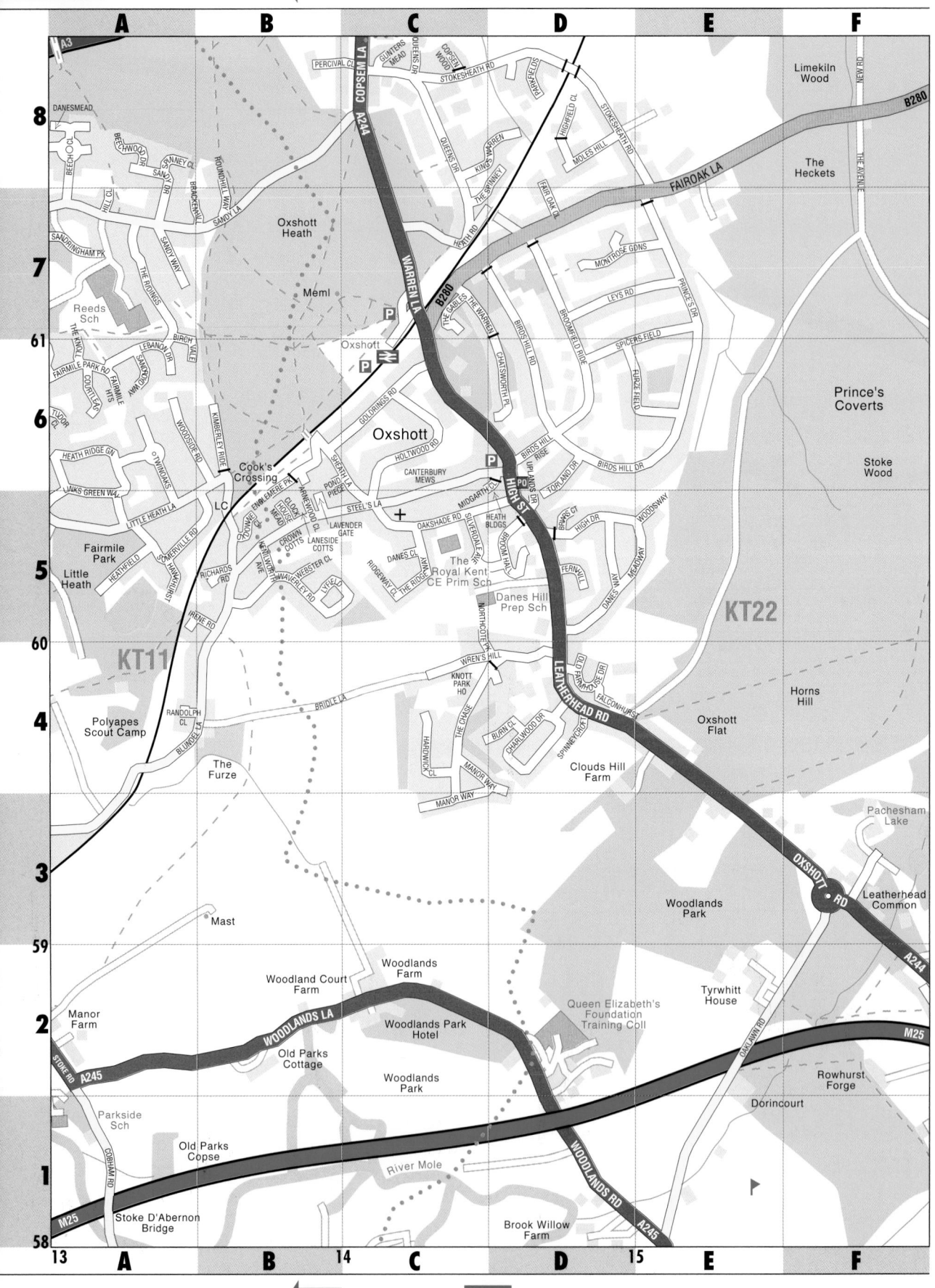

73
55
Oxshott Heath
Oxshott
Meml
Reeds Sch
Cook's Crossing
Fairmile Park
Little Heath
KT11
KT22
Polyapes Scout Camp
The Furze
Mast
Limekiln Wood
The Heckets
Prince's Coverts
Stoke Wood
The Royal Kent CE Prim Sch
Danes Hill Prep Sch
Horns Hill
Oxshott Flat
Clouds Hill Farm
Pachesham Lake
Leatherhead Common
Woodlands Park
Woodlands Farm
Woodland Court Farm
Manor Farm
Woodlands Park Hotel
Old Parks Cottage
Queen Elizabeth's Foundation Training Coll
Tyrwhitt House
Rowhurst Forge
Dorincourt
Parkside Sch
Old Parks Copse
River Mole
Stoke D'Abernon Bridge
Brook Willow Farm
COPSEM LA
WARREN LA
HIGH ST
LEATHERHEAD RD
OXSHOTT RD
FAIROAK LA
WOODLANDS LA
WOODLANDS RD
STOKE RD
COBHAM RD
OAKLAWN RD
BRIDLE LA
SANDY LA
STOKESHEATH RD
BIRDS HILL DR
STEEL'S LA
WREN'S HILL
A3
A244
A245
B280
M25
73
94

56
76

A
B
C
D
E
F
FAIROAK LA
Chessington Wood
Acre Hill Farmhouse
The New Epsom & Ewell Cottage
Horton Country Park
KT19
A243
WOODVIEW
WEST RD
Malden Rushett
New Wood
West Park
RUSHETT LA
KT9
Silverglade Bsns Pk
SILVERGLADE
WEST PARK RD
Byhurst Farm
Glanmire Farm
Fox & Hounds (PH)
Airstrip
CHRIST CHURCH RD
B280
LEATHERHEAD RD
Rushett Farm
Bunker's Hill
Great Stew Pond
Epsom Common
D'Abernon Chase Lodge
Telegraph Hill
The Forest
Newton Wood
World's End
The Star (PH)
KT18
KT22
Ashtead Common
Pachesham Park
Caen Wood
CH
KINGSTON RD
BROADHURST
CULVERHAY
OVERDALE
NEWTON WOOD RD
The Rye
THE RENMANS
GRADDOCKS AVE
BAGOT CL
Ashley Court
ASHTEAD WOODS RD
THE COMMON
Wood Field
Ashtead
PETTERS RD
ST STEPHENS AVE
KT21
WOODLANDS COPSE
LC
CHAFFERS MEAD
MEAD END
Pachesham Manor
RYE FIELD
THE RIDINGS
WOODFIELD RD
WOODFIELD LA
WOODLODGE
CRAY AVE
BRAMLEY WAY
1 WHITTAKER CT
2 ST JAMES CT
OXSHOTT RD
A244
Trevona
BIRCH CT
CRADDOCKS PAR
RUTLAND CL
MEADOW GATE
MEADOW RD
DARCY RD
DARCY PL
OLD STEDE CL
The Greville Prim Sch
LINKS CL
LINKS PL
MIENA WAY
WOODFIELD CL
ELM WOOD
ELMWOOD
PRESTON GR
LINKS RD
WARWICK GDNS
HILLSIDE RD
BERRY MEADE
STONNY CROFT
BERRY MEADE CL
B2430
FAIRHOLME CRES
TAYLOR RD
READ RD
BALQUHAIN CL
Barnett Wood Inf Sch
WALTER'S MEAD
CLAVERTON
MOAT CT
KINGSTON RD
BROOKERS CL
BROOKERS CT
Lower Ashtead
Recn Gd
Liby
TEMPLEWOOD PK
RYEBRIDGE CL
GREENDENE DR
FLORAL CT
THE CHASE
RICHBELL CL
GREEN LA
CHURCH RD
CROFTON
THE MARLD
BURNSIDE
WISHFORD CT
ASTEDE PL
WESTFIELD
BOWYERS CL
CRISPIN CL
Ashtead
Super store
WOODBRIDGE GR
RYE BROOK RD
CORFE CL
ROSEDALE
OAKHILL CL
OAKHILL RD
BARNETT WOOD LA
MULBERRY CT
GLEBE RD
OAKFIELD RD
GREVILLE PARK AVE
WOODFIELD LA
POUND CT
MARLBOROUGH RD
EPSOM RD
A24
KINGSBROOK
WOODBRIDGE AVE
SANDES PL
CLARE WOOD
CAEN WOOD RD
PADDOCKS CL
GREVILLE PARK RD
GRENVILLE PL
BERKELEY CT
West Hill Sch
BROOK WAY
Regent Pk
THE AVENUE
FAIRWAY
MERTON WALK
CLARE CRES
MERTON WAY
RYELANDS CT
M25
HEATHFIELD CL
ASTON CL
WEST FARM AVE
THE MURREYS
Murreys Court
AGATES LA
THE BYWAYS
SKINNERS LA
GLADSTONE RD
OLDFIELD GDNS
VIRGINIA CL
PADDOCKS WAY
GREVILLE CT
PARK RD
LIME TREE CT
THE STREET
PARK LA
PURCELL'S CL
ALBERT RD
GAYWOOD RD
HOWARD CL
DENE RD
16
17
18
58
59
60
61
1
2
3
4
5
6
7
8

95
76

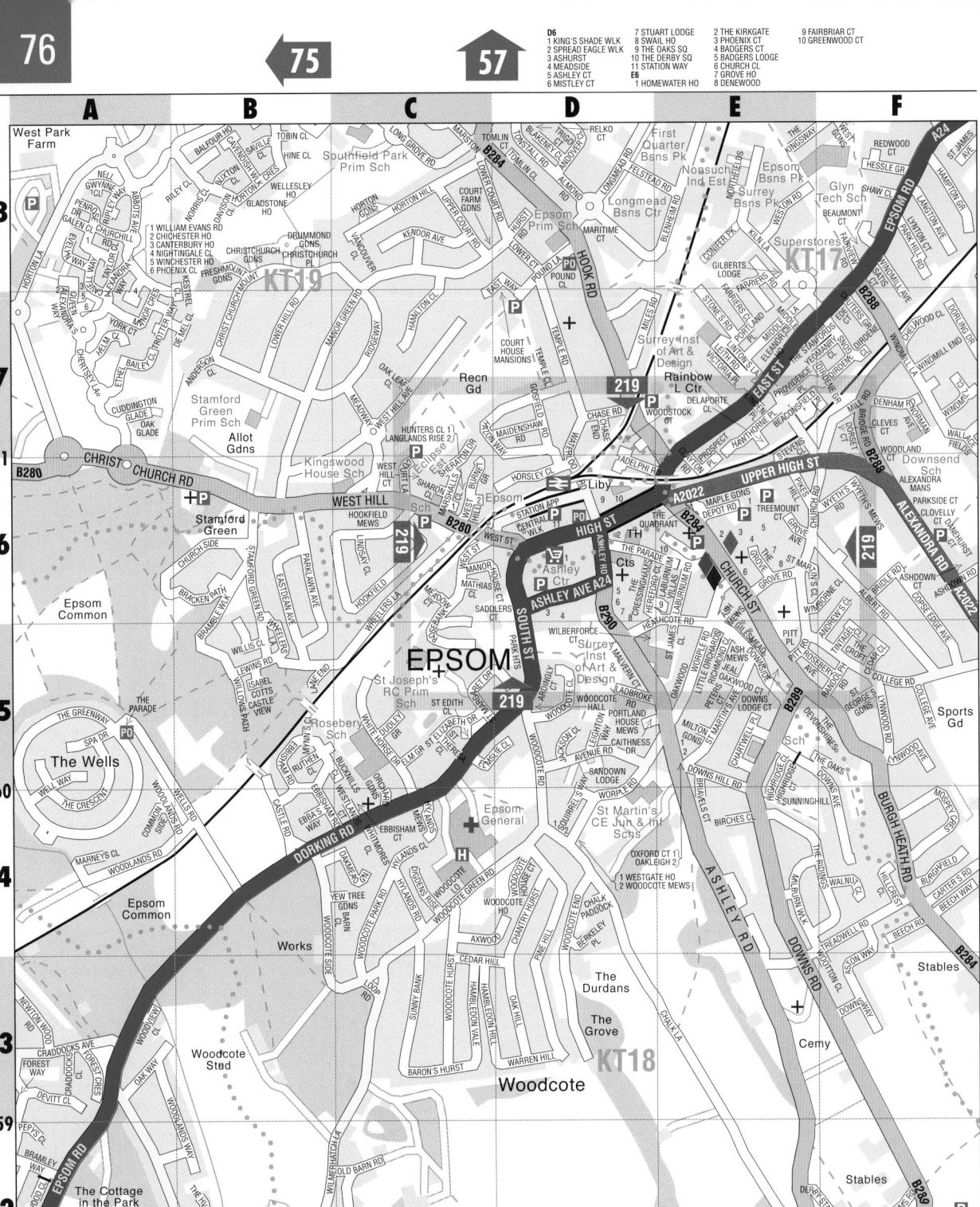

D6
1 KING'S SHADE WLK
2 SPREAD EAGLE WLK
3 ASHURST
4 MEADSIDE
5 ASHLEY CT
6 MISTLEY CT

7 STUART LODGE
8 SWAIL HO
9 THE OAKS SQ
10 THE DERBY SQ
11 STATION WAY
E6
1 HOMEWATER HO

2 THE KIRKGATE
3 PHOENIX CT
4 BADGERS CT
5 BADGERS LODGE
6 CHURCH CL
7 GROVE HO
8 DENEWOOD

9 FAIRBRIAR CT
10 GREENWOOD CT

58
78

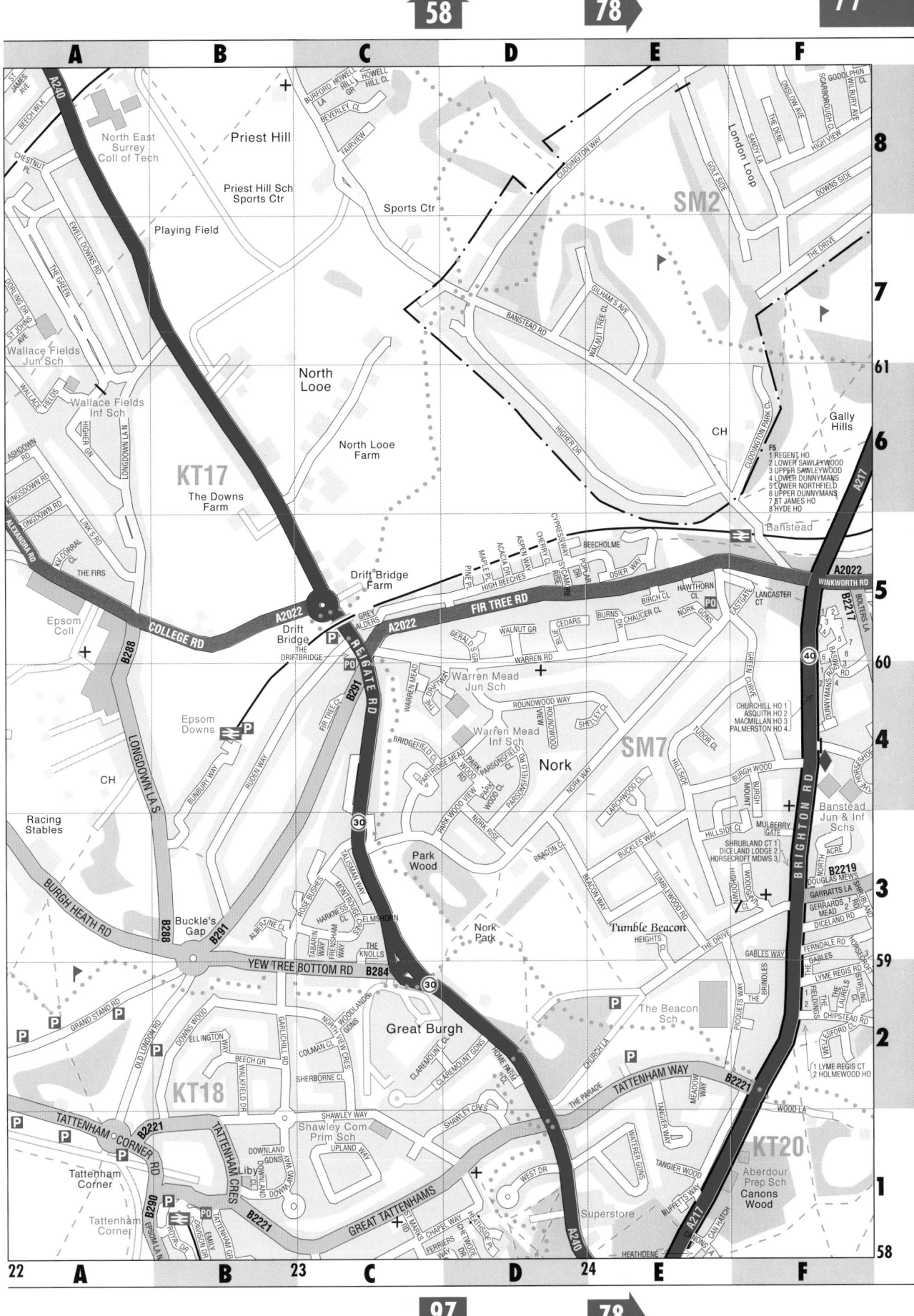
A
B
C
D
E
F
8
7
61
6
5
60
4
3
59
2
1
58
22
23
24
A240
Priest Hill
North East Surrey Coll of Tech
Priest Hill Sch Sports Ctr
Sports Ctr
Playing Field
SM2
London Loop
CUDDINGTON WAY
BANSTEAD RD
GILHAM'S AVE
WALNUT TREE CL
HIGHER DR
GOLF SIDE
SANDY LA
THE DENE
ONSLOW AVE
SCARBOROUGH CL
GODOLPHIN CL
WILBURY AVE
HIGH VIEW
DOWNS SIDE
THE DRIVE
CUDDINGTON PARK CL
CH
Gally Hills
F5
1 REGENT HO
2 LOWER SAWLEYWOOD
3 UPPER SAWLEYWOOD
4 LOWER DUNNYMANS
5 LOWER NORTHFIELD
6 UPPER DUNNYMANS
7 ST JAMES HO
8 HYDE HO
Banstead
A217
North Looe
North Looe Farm
KT17
The Downs Farm
ST JAMES AVE
BEECH WLK
CHESTNUT PL
EWELL DOWNS RD
THE GREEN
DORLING DR
ST JOHNS AVE
Wallace Fields Jun Sch
WALLACE FIELDS
Wallace Fields Inf Sch
HIGHER GN
LONGDOWN LA N
ASHDOWN RD
KINGSDOWN RD
LONGDOWN RD
LINK'S RD
KILCORRAL CL
THE FIRS
ALEXANDRA RD
Epsom Coll
COLLEGE RD
A2022
B288
Drift Bridge Farm
Drift Bridge
THE DRIFTBRIDGE
GREY ALDERS
FIR TREE RD
REIGATE RD
PINE PL
MAPLE PL
ACACIA DR
ASPEN WAY
CHERRY CL
CYPRESS WAY
SYCAMORE RISE
POPLAR DR
BEECHOLME
HIGH BEECHES
OSIER WAY
BIRCH CL
HAWTHORN CL
NORK GDNS
EASTGATE
LANCASTER CT
WINKWORTH RD
B2217
BOLTERS LA
GERALD'S GR
WALNUT GR
CEDARS
BURNS DR
CHAUCER CL
WARREN RD
Warren Mead Jun Sch
WARREN MEAD
THE DRIFTWAY
ROUNDWOOD WAY
ROUNDWOOD VIEW
SHELLEY CL
GREEN CURVE
BASING RD
DUNNYMANS RD
CHURCHILL HO 1
ASQUITH HO 2
MACMILLAN HO 3
PALMERSTON HO 4
40
Epsom Downs
B291
FIR TREE CL
Warren Mead Inf Sch
BRIDGEFIELD CL
PARTRIDGE MEAD
PARK WOOD RD
PARSONSFIELD CL
PARSONSFIELD RD
PARK WOOD VIEW
PARK WOOD CL
NORK RISE
Nork
NORK WAY
SM7
TUDOR CL
HILLSIDE
BURGH WOOD
BURGH MOUNT
Banstead Jun & Inf Schs
HORSESHOE
CH
LONGDOWN LA S
BUNBURY WAY
RUDEN WAY
Racing Stables
30
LARCHWOOD CL
BUCKLES WAY
HILLSIDE CL
MULBERRY GATE
SHRUBLAND CT 1
DICELAND LODGE 2
HORSECROFT MDWS 3
BRIGHTON RD
NORTH ACRE
B2219
DOUGLAS MEWS
GARRATTS LA
SHRUBLAND RD
GERRARDS MEAD
DICELAND RD
Park Wood
BEACON CL
BEACON WAY
TUMBLEWOOD RD
HIGHDOWN
WOODGAVIL
BURGH HEATH RD
TALISMAN WAY
ROSE BUSHES
MONTROUGE CRES
HARKNESS CL
ELMSHORN
ALBERTINE CL
TABARIN WAY
FRENSHAM WAY
THE KNOLLS
Buckle's Gap
B288
Nork Park
Tumble Beacon
HEIGHTS CL
THE DRIVE
GABLES WAY
FERNDALE RD
HORSECROFT
THE GABLES
LYME REGIS RD
THE LAURELS
STIRLING CL
FIELDINGS
THE BRINDLES
PICQUETS WAY
YEW TREE BOTTOM RD
B284
GRAND STAND RD
OLD LONDON RD
DOWNS WOOD
GARLICHILL RD
NORTH VIEW CRES
WOODLANDS GDNS
Great Burgh
The Beacon Sch
CHIPSTEAD RD
WELLESFORD CL
1 LYME REGIS CT
2 HOLMEWOOD HO
ELLINGTON WAY
BEECH GR
WALKFIELD DR
COLMAN CL
SHERBORNE CL
CLAREMOUNT CL
CLAREMOUNT GDNS
HOME FARM CL
CHURCH LA
TATTENHAM WAY
B2221
MEADOW WAY
KT18
TATTENHAM CORNER RD
B2221
TATTENHAM CRES
SHAWLEY WAY
Shawley Com Prim Sch
SHAWLEY CRES
THE PARADE
TANGIER WAY
WATERER GDNS
WOOD LA
KT20
Tattenham Corner
DOWNLAND GDNS
DOWNLAND CL
DOWNLAND WAY
UPLAND WAY
Liby
WEST DR
TANGIER WOOD
RUFFETTS WAY
Aberdour Prep Sch
Canons Wood
B290
EPSOM LA N
ROYAL DR
DAVISON DR
EMILY DAVISON DR
TATTENHAM GR
GREAT TATTENHAMS
ST MARKS RD
CHAPEL WAY
CHETWODE DR
HEATHSIDE PL
FERRIERS WAY
Superstore
A240
HEATHDENE
CANONS LA
CAN HATCH

97
78

77
59

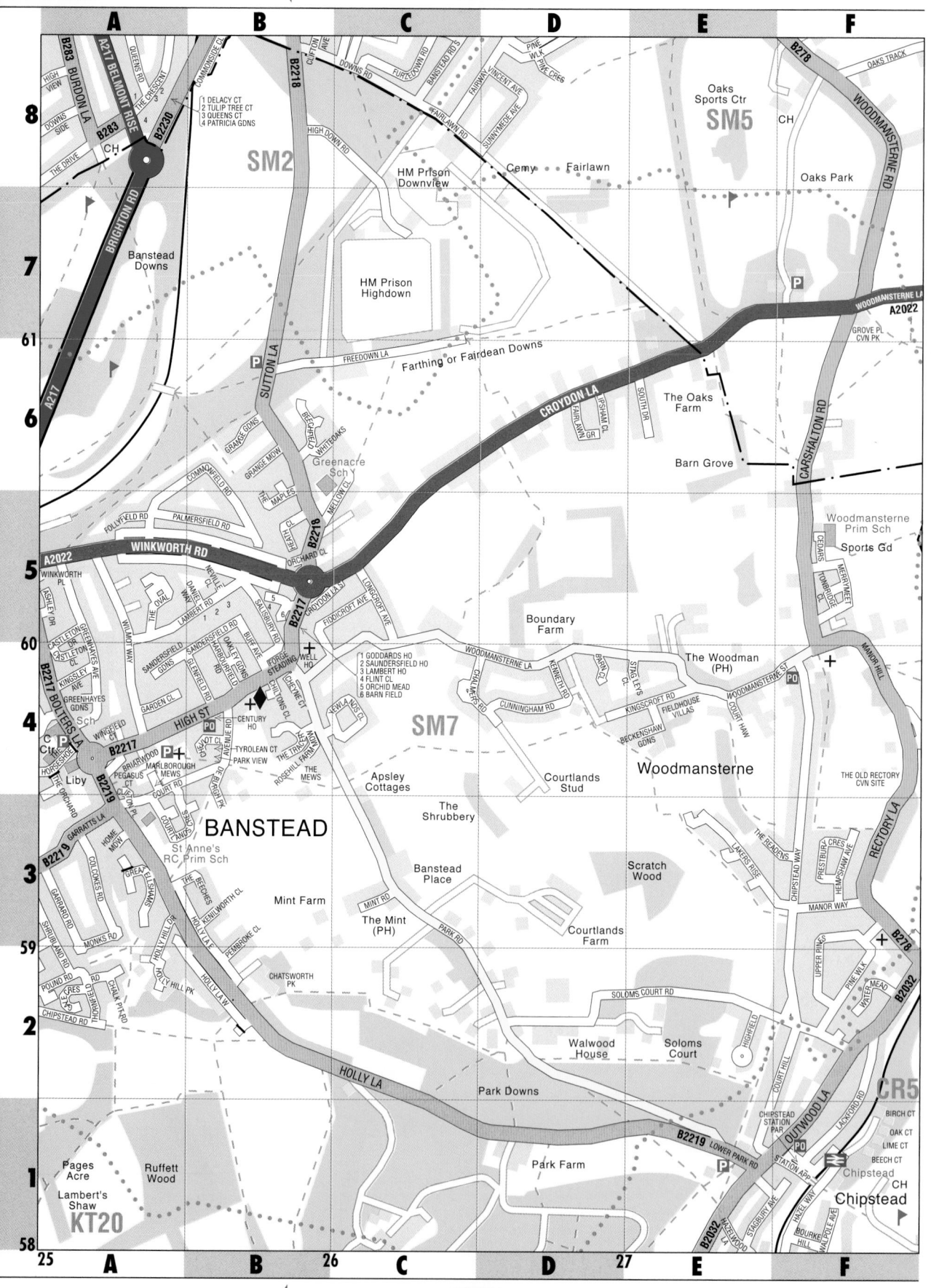
A
B
C
D
E
F
8
7
61
6
5
60
4
3
59
2
1
58
25
26
27
SM2
SM5
SM7
KT20
CR5
BANSTEAD
Woodmansterne
Chipstead
A217 BELMONT RISE
B283 BURDON LA
BRIGHTON RD
B2230
B2218
SUTTON LA
CROYDON LA
A2022
WINKWORTH RD
B2217
HIGH ST
B2217 BOLTERS LA
B2219
HOLLY LA
LOWER PARK RD
B2032
OUTWOOD LA
B278
WOODMANSTERNE RD
CARSHALTON RD
RECTORY LA
MANOR HILL
WOODMANSTERNE LA
WOODMANSTERNE ST
CHIPSTEAD WAY
MANOR WAY
COURT HILL
PARK RD
MINT RD
SOLOMS COURT RD
FREEDOWN LA
HIGH DOWN RD
FAIRLAWN RD
DOWNS RD
FURZEDOWN RD
BANSTEAD RD S
CLIFTON AVE
VINCENT AVE
SUNNYMEDE AVE
FAIRWAY
PINE WLK
PINE CRES
OAKS TRACK
COMMONSIDE CL
QUEENS RD
THE CRESCENT
HIGH VIEW
DOWNS SIDE
THE DRIVE
1 DELACY CT
2 TULIP TREE CT
3 QUEENS CT
4 PATRICIA GDNS
GRANGE GDNS
GRANGE MDW
BEECHFIELD
WHITEOAKS
THE MAPLES
HEATH CL
MELLOW CL
ORCHARD CL
COMMONFIELD RD
PALMERSFIELD RD
FOLLYFIELD RD
WINKWORTH PL
ASHLEY DR
CASTLETON DR
CASTLETON CL
GREENHAYES AVE
KINGSLEY AVE
GREENHAYES GDNS
WILMOT WAY
THE OVAL
DANIEL WAY
NEVILLE CL
LAMBERT RD
SANDERSFIELD GDNS
SANDERSFIELD RD
GLENFIELD RD
MARBOURFIELD RD
OAKLEY GDNS
BUFF AVE
SALISBURY RD
FORGE STEADING
GARDEN CL
CROYDON LA S
FIDDICROFT AVE
LONGCROFT AVE
1 GODDARDS HO
2 SAUNDERSFIELD HO
3 LAMBERT HO
4 FLINT CL
5 ORCHID MEAD
6 BARN FIELD
WELL HO
CHILTONS CL
CHEYNE CT
NEWLANDS CL
THE TRACERY
ROSEHILL FARM MDW
THE MEWS
CENTURY HO
TYROLEAN CT
PARK VIEW
CHEVIOT CL
AVENUE RD
DE BURGH PK
WINGFIELD CT
BRIARWOOD CT
MARLBOROUGH MEWS
PEGASUS CT
CLIFTON PL
COURT RD
COURTLANDS CRES
HORSESHOE
THE ORCHARD
GARRATTS LA
HOME MDW
GREAT ELSHAMS
COLCOKES RD
GARRARD RD
MONKS RD
SHRUBLAND RD
POUND RD
YEW TREE CRES
THORNFIELD RD
CHALK PIT RD
CHIPSTEAD RD
THE BEECHES
KENILWORTH CL
HOLLY LA E
HOLLY LA W
HOLLY HILL DR
HOLLY HILL PK
PEMBROKE CL
CHATSWORTH PK
CHALMERS RD
CUNNINGHAM RD
KENNETH RD
BARN CL
STAG LEYS CL
KINGSCROFT RD
FIELDHOUSE VILLAS
BECKENSHAW GDNS
COURT HAW
FAIRLAWN GR
IPSHAM CL
SOUTH DR
THE READENS
LAKERS RISE
PRESTBURY CRES
HEMPSHAW AVE
UPPER PINES
PINE WLK
WATER MEAD
CEDARS
TOMBRIDGE CL
MERRYMEET
HIGHFIELD
STATION APP
STAGBURY AVE
HAZELWOOD LA
HAZEL WAY
WALPOLE AVE
BOURKE HILL
LACKFORD RD
BIRCH CT
OAK CT
LIME CT
BEECH CT
CHIPSTEAD STATION PAR
GROVE PL CVN PK
THE OLD RECTORY CVN SITE
Oaks Sports Ctr
Oaks Park
CH
Fairlawn
Cemy
HM Prison Downview
HM Prison Highdown
Farthing or Fairdean Downs
Banstead Downs
Greenacre Sch
The Oaks Farm
Barn Grove
Woodmansterne Prim Sch
Sports Gd
Boundary Farm
The Woodman (PH)
PO
Courtlands Stud
Apsley Cottages
The Shrubbery
Banstead Place
Scratch Wood
Mint Farm
The Mint (PH)
Courtlands Farm
St Anne's RC Prim Sch
Sch
C Ctr
Liby
Walwood House
Soloms Court
Park Downs
Park Farm
Pages Acre
Ruffett Wood
Lambert's Shaw
Chipstead

77
98

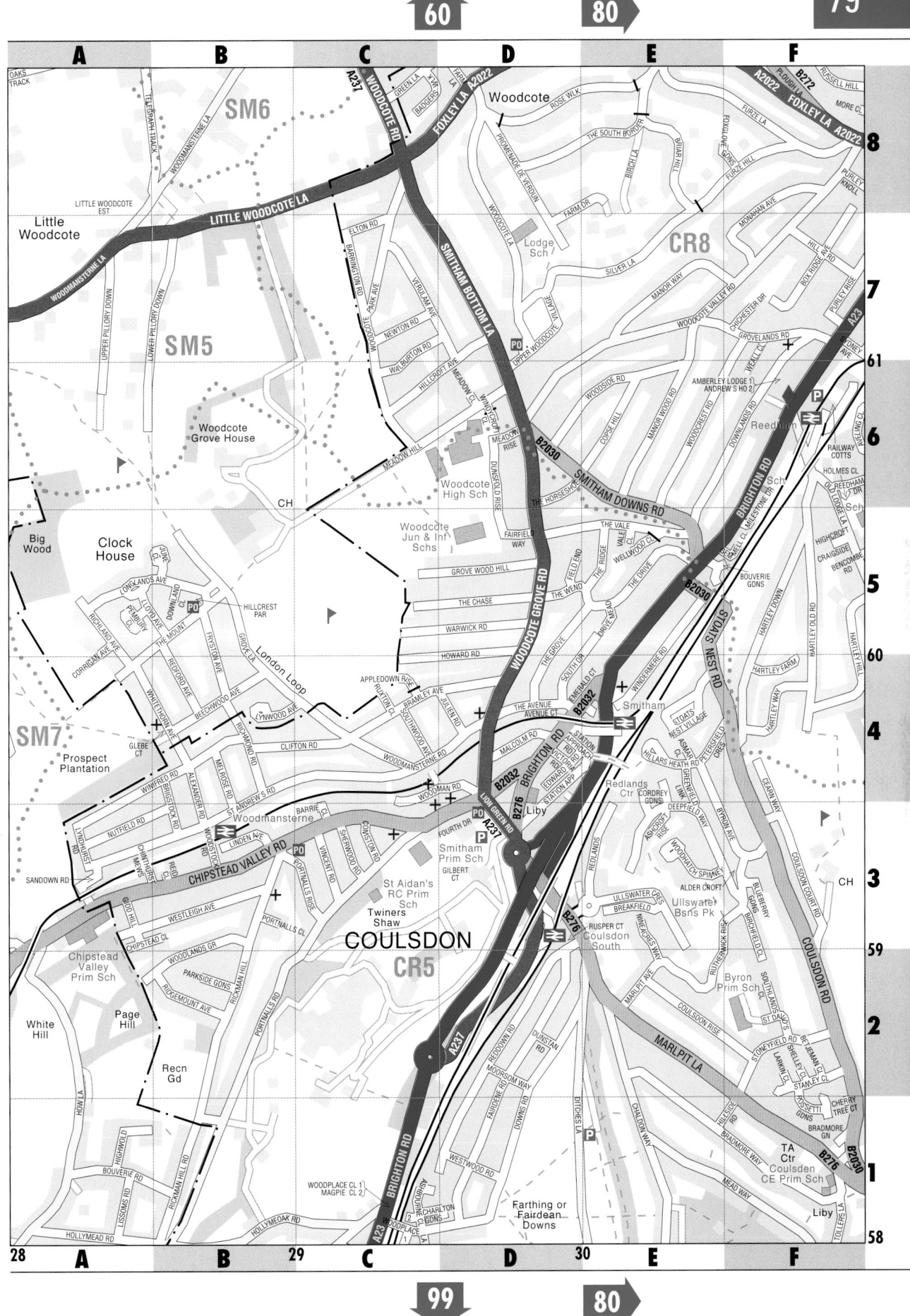
60
80
A
B
C
D
E
F
8
7
61
6
5
60
4
3
59
2
1
58
28
29
30
99
80
SM6
SM5
SM7
CR8
CR5
Woodcote
Little Woodcote
LITTLE WOODCOTE EST
LITTLE WOODCOTE LA
WOODMANSTERNE LA
FOXLEY LA A2022
WOODCOTE RD
A237
SMITHAM BOTTOM LA
WOODCOTE GROVE RD
SMITHAM DOWNS RD
B2030
BRIGHTON RD
A23
B2032
B276
COULSDON RD
MARLPIT LA
STOATS NEST RD
CHIPSTEAD VALLEY RD
Woodcote Grove House
Clock House
Big Wood
Prospect Plantation
London Loop
Woodcote High Sch
Woodcote Jun & Inf Schs
Lodge Sch
Reedham
Smitham
Woodmansterne
Smitham Prim Sch
St Aidan's RC Prim Sch
Twiners Shaw
COULSDON
Coulsdon South
Redlands Ctr
Ullswater Bsns Pk
Byron Prim Sch
Chipstead Valley Prim Sch
White Hill
Page Hill
Recn Gd
Farthing or Fairdean Downs
TA Ctr
Coulsden CE Prim Sch
Liby
CH
HILLCREST PAR
AMBERLEY LODGE 1
ANDREW'S HO 2
WOODPLACE CL 1
MAGPIE CL 2

A7
1 SILVERMERE CT
2 LIDDELL CT
3 ADAMS CT
4 BYRNE CT
5 FOXLEY LODGE

A8
1 BOURNE CT
2 COLDHARBOUR LA
3 GRESHAM CT
4 TUDOR CT
5 RUSSELL PAR
6 RUSSELL HILL PAR

79

A8
7 KIMBERLEY PL
8 THE EXCHANGE
9 PURLEY PAR
10 ASTORIA CT
11 GEMINI CT
12 REYNARD CT

61

B7
1 LISTER CT
2 NICHOLASS CT
3 GODSTONE MOUNT
4 REDWING CT

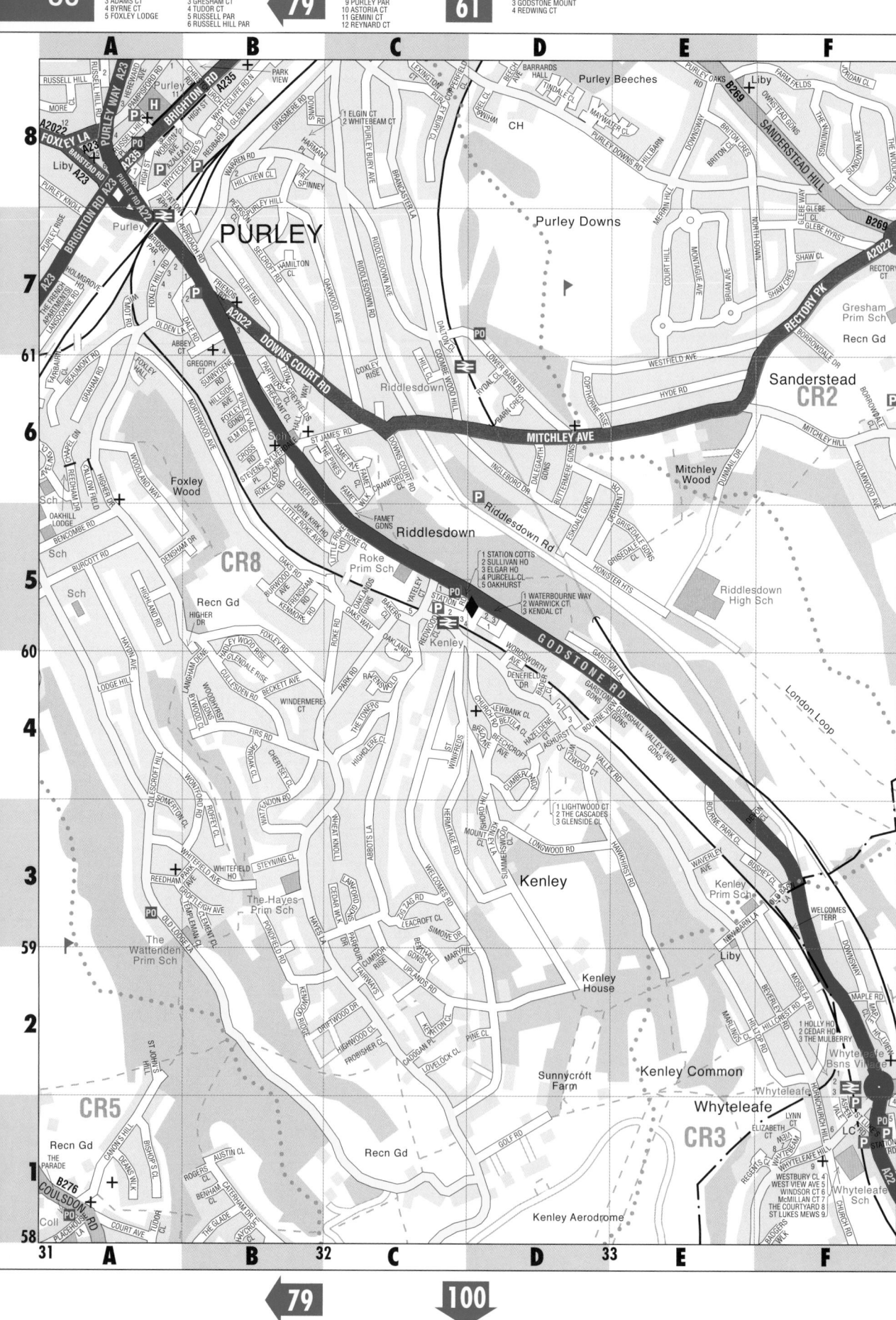

79
100

62
82

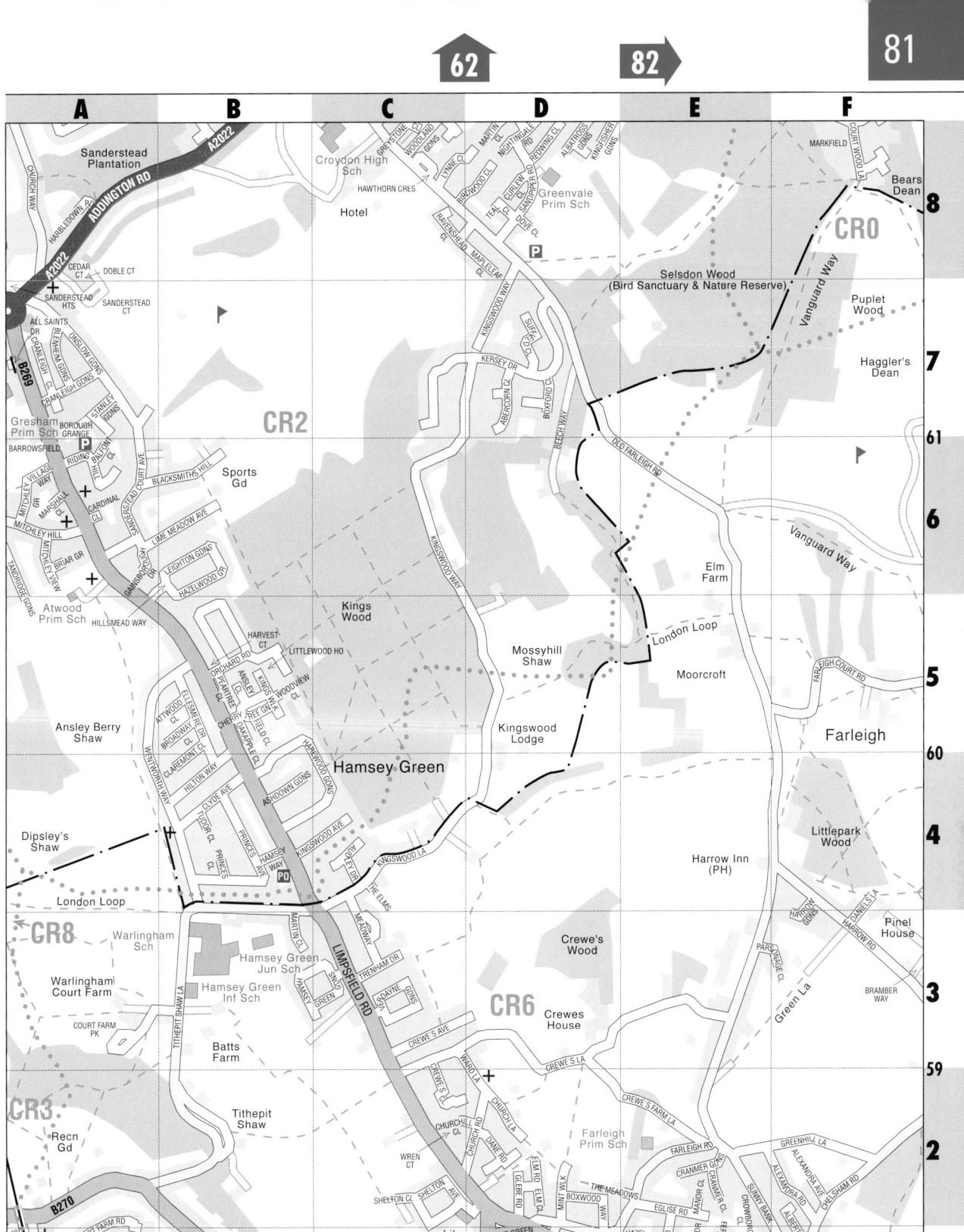
Sanderstead Plantation
ADDINGTON RD
A2022
Croydon High Sch
Hotel
Greenvale Prim Sch
Selsdon Wood (Bird Sanctuary & Nature Reserve)
Bears Dean
CR0
Vanguard Way
Puplet Wood
Haggler's Dean
CR2
Gresham Prim Sch
Sports Gd
Atwood Prim Sch
Kings Wood
Mossyhill Shaw
London Loop
Moorcroft
Elm Farm
Farleigh
Ansley Berry Shaw
Kingswood Lodge
Hamsey Green
Dipsley's Shaw
Littlepark Wood
Harrow Inn (PH)
CR8
Warlingham Sch
Hamsey Green Jun Sch
Hamsey Green Inf Sch
Warlingham Court Farm
LIMPSFIELD RD
CR6
Crewe's Wood
Crewes House
Pinel House
Batts Farm
Tithepit Shaw
CR3
Recn Gd
Farleigh Prim Sch
Green La
B270
HILLBURY RD
WARLINGHAM
Upper Warlingham
Chelsham Place Farm
Highlands Farm
B269
1 BOURNEFIELD RD
2 ALPHA CT
3 BROCKLEBANK CT

101
82

81
63

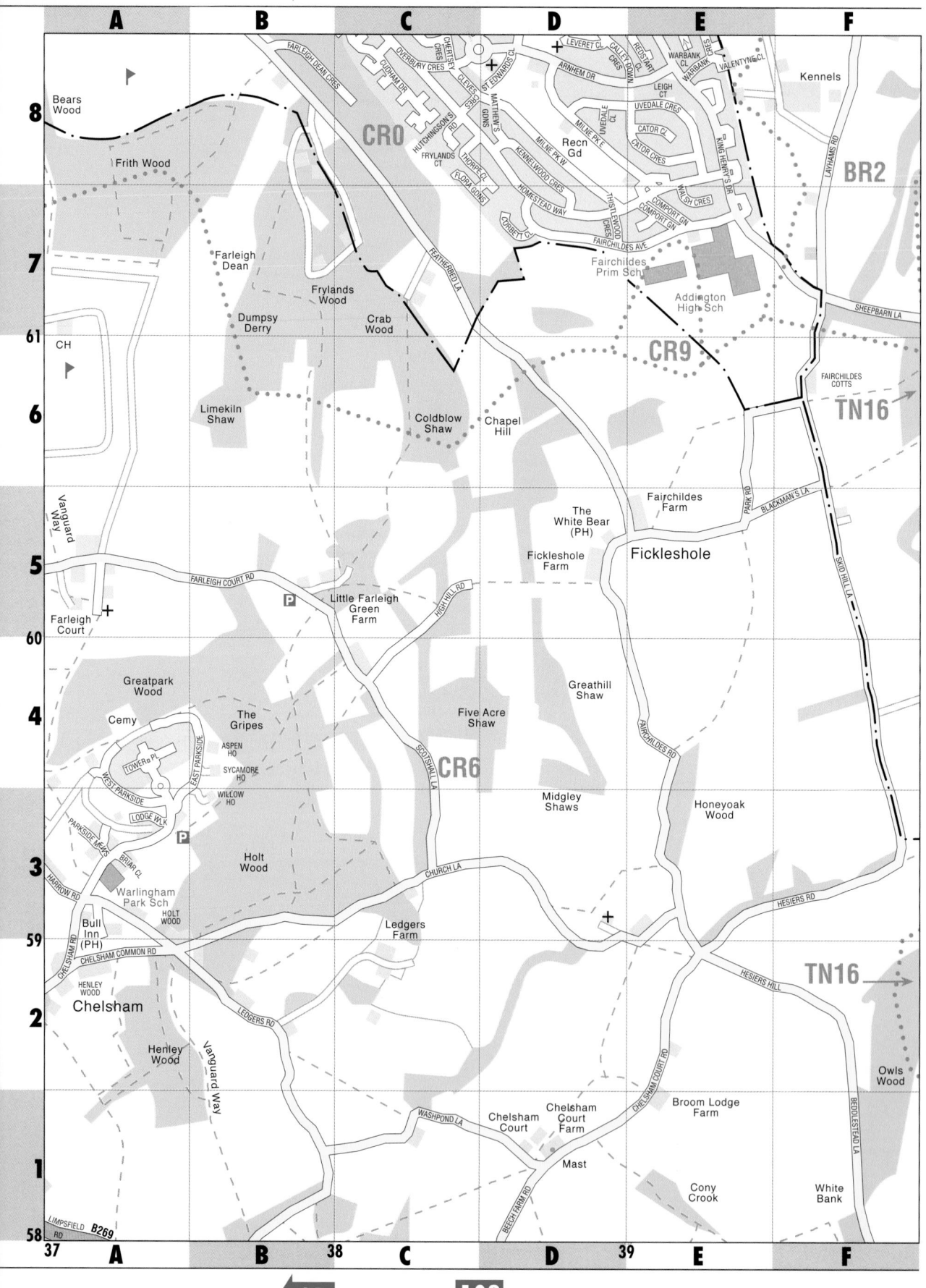
A
B
C
D
E
F
8
7
61
6
5
60
4
3
59
2
1
58
37
38
39
Bears Wood
Frith Wood
Farleigh Dean
Dumpsy Derry
Frylands Wood
Crab Wood
Limekiln Shaw
Coldblow Shaw
Chapel Hill
CH
CR0
CR9
CR6
BR2
TN16
Kennels
Recn Gd
Fairchildes Prim Sch
Addington High Sch
FAIRCHILDES COTTS
SHEEPBARN LA
LAYHAMS RD
FARLEIGH DEAN CRES
OVERBURY CRES
CUDHAM DR
CHERTSEY CRES
CLEVES CRES
ST EDWARDS CL
MATTHEW'S GDNS
LEVERET CL
CALLEY DOWN CRES
REDSTART CL
WARBANK CL
WARBANK CRES
VALENTYNE CL
ARNHEM DR
LEIGH CT
UVEDALE CRES
UVEDALE CL
CATOR CL
CATOR CRES
MILNE PK E
MILNE PK W
KING HENRY'S DR
HUTCHINGSON'S RD
FRYLANDS CT
THORPE CL
FLORA GDNS
KENNELWOOD CRES
HOMESTEAD WAY
CORBETT CL
THISTLEWOOD CRES
COMPORT GN
WALSH CRES
FAIRCHILDES AVE
FEATHERBED LA
Vanguard Way
Fairchildes Farm
The White Bear (PH)
Fickleshole Farm
Fickleshole
PARK RD
BLACKMAN'S LA
SKID HILL LA
FARLEIGH COURT RD
Little Farleigh Green Farm
HIGH HILL RD
Farleigh Court
Greatpark Wood
Cemy
The Gripes
Five Acre Shaw
Greathill Shaw
FAIRCHILDES RD
ASPEN HO
SYCAMORE HO
WILLOW HO
TOWER PL
EAST PARKSIDE
WEST PARKSIDE
LODGE WLK
PARKSIDE MEWS
SCOTSHALL LA
Midgley Shaws
Honeyoak Wood
Holt Wood
BRIAR CL
HARROW RD
Warlingham Park Sch
CHURCH LA
Ledgers Farm
HOLT WOOD
Bull Inn (PH)
CHELSHAM RD
CHELSHAM COMMON RD
HESIERS RD
HESIERS HILL
HENLEY WOOD
Chelsham
LEDGERS RD
Henley Wood
Owls Wood
CHELSHAM COURT RD
Broom Lodge Farm
BEDDLESTEAD LA
WASHPOND LA
Chelsham Court
Chelsham Court Farm
Mast
BEECH FARM RD
Cony Crook
White Bank
LIMPSFIELD RD
B269

81
102

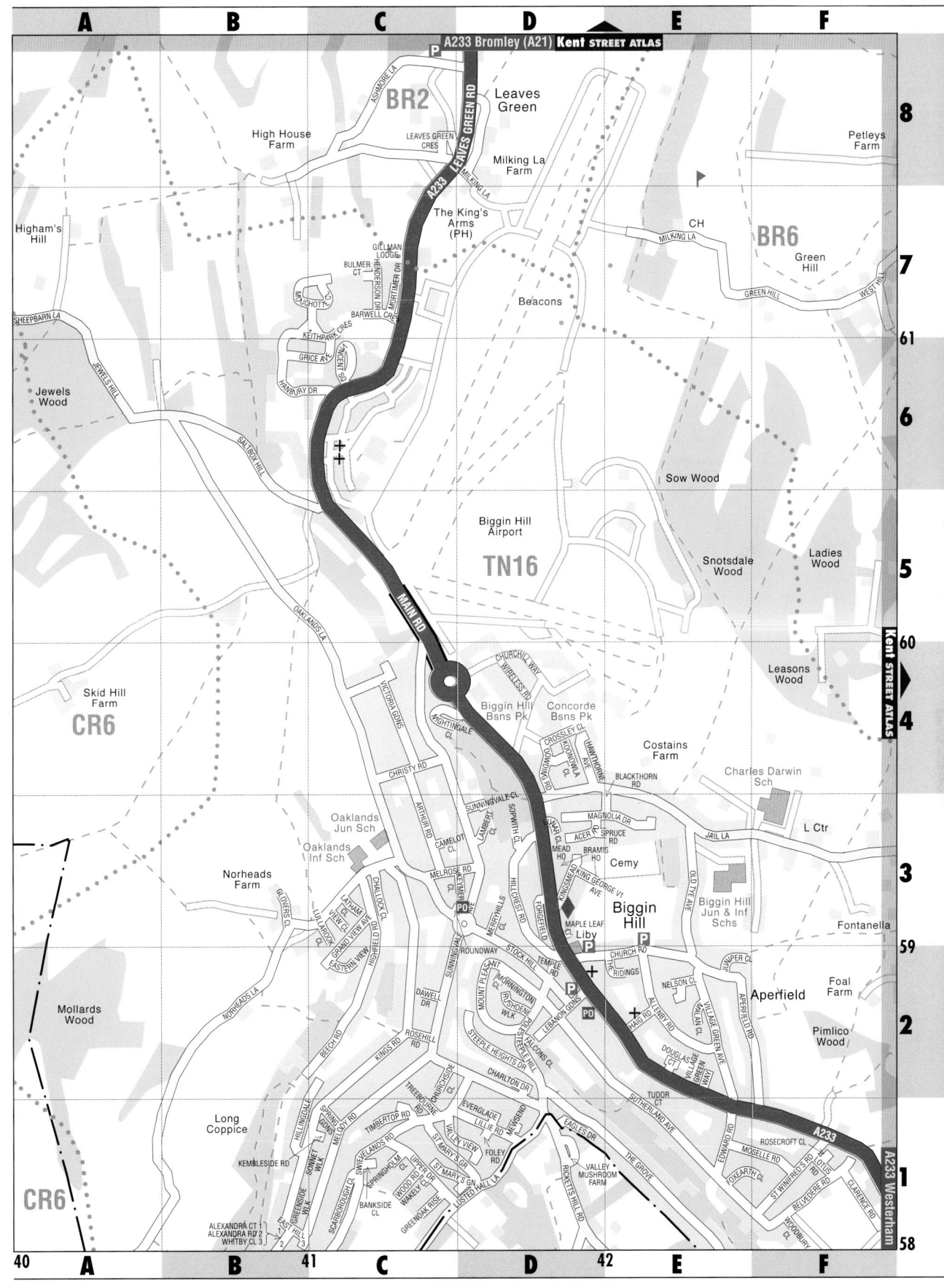
A233 Bromley (A21)
Kent STREET ATLAS
Leaves Green
BR2
High House Farm
Milking La Farm
Petleys Farm
Higham's Hill
The King's Arms (PH)
CH
BR6
Green Hill
Beacons
Jewels Wood
Sow Wood
Biggin Hill Airport
TN16
Snotsdale Wood
Ladies Wood
Leasons Wood
Skid Hill Farm
CR6
Biggin Hill Bsns Pk
Concorde Bsns Pk
Costains Farm
Charles Darwin Sch
L Ctr
Oaklands Jun Sch
Oaklands Inf Sch
Norheads Farm
Cemy
Biggin Hill
Biggin Hill Jun & Inf Schs
Fontanella
Aperfield
Foal Farm
Mollards Wood
Pimlico Wood
Long Coppice
VALLEY MUSHROOM FARM
CR6
A233 Westerham
MAIN RD
LEAVES GREEN RD
A233

64

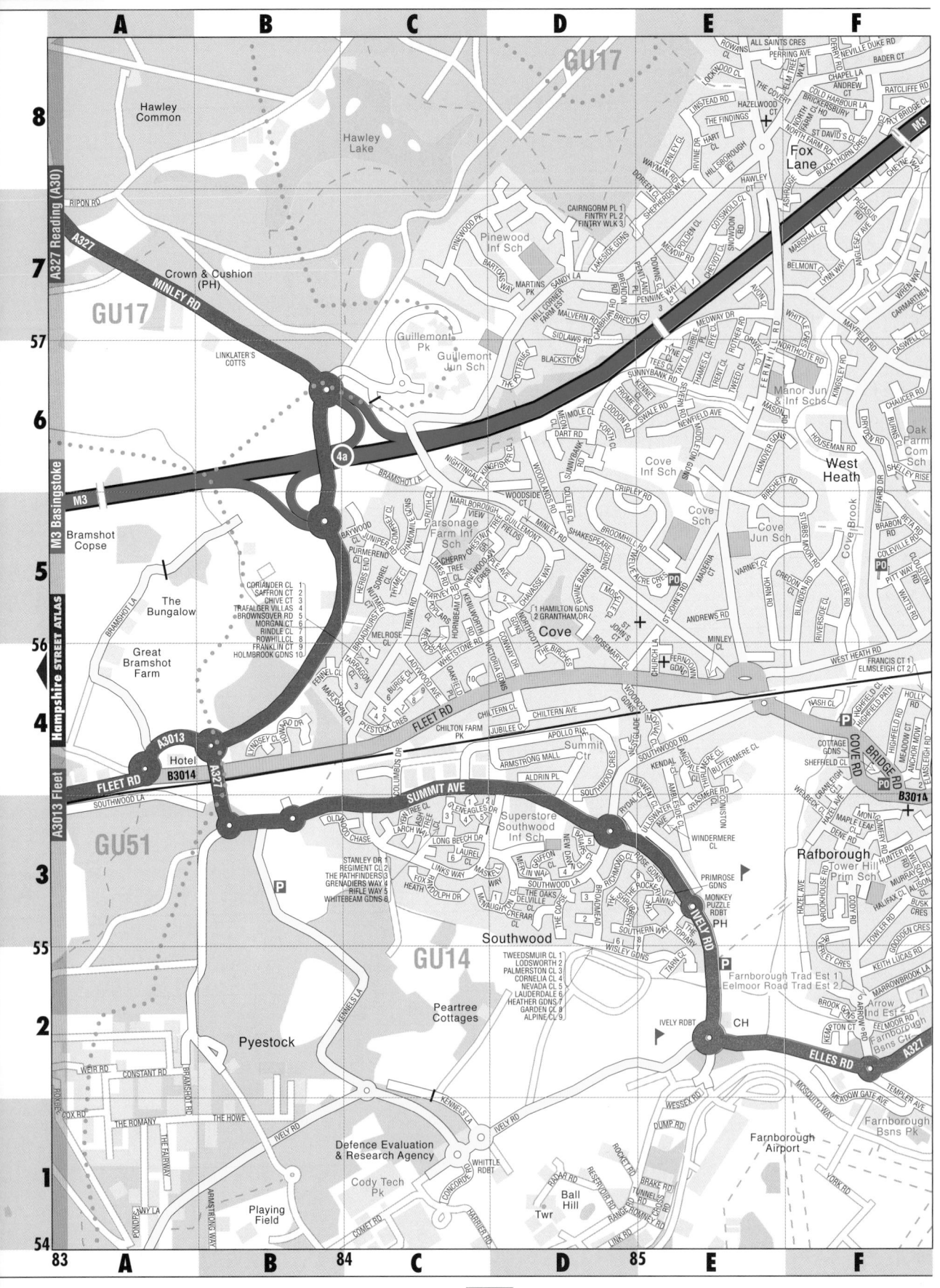
A
B
C
D
E
F
Hawley Common
Hawley Lake
GU17
Fox Lane
A327 Reading (A30)
A327
MINLEY RD
Crown & Cushion (PH)
Pinewood Inf Sch
Guillemont Pk
Guillemont Jun Sch
LINKLATER'S COTTS
M3
M3 Basingstoke
4a
Bramshot Copse
The Bungalow
Great Bramshot Farm
Parsonage Farm Inf Sch
Cove
Cove Inf Sch
Cove Sch
Cove Jun Sch
Manor Jun & Inf Schs
Oak Farm Com Sch
West Heath
Cove Brook
Hampshire STREET ATLAS
A3013
Hotel
FLEET RD
B3014
A3013 Fleet
SUMMIT AVE
Summit Ctr
Superstore
Southwood Inf Sch
Southwood
GU51
GU14
COVE RD
BRIDGE RD
Rafborough
Tower Hill Prim Sch
MONKEY PUZZLE RDBT
PH
IVELY RD
Farnborough Trad Est
Eelmoor Road Trad Est
Arrow Ind Est
Farnborough Bsns Ctr
ELLES RD
IVELY RDBT
CH
Peartree Cottages
Pyestock
Defence Evaluation & Research Agency
WHITTLE RDBT
Cody Tech Pk
Playing Field
Ball Hill
Twr
Farnborough Airport
Farnborough Bsns Pk
8
7
57
6
5
56
4
3
55
2
1
54
83
84
85

104

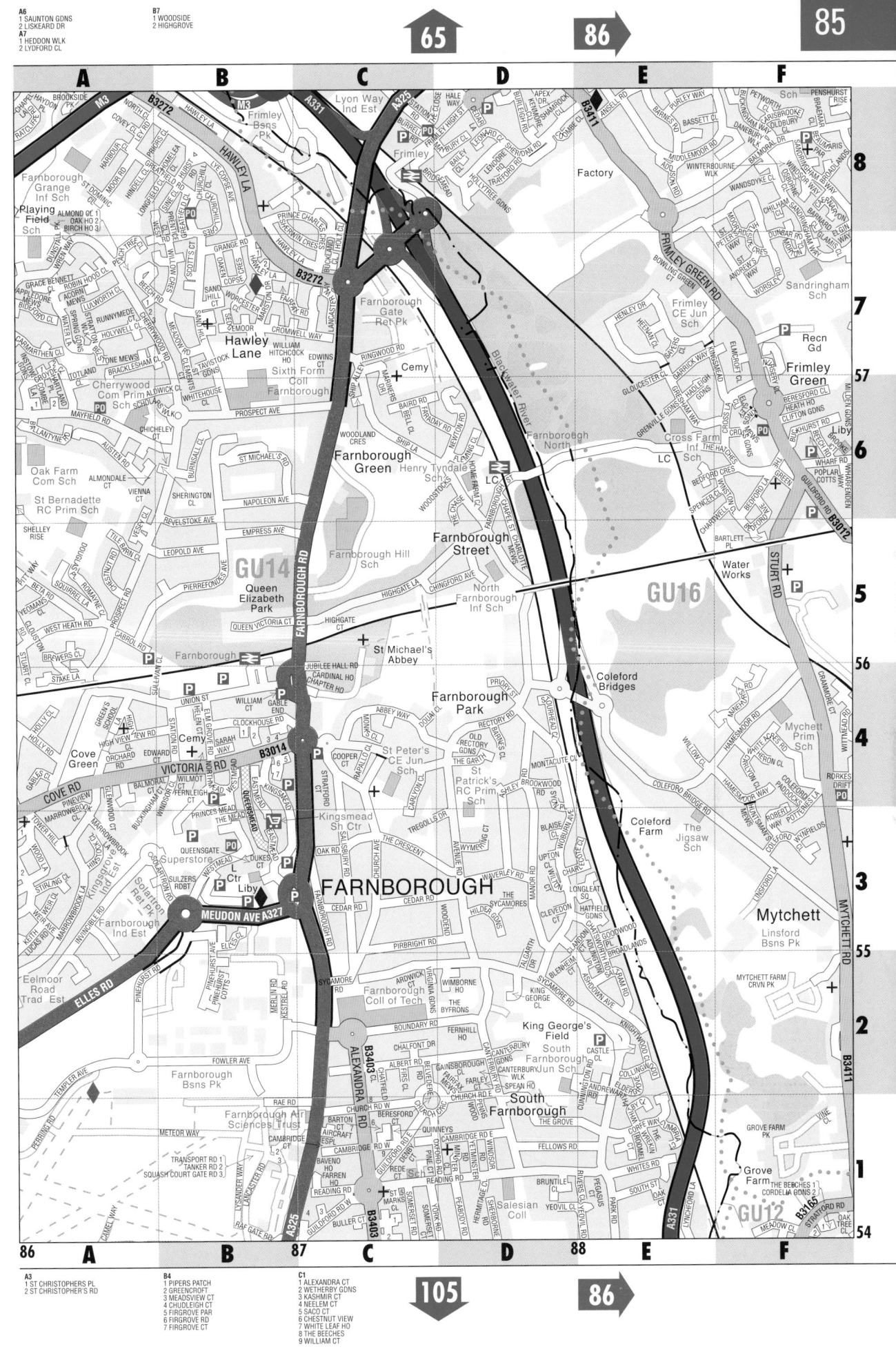
85
65
86
105
86
A6
1 SAUNTON GDNS
2 LISKEARD DR
A7
1 HEDDON WLK
2 LYDFORD CL
B7
1 WOODSIDE
2 HIGHGROVE
A B C D E F
FARNBOROUGH
Farnborough Green
Farnborough Street
Farnborough Park
South Farnborough
Hawley Lane
Frimley
Frimley Green
Mytchett
Cove Green
GU14
GU16
GU12
Blackwater River
Coleford Bridges
Queen Elizabeth Park
St Michael's Abbey
Farnborough Coll of Tech
Farnborough Air Sciences Trust
Farnborough Bsns Pk
Farnborough Ind Est
Eelmoor Road Trad Est
Solartron Ret Pk
Kingsgrove Ind Est
Kingsmead Sh Ctr
Lyon Way Ind Est
Frimley Bsns Pk
Linsford Bsns Pk
Salesian Coll
Water Works
Factory
FARNBOROUGH RD
ALEXANDRA RD
VICTORIA RD
COVE RD
MEUDON AVE
ELLES RD
HAWLEY LA
FRIMLEY GREEN RD
MYTCHETT RD
STURT RD
GUILDFORD RD
A325
A331
A327
B3272
B3014
B3403
B3411
B3012
B3165
M3
86
87
88
54
55
56
57
A3
1 ST CHRISTOPHERS PL
2 ST CHRISTOPHER'S RD
B4
1 PIPERS PATCH
2 GREENCROFT
3 MEADSVIEW CT
4 CHUDLEIGH CT
5 FIRGROVE PAR
6 FIRGROVE RD
7 FIRGROVE CT
C1
1 ALEXANDRA CT
2 WETHERBY GDNS
3 KASHMIR CT
4 NEELEM CT
5 SACO CT
6 CHESTNUT VIEW
7 WHITE LEAF HO
8 THE BEECHES
9 WILLIAM CT

85
66

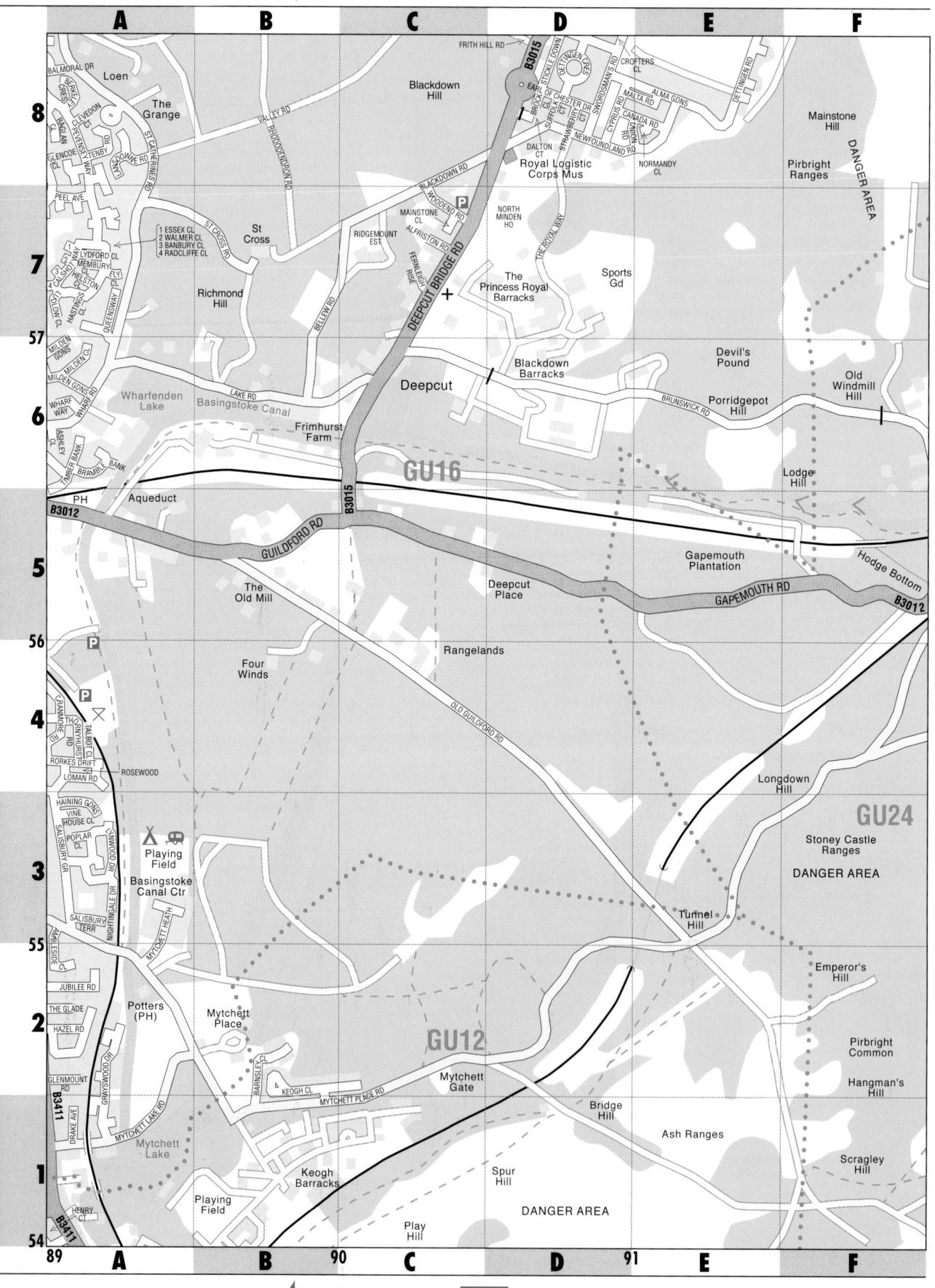
A
B
C
D
E
F
8
7
57
6
5
56
4
3
55
2
1
54
89
90
91
FRITH HILL RD
B3015
BALMORAL DR
Loen
The Grange
Blackdown Hill
VALLEY RD
RHODODENDRON RD
ST CATHERINES RD
STICKLE DOWN
DETTINGEN CRES
CROFTERS CL
DETTINGEN RD
EARL OF CHESTER DR
SWORDSMAN'S RD
MALTA RD
ALMA GDNS
CYPRUS RD
CANADA RD
UNION RD
NEWFOUNDLAND RD
DALTON CT
NORMANDY CL
Royal Logistic Corps Mus
Mainstone Hill
Pirbright Ranges
DANGER AREA
BERKELEY CRES
CLEVEDON CT
PEVENSEY WAY
TENBY RD
RAGLAN
GLENCOE CL
LANSDOWNE RD
PEEL AVE
BLACKDOWN RD
WOODEND RD
MAINSTONE CL
NORTH MINDEN HO
ST CROSS RD
St Cross
RIDGEMOUNT EST
ALFRISTON RD
1 ESSEX CL
2 WALMER CL
3 BANBURY CL
4 RADCLIFFE CL
LYDFORD CL
MEMBURY CL
ELY CL
HELSTON CL
CALSHOT WAY
HASTINGS CL
LUDLOW CL
QUEENSWAY
FERNLEIGH RISE
DEEPCUT BRIDGE RD
THE ROYAL WAY
The Princess Royal Barracks
Sports Gd
Richmond Hill
BELLEW RD
MILDEN GDNS
MILDEN CL
WHARF WAY
WHARF RD
Wharfenden Lake
Basingstoke Canal
LAKE RD
Deepcut
Blackdown Barracks
Devil's Pound
Old Windmill Hill
BRUNSWICK RD
Porridgepot Hill
Frimhurst Farm
ASHLEY CL
TIMBER BANK
BRAMBLE BANK
GU16
Lodge Hill
PH
Aqueduct
B3012
GUILDFORD RD
Gapemouth Plantation
Hodge Bottom
The Old Mill
Deepcut Place
GAPEMOUTH RD
Four Winds
Rangelands
OLD GUILDFORD RD
CRANMORE RD
THORNYHURST RD
TALBOT CL
RORKES DRIFT
LOMAN RD
ROSEWOOD
Longdown Hill
GU24
HAINING GDNS
VINE HOUSE CL
POPLAR CL
SALISBURY GR
LINWOOD DR
Playing Field
Basingstoke Canal Ctr
Stoney Castle Ranges
DANGER AREA
SALISBURY TERR
NIGHTINGALE DR
MYTCHETT HEATH
Tunnel Hill
AMBLESIDE CL
JUBILEE RD
Emperor's Hill
THE GLADE
HAZEL RD
Potters (PH)
Mytchett Place
GU12
Pirbright Common
GLENMOUNT RD
B3411
GRAYSWOOD DR
BARNSLEY CL
KEOGH CL
MYTCHETT PLACE RD
Mytchett Gate
Hangman's Hill
DRAKE AVE
MYTCHETT LAKE RD
Mytchett Lake
Bridge Hill
Ash Ranges
Keogh Barracks
Spur Hill
Scragley Hill
HENRY CT
Playing Field
DANGER AREA
Play Hill

85
106

67
88

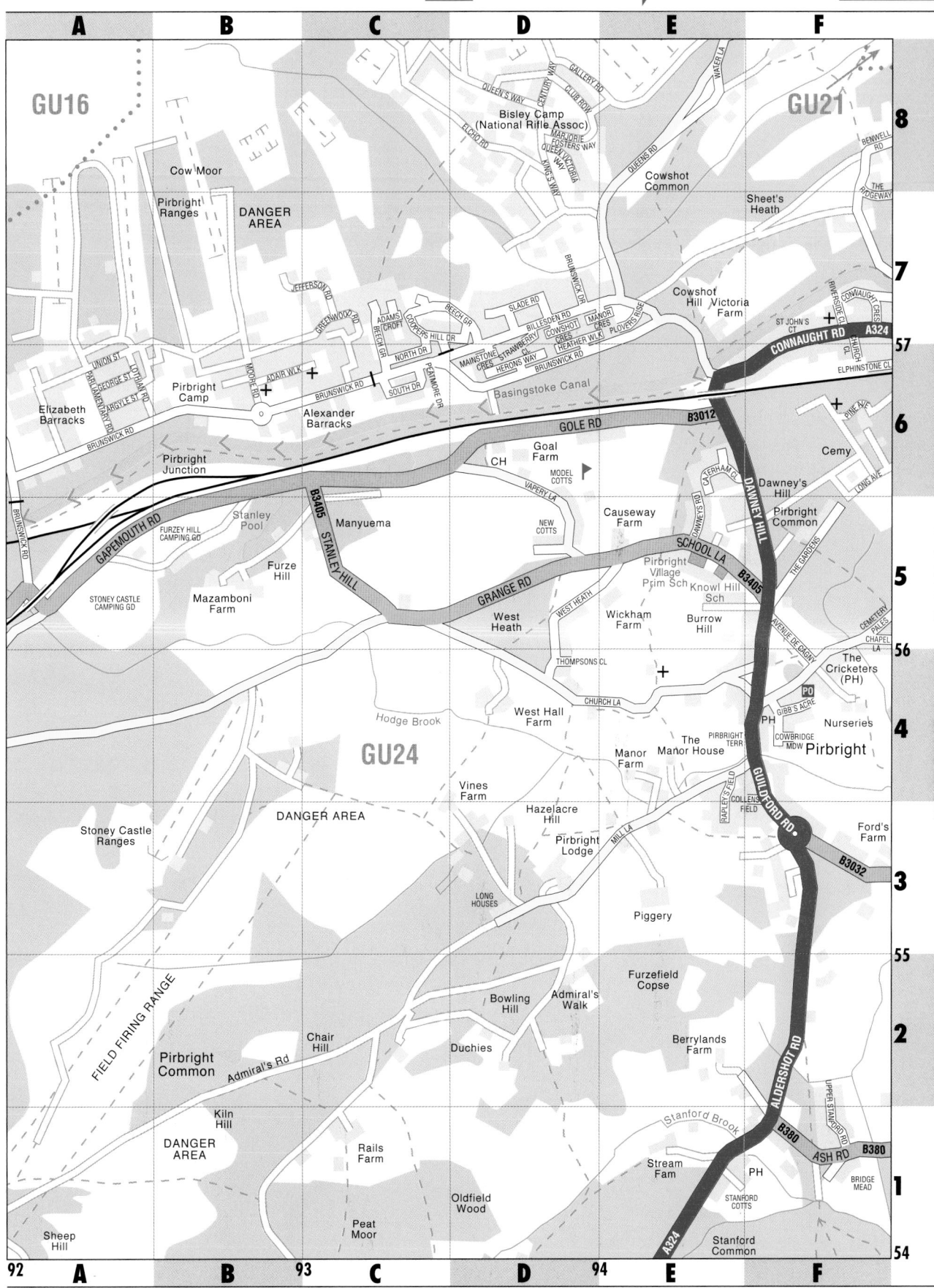

A B C D E F
8 7 6 5 4 3 2 1
57 56 55 54
92 93 94

107
88

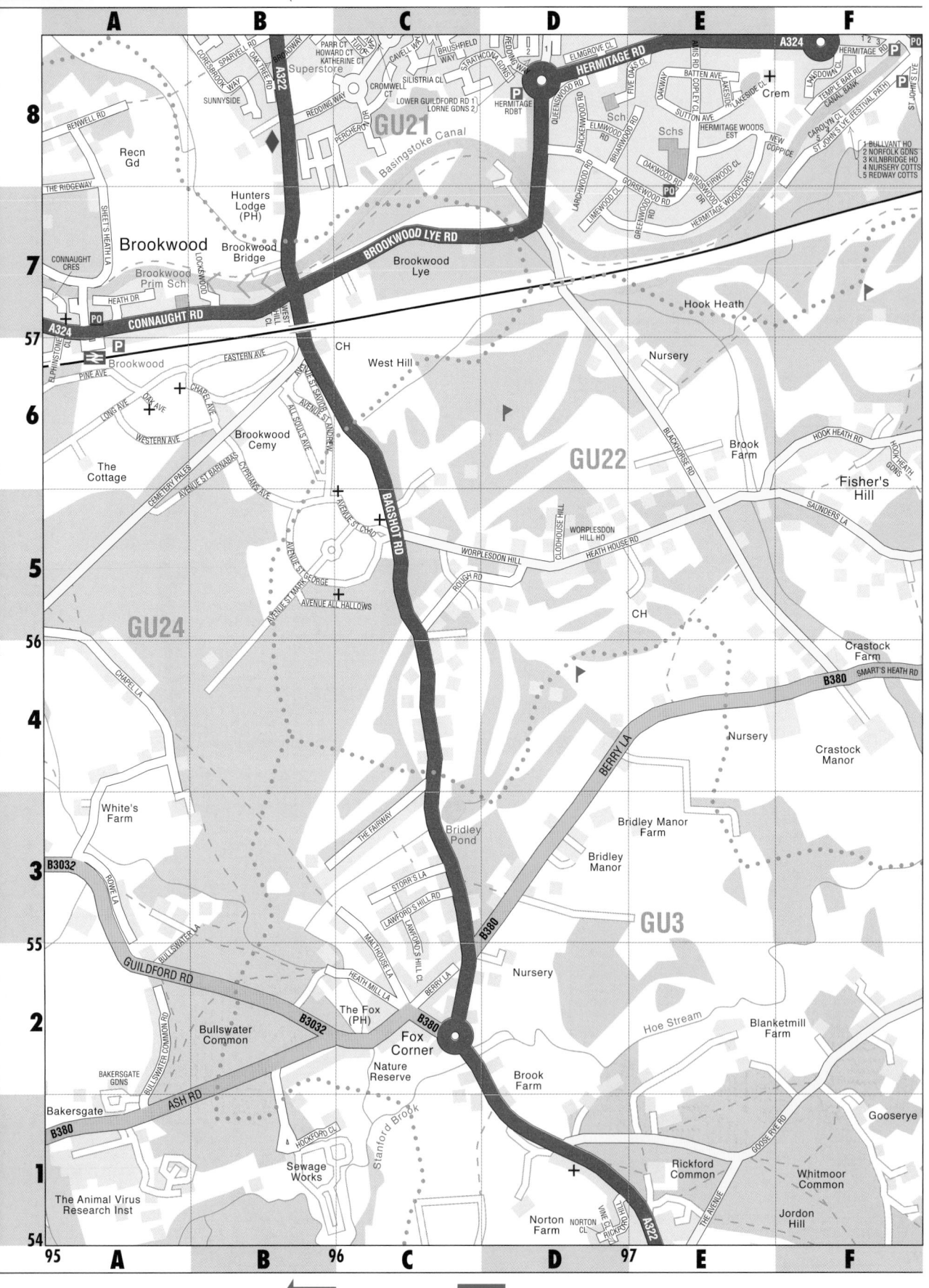
Brookwood
Recn Gd
Hunters Lodge (PH)
Brookwood Bridge
Brookwood Lye
Brookwood Prim Sch
Brookwood Cemy
The Cottage
West Hill
Hook Heath
Nursery
Brook Farm
Fisher's Hill
Crastock Farm
Crastock Manor
White's Farm
Bridley Pond
Bridley Manor Farm
Bridley Manor
Bullswater Common
The Fox (PH)
Fox Corner
Nature Reserve
Brook Farm
Blanketmill Farm
Gooserye
Bakersgate
Sewage Works
Rickford Common
Whitmoor Common
Jordon Hill
Norton Farm
The Animal Virus Research Inst
GU21
GU22
GU24
GU3
Basingstoke Canal
Stanford Brook
Hoe Stream
CONNAUGHT RD
BROOKWOOD LYE RD
HERMITAGE RD
BAGSHOT RD
BERRY LA
GUILDFORD RD
ASH RD
WORPLESDON HILL
HEATH HOUSE RD
BLACKHORSE RD
SAUNDERS LA
SMART'S HEATH RD
HOOK HEATH RD
A322
A324
B380
B3032
1 BULLVANT HO
2 NORFOLK GDNS
3 KILNBRIDGE HO
4 NURSERY COTTS
5 REDWAY COTTS

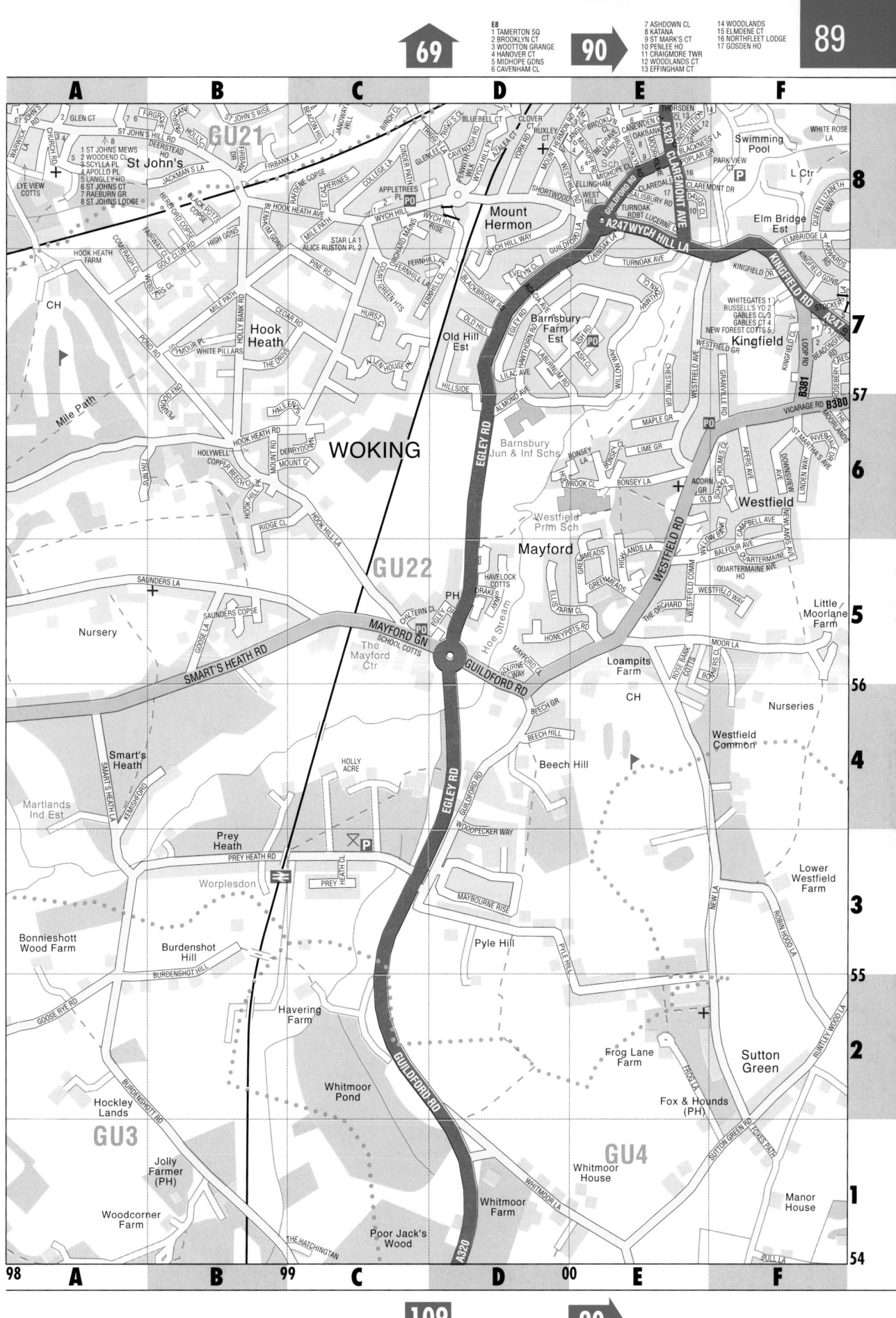

E8
1 TAMERTON SQ
2 BROOKLYN CT
3 WOOTTON GRANGE
4 HANOVER CT
5 MIDHOPE GDNS
6 CAVENHAM CL

7 ASHDOWN CL
8 KATANA
9 ST MARK'S CT
10 PENLEE HO
11 CRAIGMORE TWR
12 WOODLANDS CT
13 EFFINGHAM CT

14 WOODLANDS
15 ELMDENE CT
16 NORTHFLEET LODGE
17 GOSDEN HO

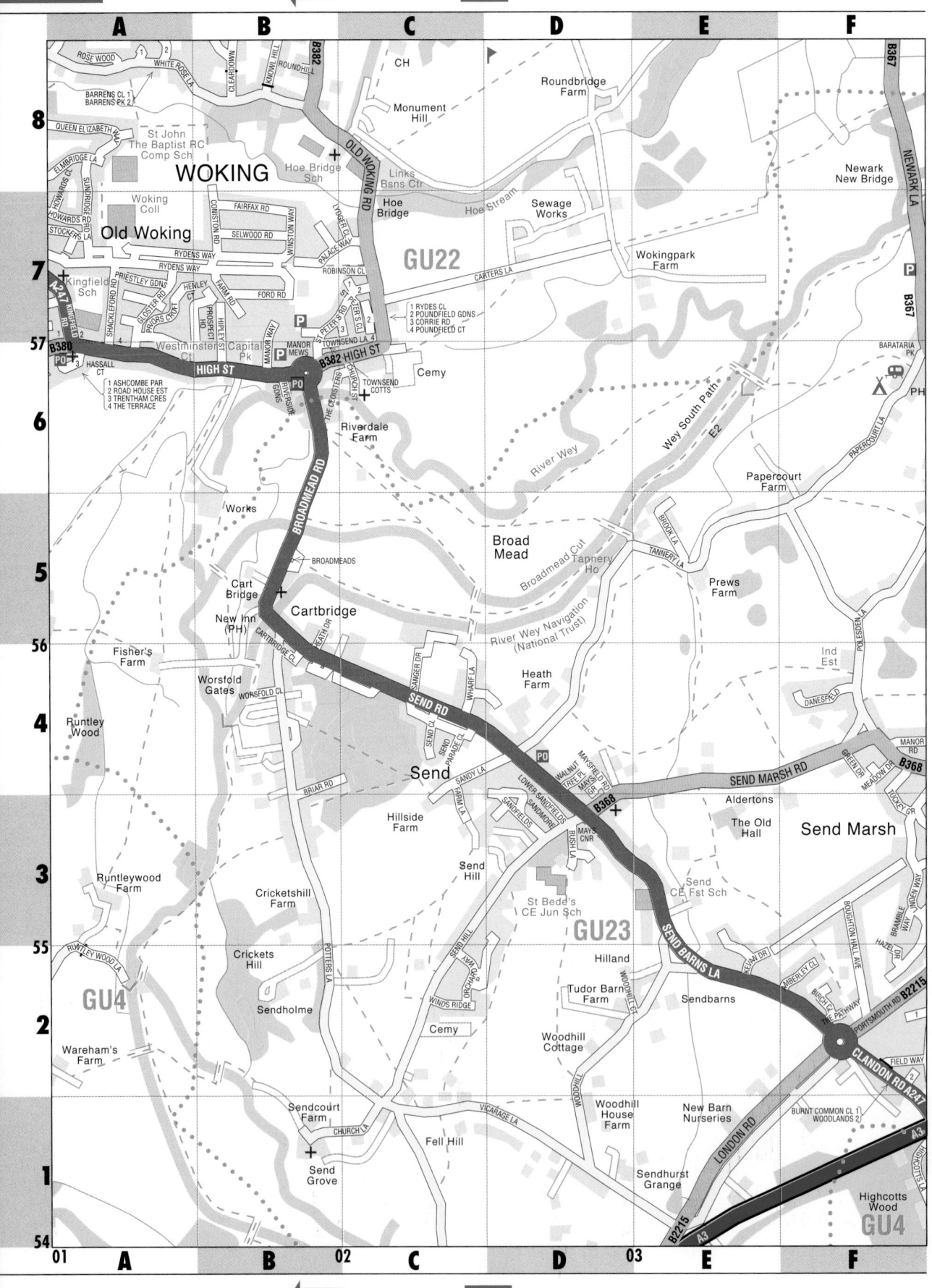
WOKING
Old Woking
Kingfield Sch
St John The Baptist RC Comp Sch
Woking Coll
Hoe Bridge Sch
Hoe Bridge
Monument Hill
Links Bsns Ctr
Roundbridge Farm
Sewage Works
Wokingpark Farm
Newark New Bridge
Hoe Stream
GU22
CARTERS LA
HIGH ST
OLD WOKING RD
BROADMEAD RD
Westminster Ct
Capital Pk
Cemy
Riverdale Farm
River Wey
Wey South Path
Papercourt Farm
Broad Mead
Broadmead Cut
Tannery Ho
Works
Cart Bridge
Cartbridge
New Inn (PH)
River Wey Navigation (National Trust)
Prews Farm
Fisher's Farm
Worsfold Gates
Heath Farm
Ind Est
Runtley Wood
SEND RD
Send
SEND MARSH RD
Aldertons
The Old Hall
Send Marsh
Hillside Farm
Send Hill
Runtleywood Farm
Cricketshill Farm
St Bede's CE Jun Sch
Send CE Fst Sch
GU23
SEND BARNS LA
Crickets Hill
Hilland
Tudor Barn Farm
Sendbarns
GU4
Sendholme
Cemy
Woodhill Cottage
Wareham's Farm
Sendcourt Farm
Fell Hill
Woodhill House Farm
New Barn Nurseries
Send Grove
Sendhurst Grange
Highcotts Wood
LONDON RD
CLANDON RD
PORTSMOUTH RD
VICARAGE LA
CHURCH LA
POTTERS LA
A B C D E F
8 7 6 5 4 3 2 1
57 56 55 54
01 02 03

A B C D E F

8 7 57 6 5 56 4 3 55 2 1 54

Ockham Mill
WARREN FARM MOBILE HOME PK
The Bourne
Abbey Stream
Newark Priory (rems of)
GU22
River Wey
E2
Wey South Path
Walsham Meadow
Dunsborough Farm
DUNSBOROUGH COTTS
Ripley Green
MILL LA
Royal Horticultural Society's Garden (Wisley)
A3
ELM LA
B2215
B2039
Wisley Airfield (disused)
Sewage Works
Bridgefoot Farm
PORTSMOUTH RD
ISLAND COTTS
GREENSIDE COTTS
Buckingham Lodge
OCKHAM RD N
Old Rectory Farm
Ripley
Homewood Farm
NEWARK CL
HEDGE CROFT COTTS
THE GREEN
RYDE CL
WHITE HORSE LA
NEWARK LA
B367
HIGH ST
DORTON WAY
WENTWORTH CL
PERSEVERANCE COTTS
Ripley CE Inf Sch
WHITE HART CT
WHITE HART MWS
Church End
Ockham Park
B2039
POLESDEN LA
GEORGELANDS
LOVELACE CT
CHURCH ROW
Ripley Court Sch
Chapel Farm
HAYNES CL
FORBENCH CL
WEST END COTTS
GRANDIS COTTS
Ockham Park House
Park Wood
Devonia Farm
ROSE LA
GUILESHILL LA
MILESTONE CL
GROVE HEATH N
GU23
HEATH MEWS
Service Area
Service Area
Guileshill Farm
RIPLEY BY-PASS
PORTSMOUTH RD
HEATHRISE
GROVE HEATH LA
MANOR RD
THE RIDINGS
Willow Farm
GROVE HEATH RD
Bachelor's Copse
TUCKEY GR
The Jovial Sailor (PH)
Grove Heath Farm
Roborow
Roborow Wood
SEND MARSH RD
B368
BIRNAM CL
GREY FRIARS RD
STRINGHAMS COPSE
ELM CL
OAKS WAY
Loveland's Copse
Ryde Farm
RIPLEY LA
Bachelor's La
HAWTHORN RD
WILLOW DR
MAPLE RD
GROVE HEATH CT
KILN LA
BEECH DR
Garlick's Arch Copse
Hangover House
HUNGRY HILL LA
Hungry Hill
Hungry Hill Cottage
Garlick's Arch
CHESTNUT CL
GAMBLES LA
Burntcommon
BURNTCOMMON LA
Oldlands Copse
Sheppardsgrove Copse
Brambleride Copse
Tithebarns Farm
The Paddocks
KT24
Tithe Barns
TITHEBARNS LA
Sussex Farm
August Hill
Holride Farm
CLANDON RD
GU4
Old Ride Farm
RIPLEY RD
Hazelhurst Cottage
Brambleride
HIGHCOTTS LA
A247

04 A B 05 C D 06 E F

111
92

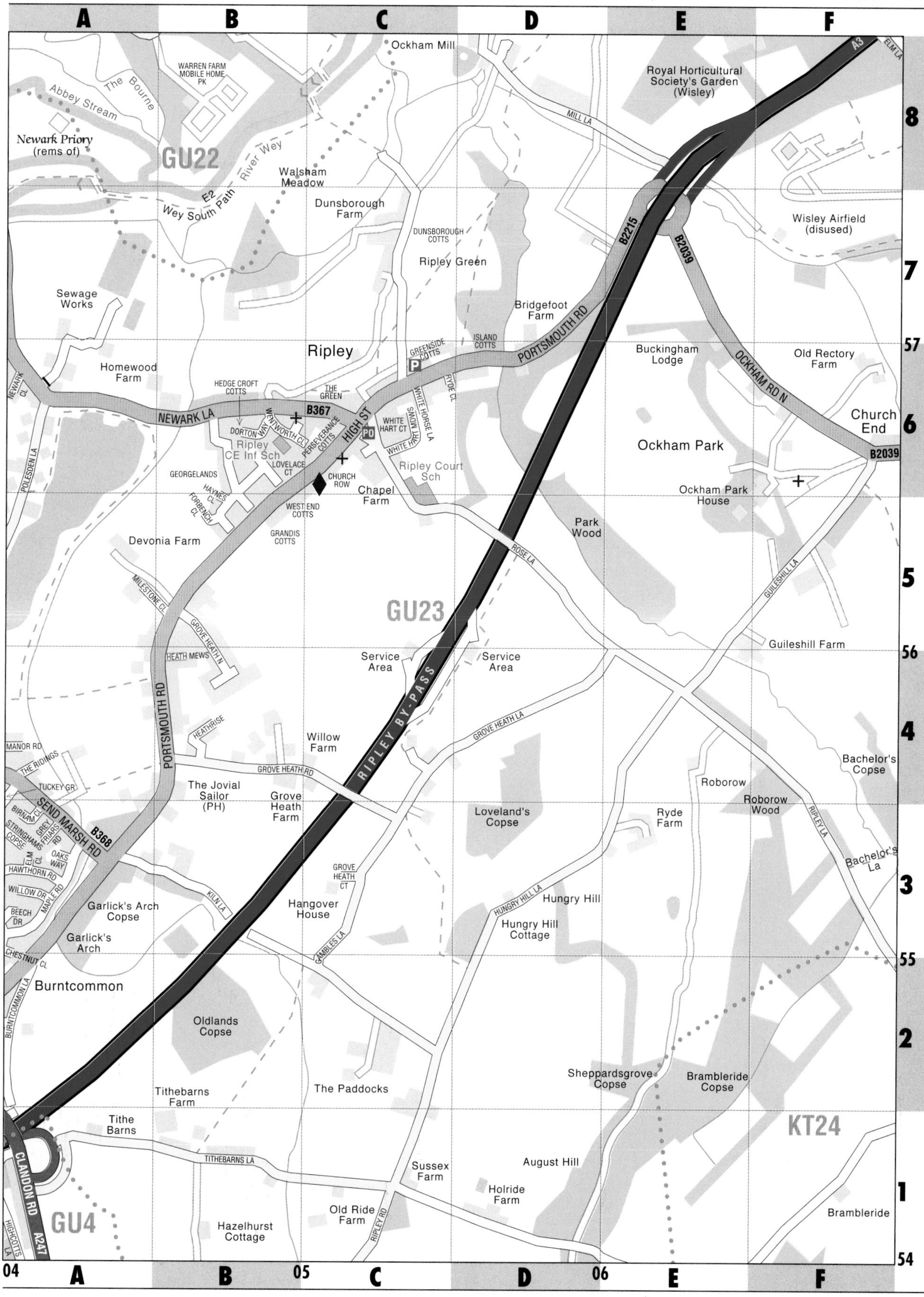

91
72

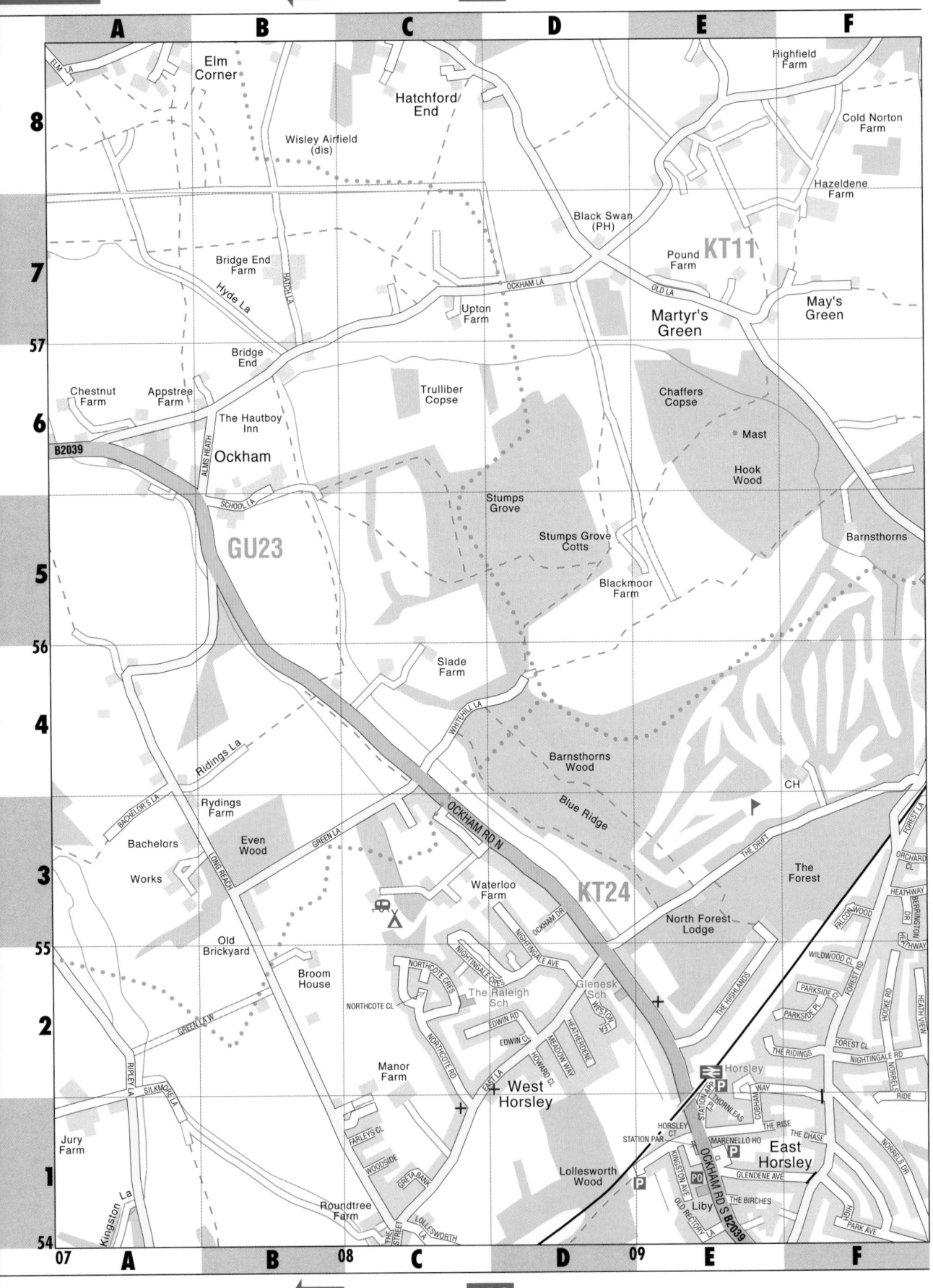
Elm Corner
Hatchford End
Wisley Airfield (dis)
Highfield Farm
Cold Norton Farm
Hazeldene Farm
Black Swan (PH)
KT11
Pound Farm
Bridge End Farm
Hyde La
HATCH LA
OCKHAM LA
OLD LA
Upton Farm
Martyr's Green
May's Green
Bridge End
Chestnut Farm
Appstree Farm
The Hautboy Inn
Trulliber Copse
Chaffers Copse
Mast
Hook Wood
B2039
ALMS HEATH
Ockham
SCHOOL LA
Stumps Grove
Stumps Grove Cotts
GU23
Barnsthorns
Blackmoor Farm
Slade Farm
WHITEHILL LA
Ridings La
Barnsthorns Wood
CH
BACHELOR'S LA
Rydings Farm
Blue Ridge
OCKHAM RD N
Bachelors
Even Wood
LONG REACH
GREEN LA
THE DRIFT
The Forest
Works
Waterloo Farm
KT24
North Forest Lodge
OCKHAM DR
NIGHTINGALE AVE
NIGHTINGALE CRES
Old Brickyard
Broom House
NORTHCOTE CRES
The Raleigh Sch
Glenesk Sch
NORTHCOTE CL
EDWIN RD
EDWIN CL
WESTON LEA
HEATHERDENE
MEADOW WAY
HOWARD CL
THE HIGHLANDS
GREEN LA W
NORTHCOTE RD
Manor Farm
EAST LA
West Horsley
Horsley
RIPLEY LA
SILKMORE LA
Jury Farm
FARLEYS CL
WOODSIDE
GRETA BANK
Lollesworth Wood
STATION PAR
HORSLEY CT
MARENELLO HO
East Horsley
KINGSTON AVE
OLD RECTORY LA
GLENDENE AVE
Liby
THE BIRCHES
OCKHAM RD S B2039
Kingston La
Roundtree Farm
THE STREET
LOLLESWORTH LA
FOREST LA
ORCHARD CL
HEATHWAY
BERRINGTON DR
FALCON WOOD
WILDWOOD CL
FOREST RD
PARKSIDE CL
PARKSIDE PL
HOOKE RD
HEATH VIEW
FOREST CL
THE RIDINGS
NIGHTINGALE RD
NORRELS RIDE
COBHAM WAY
THORNLEAS PL
STATION APP
THE RISE
THE CHASE
NORRELS DR
HIGH PARK AVE
A B C D E F
8 7 57 6 5 56 4 3 55 2 1 54
07 08 09

91
112

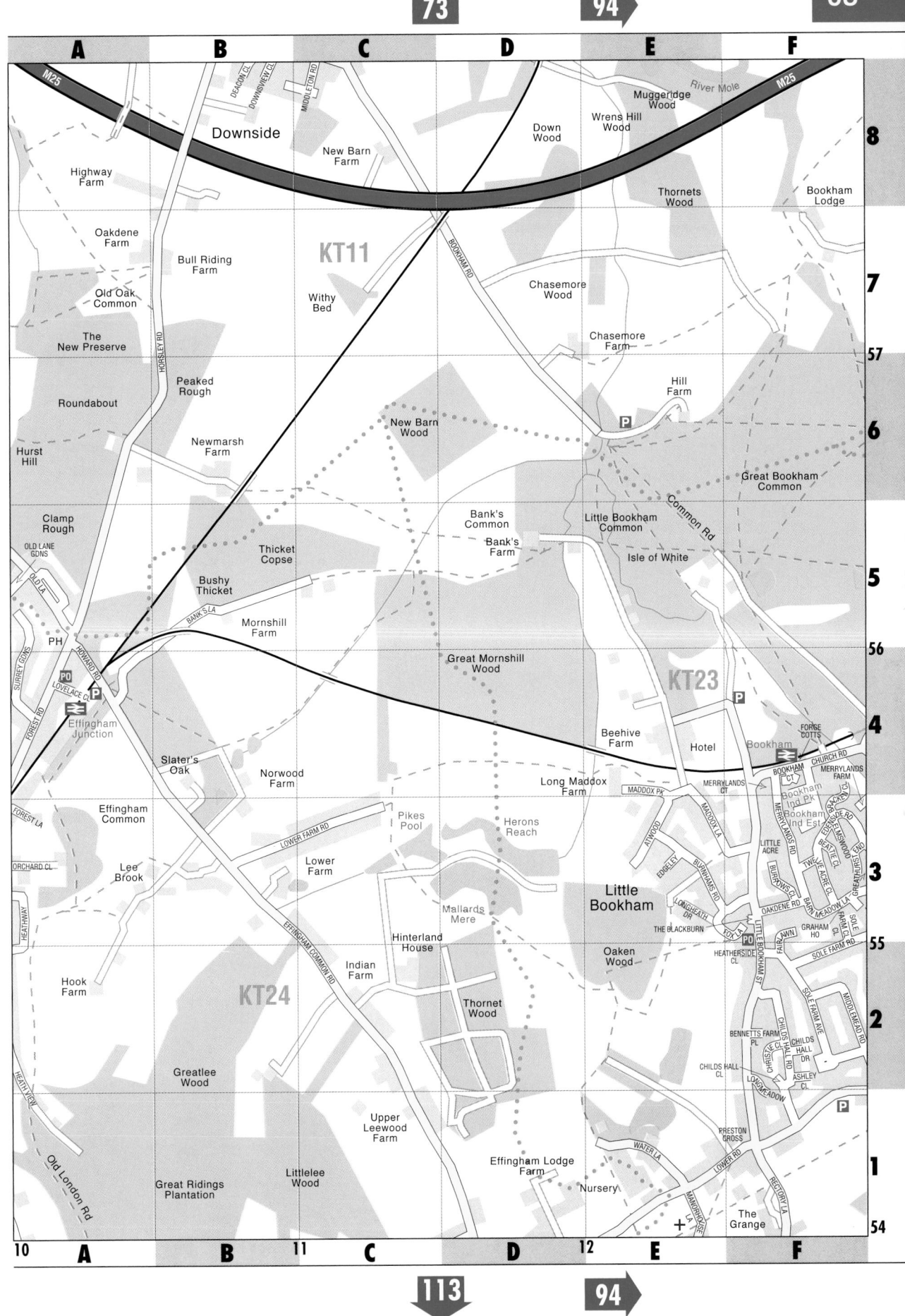
73
94
A
B
C
D
E
F
M25
Downside
Highway Farm
New Barn Farm
Down Wood
Wrens Hill Wood
Muggeridge Wood
River Mole
Thornets Wood
Bookham Lodge
Oakdene Farm
Bull Riding Farm
KT11
Withy Bed
Old Oak Common
The New Preserve
Chasemore Wood
Chasemore Farm
Peaked Rough
Roundabout
Hill Farm
New Barn Wood
Hurst Hill
Newmarsh Farm
Great Bookham Common
Clamp Rough
Bank's Common
Little Bookham Common
Common Rd
Bank's Farm
Thicket Copse
Isle of White
Bushy Thicket
Mornshill Farm
PH
Great Mornshill Wood
KT23
Effingham Junction
Beehive Farm
Hotel
Bookham
Slater's Oak
Norwood Farm
Long Maddox Farm
Effingham Common
Pikes Pool
Herons Reach
Lee Brook
Lower Farm
Little Bookham
Mallards Mere
Hinterland House
Oaken Wood
Indian Farm
Hook Farm
KT24
Thornet Wood
Greatlee Wood
Upper Leewood Farm
Effingham Lodge Farm
Nursery
Great Ridings Plantation
Littlelee Wood
Old London Rd
The Grange
8
7
57
6
5
56
4
3
55
2
1
54
10
11
12
113
94

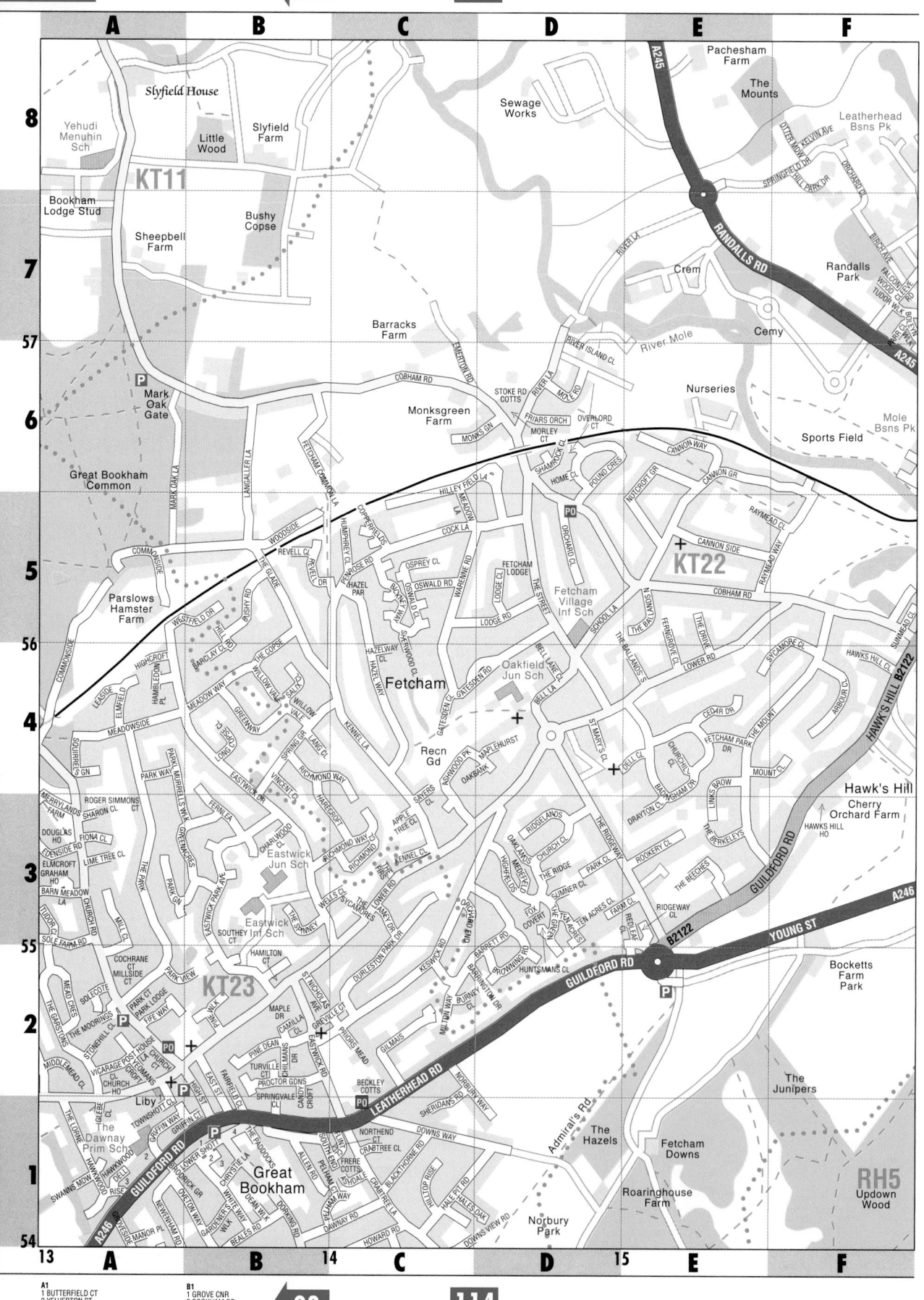

A1
1 BUTTERFIELD CT
2 YELVERTON CT
3 HAWKWOOD HO

B1
1 GROVE CNR
2 BOOKHAM GR
3 BOOKHAM GROVE HO
4 LEATHERHEAD RD

93

114

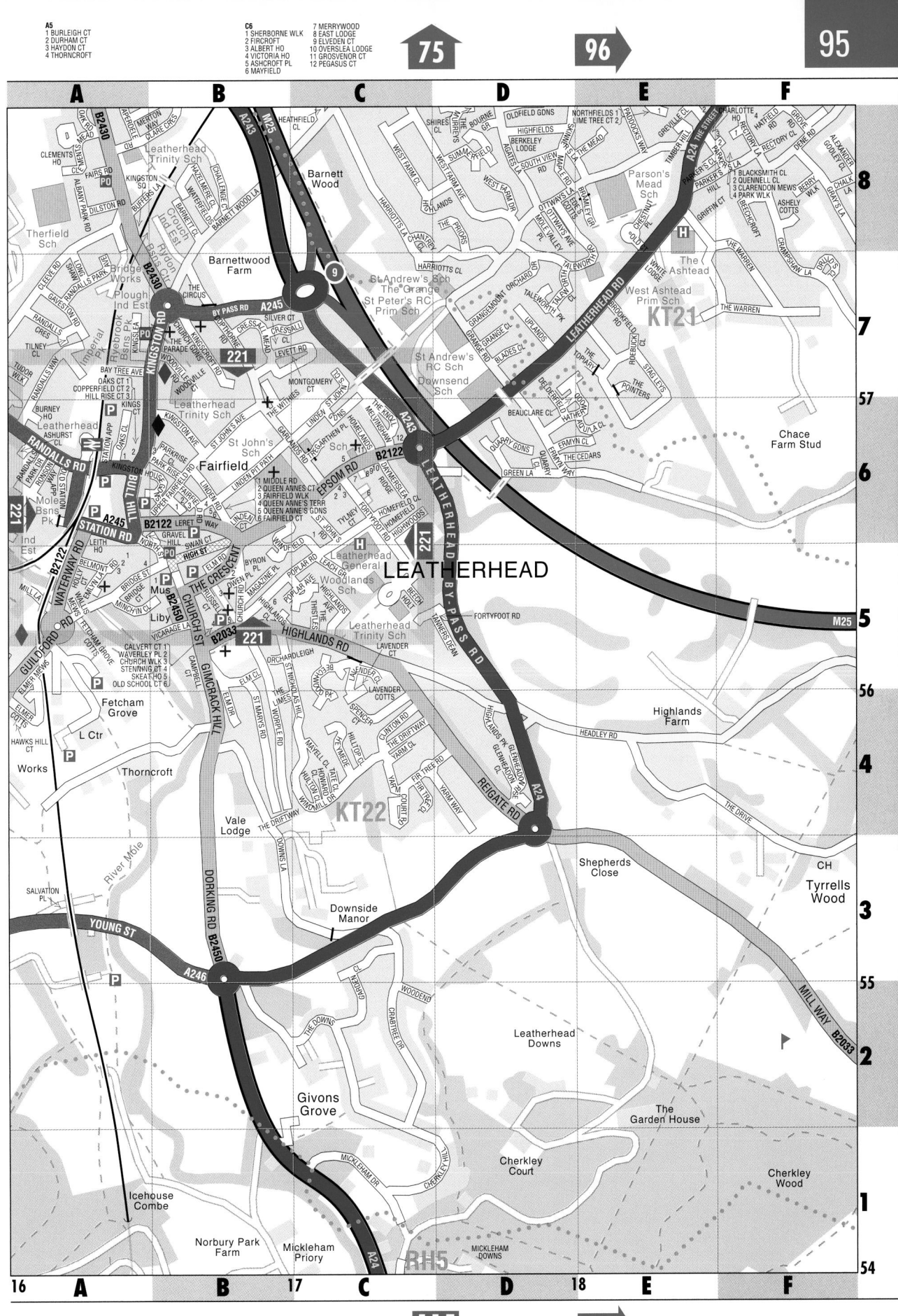
A5
1 BURLEIGH CT
2 DURHAM CT
3 HAYDON CT
4 THORNCROFT
C6
1 SHERBORNE WLK
2 FIRCROFT
3 ALBERT HO
4 VICTORIA HO
5 ASHCROFT PL
6 MAYFIELD
7 MERRYWOOD
8 EAST LODGE
9 ELVEDEN CT
10 OVERSLEA LODGE
11 GROSVENOR CT
12 PEGASUS CT
75
96
95
A B C D E F
8 7 57 6 5 56 4 3 55 2 1 54
16 17 18
LEATHERHEAD
KT21
KT22
RH5
M25
A24
A243
A245
A246
B2430
B2122
B2450
B2033
221
Barnett Wood
Barnettwood Farm
Parson's Mead Sch
The Ashtead
West Ashtead Prim Sch
St Andrew's Sch The Grange
St Peter's RC Prim Sch
St Andrew's RC Sch
Downsend Sch
Leatherhead Trinity Sch
Therfield Sch
Bridge Works
Plough Ind Est
Crouch Ind Est
Rydon Bsns Ctr
Rye Brook Bsns Pk
Imperial Pk
Mole Bsns Pk
Ind Est
Fairfield
St John's Sch
Leatherhead General
Woodlands Sch
Mus
Liby
Chace Farm Stud
Highlands Farm
Fetcham Grove
L Ctr
Works
Thorncroft
Vale Lodge
Shepherds Close
Tyrrells Wood
CH
Downside Manor
Leatherhead Downs
Givons Grove
The Garden House
Cherkley Court
Cherkley Wood
Icehouse Combe
Norbury Park Farm
Mickleham Priory
MICKLEHAM DOWNS
River Mole
YOUNG ST
DORKING RD
GIMCRACK HILL
CHURCH ST
GUILDFORD RD
RANDALLS RD
STATION RD
KINGSTON RD
BY PASS RD
LEATHERHEAD BY-PASS RD
LEATHERHEAD RD
EPSOM RD
HIGHLANDS RD
REIGATE RD
HEADLEY RD
MILL WAY
THE CRESCENT
HIGH ST
BULL HILL
FORTYFOOT RD
THE DRIVE
THE WARREN
THE STREET
CALVERT CT 1
WAVERLEY PL 2
CHURCH WLK 3
STENNING CT 4
SKEAT HO 5
OLD SCHOOL CT 6
1 MIDDLE RD
2 QUEEN ANNES CT
3 FAIRFIELD WLK
4 QUEEN ANNE'S TERR
5 QUEEN ANNE'S GDNS
6 FAIRFIELD CT
1 BLACKSMITH CL
2 QUENNELL CL
3 CLARENDON MEWS
4 PARK WLK
OAKS CT 1
COPPERFIELD CT 2
HILL RISE CT 3
115
96

95
76

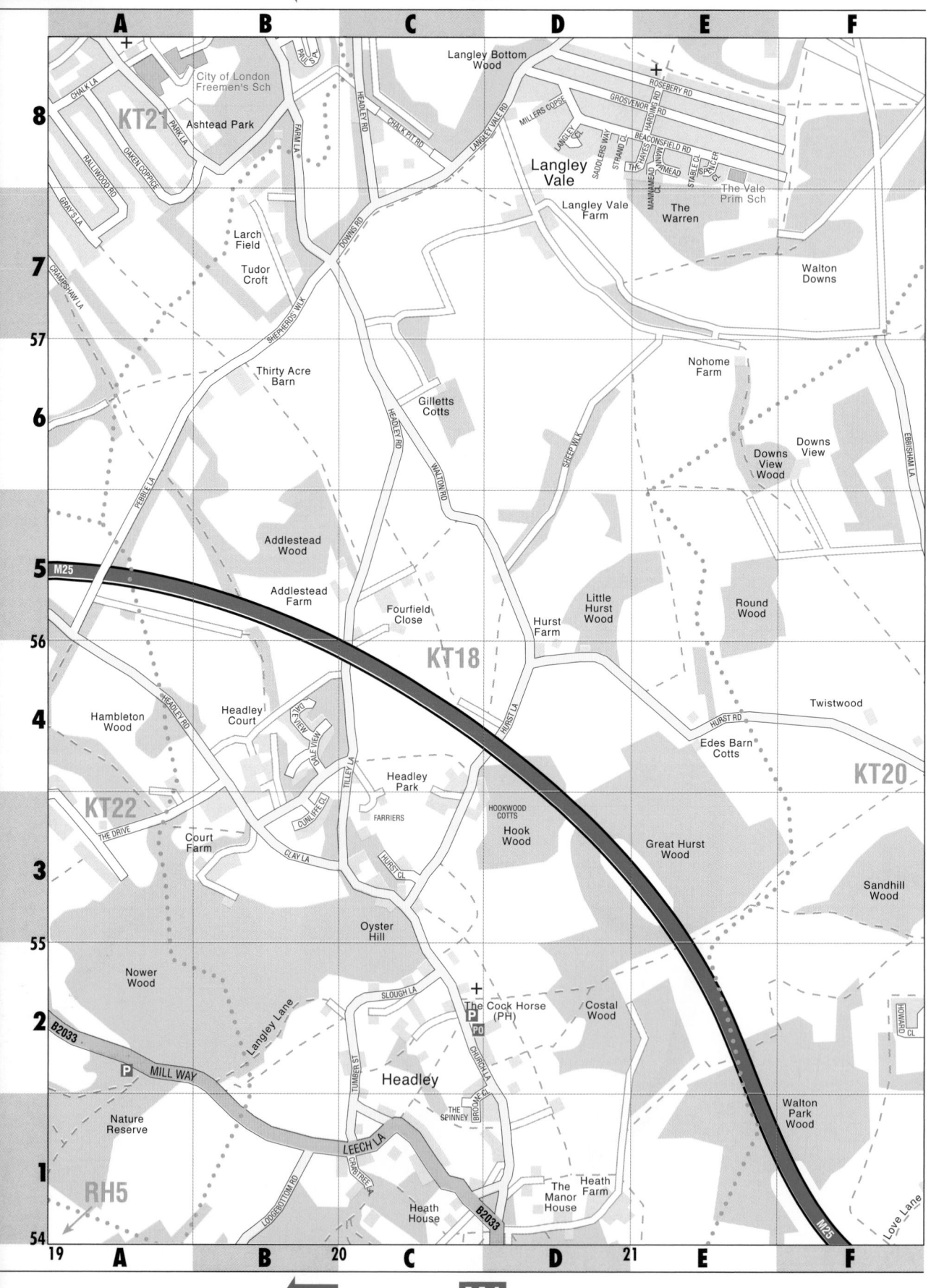
A
B
C
D
E
F
8
7
57
6
5
56
4
3
55
2
1
54
19
20
21
Langley Bottom Wood
City of London Freemen's Sch
KT21
Ashtead Park
CHALK LA
PARK LA
RALLIWOOD RD
OAKEN COPPICE
GRAY'S LA
FARM LA
HEADLEY RD
CHALK PIT RD
LANGLEY VALE RD
MILLERS COPSE
ROSEBERY RD
GROSVENOR RD
HARDING RD
BEACONSFIELD RD
LANGLEY CL
SADDLERS WAY
STRAND CL
HAYES
MANNAMEAD
MANNAMEAD CL
STABLE CL
SPENCER CL
Langley Vale
The Vale Prim Sch
Langley Vale Farm
The Warren
Larch Field
Tudor Croft
DOWNS RD
CRAMPSHAW LA
SHEPHERDS WLK
Walton Downs
Thirty Acre Barn
Nohome Farm
Gilletts Cotts
HEADLEY RD
WALTON RD
SHEEP WLK
Downs View Wood
Downs View
EBBISHAM LA
PEBBLE LA
Addlestead Wood
M25
Addlestead Farm
Fourfield Close
Hurst Farm
Little Hurst Wood
Round Wood
KT18
Hambleton Wood
HEADLEY RD
Headley Court
DALE VIEW
HURST LA
HURST RD
Twistwood
Edes Barn Cotts
KT20
TILLEY LA
Headley Park
KT22
CUNLIFFE CL
FARRIERS
HOOKWOOD COTTS
Hook Wood
THE DRIVE
Court Farm
CLAY LA
HURST CL
Great Hurst Wood
Sandhill Wood
Oyster Hill
Nower Wood
SLOUGH LA
The Cock Horse (PH)
Costal Wood
B2033
P
PO
HOWARD CL
Langley Lane
MILL WAY
CHURCH LA
TUMBER ST
Headley
Nature Reserve
THE SPINNEY
BROOME CL
Walton Park Wood
LEECH LA
CRABTREE LA
LODGEBOTTOM RD
RH5
Heath House
The Manor House
Heath Farm
Love Lane

95
116

77

98

A B C D E F
8 57 7 6 5 56 4 3 55 2 1 54
22 23 24
Race Course
KT18
Walton Downs
Burgh Heath
Canons Farm Cottages
Canons Farm
Ambrose Cottages
South Tadworth Farm
The Phoenix Ctr
Sports Ctr
Pit Wood Mast
Ind Est
Epsom Downs Metro Ctr
EPSOM LANE N
B290
A240 REIGATE RD
A217
BRIGHTON RD
Garden Farm
Kingswood
Kingswood Pk
WATERHOUSE LA
B2032
BONSOR DR
The Childrens Trust (Tadworth Court)
Tadworth
Tadworth Prim Sch
ASHURST RD
STATION APP
TADWORTH ST
KT20
NEW RD
MILL RD
MERE RD
Kingswood Warren
Transport Police Training Ctr
Chinthurst Sch
Walton on the Hill
Ebbisham Farm
Walton Manor
Bramley Sch
Walton on the Hill Prim Sch
Mere Pond
Blue Ball (PH)
Walton Mill (dis)
Kingswood Court
DORKING RD
Castle House
Hogden Bottom
The Gallops
Banstead Heath
The Red Lodge
HOLLY LODGE (MOBILE HOME PK)
Recn Gd
CHEQUERS LA
B2220

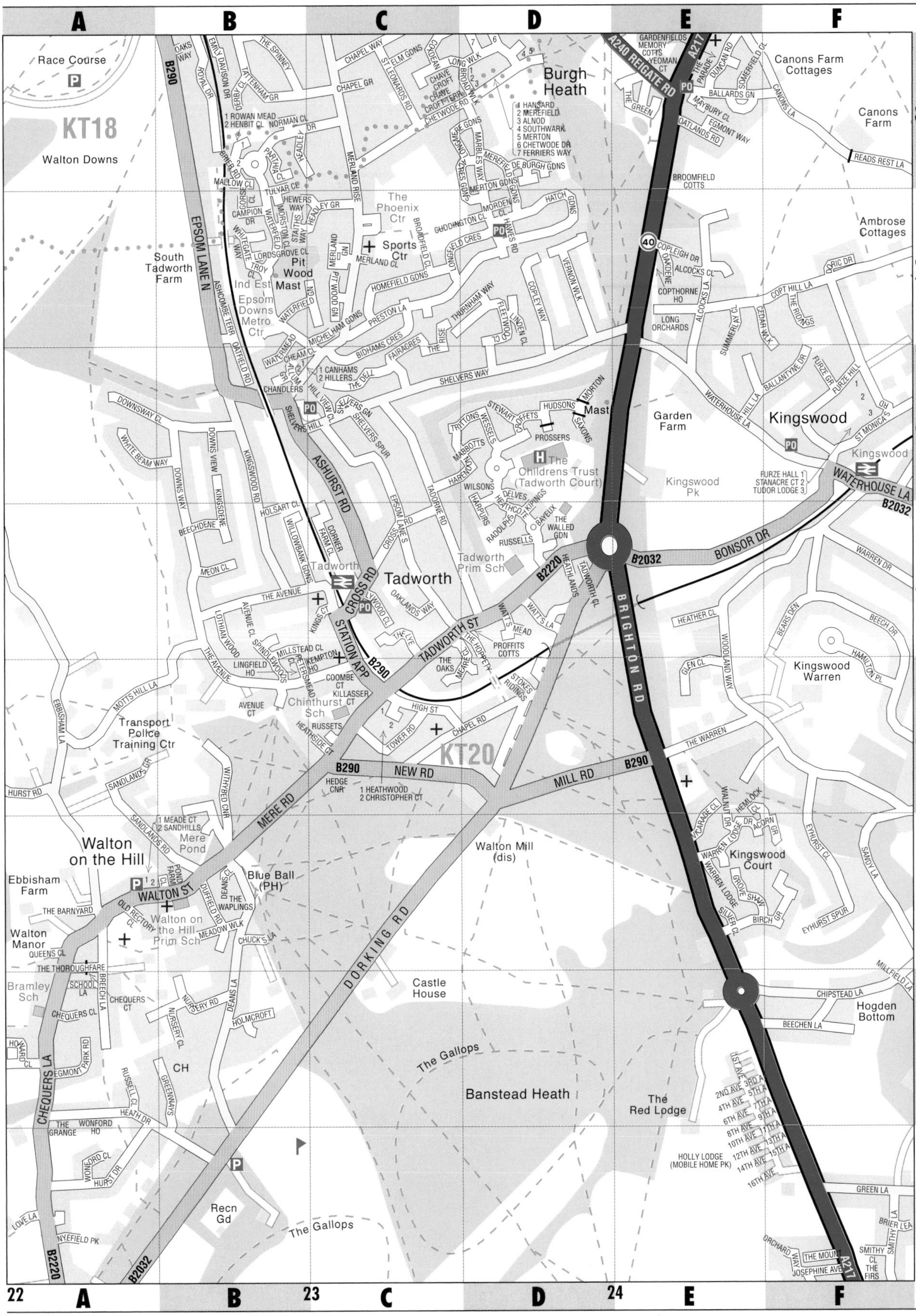

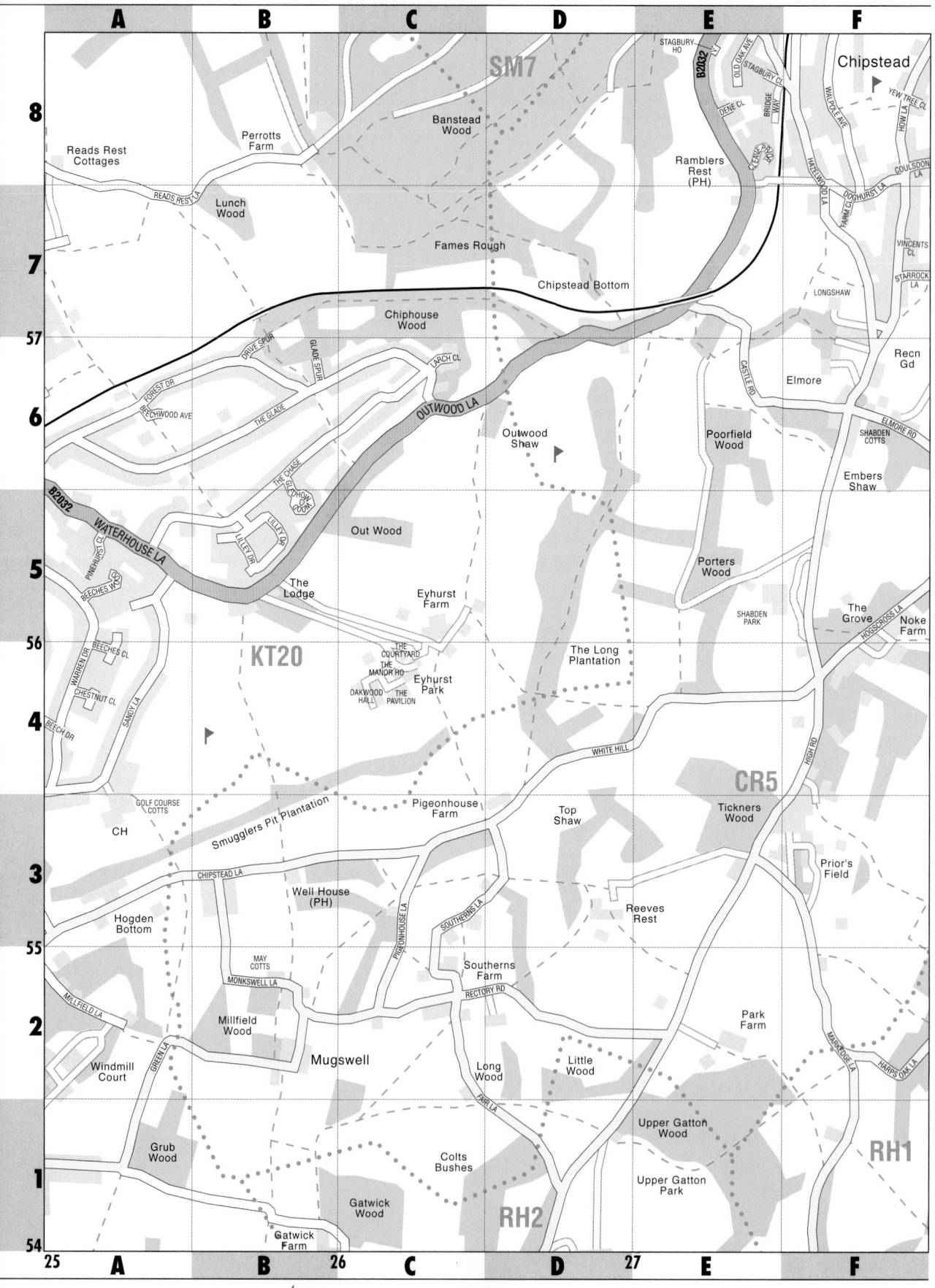

SM7

8

Reads Rest
Cottages

Perrotts
Farm

Banstead
Wood

STAGBURY
HO

B2032

OLD OAK AVE

STAGBURY CL

Chipstead

YEW TREE CL

HOW LA

WALPOLE AVE

Ramblers
Rest
(PH)

READS REST LA

Lunch
Wood

DENE CL

COULSDON LA

DRIVE SPUR

GLADE SPUR

Fames Rough

Chipstead Bottom

FARM CL

DOGHURST LA

VINCENTS
CL

7

LONGSHAW

STARROCK
LA

57

Chiphouse
Wood

Recn
Gd

FOREST DR

LARCH CL

OUTWOOD LA

CASTLE RD

Elmore

BEECHWOOD AVE

THE GLADE

Outwood
Shaw

Poorfield
Wood

ELMORE RD

SHABDEN
COTTS

6

B2032

THE CHASE

Out Wood

Embers
Shaw

WATERHOUSE LA

BEECHWOOD DR

LILLEY DR

PINEHURST CL

The
Lodge

Eyhurst
Farm

Porters
Wood

The
Grove

Noke
Farm

5

BEECHES WAY

SHABDEN
PARK

HOSSCROSS LA

56

BEECHES CL

WARREN DR

CHESTNUT CL

SANDY LA

THE
COURTYARD

THE
MANOR HO

OAKWOOD
HALL

Eyhurst
Park

THE
PAVILION

The Long
Plantation

KT20

4

BEECH DR

WHITE HILL

HIGH RD

GOLF COURSE
COTTS

CR5

3

CH

Smugglers Pit Plantation

Pigeonhouse
Farm

Top
Shaw

Tickners
Wood

Prior's
Field

CHIPSTEAD LA

Well House
(PH)

Reeves
Rest

Hogden
Bottom

PIGEONHOUSE LA

SOUTHERNS LA

55

MAY
COTTS

MONKSWELL LA

Southerns
Farm

MILLFIELD LA

Millfield
Wood

RECTORY RD

Park
Farm

HARPS OAK LA

2

Windmill
Court

GREEN LA

Mugswell

Long
Wood

Little
Wood

Upper Gatton
Wood

RH1

Grub
Wood

PAR LA

Colts
Bushes

Upper Gatton
Park

1

Gatwick
Wood

RH2

54

Gatwick
Farm

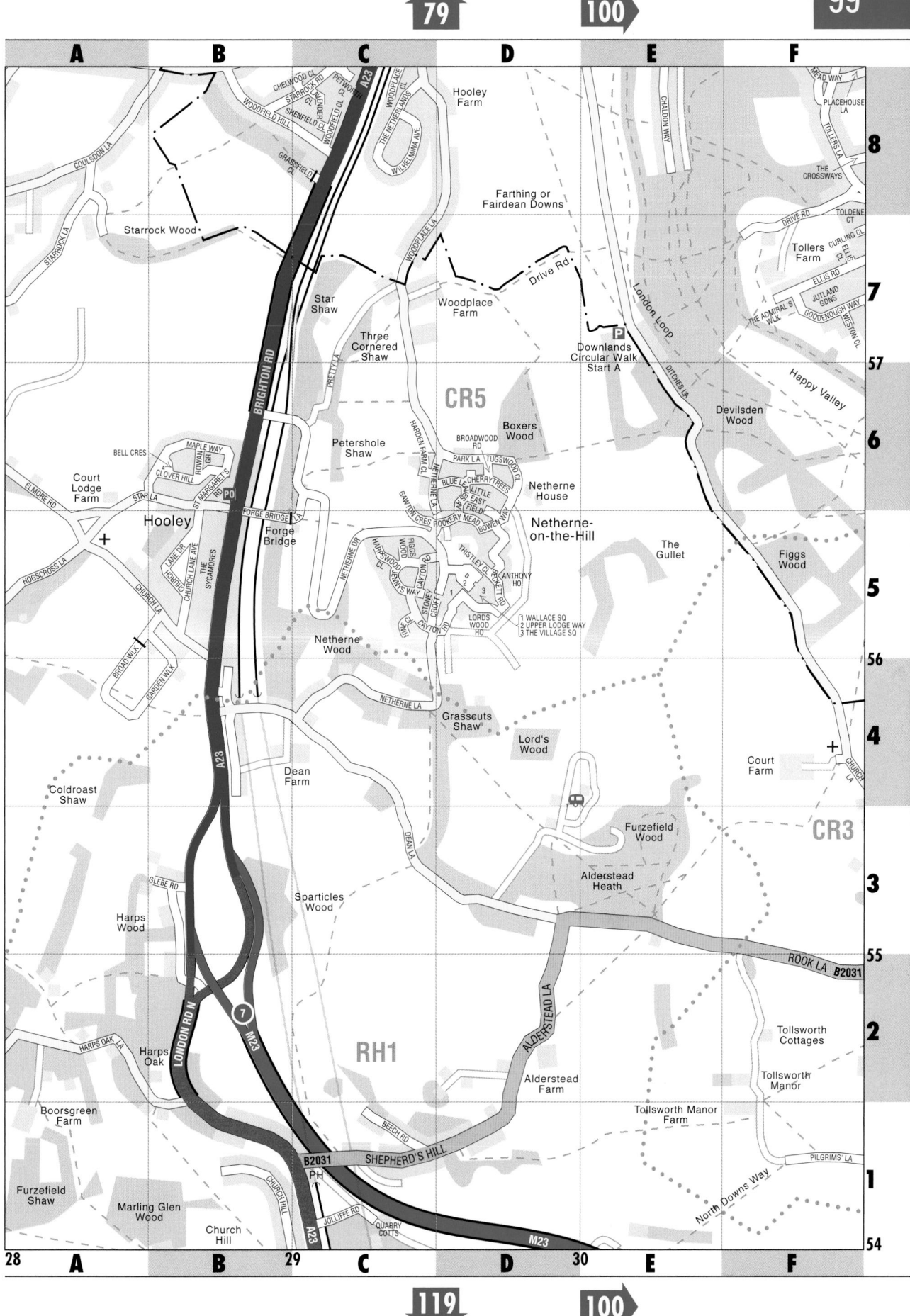

99
80

C6
1 NEWLANDS CT
2 HUNTSMANS CT
3 ALMA CT

D5
1 LE PERSONNE HOMES
2 THE FIRS
3 CHATFIELD CT
4 CHRISTIE WLK
5 CEDAR CT
6 HOLM CT

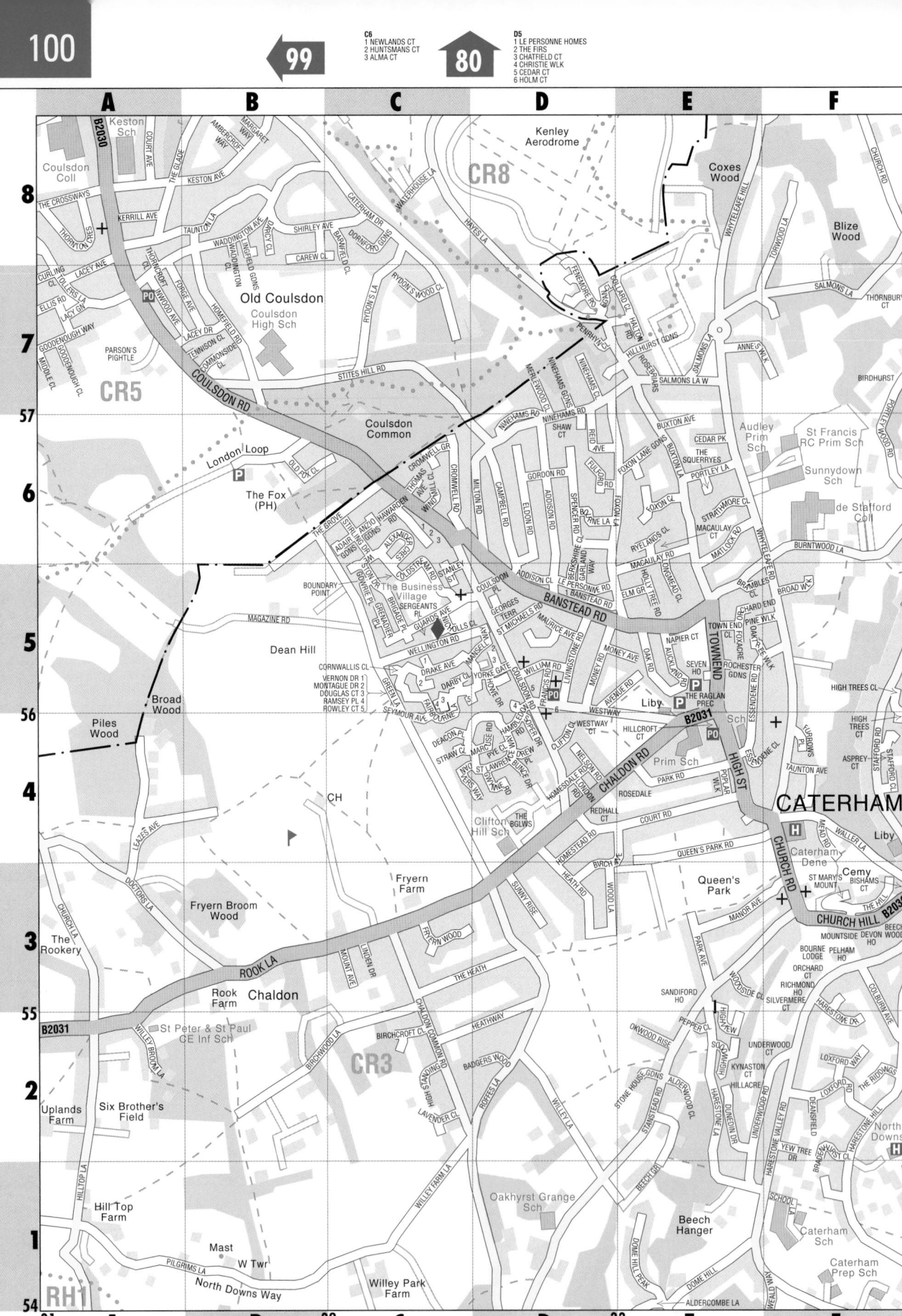

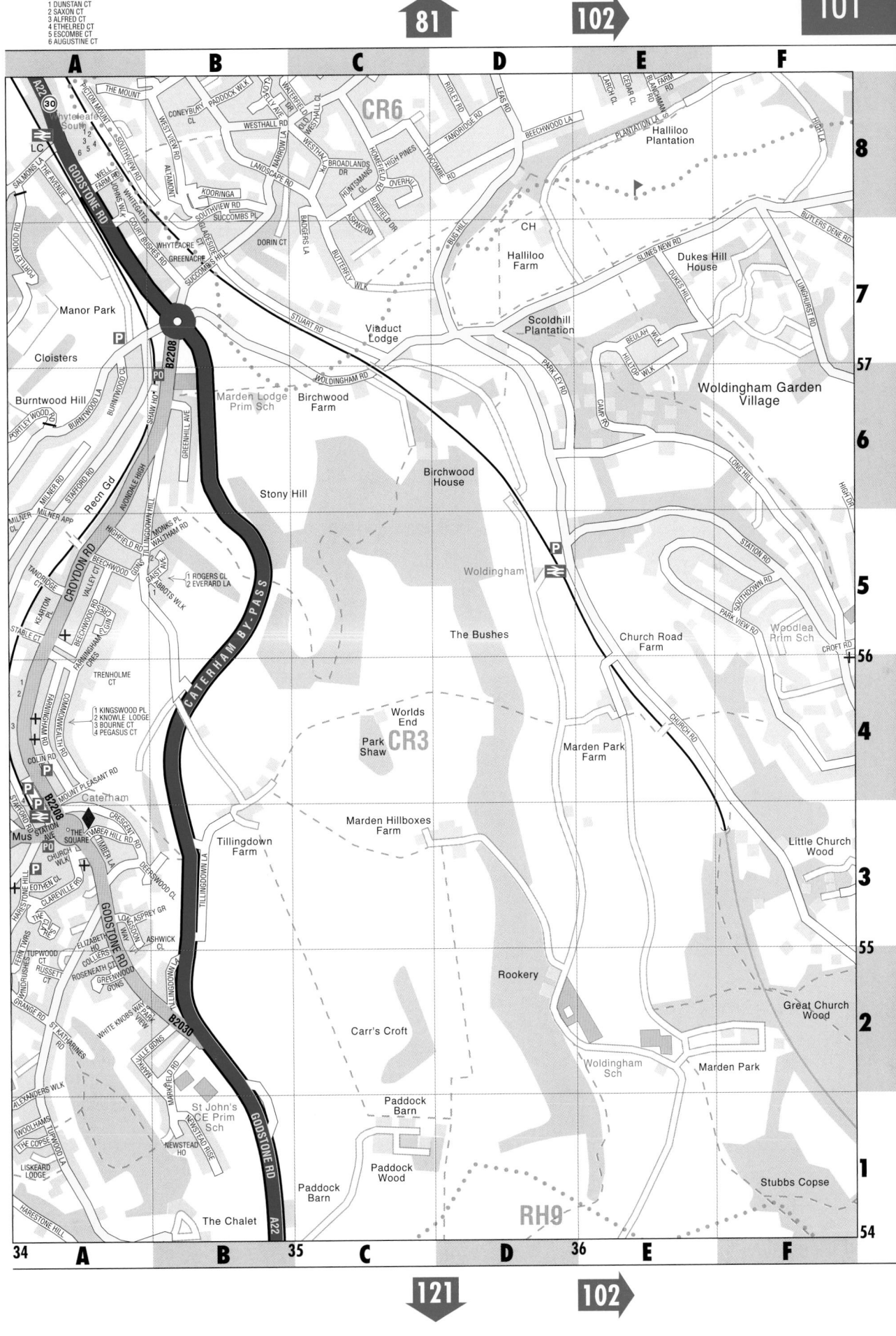

A8
1 DUNSTAN CT
2 SAXON CT
3 ALFRED CT
4 ETHELRED CT
5 ESCOMBE CT
6 AUGUSTINE CT

CR6

Whyteleafe South
LC

THE MOUNT
CONEYBURY CL
WEST VIEW RD
WESTHALL RD
LANDSCAPE RD
KOORINGA
SOUTHVIEW RD
SUCCOMBS PL
GREENACRE
WHYTEACRE
DORIN CT
PADDOCK WLK
WATERFIELD GN
CLOVELLY AVE
HIGH PINES
OVERHILL
BROADLANDS DR
HUNTSMANS CL
ASHWOOD
BURFIELD DR
BUTTERY WLK
BADGERS LA

Halliloo Plantation

Halliloo Farm
CH

Dukes Hill House
SLINES NEW RD
DUKES HILL

Manor Park
Cloisters

A22
30

GODSTONE RD
SALMONS LA
THE AVENUE
ACTION MOUNT
SOUTHVIEW RD
WHITEGATES
COURT BUSHES RD
SUCCOMBS HILL
STUART RD
WOLDINGHAM RD

Viaduct Lodge

Scoldhill Plantation

Woldingham Garden Village

Burntwood Hill
PORTLEY WOOD RD
PORTLEY RD
MILNER RD
STAFFORD RD
BURNTWOOD LA
WHITTAKER RD
B2208
SHAW RD
GREENHILL AVE
MARDEN LODGE PRIM SCH
Birchwood Farm
PARK LEY RD
CAMP RD
BEULAH WLK
HILLTOP WLK

Recn Gd
MILNER RD
MILNER APP
AVONDALE HIGH
TILLINGDOWN HILL
HIGHFIELD RD
MONKS PL
WALTHAM RD
Stony Hill
Birchwood House

LONG HILL
HIGH CR

STABLE CT
TANDRIDGE CT
KEARTON PL
FARNINGHAM CRES
BEECHWOOD RD
VALLEY CT
OAST ABBOTS WLK
1 ROGERS CL
2 EVERARD LA
CROYDON RD

CATERHAM BY-PASS

Woldingham

STATION RD
SOUTHDOWN RD
PARK VIEW RD
Woodlea Prim Sch
CROFT RD

Church Road Farm

FARNINGHAM RD
COMMONWEALTH RD
TRENHOLME CT
1 KINGSWOOD PL
2 KNOWLE LODGE
3 BOURNE CT
4 PEGASUS CT
The Bushes

Worlds End
Park Shaw
CR3

Marden Park Farm

CHURCH RD

COLIN RD
MOUNT PLEASANT RD
B2208
Caterham
Mus
STATION AVE
THE SQUARE
CRESCENT
TIMBER HILL RD
Marden Hillboxes Farm

Little Church Wood

HARESTONE HILL
CHURCH WLK
GODSTONE RD
TIMBER HILL
CLAREVILLE RD
EOTHEN CT
TILLINGDOWN LA
Tillingdown Farm

FERN TWRS
TUPWOOD CT
RUSSETT CT
COLLIERS
ROSENEATH GDNS
GREENWOOD GDNS
ELIZABETH HO
LONG ASHTON WAY
ASPREY GR
DEERSWOOD CL
ASHWICK CL
Rookery

Great Church Wood

WINDHURST
GRANGE RD
ST KATHARINES RD
ALEXANDERS WLK
WOOLHAMS
THE COPSE
LISKEARD LODGE
TUPWOOD LA
WHITE KNOBS WAY
MARKFIELD
PARK VIEW
NEVILLE GDNS
Carr's Croft

Woldingham Sch
Marden Park

St John's CE Prim Sch
NEWSTEAD RISE
NEWSTEAD HO
B2030
GODSTONE RD
Paddock Barn
Paddock Wood

Stubbs Copse

Paddock Barn
The Chalet
A22

RH9

CR3

101
82

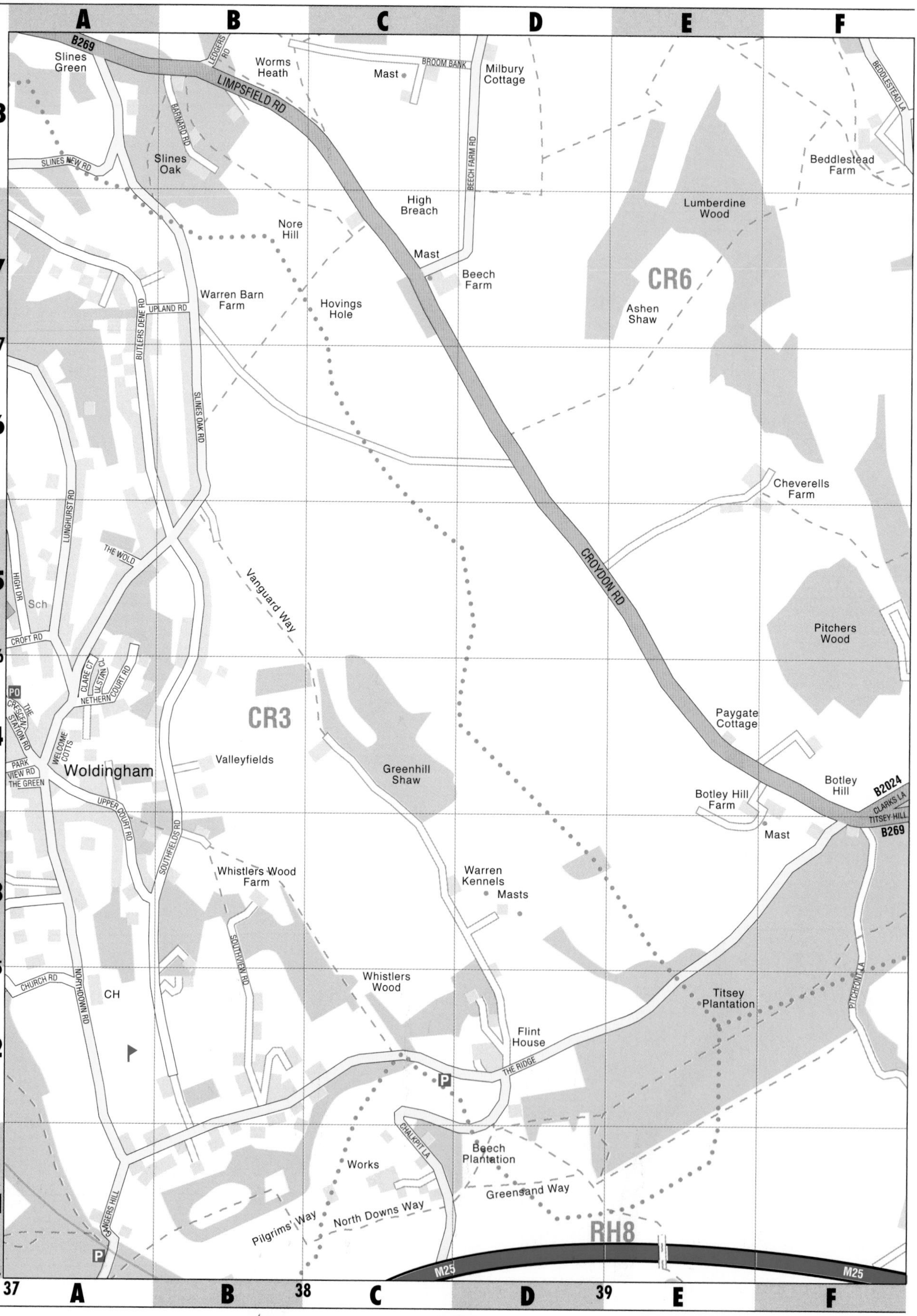

A **B** **C** **D** **E** **F**

B269
Slines Green
Worms Heath
Mast
Broom Bank
Milbury Cottage
LIMPSFIELD RD
LEGGERS RD
BARNARD RD

8

Slines Oak
Slines New Rd
High Breach
Beech Farm Rd
Lumberdine Wood
Beddlestead La

Nore Hill
Mast
Beech Farm
CR6
Beddlestead Farm

7

Warren Barn Farm
Hovings Hole
Ashen Shaw
UPLAND RD
BUTLERS DENE RD

57

SLINES OAK RD
Cheverells Farm

6

Vanguard Way
CROYDON RD
Pitchers Wood
LUNGHURST RD
THE WOLD

5

HIGH DR
Sch
Paygate Cottage

56

CROFT RD
CR3
CLARE CT
ULSTAN CL
COURT RD
NETHERN
PO
THE CRESCENT
STATION RD
Valleyfields
Greenhill Shaw
Botley Hill Farm
Botley Hill
B2024
CLARKS LA
TITSEY HILL
B269

4

PARK VIEW RD
WELCOME COTTS
THE GREEN
Woldingham
Mast

UPPER COURT RD
Whistlers Wood Farm
Warren Kennels
Masts

3

SOUTHFIELDS RD
SOUTHVIEW RD
PITCHEN LA

55

CHURCH RD
CH
Whistlers Wood
Titsey Plantation
NORTHDOWN RD
Flint House
THE RIDGE

2

CHALKPIT LA
P
Works
Beech Plantation
Greensand Way
RANGERS HILL

1

P
Pilgrims' Way
North Downs Way
RH8
M25
M25

54

37 **A** **B** 38 **C** **D** 39 **E** **F**

83

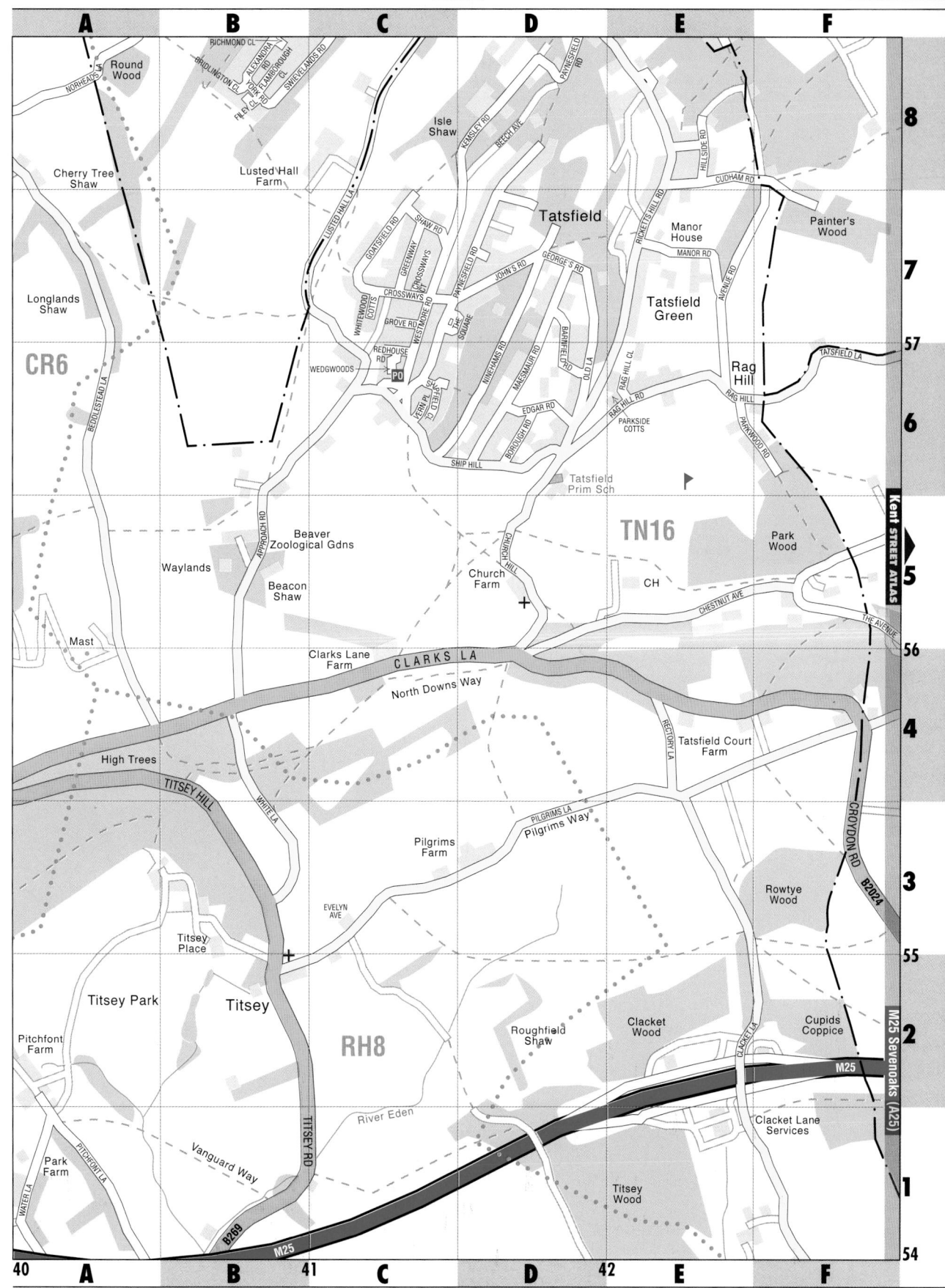
A
B
C
D
E
F
Round Wood
Cherry Tree Shaw
Lusted Hall Farm
Isle Shaw
Tatsfield
Manor House
Painter's Wood
Longlands Shaw
Tatsfield Green
CR6
Rag Hill
Tatsfield Prim Sch
TN16
Park Wood
Beaver Zoological Gdns
Waylands
Beacon Shaw
Church Farm
CH
Mast
Clarks Lane Farm
CLARKS LA
North Downs Way
High Trees
Tatsfield Court Farm
Pilgrims Farm
Pilgrims Way
Rowtye Wood
Titsey Place
Titsey Park
Titsey
RH8
Roughfield Shaw
Clacket Wood
Cupids Coppice
Pitchfont Farm
River Eden
Clacket Lane Services
Park Farm
Vanguard Way
Titsey Wood
M25
B269
B2024
CROYDON RD
TITSEY HILL
TITSEY RD
Kent STREET ATLAS
M25 Sevenoaks (A25)
8
7
57
6
5
56
4
3
55
2
1
54
40
41
42

123

84

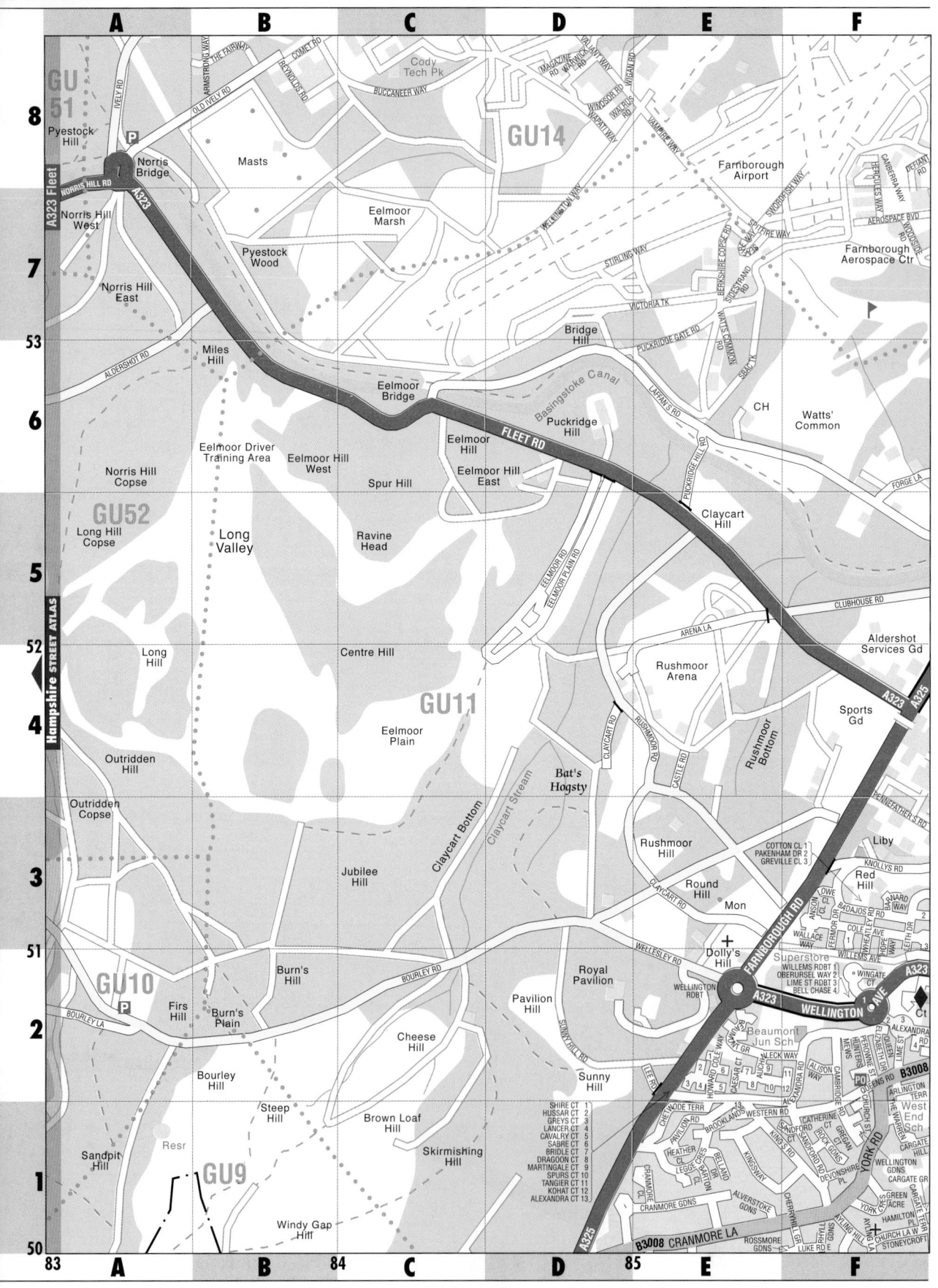
Pyestock Hill
Norris Bridge
Norris Hill West
Norris Hill East
Masts
Pyestock Wood
Eelmoor Marsh
Cody Tech Pk
GU14
Farnborough Airport
Farnborough Aerospace Ctr
Bridge Hill
Miles Hill
Eelmoor Bridge
Basingstoke Canal
Puckridge Hill
Watts' Common
Eelmoor Driver Training Area
Eelmoor Hill West
Eelmoor Hill
Eelmoor Hill East
Spur Hill
Norris Hill Copse
GU52
Long Hill Copse
Long Valley
Ravine Head
Claycart Hill
Long Hill
Centre Hill
Rushmoor Arena
Aldershot Services Gd
GU11
Eelmoor Plain
Sports Gd
Outridden Hill
Bat's Hogsty
Rushmoor Bottom
Outridden Copse
Claycart Bottom
Claycart Stream
Rushmoor Hill
Jubilee Hill
Round Hill
Red Hill
Dolly's Hill
Superstore
Royal Pavilion
Pavilion Hill
Burn's Hill
GU10
Firs Hill
Burn's Plain
Cheese Hill
Beaumont Jun Sch
Bourley Hill
Sunny Hill
Steep Hill
Brown Loaf Hill
Skirmishing Hill
West End Sch
Sandpit Hill
Resr
GU9
Windy Gap Hill
A323 Fleet
Hampshire STREET ATLAS
FLEET RD
FARNBOROUGH RD
WELLINGTON AVE
B3008 CRANMORE LA
YORK RD
SHIRE CT 1
HUSSAR CT 2
GREYS CT 3
LANCER CT 4
CAVALRY CT 5
SABRE CT 6
BRIDLE CT 7
DRAGOON CT 8
MARTINGALE CT 9
SPURS CT 10
TANGIER CT 11
KOHAT CT 12
ALEXANDRA CT 13
COTTON CL 1
PAKENHAM DR 2
GREVILLE CL 3
WILLEMS RDBT 1
OBERURSEL WAY 2
LIME ST RDBT 3
BELL CHASE 4

125

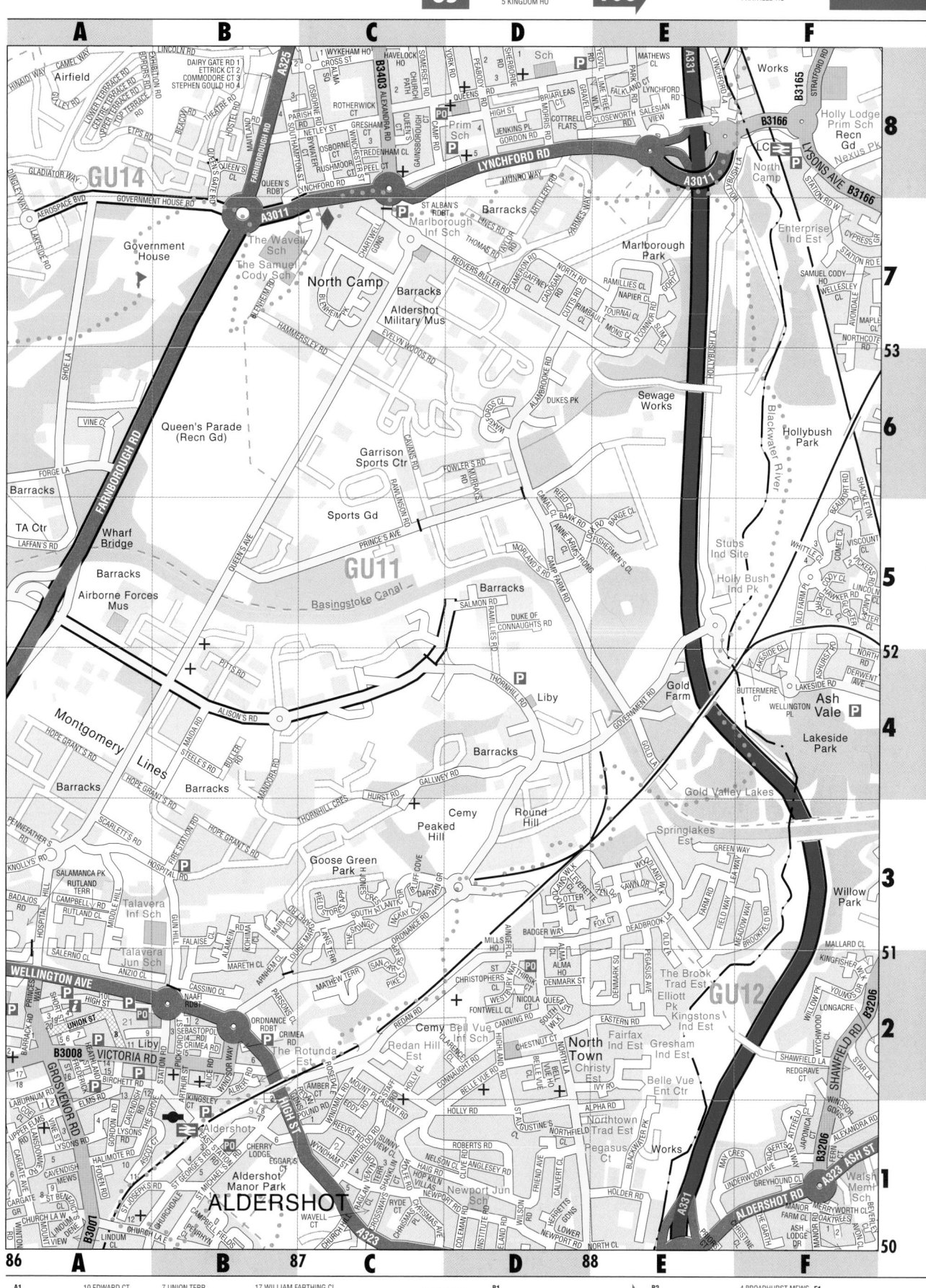

C8
1 HAWTHORN CT
2 SHAFTESBURY CT
3 PRINCESS CT

D8
1 SYLVAN CT
2 GROSVENOR HO
3 ARNELLA CT
4 THE FERNS
5 KINGDOM HO

F5
1 STIRLING CL
2 WYVERN CL
3 BALMORAL HO
4 HATFIELD HO

A1
1 LABURNUM CL
2 LABURNUM PAS
3 PARK HO
4 WOLSELEY RD
5 CULLENS MEWS
6 SALES CT
7 BURLINGTON CT
8 CHASEWATER CT
9 GARRETT MEWS
10 EDWARD CT
11 HEREFORD HO
12 HEATHER CT
A2
1 UPPER UNION ST
2 EDWARD ST
3 NELSON ST
4 LOWER NELSON ST
5 UPPER UNION TERR
6 CROSS ST
7 UNION TERR
8 WELLINGTON ST
9 LITTLE WELLINGTON ST
10 COURT RD
11 THE ARCADE
12 STRATFIELD HO
13 PHOENIX CT
14 FIR TREE ALLEY
15 MOUNTBATTEN CT
16 SEFTON HO
17 WILLIAM FARTHING CL
18 HIGH VIEW LODGE
19 NELSON HO
20 IONA HO
21 The Wellington Ctr

B1
1 MANOR WLK
2 BOULTERS RD
3 WELLESLEY GATE
4 ST DAVIDS CT
5 HERALD CT
6 ST GEORGE'S RD E
7 HARRIET CT
8 BEECHNUT RD
9 Beechnut Ind Est

B2
1 ARTILLERY RD
2 ENTERPRISE HO
3 EMARC HO
4 WALPOLE HO
5 LONDON HO
6 GABLE END
7 AVERY CT
C1
1 WINDMILL CT
2 Manor Pk Ind Est
3 BEMBRIDGE CT
4 BROADHURST MEWS
5 PEMBURY PL

F1
1 OAKTREES CT
2 WOODLANDS PK

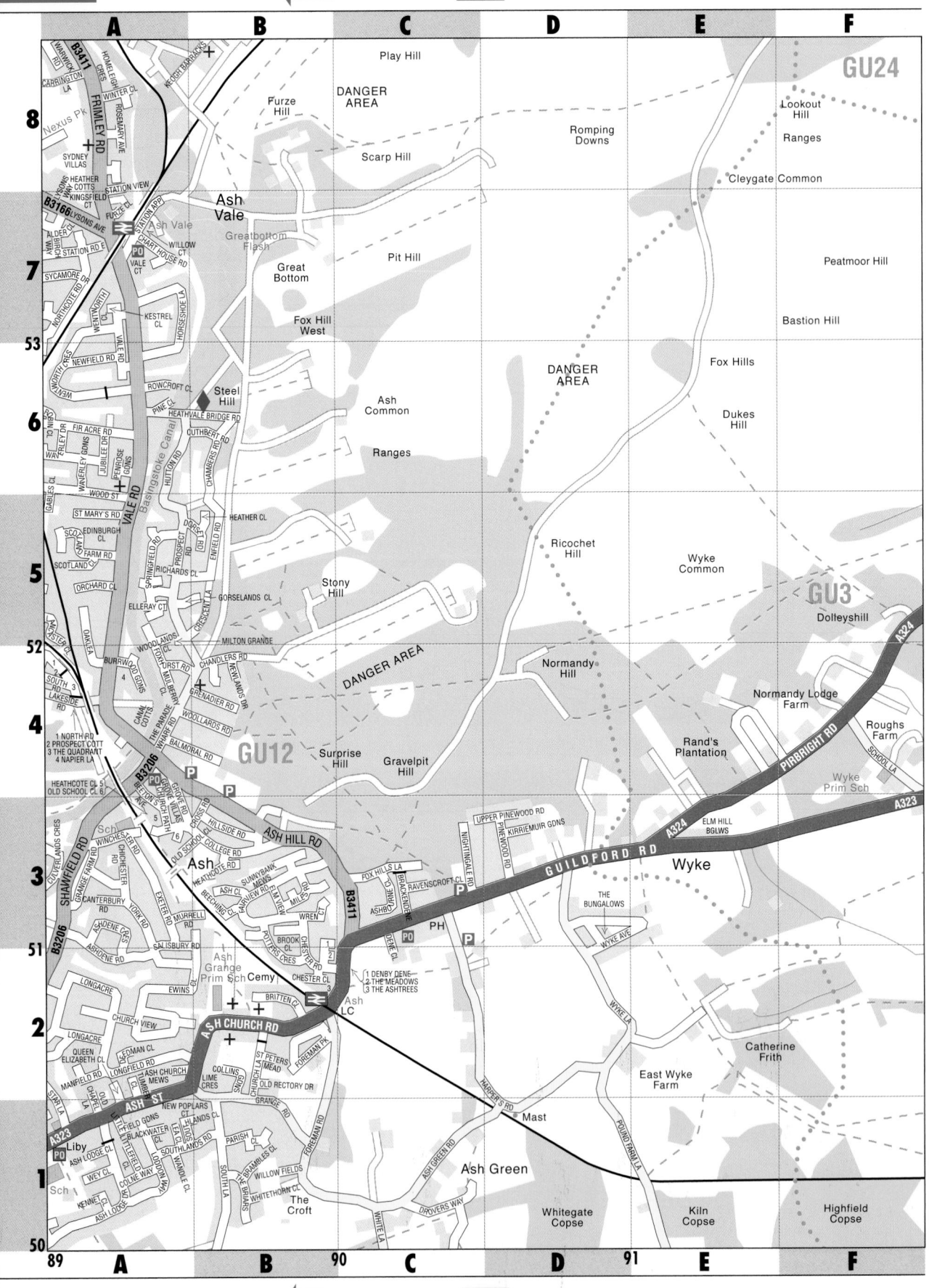

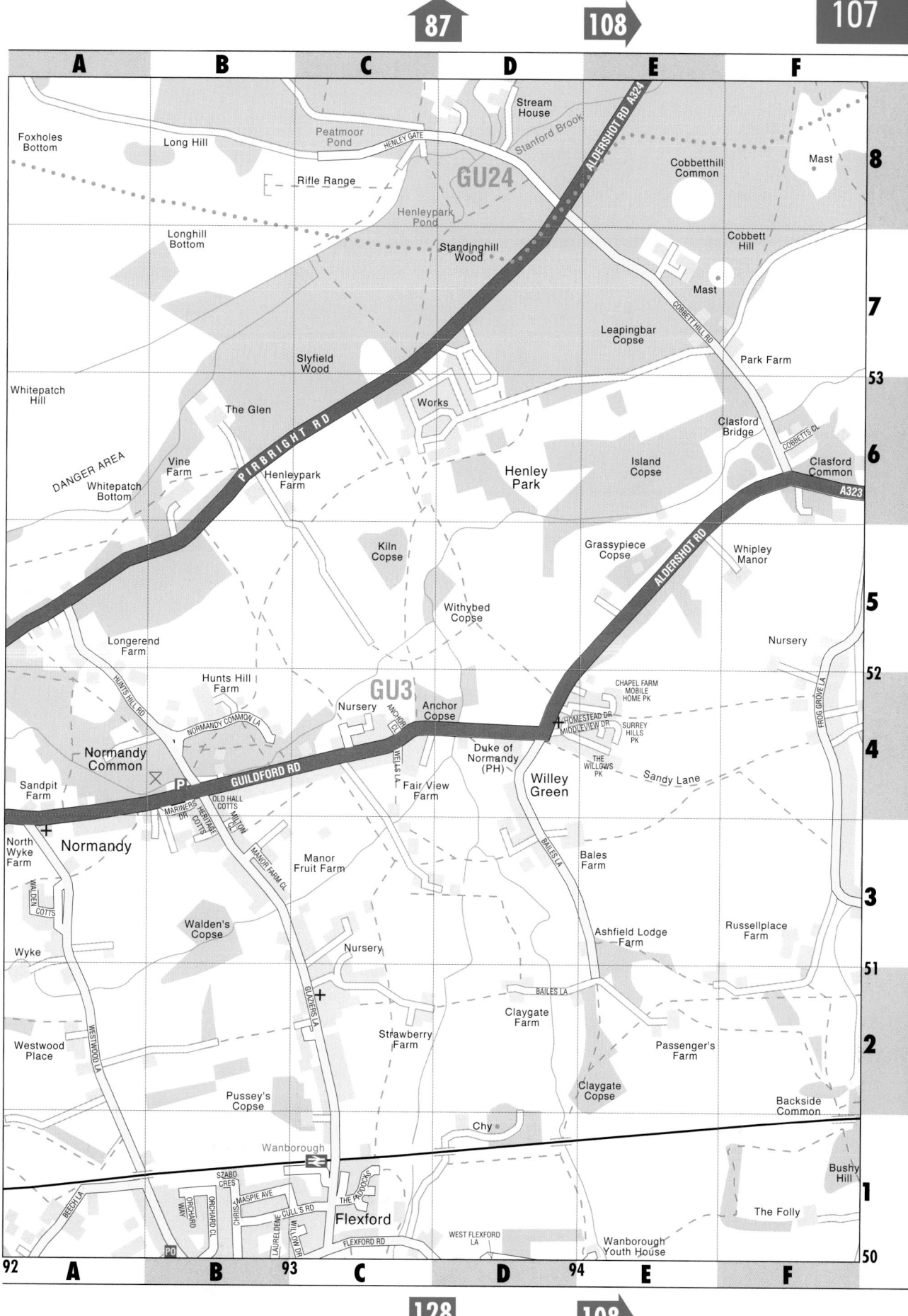

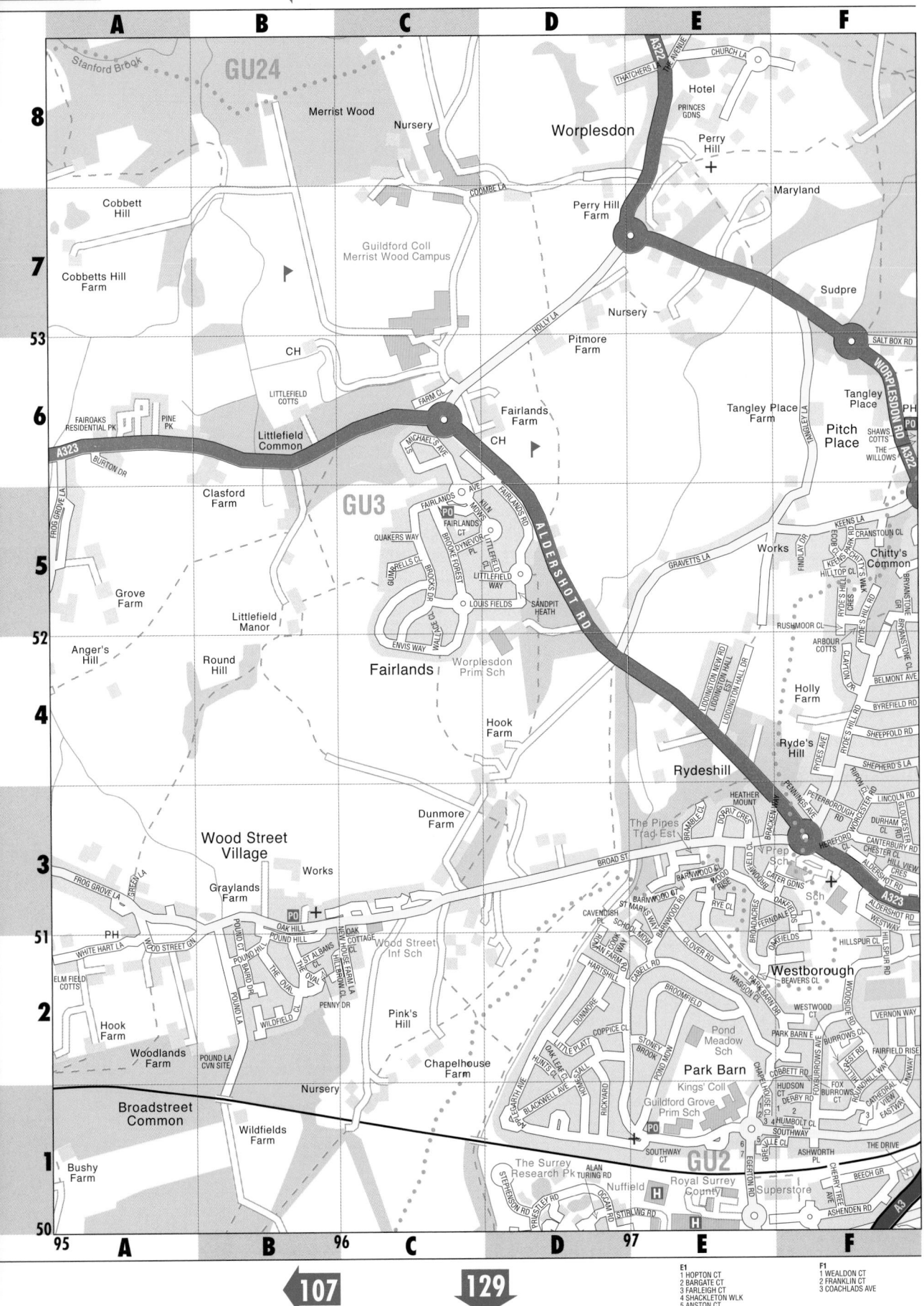

E1
1 HOPTON CT
2 BARGATE CT
3 FARLEIGH CT
4 SHACKLETON WLK
5 ANSTON CT
6 PURBECK CT
7 EGERTON CT

F1
1 WEALDON CT
2 FRANKLIN CT
3 COACHLADS AVE

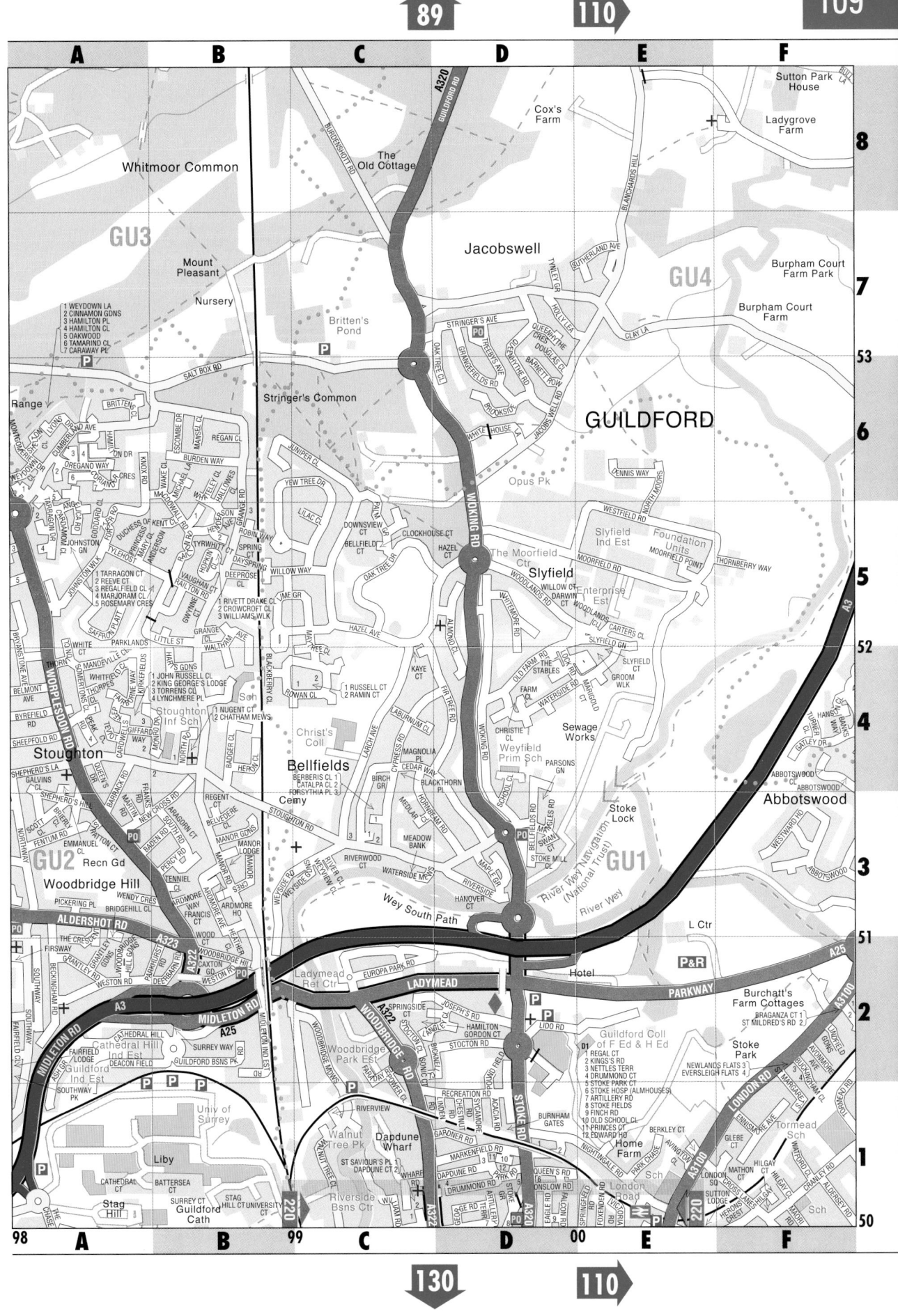

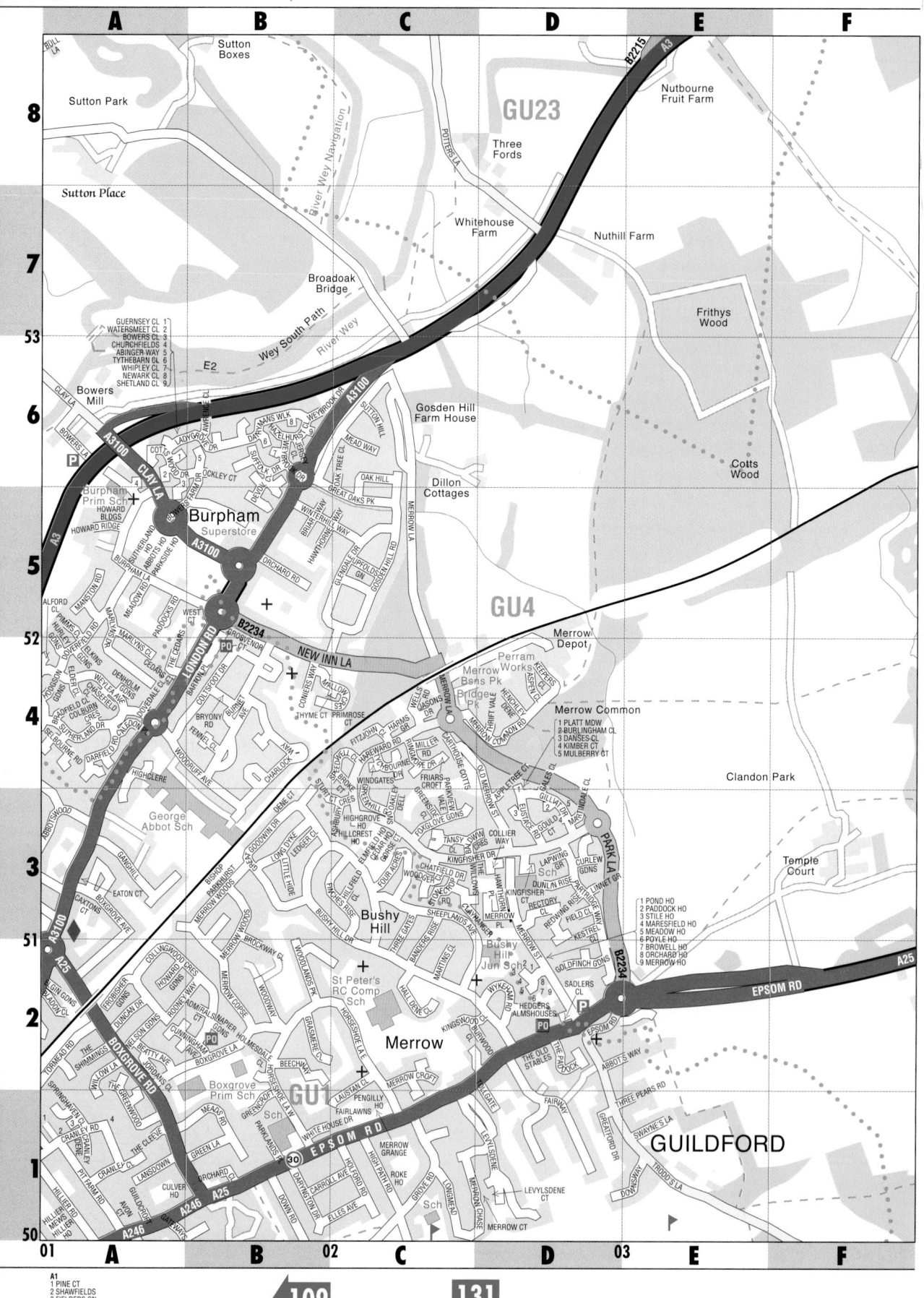

A1
1 PINE CT
2 SHAWFIELDS
3 FIELDERS GN
4 CRANLEY MANOR

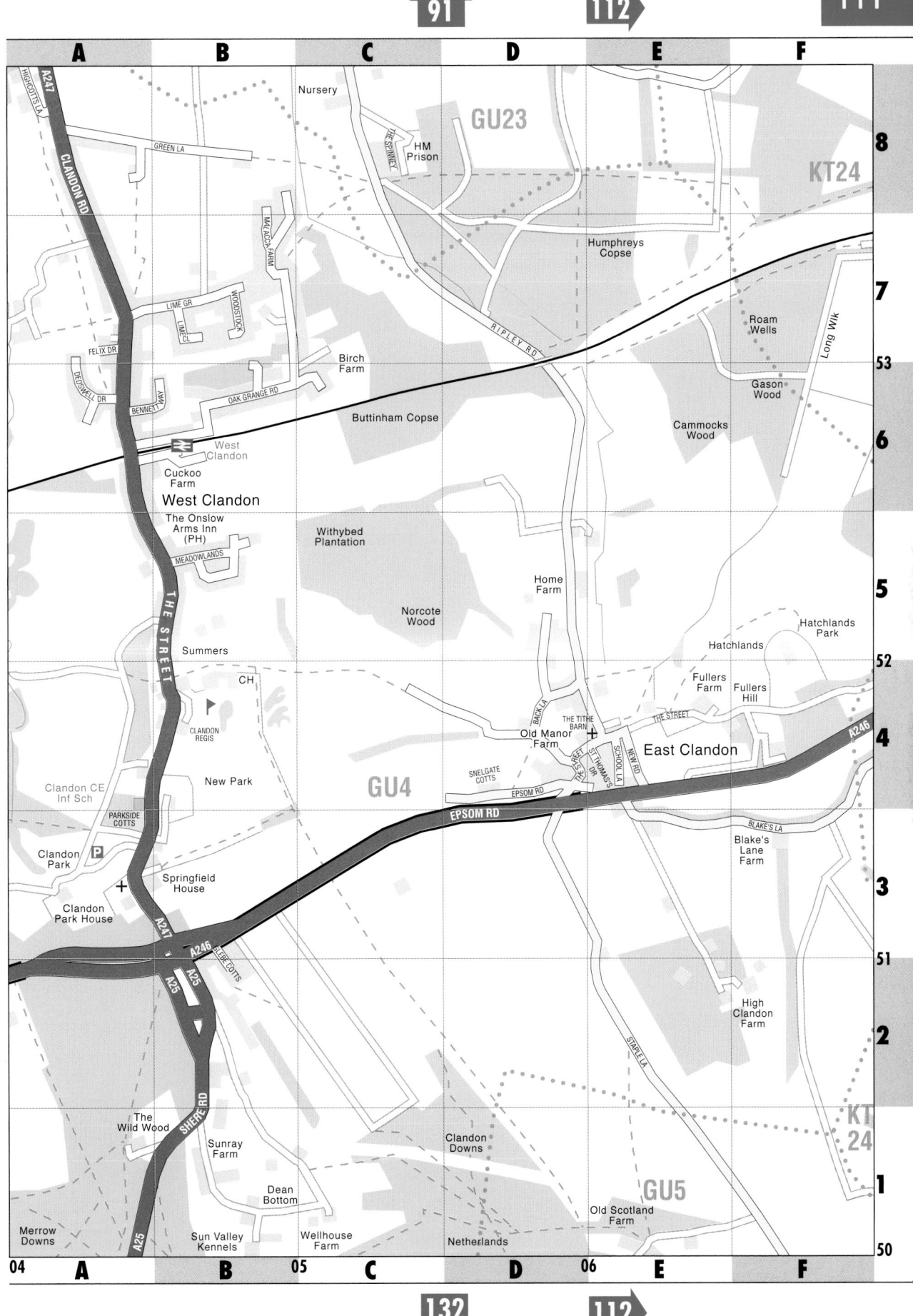

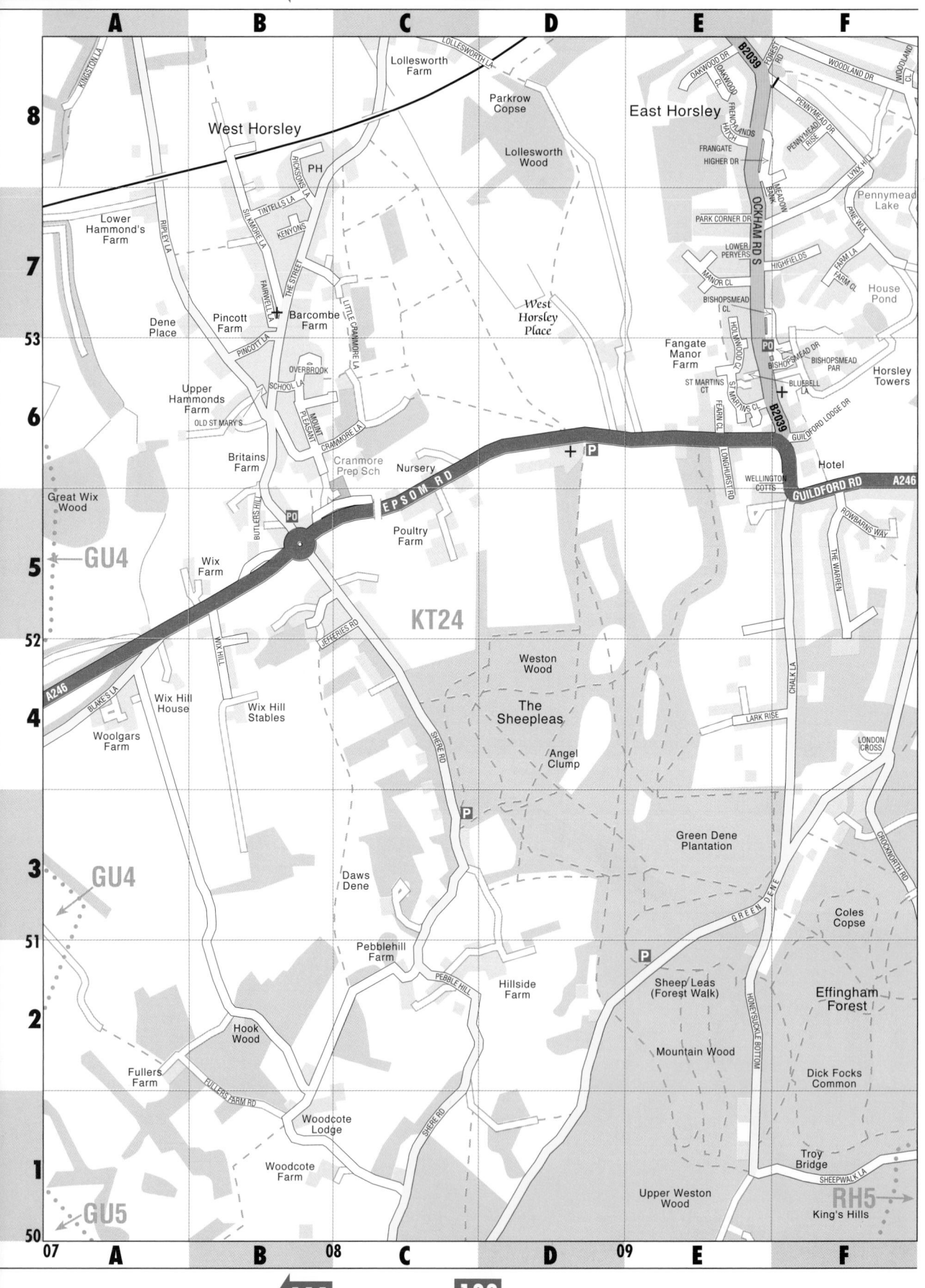

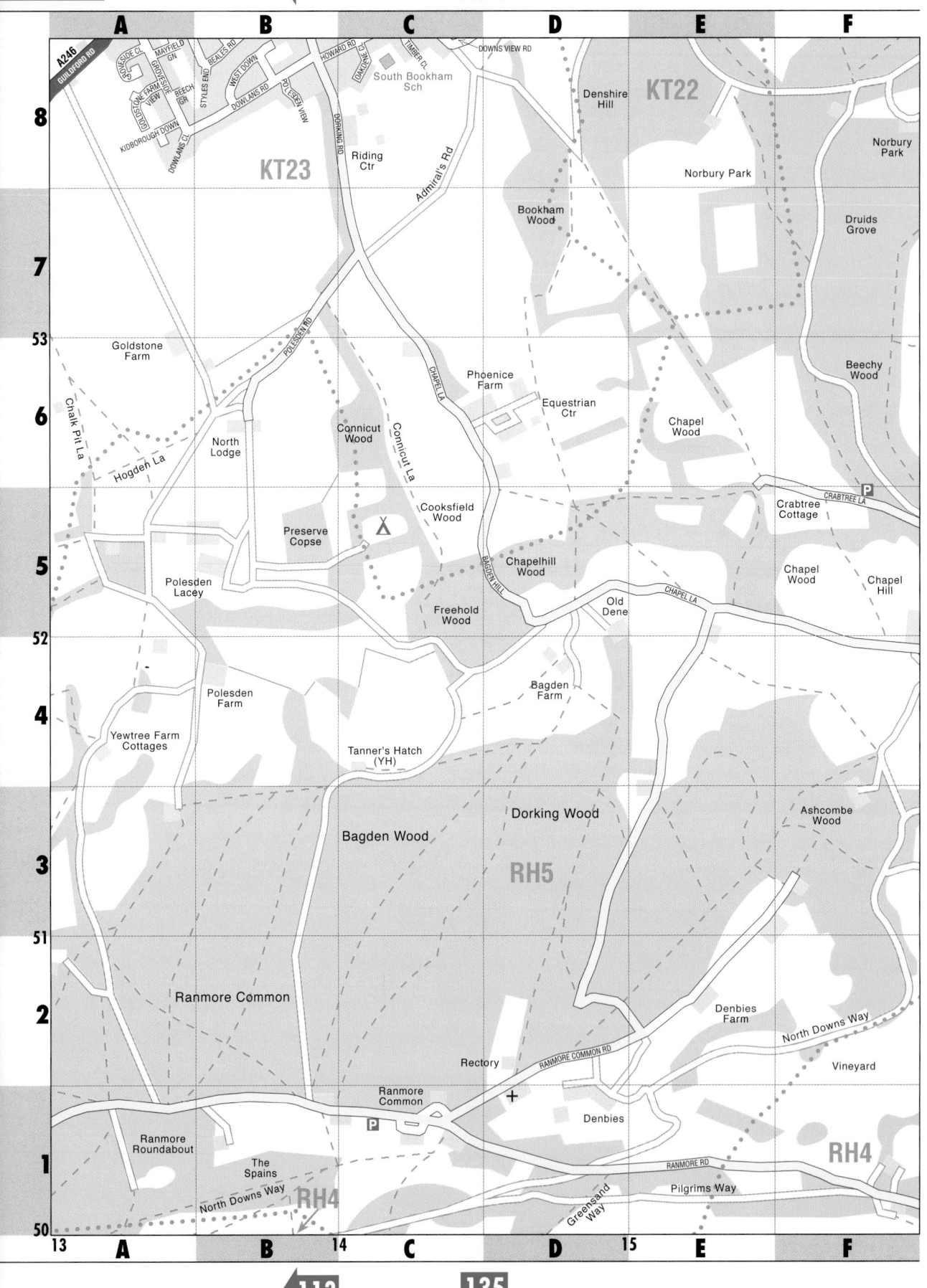

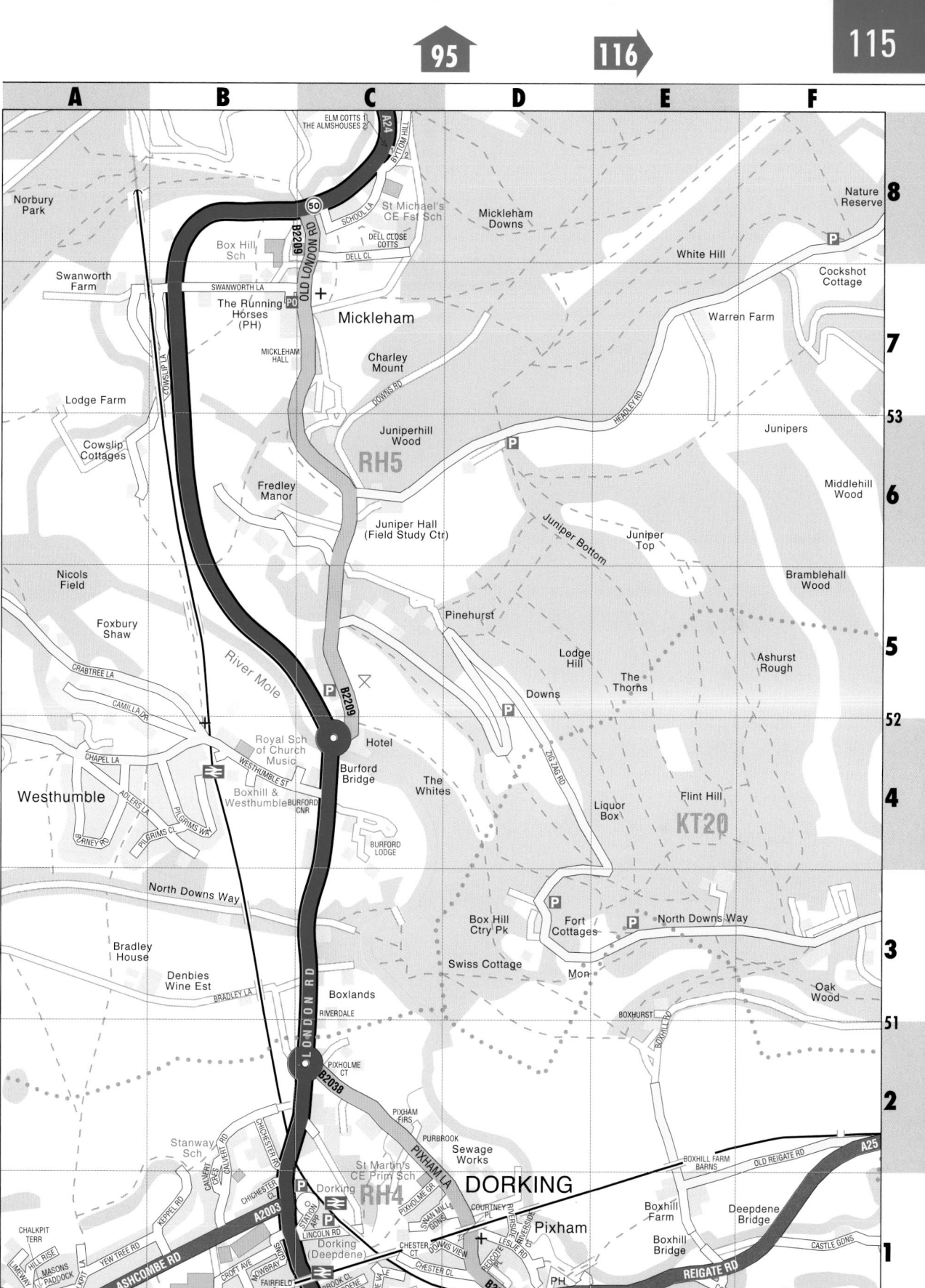
A
B
C
D
E
F
ELM COTTS
THE ALMSHOUSES
A24
BYTTOM HILL
Norbury Park
8
Nature Reserve
St Michael's CE Fst Sch
SCHOOL LA
Mickleham Downs
B2209
OLD LONDON RD
Box Hill Sch
DELL CLOSE COTTS
DELL CL
White Hill
Cockshot Cottage
Swanworth Farm
SWANWORTH LA
PO
The Running Horses (PH)
Mickleham
Warren Farm
7
MICKLEHAM HALL
Charley Mount
COWSLIP LA
Lodge Farm
DOWNS RD
HEADLEY RD
53
Juniperhill Wood
Junipers
Cowslip Cottages
RH5
Fredley Manor
Middlehill Wood
6
Juniper Hall (Field Study Ctr)
Juniper Bottom
Juniper Top
Nicols Field
Bramblehall Wood
Pinehurst
Foxbury Shaw
Lodge Hill
Ashurst Rough
5
River Mole
CRABTREE LA
The Thorns
Downs
B2209
CAMILLA DR
52
Hotel
Royal Sch of Church Music
CHAPEL LA
Burford Bridge
WESTHUMBLE ST
ZIG ZAG RD
The Whites
Westhumble
Boxhill & Westhumble
BURFORD CNR
ADLERS LA
Liquor Box
Flint Hill
4
PILGRIMS WAY
KT20
PILGRIMS CL
BURNEY RD
BURFORD LODGE
North Downs Way
Box Hill Ctry Pk
Fort Cottages
North Downs Way
Bradley House
3
Swiss Cottage
Denbies Wine Est
Mon
Oak Wood
BRADLEY LA
LONDON RD
Boxlands
RIVERDALE
BOXHURST
BOXHILL RD
51
PIXHOLME CT
B2038
2
PIXHAM FIRS
PURBROOK
Stanway Sch
CHICHESTER RD
CALVERT RD
CALVERT CRES
Sewage Works
St Martin's CE Prim Sch
BOXHILL FARM BARNS
OLD REIGATE RD
A25
KEPPEL RD
CHICHESTER CL
PIXHAM LA
DORKING
Dorking
RH4
PIXHOLME GR
A2003
STATION APP
SWAN MILL GDNS
COURTNEY PL
RIVERSIDE RD
RIVERSIDE CT
Boxhill Farm
Deepdene Bridge
CHALKPIT TERR
Pixham
LINCOLN RD
YEW TREE RD
Dorking (Deepdene)
CHESTER CT
DOWNS VIEW
REDCOTE PL
LESLIE RD
Boxhill Bridge
HILL RISE
CROFT AVE
CHESTER CL
CASTLE GDNS
1
LIMEWAY TERR
MASONS PADDOCK
ASHCOMBE RD
MOWBRAY GDNS
BROOK CL
DEEPDENE VALE
REIGATE RD
CHALKPIT TERR
CHALKPIT LA
FAIRFIELD CL
DEEPDENE AVENUE RD
PH
RANMORE RD
The Ashcombe Sch
Cemy
B2038
COACH RD
Betchworth Park
A2003
FAIRFIELD DR
FAIRFIELD CT
A24
A25
50
16
17
18

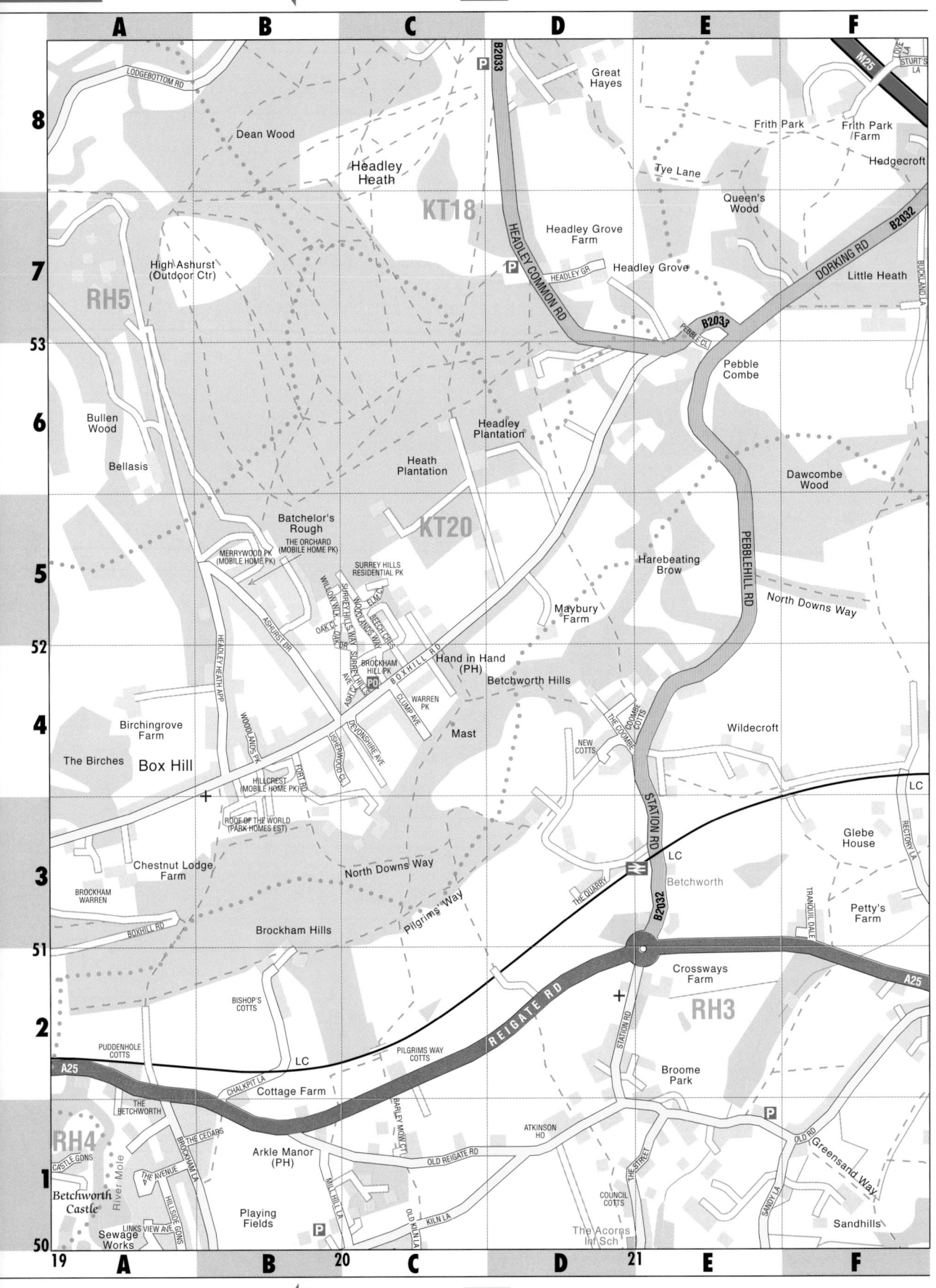

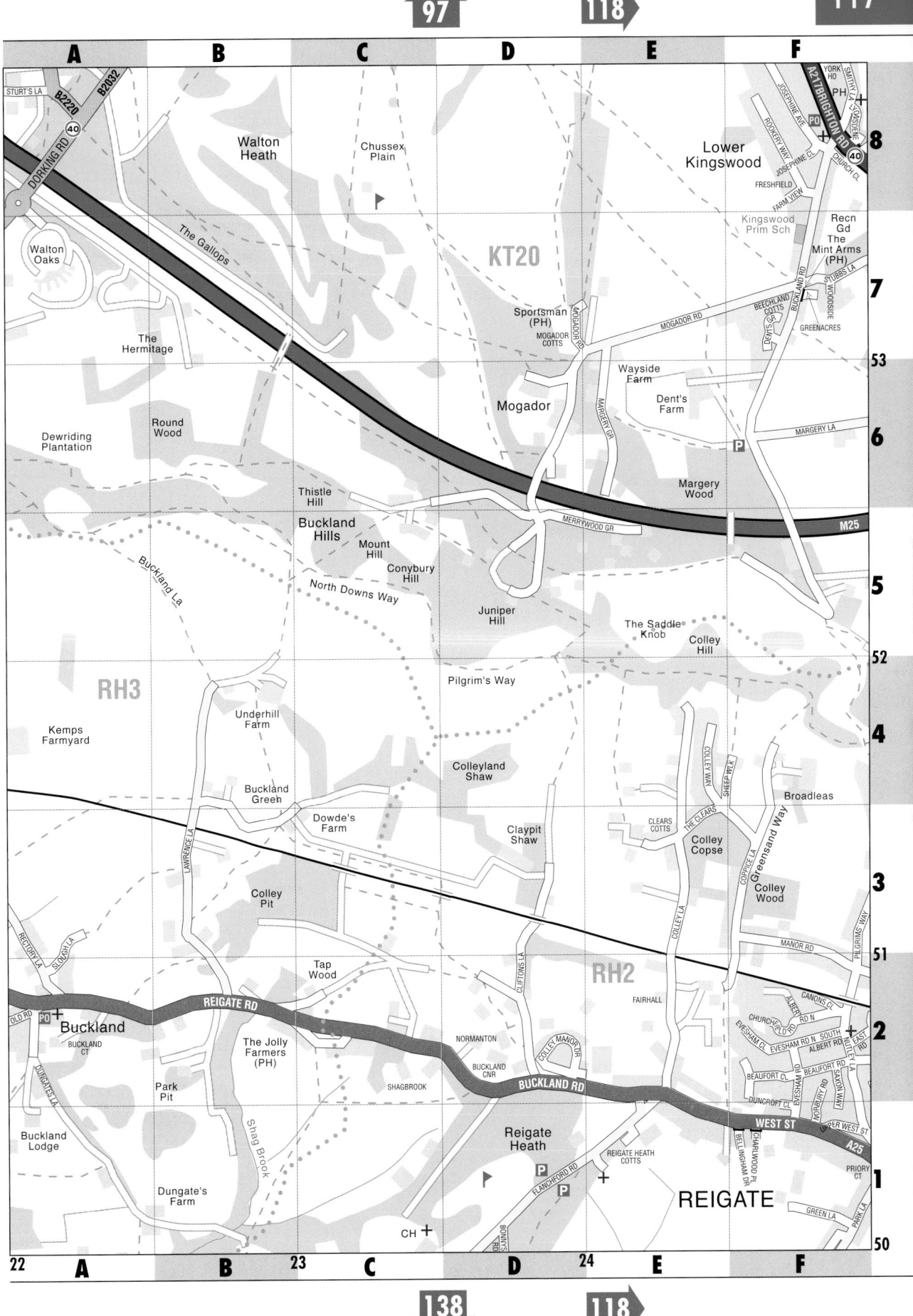
97
118
Walton Heath
Chussex Plain
Lower Kingswood
Walton Oaks
The Gallops
KT20
The Hermitage
Sportsman (PH)
Mogador
Wayside Farm
Dent's Farm
Round Wood
Dewriding Plantation
Thistle Hill
Buckland Hills
Mount Hill
Conybury Hill
Margery Wood
M25
Buckland La
North Downs Way
Juniper Hill
The Saddle Knob
Colley Hill
Pilgrim's Way
RH3
Underhill Farm
Kemps Farmyard
Colleyland Shaw
Broadleas
Buckland Green
Dowde's Farm
Claypit Shaw
Colley Copse
Greensand Way
Colley Wood
Colley Pit
Tap Wood
RH2
Buckland
The Jolly Farmers (PH)
Park Pit
Shag Brook
Reigate Heath
Buckland Lodge
Dungate's Farm
REIGATE
REIGATE RD
BUCKLAND RD
WEST ST
A25
Kingswood Prim Sch
Recn Gd
The Mint Arms (PH)
A217 BRIGHTON RD
DORKING RD
B2220
B2032
MOGADOR RD
MARGERY LA
MERRYWOOD GR
LAWRENCE LA
COLLEY LA
CLIFTONS LA
MANOR RD
FLANCHFORD RD
138
118

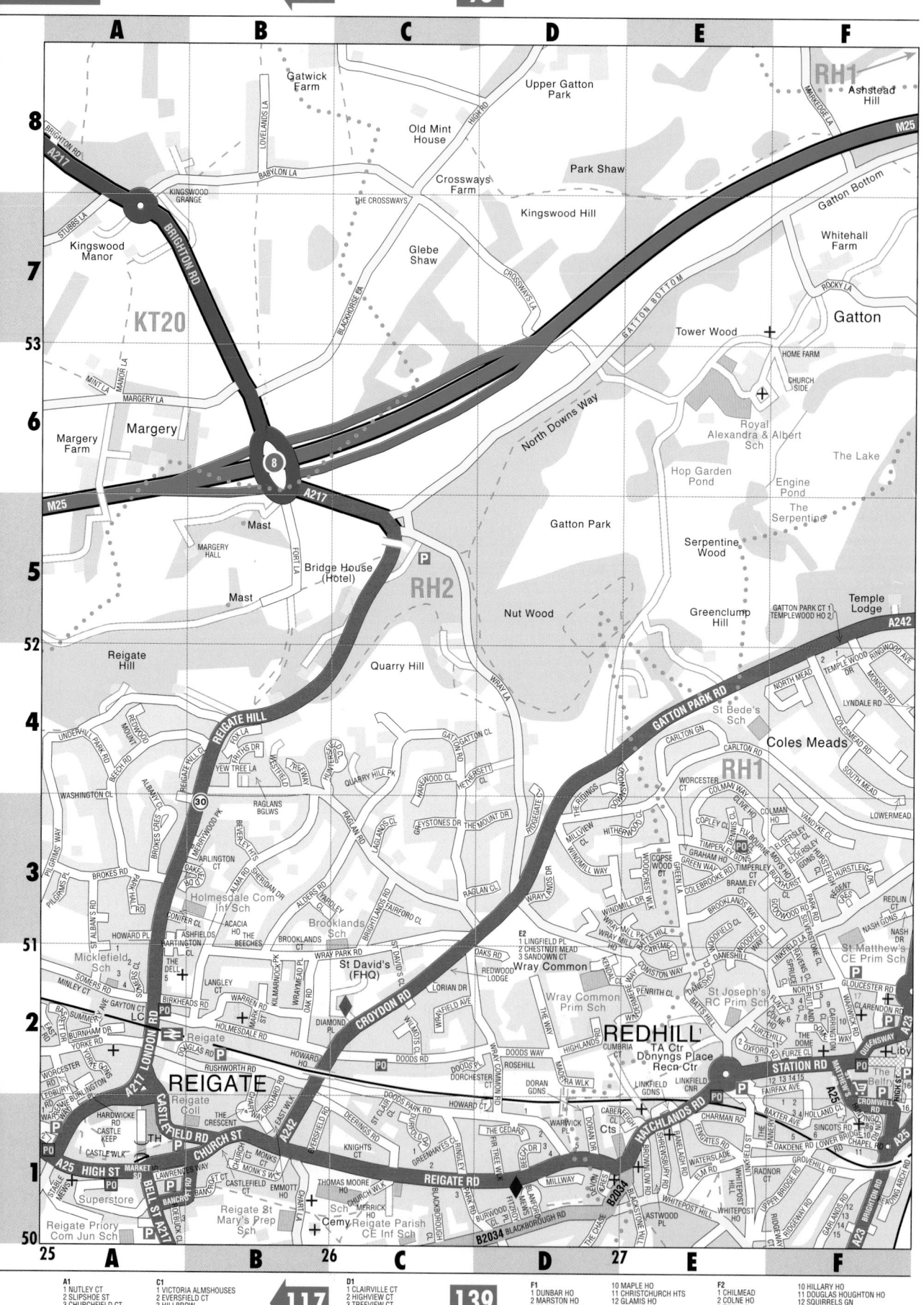

← 117   139

A1
1 NUTLEY CT
2 SLIPSHOE ST
3 CHURCHFIELD CT
A2
1 SOMERS PL
2 FLANCHFORD HO
3 CLAYHALL HO
4 LITTLETON HO
5 ELVINGTON LODGE

C1
1 VICTORIA ALMSHOUSES
2 EVERSFIELD CT
3 HILLBROW

D1
1 CLAIRVILLE CT
2 HIGHVIEW CT
3 TREEVIEW CT
4 HARLOW CT
5 WRAYMILL HO

F1
1 DUNBAR HO
2 MARSTON HO
3 CROMWELL WLK
4 EDGEHILL HO
5 MORRISS CT
6 OBSERVATORY WLK
7 WAVENEY HO
8 GROVE HO
9 ELY HO

10 MAPLE HO
11 CHRISTCHURCH HTS
12 GLAMIS HO
13 ATHOLL HO
14 DUNVEGAN HO
15 STIRLING HO
16 MARKET FIELD RD

F2
1 CHILMEAD
2 COLNE HO
3 TAVY HO
4 ROTHER HO
5 WANDLE HO
6 KENNET HO
7 ORWELL HO
8 WINDRUSH HO
9 AVON HO

10 HILLARY HO
11 DOUGLAS HOUGHTON HO
12 SQUIRRELS GN
13 CHILWORTH CT
14 THE HOLLIES
15 CROMWELL PL
16 MARYLEBONE HO
17 Abbey Bsns Ctr

A2
1 PRINCESS HO
2 LADBROKE COTTS
3 QUEENS CT
4 DIAMOND CT
5 ST ANNES WAY
6 CLEEVES CT
7 ST ANNES MOUNT
8 NIGHTINGALE CT
9 GABLE CT

10 HATHAWAY CT
11 BOLEYN CT
12 TUDOR CT
13 LENNOX CT
14 BRONTE CT
15 OAKLEY CT
16 STUART CT
17 CLYDE CT
18 LANCELOT HO
19 GUINEVERE HO

20 GALAHAD HO
21 KNIGHTS PL
22 WARWICK QUADRANT

A3
1 ALTON HO
2 SWALE HO
3 BOVEY HO
4 FRENCHES CT
5 PENRYN HO
6 NASH DR

7 LADBROKE CT
8 CONSERO CT
9 WARWICK HO
10 PEBWORTH CT
11 BARFIELD CT

5 SPEEDWELL HO
6 CAMPION HO

A4
1 RINGWOOD LODGE
2 DOWNS CT
3 LYNDALE CT
4 VICTORIA ALMSHOUSES

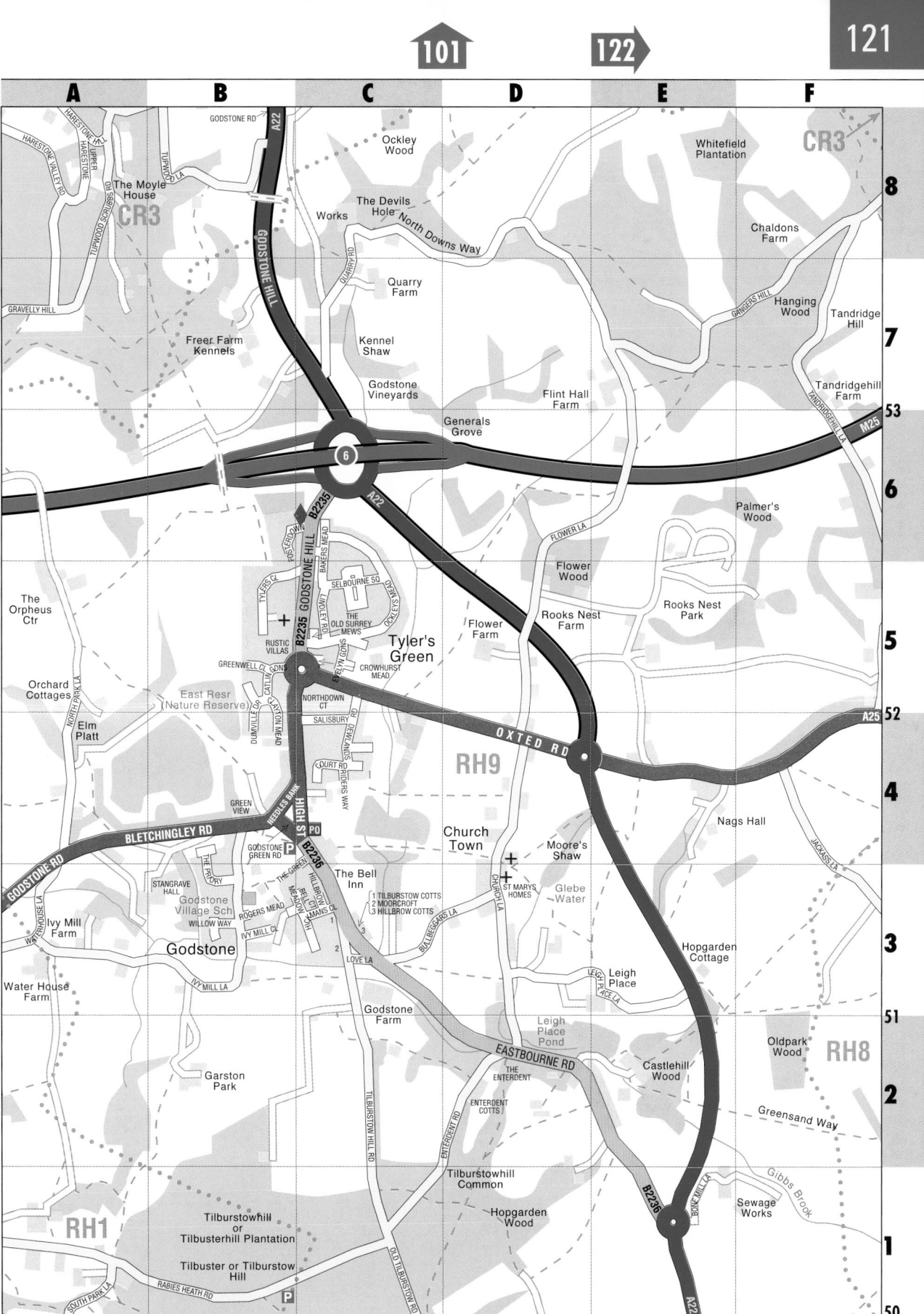

A B C D E F
8 7 6 5 4 3 2 1
53 52 51 50
37 38 39
M25
North Downs Way
South Hawke
CR3
Lodge Wood
Chalkpit Wood
Greensand Way
Five Acre Shaw
Downs Way Sch
St Mary's CE Jun Sch
Oxted Sch
Robins Grove Wood
Barrow Green Court
Laverock Sch
Cemy
The Abbeys
Barrow Green Farm
The Bogs
Oxted
Liby
The Mount
RH9
Priory Shaw
Towland Pond
L Ctr
A25
The Priory
WEST HILL
EAST HILL
Oxted
GODSTONE RD
A25 OXTED RD
CH
Mill Barn
Oxted Mill
RH8
Stonehall Farm
River Eden
The Birches
Hurst Green
Little Court Farm
Beechwood Hill
Oxted Place
Broadham Green
The Haycutter (PH)
Tanhouse Farm
Moor House Sch
Tandridge Court Farm
Tandridge
Perrysfield Farm
Greensand Way
Tandridge Park
Mill Pond
Barley Mow (PH)
Perrysfield
Reddings Wood
Coltsford Mill
St Peter's CE Inf Sch
Tandridge Hall
Stockett's Manor
Sewage Works
Southlands Wood
Rose Farm
Stockett's Manor

103

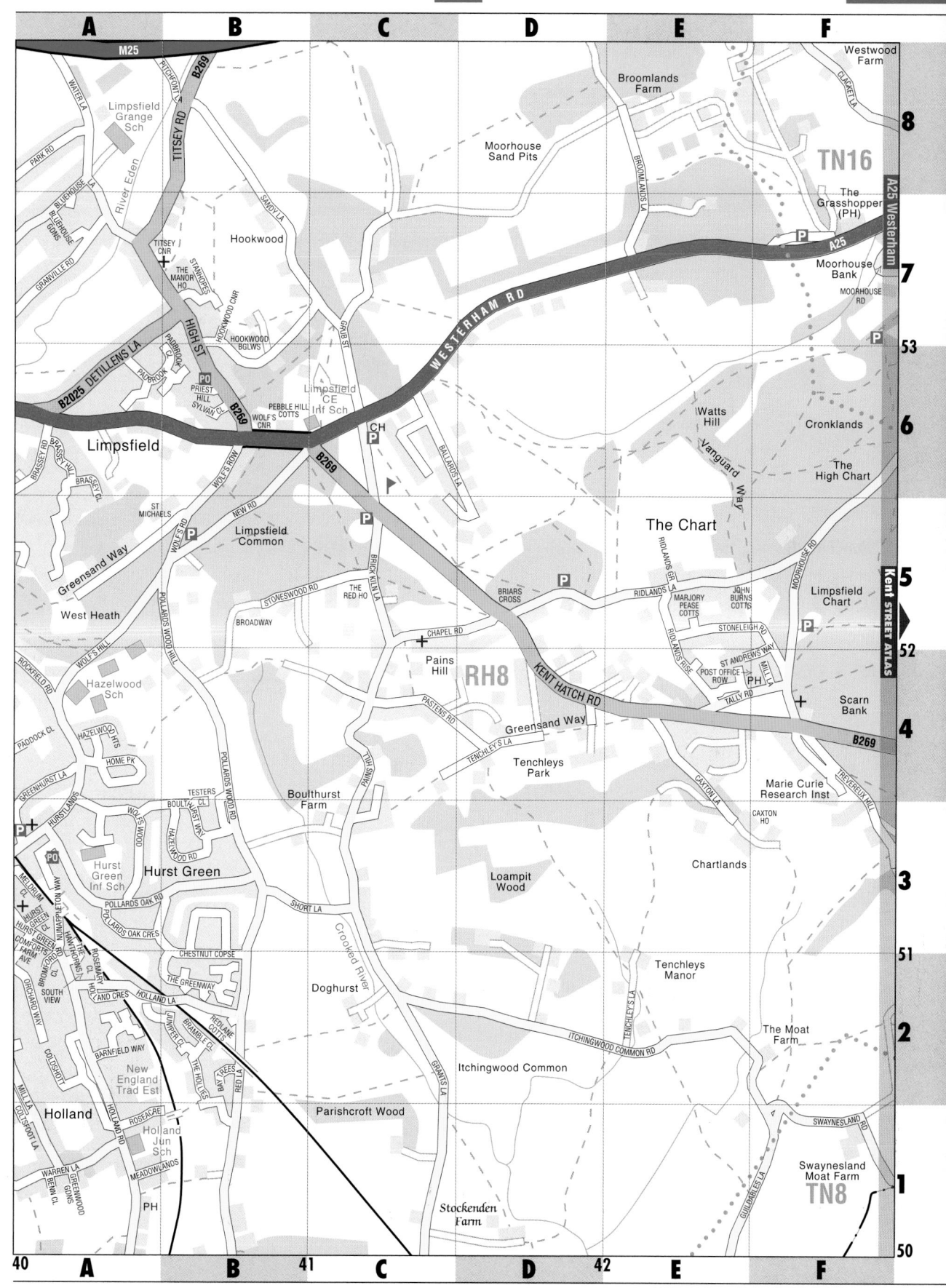

A
B
C
D
E
F
M25
B269
TITSEY RD
PITCHFONT LA
WATER LA
Limpsfield Grange Sch
River Eden
PARK RD
BLUEHOUSE LA
BLUEHOUSE GDNS
GRANVILLE RD
TITSEY CNR
THE MANOR HO
STANHOPES
HOOKWOOD CNR
HOOKWOOD BGLWS
Hookwood
SANDY LA
HIGH ST
B2025 DETILLENS LA
PADBROOK CL
PADBROOK
PO
PRIEST HILL
SYLVAN CL
PEBBLE HILL COTTS
WOLF'S CNR
Limpsfield CE Inf Sch
GRUB ST
Limpsfield
BRASSEY RD
BRASSEY HILL
BRASSEY CL
ST MICHAELS
WOLF'S ROW
NEW RD
Greensand Way
WOLF'S RD
Limpsfield Common
West Heath
WOLF'S HILL
POLLARDS WOOD HILL
Moorhouse Sand Pits
Broomlands Farm
BROOMLANDS LA
WESTERHAM RD
CH
BALLARDS LA
BRICK KILN LA
STONESWOOD RD
THE RED HO
BROADWAY
BRIARS CROSS
CHAPEL RD
Pains Hill
RH8
KENT HATCH RD
PASTENS RD
TENCHLEY'S LA
Tenchleys Park
Westwood Farm
CLACKET LA
TN16
The Grasshopper (PH)
A25
A25 Westerham
Moorhouse Bank
MOORHOUSE RD
Watts Hill
Vanguard Way
Cronklands
The High Chart
The Chart
RIDLANDS GR
RIDLANDS LA
MARJORY PEASE COTTS
JOHN BURNS COTTS
STONELEIGH RD
RIDLANDS RISE
ST ANDREWS WAY
POST OFFICE ROW
MILL LA
PH
TALLY RD
MOORHOUSE RD
Limpsfield Chart
Kent STREET ATLAS
Scarn Bank
Marie Curie Research Inst
TREVEREUX HILL
CAXTON LA
CAXTON HO
Chartlands
ROCKFIELD RD
Hazelwood Sch
PADDOCK CL
HAZELWOOD HTS
HOME PK
GREENHURST LA
HURSTLANDS
TESTERS CL
BOULTHURST WAY
WOLFS WOOD
HAZELWOOD RD
POLLARDS WOOD RD
Hurst Green Inf Sch
Hurst Green
MELDRUM CL
HURST GREEN CL
HURST GREEN RD
COMFORTS FARM AVE
NUNAPPLETON WAY
POLLARDS OAK RD
POLLARDS OAK CRES
HAWTHORNS
THE CL
ROSEMARY LA
BROMLEY RD
ORCHARD WAY
SOUTH VIEW
HOLLAND CRES
HOLLAND LA
CHESTNUT COPSE
THE GREENWAY
Boulthurst Farm
PAINS HILL
SHORT LA
Crooked River
Doghurst
Loampit Wood
Tenchleys Manor
TENCHLEY'S LA
ITCHINGWOOD COMMON RD
The Moat Farm
Itchingwood Common
REDLANE COTTS
JUNIPER CL
BRAMBLE CL
BARNFIELD WAY
COLDSHOTT
New England Trad Est
THE HOLLIES
BAY TREES
RED LA
GRANTS LA
Parishcroft Wood
Holland
MILL LA
COLTSFOOT LA
HOLLAND RD
ROSEACRE
Holland Jun Sch
WARREN LA
BENIN CL
GREENWOOD GDNS
GREENWOOD
MEADOWLANDS
PH
Stockenden Farm
SWAYNESLAND RD
Swaynesland Moat Farm
GUILDABLES LA
TN8
8
7
53
6
5
52
4
3
51
2
1
50
40
41
42

144

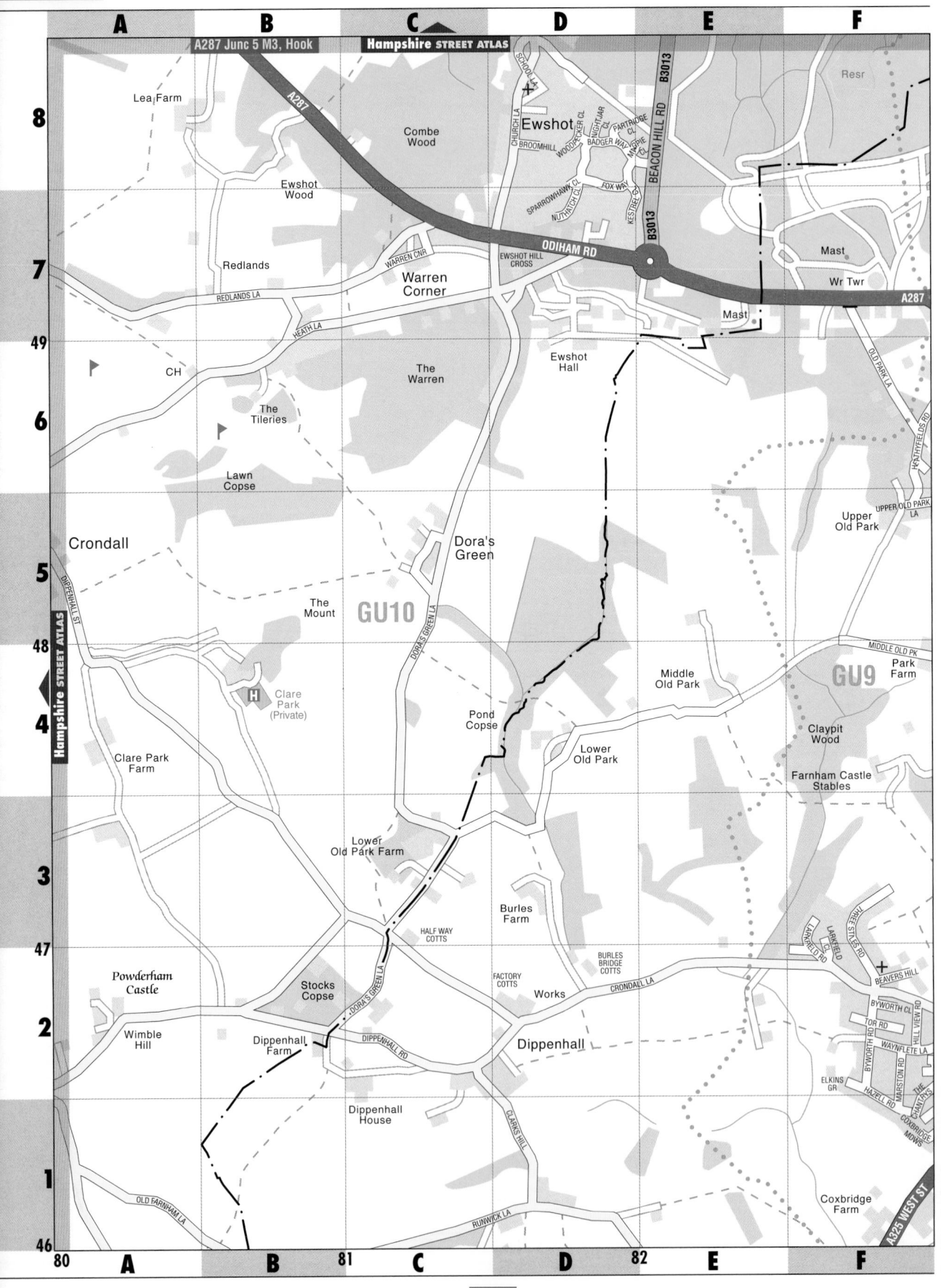

A287 Junc 5 M3, Hook

HAMPSHIRE STREET ATLAS

8

Lea Farm

Combe Wood

Ewshot Wood

Ewshot

CHURCH LA
BROOMHILL
WOODPECKER CL
NIGHTJAR CL
PARTRIDGE CL
BADGER WAY
MAGPIE
FOX WAY
KESTREL CL
SPARROWHAWK CL
NUTHATCH CL

B3013
BEACON HILL RD

Resr

Mast

7

Redlands

WARREN CNR

Warren Corner

REDLANDS LA

HEATH LA

ODIHAM RD

EWSHOT HILL CROSS

B3013

Mast

Wr Twr

A287

49

CH

The Warren

Ewshot Hall

Mast

Hampshire STREET ATLAS

6

The Tileries

Lawn Copse

OLD PARK LA

KNIGHTSFIELDS RD

UPPER OLD PARK LA

5

Crondall

Dora's Green

Upper Old Park

DIPPENHALL ST

The Mount

GU10

DORA'S GREEN LA

48

Hampshire STREET ATLAS

Clare Park (Private)

Middle Old Park

MIDDLE OLD PK

GU9

Park Farm

4

Clare Park Farm

Pond Copse

Lower Old Park

Claypit Wood

Farnham Castle Stables

3

Lower Old Park Farm

Burles Farm

THREE STILES RD

LARKFIELD

LARKFIELD RD

47

HALF WAY COTTS

BURLES BRIDGE COTTS

FACTORY COTTS

CRONDALL LA

Beavers Hill

BYWORTH CL

TOR RD

HILL VIEW RD

2

Powderham Castle

Wimble Hill

Stocks Copse

Dippenhall Farm

DORA'S GREEN LA

DIPPENHALL RD

Works

Dippenhall

WAYNFLETE LA

BYWORTH RD

MARSTON RD

HAZELL RD

ELKINS GR

THE CHANTERS

THE COXBRIDGE MEWS

1

Dippenhall House

CLARKS HILL

Coxbridge Farm

A325 WEST ST

OLD FARNHAM LA

RUNWICK LA

46

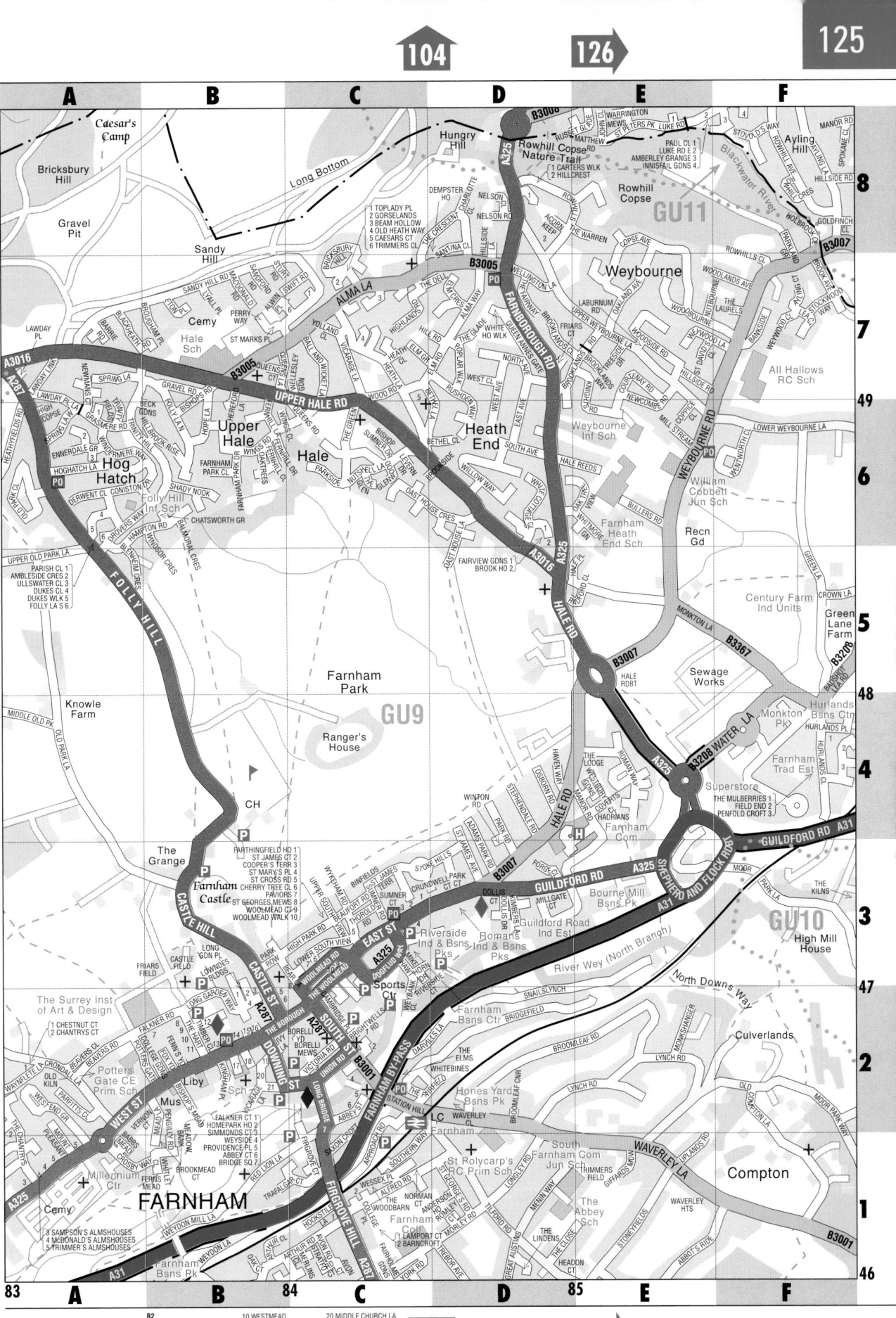

B2
1 LONG GARDEN WLK W
2 LONG GARDEN WLK E
3 LONG GARDEN MEWS
4 LONG GARDEN WLK
5 ST GEORGES YD
6 THE MEWS
7 AUSTIN'S COTTS
8 LOVETT HO
9 MOUNTBATTEN LODGE
10 WESTMEAD
11 COBBETTS MEWS
12 LION AND LAMB WAY
13 ARUNDELL PL
14 LION AND LAMB YD
15 HARTS YD
16 OLD KILN COURTYARD
17 CHURCH PAS
18 WEAVERS YD
19 UPPER CHURCH LA
20 MIDDLE CHURCH LA
21 LOWER CHURCH LA

125
105

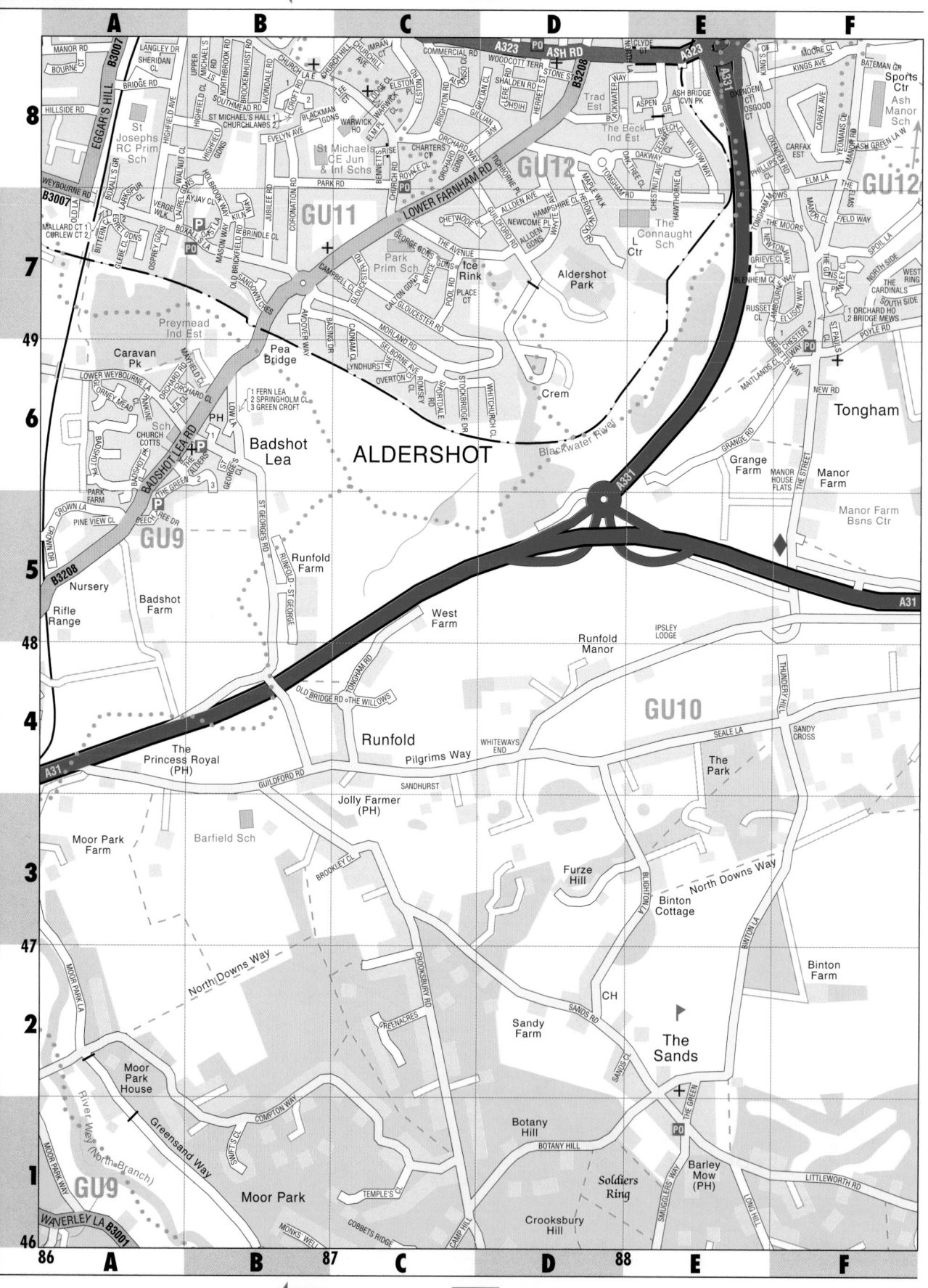

125
147

A   B   C   D   E   F

8
Ash Green

Bin Wood

Pound Farm

Week Wood

GU3

Ash Green Lane E

Ash Green Lane W

Pound Farm La

Green Lane W

GU12

Rickwood Farm

Green Lane E

Old Cross Tree Way

Pilgrims View

Farm Wk

Hazel Rd

North Side

East Ring

St Paul's CE Inf Sch

South Side

Poyle Farm

Poyle Rd

White La

Grubground Copse

7

49

Whitegrass Copse

Poyle Park

6

Inwood Farm

White Lane Farm

Hog's Back Hotel

A31

5

Nature Reserve

Wood La

Downlands

Great Down

Stony Hill

48

Manor Fields

Manor Farm Craft Ctr

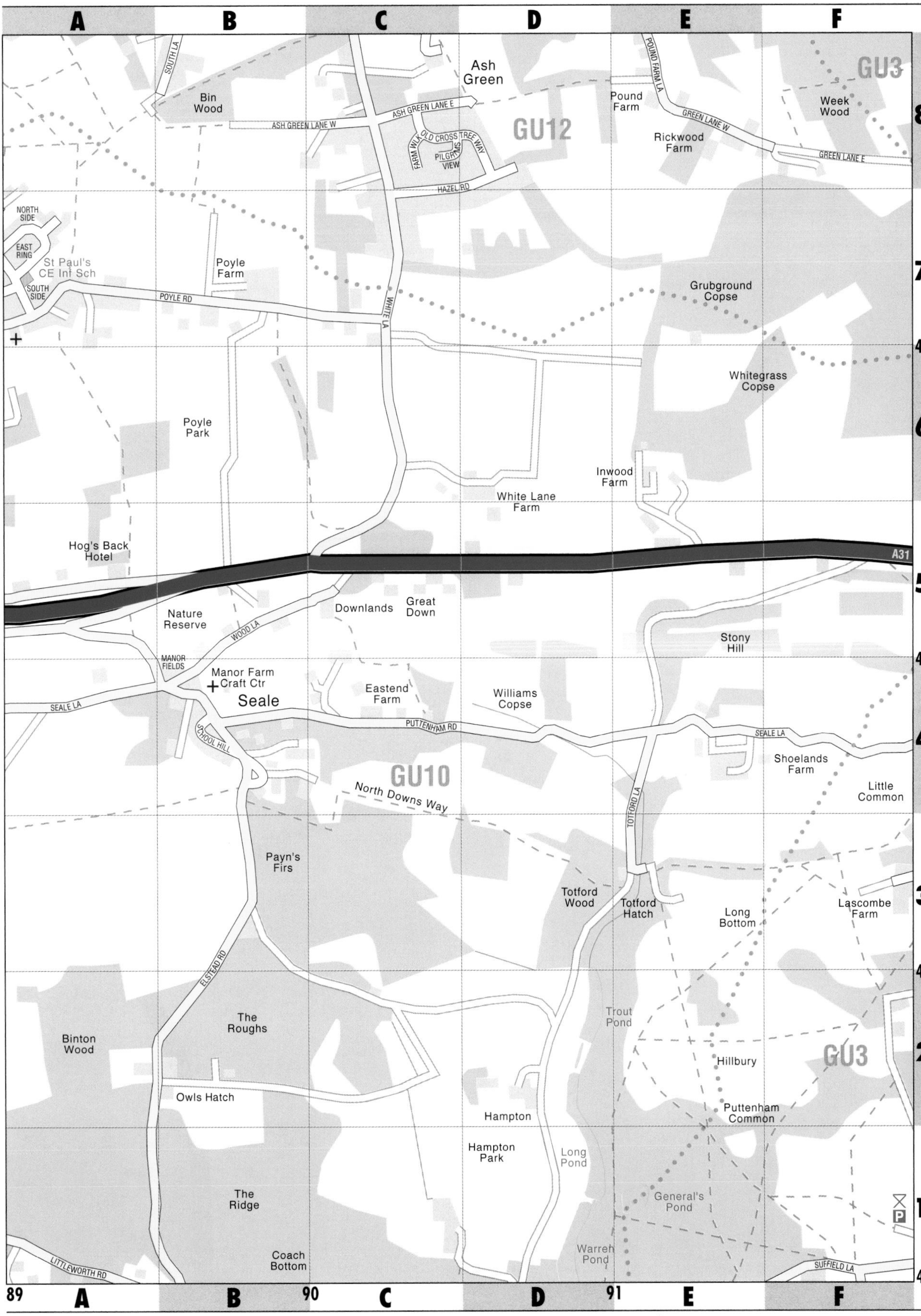

Seale

Seale La

Eastend Farm

Puttenham Rd

Williams Copse

Seale La

Shoelands Farm

Little Common

4

School Hill

GU10

North Downs Way

Totford La

Payn's Firs

Elstead Rd

Totford Wood

Totford Hatch

Long Bottom

Lascombe Farm

3

47

Trout Pond

The Roughs

Binton Wood

Hillbury

GU3

2

Owls Hatch

Puttenham Common

Hampton

Hampton Park

Long Pond

General's Pond

The Ridge

Warren Pond

Coach Bottom

Littleworth Rd

Suffield La

1

46

89   A   B   90   C   D   91   E   F

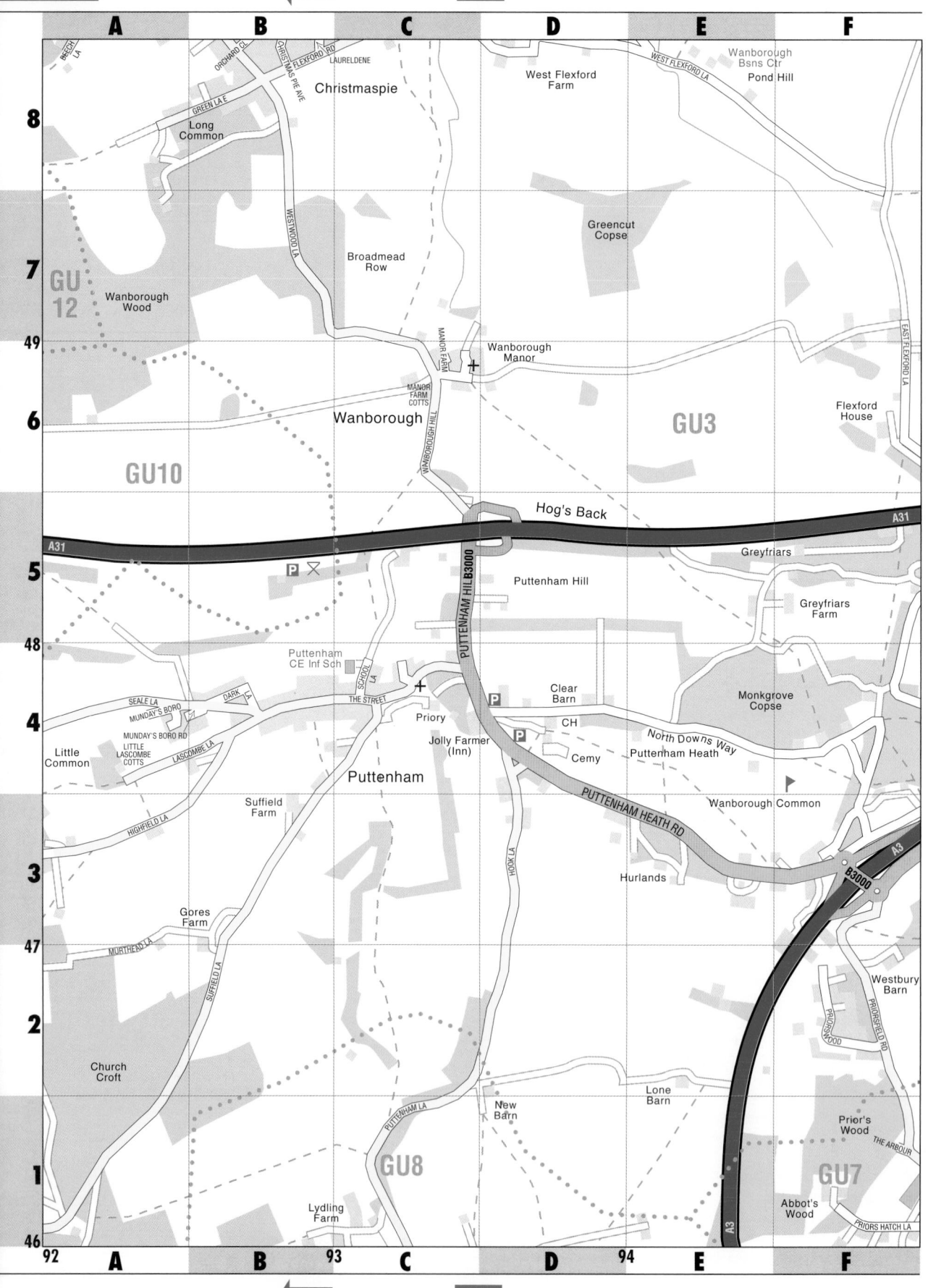

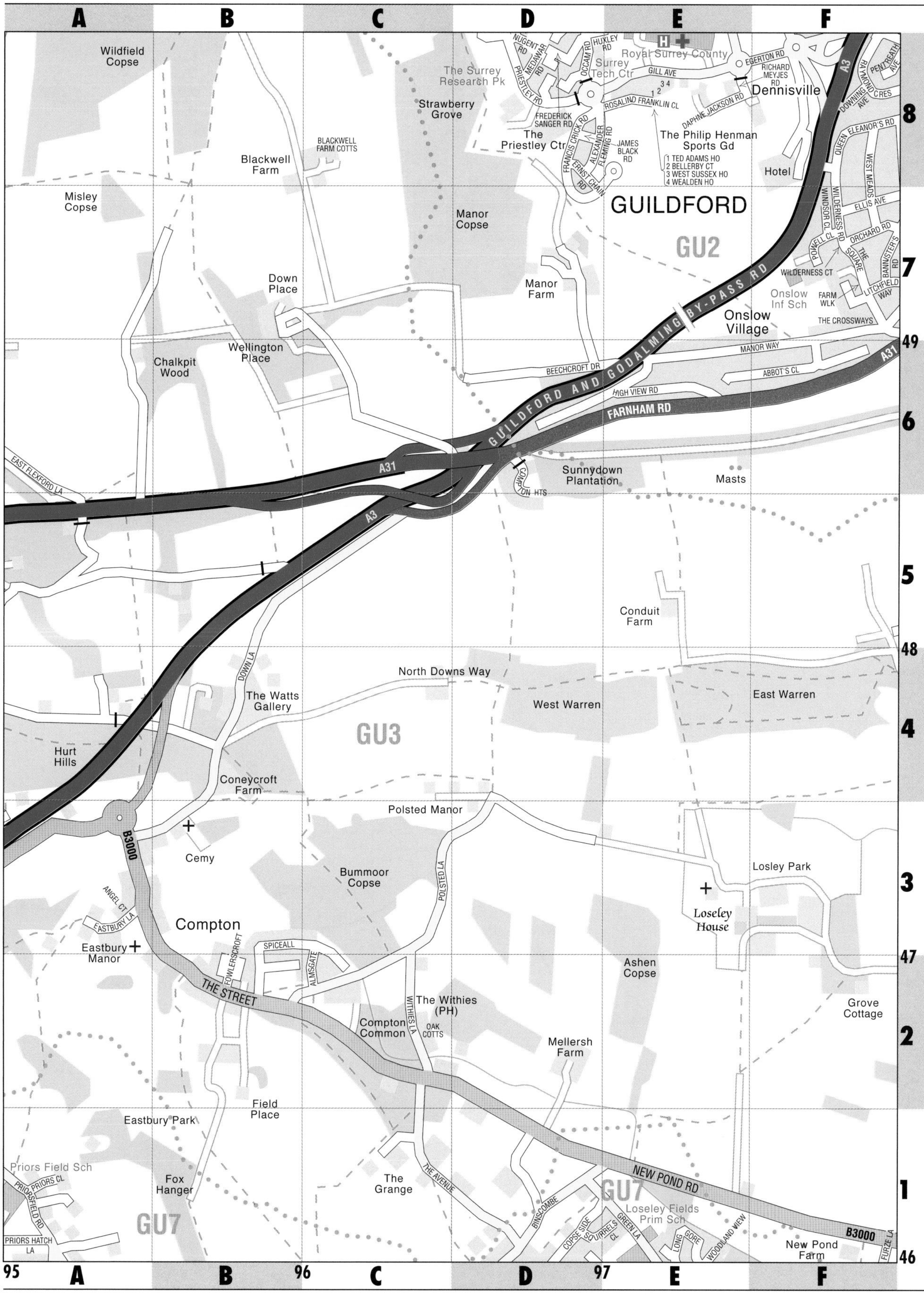

A B C D E F

8

7

49

6

5

48

4

47

3

2

1

46

95 A B 96 C D 97 E F

Wildfield Copse

Misley Copse

Blackwell Farm

BLACKWELL FARM COTTS

Strawberry Grove

The Surrey Research Pk

NUGENT RD
PRIESTLEY RD
MEDAWAR RD
OCCAM RD
HUXLEY CL
Surrey Tech Ctr
Royal Surrey County H +
GILL AVE
EGERTON RD
RICHARD MEYJES RD
RAYMOND AVE
PENTREATH AVE
DOWNING AVE

ROSALIND FRANKLIN CL
DAPHNE JACKSON RD
Dennisville

FREDERICK SANGER RD
The Priestley Ctr
ERNST CHAIN RD
ALEXANDER FLEMING RD
JAMES BLACK RD

The Philip Henman Sports Gd
1 TED ADAMS HO
2 BELLERBY CT
3 WEST SUSSEX HO
4 WEALDEN HO

Hotel

GUILDFORD

GU2

QUEEN ELEANOR'S RD
WEST MEADS AVE
ELLIS AVE
WINDSOR RD
WILDERNESS RD
ORCHARD RD
THE SQUARE
BANNISTERS RD

Manor Copse

Down Place

Manor Farm

WILDERNESS CT
POWELL CL
THE LITCHFIELD
FARM WLK
LITCHFIELD WAY
THE CROSSWAYS

Onslow Inf Sch

Onslow Village

Chalkpit Wood

Wellington Place

GUILDFORD AND GODALMING BY-PASS RD

BEECHCROFT DR
HIGH VIEW RD
MANOR WAY
ABBOT'S CL

A31

EAST FLEXFORD LA

A31

FARNHAM RD

A3

COMPTON HTS

Sunnydown Plantation

Masts

Conduit Farm

Down La

The Watts Gallery

North Downs Way

West Warren

East Warren

GU3

Hurt Hills

Coneycroft Farm

Polsted Manor

POLSTED LA

Loseley Park

B3000

Cemy

Bummoor Copse

Loseley House +

ANGEL CT
EASTBURY LA
Compton

Eastbury Manor +

SPICEALL
FOWLERSCROFT
ALMSGATE

THE STREET

Ashen Copse

Grove Cottage

The Withies (PH)

WITHIES LA
OAK COTTS

Compton Common

Mellersh Farm

47

Eastbury Park

Field Place

THE AVENUE

Fox Hanger

The Grange

NEW POND RD

GU7

Loseley Fields Prim Sch

PRIORS FIELD RD
Priors Field Sch
PRIORS CL

PRIORS HATCH LA

GU7

BINSCOMBE
COPSE SIDE
BURRELL'S CL
GREEN LA
LONG GORE
WOODLAND VIEW

B3000

New Pond Farm

FURZE LA

129

C8
1 MANGLES CT
2 BAYLISS CT
3 BEDFORD HO
4 FRIARY HO
5 THE FRIARY
6 THE MALL
7 Wey Ct
8 RECTORY CT
9 ABBOTS YD
10 AQUATICE
11 GATEWAY HO
12 FAYS PAS

109

D7
1 WHITE LION WLK
2 MILKHOUSE GATE
3 TRINITY CHURCHYARD

D8
1 THE COURTYARD

E8
1 WILLIAM SWAYNE HO
2 DENEHYRST CT
3 EASTGATE HO
4 PROSPECT CT
5 CHANTRY PL
6 HILLSIDE CT
7 SYCAMORE CT
8 HARVEY LODGE
9 TRINITY GATE

F8
1 FRESHBOROUGH CT
2 TELFORD CT
3 SHELDON CT
4 BEECH CT
5 GRAYLANDS CT
6 EDGEBOROUGH CT
7 COMPTON CT
8 GROSVENOR HO
9 ST LUKE'S SQ
10 KNIGHTSBRIDGE HO
11 CADOGAN HO
12 ALEXANDRA LODGE
13 LYNNE CT
14 CHESHAM MEWS
15 TYRELLS PL

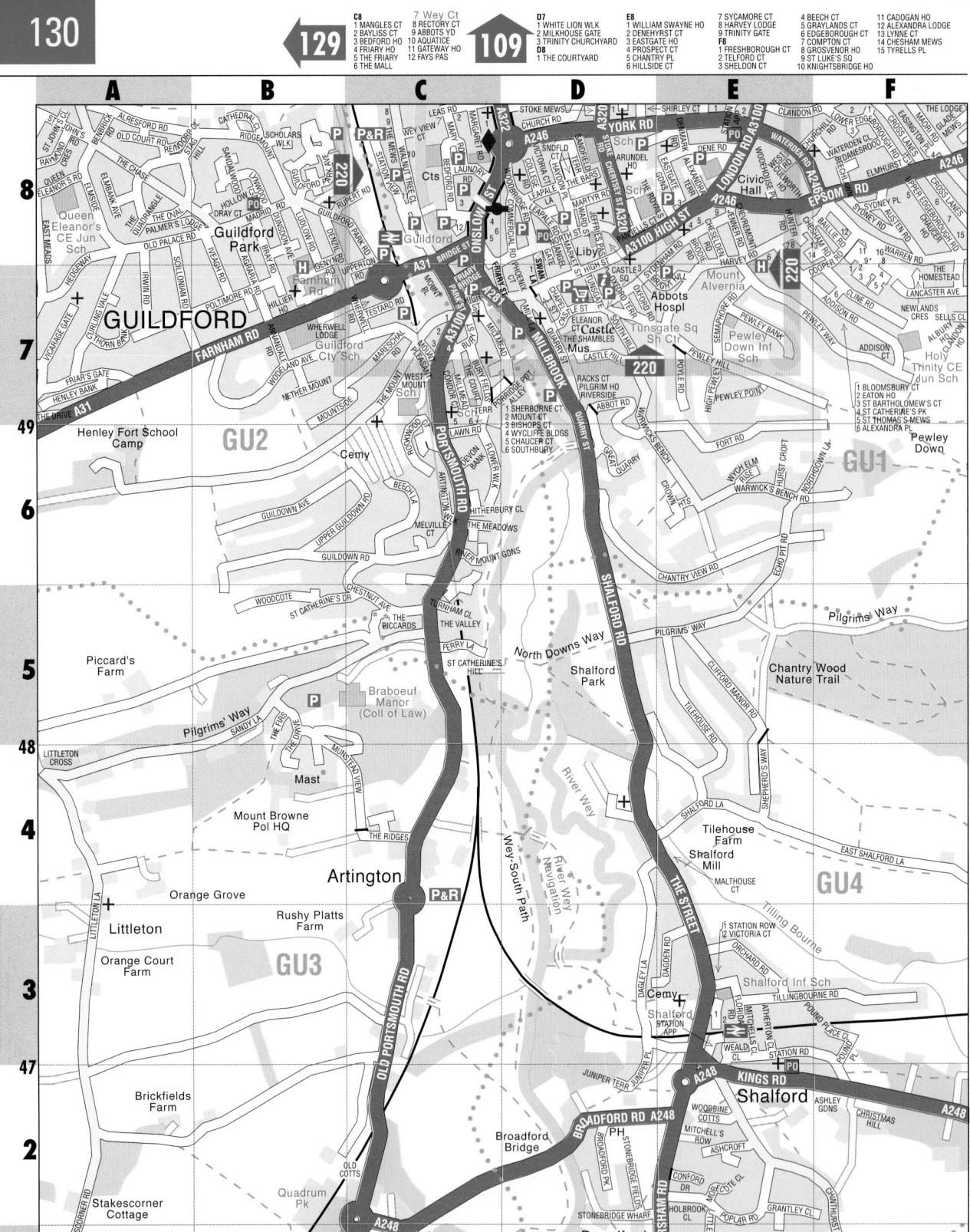

129

151

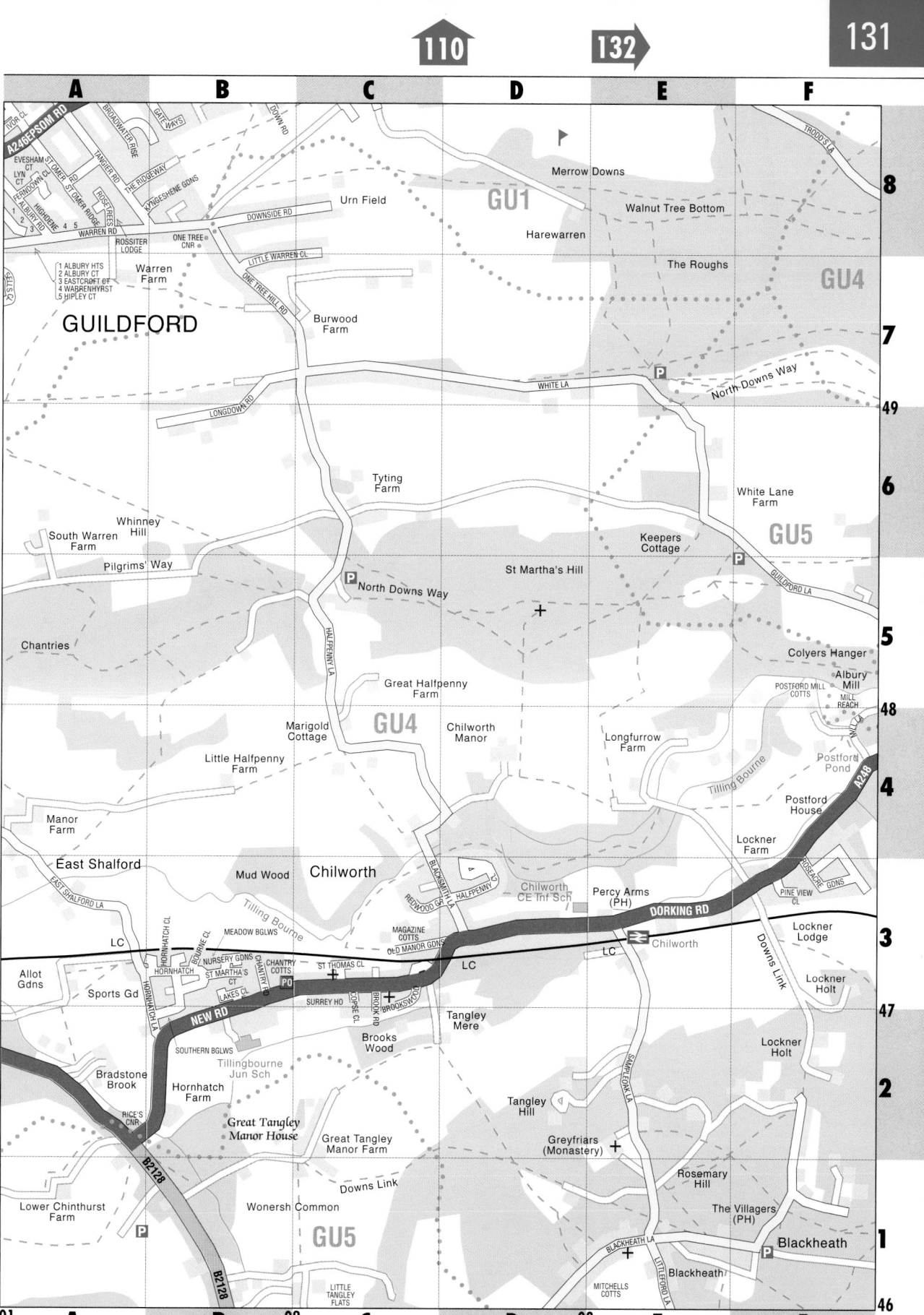
110
132
A
B
C
D
E
F
8
7
49
6
5
48
4
3
47
2
1
46
01
02
03
A246 EPSOM RD
Merrow Downs
Walnut Tree Bottom
Urn Field
GU1
Harewarren
The Roughs
GU4
Warren Farm
GUILDFORD
Burwood Farm
1 ALBURY HTS
2 ALBURY CT
3 EASTCROFT CT
4 WARRENHYRST
5 HIPLEY CT
ROSSITER LODGE
ONE TREE CNR
WARREN RD
DOWNSIDE RD
LITTLE WARREN CL
ONE TREE HILL RD
WHITE LA
North Downs Way
LONGDOWN RD
Tyting Farm
White Lane Farm
Whinney Hill
South Warren Farm
Keepers Cottage
GU5
Pilgrims' Way
St Martha's Hill
North Downs Way
GUILDFORD LA
Chantries
Colyers Hanger
Albury Mill
Great Halfpenny Farm
POSTFORD MILL COTTS
MILL REACH
Marigold Cottage
GU4
Chilworth Manor
Longfurrow Farm
Little Halfpenny Farm
Postford Pond
Tilling Bourne
Postford House
A248
Manor Farm
Lockner Farm
East Shalford
Mud Wood
Chilworth
Chilworth CE Inf Sch
Percy Arms (PH)
DORKING RD
Tilling Bourne
Lockner Lodge
Chilworth
Downs Link
Allot Gdns
Sports Gd
NEW RD
Tangley Mere
Lockner Holt
Brooks Wood
Lockner Holt
Bradstone Brook
Tillingbourne Jun Sch
Hornhatch Farm
Tangley Hill
Great Tangley Manor House
Great Tangley Manor Farm
Greyfriars (Monastery)
Rosemary Hill
Downs Link
Lower Chinthurst Farm
Wonersh Common
The Villagers (PH)
GU5
Blackheath
Blackheath
B2128
LITTLE TANGLEY FLATS
MITCHELLS COTTS
152
132

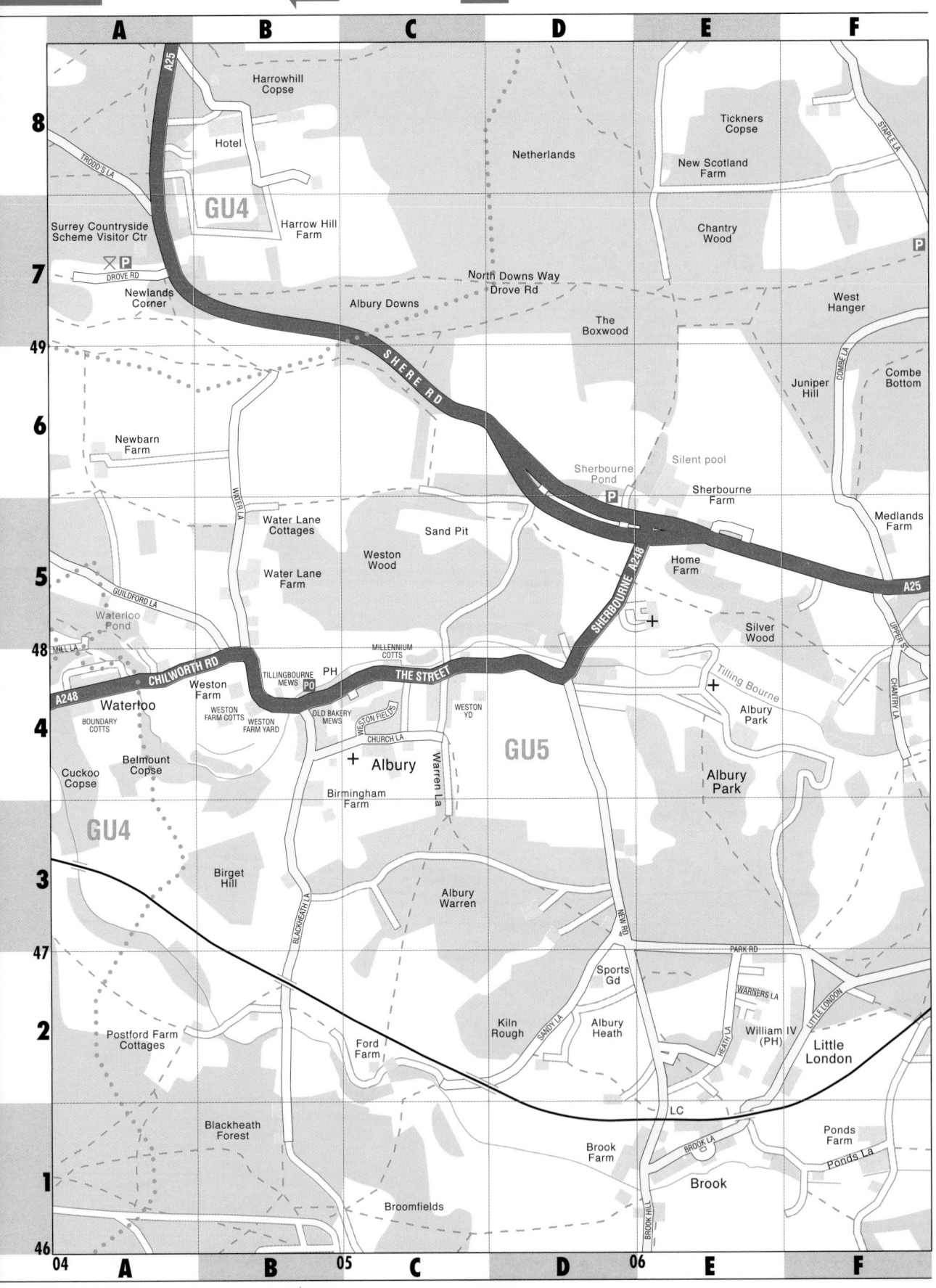

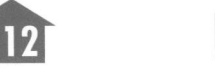

112
134

A
B
C
D
E
F
KT24
Staplelane Copse
FRANCIS CNR
COMBE LA
SHERE RD
GREEN DENE
Upper Common
West Hanger Nature Trail
STAPLE LA
COMBE LA
Netley Heath
North Downs Way
Gravelhill Gate
Drove Road
Great Kings Wood
Little Kings Wood
Hollister Farm
Colekitchen Hole
Hackhurst Downs
Colekitchen Farm
COLEKITCHEN LA
Netley Plantation
Netley Park
Hackhurst Downs
Pilgrim's Way
King's Holt
Netley House
Round Down
Kingswood Hanger
Manor House
LONDON LA
OLD DR
NETLEY CL
Churchfield Farm
Hackhurst Farm
Shere CE Inf Sch
SHERE RD
UPPER ST
GOMSHALL LA
MIDDLE ST
PO
Gomshall
ARCHERY PL
LEATHER LA
BEGGARS LA
Netley Farm
STATION RD
PO
Piney Copse
HACKHURST LA
RECTORY LA
LOWER ST
WILLOW WLK
ORCHARD RD
WELLERS CT
CHURCH LA
Shere
High House Farm
Gomshall
Gomshall Mill
DORKING RD
Hunters Moon Farm
RH5
SHERE LA
PILGRIMS WAY
THE SQUARE
CHURCH HILL
Mus
NEW RD
GRAVELPITS COTTS
QUEEN ST
GOOSE GN
Gomshall Marsh
Tilling Bourne
CRICKETTS HILL
THE SPINNING WLK
PILGRIMS CL
GU5
GRAVEL PITS LA
HIGH VIEW
FERN COTTS
Abinger Hammer Village Sch
PATHFIELDS
HEATHROW
MARSH VIEW
PO
TOWERHILL
Towerhill Farm
WONHAM WAY
Southbrook Farmhouse
GUILDFORD RD
A25
SANDY LA
LC
TOWER HILL RISE
B2126
FELDAY RD
Abinger Hammer
Towerhill Lane
Burrows Farm
BURROWS LA
HAMMERFIELD DR
P
P
SHERE CT
HOOK LA
PARKLANDS
BIRCHES LA
Parklands Farm
BURROWS CROSS
Engine Wood
Rad Lane
HOUND HOUSE RD
Hazelhatch
HORSHAM RD
Drydown Farm
Burrows Lea
LENTEN CL
WONHAM WAY
Hazel Brow
Home Farm
LAWBROOK LA
JESSIE'S HOLLOW
Burrows Cross House
PURSERS LA
RAD LA
RAD LA
B2126
Cotterells Farm
Lawbrook
LEE JESSIES LA
HOLLOW
BROADFIELD RD
CREST HILL
FULVENS
KNOBFIELD
ANNISDOWNE CL
HOE LA
Cotterell House
8
7
49
6
5
48
4
3
47
2
1
46
07
08
09

154
134

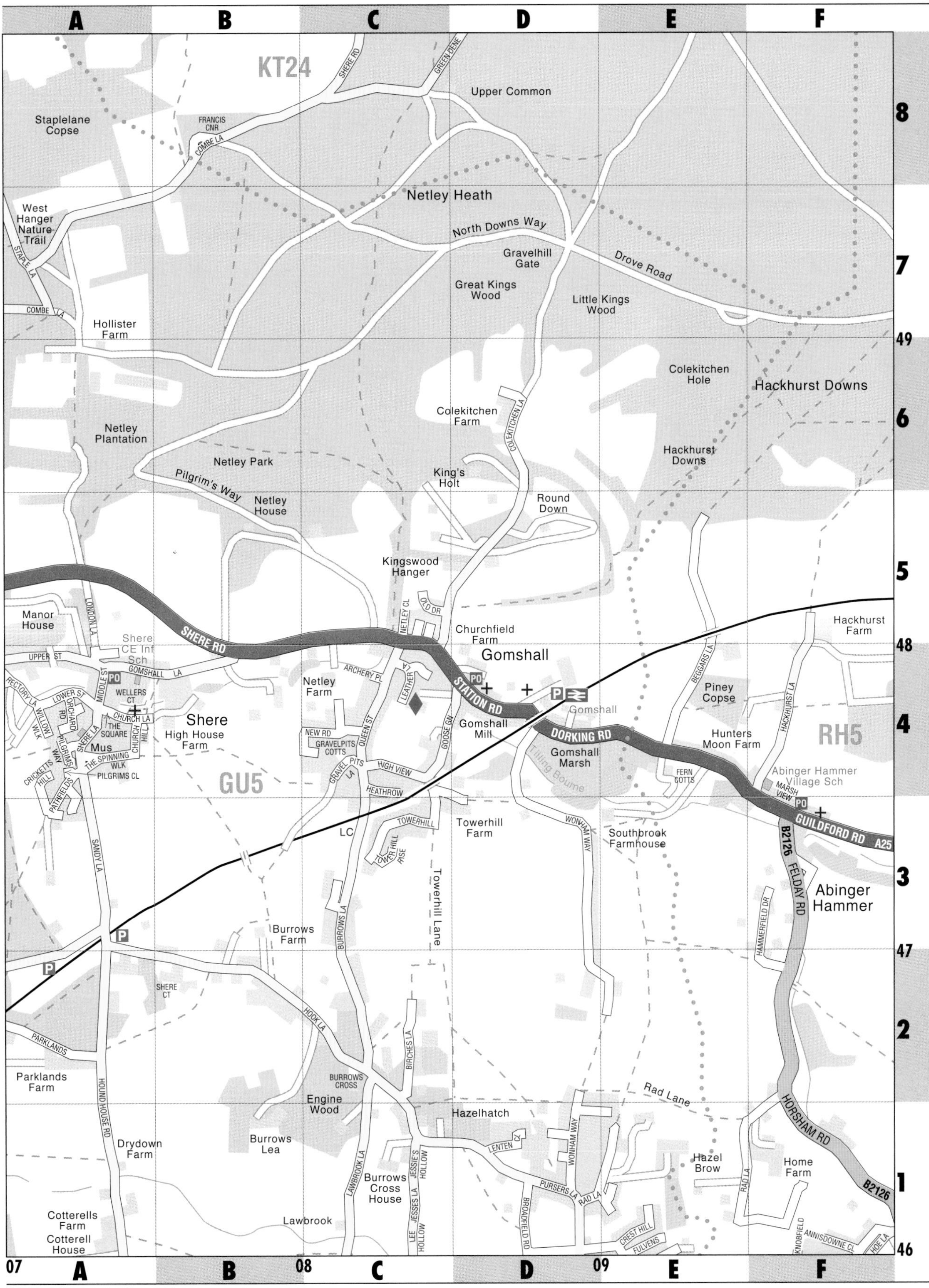

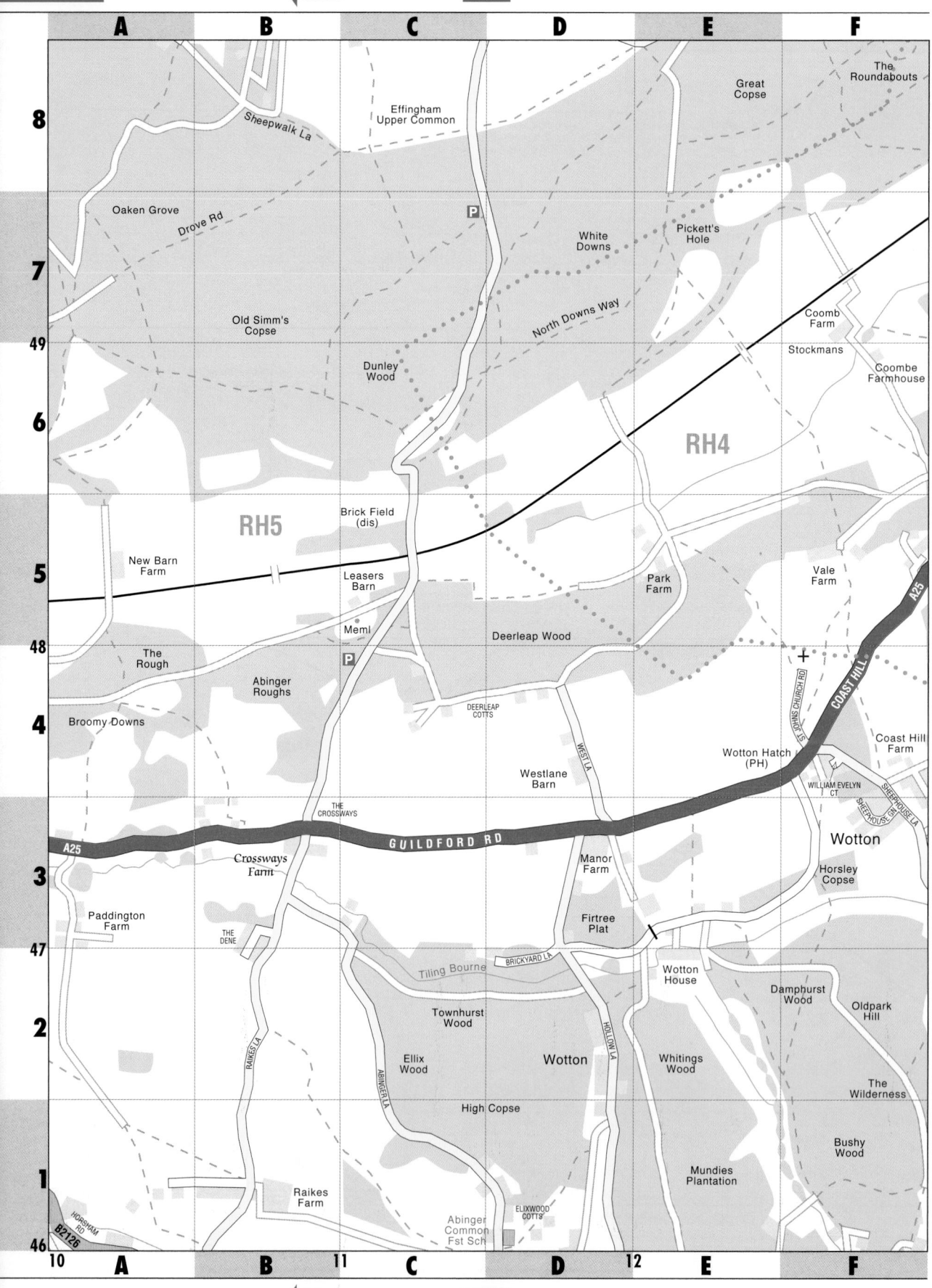

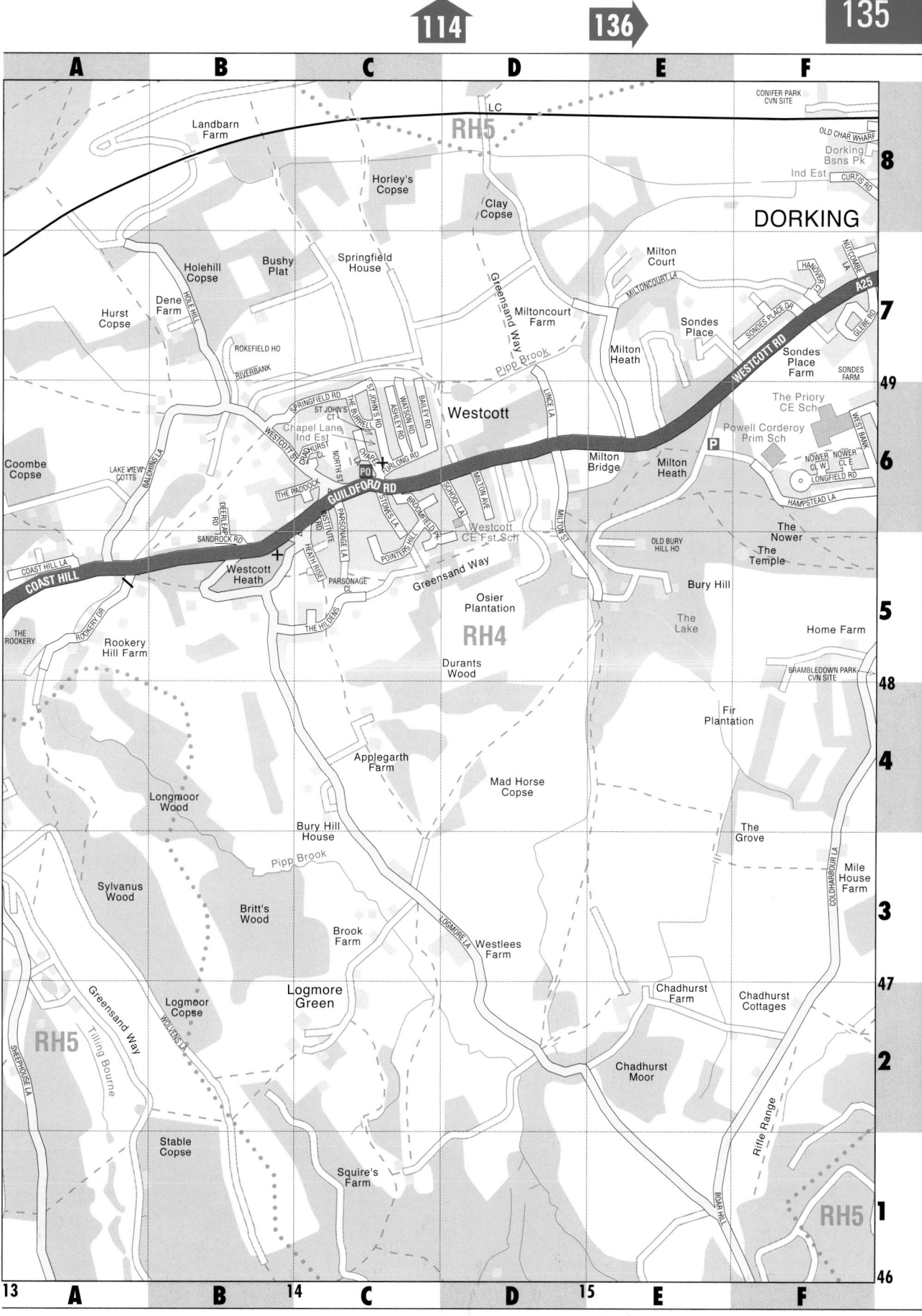

DORKING

RH5

RH4

RH5

RH5

Westcott

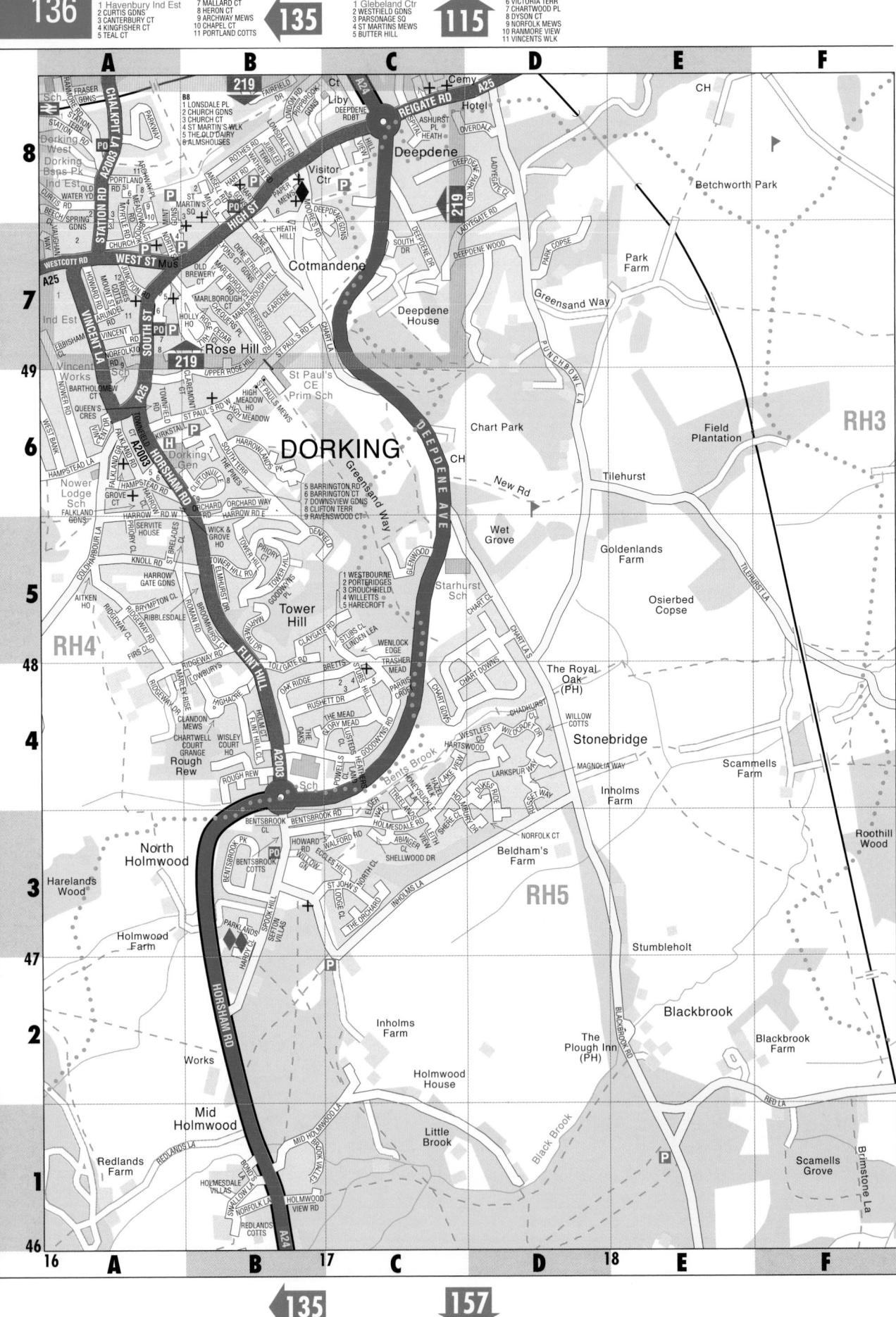

A8
1 Havenbury Ind Est
2 CURTIS GDNS
3 CANTERBURY CT
4 KINGFISHER CT
5 TEAL CT

6 WILLOW MEAD
7 MALLARD CT
8 HERON CT
9 ARCHWAY MEWS
10 CHAPEL CT
11 PORTLAND COTTS

A7
1 Glebeland Ctr
2 WESTFIELD GDNS
3 PARSONAGE SQ
4 ST MARTINS MEWS
5 BUTTER HILL

A7
6 VICTORIA TERR
7 CHARTWOOD PL
8 DYSON CT
9 NORFOLK MEWS
10 RANMORE VIEW
11 VINCENTS WLK

12 GILLIAMS HO

135
115

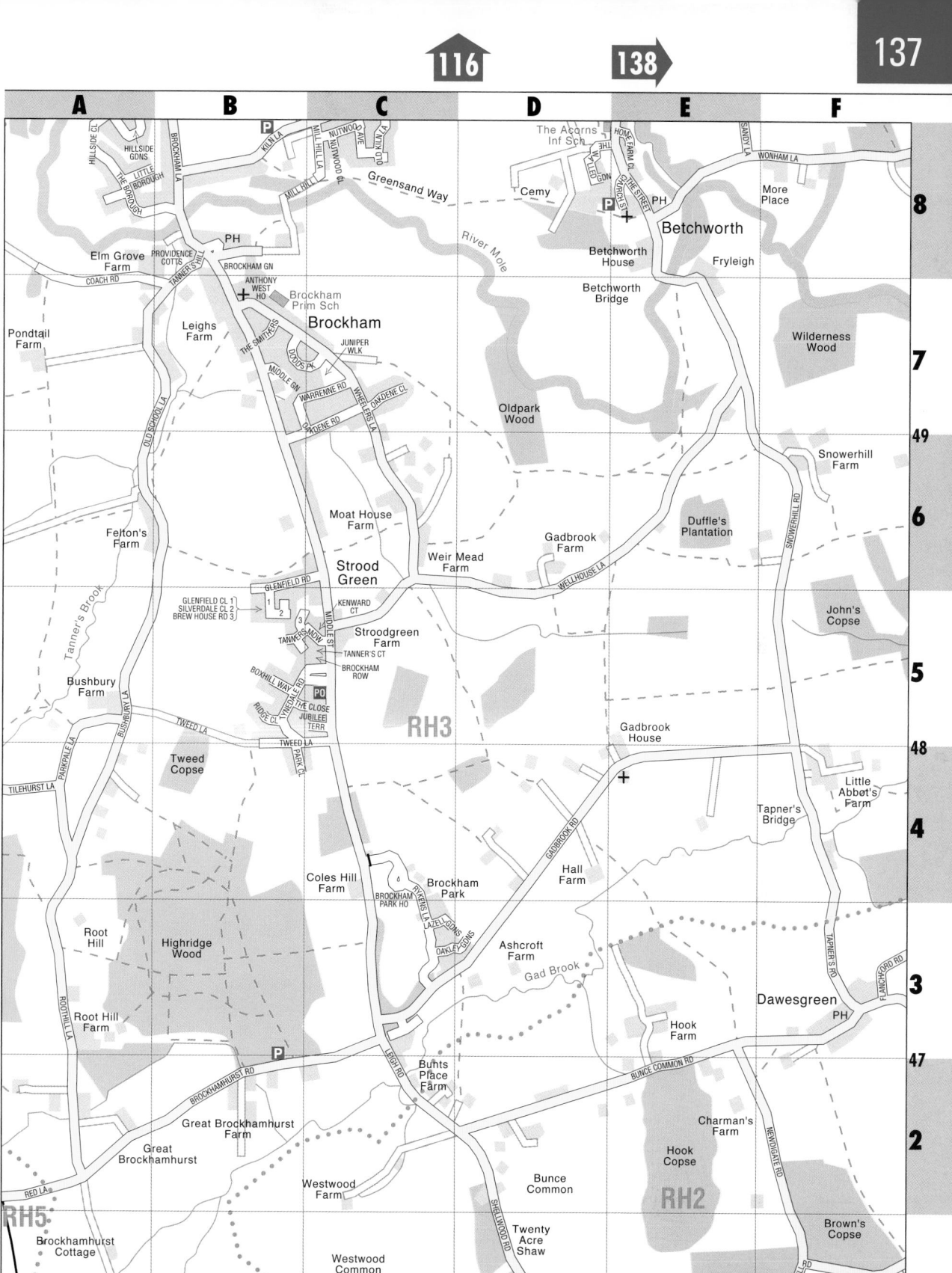

A   B   C   D   E   F

8

Hillside Gdns
HILLSIDE CL
Little Borough
THE BOROUGH
Brockham La
KILN LA
MILL HILL LA
NUTWOOD AVE
OLD KILN LA
The Acorns Inf Sch
HOME FARM LA
THE STREET
CROSS GDN
CARROLL ST
PH
WONHAM LA
SANDY LA
More Place

Greensand Way
Cemy
Betchworth House
Betchworth
Betchworth Bridge
Fryleigh

Elm Grove Farm
PROVIDENCE COTTS
TANNER'S HILL
PH
Brockham Gn
COACH RD
ANTHONY WEST HO
Brockham Prim Sch

Pondtail Farm
Leighs Farm
THE SMITHERS
Brockham
JUNIPER WLK
MIDDLE GN
WARRENNE RD
OAKDENE RD
WHEELERS LA
OAKDENE CL

7

River Mole
Oldpark Wood
Wilderness Wood
Snowerhill Farm

49

OLD SCHOOL LA
Felton's Farm
Moat House Farm
Strood Green
Weir Mead Farm
Gadbrook Farm
Duffle's Plantation

6

Tanner's Brook
GLENFIELD RD
GLENFIELD CL 1
SILVERDALE CL 2
BREW HOUSE RD 3
KENWARD CT
MIDDLE ST
TANNERS MDW
Stroodgreen Farm
TANNER'S CT
BROCKHAM ROW
WELLHOUSE LA
John's Copse

Bushbury Farm
BOXHILL WAY
RIDGE CL
TYNDALE RD
PO
THE CLOSE
JUBILEE TERR
Gadbrook House

5

BUSHBURY LA
PARKPALE LA
TWEED LA
PARK CL
TWEED LA
RH3

48

TILEHURST LA
Tweed Copse
Coles Hill Farm
BROCKHAM PARK HO
Brockham Park
RYKENS LA
LAZELL GDNS
OAKLEY GDNS
Hall Farm
GADBROOK RD
Tapner's Bridge
Little Abbot's Farm
TAPNER'S RD

4

Root Hill
Highridge Wood
Ashcroft Farm
Gad Brook
Dawesgreen
PH
FLANCHFORD RD

3

47

ROOTHILL LA
Root Hill Farm
BROCKHAMHURST RD
P
Bunts Place Farm
LEIGH RD
Hook Farm
BUNCE COMMON RD
NEWDIGATE RD

Great Brockhamhurst Farm
Great Brockhamhurst
RED LA
Westwood Farm
Charman's Farm
Hook Copse

2

RH5
Brockhamhurst Cottage
Westwood Common
SHELLWOOD RD
Bunce Common
Twenty Acre Shaw
RH2
CLAYHILL RD
Brown's Copse
Coombers Rough
Oak Farm

1

46

19   A   B   20   C   D   21   E   F

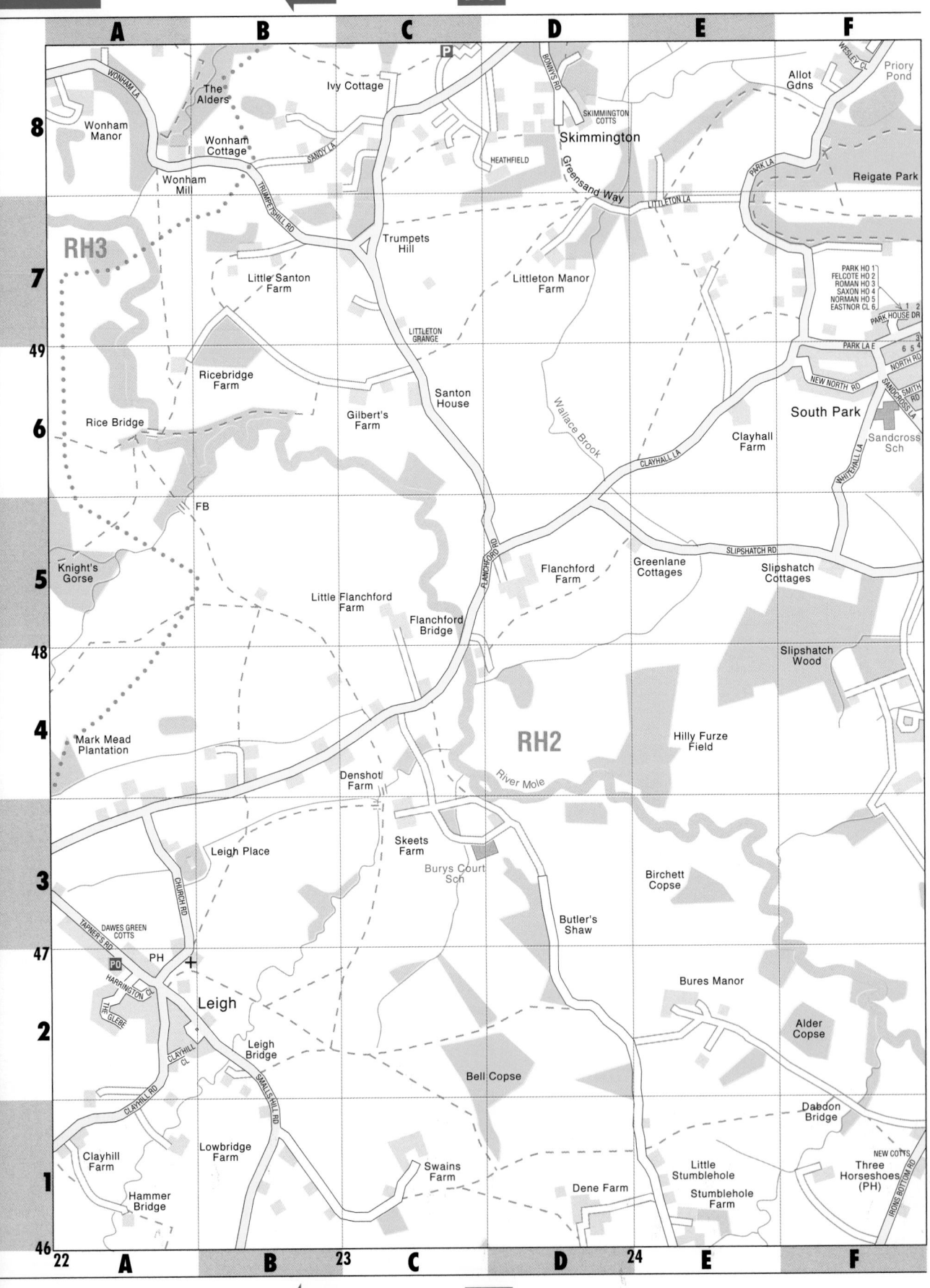
A
B
C
D
E
F
8
7
49
6
5
48
4
3
47
2
1
46
22
23
24
Wonham Manor
The Alders
Ivy Cottage
Wonham Cottage
Wonham Mill
Skimmington
SKIMMINGTON COTTS
HEATHFIELD
Greensand Way
LITTLETON LA
Allot Gdns
Priory Pond
Reigate Park
RH3
Trumpets Hill
Little Santon Farm
Littleton Manor Farm
LITTLETON GRANGE
Ricebridge Farm
Santon House
Gilbert's Farm
Rice Bridge
Wallace Brook
CLAYHALL LA
Clayhall Farm
South Park
Sandcross Sch
FB
Knight's Gorse
Flanchford Farm
Greenlane Cottages
SLIPSHATCH RD
Slipshatch Cottages
Little Flanchford Farm
Flanchford Bridge
FLANCHFORD RD
Slipshatch Wood
RH2
Hilly Furze Field
Mark Mead Plantation
River Mole
Denshot Farm
Leigh Place
Skeets Farm
Burys Court Sch
Birchett Copse
Butler's Shaw
DAWES GREEN COTTS
PH
PO
Leigh
Bures Manor
Alder Copse
Leigh Bridge
Bell Copse
Dabdon Bridge
Clayhill Farm
Lowbridge Farm
Swains Farm
Little Stumblehole
Stumblehole Farm
Dene Farm
Three Horseshoes (PH)
NEW COTTS
Hammer Bridge
WONHAM LA
SANDY LA
TRUMPETSHILL RD
BONNY'S RD
WESLEY CL
PARK LA
PARK HO 1
FELCOTE HO 2
ROMAN HO 3
SAXON HO 4
NORMAN HO 5
EASTNOR CL 6
PARK HOUSE DR
PARK LA E
NORTH RD
NEW NORTH RD
SANDCROSS LA
SMITH RD
WHITEHALL LA
CHURCH RD
TAPNER'S RD
HARRINGTON CL
THE GLEBE
CLAYHILL CL
CLAYHILL RD
SMALLS HILL RD
IRONS BOTTOM RD

118
140

F8
1 ROMANBY CT
2 THE IVIES
3 THE WILLOWS
4 GURNEY'S CL
5 WILTON HILL CT
6 BRIGHTON TERR
7 CORSTEN HOLLOW
8 THE GLEN
9 BAKERS CT
10 ARCHERS CT
11 ASPEN CT
12 BROOK TERR

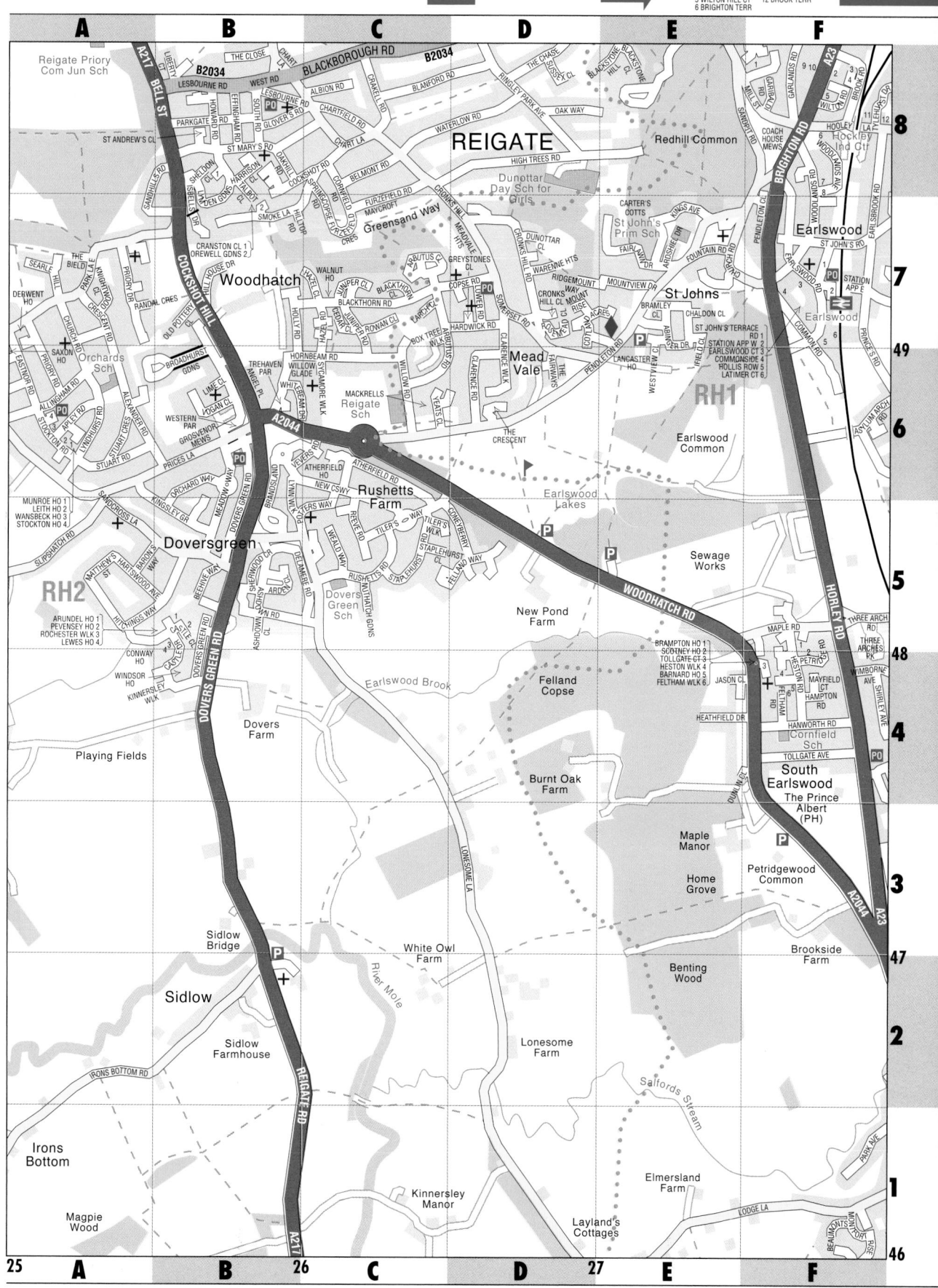

160
140

139
119

139
161

A B C D E F

8

7

49

6

5

48

4

3

RH9

47

2

1

46

31 A 32 B C 33 D E F

Coldharbour Farm
Lyttel Hall
Oakbarn Cottages
Crookedfield Shaw
Sandhills Farm
Nutfield Brook
OUTWOOD LA
Cucksey's Farm
Thepps Shaw
KINGS CROSS LA
Kennels Farm
The Park
Henhaw Farm
Poundhill Wood
Cinderhill Wood
COOPER'S HILL RD
Bransland Wood
RH1
Salfords Stream
Hope Farm
Lawn Hill
CRAB HILL LA
Burstow Park Farm
Spring Field Wood
Lodge Farm
Brownshill Shaw
PRINCE OF WALES RD
BROWN'S HILL
Harewood House
Stone House Farm
Harewood Home Farm
Shepheard's Hurst
BRICKFIELD RD
Cobbler's Corner
OUTWOOD LA
GREEN LA
Dog & Duck (PH)
Outwood Common
Greensand Way
M23

141
121

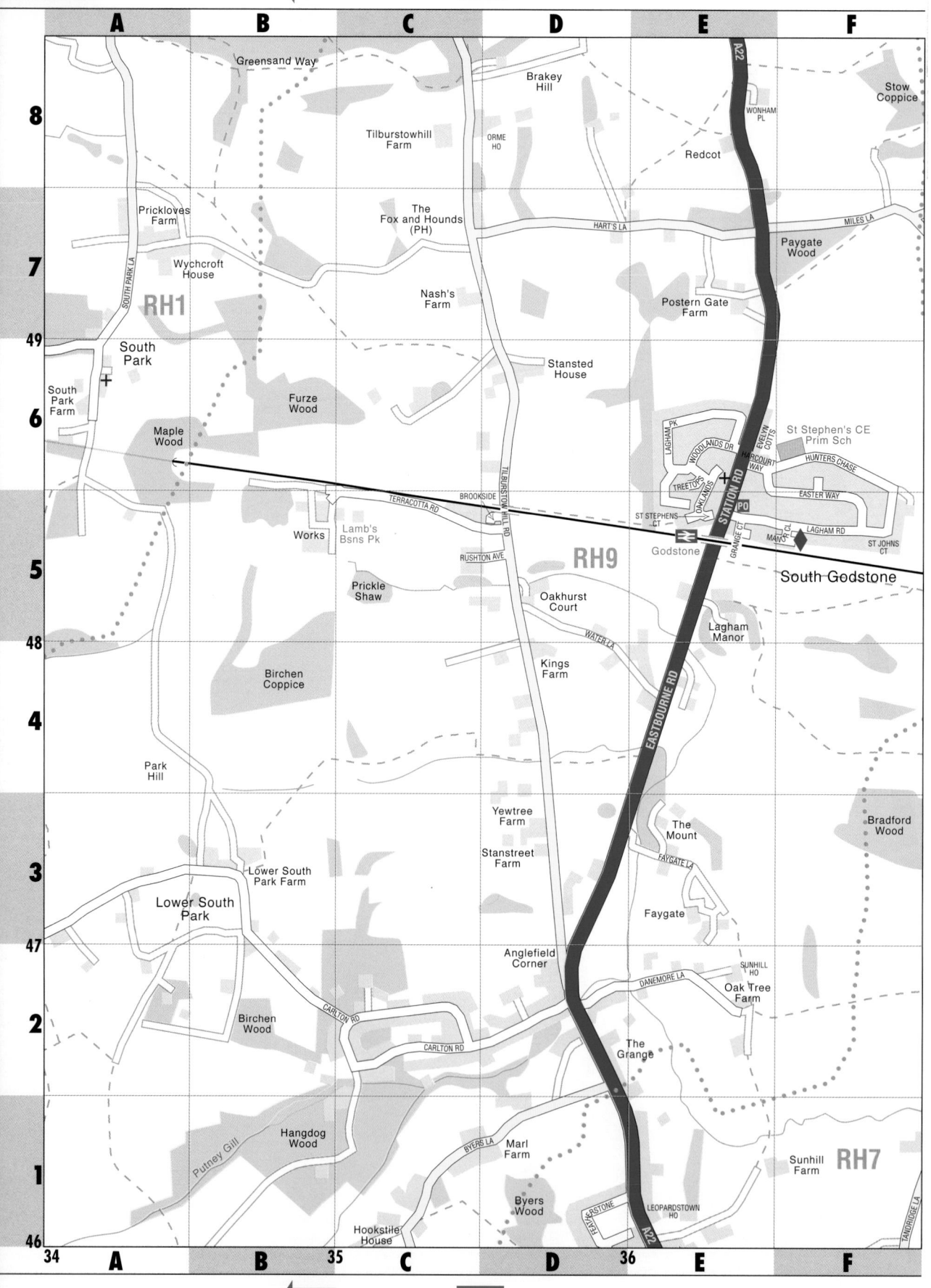

122
144

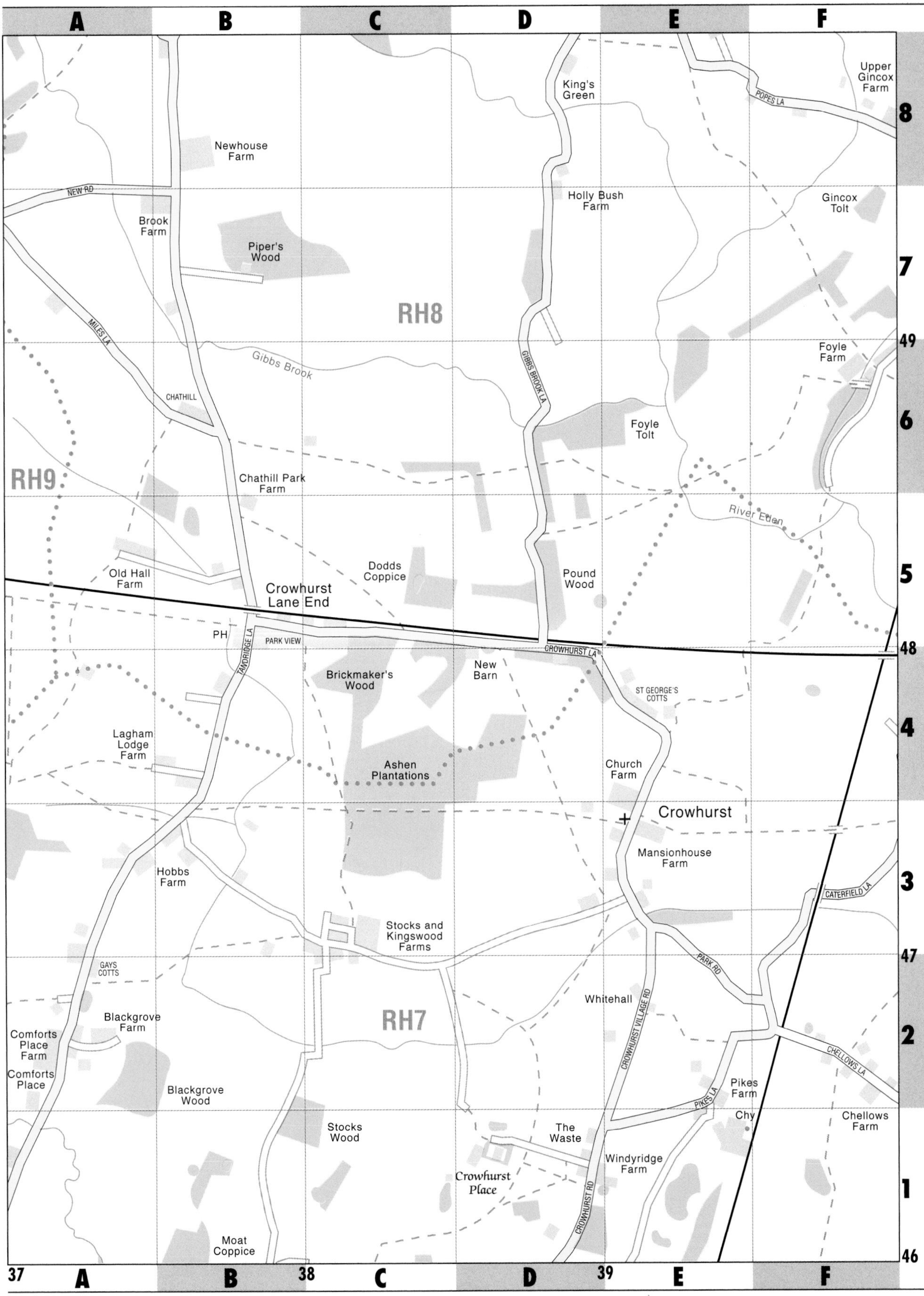
A
B
C
D
E
F
King's Green
Upper Gincox Farm
POPES LA
8
Newhouse Farm
NEW RD
Holly Bush Farm
Gincox Tolt
Brook Farm
Piper's Wood
7
RH8
MILES LA
49
Foyle Farm
Gibbs Brook
GIBBS BROOK LA
CHATHILL
6
Foyle Tolt
RH9
Chathill Park Farm
River Eden
Dodds Coppice
Old Hall Farm
Pound Wood
5
Crowhurst Lane End
PH
PARK VIEW
TANDRIDGE LA
CROWHURST LA
48
New Barn
Brickmaker's Wood
ST GEORGE'S COTTS
Lagham Lodge Farm
4
Ashen Plantations
Church Farm
Crowhurst
Mansionhouse Farm
Hobbs Farm
3
CATERFIELD LA
Stocks and Kingswood Farms
GAYS COTTS
PARK RD
47
Whitehall
CROWHURST VILLAGE RD
RH7
Blackgrove Farm
Comforts Place Farm
2
CHELLOWS LA
Comforts Place
Blackgrove Wood
Pikes Farm
PIKES LA
Chy
Chellows Farm
Stocks Wood
The Waste
Windyridge Farm
Crowhurst Place
CROWHURST RD
1
Moat Coppice
46
37
38
39

164
144

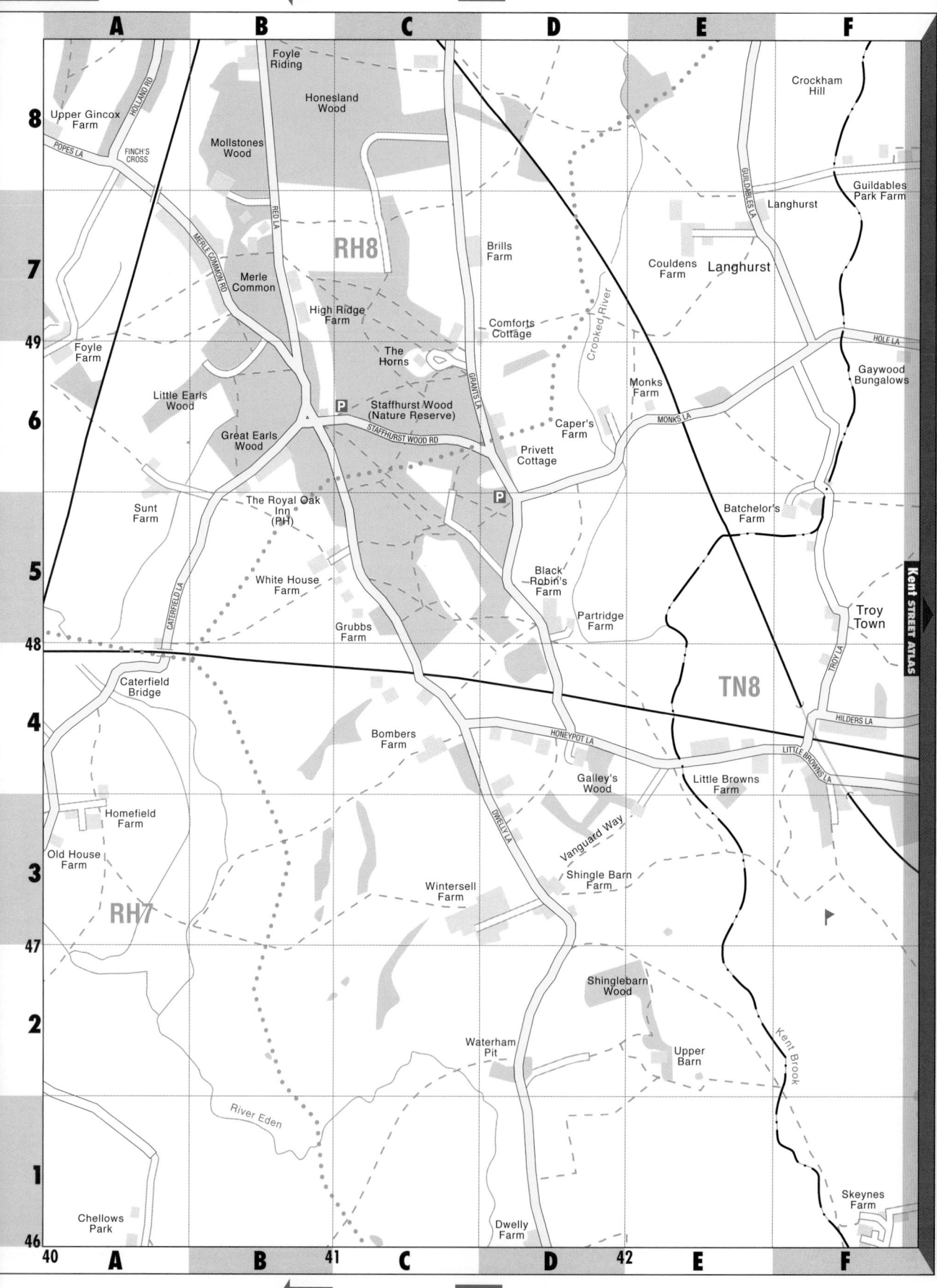

124
146

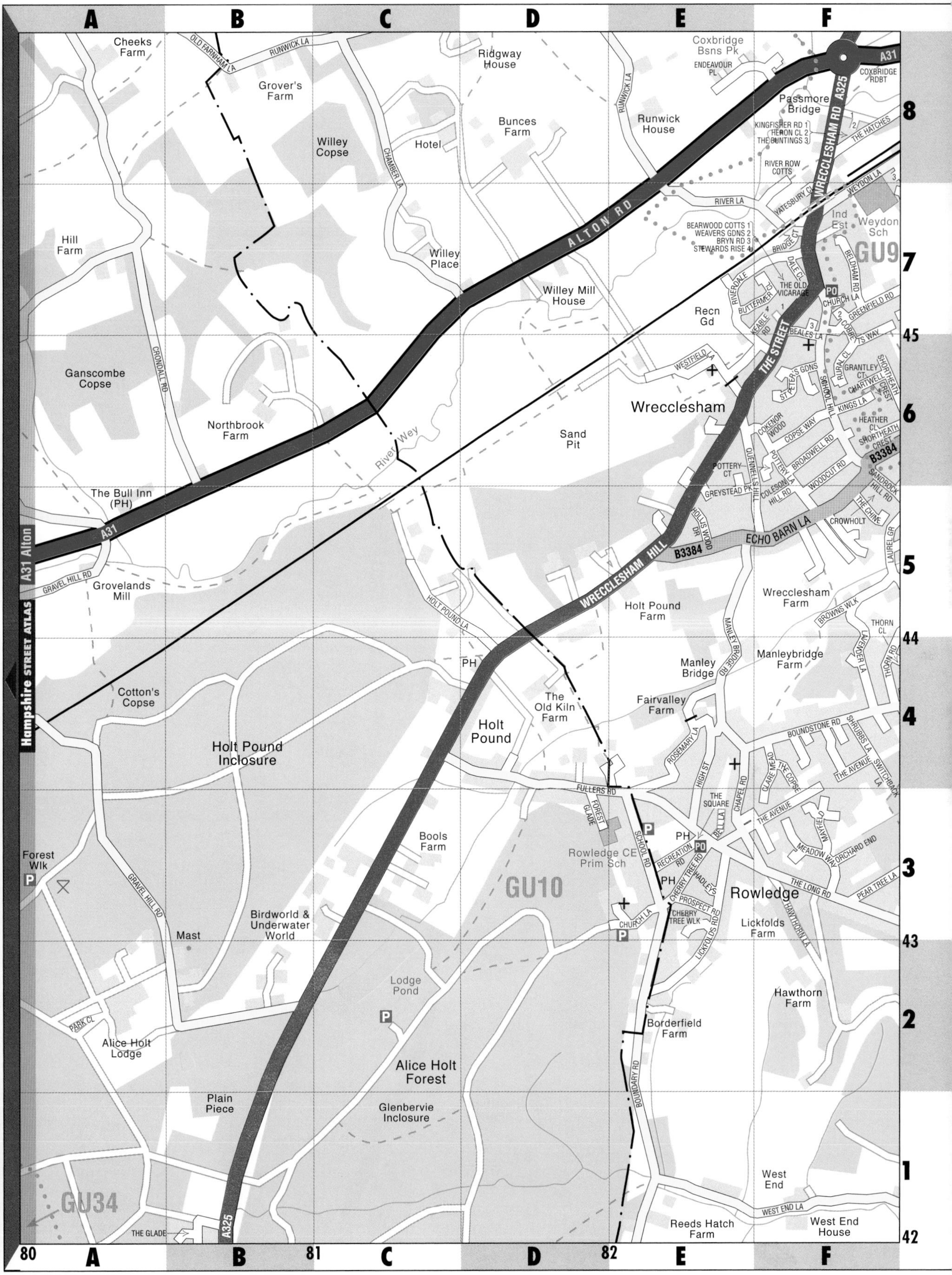
A
B
C
D
E
F
Cheeks Farm
OLD FARNHAM LA
RUNWICK LA
Grover's Farm
Ridgway House
Coxbridge Bsns Pk
ENDEAVOUR PL
A31
COXBRIDGE RDBT
Bunces Farm
RUNWICK LA
Runwick House
Passmore Bridge
A325
WRECCLESHAM RD
Willey Copse
Hotel
CHAMBER LA
KINGFISHER RD 1
HERON CL 2
THE BUNTINGS 3
THE HATCHES
RIVER ROW COTTS
WEYDON LA
RIVER LA
YATESBURY CL
Ind Est
Weydon Sch
ALTON RD
Hill Farm
BEARWOOD COTTS 1
WEAVERS GDNS 2
BRYN RD 3
STEWARDS RISE 4
BRIDGE CT
GU9
Willey Place
Willey Mill House
RIVERDALE
DALE CL
THE OLD VICARAGE
BUTTERMER
PO
CHURCH LA
BELDHAM RD
GREENFIELD RD
Recn Gd
KEABLE RD
BEALES LA
COBBETTS WAY
Ganscombe Copse
CRONDALL RD
WESTFIELD LA
THE STREET
RURAL CL
GRANTLEY CT
CHARTWELL
SHORTHEATH CREST
ST PETERS GDNS
SCHOOL HILL
KINGS LA
Wrecclesham
Northbrook Farm
River Wey
Sand Pit
COKENOR WOOD
COPSE WAY
HEATHER CL
SHORTHEATH CREST
BROADWELL RD
POTTERY LA
QUENNELLS HILL
POTTERY CT
WOODCUT RD
B3384
SANDROCK HILL RD
The Bull Inn (PH)
GREYSTEAD PK
COLESON HILL RD
THE CHINE
HOLLIS WOOD DR
CROWHOLT
ECHO BARN LA
LAUREL GR
A31
A31 Alton
GRAVEL HILL RD
Grovelands Mill
B3384
WRECCLESHAM HILL
Wrecclesham Farm
HOLT POUND LA
Holt Pound Farm
BROWNS WLK
THORN CL
MANLEY BRIDGE RD
LAVENDER LA
THORN RD
PH
Manley Bridge
Manleybridge Farm
Cotton's Copse
The Old Kiln Farm
Fairvalley Farm
Holt Pound
BOUNDSTONE RD
SHRUBBS LA
Holt Pound Inclosure
ROSEMARY LA
HIGH ST
CLARE MEAD
THE COPSE
THE AVENUE
SWITCHBACK LA
FULLERS RD
FOREST GLADE
THE SQUARE
CHAPEL RD
THE AVENUE
MAYFIELD
Bools Farm
SCHOOL RD
P
PH
BELLLA
Forest Wlk
P
Rowledge CE Prim Sch
RECREATION RD
PO
MEADOW WAY
ORCHARD END
GRAVEL HILL RD
GU10
CHERRY TREE RD
PH
HADLEYS
THE LONG RD
PEAR TREE LA
Rowledge
PROSPECT RD
CHERRY TREE WLK
Birdworld & Underwater World
CHURCH LA
Lickfolds Farm
Mast
P
LICKFOLDS RD
HAWTHORN LA
Lodge Pond
Hawthorn Farm
P
PARK CL
Borderfield Farm
Alice Holt Lodge
Alice Holt Forest
BOUNDARY RD
Plain Piece
Glenbervie Inclosure
West End
GU34
WEST END LA
A325
THE GLADE
Reeds Hatch Farm
West End House
8
7
45
6
5
44
4
3
43
2
1
42
80
81
82
Hampshire STREET ATLAS

166
146

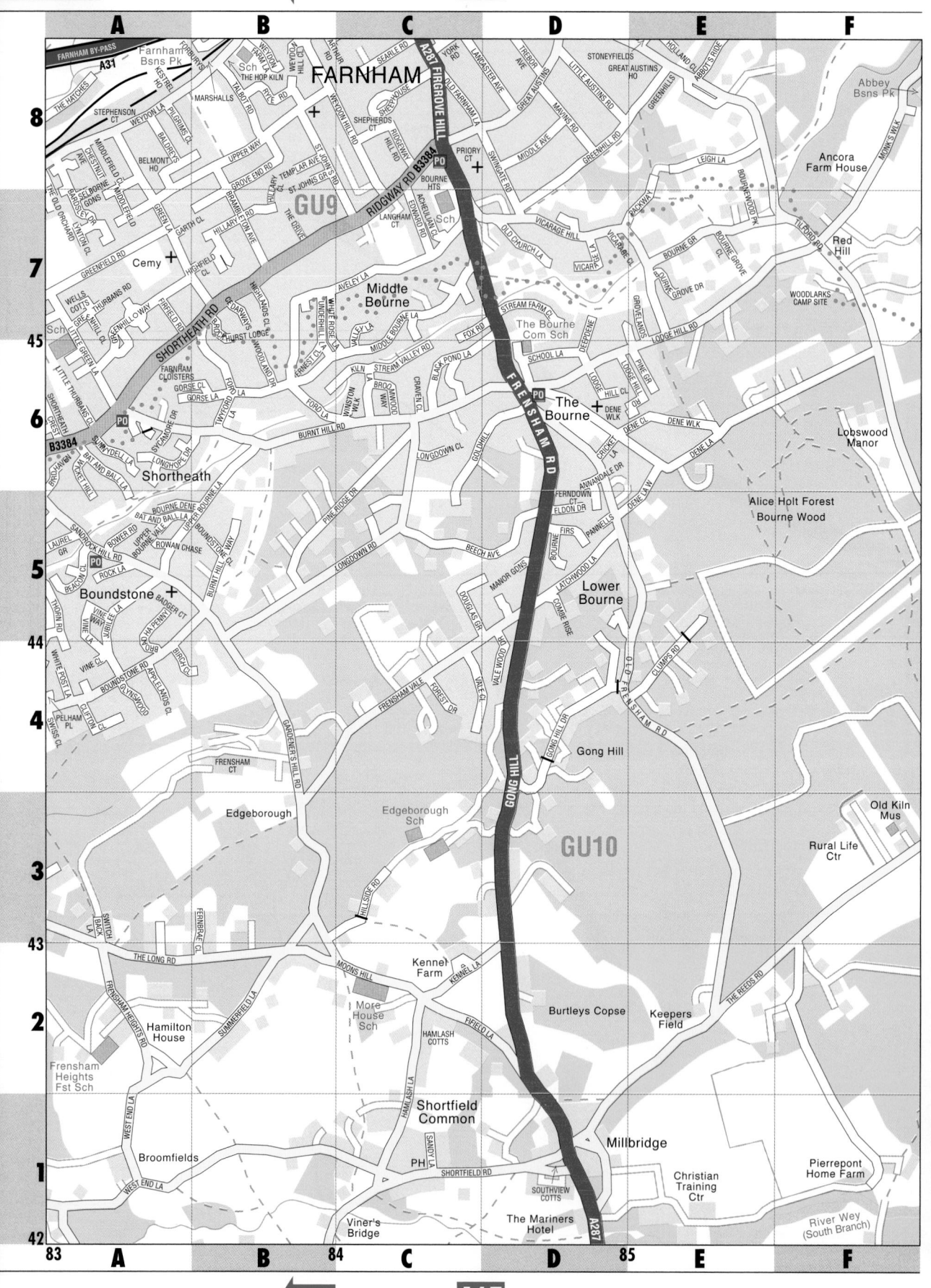

A B C D E F

8

Abbey Bsns Pk

B3001

MONKS WELL

CORBET'S RIDGE

CAMP HILL

P

CROOKSBURY RD

SMUGGLER'S WAY

Mast

Stone Hill

LONG HILL

Long Hill

Priory Farm

Waverley Abbey House

WAVERLEY LA

Waverleymill Bridge

Bishop's Firs

Monk's Walk Farm

GU9

Waverley Abbey (remains of)

Crooksbury House

Crooksbury Common

7

River Wey (North Branch)

Turner's Hill

45

Monks Hill

Charles Hill

6

Black Lake

Sheephatch Copse

Tilfordmill Bridge

SHEEPHATCH LA

Sheephatch Farm

GREEN LA

CHARLES HILL

Nursery

B3001

GU10

Starcross Farm

Waverley Abbey Jun Sch

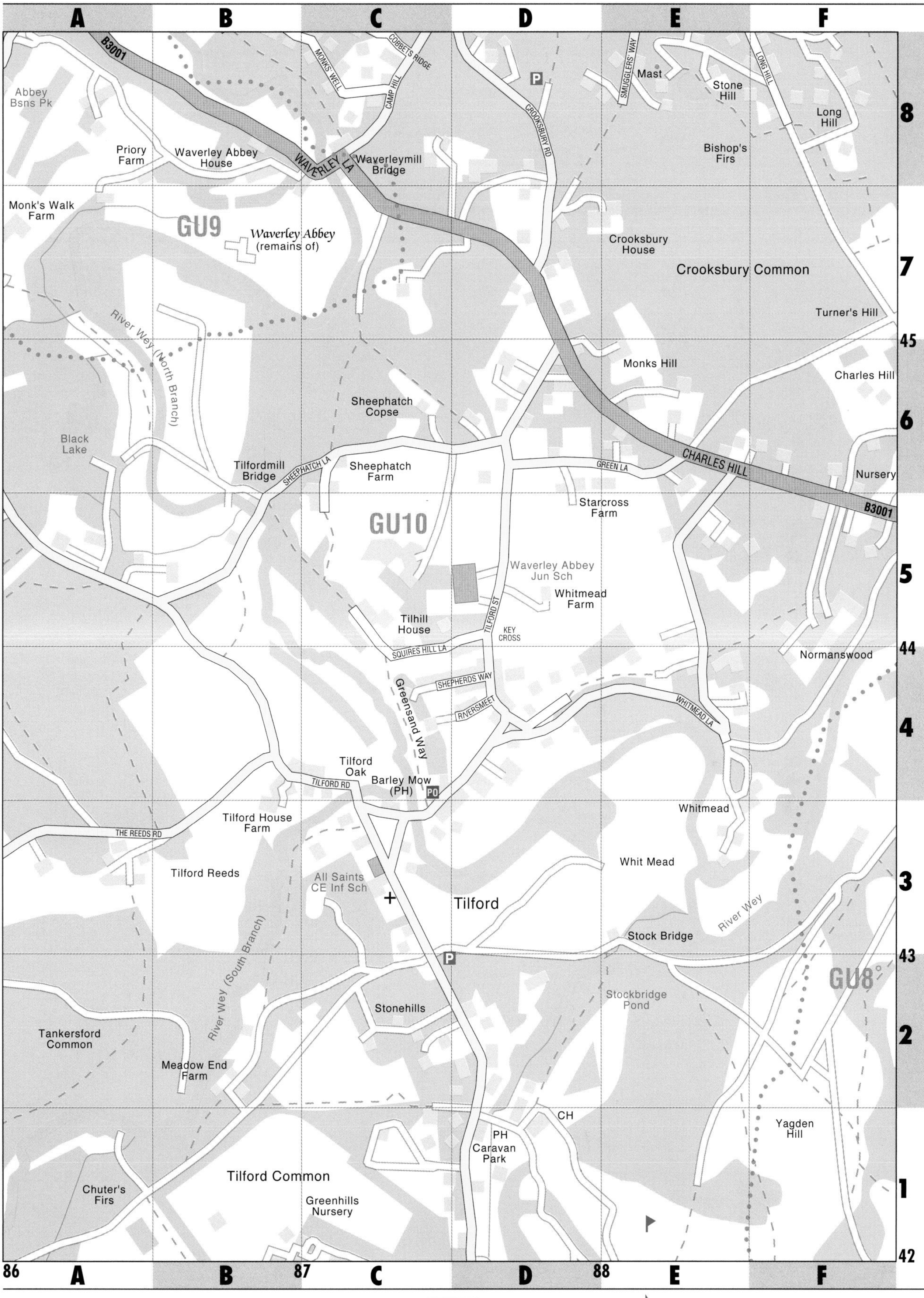

Whitmead Farm

5

Tilhill House

TILFORD ST

KEY CROSS

SQUIRES HILL LA

Normanswood

44

Greensand Way

SHEPHERDS WAY

RIVERSMEET

WHITMEAD LA

4

Tilford Oak

TILFORD RD

Barley Mow (PH)

PO

Whitmead

Tilford House Farm

THE REEDS RD

Tilford Reeds

River Wey (South Branch)

Whit Mead

3

All Saints CE Inf Sch

+

Tilford

Stock Bridge

River Wey

43

GU8

P

Stonehills

Stockbridge Pond

2

Tankersford Common

Meadow End Farm

CH

Yagden Hill

PH Caravan Park

1

Chuter's Firs

Tilford Common

Greenhills Nursery

42

86 A B 87 C D 88 E F

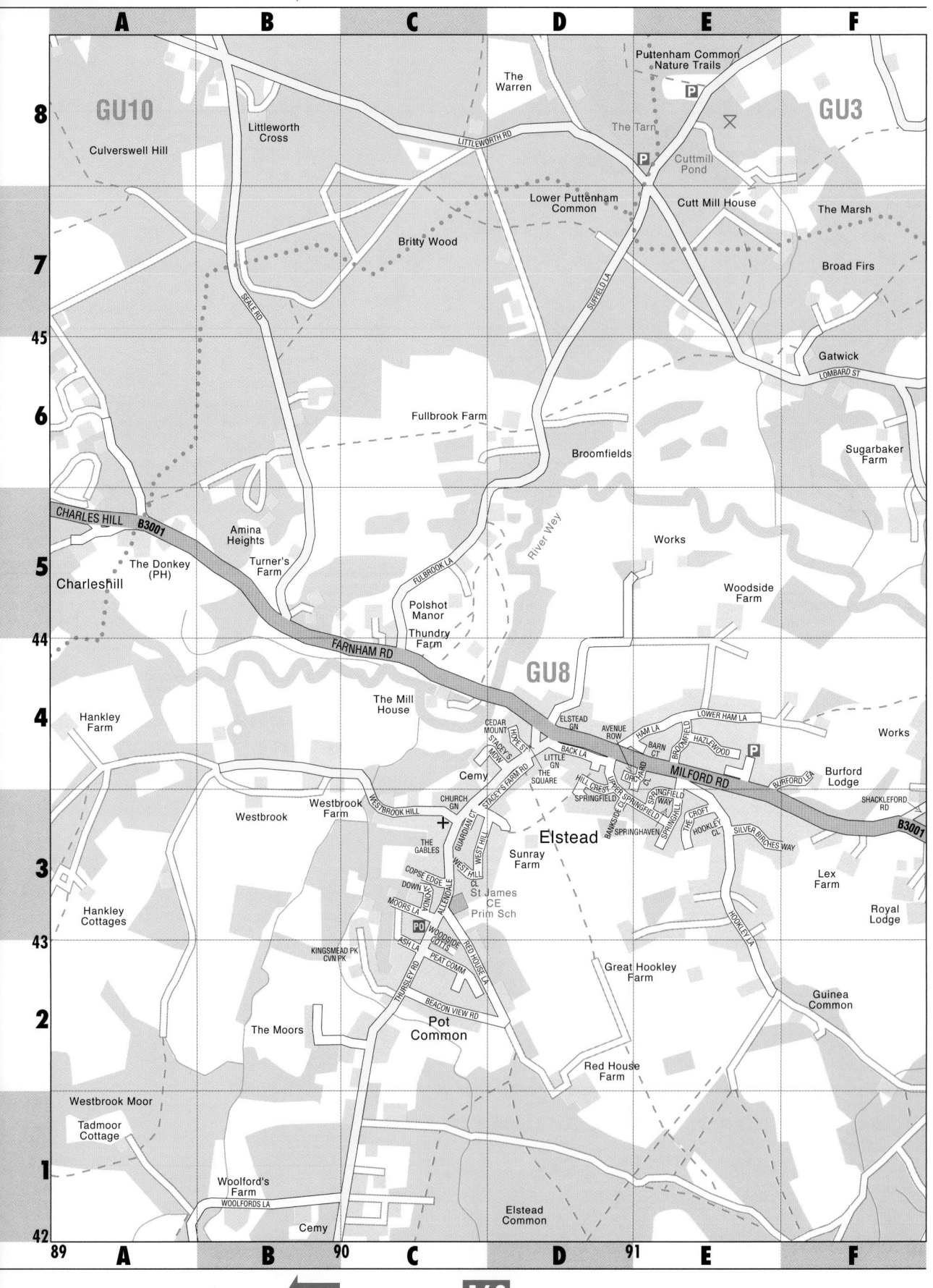

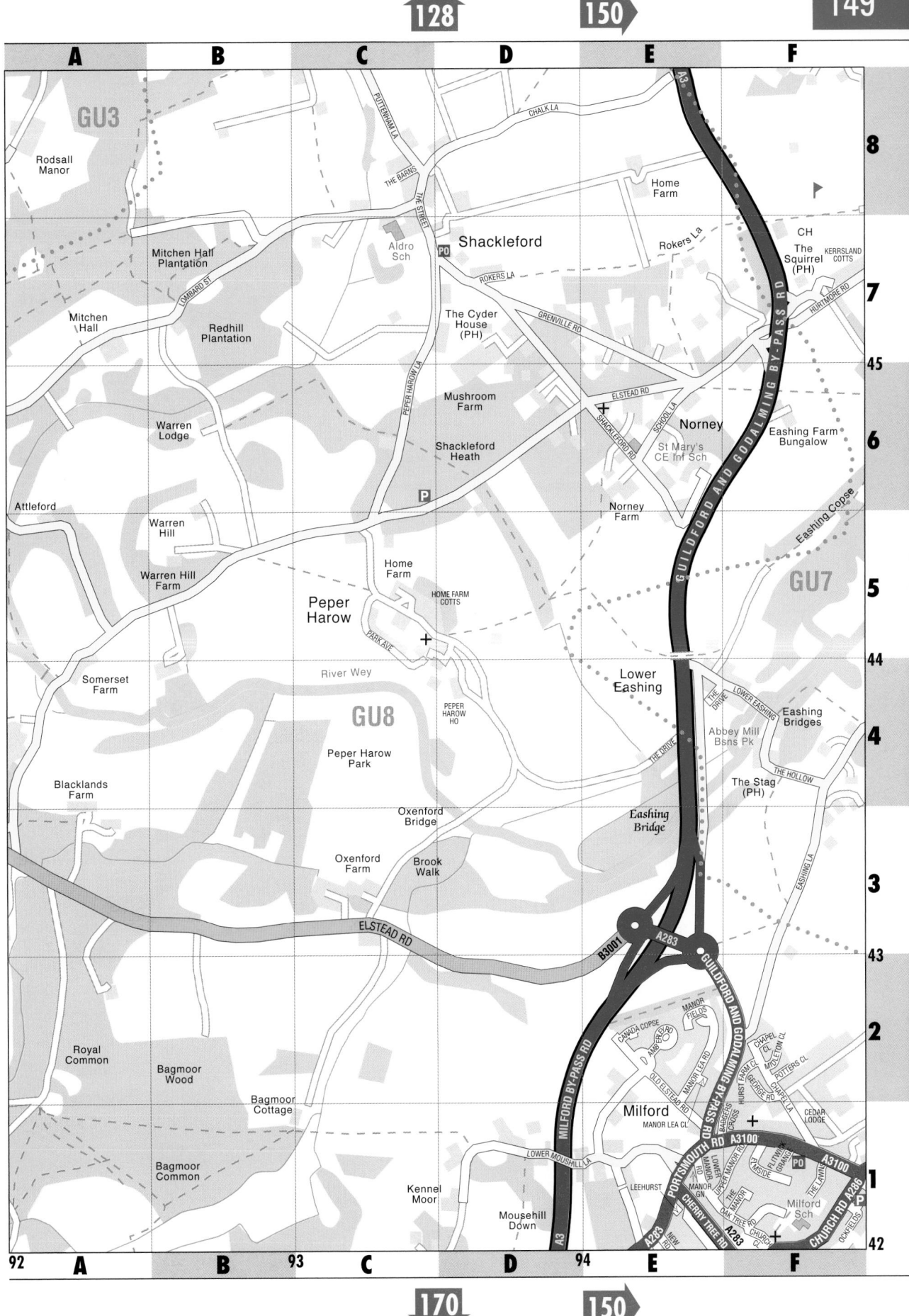

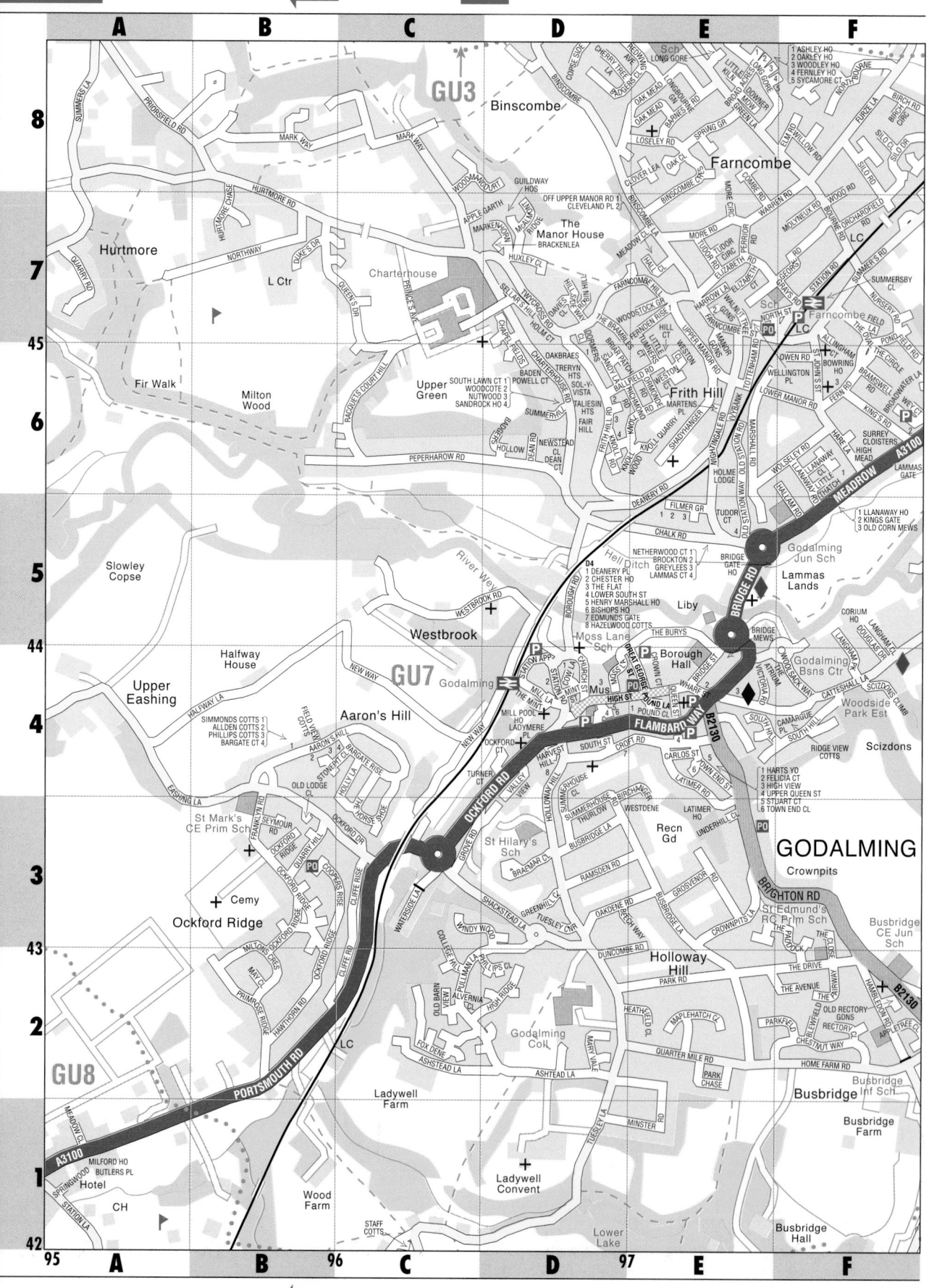
Binscombe
Farncombe
Hurtmore
Charterhouse
The Manor House
Upper Green
Frith Hill
Milton Wood
Fir Walk
Slowley Copse
Westbrook
Halfway House
Upper Eashing
Aaron's Hill
Godalming
Borough Hall
Lammas Lands
Godalming Bsns Ctr
Woodside Park Est
Scizdons
GODALMING
Crownpits
Ockford Ridge
St Mark's CE Prim Sch
St Hilary's Sch
Recn Gd
Holloway Hill
Godalming Coll
Ladywell Farm
Ladywell Convent
Wood Farm
Busbridge
Busbridge Farm
Busbridge Hall
Lower Lake
GU3
GU7
GU8
PORTSMOUTH RD
OCKFORD RD
FLAMBARD WAY
BRIDGE RD
BRIGHTON RD
MEADROW
A3100
B2130

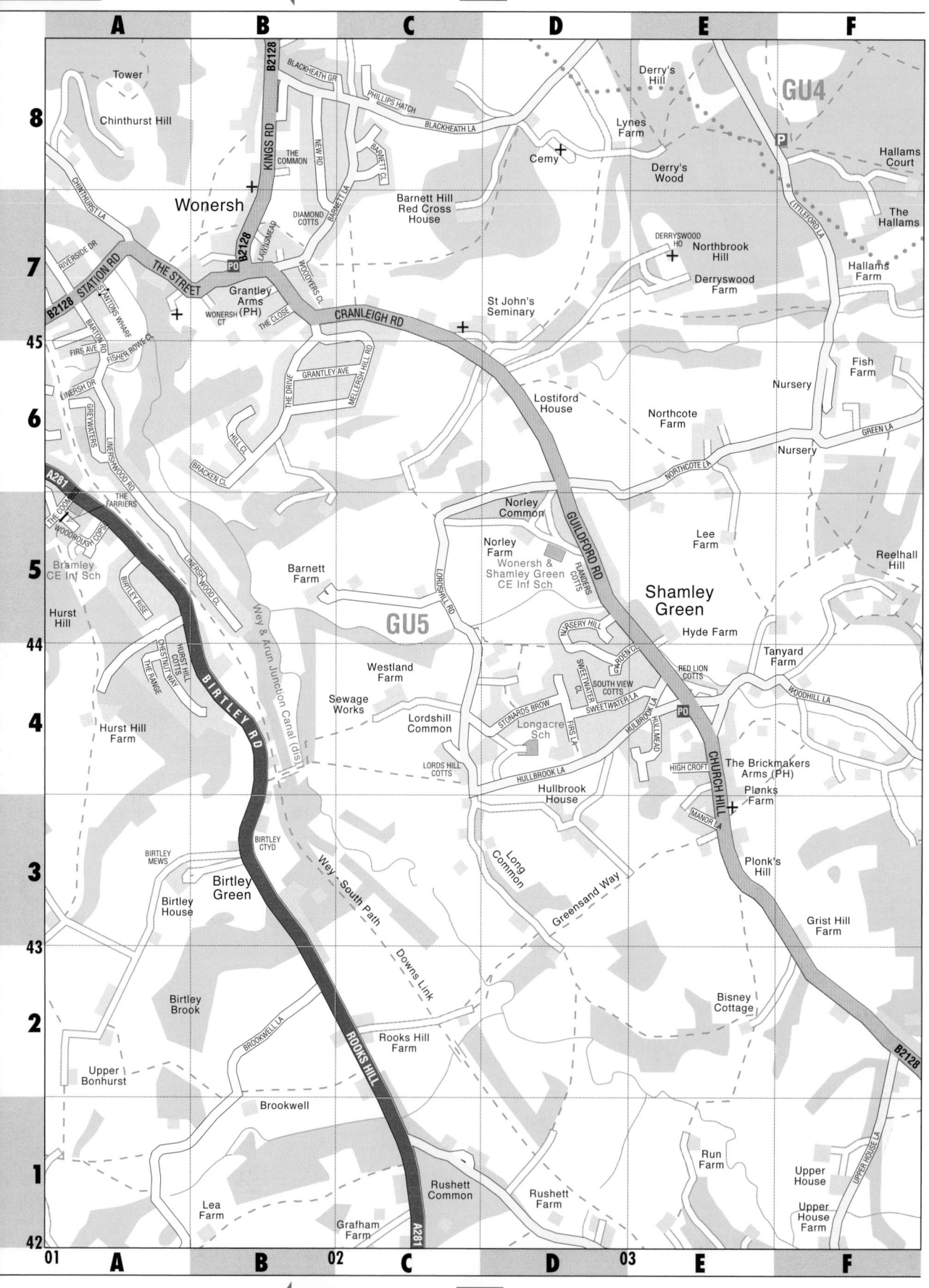

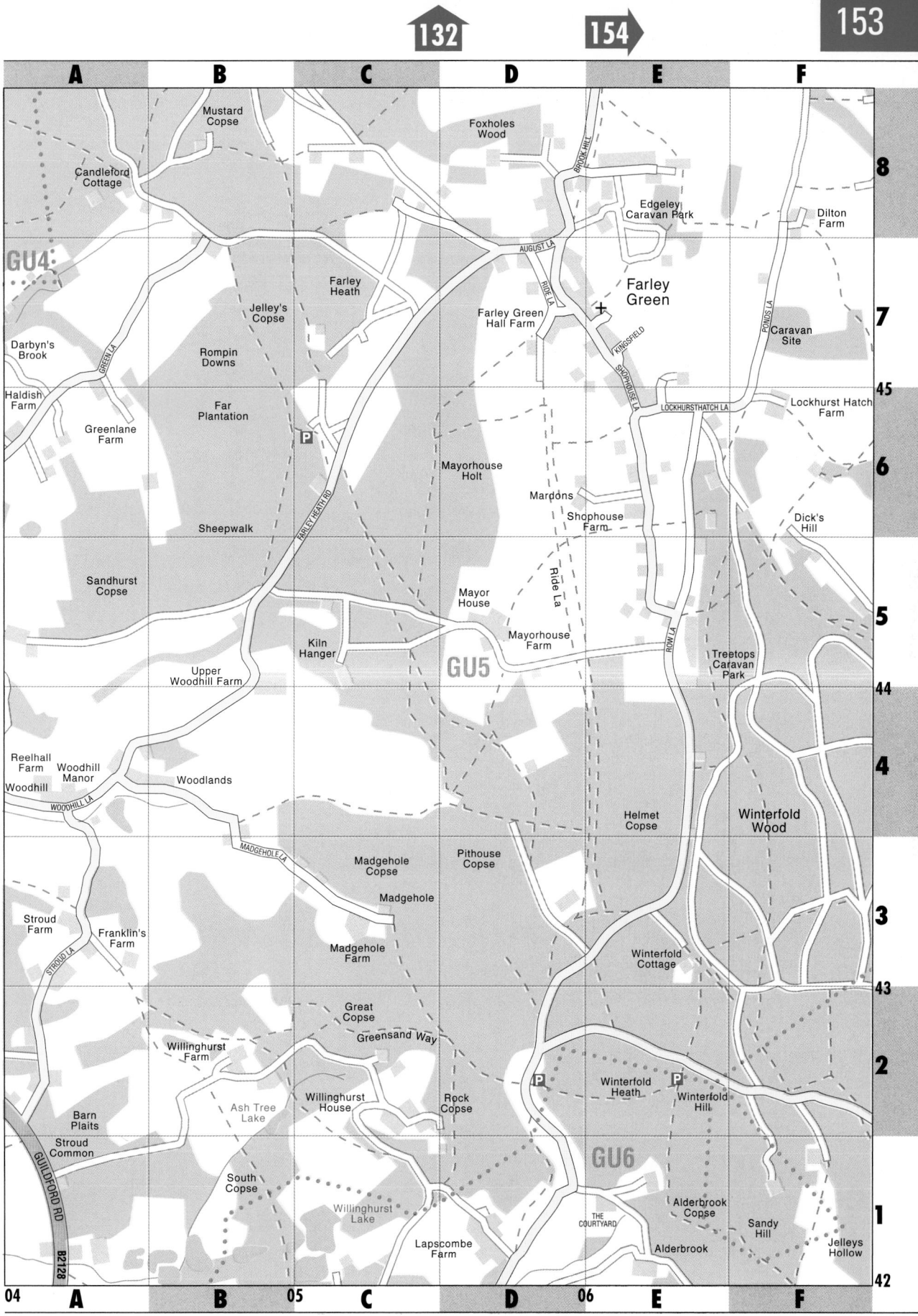

153 133

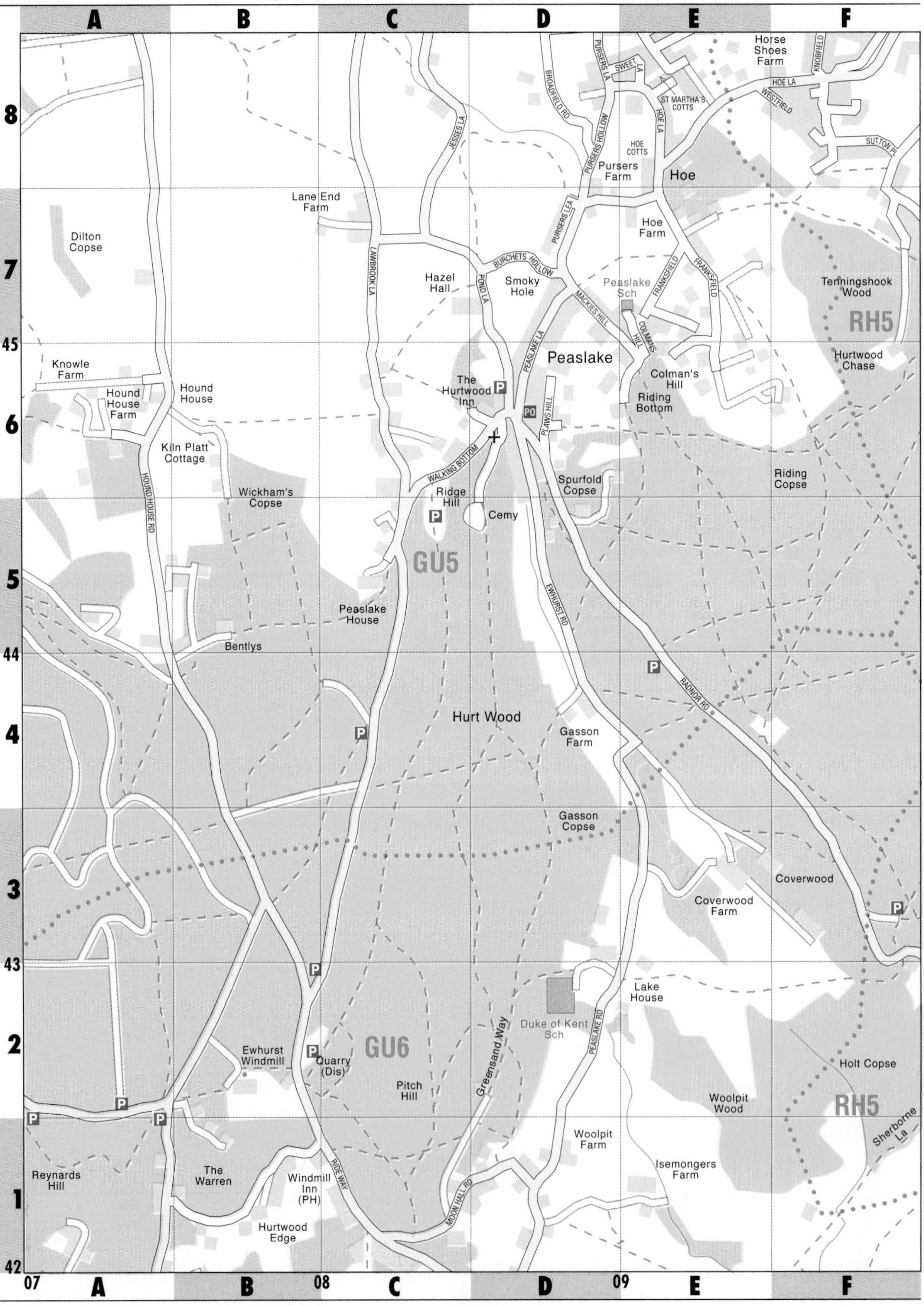

A B C D E F

8
7
45
6
5
44
4
3
43
2
1
42

Horse Shoes Farm

SWEET LA
PURSERS LA
BROADFIELD RD
PURSERS HOLLOW
HOE LA
HOE LA
WESTFIELD
KNOBFIELD
SUTTON PL

St Martha's Cotts
Hoe Cotts
Pursers Farm
Hoe

Dilton Copse

JESSES LA
Lane End Farm

LAWBROOK LA
Hazel Hall
Smoky Hole
Hoe Farm
Peaslake Sch
FRANKSFIELD
FRANKSFIELD
Tenningshook Wood

RH5

POND LA
BURCHETS HOLLOW
MACKIES HILL
COLMANS HILL

Peaslake

Knowle Farm
Hound House Farm
Hound House

The Hurtwood Inn
PEASLAKE LA
PO
PAWS HILL
Colman's Hill
Riding Bottom
Hurtwood Chase

Kiln Platt Cottage

WALKING BOTTOM
Spurfold Copse
Riding Copse

Wickham's Copse
Ridge Hill
Cemy
P

GU5

HOUND HOUSE RD

Peaslake House
Bentlys

ENHURST RD

P
RADNOR RD

Hurt Wood
Gasson Farm

P

Gasson Copse

Coverwood

Coverwood Farm

P

P
Greensand Way
Lake House
PEASLAKE RD

P
GU6
Ewhurst Windmill
P Quarry (Dis)
Pitch Hill
Duke of Kent Sch
Holt Copse

P
P
P
Reynards Hill
The Warren
RIDGE WAY
Windmill Inn (PH)
MOON HALL RD
Woolpit Farm
Woolpit Wood
Isemongers Farm
RH5
Sherborne La

Hurtwood Edge

07 A B 08 C D 09 E F

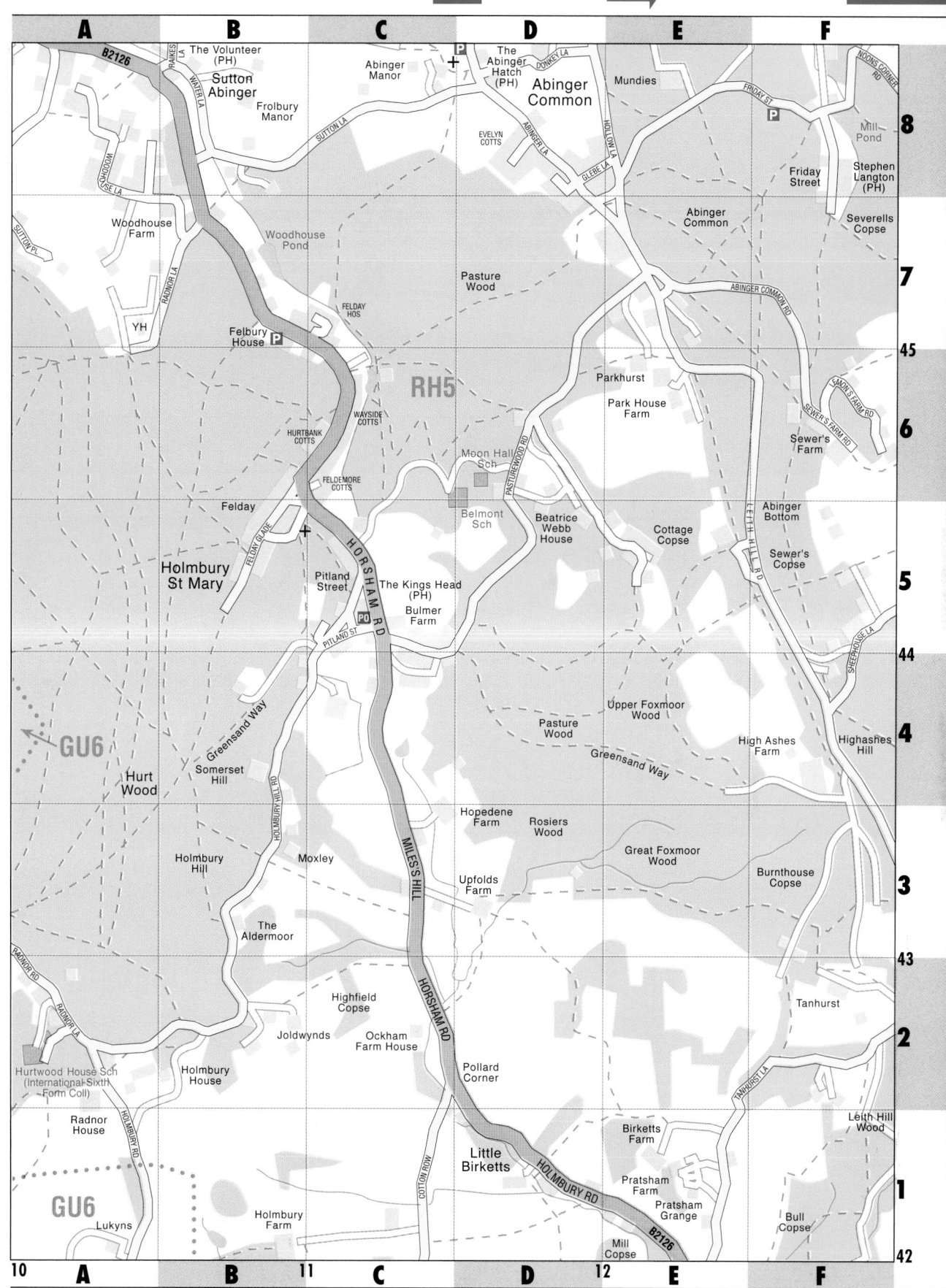

RH4

Hambridge Brow

Redlands Wood

OAKS LA

Redlands Bank House

Bushey Croft

Ashleigh Cotts

FOLLY LA

Folly Farm

Oakdale Cottage

South Holmwood

ST AUSTELLS PL

WARWICK RD

NORFOLK RD

BUCKINGHAM RD

BETCHETS GREEN RD

WARWICK CL

Meml

Holmwood Common

Mill Bottom

Mill House

Eutrie

MILL BOTTOM LA

MOORFIELD

MILL RD

Fourwents Pond

P

P

P

Brook Lodge Farm

Waterlands Farm

LODGE LA

BLACKBROOK RD

Hawesrew Farm

Wymbleton Farm

Lodge Farm

Brookfield Copse

Holmwood Park Farm

BROOKSIDE

Oakfield Farm

Redlands

Betchets Green

MILFORD CT 1
CHURCH TERR 2

Holmwood Common

HORSHAM RD

SPRING COTTS

Holmwood Corner

Grandon Lodge

Vigo Farm

ANSTIE GRANGE DR

Anstie Grange

Anstie Grange Farm

Capel Leyse

RH5

Posterns Farm

Petersfield Farm

Swires Farm

HENFOLD LA

Stockrydons

MOORHURST LA

Moorhurst Manor

OLD HORSHAM RD

Holmwood

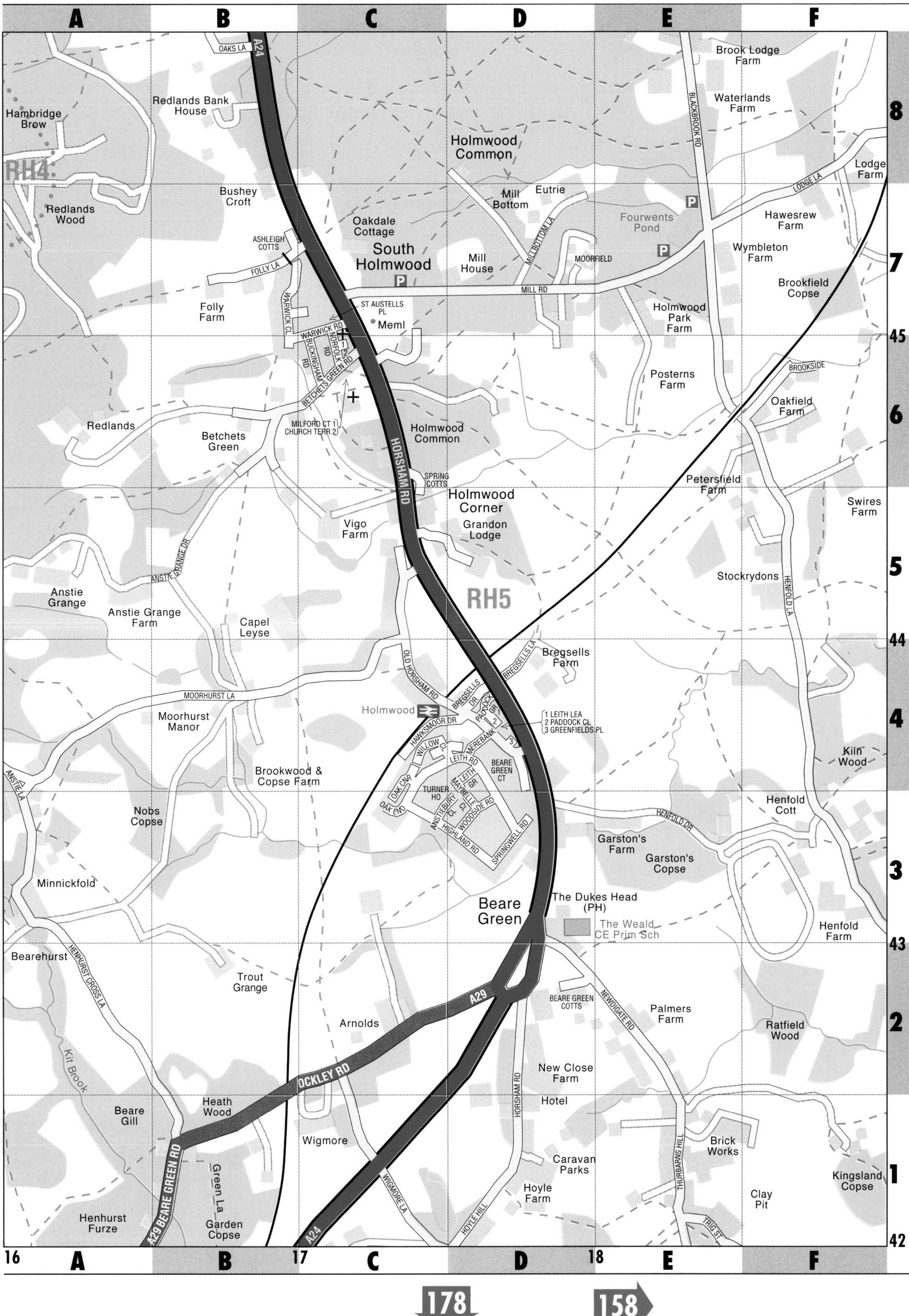

Brookwood & Copse Farm

Nobs Copse

ANSTIE LA

BREGSELLS DR

BREGSELLS LA

Bregsells Farm

HAWKSMOOR DR

WILLOW CL

PARDOCK GR

LEITH RD

LEITH GR

OAK CNR

OAK END

TURNER HO

ANSTIEBURY CL

MAYBELL CL

HIGHLAND RD

WOODSIDE RD

SPRINGWELL RD

MEREBANK

R ST

Beare Green CT

1 LEITH LEA
2 PADDOCK CL
3 GREENFIELDS PL

Garston's Farm

Garston's Copse

HENFOLD DR

Kiln Wood

Henfold Cott

Henfold Farm

Minnickfold

Bearehurst

HENHURST CROSS LA

A24 BEARE GREEN RD

Trout Grange

Beare Green

A29

OCKLEY RD

Kit Book

Arnolds

Heath Wood

Green La

Garden Copse

Wigmore

WIGMORE LA

A24

Beare Gill

Henhurst Furze

The Dukes Head (PH)

The Weald CE Prim Sch

BEARE GREEN COTTS

NEWDIGATE RD

HORSHAM RD

New Close Farm

Hotel

HOYLE HILL

Caravan Parks

Hoyle Farm

THURBANS HILL

Palmers Farm

Brick Works

TRIG ST

Ratfield Wood

Clay Pit

Kingsland Copse

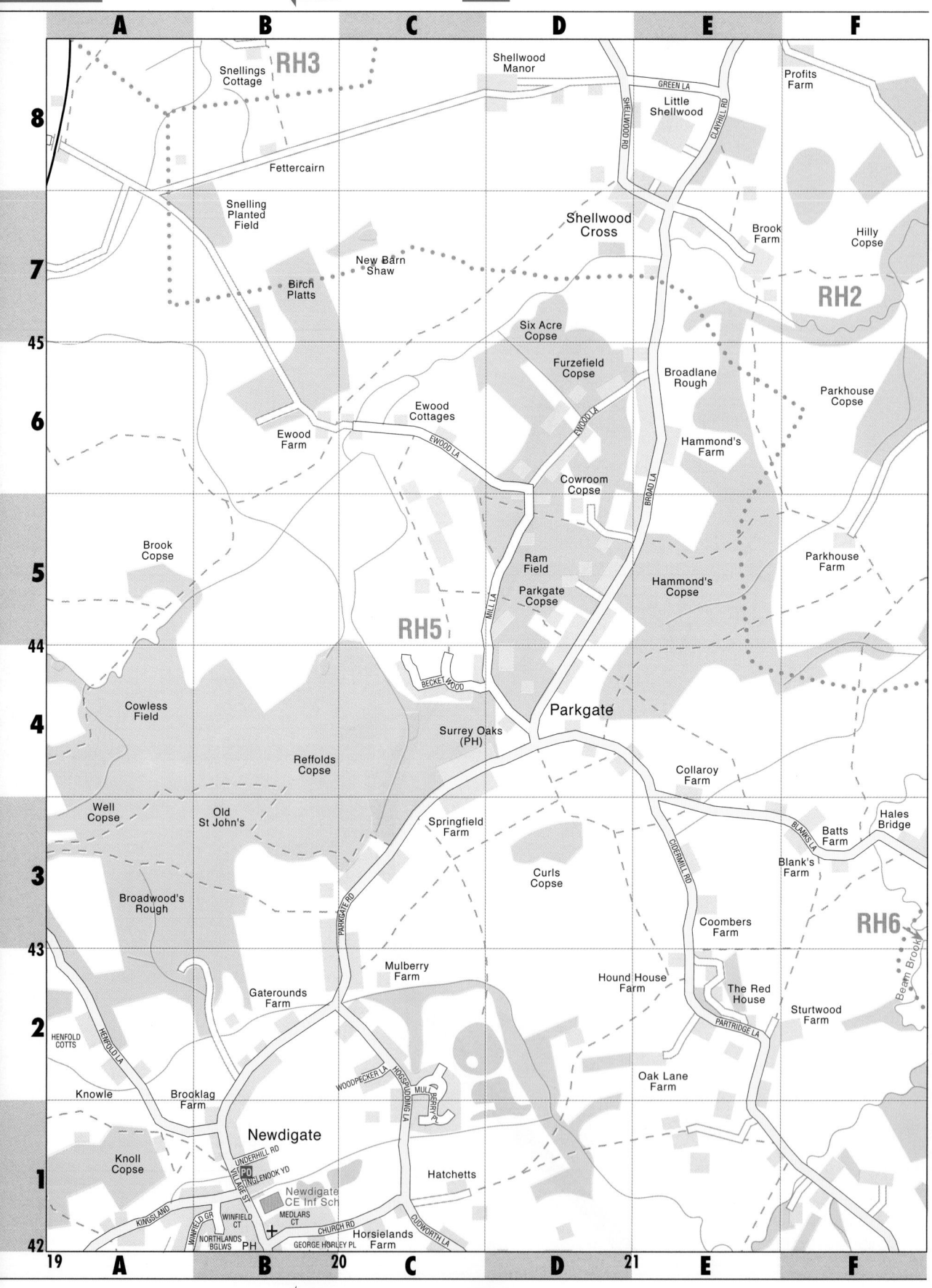

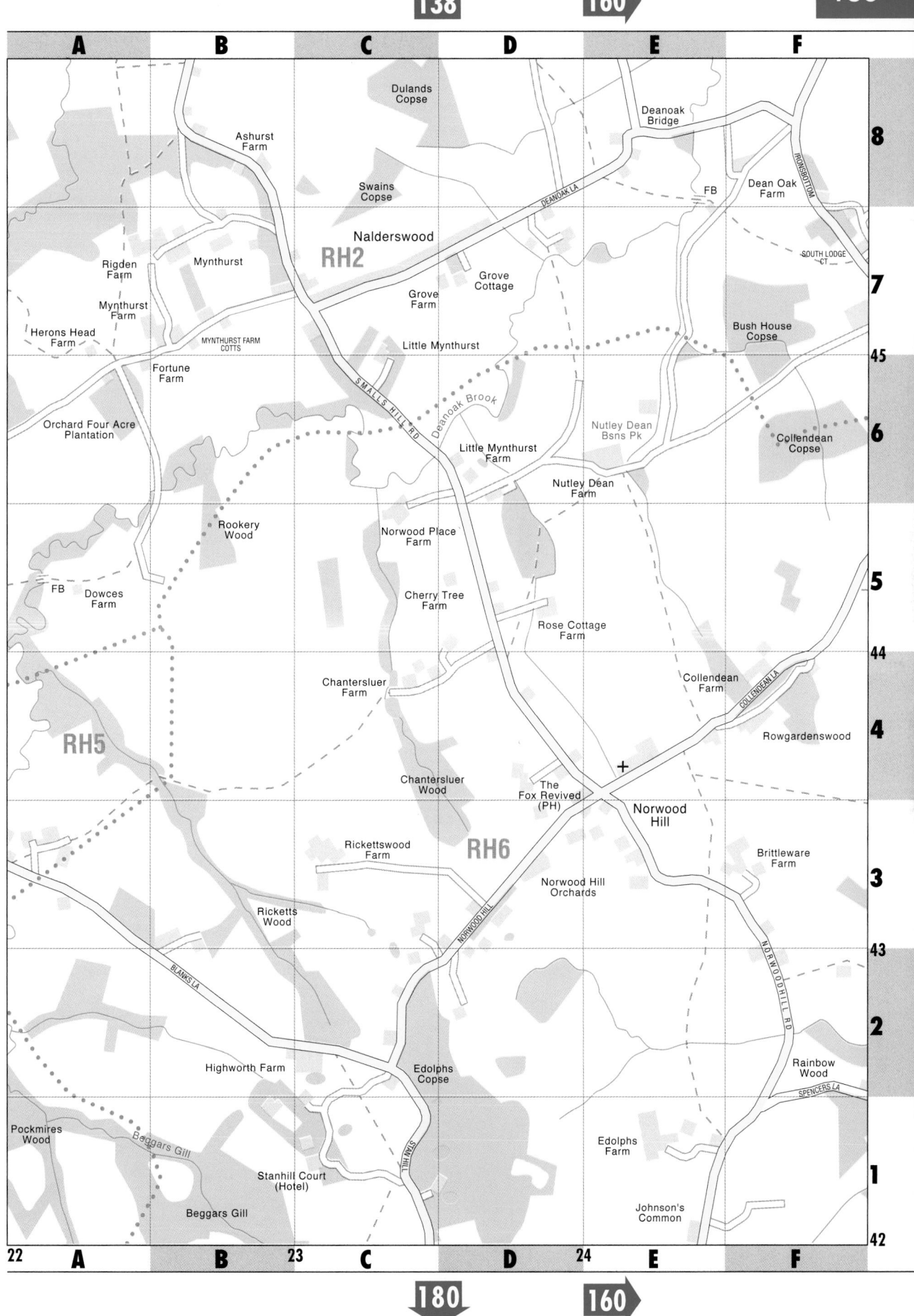

A | **B** | **C** | **D** | **E** | **F**

8

Dulands Copse
Deanoak Bridge
Ashurst Farm
Swains Copse
FB
Dean Oak Farm
IRONSBOTTOM
DEANOAK LA

Nalderswood
RH2
SOUTH LODGE CT
7

Rigden Farm
Mynthurst
Grove Cottage
Grove Farm
Bush House Copse

Mynthurst Farm
45

Herons Head Farm
MYNTHURST FARM COTTS
Little Mynthurst

Fortune Farm
SMALLS HILL RD
Deanoak Brook
Nutley Dean Bsns Pk
Collendean Copse
6

Orchard Four Acre Plantation
Little Mynthurst Farm

Nutley Dean Farm

Rookery Wood
Norwood Place Farm
5

FB
Dowces Farm
Cherry Tree Farm
Rose Cottage Farm

Collendean Farm
44

Chantersluer Farm
COLLENDEAN LA
RH5
Rowgardenswood
4

Chantersluer Wood
The Fox Revived (PH)
Norwood Hill
Brittleware Farm

Rickettswood Farm
RH6
Norwood Hill Orchards
3

Ricketts Wood
NORWOOD HILL
NORWOOD HILL RD
43

BLANKS LA
2

Highworth Farm
Edolphs Copse
Rainbow Wood
SPENCERS LA

Pockmires Wood
STANHILL
Edolphs Farm
1

Beggars Gill
Stanhill Court (Hotel)
Johnson's Common

Beggars Gill
42

22 | **A** | **B** | 23 | **C** | **D** | 24 | **E** | **F**

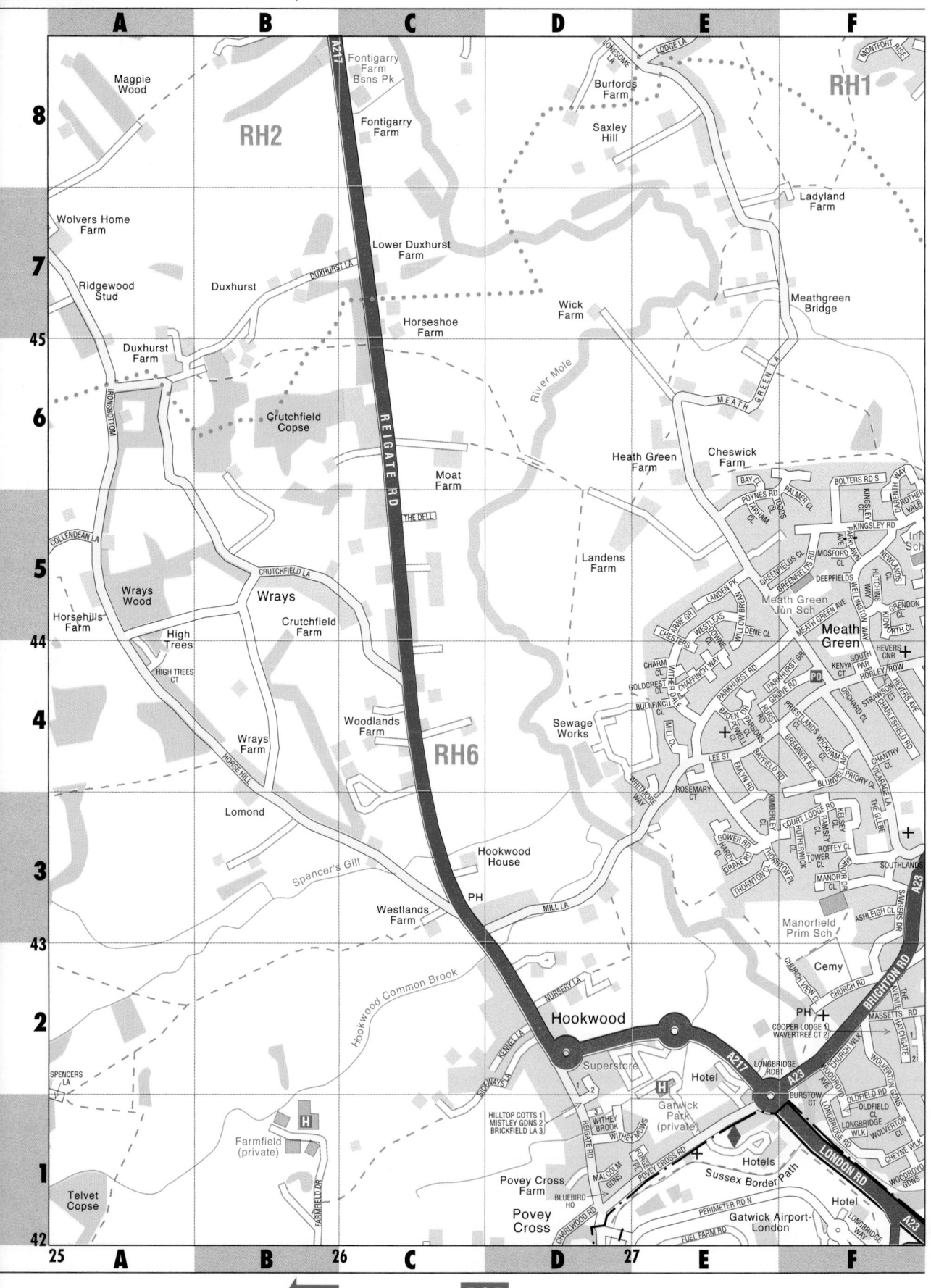

159
139
159
181

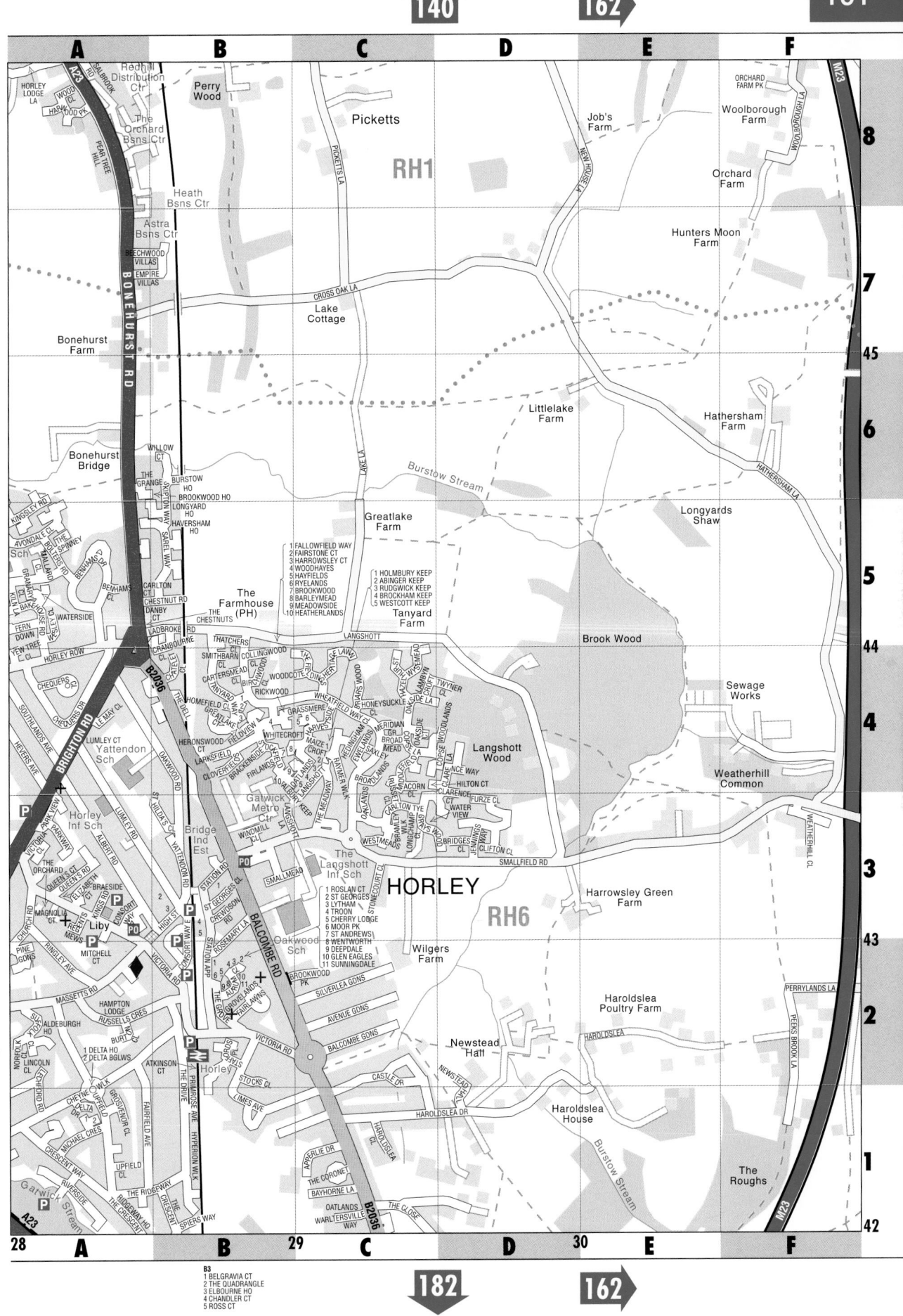

HORLEY

RH1

RH6

A23

M23

BONEHURST RD

BRIGHTON RD

BALCOMBE RD

B2036

B2037

Horley Lodge La
Redhill Distribution Ctr
Perry Wood
Picketts
Job's Farm
Orchard Farm Pk
Woolborough Farm
The Orchard Bsns Ctr
Orchard Farm
Heath Bsns Ctr
Astra Bsns Ctr
Beechwood Villas
Empire Villas
Hunters Moon Farm
Cross Oak La
Lake Cottage
Bonehurst Farm
Hathersham Farm
Littlelake Farm
Longyards Shaw
Bonehurst Bridge
Willow Ct
Burstow Ho
Brookwood Ho
Longyard Ho
Haversham Ho
Burstow Stream
Hathersham La
The Grange
Skipton Way
Sarel Way
Greatlake Farm
Carlton Cl
Chestnut Rd
Danby Ct
Ladbroke Rd
Cranbourne
The Farmhouse (PH)
The Chestnuts
1 Fallowfield Way
2 Fairstone Ct
3 Harrowsley Ct
4 Woodhayes
5 Hayfields
6 Ryelands
7 Brookwood
8 Barleymead
9 Meadowside
10 Heatherlands
1 Holmbury Keep
2 Abinger Keep
3 Rudgwick Keep
4 Brockham Keep
5 Westcott Keep
Tanyard Farm
Brook Wood
Sewage Works
Langshott
Thatchers
Smithbarn
Collingwood
Cartersmead
Tanyard
Rickwood
Homefield Ct
Greenlake
Heronswood Ct
Larksfield
Clover Fld
Whitecroft
Brackenside
Firlands
Maize Cft
Larkshot
Windmill
Gatwick Metro Ctr
Smallmead
Langshott Keep
Westmeads
The Meadway
Bridges Cl
Clifton Cl
Smallfield Rd
Langshott Wood
Twyner
Weatherhill Common
Weatherhill Cl
The Langshott Inf Sch
Stonecourt Cl
1 Roslan Ct
2 St Georges
3 Lytham
4 Troon
5 Cherry Lodge
6 Moor Pk
7 St Andrews
8 Wentworth
9 Deepdale
10 Glen Eagles
11 Sunningdale
Harrowsley Green Farm
Wilgers Farm
Haroldslea Poultry Farm
Perrylands La
Oakwood Sch
Brookwood Pk
Silverlea Gdns
Avenue Gdns
Balcombe Gdns
Newstead Hall
Haroldslea
Peeks Brook La
Victoria Rd
Castle Dr
Newstead Dr
Haroldslea Dr
Haroldslea House
Burstow Stream
The Roughs
Garwick Stream
The Ridgeway
The Crescent
Spiers Way
Apperlie Dr
The Coronet
Bayhorne La
Oatlands
Warltersville Way
The Close

B3
1 BELGRAVIA CT
2 THE QUADRANGLE
3 ELBOURNE HO
4 CHANDLER CT
5 ROSS CT

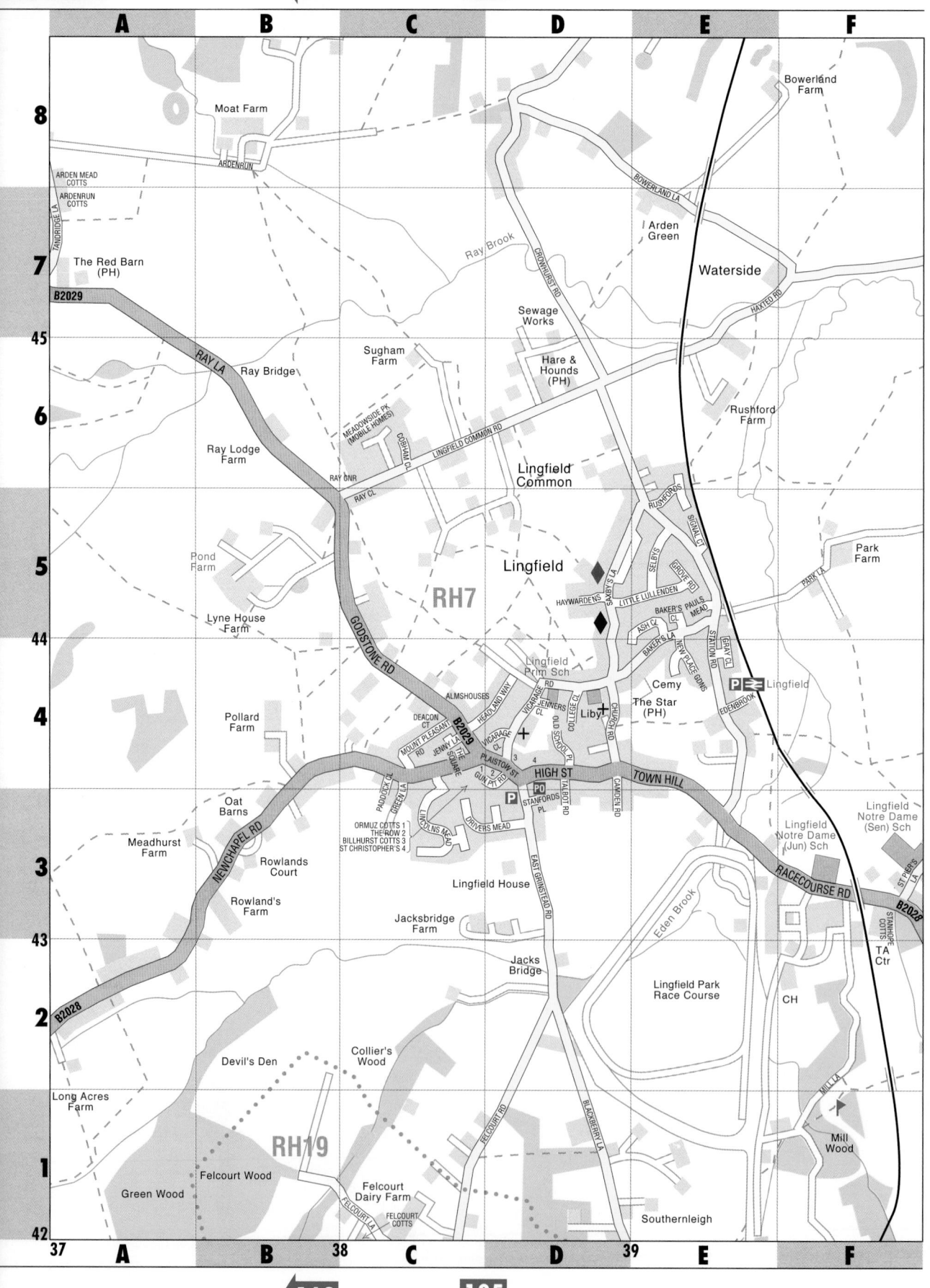

144

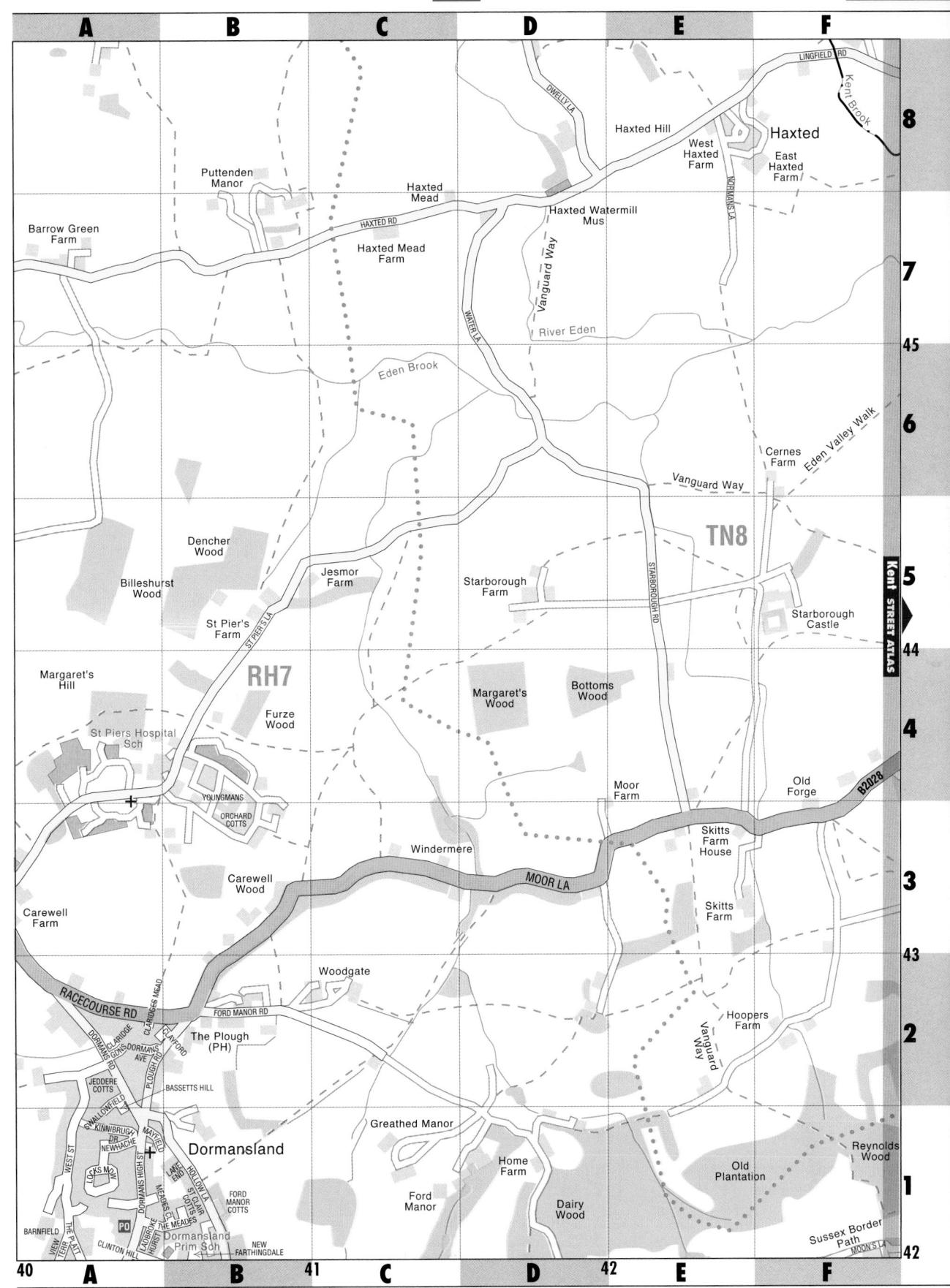
A
B
C
D
E
F
8
7
45
6
5
44
4
3
43
2
1
42
40
41
42
Lingfield Rd
Kent Brook
Haxted
Haxted Hill
West Haxted Farm
East Haxted Farm
Dwelly La
Normans La
Puttenden Manor
Haxted Mead
Haxted Rd
Haxted Watermill Mus
Barrow Green Farm
Haxted Mead Farm
Vanguard Way
Water La
River Eden
Eden Brook
Eden Valley Walk
Cernes Farm
Vanguard Way
TN8
Dencher Wood
Billeshurst Wood
Jesmor Farm
Starborough Farm
Starborough Rd
Starborough Castle
St Pier's Farm
St Pier's La
Kent Street Atlas
Margaret's Hill
RH7
Margaret's Wood
Bottoms Wood
Furze Wood
St Piers Hospital Sch
Moor Farm
Old Forge
B2028
Youngmans
Orchard Cotts
Skitts Farm House
Windermere
Carewell Wood
Moor La
Carewell Farm
Skitts Farm
Woodgate
Racecourse Rd
Claridges Mead
Ford Manor Rd
Hoopers Farm
Vanguard Way
The Plough (PH)
Dormans Gdns
Claridge
Dormans Ave
Plough Rd
Clayford
Jeddere Cotts
Bassetts Hill
Swallowfield
Kinnibrugh Dr
Newhache
Mayfield
Greathed Manor
Dormansland
Reynolds Wood
West St
Locks Mdw
Dormans High St
Lane End
Hollow La
Home Farm
Old Plantation
Meades Cl
St Clair Cotts
Ford Manor Cotts
Ford Manor
Dairy Wood
PO
The Meades
Barnfield
View Terr
The Platt
Ladbroke Hurst
Dormansland Prim Sch
Clinton Hill
New Farthingdale
Sussex Border Path
Moon's La

186

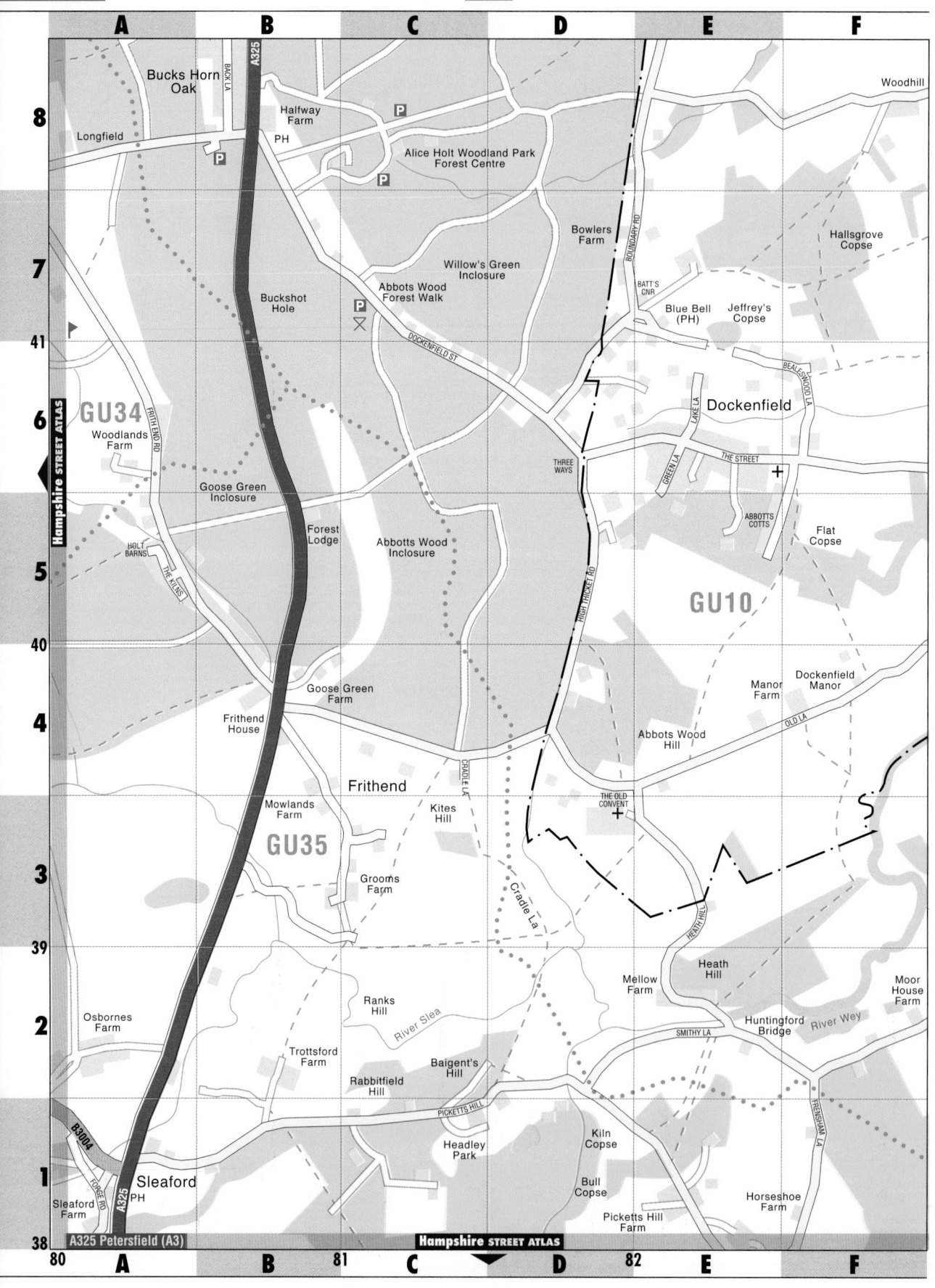

Bucks Horn Oak

Longfield

Halfway Farm

PH

P

P

Alice Holt Woodland Park Forest Centre

Willow's Green Inclosure

Bowlers Farm

Woodhill

Hallsgrove Copse

Buckshot Hole

Abbots Wood Forest Walk

P

BOUNDARY RD

BATT'S CNR

Blue Bell (PH)

Jeffrey's Copse

DOCKENFIELD ST

GU34

Woodlands Farm

Dockenfield

LAKE LA

GREEN LA

THE STREET

THREE WAYS

ABBOTTS COTTS

Flat Copse

Goose Green Inclosure

THE KILNS

FRITH END RD

HOLT BARNS

Forest Lodge

Abbotts Wood Inclosure

HIGH THICKET RD

GU10

Goose Green Farm

Frithend House

Abbots Wood Hill

OLD LA

Manor Farm

Dockenfield Manor

Frithend

CRADLE LA

Mowlands Farm

GU35

Kites Hill

THE OLD CONVENT

HEATH HILL

Grooms Farm

Cradle La

Heath Hill

Moor House Farm

Osbornes Farm

Ranks Hill

River Slea

Mellow Farm

Huntingford Bridge

River Wey

SMITHY LA

Trottsford Farm

Baigent's Hill

Rabbitfield Hill

PICKETTS HILL

FRENSHAM LA

B3004

FORGE RD

Sleaford Farm

Sleaford

A325

PH

Headley Park

Kiln Copse

Bull Copse

Picketts Hill Farm

Horseshoe Farm

A325

BACK LA

Hampshire STREET ATLAS

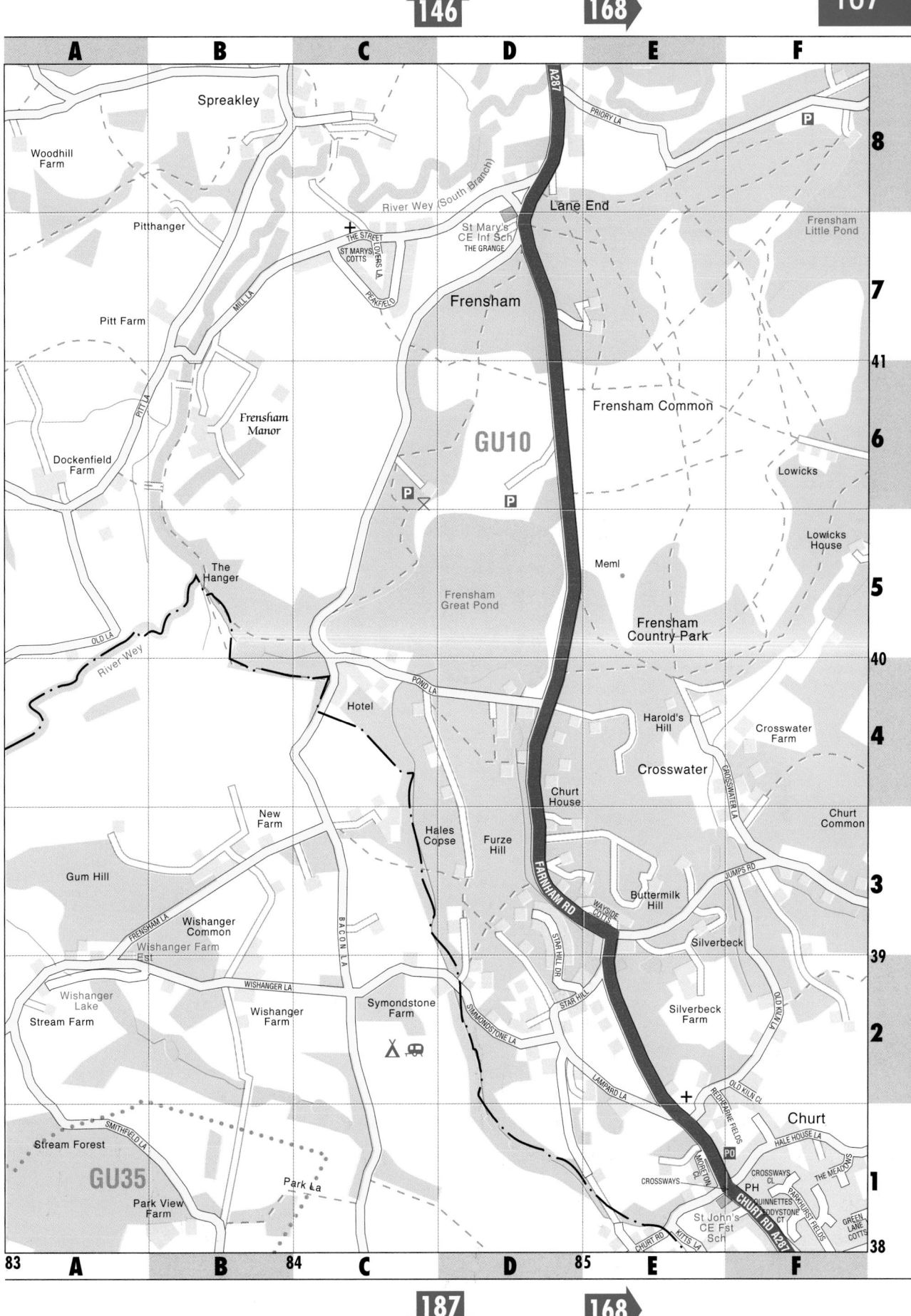

A   B   C   D   E   F

8

Chuter's Cottage

Green Hill

Abbot's Lodge

Greensand Way

Lion's Mouth

Frensham Little Pond

Greenhills Farm

GRANGE RD

The Grange

7

WINCHESTER RD

EGLINTON RD

41

CARLISLE RD

Hankley Common

WELLESLEY RD

6

LOWICKS RD

+

Grey Walls

Kettlebury Hill

SANDY LA

GLEBE LA

GU10

5

PO

Rushmoor

GU8

The Flashes

40

TILFORD RD

Gold Hill

4

The Devil's Jumps

Wychmoor Copse

THURSLEY RD

3

The Pride of the Valley (PH)

JUMPS RD

Kettlebury Farm

Churt Lea

Churt Place Farm

39

Pitch Place Farm

CRABTREE LA

Old Kiln Farm

2

HALE HOUSE LA

Hillside Farm

Hyde Farm

HYDE LA

SAILORS LA

Avalon

OLD BARN LA

Hyde Copse

Glenhead Farm

Upper Ridgeway Farm

GREEN CROSS LA

Fair View Farm

1

Green Cross Farm

Green Cross

Green Farm

Stock Farm House

Marchants Farm

SILVER BIRCH COTTS

GREEN LA

38

GREEN LA

86   87   88

A   B   C   D   E   F

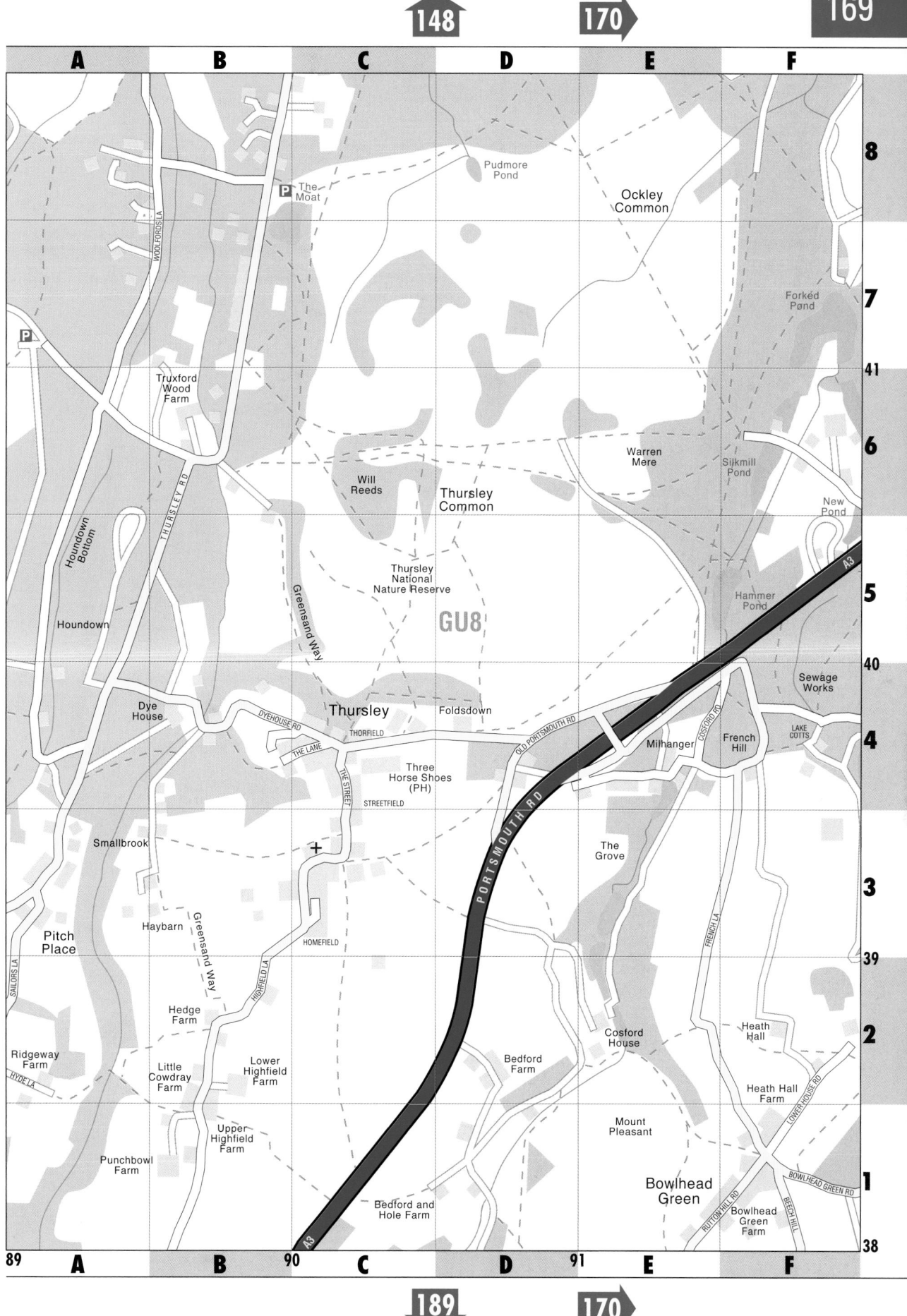

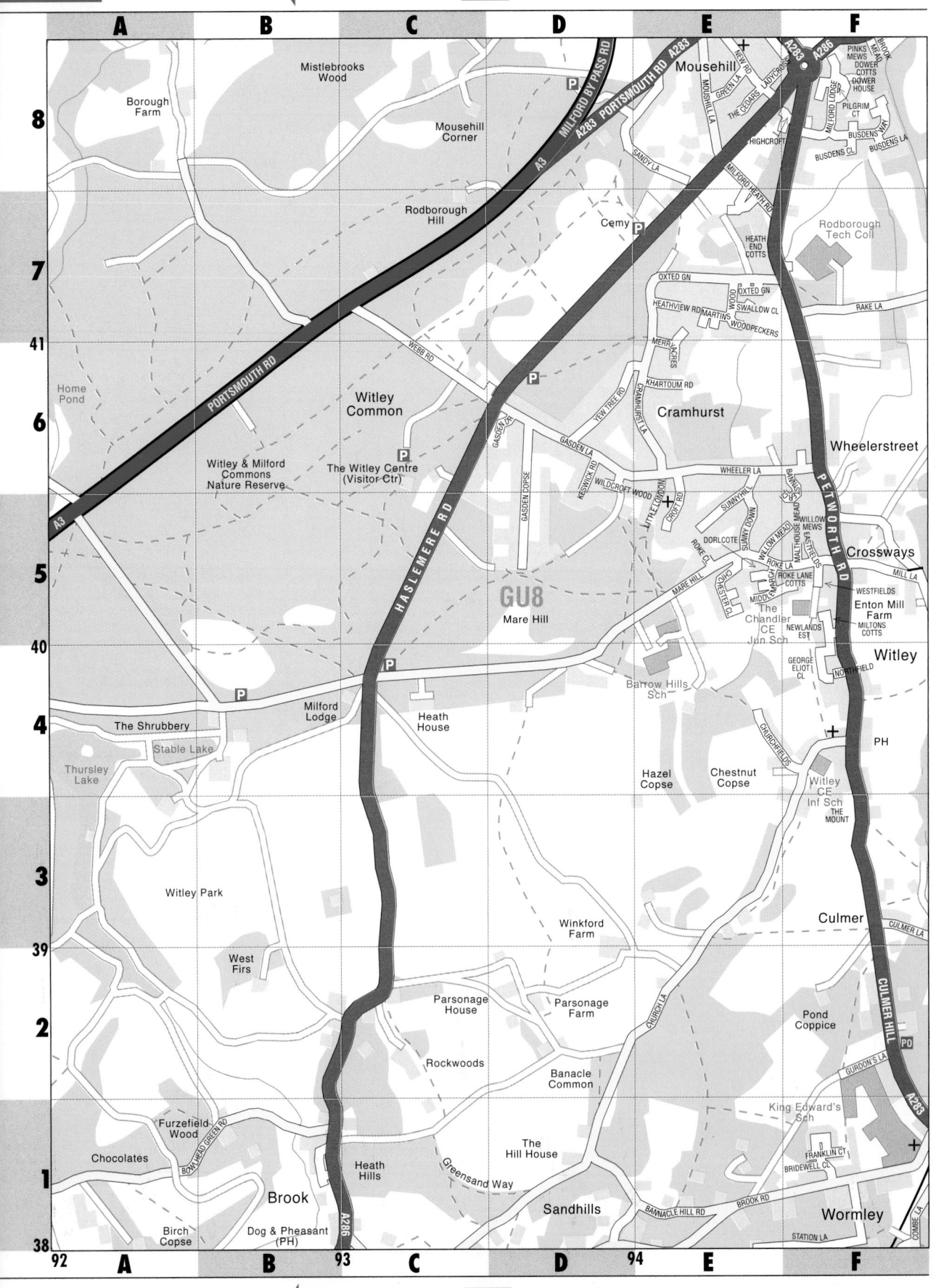

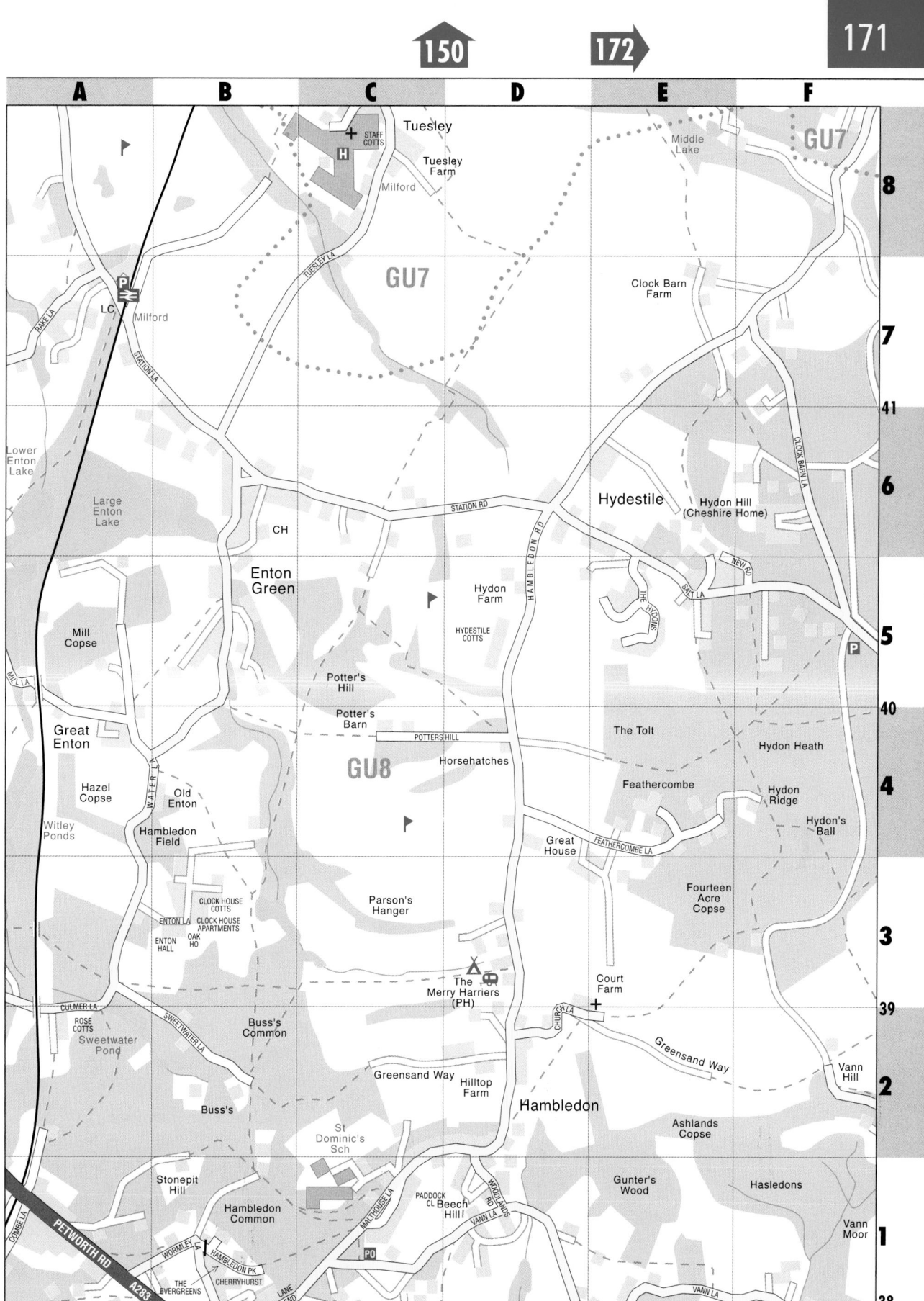

← 150
172 →

Tuesley

STAFF COTTS

Milford

Tuesley Farm

Middle Lake

GU7

Clock Barn Farm

GU7

TUESLEY LA

8

LC

Milford

STATION LA

Milford

41

7

Lower Enton Lake

Large Enton Lake

CH

STATION RD

Hydestile

Hydon Hill (Cheshire Home)

CLOCK BARN LA

6

NEW RD

SALT LA

Enton Green

Hydon Farm

HAMBLEDON RD

THE LYONS

P

5

Mill Copse

HYDESTILE COTTS

HILL LA

Potter's Hill

40

Great Enton

Potter's Barn

POTTERS HILL

The Tolt

Hydon Heath

Hazel Copse

WATER LA

Old Enton

GU8

Horsehatches

Feathercombe

Hydon Ridge

Hydon's Ball

4

Witley Ponds

Hambledon Field

Great House

FEATHERCOMBE LA

Fourteen Acre Copse

CLOCK HOUSE COTTS

CLOCK HOUSE APARTMENTS

Parson's Hanger

ENTON LA

ENTON HALL

OAK HO

CHURCH LA

Court Farm

3

CULMER LA

The Merry Harriers (PH)

39

ROSE COTTS

SWEETWATER LA

Buss's Common

Greensand Way

Greensand Way

Vann Hill

Sweetwater Pond

Greensand Way

Hilltop Farm

2

Buss's

Hambledon

Ashlands Copse

St Dominic's Sch

Gunter's Wood

Hasledons

Stonepit Hill

MALTHOUSE LA

PADDOCK CL

Beech Hill

WOODLANDS RD

VANN LA

Vann Moor

COMBE LA

Hambledon Common

PETWORTH RD

A283

WORMLEY

HAMBLEDON PK

CHERRYHURST

LANE END

PO

VANN LA

38

191
172 →

95   96   97

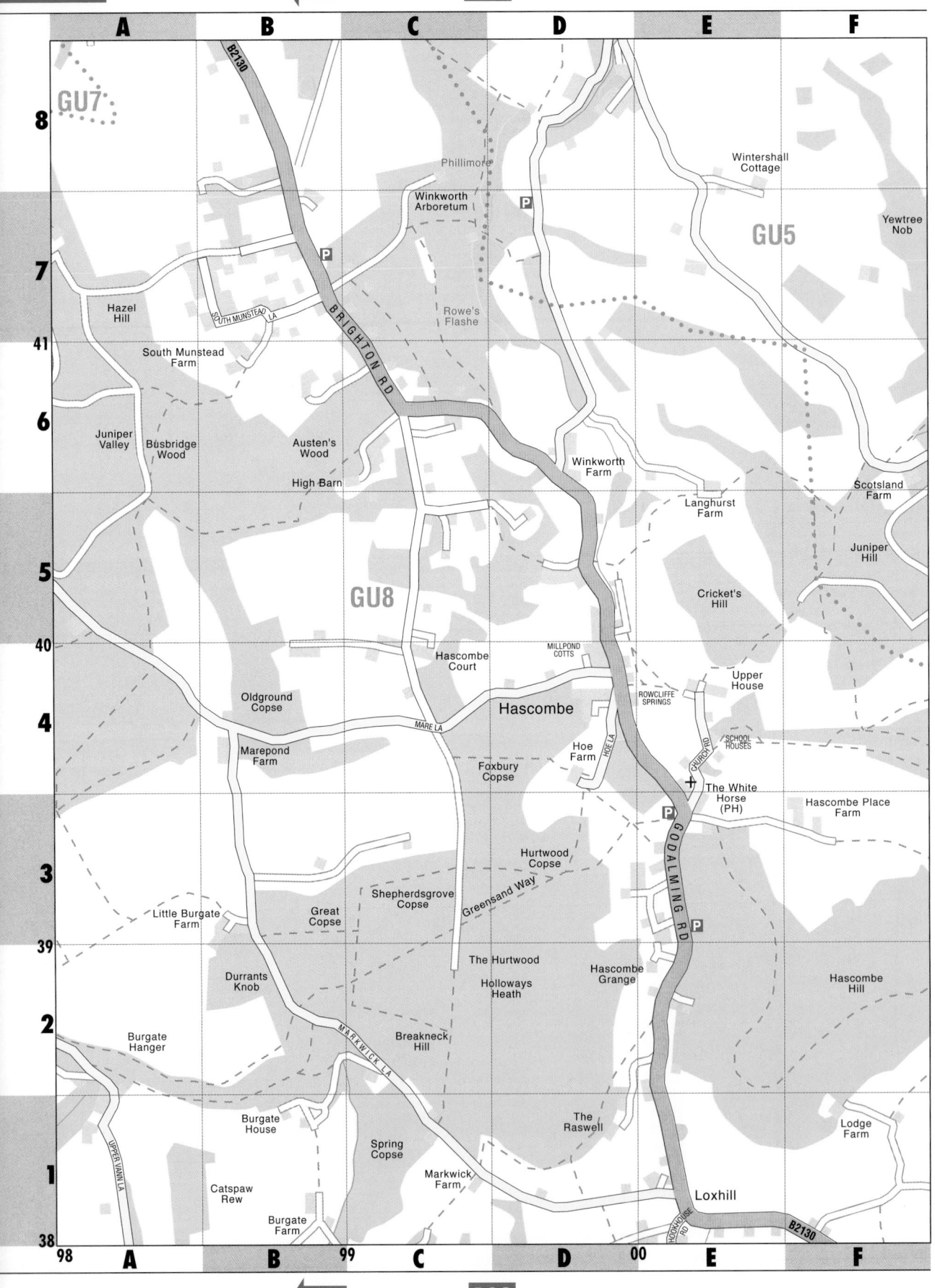

GU7

GU5

GU8

Hascombe

Hazel Hill

South Munstead Farm

Juniper Valley

Busbridge Wood

Austen's Wood

High Barn

Winkworth Arboretum

Phillimore

Rowe's Flashe

Winkworth Farm

Langhurst Farm

Wintershall Cottage

Yewtree Nob

Scotsland Farm

Juniper Hill

Cricket's Hill

Upper House

MILLPOND COTTS

ROWCLIFFE SPRINGS

SCHOOL HOUSES

The White Horse (PH)

Hascombe Place Farm

Hascombe Court

Oldground Copse

Marepond Farm

Hoe Farm

Foxbury Copse

Hurtwood Copse

Shepherdsgrove Copse

Greensand Way

Little Burgate Farm

Great Copse

Durrants Knob

The Hurtwood

Holloways Heath

Hascombe Grange

Hascombe Hill

Burgate Hanger

Breakneck Hill

The Raswell

Burgate House

Spring Copse

Markwick Farm

Lodge Farm

Catspaw Rew

Burgate Farm

Loxhill

B2130

BRIGHTON RD

GODALMING RD

MARE LA

HOE LA

CHURCH RD

MARKWICK LA

UPPER VANN LA

HORSHOUSE RD

B2130

SOUTH MUNSTEAD LA

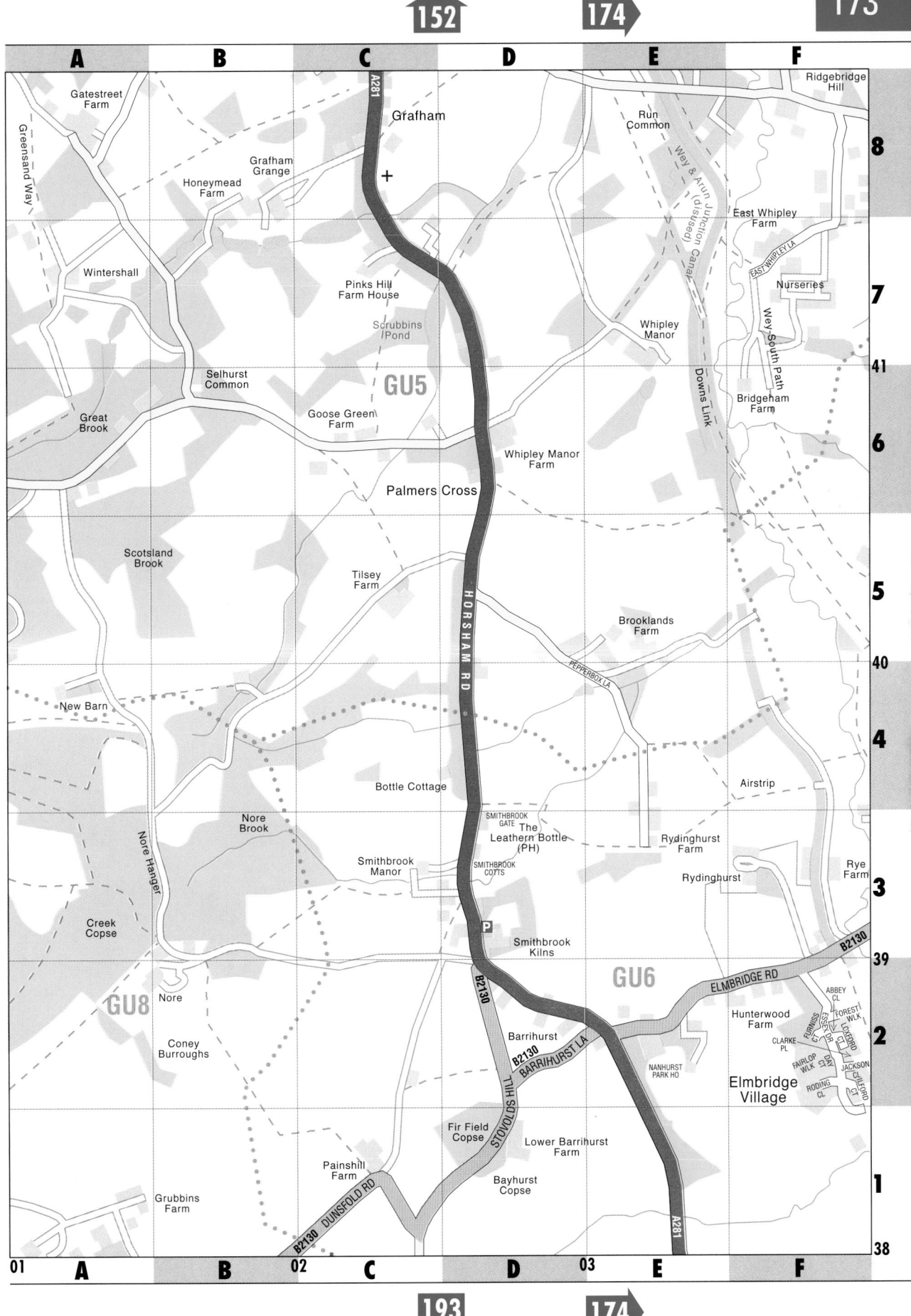

173
153

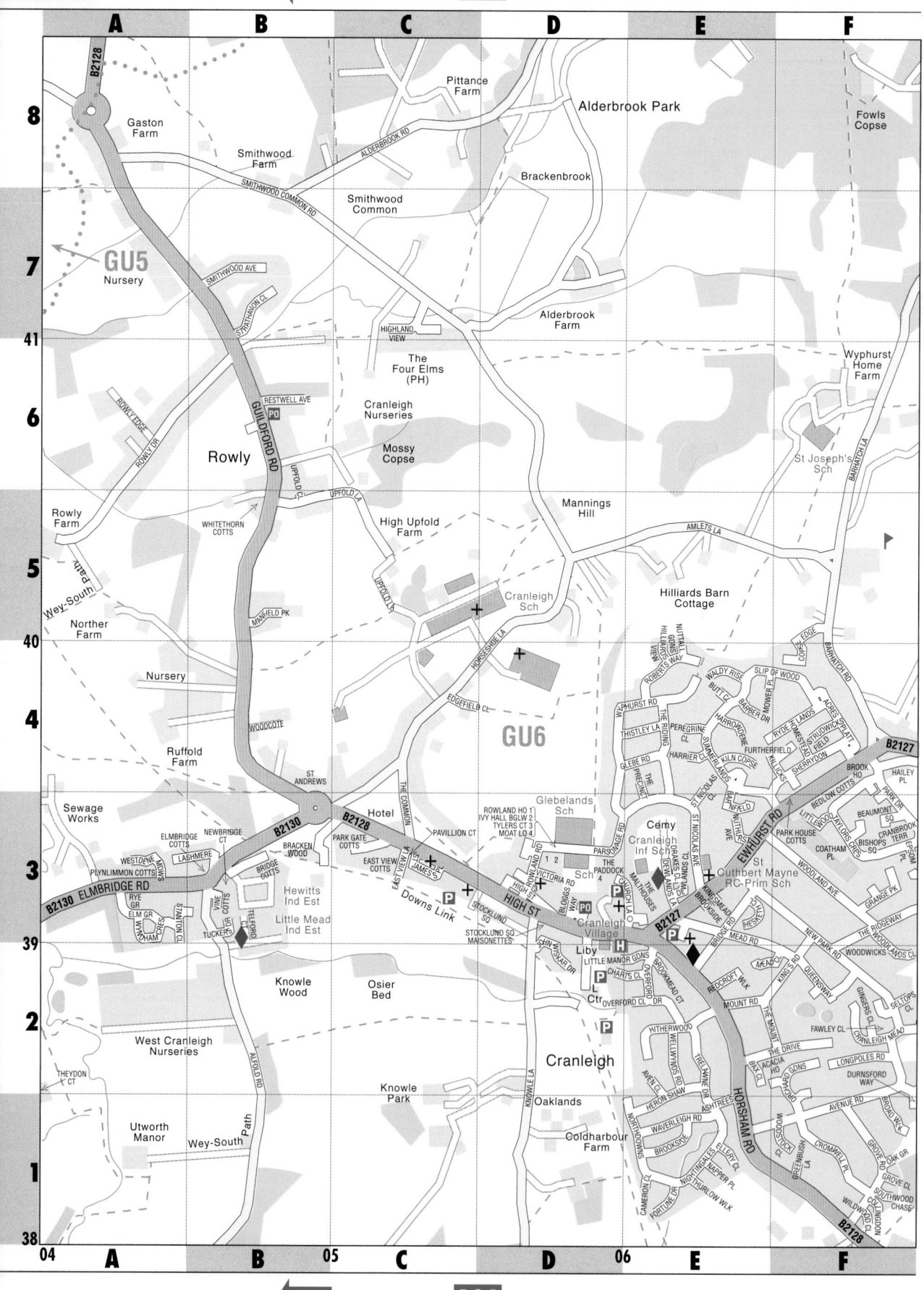

173
194

154
176

175
155

175
196

156
178

A B C D E F

8
7
41
6
5
40
4
3
39
2
1
38

Church Wood
Meares Copse
Buckinghill Farm
Cherry Tree Lodge
ABINGER RD
BROOMEHALL RD
A29
BOGNOR RD
Etherley Copse
New Barn House
Pennsylvania Copse
ETHERLEY HILL
Highfield Wood
Aviary Barn
BURYWOOD HILL
Goster Wood
COX CNR
OCKLEY RD
Sheep Green
Aviary Copse
Square Copse
Holms Gill
PARK LA
High Woods
Wellspring Pond
Hatch Park
Home Farm
Jayes Park
LAKE RD
Jayes Park
COLE'S LA
Kissing Copse
Kings Arms Inn
Ockley Court
B2126
Woodstock House
Volvens Farm
Courtbottom Wood
B2126
MOLE ST
Castle Copse
Red Lion Inn
Weavers Pond
Church Copse
RH5
PO
Ockley
PISLEY LA
Scott-Broadwood CE Inf Sch
Vann Farm
Wickney Holt
Fishfold Farm
Parkland Farmhouse
STANE ST
PRIDEAUX GDNS
Sewage Works
CRICKETERS CL
COUNCIL COTTS
FRIDAY ST
VANN FARM RD
VANN LAKE
The Cricketers Arms (PH)
Vann House
ELMERS RD
Vann Lake
BRICKYARD COPSE
Elmers Farm
RECTORY CL
VANN LAKE RD
CATHILL LA
NEW BARN LA
New Barn
Cathill Wood
LEITH VALE COTTS
Standon Homestead
Birches Wood
Leith Vale
STANDON LA
Fir Copse
Sewage Works
Hannah Peschar Gall & Gdn
Eversheds Farm
Waleys La
WEARE ST
CHURCH LA
WALEYS LA
Oakwood Mill Farm
Hopgardens Rue
Waleys
A29

13 A B 14 C D 15 E F

197
178

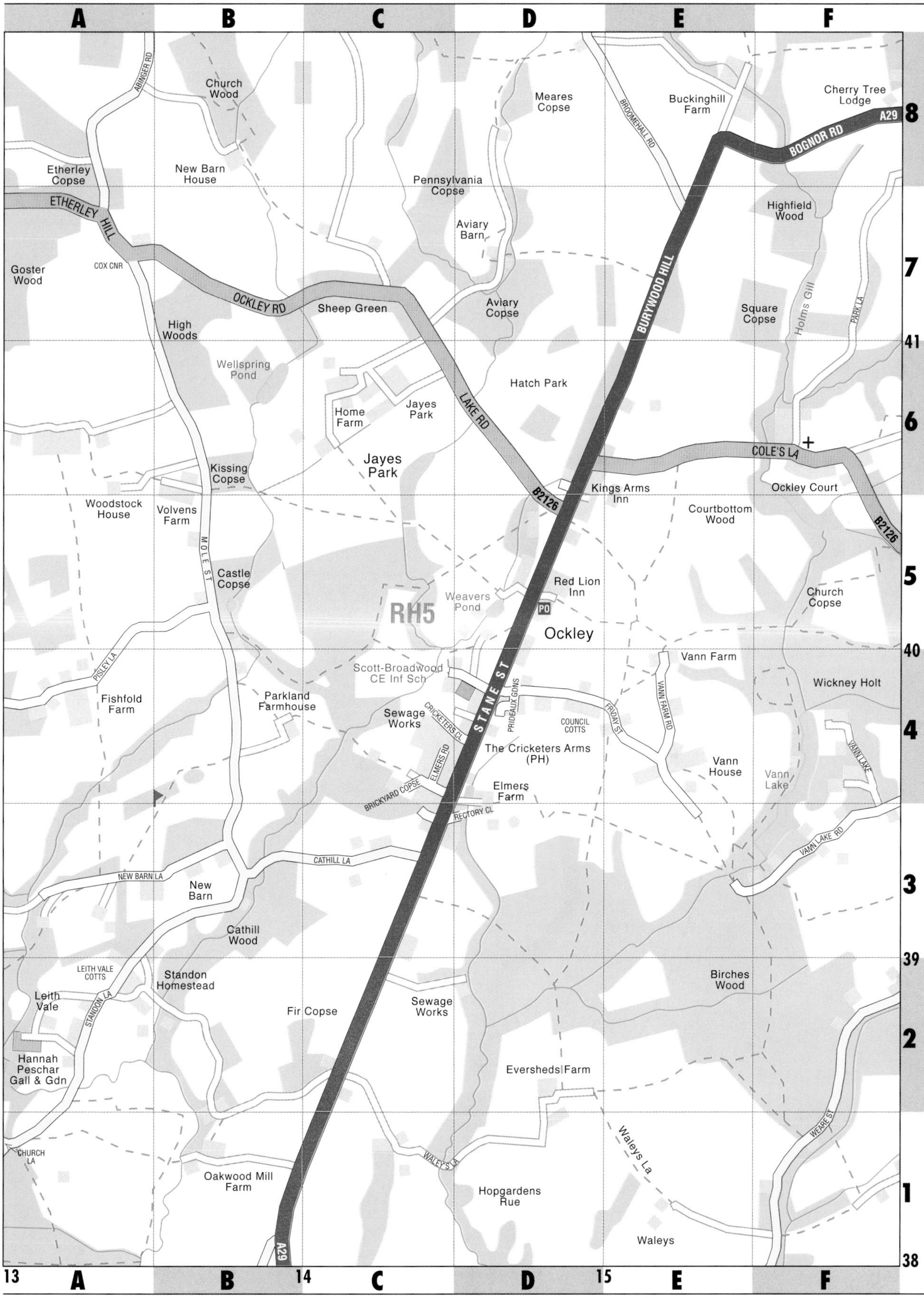

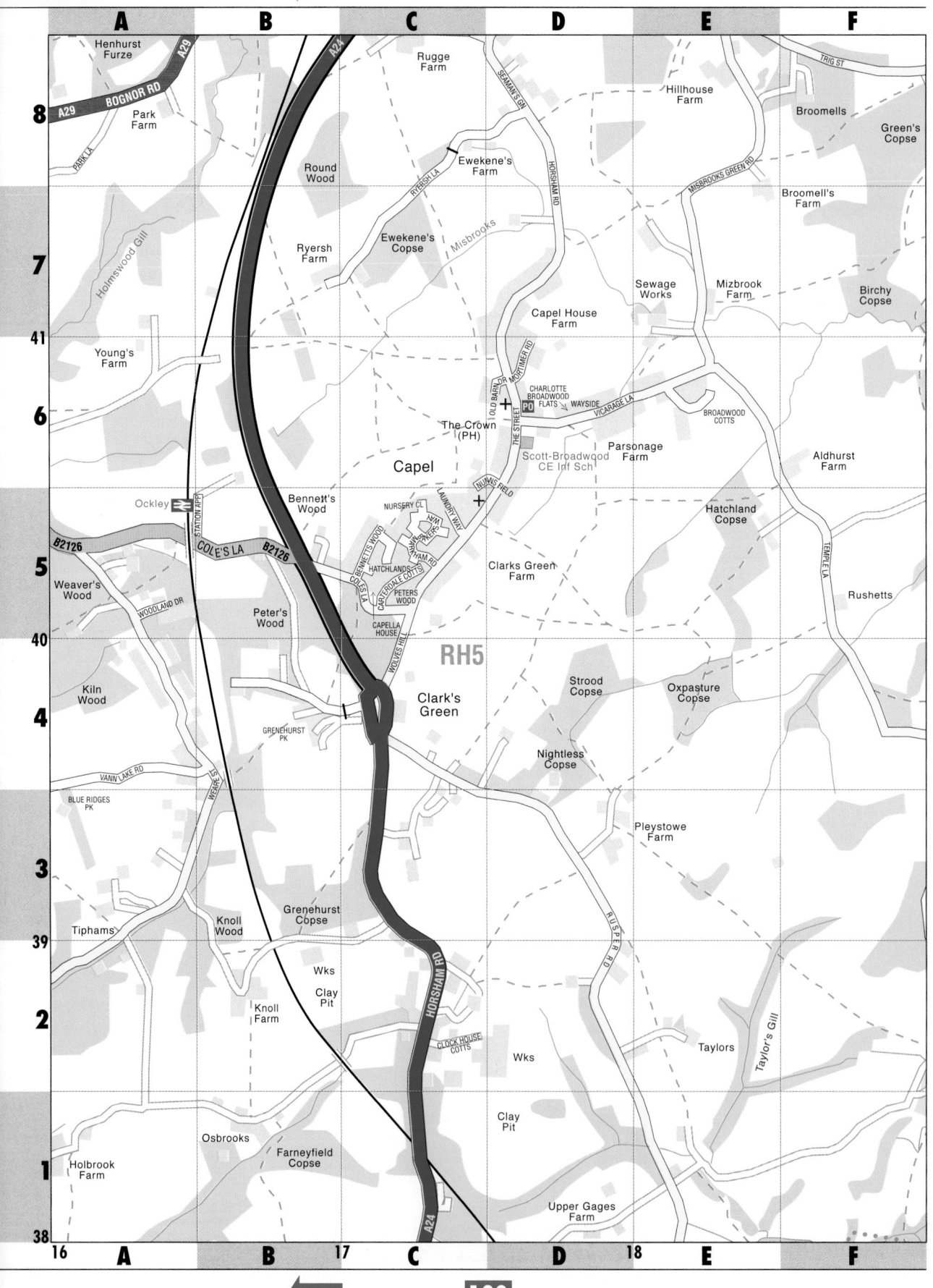

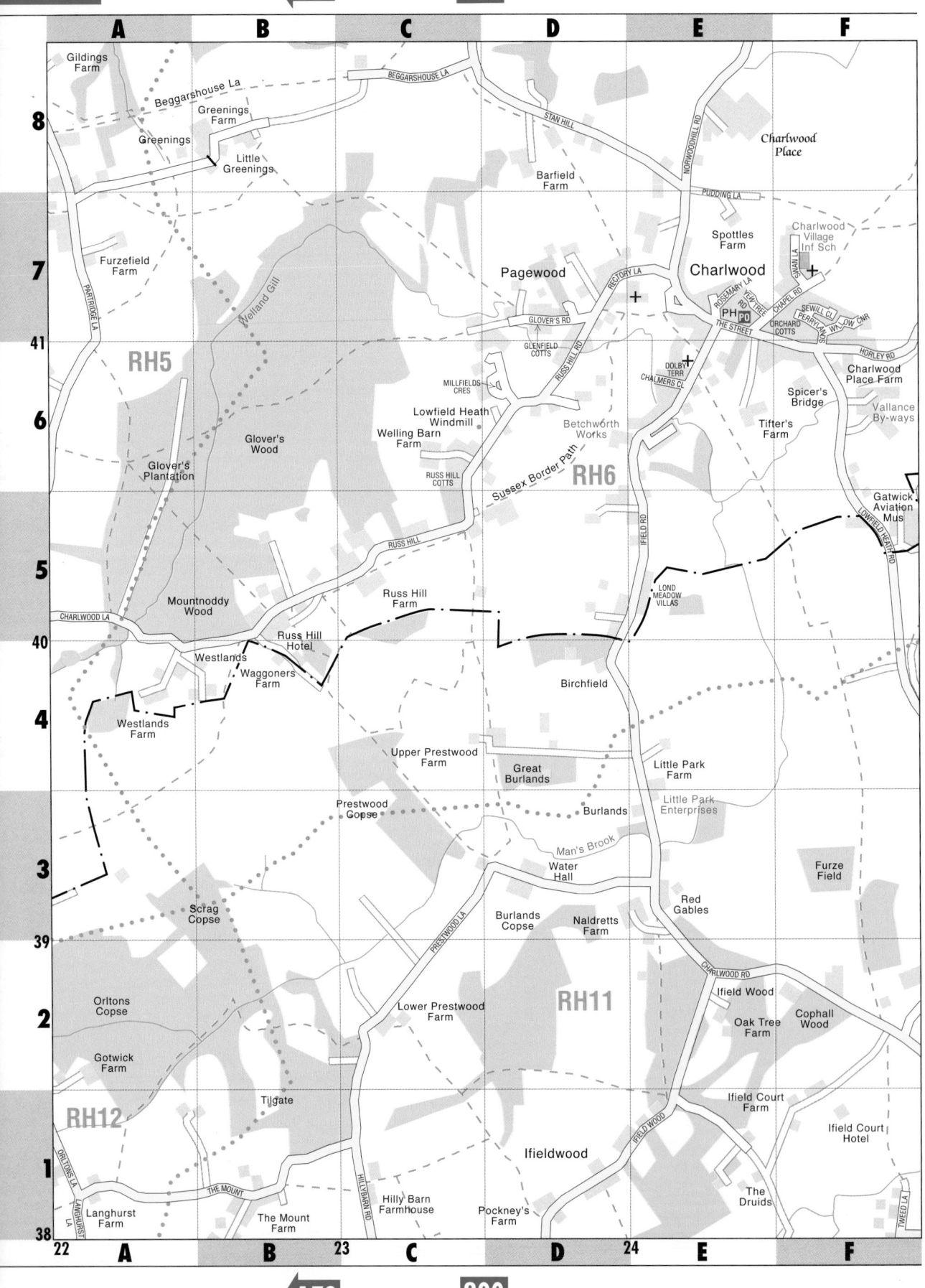

A B C D E F

8
7
41
6
5
40
4
3
39
2
1
38

Gildings Farm

Beggarshouse La

Beggarshouse La

Greenings
Farm
Greenings
Little Greenings

Stan Hill

Barfield
Farm

Norwoodhill Rd

Charlwood
Place

Pudding La

Furzefield
Farm

Welland Gill

Partridge La

RH5

Pagewood

Glover's Rd

Rectory La

Charlwood

Spottles
Farm

Charlwood
Village
Inf Sch

Glenfield
Cotts

Millfields
Cres

Lowfield Heath
Windmill
Welling Barn
Farm

Russ Hill Rd

Russ Hill
Cotts

Sussex Border Path

RH6

Betchworth
Works

Dolby
Terr
Chalmers Cl

Rosemary La

PH
PO
The Street

Orchard
Cotts

Sewill Cl
Perryfield
Low Cnr

Chapel Rd

Horley Rd

Charlwood
Place Farm

Spicer's
Bridge

Tifter's
Farm

Vallance
By-ways

Gatwick
Aviation
Mus

Glover's
Wood

Glover's
Plantation

Russ Hill

Russ Hill
Farm

Lond
Meadow
Villas

Ifield Rd

Lowfield Heath Rd

Charlwood La

Mountnoddy
Wood

Russ Hill
Hotel

Westlands

Waggoners
Farm

Birchfield

Westlands
Farm

Upper Prestwood
Farm

Great
Burlands

Little Park
Farm

Little Park
Enterprises

Furze
Field

Prestwood
Copse

Burlands

Man's Brook

Water
Hall

Red
Gables

Scrag
Copse

Burlands
Copse

Naldretts
Farm

Charlwood Rd

Prestwood La

RH11

Ifield Wood

Orltons
Copse

Lower Prestwood
Farm

Oak Tree
Farm

Cophall
Wood

Gotwick
Farm

Tilgate

Ifield Court
Farm

Ifield Court
Hotel

RH12

Ifieldwood

The
Druids

Orltons La
Langhurst La

Langhurst
Farm

The Mount

The Mount
Farm

Hilly Barn Rd

Hilly Barn
Farmhouse

Pockney's
Farm

Ifield Wood

Tweed La

22 A 23 B C 24 D E F

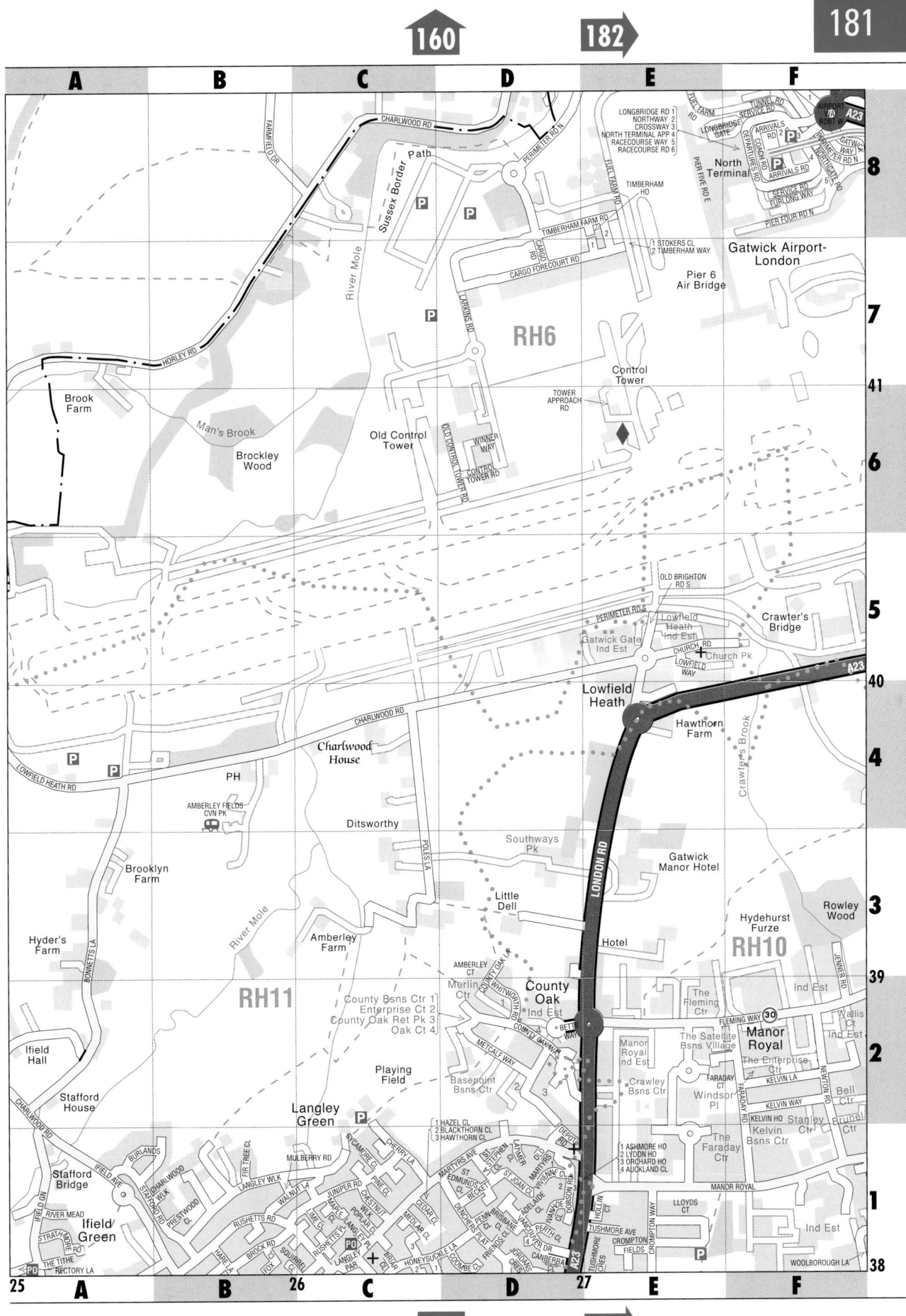

160
182
201
182

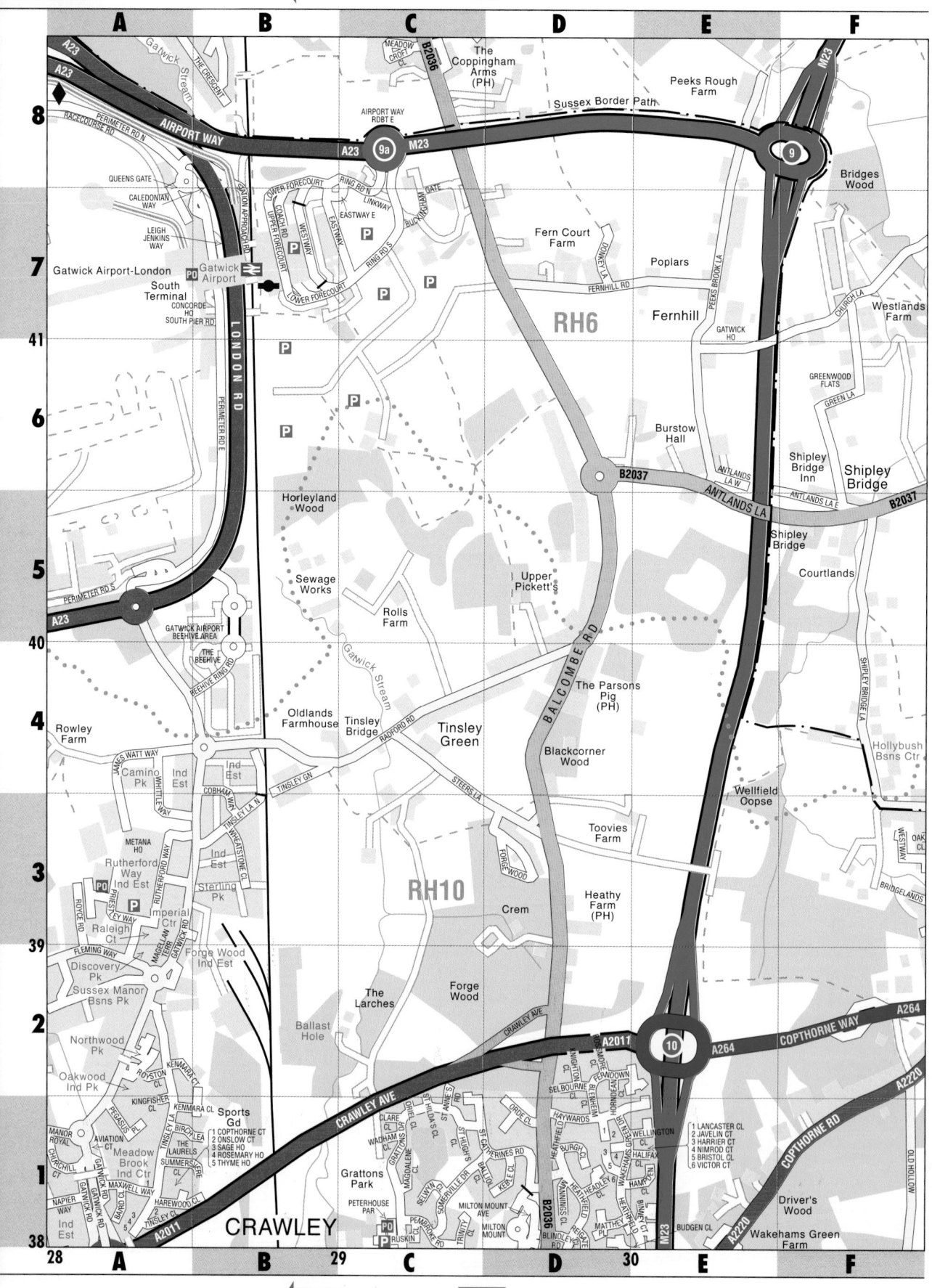

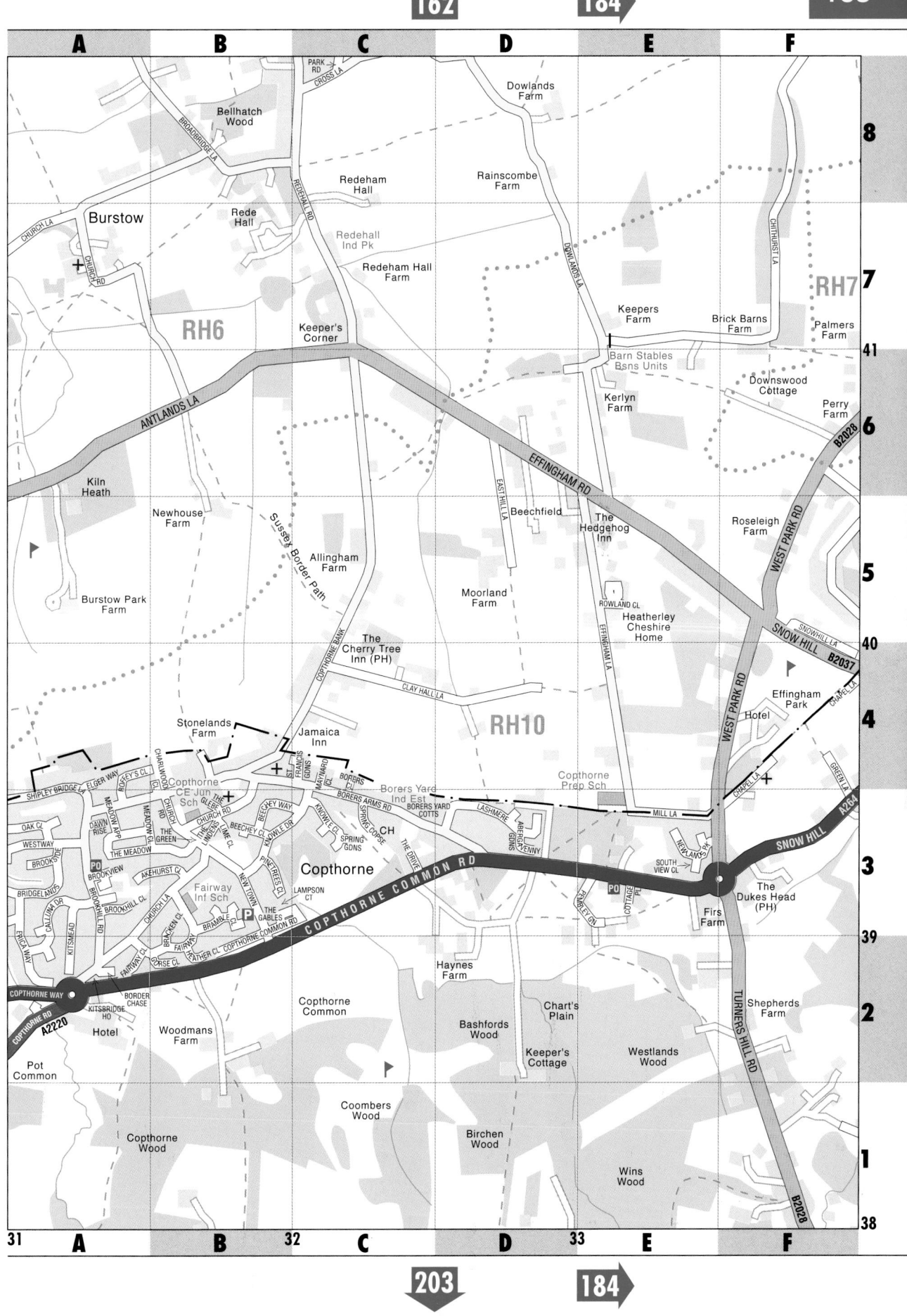
162
184
A
B
C
D
E
F
8
7
41
6
5
40
4
3
39
2
1
38
31
32
33
Bellhatch Wood
Dowlands Farm
Redeham Hall
Rainscombe Farm
Burstow
Rede Hall
Redehall Ind Pk
Redeham Hall Farm
RH6
RH7
Keeper's Corner
Keepers Farm
Brick Barns Farm
Palmers Farm
Barn Stables Bsns Units
Downswood Cottage
Kerlyn Farm
Perry Farm
ANTLANDS LA
EFFINGHAM RD
Kiln Heath
Newhouse Farm
Beechfield
The Hedgehog Inn
Roseleigh Farm
WEST PARK RD
Sussex Border Path
Allingham Farm
Burstow Park Farm
Moorland Farm
Heatherley Cheshire Home
SNOW HILL
B2037
B2028
The Cherry Tree Inn (PH)
CLAY HALL LA
Effingham Park
Hotel
RH10
Stonelands Farm
Jamaica Inn
Copthorne CE Jun Sch
Borers Yard Ind Est
Copthorne Prep Sch
MILL LA
Copthorne
CH
COPTHORNE COMMON RD
Fairway Inf Sch
The Dukes Head (PH)
Firs Farm
A264
Haynes Farm
COPTHORNE WAY
A2220
Hotel
Copthorne Common
Woodmans Farm
Chart's Plain
Bashfords Wood
Keeper's Cottage
Westlands Wood
Shepherds Farm
TURNERS HILL RD
Pot Common
Coombers Wood
Copthorne Wood
Birchen Wood
Wins Wood
203
184

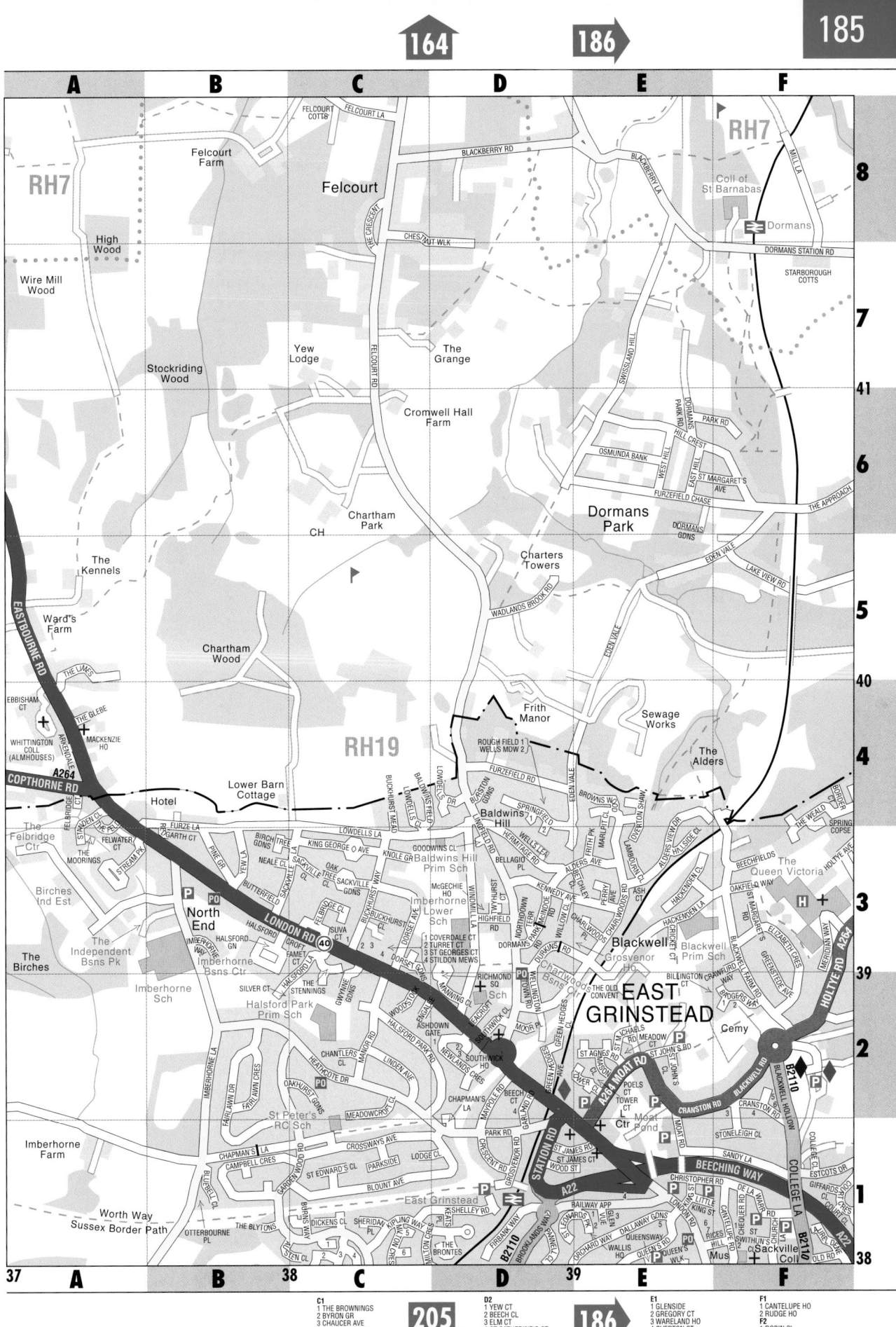

C1
1 THE BROWNINGS
2 BYRON GR
3 CHAUCER AVE
4 TENNYSON RISE
5 THE SAYERS
6 WORDSWORTH RISE

D2
1 YEW CT
2 BEECH CL
3 ELM CT
4 ST CATHERINE'S CT

E1
1 GLENSIDE
2 GREGORY CT
3 WARELAND HO
4 OVERTON CT
5 BROOKLAND HO
6 INSTITUTE WLK
7 CANTELUPE MEWS

F1
1 CANTELUPE HO
2 RUDGE HO
F2
1 ROBIN CL
2 EARLE HO
3 EASTCOURT VILLAS
4 THE OLD SURGERY
5 ST JULIAN
6 DRURY LO

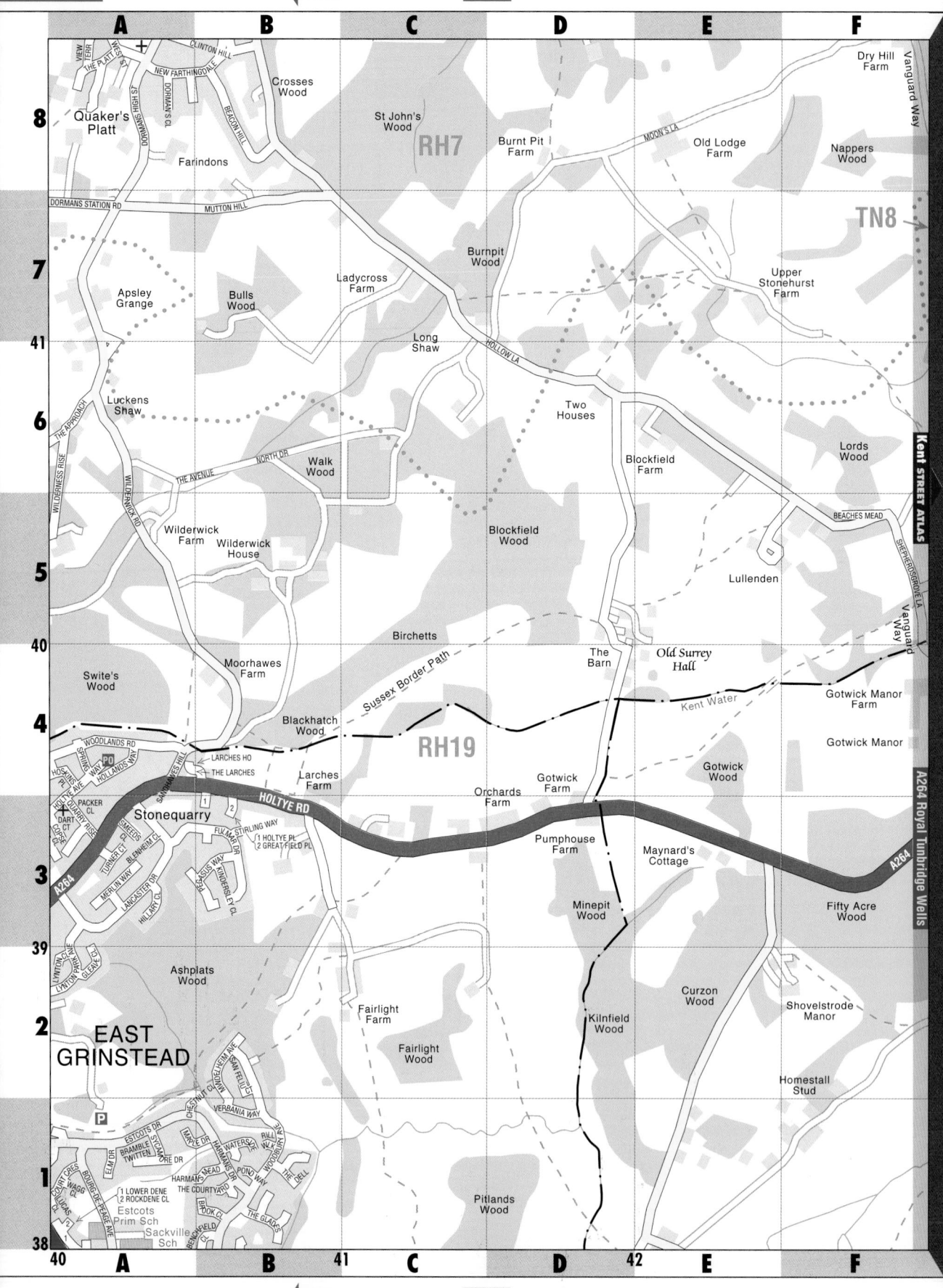

Dry Hill Farm

Vanguard Way

Quaker's Platt

Crosses Wood

St John's Wood

RH7

Burnt Pit Farm

Old Lodge Farm

Nappers Wood

Farindons

Clinton Hill

New Farthingdale

Beacon Hill

Moon's La

TN8

Dormans Station Rd

Mutton Hill

Burnpit Wood

Ladycross Farm

Upper Stonehurst Farm

41

Apsley Grange

Bulls Wood

Long Shaw

Hollow La

Two Houses

Lords Wood

Luckens Shaw

Blockfield Farm

Beaches Mead

The Approach

Wilderness Rise

North Dr

Walk Wood

Wilderwick Rd

The Avenue

Wilderwick Farm

Wilderwick House

Blockfield Wood

Lullenden

Shepherds Grove La

Vanguard Way

Kent Street Atlas

40

Birchetts

The Barn

Old Surrey Hall

Swite's Wood

Moorhawes Farm

Sussex Border Path

Kent Water

Gotwick Manor Farm

Blackhatch Wood

RH19

Gotwick Manor

Woodlands Rd

Spring Way

Hollands Way

Santhaws Hill

Larches Ho

The Larches

Larches Farm

Orchards Farm

Gotwick Farm

Gotwick Wood

A264

Stonequarry

Holtye Rd

Pumphouse Farm

Maynard's Cottage

Fifty Acre Wood

A264 Royal Tunbridge Wells

39

Ashplats Wood

Minepit Wood

Curzon Wood

Shovelstrode Manor

EAST GRINSTEAD

Fairlight Farm

Kilnfield Wood

Homestall Stud

Fairlight Wood

Estcots Prim Sch

Sackville Sch

Pitlands Wood

167
188

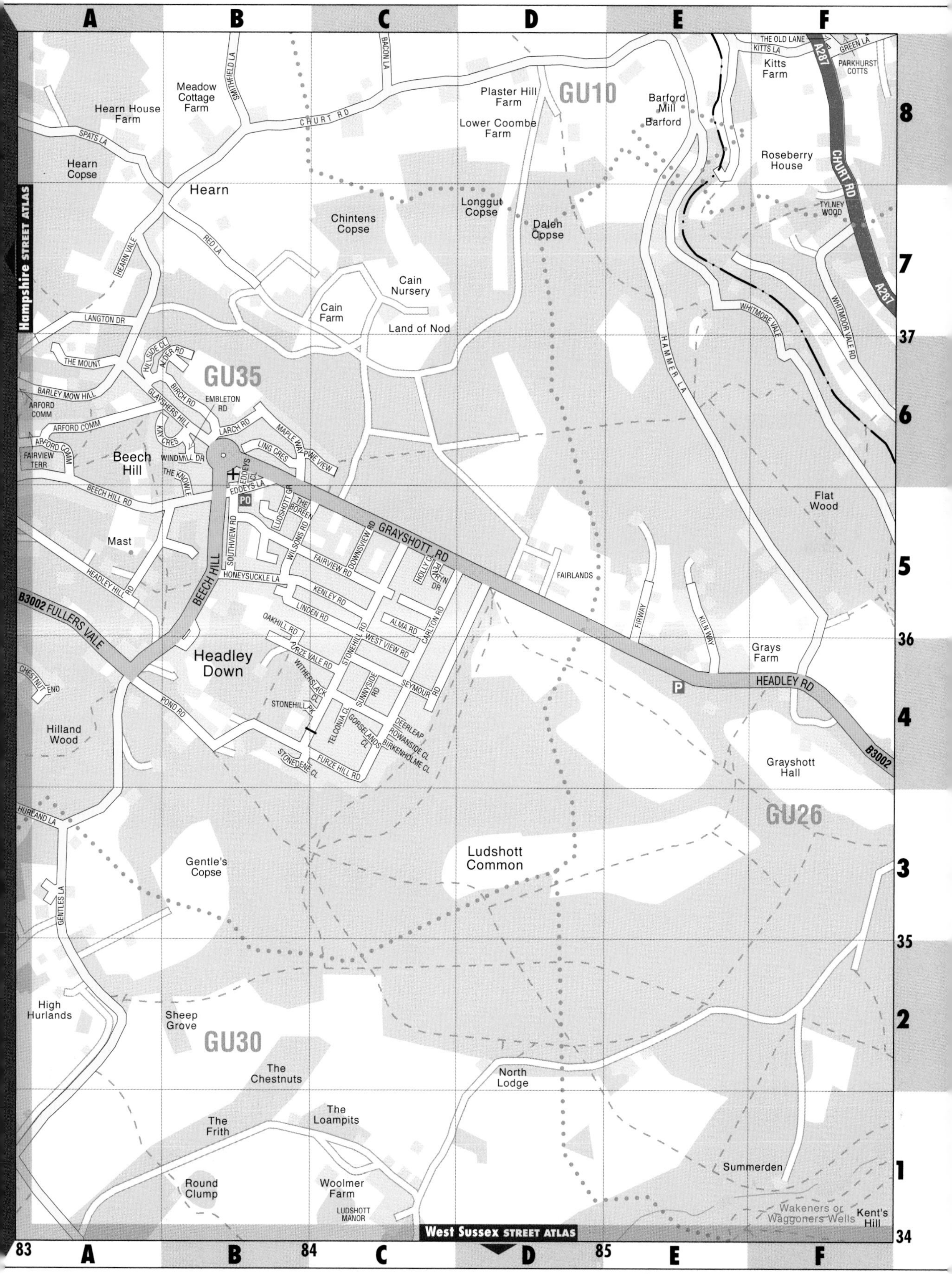
A
B
C
D
E
F
8
7
37
6
5
36
4
3
35
2
1
34
83
84
85
Hampshire STREET ATLAS
West Sussex STREET ATLAS
GU10
GU35
GU26
GU30
THE OLD LANE
KITTS LA
GREEN LA
PARKHURST COTTS
Kitts Farm
A287
CHURT RD
Meadow Cottage Farm
SMITHFIELD LA
BACON LA
Plaster Hill Farm
Barford Mill
Barford
Hearn House Farm
SPATS LA
CHURT RD
Lower Coombe Farm
Roseberry House
Hearn Copse
Hearn
Chintens Copse
Longgut Copse
Dalen Copse
TYLNEY WOOD
RED LA
HEARN VALE
Cain Nursery
Cain Farm
Land of Nod
WHITMORE VALE
WHITMOOR VALE RD
A287
LANGTON DR
HAMMER LA
HILLSIDE CL
ALDER RD
THE MOUNT
GU35
BARLEY MOW HILL
BIRCH RD
EMBLETON RD
ARFORD COMM
GLAYSHERS HILL
ARFORD COMM
LARCH RD
MAPLE WAY
KAY CRES
LING CRES
PINE VIEW
ARFORD COMM
FAIRVIEW TERR
Beech Hill
WINDMILL DR
THE KNOWLE
EDDEYS CL
EDDEYS LA
PO
BEECH HILL RD
LUDSHOTT GR
THE BOREEN
Flat Wood
GRAYSHOTT RD
DOWNSVIEW RD
Mast
SOUTHVIEW RD
WILSONS RD
FAIRVIEW RD
HOLLY CL
PENRYN DR
FAIRLANDS
HEADLEY HILL RD
BEECH HILL
HONEYSUCKLE LA
KENLEY RD
FIRWAY
KILN WAY
B3002 FULLERS VALE
LINDEN RD
ALMA RD
CARLTON RD
OAKHILL RD
WEST VIEW RD
Headley Down
STONEHILL RD
FURZE VALE RD
Grays Farm
HEADLEY RD
CHESTNUT END
WITHERSLACK CL
SUNNYSIDE RD
SEYMOUR RD
P
POND RD
STONEHILL PK
Hilland Wood
TELCONIA CL
GORSELANDS CL
DEERLEAP
ROWANSIDE CL
BIRKENHOLME CL
B3002
Grayshott Hall
STONEDENE CL
FURZE HILL RD
HURLAND LA
Ludshott Common
Gentle's Copse
GENTLES LA
High Hurlands
Sheep Grove
North Lodge
The Chestnuts
The Loampits
The Frith
Summerden
Round Clump
Woolmer Farm
LUDSHOTT MANOR
Wakeners or Waggoners Wells
Kent's Hill

188

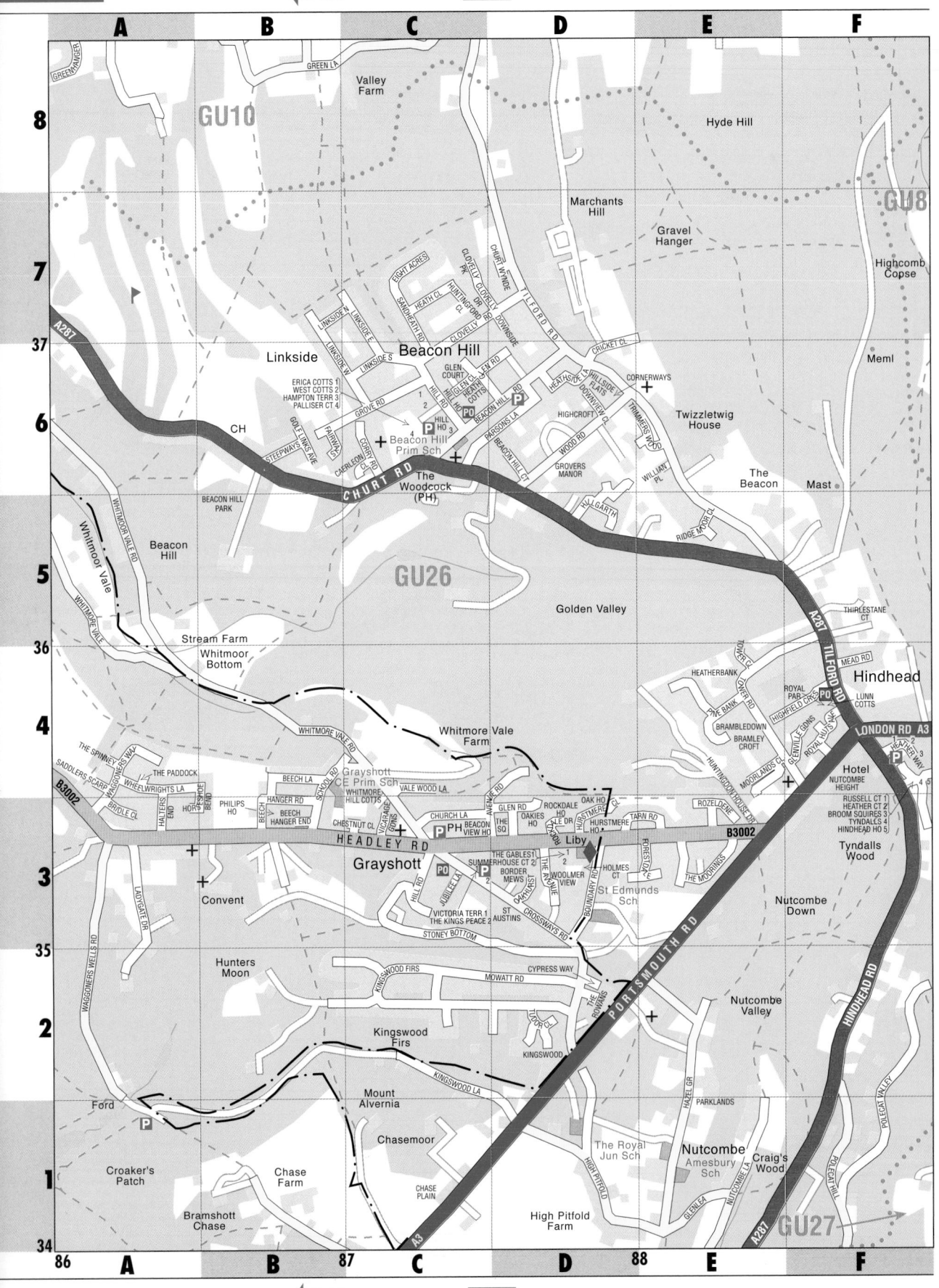

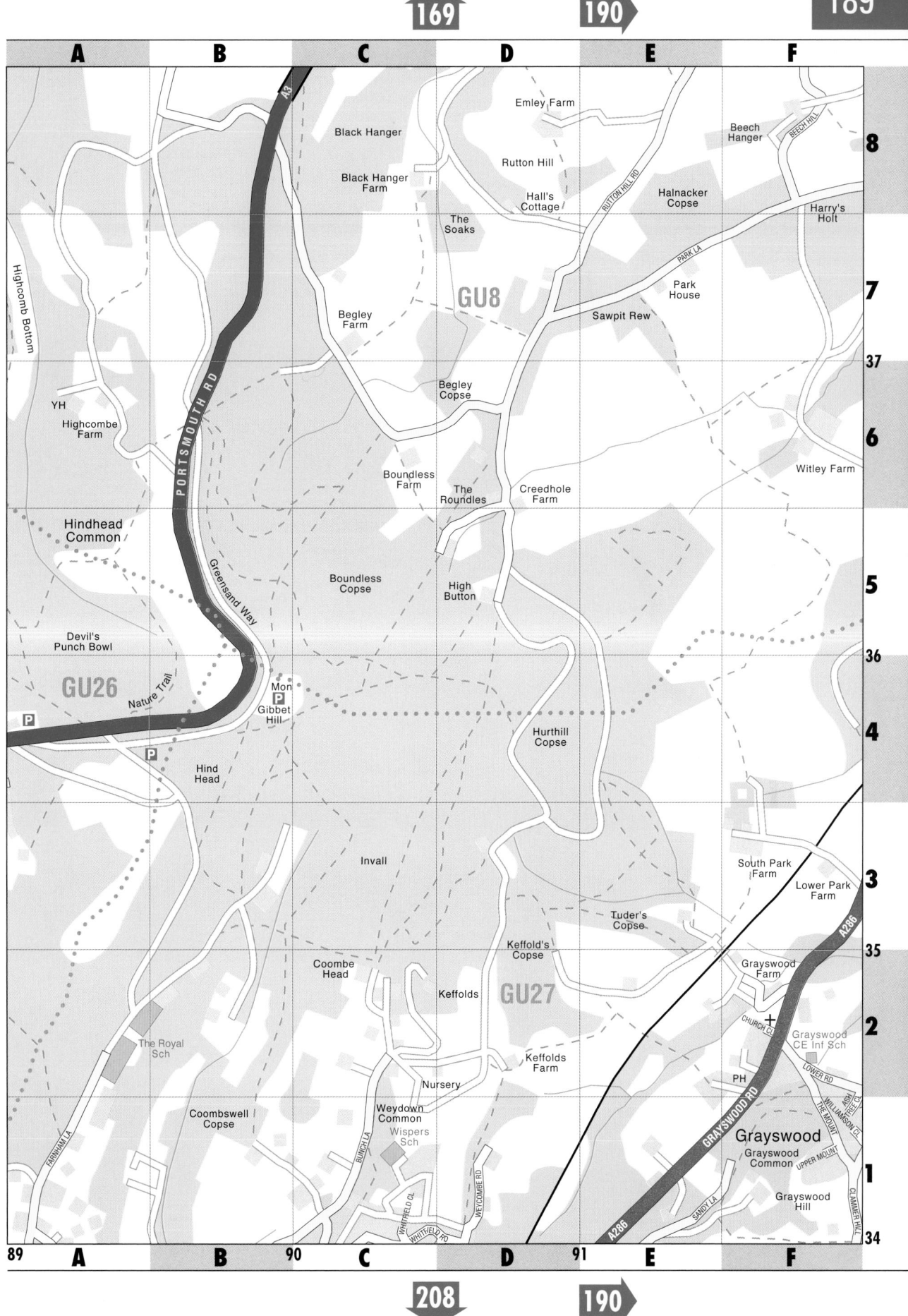

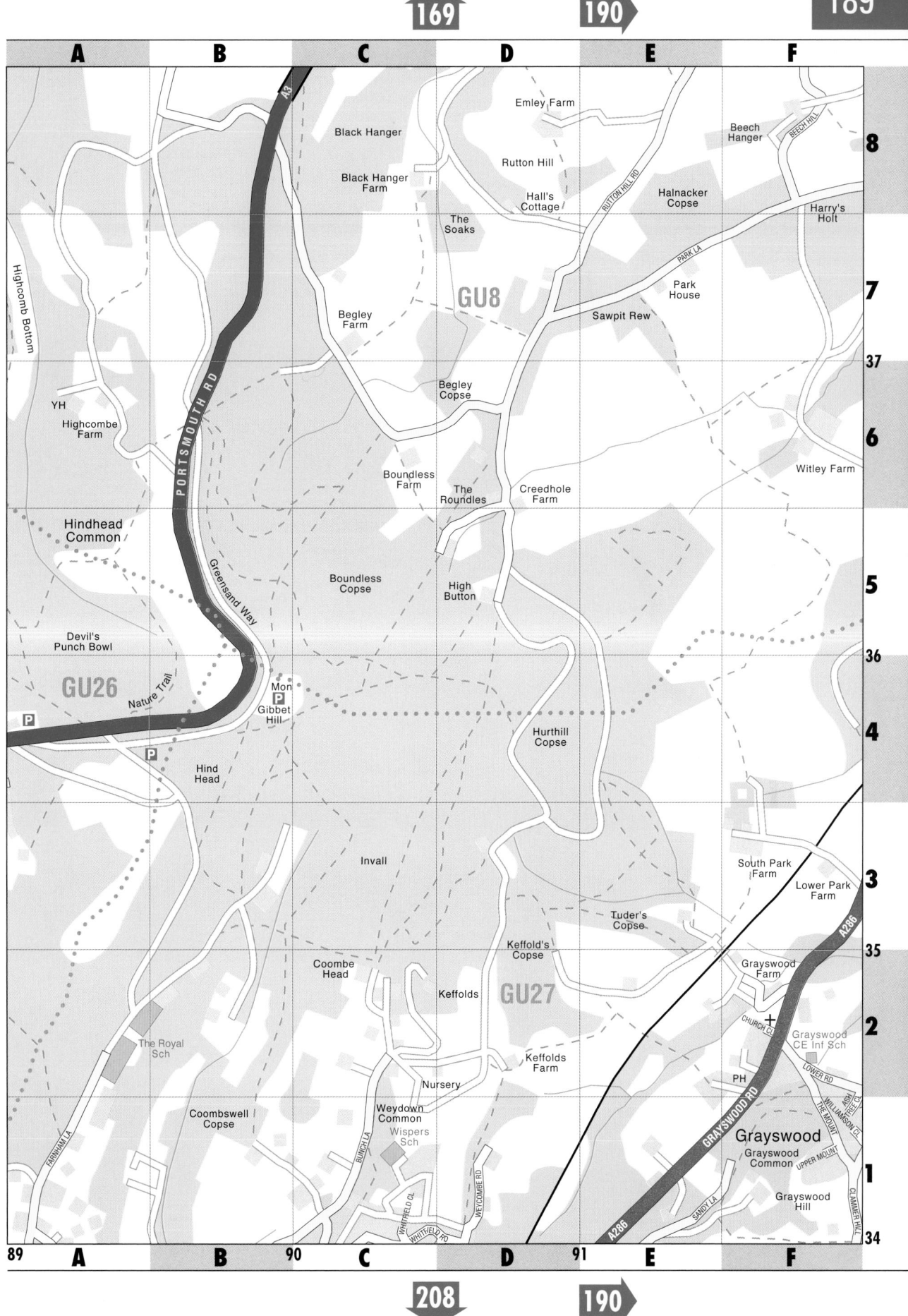

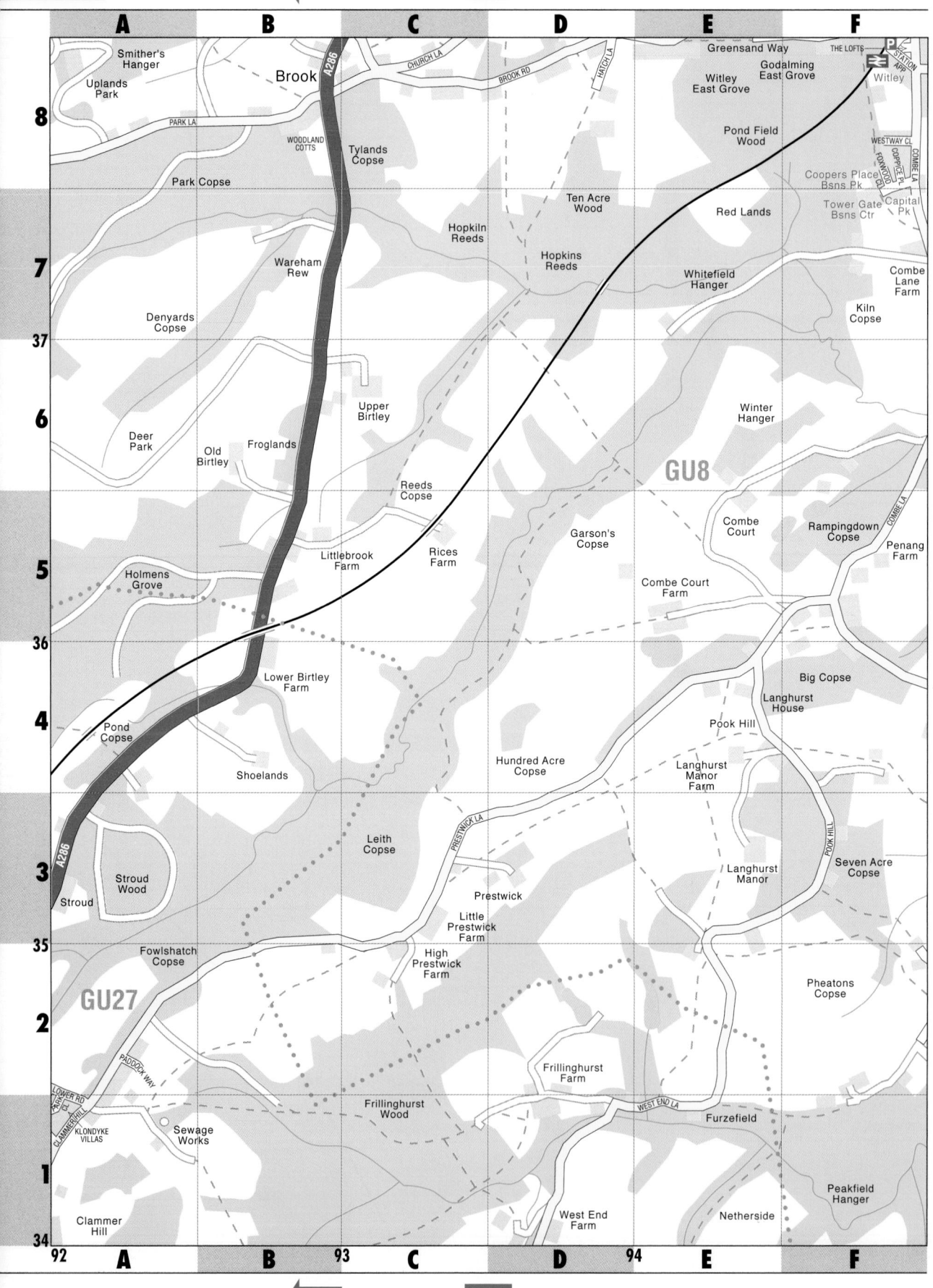

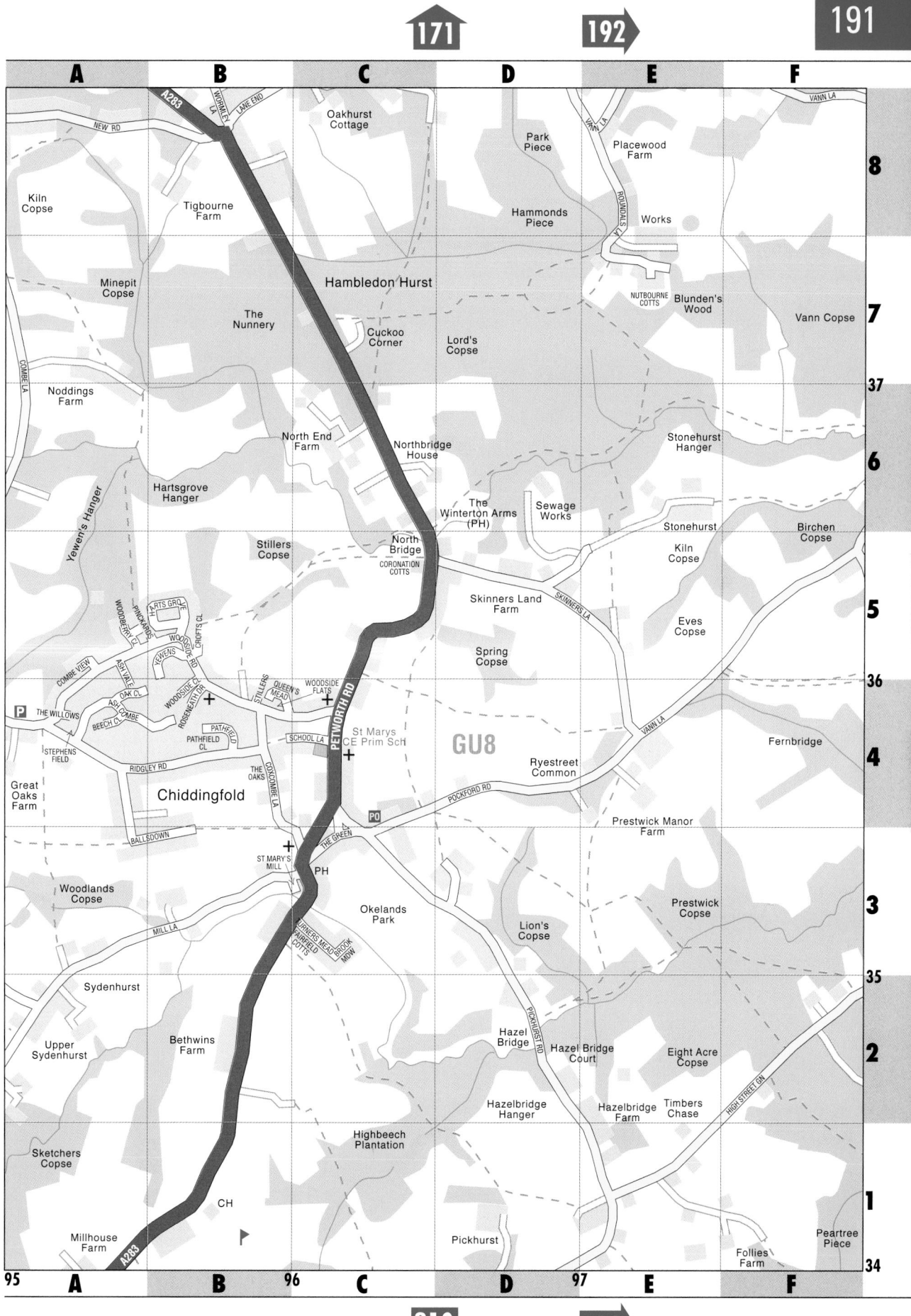

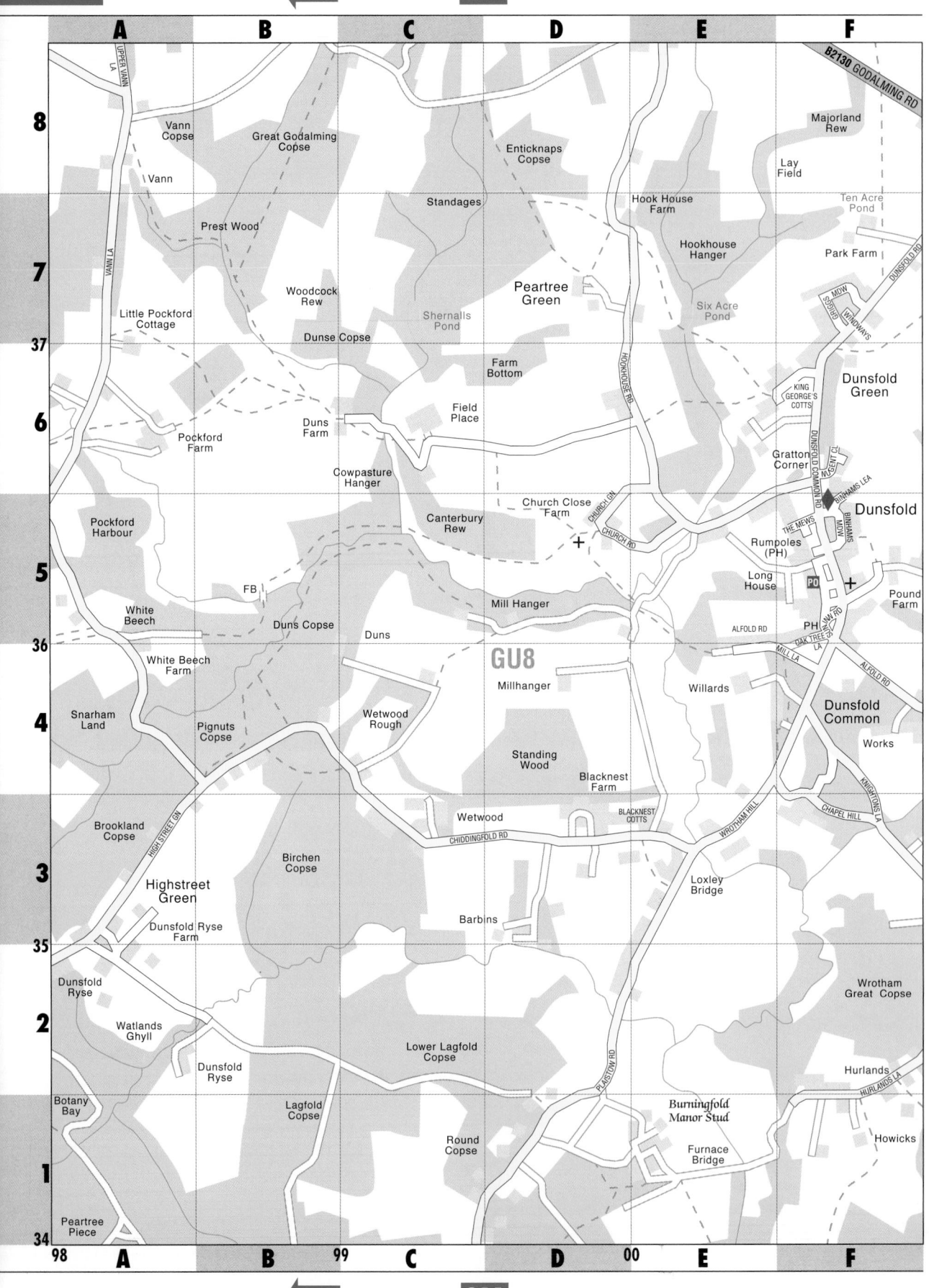

173
194

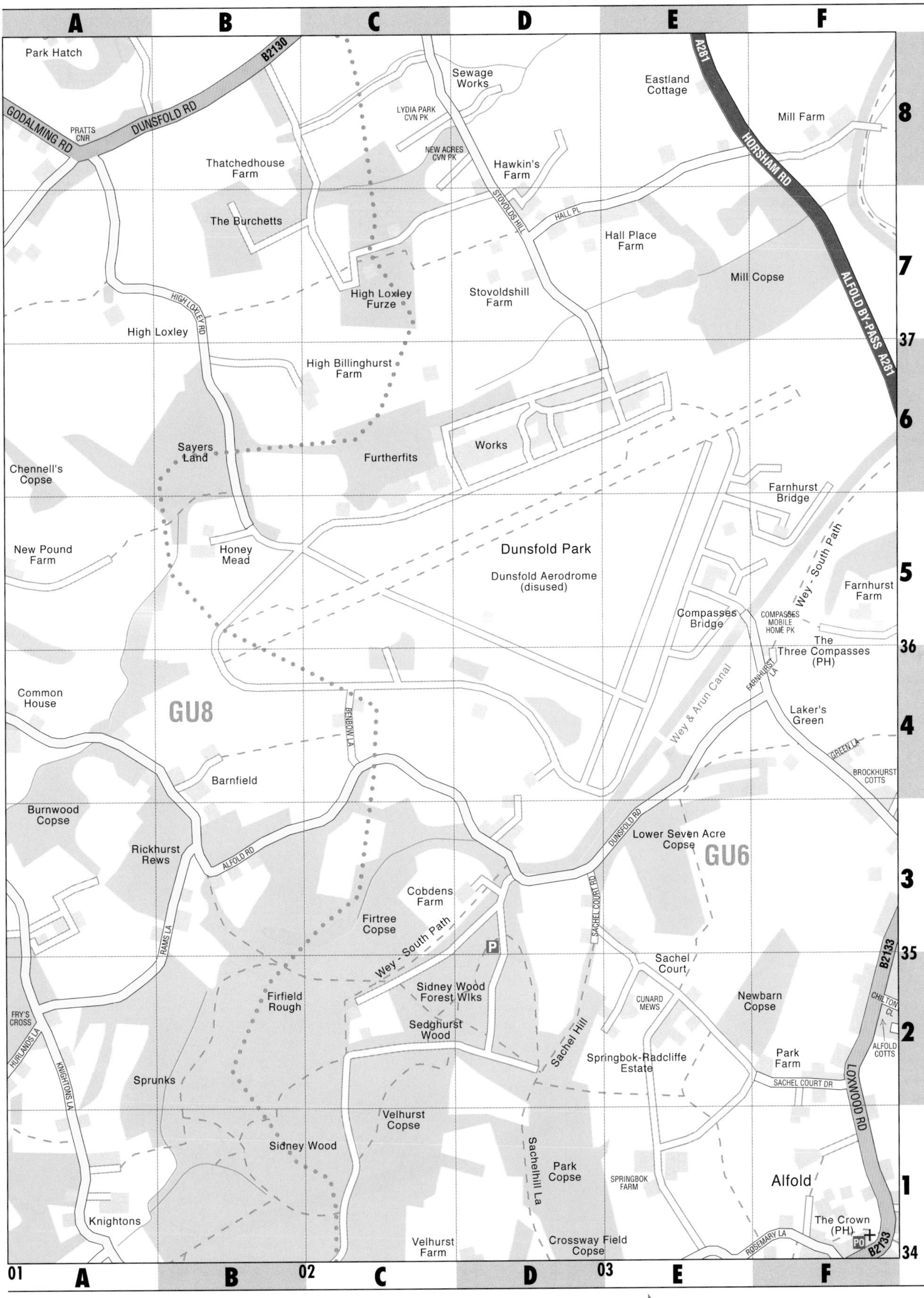

A B C D E F

8 — Park Hatch, GODALMING RD, PRATTS CNR, DUNSFOLD RD, B2130, Sewage Works, LYDIA PARK CVN PK, NEW ACRES CVN PK, Hawkin's Farm, STOVOLDS HILL, HALL PL, Eastland Cottage, HORSHAM RD, A281, Mill Farm

7 — Thatchedhouse Farm, The Burchetts, High Loxley Furze, Stovoldshill Farm, Hall Place Farm, Mill Copse, ALFOLD BY-PASS A281

37 — HIGH LOXLEY RD, High Loxley

6 — High Billinghurst Farm, Sayers Land, Furtherfits, Works

Chennell's Copse, Honey Mead, Farnhurst Bridge, Wey - South Path

5 — New Pound Farm, Dunsfold Park, Dunsfold Aerodrome (disused), Compasses Bridge, COMPASSES MOBILE HOME PK, Farnhurst Farm

36 — The Three Compasses (PH)

Common House, GU8, BENBOW LA, FARNHURST LA, Laker's Green

4 — Wey & Arun Canal, GREEN LA, BROCKHURST COTTS

Barnfield, Burnwood Copse, Rickhurst Rews, ALFOLD RD, RAMS LA, DUNSFOLD RD, Lower Seven Acre Copse, GU6

3 — Cobdens Farm, Firtree Copse, Wey - South Path, SACHEL COURT RD, Sachel Hill, Sachel Court, B2133

35 — FRY'S CROSS, HURLANDS LA, KNIGHTONS LA, Firfield Rough, Sidney Wood Forest Wlks, Sedghurst Wood, CUNARD MEWS, Springbok-Radcliffe Estate, Newbarn Copse, CHILTON CL, ALFOLD COTTS

2 — Sprunks, Velhurst Copse, SACHELHILL LA, Park Farm, SACHEL COURT DR

Sidney Wood, Park Copse, SPRINGBOK FARM, Alfold, LOXWOOD RD

1 — Knightons, Velhurst Farm, Crossway Field Copse, ROSEMARY LA, The Crown (PH), PO, B2133

34

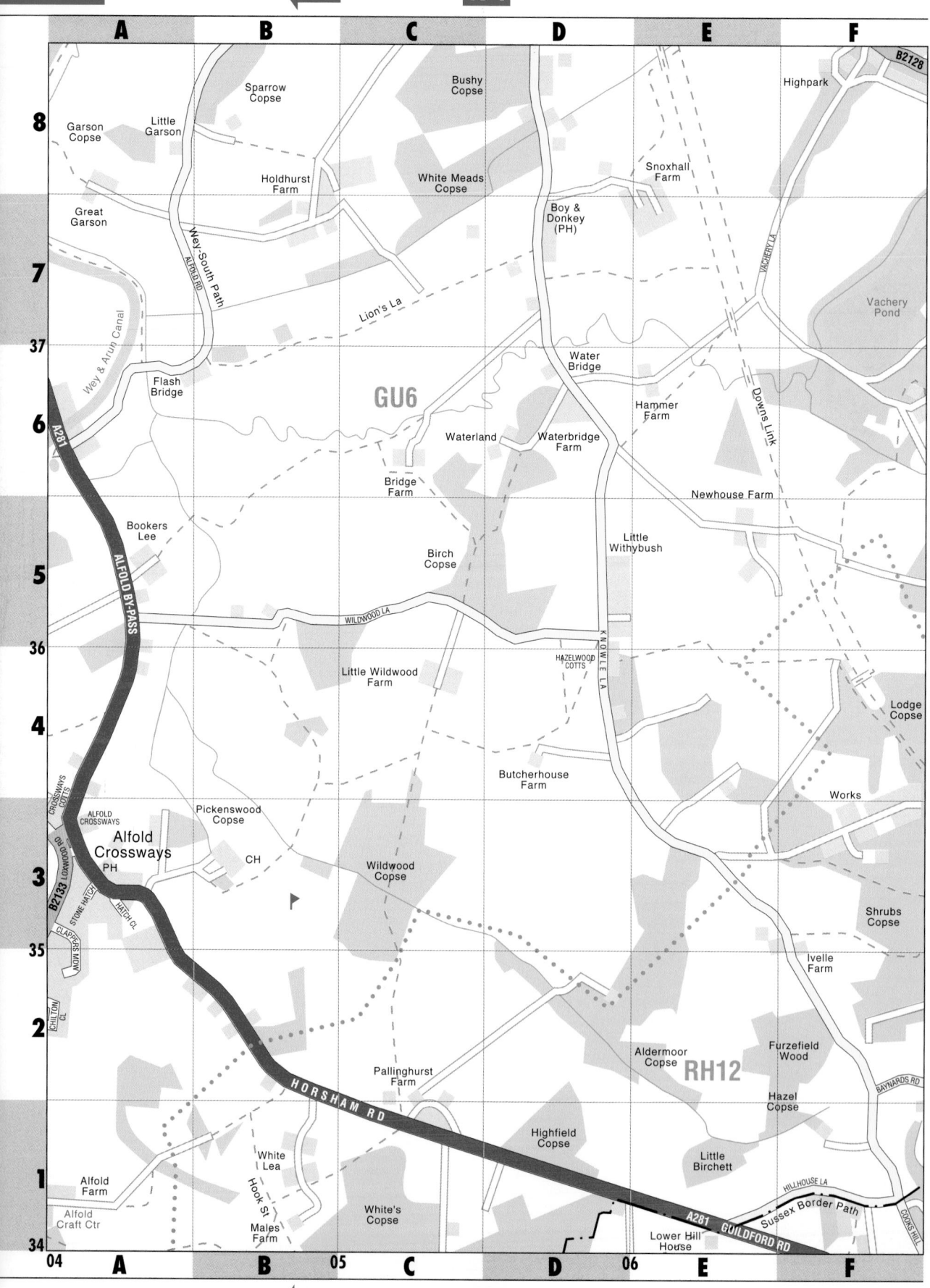

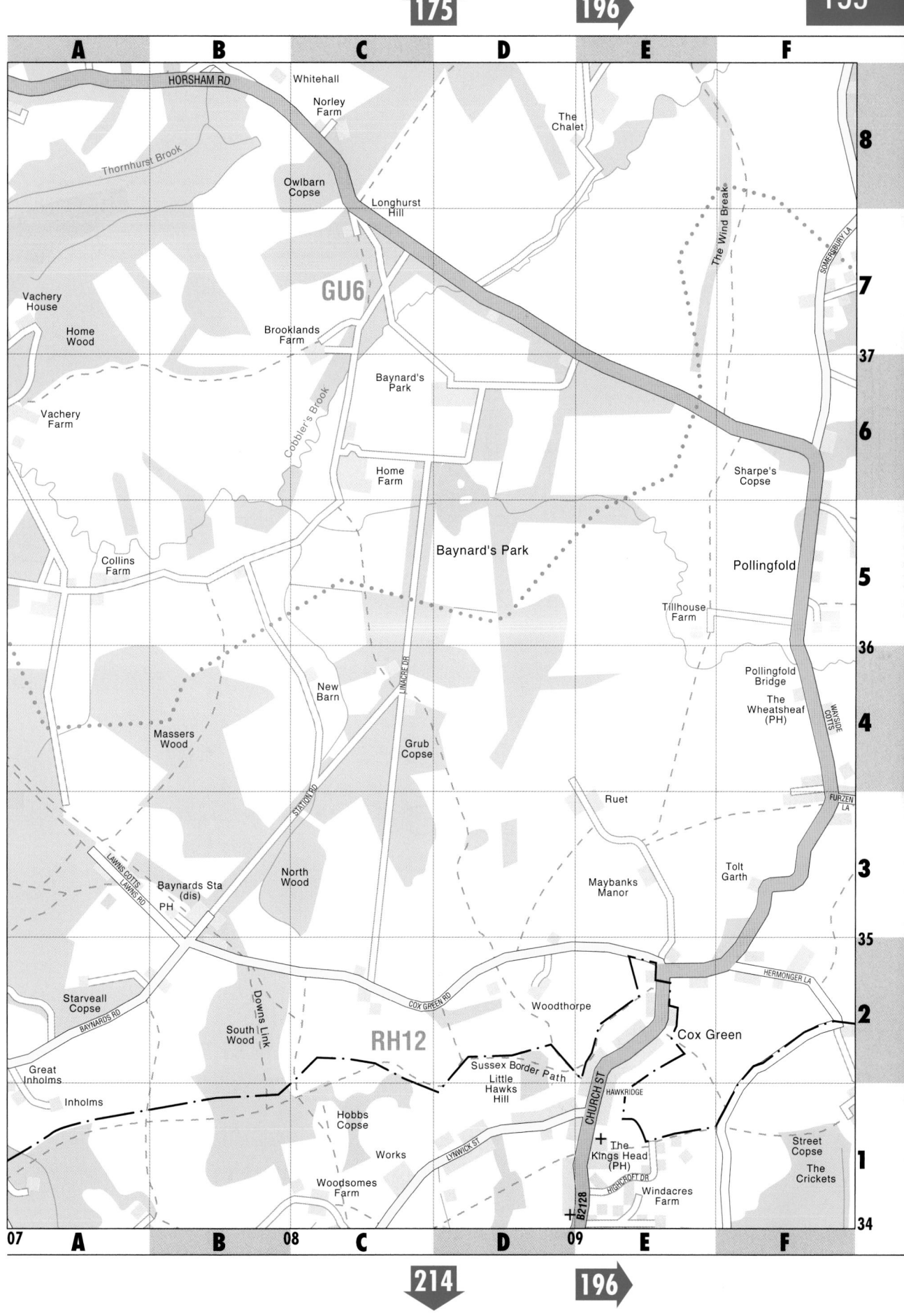

A B C D E F

8

7

37

6

5

36

4

3

35

2

1

34

HORSHAM RD

Whitehall

Norley Farm

The Chalet

Thornhurst Brook

Owlbarn Copse

Longhurst Hill

The Wind Break

SOMERSBURY LA

GU6

Vachery House

Home Wood

Brooklands Farm

Cobbler's Brook

Baynard's Park

Vachery Farm

Home Farm

Sharpe's Copse

Pollingfold

Collins Farm

Baynard's Park

Tillhouse Farm

Pollingfold Bridge

The Wheatsheaf (PH)

WAYSIDE COTTS

New Barn

Massers Wood

Grub Copse

LINACRE DR

FURZEN LA

Ruet

STATION RD

North Wood

Maybanks Manor

Tolt Garth

LAWNS COTTS

LAWNS RD

Baynards Sta (dis)

PH

HERMONGER LA

Starveall Copse

Downs Link

South Wood

COX GREEN RD

Woodthorpe

Cox Green

BAYNARDS RD

RH12

Sussex Border Path

Little Hawks Hill

HAWKRIDGE

CHURCH ST

Great Inholms

Inholms

Hobbs Copse

Works

LYNWICK ST

The Kings Head (PH)

HIGHCROFT DR

Windacres Farm

Street Copse

The Crickets

Woodsomes Farm

B2128

A B C D E F

07 08 09

214 196

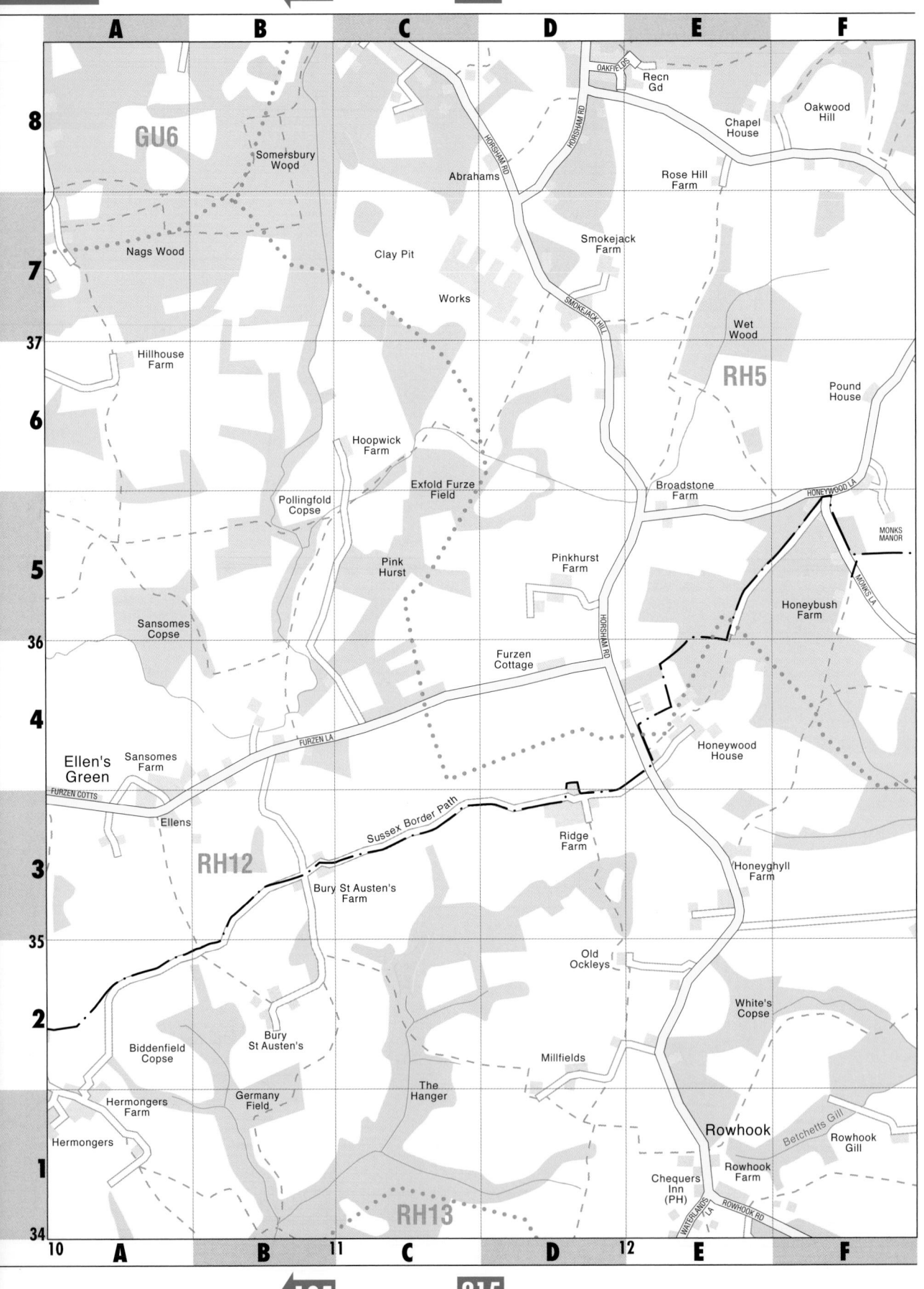

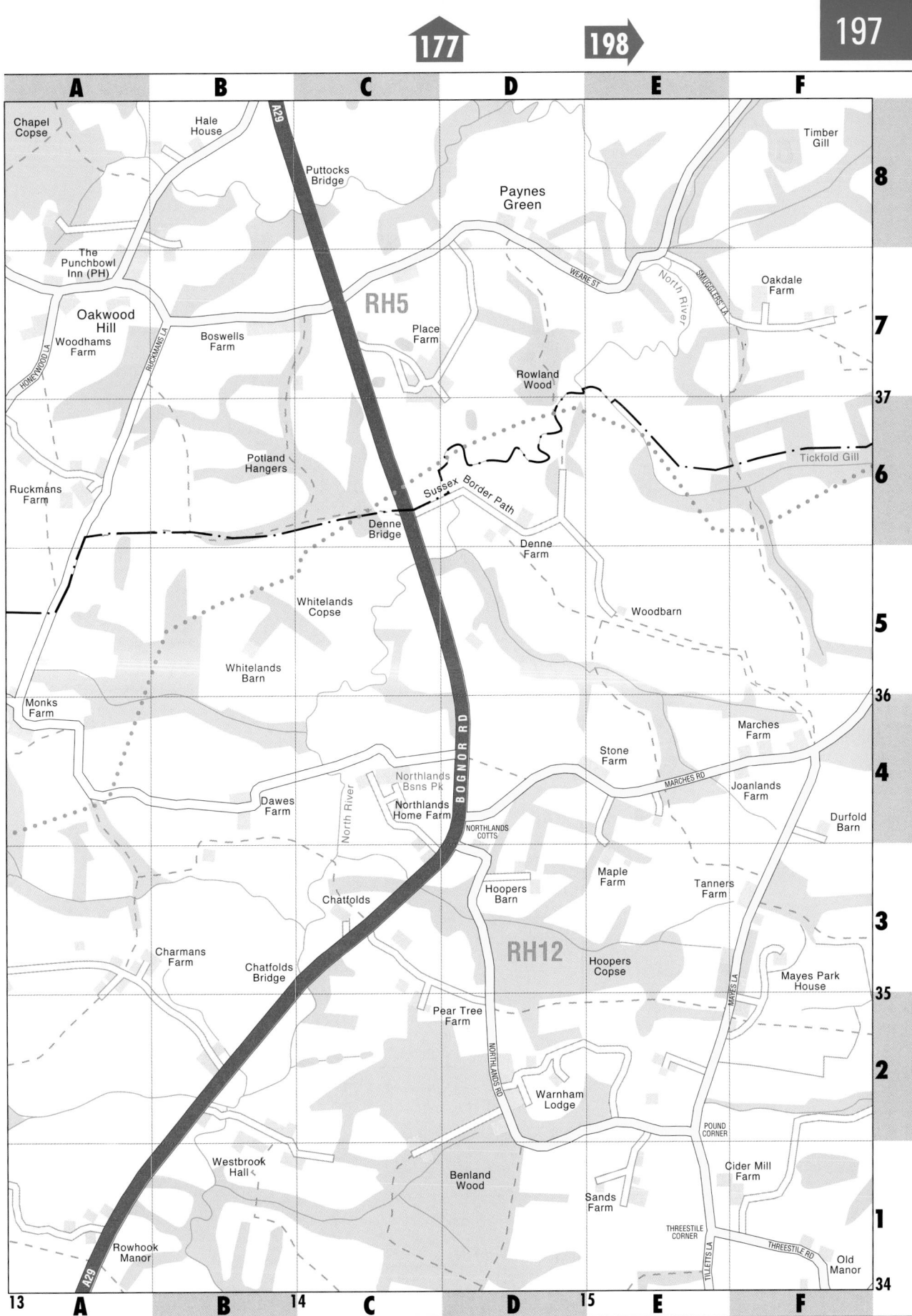
177
198
A
B
C
D
E
F
Chapel Copse
Hale House
A29
Puttocks Bridge
Paynes Green
Timber Gill
The Punchbowl Inn (PH)
Oakwood Hill
Woodhams Farm
HONEYWOOD LA
RUCKMANS LA
Boswells Farm
RH5
Place Farm
WEARE ST
North River
SMUGGLERS LA
Oakdale Farm
Rowland Wood
Potland Hangers
Ruckmans Farm
Sussex Border Path
Tickfold Gill
Denne Bridge
Denne Farm
Whitelands Copse
Woodbarn
Whitelands Barn
Monks Farm
BOGNOR RD
Marches Farm
Stone Farm
MARCHES RD
Joanlands Farm
Northlands Bsns Pk
Northlands Home Farm
Dawes Farm
NORTHLANDS COTTS
Durfold Barn
Hoopers Barn
Maple Farm
Tanners Farm
Chatfolds
RH12
Charmans Farm
Chatfolds Bridge
Hoopers Copse
Mayes Park House
MAYES LA
Pear Tree Farm
NORTHLANDS RD
Warnham Lodge
POUND CORNER
Westbrook Hall
Benland Wood
Cider Mill Farm
Sands Farm
THREESTILE CORNER
TILLETTS LA
THREESTILE RD
Rowhook Manor
Old Manor
8
7
37
6
5
36
4
3
35
2
1
34
13
14
15
216
198

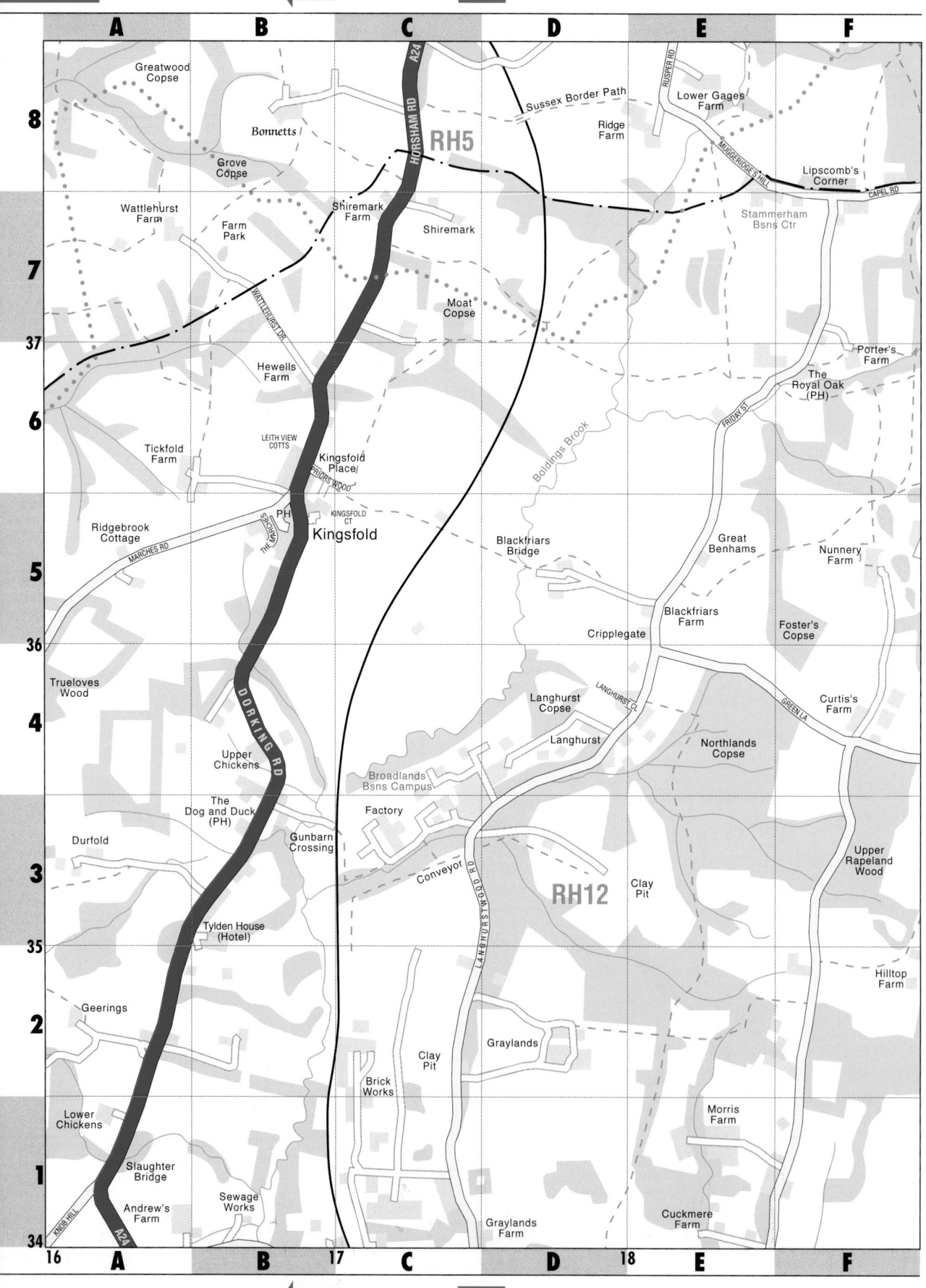

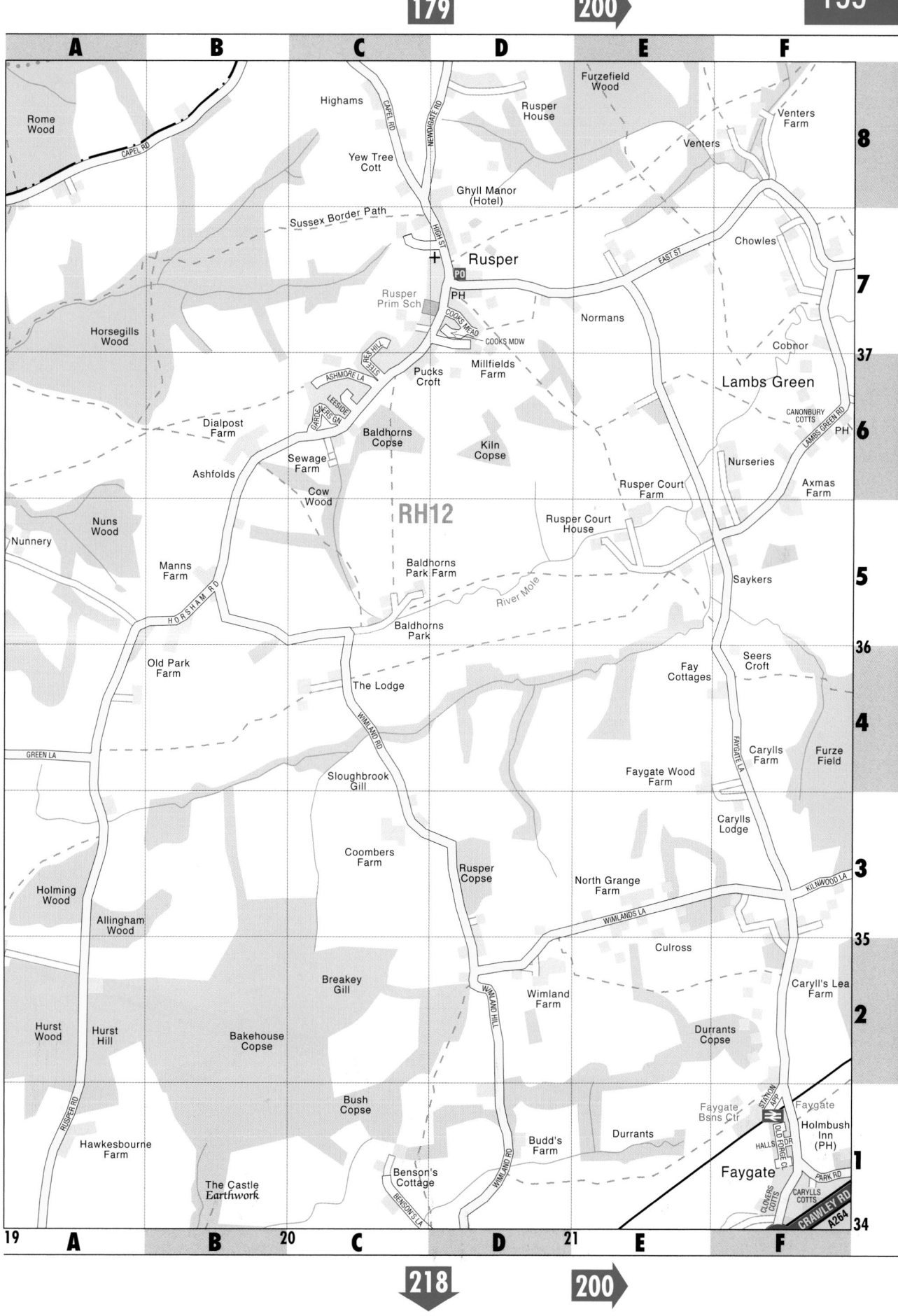
179
200
A
B
C
D
E
F
8
7
37
6
5
36
4
3
35
2
1
34
19
20
21
218
Rome Wood
CAPEL RD
Highams
CAPEL RD
NEWDIGATE RD
Yew Tree Cott
Rusper House
Furzefield Wood
Venters Farm
Venters
Ghyll Manor (Hotel)
Sussex Border Path
HIGH ST
Rusper
PO
PH
EAST ST
Chowles
Rusper Prim Sch
COOKS MEAD
COOKS MDW
Normans
Horsegills Wood
Cobnor
Pucks Croft
Millfields Farm
Lambs Green
ASHMORE LA
LEESIDE
CANONBURY COTTS
LAMBS GREEN RD
PH
Dialpost Farm
Baldhorns Copse
Kiln Copse
Sewage Farm
Ashfolds
Nurseries
Rusper Court Farm
Axmas Farm
Cow Wood
RH12
Nuns Wood
Nunnery
Rusper Court House
Manns Farm
Baldhorns Park Farm
Saykers
HORSHAM RD
River Mole
Baldhorns Park
Old Park Farm
Seers Croft
Fay Cottages
The Lodge
WIMLAND RD
GREEN LA
Carylls Farm
Furze Field
FAYGATE LA
Faygate Wood Farm
Sloughbrook Gill
Carylls Lodge
Coombers Farm
Rusper Copse
North Grange Farm
Holming Wood
KILNWOOD LA
WIMLANDS LA
Allingham Wood
Culross
Breakey Gill
Wimland Farm
Caryll's Lea Farm
WIMLAND HILL
Hurst Wood
Hurst Hill
Bakehouse Copse
Durrants Copse
RUSPER RD
Bush Copse
Faygate Bsns Ctr
STATION APP
Faygate
Holmbush Inn (PH)
Hawkesbourne Farm
Budd's Farm
Durrants
HALLS DR
OLD FORGE CL
Benson's Cottage
WIMLAND RD
Faygate
PARK RD
The Castle
Earthwork
BENSON'S LA
CLOVERS COTTS
CARYLLS COTTS
CRAWLEY RD
A264
200

199
180

E5
1 LOVELL PATH
2 DEWAR CL
3 BEAUMONT CL
4 STRICKLAND CL
5 WEAVER CL
6 BERRYMEADE WLK
7 TUNNMEADE
8 HUNTERS LODGE

Labels and place names on map:

Bridgehill Farm
Langhurst Hill
THE MOUNT
Kirk Farm
LANGHURST LA
BURNT HOUSE LA
HILLYBARN RD
IFIELD WOOD
RECTORY LA
Bonwycks Place
River Mole
Rectory Farmhouse
IFIELD ST
PLOUGH LA
PARHAM RD
PATCHING CL
The Gate (PH)
Broomhill House
Mount Cottages
The Grove
RUSPERS KEEP
ALDWICK CL
Works
Granthams Bridge
Lower Barn
Ifield Brook
RUDGWICK RD
Sandalwood
Furlong Farm
Stumbleholm Farm
RUSPER RD
COOLHAM CT
TANGMERE RD
TREYFORD CL
RH11
Golf and Country Club
CAMELOT CT
AARPTHORNE CL
Ifield Park
WOODROFFE
BENTON HO
CH
MERLIN CL
ARTHUR RD
THE MILLBANK
HILLMEAD
PARKFIELD CL
Hyde Hill
D5
1 FULMAR CL
2 GUILLEMOT PATH
3 STONEYCROFT WLK
4 THE ORCHARDS
5 REDSHANK CT
6 SHEARWATER CT
7 BOWNESS CL
8 HUNSTANTON CL
LANCELOT CL
STANBRIDGE CL
GALAHAD RD
MIDDLETON WAY
Ifield Mill
MEADOWCROFT
THE HOLLOW
HIGHAMS HILL
AVON WLK
Hyde Hill Brook
GARTON CL
HYDE DR
BINMEAD
CHERWELL WLK
ST ANDREWS RD
IVYLAKE DR
TROON CL
GRIER
DERWENT CL
CUCKMERE
CAPEL LA
GOSSOPS PARO
KEKENNET
MEDWAY RD
MDDR PARK CRES
PUFFIN RD
BITTERN CL
LAWS
HANVRY
BEHENNA
COMPASSION
LEA CL
COBNOR CL
LAVANT CL
WOLD CL
KITTIWAKE
ABBOTSDALE RD
PAK CL
COLLINS RD
Ifield Mill Pond
TRENT CL
EDEN CL
Upper Bewbush
CONISTON CL
SANDPIPER CL
FAIRWAY
REEDINGS
SAMARITAN
WATERFIELD
Waterfield Prim Sch
HURST CL
RH12
House Copse
THIRLMERE
RYDAL CL
KESWICK CL
YEWLANDS WLK
HARMONY
WATERSIDE
HAWKESMOOR RD
CHEYNELL WLK
MORECAMBE CL
ELLISON
JUXON
MONKMEAD
Burnt Stubbs
Kilnwood Farm
Bewbush Brook
ANDROMEDA CL
PEGASUS CT
NEPTUNE CL
PADSTOW WLK
COMPER CL
FILEY
HENSHAW
APSLEY CL
TWYNE
BURRELL RD
KILNWOOD LA
Capon Grove
Spruce Hill Brook
HINDON WLK
GEMINI RD
ORION CL
SATURN CL
LUTYENS CL
CAPRICORN CL
WICKLOW WLK
PEGWELL
COLWYN CL
Kilnwood
GANYMEDE CT
CALLISTO CL
MERCURY CL
OBERON WAY
WYCLIFFE
VANBRUGH
BEWBUSH DR
ARNE CL
BYRD CL
COWFOLD CT
WISBROUGH HARTING
Kilnwood Copse
RANSOME CL
BOOTH RD
GOODWYN CL
DORSTEN SQ
PO SQ
MANCHESTER RD
SLAUGHAM
WISTON
Pondtail Shaw
NESBIT CL
CALVIN RD
Sch
WALLCOTT CL
WEST EY CL
TALLIS RD
PURCELL RD
CUCKFIELD
Bewbush
MASEFIELD CL
LETCHWORTH RD
BREEZEHURST DR
SALVINGTON RD
JOLESFIELD CT
HENTY CL
SULLIVAN DR
CORBY CL
BRACKNELL WLK
L Ctr
Millennium
NINFIELD CT
Fullers Shaw
WELWYN
WASHINGTON
RUNCORN CL
MERIDIAN WAY
A2220
HOWARD RD 1
BEWBUSH MANOR 2
SHIRLEY CL 3
WARRINGTON CL 4
PETERLEE WLK 5
GUMBERNAULD WLK 6
THETFORD WLK 7
HATFIELD WLK 8
MANORFIELDS
NORFOLK CL
FRANCIS EDWARDS WAY
SKELMERSDALE CL
PUNNETTS CT
HORSHAM RD
ST AUBIN
ST SAMPSON RD
ST BREALES RD
ERSKINE CL
CHECKWOOD RD
BERKELEY CL
A2220
A264
ST CLEMENT CL
MILLAIS CT
Buchan Park
CRAWLEY RD
BURNS WAY
Hopper Farm
Ind Est
Creasy's Forest
A264
Holmbush Farm World
Holmbush Farm
Spruce Hill
Buchan Country Park
Douster Pond
Target Hill
A264
Silver Hill
Island Pond
Middle Covert
Island Pond

199

F3
1 BERSTEAD WLK
2 DONNINGTON CT
3 HASSOCKS CT
4 PYECOMBE CT
5 TELHAM CT
6 WARBLETON HO
7 CALDBECK HO
8 HALNAKER WLK
9 ICKLESHAM HO

181

D5
1 THE COURTYARD
2 WALSTEAD HO
3 RAVENDENE CT
4 WILLOWFIELD
5 ASHWOOD
6 PARISH HO

202

7 PERRYFIELD HO
8 HANDSWORTH HO
9 GLENDON HO
10 ALEXANDRA CT
11 SPRING CL

201

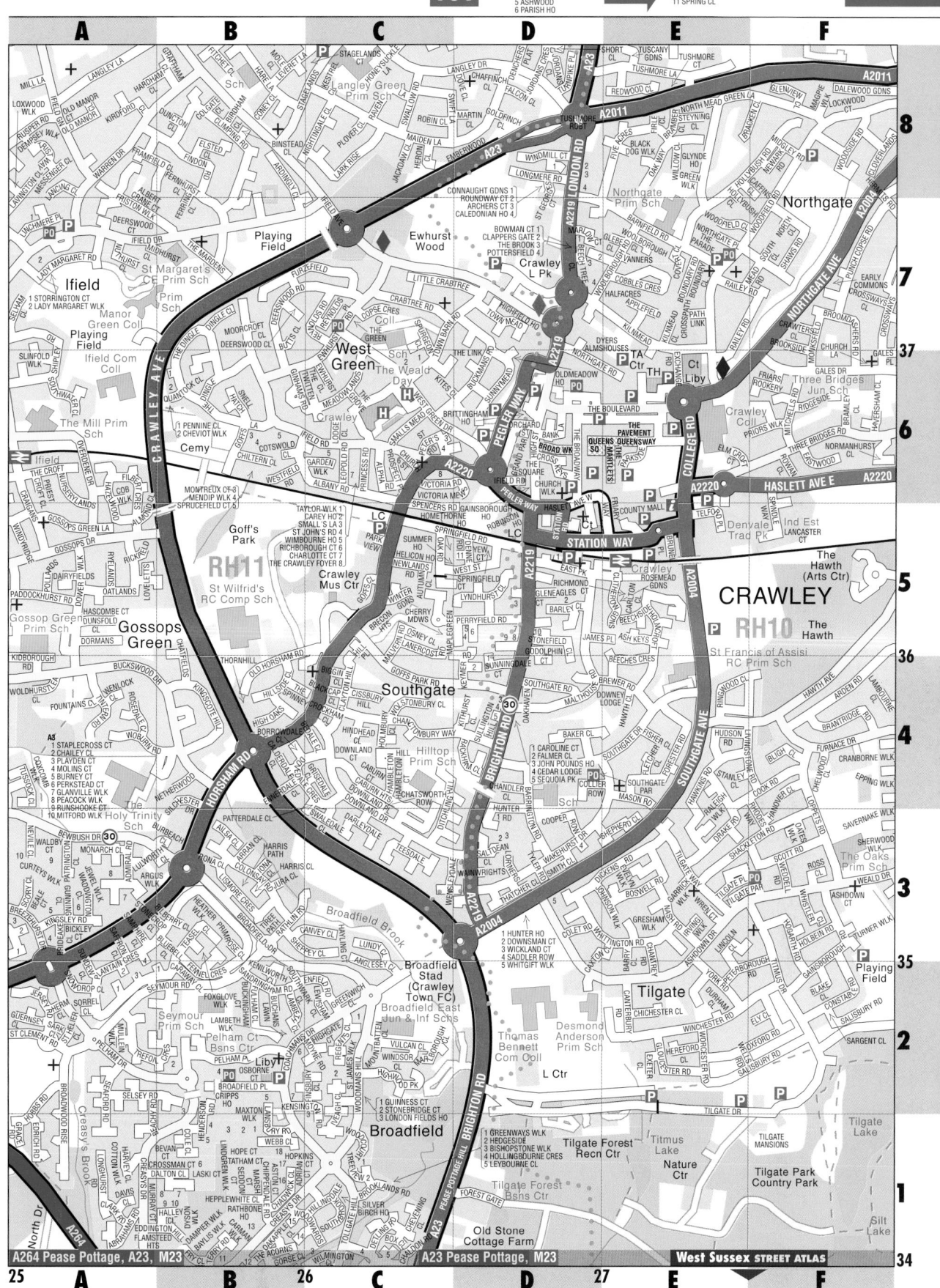

A2
1 CROWBERRY CL
2 BURDOCK CL
3 CHARLOCK CL
4 BORAGE CL

B1
1 STRACHEY CT
2 GREENWOOD CT
3 SHINWELL WLK
4 WILKINSON CT
5 MORRISON CT
6 ADAMSON CT
7 KEIR HARDIE HO
8 SILKIN WLK
9 HERSCHEL WLK

10 JEANS CT
11 PANKHURST CT
12 RAMBLERS WAY
13 SHERATON WLK
14 TIMBERLANDS
15 WOODING GR
16 THOMSON CT
17 RICHARDSON CT
18 RAMSEY CT

B2
1 CELANDINE CL
2 HENBANE CT
3 SELSEY CT
4 BROADFIELD BARTON
5 ATTLEE HO
6 BALMORAL CT
7 ISLINGTON HO

201
182

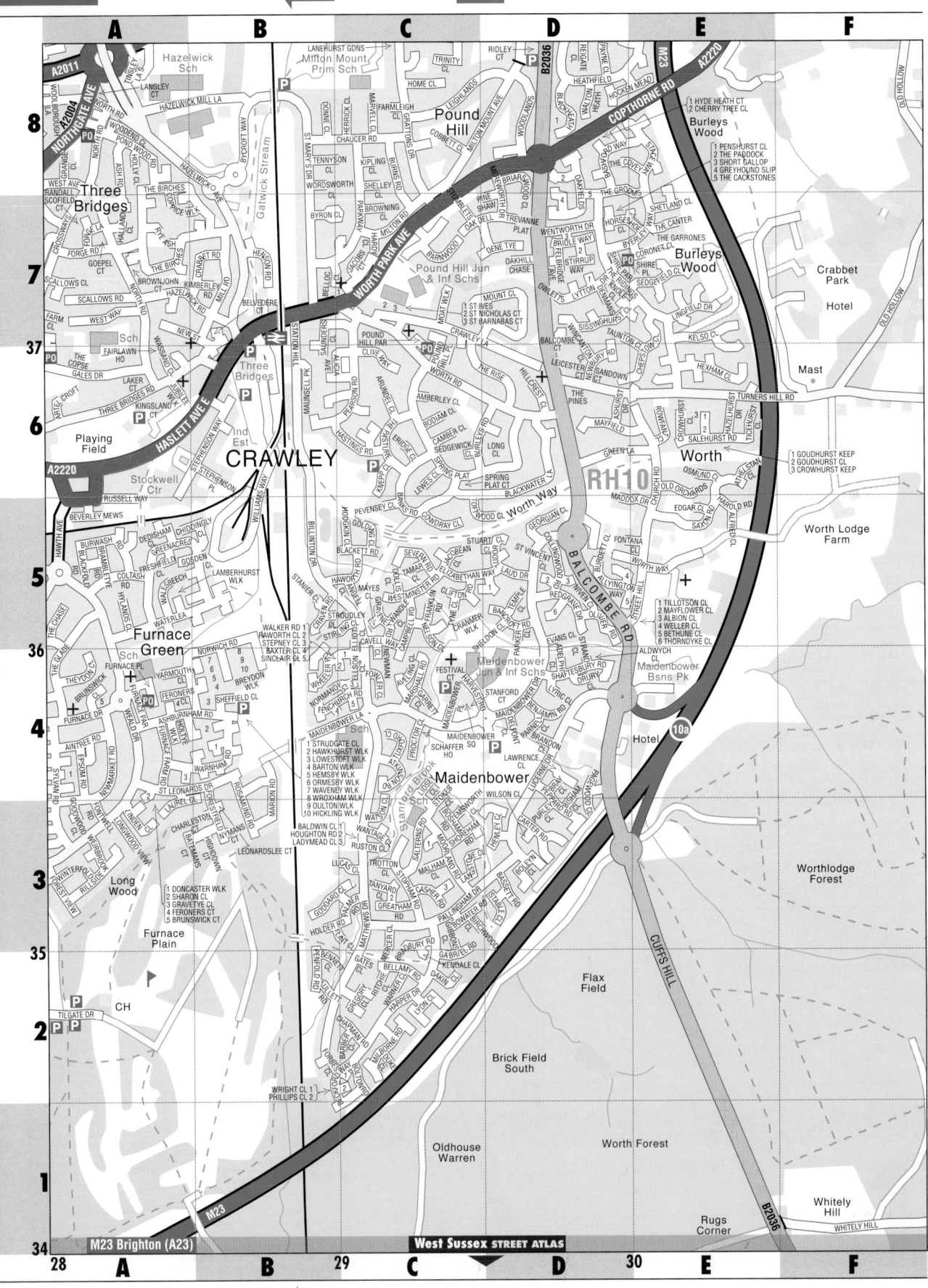
A
B
C
D
E
F
8
7
37
6
5
36
4
3
35
2
1
34
28
29
30
Hazelwick Sch
Milton Mount Prim Sch
LANEHURST GDNS
RIDLEY CT
TRINITY CL
HOME CL
B2036
M23
A2220
A2011
A2004
NORTHGATE AVE
TINSLEY LA S
LANGLEY CT
HAZELWICK MILL LA
WOOLBOROUGH LA
HEATHFIELD
HOCKEN MEAD
REIGATE
PAYNE CL
COPTHORNE RD
1 HYDE HEATH CT
2 CHERRY TREE CL
Burleys Wood
1 PENSHURST CL
2 THE PADDOCK
3 SHORT GALLOP
4 GREYHOUND SLIP
5 THE CACKSTONES
OLD HOLLOW
Pound Hill
LEIGHLANDS
FARMLEIGH CL
DONNE CL
HERRICK CL
MARVELL CL
GRATTONS DR
CHAUCER RD
COBBETT CL
MILTON MOUNT AVE
WOODLANDS
ST MARY'S DR
TENNYSON CL
KIPLING CL
BURNS RD
WORDSWORTH CL
SHELLEY CL
BROWNING CL
BYRON CL
PARKWAY
MILTON RD
HARDY CL
Three Bridges
NORTH RD
WOODEND CL
POND WOOD RD
HOLLY CL
ASH RD
WEST AVE
RANDALL SCOFIELD CT
THE BIRCHES
COPPICE WLK
RYE ASH
HAZELWICK AVE
BYCROFT WAY
Gatwick Stream
CROSSWAYS
FORGE CL
FORGE RD
GOEPEL CT
SCALLOWS CL
SCALLOWS RD
WEST WAY
BROWNJOHN CT
KIMBERLEY RD
HAZELWICK RD
CRABBET RD
MILL RD
HENSON RD
BELVEDERE CT
NEW ST
WORTH PARK AVE
FARM CL
Sch
FAIRLAWN HO
THE COPSE
GALES DR
LAKER CT
THREE BRIDGES RD
KINGSLAND CT
WASSAND CL
JUBILEE WLK
Three Bridges
STATION HILL
ARTEL CROFT
Playing Field
HASLETT AVE E
Ind Est
STEPHENSON WAY
CRAWLEY
A2220
Stockwell Ctr
STEPHENSON PL
WILLIAMS WAY
RUSSELL WAY
BEVERLEY MEWS
HAWTH AVE
MAUNSELL PK
BILLINTON DR
JACOBS CT
BELLOC CT
Pound Hill Jun & Inf Schs
MOAT WLK
SAUNDERS CL
ALICIA AVE
POUND HILL PAR
CLIVE WAY
POUND HILL PL
PEARSON RD
ARUNDEL CL
WORTH RD
AMBERLEY CL
BODIAM CL
CAMBER CL
SEDGEWICK CL
BURLEYS RD
LONG CL
HASTINGS RD
THE PASTURE
ERIDGE CL
SPRING PLAT
SPRING PLAT CT
KNEPP CL
LEWES CL
PEVENSEY CL
BANKS RD
COWDRAY CL
TOFTWOOD CL
Worth Way
BLACKWATER LA
HILLCREST CL
THE RISE
CRAWLEY LA
MOUNT CL
1 ST IVES
2 ST NICHOLAS CT
3 ST BARNABAS CT
BRIARS WOOD
MERSEWORTH DR
STUMBLETS
PINE SHAW
OAK DELL
TREVANNE PLAT
DENE TYE
BARNWOOD
OAKHILL CHASE
WENTWORTH DR
BRIDLE WAY
FELBRIDGE AVE
STIRRUP WAY
OWLETTS
LYTTON DR
DENMANS
THE KNOLLS
SISSINGHURST CL
BALCOMBE CT
LEICESTER CT
WINCANTON CL
NEWBURY RD
SANDOWN CT
CHEPSTOW CL
TAUNTON CL
THE PINES
BASFORD WAY
THE COVEY
OAKFIELDS
THE GROOMS
HORSESHOE CL
SHETLAND CL
THE CANTER
THE GARRONES
CORONET CL
BYERLEY WAY
SHIRE PAR
SHIRE PL
SEDGEFIELD CL
THE RIDINGS
Burleys Wood
LINGFIELD DR
KELSO CL
HEXHAM CL
Crabbet Park
Hotel
Mast
TURNERS HILL RD
OLD HOLLOW
ASHURST DR
MAYFIELD
ROWFANT CL
CROWHURST CL
HAZELHURST CL
TICEHURST CL
SALEHURST RD
Worth
GREEN LA
RH10
OSMUND CL
OLD ORCHARDS
ATHELSTAN CL
1 GOUDHURST KEEP
2 GOUDHURST CL
3 CROWHURST KEEP
MADDOX DR
CHURCH RD
EDGAR CL
SAXON RD
HAROLD RD
ALFRED CL
Worth Lodge Farm
FONTANA CL
WORTH WAY
ALLYINGTON WAY
BURDETT CL
STREET HILL
1 TILLOTSON CL
2 MAYFLOWER CL
3 ALBION CL
4 WELLER CL
5 BETHUNE CL
6 THORNDYKE CL
BALCOMBE RD
GEORGIAN CL
COLLINGWOOD CL
ST VINCENT CL
NIVEN CL
OLIVER RD
REDGRAVE DR
EVANS CL
STRAND CL
ADELPHI CL
SHAFTESBURY RD
DRURY CL
ALDWYCH CL
Maidenbower Bsns Pk
LYRIC CL
Hotel
10a
GOLDINGS CL
HODGKIN CL
BLACKETT RD
STUART CL
JACOBEAN CL
SEVERN RD
TAMAR CL
ELIZABETHAN WAY
TUDOR CL
LAUD DR
DOLLIS CL
WESTMINSTER RD
FRANKLIN RD
CLIFTON RD
BANCROFT RD
TEMPLE CL
PARKER RD
STANIER CL
HAWORTH RD
MAYES CL
STROUDLEY CL
STIRLING CL
CRAVEN RD
CAVELL WAY
CAMPBELL RD
NELSON CL
CRAMMER WLK
SHELDON CL
WALKER RD 1
HAWORTH CL 2
STEPNEY CL 3
BAXTER CL 4
SINCLAIR CL 5
WHEELER RD
TELSTON CL
ELLIOT CL
NEWMAN
FOWLER CL
AVELING CL
MARSHALL RD
GARRETT CL
FESTIVAL CT
Maidenbower Jun & Inf Schs
HARVEST RD
STANFORD CT
MAIDENBOWER DR
BENJAMIN RD
NORMANDY CL
FENCHURCH RD
MAIDENBOWER LA
Sch
TURPIN CL
PROCTOR CL
MAIDENBOWER PL
MAIDENBOWER SQ
SCHAFFER HO
DELFONT CL
PARNELL CL
BRANDON CL
LAWRENCE CL
1 STRUDGATE CL
2 HAWKHURST WLK
3 LOWESTOFT WLK
4 BARTON WLK
5 HEMSBY WLK
6 ORMESBY WLK
7 WAVENEY WLK
8 WROXHAM WLK
9 OULTON WLK
10 HICKLING WLK
ATKINSON RD
Maidenbower
Stanford Brook Sch
WILSON CL
LUCERNE DR
PEBBLE CL
PEPPARD RD
CARTER RD
PURLEY CL
PAGEWOOD CL
BALDWIN CL
HOUGHTON RD 2
LADYMEAD CL 3
WANTAGE CL
RUSTON CL
SALTERNS RD
BOSHAM RD
SHOREHAM RD
MOORLAND RD
HEMLEY CL
BOLEYN CL
LUCAS CL
TROTTON CL
MALHAM CL
STOPHAM RD
TANYARD CL
GREATHAM RD
CASHER RD
BASSETT RD
STABLE CL
GODDARD CL
PALMER RD
HOLDER RD
FLINT CL
MATTHEWS DR
PALLINGHAM DR
BIRCHWOOD CL
BOWATER RD
GIBBONS CL
GABRIEL RD
KENDALE CL
DAKIN CL
BRADBURY RD
BENNETT CL
PENFOLD RD
GATES CL
MERCER CL
BELLAMY RD
RITCHIE CL
WARNER CL
HARPER DR
LYON CL
GREGORY CL
JULLETT
CHAPMAN RD
BARBER CL
MILBORNE RD
DUKE CL
FORBES CL
BECKFORD WAY
BOLTON RD
WRIGHT CL 1
PHILLIPS CL 2
Furnace Green
BURWASH RD
BLACKFOLD RD
BRAMBLETYE CL
DEDISHAM CL
CHIDDINGLY CL
GREENACRES
FRESHFIELD CL
GOSDEN CL
COLTASH RD
WALESBEECH
LAMBERHURST WLK
HYLANDS CL
WATERLEA
THE CHASE
THE GLADE
Sch
FURNACE PL
NORWICH RD
YARMOUTH CL
THEYDON CL
BRUINSWICK
FURNACE DR
FURNACE PAR
WEALD DR
FERONERS
SHEFFIELD CL
BREYDON WLK
ASHBURNHAM RD
HOLLYE WLK
FURNACE FARM RD
AINTREE RD
EPSOM RD
NEWMARKET RD
SYLVAN RD
WARNHAM CT
ST LEONARDS DR
LAUREL CL
FORESTFIELD
ROSAMUND RD
MARION RD
GOODWOOD CL
FONTWELL
LINDEN CL
LONGWOOD VIEW
CHARLESTON CT
NYMANS CT
BATEMANS CT
HIGHDOWN CT
LEONARDSLEE CT
WEIRBROOK
RILLSIDE
WINTERFOLD
FOREST VIEW
Long Wood
1 DONCASTER WLK
2 SHARON CL
3 GRAVETYE CL
4 FERONERS CT
5 BRUNSWICK CT
Furnace Plain
CH
TILGATE DR
Flax Field
CUFFS HILL
Worthlodge Forest
Brick Field South
Oldhouse Warren
Worth Forest
Whitely Hill
WHITELY HILL
Rugs Corner
B2036
M23
M23 Brighton (A23)
West Sussex STREET ATLAS

201

	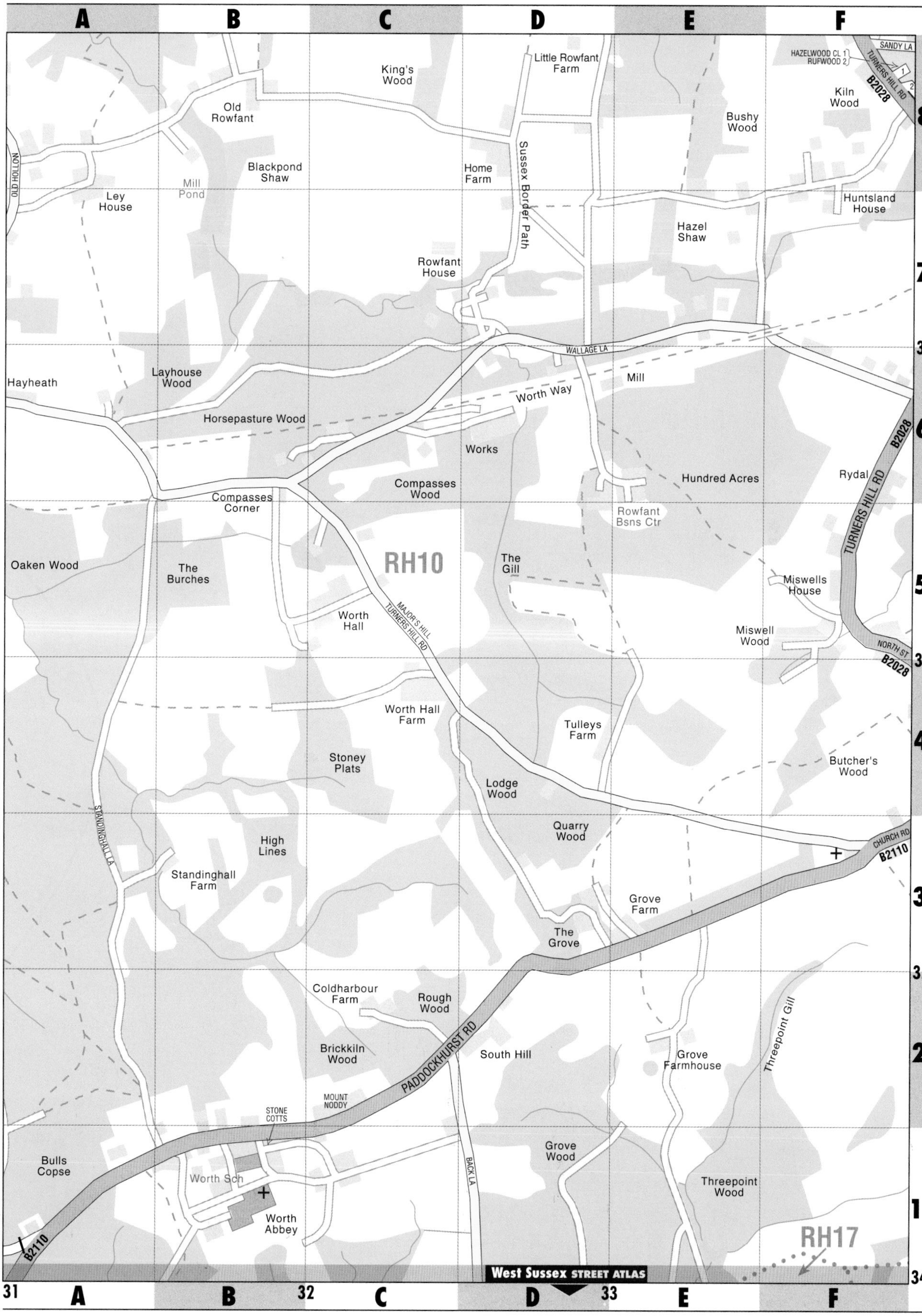 A	B	C	D	E	F

8

Old Rowfant

King's Wood

Little Rowfant Farm

HAZELWOOD CL 1
RUFWOOD 2

SANDY LA

Kiln Wood

B2028

TURNERS HILL RD

Ley House

Mill Pond

Blackpond Shaw

Home Farm

Sussex Border Path

Bushy Wood

Hazel Shaw

Huntsland House

7

Rowfant House

WALLAGE LA

37

Hayheath

Layhouse Wood

Horsepasture Wood

Worth Way

Mill

B2028

TURNERS HILL RD

6

Works

Compasses Wood

Hundred Acres

Rydal

Oaken Wood

The Burches

Compasses Corner

RH10

The Gill

Rowfant Bsns Ctr

Miswells House

5

Worth Hall

MAJOR'S HILL
TURNERS HILL RD

Miswell Wood

NORTH ST
B2028

36

Worth Hall Farm

Tulleys Farm

Butcher's Wood

4

Stoney Plats

Lodge Wood

STANDINGHALL LA

Quarry Wood

Grove Farm

CHURCH RD
B2110

3

Standinghall Farm

High Lines

The Grove

35

Coldharbour Farm

Rough Wood

Threepoint Gill

2

Brickkiln Wood

South Hill

PADDOCKHURST RD

BACK LA

Grove Farmhouse

MOUNT NODDY

STONE COTTS

Bulls Copse

Worth Sch

Grove Wood

Threepoint Wood

Worth Abbey

B2110

RH17

1

34

31	A		B	32	C		D	33	E		F

Crawley Down

RH10

Turners Hill Park

Peartree Shaw
1 LINNET CL
2 TURTLEDOVE AVE
3 LARK RISE
4 FINCH CRES
5 KINGFISHER LA
6 ROBIN ROW
7 TOMTIT CRES
8 NIGHTINGALE LA
9 PIGEON PASS
10 WREN ST

PUFFIN HILL 11
SWALLOW ST 12
NUTHATCH WAY 13
JAY WLK 14
RAVEN CL 15
KESTREL WLK 16
BLACKBIRD HILL 17

Alexander House (Hotel)

RH19

Turners Hill

Withypitts

Worth Way

Sussex Border Path

Gulledge Wood

French Wood

Tilkhurst Farm

Front Wood

Bankton

RIDGEDALE 1
AUCHINLECK CT 2
ROYAL OAK HO 3

Grange Farm

The Grange

Sandhill

Rainbow Shaw

Warren Wood

Little Nobs

Burleigh Arches Wood

Burleigh Oaks House

Fen Place Mill

River Medway

Moat Shaw

Mill Wood

Hurley Farm

Ash Lea Farm

Furze Field

EAST ST

Furzewood Farm

Castle Shaw

Target Shaw

Tickeridge Farm

Kingscote

RAILWAY COTTS

Burleigh Farm

MANTELMAS COTTS

Willow Ridge

Rashes Farm

Spring Wood

Rookery Wood

Holstein Wood

Tickeridge Shaw

South Wood

Bluebell Rly

Stone Wood

Withypitts Farm

Coomberdean Wood

Great Wildgoose Wood

Vowels Forest Wlk

Minepit Wood

Vowels Gill

Mill Place Wood

The Punch Bowl (PH)

Thornhill Cottages

Selsfield Place

Drive Shaw

Bushy Wood

Bramblehill

Selsfield Common

Moatlands

Pine Wood

Warren's Wood

Home Farm

Hastings Wood

Selsfield House

Ducknell's Wood

Gravetye Manor (Hotel)

Lower Lake

Crawley Down Village CE Prim Sch

Burleigh House Farm

F8
1 MIDDLE ROW
2 FOREST LODGE
3 SACKVILLE CT
4 GREAT HOUSE CT
5 PORTLAND HO
6 CORNWALL GDNS
7 NORMANDY CL
8 WILLOW MEAD
9 KINGS COPSE
10 REGAL DR
11 BECKETT WAY
12 TOLLGATE PL
13 FAIRVIEW CT

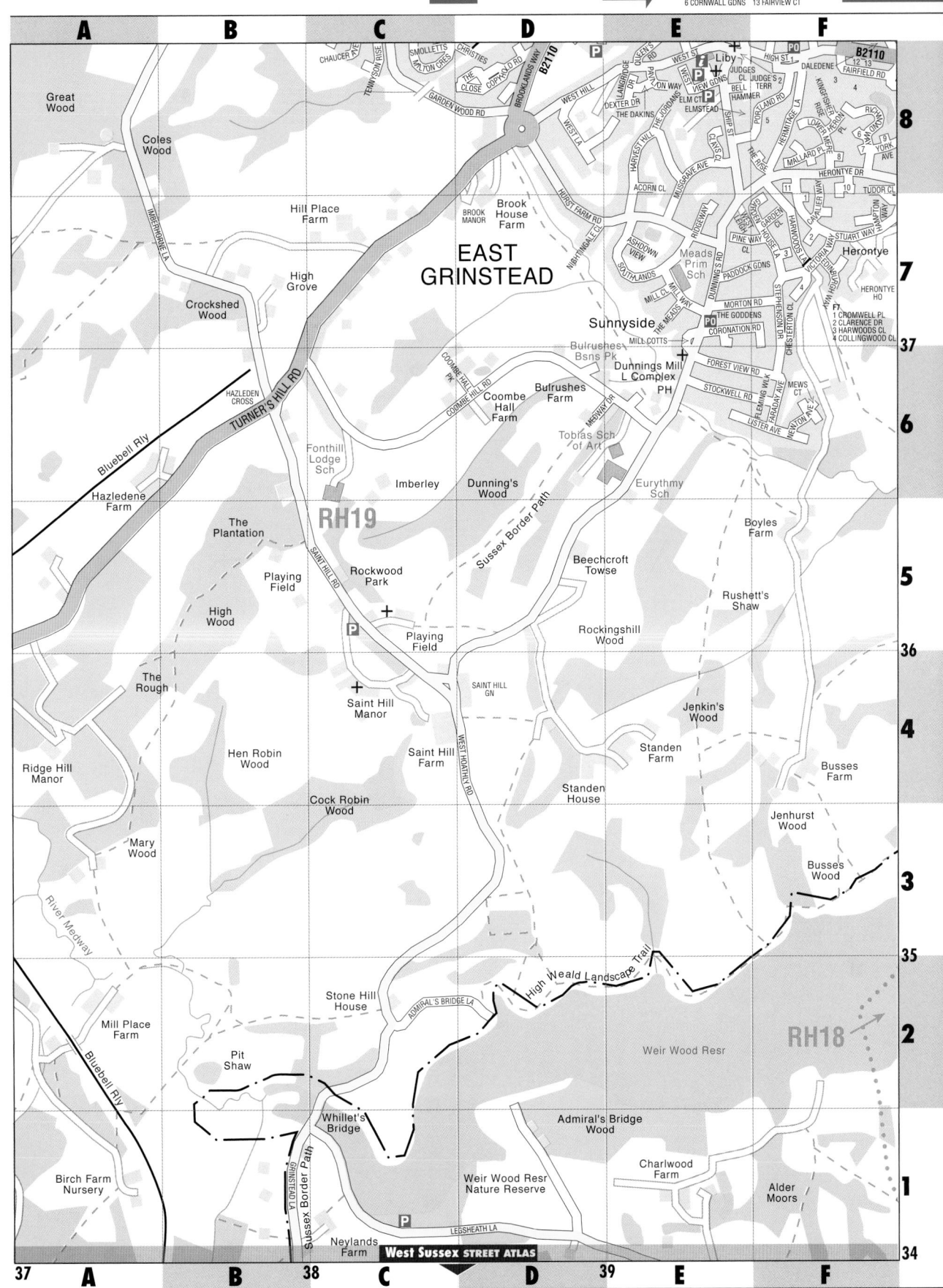

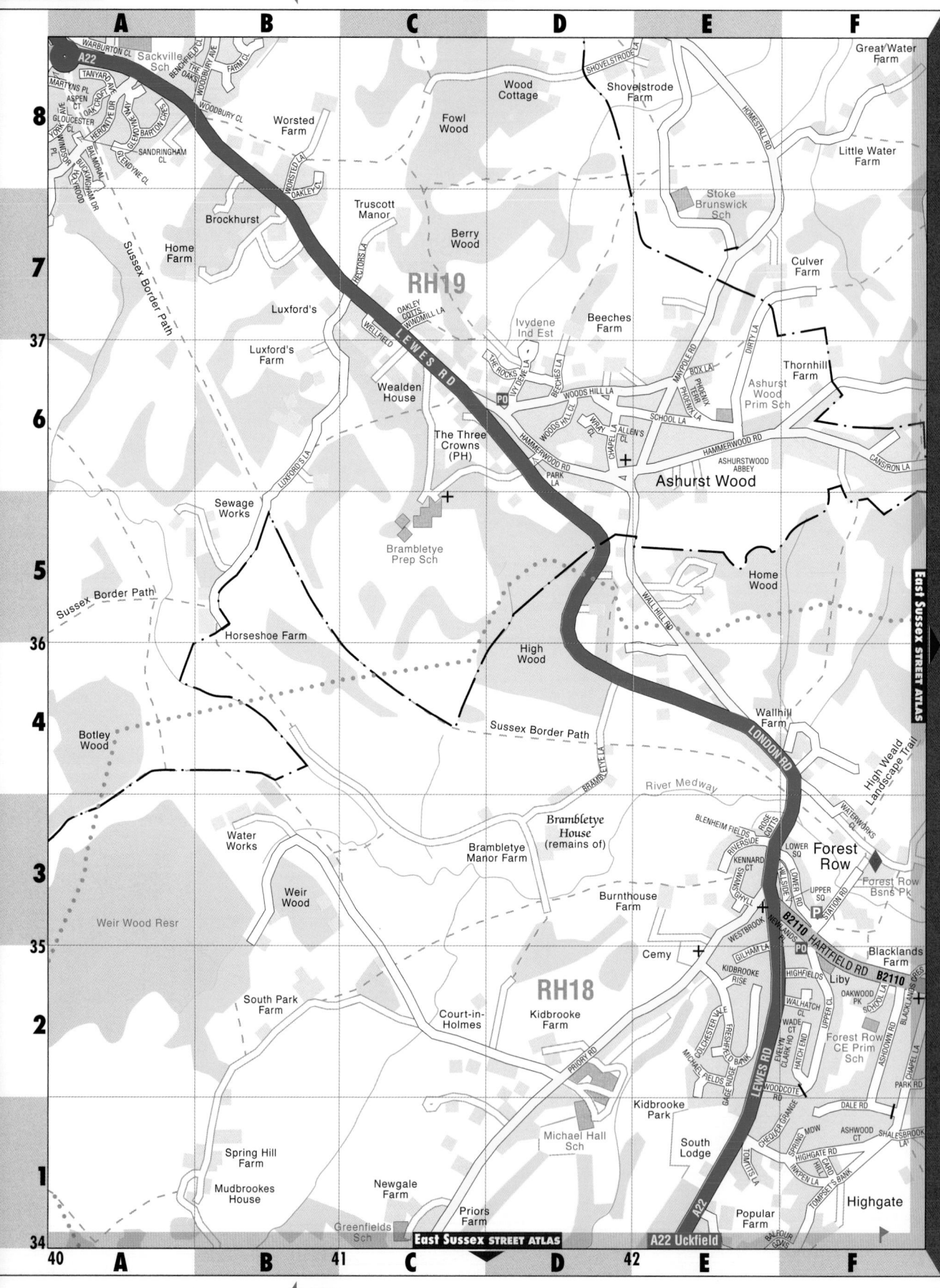

A   B   C   D   E   F

8

7

37

6

5

36

4

3

35

2

1

34

40   A   B   41   C   D   42   E   F

RH19

RH18

Sussex Border Path

A22

Sackville Sch
WARBURTON CL
TANYARD
MARTYNS PL
ASPEN CT
OAK
GLOUCESTER
YORK
WINDSOR PL
BLACKWIGHAM CT
HERONS WOOD
GLENDYNE CL
BALMORAL
BARTON CRES
HEATHER WAY
WILLIAMS WAY
HEROLYE DR
BENFIELD CL
THE OAKS
WOODBURY AVE
WOODBURY CL
FARM CL
SANDRINGHAM CL

Worsted Farm
Brockhurst
Home Farm
Luxford's
Luxford's Farm
WORSTED LA
OAKLEY
HECTORS LA
WELLFIELD
LEWES RD
OAKLEY
COLTS
WINDMILL LA
Wealden House
LUXFORD'S LA
Sewage Works
Horseshoe Farm
Botley Wood
Truscott Manor
Fowl Wood
Berry Wood
Wood Cottage
Shovelstrode Farm
SHOVELSTRODE LA
Great Water Farm
Little Water Farm
HOMESTALL RD
Stoke Brunswick Sch
Culver Farm
Thornhill Farm
DIRTY LA
Ashurst Wood Prim Sch
CANSIRON LA
Ashurst Wood
ASHURSTWOOD ABBEY
HAMMERWOOD RD
SCHOOL LA
MAYPOLE RD
BOX LA
PHOENIX TERR
PHOENIX LA
CHAPEL LA
ALLEN'S CL
WRAY CL
WOODS HILL LA
WOODS HILL CL
BEECHES LA
LYDENE LA
THE ROCKS
Ivydene Ind Est
Beeches Farm
The Three Crowns (PH)
PO
PARK LA
HAMMERWOOD RD
BRAMBLETYE LA
High Wood
Home Wood
WALL HILL RD
Wallhill Farm
LONDON RD
High Weald Landscape Trail
WATERWORKS
Forest Row
Forest Row Bsns Pk
BLENHEIM FIELDS
ROSE COTTS
RIVERSIDE
KENNARD CT
LOWER SQ
UPPER SQ
STATION RD
LOWER RD
SWAINS
NEWLANDS
B2110
HARTFIELD RD
B2110
PO
Blacklands Farm
Liby
OAKWOOD PK
SCHOOL LA
ASHDOWN RD
CHAPEL LA
PARK RD
Forest Row CE Prim Sch
GILHAMS
HIGHFIELDS
KIDBROOKE RISE
Cemy
Westbrook
WALHATCH CL
HIGHFIELDS
Burnthouse Farm
Brambletye House (remains of)
Brambletye Manor Farm
River Medway
Sussex Border Path
PRIORY RD
Court-in-Holmes
Kidbrooke Farm
Newgale Farm
Michael Hall Sch
Priors Farm
Kidbrooke Park
South Lodge
Highgate
Popular Farm
BALFOUR
LEWES RD
A22
IMPENS CL
TOMPSETS BANK
HIGHGATE RD
SPRINGS MDW
CARD HILL
CHEQUER GRANGE
WOODCOTE RD
WADE CT
EVELYN CLARK RD
HATCH END
UPPER CL
MICHAEL FIELDS
GAGE RIDGE
FRESHFIELD
COLCHESTER VALE
TOMLINSCOTE
DALE RD
ASHWOOD CT
SHALESBROOK LA
BLACKLANDS CRES
Water Works
Weir Wood
Weir Wood Resr
South Park Farm
Spring Hill Farm
Mudbrookes House
Greenfields Sch

East Sussex STREET ATLAS

A22 Uckfield

East Sussex STREET ATLAS

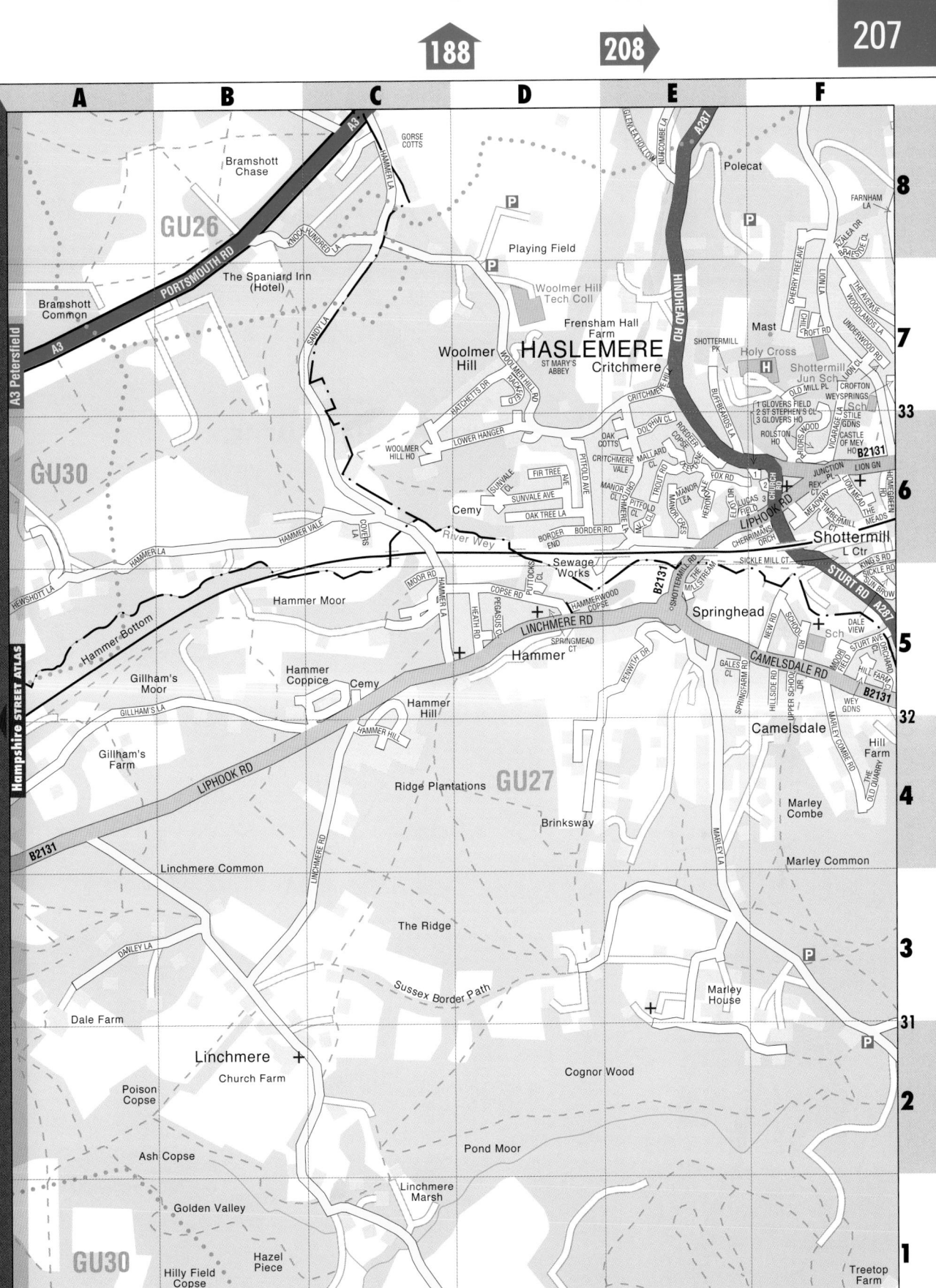
188
208
A
B
C
D
E
F
Bramshott Chase
GU26
PORTSMOUTH RD
A3
The Spaniard Inn (Hotel)
Bramshott Common
A3 Petersfield
Playing Field
Woolmer Hill Tech Coll
Frensham Hall Farm
HASLEMERE
Woolmer Hill
Critchmere
Polecat
HINDHEAD RD
A287
Mast
Holy Cross
Shottermill Jun Sch
GU30
Cemy
River Wey
Shottermill
L Ctr
Sewage Works
Hammer Moor
Springhead
LINCHMERE RD
Hammer
Hammer Bottom
Gillham's Moor
Hammer Coppice
Hammer Hill
Camelsdale
CAMELSDALE RD
Gillham's Farm
LIPHOOK RD
Ridge Plantations
GU27
Brinksway
Hill Farm
Marley Combe
B2131
Linchmere Common
Marley Common
The Ridge
Sussex Border Path
Marley House
Dale Farm
Linchmere
Church Farm
Cognor Wood
Poison Copse
Ash Copse
Pond Moor
Linchmere Marsh
Golden Valley
GU30
Hilly Field Copse
Hazel Piece
Treetop Farm
Hampshire STREET ATLAS
West Sussex STREET ATLAS
8
7
33
6
5
32
4
3
31
2
1
30
86
87
88

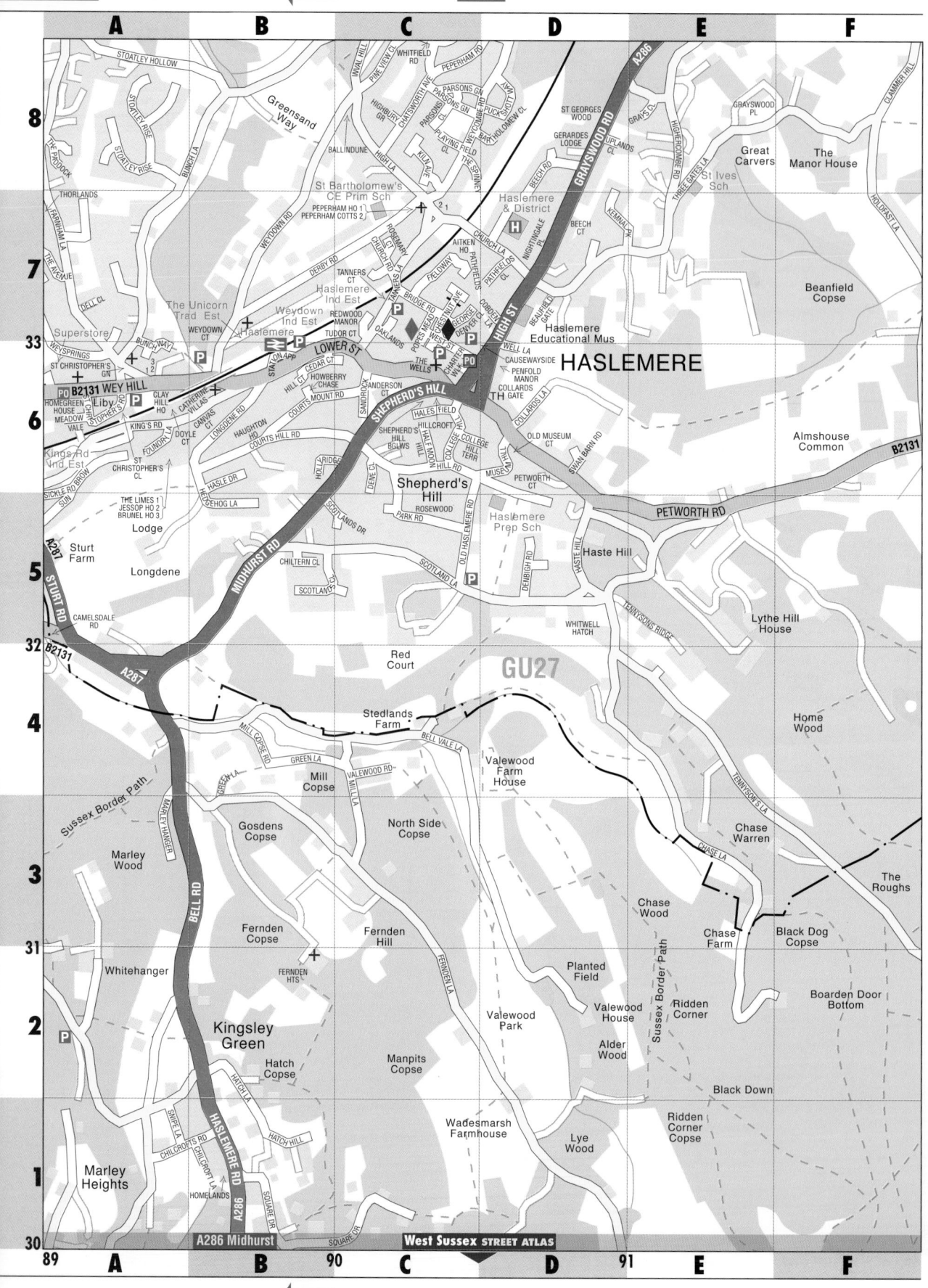

A B C D E F

8

7

33

6

5

32

4

31

3

2

1

30

HASLEMERE

GU27

A286 Midhurst

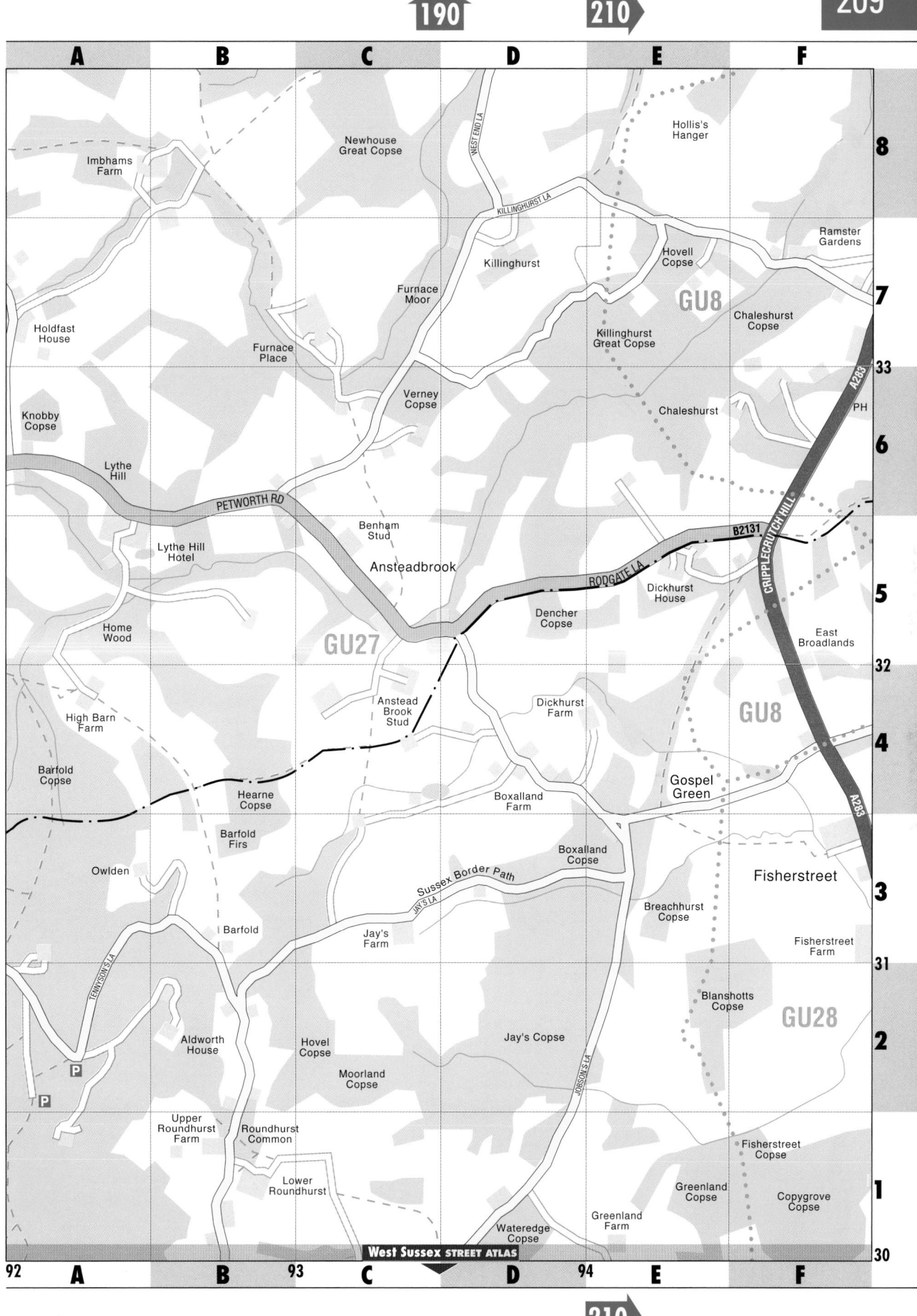

A B C D E F

8
7
33
6
32
4
3
31
2
1
30

Imbhams Farm

Newhouse Great Copse

WEST END LA

Hollis's Hanger

KILLINGHURST LA

Killinghurst

Hovell Copse

Ramster Gardens

GU8

Holdfast House

Furnace Moor

Chaleshurst Copse

Knobby Copse

Furnace Place

Killinghurst Great Copse

A283

PH

Lythe Hill

Verney Copse

Chaleshurst

PETWORTH RD

Benham Stud

B2131

CRIPPLECRUTCH HILL

Lythe Hill Hotel

Ansteadbrook

RODGATE LA

Dickhurst House

East Broadlands

Home Wood

GU27

Dencher Copse

GU8

High Barn Farm

Anstead Brook Stud

Dickhurst Farm

Barfold Copse

Hearne Copse

Boxalland Farm

Gospel Green

Barfold Firs

Boxalland Copse

Fisherstreet

Owlden

Sussex Border Path

Breachhurst Copse

Fisherstreet Farm

TENNYSON'S LA

Barfold

JAY'S LA

Jay's Farm

Blanshotts Copse

GU28

P

Aldworth House

Hovel Copse

Jay's Copse

P

JOBSON'S LA

Moorland Copse

Fisherstreet Copse

Upper Roundhurst Farm

Roundhurst Common

Greenland Copse

Copygrove Copse

Lower Roundhurst

Greenland Farm

Wateredge Copse

A283

92 A B 93 C D 94 E F

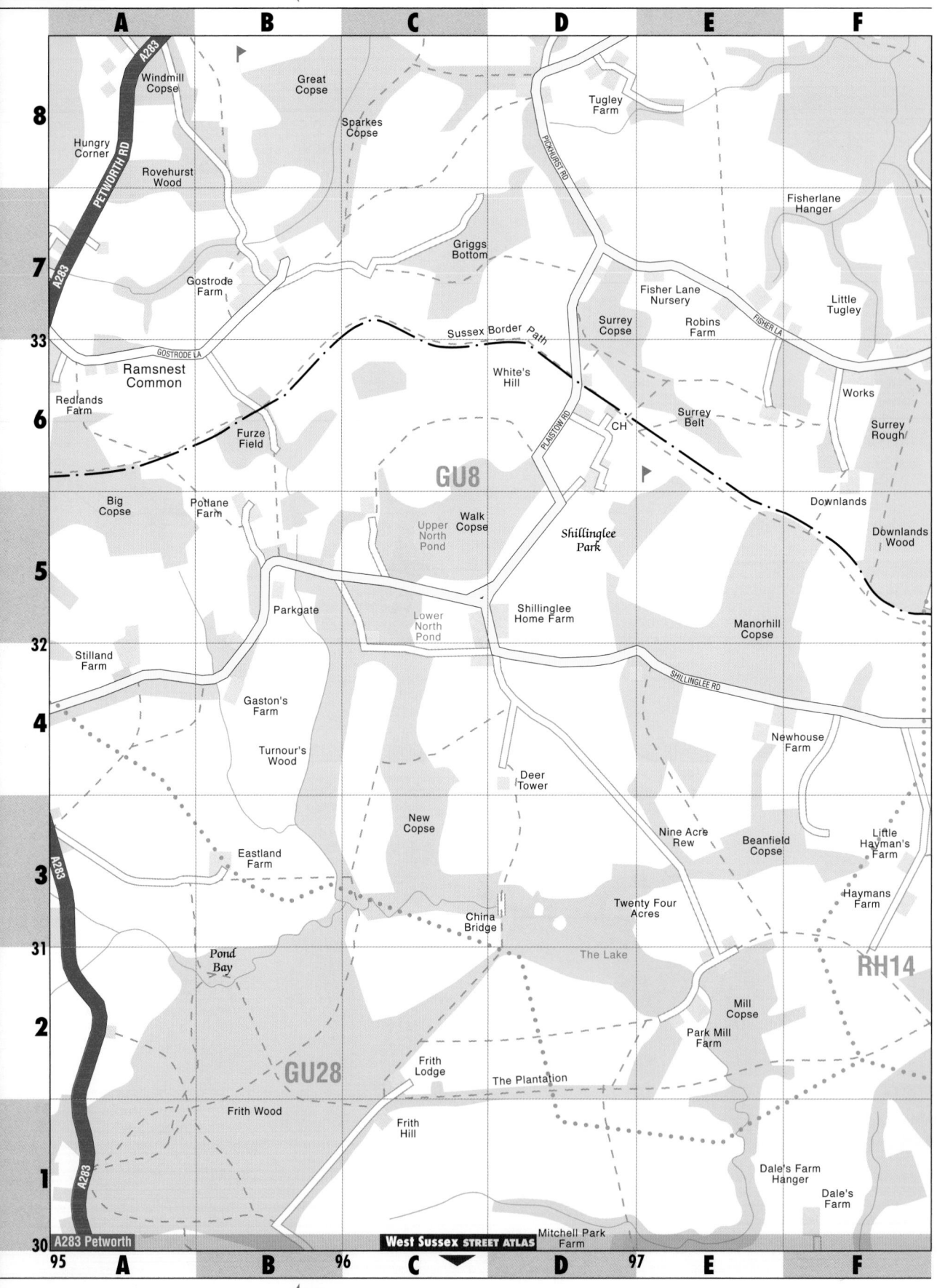

A283

Windmill Copse

Great Copse

Tugley Farm

8

Hungry Corner

PETWORTH RD

Rovehurst Wood

Sparkes Copse

PICKHURST RD

Fisherlane Hanger

7

A283

Gostrode Farm

Griggs Bottom

Fisher Lane Nursery

Little Tugley

FISHER LA

33

GOSTRODE LA

Sussex Border Path

Surrey Copse

Robins Farm

Ramsnest Common

White's Hill

Works

Redlands Farm

Furze Field

PLAISTOW RD

CH

Surrey Belt

Surrey Rough

6

GU8

Surrey Rough

Downlands

Big Copse

Potlane Farm

Upper North Pond

Walk Copse

Shillinglee Park

Downlands Wood

5

Parkgate

Lower North Pond

Shillinglee Home Farm

Manorhill Copse

32

Stilland Farm

SHILLINGLEE RD

Gaston's Farm

4

Newhouse Farm

Turnour's Wood

Deer Tower

New Copse

Nine Acre Rew

Beanfield Copse

Little Hayman's Farm

3

Eastland Farm

China Bridge

Twenty Four Acres

Haymans Farm

31

Pond Bay

The Lake

RH14

2

Mill Copse

GU28

Frith Lodge

Park Mill Farm

Frith Wood

The Plantation

Frith Hill

Dale's Farm Hanger

1

A283

Dale's Farm

30

A | B | C | D | E | F

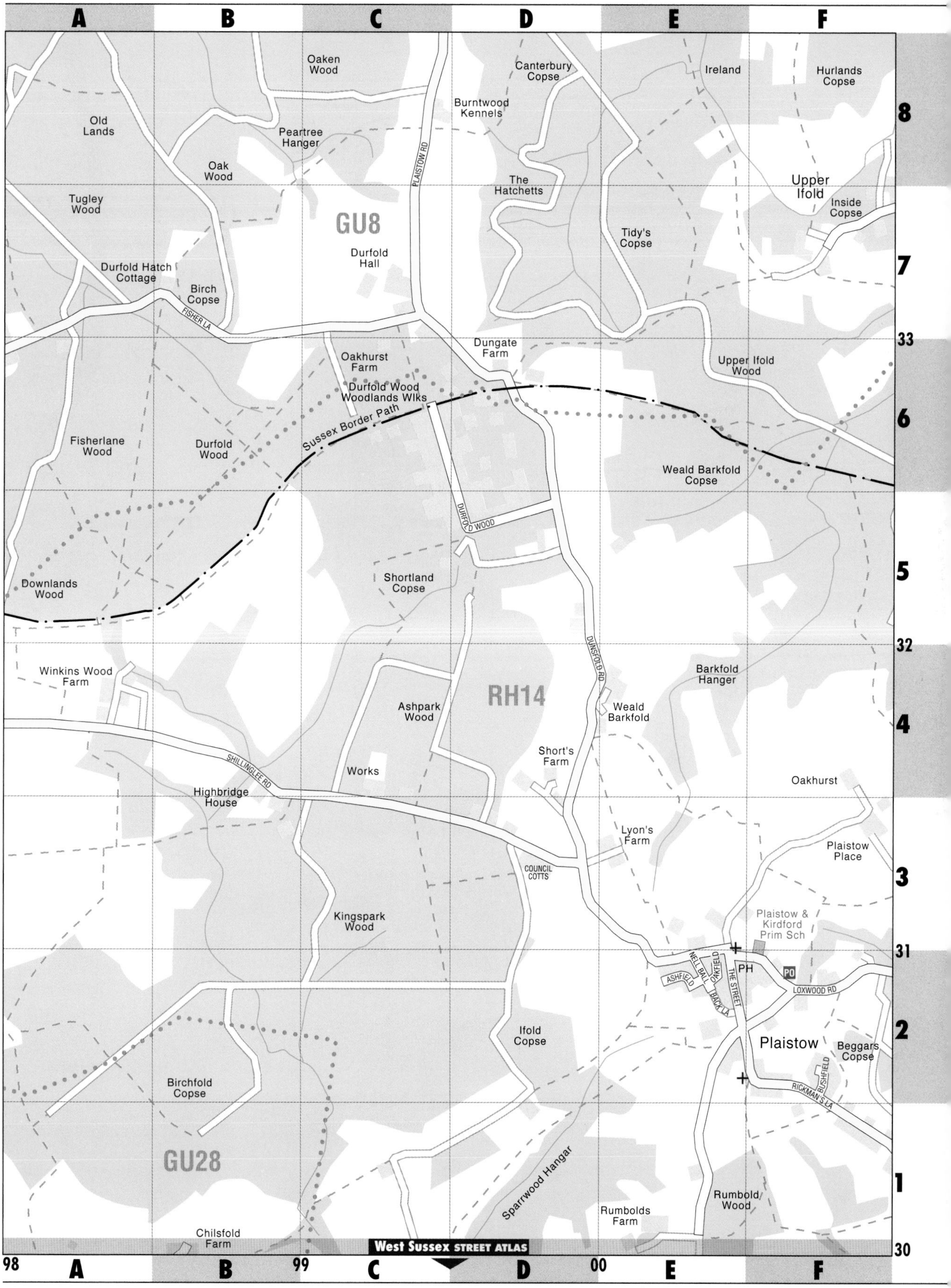

Oaken Wood

Canterbury Copse

Ireland

Hurlands Copse

8

Old Lands

Burntwood Kennels

Peartree Hanger

Upper Ifold

Inside Copse

Oak Wood

The Hatchetts

GU8

Tugley Wood

Durfold Hall

Tidy's Copse

7

Durfold Hatch Cottage

Birch Copse

FISHER LA

Dungate Farm

Upper Ifold Wood

33

Oakhurst Farm

Durfold Wood Woodlands Wlks

Sussex Border Path

6

Fisherlane Wood

Durfold Wood

Weald Barkfold Copse

DURFOLD WOOD

DUNSFOLD RD

Downlands Wood

Shortland Copse

5

32

Winkins Wood Farm

RH14

Barkfold Hanger

Ashpark Wood

Weald Barkfold

4

SHILLINGLEE RD

Works

Short's Farm

Oakhurst

Highbridge House

Plaistow Place

Lyon's Farm

3

Kingspark Wood

COUNCIL COTTS

Plaistow & Kirdford Prim Sch

31

NELL BALL

ASHFIELD

PARKFIELD

BACK LA

THE STREET

PH

PO

LOXWOOD RD

Ifold Copse

Plaistow

Beggars Copse

2

Birchfold Copse

BUSHFIELD

RICKMAN'S LA

GU28

Sparrwood Hangar

Rumbold Wood

1

Chilsfold Farm

Rumbolds Farm

98 | A | B | 99 | C | D | 00 | E | F

West Sussex STREET ATLAS

211
193
B
C
D
F
8
7
33
6
5
32
4
3
31
2
1
30
01
02
03
Old Knightons
Priorswood
Glasshouse Copse
Old Lock House
GU8
Upper Ifold Farm
ROSEMARY LA
GU6
Turtles Farm
High Bridge
B2133
LOXWOOD RD
Sydney Wood Cott
Westland Copse
Sir Roger Tichbourne (PH)
Alfold Bars
PIGBUSH LA
THE WALLED GDN
Loxwood Hall
Gennets Wood
OAKHURST LA
Oakhurst Farm
Tokens Farm
Thirds Copse
Sydney Farm
Lee House Farm
Gennets Wood
The Rookery
Barberry Furze
Sussex Border Path
Barberry Bridge
Gennets Furze
Pawlies Farm
Wey-South Path
Hog Wood
Oxoncroft Copse
Pond Copse
Hog Copse
Gennets Farm
Furzen Wood
POND COPSE LA
SPY LA
POUND CL
THE RETREAT
IFOLD BRIDGE LA
Loxwood
GUILDFORD RD
POND CL
THE LANE
Hogwood Farm
RH14
THE PARADE
NICHOLSFIELD
Barn Wood
THISTLEDOWN VALE
LOXWOOD PLACE FARM
PO
GLEBELANDS
STATION RD
HOGWOOD RD
LOXMEADOWS
Devil's Hole
HIGH ST
WILLETTS WAY
PANNELLS ASH
Wey & Arun Canal
B2133
POUNDFIELD LA
Ifold
CHALK RD
WYCHWOOD
WILDACRE CL
Loxwoodhills Pond
THE CLOSE
BIRCHWOOD CL
THE RIDE
LOXWOOD RD
Charleshurst
OAK WAY
THE DRIVE
Quennells Farm
Spring Copse
IFOLDHURST
Headfoldswood Farm
Corner Copse
PLAISTOW RD
Flitchings Farm
LAKERS LEA
FOXBRIDGE LA
RICKMAN'S LA
Foxbridge Hanger
Little Headfoldswood Copse
Foxbridge Farm
Woodlands Farm
CH
211

194
214

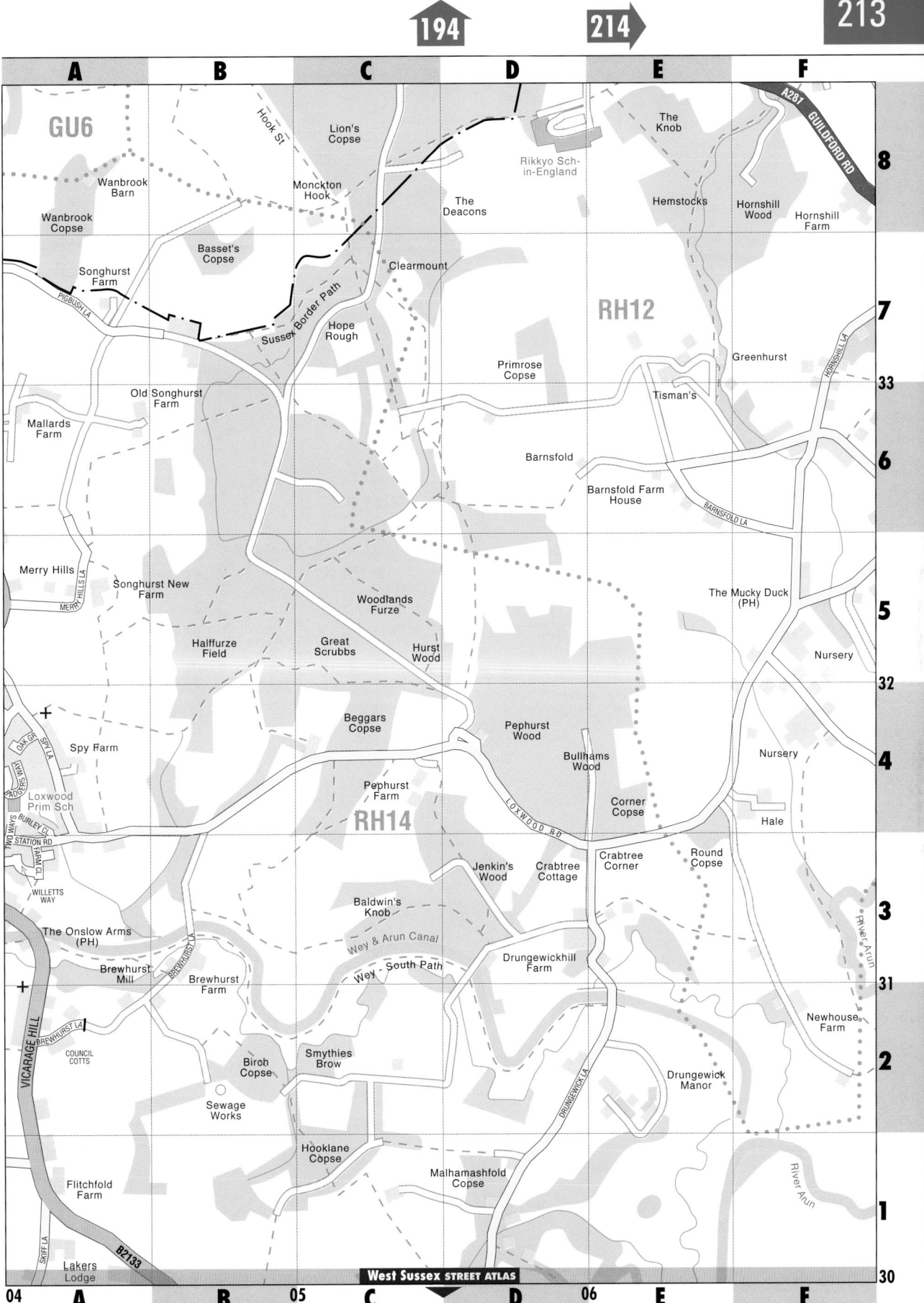
GU6
RH12
RH14
Lion's Copse
Hook St
Wanbrook Barn
Wanbrook Copse
Monckton Hook
Rikkyo Sch-in-England
The Knob
Hemstocks
Hornshill Wood
Hornshill Farm
A281 GUILDFORD RD
The Deacons
Basset's Copse
Clearmount
Songhurst Farm
PIGBUSH LA
Sussex Border Path
Hope Rough
Primrose Copse
Greenhurst
HORNSHILL LA
Tisman's
Old Songhurst Farm
Mallards Farm
Barnsfold
Barnsfold Farm House
BARNSFOLD LA
Merry Hills
MERRY HILLS LA
Songhurst New Farm
Woodlands Furze
The Mucky Duck (PH)
Halffurze Field
Great Scrubbs
Hurst Wood
Nursery
Spy Farm
OAK GR
SPY LA
Beggars Copse
Pephurst Wood
Bullhams Wood
Nursery
Loxwood Prim Sch
BADGERS WAY
Pephurst Farm
LOXWOOD RD
Corner Copse
Hale
TWO WAYS
BURLEY CL
STATION RD
FARM CL
WILLETTS WAY
Jenkin's Wood
Crabtree Cottage
Crabtree Corner
Round Copse
Baldwin's Knob
The Onslow Arms (PH)
Wey & Arun Canal
River Arun
Brewhurst Mill
BREWHURST LA
Brewhurst Farm
Wey - South Path
Drungewickhill Farm
Newhouse Farm
VICARAGE HILL
BREWHURST LA
COUNCIL COTTS
Birch Copse
Smythies Brow
Drungewick Manor
DRUNGEWICK LA
Sewage Works
Hooklane Copse
Malhamashfold Copse
Flitchfold Farm
River Arun
SKIFF LA
Lakers Lodge
B2133
A
B
C
D
E
F
8
7
33
6
5
32
4
3
31
2
1
30
04
05
06

214

213
195

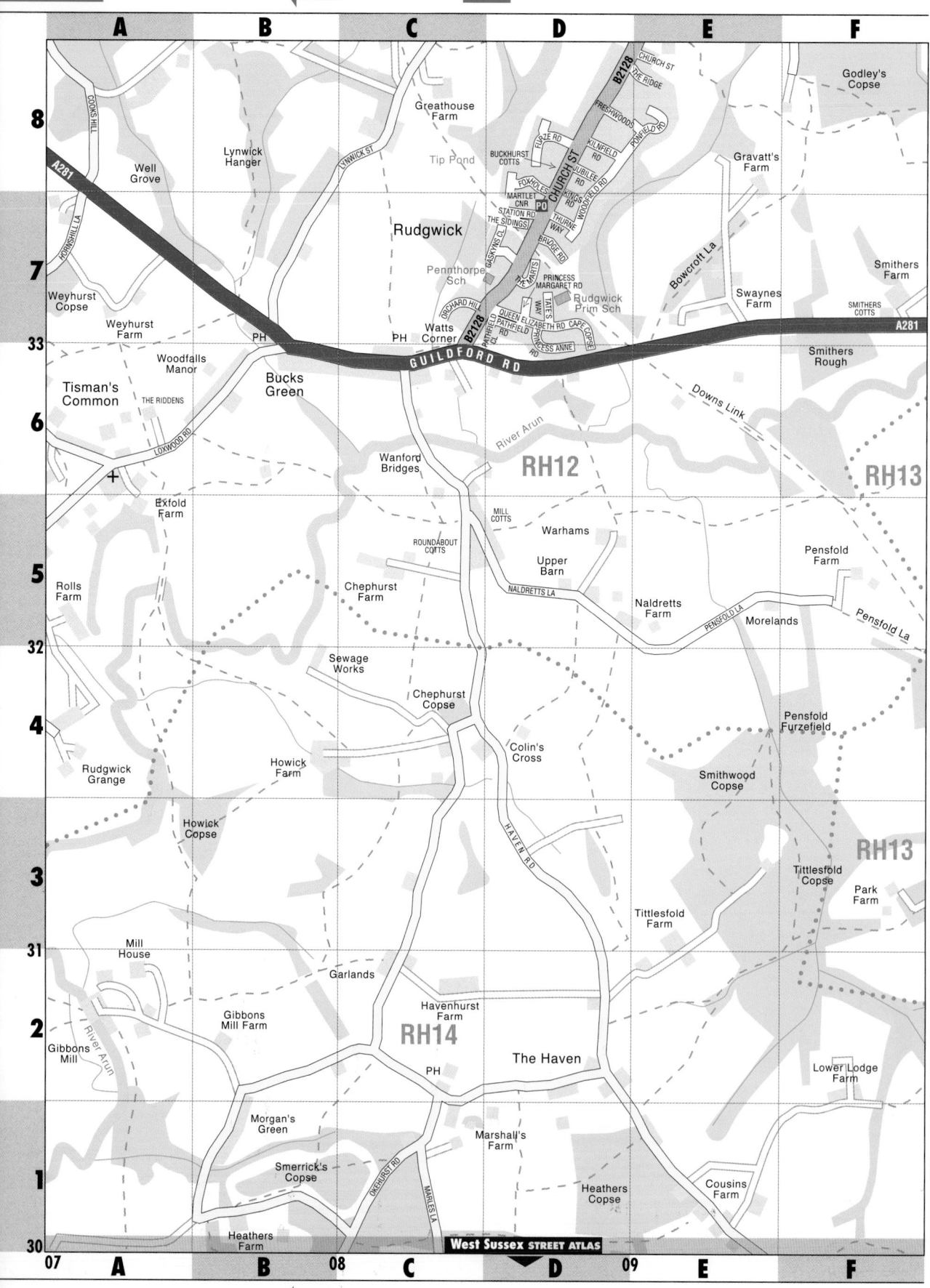
A
B
C
D
E
F
8
7
33
6
5
32
4
3
31
2
1
30
07
08
09
A281
COOKS HILL
Well Grove
Lynwick Hanger
LYNWICK ST
Greathouse Farm
Tip Pond
Rudgwick
Pennthorpe Sch
B2128
CHURCH ST
THE RIDGE
FRESHWOODS
PONFIELD RD
FURZE RD
KILNFIELD RD
BUCKHURST COTTS
JUBILEE RD
FOXHOLES
MARTLET CNR
KINGS RD
WOODFIELD RD
STATION RD
THE SIDINGS
THURNE WAY
GASKYNS CL
BRIDGE RD
THE MARTS
PRINCESS MARGARET RD
Rudgwick Prim Sch
ORCHARD HILL
TATE'S WAY
QUEEN ELIZABETH RD
CAPE COPSE
PATHFIELD RD
PATHFIELD CL
PRINCESS ANNE RD
PO
Godley's Copse
Gravatt's Farm
Bowcroft La
Swaynes Farm
Smithers Farm
SMITHERS COTTS
Smithers Rough
HORNSHILL LA
Weyhurst Copse
Weyhurst Farm
PH
Watts Corner
GUILDFORD RD
Woodfalls Manor
Tisman's Common
THE RIDDENS
Bucks Green
LOXWOOD RD
Downs Link
River Arun
RH12
RH13
Wanford Bridges
Exfold Farm
MILL COTTS
Warhams
ROUNDABOUT COTTS
Upper Barn
Pensfold Farm
Rolls Farm
Chephurst Farm
NALDRETTS LA
Naldretts Farm
PENSFOLD LA
Morelands
Pensfold La
Sewage Works
Chephurst Copse
Pensfold Furzefield
Rudgwick Grange
Howick Farm
Colin's Cross
Smithwood Copse
Howick Copse
HAVEN RD
Tittlesfold Copse
Park Farm
Tittlesfold Farm
Mill House
Garlands
Havenhurst Farm
Gibbons Mill Farm
Gibbons Mill
RH14
The Haven
Lower Lodge Farm
Morgan's Green
Marshall's Farm
Smerrick's Copse
OKEHURST RD
MARLES LA
Heathers Copse
Cousins Farm
Heathers Farm

213

	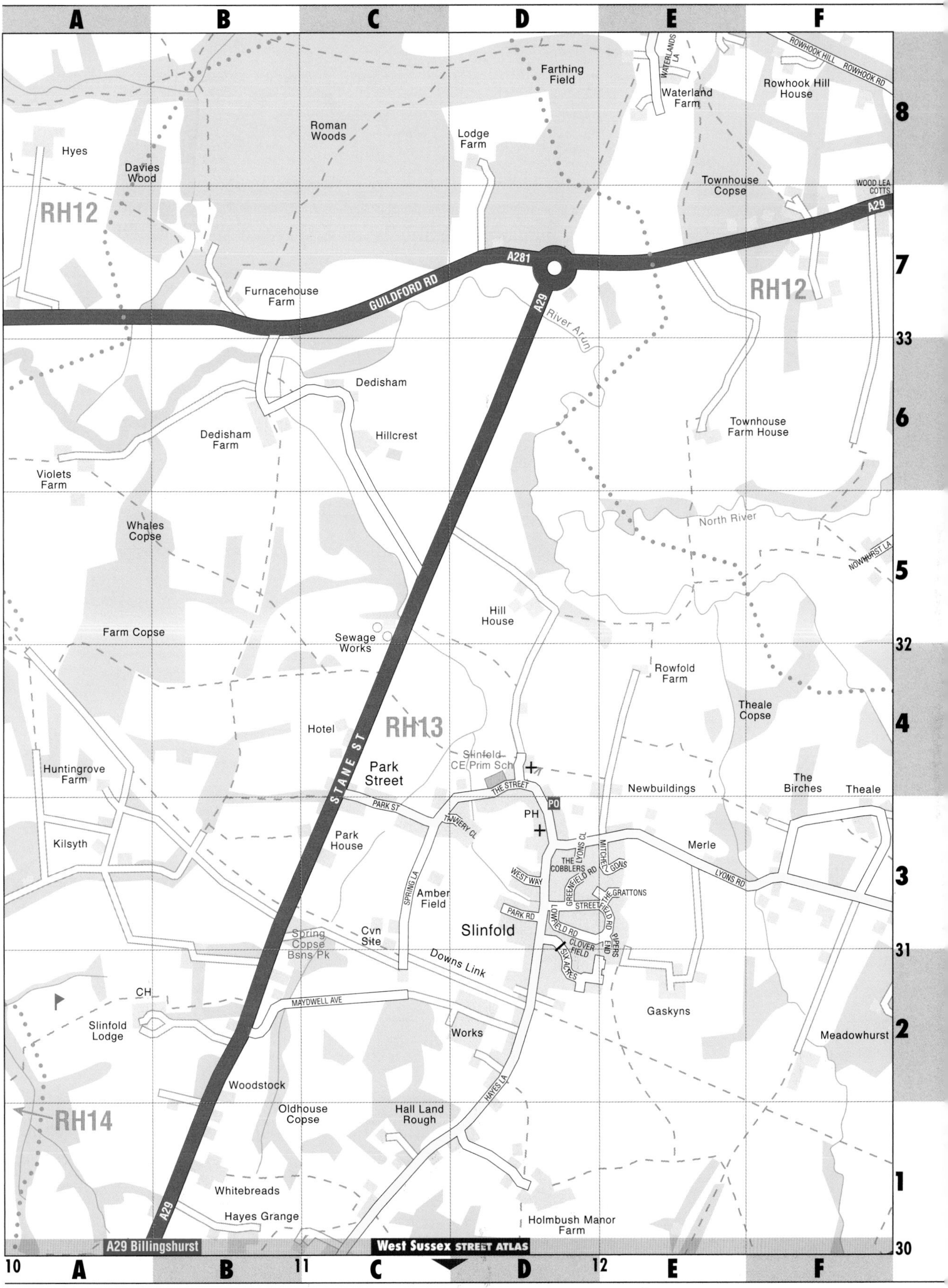 **A**	**B**	**C**	**D**	**E**	**F**	

Rowhook Hill ROWHOOK RD

8

Farthing Field

Waterlands La

Roman Woods

Lodge Farm

Waterland Farm

Rowhook Hill House

Hyes

Davies Wood

Townhouse Copse

WOOD LEA COTTS

RH12

A29

7

Furnacehouse Farm

GUILDFORD RD

A281

A29

River Arun

RH12

33

Dedisham

6

Townhouse Farm House

Dedisham Farm

Hillcrest

Violets Farm

North River

5

Whales Copse

NOWHURST LA

Farm Copse

Sewage Works

Hill House

32

Rowfold Farm

Theale Copse

RH13

Hotel

4

Park Street

Slinfold CE Prim Sch

Newbuildings

The Birches Theale

Huntingrove Farm

PARK ST

STANE ST

THE STREET

PO

PH

Kilsyth

Park House

TANNERY CL

THE COBBLERS

WEST WAY

GREENFIELD

LYONS CL

MITCHEL

L GDNS

Merle

LYONS RD

3

Spring Copse Bsns Pk

Amber Field

SPRING LA

STREET

FIELD RD

THE GRATTONS

PIPERS

Cvn Site

PARK RD

Slinfold

LINFIELD RD

CLOVER FIELD

31

CH

Downs Link

SIX ACRES

MAYDWELL AVE

Gaskyns

Meadowhurst

2

Slinfold Lodge

Works

Woodstock

HAYES LA

Oldhouse Copse

Hall Land Rough

1

RH14

Whitebreads

Hayes Grange

Holmbush Manor Farm

30

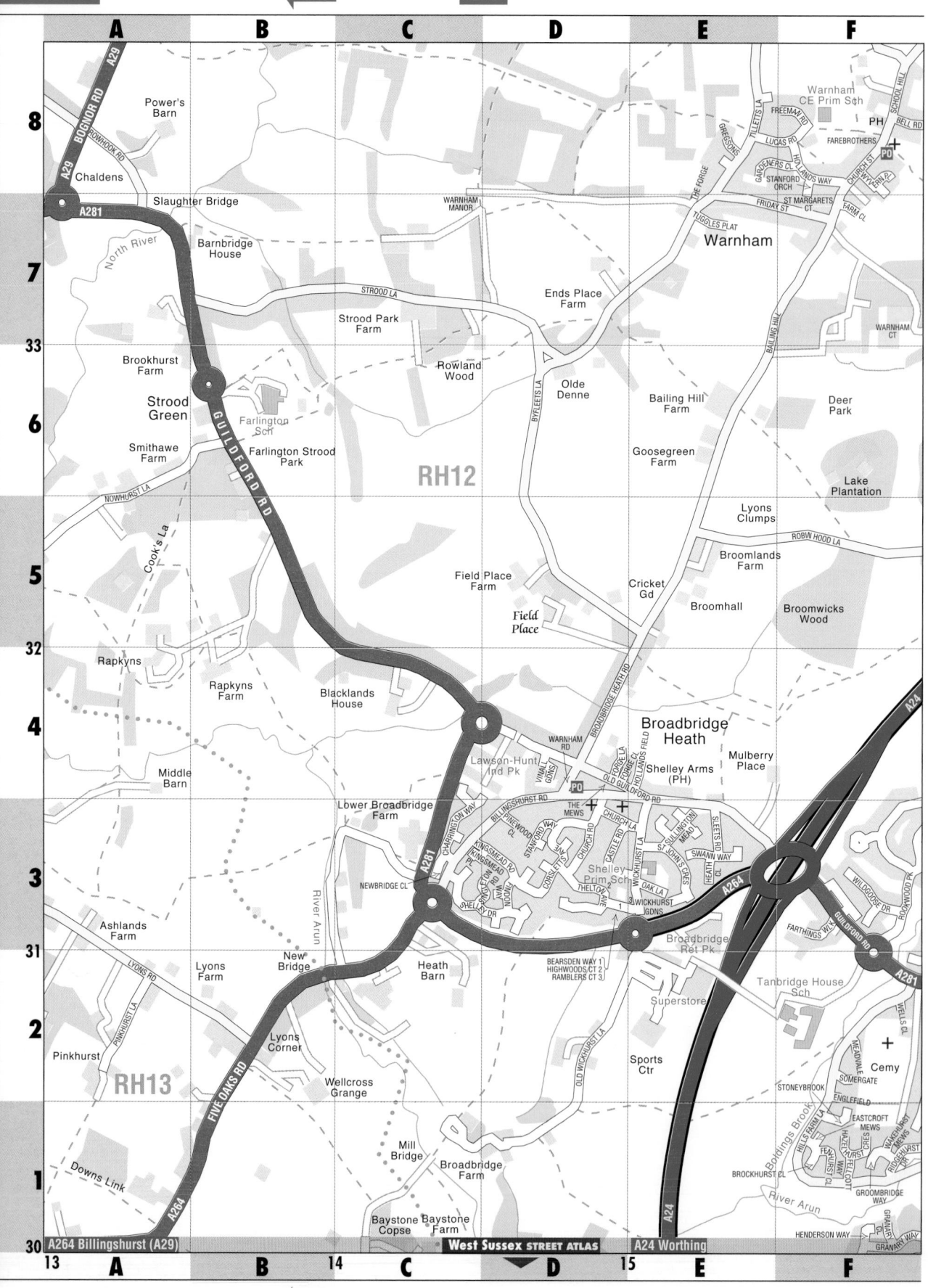
A
B
C
D
E
F
8
7
33
6
5
32
4
3
31
2
1
30
Power's Barn
Chaldens
Slaughter Bridge
Barnbridge House
North River
Strood Park Farm
Ends Place Farm
Warnham
Warnham CE Prim Sch
PH
Brookhurst Farm
Strood Green
Farlington Sch
Farlington Strood Park
Smithawe Farm
Rowland Wood
Olde Denne
Bailing Hill Farm
Goosegreen Farm
Deer Park
Lake Plantation
RH12
Lyons Clumps
Broomlands Farm
Field Place Farm
Field Place
Cricket Gd
Broomhall
Broomwicks Wood
Rapkyns
Rapkyns Farm
Blacklands House
Broadbridge Heath
Mulberry Place
Middle Barn
Lawson-Hunt Ind Pk
Shelley Arms (PH)
Lower Broadbridge Farm
Shelley Prim Sch
River Arun
Ashlands Farm
Lyons Farm
New Bridge
Heath Barn
Broadbridge Ret Pk
Tanbridge House Sch
Superstore
Pinkhurst
Lyons Corner
RH13
Wellcross Grange
Sports Ctr
Cemy
Mill Bridge
Broadbridge Farm
Downs Link
Boldings Brook
River Arun
Baystone Copse
Baystone Farm
A29
BOGNOR RD
ROWHOOK RD
A281
STROOD LA
GUILDFORD RD
NOWHURST LA
Cook's La
BYFLEETS LA
BAILING HILL
ROBIN HOOD LA
BROADBRIDGE HEATH RD
WARNHAM MANOR
THE FORGE
TUGGLES PLAT
FRIDAY ST
ST MARGARETS CT
FARM CL
GREGSONS
TILLETTS LA
FREEMAN RD
LUCAS RD
GARDENERS CL
HOLLANDS WAY
STANFORD ORCH
CHURCH ST
SCHOOL HILL
BELL RD
FAREBROTHERS
WARNHAM CT
WARNHAM RD
VINALL GDNS
FORGE LA
FORGE CL
HOLLANDS FIELD
OLD GUILDFORD RD
BILLINGSHURST RD
THE MEWS
CHARRINGTON WAY
PINEWOOD CL
STANFORD WAY
KINGSMEAD RD
KINGSMEAD PL
CORSLETTS AVE
CHURCH RD
CHURCH LA
CASTLE RD
WICKHURST LA
SULLINGTON MEAD
ST JOHN'S CRES
SWANN WAY
SLEETS RD
HEATH CL
OAK LA
THELTON AVE
WICKHURST GDNS
SHELLEY DR
FINDON WAY
NEWBRIDGE CL
A264
BEARSDEN WAY 1
HIGHWOODS CT 2
RAMBLERS CT 3
A24
WILDGOOSE DR
ROOKWOOD PK
FARTHINGS WLK
LYONS RD
PINKHURST LA
FIVE OAKS RD
OLD WICKHURST LA
WELLS CL
MEADVALE
SOMERGATE
STONEYBROOK
ENGLEFIELD
EASTCROFT MEWS
HILLS FARM LA
HAZELHURST CRES
FENHURST CL
FELCOTT WAY
WAKEHURST MEWS
RIDGEHURST DR
BROCKHURST CL
GROOMBRIDGE WAY
HENDERSON WAY
GRANARY CL
GRANARY WAY

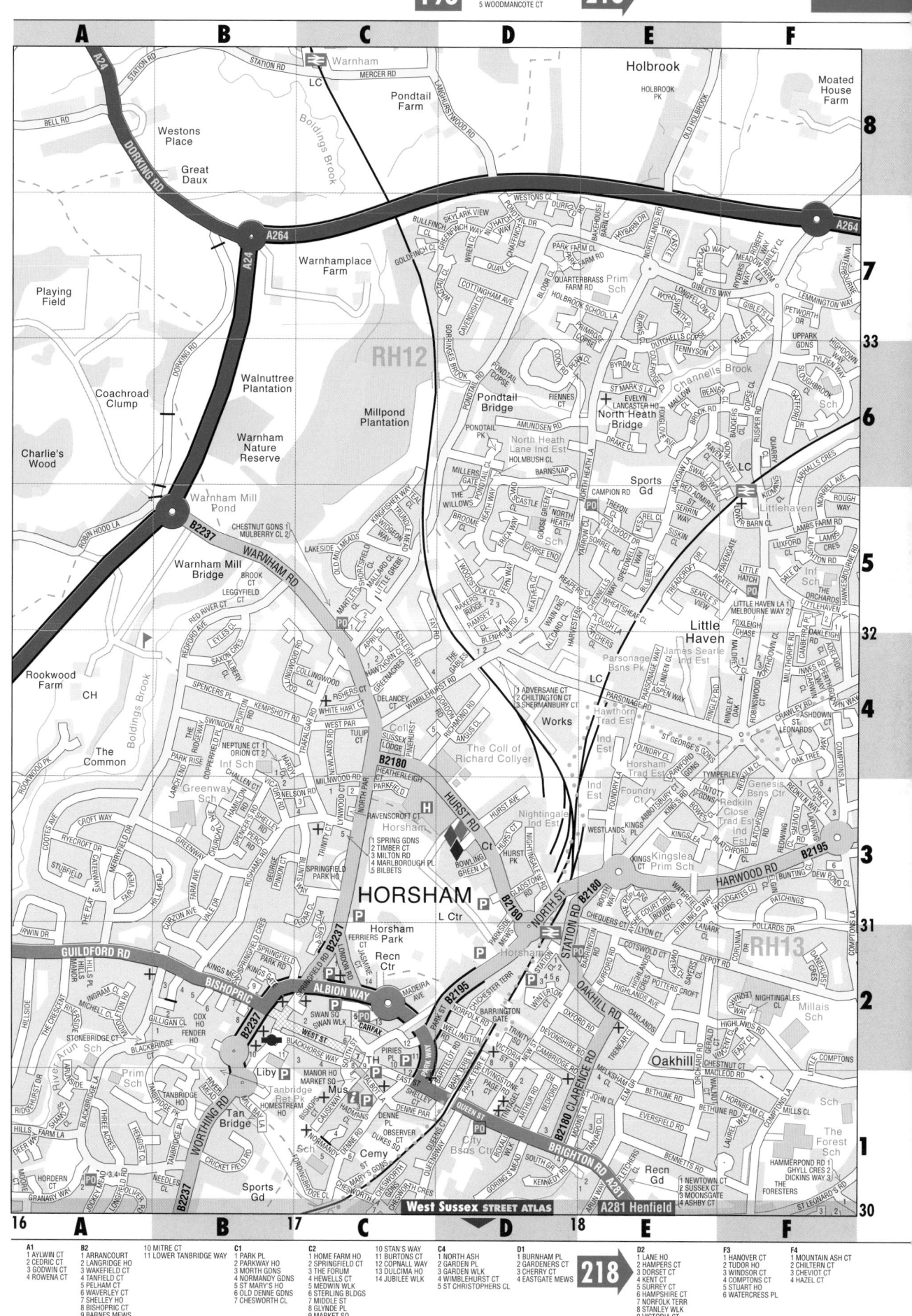

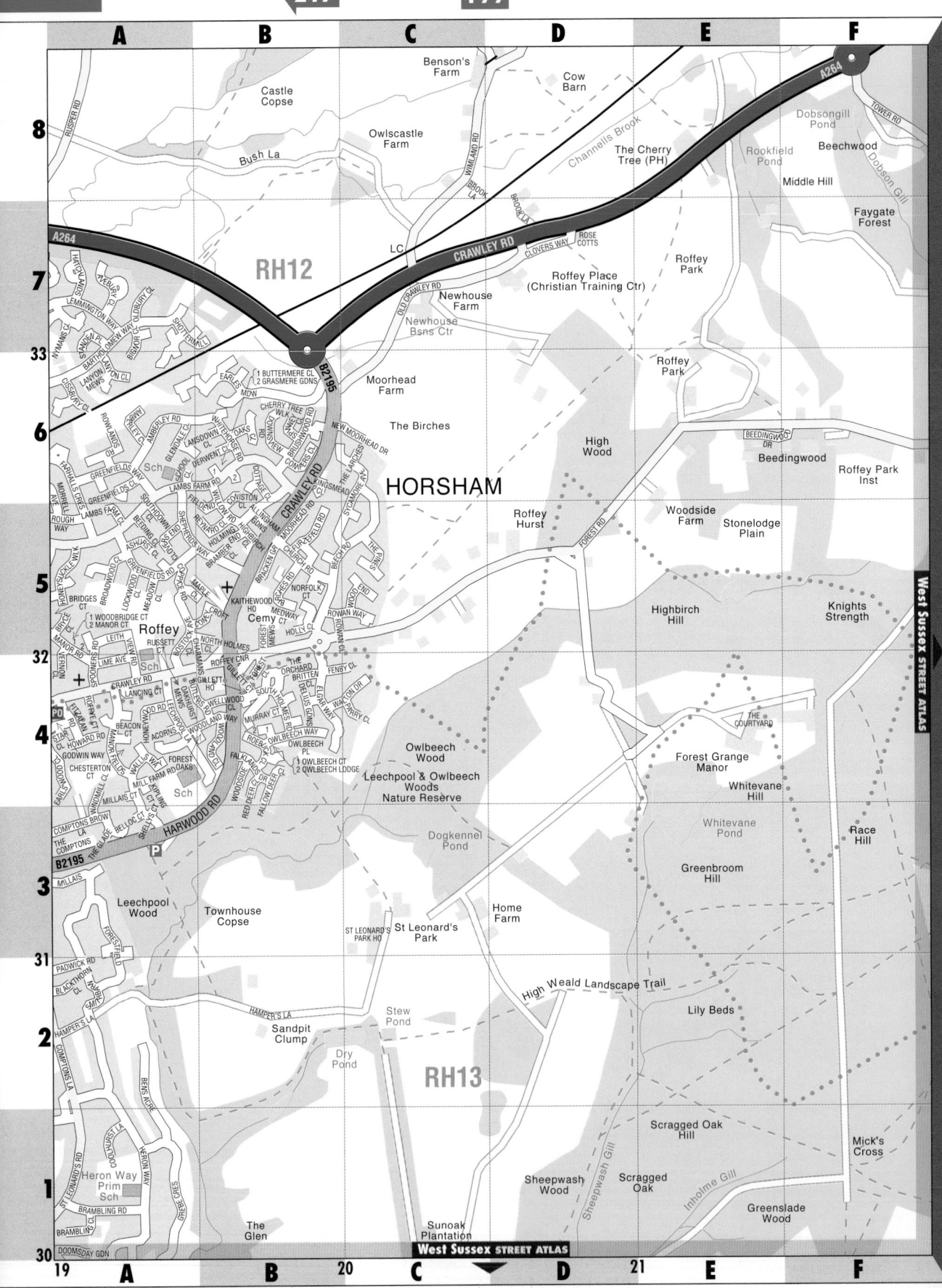

A264
RH12
B2195
HORSHAM
Roffey
RH13

West Sussex STREET ATLAS

Scale: 7 inches to 1 mile

0   110 yards   220 yards
0   125 m   250 m

One-way Streets

House numbers
1   59
HIGH ST

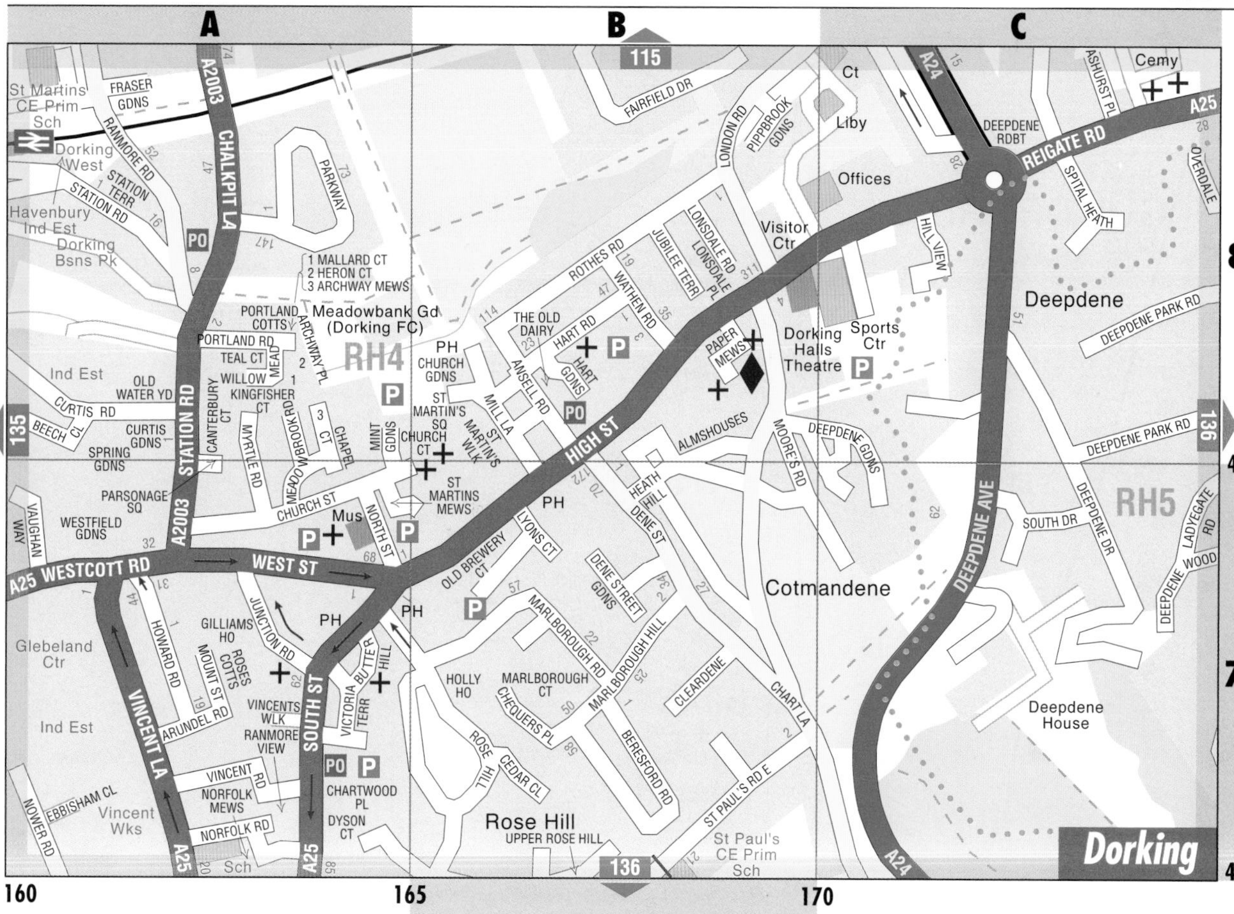

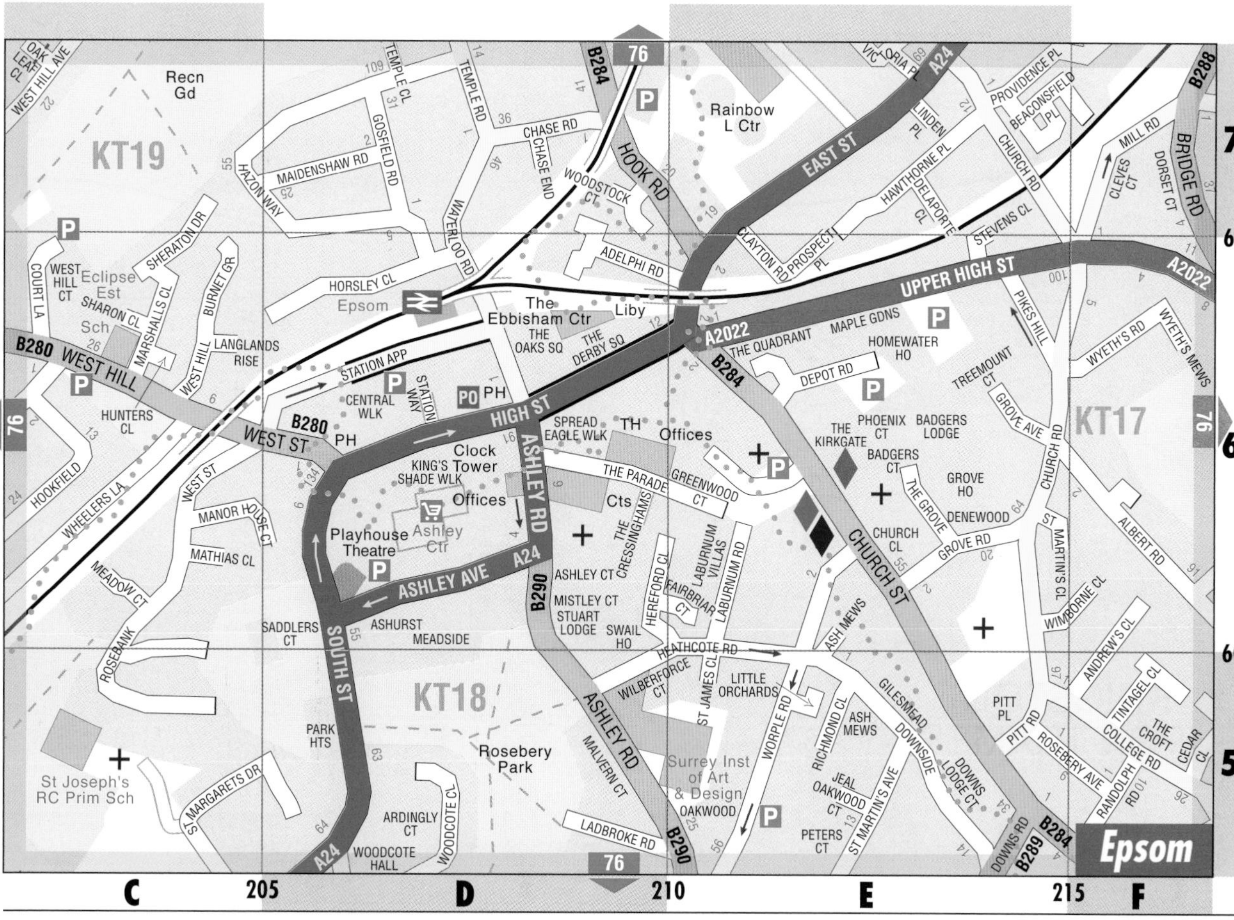

Dorking (top map)

A   B   115   C

8
495
7
490

135   136

St Martins CE Prim Sch
FRASER GDNS
A2003
CHALKPIT LA
RANMORE RD
Dorking West STATION TERR
STATION RD
Havenbury Ind Est
Dorking Bsns Pk
PO
PARKWAY
PORTLAND COTTS
PORTLAND RD
TEAL CT
ARCHWAY PL
MEAD
WILLOW
KINGFISHER
CANTERBURY
MYRTLE RD
CHAPEL
MINT
NSGS
1 MALLARD CT
2 HERON CT
3 ARCHWAY MEWS
Meadowbank Gd (Dorking FC)
RH4
Ind Est
OLD WATER YD
CURTIS RD
BEECH CL
CURTIS GDNS
SPRING GDNS
PARSONAGE SQ
WESTFIELD GDNS
A2003
STATION RD
MEADOWBROOK RD
CHURCH ST
NORTH ST
Mus
ST MARTIN'S SQ
CHURCH CT
ST MARTINS WLK
ST MARTINS MEWS
MILL LA
ANSELL RD
HIGH ST
FAIRFIELD DR
LONDON RD
PIPPBROOK GDNS
ROTHES RD
WATHEN RD
HART RD
JUBILEE TERR
LONSDALE RD
LONSDALE PL
THE OLD DAIRY
PH
CHURCH GDNS
PAPER MEWS
Visitor Ctr
Dorking Halls Theatre
Sports Ctr
HILL VIEW
A24
REIGATE RD
DEEPDENE RDBT
Cemy
ASHURST RD
A25
OVERDALE
SPITAL HEATH
Deepdene
DEEPDENE PARK RD
RH5
DEEPDENE PARK RD
DEEPDENE AVE
SOUTH DR
DEEPDENE DR
DEEPDENE WOOD
LADYGATE
Deepdene House
VAUGHAN WAY
A25 WESTCOTT RD
WEST ST
Glebeland Ctr
Ind Est
VINCENT LA
HOWARD RD
GILLIAMS HO
ROSES COTTS
JUNCTION RD
MOUNT ST
RANMORE VIEW
VINCENTS WLK
ARUNDEL RD
VINCENT RD
NORFOLK MEWS
NORFOLK RD
Vincent Wks
EBBISHAM CL
NOWER RD
A25
SOUTH ST
VICTORIA TERR
BUTTER HILL
PH
PH
PH
OLD BREWERY
LYONS CT
DENE ST
HEATH HILL
DENE STREET
DENE GDNS
MARLBOROUGH RD
MARLBOROUGH HILL
HOLLY HO
MARLBOROUGH CT
CHEQUERS PL
BERESFORD RD
CLEARDENE
CHART LA
Cotmandene
MOORE'S RD
DEEPDENE GDNS
ALMSHOUSES
ROSE HILL
CEDAR CL
CHARTWOOD PL
DYSON CT
PO
Rose Hill
UPPER ROSE HILL
ST PAUL'S RD E
St Paul's CE Prim Sch
A24
136
Dorking

160   165   170

Epsom (bottom map)

C   B284   76   D   210   E   215   F

7
610
6
605
5

KT19
Recn Gd
WEST HILL AVE
OAK CL
HAZON WAY
MAIDENSHAW RD
SHERATON DR
TEMPLE CL
TEMPLE RD
GOSFIELD RD
CHASE RD
CHASE END
WOODSTOCK CL
WATERLOO RD
HOOK RD
Rainbow L Ctr
VICTORIA PL
EAST ST
A24
LINDEN PL
HAWTHORNE PL
DELAPORTE RD
CHURCH RD
PROVIDENCE PL
BEACONSFIELD
MILL HILL
BRIDGE RD
DORSET RD
CLEVES CT
B288
B280 WEST HILL
WEST HILL COURT LA
Eclipse Est
SHARON CL
Sch
BURNET GR
WEST HILL
MARSHALL'S CL
LANGLANDS RISE
HORSLEY CL
Epsom
ADELPHI RD
The Ebbisham Ctr
THE OAKS SQ
THE DERBY SQ
Liby
CLAYTON RD
PROSPECT PL
STEVENS CL
UPPER HIGH ST
A2022
PIKES HILL
WYETH'S RD
WYETH'S MEWS
TREEMOUNT
GROVE AVE
KT17
A2022
76
76
610
HUNTERS CL
B280
STATION APP
CENTRAL WLK
STATION WAY
PO
PH
HIGH ST
HOOKFIELD
WHEELERS LA
WEST ST
WEST ST
PH
Clock
KING'S Tower
SHADE WLK
Offices
Ashley Ctr
Playhouse Theatre
ASHLEY RD
A24
SPREAD EAGLE WLK
THE PARADE
Cts
GREENWOOD CT
THE CHESSINGHAMS
Offices
TH
A2022
A2022
THE QUADRANT
MAPLE GDNS
HOMEWATER HO
DEPOT RD
THE KIRKGATE
PHOENIX CT
BADGERS LODGE
BADGERS CT
GROVE HO
THE GROVE
DENEWOOD
GROVE RD
MARTIN'S CL
ALBERT RD
WIMBORNE CL
MEADOW CT
MANOR HOUSE CT
MATHIAS CL
ASHLEY AVE
SADDLERS CT
ASHURST MEADSIDE
B290
MISTLEY CT
STUART LODGE
SWAIL HO
LABURNUM VILLAS
LABURNUM RD
HEREFORD CL
FAIRBRIAR
HEATHCOTE RD
WILBERFORCE
ST JAMES CL
LITTLE ORCHARDS
WORPLE RD
RICHMOND CL
ASH MEWS
ASH MEWS
GILESMEAD
DOWNSIDE
CHURCH CL
CHURCH ST
ANDREW'S CL
TINTAGEL CT
THE CROFT
CEDAR
COLLEGE RD
ROSEBERY AVE
RANDOLPH RD
PITT PL
PITT RD
B280
B290
SOUTH ST
KT18
PARK HTS
ST MARGARETS DR
St Joseph's RC Prim Sch
ARDINGLY CT
WOODCOTE HALL
A24
Rosebery Park
WOODCOTE RD
MALVERN CT
LADBROKE RD
B290
ASHLEY RD
Surrey Inst of Art & Design
OAKWOOD
JEAL CT
OAKWOOD
DOWNS RD
LODGE CT
PETERS CT
ST MARTIN'S AVE
DOWNS RD
B289
B284
Epsom

C   205   D   210   E   215   F

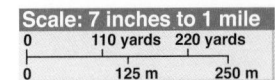

Scale: 7 inches to 1 mile

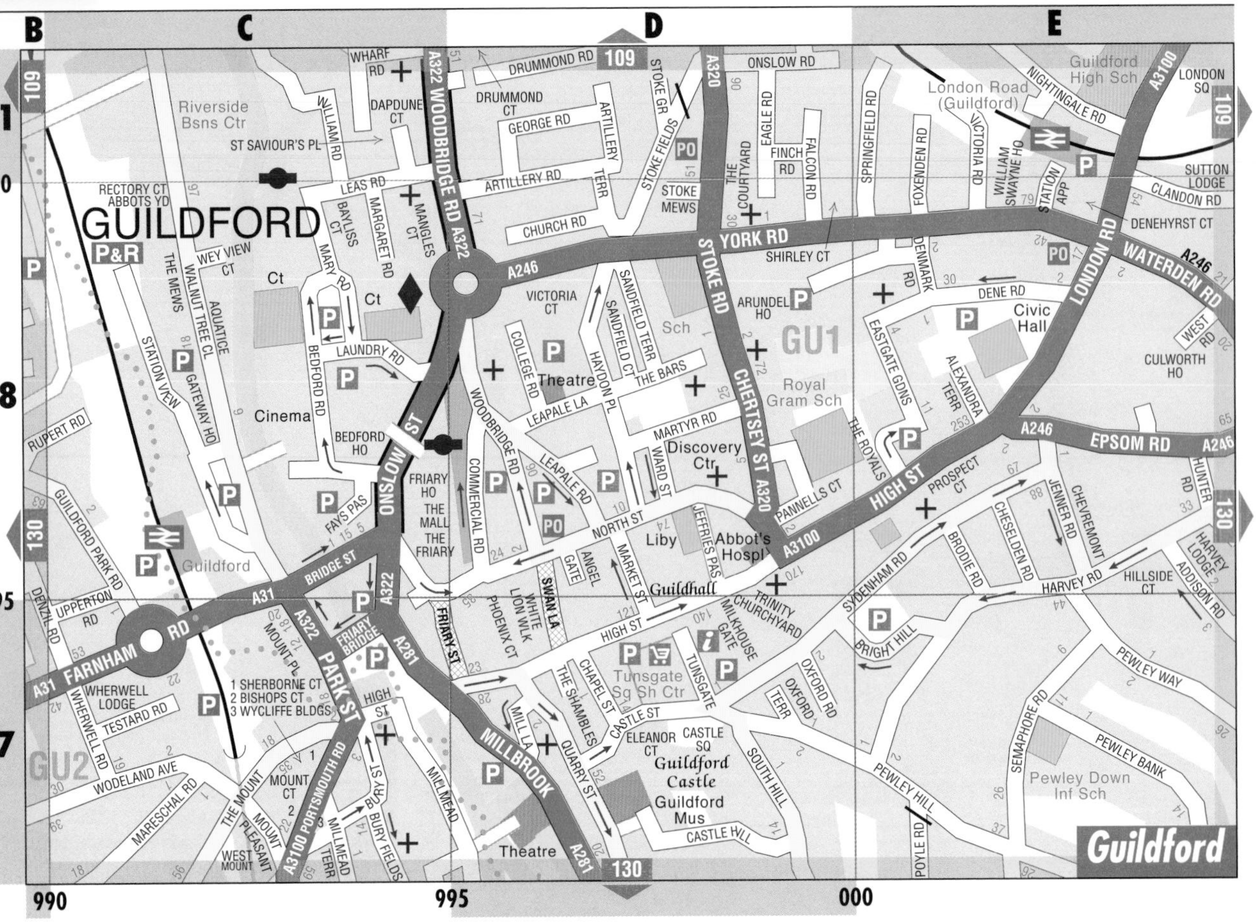

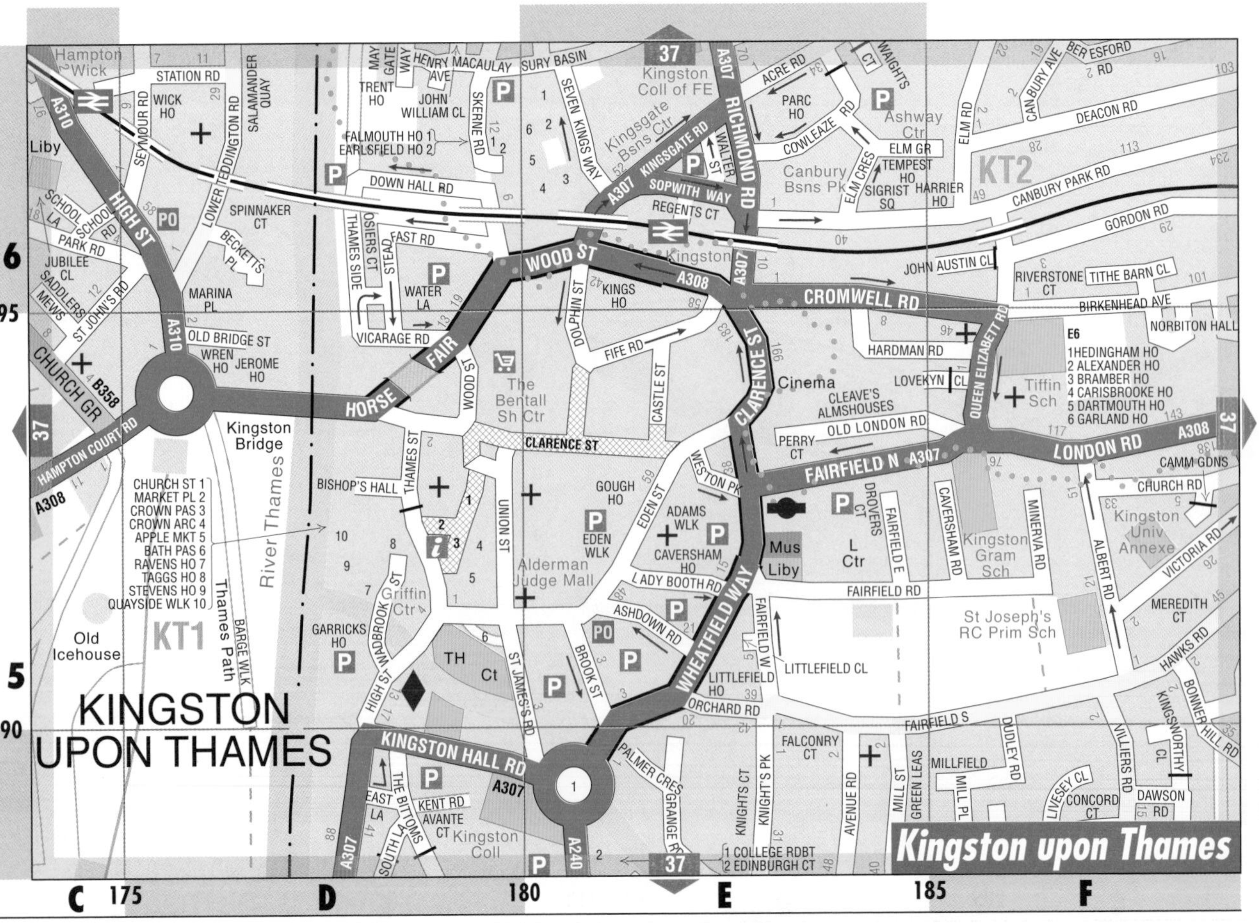

Guildford
GUILDFORD
1 SHERBORNE CT
2 BISHOPS CT
3 WYCLIFFE BLDGS
Kingston upon Thames
KINGSTON UPON THAMES
CHURCH ST 1
MARKET PL 2
CROWN PAS 3
CROWN ARC 4
APPLE MKT 5
BATH PAS 6
RAVENS HO 7
TAGGS HO 8
STEVENS HO 9
QUAYSIDE WLK 10
E6
1 HEDINGHAM HO
2 ALEXANDER HO
3 BRAMBER HO
4 CARISBROOKE HO
5 DARTMOUTH HO
6 GARLAND HO
1 COLLEGE RDBT
2 EDINBURGH CT

A B C

7 6 5

570 565

160 165 170

95 94

Leatherhead

Imperial Pk
Ryebrook Bsns Pk
TUDOR WLK
RANDALLS WAY
BURNEY HO
A245
RANDALLS RD
Leatherhead
OAKS CT
OAKS CL
STATION APP
COPPERFIELD CT
KINGS CT
BAY TREE AVE
KINGSTON RD
BULL HILL
ASHURST CL
RANDALLS PARK DR
RONSON WAY
OLD STATION APP
Mole Bsns Pk
Leatherhead Ind Est
STATION RD
LEITH HO
PH
B2122
WATERWAY RD
River Mole
MILL LA
WALLIS MEWS
GUILDFORD RD
FETCHAM GROVE COTTS
BELMONT RD
HOLLY CT
EMLYN LA
HAYDON CT
DURHAM CT
BURLEIGH CT
THORNCROFT
BRIDGE ST
BRIDGE CT
MINCHIN CL
WOODVILLE RD
WOODVILLE CT
KINGSCROFT RD
Leatherhead Trinity Sch
COPTHORNE RD
MONTGOMERY CT
LEVETT RD
THE WITHIES
HILL RISE CT
PARK RISE CL
KINGSTON AVE
ST JOHN'S AVE
KT22
PARK RISE
KINGSTON GDNS
KINGSTON HOUSE
UPPER FAIRFIELD RD
FAIRFIELD RD
MIDDLE RD
LINDEN RD
1 QUEEN ANNES CT
2 FAIRFIELD WLK
3 QUEEN ANNE'S TERR
4 QUEEN ANNE'S GDNS
5 FAIRFIELD CT
Fairfield
LINDEN PIT PATH
LINDEN CT
St John's Sch
GARLANDS RD
LINDEN GDNS
ST JOHN'S CL
TREGARTHEN PL
Downsend Sch
ASHCROFT PL
HOMELANDS
GROSVENOR CT
MELVINSHAW
THE KNOLL
PEGASUS CT
A243
M25
B2122
A24
EPSOM RD
VICTORIA HO
FIRCROFT
ALBERT HO
MERRYWOOD
ELVEDEN CT
EAST LODGE
OVERSLEA LODGE
MAYFIELD
DAYMERSLEA RIDGE
TYLNEY CT
FORTYFOOT RD
HOMEFIELD CL
HOMEFIELD
HIGHWOODS
LERET WAY
GRAVEL HILL
NORTH ST
SWAN CT
HIGH ST
PO
ELM RD
B2450
THE CRESCENT
Thorndike Theatre
CALVERT CT
Leatherhead Mus of Local History
The Mansion
Mansion Gdn
Liby
CHURCH ST
RUSSELL CT
CHURCH WLK
OWEN PL
WAVERLEY PL
BYRON PL
CHURCH RD
MAGAZINE PL
SKEAT HO
STENNING CT
VICARAGE LA
B2033
HIGHLANDS RD
ST JOHN'S RD
SHERBORNE WLK
WINDFIELD
POPLAR RD
LEACH GR
POPLAR AVE
OLD SCHOOL CT
HIGHLANDS CL
THE THISTLES
HIGHLANDS AVE
H
Leatherhead General
Woodlands Sch
BEECH HOLT
TANNERS DEAN
Leatherhead Trinity Sch

3 2 1

590 585

005 010 015

69 70

Woking

THE LARCHES
HORSELL PK
GRAYLANDS
BROOMHALL LA
1 THURLTON CT
2 BROOMHALL END
A3046
CHOBHAM RD
FERNDALE RD
EXETER HO
BARGATE HO
THE GROVE
Basingstoke Canal
NAPIER CT
BROOMHALL RD
HEATHVIEW
ALWYNE CT
CENTURY CT
KINGSWOOD CT
BREWERY RD
VICTORIA WAY
1 BRIDGEWATER PL
2 KENNET CT
3 STRATFORD CT
4 ASHTON CT
5 REGENTS CT
A320
BOUNDARY RD
PINEWOOD CT
KINGSOAK HO
BOARD SCHOOL RD
VICTORIA PL
BEDSER CL
WESCO CT
COURTENAY MEWS
NORTH RD
EASTBROOK CL
THE CLOCK TWR
KINGS RD
KINGSMEAD
Lion Ret Pk
ELLIOTT CT
HALL PL
THE LIMES
ROSEWOOD CT
PALACE CT
LANCASTER CL
MAYBURY RD
Maybury Inf Sch
WALTON RD
THE VILLAS
PORTUGAL RD
MARLBOROUGH RD
Bsns Ctr
HANNAH CT
BURLEIGH GDNS
GLOSTER CT
GROVE RD
BRAMWELL PL
GU21
CENTRAL BLDGS
CHOBHAM RD
CHURCH ST E
CHRISTCHURCH WAY
WEST ST
CHERTSEY RD
STANLEY RD
GROSVENOR RD
The Woking Martian
Liby
DUKE ST
LOCKE WAY
ADDISON RD
THE BROADWAY
COMMERCIAL WAY
The Victoria Entertainment Ctr
TOWN SQ
MERCIA WLK
WOLSEY WLK
ALBION HO
CHURCH PATH
The Peacocks Sh Ctr
Wolsey Pl Sh Ctr
LOCKFIELD DR
A324
FORGE END
CHURCH ST W
CAWSEY WAY
CHAPEL ST
HIGH ST
Woking
EASTGATE
STATION APP
THE EXCHANGE
CENTRIUM
Mkt
GOLDSWORTH RD
BUTTS RD
VICTORIA RD
GUILDFORD RD
Ct
THE BIRCHES
BRADFIELD CL
SOMERSET HO
HEATHSIDE CRES
HOLLY LODGE
OAK HO
COPPER BEECH HO
CALLUNA CT
HOLBRECK PL
MARCUS CT
WHITE ROSE LA
GREENHEYS PL
HEATHSIDE RD
JARMAN CT
AARRON CT
ORIENTAL CL
ORIENTAL RD
St Dunstan's RC Prim Sch
TUDOR CL
The Park Sch
PARK RD
GU22
Harven Sch
DOWNSIDE ORCH
NORTHBURY HO
MARIE CARLILE
BRACKEN CL
DINSDALE CL
HEATHSIDE GDNS
HEATHFIELD RD
HOCKERING RD
PEMBROKE GDNS
HOCKERING GDNS
ONSLOW CRES
ONSLOW CL
ABBOTSFORD CL
RUSCOE DR
FOXHANGER GDNS
THE FURLOUGH
TINTAGEL WAY
DORCHESTER CT
TEMPLECOMBE MEWS
PEMBROKE CT
LYTTON RD
MILFORD HO
PINEACRE CT
ELLERAY
PEMBROKE RD
ST PAULS RD
THE CLOSE
RIDGE WAY HO
THE RIDGE
Maybury Bsns Ctr
SHAFTESBURY RD
MAYBURY CT
PARK RD

C D E F

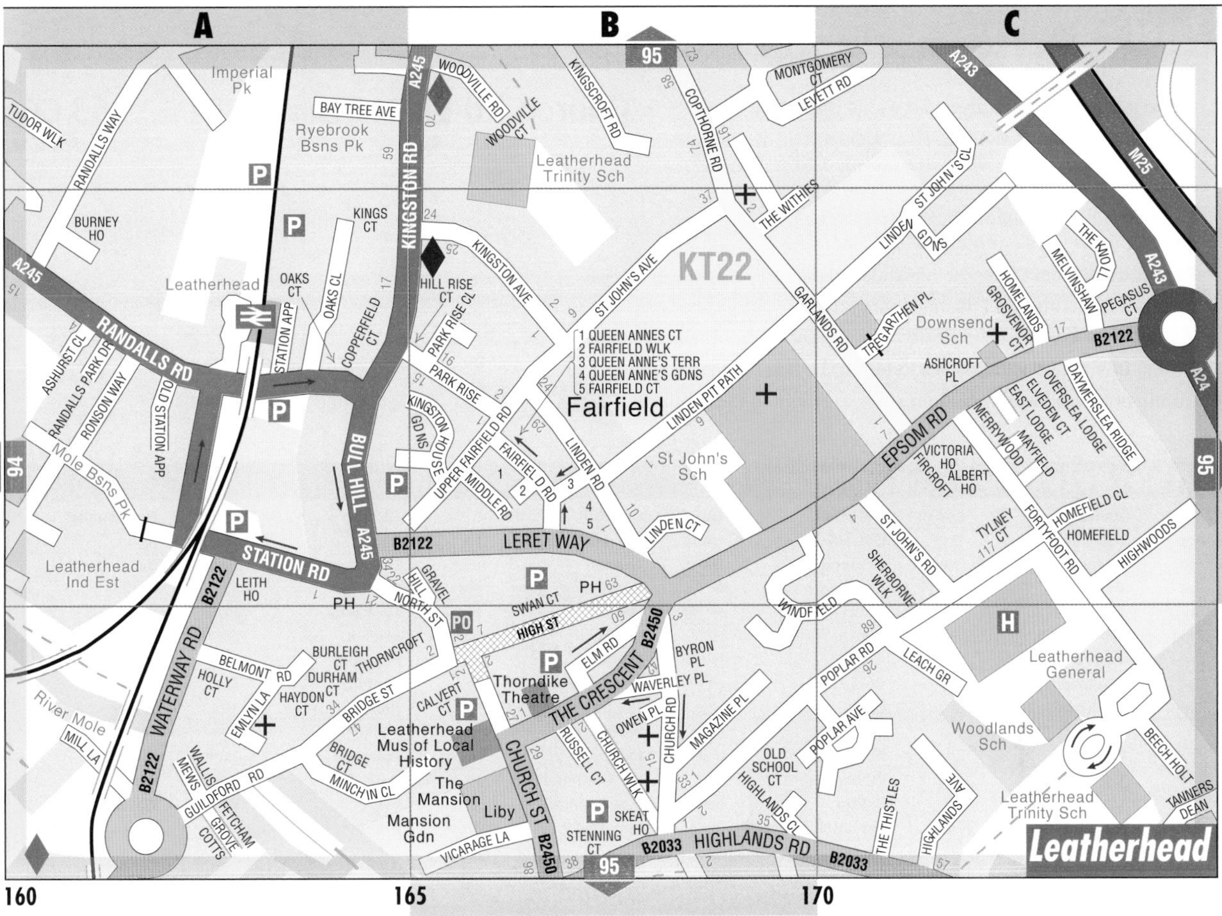

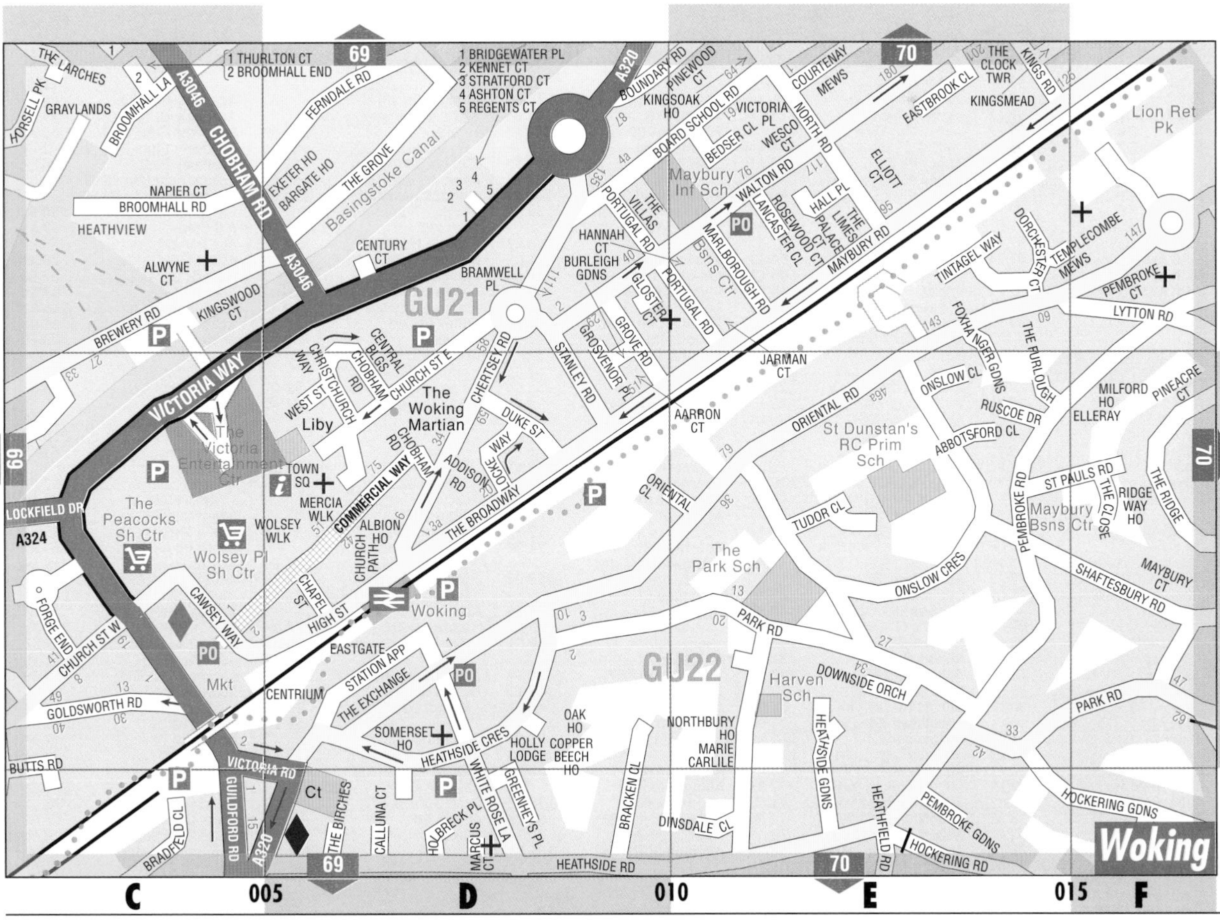

Index

Place name May be abbreviated on the map

Church Rd 6 Beckenham BR2..........**53** C6

Location number Present when a number indicates the place's position in a crowded area of mapping

Locality, town or village Shown when more than one place has the same name

Postcode district District for the indexed place

Page and grid square Page number and grid reference for the standard mapping

Cities, towns and villages are listed in CAPITAL LETTERS

Public and commercial buildings are highlighted in magenta   Places of interest are highlighted in blue with a star ★

Abbreviations used in the index

Acad	Academy	Comm	Common	Gd	Ground	L	Leisure	Prom	Promenade
App	Approach	Cott	Cottage	Gdn	Garden	La	Lane	Rd	Road
Arc	Arcade	Cres	Crescent	Gn	Green	Liby	Library	Recn	Recreation
Ave	Avenue	Cswy	Causeway	Gr	Grove	Mdw	Meadow	Ret	Retail
Bglw	Bungalow	Ct	Court	H	Hall	Meml	Memorial	Sh	Shopping
Bldg	Building	Ctr	Centre	Ho	House	Mkt	Market	Sq	Square
Bsns, Bus	Business	Ctry	Country	Hospl	Hospital	Mus	Museum	St	Street
Bvd	Boulevard	Cty	County	HQ	Headquarters	Orch	Orchard	Sta	Station
Cath	Cathedral	Dr	Drive	Hts	Heights	Pal	Palace	Terr	Terrace
Cir	Circus	Dro	Drove	Ind	Industrial	Par	Parade	TH	Town Hall
Cl	Close	Ed	Education	Inst	Institute	Pas	Passage	Univ	University
Cnr	Corner	Emb	Embankment	Int	International	Pk	Park	Wk, Wlk	Walk
Coll	College	Est	Estate	Intc	Interchange	Pl	Place	Wr	Water
Com	Community	Ex	Exhibition	Junc	Junction	Prec	Precinct	Yd	Yard

Index of towns, villages, streets, hospitals, industrial estates, railway stations, schools, shopping centres, universities and places of interest

1st–ACS

1st Ave KT20 . . . . 97 E2
2nd Ave KT20 . . . . 97 E2
3rd Ave KT20 . . . . 97 E2
4th Ave KT20 . . . . 97 E2
5th Ave KT20 . . . . 97 E2
6th Ave KT20 . . . . 97 E2
7th Ave KT20 . . . . 97 E2
8th Ave KT20 . . . . 97 E2
9th Ave KT20 . . . . 97 F2
10th Ave KT20 . . . . 97 E1
11th Ave KT20 . . . . 97 F1
12th Ave KT20 . . . . 97 F1
13th Ave KT20 . . . . 97 F1
14th Ave KT20 . . . . 97 F1
15th Ave KT20 . . . . 97 F1
16th Ave KT20 . . . . 97 F1

A

Aaron Ct BR3 . . . . 44 B6
AARON'S HILL 150 C4
Aaron's Hill GU7 . . . . . . 150 B4
Aarron Ct GU21 . . . . 69 F2
Abbess Cl SW2 . . . . 22 B7
Abbetts La GU15 . . . . 65 B3
Abbey Bsns Ctr **17**
RH1 . . . . 118 F2
Abbey Cl
Bracknell RG12 . . . . 27 D4
Elmbridge Village GU6 . . 173 F2
Pyrford GU22 . . . . 70 E3
Wokingham RG40 . . . . . . 25 C7
Abbey Ct
Camberley GU15 . . . . 65 D5
Chertsey KT16 . . . . 33 B2
Farnham GU9 . . . . 125 C2
1 Hampton TW12 . . . . . . 16 A1
Laleham TW18 . . . . 33 C5
Purley CR8 . . . . 80 B7
Abbey Dr
Laleham TW18 . . . . 33 C5
Upper Tooting SW17 . . . . . 21 A3
Abbeyfield Cl CR4 . . . . . . 40 E7
Abbeyfield Ho RH8 . . . . . 122 E5
Abbeyfields Pk KT16 . . . . 33 C2
Abbey Gdns KT16 . . . . . . 33 A3
Abbey Gn KT16 . . . . 33 A3
Abbey Ind Est CR4 . . . . . . 40 F4
Abbey La BR3 . . . . 24 A1

Abbeylands KT13 . . . . 53 B3
Abbey Lo **3** TW18 . . . . . . 12 F3
Abbey Mdws KT16 . . . . . . 33 C2
Abbey Mews
Brentford TW7 . . . . 6 B6
Laleham TW18 . . . . 33 C5
Abbey Mill Bsns Pk
GU7 . . . . 149 F4
Abbey Pk BR3 . . . . 24 A1
Abbey Pl KT16 . . . . 33 A6
Abbey Prim Sch SM4 . . . . 40 A2
Abbey Rd
Chertsey KT16 . . . . 33 B2
Croydon CR0, CR9 . . . . . . 61 B7
Lower Halliford TW17 . . . . 34 A1
Merton SW19 . . . . 40 C8
Selsdon CR2 . . . . 62 D1
Virginia Water GU25 . . . . . 31 D5
Woking GU21 . . . . 69 D2
Abbey River Cotts
KT16 . . . . 33 C3
Abbey Sch The GU9 . . . . 125 D1
Abbey St GU9 . . . . 125 C2
Abbey Trad Est SE26 . . . . 23 F3
Abbey Way GU14 . . . . 85 C4
Abbey Wlk KT8 . . . . 36 B5
Abbey Wood SL5 . . . . 30 A2
Abbot Cl KT14 . . . . 71 D8
Abbots Ave KT19 . . . . 76 A8
Abbotsbury RG12 . . . . 26 F4
Abbotsbury Ct RH13 . . . . 217 E3
Abbotsbury Prim Sch
SM4 . . . . 40 B4
Abbotsbury Rd
Coney Hall BR2, BR4 . . . . . 63 F8
Morden SM4, SW19 . . . . . . 40 B5
Abbot's Cl GU2 . . . . 129 F6
Abbots Ct SE25 . . . . 42 E6
Abbots Dr GU25 . . . . 31 C5
Abbotsfield Rd RH11 . . . . 200 D4
Abbotsford Cl GU22 . . . . . 70 A2
Abbots Gn CR0, CR2 . . . . . 62 D4
Abbotshall Rd SE6 . . . . . . 24 D6
Abbots Ho GU4 . . . . 110 A5
Abbots La CR8 . . . . 80 C3
Abbotsleigh Cl SM2 . . . . . 59 B3
Abbotsleigh Rd SW16 . . . . 21 C3
Abbotsmede Cl TW1 . . . . . 16 F6
Abbots Pk SW2 . . . . 22 A7
Abbots Rd SM1, SM3 . . . . 58 E6
Abbot's Ride GU9 . . . . . . 125 E1

Abbots Rise RH1 . . . . 119 A3
Abbots Way
Beckenham BR3 . . . . 43 E4
Chertsey KT16 . . . . 32 F2
Abbot's Way GU1 . . . . . . 110 D2
Abbots Wlk CR3 . . . . 101 B5
ABBOTSWOOD 109 F3
Abbotswood
Guildford GU1 . . . . 109 F3
Walton-on-T KT13 . . . . 53 F7
Abbotswood Cl GU1 . . . . 109 F4
Abbotswood Dr KT13 . . . . 53 D1
Abbots Wood Forest Wlk ★
GU10 . . . . 166 C7
Abbotswood Rd SW16 . . . . 21 D5
Abbots Yd **9** GU1 . . . . . 130 C8
Abbott Ave SW20 . . . . 39 D8
Abbott Ho SW12 . . . . 20 F8
Abbotts Cotts GU10 . . . . 166 C5
Abbotts Rd CR4, SW16 . . . 41 C5
Abbotts Tilt KT12 . . . . 54 E7
Abelia Cl GU24 . . . . 67 E6
Abell Ct KT15 . . . . 52 C6
Abercairn Rd SW16 . . . . . 21 C1
Aberconway Rd SM4 . . . . . 40 B5
Abercorn Cl CR2 . . . . 81 D7
Abercorn Mews TW10 . . . . . 6 E3
Abercorn Way GU21 . . . . . 69 A1
Aberdare Cl BR4 . . . . 63 C8
Aberdeen Rd CR0 . . . . 61 D6
Aberdour Prep Sch
KT20 . . . . 77 F1
Aberfoyle Rd SW16 . . . . . 21 D2
Abergavenny Gdns
RH10 . . . . 183 D3
Abingdon Cl
Bracknell RG12 . . . . 27 E4
Merton SW19 . . . . 20 C2
Woking GU21 . . . . 69 C1
Abingdon Ct
Upper Tooting SW17 . . . . . 20 F2
16 Woking GU22 . . . . . . 69 F1
Abingdon Lo BR2 . . . . 44 F7
Abingdon Rd
Sandhurst GU47 . . . . 45 C1
Thornton Heath SW16 . . . . 41 E8
Abinger Ave SM2 . . . . 58 D2
Abinger Cl
Dorking RH5 . . . . 136 C3
New Addington CR0 . . . . . . 63 C4
Wallington SM6 . . . . 60 E5
ABINGER COMMON 155 D8

Abinger Common Fst Sch
RH5 . . . . 134 D1
Abinger Common Rd
RH5 . . . . 155 F7
Abinger Ct
3 Thornton Heath
CR0 . . . . 42 B2
Wallington SM6 . . . . 60 E5
Abinger Dr RH1 . . . . 139 E7
Abinger Gdns TW7 . . . . 5 E4
ABINGER HAMMER 133 F3
Abinger Hammer Village
Sch RH5 . . . . 133 F4
Abinger Ho **2** KT2 . . . . . 18 B1
Abinger Keep RH6 . . . . . . 161 C4
Abinger La RH5 . . . . 134 C2
Abinger Rd RH5 . . . . 156 C3
Abinger Way GU4 . . . . . . 110 B6
Abney Ct TW2 . . . . 16 C6
Aboyne Dr SW20 . . . . 39 A7
Aboyne Rd SW17 . . . . 20 D5
Abraham Cowley Day
Hospl KT16 . . . . 51 D7
Abrahams Rd RH11 . . . . . 201 A1
Acacia Ave
Brentford TW8 . . . . 6 B7
Littleton TW17 . . . . 34 A4
Sandhurst GU47 . . . . 45 D1
Woking GU22 . . . . 89 D7
Acacia Cl
Penge SE20 . . . . 43 A7
Woodham KT15 . . . . 51 F1
Acacia Ct
Bracknell RG12 . . . . 27 B6
4 Richmond TW9 . . . . 6 F3
6 West Norwood SW16 . . 22 A3
Acacia Dr
Banstead KT17 . . . . 77 D5
Cheam SM3 . . . . 40 A1
Woodham KT15 . . . . 51 F1
Acacia Gdns BR4 . . . . 63 C8
Acacia Gr
Dulwich SE21 . . . . 22 D6
Kingston u T KT3 . . . . 38 E6
Acacia Ho
Cranleigh GU6 . . . . 174 E2
1 New Malden KT3 . . . . . 38 E5
Reigate RH2 . . . . 118 A3
Acacia Mews UB7 . . . . 2 D8
Acacia Rd
Beckenham BR3 . . . . 43 F6
Guildford GU1 . . . . 109 D1
Hampton TW12 . . . . 16 A2

Acacia Rd continued
Mitcham CR4 . . . . 41 B7
Staines TW18 . . . . 13 B3
Thornton Heath SW16 . . . . 41 E8
Academy Cl GU15 . . . . 65 E8
Academy Ct TW16 . . . . 35 A5
Academy Gate GU15 . . . . . 65 B6
Academy Gdns CR0 . . . . . . 42 F1
Academy Pl GU47 . . . . 64 E7
Accommodation La UB7 . . . 2 C8
Accommodation Rd
KT16 . . . . 50 E6
A C Ct KT7 . . . . 37 A3
Ace Par KT9 . . . . 56 E7
Acer Cl RG42 . . . . 28 A8
Acer Dr GU24 . . . . 67 F6
Acer Rd TN16 . . . . 83 D3
Acheulian Cl GU9 . . . . . . 146 C7
Ackroyd Rd SE23 . . . . 23 E8
Acorn Cl
East Grinstead RH19 . . . . 205 E6
1 Hampton TW12 . . . . . . 16 B2
Horley RH6 . . . . 161 C4
Acorn Ct TW12 . . . . 15 F3
Acorn Dr RG40 . . . . 25 C7
Acorn Gdns SE19 . . . . 42 E8
Acorn Gr
Kingswood KT20 . . . . 97 F3
Woking GU22 . . . . 89 E6
Acorn Keep GU9 . . . . 125 E8
Acorn Mews GU14 . . . . . . 85 A7
Acorn Rd GU17 . . . . 64 B5
Acorns RH13 . . . . 218 A4
Acorns Inf Sch The
RH3 . . . . 116 D1
Acorns The
Crawley RH11 . . . . 201 B1
21 Putney SW19 . . . . 19 D7
Smallfield RH6 . . . . 162 B3
Acorns Way KT10 . . . . 55 C5
Acorn Way
Beckenham BR3 . . . . 44 C4
Forest Hill SE23 . . . . 23 D5
Acqua Ho TW9 . . . . 7 B7
Acre La SM5 . . . . 60 A6
Acre Rd
Kingston u T KT2 . . . . 37 E8
Mitcham SW19 . . . . 20 D2
Acres Gdns KT20 . . . . 97 D8
Acres Platt GU6 . . . . 174 F4
ACS Egham International
Sch TW20 . . . . 31 C7

Act–All 223

Action Ct TW15 34 C8
Acuba Ho SW18 20 B7
Acuba Rd SW18 20 B6
Adair Cl SE25 43 B6
Adair Gdns CR3 100 C6
Adair Wlk GU24 87 B6
Adam Cl SE6 24 A5
Adam Ct 4 SM1 59 C6
Adams Cl KT5 37 F3
Adams Croft GU24 87 C7
Adams Ct 3 CR8 80 A7
Adams Ho 3 SW16 21 C3
Adams Mews SW17 20 F6
Adamson Ct 6 RH11 201 B1
Adamson Way BR3 44 C4
Adams Park Rd GU9 125 D3
Adams Qtr TW8 6 C8
Adams Rd BR3 43 E4
Adamsrill Prim Sch SE26 23 E5
Adamsrill Rd SE23, SE26 23 E4
Adams Way SE25, CR0 43 A3
Adams Wlk 11 KT1 37 E7
Adare Wlk SW16, SW2 21 F6
ADDINGTON 63 A5
Addington Bsns Ctr CR0 63 E1
Addington Ct 8 SW14 7 D4
Addington Gr SE26 23 E4
Addington High Sch CR0 82 E7
Addington Rd
Sanderstead CR2 81 A8
Selsdon CR2 62 C1
Thornton Heath CR0 42 A1
West Wickham BR4, CR0 63 D6
Addington Village Rd CR0 63 A5
ADDISCOMBE 43 B1
Addiscombe Ave CR0 43 A2
Addiscombe Court Rd CR0, CR9 61 E8
Addiscombe Rd
Crowthorne RG45 45 C4
Croydon CR0, CR9 61 E8
Addison Ave TW3 5 C6
Addison Cl CR3 100 D5
Addison Ct
16 Belmont SM2 59 B3
Guildford GU1 130 F7
Twickenham TW1 17 A7
Addison Gdns KT5 37 F5
Addison Rd
Caterham CR3 100 D6
Croydon SE25 43 A5
Farnborough GU16 85 E8
Guildford GU1 130 F7
Teddington TW11 17 B2
4 Woking GU21 69 F2
Addison's Cl CR0 62 F8
ADDLESTONE 52 A6
Addlestone Ho KT15 52 B7
ADDLESTONEMOOR 52 C8
Addlestone Moor KT15 52 C8
Addlestone Pk KT15 52 B5
Addlestone Rd KT13, KT15 52 E6
Addlestone Sta KT15 52 D6
Adecroft Way KT8 36 C6
Adela Ave KT3 39 B5
Adelaide Cl
Crawley RH11 181 D1
Horsham RH12 217 F4
Adelaide Ct 15 BR3 24 A1
Adelaide Pl KT13 53 D6
Adelaide Rd
Ashford TW15 13 D3
Heston TW5 4 E6
Kingston u T KT6 37 E4
Richmond TW9 6 F3
Teddington TW11 16 F2
Walton-on-T KT12 54 B7
Adelina Mews SW12 21 D7
Adelphi Cl RH10 202 D4
Adelphi Rd KT17 76 D6
Adenmore Rd SE6 24 A8
Adlers La RH5 115 A4
Adlington Pl GU14 85 E2
Admiral Ct SM5 40 E1
Admiral Ho TW11 17 B3
Admiral Rd RH11 201 A3
Admiral's Bridge La RH19 205 C2
Admirals Ct
Guildford GU1 110 B2
32 Putney SW19 19 D7
Admiral Stirling Ct KT13 52 F6
Admiral's Wlk The CR5 99 F7
Admiralty Rd TW11 16 F2
Admiralty Way
Camberley GU15 64 F4
Teddington TW11 16 F2
Adolf St SE6 24 B4
Adrian Ct RH11 201 B1
Advance Rd SE27 22 C4
Adversane Ct RH12 217 D4
Adyar Ct 7 SW19 19 E1
Aerodrome Way TW5 4 C8
Aerospace Bvd GU14 105 A7
Agar Cl KT6 56 F8
Agar Ho 6 KT1 37 E6
Agate Ho
New Malden KT4 38 E1
12 Penge SE26 23 B3
Agate La RH12 217 F5
Agates La KT21 95 D8
Agincourt SL5 29 C6
Agnes Scott Ct 5 KT13 53 B7
Agnew Rd SE23 23 D8
Agraria Rd GU2 130 B7
Ailsa Ave TW1 6 B2
Ailsa Cl RH11 201 B3
Ailsa Rd TW1 6 B2
Ainger Cl GU12 105 D2
Ainsdale Way GU21 69 A1
Ainsworth Rd CR0, CR9 61 B8
Aintree Cl SL3 1 E6
Aintree Ho SE26 23 B2
Aintree Rd RH10 202 A4
Airborne Forces Mus★ GU11 105 A5
Airborne Ho 10 SM6 60 B6
Aircraft Espl GU14 85 C1
Aird Ct TW12 36 B8
Airedale Rd SW12 20 F8
Air Forces Meml★ TW20 11 D4
Air Park Way TW13 15 B6
Airport Ho CR0 61 A4
Airport Way
Horley RH6 182 B8
Stanwell TW19 2 A3
Airport Way Rdbt E RH6 182 C8
Airport Way Rdbt W RH6 181 F8
Aisne Rd GU16 66 E1
Aitken Cl CR4 40 F2
Aitken Ho
Dorking RH4 136 A5
Haslemere GU27 208 C7
Aitken Rd SE6 24 B6
Aits View KT8 36 B6
Akabusi Cl SE25 43 A3
Akehurst Cl RH10 183 B3
Akehurst St SW15 19 A8
Akerman Rd KT6 37 C3
Alamein Rd GU11 105 B3
Alanbrooke Cl GU21 68 C1
Alanbrooke Rd GU11 105 D6
Alan Hilton Ct KT16 51 D4
Alan Rd SW19 19 E3
Alan Turing Rd GU2 108 D1
Albain Cres TW15 13 E6
Alba Mews SW18 20 A6
Albans Cl SW16 21 E5
Albany Cl
Esher KT10 55 A2
Mortlake SW14 7 B3
Reigate RH2 118 A3
Albany Cres KT10 55 E4
Albany Ct
Ashford TW15 14 D2
Cheam SM1 58 F6
Frimley GU16 65 C1
Kingston u T KT2 17 E2
Oatlands Park KT13 53 E8
Richmond TW10 17 B5
Surbiton KT6 37 D2
3 Weybridge KT13 53 B6
Albany Hall KT4 39 B2
Albany Ho 6 TW8 6 E8
Albany Mews
Kingston u T KT2 17 D2
Sutton SM1 59 B5
Albany Par 4 TW8 6 E8
Albany Park Ind Est GU15 65 C1
Albany Park Rd
Kingston u T KT2 17 E2
Leatherhead KT22 95 A8
Albany Pas 14 TW10 6 E2
Albany Pk
Frimley GU15 65 C1
Poyle SL3 1 D7
Albany Pl
Brentford TW8 6 D8
Egham TW20 12 B4
Albany Rd
Brentford TW8 6 D8
Crawley RH11 201 C6
Hersham KT12 54 D6
New Malden KT3 38 D5
Richmond TW10 6 F2
Wimbledon SW19 20 B3
Albany Reach KT7 36 F4
Albany Terr 6 TW10 6 F2
Albatross Gdns CR2 81 D8
Albemarle SW19 19 D6
Albemarle Ave TW2 15 F7
Albemarle Gdns KT3 38 D5
Albemarle Lo SE26 23 E3
Albemarle Pk BR3 44 B8
Albemarle Rd BR2, BR3 44 C8
Albermarle Prim Sch SW19 19 E6
Alberta Ave SM1 58 F5
Alberta Ct 1 TW10 6 F2
Alberta Dr RH6 162 A3
Albert Ave KT16 33 A6
Albert Carr Gdns SW16 21 E3
Albert Crane Ct RH11 201 A8
Albert Ct 9 SW19 19 E7
Albert Dr
Putney SW19 19 E6
Sheerwater GU21, KT14 70 D5
1 Staines TW18 13 A3
Albert Gr SW20 39 D8
Albert Ho 3 KT22 95 C6
Albertine Cl KT17 77 B3
Albert Mews RH1 140 A6
Albert Rd
Addlestone KT15 52 D6
Albert Rd *continued*
Aldershot GU11 105 B2
Ashford TW15 13 F3
Ashtead KT21 75 F1
Bagshot GU19 47 E1
Bracknell RG42 27 B8
Camberley GU15 65 C5
Carshalton SM1 59 D5
Crowthorne RG45 45 B5
Croydon CR0, SE25 43 B5
Englefield Green TW20 11 D2
Epsom KT17 76 F6
Farnborough GU14 85 C2
Hampton TW12 16 C3
Horley RH6 161 A3
Hounslow TW3 5 A3
Kingston u T KT1 37 F7
Merstham RH1 119 C6
Mitcham CR4 40 F6
New Malden KT3 38 F5
Penge SE20 23 D2
Richmond TW10 6 F2
Teddington TW11 16 F2
Twickenham TW1 16 F7
Warlingham CR6 81 F2
Wokingham RG40 25 B5
Albert Rd N RH2 117 F2
Albert Wlk RG45 45 B5
Albery Cl RH12 217 B4
Albion Cl RH10 202 D5
Albion Ct
Streatham SW2 22 A6
Sutton SM2 59 D3
Albion Ho 10 GU21 69 F2
Albion Par GU21 68 C2
Albion Pl SE25 43 A6
Albion Rd
Hounslow TW3 5 A3
Kingston u T KT2 38 C8
Reigate RH2 139 C8
Sandhurst GU47 64 B8
Sutton SM2 59 D3
Twickenham TW2 16 E7
Albion St CR0, CR9 42 B1
Albion Villas Rd SE23, SE26 23 C5
Albion Way RH12 217 C2
ALBURY 132 C4
Albury Ave
East Ewell SM2 58 C1
Hounslow TW7 5 F7
Albury Cl
Epsom KT19 57 B2
Hampton TW12 16 B2
Longcross KT16 50 A7
Albury Ct
4 Croydon CR0 61 C6
Guildford GU1 131 A8
Mitcham CR4 40 D7
Sutton SM1 59 C6
Albury Ho GU1 130 F7
Albury Hts GU1 131 A8
Albury Keep RH6 161 B4
Albury Lo 10 SW2 21 F8
Albury Pl RH1 119 C6
Albury Rd
Chessington KT9 56 E5
Guildford GU1 131 A8
Hersham KT12 53 F4
Merstham RH1 119 C6
Alcester Ct 4 SM6 60 B6
Alcester Rd SM6 60 B6
Alcock Cl SM6 60 D3
Alcock Rd TW5 4 D7
Alcocks Cl KT20 97 E7
Alcocks La KT20 97 E7
Alcorn Cl SM3 59 A8
Alcot Cl RG45 45 B4
Aldeburgh Ho RH6 161 A2
Alden Ct
South Croydon CR0 61 D7
5 Wimbledon SW19 20 A2
Aldenham Terr RG12 27 C3
Aldenholme KT13 53 E4
Alderbrook Ct BR4 63 B8
Alderbrook Prim Sch SW12 21 B8
Alderbrook Rd
Balham SW12 21 B8
Cranleigh GU6 174 C8
Alder Cl
Ash Vale GU12 106 A7
Crawley Down RH10 204 B8
Englefield Green TW20 11 E3
Aldercombe La CR3 100 E1
Alder Croft CR5 79 F3
Alder Ct
Bracknell RG12 27 B6
4 West Norwood SW16 22 A3
Aldergrove Gdns TW4 4 E5
Alderman Judge Mall 6 KT1 37 E7
Alderman Willey Cl RG41 25 B6
Aldermead TW3 5 B3
Aldermoor Rd SE6 23 F5
Alderney Ave TW5 5 B7
Alder Rd
Headley Down GU35 187 B6
Mortlake SW14 7 D4
Alders Ave RH19 185 E3
Aldersbrook Dr KT2 17 F2
Aldersey Rd GU1 109 F1
Aldersgrove KT8 36 D4
ALDERSHOT 105 B1
Aldershot Military Mus★ GU11 105 C7
Aldershot Rd
Ash GU12 105 F1
Fairlands GU3 108 D5
Fleet GU14, GU52 104 A6
Pirbright GU24 87 F2
Wood St V GU3 107 E5
Aldershot Sta GU11 105 B1
Alderside Wlk TW20 11 E3
Aldersmead Ave CR0 43 D3
Aldersmead Rd BR3 23 E1
Alders Rd RH2 118 B3
Alderstead La RH1 99 D2
Alders The
Badshot Lea GU9 126 B6
Feltham TW13 15 E4
Heston TW5 4 F8
Streatham SW16 21 C4
West Byfleet KT14 71 C7
West Wickham BR4 63 B8
Alders View Dr RH19 185 E3
Alderton KT2 38 B8
Alderton Ct KT8 35 F5
Alderton Rd CR0 43 A2
Alderwick Dr TW3 5 D4
Alderwood Cl CR3 100 E2
Aldingbourne Cl RH11 200 F7
Aldis Mews SW17 20 E3
Aldis St SW17 20 E3
Aldous Ho TW18 12 E4
Aldren Rd SW17 20 C5
Aldrich Cres CR0 63 C2
Aldrich Gdns SM3 58 F7
Aldrich Terr SW18 20 C6
Aldridge Pk RG42 8 B2
Aldridge Rise KT3 38 E3
Aldrington Rd SW16 21 C4
Aldrin Pl GU14 84 D4
Aldro Sch GU8 149 C7
Aldwick Cl GU14 85 A6
Aldwick Rd CR0 60 F6
Aldworth Cl RG12 27 A5
Aldworth Gdns RG45 45 A5
Aldwych Cl RH10 202 D4
Alexa Ct 3 SM2 59 A4
Alexander Cl TW2 16 F6
Alexander Cres CR3 100 C6
Alexander Ct
Beckenham BR2 44 D8
14 Surbiton KT6 37 D2
Alexander Evans Mews SE23 23 D6
Alexander Fleming Rd GU2 129 D8
Alexander Godley Cl KT21 95 F8
Alexander Ho
14 Kingston u T KT2 37 E8
19 Sutton SM2 59 C4
Alexander Lo SM1 58 F5
Alexander Pl RH8 122 E7
Alexander Rd
Coulsdon CR5 79 B4
Egham TW20 12 C3
Reigate RH2 139 A6
Alexanders Wlk CR3 101 A1
Alexander Wlk RG12 27 B4
Alexandra Ave
Camberley GU15 65 A5
Sutton SM1 59 A7
Warlingham CR6 81 F2
Alexandra Cl
Staines TW18 13 D2
Walton-on-T KT12 54 A8
Alexandra Cotts SE20 23 D2
Alexandra Cres BR1 24 F2
Alexandra Ct
Aldershot GU11 104 E1
Biggin Hill TN16 83 B1
10 Crawley RH10 201 D5
1 Farnborough GU14 85 C1
Alexandra Dr
Surbiton KT5 38 A2
West Norwood SE19 22 E3
Alexandra Gdns
Chiswick W4 7 E7
Hounslow TW3 5 B5
Knaphill GU21 68 D1
Wallington SM5 60 A2
Alexandra Ho SL5 29 B6
Alexandra Inf Sch
Kingston u T KT2 18 A1
Penge BR3 23 D1
Alexandra Jun & Inf Sch TW3 5 B5
Alexandra Jun Sch SE26 23 D2
Alexandra Lo
12 Guildford GU1 130 F8
1 Weybridge KT13 53 B6
Alexandra Mans KT17 76 F6
Alexandra Pl
Croydon CR0 42 E1
Guildford GU1 130 F7
South Norwood SE25 42 D4
Alexandra Rd
Addlestone KT15 52 D6
Aldershot GU11 104 F2
Ashford TW15 14 E2
Ash GU12 105 F1
Biggin Hill TN16 103 B8
12 Brentford TW8 6 D8
Croydon CR0 42 E2
Englefield Green TW20 11 C2
Epsom KT17 76 F6
Farnborough GU14, GU11 85 C1
Hounslow TW3 5 B5
Alexandra Rd *continued*
Kingston u T KT2 18 A1
Mitcham CR4 20 E1
Mortlake SW14 7 D4
Penge SE26 23 D2
Richmond TW9 6 F5
Thames Ditton KT7 36 F4
Twickenham TW1 6 C1
Warlingham CR6 81 F2
Wimbledon SW19 20 A3
Alexandra Sq SM4 40 A4
Alexandra Terr GU1 130 E8
Alexandra Way KT19 76 A8
Alexandra Wlk 8 SE19 22 E3
ALFOLD 193 F1
ALFOLD BARS 212 E7
Alfold By-Pass
Alfold Crossways GU6 194 A5
Alfold GU6 193 F7
Alfold Cotts GU6 193 F2
Alfold Craft Ctr GU6 194 A1
ALFOLD CROSSWAYS 194 A3
Alfold Crossways GU6 194 A3
Alfold Rd
Cranleigh GU6 194 B7
Dunsfold GU8 193 B3
Alfonso Cl GU12 126 C8
Alford Cl
Guildford GU4 110 A4
Sandhurst GU47 64 A7
Alford Ct 4 SM2 59 B3
Alford Gn CR0 63 D4
Alfred Butt Ho SW17 20 F5
Alfred Cl RH10 202 E5
Alfred Ct 3 CR3 101 A8
Alfred Hurley Ho SW17 20 C4
Alfred Rd
Croydon SE25 43 A4
Farnham GU9 125 C1
Feltham TW13 15 C6
Kingston u T KT1 37 F6
Sutton SM1 59 C5
Alfreton Cl SW19 19 D5
Alfriston KT5 37 F3
Alfriston Ave CR0 41 E2
Alfriston Cl KT5 37 F3
Alfriston Rd GU16 86 C7
Algar Cl TW7 6 A4
Algar Ct TW12 36 B8
Algar Rd TW7 6 A4
Algarve Rd SW18 20 B7
Algernon Tollemache Almshos The TW10 17 C5
Alice Gough Meml Homes RG12 27 B6
Alice Ho TW18 13 A2
Alice Holt Woodland Park Forest Ctr★ GU10 166 C8
Alice Mews 4 TW11 16 F3
Alice Rd GU11 105 B2
Alice Ruston Pl GU22 89 C8
Alice Way TW3 5 B3
Alicia Ave RH10 202 C6
Alington Gr SM6 60 D2
Alison Cl
Croydon CR0 43 D1
Farnborough GU14 84 F3
Woking GU21 69 E4
Alison Dr GU15 65 F5
Alison's Rd GU11 105 B4
Alison Way GU11 104 F2
Allan Cl KT3 38 D4
Allbrook Cl TW11 16 E3
Allbrook Ho 5 SW15 19 A8
Allcard Cl RH12 217 D4
Allcot Cl
Crawley RH11 200 E3
East Bedfont TW14 14 F7
Allcott Ho TW7 5 F4
Allden Ave GU12 126 D7
Allden Cotts GU7 150 B4
Allden Gdns GU12 126 D7
Alldens Hill GU5, GU8 151 D1
Alldens La GU8 151 B1
Allder Way CR2 61 B3
Allenby Ave CR2 61 C2
Allenby Rd
Biggin Hill TN16 83 E2
Forest Hill SE23 23 E5
Sandhurst GU15 65 A6
Allen Cl
Mitcham CR4 41 C8
Sunbury TW16 35 B8
Allendale GU8 148 C3
Allendale Cl
Forest Hill SE26 23 D3
Sandhurst GU47 45 A2
Allenford Ho SW15 7 F1
All England Lawn Tennis & Croquet Club The★ SW19 19 E5
Allen House Pk GU22 89 C7
Allen Rd
Great Bookham KT23 94 B1
Penge BR3 43 D7
Sunbury TW16 35 B7
Thornton Heath CR0 42 A1
Allen's Cl RH19 206 D6
Allenswood 12 SW19 19 E7
Allerford Ct SE6 24 B5
Allerford Rd SE6 24 B4

Allerton Ct SM3. . . . . 58 D8
Allerton Ho 4 SW19 . . . . 20 C1
Alleyn Cres SE21. . . . . 22 D6
Alleyn Pk SE21 . . . . 22 E5
Alleyn Rd SE21 . . . . 22 E5
Allgood Cl SM4. . . . . 39 D3
All Hallows RC Sch
GU9. . . . . 125 F7
Alliance Cl TW4 . . . . .4 F2
Alliance Ct TW15 . . . . 14 C4
Allingham Ct GU7. . . . . . 150 F7
Allingham Gdns RH12 . . . 218 B5
Allingham Rd RH2 . . . . . . 139 A6
Allington Ave TW17. . . . . . 34 E6
Allington Cl SW19 . . . . . . 19 D3
Allington Ct CR0. . . . . 43 C3
Allison Gr SE21. . . . . 22 E7
Alloway Cl 4 GU21 . . . . . 69 B1
All Saints' Benhilton CE
Prim Sch SM1. . . . . 59 B7
All Saints CE Inf Sch
GU10. . . . . 147 C3
All Saint's CE Jun Sch
SE19. . . . . 42 E8
All Saints CE Prim Sch
Horsham RH12 . . . . 217 F6
Merton SW19 . . . . 20 C1
Wallington SM5. . . . . 60 A5
All Saints Cl RG40. . . . . . . 25 C7
All Saints Cres GU14 . . . . 64 E1
All Saints Ct TW5. . . . . 4 D6
All Saints Dr CR2 . . . . 81 A7
All Saints RC Sch BR4. . . . 63 D6
All Saints Rd
Lightwater GU18 . . . . 48 C1
Merton SW19 . . . . 20 C1
Sutton SM1 . . . . 59 C7
Allsmoor La RG12. . . . . 27 F6
All Souls Ave GU24. . . . . . . 88 B6
All Souls' Rd SL5 . . . . 29 A5
Allum Gr KT20. . . . . 97 B6
Allwood Cl SE26 . . . . 23 D4
Allyington Way RH10. . . . 202 D5
Allyn Cl TW18 . . . . 12 F2
Alma Cl
Aldershot GU12. . . . . 105 D2
Knaphill GU21 . . . . 68 E1
Alma Cres SM1 . . . . 58 E5
Alma Ct
3 Caterham CR3 . . . . 100 C6
Wokingham RG41 . . . . 25 A5
Alma Gdns GU16. . . . . 86 E8
Alma Ho
Aldershot GU12. . . . . 105 D2
7 Brentford TW8. . . . . 6 E8
Alma La GU9 . . . . 125 C7
Alma Pl
Penge SE19. . . . . 22 F1
Thornton Heath CR7 . . . . . 42 A4
Alma Rd
Carshalton SM5. . . . . 59 E5
Headley Down GU35 . . . . . 187 C5
Reigate RH2. . . . . 118 B3
Thames Ditton KT10, KT7 . . 36 E1
Alma Sq GU14 . . . . 105 C8
Alma Terr SW18 . . . . 20 D8
Alma Way GU9. . . . . 125 D7
Almer Rd SW20. . . . . 19 A1
Almners Rd
Chertsey KT16. . . . . 32 C2
Lyne KT16 . . . . 32 B1
Almondale Ct GU14 . . . . . . 85 A6
Almond Ave
Carshalton SM5. . . . . 59 F8
Woking GU22. . . . . 89 D6
Almond Cl
Charlton TW17. . . . . 34 C7
Crawley RH11 . . . . 201 A5
Englefield Green TW20 . . . . 11 B2
Farnborough GU14 . . . . . . 85 A7
Feltham TW13 . . . . 15 A7
Guildford GU1 . . . . 109 D5
Almond Gr TW8 . . . . 6 B7
Almond Rd KT19. . . . . 76 D8
Almond Way CR4 . . . . 41 D5
Almorah Rd TW5 . . . . 4 D6
Almsgate GU3 . . . . 129 C2
Alms Heath GU23 . . . . 92 B6
Almshouse La KT9 . . . . 56 D2
Almshouses
6 Dorking RH4. . . . . 136 B8
Lingfield RH7. . . . . 164 C4
Sunbury TW16. . . . . 34 F8
Almshouses The RH5 . . . 115 C8
Alnod KT18. . . . . 97 D8
Alnwick Gr SM4 . . . . 40 B5
Alphabet Gdns SM5 . . . . . . 40 D3
Alpha Ct CR6 . . . . 81 A1
Alpha Hospl GU21 . . . . 68 D1
Alpha Rd
Aldershot GU12. . . . . 105 E1
Chobham GU24 . . . . 49 F1
Crawley RH11 . . . . 201 C6
Croydon CR0 . . . . 42 E1
Surbiton KT5. . . . . 37 F3
Teddington TW11. . . . . 16 D3
Woking GU22. . . . . 70 C4
Alpha Way TW20. . . . . 32 C8
Alphea Cl SW19. . . . . 20 E1
Alphington Ave GU16 . . . . 65 F1
Alphington Gn GU16 . . . . . 65 F1
Alpine Ave KT5 . . . . 57 C8
Alpine Cl
Farnborough GU14 . . . . 84 D3
South Croydon CR0 . . . . 61 E7
Alpine Rd
Redhill RH1 . . . . 119 A4
Walton-on-T KT12 . . . . 35 A2
Alpine View SM5. . . . . 59 E5
Alresford Rd GU2 . . . . . . 130 A8
Alric Ave KT3. . . . . 38 F6
Alsace Wlk GU15. . . . . 65 B1
Alsford Cl GU18. . . . . 66 F7
Alsom Ave KT4 . . . . 58 A6
Alston Cl KT7. . . . . 37 B2
Alstonfield KT10. . . . . 55 B5
Alston Rd SW17. . . . . 20 D4
Altamont CR6 . . . . 101 B8
Altdam Farm RH1. . . . . . . 140 A2
Alterton Cl GU21. . . . . 69 A2
Alt Gr SW19 . . . . 19 E1
Althorne Rd RH1. . . . . . . 140 A7
Althorp Rd SW17 . . . . 20 F7
Alton Cl TW7 . . . . .5 F5
Alton Ct
19 Beckenham BR3. . . . . . . 24 A1
Egham TW18 . . . . 32 E8
Alton Gdns
Beckenham BR3. . . . . 24 A1
Twickenham TW2. . . . . 16 D8
Alton Ho 1 RH1 . . . . 119 A3
Alton Rd
Croydon CR0, CR9 . . . . 61 A7
Farnham GU10, GU9 . . . . . 145 D7
Richmond TW10, TW9 . . . . . . 6 E3
Roehampton SW15 . . . . 19 A7
Alton Ride GU17 . . . . 64 C6
Altyre Cl BR3 . . . . 43 F4
Altyre Rd CR0, CR9 . . . . . . 61 D8
Altyre Way BR3. . . . . 43 F4
Alvernia Cl GU7. . . . . 150 C2
Alvernia Lo 4 SM1 . . . . . . 59 B7
Alverstoke Gdns
GU11 . . . . 104 E1
Alverstone Ave SW18,
SW19. . . . . 20 A6
Alverstone Rd KT3 . . . . 38 F5
Alverston Gdns SE25. . . . . 42 E4
Alvia Gdns SM1. . . . . 59 C6
Alway Ave KT19. . . . . 57 D5
Alwen Cotts CR0. . . . . 62 D6
Alwin Pl GU9 . . . . 125 B7
Alwyn Cl CR0 . . . . 63 B3
Alwyne Ct GU21. . . . . 69 E3
Alwyne Mans SW19 . . . . . . 19 F2
Alwyne Rd SW19. . . . . 19 F2
Alwyns Cl 3 KT16. . . . . 33 A3
Alwyns La 4 KT16 . . . . 33 A3
Amalgamated Dr TW8. . . . . .6 B8
Amanda Ct TW15 . . . . 13 F6
Aman Dalvi Ho SW18. . . . . 19 E8
Ambassador RG12 . . . . 26 F4
Ambassador Cl TW3 . . . . . . .4 E5
Ambassador The SL5. . . . . 30 B2
Ambercroft Way CR5. . . . 100 B8
Amber Ct
Aldershot GU12. . . . . 105 C2
Feltham TW13 . . . . 14 E5
Mitcham CR4 . . . . 40 E5
5 Staines TW18. . . . . 12 F3
Amber Hill GU15. . . . . 66 B4
Amberley Cl
Crawley RH10 . . . . 202 C6
Horsham RH12 . . . . 218 A6
Send Marsh GU23 . . . . 90 F2
Amberley Ct
Beckenham BR3. . . . . 23 F1
Sutton SM2 . . . . 59 C3
Amberley Dr KT15 . . . . 70 F8
Amberley Fields Cvn Pk
RH11 . . . . 181 B4
Amberley Gdns KT19. . . . . 57 F6
Amberley Gr
Croydon CR0 . . . . 42 F2
Forest Hill SE26. . . . . 23 B3
Amberley Grange
GU11 . . . . 125 F8
Amberley Lo CR8 . . . . 79 F6
Amberley Rd
Horsham RH12 . . . . 218 A6
Milford GU8. . . . . 149 E2
Amberley Way
Heston TW4. . . . . 4 C2
Morden SM4 . . . . 39 F2
Amberside Cl TW2. . . . . 5 D1
Amberwood Cl SM6. . . . . . 60 E5
Amberwood Dr GU15. . . . . 65 F7
Amberwood Rise KT3 . . . . 38 E3
Amblecote KT11 . . . . 73 E7
Ambleside
Catford BR1. . . . . 24 D2
Crowthorne RG45 . . . . 45 C4
Godalming GU7 . . . . 151 A5
13 Putney SW19 . . . . 19 E7
Ambleside Ave
Beckenham BR3. . . . . 43 E4
Streatham SW16. . . . . 21 D4
Walton-on-T KT12 . . . . 35 C1
Ambleside Cl
Crawley RH11 . . . . 200 D5
Farnborough GU14 . . . . 84 E3
Mytchett GU16. . . . . 86 A2
Redhill RH1 . . . . 140 B4
Ambleside Cres GU9 . . . . 125 A6
Ambleside Dr TW14. . . . . . 14 F7
Ambleside Gdns
Selsdon CR2 . . . . 62 D1
Streatham SW16. . . . . 21 D3
Sutton SM2 . . . . 59 C4
Ambleside Rd GU18. . . . . . 67 B8
Ambleside Way TW20 . . . . 12 B1
Ambrey Way CR8, SM6. . . . 60 D2
Ambrook Ct SM1. . . . . 59 D5
Amen Cnr
Bracknell RG12 . . . . 26 D7
Streatham SW17 . . . . 21 A2
Amen Corner Bsns Pk
RG12. . . . . 26 D7
Amenity Way SM4 . . . . 39 C2
American Com Sch
KT11. . . . . 54 C1
American Magna Carta
Meml★ TW20 . . . . 11 D6
American Sch in
Switzerland (English
Branch) The TW20 . . . . . . 32 C6
Amersham Rd CR0. . . . . . . 42 D3
Amesbury Ave SW2 . . . . . . 21 F6
Amesbury Cl KT4 . . . . 39 C1
Amesbury Rd TW13 . . . . . . 15 D6
Amesbury Sch GU26 . . . . 188 E1
Amey Dr KT23 . . . . 94 C3
Amhurst Gdns TW7. . . . . . . 6 A5
Amis Ave
Chessington KT19 . . . . 57 B5
Woodham KT15 . . . . 52 A1
Amis Rd GU21 . . . . 88 E8
Amity Gr SW20 . . . . 39 C8
Amlets La GU6. . . . . 174 E5
Ampere Way CR0, CR9 . . . . 41 F1
Amroth Cl SE23. . . . . 23 B7
Amstel Way GU21. . . . . 68 F1
Amundsen Rd RH12. . . . . 217 D6
Amyand Cotts 12 TW1. . . . . .6 B1
Amyand Park Gdns 3
TW1. . . . . 17 B8
Amyand Park Rd TW1. . . . 17 A8
Amy Cl SM6 . . . . 60 E3
Amy Johnson Prim Sch
SM6 . . . . 60 E3
Amy Rd RH8. . . . . 122 E6
Anarth Ct KT13 . . . . 34 E1
Ancaster Cres KT3. . . . . . . 39 A3
Ancaster Dr SL5 . . . . 28 E8
Ancaster Rd BR3. . . . . 43 D6
Anchester Mews BR3 . . . . 43 D6
Anchorage Cl SW19. . . . . . 20 A3
Anchor Cl GU3. . . . . 107 C4
Anchor Cotts RH7. . . . . . . 163 E8
Anchor Cres 7 GU21. . . . . 68 D2
Anchor Hill GU21 . . . . 68 D2
Anchor Mdw GU14. . . . . . . 84 F4
Anders Cnr RG42 . . . . 26 F8
Anderson Cl
Cheam SM3 . . . . 40 A1
Epsom KT19. . . . . 76 B7
Guildford GU2 . . . . 109 B5
Anderson Ct
Haslemere GU27 . . . . 208 C6
Redhill RH1 . . . . 140 A6
Anderson Dr TW15. . . . . . . 14 C4
Anderson Ho
Farnham GU9. . . . . 125 D1
Upper Tooting SW17 . . . . . 20 D3
Anderson Pl GU19 . . . . 47 E4
Anderson Rd KT13 . . . . 53 D7
Anderson's Pl TW3 . . . . .5 B3
Andhurst Ct KT2. . . . . 38 B8
Andon Ct BR3 . . . . 43 E6
Andover Cl
East Bedfont TW14 . . . . . . 14 F7
Epsom KT19. . . . . 76 D8
Andover Ct
North Cheam KT4 . . . . 58 B8
Stanwell TW19. . . . . 13 D8
Andover Rd
Blackwater GU17. . . . . 64 C6
Twickenham TW2. . . . . 16 D7
Andover Way GU11 . . . . . 126 B7
Andrecht Terr CR4. . . . . . . 41 D5
Andreck Ct BR3. . . . . 44 C7
Andrewartha Rd GU14. . . . 85 E2
Andrew Cl RG40 . . . . 25 E5
Andrew Ct
Beckenham BR3. . . . . 44 B6
Farnborough GU14 . . . . 84 F8
Forest Hill SE23. . . . . 23 D6
Andrewes Ho SM1 . . . . 59 A6
Andrew Ewing Prim Sch
TW5 . . . . .4 F7
Andrew Reed Ho SW18. . . . 19 E8
Andrews Cl KT4. . . . . 58 D8
Andrew's Cl KT17 . . . . 76 F6
Andrew's Ho CR8 . . . . 79 F6
Andrews Rd GU14. . . . . 84 E5
Andrew Wilmot Ct
SW19. . . . . 20 C7
Andromeda Cl RH11 . . . . 200 E4
ANERLEY 43 B8
Anerley Ct SE20 . . . . 23 B1
Anerley Gr SE19 . . . . 22 F1
Anerley Hill SE19 . . . . 22 F2
Anerley Park Rd SE20 . . . . 23 B1
Anerley Pk SE20 . . . . 23 B1
Anerley Rd SE20, SE19 . . . . 43 B8
Anerley Sta SE20 . . . . 43 B8
Anerley Station Rd
SE20. . . . . 43 B8
Anerley Vale 3 SE19. . . . . 23 A1
Anfield Cl SW12 . . . . 21 C8
Angas Ct 1 KT13 . . . . 53 C5
Angela Ct 2 SE23. . . . . 23 C7
Angel Ct GU3. . . . . 129 A3
Angelfield TW3. . . . . .5 B2
Angel Gate GU1. . . . . 130 D8
Angel Hill SM1. . . . . 59 B7
Angel Hill Ct 2 SM1 . . . . . 59 B7
Angel Hill Dr SM1. . . . . 59 B7
Angelica Gdns CR0 . . . . . . 43 D1
Angelica Rd
Bisley GU24. . . . . 68 A4
Angelica Rd *continued*
Guildford GU2 . . . . 109 A5
Angell Cl RH10 . . . . 202 C5
Angell Ho TW7 . . . . 6 A6
Angel Mews SW15 . . . . 19 A8
Angel Pl RH2 . . . . 139 B6
Angel Rd KT7. . . . . 37 A1
Angers Cl GU15. . . . . 66 C7
Anglers Reach KT6. . . . . . . 37 D4
Anglesea Ho KT1 . . . . 37 D5
Anglesea Rd KT1 . . . . 37 D5
Anglesey Ave GU14 . . . . . . 84 F7
Anglesey Cl
Ashford TW15 . . . . 14 A5
Crawley RH11 . . . . 201 C2
Anglesey Court Rd
SM5. . . . . 60 A4
Anglesey Gdns SM5. . . . . . 60 A4
Anglesey Rd GU12 . . . . . . 105 D1
Angles Rd SW16 . . . . 21 E4
Anglo American Laundry
SW17. . . . . 20 C5
Angus Cl
Chessington KT9 . . . . 57 A5
Horsham RH12 . . . . 217 D4
Angus Ho 10 SW12. . . . . . . 21 D8
Anlaby Rd TW11 . . . . 16 E3
Annandale Dr GU10 . . . . . 146 D6
Annandale Rd
Croydon CR0 . . . . 62 A8
Guildford GU2 . . . . 130 B7
Anne Armstrong Cl
GU11 . . . . 105 D5
Anne Boleyn's Wlk
Cheam SM3 . . . . 58 E3
Kingston u T KT2 . . . . 17 E3
Anne Compton Mews 2
SE12. . . . . 24 F8
Anners Cl TW20. . . . . 32 C6
Annes Ct SE6 . . . . 24 A3
Annesley Dr CR0. . . . . 62 F7
Anne's Wlk CR3. . . . . 100 E7
Annett Cl TW17. . . . . 34 E5
Annett Rd KT12 . . . . 35 A2
Anne Way KT8. . . . . 36 B5
Annie Brookes Cl
TW18. . . . . 12 D5
Anningsley Pk KT16. . . . . . 51 C1
Annisdowne Cl RH5. . . . . 133 F1
Ann Parkes Ct TW5 . . . . . . 4 D5
Annsworthy Ave CR7,
SE25. . . . . 42 D6
Annsworthy Cres CR7 . . . . 42 D7
Ansell Gr SM5 . . . . 41 A1
Ansell Rd
Dorking RH4 . . . . 136 B8
Frimley GU16. . . . . 65 E1
Upper Tooting SW17 . . . . . 20 F5
Anselm Cl CR0. . . . . 61 F7
Ansford Rd BR1, SE6. . . . . . 24 D4
Ansley Cl CR2 . . . . 81 B5
Anslie Wlk 9 SW12. . . . . . 21 B8
Anson Cl GU11. . . . . 104 F3
Anson Ct TW19 . . . . 13 E8
ANSTEADBROOK 209 C5
Anstice Cl W4 . . . . .7 E7
Anstiebury Cl RH5 . . . . . . 157 C3
Anstie Grange Dr
RH5 . . . . 157 B5
Anstie La RH5 . . . . 156 F4
Anston Ct 6 GU2 . . . . 108 E1
Anthony Ct TW7 . . . . .5 F4
Anthony Ho CR5 . . . . 99 D5
Anthony Rd CR0, SE25 . . . . 43 A3
ANTHONYS 70 A7
Anthony West Ho
RH3 . . . . 137 B7
Antigua Wlk SE19. . . . . 22 D3
Antlands La RH6. . . . . 182 E5
Antlands La E RH6 . . . . . . 182 F5
Antlands La W RH6 . . . . . 182 E6
Anton Cres SM1 . . . . 59 A7
Antrobus Cl SM1. . . . . 58 F5
Anvil Cl SW16 . . . . 21 C1
Anvil La KT11. . . . . 73 A5
Anvil Rd TW16 . . . . 35 A6
Anyards Rd KT11. . . . . 73 B5
Anzio Cl GU11 . . . . 105 A2
Anzio Gdns CR3. . . . . 100 C6
Aostle Way CR7. . . . . 42 B7
Apeldoorn Dr SM6 . . . . 60 E2
Aperdele Rd KT22. . . . . 75 A1
APERFIELD 83 F2
Aperfield Rd TN16 . . . . 83 E2
Apers Ave GU22 . . . . 89 F6
Apex Cl BR3 . . . . 44 B8
Apex Dr GU16 . . . . 65 D1
Apex Ret Pk TW13 . . . . 15 F5
Apley Rd RH2. . . . . 139 A6
Aplin Ct SM1 . . . . 59 B4
Aplin Way
Hounslow TW7. . . . . 5 E6
Lightwater GU18 . . . . 48 A1
Apollo Pl GU21 . . . . 89 A8
Apollo Rise GU14 . . . . 84 D4
Apperlie Dr RH6 . . . . 161 C1
Appleby Cl TW2 . . . . 16 D6
Appleby Ct GU15. . . . . 65 B6
Appleby Gdns TW14. . . . . . 14 F7
Appledore RG12 . . . . 26 F3
Appledore Cl
1 Hayes BR2 . . . . 44 F4
Upper Tooting SW12,
SW17 . . . . 20 F6
Appledore Mews GU14 . . . 85 A7
Appledown Rise CR5. . . . . 79 C4
Applefield RH10 . . . . 201 E7
Applegarth
Claygate KT10 . . . . 55 F5
New Addington CR0. . . . . . . 63 B3
Apple Garth GU7. . . . . 150 C7
Applegarth Ave GU2 . . . . 108 D1
Applegarth Inf & Jun Schs
CR0. . . . . 63 B4
Apple Gr KT9 . . . . 56 E6
Applelands Cl GU10. . . . . 146 A4
Apple Mkt KT1. . . . . 37 D7
Appleton Gdns KT3 . . . . . . 39 A3
Appleton Sq CR4. . . . . 40 E8
Appletree Cl
Godalming GU7 . . . . 150 F2
6 Penge SE20 . . . . 43 B8
Apple Tree Cl KT23 . . . . . . 94 C3
Appletree Ct GU4 . . . . 110 D3
Appletree Pl 4 RG42. . . . . 27 A8
Appletrees Pl GU22 . . . . . . 89 C8
Apple Tree Way GU47 . . . . 45 D1
Appley Dr GU15. . . . . 65 B6
Approach Rd
Ashford TW15 . . . . 14 C2
East Molesey KT8 . . . . 36 A4
Farnham GU9. . . . . 125 C1
Merton SW20 . . . . 39 C7
Purley CR8. . . . . 80 B7
Tatsfield TN16 . . . . 103 B5
Approach The RH19. . . . . 185 F6
April Cl
Ashtead KT21 . . . . 75 F1
Camberley GU15 . . . . 65 C2
Feltham TW13 . . . . 15 A5
Horsham RH12 . . . . 217 C4
April Glen SE23. . . . . 23 D5
Aprilwood Cl KT15 . . . . 70 F8
Apsley Ct
Crawley RH11 . . . . 200 F4
Sutton SM2 . . . . 59 C4
Apsley Ho 1 TW4. . . . . .4 F3
Apsley Rd
Croydon SE25 . . . . 43 B5
Kingston u T KT3 . . . . 38 C6
Aqua Ho KT16 . . . . 33 C2
Aquarius TW1 . . . . 17 B7
Aquarius Ct RH11 . . . . . . 200 E4
Aquatice 10 GU1. . . . . 130 C8
Aquila Cl KT21. . . . . 95 E6
Arabella Dr SW15. . . . . .7 E3
Aragon Ave
Ewell KT17. . . . . 58 B2
Thames Ditton KT7 . . . . 36 F4
Aragon Cl
Ashford TW16 . . . . 14 F1
New Addington CR0. . . . . . . 63 E1
Aragon Ct
Bracknell RG12 . . . . 27 C5
East Molesey KT8 . . . . 36 C5
Epsom KT19. . . . . 57 E1
4 Knaphill GU21 . . . . 68 D2
Aragon Pl SM4 . . . . 39 E2
Aragon Prim Sch SM4 . . . . 39 D2
Aragon Rd
Kingston u T KT2 . . . . 17 E3
West Barnes SM4 . . . . 39 E2
Aragon Wlk KT14 . . . . 71 F6
Aragorn Ct GU2. . . . . 109 B3
Aram Ct GU22 . . . . 70 B4
Arbor Cl BR3 . . . . 44 B7
Arborfield Cl SW2 . . . . 21 F7
Arbour Cl KT22 . . . . 94 F4
Arbour Cotts GU2. . . . . . . 108 F5
Arbour The GU7 . . . . 128 F1
Arbrook Chase KT10 . . . . . 55 C4
Arbrook Ct KT9 . . . . 56 D5
Arbrook Hall KT10 . . . . 55 F4
Arbrook La KT10. . . . . 55 D4
Arbury Terr SE26 . . . . 23 B5
Arbutus Cl RH1 . . . . 139 C7
Arbutus Rd RH1 . . . . 139 C6
Arcade The
11 Aldershot GU11 . . . . . . 105 A2
5 Croydon CR0). 61 C7
Arcadia Cl SM5 . . . . 60 A6
Arcadian Pl SW18. . . . . 19 F8
Archbishop Lanfranc Sch
The CR0. . . . . 41 E3
Archbishop's Pl 3
SW2. . . . . 21 F8
Archbishop Tenison's CE
Sch CR0. . . . . 61 F7
Archdale Pl KT3 . . . . 38 B6
Archdeacon Cambridge's
CE Prim Sch TW2. . . . . . . 16 E6
Archer Cl KT2 . . . . 17 E1
Archer Ct TW13. . . . . 15 A7
Archer Ho TW10 . . . . 7 A3
Archer Mews TW12 . . . . . . 16 C2
Archer Rd SE25 . . . . 43 B5
Archers Ct
Crawley RH10 . . . . 201 D8
3 Croydon CR2 . . . . 61 C5
10 Redhill RH1 . . . . 139 F8
Archery Pl GU5 . . . . 133 C4
Arch Rd KT12. . . . . 54 D7
Archway Cl
Wallington SM6. . . . . 60 E7
Wimbledon SW19 . . . . 20 B4
Archway Mews 9
RH4 . . . . 136 A8
Archway Pl RH4 . . . . 136 A8
Archway St SW13, SW14 . . . .7 E4
Arcturus Rd RH11. . . . . . . 200 E3
Arcus Rd BR1. . . . . 24 E2
Arden 17 SW19 . . . . 19 D7
Arden Cl
Bracknell RG12 . . . . 28 A7
Reigate RH2. . . . . 139 B5

Arden Mead Cotts RH7 164 A8
Arden Rd RH10 201 F4
Ardenrun RH7 164 B8
Ardenrun Cotts RH7 164 A7
Ardent Cl SE25 42 E6
Ardesley Wood KT13 53 E6
Ardfern Ave SW16 42 A6
Ardfillan Rd SE6 24 D6
Ardgowan Rd SE6 24 E7
Ardingly RG12 27 A4
Ardingly Cl
Crawley RH11 201 B8
South Croydon CR0 62 D7
Ardingly Ct KT18 76 D5
Ardleigh Gdns SM3 40 A2
Ardley Cl SE23, SE6 23 E5
Ardlui Rd SE27 22 C6
Ardmay Gdns KT6 37 E4
Ardmore Ave GU2 109 B3
Ardmore Ho GU2 109 B3
Ardmore Way GU2 109 B3
Ardoch Rd SE6 24 D6
Ardrossan Ave GU15 66 A5
Ardrossan Gdns KT4 58 A7
Ardshiel Dr RH1 139 E7
Ardwell Rd SW2 21 E6
Ardwick Ct GU14 85 C2
Arena La GU11 104 E5
Arenal Dr RG45 45 C3
Arena The RG12 27 A7
Arethusa Way GU24 67 F3
Arford Comm GU35 187 A6
Argent Cl TW20 12 C2
Argent Ct KT6 57 A7
Argent Terr GU47 64 E8
Argonaut Pk SL3 1 F6
Argosy Gdns TW18 12 F2
Argosy La TW19 13 D8
Argus Wlk RH11 201 A3
Argyle Ave TW2, TW3 5 A1
Argyle Ct TW11 16 E3
Argyle Ho SM2 59 C4
Argyle Rd TW3 5 B2
Argyle St GU24 87 A6
Argyll Ct 15 SW2 21 E8
Argyll Ho TW10 17 C6
Ariel Way TW4 4 B4
Arista Ct TW20 11 D2
Arkell Gr SE19 22 B1
Arkendale RH19 185 A4
Arkindale Rd SE6 24 C5
Arklow Mews 3 KT6 56 E8
Arkwright Dr RG42 26 D7
Arkwright Ho 22 SW2 21 E8
Arkwright Rd
Poyle SL3 1 E5
South Croydon CR2 61 F2
Arlington Cl
Bracknell RG42 27 A8
Sutton SM1 59 A8
Twickenham TW1 6 C1
Arlington Ct
Reigate RH2 118 A3
4 Twickenham TW1 6 C1
Arlington Dr SM5 59 F8
Arlington Lo KT13 53 B6
Arlington Rd
Ashford TW15 13 F3
Richmond TW10 17 D6
Surbiton KT6 37 D3
Teddington TW11 16 F4
Twickenham TW1 6 C1
Arlington Sq RG12 27 A7
Arlington Terr GU11 104 F2
Armadale Rd
Feltham TW14 4 A2
Woking GU21 69 A2
Armeston KT3 38 D2
Armfield Cl KT8 35 F4
Armfield Cotts 5 CR4 40 F7
Armfield Cres CR4 40 F7
Armistice Gdns SE25 43 A6
Armitage Ct SL5 29 C3
Armitage Dr GU16 65 F1
Armstrong Cl KT12 35 A3
Armstrong Mall GU14 84 D4
Armstrong Rd
Englefield Green TW20 11 C2
Feltham TW13 15 E3
Armstrong Way GU14 84 B1
Armytage Rd TW5 4 D7
Arnal Cres SW18 19 E8
Arncliffe RG12 27 A4
Arndale Way TW20 12 A3
Arndell Ho 3 SM1 59 C6
Arne Cl RH11 200 F3
Arne Gr RH6 160 E5
Arnella Ct 3 GU14 105 D8
Arnewood Cl
Oxshott KT22 74 B5
Roehampton SW15 19 A7
Arney's La CR4 41 A3
Arnfield Cl RH11 200 E5
Arngask Rd SE6 24 D8
Arnhem Cl GU11 105 B2
Arnhem Dr CR0 82 D8
Arnison Rd KT8 36 D5
Arnold Cres TW7 5 D2
Arnold Dr KT9 56 D4
Arnold Ho CR0 61 B6
Arnold Rd
Mitcham SW17 20 F1
Sheerwater GU21 70 B4
Staines TW18 13 C1
Arnulf St SE6 24 B4
Arnull's Rd SW16 22 B2
Arona Ho TW16 35 A8
Arosa Rd 16 TW1 6 D1
Arragon Gdns
Streatham SW16 21 E1
West Wickham BR4 63 B7
Arragon Rd
Twickenham TW1 17 A8
Wandsworth SW18 20 A7
Arran Cl
Crawley RH11 201 B3
Wallington SM6 60 C6
Arrancourt 1 RH12 217 B2
Arran Rd SE6 24 C6
Arran Way KT10 55 B8
Arras Ave SM4 40 C4
Arreton Mead GU21 69 F5
Arrivals Rd RH6 181 F8
Arrol Rd BR3 43 D6
Arrow Ind Est GU14 84 F2
Arrow Rd GU14 84 F2
Artel Croft RH10 202 A6
Artemis Pl SW18 19 F8
Arterberry Rd SW20, SW19 39 D8
Arthur Cl
Bagshot GU19 47 E1
Farnham GU9 125 B1
Arthur Ct CR0 61 D7
Arthur Rd
Biggin Hill TN16 83 C3
Crawley RH11 200 E6
Farnham GU9 125 C1
Horsham RH13 217 D1
6 Kingston u T KT2 18 A1
West Barnes KT3 39 B4
Wimbledon SW19 20 A5
Wokingham RG41 25 A6
Arthur's Bridge Rd GU21 69 D2
Arthur St GU11 105 B2
Artillery Rd
1 Aldershot GU11 105 B2
Farnborough GU11, GU14 105 D8
7 Guildford GU1 109 D1
Artillery Terr GU1 109 D1
ARTINGTON 130 C4
Artington Wlk GU2 130 C6
Arundale KT1 37 D5
Arundel Ave
Ewell KT17 58 B1
Merton SM4 39 F5
South Croydon CR2 62 A1
Arundel Cl
Crawley RH10 202 C6
Croydon CR0, CR9 61 B7
Hampton TW12 16 B3
Arundel Ct
4 Beckenham BR2 44 E7
Croydon CR0 61 B7
Arundel Ho
Croydon CR0 61 D5
Guildford GU1 130 D8
Reigate RH2 139 B5
Richmond TW10 7 A2
Arundell Pl 13 GU9 125 B2
Arundel Rd
Belmont SM2 58 F3
Dorking RH4 136 A7
Frimley GU15 66 C4
Hounslow TW4 4 C4
Kingston u T KT1 38 C7
Thornton Heath CR0 42 D3
Arun Ho
8 New Malden KT3 38 E5
7 Teddington KT2 37 D8
Arunside RH12 217 A1
Arunside Sch RH12 217 A2
Arun Way RH13 217 E1
Ascalon Ct 19 SW2 21 F8
Ascent Ho KT13 53 E5
Aschurch Rd CR0 42 F2
ASCOT 29 A6
Ascot Ct GU11 105 A1
Ascot Heath CE Jun Sch SL5 8 E1
Ascot Heath Inf Sch SL5 8 E1
Ascot Ho
8 Egham TW20 12 A3
Penge SE26 23 B2
Ascot Mews SM6 60 C2
Ascot Race Course SL5 28 F6
Ascot Rd
East Bedfont TW14 14 B6
Mitcham SW17 21 A2
Ascot Sta SL5 29 A5
Ascot Twrs SL5 28 F7
Ascot Wood SL5 29 A6
ASH 106 B3
Ashbourne RG12 26 F3
Ashbourne Cl
Ash GU12 106 C3
Coulsdon CR5 79 C1
Ashbourne Rd CR4, SW17 21 A1
Ashbourne Terr 1 SW19 20 A1
Ash Bridge Cvn Pk GU12 126 E8
Ashbrook Rd SL4 11 B8
Ashburnham Pk KT10 55 C6
Ashburnham Rd
Crawley RH10 202 A4
Richmond TW10 17 B5
Ashburton Ave CR0 43 B1
Ashburton Cl CR0 43 A1
Ashburton Com Sch CR0 43 B2
Ashburton Gdns CR0 62 A8
Ashburton Ho SM6 60 D5
Ashburton Jun & Inf Sch CR0 43 B3
Ashburton Rd CR0, CR9 62 A8
Ashbury Cres GU4 110 C3
Ashbury Dr GU17 65 A1
Ashbury Pl SW19 20 C2
Ashby Ave KT9 57 A4
Ashby Ct RH13 217 E1
Ashby Grange 7 SM6 60 C4
Ashby Ho 13 KT6 37 E3
Ashby Way UB7 3 A7
Ashby Wlk CR0 42 C3
Ash Church Mews GU12 106 A2
Ash Church Rd GU12 106 B2
Ash Cl
Ash GU12 106 B3
Blackwater GU17 64 C5
Box Hill KT20 116 C4
Carshalton SM5 59 F8
Crawley Down RH10 204 C8
Kingston u T KT3 38 D7
Lingfield RH7 164 E5
Merstham RH1 119 C5
Penge SE20 43 C7
Pyrford GU22 71 A4
Woking GU22 89 E7
Ash Combe GU8 191 A4
Ashcombe Ave KT6 37 D2
Ashcombe Par GU22 90 A7
Ashcombe Rd
Dorking RH4 115 A1
Merstham RH1 119 C8
Wallington SM5 60 A4
Wimbledon SW19 20 A3
Ashcombe Sch The RH4 115 B1
Ashcombe Sq KT3 38 C6
Ashcombe Terr KT20 97 B7
Ashcroft GU4 130 E2
Ashcroft Ct SE26 23 C5
Ashcroft Pk KT11 73 E6
Ashcroft Pl 5 KT22 95 C6
Ashcroft Rd KT9 56 F7
Ashcroft Rise CR5 79 E3
Ash Ct
Addlestone KT15 52 B5
Ashford TW15 14 C3
East Grinstead RH19 185 E3
9 Merton SW19 19 E1
Ottershaw KT16 51 C5
West Ewell KT19 57 C6
3 West Norwood SW16 22 A3
Ashdale KT23 94 C1
Ashdale Cl
Stanwell TW19 13 E6
Twickenham TW2 16 C8
Ashdale Way TW2 16 B8
Ashdene Cl TW15 14 C1
Ashdene Cres GU12 106 A3
Ashdene Ho TW20 11 C2
Ashdene Rd GU12 106 A2
Ashdown Ave GU14 85 E2
Ashdown Cl
13 Beckenham BR3 44 B7
Bracknell RG12 28 A7
Reigate RH2 139 B5
7 Woking GU22 89 E8
Ashdown Ct
Crawley RH10 201 F3
Dulwich SE22 23 A7
Epsom KT17 76 F6
Horsham RH13 217 F4
New Malden KT4 38 F2
Sutton SM2 59 C4
Ashdown Dr RH10 201 E3
Ashdown Gate RH19 185 D2
Ashdown Gdns CR2 81 B4
Ashdown Pl
Ewell KT17 57 F3
Thames Ditton KT7 37 A2
Ashdown Rd
Ewell KT17 77 A6
Forest Row RH18 206 F2
Kingston u T KT1 37 E7
Reigate RH2 139 B5
Ashdown View RH19 205 E7
Ashdown Way SW17 21 A6
Ash Dr RH1 140 B7
Ashe Ho 21 TW1 6 D1
Ashely Cotts KT21 95 F8
Ashenden Rd GU2 108 F1
Ashen Gr SW19 20 A6
Ashen Vale CR2 62 D2
Asher Dr SL5 28 C8
Ashfield RH14 211 E2
Ashfield Ave TW13 15 B7
Ashfield Cl
Beckenham BR3 24 A1
Richmond TW10 17 E7
Ashfields RH2 118 B3
ASHFORD 13 F2
Ashford Ave TW15 14 B2
Ashford Bsns Complex TW15 14 C4
Ashford CE Prim Sch TW15 14 B2
Ashford Cl TW15 13 E4
ASHFORD COMMON 14 D2
Ashford Cres TW15 13 E5
Ashford Gdns KT11 73 D3
Ashford Hospl TW15 13 E6
Ashford Ind Est TW15 14 C4
Ashford Park Prim Sch TW15 13 D4
Ashford Rd
Feltham TW13, TW15 14 E5
Ashford Rd *continued*
Littleton Common TW15, TW17 14 C1
Staines TW18 33 D8
Ashford Sta TW15 13 F5
Ash Gr
East Bedfont TW14 14 E7
Guildford GU2 109 A2
Heston TW5 4 D7
Penge SE20 43 C7
Staines TW18 13 C2
West Wickham BR4 44 C1
Ash Grange Prim Sch GU12 106 B2
ASH GREEN 106 C1
Ash Green Lane E GU12 127 C8
Ash Green Lane W GU12 127 C8
Ash Green La W GU12 126 F8
Ash Green Rd GU12 106 C1
Ashgrove Rd
Ashford TW15 14 D3
Catford BR1 24 D2
Ash Hill Rd GU12 106 B3
Ash Ho TW11 17 C1
Ashington Ct 3 RH12 217 D5
Ash Keys RH10 201 E5
Ash La GU8 148 C2
Ashlake Rd SW16 21 E4
Ashlea Ct CR6 81 A1
Ashlea Ho TW15 13 F3
Ashleigh Ave TW20 12 C1
Ashleigh Cl RH6 160 F3
Ashleigh Cotts RH5 157 B7
Ashleigh Ct SE26 23 B2
Ashleigh Gdns SM1 59 B8
Ashleigh Ho
1 Mortlake SW14 7 E4
Streatham SW16 21 F4
Ashleigh Point 8 SE26 23 D5
Ashleigh Rd
Horsham RH12 217 C4
Mortlake SW14 7 E4
Penge SE20 43 B6
Ashley Ave
Epsom KT18 76 D6
Morden SM4 40 A4
Ashley CE Prim Sch KT12 35 A1
Ashley Cl
Frimley GU16 86 A6
Little Bookham KT23 93 F2
Oatlands Park KT12, KT13 34 F1
Ashley Ct
5 Epsom KT18 76 D6
Knaphill GU21 68 F1
Ashley Ctr KT18 76 D6
Ashley Dr
Banstead SM7 78 A5
Blackwater GU17 64 C4
Hounslow TW7 5 E8
Twickenham TW2 16 B7
Walton-on-T KT12 54 A7
Ashley Gdns
Richmond TW10 17 D6
Shalford GU4 130 F2
Ashley Ho GU7 150 E8
Ashley La CR0 61 B6
ASHLEY PARK 54 A7
Ashley Park Ave KT12 53 F8
Ashley Park Cres KT12 35 A1
Ashley Park Rd KT12 54 A7
Ashley Pl 5 KT12 35 A1
Ashley Rd
Epsom KT18 76 E4
Farnborough GU14 85 D4
Hampton TW12 36 A8
Knaphill GU21 68 F1
Richmond TW9 6 E4
Thames Ditton KT7 36 F3
Thornton Heath CR7 41 F5
Walton-on-T KT12 54 A8
Westcott RH4 135 C6
Wimbledon SW19 20 B2
Ashley Rise KT12 54 A7
Ashley Way GU24 67 D6
Ashling Rd CR0, CR9 43 A1
Ash Lo 2 TW16 14 F1
Ash Lodge Cl GU12 106 A1
Ash Lodge Dr GU12 106 A1
Ashlyn's Pk KT11 73 E6
Ashlyns Way KT9 56 D4
Ashman Ct CR2 61 B2
Ash Manor Sch GU12 126 F8
Ashmead Rd TW14 15 A7
Ashmere Ave BR3 44 D7
Ashmere Cl SM3 58 D5
Ash Mews KT18 76 E5
Ashmill Ct CR0 42 C3
Ashmore Ct
Catford SE6 24 E7
Heston TW5 5 A8
Ashmore Ho RH11 181 D1
Ashmore La
Biggin Hill BR2 83 C8
Rusper RH12 199 C6
Ash Rd
Aldershot GU12 126 D8
Cheam SM3, SM4 39 F1
Crawley RH10 202 A8
Croydon CR0 63 A8
Littleton TW17 34 A5
Pirbright GU24 88 A1
Woking GU22 89 E7
Ashridge GU14 84 F7
Ashridge Gn 2 RG42 27 B8
Ashridge Rd RG40 25 D8
Ashridge Way
Ashford TW16 15 A2
Merton SM4, SW20 39 F5
Ash St GU12 106 A1
Ash Sta GU12 106 B2
Ashstead La GU7 150 C2
Ashstead Sta KT21 75 E3
ASHTEAD 75 E1
Ashtead Ct 15 SW19 19 D7
Ashtead Hospl The KT21 95 E8
Ashtead La GU7 150 D2
Ashtead Woods Rd KT21 75 C3
Ash Tech Coll The TW15 13 E5
Ashton Cl
Cheam SM1 59 A6
Hersham KT12 54 B4
Ashton Ct
1 Beckenham BR3 43 F8
Woking GU21 69 F3
Ashton Gdns TW4 4 F3
Ashton Ho SW15 19 B8
Ashton Rd 2 GU21 68 F2
Ashtree Ave CR4 40 D7
Ash Tree Cl
Croydon BR3, CR0 43 E3
Farnborough GU14 84 C3
Grayswood GU27 189 F1
1 Surbiton KT6 37 E1
Ashtree Ct TW15 14 B3
Ashtrees GU6 174 E1
Ashtrees The GU12 106 B2
Ash Tree Villas CR0 41 F3
Ash Tree Way CR0 43 E3
Ashurst 3 KT18 76 D6
Ashurst Cl
Horsham RH12 218 A5
Kenley CR8 80 D4
Leatherhead KT22 95 A6
Penge SE20 43 B8
Ashurst Dr
Box Hill KT20 116 B5
Crawley RH10 202 D6
Littleton TW17 33 E5
Ashurst Gdns SW2 22 A7
Ashurst Pl RH4 136 C8
Ashurst Rd
Ash Vale GU12 105 F4
Tadworth KT20 97 C6
Ashurst Wlk CR0 62 B8
ASHURST WOOD 206 E6
Ashurstwood Abbey RH19 206 F6
Ashurst Wood Prim Sch RH19 206 E6
ASH VALE 106 B7
Ash Vale GU8 191 A5
Ashvale Rd SW17 20 F3
Ash Vale Sta GU12 106 A7
Ashview Cl TW15 13 E3
Ashview Gdns TW15 13 E3
Ashville Pk RG41 25 B5
Ashville Way RG41 25 A5
Ashway Ctr 5 KT2 37 E8
Ashwell Ave GU15 65 F6
Ashwell Ct TW15 13 E6
Ashwick Cl CR3 101 A3
Ashwood
5 Crawley RH11 201 D5
Warlingham CR6 101 C7
Ashwood Ct
Forest Row RH18 206 F1
Knaphill GU21 68 C2
Ashwood Gdns CR0 63 C4
Ashwood Pk
11 Belmont SM2 59 A3
Fetcham KT22 94 C4
Woking GU22 70 A1
Ashwood Pl GU22 70 A1
Ashwood Rd
Englefield Green TW20 11 B2
Woking GU22 70 A1
Ashworth Pl GU2 108 F1
Aslett St SW18 20 C8
Asmar Cl CR5 79 E4
Aspects SM1 59 B5
Aspen Cl
Guildford GU4 110 D4
Staines TW18 12 F5
Stoke D'Abernon KT11 73 E3
Aspen Ct
East Grinstead RH19 206 A8
11 Redhill RH1 139 F8
Richmond TW9 7 A7
South Croydon CR2 61 D2
Virginia Water GU25 31 E5
Aspen Gdns
Ashford TW15 14 C3
Mitcham CR4 41 A4
Aspen Gr GU12 126 E8
Aspen Ho
Chelsham CR6 82 B4
Richmond TW9 7 A7
Aspen Lo 1 SW19 19 F2
Aspen Sq KT13 53 D7
Aspen Vale CR3 80 F1
Aspen Way
Banstead KT17 77 D5
Feltham TW13 15 B5
Horsham RH12 217 E4
Aspinall Ho SW12 21 E7

Aspin Way GU17 . . . . 64 B5
Asprey Ct CR3 . . . . 100 F4
Asprey Gr CR3 . . . . 101 A3
Asprey Ho CR4 . . . . 40 E6
Asquith Ho SM7 . . . . 77 F4
Assembly Wlk SM5 . . . . . . 40 E2
Assher Rd KT12 . . . . 54 E7
Assheton-Bennett Ho 15 KT6 . . . . 37 E4
Assisi Ct SW12 . . . . 20 F7
Astede Pl KT21 . . . . 75 F1
Astleham Rd TW17 . . . . . . 33 E6
Astleham Way TW17 . . . . 33 F6
Astley Ho 8 SE27 . . . . 22 C4
Astolat Bsns Pk The GU3 . . . . 130 C1
Aston Cl KT21 . . . . 75 C1
Aston Cotts SL4 . . . . 9 A4
Aston Ct
Crawley RH11 . . . . 201 B1
Wimbledon SW20 . . . . 19 C1
Aston Gn TW5 . . . . 4 C5
Aston Pl SW16 . . . . 22 B2
Aston Rd
Claygate KT10 . . . . 55 E5
Merton SW20 . . . . 39 C7
Astonville St SW18 . . . . . . 20 A7
Aston Way KT18 . . . . 76 F3
Astor Cl
Addlestone KT15 . . . . 52 D6
Kingston u T KT2 . . . . 18 B2
Astoria Ct 10 CR8 . . . . 80 A8
Astoria Mans 18 SW16 . . . . 21 E5
Astoria Par SW16 . . . . 21 E5
Astra Bsns Ctr RH1 . . . . . 161 A7
Astra Mead RG42 . . . . 8 B2
Astrid Ho TW13 . . . . 15 C6
Astwood Pl RH1 . . . . 118 E1
Asylum Arch Rd RH1 . . . . 139 F6
Atalanta Cl CR8 . . . . 61 A1
Atbara Ct TW11 . . . . 17 B2
Atbara Rd TW11 . . . . 17 B2
Atcham Rd TW3 . . . . 5 C3
Atfield Gr GU20 . . . . 48 D4
Atheldene Rd SW18 . . . . . . 20 C7
Athelney Prim Sch SE6 . . . . 24 A5
Athelney St SE6 . . . . 24 A5
Athelstan Cl RH10 . . . . . . 202 E6
Athelstan Ho KT1 . . . . 37 F5
Athelstan House Sch TW12 . . . . 36 A8
Athelstan Rd KT1 . . . . 37 F5
Athena Cl KT1 . . . . 37 F6
Atherfield Ho RH2 . . . . . . 139 C6
Atherfield Rd RH2 . . . . . . 139 C6
Atherley Way TW4 . . . . 15 F8
Atherton Cl
Shalford GU4 . . . . 130 E3
Stanwell TW19 . . . . 2 D1
Atherton Dr SW19 . . . . 19 D4
Atherton Ho CR2 . . . . 61 E4
Athlone KT10 . . . . 55 E4
Athlone Ct 4 SE6 . . . . 24 D8
Athlone Rd SW2 . . . . 22 A8
Atholl Ho 13 RH1 . . . . 118 F1
Atkins Cl GU21 . . . . 69 A1
Atkins Dr BR4 . . . . 63 D8
Atkinson Ct RH6 . . . . 161 B2
Atkinson Ho RH3 . . . . 116 D1
Atkinson Rd RH10 . . . . . . 202 C4
Atkins Rd SW4, SW12 . . . . . 21 D8
Atlanta Ct CR7 . . . . 42 C6
Atrebatti Rd GU47 . . . . 45 C1
Atrium The GU7 . . . . 150 E4
Attebrouche Ct RG12 . . . . . 27 D2
Attfield Cl GU12 . . . . 105 F1
Attleborough Ct SE21 . . . . 23 B6
Attlee Cl CR7 . . . . 42 C4
Attlee Ho
5 Crawley RH11 . . . . 201 B2
Feltham TW13 . . . . 15 A5
Attwood Cl CR2 . . . . 81 B5
Atwater Cl SW2 . . . . 22 A7
Atwell Pl KT7 . . . . 37 A1
Atwood KT23 . . . . 93 E3
Atwood Ave TW9 . . . . 7 A5
Atwood Ho SE21 . . . . 22 E5
Atwood Prim Sch CR2 . . . 81 A6
Aubyn Hill SE27 . . . . 22 D4
Auchinleck Ct RH10 . . . . . 204 B7
Auchinleck Way GU11 . . . . 104 E2
Auckland Cl
Crawley RH11 . . . . 181 D1
South Norwood SE19 . . . . . . 42 F8
Auckland Ct SE27 . . . . 22 C4
Auckland Gdns SE19 . . . . . 42 F8
Auckland Hill SE27 . . . . 22 C4
Auckland Ho BR3 . . . . 43 E4
Auckland Rd
Caterham CR3 . . . . 100 E5
Kingston u T KT1 . . . . 37 F5
South Norwood SE19, SE25 . . . . 42 F8
Auckland Rise SE19 . . . . . . 42 E8
Auden Pl SM3 . . . . 58 C6
Audley Cl KT15 . . . . 52 B5
Audley Ct
Surbiton KT5 . . . . 37 F3
Twickenham TW2 . . . . 16 D5
Audley Dr CR6 . . . . 81 C4
Audley Firs KT12 . . . . 54 C6
Audley Ho KT15 . . . . 52 B5
Audley Pl SM2 . . . . 59 B3
Audley Prim Sch CR3 . . . 100 F6
Audley Rd TW10 . . . . 6 F2
Audley Way SL5 . . . . 28 D6
Audrey Cl BR3 . . . . 44 B3
Audric Cl KT2 . . . . 38 A8
Augur Cl TW18 . . . . 12 F3
Augusta Cl KT8 . . . . 35 F6
Augusta Rd TW2 . . . . 16 C6
Augustine Cl SL3 . . . . 1 E4
Augustine Ct 6 CR3 . . . . 101 A8
August La GU5 . . . . 153 D7
Augustus Cl TW8 . . . . 6 D7
Augustus Ct
Feltham TW13 . . . . 15 F4
Hounslow TW3 . . . . 5 C3
8 Putney SW19 . . . . 19 E7
South Norwood SE19 . . . . . . 22 E1
Streatham SW16 . . . . 21 D6
Augustus Gdns GU15 . . . . . 66 C5
Augustus Rd SW19 . . . . 19 E7
Aultone Way
Carshalton SM5 . . . . 59 F7
Sutton SM1 . . . . 59 C8
Aultone Yd Ind Est SM5 . . . . 59 F7
Aura Ho 3 TW9 . . . . 7 B6
Aurelia Gdns CR7 . . . . 41 F3
Aurelia Rd CR0, CR7, CR9 . . . . 41 F3
Auriol Cl KT4 . . . . 57 E7
Auriol Jun Sch KT19 . . . . . 57 F6
Auriol Park Rd KT4 . . . . . . 57 E7
Aurum Cl RH6 . . . . 161 B2
Austen Cl RH19 . . . . 185 B1
Austen Rd
Farnborough GU14 . . . . 85 A6
Guildford GU1 . . . . 130 F8
Austin Cl
Coulsdon CR8 . . . . 80 B1
Forest Hill SE23, SE6 . . . . 23 F8
Twickenham TW1 . . . . 6 C2
Austin Ho 19 KT6 . . . . 37 E4
Austin's Cotts 7 GU9 . . . 125 B2
Austyn Gdns KT5 . . . . 38 B1
Austyns Pl 2 KT17 . . . . 57 F2
Autumn Cl
Crawley RH11 . . . . 201 C5
Wimbledon SW19 . . . . 20 C2
Autumn Dr SM2 . . . . 59 B2
Autumn Lo 1 CR2 . . . . 61 E6
Avalon Cl SW20 . . . . 39 E7
Avalon Ct CR0 . . . . 42 F2
Avante Ct KT1 . . . . 37 D6
Avarn Rd SW17 . . . . 20 F2
Avebury RG12 . . . . 27 A3
Avebury Cl RH12 . . . . 218 A7
Avebury Rd SW19 . . . . 39 F8
Aveley La GU9 . . . . 146 C7
Aveling Cl
Crawley RH10 . . . . 202 C4
Purley CR8 . . . . 79 F6
Aven Cl GU6 . . . . 174 E2
Avening Rd SW18 . . . . 20 A8
Avening Terr SW18 . . . . . . 20 A8
Avenue All Hallows GU24 . . . . 88 B5
Avenue C KT15 . . . . 52 E7
Avenue Cl
Cranford TW5 . . . . 4 B6
Tadworth KT20 . . . . 97 B5
Avenue Cres TW5 . . . . 4 B7
Avenue Ct
Coulsdon CR5 . . . . 79 D4
Penge SE20 . . . . 43 C8
Tadworth KT20 . . . . 97 B4
Avenue De Cagny GU24 . . . . 87 F5
Avenue Elmers KT6 . . . . . . 37 E4
Avenue Gdns
Cranford TW5 . . . . 4 B7
Horley RH6 . . . . 161 C2
Mortlake SW14 . . . . 7 E4
South Norwood SE25 . . . . . . 43 A7
Teddington TW11 . . . . 16 F2
Avenue One KT15 . . . . 52 E6
Avenue Par TW16 . . . . 35 B6
Avenue Park Rd SE21, SE27 . . . . 22 B6
Avenue Prim Sch SM2 . . . 59 A1
Avenue Rd
Banstead SM7 . . . . 78 B4
Belmont SM2 . . . . 59 A1
Caterham CR3 . . . . 100 E5
Cobham KT11 . . . . 73 D3
Cranleigh GU6 . . . . 174 F1
Egham TW18 . . . . 12 D3
Epsom KT18 . . . . 76 D5
Farnborough GU14 . . . . 85 D3
Feltham TW13 . . . . 14 F5
Grayshott GU26 . . . . 188 C3
Hampton TW12 . . . . 36 B8
Hounslow TW7 . . . . 5 F6
Kingston u T KT1 . . . . 37 E6
Mitcham SW16 . . . . 41 D7
New Malden KT3 . . . . 38 E5
South Norwood, Anerley SE25 . . . . 43 A7
Tatsfield TN16 . . . . 103 E7
Teddington TW11 . . . . 17 A2
Wallington SM6 . . . . 60 C3
Wimbledon SW20 . . . . 39 B7
Avenue Row GU8 . . . . 148 D4
Avenue S KT5 . . . . 38 A2
Avenue St Andrew GU24 . . . . 88 B6
Avenue St Barnabas GU24 . . . . 88 B6
Avenue St Chad GU22 . . . . 88 C5
Avenue St George GU22 . . . . 88 B5
Avenue St Mark GU22, GU24 . . . . 88 B5
Avenue St Savior GU24 . . . 88 B6
Avenue Sucy GU15 . . . . 65 B4
Avenue Terr KT3 . . . . 38 C6
Avenue The
Aldershot GU12 . . . . 126 C7
Beckenham BR3 . . . . 44 C8
Belmont SM2 . . . . 58 F2
Biggin Hill TN16 . . . . 103 F5
Brockham RH3 . . . . 116 A1
Camberley GU15 . . . . 65 B5
Chobham GU24 . . . . 50 A2
Claygate KT10 . . . . 55 E5
Compton GU3, GU7 . . . . . . 129 C1
Coulsdon CR5 . . . . 79 D4
Cranford TW5 . . . . 4 A6
Crowthorne RG45 . . . . 45 B5
Dormansland RH19 . . . . . . 186 B6
Egham TW20 . . . . 12 B4
Ewhurst GU6 . . . . 175 E6
Godalming GU7 . . . . 150 F2
Grayshott GU26 . . . . 188 D3
Hampton TW12 . . . . 15 F2
Haslemere GU27 . . . . 207 F7
Horley RH6 . . . . 160 F2
Hounslow TW3 . . . . 5 B2
Lightwater GU18 . . . . 48 A1
4 New Malden KT4 . . . . . . 39 A1
North Ascot SL5 . . . . 8 F1
Oxshott KT22 . . . . 74 F8
Richmond TW9 . . . . 6 F5
Rowledge GU10 . . . . 145 F3
South Croydon CR0 . . . . 61 E7
South Nutfield RH1 . . . . . . 140 E6
Staines TW18 . . . . 33 B8
Stoneleigh KT17, SM3 . . . . . 58 C3
Sunbury TW16 . . . . 35 B7
Surbiton KT5 . . . . 37 F3
Tadworth KT20 . . . . 97 B5
Twickenham TW1 . . . . 6 B2
West Wickham BR4 . . . . 44 E2
Whyteleafe CR3 . . . . 101 A8
Woodham KT15 . . . . 52 A1
Worcester Park KT4 . . . . . . 57 F8
Worplesdon GU3 . . . . 88 E1
Avenue Three KT15 . . . . . . 52 E7
Avenue Two KT15 . . . . 52 E6
Averil Gr SW16 . . . . 22 B2
Avern Gdns KT8 . . . . 36 B5
Avern Rd KT8 . . . . 36 B5
Avery Ct
7 Aldershot GU11 . . . . . . 105 B2
Penge SE20 . . . . 23 B1
Aviary Rd GU22 . . . . 71 A3
Aviary Way RH10 . . . . 184 C1
Aviation Ct RH10 . . . . 182 A1
Aviator Pk KT15 . . . . 52 D7
Aviemore Cl BR3 . . . . 43 F4
Aviemore Way BR3 . . . . . . 43 E4
Avington Cl GU1 . . . . 109 E1
Avington Gr SE20 . . . . 23 C1
Avoca Rd SW17 . . . . 21 A4
Avocet Cres GU47 . . . . 64 E8
Avon Cl
Addlestone KT15 . . . . 52 A4
Ash GU12 . . . . 105 F1
Farnborough GU14 . . . . 84 E7
Sutton SM1 . . . . 59 C6
Worcester Park KT4 . . . . . . 58 A8
Avon Ct
Farnham GU9 . . . . 125 C1
Guildford GU1 . . . . 110 A1
Avondale GU12 . . . . 105 F7
Avondale Ave
Hinchley Wood KT10 . . . . . . 56 A7
New Malden KT4 . . . . 38 F1
Staines TW18 . . . . 12 F1
Avondale Cl
Hersham KT12 . . . . 54 C5
Horley RH6 . . . . 161 A5
Avondale Ct 9 SM2 . . . . . . 59 C3
Avondale Gdns TW4 . . . . 4 F2
Avondale High CR3 . . . . . 101 A6
Avondale Ho 6 SW14 . . . . . 7 D4
Avondale Rd
Aldershot GU11 . . . . 126 B8
Ashford TW15, TW19 . . . . . . 13 D5
Bromley BR1 . . . . 24 F2
Mortlake SW14 . . . . 7 D4
South Croydon CR2 . . . . 61 C4
Wimbledon SW19 . . . . 20 B3
Avon Ho
9 Redhill RH1 . . . . 118 F2
5 Teddington KT2 . . . . 37 D8
Avonmead GU21 . . . . 69 C1
Avonmore Ave GU1 . . . . . 109 F2
Avon Path CR2 . . . . 61 C3
Avon Rd
Ashford TW16 . . . . 14 F1
Farnham GU9 . . . . 125 C1
Avonwick Rd TW3 . . . . 5 B5
Avon Wlk RH11 . . . . 200 F5
Avro Way
Byfleet KT13 . . . . 52 E1
Wallington SM6 . . . . 60 E3
Axbridge RG12 . . . . 27 E4
Axes La RH1 . . . . 140 D2
Axford Ho SW2 . . . . 22 B7
Axwood KT18 . . . . 76 C4
Ayebridges Ave TW20 . . . . 12 C1
Ayjay Cl GU11 . . . . 126 A7
Aylesbury Ct SM1 . . . . 59 C7
Aylesford Ave BR3 . . . . 43 E4
Aylesworth Spur SL4 . . . . . 11 B8
Aylett Rd
Croydon SE25 . . . . 43 B5
Isleworth TW7 . . . . 5 E5
Ayliffe Cl KT1 . . . . 38 A7
Ayling Ct GU9 . . . . 125 F7
Ayling Hill GU11 . . . . 104 F1
Ayling La GU11 . . . . 125 F8
Aylward Rd
Forest Hill SE23 . . . . 23 D6
Merton SW20 . . . . 39 F6
Aylwin Ct 1 RH12 . . . . . . 217 A1
Aymer Cl TW18 . . . . 32 E8
Aymer Dr TW18 . . . . 32 E8
Aysgarth RG12 . . . . 27 A3
Aysgarth Ct SM1 . . . . 59 B7
Aysgarth Rd SE21 . . . . 22 E8
Ayshe Court Dr RH13 . . . . 217 E3
Azalea Ct
Purley CR8 . . . . 80 B8
Woking GU22 . . . . 89 D8
Azalea Dr GU27 . . . . 207 F8
Azalea Ho TW13 . . . . 15 B7
Azalea Way GU15 . . . . 66 B6
Azriel Terr 3 BR4 . . . . 44 B1
Azure Ct TW13 . . . . 14 F5

B

Babbacombe Cl KT9 . . . . . 56 D5
Babbage Way RG12 . . . . . . 27 A3
Babbs Mead GU9 . . . . 125 A1
Baber Dr TW14 . . . . 4 C1
Babington Ct SW16 . . . . . . 21 D3
Babington Rd SW16 . . . . . . 21 D3
Babylon La KT20, RH2 . . . . 118 B8
Bachelor's La GU23 . . . . . . 92 A3
Back Gn KT12 . . . . 54 C4
Back La
Brentford TW8 . . . . 6 D8
Crawley RH10 . . . . 203 D1
East Clandon GU4 . . . . 111 D4
Elstead GU8 . . . . 148 D4
Frithend GU10 . . . . 166 B8
Plaistow RH14 . . . . 211 E2
Richmond TW10 . . . . 17 C6
Backley Gdns CR0 . . . . 43 A3
Back Rd TW11 . . . . 16 E2
Bacon Cl GU47 . . . . 64 D6
Bacon La GU10 . . . . 167 C3
Badajos Rd GU11 . . . . 104 F3
Baddeley Ho KT8 . . . . 36 A4
Baden Cl TW18 . . . . 13 B1
Baden Dr RH6 . . . . 160 E4
Baden Powell Cl KT6 . . . . . 56 F8
Baden Powell Ct GU7 . . . 150 D6
Baden Rd GU2 . . . . 109 B3
Bader Cl CR8 . . . . 80 D4
Bader Ct GU14 . . . . 84 F8
Badger Cl
Feltham TW13 . . . . 15 B5
Guildford GU2 . . . . 109 B4
Hounslow TW4 . . . . 4 C4
Badger Ct GU10 . . . . 146 A5
Badger Dr GU18 . . . . 48 A1
Badgers Cl
Ashford TW15 . . . . 13 F3
Farncombe GU7 . . . . 150 D8
Horsham RH12 . . . . 217 F6
Woking GU21 . . . . 69 C1
Badgers Copse
Frimley GU15 . . . . 65 E4
Worcester Park KT4 . . . . . . 57 F8
Badgers Cross GU8 . . . . . 149 E1
Badgers Ct
4 Epsom KT17 . . . . 76 E6
Worcester Park KT4 . . . . . . 57 F8
Badgers Hill GU25 . . . . 31 C4
Badgers Hole CR0 . . . . 62 D6
Badgers Hollow GU7 . . . . 150 D6
Badgers La CR6 . . . . 101 C8
Badgers Lo 5 KT17 . . . . . . 76 E6
Badger's Mount CR8 . . . . . 61 B1
Badgers Way
Bracknell RG12 . . . . 27 F7
East Grinstead RH19 . . . . . 185 F2
Loxwood RH14 . . . . 213 A4
Badgers Wlk
Kingston u T KT3 . . . . 38 E7
Purley CR8 . . . . 79 C8
Whyteleafe CR3 . . . . 80 F1
Badgers Wood CR3 . . . . . 100 D2
Badger Way
Aldershot GU12 . . . . 105 D3
Crondall GU10 . . . . 124 D8
Badgerwood Dr GU16 . . . . 65 D2
Badingham Dr KT22 . . . . . . 94 E4
Badminton Rd SW12 . . . . . 21 A8
BADSHOT LEA 126 B6
Badshot Lea Rd GU11, GU9 . . . . 126 A6
Badshot Lea Village Inf Sch GU9 . . . . 126 A6
Badshot Pk GU9 . . . . 126 A6
Bagden Hill KT23, RH5 . . . . 114 D5
Bagot Cl KT21 . . . . 75 F3
BAGSHOT 47 D3
Bagshot Gn GU19 . . . . 47 E3
Bagshot Inf Sch GU19 . . . . 47 E2
Bagshot Rd
Ascot SL5 . . . . 29 C2
Bracknell RG12 . . . . 27 C4
Brookwood GU21, GU22, GU24, GU3 . . . . 88 C5
Englefield Green TW20 . . . . 11 C2
West End GU24 . . . . 68 C8
Bagshot Sta GU19 . . . . 47 E4
Bahram Rd KT19 . . . . 57 D1
Baigents La GU20 . . . . 48 D4
Bailes La GU3 . . . . 107 D3
Bailey Cl
Frimley GU16 . . . . 85 D8
Horsham RH12 . . . . 217 F7
Bailey Cres KT9 . . . . 56 D3
Bailey Ho
Mitcham CR4 . . . . 40 E6
11 Penge SE26 . . . . 23 B3
Bailey Mews W4 . . . . 7 B8
Bailey Pl SE26 . . . . 23 D2
Bailey Rd RH4 . . . . 135 C6
Baileys Cl GU17 . . . . 64 C4
Bailing Hill RH12 . . . . 216 E7
Baillie Rd GU1 . . . . 130 F8
Bain Ave GU15 . . . . 65 B2
Bainbridge Cl KT2 . . . . 17 E3
Baines Cl CR0 . . . . 61 D5
Bainton Mead GU21 . . . . . . 69 A2
Baird Cl RH10 . . . . 182 A1
Baird Dr GU3 . . . . 108 B2
Baird Gdns SE19 . . . . 22 E4
Baird Rd GU14 . . . . 85 C6
Bakeham La TW20 . . . . 11 D1
Bakehouse Barn Cl RH12 . . . . 217 E7
Bakehouse Ct SL5 . . . . 28 B8
Bakehouse Rd RH6 . . . . . 161 A5
Baker Cl RH10 . . . . 201 D4
Baker La CR4 . . . . 41 A7
Bakers Cl CR8 . . . . 80 C5
Baker's Cl RH7 . . . . 164 E5
Bakers Ct
9 Redhill RH1 . . . . 139 F8
South Norwood SE25 . . . . . . 42 E6
Bakers End SW20 . . . . 39 E7
Bakersgate Gdns GU24 . . . 88 A2
Bakers Gdns SM5 . . . . 59 E8
Baker's La RH7 . . . . 164 E4
Bakers Mead RH9 . . . . 121 C6
Baker St KT13 . . . . 53 B6
Bakers Way RH5 . . . . 178 C5
Bakery Mews KT6 . . . . 38 A1
Bakewell Dr KT3 . . . . 38 E7
Balaam Ho SM1 . . . . 59 A6
Balaclava Rd KT6 . . . . 37 C2
Balchins La RH4 . . . . 135 B6
Balcombe Ct RH10 . . . . . . 202 D7
Balcombe Gdns RH6 . . . . 161 C2
Balcombe Ho 3 SW2 . . . . . 21 F7
Balcombe Rd
Crawley, Tinsley Green RH6, RH10 . . . . 182 D5
Crawley, Worth RH10 . . . . . 202 D5
Horley RH6 . . . . 161 B2
Baldreys GU9 . . . . 146 A8
Baldry Gdns SW16 . . . . 21 F2
Baldwin Cl RH10 . . . . 202 C3
Baldwin Cres GU4 . . . . . . 110 C3
Baldwin Gdns TW3 . . . . 5 C6
Baldwin Ho 15 SW2 . . . . . . 22 A7
Baldwins Field RH19 . . . . 185 C4
Baldwins Hill Prim Sch RH19 . . . . 185 D3
Balfont Cl CR2 . . . . 81 A6
Balfour Ave GU22 . . . . 89 F5
Balfour Cres RG12 . . . . 27 B4
Balfour Gdns RH18 . . . . . . 206 E1
Balfour Ho KT19 . . . . 76 B8
Balfour Rd
Croydon SE25 . . . . 43 A5
Hounslow TW3 . . . . 5 B4
Merton SW19 . . . . 20 B1
Wallington SM5 . . . . 59 F3
Weybridge KT13 . . . . 53 A6
Balgowan Cl KT3 . . . . 38 E5
Balgowan Prim Sch BR3 . . . . 43 E7
Balgowan Rd BR3 . . . . 43 F7
BALHAM 21 A7
Balham Gr SW12 . . . . 21 A8
Balham High Rd SW12, SW17 . . . . 21 A7
Balham Hill SW12 . . . . 21 B8
Balham New Rd SW12 . . . . 21 B8
Balham Park Mans SW12 . . . . 20 F7
Balham Park Rd SW12, SW17 . . . . 21 A7
Balham Sta SW12 . . . . 21 B7
Balham Station Rd SW12 . . . . 21 B7
Balintore Ct 8 GU47 . . . . . 64 D8
Ballands N The KT22 . . . . . 94 E5
Ballands' S The KT22 . . . . . 94 E4
Ballantyne Dr KT20 . . . . . . 97 F6
Ballantyne Rd GU14 . . . . . . 85 A6
Ballard Cl KT2 . . . . 18 D1
Ballard Ct GU15 . . . . 66 A8
Ballard Rd GU15 . . . . 66 A8
Ballards Farm Rd CR0, CR2 . . . . 62 A4
Ballards Gn KT20 . . . . 97 E8
Ballards La RH8 . . . . 123 C6
Ballards Rise CR2 . . . . 62 A4
Ballards Way CR0, CR2 . . . . 62 C4
Ballater Rd CR2 . . . . 61 F5
Ballencrieff Rd SL5 . . . . . . 29 F2
Ballfield Rd GU7 . . . . 150 E6
Ballina St SE23 . . . . 23 D8
Ballindune GU27 . . . . 208 C8
Balliol Cl RH10 . . . . 182 D1
Balliol Way GU47 . . . . 45 E1
Balloch Rd SE6 . . . . 24 D6
Ballsdown GU8 . . . . 191 A3
Ball & Wicket La GU9 . . . . 125 C7
Balmain Ct TW3 . . . . 5 B6

Balmoral RH19 206 A8
Balmoral Ave BR3 43 E5
Balmoral Cres
East Molesey KT8 36 A6
Hale GU9 125 B6
Balmoral Ct
15 Belmont SM2 59 A3
6 Crawley RH11 201 B2
Farnborough GU14 85 B4
North Cheam KT4 58 B8
West Norwood SE27 22 C4
Balmoral Dr
Frimley GU16 85 F8
Woking GU22 70 C3
Balmoral Gdns CR2 61 D1
Balmoral Grange TW18 33 B7
Balmoral Ho 3 GU12 105 F5
Balmoral Mans 3 TW1 6 D1
Balmoral Rd
Ash GU12 106 B4
Kingston u T KT1 37 F5
North Cheam KT4 58 B8
Balmoral Way SM2 59 A1
Balquhain Cl KT21 75 D2
Baltic Cl SW19 20 D1
Baltimore Ho SW19 20 B1
Balvernie Gr SW18 20 A8
Bamford Rd BR1 24 D3
Bampfylde Cl SM6 60 C7
Bampton Rd SE23 23 D5
Bampton Way GU21 69 A2
Banavie Gdns BR3 44 C8
Banbury RG12 27 E2
Banbury Cl
Frimley GU16 86 A7
Wokingham RG41 25 A6
Banbury Ct 13 SM2 59 A3
Bancroft Cl TW15 14 A3
Bancroft Ct RH2 118 B1
Bancroft Rd
Crawley RH10 202 D5
Reigate RH2 118 B1
Banders Rise GU1 110 C2
Band La 1 TW20 12 A3
BANDONHILL 60 D5
Bandon Hill Prim Sch SM6 60 D4
Bandon Rise SM6 60 D5
Banfor Ct SM6 60 C4
Bank Ave CR4 40 D7
Bank Bldgs 13 SW16 21 C3
Bankfoot Rd BR1 24 E4
Bank Ho
Addlestone KT15 52 B6
1 Sutton SM1 59 C4
Bankhurst Rd SE4, SE6 23 F8
Bank La
Crawley RH10 201 D6
Kingston u T KT2 17 E1
Roehampton SW15 7 E2
Bank Mews SM1 59 C4
Bank Rd GU11 105 D5
Banks Ho TW7 5 E5
Bankside
Heath End GU9 125 F7
South Croydon CR2 61 F4
Woking GU21 69 B1
Bankside Cl
Biggin Hill TN16 83 C1
Carshalton SM5 59 E4
Elstead GU8 148 D3
Isleworth TW7 5 F3
Bankside Dr KT7 56 B8
Bankside Way 7 SE19 22 E2
Bank's La KT24 93 B5
Banks Rd RH10 202 C5
Banks Way GU1 109 F4
Bannacle Hill Rd GU8 170 E1
Banning Ho 4 SW19 19 D7
Bannister Cl
Streatham SW2 22 A7
Witley GU8 170 F6
Bannister's Rd GU2 129 F7
Bannow Cl KT19 57 E6
BANSTEAD 78 B3
Banstead Com Jun Sch SM7 77 F4
Banstead Inf Sch SM7 77 F4
Banstead Rd
Belmont KT17, SM7 77 D7
Caterham CR3 100 D5
Purley CR8 80 A8
Sutton SM5 59 E3
Banstead Rd S SM2 59 D1
Banstead Sta SM7 77 F5
Banstead Way SM6 60 E5
Bapel Ct BR3 24 A1
Barataria Pk GU23 90 F6
Barbara Cl TW17 34 B4
Barber Cl RH10 202 C2
Barber Dr GU6 174 E4
Barberry Way GU17 64 F2
Barbon Cl GU15 66 D3
Barclay Cl KT23 94 B4
Barclay Rd CR0, CR9 61 D7
Barcombe Ave SW2 21 F6
Barcom Trad Est CR0 41 E2
Bardeen Pl RG12 27 D6
Bardney Rd SM4 40 B5
Bardolph Ave CR0 62 F2
Bardolph Rd TW9 6 F4
Bardon Wlk GU21 69 B2
Bardsley Cl CR0 61 F7
Bardsley Dr GU9 146 A7
Barfield Ct 11 RH1 119 A3
Barfields RH1 120 C2
Barfield Sch GU10 126 B3
Barfreston Way SE20 43 B8
Bargate Cl KT3 39 A2
Bargate Ct
Godalming GU7 150 C4
2 Guildford GU2 108 E1
Bargate Ho GU21 69 F3
Bargate Rise GU7 150 C4
Barge Cl GU11 105 E5
Bargery Rd SE6 24 B7
Barge Wlk KT1, KT6, KT7 37 D5
Bargrove Cl 7 SE20 23 A1
Bargrove Cres SE6 23 F6
Barham Cl KT13 53 C6
Barham Ct 8 CR0 61 C6
Barham Rd
Croydon CR0, CR2 61 C5
Wimbledon SW20 19 A1
Barhatch La GU6 174 F6
Barhatch Rd GU6 174 F4
Baring Rd CR0, CR9 43 A1
Barker Cl
Chertsey KT16 32 E2
Kingston u T KT3 38 B5
Richmond TW9 7 B5
Barker Gn RG12 27 B4
Barker Ho SE21 22 E5
Barker Rd KT16 32 F2
Barkers Mdw SL5 28 D8
Barker Wlk SW16 21 D5
Barkham Rd RG41 25 A5
Barkhart Dr RG40 25 C7
Barkhart Gdns RG40 25 C7
Barkis Mead GU47 45 E2
Barley Cl RH10 201 D5
Barley Ct TW19 13 E7
Barleymead RH6 161 B4
Barley Mow Cl GU21 68 D2
Barley Mow Ct RH3 116 C1
Barley Mow Hill GU35 187 A6
Barley Mow La GU21 68 D3
Barley Mow Rd TW20 11 C3
Barley Mow Way TW17 34 A5
Barlow Cl SM6 60 E3
Barlow Rd
Crawley RH11 200 E3
Hampton TW12 16 A1
Barmeston Rd SE6 24 B6
Barmouth Rd CR0 62 D8
Barnard Cl
Frimley GU16 85 F8
Sunbury TW16 15 B1
Wallington SM6 60 D3
Barnard Ct
1 Knaphill GU21 68 E1
Streatham SW16 21 F5
Barnard Gdns KT3 39 A5
Barnard Ho RH1 139 F4
Barnard Pl KT17 58 C1
Barnard Rd
Chelsham CR6 102 B8
Mitcham CR4 41 A7
Barnards Pl CR2 61 B2
Barnard Way GU11 104 F3
Barnato Cl KT14 71 E7
Barnby Rd GU21 68 D2
Barn Cl
Ashford TW15 14 B3
Bracknell RG12 27 D7
Camberley GU15 65 E6
Epsom KT18 76 C4
Woodmansterne SM7 78 D4
Barn Cres CR8 80 D6
Barncroft GU9 125 C1
Barn Ct GU8 148 E4
Barneby Cl TW2 16 E7
BARNES 7 F6
Barnes Bridge Sta SW13 7 E5
Barnes Cl GU14 85 D4
Barnes Ct CR7 42 C6
Barnes End KT3 39 A4
Barnes High St SW13 7 F5
Barnes Hospl SW14 7 E4
Barnes Mews 9 RH12 217 B2
Barnes Prim Sch SW13 7 F4
Barnes Qtr 6 TW8 6 C7
Barnes Rd
Farncombe GU7 150 E8
Frimley GU16 85 E8
Barnes Wallis Cl KT24 113 D8
Barnes Wallis Dr KT13, KT14 71 E8
Barnett Cl
Leatherhead KT22 95 B8
Wonersh GU5 152 C8
Barnett Ct RG12 27 C7
Barnett Gn RG12 27 B3
Barnett La
Lightwater GU18 66 F7
Wonersh GU5 152 C7
Barnett Row GU4 109 D6
Barnett's Shaw RH8 122 D8
Barnetts Way RH8 122 D8
Barnett Wood Inf Sch KT21 75 D2
Barnett Wood La
Ashtead KT21, KT22 75 D1
Leatherhead KT22 95 B8
Barnfield
Cranleigh GU6 174 E3
Dormansland RH7 165 A1
New Malden KT3 38 E3
Barn Field SM7 78 B5
Barnfield Ave
Croydon CR0 62 C8
Barnfield Ave *continued*
Kingston u T KT2 17 E3
Mitcham CR4 41 B6
Barnfield Cl
Coulsdon CR5 100 C8
Wandsworth SW17 20 C5
Barnfield Gdns KT2 17 E3
Barnfield Rd
Crawley RH10 201 E7
South Croydon CR2 61 E2
Tatsfield TN16 103 D6
Barnfield Way RH8 123 A2
Barnfield Wood Cl BR3 44 D3
Barnfield Wood Rd BR3 44 D3
Barnhill Ave BR2 44 F4
Barnlea Cl TW13 15 E6
Barnmead GU24 49 F1
Barn Meadow La KT23 93 F3
Barnmead Rd BR3 43 E8
Barn Rd KT15 52 B2
Barnsbury Cl KT3 38 C5
Barnsbury Cres KT5 38 C1
Barnsbury Jun & Inf Schs GU22 89 D6
Barnsbury La KT5 38 C1
Barnscroft SW20 39 B6
Barnsfold La RH12 213 E6
Barnsford Cres GU24 68 A6
Barnsley Cl GU12 86 B2
Barnsnap Cl RH12 217 D6
Barn Stables Bsns Units RH10 183 E6
Barns The GU8 149 C8
Barnway TW20 11 C3
Barnwood RH10 202 C7
Barnwood Cl GU3 108 E3
Barnwood Ct GU2, GU3 108 E3
Barnwood Rd GU2, GU3 108 E3
Barnyard The KT20 97 A3
Baron Cl SM2 59 B1
Baron Ct CR4 40 E5
Baron Gr CR4 40 E5
Baron Ho 6 SW19 40 D8
Barons BR3 44 B7
Barons Ct SM6 60 D7
Baronsfield Rd TW1 6 B1
Baron's Hurst KT18 76 C3
Barons The TW1 6 B1
Barons Way TW20 12 D2
Baron's Way RH2 139 A5
Baron's Wlk CR0 43 E3
Barossa Rd GU15 65 D7
Barracane Dr RG45 45 B5
Barrack Path 9 GU21 68 F1
Barrack Rd
Aldershot GU11 105 A2
Guildford GU2 109 A4
Hounslow TW4 4 E3
Barrads Hall CR2 61 D1
Barrards Hall CR2 80 D8
Barr Beacon SE23 23 C8
Barrens Brae GU22 70 A1
Barrens Cl GU22 90 A8
Barrens Pk GU22 90 A8
Barrett Cres RG40 25 E6
Barrett Rd KT22 94 D3
Barrhill Rd SW2 21 E6
Barricane GU21 89 B8
Barrie Cl CR5 79 C3
Barrie Rd GU9 125 A7
Barrihurst La GU6 173 D2
Barringer Sq SW17 21 A4
Barrington Ct
Dorking RH4 136 A6
Staines TW18 12 F2
Barrington Dr KT22 94 D2
Barrington Gate RH12 217 D2
Barrington Lo KT13 53 C5
Barrington Rd
Cheam SM3 40 A1
Crawley RH10 201 D3
Dorking RH4 136 A6
Horsham RH13 217 E2
Purley CR8 79 C7
Barrington Wlk 10 SE19 22 E2
Barrow Ave SM5 59 F3
Barrow Ct SE6 24 F7
Barrow Green Rd RH8 122 C6
Barrow Hedges Cl SM5 59 E3
Barrow Hedges Prim Sch SM5 59 E3
Barrow Hedges Way SM5 59 E3
Barrow Hill KT4 57 E8
Barrow Hill Cl KT4 57 E8
Barrow Hills Sch GU8 170 E4
Barrow Rd
Croydon CR0 61 A5
Streatham SW16 21 D2
Barrowsfield CR2 81 A7
Barrsbrook Farm Rd KT16 32 E1
Barrsbrook Hall KT16 32 E1
Barr's La GU21 68 D3
Barry Cl RH10 201 E3
Barry Sq RG12 27 D2
Barry Terr TW15 13 F6
Barsons Cl SE20 23 C1
Bars The GU1 130 D8
Barston Rd SE27 22 C5
Barstow Cres SW2 21 F7
Bartholomew Cl GU27 208 D8
Bartholomew Ct RH4 136 A6
Bartholomew Way RH12 218 A7
Bartlett Pl GU16 85 F5
Bartlett St CR0, CR2 61 D5
Barton Cl
Addlestone KT15 52 A4
Aldershot GU11 104 E1
Knaphill GU21 68 C1
Shepperton TW17 34 B3
Barton Cres RH19 206 A8
Barton Ct
Beckenham BR2 44 D6
Farnborough GU14 85 C1
Sutton SM1 59 B4
Barton Gn KT3 38 D7
Barton Pl GU1 110 B4
Barton Rd GU5 152 A7
Bartons Way GU14 84 D7
Barton The KT11 73 D7
Barton Wlk RH10 202 B4
Barts Cl BR3 44 A4
Barttelot Rd RH12 217 D2
Barwell Bsns Pk KT9 56 D2
Barwell La KT9 56 C3
Barwood Ave BR4 44 B1
Basden Gr TW13 16 A6
Basemoors RG12 27 E7
Basepoint Bsns Ctr RH11 181 D2
Bashford Way RH10 202 D8
Basildene Rd TW4, TW5 4 D4
Basildon Cl SM2 59 B2
Basildon Way RH11 200 E2
Basil Gdns
Croydon CR0 43 D1
West Norwood SE27 22 C3
Basing Cl KT7 36 F2
Basing Dr GU11 126 B7
Basingfield Rd KT7 36 F2
Basinghall Gdns SM2 59 B2
Basing Ho SE6 24 A4
Basing Rd SM7 77 F4
Basingstoke Canal Ctr* GU16 86 A3
Basing Way KT7 36 F2
Baskerville Ct
Croydon SE25 42 E4
Wandsworth SW18 20 E8
Baskerville Rd SW18 20 E8
Basset Cl KT15 52 C1
Bassett Cl
Belmont SM2 59 B2
Frimley GU16 85 E8
Bassett Dr RH2 118 A2
Bassett Gdns TW7 5 C7
Bassett Rd
Crawley RH10 202 D3
Woking GU22 70 C3
Bassetts Hill RH7 165 A2
Bassingham Rd SW18 20 C8
Batavia Cl TW16 35 C8
Batavia Rd TW16 35 B8
Bat & Ball La
Rowledge GU10 146 A5
Wrecclesham GU10 146 A6
Batcombe Mead RG12 27 E2
Bateman Gr GU12 126 F8
Batemans Ct RH10 202 A3
Bates Cres
Croydon CR0 61 A5
Streatham SW16 21 C1
Bateson Way GU21 70 C5
Bates Wlk KT15 52 C4
Bath Ct 3 SE26 23 A5
Bathgate Rd SW19 19 D5
Bath House Rd CR0 41 E1
Bath Pas KT1 37 D7
Bath Rd
Camberley GU15 65 D6
Cranford, Hounslow TW3, TW4, TW5 4 E5
Harlington TW6, UB7, TW5 3 D6
Harmondsworth TW6, UB7 2 E6
Poyle SL3, UB7, TW6 1 E6
Bath Road Cotts SL3 1 E6
Bathurst Ave SW19 40 B8
Batley Cl CR4 40 F2
Batsworth Rd CR4 40 D6
Batten Ave GU21 88 E8
Battenberg Wlk 10 SE19 22 E3
Battersby Rd SE6 24 D5
Battersea Ct GU2 109 B1
Battlebridge La RH1 119 B5
Battle Cl SW19 20 C2
Batt's Cnr GU10 166 E7
Batts Hill RH2 118 E3
Batty's Barn Cl RG40 25 D5
Baty Ho SW2 21 F7
Baudwin Rd SE6 24 E6
Baulk The SW18 20 A8
Bavant Rd SW16 41 F7
Baveno Ho GU14 85 C1
Bawtree Cl SM2 59 C1
Bax Cl GU6 174 E2
Baxter Ave RH1 118 F1
Baxter Cl RH10 202 B4
Bayards CR6 81 C1
Bay Cl RH6 160 E6
Baydon Ct BR2 44 F6
Bay Dr RG12 27 E7
Bayeux KT20 97 D5
Bayfield Ave GU16 65 E2
Bayfield Rd RH6 160 E4
Bayford Cl GU17 65 A1
Baygrove Mews KT1 37 C8
Bayham Rd SM4 40 C5
Bay Ho RG12 27 E7
Bayhorne La RH6 161 C1
Bayleaf Cl TW12 16 D3
Baylis Mews TW1 17 A8
Bayliss Ct 2 GU1 130 C8
Baylis Wlk RH11 201 B1
Baynards Rd RH12 195 A2
Bay Rd RG12 27 E8
Bays Cl SE26 23 C3
Baysfarm Ct UB7 2 C6
Bay Tree Ave KT22 95 A7
Bay Trees RH8 123 B2
Baywood Cl GU14 84 C5
Bazalgette Cl KT3 38 D4
Bazalgette Gdns KT3 38 D4
Beachborough Rd BR1 24 C4
Beach Gr TW13 16 A6
Beach's Ho 2 TW18 13 A3
Beachy Rd RH11 201 A1
Beacon Cl
Banstead SM7 77 D3
Rowledge GU10 146 A5
Beacon Ct
Colnbrook SL3 1 C7
Horsham RH13 218 A4
Beacon Gr SM5 60 A6
BEACON HILL 188 C6
Beacon Hill
Dormansland RH7 186 B8
Woking GU21 89 C8
Beacon Hill Com Sch GU26 188 C6
Beacon Hill Ct GU26 188 D6
Beacon Hill Pk GU26 188 B6
Beacon Hill Rd
Beacon Hill GU26 188 D6
Crondall GU10 124 E8
Beacon Ho 10 SE26 23 B3
Beacon Pl SM6 60 E7
Beacon Rd
Farnborough GU14 105 B8
Harlington TW19, TW6 3 A1
Beacon Rdbt TW6 3 A1
Beacon Sch The KT20 77 E2
Beaconsfield Gdns KT10 55 E3
Beaconsfield Pl KT17 76 E7
Beaconsfield Rd
Claygate KT10 55 E3
Kingston u T KT3 38 D7
Langley Vale KT18 96 E8
Old Woking GU22 89 F7
Surbiton KT5 37 F2
Thornton Heath CR0 42 D3
Twickenham TW1 6 B1
Beaconshaw BR1 24 E1
Beacon View Ho GU26 188 C3
Beacon View Rd GU8 148 C2
Beacon Way SM7 77 E3
Beadle Ct CR4 40 E6
Beadles La RH8 122 D4
Beadlow Cl SM4 40 D3
Beadman Pl SE27 22 B4
Beadman St SE27 22 B4
Beadnell Rd SE23 23 D7
Beaford Gr SW20 39 F6
Beagle Cl TW13 15 B4
Beale Cl RG40 25 B7
Beale Ct RH11 201 A3
Beales La
Weybridge KT13 53 B7
Wrecclesham GU10 145 F7
Beales Rd KT23 94 B1
Bealeswood La GU10 166 F6
Beam Hollow GU9 125 C7
Bean Oak Rd RG40 25 F6
Beardell St SE19 22 F2
Beard Rd TW10 17 F3
Beard's Hill TW12 36 A8
Beards Hill Cl TW12 36 A8
Beard's Rd TW15, TW16 14 E2
BEARE GREEN 157 D3
Beare Green Cotts RH5 157 D2
Beare Green Ct RH5 157 D4
Beare Green Rd RH5 157 B1
Bearfield Rd KT2 17 E1
Bear La GU9 125 C3
Bear Rd TW13 15 D4
Bears Den KT20 97 F5
Bearsden Ct SL5 29 F2
Bearsden Way RH12 216 D3
Bears Rail Pk SL4 10 F8
Bearsted Terr 7 BR3 44 A8
Bearwood Cl KT15 52 A4
Bearwood Cotts GU10 145 F7
Beasley's Ait La TW16, TW17 34 F3
Beatrice Ave SW16 41 F7
Beatrice Ho SE6 24 A6
Beatrice Rd
Oxted RH8 122 E6
2 Richmond TW10 6 F2
Beatrix Potter Prim Sch SW18 20 C7
Beattie Cl
East Bedfont TW14 14 F7
Little Bookham KT23 93 F3
Beatty Ave GU1 110 A2
Beauchamp Rd
East Molesey KT8 36 C4

Beauchamp Rd *continued*
South Norwood CR7, SE25 42 D8
Sutton SM1 59 A6
Twickenham TW1 17 A8
Beauchamp Villas KT2 17 F1
Beauclare Cl KT21 95 D6
Beauclerc Ct TW16 35 C6
Beauclerc Inf Sch TW16 35 C6
Beauclere Ho 1 SM2 59 C3
Beauclerk Cl TW13 15 B7
Beauclerk Ho 10 SW16 21 E5
Beaufield Gate GU27 208 D7
Beaufort Cl
Putney SW19 19 B8
Reigate RH2 117 F2
Woking GU22 70 C3
Beaufort Com Prim Sch GU21 68 F3
Beaufort Ct TW10 17 C4
Beaufort Gdns
Heston TW5 4 E6
North Ascot SL5 28 E8
South Norwood SW16 21 F1
Beaufort Ho
Ashford TW15 14 B3
9 Wimbledon SW20 39 D8
Beaufort Lo CR2 61 D1
Beaufort Mews GU21 69 D2
Beaufort Rd
Ash Vale GU12 105 F6
Farnham GU9 125 C3
Kingston u T KT1, KT5, KT6 37 E5
Reigate RH2 117 F2
Richmond TW10 17 C4
Twickenham TW1 17 C8
Woking GU22 70 C3
Beauforts TW20 11 C3
Beaufort Way KT17 58 A3
Beaufoy Ho 3 SE27 22 B5
Beaufront Cl GU15 66 A7
Beaufront Rd GU15 66 B7
Beaulieu Ave SE26 23 B4
Beaulieu Cl
Bracknell RG12 28 A6
Hounslow TW4 4 F2
Mitcham CR4 41 A8
26 Twickenham TW1 6 D1
Beaulieu Gdns GU17 64 C5
Beaulieu Hts SE25 42 E8
Beaumaris Par GU16 85 F8
Beaumont Ave TW9 6 F4
Beaumont Cl 3 RH11 200 E5
Beaumont Ct
Ascot SL5 28 F5
Ewell KT17 76 F8
Mitcham CR4 41 A7
5 Wimbledon SW20 19 D1
Beaumont Dr
Ashford TW15 14 D3
New Malden KT4 39 B2
Beaumont Gdns RG12 27 E4
Beaumont Gr GU11 104 E2
Beaumont Ho
1 Streatham SW2 21 E7
Wimbledon SW19 20 A5
Beaumont Jun Sch GU11 104 F2
Beaumont Lo BR4 63 E7
Beaumont Pl TW7 5 F2
Beaumont Prim Sch CR8 80 A5
Beaumont Rd
Purley CR8 80 A6
Putney SW15, SW19 19 E8
South Norwood SE19 22 C2
Beaumonts RH1 139 F1
Beaumont Sq GU6 174 F3
Beaumont Terr 1 SE13 24 E8
Beaver Cl
Hampton TW12 36 B8
Horsham RH12 217 F6
8 Penge SE20 23 A1
West Barnes SM4 39 C2
Wokingham RG41 25 B3
Beavers Cl
Farnham GU9 125 A2
Guildford GU3 108 E2
Beavers Com Prim Sch TW4 4 C4
Beavers Cres TW4 4 D3
Beavers Hill GU9 124 F2
Beavers La TW4 4 C4
Beavers Rd GU9 125 A2
Beaver Zoological Gdns* TN16 103 B5
Beck Ct BR3 43 D6
BECKENHAM 44 A7
Beckenham Bsns Ctr BR3 23 E2
Beckenham Ct BR3 44 A8
Beckenham Gr BR2 44 D7
Beckenham Hill Rd BR3, SE6 24 C3
Beckenham Hill Sta SE6 24 C3
Beckenham Hospl BR3 43 F7
Beckenham Junction Sta BR3 44 A8
Beckenham La BR2 44 F7
Beckenham Place Pk BR3 24 B1
Beckenham Rd
Beckenham BR3 43 E8
West Wickham BR3, BR4 44 C2
Beckenshaw Gdns SM7 78 E4
Becket Cl
Croydon SE25 43 A3
2 Merton SW19 40 B8
Beckett Ave CR8 80 B4
Beckett Cl
Streatham SW16 21 D6
Wokingham RG40 25 E6
Beckett Ho SM3 58 D7
Beckett La RH11 181 D1
Beckett Rd CR5 99 D5
Becketts Cl TW14 4 B1
Becketts Pl KT1 37 D8
Beckett Way 11 RH19 205 F8
Beckett Wlk BR3 23 E2
Becket Wood RH5 158 C4
Beckford Ave RG12 27 B3
Beckford Rd CR0, SE25 42 F3
Beckford Way RH10 202 B2
Beck Gdns GU9 125 A6
Beck Ind Est The GU12 126 D8
Beckingham Rd GU2 109 A2
Beck La BR3 43 D6
Beckley Cotts KT23 94 C1
Beckmead Sch BR3 44 A1
Beck River Pk 8 BR3 44 A8
Beck Way BR3 44 A6
Beckway Rd SW16 41 D7
Beckworth Pl KT13 53 E8
Beclands Rd SW17 21 A2
Becmead Ave SW16 21 D4
Becondale Rd SE19 22 E3
Bedale Cl RH11 201 C4
BEDDINGTON CORNER 41 A2
BEDDINGTON 60 E8
Beddington Cross CR0 41 E2
Beddington Farm Rd
Croydon CR0 60 F8
Wallington CR0, CR9 41 E1
Beddington Gdns SM5, SM6 60 A4
Beddington Gr SM6 60 D5
Beddington Ind Est CR0 41 E1
Beddington Inf Sch SM6 60 C6
Beddington La CR0 60 E8
Beddington Manor SM2 59 D4
Beddington Park Cotts SM6 60 D7
Beddington Park Prim Sch CR0 60 D7
Beddlestead La CR6, TN16 103 A6
Bedelsford Sch KT1 37 E6
Bedfont Cl
East Bedfont TW14 3 C1
Mitcham CR4 41 A7
Bedfont Court Est TW19 2 B4
Bedfont Ct TW19 2 B4
Bedfont Green Cl TW14 14 C7
Bedfont Ind Pk TW15 14 D5
Bedfont Ind Pk N TW15 14 C5
Bedfont Inf Sch TW14 3 E1
Bedfont Jun Sch TW14 3 E1
Bedfont La TW14, TW13 14 F8
Bedfont Lakes Ctry Pk* TW14 14 C6
Bedfont Rd
East Bedfont TW14, TW13 14 D6
Stanwell TW19 2 F1
Bedford Ave GU16 85 F5
Bedford Cl
13 Chiswick W4 7 E8
Woking GU21 69 C4
Bedford Cres GU16 85 F6
Bedford Ct
9 Richmond TW9 6 F3
South Norwood SE19 42 F8
Bedford Hill SW12, SW16, SW17 21 B6
Bedford Ho 3 GU1 130 C8
Bedford La
Frimley GU16 85 F6
Sunningdale SL5 30 B4
Bedford Mews SE6 24 B6
Bedford Pk CR0 42 C1
Bedford Pl CR0 42 D1
Bedford Rd
Guildford GU1 130 C8
Horsham RH13 217 D1
North Cheam KT4 58 C8
Twickenham TW2 16 D5
Bedford Terr 11 SM2 59 C4
Bedford Villas SM5 59 F7
Bedgebury Gdns SW19 19 E6
Bedlow Cotts GU6 174 F3
Bedlow Way CR0 60 F6
Bedser Cl
South Norwood CR7 42 C6
Woking GU21 70 A3
Bedster Gdns KT8 36 B6
Bedwardine Rd SE19 22 E1
Beech Ave
Brentford TW8 6 B7
Camberley GU15 65 D4
Effingham KT24 113 D6
Farnham GU10 146 C5
Beech Ave *continued*
South Croydon CR2 61 D1
Tatsfield TN16 103 D8
Beech Cl
Aldershot GU12 126 E8
Ashford TW15 14 D3
Blindley Heath RH7 163 E8
Byfleet KT14 71 E7
Carshalton SM5 59 F8
Chiddingfold GU8 191 A4
Cobham KT11 74 A8
Dorking RH4 136 A8
2 East Grinstead RH19 185 D2
Effingham KT24 113 D7
Hersham KT12 54 C6
Putney SW15 19 A8
Stanwell TW19 13 D8
Sunbury TW16 35 D7
Wimbledon SW19 19 C2
Beech Close Ct KT11 73 F8
Beech Copse CR2 61 E5
Beech Cres KT20 116 C5
Beechcroft
Ashtead KT21 95 F8
Kingston u T KT2 38 B8
Beechcroft Ave
Kenley CR8 80 D4
Kingston u T KT1, KT3 38 C7
Beechcroft Cl
Ascot SL5 29 D5
Heston TW5 4 E7
Streatham SW16 21 F3
Beechcroft Ct RG12 27 B6
Beechcroft Dr GU2 129 D6
Beechcroft Lo 12 SM2 59 C3
Beechcroft Manor KT13 53 D7
Beechcroft Mans SW16 21 F3
Beechcroft Rd
Chessington KT9 56 F7
Mortlake SW14 7 C4
Upper Tooting SW17 20 E6
Beech Ct
Beckenham BR3 23 F1
Chipstead CR5 78 F1
East Grinstead RH19 185 D2
4 Guildford GU1 130 F8
Haslemere GU27 208 D7
Teddington TW11 17 C2
5 West Norwood SW16 22 A3
Beechdene KT20 97 B5
Beech Dr
Blackwater GU17 64 D4
Kingswood KT20 97 F5
Reigate RH2 118 D1
Send Marsh GU23 91 A3
Beechen Cliff Way TW7 5 F5
Beechen La KT20 97 F2
Beechen Pl SE23 23 C6
Beeches Ave SM5 59 E3
Beeches Cl
Kingswood KT20 98 A4
Penge SE20 43 C8
Beeches Cres RH10 201 E4
Beeches La RH19 206 D6
Beeches Mead RH19 186 F5
Beeches Rd
Cheam SM3 39 E1
Upper Tooting SW17 20 F5
Beeches The
Ash Vale GU12 85 F1
Banstead SM7 78 B3
Bramley GU5 151 F6
8 Farnborough GU14 85 C1
Fetcham KT22 94 E3
Hounslow TW3 5 B6
Mitcham CR4 40 E4
Reigate RH2 118 B2
South Croydon CR2 61 C4
Staines TW18 13 A3
Beeches Wlk SM2, SM5 59 E2
Beeches Wood KT20 98 A5
Beechey Cl RH10 183 B3
Beechey Way RH10 183 B3
Beech Farm Rd CR6 102 D8
Beechfield SM7 78 B6
Beechfield Ct 7 CR0 61 C6
Beechfield Rd SE6 23 F7
Beechfields RH19 185 F3
Beech Gdns
Crawley Down RH10 204 A8
Woking GU21 69 E4
Beech Glen RG12 27 B5
Beech Gr
Addlestone KT15 52 B6
Burgh Heath KT18 77 B2
Caterham CR3 100 E1
Great Bookham KT23 114 A8
Guildford GU2 108 F1
Kingston u T KT3 38 D6
Mitcham CR4 41 D5
Pirbright GU24 87 D7
Woking GU22 89 D4
Beech Hall KT16 51 C3
Beech Hanger End GU26 188 B3
BEECH HILL 187 A6
Beech Hill
Bowlhead Green GU8 189 F8
Headley Down GU35 187 B5
Woking GU22 89 D4
Beech Hill Rd
Headley Down GU35 187 A5
Sunningdale SL5 29 F3
Beech Ho
Beckenham BR2 44 E8
Beech Ho *continued*
Heston TW5 4 E7
New Addington CR0 63 B4
Beech Holme RH10 204 B8
Beech Holt KT22 95 C5
Beech House Rd CR0, CR9 61 D7
Beeching Cl GU12 106 B3
Beeching Way RH19 185 E1
Beech La
Flexford GU3 107 A1
Grayshott GU26 188 B4
Guildford GU2 130 C6
Beechland Cotts KT20 117 F7
Beechlawn GU1 130 F8
Beech Lo TW18 12 E3
Beechmeads KT11 73 D6
Beechmont Ave GU25 31 D4
Beechmont Cl BR1 24 E3
Beechmore Gdns SM3 58 D8
Beechnut Dr GU17 64 B6
Beechnut Ind Est 9 GU12 105 B1
Beechnut Rd 8 GU12 105 B1
Beecholme KT17 77 E5
Beecholme Ave CR4 41 B8
Beecholme Prim Sch CR4 41 B8
Beech Rd
Biggin Hill TN16 83 C2
East Bedfont TW14 14 E8
Epsom KT18 76 F4
Farnborough GU14 85 A7
Frimley GU16 85 F6
Haslemere GU27 208 D8
Horsham RH12 218 B5
Merstham RH1 99 C1
Oatlands Park KT13 53 D6
Reigate RH2 118 A4
Thornton Heath SW16 41 F6
Beech Ride GU47 45 B1
Beechrow KT2 17 E4
Beechside RH10 201 E5
Beechtree Ave TW20 11 B2
Beech Tree Cl RH10 201 D7
Beech Tree Ct BR2 44 E7
Beech Tree Dr GU9 126 A5
Beech Tree La TW18 33 B7
Beech Tree Pl SM1 59 B5
Beechvale 3 GU22 69 F1
Beechway GU1 110 B2
Beech Way
Epsom KT17 76 F4
Godalming GU7 150 D3
Selsdon CR2 81 D7
Twickenham TW2 16 A5
Beech Wlk KT17 77 A8
Beech Wood CR3 100 F3
Beechwood Ave
Ashford TW16 15 A2
Kingswood KT20 98 A6
Oatlands Park KT13 53 E6
Richmond TW9 7 A6
Staines TW18 13 B2
Thornton Heath CR7 42 B5
Wallington CR5 79 B4
Beechwood Cl
Knaphill GU21 68 E2
Long Ditton KT6 37 D2
North Ascot SL5 8 F1
Oatlands Park KT13 53 E6
Beechwood Ct
Ashford TW16 15 A3
Carshalton SM5 59 F6
Cheam SM1 59 A5
Chiswick W4 7 D8
Sutton SM2 59 D4
Walton-on-T KT12 54 A7
Beechwood Dr KT11 74 A8
Beechwood Gdns CR3 101 A5
Beechwood La CR6 101 D8
Beechwood Manor KT13 53 E6
Beechwood Pk KT22 95 C5
Beechwood Rd
Caterham CR3 101 A5
Knaphill GU21 68 D2
South Croydon CR2 61 E2
Wentworth GU25 31 B1
Beechwoods Ct SE19 22 F3
Beechwood Villas RH1 161 A7
Beecot La KT12 54 C8
Beeding Cl RH12 218 A5
Beedingwood Dr RH12 218 E6
Beedon Dr RG12 26 E3
Beehive La RG12 26 C7
Beehive Rd
Bracknell RG12, RG42 26 D7
Staines TW18 12 F3
Beehive Ring Rd RH6 182 B4
Beehive The RH6 182 B4
Beehive Way RH2 139 B5
Beeleigh Rd SM4 40 B5
Beemans Row 1 SW18 20 C6
Beeston Way TW14 4 C1
Beeton's Ave GU12 106 A4
Beggarshouse La RH6 180 C8
Beggars La
Chobham GU24 68 C8
Gomshall RH5 133 E4
Beggar's Roost La SM1 59 A4
Begonia Pl 1 TW12 16 A2
Beharrell Ho SL5 29 E4
Behenna Cl RH11 200 E5
Beira St SW12 21 B8
Belcroft Cl BR1 24 F1
Beldam Bridge Rd GU24 68 A6
Beldham Gdns KT8 36 B6
Beldham Rd GU9 145 F7
Belenoyd Ct SW16 21 F5
Belfast Rd SE25 43 B5
Belfield Rd KT19 57 E3
Belfry Shp Ctr The RH1 118 F2
Belgrade Rd TW12 36 B8
Belgrave Cl KT12 54 B6
Belgrave Cres TW16 35 B8
Belgrave Ct GU17 64 D3
Belgrave Manor GU22 89 E8
Belgrave Rd
Barnes SW13 7 F7
Hounslow TW4 4 F4
Mitcham CR4 40 D6
South Norwood SE25 42 F5
Sunbury TW16 35 B8
Belgrave Wlk CR4 40 D6
Belgravia Ct 1 RH6 161 B3
Belgravia Gdns BR1 24 E2
Belgravia Ho 1 TW11 17 C1
Belgravia Mews KT1 37 D5
Bel La 2 TW13 15 F5
Bellagio Pl RH19 185 D3
Bellamy Ho
Heston TW5 5 A8
Upper Tooting SW17 20 D4
Bellamy Rd RH10 202 C2
Bellamy St SW12 21 B8
Belland Dr GU11 104 E1
Bellasis Ave SW2 21 E6
Bell Bridge Rd KT16 32 F1
Bell Chase GU11 104 F2
Bell Cl GU14 85 C6
Bell Cnr KT16 32 F2
Bell Cres CR5 99 B6
Bell Ct
Tolworth KT5 57 B8
13 Woking GU22 69 F1
Bell Ctr RH10 181 F2
Bell Dr SW18 19 E8
Bellerby Ct GU2 129 E8
Bellever Hill GU15 65 E5
Belle Vue Cl
Aldershot GU12 105 D2
Staines TW18 33 A8
Belle Vue Ent Ctr GU12 105 E2
Belle Vue Inf Sch GU12 105 D2
Bellevue Pk CR7 42 C5
Bellevue Rd
Kingston u T KT1 37 E6
Upper Tooting SW17 20 F7
Belle Vue Rd GU12 105 D2
Bellew Rd GU16 86 B7
Bellew St SW17 20 C5
Bell Farm Jun Sch KT12 54 C6
Bellfield CR0 62 F3
BELLFIELDS 109 C4
Bellfields Ct GU1 109 C5
Bellfields Rd GU1 109 D3
Bell Foundry La RG40 25 C8
Bell Gn SE6 23 F4
BELL GREEN 23 F4
Bell Green La BR3, SE26, SE6 23 F4
Bell Hammer RH19 205 E8
Bell Ho 15 SW2 22 A8
Bell House Gdns RG41 25 B6
BELLINGHAM 24 A3
Bellingham Cl GU15 66 C4
Bellingham Dr RH2 117 F1
Bellingham Gn SE6 24 A5
Bellingham Rd SE6 24 C5
Bellingham Sta SE6 24 B5
Bellingham Trad Est SE6 24 B6
Bell La
Blackwater GU17 64 C5
Fetcham KT22 94 D4
Rowledge GU10 145 E3
Twickenham TW1 17 A7
Bell Lane Cl KT22 94 D4
Bellmarsh Rd KT15 52 B6
Bell Mdw
Dulwich SE19 22 E4
Godstone RH9 121 C3
Bellmore Ct 5 CR0 42 F1
Belloc Cl RH10 202 C7
Belloc Ct RH13 218 A3
Bello Cl SE24 22 B7
Bell Pl GU19 47 F3
Bell Rd
East Molesey KT8 36 D4
Hounslow TW3 5 B3
Kingsley Green GU27 208 B3
Warnham RH12 217 A8
Bells La SL3 1 B4
Bell St RH2 139 B8
Belltrees Gr 1 SW16 22 A3
Bell Vale La GU27 208 C4
Bell View BR3 23 F1
Bellview Ct TW3 5 B3
Bell Vue Ho GU12 105 D2
Bell Weir Cl TW19 12 B6
Bellwether La RH1 162 B7
BELMONT 59 A2
Belmont KT13 53 C4

Belmont Ave
Guildford GU2 . . . . 108 F4
West Barnes KT3. . . . . 39 A5
Belmont Cl GU14 . . . . 84 F7
Belmont Cotts SL3. . . . . 1 C7
Belmont Ho GU9. . . . . 146 A8
Belmont Mews
Camberley GU15 . . . . 65 C3
Putney SW19. . . . . 19 D6
Belmont Rd
Beckenham BR3. . . . . 43 F7
Belmont SM2. . . . . 59 A1
Camberley GU15 . . . . 65 C4
Crowthorne RG45 . . . . 45 B6
Croydon SE25 . . . . 43 B4
Leatherhead KT22. . . . . 95 A5
Reigate RH2. . . . . 139 C8
Twickenham TW2. . . . . 16 D6
Wallington SM6 . . . . 60 C5
Belmont Rise SM1, SM2. . . 58 F3
Belmont Sch RH5. . . . . . . 155 D6
Belmont Sta SM2 . . . . 59 B1
Belmore Ave GU22. . . . . . . 70 D3
Belsize Gdns SM1. . . . . . . 59 B6
Belsize Grange KT16 . . . . . 33 C2
Belstone Mews GU14. . . . . 85 A7
Beltane Dr SW19. . . . . 19 D5
Belthorn Cres SW12. . . . . . 21 C8
Belton Rd GU15. . . . . 65 E5
Belvedere Ave SW19 . . . . . 19 E3
Belvedere Cl
Esher KT10 . . . . 55 B5
Guildford GU2 . . . . 109 B3
Teddington TW11. . . . . 16 E3
Weybridge KT13 . . . . 53 A5
Belvedere Ct
Blackwater GU17. . . . . 64 D3
Crawley RH10 . . . . 202 B7
8 Kingston u T KT2 . . . . . . 18 A1
Redhill RH1 . . . . 119 A5
Belvedere Dr SW19 . . . . . . 19 E3
Belvedere Gdns KT8 . . . . . 36 A4
Belvedere Gr SW19 . . . . . . 19 E3
Belvedere Grange SL5 . . . . 30 A1
Belvedere Ho
Feltham TW13 . . . . 15 A7
Weybridge KT13 . . . . 53 B5
Belvedere Rd
Biggin Hill TN16. . . . . 83 F1
Farnborough GU14 . . . . 85 C2
Penge SE19. . . . . 22 F1
Belvedere Sq SW19 . . . . . . 19 E3
Belvoir Cl GU16. . . . . 65 F1
Belvoir Lo SE22. . . . . 23 A8
Belvoir Rd SE22. . . . . 23 A8
Bembridge Ct 3
GU12 . . . . 105 C1
Benbow La GU8. . . . . 193 C4
Benbrick Rd GU2 . . . . 130 A8
Benbury Cl BR1. . . . . 24 C3
Bence The TW20. . . . . 32 B6
Bench Field CR2. . . . . 61 F5
Benchfield Cl RH19 . . . . . 186 B1
Bencombe Rd CR8. . . . . . . 80 A5
Bencroft Rd SW16 . . . . 21 C1
Bencurtis Pk BR4. . . . . 63 D8
Bendon Valley SW18 . . . . . 20 B8
Benedict Dr TW14 . . . . 14 D8
Benedict Prim Sch
CR4. . . . . 40 D6
Benedict Rd CR4. . . . . 40 D6
Benedict Wharf CR4 . . . . . 40 E6
Benen-Stock Rd TW19 . . . . 2 A2
Benett Gdns SW16 . . . . 41 E7
Beney Ct BR3. . . . . 44 A7
Benfleet Cl
Cobham KT11. . . . . 73 E7
Sutton SM1 . . . . 59 C7
Benham Cl
Chessington KT9 . . . . 56 C4
Coulsdon CR5 . . . . 80 B1
Benham Gdns TW3, TW4. . . . 4 F2
Benhams Cl RH6. . . . . 161 A5
Benhams Dr RH6 . . . . 161 A5
Benhill Ave SM1 . . . . 59 C6
Benhill Ct SM1. . . . . 59 D6
Benhill Rd SM1 . . . . 59 D6
Benhill Wood Rd SM1. . . . 59 C6
BENHILTON 59 C7
Benhilton Ct SM1 . . . . 59 C7
Benhilton Gdns SM1 . . . . . 59 B7
Benhurst Cl CR2 . . . . 62 D1
Benhurst Ct
13 Penge SE20 . . . . 43 B8
Streatham SW16. . . . . 22 A3
Benhurst Gdns CR2 . . . . . . 62 C1
Benhurst La SW16 . . . . 22 A3
Benin St SE13 . . . . 24 D8
Benjamin Ct TW15 . . . . 14 C1
Benjamin Mews SW17. . . . 21 C8
Benjamin Rd RH10 . . . . . . 202 D4
Benn Cl RH8. . . . . 123 A1
Benner La GU24 . . . . 68 A7
Bennet Cl KT1 . . . . 37 C8
Bennets Ct SW19 . . . . 40 C8
Bennett Cl
Cobham KT11. . . . . 73 A6
Crawley RH10 . . . . 202 B2
Hounslow TW4. . . . . 4 E2
Bennett Ct GU15 . . . . 65 C5
Bennetts Ave CR0. . . . . 62 E8
Bennetts Cl CR4, SW16. . . . 41 B8
Bennetts Farm Pl KT23. . . . 93 F2
Bennetts Rd RH13 . . . . 217 E1
Bennetts Rise GU11. . . . . . 126 C8
Bennett St 2 W4 . . . . 7 E8
Bennetts Way CR0 . . . . 62 F8
Bennetts Wood RH5 . . . . 178 C5
Bennett Way GU4. . . . . . . 111 B6
Benning Way RG40. . . . . . . 25 D8
Benns Wlk 5 TW9 . . . . 6 E3
Bens Acre RH13 . . . . 218 A2
Bensbury Cl SW15 . . . . 19 C8
Bensham Cl CR7. . . . . 42 C5
Bensham Gr CR7. . . . . 42 C7
Bensham La CR0, CR7. . . . . 42 B3
Bensham Manor Rd CR0,
CR7 . . . . 42 C5
Bensham Manor Sch
CR7. . . . . 42 C4
Bensington Ct TW14 . . . . . . 3 D1
Benson Cl TW3 . . . . 5 A3
Benson Ho 1 TW10. . . . . . 17 C5
Benson Prim sch CR0. . . . . 62 E7
Benson Rd
Croydon CR0, CR9 . . . . 61 A7
Forest Hill SE23. . . . . 23 C7
Benson's La RH12. . . . . . 199 C1
Bentall Sh Ctr The 10
KT2. . . . . 37 E7
Benthall Gdns CR8. . . . . . . 80 C2
Bentham Ave GU21 . . . . . . 70 C4
Bentinck Ho 4 TW10 . . . . 17 C5
Bentley Cl SW19 . . . . 20 A5
Bentley Copse GU15 . . . . . 66 B4
Bentley Ct 4 GU15. . . . . . . 65 D5
Bentley Dr KT13 . . . . 53 A2
Bentley Pl KT13. . . . . 53 A6
Benton's La SE27 . . . . 22 C4
Benton's Rise SE27 . . . . . . 22 D3
Bentsbrook Cl RH5. . . . . . 136 B3
Bentsbrook Cotts
RH5 . . . . 136 B3
Bentsbrook Pk RH5 . . . . . 136 B3
Bentsbrook Rd RH5 . . . . . 136 B3
Benwell Ct TW16 . . . . 35 A8
Benwell Rd GU24 . . . . 88 A8
Benwick Ct SE20. . . . . 43 C8
Benwood Ct SM1 . . . . 59 C7
Beomonds 5 KT16. . . . . . . 33 A2
Beomonds Row 4
KT16 . . . . 33 A2
Berberis Cl GU1 . . . . 109 C3
Bere Rd RG12. . . . . 27 E3
Beresford Ave
Tolworth KT5. . . . . 38 C2
Twickenham TW1. . . . . 6 C1
Beresford Cl GU16 . . . . 85 F6
Beresford Ct
Farnborough GU14 . . . . 85 C1
Kingston u T KT3 . . . . 38 C5
11 Twickenham TW1 . . . . 6 C1
Beresford Gdns TW4 . . . . . . 4 F2
Beresford Ho SE21. . . . . . . 22 E5
Beresford Rd
Belmont SM2. . . . . 58 F3
Dorking RH4 . . . . 136 B7
Kingston u T KT2 . . . . 37 F8
Kingston u T, Norbiton
KT3. . . . . 38 C5
Bergenia Ct GU24. . . . . 67 E6
Bergenia Ho TW13. . . . . . . 15 B7
Berkeley Ave TW4 . . . . 4 A5
Berkeley Cl
Crawley RH11 . . . . 200 E2
2 Kingston u T KT2 . . . . . . 17 E1
Stanwell TW19. . . . . 12 D6
Berkeley Cres GU16. . . . . . 86 A8
Berkeley Ct
Ashtead KT21 . . . . 75 F1
3 Croydon CR0 . . . . 61 D6
Oatlands Park KT13. . . . . . . 53 E8
Wallington SM6 . . . . 60 C6
Berkeley Dr
Cranbourne SL4. . . . . 9 B7
East Molesey KT8 . . . . 36 A6
Berkeley Gdns
Claygate KT10 . . . . 56 A4
Pyrford KT14 . . . . 70 F5
Walton-on-T KT12 . . . . 34 F2
Berkeley Ho 13 TW8 . . . . . . 6 D8
Berkeley Lo
Ashtead KT21 . . . . 95 D8
New Malden KT3 . . . . 38 E5
Berkeley Pl
Epsom KT18. . . . . 76 D4
Wimbledon SW19 . . . . 19 D2
Berkeley Prim Sch TW5. . . 4 D7
Berkeleys The KT22. . . . . . 94 E3
Berkeley Waye TW5. . . . . . . 4 D7
Berkley Cl TW2 . . . . 16 E5
Berkley Ct
Guildford GU1 . . . . 109 E1
10 Twickenham TW1 . . . . . . 17 A8
Berkley Mews TW16 . . . . . 35 C6
Berkshire Cl CR3 . . . . 100 D5
Berkshire Copse Rd
GU11 . . . . 104 E7
Berkshire Ho SE6. . . . . 24 A4
Berkshire Rd GU15. . . . . . . 65 F8
Berkshire Way
Bracknell RG12 . . . . 26 D6
Mitcham CR4 . . . . 41 E5
Bernard Ct GU15. . . . . 65 B4
Bernard Gdns 12 SW19 . . . 19 F3
Bernard Rd SM6 . . . . 60 B6
Bernel Dr CR0 . . . . 62 F7
Berne Rd CR7 . . . . 42 C4
Bernersh Cl GU47. . . . . 45 C1
Berney Ho BR3 . . . . 43 E4
Berney Rd CR0 . . . . 42 D2
Berridge Rd SE19. . . . . 22 E3
Berrington Dr KT24 . . . . . . 92 F3
Berrybank GU47 . . . . 64 E6
Berrycroft RG12 . . . . 27 D8
Berry Ct TW4 . . . . 4 F2
Berry La
Hersham KT12. . . . . 54 D5
Pirbright GU3. . . . . 88 C2
West Norwood SE21,
SE27 . . . . 22 D4
Woking GU22, GU3 . . . . 88 D4
BERRYLANDS 38 A3
Berrylands
Surbiton KT5 . . . . 37 F3
West Barnes SW20. . . . . 39 C5
Berrylands Ct 6 SM2 . . . . 59 B3
Berrylands Rd KT5. . . . . . . 37 F3
Berrylands Sta KT5 . . . . . . 38 B5
Berryman's La SE26. . . . . . 23 D4
Berry Meade KT21 . . . . 75 F2
Berrymeade Wlk 6
RH11 . . . . 200 E5
Berryscourt KT14 . . . . 71 D8
Berryscroft Ct TW18 . . . . . 13 C1
Berryscroft Rd TW18. . . . . 13 C1
Berry's La KT14. . . . . 71 D8
Berry Wlk KT21. . . . . 95 F8
Berstead Wlk 1
RH11 . . . . 200 F3
Bertal Rd SW17. . . . . 20 D4
Bertie Rd SE26 . . . . 23 D2
Bertram Cotts SW19 . . . . . 20 A1
Bertram Rd KT2 . . . . 18 A1
Bertrand Ho 11 SW16 . . . . 21 E5
Bert Rd CR7 . . . . 42 C4
Bertrum House Sch
SW17 . . . . 21 A6
Berwick Cl TW2 . . . . 16 A7
Berwick Ct KT4. . . . . 57 F8
Berwick Gdns SM1. . . . . . . 59 C7
Berwyn Ave TW3. . . . . 5 B6
Berwyn Rd
Mortlake SW14, TW10. . . . . . 7 B3
Streatham SE24. . . . . 22 B7
Beryl Harding Ho 10
SW20. . . . . 19 D1
Berystede KT2. . . . . 18 B1
Besley St SW16 . . . . 21 C2
Bessant Dr TW9 . . . . 7 B6
Bessborough Rd SW15. . . . 19 A7
Bessborough Wks KT8 . . . 35 F4
Beswick Gdns RG12. . . . . . 27 F8
Beta Rd
Chobham GU24 . . . . 49 F1
Farnborough GU14 . . . . 85 A5
Woking GU22. . . . . 70 B3
Beta Way TW20. . . . . 32 C8
Betchets Green Rd
RH5 . . . . 157 C6
Betchley Cl RH19 . . . . 185 E3
BETCHWORTH 137 E8
Betchworth Cl SM1 . . . . . . 59 D5
Betchworth Sta RH3 . . . . 116 E3
Betchworth The RH4. . . . 116 A1
Betchworth Way CR0 . . . . 63 C2
Betchworth Works
RH6. . . . . 180 D6
Bethany Waye TW14 . . . . . 14 E8
Bethel Cl GU9 . . . . 125 D6
Bethel La GU9 . . . . 125 D6
Bethersden Cl BR3. . . . . . . 23 F1
Bethesda Ct 6 SE20 . . . . . 23 C1
Bethlem Royal Hospl The
BR3. . . . . 44 A2
Bethune Cl RH10. . . . . 202 D5
Bethune Rd RH13 . . . . 217 E1
Betjeman Cl CR5. . . . . 79 F2
Betley Ct KT12. . . . . 54 B7
Betony Cl CR0 . . . . 43 D1
Betts Cl BR3 . . . . 43 E7
Betts Way
Crawley RH10 . . . . 181 D2
Long Ditton KT6. . . . . 37 B1
Penge SE20 . . . . 43 B8
Bettswood Ct 16 SE20. . . . 43 B8
Betula Cl CR8. . . . . 80 D4
Between Streets KT11. . . . 73 A5
Beulah Ave CR7. . . . . 42 C7
Beulah Cres CR7. . . . . 42 C7
Beulah Gr CR0. . . . . 42 C3
Beulah Hill SE19, SW16 . . . 22 C1
Beulah Inf Sch CR7 . . . . . . 42 C6
Beulah Jun Sch CR7 . . . . . 42 C6
Beulah Rd
Merton SW19 . . . . 19 F1
South Norwood CR7 . . . . . . 42 C6
Sutton SM1 . . . . 59 A6
Beulah Wlk CR3 . . . . 101 E7
Bevan Ct
Crawley RH11 . . . . 201 B1
Croydon CR0 . . . . 61 A5
22 Twickenham TW1 . . . . 6 D1
Bevan Gate RG42 . . . . 27 A8
Bevan Ho TW13. . . . . 15 A5
Bevan Pk KT17. . . . . 57 F1
Beverley Ave
Hounslow TW4. . . . . 4 F3
Wimbledon SW20 . . . . 38 F8
Beverley Cl
Addlestone KT15 . . . . 52 D5
Ash GU12. . . . . 105 F1
Chessington KT9 . . . . 56 C6
East Ewell KT17. . . . . 77 C8
Frimley GU15. . . . . 66 D6
Oatlands Park KT13. . . . . . . 53 E8
Beverley Cotts SW15. . . . . 18 E5
Beverley Cres GU14. . . . . . 84 F2
Beverley Ct
5 Belmont SM2 . . . . 59 A4
5 Hounslow TW4. . . . . 4 F3
Kingston u T SW20 . . . . 38 F8
Beverley Gdns
Barnes SW13. . . . . 7 F4
Beverley Gdns *continued*
2 North Cheam KT4. . . . . . 39 A1
Beverley Ho
Beckenham BR3. . . . . 24 C1
Catford BR1. . . . . 24 D3
Beverley Hts RH2 . . . . 118 B3
Beverley Hyrst 10 CR0. . . . 61 F8
Beverley La KT2 . . . . 18 E1
Beverley Lo 6 TW10. . . . . . . 6 E2
Beverley Mans 2 TW4 . . . . . 4 F3
Beverley Mews RH10. . . . 202 A5
Beverley Rd
Barnes SW13. . . . . 7 F4
Kenley CR3 . . . . 80 F2
Mitcham CR4 . . . . 41 D5
New Malden KT3 . . . . 39 A5
North Cheam KT4 . . . . 58 C8
Penge SE20 . . . . 43 B7
Sunbury TW16 . . . . 34 F8
Teddington KT1 . . . . 37 C8
Beverley Trad Est SM4 . . . 39 D2
Beverley Way
Kingston u T KT3, SW20,
KT2 . . . . 38 F8
Wimbledon KT3, SW20 . . . . 39 A6
Beverley Way Kingston Bypass KT3 . . . . 38 F8
Beverley Way (Kingston By Pass) KT3, SW20 . . . . . 39 A6
Beverstone Rd CR7 . . . . . . 42 B5
Bevill Allen Cl SW17 . . . . . 20 F3
Bevill Cl SE25. . . . . 43 A6
Bevington Rd BR3 . . . . 44 B7
Bevin Sq SW17 . . . . 20 F5
BEWBUSH 200 F3
Bewbush Com Prim Sch
RH11. . . . . 200 F3
Bewbush Dr RH11. . . . . . . 200 F3
Bewbush Manor
RH11 . . . . 200 E2
Bew Ct SE21. . . . . 23 A8
Bewley St SW19 . . . . 20 C2
Bewlys Rd SE27. . . . . 22 B3
Bexhill Cl TW13. . . . . 15 E6
Bexhill Rd
Forest Hill SE4. . . . . 23 F8
Mortlake SW14 . . . . 7 C4
Beynon Rd SM5. . . . . 59 F5
Bicester Rd TW9. . . . . 7 B4
Bickersteth Rd SW17. . . . . 20 F2
Bickley Ct
Crawley RH11 . . . . 201 A3
10 Wimbledon SW19. . . . . . 20 A1
Bickley St SW17 . . . . 20 F3
Bicknell Cl GU1. . . . . 109 C2
Bicknell Rd GU16 . . . . 65 E2
Bickney Way KT22 . . . . 94 C5
Bicknoller Cl SM2. . . . . 59 B1
Bidborough Cl 5 BR2. . . . . 44 F4
Biddulph Rd CR2 . . . . 61 C2
Bideford Cl
Farnborough GU14 . . . . 85 A7
Feltham TW13 . . . . 15 F5
Bideford Rd BR1. . . . . 24 F5
Bidhams Cres KT20 . . . . . . 97 C6
Bidmead Ct KT6 . . . . 56 E7
Bield The RH2 . . . . 139 A7
Bietigheim Way GU15. . . . . 65 C6
Big Common La RH1 . . . . 120 B3
Biggin Ave CR4. . . . . 40 F8
Biggin Cl RH11 . . . . 201 C4
BIGGIN HILL 83 E3
Biggin Hill SE19 . . . . 22 B1
Biggin Hill Airport
TN16. . . . . 83 D5
Biggin Hill Bsns Pk
TN16. . . . . 83 D4
Biggin Hill Cl KT2. . . . . 17 C3
Biggin Hill Jun & Inf Schs
TN16. . . . . 83 E3
Biggin Way SE19. . . . . 22 C1
Bigginwood Rd SW16 . . . . 42 B8
Bignor Cl RH12 . . . . 218 A7
Bilberry Cl RH11 . . . . 201 B3
Bilberry Manor SM2 . . . . . 59 C3
Bilbets RH12 . . . . 217 C3
Billesden Rd GU24 . . . . 87 D7
Billet Rd TW18, TW19 . . . . . 13 A5
Billhurst Cotts RH7 . . . . . 164 D4
Billingshurst Rd
RH12 . . . . 216 D3
Billington Ct RH19 . . . . . . 185 E2
Billinton Dr RH10 . . . . 202 B5
Billinton Hill CR0 . . . . 61 D8
Billockby Cl KT9 . . . . 56 F4
Billsley Ct SE25. . . . . 42 E5
Bilton Ind Est RG12 . . . . . . 26 E5
Binbury Row TW18. . . . . . . 12 E4
Bindon Gn SM4. . . . . 40 B5
Binfield Rd
Bracknell, Dowlesgreen
RG40. . . . . 25 F7
Bracknell, Priestwood
RG42. . . . . 27 A8
Byfleet KT14 . . . . 71 E7
South Croydon CR2 . . . . 61 F5
Binfields GU9. . . . . 125 C3
Bingham Cnr CR0. . . . . 43 A1
Bingham Dr
Knaphill GU21 . . . . 68 F1
Staines TW18. . . . . 13 D1
Bingham Rd CR0, CR9. . . . . 43 B1
Bingley Rd TW16 . . . . 15 A1
Binhams Lea GU8. . . . . . . 192 F5
Binhams Mdw GU8. . . . . . 192 F5
Binley Ho SW15. . . . . 7 F1
Binney Ct RH10. . . . . 182 E1
BINSCOMBE 150 D8
Binscombe Cres GU7. . . . . 150 E8
Binscombe La GU7. . . . . . 150 E7
Binstead Cl RH11 . . . . 201 B8
Binsted Dr GU17 . . . . 64 D5
Binton La GU10 . . . . 126 E3
Birchanger GU7 . . . . 150 E4
Birchanger Rd SE25. . . . . . 43 A4
Birch Ave
Caterham CR3 . . . . 100 D3
Leatherhead KT22. . . . . 94 F7
Birch Circ GU7 . . . . 150 F8
Birch Cl
Banstead SM7. . . . . 77 E5
Brentford TW8. . . . . 6 B7
Camberley GU15 . . . . 65 E8
Crawley Down RH10 . . . . . 204 C8
Hounslow TW3. . . . . 5 D5
New Haw KT15 . . . . 52 D2
Rowledge GU10. . . . . 146 A4
Send Marsh GU23 . . . . 90 F2
Teddington TW11. . . . . 17 A3
Woking GU21. . . . . 89 C8
Birchcroft Cl CR3 . . . . 100 C2
Birch Ct
Ashtead KT21 . . . . 75 D2
Chipstead CR5. . . . . 78 F1
Croydon CR0 . . . . 61 F8
Sutton SM1 . . . . 59 C6
9 Wallington SM6 . . . . 60 B6
Birchdale Cl KT14. . . . . 71 C8
Birch Dr GU17 . . . . 64 D3
Birchend Cl CR2 . . . . 61 D4
Birches Cl
Epsom KT18. . . . . 76 E4
Mitcham CR4 . . . . 40 F6
Birches Ind Est RH19. . . . 185 A3
Birches La GU5 . . . . 133 C2
Birches Rd RH12. . . . . 218 B5
Birches The
Blackwater GU17. . . . . 64 B5
5 Bromley BR2 . . . . 44 F5
Crawley RH10 . . . . 202 A7
East Horsley KT24. . . . . 92 E1
Farnborough GU14 . . . . 84 D4
South Norwood SE25. . . . . . 42 F7
Twickenham TW4. . . . . 15 F8
Woking GU22. . . . . 69 F1
Birchett Rd
Aldershot GU11. . . . . 105 A2
Farnborough GU14 . . . . 84 E6
Birchetts Cl 1 RG42 . . . . . 27 B8
Birchfield Cl
Addlestone KT15 . . . . 52 B6
Coulsdon CR5 . . . . 79 F3
Birchfield Gr KT17 . . . . 58 C1
Birchfields GU15. . . . . 65 C4
Birch Gn TW18 . . . . 13 A4
Birch Gr
Bracknell RG12 . . . . 27 C5
Cobham KT11. . . . . 73 D5
Guildford GU1 . . . . 109 C4
Kingswood KT20 . . . . 97 F3
Lewisham SE12 . . . . 24 F8
Upper Halliford TW17 . . . . . 34 E7
Woking GU22. . . . . 70 D4
BIRCH GREEN 13 A4
Birchgrove Ho TW9 . . . . 7 B7
BIRCH HILL 27 C2
Birch Hill CR0 . . . . 62 D5
Birch Hill Prim Sch
RG12. . . . . 27 B1
Birch Hill Rd RG12 . . . . 27 B2
Birch Ho
Farnborough GU14 . . . . 85 A7
Teddington TW11. . . . . 17 C1
Birchington Rd KT5. . . . . . 37 F2
Birch La
Purley CR8. . . . . 79 E8
West End GU24 . . . . 67 D7
Winkfield SL5. . . . . 28 A8
Birchlands Ave SW12 . . . . 20 F8
Birchlands Ct GU47 . . . . . . 45 E2
Birch Lea RH10 . . . . 182 A1
Birch Platt GU24. . . . . 67 D6
Birch Rd
Farncombe GU7. . . . . 151 A8
Feltham TW13 . . . . 15 D3
Headley Down GU35 . . . . . 187 B6
Windlesham GU20. . . . . 48 E4
Birch Side RG45 . . . . 45 A6
Birch Tree Ave BR4 . . . . . . 63 F6
Birch Tree Gdns
RH19 . . . . 185 B3
Birch Tree View GU18. . . . 48 A1
Birch Tree Way CR0. . . . . . 62 B8
Birch Vale KT11. . . . . 74 A6
Birch Way
Ash Vale GU12. . . . . 106 A7
Redhill RH1 . . . . 140 B7
Warlingham CR6 . . . . 81 E1
Birch Wlk
Mitcham CR4 . . . . 41 B8
West Byfleet KT14. . . . . 71 A7
Birchwood Ave
Beckenham BR3. . . . . 43 F5
Hackbridge SM6 . . . . 60 B7
Birchwood Cl
Crawley RH10 . . . . 202 C3
Horley RH6 . . . . 161 B4
Ifold RH14. . . . . 212 D3
Morden SM4 . . . . 40 B5
Birchwood Ct KT13 . . . . . . 53 C5
Birchwood Dr
Lightwater GU18 . . . . 48 C1
West Byfleet KT14. . . . . 71 A7

Birchwood Gr TW12 16 A2
Birchwood La
 Caterham CR3 100 B2
 Oxshott KT10, KT22 55 E1
Birchwood Rd
 Streatham SW17 21 B3
 West Byfleet KT14 71 A7
Birdham Cl RH11 201 B8
Birdhaven GU10 146 A6
Birdhurst CR3 100 F7
Birdhurst Ave CR2 61 D6
Birdhurst Ct SM6 60 C3
Birdhurst Gdns CR2 61 D6
Birdhurst Rd
 Mitcham SW19 20 E2
 South Croydon CR2 61 E5
Birdhurst Rise CR2 61 E5
Bird-In-Hand Pas SE23 23 C6
Bird Mews RG40 25 B6
Birds Gr GU21 68 B1
Birds Hill Dr KT22 74 D6
Birds Hill Rd KT22 74 D6
Birds Hill Rise KT22 74 D6
Birdswood Dr GU21 88 E7
Birdwell Ct CR2 61 D6
Bird Wlk TW2 15 F7
Birdwood Cl
 Selsdon CR2 81 D8
 Teddington TW11 16 E4
Birdwood Rd GU15 64 F6
Birdworld & Underwater World★ GU10 145 B3
Birkbeck Hill SE21 22 B7
Birkbeck Pl
 Sandhurst GU47 45 E1
 West Norwood SE21 22 C6
Birkbeck Rd
 Penge BR3 43 D7
 Wimbledon SW19 20 B2
Birkbeck Sta SE20 43 C6
Birkdale RG12 26 E2
Birkdale Ct SL5 29 C4
Birkdale Dr RH11 200 D5
Birkdale Gdns CR0 62 D6
Birkenhead Ave KT2 37 F8
Birkenholme Cl GU35 187 C4
Birkhall Rd SE6 24 D6
Birkheads Rd RH2 118 A2
Birkin Ct KT14 71 D8
Birkwood Cl SW12 21 D8
Birnam Cl GU23 91 A3
Birnham Ho TW1 17 C8
Birtley Ctyd GU5 152 B3
BIRTLEY GREEN 152 B3
Birtley Mews GU5 152 A3
Birtley Rd GU5 152 B4
Birtley Rise GU5 152 A5
Birtway Ct 15 SM1 59 C6
Biscoe Cl TW5 5 A8
Bisenden Rd CR0 61 E8
Bisham Cl
 Carshalton CR4 40 F1
 Crawley RH10 202 D3
Bishams Ct CR3 100 F3
Bishop Challoner Sch BR2 44 D7
Bishopdale RG12 27 A5
Bishop David Brown Sch The GU21 70 D6
Bishop Duppa's Almshouses 8 TW10 6 E2
Bishop Duppas Pk TW17 34 E2
Bishop Fox Way KT8 35 F5
Bishop Gilpin CE Prim Sch SW19 19 F3
Bishop Parkhurst GU1 110 B3
Bishop Perrin CE Prim Sch TW2 16 B7
Bishopric RH12 217 B2
Bishopric Ct 3 RH12 217 B2
Bishops Cl
 Richmond TW10 17 D5
 Sutton SM1 59 A7
Bishop's Cl CR5 80 A1
Bishop's Cotts RH3 116 B2
Bishopscourt 3 CR0 61 F8
Bishops Ct
 1 Ashford TW16 14 F1
 Guildford GU2 130 C7
 Horsham RH12 217 C1
 North Ascot SL5 8 F2
 Richmond TW9 6 E4
Bishops Dr
 East Bedfont TW14 3 D1
 Wokingham RG40 25 C7
Bishopsford Com Sch SM4 40 D3
Bishopsford Ho SM4 40 E3
Bishopsford Rd SM4 40 D3
BISHOPSGATE 10 F4
Bishopsgate Rd TW20 11 B5
Bishopsgate Sch TW20 11 A5
Bishops Gr
 Hampton TW12 15 F4
 Windlesham GU20 48 C4
Bishop's Hall KT1 37 D7
Bishops Hill KT12 35 A2
Bishops Ho 6 GU7 150 D4
Bishop's La SL4 8 B7
Bishop's Mead GU9 125 B2
Bishopsmead Cl
 East Horsley KT24 112 E7
Bishopsmead Cl *continued*
 Epsom KT19 57 D1
Bishopsmead Ct KT19 57 E1
Bishopsmead Dr KT24 112 F6
Bishopsmead Par KT24 112 F6
Bishops Park Rd SW16 41 E8
Bishop's Pl SM1 59 C5
Bishops Rd GU9 125 B7
Bishop's Rd CR0 42 B2
Bishops Sq GU6 174 F3
Bishopsthorpe Rd SE26 23 D4
Bishopstone Wlk RH11 201 C1
Bishop Sumner Dr GU9 125 C6
Bishops Way TW20 12 D2
Bishops Wlk CR0, CR9 62 E5
Bishops Wood GU21 68 F2
Bishop Thomas Grant RC Sec Sch SW16 21 F3
Bishop Wand CE Sch The TW16 34 F7
BISLEY 68 B3
Bisley CE Prim Sch GU24 68 A3
Bisley Cl KT4 39 C1
Bisley Ho SW19 19 D6
Bison Ct TW14 15 B8
Bitmead Cl RH11 200 E5
Bittams La KT16 51 E6
Bittern Cl
 Aldershot GU11 126 A7
 Crawley RH11 200 D5
 Sandhurst GU47 64 D8
Bitterne Dr GU21 69 A2
Bittoms The KT1 37 D6
Blackberry Cl
 Guildford GU1 109 B4
 Upper Halliford TW17 34 E5
Blackberry Farm Cl TW5 4 E7
Blackberry La RH7 185 E8
Blackberry Rd RH19, RH7 185 D8
Blackbird Cl GU47 64 D8
Blackbird Hill RH10 204 C5
Blackborough Cl RH2 118 C1
Blackborough Rd RH2 118 D1
Blackbridge Ct RH12 217 A2
Blackbridge La RH12 217 A1
Blackbridge Rd GU22 89 D7
BLACKBROOK 136 E2
Blackbrook Rd
 Dorking RH5 136 E2
 South Holmwood RH5 157 E8
Blackburn The KT23 93 F3
Blackburn Trad Est TW19 2 F1
Blackburn Way
 Godalming GU7 151 A5
 Hounslow TW4 4 E2
Blackbush Cl SM2 59 B3
Blackcap Cl RH11 201 C4
Blackcap Pl GU47 64 E8
Black Cnr RH10 182 D4
Black Dog Wlk RH10 201 E8
Blackdown Ave GU22 70 E4
Blackdown Cl GU22 70 D3
Blackdown Rd GU16 86 C8
Blackenham Rd SW17 20 F4
Blackett Cl TW18 32 F7
Blackett Rd RH10 202 C5
Blackfold Rd RH10 202 A5
Blackford Cl CR2 61 B2
Blackham Ho SW19 19 E2
BLACKHEATH 131 F1
Blackheath RH10 202 D8
Blackheath Gr GU5 152 B8
Blackheath La
 Albury GU5 132 B3
 Wonersh GU5, GU4 152 C8
Blackheath Rd GU9 125 A7
Blackhills KT10 55 A2
Blackhorse La
 Croydon CR0 43 A2
 Lower Kingswood KT20, RH2 118 C7
Blackhorse Rd GU21, GU22 88 E6
Black Horse Way RH12 217 C2
Black Lake Cl TW20 32 A8
Blacklands Cres RH18 206 F2
Blacklands Mdw RH1 119 E2
Blacklands Rd SE6 24 C4
Blackman Gdns GU11 126 B8
Blackman's La CR6 82 F5
Blackmeadows RG12 27 C3
Blackmoor Cl SL5 28 D7
Blackmoor Wood SL5 28 D7
Blackmore Cres GU21 70 C5
Blackmore Ho SE23 23 F7
Blackmore's Gr TW11 17 A2
Blackness La GU22 89 E8
BLACKNEST 30 B6
Blacknest Cotts GU8 192 E3
Blacknest Gate Rd SL5 30 B6
Blacknest Rd GU25, SL5 30 E6
Black Pond La GU10 146 C6
Black Potts Copse GU22 89 B8
Black Prince Cl KT14 71 F5
Blackshaw Rd SW17 20 D3
Blacksmith Cl KT21 95 F8
Blacksmith La GU4 131 D3
Blacksmiths Hill CR2 81 B6
Blacksmiths La KT16 33 A2
Blacksmith's La TW18 33 C6
Blackstone Cl
 Farnborough GU14 84 D6
 Reigate RH1 139 E8
Blackstone Hill RH1, RH2 118 E1
Blackstone Ho SE21 22 E5
Blackstroud La E GU18, GU24 67 E8
Blackstroud La W GU18 67 D8
Blackthorn Cl
 Crawley RH11 181 C1
 Horsham RH13 218 A2
 Reigate RH2 139 C7
Blackthorn Cres GU14 84 F8
Blackthorn Ct
 Heston TW5 4 E7
 7 West Norwood SW16 22 A3
Blackthorn Dr GU18 67 B7
Blackthorne Ave CR0 43 C1
Blackthorne Cres SL3 1 E5
Blackthorne Ct TW15 14 C1
Blackthorne Rd
 Great Bookham KT23 94 C1
 Poyle SL3 1 E4
Blackthorn Pl GU1 109 C4
Blackthorn Rd
 Biggin Hill TN16 83 E3
 Reigate RH2 139 C7
BLACKWATER 64 D5
Blackwater Cl GU12 106 A1
Blackwater La RH10 202 D6
Blackwater Pk GU12 105 E1
Blackwater Sta GU17 64 E4
Blackwater Trad Est GU12 126 D8
Blackwater Way GU12 126 D8
BLACKWELL 185 E3
Blackwell Ave GU2 108 D1
Blackwell Farm Cotts GU3 129 C8
Blackwell Farm Rd RH19 185 F3
Blackwell Hollow RH19 185 F2
Blackwell Prim Sch RH19 185 E3
Blackwell Rd RH19 185 F2
Blackwood Cl KT14 71 C7
Bladen Cl KT13 53 E4
Blades Cl KT22 95 D7
Bladon Cl GU1 110 A2
Bladon Ct
 Beckenham BR2 44 E7
 Streatham SW16 21 E2
Blagdon Rd KT3 38 F5
Blagdon Wlk TW11 17 C2
Blair Ave KT10 55 C8
Blair Ct
 Beckenham BR3 44 B8
 Carshalton SM5 59 F7
 Catford SE6 24 F7
Blairderry Rd SW2 21 E6
Blaise Cl GU14 85 D3
Blake Cl
 Carshalton SM5 40 E1
 Crawley RH10 201 F2
 Crowthorne RG45 45 C4
 Wokingham RG40 25 E8
Blake Ct CR0 61 B5
Blakeden Dr KT10 55 F4
Blakehall Rd SM5 59 F4
Blake Ho BR3 24 B2
Blake Mews 15 TW9 7 A6
Blakemore Rd
 Streatham SW16 21 E5
 Thornton Heath CR7 41 F4
Blakeney Ave BR3 43 F8
Blakeney Cl KT19 76 D8
Blakeney Rd BR3 43 F8
Blake Rd
 Croydon CR0 61 E8
 Mitcham CR4 40 E6
Blakes Ave KT3 38 F3
Blake's Gn BR4 44 C1
Blakes La KT3 38 F4
Blake's La GU4 111 F3
Blakes Terr KT3 39 A4
Blakewood Cl TW13 15 C4
Blakewood Ct SE20 23 B1
Blanchard Ho 13 TW1 6 D1
Blanchards Hill GU4 109 E8
Blanchland Rd SM4 40 B4
Blanchman's Rd CR6 81 E1
Blandfield Rd SW12 21 A8
Blandford Ave
 Penge BR3 43 E7
 Twickenham TW2 16 B7
Blandford Cl
 Wallington CR0 60 E7
 Woking GU22 70 B2
Blandford Rd
 Penge BR3 43 D7
 Teddington TW11 16 E3
Blane's La SL5 28 C3
Blanford Mews RH2 118 D1
Blanford Rd RH2 139 C8
Blanks La RH5, RH6 159 B2
Blashford St SE13 24 D8
Blatchford Cl RH13 217 F3
Blatchford Ct 6 KT12 35 A1
Blatchford Rd RH13 217 F3
Blays Cl TW20 11 C2
Blay's La TW20 11 B2
Blean Gr SE20 23 C1
Blegborough Rd SW16 21 C2
Blencarn Cl GU21 68 F3
Blendworth Point 4 SW15 19 B7
Blenheim 26 SW19 19 D7
Blenheim Bsns Ctr CR4 40 F7
Blenheim Cl
 Crawley RH10 182 D1
 East Grinstead RH19 186 A3
 Tongham GU10 126 E7
 Wallington SM6 60 C3
 West Barnes SW20 39 C6
 West Byfleet KT14 70 F6
Blenheim Cres
 Hale GU9 125 A5
 South Croydon CR2 61 C3
Blenheim Ct
 Bromley BR2 44 F5
 Egham TW18 12 D4
 Farnborough GU14 85 D2
 8 Hampton TW12 36 A8
 Richmond TW9 6 F4
 South Norwood SE19 42 E8
 Sutton SM2 59 C4
Blenheim Ctr TW3 5 B4
Blenheim Ctr SE26 23 D1
Blenheim Fields RH18 206 E3
Blenheim Gdns
 Kingston u T KT2 18 B1
 Sanderstead CR2 81 A7
 Wallington SM6 60 C3
 Woking GU22 89 B8
Blenheim High Sch KT19 57 D1
Blenheim Ho TW3 5 A4
Blenheim Park Rd CR2 61 C2
Blenheim Pk GU11 105 C7
Blenheim Pl TW11 16 F3
Blenheim Rd
 Epsom KT19 76 E8
 Farnborough GU14 105 B7
 Horsham RH12 217 D4
 Penge SE20 23 C1
 Sutton SM1 59 B7
 West Barnes SW20 39 C6
Blenheim Way TW7 6 A6
Blenhiem Pl GU15 65 C3
Bleriot Rd TW5 4 C7
BLETCHINGLEY 120 D2
Bletchingley Cl RH1 119 C6
Bletchingley Rd
 Godstone RH9 121 B4
 Merstham RH1 119 E6
 Nutfield RH1 120 A2
Bletchingly Cl CR7 42 B5
Bletchmore Cl UB3 3 D8
Blewburton Wlk RG12 27 E5
Blewfield GU7 150 F2
Bligh Cl RH10 201 F4
Bligh Ho 4 SE27 22 C4
Blighton La GU10 126 E3
Blincoe Cl SW19 19 D6
Blind Cnr SE25 43 B5
Blindley Ct RH7 163 E8
BLINDLEY HEATH 163 D8
Blindley Rd RH10 182 D1
Bloggs Way GU6 174 D3
Blomfield Dale RG42 26 D7
Blondell Cl UB7 2 D8
Bloomfield Cl GU21 68 E1
Bloomfield Rd KT1 37 E6
Bloom Gr SE27 22 B5
Bloomhall Rd SE19 22 D3
Bloomsbury Cl KT19 57 D1
Bloomsbury Ct
 Cranford TW5 4 B6
 Guildford GU1 130 F7
Bloomsbury Way GU17 64 D3
Bloor Cl RH12 217 D7
Blossom Cl CR2 61 F5
Blossom Waye TW5 4 E7
Blount Ave RH19 185 C1
Bloxham Cres TW12 35 F8
Bloxham Rd GU6 175 A3
Bloxworth Cl
 9 Bracknell RG12 27 F5
 Wallington SM6 60 C7
Blue Anchor Alley 7 TW9 6 E3
Blue Ball La TW20 11 F3
Blue Barn La KT13 72 A8
Bluebell Cl
 Carshalton CR4 41 B1
 Crawley RH11 201 B3
 East Grinstead RH19 185 B1
 Forest Hill SE26 22 F4
 Horsham RH12 217 E5
Bluebell Ct GU22 89 D8
Bluebell Hill RG12 27 E8
Bluebell La KT24 112 E6
Bluebell Mews GU15 65 D7
Bluebell Rise GU18 67 B8
Blueberry Gdns CR5 79 F3
Bluebird Ho RH6 160 D1
Blue Cedars SM7 77 D5
Blue Cedars Pl KT11 73 D7
Blue Coat Wlk RG12 27 D4
Bluefield Cl TW12 16 A3
Bluegates
 Stoneleigh KT17 58 A3
 Wimbledon SW19 19 E3
Bluehouse Gdns RH8 123 A7
Bluehouse La RH8 122 F7
Blue Leaves Ave CR5 99 D6
Blueprint Apartments SW12 21 B8
Blue Ridges Pk RH5 178 A3
Blue Sch The TW7 6 A4
Bluethroat Cl GU47 64 E8
Bluff Cove GU11 105 C3
Blundel La KT11 74 B4
Blundell Ave RH6 160 F4
Blunden Rd GU14 84 F5
Blunt Rd CR0 61 D5
Blunts Ave UB7 3 A7
Blunts Way RH12 217 C3
Blyth Cl TW1 5 F1
Blythe Cl SE23 23 F8
Blythe Hill SE23, SE6 23 F8
Blythe Hill La SE23, SE6 23 F7
Blythe Ho RG12 26 F3
Blytheswood Pl SW16 21 F4
Blythe Vale SE23, SE6 23 F7
Blythewood 9 SM1 59 D5
Blythewood La SL5 28 E7
Blyth Rd BR1 44 F8
Blythwood Dr GU16 65 D2
Blythwood Pk 12 BR1 44 F8
Blyton Ct BR3 24 A2
Blytons The RH19 185 B1
Board School Rd GU21 69 F3
Boar Hill RH5 135 E1
Bocketts Farm Pk★ KT22 94 F2
Bockhampton Rd KT2 17 F1
Boddicott Cl SW19 19 E6
Bodens Ride SL5 28 F1
Bodiam Cl RH10 202 C6
Bodiam Ct
 Carshalton SM1 59 D6
 Hayes BR2 44 F5
Bodiam Rd SW16 21 D1
Bodicea Mews TW4 5 A1
Bodley Cl KT3 38 E4
Bodley Manor Way SE24 22 A8
Bodley Rd KT3 38 E4
Bodmin Gr SM4 40 B4
Bodmin St SW18 20 A7
Bodnant Gdns SW20 39 B6
Bofors Rd GU14 105 A8
Bog La RG12 28 A5
Bognor Rd RH12, RH5 197 D4
Bois Hall Rd KT15 52 D5
Bolderwood Way BR4 63 B8
Bolding House La GU24 67 F7
Boleyn Ave KT17 58 B1
Boleyn Cl
 Crawley RH10 202 D3
 Egham TW18 12 E3
Boleyn Ct
 East Molesey KT8 36 D5
 5 Knaphill GU21 68 C1
 11 Redhill RH1 119 A2
Boleyn Dr KT8 35 F6
Boleyn Gdns BR4 63 B8
Boleyn Lo SW19 19 D3
Boleyn Wlk KT22 94 F7
Bolingbroke Gr SW11 20 F8
Bolingbroke Ho
 Beckenham BR3 43 E4
 Catford BR3 24 B3
Bolney Ct
 Crawley RH11 200 F3
 Kingston u T KT6 37 C4
Bolsover Gr RH1 119 E6
Bolstead Rd CR4 41 B8
Bolters La SM7 78 A4
Bolters Rd RH6 161 A5
Bolters Rd S RH6 160 F6
Bolton Cl
 Chessington KT9 56 E4
 Penge SE20 43 A7
Bolton Dr SM4 40 D2
Bolton Gdns
 Bromley BR1 24 F2
 Teddington TW11 17 A2
Bolton Rd
 Chessington KT9 56 E4
 Chiswick W4 7 C7
 Crawley RH10 202 C2
Boltons Cl GU22 71 A3
Bolton's La
 Harlington UB3 3 B7
 Pyrford GU22 71 A3
Bomer Cl UB7 3 A7
Bonaly Ho RH8 122 C4
Bonchurch Cl SM2 59 B3
Bond Gdns SM6 60 C6
Bond Prim Sch CR4 40 F7
Bond Rd
 Mitcham CR4 40 F7
 Surbiton KT6 56 F8
 Warlingham CR6 81 E1
Bond's La RH5 136 B1
Bond St TW20 11 C3
Bond Way RG12 27 B8
Bonehurst Rd RH1, RH6 161 A7
Bone Mill La RH9 121 E1
Bones La RH6, RH7 163 B2
Bonner Hill Rd KT1 38 A6
Bonners Cl GU22 89 F5
Bonnetts La RH11 181 A3
Bonnington Ho 11 SM2 59 B4
Bonnys Rd RH2 138 D8
Bonser Rd TW1 16 F6
Bonsey Cl GU22 89 E6
Bonsey La GU22 89 E6
Bonsey's La GU24, KT16 50 F2
Bonsor Dr KT20 97 E5

Bonus Pastor RC Sch BR1 . . . 24 E4
Bonville Rd BR1 . . . 24 F3
Bookham Ct
 Little Bookham KT23 . . . 93 F4
 Mitcham CR4 . . . 40 D6
Bookham Gr 2 KT23 . . . 94 B1
Bookham Grove Ho 3 KT23 . . . 94 B1
Bookham Ind Est KT23 . . . 93 F3
Bookham Ind Pk KT23 . . . 93 F4
Bookham Rd KT11 . . . 93 D7
Bookham Sta KT23 . . . 93 F4
Bookhurst Hill GU6 . . . 175 A4
Bookhurst Rd GU6 . . . 175 B4
Boole Hts RG12 . . . 27 A4
Boothby Ho 2 SW16 . . . 21 C3
Booth Dr TW18 . . . 13 D2
Booth Ho 9 TW8 . . . 6 C7
Booth Rd
 Crawley RH11 . . . 200 E3
 Croydon CR0, CR9 . . . 61 B8
Boothroyd Ho TW7 . . . 5 F4
Booth Way RH13 . . . 217 E3
Borage Cl 4 RH11 . . . 201 A2
Border Chase RH10 . . . 183 A2
Border Cres SE26 . . . 23 B3
Border Ct RH19 . . . 185 F4
Border End GU27 . . . 207 D6
Border Gate CR4 . . . 40 F8
Border Gdns CR0 . . . 63 B6
Border Mews GU26 . . . 188 D3
Border Rd
 Forest Hill SE26 . . . 23 B3
 Haslemere GU27 . . . 207 D6
Bordesley Rd SM4 . . . 40 B5
Bordeston Ct 11 TW8 . . . 6 C7
Bordon Wlk 6 SW15 . . . 19 A8
Boreen The GU35 . . . 187 B5
Borelli Mews GU9 . . . 125 C2
Borelli Yd GU9 . . . 125 C2
Borers Arms Rd RH10 . . . 183 C3
Borers Cl RH10 . . . 183 C4
Borers Yard Cotts RH10 . . . 183 C3
Borers Yard Ind Est RH10 . . . 183 C3
Borland Rd TW11 . . . 17 B1
Borough Grange CR2 . . . 81 A7
Borough Hill CR0, CR9 . . . 61 B7
Borough Rd
 Godalming GU7 . . . 150 D5
 Hounslow TW7 . . . 5 F6
 7 Kingston u T KT2 . . . 18 A1
 Mitcham CR4 . . . 40 E7
 Tatsfield TN16 . . . 103 D6
Borough The
 Brockham RH3 . . . 137 A8
 Farnham GU9 . . . 125 B2
Borrowdale Cl
 Crawley RH11 . . . 201 B4
 Sanderstead CR2 . . . 80 F6
 3 Thorpe Lea TW20 . . . 12 B1
Borrowdale Dr CR2 . . . 80 F7
Borrowdale Gdns GU15 . . . 66 D4
Bosbury Rd SE6 . . . 24 C5
Boscombe Cl TW20 . . . 32 C8
Boscombe Gdns SW16 . . . 21 E2
Boscombe Ho CR0 . . . 42 D1
Boscombe Rd
 Merton SW19 . . . 40 B8
 Mitcham SW17 . . . 21 A2
 North Cheam KT4 . . . 39 D1
Bosham Rd RH10 . . . 202 C3
Boshers Gdns TW20 . . . 11 F2
Bosman Dr GU20 . . . 48 B6
Bostock Ave RH12 . . . 218 A5
Bostock Ho TW5 . . . 5 A8
Boston Ct
 South Norwood SE25 . . . 42 F5
 Sutton SM2 . . . 59 C3
Boston Gdns W4 . . . 7 E8
Boston Manor Rd TW8 . . . 6 C8
Boston Rd CR0 . . . 42 A3
Boswell Ho 5 SW16 . . . 21 C3
Boswell Rd
 Crawley RH10 . . . 201 E3
 Thornton Heath CR7 . . . 42 C5
Boswood Ct TW4 . . . 4 F4
Botany Hill GU10 . . . 126 D1
Botery's Cross RH1 . . . 120 B2
Bothwell Rd CR0 . . . 63 C1
Bothy The GU22 . . . 70 F2
Botsford Rd SW20 . . . 39 E7
Boucher Cl TW11 . . . 16 F3
Boughton Ave BR2 . . . 44 F2
Boughton Hall Ave GU23 . . . 90 F3
Bouldish Farm Rd SL5 . . . 29 A5
Boulevard The
 Crawley RH10 . . . 201 E6
 4 Upper Tooting SW17 . . . 21 A6
Boullen Ct SM1 . . . 59 C6
Boulogne Rd CR0 . . . 42 C3
Boulters Ho RG12 . . . 27 E5
Boulters Rd 2 GU11 . . . 105 B1
Boulthurst Way RH8 . . . 123 B3
Boundaries Mans 3 SW12 . . . 21 A7
Boundaries Rd
 Feltham TW13 . . . 15 C7
 Upper Tooting SW12, SW17 . . . 21 A7
Boundary Bsns Ct CR4 . . . 40 D6
Boundary Bsns Ctr GU21 . . . 70 A4
Boundary Cl
 Crawley RH10 . . . 201 E7
 Kingston u T KT1 . . . 38 B6
 Penge SE20 . . . 43 A7
Boundary Cotts GU4 . . . 132 A4
Boundary Ho
 6 Balham SW12 . . . 21 B7
 Twickenham TW1 . . . 6 B2
Boundary Pk KT13 . . . 53 E7
Boundary Point CR3 . . . 100 C5
Boundary Rd
 Crawley RH10 . . . 201 E7
 Dockenfield GU10 . . . 166 D7
 Farnborough GU14 . . . 85 C2
 Grayshott GU26 . . . 188 D3
 Mitcham SW19 . . . 20 D2
 Rowledge GU10 . . . 145 E2
 Staines TW15 . . . 13 C3
 Wallington SM5, SM6 . . . 60 A3
 Woking GU21 . . . 70 A4
Boundary Rd E KT15 . . . 52 B2
Boundary Rd N KT15 . . . 52 B2
Boundary Rd W KT15 . . . 52 B2
Boundary Way
 Addington CR0 . . . 63 A5
 Woking GU21 . . . 70 A4
Boundfield Rd SE6 . . . 24 E6
BOUNDSTONE . . . 146 A5
Boundstone Cl GU10 . . . 146 B5
Boundstone Rd GU10 . . . 146 A4
Bourbon Ho SE6 . . . 24 C4
Bourdon Rd SE20 . . . 43 C7
Bourg-de-Peage Ave RH19 . . . 186 A1
Bourke Hill CR5 . . . 78 F1
Bourley La GU10 . . . 104 A2
Bourley Rd
 Aldershot GU11 . . . 104 C2
 Crondall GU10 . . . 104 C2
Bourne Ave KT16 . . . 33 A6
Bourne Bsns Pk KT15 . . . 52 E6
Bourne Cl
 Chilworth GU4 . . . 131 B3
 Hinchley Wood KT7 . . . 55 F8
 Hounslow TW7 . . . 5 E4
 West Byfleet KT14 . . . 71 B6
Bourne Com Sch The GU10 . . . 146 D6
Bourne Ct
 Aldershot GU11 . . . 126 A8
 Caterham CR3 . . . 101 A4
 Chiswick W4 . . . 7 C8
 1 Purley CR8 . . . 80 A8
 West Byfleet KT14 . . . 71 E6
Bourne Dene GU10 . . . 146 A5
Bourne Dr CR4 . . . 40 D7
Bournefield Rd CR3 . . . 81 A1
Bourne Firs GU10 . . . 146 D5
Bourne Gr
 Ashtead KT21 . . . 95 D8
 Farnham GU10 . . . 146 E7
Bourne Grove Cl GU10 . . . 146 E7
Bourne Grove Dr GU10 . . . 146 E7
Bourne Hall Mus* KT17 . . . 57 F2
Bourne Ho 6 TW15 . . . 14 A3
Bourne Hts GU9 . . . 146 C8
Bourne La CR3 . . . 100 D6
Bourne Lo CR3 . . . 100 F3
Bourne Mdw TW20 . . . 32 B5
Bourne Mill Bsns Pk GU9 . . . 125 E3
Bournemouth Ct SM1 . . . 59 C5
Bournemouth Rd SW19 . . . 40 A8
Bourne Park Cl CR8 . . . 80 E3
Bourne Rd
 Farncombe GU7 . . . 150 F7
 Merstham RH1 . . . 119 C5
 Virginia Water GU25 . . . 31 D4
 Woodham KT15 . . . 52 B2
Bourneside GU25 . . . 31 A2
Bourneside Gdns SE6 . . . 24 C3
Bourneside Rd KT15 . . . 52 D5
Bourne St CR0, CR9 . . . 61 B8
Bourne Vale BR2 . . . 44 F1
Bournevale Rd SW16 . . . 21 E4
Bourne View CR8 . . . 80 D4
Bourne Way
 Addlestone KT15 . . . 52 C5
 Cheam SM1 . . . 58 F5
 Coney Hall BR2, BR4 . . . 63 F8
 West Ewell KT19 . . . 57 C6
 Woking GU22 . . . 89 D5
Bournewood Pk GU10 . . . 146 E7
Bourns Ct RH13 . . . 217 E3
Bournville Rd SE13, SE6 . . . 24 A8
Bousley Rise KT16 . . . 51 D4
Bouverie Ct SW16 . . . 21 E3
Bouverie Gdns CR8 . . . 79 F5
Bouverie Rd CR5 . . . 79 A1
Boveney Ho RG12 . . . 27 E5
Boveney Rd SE23 . . . 23 D8
Bovey Ho 3 RH1 . . . 119 A3
Bovill Rd SE23 . . . 23 D8
Bovingdon Sq CR4 . . . 41 E5
Bowater Gdns TW16 . . . 35 C7
Bowater Rd RH10 . . . 202 C3
Bowater Ridge KT13 . . . 53 D1
Bow Cnr 1 TW2 . . . 16 E6
Bowden Cl TW14 . . . 14 E7
Bowden Rd SL5 . . . 29 D4
Bowen Dr SE21 . . . 22 E5
Bowen Way CR5 . . . 99 D5
Bower Ct GU22 . . . 70 B3
Bower Hill Cl RH1 . . . 140 E6
Bower Hill La RH1 . . . 140 D7
Bowerland La RH7 . . . 164 E7
Bower Rd GU10 . . . 146 A5
Bowers Cl GU4 . . . 110 A6
Bowers Farm Dr GU4 . . . 110 B5
Bowers La GU4 . . . 110 A6
Bowers Pl RH10 . . . 204 B8
Bowers The RG40 . . . 25 A1
Bowes Cl RH13 . . . 217 E3
Bowes Lyon Ho 2 TW10 . . . 17 C5
Bowes Rd
 Egham TW18 . . . 12 E2
 Walton-on-T KT12 . . . 54 B8
Bowie Cl SW4 . . . 21 D8
Bowland Dr RG12 . . . 27 E2
Bowley Cl SE19 . . . 22 F2
Bowley La SE19 . . . 22 F3
BOWLHEAD GREEN . . . 169 E1
Bowlhead Green Rd GU8 . . . 170 B1
Bowling Green Cl SW19 . . . 19 B8
Bowling Green Ct GU16 . . . 85 E7
Bowling Green La RH12 . . . 217 D3
Bowling Green Rd GU24 . . . 49 E2
Bowlings The GU15 . . . 65 C6
Bowman Ct RH10 . . . 201 D7
Bowman Mews SW18 . . . 19 F7
Bowmans Lea SE23 . . . 23 C8
Bowman's Mdw SM6 . . . 60 B7
Bowness Cl 7 RH11 . . . 200 D5
Bowness Cres SW15 . . . 18 E3
Bowness Dr TW4 . . . 4 E3
Bowness Rd SE6 . . . 24 B8
Bowring Ho GU7 . . . 150 F6
Bowsley Ct TW13 . . . 15 A6
Bowsprit The KT11 . . . 73 C4
Bowyer Cres RG40 . . . 25 C8
Bowyer Ho CR4 . . . 40 E6
Bowyers Cl KT21 . . . 75 F1
Bowyer Wlk SL5 . . . 28 E8
Boxall Rd SE21 . . . 22 E8
Boxall's Gr GU11 . . . 126 A8
Boxall's La GU11 . . . 126 A7
Boxall Wlk RH13 . . . 217 D1
Box Cl RH11 . . . 201 C1
Boxford Cl CR2 . . . 81 D7
Boxford Ridge RG12 . . . 27 B6
Boxgrove Ave GU1 . . . 110 A3
Boxgrove La GU1 . . . 110 B2
Boxgrove Prim Sch GU1 . . . 110 B2
Boxgrove Rd GU1 . . . 110 A2
BOX HILL . . . 116 A4
Box Hill Ctry Pk* KT20 . . . 115 D3
Boxhill Farm Barns RH4 . . . 115 E2
Boxhill Rd RH4 . . . 115 E3
Box Hill Sch RH5 . . . 115 B8
Boxhill Way RH3 . . . 137 B5
Boxhill & Westhumble Sta RH5 . . . 115 B4
Boxhurst RH4 . . . 115 E3
Box La RH19 . . . 206 E6
Boxley Rd SM4, SW19 . . . 40 C5
Box Ridge Ave CR8 . . . 79 F7
Box Tree Wlk RH1 . . . 139 C7
Boxwood Way CR6 . . . 81 D2
Boyce Ho SW16 . . . 21 C3
Boyd Cl KT2 . . . 18 A1
Boyd Ct RG42 . . . 27 A8
Boyd Rd SW19 . . . 20 D2
Boyland Rd BR1 . . . 24 F3
Boyle Farm Rd KT7 . . . 37 A3
Brabazon Ave SM6 . . . 60 E3
Brabazon Rd TW5 . . . 4 D7
Brabham Ct KT4 . . . 58 B8
Braboeuf Manor (Coll of Law) GU2 . . . 130 C5
Brabon Rd GU14 . . . 84 F5
Brabourne Cl 7 SE19 . . . 22 E3
Brabourne Ct SM2 . . . 59 B4
Brabourne Rise BR3 . . . 44 D4
Brabrook Ct SM6 . . . 60 B5
Bracebridge GU15 . . . 65 A5
Bracewood Gdns CR0 . . . 61 F7
Bracken Ave
 Balham SW12 . . . 21 A8
 West Wickham CR0 . . . 63 B7
Bracken Bank SL5 . . . 28 C8
Bracken Cl
 Ashford TW16 . . . 14 F2
 Copthorne RH10 . . . 183 B2
 Crawley RH10 . . . 201 F8
 Little Bookham KT23 . . . 93 F3
 Twickenham TW2 . . . 16 A8
 Woking GU22 . . . 69 F1
 Wonersh GU5 . . . 152 B6
Brackendale KT1 . . . 38 B7
Brackendale Cl
 Frimley GU15 . . . 65 E3
 Hounslow TW5 . . . 5 B6
Brackendale Ct 2 BR3 . . . 24 A1
Brackendale Rd GU15 . . . 65 D4
Brackendene GU12 . . . 106 C3
Brackendene Cl GU21 . . . 70 A4
Bracken End TW7 . . . 5 D2
Bracken Gr RH12 . . . 218 B5
Brackenhill KT11 . . . 74 B7
Bracken Hill Cl 7 BR1 . . . 44 F8
Bracken Hill La BR1 . . . 44 F8
Brackenlea GU7 . . . 150 D7
Bracken Path KT18 . . . 76 B6
Brackens BR3 . . . 24 A1
Brackenside RH6 . . . 161 B4
Brackens The RG45 . . . 45 A7
Bracken Way
 Chobham GU24 . . . 49 F1
 Guildford GU3 . . . 108 E3
Brackenwood
 Cranleigh GU6 . . . 174 B3
 Frimley GU15 . . . 66 D5
 Sunbury TW16 . . . 35 A8
Brackenwood Rd GU21 . . . 88 D8
Bracklesham Cl GU14 . . . 85 A7
Bracklesham Ho GU21 . . . 68 C1
Brackley KT13 . . . 53 D5
Brackley Cl SM6 . . . 60 E3
Brackley Rd BR3 . . . 24 A1
BRACKNELL . . . 27 D6
Bracknell Beeches RG12 . . . 27 B6
Bracknell Bsns Ctr The RG12 . . . 26 F7
Bracknell Cl GU15 . . . 46 F1
Bracknell Coll RG12 . . . 27 C7
Bracknell Enterprise Ctr RG12 . . . 27 A7
Bracknell Rd
 Bracknell GU19 . . . 47 E5
 Camberley GU15 . . . 47 A1
 Crowthorne RG45 . . . 45 D6
 Winkfield RG42 . . . 8 A5
Bracknell Sta RG12 . . . 27 B6
Bracknell Wlk RH11 . . . 200 E3
Bracknell & Workingham Coll RG12 . . . 27 C8
Bracondale KT10 . . . 55 C5
Bradbury Ct SW20 . . . 39 C7
Bradbury Rd RH10 . . . 202 C3
Braddock Cl TW7 . . . 5 F5
Braddon Rd TW9 . . . 6 F4
Bradenhurst Cl CR3 . . . 100 F2
Bradfield Cl
 Guildford GU4 . . . 110 A4
 Woking GU22 . . . 69 E1
Bradfields RG12 . . . 27 D4
Bradford Cl SE26 . . . 23 B4
Bradford Dr KT19 . . . 57 F4
Brading Rd
 Streatham SW2 . . . 21 F8
 Thornton Heath CR0 . . . 41 F3
Bradley Cl SM2 . . . 59 B1
Bradley Ct CR0 . . . 61 A6
Bradley Dr RG40 . . . 25 A2
Bradley La RH4, RH5 . . . 115 B3
Bradley Mews SW12 . . . 20 F7
Bradley Rd SE19 . . . 22 C2
Bradlord Ho SE21 . . . 22 E5
Bradmore Gn CR5 . . . 79 F1
Bradmore Way CR5 . . . 79 F1
Bradshaw Cl SW19 . . . 20 A2
Bradshaws Cl SE25 . . . 43 A6
Bradsole Ho 13 BR3 . . . 24 A1
Bradstock Rd KT17 . . . 58 B5
Brae Ct
 2 Kingston u T KT2 . . . 38 A8
 South Norwood SE25 . . . 42 E8
Braemar Ave
 South Croydon CR2 . . . 61 C2
 Thornton Heath CR7 . . . 42 B6
 Wimbledon SW18, SW19 . . . 20 A6
Braemar Cl
 Frimley GU16 . . . 85 F8
 Godalming GU7 . . . 150 D3
Braemar Ct
 5 Brentford TW8 . . . 6 D8
 Catford SE6 . . . 24 F7
Braemar Gdns BR4 . . . 44 C1
Braemar Ho TW11 . . . 17 B3
Braemar Rd
 Brentford TW8 . . . 6 D8
 North Cheam KT4 . . . 58 B7
Braeside
 Beckenham BR3 . . . 24 B3
 Bracknell RG12 . . . 26 C7
 Horley RH6 . . . 161 A3
 Woodham KT15 . . . 71 B8
Braeside Ave SW19 . . . 39 E8
Braeside Cl GU27 . . . 207 F8
Braeside Rd SW16 . . . 21 C1
Braes Mead RH1 . . . 140 E8
Brafferton Rd CR0 . . . 61 C6
Braganza Ct GU1 . . . 109 F2
Bragg Rd TW11 . . . 16 F2
Braid Cl TW13 . . . 15 F6
Braidwood Ho 2 CR7 . . . 42 B5
Braidwood Rd SE6 . . . 24 D7
Brailsford Cl CR4 . . . 20 E1
Brainton Ave TW14 . . . 15 C8
Brakenhale Sch The RG12 . . . 27 B5
Brake Rd GU14 . . . 84 E1
Brakes Rise GU47 . . . 64 E8
Brakey Hill RH1 . . . 120 E1
Bramber Cl
 Crawley RH10 . . . 201 E8
 Horsham RH12 . . . 218 B5
Bramber Ho 15 KT2 . . . 37 E8
Bramber Way CR6 . . . 81 F3
Bramble Acres Cl SM2 . . . 59 A3
Bramble Bank GU16 . . . 86 A6
Bramble Banks SM5 . . . 60 A2
Bramble Cl
 Beckenham BR3 . . . 44 C4
 Copthorne RH10 . . . 183 B3
 Croydon CR0 . . . 63 B6
 Guildford GU3 . . . 108 E3
 Oxted RH8 . . . 123 B2
Bramble Cl *continued*
 Redhill RH1 . . . 140 A7
 Upper Halliford TW17 . . . 34 D6
Bramble Ct GU6 . . . 175 E6
Brambledene Cl GU21 . . . 69 C1
Brambledown
 Hindhead GU26 . . . 188 E4
 Staines TW18 . . . 33 B8
Brambledown Cl BR2, BR4 . . . 44 E4
Brambledown Park Cvn Site RH4 . . . 135 F5
Brambledown Rd
 South Croydon CR2 . . . 61 E3
 Wallington SM5, SM6 . . . 60 B3
Bramblegate RG45 . . . 45 A6
Bramble Hedge Farm (Ind Est) KT11 . . . 72 C5
Bramble La TW12 . . . 15 F2
Bramble Rise KT11 . . . 73 C5
Brambles Cl
 Ash GU12 . . . 106 B1
 Brentford TW7, TW8 . . . 6 B7
 Caterham CR3 . . . 100 E5
Brambles Pk GU5 . . . 151 F6
Brambles The
 Farncombe GU7 . . . 150 D7
 8 Wimbledon SW19 . . . 19 F3
Brambleton Ave GU9 . . . 146 B7
Bramble Twitten RH19 . . . 186 A1
Brambletye Jun Sch RH1 . . . 140 A7
Brambletye La RH18 . . . 206 D4
Brambletye Park Rd RH1 . . . 140 A7
Brambletye Prep Sch RH19 . . . 206 C5
Brambletye Rd RH10 . . . 202 A5
Bramble Way GU23 . . . 90 F3
Bramble Wlk KT18 . . . 76 B6
Bramblewood RH2 . . . 119 B6
Bramblewood Cl SM5 . . . 40 E1
Brambling Cl RH13 . . . 218 A1
Brambling Ct SE25 . . . 42 F5
Brambling Rd RH13 . . . 218 A1
Bramcote
 Frimley GU15 . . . 66 C5
 Weybridge KT13 . . . 53 C6
Bramcote Ave CR4 . . . 40 F5
Bramcote Ct CR4 . . . 40 F5
Bramerton Rd BR3 . . . 43 F6
Bramham Gdns KT9 . . . 56 D6
Bramis Ho TN16 . . . 83 D3
BRAMLEY . . . 151 F6
Bramley Ave
 Coulsdon CR5 . . . 79 C4
 Upper Halliford TW17 . . . 34 E6
Bramley Bsns Ctr The GU5 . . . 151 F7
Bramley CE Inf Sch GU5 . . . 152 A5
Bramley Cl
 Chertsey KT16 . . . 33 B1
 Crawley RH10 . . . 201 F6
 Croydon CR2 . . . 61 C5
 Redhill RH1 . . . 139 E7
 Staines TW18 . . . 13 C2
 Twickenham TW2 . . . 5 C1
Bramley Croft GU26 . . . 188 E4
Bramley Ct
 Feltham TW14 . . . 3 E1
 Mitcham CR4 . . . 40 D7
 Redhill RH1 . . . 118 E3
 Wallington SM6 . . . 60 C5
Bramley Gr KT21 . . . 95 E8
Bramley Grange GU5 . . . 151 F6
Bramley Hill CR0, CR2 . . . 61 C6
Bramley Ho
 3 Hounslow TW3 . . . 4 F3
 1 Kingston u T KT2 . . . 18 B1
 Redhill RH1 . . . 140 A8
 Roehampton SW15 . . . 7 F1
Bramleyhyrst CR2 . . . 61 C5
Bramley La GU17 . . . 64 B5
Bramley Park Ct GU5 . . . 151 F6
Bramley Rd
 Camberley GU15 . . . 65 B2
 Carshalton SM1 . . . 59 D5
 East Ewell SM2 . . . 58 D2
Bramley Sch KT20 . . . 97 A2
Bramley Way
 Ashtead KT21 . . . 75 F2
 Hounslow TW4 . . . 4 F2
 West Wickham BR4 . . . 63 B8
Bramley Wlk RH6 . . . 161 C3
Brampton Gdns KT12 . . . 54 C5
Brampton Ho RH1 . . . 139 F5
Brampton Rd CR0 . . . 42 F3
Bramshaw Rise KT3 . . . 38 E3
Bramshot La
 Blackwater GU14 . . . 84 A5
 Farnborough GU14 . . . 84 C6
Bramshot Rd GU14 . . . 84 A2
Bramshott Ct 3 KT6 . . . 37 E3
Bramston Rd SW17 . . . 20 C5
Bramswell Rd GU7 . . . 150 F6
Bramwell Cl TW16 . . . 35 D7
Bramwell Pl GU21 . . . 69 F3
Brancaster La CR8 . . . 80 C8
Brancaster Rd SW16 . . . 21 E5
Branch Ho 19 SM1 . . . 59 C6
Brandon Cl
 Crawley RH10 . . . 202 D4
 Frimley GU15 . . . 66 D4

Brandon Ho BR3......... 24 B3
Brandon Rd SM1........ 59 B6
Brandreth Rd SW17.... 21 B6
Brandries The SM6..... 60 D7
BRANDS HILL 1 A8
Brandsland RH2...... 139 B6
Brands Rd SL3........... 1 B8
Brandy Way SM2....... 59 A3
Brangbourne Rd BR1 .. 24 C3
Brangwyn Cres SW19 .. 40 D7
Branksome KT13....... 53 D4
Branksome Cl
  Camberley GU15 .... 65 E6
  Teddington TW11....... 16 D4
  Walton-on-T KT12 .... 54 D8
Branksome Hill Rd
  GU47.................... 64 E8
Branksome Park Rd
  GU15.................... 65 E6
Branksome Rd SW19.... 40 A8
Branksome Way KT3.... 38 D8
Bransby Rd KT9......... 56 E4
Branscombe Ct BR2..... 44 E4
Branstone Ct 9 TW9.....6 F6
Branstone Rd TW9......6 F6
Brantridge Rd RH10... 201 F4
Brants Bridge RG12.... 27 E7
Brantwood Ave TW7 ....6 A3
Brantwood Cl 1 KT14.. 71 A6
Brantwood Ct KT14.... 70 F6
Brantwood Dr KT14.... 70 F6
Brantwood Gdns 2
  KT14.................... 71 A6
Brantwood Rd CR2...... 61 D2
Branxholme Ct BR1 .... 44 F8
Brassey Cl
  East Bedfont TW14 .... 15 A7
  Limpsfield RH8 .... 123 A6
Brassey Hill RH8...... 123 A6
Brassey Ho KT12....... 35 A1
Brassey Rd RH8........ 123 A6
Brasted Cl
  Belmont SM2.......... 59 A1
  Forest Hill SE26....... 23 C4
Brasted Lo 11 BR3...... 24 A1
Brathway Rd SW18..... 20 A8
Brattain Ct RG12....... 27 D6
Bratten Ct CR0......... 42 D3
Braunston Ho TW8.......6 C8
Bravington Cl TW17.... 33 F4
Braxted Pk SW16....... 21 F2
Braybourne Dr TW7.....5 F7
Braybrook RG41........ 25 B4
Braybrooke Gdns SE19 .. 22 E1
Bray Cl RH10........... 202 D4
Braycourt Ave KT12.... 35 C2
Bray Ct
  Chessington KT9 ...... 56 F5
  Streatham SW16....... 21 E3
Braye Cl GU47.......... 45 C1
Bray Gdns GU22........ 70 E3
Bray Rd
  Guildford GU2........ 130 B8
  Stoke D'Abernon KT11... 73 E3
Braywick Ct 8 KT2 .... 18 A1
Braywood Ave TW20 ... 12 A2
Braziers La RG42, SL4.... 8 D4
Brazil Cl CR0.......... 41 E2
Breakfield CR5......... 79 E3
Breakspeare SE21...... 22 F5
Breamore Cl SW15..... 19 A7
Breamwater Gdns
  TW10................... 17 B5
Brecon Cl
  Farnborough GU14 .... 84 D7
  Mitcham CR4 .... 41 E6
  North Cheam KT4 ...... 58 C8
Brecon Ho SW18....... 20 A8
Brecon Hts RH11...... 201 C5
Brecons The KT13..... 53 D6
Bredhurst Cl SE20..... 23 C2
Bredinghurst SE22..... 23 A8
Bredon Rd CR0........ 42 F2
Bredune CR8........... 80 D4
Breech La KT20........ 97 A2
Breech The GU47...... 64 E7
Breezehurst Dr RH11... 200 F3
Bregsells Dr RH5...... 157 D4
Bregsells La RH5...... 157 D4
Bremer Rd TW18, TW19... 13 A5
Bremner Ave RH6..... 160 F4
Brenchley Cl BR2...... 44 F3
Brenda Rd SW17....... 20 F6
Brende Gdns KT8...... 36 B5
Brendon Cl
  Esher KT10............ 55 C4
  Harlington UB7......... 3 C7
Brendon Dr KT10...... 55 C4
Brendon Ho SM2 ...... 59 C4
Brendon Rd GU14..... 84 D7
Brenley Cl CR4........ 41 A6
BRENTFORD 6 D7
Brentford Bsns Ctr TW8... 6 C7
BRENTFORD END 6 C7
Brentford Ho 7 TW1... 17 B8
Brentford Sch for Girls
  TW8..................... 6 D8
Brentford Sta TW8........ 6 C8
Brent Ho BR1........... 24 D3
Brent Knoll Specl Sch
  SE26................... 23 D5
Brent Lea TW8.......... 6 C7
Brentmoor Rd GU24.... 67 D6
Brent Rd
  Brentford TW8.......... 6 C8

Brent Rd continued
  South Croydon CR2 .... 62 B2
Brentside TW8.......... 6 C8
Brentside Executive Ctr
  TW8..................... 6 B8
Brentwaters Bsns Pk
  TW8..................... 6 C7
Brent Way TW8.......... 6 D7
Brentwood Ct KT15.... 52 B6
Brereton Ho 3 SW2 ... 22 A8
Bret Harte Rd GU16.... 65 E1
Bretherton Ct CR2..... 61 E4
Bretlands Rd KT16..... 51 E8
Brettgrave KT19....... 57 C1
Brett Ho 1 SW15...... 19 D8
Brett House Cl 2
  SW15.................. 19 D8
Brettingham Cl RH11.... 200 E3
Bretts RH4............ 136 C4
Brewer Rd RH10...... 201 E4
Brewers Cl GU14....... 85 A5
Brewers La 10 TW9 ..... 6 D2
Brewery La TW1....... 71 E6
Brewery Mews Bsns Ctr 1
  TW7..................... 6 A4
Brewery Rd GU21...... 69 E2
Brew House Rd RH3... 137 B5
Brewhurst La RH14.... 213 A2
Breydon Wlk RH10.... 202 B4
Brian Ave CR2.......... 80 E7
Briane Rd KT19........ 57 C1
Briar Ave
  Lightwater GU18....... 67 A8
  South Norwood SW16... 21 F1
Briar Banks SM5....... 60 A2
Briar Cl
  Chelsham CR6 .... 82 A3
  Crawley RH11 .... 181 C1
  Hampton TW12 .... 15 F3
  Isleworth TW7.......... 5 E4
  West Byfleet KT14..... 71 C8
Briar Ct
  Cheam SM3 .... 58 C6
  Hampton TW12 .... 16 B3
Briardale SW19....... 19 F7
Briar Gdns BR2........ 44 F1
Briar Gr CR2........... 81 A6
Briar Hill CR8.......... 79 E8
Briar La
  Croydon CR0 .... 63 B6
  Wallington SM5....... 60 A2
Briarleas Ct GU14..... 105 D8
Briar Patch GU7...... 150 D6
Briar Rd
  Littleton TW17........ 34 A4
  Send GU23............ 90 B4
  Thornton Heath SW16... 41 F6
  Twickenham TW2...... 16 E7
Briars Cl GU14........ 84 D3
Briars Cross RH8..... 123 D5
Briars Ct KT22........ 74 D5
Briars The
  Ash GU12............ 106 B1
  Chessington KT9 ...... 57 A4
Briars Wood RH6..... 161 C4
Briarswood Cl RH10.... 202 D8
Briar The 17 SM1..... 59 C6
Briar Way GU4........ 110 B5
Briar Wlk KT14........ 71 A7
Briarwood SM7........ 78 A4
Briarwood Cl 1 TW13.. 14 E5
Briarwood Ct 6 KT4... 39 A1
Briarwood Rd
  Knaphill GU21........ 88 D8
  Stoneleigh KT17...... 58 A4
Briary Lo BR3.......... 44 C8
Briavels Ct KT18....... 76 E4
Brickersbury Ho GU14.. 84 F8
Brick Farm Cl TW9......7 B6
Brickfield Cl TW8....... 6 C7
Brickfield La
  Harlington UB3 .... 3 D8
  Hookwood RH6....... 160 D1
Brickfield Rd
  Outwood RH1........ 162 C8
  South Norwood CR7,
  SW16................ 42 B8
  Wimbledon SW19 ..... 20 B4
Brickfields Ind Pk
  RG12.................... 27 A7
Brick Hill GU24........ 49 C6
Brickhouse La RH7,
  RH9.................. 163 C4
Brick Kiln La RH8..... 123 C5
Bricklands RH10...... 204 B7
Bricksbury Hill GU9... 125 C7
Brickwood Cl SE26.... 23 B5
Brickwood Rd CR0..... 61 E8
Brickyard Copse RH5... 177 C4
Brickyard La
  Crawley Down RH10... 204 B8
  Wotton RH5......... 134 D2
Brideake Cl RH11..... 201 A3
Bridewell Cl GU8..... 170 F1
Bridge Barn La GU21.. 69 D1
Bridge Cl
  Byfleet KT14.......... 71 F7
  Lower Halliford KT12... 34 F1
  Staines TW18.......... 12 E4
  Teddington TW11...... 16 F4
  Woking GU21.......... 69 C2
Bridge Cotts GU6..... 174 B3
Bridge Ct
  Leatherhead KT22 .... 95 A5
  Walton-on-T KT12 .... 34 F1
  5 Weybridge KT13.... 53 B6
  Woking GU21.......... 69 D2

Bridge Ct continued
  Wrecclesham GU10..... 145 F7
Bridge End GU15...... 65 B4
Bridge Gdns GU9..... 125 D2
Bridgefield Cl SM7.... 77 C4
Bridgefield Rd SM1.... 59 A4
Bridge Gate Ho GU7.. 150 E5
Bridge Gdns
  East Molesey KT8 .... 36 D5
  Littleton Common TW15... 14 C1
Bridgeham Cl KT13.... 53 A5
Bridgeham Way RH6... 162 B2
Bridgehill Cl GU2..... 109 A3
Bridge Ho
  Chertsey KT16........ 33 C2
  4 Sutton SM2........ 59 B4
Bridge Ind Est RH6 ... 161 B3
Bridge La GU25........ 31 F3
Bridgelands RH10.... 183 A3
Bridgelands Cl BR3.... 23 F1
Bridgeman Rd TW11... 17 A2
Bridgemead GU16..... 85 D8
Bridge Mead GU24.... 87 F1
Bridge Mews
  Godalming GU7...... 150 E4
  Tongham GU10...... 126 F7
  Woking GU21.......... 69 D2
Bridge Par
  Croydon CR0 .... 61 B7
  Purley CR8............ 80 A7
  Streatham SW16...... 21 E3
Bridge Pk GU4........ 110 C4
Bridge Pl CR0......... 42 D1
Bridge Rd
  Aldershot GU11...... 126 A4
  Ascot SL5............. 29 D4
  Bagshot GU19......... 47 E3
  Camberley GU15 ...... 65 B3
  Chertsey KT16......... 33 B2
  Chessington KT9 ...... 56 E5
  Cobham KT11......... 73 B4
  Cranleigh GU6....... 174 E3
  East Molesey KT8 .... 36 E5
  Epsom KT17........... 76 F7
  Farnborough GU14 .... 84 F4
  Farncombe GU7...... 150 E5
  Haslemere GU27..... 208 C7
  Isleworth TW3, TW7 ... 5 D4
  Penge BR3............ 23 F1
  Rudgwick RH12...... 214 D7
  Sutton SM2.......... 59 B4
  Twickenham TW1........ 6 B1
  Wallington SM6....... 60 C5
  Weybridge KT13...... 52 F6
Bridge Ret Pk RG40.... 25 B5
Bridge Row CR0....... 42 D1
Bridges Cl RH6....... 161 C1
Bridges Ct RH12...... 218 A5
Bridges La CR0........ 60 E6
Bridge Sq GU9....... 125 C2
Bridges Rd SW19..... 20 B2
Bridges Road Mews
  SW19.................. 20 B2
Bridge St
  Colnbrook SL3........... 1 D7
  Godalming GU7...... 150 E4
  Guildford GU1....... 130 C8
  Leatherhead KT22 .... 95 A5
  Richmond TW10........ 6 D2
  Staines TW18.......... 12 E4
  Walton-on-T KT12 .... 34 F2
Bridgetown Cl 5 SE19... 22 E3
Bridge View SL5....... 30 B2
Bridgewater Pl GU21.. 69 F3
Bridgewater Rd KT13... 53 D4
Bridge Way
  Chipstead CR5........ 98 E8
  Twickenham TW2...... 16 C8
Bridgewood Cl SE20... 23 B1
Bridgewood Rd
  North Cheam KT4 .... 58 A6
  Streatham SW16...... 21 D1
Bridge Works
  Camberley GU15 ...... 65 B3
  Leatherhead KT22 .... 95 A4
Bridgford St SW17,
  SW18................. 20 C5
Bridle Cl
  Grayshott GU26..... 188 A3
  Kingston u T KT1...... 37 D5
  Sunbury TW16........ 35 A6
  West Ewell KT19...... 57 D5
Bridle Ct GU11....... 104 E2
Bridle La
  Oxshott KT11, KT22.... 74 B4
  Twickenham TW1........ 6 B1
Bridle Path CR0....... 60 E7
Bridle Path The KT17... 58 C1
Bridlepath Way TW14... 14 E7
Bridle Rd
  Addington CR0........ 63 A6
  Claygate KT10........ 56 B4
  Epsom KT17........... 76 F6
Bridle Rd The CR8.... 60 E1
Bridle Way
  Crawley RH10........ 202 D7
  Croydon CR0 .... 63 A6
Bridle Way The SM6... 60 C1
Bridlington Cl TN16... 103 B8
Bridport Rd CR7....... 42 B6
Brier Lea KT20........ 97 F1
Brierley CR0........... 63 B4
Brierley Cl SE25....... 43 A5
Brierley Rd SW12..... 21 C6
Brierly Cl GU2........ 109 A3
Brier Rd KT20......... 97 B8
Brigade Pl CR3....... 100 C5

Briggs Cl CR4........... 41 B8
Brighthampton KT13.... 53 F6
Bright Hill GU1....... 130 E7
Brightlands Rd RH2... 118 C3
Brightman Rd SW18... 20 D7
Brighton Cl KT15...... 52 C5
Brighton Rd
  Addlestone KT15...... 52 C5
  Aldershot GU11...... 126 C8
  Banstead KT20, SM2,
  SM7................ 77 F3
  Belmont SM2.......... 59 B2
  Coulsdon CR5, CR8.... 79 D4
  Crawley RH11........ 201 D4
  Croydon CR2, CR8 .... 61 C3
  Godalming GU7, GU8... 151 A1
  Hooley CR5, RH1...... 99 B6
  Horley RH6........... 160 F2
  Horsham RH13....... 217 E1
  Kingston u T KT6...... 37 D3
  Kingswood KT20 ..... 97 F8
  Lower Kingswood KT20... 117 F8
  Purley CR8............ 80 B8
  Redhill RH1.......... 139 F8
  Salfords RH1......... 140 A2
  South Croydon CR2 ... 61 C3
Brighton Terr 6 RH1... 139 F8
Brightside Ave TW18... 13 C3
Brightwell Cl CR0...... 42 A1
Brightwell Cres SW17... 20 F3
Brightwells Rd GU9... 125 C2
Brigstock Par 1 CR7... 42 A4
Brigstock Rd
  Coulsdon CR5........ 79 B3
  Thornton Heath CR7 ... 42 B5
Brimshot La GU24..... 49 E2
Brindle Cl GU11...... 126 B7
Brindles The SM7..... 77 F2
Brindley Ho
  Carshalton SM1....... 59 E5
  21 Streatham SW12 ... 21 E8
Brine Ct KT4........... 37 D4
Brinkley Ct KT4........ 58 B8
Brinkley Rd KT4....... 58 B8
Brinkworth Pl SL4..... 11 B8
Brinn's La GU17....... 64 C5
Brinsworth Cl TW2.... 16 D6
Brisbane Ave SW19.... 40 B8
Brisbane Cl RH11..... 181 D1
Briscoe Rd SW19..... 20 D2
Brisson Cl KT10....... 54 F4
Bristol Cl
  Crawley RH10........ 182 D1
  Stanwell TW19.......... 2 E1
  Wallington SM6....... 60 E3
Bristol Ct 11 TW19 ..... 2 E1
Bristol Gdns SW15.... 19 C8
Bristol Rd SM4........ 40 C4
Bristow Inf Sch GU15... 65 B2
Bristow Rd
  Camberley GU15 ...... 65 B3
  Hounslow TW3.......... 5 C4
  Wallington CR0....... 60 E6
  West Norwood SE19 ... 22 E3
Britannia Ind Est SL3 ..1 E5
Britannia Rd KT5....... 37 F2
Britannia Way TW19... 13 D8
British Home & Hospl for
  Incurables SE27....... 22 B3
British Wildlife Ctr*
  RH7.................. 163 E3
Briton Cl CR2.......... 80 E8
Briton Cres CR2....... 80 E8
Briton Hill Rd CR2.... 61 F1
Brittain Ct GU47...... 64 C7
Brittain Rd KT12....... 54 D5
Britten Cl
  Ash GU12............ 106 B2
  Crawley RH11........ 200 F3
  Horsham RH13....... 218 B4
Brittens Cl GU2, GU3... 109 A6
Brittingham Ho RH11 ... 201 D6
Britton Cl SE6........ 24 D8
Brixton Hill SW2...... 21 E8
Brixton Hill Pl SW2 ... 21 E8
Broadacre TW18....... 13 A3
Broadacres GU3...... 108 E2
Broad Acres GU7..... 150 E8
BROADBRIDGE HEATH
  .... 216 E4
Broadbridge Heath Rd
  RH12................ 216 D4
Broadbridge La
  Burstow RH6......... 183 B8
  Smallfield RH6....... 162 A2
Broadbridge Ret Pk
  RH12................ 216 E3
Broad Cl KT12.......... 54 E7
Broadcoombe CR2..... 62 D3
Broadeaves Cl
  South Croydon CR2 ... 61 E5
BROADFIELD 201 C1
Broadfield Barton 4
  RH11................ 201 B2
Broadfield Cl
  Burgh Heath KT20.... 97 C2
  Croydon CR0 .... 60 F8
Broadfield Dr RH11.... 201 B3
Broadfield East Jun & Inf
  Schs RH11........... 201 C2
Broadfield Pl RH11.... 201 B2
Broadfield Rd
  Catford SE6........... 24 E7
  Peaslake GU5........ 154 D8
Broadfields KT8........ 36 E3
BROADFORD 130 D1
Broadford La GU24.... 68 E7

Broadford Pk GU4..... 130 D2
Broadford Rd GU4.... 130 D2
Broadgates Rd SW18... 20 D7
Broad Green Ave CR0... 42 B2
BROADHAM GREEN ... 122 D3
Broadham Green Rd
  RH8.................. 122 D2
Broadham Pl RH8..... 122 D4
Broad Ha'penny GU10... 146 A5
Broad Highway KT11... 73 D5
Broadhurst
  Ashtead KT21........ 75 E3
  Farnborough GU14 ... 84 C5
Broadhurst Cl 9 TW10.... 6 E2
Broadhurst Gdns RH2... 139 B6
Broadhurst Mews 4
  GU12................ 105 C1
Broad La
  Bracknell RG12....... 27 D6
  Hampton TW12 ...... 16 A2
  Parkgate RH2, RH5... 158 E6
Broadlands
  Farnborough GU14 ... 85 E2
  Feltham TW13 .... 16 A5
  Frimley GU16......... 85 F8
  Horley RH6.......... 161 C4
Broadlands Ave
  Shepperton TW17 .... 34 C3
  Streatham SW16...... 21 E6
Broadlands Bsns Campus
  RH12................ 198 C4
Broadlands Cl SW16... 21 E6
Broadlands Ct
  Bracknell RG42....... 26 E8
  Richmond TW9.......... 7 A7
Broadlands Dr
  Sunningdale SL5...... 29 D2
  Warlingham CR6..... 101 C8
Broadlands Mans 2
  SW16................. 21 E6
Broadlands Way KT3... 38 F3
Broadley Gn GU20.... 48 D4
Broadmead
  Ashtead KT21........ 75 F2
  Catford SE6........... 24 A5
  Farnborough GU14 ... 84 D3
  Hampton TW12 ...... 16 A2
  Horley RH6.......... 161 C4
  Merstham RH1....... 119 C2
Broadmead Ave KT4... 39 A2
Broadmead Cl TW12... 16 A2
Broadmead Inf Sch
  CR0.................. 42 D3
Broadmead Jun Sch
  CR0.................. 42 D3
Broadmead Rd GU23... 90 B5
Broadmeads GU23.... 90 B5
Broadmere Com Prim Sch
  GU21................. 70 D6
Broadmoor Cotts
  RH5................. 156 A8
Broadmoor Est RG45... 45 D4
Broadmoor Hospl
  RG45................ 45 D4
Broadmoor Prim Sch
  RG45................ 45 D4
Broad Oak TW16...... 14 F2
Broad Oaks KT6....... 57 B8
Broadoaks Cres KT14... 71 B6
Broad Oaks Way BR2... 44 F4
Broadpool Cotts SL5.... 9 A1
Broad St Wlk RG40.... 25 C6
Broad St
  Guildford GU3....... 108 D3
  Teddington TW11..... 16 F2
  West End GU24....... 67 D6
  Wokingham RG40 .... 25 C6
Broadview Est TW19... 14 A8
Broadview Rd SW16... 21 D1
Broadwater Cl
  Hersham KT12....... 54 A5
  Sheerwater GU21..... 70 D7
  Wraysbury TW19...... 11 E8
Broadwater Ho 1
  KT13................. 53 B7
Broadwater La GU7... 150 F6
Broadwater Pl KT13... 53 B7
Broadwater Prim Sch
  SW17................ 20 E4
Broadwater Rd SW17... 20 E4
Broadwater Rd N KT12... 54 A5
Broadwater Rd S KT12... 54 A5
Broadwater Rise GU1... 131 A8
Broadwater Sch GU7... 151 A8
Broadway
  Bracknell RG12....... 27 C7
  Cranbourne SL4........ 9 B7
  Knaphill GU21........ 68 C1
  Limpsfield RH8...... 123 B5
  Tolworth KT6......... 38 B1
Broadway Ave
  Thornton Heath CR0 ... 42 D4
  Twickenham TW1........ 6 B1
Broadway Cl CR2...... 81 B5
Broadway Ct
  Beckenham BR3...... 44 C6
  Wimbledon SW19 .... 20 A2
Broadway Gdns CR4... 40 E5
Broadway Ho GU21... 68 C1
Broadway Ho 5 SW19... 20 A1
Broadway Ho GU47... 64 B7
Broadway Lofts SW17... 20 E4
Broadway Mkt SW17... 20 F4
Broadway Par BR1.... 24 D3
Broadway Pl 5 SW19... 19 F2
Broadway Rd GU18,
  GU20................ 48 C2

Broadway The
Cheam SM3 58 E4
Crawley RH10 201 D6
Laleham TW18 33 C7
Mortlake SW13 7 E5
Sandhurst GU47 64 B8
Sutton SM1 59 C6
Thames Ditton KT10 36 E1
Tolworth KT6 38 A1
Wallington CR0 60 E6
Wimbledon SW19 19 F2
Woking GU21 69 F2
Woodham KT15 52 A1
Broadwell Ct TW5 4 D6
Broadwell Rd GU10 145 F6
Broad Wlk
Burgh Heath KT18 97 D8
Caterham CR3 100 F5
Cranleigh GU6 174 F1
Crawley RH10 201 D6
Frimley GU16 65 E2
Heston TW5 4 E6
Lower Kingswood CR5 99 A4
Richmond TW9 6 F7
Broadwood Cl RH12 218 A5
Broadwood Cotts RH5 178 E6
Broadwood Rd CR5 99 D6
Broadwood Rise RH11 201 A2
Brockbridge Ho SW15 7 F1
Brock Cl GU16 86 D8
Brockenhurst KT8 35 F3
Brockenhurst Ave KT4 38 E1
Brockenhurst Cl GU21 69 F5
Brockenhurst Rd
Aldershot GU11 126 B8
Ascot SL5 29 B3
Bracknell RG12 28 A6
Croydon CR0 43 B2
Brockenhurst Way SW16 41 D7
BROCKHAM 137 C7
Brockham Cl SW19 19 F3
Brockham Cres CR0 63 D3
Brockham Ct
5 Belmont SM2 59 B3
8 Croydon CR2 61 C5
Brockham Dr SW2 21 F8
Brockham Gn RH3 137 B8
Brockham Hill Pk KT20 116 C4
Brockham Ho 14 SW2 21 F8
Brockhamhurst Rd RH3 137 B2
Brockham Keep RH6 161 C4
Brockham La RH3 116 A1
Brockham Park Ho RH3 137 C4
Brockham Prim Sch RH3 137 B7
Brockham Row RH3 137 C5
Brockham Warren KT20 116 A3
Brockholes Cross KT24 113 A6
Brockhurst Cl RH12 216 F1
Brockhurst Cotts GU6 193 F4
Brockhurst Lo GU9 146 B7
Brocklebank Ct CR6 81 A1
Brocklebank Rd SW18 20 C8
Brocklesby Rd SE25 43 B5
Brockley Combe KT13 53 D6
Brockley Pk SE23 23 E8
Brockley Rise SE23 23 E8
Brockley View SE23 23 E8
Brockman Rise BR1 24 D4
Brock Rd RH11 181 B1
Brock's Cl GU7 151 A5
Brocks Dr
Cheam SM3 58 E7
Fairlands GU3 108 C5
Brockshot Cl 1 TW8 6 D8
Brockton GU7 150 E5
Brock Way GU25 31 C5
Brockway Cl GU1 110 B2
Brockwell Ave BR3 44 B4
Brockwell Ct 2 CR0 42 B2
Brockwell Park Gdns SE24 22 B8
Brockwell Park Row 9 SW2 22 A8
Brockworth KT2 38 B8
Broderick Ho SE21 22 E5
Brodie Ho 7 SM6 60 B6
Brodie Rd GU1 130 E8
Brodrick Gr KT23 94 A1
Brodrick Rd SW17 20 E6
Brograve Gdns BR3 44 B7
Broke Ct GU4 110 C4
Brokes Cres RH2 118 A3
Brokes Rd RH2 118 A3
Bromford Cl RH8 123 A2
Bromleigh Ct SE21, SE22 23 B6
BROMLEY 44 E8
Bromley Ave BR1 24 E1
Bromley Cres BR2 44 F6
Bromley Ct BR1 24 F1
Bromley Gdns BR2 44 F6
Bromley Gr BR2 44 D7
Bromley Hill BR1 24 E2
BROMLEY PARK 44 F8
Bromley Pk 13 BR1 44 F8
Bromley Rd
Beckenham BR3 44 B8
Bromley BR2, BR3 44 D7
Catford SE6, BR1 24 B5
Bromley Road Inf Sch BR3 44 B8
Bromley Road Ret Pk SE6 24 B6
Brompton Cl
Hounslow TW4 4 F2
Penge SE20 43 A7
Bromwich Ho TW10 6 E1
Bronson Rd SW20 39 E7
Bronte Ct 14 RH1 119 A2
Brontes The RH19 185 D1
BROOK
Guildford 132 E1
Witley 170 B1
Brook Ave GU9 125 F7
Brook Cl
Ash GU12 106 B3
Dorking RH4 115 C1
East Grinstead RH19 186 B1
Epsom KT19 57 E2
Sandhurst GU47 45 E1
Stanwell TW19 13 F8
Upper Tooting SW17 21 A6
West Barnes SW20 39 B6
Wokingham RG41 25 A8
Brook Ct
Beckenham BR3 43 F8
6 Brentford TW8 6 D8
Cheam SM3 58 C6
Horsham RH12 217 B5
7 Mortlake SW14 7 E4
Brookdale Rd SE6 24 B8
Brook Dr
Ashford TW16 14 E2
Bracknell RG12 27 E5
Brooke Ct
Frimley GU16 85 F6
7 Kingston u T KT2 17 D4
Brooke Forest GU3 108 C5
Brookehowse Rd SE6 24 B5
Brookers Cl KT21 75 D2
Brookers Cnr RG45 45 C5
Brookers Ho KT21 75 D2
Brookers Row RG45 45 C6
Brook Farm Rd KT11 73 D4
Brookfield
Farncombe GU7 151 A8
Woking GU21 69 B3
Brookfield Ave SM1 59 E7
Brookfield Cl
Ottershaw KT16 51 D4
Redhill RH1 140 A3
Brookfield Ct GU18 48 C1
Brookfield Gdns KT10 55 F4
Brookfield Pl KT11 73 E4
Brookfield Prim Sch SM3 39 E1
Brookfield Rd
Aldershot GU12 105 F3
Ashtead KT21 95 E7
Brookfields Ave CR4 40 E4
Brook Gdns
Barnes SW13 7 F4
Farnborough GU14 84 F2
Kingston u T KT2 38 C8
Brook Gn
Bracknell RG42 26 F8
Chobham GU24 49 F1
Brook Hill
Farley Green GU5 153 D8
Oxted RH8 122 C5
Brookhill Cl RH10 183 A3
Brookhill Rd RH10 183 A3
Brook Ho
Cranleigh GU6 174 F4
Heath End GU9 125 D6
5 Twickenham TW1 17 A8
Brookhouse 2 SW19 20 A2
Brookhouse Rd GU14 84 F3
Brookhurst Rd KT15 52 B4
Brook La
Chobham GU24 68 D8
Farley Green GU5 132 E1
Faygate RH12 218 C8
Send GU23 90 E5
Brook La Bns Ctr 4 TW8 6 D8
Brook La N 3 TW8 6 D8
Brookland Ho 5 RH19 185 E1
Brooklands GU11 104 E1
Brooklands Ave SW18 20 B6
Brooklands Cl
Charlton TW16 34 E8
Heath End GU9 125 D7
Stoke D'Abernon KT11 73 E4
Brooklands Ct
Kingston u T KT1 37 D5
Mitcham CR4 40 D7
New Haw KT15 52 D1
Reigate RH2 118 B3
Brooklands Ind Est
Byfleet KT13 52 E1
West Byfleet KT13 71 E8
Brooklands La KT13 52 F4
Brooklands Motoring & Aviation Mus* KT13 53 A2
Brooklands Pl TW12 16 B3
Brooklands Rd
Crawley RH11 201 C1
Heath End GU9 125 E7
Thames Ditton KT7 37 A1
Weybridge KT13 53 B3
Brooklands Sch RH2 118 B3
Brooklands Tech Coll KT13 52 F4
Brooklands Terr TW16 35 A5
Brooklands The TW7 5 D6
Brooklands Way
East Grinstead RH19 205 D8
Heath End GU9 125 E7
Redhill RH1 118 E3
Brookley Cl GU10 126 C3
Brookleys GU24 49 F1
Brooklyn 9 SE20 23 A1
Brooklyn Ave SE25 43 B5
Brooklyn Cl
Carshalton SM5 59 E8
Woking GU22 89 E8
Brooklyn Ct
Feltham TW13 15 B6
2 Woking GU22 89 E8
Brooklyn Gr SE25 43 B5
Brooklyn Rd
Croydon SE25 43 B5
Woking GU22 89 E8
Brook Manor RH19 205 D7
Brook Mdw GU8 191 C3
Brookmead CR4 41 C3
Brook Mead
Milford GU8 170 F8
West Ewell KT19 57 E4
Brookmead Ct
Cranleigh GU6 174 E2
Farnham GU9 125 B1
Brookmead Ind Est CR0 41 C3
Brookmead Rd CR0 41 C3
Brook Rd
Bagshot GU19 47 E2
Brook GU8 190 D8
Camberley GU15 65 B4
Chilworth GU4 131 C3
Horsham RH12 217 E6
Merstham RH1 119 C7
Redhill RH1 139 F8
Surbiton KT6 56 E8
Thornton Heath CR7 42 C5
Twickenham TW1 6 A1
Wormley GU8 170 E1
Brook Rd S TW8 6 D8
Brooksby Cl GU17 64 B5
Brook Sch The RH10 202 C3
Brooks Cl KT13 53 A1
Brookscroft CR0 62 E1
Brooks Ho 6 SW2 22 A7
BROOKSIDE 8 F2
Brookside
Beare Green RH5 157 F6
Chertsey KT16 32 E2
Colnbrook SL3 1 C7
Copthorne RH10 183 A3
Cranleigh GU6 174 E1
Cranleigh GU6 174 E3
Crawley Down RH10 204 B8
Crawley RH10 201 F7
Guildford GU4 109 D6
Hale GU9 125 D6
Sandhurst GU47 64 C8
South Godstone RH9 142 D5
Wallington SM5 60 A5
Brookside Ave TW15 13 D3
Brookside Cl TW13 15 A5
Brookside Cres 1 KT4 39 A1
Brookside Ct 1 SW16 21 C1
Brookside Pk GU14 65 A1
Brookside Way CR0 43 D3
Brooks La W4 7 A8
Brooks Rd W4 7 A8
Brook St KT1 37 E7
Brookswood GU4 131 C3
Brook Terr 12 RH1 139 F8
Brook The RH10 201 D7
Brook Trad Est The GU12 105 E2
Brook Valley RH5 136 B1
Brookview RH10 183 A3
Brook View Lo KT4 39 A1
Brookview Rd SW16, SW17 21 C3
Brook Way KT22 75 A1
Brookwell La GU5 152 B2
BROOKWOOD 88 A7
Brookwood RH6 161 B4
Brookwood Ave SW13 7 F5
Brookwood Cl BR2 44 F5
Brookwood Ho RH6 161 B6
Brookwood Lye Rd GU21, GU24 88 C7
Brookwood Pk RH6 161 B2
Brookwood Prim Sch GU24 88 A7
Brookwood Rd
Farnborough GU14 85 D4
Hounslow TW3 5 B6
Wandsworth SW18 20 A7
Brookwood Sta GU24 88 A6
Broom Acres GU47 45 B1
Broom Bank CR6 102 C8
Broom Cl
Esher KT10 55 B5
Teddington TW11 17 D1
Broomcroft Cl GU22 70 D3
Broomcroft Dr GU22 70 D3
Broomdashers Rd RH10 201 F7
Broome Cl
Headley KT18 96 C1
Horsham RH12 217 D5
Broome Ct 3 TW9 7 A6
Broome Hall RH5 156 D2
Broomehall Rd
Coldharbour RH5 156 D2
Ockley RH5 177 E8
Broome Lo
Ascot SL5 29 D4
Broome Lo *continued*
Staines TW18 13 B3
Broome Rd TW12 35 F8
Broomers La GU6 175 E5
Broomfield
Elstead GU8 148 E4
Guildford GU2 108 E2
Staines TW18 13 A2
Sunbury TW16 35 A8
Broom Field GU18 67 A7
Broomfield Cl
Guildford GU3 108 E3
Sunningdale SL5 30 B2
Broomfield Cotts KT20 97 E8
Broomfield Ct
Sunningdale SL5 30 B3
Weybridge KT13 53 B4
Broomfield House Sch TW9 6 F6
Broomfield La GU10 146 A1
Broomfield Pk
Sunningdale SL5 30 B2
Westcott RH4 135 C6
Broomfield Rd
Beckenham BR3 43 F6
Richmond TW9 6 F6
Surbiton KT5 37 F1
Teddington TW11 17 C2
Woodham KT15 71 B8
Broomfield Ride KT22 74 D7
Broomfields KT10 55 C5
Broom Gdns CR0 63 A7
BROOMHALL 30 B2
Broom Hall KT22 74 D5
Broomhall Bldgs 1 SL5 30 B2
Broomhall End GU21 69 E3
Broomhall La
Sunningdale SL5 30 A3
Woking GU21 69 E3
Broomhall Rd
South Croydon CR2 61 D2
Woking GU21 69 E3
Broomhill GU10 124 D8
Broomhill Ct KT10 55 B5
Broomhill Rd GU14 84 D5
Broomhurst Ct RH4 136 B5
Broom La GU24 49 E3
Broomlands La RH8 123 E8
Broomleaf Cnr GU9 125 D2
Broomleaf Rd GU9 125 E2
Broomloan La SM1 59 A8
Broom Lock TW11 17 C2
Broom Pk KT1 17 D1
Broom Rd
Croydon CR0 63 A7
Richmond TW11 17 C3
Broomsleigh Bsns Pk SE26 23 F3
Broom Squires GU26 188 F4
Broomsquires Rd GU19 47 F2
Broom Water TW11 17 C3
Broom Water W TW11 17 C3
Broom Way
Blackwater GU17 64 E4
Oatlands Park KT13 53 E6
Broomwood Cl CR0 43 D4
Broomwood Way GU10 146 C6
Broseley Gr SE26 23 E3
Broster Gdns SE25 42 F6
Brougham Pl GU9 125 B7
Brough Cl KT2 17 D3
Broughton Ave TW10 17 C4
Broughton Ho 10 SW19 19 E1
Broughton Mews GU16 65 F1
Broughton Rd CR7 42 A3
Browell Ho GU4 110 D2
Browells La TW13 15 B6
Brown Bear Ct TW13 15 D4
Brown Cl SM6 60 E3
Browne Ho 9 SE26 23 B3
Browngraves Rd UB7 3 C7
Brownhill Rd SE6 24 C8
Browning Ave
Carshalton SM1 59 E6
North Cheam KT4 39 B1
Browning Cl
Crawley RH10 202 C7
Frimley GU15 66 C4
Hampton TW12 15 F4
Browning Rd KT22 94 D2
Brownings The 1 RH19 185 C1
Browning Way TW5 4 D6
Brownjohn Ct RH10 202 A7
Brownlow Rd
Redhill RH1 118 E1
South Croydon CR0 61 F6
Brownrigg Cres RG12 27 E8
Brownrigg Rd TW15 14 A4
Brown's Hill RH1 141 D2
Browns La KT24 113 D8
Brownsover Rd GU14 84 C4
Brown's Rd KT5, KT6 37 F2
Browns Wlk GU10 145 F5
Browns Wood RH19 185 E4
Brow The RH1 140 A4
Broxholm Rd SE27, SW16 22 A5
Brox La KT15, KT16 51 D2
Brox Mews KT16 51 C4
Brox Rd KT16 51 D4
Broxted Rd SE23, SE6 23 F6
Bruce Ave TW17 34 C3
Bruce Cl KT14 71 E6
Bruce Dr CR2 62 D2
Bruce Hall Mews SW17 21 A4
Bruce Lawns SW17 21 A4
Bruce Rd
Mitcham CR4 21 A1
South Norwood SE25 42 D5
Brudenell Rd SW17 21 A4
Brumana Cl KT13 53 B4
Brumfield Rd KT19 57 C5
Brunel Cl
Cranford TW5 4 B7
South Norwood SE19 22 F2
Brunel Ct SW13 7 F5
Brunel Ctr RH10 181 F2
Brunel Dr RG45 45 C8
Brunel Ho
Haslemere GU27 208 A6
24 Streatham SW2 21 E8
Brunel Pl RH10 201 E5
Brunel Univ Coll Osterley Campus TW7 5 F7
Brunel Univ (Runnymede Campus) TW20 11 C5
Brunel Wlk TW2 16 A8
Brunner Ct KT16 51 C5
Brunner Ho SE6 24 C4
Brunswick RG12 27 A2
Brunswick Cl
Crawley RH10 202 A4
Thames Ditton KT7 36 F1
Twickenham TW2 16 D5
Walton-on-T KT12 54 C8
Brunswick Ct
Crawley RH10 202 A4
Kingston u T KT2 17 D2
2 Merton SW19 19 E1
2 Penge SE19 23 A1
Brunswick Dr GU24 87 D7
Brunswick Gr KT11 73 C6
Brunswick Manor SM1 59 C6
Brunswick Mews SW16 21 D2
Brunswick Pl SE19 23 A1
Brunswick Rd
Kingston u T KT2 38 A8
Pirbright, Alexander Barracks GU24 87 C6
Pirbright, Blackdown Barracks GU16, GU24 86 E6
Sutton SM1 59 B6
Brunswick Terr BR3 44 B8
Bruntile Cl GU14 85 D1
Brushfield Way GU21 68 C1
Brushwood Rd RH12 218 B6
Bruton Rd SM4 40 C5
Bruton Way RG12 27 E2
Bryan Cl TW16 15 A1
Bryanston Ave TW2 16 B7
Bryanstone Ave GU2 109 A4
Bryanstone Cl GU2 108 F4
Bryanstone Ct SM1 59 C7
Bryanstone Gr GU2 108 F5
Bryce Cl RH12 218 A5
Bryce Gdns GU11 126 C7
Bryden Cl SE26 23 E3
Brympton Cl RH4 136 A5
Brynford Cl GU21 69 E4
Bryn Rd GU10 145 F7
Bryony Ho RG42 26 E8
Bryony Rd GU1 110 B4
Bryony Way TW16 15 A2
Buccaneer Way GU14 104 C8
Buchanan Ho
Dulwich SE21 22 E5
Wandsworth SW18 20 A8
Buchan Ctry Pk* RH11 200 E1
Buchans Lawn RH11 201 B2
Buchan The GU15 66 A8
Bucharest Rd SW18 20 C8
Buckfast Rd SM4 40 B5
Buckhurst Ave CR4, SM5 40 F1
Buckhurst Cl
East Grinstead RH19 185 C3
Redhill RH1 118 F3
Buckhurst Cotts RH12 214 D8
Buckhurst Gr RG40 25 F5
Buckhurst Hill RG12 27 F5
Buckhurst La SL5 30 A6
Buckhurst Mead RH19 185 C4
Buckhurst Moors RG12 26 C6
Buckhurst Rd
Ascot SL5 29 F7
Frimley GU16 85 F6
Buckhurst Way RH19 185 C3
Buckingham Ave
East Molesey KT8 36 B7
Feltham TW14 4 B1
South Norwood CR7 42 A8
Buckingham Cl
Guildford GU1 109 F2
Hampton TW12 15 F3
Buckingham Ct
Belmont SM2 59 A2
Camberley GU15 65 D5
Crawley RH11 201 B2
Farnborough GU14 85 B4
Mitcham CR4 41 E4
3 Staines TW18 13 A4
Wokingham RG40 25 C6
Buckingham Dr RH19 206 A8

Buckingham Gate RH6 182 C7
Buckingham Gdns
- Hampton KT8 36 B7
- South Norwood CR7 42 A7
Buckingham Ho TW10 7 A2
Buckingham La SE23 23 E8
Buckingham Prim Sch TW12 15 F3
Buckingham Rd
- Hampton TW12 15 F3
- Kingston u T KT1 37 F5
- Mitcham CR4 41 E4
- Richmond TW10 17 D6
- South Holmwood RH5 157 C6
Buckingham Way SM6 60 C2
BUCKLAND 117 A2
Buckland Cl GU14 85 C7
Buckland Cnr RH2 117 D2
Buckland Ct RH3 117 A2
Buckland Inf Sch KT9 56 F5
Buckland Jun & Inf Sch TW18 13 C1
Buckland Rd
- Chessington KT9 56 F5
- East Ewell SM2 58 D2
- Lower Kingswood KT20 117 F7
- Reigate RH2 117 D2
Bucklands Rd TW11 17 C2
Buckland Way KT4 39 C1
Buckland Wlk SM4 40 C5
Bucklebury RG12 27 A2
Buckleigh Ave SW20 39 F6
Buckleigh Ho SW19 20 D3
Buckleigh Rd SW16 21 E1
Buckleigh Way SE19 22 F1
Bucklers' Way SM5 59 F7
Buckles Way SM7 77 E3
Buckley Cl SE23 23 B8
Buckley Pl RH10 204 A8
Buckmans Rd RH11 201 D6
Bucknall Way BR3 44 C4
Bucknills Cl KT18 76 C5
Bucks Cl KT14 71 B5
Bucks Copse RG41 25 A5
BUCKS GREEN 214 B6
Buckswood Dr RH11 201 A4
Buckthorn Cl RG40 25 E7
Buddhapadipa Temple The SW19 19 D4
Budebury Rd TW18 13 A3
Budge La CR4 40 F2
Budgen Cl RH10 182 D1
Budgen Dr RH1 119 A3
Budge's Cotts RG40 25 E8
Budge's Gdns RG40 25 E7
Budge's Rd RG40 25 D7
Budham Way RG12 27 B3
Buff Ave SM7 78 B4
Buffbeards La GU27 207 E6
Buffers La KT22 95 A8
Bug Hill CR3, CR6 101 D7
Bugkingham Way GU16 65 F1
Bulganak Rd CR7 42 C5
Bulkeley Cl TW20 11 C3
Bullard Rd TW11 16 F2
Bullbeggars La
- Godstone RH9 121 C3
- Woking GU21 69 B3
BULLBROOK 27 E7
Bullbrook Dr RG12 27 F8
Bullbrook Row RG12 27 E7
Buller Ct GU14 85 C1
Buller Rd
- Aldershot GU11 105 B4
- South Norwood CR7 42 D6
Bullers Rd GU9 125 E6
Bullfinch Cl
- Horley RH6 160 E4
- Horsham RH12 217 C7
- Sandhurst GU47 64 E8
Bullfinch Ct 4 SE21 22 D6
Bullfinch Rd CR2 62 D1
Bull Hill KT22 95 A6
Bullhousen Farm GU24 67 E3
Bull La
- Bracknell RG42 27 B8
- Woking GU4 89 F1
Bullrush Cl
- Carshalton SM5 59 E8
- Thornton Heath CR0 42 E3
Bulls Alley SW14 7 D5
Bullswater Common Rd GU24, GU3 88 A2
Bullswater La GU24 88 A2
Bullvant Ho GU21 88 F8
Bulmer Ct TN16 83 C7
Bulrushes Bsns Pk RH19 205 D6
Bulstrode Ave TW3 5 A4
Bulstrode Gdns TW3 5 A4
Bulstrode Rd TW3 5 A4
Bunbury Way KT17 77 B4
Bunce Common Rd RH2 137 E2
Bunce Dr CR3 100 D4
Bunch La GU27 208 B8
Bunch Way GU27 208 A6
Bundy's Way TW18 12 F2
Bungalow Rd SE25 42 E5
Bungalows The
- Caterham CR3 100 D4
- Mitcham SW16 21 B1
- Normandy GU12 106 D3
Bungalows The *continued*
- Wallington SM6 60 B5
Bunting Cl
- Horsham RH13 217 F3
- Mitcham CR4 40 F4
Buntings The GU9 145 F8
Bunyan Cl RH11 200 E3
Bunyard Dr GU21 70 C5
Burbage Gn RG12 27 F4
Burbage Rd SE21, SE24 22 D8
Burbank KT3 38 F6
Burbeach Cl RH11 201 B3
Burberry Cl KT3 38 E7
Burbidge Rd TW17 34 A5
Burbury Woods GU15 65 E6
Burchets Hollow GU5 154 D7
Burchetts Way TW17 34 B3
Burcote 6 KT13 53 D4
Burcote Rd SW18 20 D8
Burcott Gdns KT15 52 D4
Burcott Rd CR8 80 A5
Burdenshot Hill GU3 89 B3
Burdenshott Ave TW10 7 B3
Burdenshott Rd
- Guildford GU4 109 C8
- Woking GU22, GU3, GU4 89 A2
Burden Way GU2 109 B6
Burdett Ave SW20 39 A8
Burdett Cl RH10 202 D5
Burdett Rd
- Richmond TW9 6 F4
- Thornton Heath CR0 42 D3
Burdock Cl
- 2 Crawley RH11 201 A2
- Croydon CR0 43 D1
- Lightwater GU18 67 B8
Burdon La SM2 58 F2
Burdon Pk SM2 58 F2
Burfield Cl SW17 20 D4
Burfield Dr CR6 101 C8
Burfield Rd SL4 11 B8
Burford Cnr RH5 115 C4
Burford Ct RG40 25 E5
Burford La KT17 77 C8
Burford Lea GU8 148 E4
Burford Lo RH5 115 C4
Burford Rd
- Camberley GU15 65 B4
- Forest Hill SE6 23 F6
- Horsham RH13 217 E2
- New Malden KT4 39 A2
- Sutton SM1 59 A8
Burford Way CR0 63 C4
Burge Cl GU14 84 C4
Burgess Cl TW13 15 E4
Burgess Mews SW19 20 B2
Burgess Rd SM1 59 B6
Burges Way TW18 13 A3
Burgh Cl RH10 182 D1
Burghead Cl GU47 64 D7
Burghfield KT17 76 F4
BURGH HEATH 97 D8
Burgh Heath Rd KT17, KT18 76 F4
Burghhill Rd SE26 23 E4
Burghley Ave KT3 38 D8
Burghley Ct SW19 19 E3
Burghley Ho SW19 19 E5
Burghley Pl CR4 40 F5
Burghley Rd SW19 19 E4
Burgh Mount SM7 77 F4
Burgh Wood SM7 77 E4
Burgos Cl CR0 61 A4
Burgoyne Rd
- Ashford TW16 14 F2
- Camberley GU15 66 A6
- South Norwood SE25 42 F5
Burham Cl SE20 23 C1
Burhill Com Inf Sch KT12 54 D4
Burhill Rd KT12 54 C3
Buriton Ho 9 SW15 19 B7
Burke Cl SW15 7 E3
Burlands RH11 181 A1
Burlea Cl KT12 54 B5
Burleigh Ave SM6 60 B7
Burleigh Cl
- Addlestone KT15 52 B5
- Crawley Down RH10 204 B8
Burleigh Ct 1 KT22 95 A5
Burleigh Gdns
- Ashford TW15 14 C3
- Woking GU21 69 F2
Burleigh Ho SM4 39 E1
Burleigh La
- Crawley Down RH10 204 C7
- North Ascot SL5 28 E8
Burleigh Lo 3 SW19 20 B1
Burleigh Pk KT11 73 E7
Burleigh Rd
- Addlestone KT15 52 B5
- Cheam SM3, SM4 39 E1
- Frimley GU16 85 D8
- North Ascot SL5 28 E7
Burleigh Way RH10 204 B8
Burleigh Wlk SE6 24 C7
Burles Bridge Cotts GU10 124 D2
Burley Cl
- Loxwood RH14 213 A4
- Mitcham SW16 41 D7
Burley Orch KT16 33 A3
Burleys Rd RH10 202 C6
BURLEYS WOOD 202 E7
Burley Way GU17 64 C6
Burlingham Cl GU4 110 D3
Burlings The SL5 28 F7
Burlington Apartments SE20 23 B1
Burlington Ave TW9 7 A6
Burlington Cl TW14 14 D8
Burlington Ct
- 7 Aldershot GU11 105 A1
- Blackwater GU17 64 D3
- Chiswick W4 7 C7
Burlington Ho TW10 6 F1
Burlington Inf Sch KT3 38 F5
Burlington Jun Sch KT3 38 F5
Burlington La W4 7 E8
Burlington Pl RH2 118 A2
Burlington Rd
- Hounslow TW7 5 D6
- New Malden KT3 38 F5
- South Norwood CR7 42 D7
Burlsdon Way RG12 27 E8
Burma Rd GU24, KT16 49 F8
Burmarsh Ct SE20 43 C8
Burma Terr 11 SE19 22 E3
Burmester Ho SW17 20 C5
Burmester Rd SW17 20 C5
Burnaby Cres W4 7 C8
Burnaby Gdns W4 7 B8
Burnbury Rd SW12 21 C7
Burn Cl
- Addlestone KT15 52 D6
- Oxshott KT22 74 D4
Burne-Jones Dr GU47 64 D6
Burnell Ave TW10 17 C3
Burnell Ho 19 SW2 22 A7
Burnell Rd SM1 59 B6
Burnet Ave GU1 110 B4
Burnet Cl GU24 67 E6
Burnet Gr KT19 76 C6
Burney Ave KT5 37 F4
Burney Cl KT23 94 C2
Burney Ct 5 RH11 201 A3
Burney Ho
- Leatherhead KT22 95 A6
- 4 Streatham SW16 21 C3
Burney Rd RH5 115 A4
Burnham Cl GU21 68 D1
Burnham Dr
- North Cheam KT4 58 D8
- Reigate RH2 118 A2
Burnham Gates GU1 109 D1
Burnham Gdns
- Cranford TW5 4 B6
- Croydon CR0 42 F2
Burnham Manor GU15 66 A8
Burnham Pl 1 RH13 217 D1
Burnham Rd
- Knaphill GU21 68 D1
- Morden SM4 40 B5
Burnhams Rd KT23 93 E3
Burnham St KT2 38 A8
Burnham Way SE26 23 F3
Burnhill Rd BR3 44 A7
Burn Moor Chase RG12 27 E2
Burnsall Cl GU14 85 B6
Burns Ave TW14 4 A1
Burns Cl
- Farnborough GU14 84 F6
- Horsham RH12 217 E7
- Mitcham SW17 20 D2
- Wallington SM5 60 A2
Burns Ct SM6 60 B3
Burns Dr SM7 77 E5
Burnside KT21 75 F1
Burnside Cl TW1 6 A1
Burnside Ct SM6 60 A7
Burns Rd RH10 202 C8
Burns Way
- Crawley RH12 200 C1
- East Grinstead RH19 185 C1
- Heston TW5 4 D6
Burnt Ash Prim Sch BR1 24 F3
Burnt Common Cl GU23 90 F2
Burntcommon La GU23 91 A2
Burnt Hill Rd GU10 146 B6
Burnt Hill Way GU10 146 B5
Burnt House La RH12 200 A7
Burnt Oak La RH5 179 F1
Burnt Pollard La GU24 48 E1
Burntwood Cl
- Caterham CR3 101 A6
- Wandsworth SW18 20 E7
Burntwood Ct SW17 20 C5
Burntwood Grange Rd SW18 20 E7
Burntwood La
- Caterham CR3 101 A6
- Wandsworth SW17 20 D6
Burntwood Sch SW17 20 D6
Burntwood View SE19 22 F3
BURPHAM 110 B5
Burpham Court Farm Pk* GU4 109 F7
Burpham La GU4 110 A5
Burpham Prim Sch GU4 110 A5
Burrell Cl CR0 43 E3
Burrell Ct RH11 200 F4
Burrell Ho 5 TW1 17 B8
Burrell Rd GU16 85 C8
Burrell Row BR3 44 A7
Burrells 9 BR3 44 B7
Burrell The RH4 135 C6
Burr Hill La GU24 49 F2
Burritt Rd KT1 38 A7
BURROWHILL 49 E3
Burrow Hill Gn GU24 49 E2
Burrows Cl
- Guildford GU2 108 F2
- Little Bookham KT23 93 F3
Burrows Cross GU5 133 C2
Burrows La GU5 133 C3
Burrow Wlk SE21 22 C8
Burr Rd SW18 20 A8
Burrwood Gdns GU12 106 A4
Burstead Cl KT11 73 D7
Burston Gdns RH19 185 D4
BURSTOW 183 A7
Burstow Ct RH6 160 F1
Burstow Ho RH6 161 B6
Burstow Lodge Bsns Ctr RH6 162 B4
Burstow Prim Sch RH6 162 B3
Burstow Rd SW20 39 E8
Burtenshaw Rd KT7 37 A3
Burton Cl
- Chessington KT9 56 D3
- Horley RH6 161 A2
- South Norwood CR7 42 D6
- Windlesham GU20 48 D4
Burton Ct KT7 37 A3
Burton Dr GU3 108 A6
Burton Gdns TW5 4 F6
Burton Ho SE26 23 B3
Burton Rd KT2 17 E1
Burtons Ct 11 RH12 217 C2
Burton's Rd TW12 16 C4
Burtwell La SE21, SE27 22 D4
Burvill Ct SW20 39 C8
Burwash Rd RH10 202 A5
Burway Cres KT16 33 A5
Burwood Ave CR8 80 B5
Burwood Cl
- Guildford GU1 110 D2
- Hersham KT12 54 C4
- Reigate RH2 118 D1
- Tolworth KT6 38 A1
Burwood Ct SE23 23 C8
Burwood Ho RH8 122 E5
Burwood Lo SW19 19 F4
Burwood Par 3 KT16 33 A2
BURWOOD PARK 54 A5
Burwood Park Rd KT12 54 B6
Burwood Rd
- Hersham, Burwood Park KT12 54 B4
- Hersham KT12 54 D5
Bury Cl GU21 69 D3
Bury Fields GU2 130 C7
Bury Gr SM4 40 B4
Bury La GU21 69 C3
Burys Court Sch RH2 138 C3
Bury St GU2 130 C7
Burys The GU7 150 E5
Burywood Hill RH5 177 E7
BUSBRIDGE 150 F2
Busbridge CE Jun Sch GU7 150 F2
Busbridge Inf Sch GU7 150 F2
Busbridge La GU7 150 E3
Busby Ho SW16 21 C4
Busch Cl TW7 6 B6
Busch Cnr TW7 6 B6
Busdens Cl GU8 170 F8
Busdens La GU8 170 F8
Busdens Way GU8 170 F8
Bushbury La RH3 137 A5
Bush Cl KT15 52 C5
Bushell Cl SW2 21 F6
Bushell Ho 3 SE27 22 C4
Bushetts Gr RH1 119 B6
Bushey Cl CR3 80 F3
Bushey Croft RH8 122 C5
Bushey Ct SW20 39 B7
Bushey Down SW12 21 B6
Bushey La SM1 59 A6
Bushey Mans SW20 39 C6
BUSHEY MEAD 39 D6
Bushey Rd
- Croydon CR0 63 A8
- Merton SW20 39 D7
- Sutton SM1 59 A6
- Sutton SM1 59 B6
Bushey Way BR3 44 D4
Bushfield RH14 211 F2
Bushfield Dr RH1 140 A4
Bush La GU23 90 D3
Bushnell Rd SW17 21 B5
Bush Rd
- Littleton TW17 33 F4
- Richmond TW9 6 F8
Bush Wlk RG40 25 C6
Bushwood Rd TW9 7 A8
Bushy Ct KT1 37 C8
BUSHY HILL 110 C3
Bushy Hill Dr GU1 110 C3
Bushy Hill Jun Sch GU1 110 D2
Bushy Park Gdns TW11 16 D3
Bushy Park Rd TW11 17 B1
Bushy Rd
- Fetcham KT22 94 B5
- Teddington TW11 16 F1
Bushy Shaw KT21 75 C2
Business Ctr The RG41 25 B4
Business Village The CR3 100 C5
Busk Cres GU14 84 F3
Bute Ave TW10 17 E6
Bute Ct SM6 60 C5
Bute Gardens W SM6 60 C5
Bute Gdns SM6 60 C5
Bute Rd
- Thornton Heath CR0 42 A1
- Wallington SM6 60 C6
Butler Rd
- Bagshot GU19 47 F2
- Crowthorne RG45 45 B6
Butlers Cl TW4 4 F3
Butlers Dene Rd CR3 102 A7
Butlers Hill KT24 112 B5
Butlers Pl GU8 150 A1
Butlers Rd RH13 218 B4
Butt Cl GU6 174 E4
Butt Ct SM4 40 C3
Buttercup Cl RG40 26 A6
Buttercup Sq TW19 13 D7
Butterfield
- Camberley GU15 65 B4
- East Grinstead RH19 185 B3
Butterfield Cl TW1 5 F1
Butterfield Ct 1 KT23 94 A1
Butterfly Wlk CR6 101 C7
Butter Hill
- 5 Dorking RH4 136 A7
- Hackbridge SM5, SM6 60 A6
Buttermer Cl GU10 145 F7
Buttermere Cl
- East Bedfont TW14 14 F7
- Farnborough GU14 84 E4
- Horsham RH12 218 B6
- West Barnes SM4 39 D3
Buttermere Ct GU12 105 F4
Buttermere Dr GU15 66 D4
Buttermere Gdns
- Bracknell RG12 27 C6
- Sanderstead CR8 80 D6
Buttermere Way 4 TW20 12 B1
Buttersteep Rise SL5 28 C1
Butterworth Ct SW16 21 E5
Butts Cl RH11 201 B7
Butts Cotts
- 3 Feltham TW13 15 F5
- 4 Woking GU21 69 A1
Butts Cres TW13 16 A5
Butts Ho TW13 16 A5
Butts Rd
- Catford BR1 24 E3
- Woking GU21 69 E2
Butts The TW8 6 D8
Buxton Ave CR3 100 E6
Buxton Cl KT19 76 B8
Buxton Cres SM3 58 E6
Buxton Dr KT3 38 D7
Buxton La CR3 100 E6
Buxton Rd
- Ashford TW15 13 D3
- 4 Mortlake SW14 7 E4
- Thornton Heath CR7 42 B4
Byards Croft SW16 41 D8
Byatt Wlk TW12 15 E2
Bychurch End 13 TW11 16 F3
Bycroft St SE20 23 D1
Bycroft Way RH10 202 B8
Byerley Way RH10 202 E7
Byers La RH9 142 C1
Bye Ways TW2 16 B5
Byeways The KT5 38 B4
Byeway The SW14 7 C4
Byfield Ct KT3 39 A5
Byfield Rd TW7 6 A4
BYFLEET 71 D7
Byfleet Cnr KT14 71 A6
Byfleet Ind Est KT14 71 D8
Byfleet & New Haw Sta KT15 52 D1
Byfleet Prim Sch KT14 71 D8
Byfleet Rd
- New Haw KT14, KT15 52 D2
- Weybridge KT11, KT13 72 C7
Byfleets La RH12 216 D6
Byfleet Tech Ctr The KT14 71 D8
Byfrons The GU14 85 D2
Bygrove CR0 63 B3
Bygrove Ct SW19 20 D2
Bygrove Rd SW19 20 D2
Byland Cl SM4 40 D2
Bylands GU22 70 A1
Byne Rd
- Carshalton SM5 59 E8
- Penge SE20, E26 23 C3
Bynes Rd CR2 61 D3
By Pass Rd KT22 95 B7
Byrd Rd RH11 200 F3
Byrefield Rd GU2 108 F4
Byrne Ct 4 CR8 80 A7
Byrne Rd SW12 21 B6
Byron Ave
- Carshalton SM1 59 D6
- Coulsdon CR5 79 F3
- Cranford TW4 4 B5
- Frimley GU15 66 B3
- West Barnes KT3 39 A4
Byron Ave E SM1 59 D6
Byron Cl
- Crawley RH10 202 B7
- Forest Hill SE26 23 E4
- Hampton TW12 15 F4
- Horsham RH12 217 E6
- Knaphill GU21 68 E2
- Streatham SW16 21 E2
- Walton-on-T KT12 35 E1
Byron Ct
- Dulwich SE21 23 A7
- 1 Richmond TW10 17 D4
- South Norwood CR7 42 C7

Byron Dr RG45 45 B3
Byron Gdns SM1 59 D6
Byron Gr 2 RH19 185 C1
Byron Ho BR3 24 B2
Byron Pl KT22 95 B5
Byron Prim Sch CR5 79 F2
Byron Rd
Addlestone KT15 52 E6
South Croydon CR2 62 B1
Byton Rd SW17 20 F2
Byttom Hill RH5 115 C8
Byward Ave TW14 4 C1
Bywater Ct GU14 105 C8
Byways The KT21 75 D1
Byway The
Sutton SM2 59 D2
Worcester Park KT19 57 F6
Bywood RG12 27 A2
Bywood Ave CR0 43 D3
Bywood Cl CR8 80 B4
Bywood Terr CR0 43 C3
Byworth Cl GU9 124 F2
Byworth Rd GU9 124 F2

C

Cabbell Pl KT15 52 C6
Cabell Rd GU2 108 E2
Caberfeigh Cl RH1 118 E1
Cabin Moss RG12 27 E2
Cable House Ct GU21 69 E4
Cabrera Ave GU25 31 D3
Cabrera Cl GU25 31 D3
Cabrol Rd GU14 85 A5
Caburn Ct RH11 201 C4
Caburn Hts RH11 201 C4
Cackstones The RH10 202 D7
Cadbury Cl
Ashford TW16 14 E1
Isleworth TW7 6 A6
Cadbury Rd TW16 14 E2
Caddy Cl 13 TW20 12 A3
Cadley Terr SE23 23 C6
Cadmer Cl KT3 38 E5
Cadnam Cl GU11 126 C6
Cadnam Point 14
SW15 19 B7
Cadogan Cl
Beckenham BR3 44 D7
Teddington TW11 16 E3
Cadogan Ct
Frimley GU15 65 E3
New Malden KT3 38 E5
Sutton SM2 59 B4
Cadogan Ho 11 GU1 130 F8
Cadogan Pl CR8 80 C2
Cadogan Rd
Farnborough GU11 105 D7
Kingston u T KT6 37 D4
Caenshill Ho KT13 53 A3
Caenshill Pl KT13 53 A3
Caenshill Rd KT13 53 A3
Caenswood Hill KT13 53 A1
Caenwood Cl KT13 53 A4
Caen Wood Rd KT21 75 C1
Caerleon Cl
Beacon Hill GU26 188 C6
Claygate KT10 56 B3
Caernarvon GU16 85 F8
Caernarvon Cl CR4 41 E6
Caernarvon Ct 3 KT5 37 F4
Caesar Ct GU11 104 E2
Caesar's Camp Rd
GU15 66 A8
Caesar's Cl GU15 66 A8
Caesars Ct GU9 125 C7
Caesar's Way TW17 34 D3
Caesars Wlk CR4 40 F4
Caffins Cl RH10 201 E8
Caillard Rd KT14 71 E8
Cain Rd RG12 26 D7
Cain's La TW14 3 E2
Cairn Cl GU15 66 B3
Cairndale Cl BR1 24 F1
Cairngorm Cl 4 TW11 17 A3
Cairngorm Pl GU14 84 E7
Cairn Ho SW19 20 E1
Cairo New Rd CR0, CR9 61 B8
Caister Ho 11 SW12 21 B8
Caistor Mews SW12 21 B8
Caistor Rd SW12 21 B8
Caithness Dr KT18 76 D5
Caithness Rd CR4 21 B1
Calbourne Rd SW12 21 A8
Caldbeck Ave KT4 39 B1
Caldbeck Ho 7 RH11 200 F3
Calderdale Cl RH11 201 B4
Calder Rd SM4 40 C4
Calder Way SL3 1 E4
Caldwell Rd GU20 48 D5
Caledonian Ho RH10 201 D8
Caledonian Way RH6 182 B7
Caledonia Rd TW19 13 E7
Caledon Pl GU4 110 A4
Caledon Rd SM6 60 A6
Calfridus Way RG12 27 F6
California Cl SM2 59 A1
California Ct SM2 59 B1
California Rd KT3 38 C6
Callander Rd SE6 24 C6
Calley Down Cres CR0 63 D1
Callis Farm Cl TW19 2 E1
Callisto Cl RH11 200 E3
Callow Field CR8 80 A6
Callow Hill GU25 31 C7
Calluna Ct GU22 69 F1
Calluna Dr RH10 183 A3
Calmont Rd BR1 24 E2
Calonne Rd SW19 19 D4
Calshot Rd TW6 3 B5
Calshot Way
Frimley GU16 86 A7
Harlington TW6 3 A5
Calthorpe Gdns SM1 59 C7
Calton Gdns GU11 126 C7
Calumet Ct SW17 20 E2
Calverley Cl BR3 24 B2
Calverley Ct BR3 44 D7
Calverley Rd KT17 58 A4
Calvert Cl
Aldershot GU12 105 D1
Epsom KT19 57 B1
Calvert Cres RH4 115 B1
Calvert Ct
Leatherhead KT22 95 B5
8 Richmond TW9 6 F3
Calvert Rd
Dorking RH4 115 B2
Effingham KT24 113 B7
Calvin Cl GU15 66 B4
Calvin Wlk RH11 200 E3
Camac Rd TW2 16 D7
Camargue Pl GU7 150 F4
Camber Cl RH10 202 C6
CAMBERLEY 65 D6
Camberley Ave SW20 39 B7
Camberley Bsns Ctr
GU15 65 A5
Camberley Cl SM3 58 D7
Camberley Ct 7 SM2 59 B3
Camberley Inf Sch
GU15 65 C5
Camberley Rd TW6 3 A4
Camberley Sta GU15 65 D5
Camberley Twrs 1
GU15 65 D5
Cambisgate SW19 19 E3
Camborne Cl TW6 3 A4
Camborne Ho 9 SM2 59 B3
Camborne Rd
Belmont SM2 59 B3
Croydon CR0 43 A2
Wandsworth SW18 20 A8
West Barnes SM4 39 D4
Camborne Rd S TW6 3 A4
Camborne Way
Harmondsworth TW6 3 A4
Heston TW5 5 A6
Cambray Rd SW12 21 C7
Cambria 6 BR3 44 B7
Cambria Cl TW3 5 A3
Cambria Ct
Feltham TW14 15 B8
Staines TW18 12 E4
Cambria Gdns TW19 13 E8
Cambria Ho SE26 23 A4
Cambrian Cl
Camberley GU15 65 B5
West Norwood SE27 22 B5
Cambrian Ct 8 CR2 61 E6
Cambrian Rd
Farnborough GU14 84 D7
Richmond TW10 6 F1
Cambridge Ave KT3,
SW20 38 F7
Cambridge Cl
Harmondsworth UB7 2 D8
Hounslow TW4 4 E3
Knaphill GU21 68 F1
Wimbledon SW20 39 B8
Cambridge Cotts TW9 7 A8
Cambridge Cres TW11 17 A3
Cambridge Ct
Farnborough GU14 85 C1
7 Twickenham TW1 6 D1
Wimbledon SW20 39 B8
Cambridge Gdns KT1 38 A7
Cambridge Gr SE20 43 B8
Cambridge Grove Rd
Kingston u T KT1 38 A6
5 Kingston u T, Norbiton
KT1 38 A7
Cambridge Ho 2
TW11 17 A3
CAMBRIDGE PARK 6 D1
Cambridge Park Ct
TW1 17 D8
Cambridge Pk TW1 6 C1
Cambridge Pl GU9 125 C2
Cambridge Rd
Aldershot GU11 104 F2
Barnes SW13 7 F5
Carshalton SM5 59 E5
Crowthorne RG45 45 C4
Croydon SE20, SE25 43 B6
East Molesey KT8 35 F5
Hampton TW12 15 F1
Horsham RH13 217 D2
Hounslow TW4 4 E3
Kingston u T KT1 38 A7
Littleton Common TW15,
TW17 14 C1
Mitcham CR4 41 C6
New Malden KT3 38 E5
Richmond TW9 7 A7
Sandhurst GU47 45 E1
Teddington TW11 17 A3
Twickenham TW1 6 D1
Walton-on-T KT12 35 B3
Wimbledon SW20 39 B8
Cambridge Rd E GU14 85 D1
Cambridge Rd W GU14 85 C1
Cambridge Sq
Camberley GU15 65 C6
Redhill RH1 140 A6
Cambridge Tutors Coll
CR0 61 E6
Cambridge Wlk GU15 65 C6
Camden Ave TW13 15 C7
Camden Cotts KT13 53 A7
Camden Gdns
South Norwood CR7 42 B6
Sutton SM1 59 B5
Camden Hill Rd SE19 22 E2
Camden Ho SM6 60 E7
Camden Jun Sch SM5 59 F6
Camden Rd
Carshalton SM5 59 F6
Lingfield RH7 164 D4
Sutton SM1 59 B5
Camden Way CR7 42 B6
Cameford Ct 19 SW12 21 E8
Camel Cl KT2 17 D3
Camellia Ct
21 Beckenham BR3 24 A1
West End GU24 67 F6
Camellia Ho TW13 15 A7
Camellia Pl TW2 16 B8
Camelot Cl
Biggin Hill TN16 83 C3
Wimbledon SW19 20 A4
Camelot Ct RH11 200 E6
Camelsdale Fst Sch
GU27 207 F5
Camelsdale Rd GU27 207 F5
CAMELSIDE 207 F4
Camel Way GU14 105 A8
Cameron Cl GU6 174 E1
Cameron Ct 3 SW19 19 E7
Cameron Ho 10 BR1 44 F8
Cameron Lo TW3 5 C3
Cameron Pl SW16 22 A5
Cameron Rd
Farnborough GU11 105 D7
Forest Hill SE6 23 F6
Thornton Heath CR0 42 B3
Cameron Sq CR4 40 E8
Camgate Ctr The TW19 13 F8
Camilla Cl
Ashford TW16 14 F2
Great Bookham KT23 94 B2
Camilla Ct 9 SM2 59 A3
Camilla Dr RH5 115 A5
Camille Cl SE25 43 A6
Camino Pk RH10 182 A4
Camlan Rd BR1 24 F4
Camm Gdns
6 Kingston u T KT1 37 F7
Thames Ditton KT7 36 F2
Camomile Ave CR4 40 F8
Campaspe Bsns Pk
TW16 34 F4
Campbell Ave GU22 89 F6
Campbell Cl
Aldershot GU11 126 C7
Streatham SW16 21 D4
Twickenham TW2 16 D7
West Byfleet KT14 71 D7
Campbell Cres RH19 185 B1
Campbell Ct
Dulwich SE21 23 A7
Leatherhead KT22 95 B5
Campbell Fields
GU12 105 B1
Campbell Ho 6 SM6 60 B6
Campbell Pl GU16 65 F3
Campbell Rd
Aldershot GU11 105 A3
Caterham CR3 100 D6
Crawley RH10 202 C5
Thornton Heath CR0 42 B3
Twickenham TW2 16 D6
Weybridge KT13 53 A3
Campden Rd CR0, CR2 61 E5
Campen Cl SW19 19 E6
Camp End Rd KT11,
KT13 72 C8
Camp Farm Rd GU11 105 D5
Camp Hill GU10 147 C8
Camphill Ct KT14 71 A7
Camphill Ind Est KT14 71 B8
Camphill Rd KT14, KT15 71 B7
Campion Cl
Blackwater GU17 64 F3
South Croydon CR2 61 E6
Campion Dr KT20 97 B7
Campion Ho
Bracknell RG42 26 E8
6 Redhill RH1 119 A4
Campion House
(Seminary) TW7 5 D6
Campion Rd
Horsham RH12 217 E5
Hounslow TW7 5 F6
Campion Way RG40 25 E7
Camp Rd
Farnborough GU14 105 C8
Wimbledon SW19 19 C3
Woldingham CR3 101 E6
Camps Ho TW12 16 C3
Camp View SW19 19 B3
Camrose Ave TW13 15 C4
Camrose Cl
Croydon CR0 43 E2
Morden SM4 40 A5
Camrose Ct CR2 61 E4
Canada Ave RH1 140 A5
Canada Copse GU8 149 E2
Canada Dr RH1 140 A5
Canada Ho RH1 140 A5
Canada Rd
Byfleet KT14 71 D8
Cobham KT11 73 C6
Canada Rd *continued*
Frimley GU16 86 E8
Canadian Ave SE6 24 B7
Canal Bank GU21 88 F8
Canal Bank Mews
GU21 69 E2
Canal Cl GU11 105 D5
Canal Cotts GU12 106 A4
Canal Wlk
Croydon CR0 42 F3
Forest Hill SE26 23 C3
Canberra Cl RH11 181 D1
Canberra Pl RH12 217 F4
Canberra Rd TW6 3 A4
Canberra Way GU14 104 F8
Canbury Ave KT2 37 F8
Canbury Bsns Pk 3
KT2 37 E8
Canbury Ct 3 KT2 17 E1
Canbury Mews SE26 23 A5
Canbury Park Rd KT2 37 F8
Candler Mews TW1 17 A8
Candlerush Cl GU22 70 B2
Candover Cl UB7 2 D7
Candy Croft KT23 94 B2
Canewden Cl GU22 89 E8
Canfold Cotts GU6 175 B4
Canford Dr KT15 52 B8
Canford Gdns KT3 38 E3
Canford Pl TW11 17 B2
Canham Rd SE25 42 E6
Canhams KT20 97 B6
Can Hatch KT20 77 E1
Canmore Gdns SW16 21 C1
Canning Rd
Aldershot GU12 105 D2
Croydon CR0, CR9 61 F8
Cannizaro Rd SW19 19 D3
Cannon Cl
Hampton TW12 16 B2
Sandhurst GU47 64 F8
West Barnes SW20 39 C6
Cannon Cres GU24 68 E8
Cannon Gr KT22 94 E6
Cannon Hill RG12 27 C3
Cannon Hill La KT3, SM4,
SW20 39 E5
Cannon Ho SE26 23 B2
Cannon Mews SL5 28 B8
Cannon Side KT22 94 E5
Cannon Way
East Molesey KT8 36 B5
Fetcham KT22 94 E6
Canonbie Rd SE23 23 C8
Canonbury Cotts
RH12 199 F6
Canons Cl RH2 117 F2
Canon's Hill CR5 80 A1
Canons La KT20 97 F8
Canon's Wlk CR0 62 D7
Canon (W End of General
Roy's Base Line)*
TW6 3 B6
Canopus Way TW19 13 E8
Cansiron La RH19 206 F6
Cantelupe Ho 1
RH19 185 F1
Cantelupe Mews 7
RH19 185 E1
Cantelupe Rd RH19 185 F1
Canterbury Cl
Beckenham BR3 44 B8
North Cheam KT4 58 D8
Canterbury Ct
4 Ashford TW15 13 F4
3 Dorking RH4 136 A8
South Croydon CR2 61 C3
Thornton Heath CR0 42 A2
Canterbury Gdns GU14 85 D2
Canterbury Gr SE27,
SW16 22 A5
Canterbury Hall KT4 39 B2
Canterbury Ho KT19 76 A8
Canterbury Mews
KT22 74 C6
Canterbury Rd
Ash GU12 106 A3
Crawley RH10 201 E2
Farnborough GU14 85 D2
Feltham TW13 15 E6
Guildford GU2 108 F3
Morden SM4 40 C3
Thornton Heath CR0,
CR7 42 A2
Canterbury Wlk GU14 85 D2
Canter The RH10 202 E7
Cantley Cres RG41 25 A8
Cantley Gdns SE19 42 F8
Canute Ct SW16 22 A5
Canute Ho 1 TW8 6 C7
Canvas Ct GU27 208 B6
Canvey Cl RH11 201 C3
Capatus Ho SW14 7 D5
Cape Copse RH12 214 D7
CAPEL 178 C6
Capel KT5 37 F2
Capel Ave SM6 60 F5
Capel Ct
7 Mortlake SW14 7 D4
Penge SE20 43 C8
Capel La RH11 200 F5
Capella Ho RH5 178 C5
Capel Lo
5 Richmond TW9 6 F6
15 Streatham SW2 21 F8
Capel Rd RH12 199 A8
Capern Rd SW18 20 C7
Capital Bsns Ctr CR2 61 D3
Capital Ind Est CR4 40 F4
Capital Pk
Old Woking GU22 90 B6
Wormley GU8 190 F7
Caplan Ct TW10 6 F1
Caplan Est CR4 41 C8
Capper Rd GU15 65 A7
Capricorn Cl RH11 200 E4
Capri Rd CR0 42 F2
Capsey Rd RH11 200 E5
Capstans Wharf 8
GU21 68 F1
Capstone Rd BR1 24 F4
Caradon Cl GU21 69 B1
Caradon Ct 7 TW1 6 C1
Caraway Cl RH11 201 B2
Caraway Pl
Guildford GU2 109 A6
Hackbridge SM6 60 B7
Carberry Rd 13 SE19 22 E2
Carbery La SL5 29 B6
Cardamom Cl GU2 109 A5
Card Hill RH18 206 F1
Cardigan Cl GU21 68 F1
Cardigan Ct
North Cheam KT4 39 E1
7 Richmond TW10 6 E1
Cardigan Rd
Richmond TW10 6 E1
Wimbledon SW19 20 C2
Cardinal Ave
Kingston u T KT2 17 E2
West Barnes SM4 39 E3
Cardinal Cl
Sanderstead CR2 81 A6
West Barnes SM4 39 E3
Worcester Park KT4 58 A6
Cardinal Cres KT3 38 C7
Cardinal Ct KT8 36 D5
Cardinal Dr KT12 35 D1
Cardinal Ho GU14 85 C4
Cardinal Newman RC Prim
Sch KT12 54 D7
Cardinal Rd TW13 15 B7
Cardinal Road Inf Sch
TW13 15 B7
Cardinals The GU10 126 F7
Cardinal's Wlk
Ashford TW16 14 E2
Hampton TW12 16 C1
Cardingham GU21 69 B2
Cardington Sq TW4 4 D3
Cardwell Cres SL5 29 C4
Cardwells Keep GU2 109 A4
Carew Cl CR5 100 B8
Carew Ct SM2 59 B2
Carew Ho SW16 22 A5
Carew Manor Sch SM6 60 D7
Carew Rd
Ashford TW15 14 C2
Mitcham CR4 41 A7
Thornton Heath CR7 42 B5
Wallington SM6 60 C4
Carey Ho RH11 201 C6
Carey Rd RG40 25 C5
Carey's Wood RH6 162 B3
Carfax RH12 217 C2
Carfax Ave GU10 126 F8
Carfax Est GU10 126 F8
Cargate Ave GU11 105 A1
Cargate Gr GU11 105 A1
Cargate Hill GU11 104 F1
Cargate Terr GU11 104 F1
Cargill Rd SW18 20 C7
Cargo Forecourt Rd
RH6 181 D7
Cargo Rd RH6 181 D7
Cargreen Rd SE25 42 F5
Carholme Rd SE23 23 F7
Carisbrook Ct 1 SW16 21 F5
Carisbrooke GU16 85 F8
Carisbrooke Cl TW4 15 E8
Carisbrooke Ct SM2 58 F3
Carisbrooke Ho
16 Kingston u T KT2 37 E8
Richmond TW10 7 A2
Carisbrooke Rd CR4 41 E5
Carleton Ave SM6 60 D2
Carleton Cl KT10 36 D1
Carling Ct TW1 16 F7
Carlingford Gdns CR4 21 A1
Carlingford Rd SM4 39 D3
Carlington Ho CR0 61 E5
Carlin Pl GU15 65 C4
Carlinwark Dr GU15 65 F7
Carlisle Cl KT2 38 A8
Carlisle Inf Sch TW12 16 B2
Carlisle Rd
Cheam SM1 58 F4
Hampton TW12 16 B1
Rushmoor GU10 168 C6
Carlisle Way SW17 21 A3
Carlos St GU7 150 E4
Carlton Ave
Feltham TW14 4 C1
South Croydon CR2 61 E3
Carlton Cl
Chessington KT9 56 D4
Crawley RH10 201 E5
Frimley GU15 66 B3
Woking GU21 70 A5
Carlton Cres SM3 58 E6
Carlton Ct
Horley RH6 161 A5
12 Penge SE20 43 B8

Carlton Ct continued
South Norwood SE19...... 42 F8
Staines TW18............. 13 A3
Carlton Gn RH1........... 118 E4
Carlton Ho
Cheam SM1.............. 58 F4
Feltham TW14............. 3 F1
Hounslow TW4............. 5 A1
Carlton Park Ave
SW20................... 39 D7
Carlton Pl 2 KT13....... 53 B6
Carlton Rd
Ashford TW16............ 14 F1
Blindley Heath RH9....... 142 C2
Headley Down GU35...... 187 C5
Kingston u T KT3........ 38 E7
Mortlake SW14............ 7 C3
Redhill RH1, RH2........ 118 E4
South Croydon CR2...... 61 D3
Walton-on-T KT12........ 35 B2
Woking GU21............. 70 A5
Carlton Terr SE26........ 23 C5
Carlton Twrs SM5........ 59 F7
Carlton Tye RH6......... 161 C3
Carlwell St SW17........ 20 E3
Carlyle Ct KT8.......... 36 B7
Carlyle Ct RG45......... 45 C5
Carlyle Ho KT8.......... 36 A4
Carlyle Rd
Croydon CR0............ 62 A8
Staines TW18............ 13 A1
Carlyon Cl
Farnborough GU14....... 85 C4
Mytchett GU16.......... 85 C4
Carlys Cl BR3........... 43 D7
Carmalt Gdns KT12...... 54 C5
Carman Wlk RH11....... 201 B1
Carmarthen Cl GU14.... 85 A7
Carmel Cl 9 GU22...... 69 E1
Carmella Ct TW15....... 14 D1
Carmichael Ct SW13..... 7 F5
Carmichael Ho 17
SE21................... 22 E4
Carmichael Mews
SW18.................. 20 D8
Carmichael Rd SE25..... 43 A5
Carminia Rd SW17...... 21 B6
Carnac St SE21, SE27.... 22 D5
Carna Ct TW9............ 7 A5
Carnation Cl RG45....... 45 B8
Carnation Dr RG42........ 8 B2
Carnegie Cl KT6......... 56 F8
Carnegie Pl SW19........ 19 D5
Carnforth Cl KT19....... 57 B4
Carnforth Rd SW16...... 21 D1
Carnoustie RG12......... 26 E2
Carole Ho 14 SE20....... 43 B8
Carolina Rd CR7........ 42 C8
Caroline Cl
Hounslow TW7............ 5 E7
South Croydon CR0...... 61 E6
Streatham SW16........ 21 F5
Caroline Ct
Ashford TW15........... 14 B2
Catford SE6............. 24 A4
Crawley RH11........... 201 D4
17 Surbiton KT6......... 37 D2
Caroline Dr RG41........ 25 A7
Caroline Pl UB3.......... 3 E7
Caroline Rd SW19....... 19 F1
Carolyn Cl GU21......... 88 F8
Carpenter Cl KT17....... 57 F2
Carpenters Ct TW2...... 16 E6
Carrara Villas KT1....... 37 F6
Carriage Pl 14 SW16.... 21 C3
Carrick Cl TW7........... 6 A4
Carrick Gate KT10....... 55 C7
Carrigshaun KT13....... 53 D4
Carrington Ave TW3...... 5 B2
Carrington Cl
Croydon CR0............ 43 E2
Redhill RH1............ 118 F2
Carrington Ct 3 KT3.... 38 E5
Carrington Ho 7
SW19.................. 20 A1
Carrington La GU12..... 106 A8
Carrington Lo 3 TW10.... 6 E2
Carrington Pl KT10...... 55 C6
Carrington Rd TW10...... 7 A3
Carroll Ave GU1......... 110 B1
Carroll Cres SL5......... 28 F5
Carrow Rd KT12......... 54 D7
CARSHALTON............ 59 E7
Carshalton, Beddington &
  Wallington War Meml
  Hospl SM5............. 59 F4
CARSHALTON BEECHES
  .... 59 E2
Carshalton Beeches Sta
  SM5.................. 59 F4
Carshalton Boys Sports
  Coll SM5.............. 59 E8
Carshalton Coll SM5..... 59 F7
Carshalton Gr SM1...... 59 D5
Carshalton High Sch for
  Girls SM5............. 59 E7
Carshalton Lo 1 KT13... 53 E7
CARSHALTON ON THE
  HILL................ 60 B3
Carshalton Park Rd
  SM5.................. 59 F5
Carshalton Pl SM5....... 60 A5
Carshalton Rd
Camberley GU15........ 47 A1
Carshalton SM1, SM5.... 59 D5

Carshalton Rd continued
Mitcham CR4............ 41 A4
Wallington SM7......... 78 F6
Carshalton Sta SM5...... 59 F6
Carson Rd SE21......... 22 D6
Carstairs Rd SE6........ 24 C5
Carswell Rd SE6......... 24 C8
Cartbridge Cl GU23..... 90 B4
Carter Cl SM6........... 60 D3
Carterdale Cotts RH5... 178 C5
Carter Rd
Crawley RH10.......... 202 D3
Mitcham SW19.......... 20 D2
Carters Cl
Guildford GU1......... 109 E5
North Cheam KT4....... 39 D1
Carter's Cotts RH1..... 139 E7
Carters La
Forest Hill SE23........ 23 F5
Woking GU22........... 90 D7
Cartersmead Cl RH6.... 161 B4
Carter's Rd KT17........ 76 F4
Carters Wlk GU9....... 125 D8
Carthouse Cotts GU4... 110 C4
Carthouse La GU21..... 68 E5
Cartmel Cl RH2......... 118 E3
Cartmel Ct BR2......... 44 E7
Cartmel Gdns SM4...... 40 C4
Carwarden House Com
  Sch GU15............. 66 A3
Caryl Ho 6 SW19....... 19 D7
Carylls Cotts RH12..... 199 F1
Cascades CR0........... 62 F1
Cascades Ct SW19...... 19 F1
Cascadia Ho 11 KT1.... 38 A7
Caselden Cl KT15....... 52 C5
Casewick Rd SE27...... 22 B4
Casher Rd RH10........ 202 C3
Cassel Hospl The
  TW10................. 17 D4
Cassilis Rd TW1.......... 6 B1
Cassino Cl GU11....... 105 B2
Cassiobury Ave TW14... 14 F8
Cassland Rd CR7........ 42 D5
Casslee Rd SE6......... 23 F8
Cassocks Sq SW17...... 34 D2
Castillon Rd SE6........ 24 E6
Castlands Rd SE6........ 23 F6
Castle Ave KT17......... 58 B2
Castle Bsns Village
  TW12................. 36 B8
Castle Cl
Beckenham BR2......... 44 E6
Bletchingley RH1....... 120 C2
Camberley GU15........ 65 F4
3 Charlton TW16........ 14 E1
Farnborough GU14...... 85 E2
Reigate RH2........... 139 B5
Wimbledon SW19....... 19 D5
Castlecombe Dr SW19... 19 D8
Castlecraig Ct GU47..... 64 D7
Castle Ct
Belmont SM2........... 59 A4
Forest Hill SE26........ 23 E4
Morden SM4........... 40 D4
Castledine Rd SE20...... 23 B1
Castle Dr
Horley RH6............ 161 C2
Reigate RH2........... 139 B4
Castle Field GU9....... 125 B3
Castlefield Ct RH2...... 118 B1
Castlefield Rd RH2...... 118 A1
Castlegate TW9........... 6 F4
Castle Gdns RH4....... 115 F1
Castle Gn KT13.......... 53 E7
CASTLE GREEN.......... 68 D7
Castle Grove Rd GU24... 68 E7
Castle Hill
Farnham GU9.......... 125 B3
Guildford GU1......... 130 D7
Castle Hill Ave CR0...... 63 C2
Castle Hill Prim Sch
  CR0.................. 63 C4
Castle Hill Rd TW20..... 11 C5
Castle Ho 3 SM2........ 59 A3
Castle Keep RH2........ 118 A1
Castlemaine Ave
  Ewell KT17............ 58 B2
  South Croydon CR2, CR1. 61 F5
Castleman Ho SL5....... 29 D4
Castle Mews KT13....... 53 E7
Castle Of Mey Ho
  GU27................ 207 F6
Castle Par KT17......... 58 A3
Castle Rd
Aldershot GU11........ 104 E4
Broadbridge Heath
  RH12................ 216 D3
Camberley GU15........ 65 F4
Epsom KT18............ 76 B4
Isleworth TW7........... 5 F5
Kingswood CR5......... 98 E6
Oatlands Park KT13..... 53 E7
Woking GU21........... 69 F5
Castle Sq
Bletchingley RH1....... 120 C2
Guildford GU1......... 130 D7
Castle St
Bletchingley RH1....... 120 C2
Farnham GU9.......... 125 B3
Guildford GU1......... 130 D7
Kingston u T KT2........ 37 E7
Castle The RH12....... 217 E7
Castleton Cl
Banstead SM7.......... 78 A4
Croydon CR0........... 43 E3
Castleton Ct KT5........ 37 F4
Castleton Dr SM7....... 78 A5

Castleton Rd CR4........ 41 D5
Castle View KT18........ 76 B5
Castleview Rd KT13...... 53 B6
Castle Way
Ewell KT17............. 58 A2
Feltham TW13........... 15 C4
Wimbledon SW19........ 19 D5
Castle Wlk
Reigate RH2........... 118 A1
Sunbury TW16.......... 35 C6
Castle Yd 19 TW10........ 6 D2
Caswell Cl GU14......... 84 F6
Catalina Rd TW6......... 3 B5
Catalpa Cl GU1........ 109 C3
Catena Rise GU18....... 48 B1
Caterfield La
Crowhurst RH7......... 143 F3
Oxted RH7, RH8........ 144 A3
Cater Gdns GU3........ 108 F3
CATERHAM............. 100 F4
Caterham By-Pass
  CR3.................. 101 B4
Caterham Cl GU24....... 87 A6
Caterham Dene Hospl
  CR3.................. 100 F4
Caterham Dr CR5....... 100 C8
Caterham Prep Sch
  CR3.................. 100 F1
Caterham Sch CR3...... 100 F1
Caterham Sta CR3...... 101 A3
Caterways RH12........ 217 A3
CATFORD................ 24 A7
Catford Br SE6.......... 24 A8
Catford Bridge Sta
  SE6................... 24 A8
Catford Broadway SE6... 24 B8
Catford Gyratory SE6.... 24 B8
Catford High St SE6..... 24 C5
Catford High Sch
  (Annexe) BR1......... 24 E4
Catford Hill SE6......... 24 A7
Catford Rd SE6.......... 24 A8
Catford Sh Ctr SE6...... 24 B8
Catford Sta SE6......... 24 A8
Cathedral Cl GU2...... 130 B8
Cathedral Ct GU2...... 109 A1
Cathedral Hill GU2..... 109 A2
Cathedral Hill Ind Est
  GU2.................. 109 A2
Cathedral View GU2.... 108 F1
Catherine Baird Ct 13
  SW12................ 21 B8
Catherine Cl KT14...... 71 F5
Catherine Dr
Aldershot GU11........ 104 F1
3 Wimbledon SW19..... 19 F3
Catherine Dr
Ashford TW16.......... 14 F2
Richmond TW9........... 6 E3
Catherine Gdns TW3..... 5 D3
Catherine Ho
Ascot SL5............. 29 B6
Isleworth TW7........... 6 B6
Catherine Howard Ct 8
KT13................. 53 B7
Catherine Rd KT6....... 37 D4
Catherine Villas GU27.. 208 B6
Catherine Wheel Rd
  TW8................... 6 D7
Cathill La RH5......... 177 C3
Cathles Rd SW12........ 21 C8
Catlin Cres TW17....... 34 D4
Catling Cl SE23......... 23 D5
Catlin Gdns RH9....... 121 B5
Caton Ct BR2........... 44 E7
Cator Cl CR0........... 82 E8
Cator Cres CR0......... 82 E8
Cator La BR3........... 43 F8
Cator Park Sch BR3..... 23 E1
Cator Rd
Penge SE20, SE26....... 23 D2
Wallington SM5......... 59 F5
CATTESHALL........... 151 A5
Catteshall Hatch GU7... 151 A6
Catteshall La GU7...... 150 F4
Catteshall Rd GU7...... 151 A5
Catteshall Terr GU7.... 151 A5
Causeway
Feltham TW14, TW4....... 4 B3
Horsham RH12......... 217 C1
Causeway Ct 1 GU21.... 68 F1
Causeway Est SW20..... 12 C4
Causewayside GU27.... 208 D6
Causeway The
Carshalton SM5......... 60 A8
Claygate KT10.......... 55 F3
Egham TW18, TW20...... 12 D4
Sutton SM2............ 59 C2
Teddington TW11........ 16 F2
Wimbledon SW19........ 19 C3
Cavalier Ct TW15....... 14 D1
Cavalier Way RH19..... 205 F7
Cavalry Cres TW4........ 4 D3
Cavalry Ct GU11....... 104 E2
Cavans Rd GU11....... 105 C2
Cavell Way
Crawley RH10.......... 202 C5
Epsom KT19............ 76 A8
Knaphill GU21.......... 88 C8
Cavendish Apartments
  The 4 BR1............ 24 F1
Cavendish Ave KT3...... 39 B5
Cavendish Cl
Ashford TW16.......... 14 F2
Horsham RH12......... 217 D7
Cavendish Ct
Ashford TW16.......... 14 F2
Blackwater GU17........ 64 D3

Cavendish Ct continued
Catford SE6............ 24 B7
Poyle SL3.............. 1 E6
6 Richmond TW10........ 6 E1
17 Wallington SM6...... 60 B4
Weybridge KT13......... 53 C4
Cavendish Dr KT10...... 55 E5
Cavendish Gdns RH1... 119 A2
Cavendish Ho
3 Richmond TW10...... 17 C5
Twickenham TW1......... 6 A1
Cavendish Meads SL5... 29 D3
Cavendish Mews
GU11................ 105 A1
Cavendish Par TW4...... 4 E5
Cavendish Pk GU47..... 64 E6
Cavendish Pl
Guildford GU2......... 108 D3
Streatham SW12........ 21 C7
Cavendish Prim Sch W4... 7 E7
Cavendish Rd
Aldershot GU11........ 105 A1
Ashford TW16.......... 14 F2
Balham SW12........... 21 B8
Chiswick W4............ 7 C6
Mitcham SW19.......... 20 E1
New Malden KT3........ 38 F5
Redhill RH1........... 119 A2
Sutton SM2............ 59 C3
Thornton Heath CR0..... 42 B1
Weybridge KT13......... 53 C3
Woking GU22........... 89 D8
Cavendish Terr TW13.... 15 A6
Cavendish Way BR4..... 44 B1
Cavendish Wlk KT19.... 76 B8
Cavenham Cl 6 GU22... 89 E8
Cave Rd TW10........... 17 C4
Caverleigh Way KT4.... 39 B2
Caversham Ave SM3..... 58 E8
Caversham Ho
8 Kingston u T KT1..... 37 E7
Wallington SM6......... 60 E7
Caversham Rd KT1...... 37 F7
Caves Farm Cl GU47.... 64 A8
Cawnpore St SE19...... 22 E3
Cawsey Way GU21...... 69 E2
Cawston Ct 12 RH1..... 24 F1
Caxton Ave KT15........ 52 A4
Caxton Cl RH10........ 201 E3
Caxton Gdns GU2...... 109 B2
Caxton Ho RH8......... 123 F3
Caxton La RH8......... 123 E4
Caxton Rd SW19......... 20 C3
Caxton Rise RH1....... 119 A2
Caxtons Ct GU1........ 110 A3
Caygill Cl BR2.......... 44 F5
Cayton Rd CR5.......... 99 C5
Cearn Way CR5......... 79 F4
Ceasors Ct TW2......... 16 F6
Cecil Cl
Ashford TW15.......... 14 C1
Chessington KT9........ 56 D6
Cecil Ct 12 CR0......... 61 F8
Cecil Lo KT9........... 56 D6
Cecil Mans 2 SW17..... 21 A6
Cecil Pl CR4........... 40 F4
Cecil Rd
Ashford TW15.......... 14 C2
Cheam SM1............ 58 F4
Hounslow TW3........... 5 D5
Merton SW19........... 20 B1
Thornton Heath CR0..... 41 F3
Cedar Ave
Blackwater GU17........ 64 D5
Cobham KT11........... 73 C4
Twickenham TW2......... 5 C1
Cedar Cl
Aldershot GU12........ 126 E8
Bagshot GU19.......... 47 E3
Crawley RH11.......... 181 C1
Dorking RH4........... 136 B7
East Molesey KT8....... 36 E5
Epsom KT17............ 76 F5
Esher KT10............. 54 F3
Horsham RH12......... 217 C3
Kingston u T KT2....... 18 D4
Laleham TW18.......... 33 C6
Reigate RH2........... 139 C7
Wallington SM5......... 59 F4
Warlingham CR6........ 101 E8
West Norwood SE21..... 22 C6
Wokingham RG40........ 25 C6
Cedarcroft Rd KT9...... 56 F6
Cedar Ct
Addlestone KT15........ 52 C5
Bagshot GU19.......... 47 E3
9 Brentford TW8........ 6 D8
5 Caterham CR3....... 100 D5
Cobham KT11.......... 73 A6
Egham TW20............ 12 A4
Haslemere GU27....... 208 B6
2 Kingston u T KT3..... 38 E6
Mortlake SW14.......... 7 C3
Ottershaw KT16......... 51 C5
Sanderstead CR2....... 81 A8
Stoneleigh KT17........ 58 A3
4 Sutton SM2........... 59 C4
Wimbledon SW19........ 19 D5
Cedar Dr
Fetcham KT22.......... 94 E4
Sunningdale SL5........ 30 A2
Cedar Gdns
Chobham GU24......... 49 F1
Sutton SM2............ 59 C4
Woking GU21........... 69 B1
Cedar Gr
Bisley GU24............ 68 A4
Weybridge KT13......... 53 C6

Cedar Hill KT18......... 76 C3
Cedar Ho
Charlton TW16.......... 14 F1
Guildford GU4......... 110 C3
New Addington CR0..... 63 B4
5 Richmond TW9......... 7 B6
Whyteleafe CR3......... 80 F2
Cedar Hts TW10......... 17 E7
Cedarhurst 1 BR1....... 24 E1
Cedar La GU16.......... 85 D8
Cedarland Terr SW20.... 19 B1
Cedar Lo
Crawley RH11.......... 201 D4
Weybridge KT13......... 53 A7
Cedar Mount GU8....... 148 C4
Cedar Pk CR3.......... 100 E6
Cedar Rd
Cobham KT11........... 73 B5
Cranford TW5............ 4 C5
Croydon CR0, CR9....... 61 E8
East Bedfont TW14...... 14 D7
East Molesey KT8....... 36 E5
Farnborough GU14...... 85 C3
Sutton SM2............ 59 C4
Teddington TW11........ 17 A3
Weybridge KT13......... 53 A6
Woking GU22........... 89 C7
Cedars
2 Bracknell RG12...... 27 F5
Woodmansterne SM7.... 78 F5
Cedars Ave CR4......... 41 A6
Cedars Ct GU1......... 110 A4
Cedars Ho 5 SW27...... 22 B3
Cedars Prim Sch The
  TW5................... 4 A7
Cedars Rd
Barnes SW13............ 7 F5
Beckenham BR3......... 43 F7
Morden SM4........... 40 A5
Teddington KT8......... 37 C8
Wallington CR0......... 60 E6
Cedars The
Ashtead KT22.......... 95 D6
Brockham RH3......... 116 A1
Byfleet KT14........... 71 F7
Guildford GU1......... 110 A4
Milford GU8........... 170 E8
Reigate RH2........... 118 D1
Teddington TW11........ 16 F2
Wallington SM6......... 60 C6
Cedar Terr TW9.......... 6 E3
Cedar Tree Gr SE27..... 22 B3
Cedarville Gdns SW16... 21 F2
Cedar Way
Charlton TW16.......... 14 E1
Guildford GU1......... 109 C4
Cedarways GU9......... 146 B7
Cedar Wlk
Claygate KT10.......... 55 F4
Kenley CR8............ 80 C3
Kingswood KT20........ 97 E7
Cedarwood BR3......... 23 F1
Cedric Ct 2 RH12...... 217 A1
Celandine
1 Crawley RH11........ 201 B2
Crowthorne RG45....... 45 C6
Celandine Rd KT12...... 54 E6
Celia Cres TW15........ 13 D2
Celia Ct
Ewell KT17............. 57 F2
7 Richmond TW9........ 6 F6
Celtic Ave BR2.......... 44 E6
Celtic Rd KT14.......... 71 F5
Cemetery La TW17....... 34 B2
Cemetery Pales
  Brookwood GU24....... 88 A6
  Pirbright GU24........ 87 F5
Centaurs Bsns Pk TW7.... 6 A8
Centenary Ct BR3....... 44 C8
Central Ave
East Molesey KT8....... 35 F4
Isleworth TW3, TW7...... 5 C3
Wallington SM6......... 60 E5
Central Blgs 2 GU21.... 69 F2
Central Ct KT15......... 52 B6
Centrale Croydon CR0.... 61 C2
Central Gdns SM4....... 40 B4
Central Hill SE19....... 22 D2
Central La SL4........... 9 B7
Central Mans SW16...... 21 E4
Central Par
Croydon CR0............ 61 A6
East Molesey KT8....... 35 F5
Feltham TW14........... 15 C8
Heston TW5............. 5 A7
Kingston u T KT6....... 37 E3
New Addington CR0..... 63 C1
Penge SE20............ 23 D1
Streatham SW16........ 21 E4
Central Pk Est TW4...... 4 D3
Central Rd
Morden SM4........... 40 B4
North Cheam KT4....... 58 A8
Central Sq KT8.......... 35 F5
Central Terr BR3........ 43 D6
Central Veterinary
  Laboratory KT15...... 52 B2
Central Way
Cranbourne SL4......... 9 B7
Feltham TW14........... 4 B2
Oxted RH8............ 122 D8
Sutton SM5............ 59 E3
Central Wlk
Epsom KT19............ 76 D6
Wokingham RG40........ 25 C6
Centre Court Sh Ctr 3
SW19.................. 19 F2

Centre Terrace Rd
GU14 . . . . **105** A8
Centre The TW13 . . . . **15** B7
Centrium 13 GU21 . . . . **69** F2
Centurion Cl 4 GU47 . . . . **64** D8
Centurion Ct SM6. . . . . **60** B8
Century Ct
Teddington TW11. . . . . **17** A4
Woking GU21. . . . . **69** F3
Century Farm Ind Units
GU9. . . . . **125** F5
Century Ho SM7 . . . . **78** B4
Century Rd TW18,
TW20. . . . . **12** C3
Century Way GU24 . . . . **87** D8
Century Yd SE23. . . . . **23** C6
Cerne Rd SM4 . . . . **40** C3
Cerotus Pl KT16 . . . . **32** F2
Chadacre Rd KT17 . . . . **58** B5
Chaddesley KT13 . . . . **53** A6
Chadhurst Cl RH5. . . . . . . **136** D4
Chadwick Ave SW19 . . . . . **20** A2
Chadwick Cl
Crawley RH11 . . . . **201** B1
Roehampton SW15 . . . . **18** F8
Teddington TW11. . . . . **17** A2
Chadwick Pl KT6. . . . . **37** C3
Chadworth Way KT10 . . . . **55** D5
Chaffers Mead KT21 . . . . . **75** F3
Chaffinch Ave CR0 . . . . **43** D3
Chaffinch Bsns Pk
BR3. **43** D5
Chaffinch Cl
Crawley RH11 . . . . **201** D8
Croydon CR0 . . . . **43** D3
Horsham RH12 . . . . **217** D7
5 Sandhurst GU47. . . . . . . **64** D8
Tolworth KT6. . . . . **57** A7
Chaffinch Rd BR3. . . . . **43** E8
Chaffinch Way RH6 . . . . . **160** E4
Chagford Ct SW19 . . . . **20** E1
Chailey Cl
2 Crawley RH11 . . . . **201** A3
Heston TW5. . . . . **4** D6
Chailey Ct CR0. . . . . **60** E7
Chailey Pl KT12. . . . . **54** E6
Chalcot Cl SM2 . . . . **59** A3
Chalcot Mews SW16 . . . . . **21** E5
Chalcott Gdns KT6. . . . . . . **37** C1
CHALDON **100** B3
Chaldon Cl RH1. . . . . **139** E7
Chaldon Common Rd
CR3 . . . . **100** C2
Chaldon Rd
Caterham CR3. . . . . **100** D4
Crawley RH11 . . . . **201** C1
Chaldon Way CR5. . . . . **79** E1
Chale Wlk SM2 . . . . **59** B2
Chalfont Dr GU14 . . . . **85** C2
Chalfont Rd SE25 . . . . **42** F6
Chalford Cl KT8. . . . . **36** A5
Chalford Ct KT6 . . . . **37** F2
Chalford Rd SE21 . . . . **22** D4
Chalgrove Ave SM4 . . . . . . **40** A4
Chalgrove Rd SM2 . . . . **59** D3
Chalice Cl SM6 . . . . **60** D4
Chalkenden Cl SE20. . . . . . **23** B1
Chalkers Cnr SW14 . . . . **7** B4
Chalk La
Ashtead KT21 . . . . **96** A8
East Horsley KT24. . . . . . . **112** F4
Epsom KT18. . . . . **76** E3
Shackleford GU8 . . . . **149** D8
Chalkley Cl CR4. . . . . **41** A7
Chalk Paddock KT18 . . . . . **76** D4
Chalkpit La
Brockham RH3. . . . . **116** B2
Dorking RH4 . . . . **115** A1
Dorking RH4 . . . . **136** A8
Oxted RH8 . . . . **122** D8
Woldingham CR3, CR8. . . . **102** C1
Chalk Pit La KT23. . . . . . . **113** F8
Chalk Pit Rd
Banstead SM7. . . . . **78** A2
Langley Vale KT18. . . . . **96** C8
Sutton SM1 . . . . **59** C4
Chalkpit Terr RH4 . . . . . . **115** A1
Chalkpit Wood RH8 . . . . . **122** D8
Chalk Rd
Farncombe GU7. . . . . **150** E5
Ifold RH14. . . . . **212** C3
Chalky La KT9 . . . . **56** D1
Challen Ct RH12 . . . . **217** B3
Challenge Ct
Leatherhead KT22. . . . . **95** B8
Twickenham TW2. . . . . **16** E8
Challenge Rd TW15 . . . . . . **14** D5
Challice Way SW2 . . . . **21** F7
Challin St SE20 . . . . **43** C8
Challis Pl RG42 . . . . **26** E8
Challock Cl TN16 . . . . **83** C3
Challoner Ct BR2 . . . . **44** D7
Challoners Cl KT8. . . . . **36** D5
Chalmers Cl RH6 . . . . **180** E6
Chalmers Rd
Ashford TW15 . . . . **14** B3
Banstead SM7. . . . . **78** C4
Chalmers Rd E TW15. . . . . **14** C3
Chalmers Way TW14 . . . . **4** B2
Chalner Ho 21 SW2 . . . . . . **22** A7
Chamber La GU10. . . . . . . **145** C7
Chamberlain Cres BR4 . . . **44** B2
Chamberlain Gdns TW3 . . . **5** C6
Chamberlain Way KT6 . . . **37** E2
Chamberlain Wlk
TW13 . . . . **15** E4
Chambers Ho 2 SW16 . . . **21** C4
Chambers Pl CR2 . . . . **61** D3
Chambers Rd GU12 . . . . . **106** B6
Chamomile Gdns GU14. . . **84** C5
Champion Cres SE26. . . . . **23** E4
Champion Down
KT24 . . . . **113** E7
Champion Rd SE26. . . . . . . **23** E4
Champness Cl 9 SE27 . . . **22** D4
Champney Cl SL3 . . . . **1** A4
Champneys Cl SM2 . . . . . . **58** F3
Chancellor Gdns CR2 . . . . **61** B2
Chancellor Gr SE21 . . . . . . **22** C5
Chancery Ct 13 TW20 . . . . **12** A3
Chancerygate Bsns Ctr
RG41. . . . . **25** A5
Chancery Gate Bsns Ctr
CR4. **40** F4
Chancery La BR3 . . . . **44** B7
Chancery Mews SW17. . . . **20** E6
Chanctonbury Chase
RH1 . . . . **119** A1
Chanctonbury Dr SL5 . . . . **29** E1
Chanctonbury Gdns
SM2 . . . . **59** B3
Chanctonbury Way
RH11 . . . . **201** C4
Chanderie Ct 1 CR0 . . . . . **61** C7
Chandler CE Jun Sch The
GU8. . . . . **170** F5
Chandler Cl
Crawley RH10 . . . . **201** D4
Hampton TW12 . . . . **36** A8
Chandler Ct
4 Horley RH6. . . . . **161** B3
Thornton Heath CR7 . . . . . . **42** B4
2 Tolworth KT5 . . . . **38** B1
8 Wallington SM6 . . . . **60** B4
Chandlers KT20. . . . . **97** B6
Chandlers Cl TW14. . . . . . . **14** F8
Chandlers Field Prim Sch
KT8. **36** B4
Chandlers Rd GU12 . . . . . **106** B4
Chandlers Way 11
SW2. **22** A8
Chandon Lo SM2. . . . . **59** C3
Chandos Bsns Ctr 11
SM6 . . . . **60** C4
Chandos Mans CR0 . . . . . . **43** A5
Chandos Rd TW18 . . . . **12** D3
Channel Cl TW5 . . . . **5** A6
Channings GU21. . . . . **69** E4
Channon Ct 8 KT6. . . . . . . **37** E4
Chantilly Way KT19 . . . . . . **57** B1
Chantlers Cl RH19 . . . . . . **185** C2
Chanton Dr SM2. . . . . **58** C1
Chantrey Cl KT21 . . . . **95** C8
Chantrey Rd RH10 . . . . . . **201** E3
Chantry Cl
Horley RH6 . . . . **160** F4
Sunbury TW16 . . . . **15** A1
Chantry Cotts GU4 . . . . . . **131** B3
Chantry Ct SM5. . . . . **59** E7
Chantry Ct GU16 . . . . **65** D1
Chantry Hurst KT18 . . . . . . **76** D4
Chantry La GU5. . . . . **132** F4
Chantry Pl 5 GU1 . . . . . . **130** E8
Chantry Rd
Bagshot GU19 . . . . **47** D2
Chertsey KT16. . . . . **33** C2
Chessington KT9 . . . . **57** A5
Chilworth GU4 . . . . **131** B3
Chantrys Ct GU9 . . . . **125** A2
Chantrys The GU9 . . . . . . **125** A1
Chantry View Rd GU1 . . . **130** E6
Chantry Way CR4 . . . . **40** D6
Chantry Wood Nature
Trail★ GU1 . . . . **130** E5
Chapel Ave
Addlestone KT15 . . . . **52** B6
Brookwood GU24. . . . . **88** B6
Chapel Cl
Bracknell RG12 . . . . **27** D6
Milford GU8. . . . . **149** F2
Chapel Ct 10 RH4 . . . . **136** A8
Chapel Farm Mobile Home
Pk GU3 . . . . **107** E4
Chapel Fields GU7 . . . . . . **150** D7
Chapel Gn CR8 . . . . **80** A6
Chapel Gr
Addlestone KT15 . . . . **52** B6
Burgh Heath KT18. . . . . **97** C8
CHAPEL GREEN **25** C4
Chapel Hill
Dunsfold GU8 . . . . **192** F3
Effingham KT24 . . . . **113** D8
Chapelhouse Cl GU2 . . . . **108** E1
Chapel La
Ashurst Wood RH19 . . . . . **206** D6
Bagshot GU19 . . . . **47** D2
Copthorne RH10 . . . . **183** F4
Farnborough GU14 . . . . **84** F8
Forest Row RH18. . . . . **206** F2
Great Bookham KT23. . . . . **114** C6
Milford GU8. . . . . **149** F2
Pirbright GU24. . . . . **88** A4
Westcott RH4 . . . . **135** C6
Westhumble RH5. . . . . **114** E5
Chapel Lane Ind Est
RH4. . . . . **135** C6
Chapel Mill Rd KT1 . . . . . . **37** F6
Chapel Park Rd KT15. . . . . **52** B6
Chapel Rd
Camberley GU15 . . . . **65** B5
Charlwood RH6 . . . . **180** F7
Hounslow TW3. . . . . **5** B4
Limpsfield RH8 . . . . **123** C5
Redhill RH1 . . . . **118** F1
Rowledge GU10. . . . . **145** E3
Smallfield RH6. . . . . **162** B4
Chapel Rd *continued*
Tadworth KT20 . . . . **97** D4
Twickenham TW1. . . . . **17** B8
Warlingham CR6 . . . . **81** D1
West Norwood SE27 . . . . . . **22** B4
Chapel Sq
Sandhurst GU15 . . . . **64** F6
Virginia Water GU25 . . . . . . **31** E5
Chapel St
Farnborough GU14 . . . . **85** D6
Guildford GU1 . . . . **130** D7
11 Woking GU21. . . . . **69** F2
Chapel View CR2 . . . . **62** C3
Chapel Way KT18, KT20 . . . **77** C1
Chaplain's Hill RG45 . . . . . **45** D4
Chaplin Cres TW16. . . . . . . **14** E2
Chapman Ho 2 SE27. . . . . . **22** B5
Chapman Rd
Crawley RH10 . . . . **202** C2
Thornton Heath CR0 . . . . . . **42** A1
Chapman's La
East Grinstead RH19. . . . . **185** B1
East Grinstead RH19. . . . . **185** D1
Chapman Sq SW19. . . . . . . **19** D6
Chapter Ct 15 TW20. . . . . . **12** A3
Chapter Ho GU14 . . . . **85** C4
Chapter Way TW12. . . . . . . **16** A4
Chara Pl W4. . . . . **7** D8
Charcot Ho SW15 . . . . **7** F1
Chargate Cl KT12 . . . . **54** A4
Charing Ct BR2 . . . . **44** E7
Charlbury Cl 7 RG12. . . . . **27** F5
Charlecombe Ct TW18 . . . **13** B3
Charlecote Cl GU14 . . . . . . **85** D3
Charlecote Gr SE26 . . . . . . **23** B5
Charles Babbage Cl
KT9 . . . . **56** D3
Charles Cobb Gdns
CR0 . . . . **61** A5
Charles Ct
South Croydon CR2 . . . . **61** D5
5 Teddington TW11 . . . . . . **16** E3
Charles Darwin Sch
TN16. . . . . **83** F3
Charles Dickens Ct
SE25. . . . . **43** A5
Charlesfield Rd RH6 . . . . **160** F4
Charles Haller St 8
SW2. **22** A8
CHARLESHILL **148** A5
Charles Hill GU10 . . . . **147** E6
Charles Ho
Chertsey KT16. . . . . **32** F1
Englefield Green TW20 . . . . **11** C1
Charles Lesser KT9 . . . . . . **56** D5
Charles Mills Ct SW16. . . . **21** E2
Charles Rd
Merton SW19 . . . . **40** A8
Staines TW18. . . . . **13** D2
Charles Sq RG12. . . . . **27** C7
Charles St
Chertsey KT16. . . . . **32** F1
Croydon CR0, CR9 . . . . **61** C7
Hounslow TW3. . . . . **4** F5
Mortlake SW13, SW14 . . . . . . **7** E5
Charles Staunton Ho 3
SE27. . . . . **22** D4
Charleston Cl TW13. . . . . . **15** A5
Charleston Ct RH10 . . . . . **202** B3
Charleville Cir SE19,
SE26. . . . . **23** A3
Charleville Mews TW7 . . . . . **6** B3
Charlewood Mans
SW12. . . . . **21** C8
Charlmont Rd SW17 . . . . . **20** F2
Charlock Cl 3 RH11 . . . . **201** A2
Charlock Way GU1. . . . . . **110** B4
Charlotte Broadwood
Flats RH5. . . . . **178** D6
Charlotte Cl GU9. . . . . **125** D8
Charlotte Ct
Crawley RH11 . . . . **201** C6
Esher KT10 . . . . **55** C5
Charlotte Gr RH6 . . . . **162** A4
Charlotte Ho KT21 . . . . **95** E8
Charlotte Lo KT10. . . . . **55** E4
Charlotte Mews
Esher KT10 . . . . **55** B6
Farnborough GU14 . . . . **85** D5
Charlotte Par SE23. . . . . . . **23** E6
Charlotte Rd
Barnes SW13. . . . . **7** F6
Wallington SM6 . . . . **60** C4
Charlotte Sq 5 TW10 . . . . . . **6** F1
CHARLTON **34** D7
Charlton Ave KT12 . . . . **54** B6
Charlton Ct GU47 . . . . **45** D1
Charlton Dr TN16 . . . . **83** D2
Charlton Gdns CR5. . . . . . . **79** C1
Charlton Ho
5 Brentford TW8 . . . . **6** E8
Charlton TW17. . . . . **34** C7
Charlton Kings KT13 . . . . . **53** E7
Charlton La TW17. . . . . **34** D5
Charlton Rd TW17 . . . . **34** C7
CHARLWOOD **180** E7
Charlwood CR0. . . . . **62** F2
Charlwood Cl
Copthorne RH10 . . . . **183** B4
Little Bookham KT23 . . . . . . **94** B3
Charlwood Dr KT22 . . . . . . **74** D4
Charlwood Ho
Richmond TW9. . . . . **7** B7
1 Streatham SW2 . . . . **21** F7
Charlwood La RH5 . . . . . . **180** A5
Charlwood Pl RH2 . . . . . . **117** F1
Charlwood Rd
Crawley RH6, RH11 . . . . . . **181** C4
Charlwood Rd *continued*
Hookwood RH6, RH11 . . . . **181** C8
Rusper RH11, RH6. . . . . . . **180** E2
Charlwoods Bsns Ctr
RH19. . . . . **185** D2
Charlwoods Pl RH19 . . . . **185** E3
Charlwoods Rd RH19. . . . **185** E3
Charlwood Village Inf Sch
RH6. . . . . **180** F7
Charlwood Wlk RH11 . . . **181** B1
Charman Rd RH1 . . . . **118** E1
Charmans Cl RH12 . . . . . . **218** B5
Charm Cl RH6 . . . . **160** E4
Charmile Ct 1 TW16. . . . . . **14** E1
Charminster Ave SW19. . . **40** B7
Charminster Ct 3 KT6 . . . **37** D2
Charminster Rd KT4 . . . . . **39** D1
Charmouth Ct TW10 . . . . **6** F2
Charnwood SL5. . . . . **29** F3
Charnwood Ave SW19. . . . **40** B7
Charnwood Cl KT3. . . . . . . **38** E5
Charnwood Rd SE25 . . . . . **42** D5
Charrington Rd 2 CR0,
CR9 . . . . **61** C8
Charrington Way
RH12 . . . . **216** C3
Charsley Rd SE6 . . . . **24** B6
Charta Rd TW20 . . . . **12** C2
Charta Rd W TW20. . . . . . . **12** C3
Chart Cl
Bromley BR2 . . . . **44** E8
Croydon CR0 . . . . **43** C3
Dorking RH5 . . . . **136** D5
Mitcham CR4 . . . . **40** F5
Chart Downs RH5. . . . . . . **136** D4
Charter Cres TW4. . . . . **4** E3
Charter Ct KT3 . . . . **38** E6
Charter Ho 5 SM2. . . . . **59** B4
Charterhouse GU7 . . . . . . **150** C7
Charterhouse Cl RG12. . . . **27** E4
Charterhouse Rd
GU7 . . . . **150** D6
Charter Pl TW18 . . . . **13** A2
Charter Rd KT1 . . . . **38** B6
Charters Cl
Ascot SL5. . . . . **29** D4
West Norwood SE19 . . . . . . **22** E3
Charters Ct GU12 . . . . **126** C8
Charters La SL5. . . . . **29** D4
Charter Sq KT1 . . . . **38** B7
Charters Rd SL5 . . . . **29** E2
Charters Sch SL5 . . . . **29** D2
Charters Way SL5. . . . . **29** F2
Charter Wlk GU27. . . . . . . **208** C6
Chartfield Pl KT13 . . . . **53** B5
Chartfield Rd RH2 . . . . . . **139** C8
Chart Gdns RH5 . . . . **136** C4
Chartham Gr SE27 . . . . **22** B5
Chartham Rd SE25 . . . . **43** B6
Chart Ho 1 CR4 . . . . **40** F7
Chart House Rd GU12 . . . **106** A7
Chart La
Dorking RH4 . . . . **136** C7
Reigate RH2. . . . . **139** C8
Chart La S RH5 . . . . **136** D5
Charts Cl GU6 . . . . **174** E2
Chartway RH2 . . . . **118** B1
Chartwell
Frimley GU16. . . . . **85** F6
25 Putney SW19 . . . . **19** D7
5 Woking GU22 . . . . **69** E1
Wrecclesham GU9. . . . . . . **145** F6
Chartwell Cl 2 CR0. . . . . . **42** D1
Chartwell Court Grange
RH4 . . . . **136** B4
Chartwell Gdns
Cheam SM3 . . . . **58** E6
Farnborough GU11 . . . . . . **105** C7
Chartwell Lo 5 BR3 . . . . . **24** A1
Chartwell Pl
Cheam SM3 . . . . **58** F6
Epsom KT18. . . . . **76** E5
Chartwell Way 4 SE20 . . . **43** B8
Chartwood Pl 7 RH4 . . . **136** A7
Charwood SW16 . . . . **22** A4
Charwood Rd RG40 . . . . **25** F7
Chase Bridge Prim Sch
TW2 . . . . **5** E1
Chase Ct
Isleworth TW7. . . . . **6** A5
Merton SW20 . . . . **39** E7
Chase End KT19 . . . . **76** D7
Chasefield Cl GU4 . . . . . . **110** A4
Chasefield Rd SW17 . . . . . **20** F4
Chase Gdns TW2. . . . . **16** D8
Chase La GU27 . . . . **208** E3
Chaseley Ct KT13 . . . . **34** E1
Chasemore Cl CR4. . . . . **40** F2
Chasemore Gdns CR0 . . . . . **61** A5
Chase Plain GU26 . . . . **188** C1
Chase Rd KT17, KT19. . . . . . **76** D7
Chaseside Ave SW20 . . . . . **39** E7
Chaseside Gdns KT16 . . . . **33** B2
Chase The
Ascot SL5. . . . . **9** A1
Ashtead KT21 . . . . **75** C1
Coulsdon CR5 . . . . **79** D5
Crawley RH10 . . . . **202** A5
Crowthorne RG45 . . . . **45** A6
East Horsley KT24. . . . . **92** F1
Farnborough GU14 . . . . **85** D6
Guildford GU2 . . . . **130** A8
Kingswood KT20 . . . . **98** B6
Oxshott KT22. . . . . **74** C4
Reigate RH2. . . . . **139** D8
South Norwood SW16 . . . . . **22** A1
Sunbury TW16 . . . . **35** B8
Wallington SM6 . . . . **60** F5
Chasewater Ct 8
GU11 . . . . **105** A1
Chateau The SM5. . . . . **59** F7
Chatelet Cl RH6. . . . . **161** B4
Chatfield Cl GU14. . . . . **85** C2
Chatfield Ct 3 CR3 . . . . . **100** D5
Chatfield Dr GU4 . . . . **110** C3
Chatfield Rd CR0 . . . . **42** B1
Chatfields RH11 . . . . **201** B4
Chatham Ave BR2. . . . . **44** F2
Chatham Cl SM3. . . . . **39** F2
Chatham Ho 6 SM6 . . . . . . **60** B5
Chatham Mews GU2 . . . . **109** B4
Chatham Rd KT1, KT2. . . . . **38** A7
Chathill RH8. . . . . **143** B6
Chatley Heath Semaphore
Twr★ KT11 . . . . **72** D1
Chatsfield KT17. . . . . **58** A1
Chatsworth Ave
Haslemere GU27 . . . . **208** C8
Merton SW20 . . . . **39** E7
Chatsworth Cl BR2, BR4. . . **63** F8
Chatsworth Cres TW3,
TW7. . . . . **5** D4
Chatsworth Ct SW16 . . . . . **41** F6
Chatsworth Gdns KT3 . . . . **38** F4
Chatsworth Gr GU9 . . . . . **125** B6
Chatsworth Ho KT6 . . . . . . **37** D4
Chatsworth Hts GU15 . . . . **66** B7
Chatsworth Inf Sch
TW3 . . . . **5** C3
Chatsworth Jun Sch
TW3 . . . . **5** C3
Chatsworth Lo BR4 . . . . . . **63** C8
Chatsworth Pk SM7 . . . . . . **78** B2
Chatsworth Pl
Mitcham CR4 . . . . **40** F6
Oxshott KT22. . . . . **74** D6
Teddington TW11. . . . . **17** A4
Chatsworth Rd
Cheam SM3 . . . . **58** E6
Chiswick W4 . . . . **7** C8
Croydon CR0, CR9 . . . . **61** D7
Farnborough GU14 . . . . **85** E3
Chatsworth Row
RH11 . . . . **201** C4
Chatsworth Way SE27. . . . **22** C5
Chattern Ct TW15. . . . . **14** B4
CHATTERN HILL **14** B4
Chattern Hill TW15. . . . . . . **14** B4
Chattern Rd TW15 . . . . **14** C4
Chatterton Ct TW9. . . . . **6** F5
Chatton Row GU24. . . . . . . **68** A2
Chaucer Ave
Cranford TW4 . . . . **4** B5
3 East Grinstead
RH19. . . . . **185** C1
Richmond TW9. . . . . **7** A5
Weybridge KT13 . . . . **53** A3
Chaucer Cl
Banstead SM7. . . . . **77** E5
Wokingham RG40 . . . . **25** F6
Chaucer Ct
Guildford GU2 . . . . **130** C7
Redhill RH1 . . . . **119** A4
Chaucer Gdns SM1. . . . . . . **59** A7
Chaucer Gn CR0 . . . . **43** C2
Chaucer Gr GU15 . . . . **65** D5
Chaucer Ho
Guildford GU1 . . . . **130** F8
Sutton SM1 . . . . **59** A7
2 West Norwood SE27 . . . **22** C4
Chaucer Rd
Ashford TW15 . . . . **13** F4
Crawley RH10 . . . . **202** C8
Crowthorne RG45 . . . . **45** B4
Farnborough GU14 . . . . **84** F6
Sutton SM1 . . . . **59** A6
Chaucer Way
Addlestone KT15 . . . . **52** A4
Mitcham SW19 . . . . **20** D2
Chavasse Way GU14. . . . . . **84** D5
Chave Croft KT18 . . . . **97** C8
Chave Croft Terr KT18 . . . **97** C8
CHAVEY DOWN **28** A8
Chavey Down Rd RG42 . . . . . **8** B2
Chaworth Cl KT16. . . . . **51** C4
Chaworth Rd KT16 . . . . **51** C4
Chawridge La SL4 . . . . **8** C7
CHEAM **58** F5
Cheam Cl
Bracknell RG12 . . . . **27** D4
Burgh Heath KT20. . . . . **97** B6
Cheam Common Inf Sch
KT4. **58** B8
Cheam Common Jun Sch
KT4. **58** B8
Cheam Common Rd
KT4 . . . . **58** C7
Cheam Court Flats
SM3. **58** E4
Cheam Fields Prim Sch
SM3 . . . . **58** E5
Cheam High Sch SM3. . . . . **58** E6
Cheam Mans SM3. . . . . **58** E3
Cheam Park Farm Inf Sch
SM3 . . . . **58** E7
Cheam Park Farm Jun Sch
SM3 . . . . **58** E7
Cheam Park Way SM3. . . . **58** E4
Cheam Rd
Cheam SM1 . . . . **59** A4
East Ewell KT17, SM2 . . . . . **58** C1
Cheam Sta SM2. . . . . **58** E3
Cheapside GU21 . . . . **69** D5

Cheapside CE Prim Sch SL5 29 E8
Cheapside Ct SL5 29 E8
Cheapside Rd SL5 29 D7
Cheddar Rd TW6 3 B5
Cheeseman Cl
Hampton TW12 15 E2
Wokingham RG40 25 D7
Cheffrey Ct TW15 14 B2
Chelford Rd BR1, E6 24 D3
Chellows La RH7 143 F2
Chelmsford Cl SM2 59 A2
Chelsea Cl
Hampton TW12 16 C3
New Malden KT4 39 A2
Chelsea Ct SM2 59 B4
Chelsea Fields SW19 40 D8
Chelsea Gdns SM3 58 E6
Chelsfield Gdns SE26 23 C5
CHELSHAM 82 A2
Chelsham Common Rd CR6 82 A2
Chelsham Court Rd CR6 82 E2
Chelsham Rd
Croydon CR2 61 D4
Warlingham CR6 81 F2
Chelsham Terr CR6 81 F1
Cheltenham Ave 12 TW1 17 A8
Cheltenham Cl KT3 38 C6
Cheltenham Villas CR7 42 A3
Chelwood Cl
Coulsdon CR5 99 C8
Crawley RH10 201 F4
Ewell KT17 76 F7
Chelwood Ct 9 CR2 61 C5
Chelwood Gdns TW9 7 A5
Cheney Ct
Crowthorne RG45 45 C5
Forest Hill SE23 23 D7
Cheniston Cl KT14 71 A6
Cheniston Ct SL5 30 A2
Chennells Way RH12 217 E5
Chennestone Prim Sch TW16 35 B7
Chepstow Cl RH10 202 E6
Chepstow Rd CR0 61 F8
Chepstow Rise CR0 61 E7
Chequer Grange RH18 206 E1
Chequer Rd RH19 185 F1
Chequers Cl
Horley RH6 161 A4
Walton on t H KT20 97 A2
Chequers Ct
7 Croydon CR0 42 F1
Horsham RH13 217 E2
Walton on t H KT20 97 A2
Chequers Dr RH6 161 A4
Chequers La KT20 97 A2
Chequers Pl RH4 136 B7
Chequer Tree Cl GU21 68 E3
Cherbury Cl RG12 27 E5
Cherimoya Gdns KT8 36 B6
Cherington Way SL5 28 E7
Cheriton Ave 3 BR2 44 F4
Cheriton Ct
South Norwood SE25 42 E4
Walton-on-T KT12 35 C1
Cheriton Sq SW17 21 A6
Cheriton Way GU17 64 D5
Cherkley Hill KT22, RH5 95 D1
Cherrimans Orch GU27 207 F6
Cherry Cl
Banstead KT17 77 D5
Carshalton SM5 59 F8
Merton SM4 39 E5
5 Streatham SW2 22 A8
Cherry Cres TW8 6 B7
Cherry Ct
Carshalton CR4 41 A1
3 Horsham RH13 217 D1
Cherrydale Rd GU15 66 D5
Cherry Green Cl RH1 140 B7
Cherry Hill Gdns CR0 60 F6
Cherryhill Gr GU11 104 F1
Cherryhurst GU8 171 B1
Cherry La RH11 181 C1
Cherry Lo
Aldershot GU12 105 B1
Horley RH6 161 B2
Cherry Mdws RH11 201 C5
Cherry Orch
Ashtead KT21 76 B1
Staines TW18 13 A3
Cherry Orchard Gdns
6 Croydon CR0 61 D8
East Molesey KT8 35 F6
Cherry Orchard Rd
Croydon CR0 42 E1
East Molesey KT8 36 A6
Cherry St GU21 69 E1
Cherry Tree Ave
Guildford GU2 108 F1
Haslemere GU27 207 F7
Staines TW18 13 B2
Cherry Tree Cl
Crawley RH10 202 D8
Farnborough GU14 84 C5
Farnham GU9 125 C3
Sandhurst GU47 45 D1
Cherry Tree Ct
Coulsdon CR5 79 F1
5 Richmond TW9 6 F3
Cherry Tree Dr
Bracknell RG12 27 D6
Streatham SW16 21 E5
Cherry Tree Gn CR2 81 B5
Cherry Tree Ho TW2 16 D6
Cherry Tree La GU7 150 D8
Cherry Tree Rd
Milford GU8 149 E1
Rowledge GU10 145 E3
Cherrytrees CR5 99 D6
Cherry Tree Wlk
Beckenham BR3 43 F5
Coney Hall BR4 63 F6
Horsham RH12 218 B6
Rowledge GU10 145 E3
Cherry Way
Horton SL3 1 C4
Upper Halliford TW17 34 E5
West Ewell KT19 57 D4
Cherrywood Ave TW20 11 B1
Cherrywood Cl KT2 18 A1
Cherrywood Com Prim Sch GU14 85 A6
Cherrywood Ct 1 TW11 17 A3
Cherrywood La SM4, SW20 39 E5
Cherrywood Rd GU14 85 B7
CHERTSEY 33 B2
Chertsey Bridge Rd KT16, TW18 33 D2
Chertsey Bvd KT16 32 F1
Chertsey Cl CR8 80 B4
Chertsey Cres CR0 63 C1
Chertsey Ct SW14 7 B4
Chertsey Dr SM3 58 E8
Chertsey Ho TW13 16 A5
Chertsey La
Egham TW18 12 F2
Epsom KT19 76 A7
Chertsey Mus★ KT15 33 A3
Chertsey Rd
Addlestone KT15 52 B8
Ashford TW15, TW16 14 D2
Burrowhill GU20, GU24 49 C6
Byfleet KT14 71 D8
Chobham GU24, KT16, GU21 50 D1
Feltham, Ashford Common TW13, TW16 14 D2
Feltham TW13, TW16 14 E4
Lower Halliford TW17 34 A2
Shepperton TW17 33 F2
Twickenham TW2 16 D7
Windlesham GU20 48 E5
Woking GU21 69 F3
Chertsey St
Guildford GU1 130 D8
Upper Tooting SW17 21 A3
Chertsey Sta KT16 32 F1
Chertsey Wlk 7 KT16 33 A2
Chervil Cl TW13 15 A5
Cherwell Cl SL3 1 B8
Cherwell Ct
Teddington KT1 17 D1
West Ewell KT19 57 C6
Cherwell Wlk RH11 200 F5
Cheselden Rd GU1 130 E8
Cheseman St SE26 23 B5
Chesfield Rd KT2 17 E1
Chesham Cl SM2 58 E1
Chesham Cres SE20 43 C8
Chesham Ct
Kingston u T KT6 37 D3
Wandsworth SW18 20 D8
Chesham Mews 14 GU1 130 F8
Chesham Rd
Guildford GU1 130 F8
Kingston u T KT1, KT2 38 A7
Mitcham SW17 20 D2
Penge SE20 43 C8
Cheshire Cl
Mitcham CR4, SW16 41 E6
Ottershaw KT16 51 D4
Cheshire Gdns KT9 56 D4
Cheshire Ho
Cheam SM4 40 B2
Ottershaw KT16 51 D4
Chesney Cres CR0 63 C3
Chessholme Ct TW16 14 E1
Chessholme Rd TW15 14 C2
CHESSINGTON 56 E4
Chessington Cl KT19 57 C4
Chessington Com Coll KT9 56 D3
Chessington Hall Gdns KT9 56 D4
Chessington Hill Pk KT9 57 A5
Chessington North Sta KT9 56 E5
Chessington Par KT9 56 D5
Chessington Pk KT9 57 A6
Chessington Rd KT19 57 D3
Chessington South Sta KT9 56 D3
Chessington Trade Pk KT9 57 A6
Chessington Way BR4 63 B8
Chessington World of Adventures★ KT9 56 C1
Chester Ave
Richmond TW10 6 F1
Twickenham TW2 15 F7
Chesterblade La RG12 27 E2
Chester Cl
Ashford TW15 14 D3
Ash GU12 106 B2
Dorking RH4 115 C1
Guildford GU2 108 F3
1 Richmond TW10 6 F1
Sutton SM1 59 A8
Chester Ct
2 Bromley BR2 44 F5
Dorking RH4 115 C1
Chesterfield Cl RH19 184 C4
Chesterfield Ct
Ashford TW15 13 E4
Kingston u T KT6 37 E4
Chesterfield Dr KT10 56 A8
Chesterfield Ho 6 SW16 21 C3
Chesterfield Mews TW15 13 E4
Chesterfield Rd
Ashford TW15 13 E3
Chiswick W4 7 C8
West Ewell KT19 57 D3
Chester Gdns SM4 40 C3
Chester Ho
2 Godalming GU7 150 D4
Kingston u T KT1 38 B7
Chesterman Ct 8 W4 7 E7
Chester Rd
Ash GU12 106 B2
Effingham KT24 113 B7
Harlington TW6 3 A4
Hounslow TW4 4 B4
Wimbledon SW19 19 C2
Chesters RH6 160 E5
Chesters Rd GU15 66 B5
Chesters The KT3 38 E8
Chesterton Cl RH19 205 F7
Chesterton Ct RH13 218 A4
Chesterton Dr
Merstham RH1 119 E7
Stanwell TW19 13 F7
Chesterton Ho
5 Croydon CR0 61 D6
6 Sutton SM1 59 C6
Chesterton Terr KT1 38 A7
Chester Way GU10 126 F6
Chestnut Ave
Aldershot GU12 126 E8
Camberley GU15 66 A6
Coney Hall BR4 63 E6
Farnham GU9 146 A8
Guildford GU2 130 C5
Hampton TW12 16 A1
Haslemere GU27 208 C7
Kingston u T KT8, KT11 36 F7
12 Mortlake SW14 7 D4
Tatsfield TN16 103 E5
Thames Ditton KT10 36 D1
Wentworth GU25 30 F5
Weybridge KT13 53 C3
Whiteley Village KT12 53 E2
Worcester Park KT19 57 E6
Chestnut Chase RG42 8 A1
Chestnut Cl
Addlestone KT15 52 D5
Ashford, Chattern Hill TW15 14 B4
Ashford, Felthamhill TW16 14 F2
Blackwater GU17 64 E4
Carshalton SM5 40 F1
Catford SE6 24 C4
East Grinstead RH19 186 A1
Englefield Green TW20 11 C2
Grayshott GU26 188 C3
Harlington UB7 3 B7
Kingswood KT20 98 A4
Redhill RH1 140 B7
Send Marsh GU23 91 A3
West Norwood SW16 22 A4
Chestnut Copse RH8 123 B2
Chestnut Cres KT12 53 E2
Chestnut Ct
Aldershot GU12 105 D2
Beckenham BR3 24 A1
6 Belmont SM2 59 A4
5 Croydon CR0 61 C6
Farnham GU9 125 A2
Feltham TW13 15 D3
Horsham RH13 217 E2
Hounslow TW3 5 A4
Kingston u T KT3 38 E6
Chestnut Dr TW20 11 D2
Chestnut End GU35 187 A4
Chestnut Gdns RH12 217 C5
Chestnut Gr
Balham SW12 21 A7
Isleworth TW7 6 A3
Kingston u T KT3 38 D6
Mitcham CR4 41 D5
Penge SE20 23 B1
South Croydon CR2 62 C3
Staines TW18 13 C2
Woking GU22 89 E7
Chestnut Grove Sch SW12 21 A7
Chestnut Ho
Crowthorne RG45 45 C5
West Norwood SE27 22 C5
Chestnut La
Chobham GU24 49 C4
Weybridge KT13 53 B5
Chestnut Manor Cl TW18 13 B3
Chestnut Mead 2 RH1 118 E2
Chestnut Pl
Ashtead Kt21 95 E8
Dulwich SE26 22 F4
Ewell KT17 77 A8
Chestnut Rd
Ashford TW15 14 B4
Farnborough GU14 85 A5
Guildford GU1 109 D1
Horley RH6 161 B5
Kingston u T KT2 17 E1
Merton SW20 39 D7
Twickenham TW2 16 E6
West Norwood SE27 22 C5
Chestnuts The
Dulwich SE21 22 E7
Horley RH6 161 A5
Penge BR3 43 D6
Walton-on-T KT12 54 A8
Chestnut Tree Gr GU14 84 C5
Chestnut View 6 GU14 85 C1
Chestnut Way
Bramley GU5 152 A4
Feltham TW13 15 B5
Godalming GU7 150 F2
Chestnut Wlk
Crawley RH11 181 C1
Felcourt RH19 185 C8
Upper Halliford TW17 34 E5
West Byfleet KT14 71 E7
Whiteley Village KT12 53 E2
Cheston Ave CR0 43 F1
Chesworth Cl 7 RH13 217 C1
Chesworth Cres RH13 217 C1
Chesworth Gdns RH13 217 C1
Chesworth La RH12, RH13 217 C1
Chetwode Cl RG40 25 E6
Chetwode Dr KT20 77 D1
Chetwode Pl GU11 126 C7
Chetwode Rd
Burgh Heath KT18, KT20 97 C8
Upper Tooting SW17 20 F5
Chetwode Terr GU11 104 E1
Chetwood Rd RH11 200 D2
Chevening Cl RH11 201 C1
Chevening Rd SE19 22 D2
Chevington Villas RH1 120 F3
Cheviot Cl
Banstead SM7 78 B4
Farnborough GU14 84 E7
Frimley GU15 66 C4
Harlington UB3 3 D7
Sutton SM2 59 D2
Cheviot Ct 3 RH12 217 F4
Cheviot Gdns SE27 22 B4
Cheviot Rd SE27 22 B3
Cheviot Wlk RH11 201 B6
Chevremont GU1 130 E8
Chewter Cl GU19 47 F3
Chewter La GU20 48 B6
Cheyham Gdns SM2 58 D1
Cheyham Way SM2 58 E1
Cheylesmore Dr GU16 66 D3
Cheyne Ave TW2 15 F7
Cheyne Ct
Banstead SM7 78 B4
1 Croydon CR0 61 F8
4 Wallington SM6 60 B4
Cheyne Hill KT5 37 F5
Cheynell Wlk RH11 200 F4
Cheyne Park Dr BR4 63 C7
Cheyne Rd TW15 14 D2
Cheyne Way GU14 84 F8
Cheyne Wlk
Croydon CR0 62 A8
Horley RH6 161 A1
Chichele Gdns CR0 61 E6
Chichele Rd RH8 122 E7
Chicheley Ct GU14 85 B6
Chichester Cl
Crawley RH10 201 E2
Dorking RH4 115 B1
Hampton TW12 15 F2
Witley GU8 170 E5
Chichester Ct
Ewell KT17 57 F2
Stanwell TW19 13 E7
Chichester Dr CR8 79 F7
Chichester Ho KT19 76 A8
Chichester Mews SE27 22 A4
Chichester Rd
Ash GU12 106 A3
Dorking RH4 115 B2
South Croydon CR0 61 E7
Chichester Terr RH12 217 D2
Chichester Way TW14 15 C8
CHIDDINGFOLD 191 B4
Chiddingfold Rd GU8 192 C3
Chiddingly Cl RH10 202 B5
Chiddingstone Cl SM2 59 A1
Chieveley Mews SL5 30 A2
Chilberton Dr RH1 119 C5
Chilbolton TW20 11 E3
Chilbrook Rd KT11 73 A1
Chilchester Ct BR3 44 B6
Chilcombe Ho 7 SW15 19 A8
Chilcroft La GU27 208 B1
Chilcroft Rd GU27 207 F7
Chilcrofts Rd GU27 208 A1
Child Cl RG40 25 D8
Childebert Rd SW17 21 B6
Childerly KT1 38 A6
Childrens Trust (Tadworth Court) The KT20 97 D6
Childs Hall Cl KT23 93 F2
Childs Hall Dr KT23 93 F2
Childs Hall Rd KT23 93 F2
Childs La 12 SE19 22 E2
Chilham Cl GU16 85 F8
Chillerton Rd SW17 21 B3
Chillingford Ho SW17 20 C4
Chillingham Way GU15 65 C4
Chillingworth Gdns TW1 16 F5
Chilmans Dr KT23 94 B2
Chilmark Gdns
Merstham RH1 119 E6
New Malden KT3 39 A3
Chilmark Rd SW16 41 D8
Chilmead 1 RH1 118 F2
Chilmead La RH1 119 D3
Chilsey Green Rd KT16 32 E2
Chiltern Ave
Farnborough GU14 84 D4
Twickenham TW2 16 A7
Chiltern Cl
Crawley RH11 201 B6
Farnborough GU14 84 D4
Haslemere GU27 208 B5
North Cheam KT4 58 C8
South Croydon CR0 61 E7
Staines TW18 13 A3
Woking GU22 89 C5
Chiltern Ct 2 RH12 217 F4
Chiltern Dr KT5 38 B4
Chiltern Gdns BR2 44 F5
Chiltern Rd
Sandhurst GU47 45 A1
Sutton SM2 59 C1
Chilterns The SM2 59 B2
Chilthorne Cl SE6 23 F8
Chiltington Ct RH12 217 D4
Chilton Cl GU6 193 F2
Chilton Ct KT12 54 A6
Chilton Farm Pk GU14 84 C4
Chilton Rd TW9 7 A4
Chiltons Cl SM7 78 B4
CHILWORTH 131 C3
Chilworth CE Inf Sch GU4 131 D3
Chilworth Ct
8 Putney SW19 19 D7
13 Redhill RH1 118 F2
Chilworth Gdns SM1 59 C7
Chilworth Rd GU4, GU5 132 A4
Chilworth Sta GU4 131 E3
Chimneys Ct SW19 19 C1
China Mews SW2 21 F8
Chinchilla Dr TW4 4 C5
Chine The GU10 145 F5
Chingford Ave GU14 85 D5
Chingley Cl BR1 24 E2
Chinthurst La
Shalford GU4, GU5 130 F2
Wonersh GU5 152 A7
Chinthurst Mews CR5 79 A3
Chinthurst Pk GU4 130 E1
Chinthurst Sch KT20 97 C4
Chippendale Cl GU17 64 E4
Chippendale Rd RH11 201 B1
Chippenham 5 KT1 37 F7
CHIPSTEAD 78 F1
Chipstead Ave CR7 42 B5
Chipstead Cl
Belmont SM2 59 B2
Coulsdon CR5 79 A3
Penge SE19 22 F1
Redhill RH1 140 A7
Chipstead Ct GU21 68 E2
Chipstead Ho 4 SW2 21 E7
Chipstead La CR5, KT20 98 B3
Chipstead Rd SM7 78 A2
Chipstead Sta CR5 78 F1
Chipstead Station Par CR5 78 F1
Chipstead Valley Prim Sch CR5 79 A3
Chipstead Valley Rd CR5 79 B3
Chipstead Way CR5, SM7 78 F3
Chirton Wlk GU21 69 A1
Chisbury Cl RG12 27 E3
Chisholm Rd
Croydon CR0 61 E8
14 Richmond TW10 6 F1
Chislehurst Rd TW10 6 E2
Chislet Cl BR3 24 A1
CHISWICK 7 D7
Chiswick Cl CR0 60 F7
Chiswick Comm Sch W4 7 D7
Chiswick Ho★ W4 7 E8
Chiswick La S W4 7 F8
Chiswick Mall W4 7 F8
Chiswick Plaza W4 7 C8
Chiswick Quay W4 7 C6
Chiswick Sq 10 W4 7 E8
Chiswick Sta W4 7 C7
Chiswick Staithe W4 7 C6
Chiswick Village W4 7 B8
Chiswick Wharf 3 W4 7 F8
Chithurst La RH6, RH7 162 F2
Chittenden Cotts GU23 71 E3
Chitterfield Gate UB7 3 A7
Chitty's Wlk GU3 108 F5
Chive Ct GU14 84 C4
Chivelston 27 SW19 19 D7

Chivenor Gr KT2 . . . . 17 D3
CHOBHAM 49 F2
Chobham Cl KT16. . . . . . . 51 B4
Chobham Common ★
(Nature Reserve)★
KT16 . . . . 49 F6
Chobham Gdns SW19 . . . 19 D6
Chobham La KT16,
GU24 . . . . 50 A8
Chobham Mus The
GU24 . . . . 68 E8
Chobham Park La
GU24 . . . . 50 B2
Chobham Rd
Burrowhill GU24, SL5 . . . 49 C7
Chobham GU21 . . . . 69 E3
Frimley GU16 . . . . 66 A2
Knaphill GU21 . . . . 68 D3
Ottershaw KT16. . . . . 51 B4
3 Woking GU21. . . . . 69 F2
Woking, Horsell Common
GU21, GU24 . . . . 69 D5
Chobham St Lawrence CE
Prim Sch GU24 . . . . 68 E8
Choir Gn GU21 . . . . 68 E2
Cholmley Rd KT7 . . . . 37 B3
Cholmondeley Wlk TW9 . . 6 C2
Chrislaine Cl TW19 . . . . . . 2 D1
Chrismas Ave GU12 . . . . . 105 C1
Chrismas Pl GU12 . . . . 105 C1
Christabel Cl TW7 . . . . 5 E4
Christ Church TW9 . . . . 6 E4
Christchurch Ave **5**
TW11 . . . . 17 A3
Christ Church CE Inf Sch
GU25 . . . . 31 B6
Christ Church CE Jun Sch
KT16 . . . . 51 D4
Christ Church CE Prim
Sch
Forest Hill SE23 . . . . 23 D6
Purley CR8 . . . . 61 B1
Surbiton KT5 . . . . 38 A3
Christchurch Cl SW19 . . . 20 D1
Christchurch Cotts
GU25 . . . . 31 B6
Christchurch Dr GU47 . . . 64 D6
Christchurch Gdns
KT19 . . . . 76 B8
Christchurch Ho **2**
SW2 . . . . 21 E7
Christchurch Hts **11**
RH2 . . . . 118 F1
Christ Church Mount
KT19 . . . . 76 B7
Christ Church New
Malden CE Prim Sch
KT3 . . . . 38 E6
Christchurch Pk SM2 . . . . 59 C3
Christchurch Pl KT19 . . . . 76 B8
Christchurch Rd
Mitcham SW19 . . . . 20 D1
Mortlake SW14 . . . . 7 C2
Purley CR8 . . . . 80 B8
Streatham SW2 . . . . 21 F7
Virginia Water GU25 . . . . . 31 C5
Christ Church Rd
Beckenham BR3. . . . . 44 A7
Epsom KT18 . . . . 76 A6
Surbiton KT5 . . . . 37 F3
Christ Church Streatham
CE Prim Sch SW2 . . . . . . 21 F7
Christchurch Way **5**
GU21 . . . . 69 F2
Christian Fields SW16 . . . 22 A1
Christie Cl
Guildford GU1 . . . . 109 D4
Lightwater GU18 . . . . 48 C1
Little Bookham KT23 . . . . 93 F3
Christie Dr SE25 . . . . 43 A4
Christie Ho **7** BR4. . . . . . 44 B1
Christies RH19 . . . . 205 D8
Christie Wlk **4** CR3 . . . . 100 D5
Christine Cl GU12 . . . . 105 F1
Christmas Hill GU4. . . . . . 130 F1
CHRISTMASPIE 128 C8
Christmaspie Ave
GU3 . . . . 107 B1
Christopher Ct
Ashford TW15 . . . . 13 E3
6 Croydon CR0 . . . . 43 A1
24 Kingston u T KT6 . . . 37 E4
Sutton SM1 . . . . 59 A5
Tadworth KT20 . . . . 97 C4
Christopher Rd RH19. . . . 185 E1
Christ's Coll GU1 . . . . 109 C4
Christ's Sch TW10 . . . . 7 A2
Christ the King RC Fst Sch
TW19 . . . . 2 E1
Christy Est GU12 . . . . 105 E2
Christy Rd TN16 . . . . 83 C4
Chrystie La KT23 . . . . 94 B1
Chuck's La KT20 . . . . 97 B3
Chudleigh Ct **4** GU14 . . . 85 B4
Chudleigh Gdns SM1. . . . 59 C7
Chudleigh Rd TW2 . . . . . . 16 F8
Chulsa Rd SE26 . . . . 23 B3
Chumleigh Wlk KT5 . . . . . 37 F5
Church App
Dulwich SE21 . . . . 22 D5
Thorpe TW20 . . . . 32 C6
Church Ave
Beckenham BR3 . . . . 44 A8
Farnborough GU14 . . . . . . 85 C3
Mortlake SW14 . . . . 7 D4
Church Circ GU14 . . . . 85 C1
Church Cl
Addlestone KT15 . . . . 52 B6

Church Cl *continued*
6 Epsom KT17 . . . . 76 E6
Fetcham KT22 . . . . 94 D3
Grayswood GU27 . . . . 189 F2
Hounslow TW4 . . . . 4 F5
Laleham TW18 . . . . 33 C6
Lower Kingswood KT20. . . 117 F8
Milford GU8 . . . . 149 F1
Pirbright GU24 . . . . 87 F6
Woking GU21 . . . . 69 E3
Church Cotts
Badshot Lea GU9 . . . . 126 A6
Effingham KT24 . . . . 113 D8
Churchcroft Cl SW12 . . . . 21 A8
Church Ct
3 Dorking RH4 . . . . 136 B8
Forest Hill SE26 . . . . 23 E3
Great Bookham KT23. . . . . 94 A2
Harmondsworth UB7 . . . . . 3 A8
Reigate RH2. . . . . 118 B1
15 Richmond TW10 . . . . 6 D2
West Norwood SE27 . . . . . 22 B4
Churchdale GU12 . . . . 105 B1
Churchdown BR1. . . . . 24 E4
Church Dr BR4 . . . . 63 E7
CHURCH END 91 F6
Church Est Almshouses **11**
TW9 . . . . 6 F3
Church Farm La SM3. . . . . 58 E4
Churchfield Cotts SL5 . . . 30 B3
Churchfield Ct **3**
RH2 . . . . 118 A1
Churchfield Ho KT11 . . . . 73 B5
Churchfield Pl
Lower Halliford TW17 . . . . 34 B2
Weybridge KT13 . . . . 53 A6
Churchfield Rd
Reigate RH2. . . . . 117 F2
Walton-on-T KT12 . . . . 35 A1
Weybridge KT13 . . . . 53 A6
Churchfields
East Molesey KT8 . . . . 36 A6
Guildford GU4 . . . . 110 A6
Witley GU8 . . . . 170 E4
Woking GU21 . . . . 69 E3
Churchfields Ave
Feltham TW13 . . . . 16 A5
Weybridge KT13 . . . . 53 B5
Churchfields Prim Sch
BR3 . . . . 43 D6
Churchfields Rd BR3 . . . . 43 E7
Church Gdns
2 Dorking RH4. . . . . . . 136 B8
Leatherhead KT22 . . . . 95 B7
Church Gn
Dunsfold GU8 . . . . 192 D5
Elstead GU8 . . . . 148 C3
Hersham KT12 . . . . 54 C4
Church Gr KT1. . . . . 37 C3
Church Hill
Aldershot GU11,
GU12. . . . . 126 C8
Camberley GU15 . . . . 65 E5
Caterham CR3 . . . . 100 F3
Merstham RH1. . . . . 99 B1
Nutfield RH1 . . . . 119 F2
Purley CR8 . . . . 60 E1
Pyrford GU22. . . . . 71 A1
Shamley Green GU5 . . . . . 152 E4
Shere GU5. . . . . 133 A4
Tatsfield TN16 . . . . 103 D5
Wallington SM5 . . . . 59 F5
Wimbledon SW19 . . . . 19 F3
Woking GU21 . . . . 69 D3
Church Hill Rd
Cheam SM3 . . . . 58 E6
Kingston u T KT6 . . . . 37 E4
Church Ho KT23 . . . . 94 A2
Churchill Ave
Aldershot GU12 . . . . 126 C8
Horsham RH12 . . . . 217 B3
Churchill Cl
East Bedfont TW14 . . . . . . 14 F7
Farnborough GU14 . . . . . . 85 B8
Fetcham KT22 . . . . 94 E4
Warlingham CR6 . . . . 81 D2
Churchill Cres GU14 . . . . . 85 B8
Churchill Ct
Crawley RH10 . . . . 182 A1
Staines TW18. . . . . 13 C2
Churchill Dr KT13. . . . . . . 53 C6
Churchill Ho
Banstead SM7 . . . . 77 F4
7 Hampton TW12. . . . . . 36 A8
Mitcham CR4 . . . . 40 F8
Churchill Lo **6** SW16 . . . 21 D3
Churchill Rd
Epsom KT19 . . . . 76 A8
Guildford GU1 . . . . 130 F8
North Ascot SL5 . . . . 28 F7
Smallfield RH6. . . . . 162 B3
South Croydon CR2 . . . . . . 61 C3
Churchill Way
Ashford TW15 . . . . 15 A2
Biggin Hill TN16. . . . . 83 D4
Church La
Albury GU5 . . . . 132 C4
Ascot SL5. . . . . 29 D5
Ash GU12. . . . . 106 B2
Bisley GU21, GU24 . . . . . . 68 A4
Bletchingley RH1 . . . . 120 D3
Broadbridge Heath
RH12. . . . . 216 D3
Brook GU8 . . . . 190 C8
Burgh Heath KT18, SM7 . . 77 E2
Burstow RH6 . . . . 182 F7
Caterham CR3 . . . . 100 A3
Chelsham CR6 . . . . 82 C3

Church La *continued*
Chessington KT9 . . . . 56 F4
Copthorne RH10 . . . . 183 B3
Cranleigh GU6 . . . . 174 E3
Crawley RH10 . . . . 201 F6
Crondall GU10 . . . . 124 D8
East Grinstead RH19 . . . . 185 F1
Farnborough GU14 . . . . . . 84 E4
Godstone RH9 . . . . 121 D3
Grayshott GU26. . . . . 188 C3
Hambledon GU8 . . . . 171 D2
Haslemere GU27 . . . . 208 D7
Headley KT18 . . . . 96 C2
Hooley CR5 . . . . 99 B5
Merton SW19 . . . . 39 F8
Oxted RH8 . . . . 122 E6
Pirbright GU24. . . . . 87 D4
Rowledge GU10 . . . . 145 E3
Send GU23 . . . . 90 C1
Shere GU5 . . . . 133 A4
Sunningdale SL5 . . . . 30 B4
Teddington TW11 . . . . 16 F3
Thames Ditton KT7 . . . . . . 37 A3
Twickenham TW1. . . . . 17 A7
Upper Tooting, Furzedown
SW17 . . . . 21 B4
Upper Tooting SW17 . . . . . 21 A3
Wallington SM6 . . . . 60 D7
Wallis Wood RH5 . . . . 176 F1
Warlingham CR6 . . . . 81 D2
Weybridge KT13 . . . . 53 A6
Witley GU8. . . . . 170 E2
Worplesdon GU3 . . . . 108 E8
Wrecclesham GU10. . . . . . 145 F7
Church La E GU11. . . . . . . 126 B8
Churchlands GU11 . . . . . . 126 B8
Church Lane Ave CR5 . . . . 99 B5
Church Lane Dr CR5 . . . . . 99 B5
Church La W GU11. . . . . . 105 A1
Churchley Rd SE26 . . . . . . 23 B4
Churchley Villas SE26 . . . 23 B4
Church Mdw KT6 . . . . 56 C8
Church Mews KT15 . . . . . . 52 C6
Churchmore Rd SW16 . . . 41 D8
Church Paddock Ct
SM6 . . . . 60 D7
Church Par **6** TW15 . . . . 13 F4
Church Pas **17** GU9 . . . . 125 B2
Church Path
Ash GU12. . . . . 106 A3
Farnborough GU14 . . . . . 105 C8
Merton SW19 . . . . 40 E6
Mitcham CR4 . . . . 40 E6
9 Woking GU21 . . . . 69 F2
Church Pk RH11 . . . . 181 E5
Church Pl **1** CR4 . . . . 40 E6
Church Rd
Addlestone KT15 . . . . 52 B5
Aldershot GU11 . . . . 126 C8
Ascot SL5. . . . . 29 A5
Ashford TW15 . . . . 13 F4
Ashtead KT21 . . . . 75 D1
Bagshot GU19 . . . . 47 D3
Barnes SW13. . . . . 7 F5
Beckenham BR3. . . . . 44 E6
Biggin Hill TN16. . . . . 83 C7
Bracknell RG12 . . . . 27 C7
Broadbridge Heath
RH12. . . . . 216 D3
Burstow RH6 . . . . 183 A7
Byfleet KT14 . . . . 71 E6
Caterham CR3 . . . . 100 F3
Cheam SM3 . . . . 58 E4
Claygate KT10 . . . . 55 F3
Copthorne RH10 . . . . 183 B3
Cranford TW5 . . . . 4 B8
Crawley, Lowfield Heath
RH11. . . . . 181 E5
Crawley, Worth RH10. . . . 202 E6
Croydon CR0, CR9 . . . . . . 61 C7
Dunsfold GU8 . . . . 192 D5
East Molesey KT8 . . . . 36 D6
Egham TW20 . . . . 12 A3
Epsom KT17 . . . . 76 E6
Feltham TW13 . . . . 15 D3
Fetcham KT23 . . . . 94 A3
Frimley GU16. . . . . 65 D1
Guildford GU1 . . . . 130 D8
Hascombe GU8 . . . . 172 E4
Haslemere GU27 . . . . 208 C7
Haslemere, Shottermill
GU27. . . . . 207 F6
Heston TW5 . . . . 5 A7
Horley RH6 . . . . 160 F2
Horley RH6 . . . . 161 A3
Horne RH6. . . . . 162 F5
Horsham RH12 . . . . 218 B5
Hounslow TW7 . . . . 5 E7
Kenley CR8 . . . . 80 D4
Kingston u T KT1 . . . . 37 F7
Leatherhead KT22 . . . . 95 B5
Leigh RH2 . . . . 138 A3
Lingfield RH7 . . . . 164 D4
Little Bookham KT23 . . . . 93 F4
Long Ditton KT6 . . . . 37 C1
Lower Halliford TW17 . . . . 34 B2
Milford GU8 . . . . 149 F1
Mitcham CR4, SW19 . . . . . 40 D7
Newdigate RH5 . . . . 158 B1
New Malden KT4 . . . . 38 E1
Purley CR8 . . . . 60 E1
Redhill RH1 . . . . 139 E7
Richmond, Ham TW10 . . . 17 E4
Richmond TW10, TW9 . . . . 6 E2
Sandhurst GU15 . . . . 64 F7
Sandhurst, Owlsmoor
GU47. . . . . 45 A1
South Norwood SE19. . . . . 22 E1

Church Rd *continued*
Sunningdale SL5 . . . . 30 A3
Teddington TW11 . . . . 16 F3
Turners Hill RH10 . . . . 204 A3
Wallington SM6 . . . . 60 D7
Warlingham CR6 . . . . 81 D2
West End GU24 . . . . 67 F7
West Ewell KT19 . . . . 57 D3
Whyteleafe CR3 . . . . 100 F8
Wimbledon SW19 . . . . 19 E4
Windlesham GU20 . . . . . . 48 C4
Winkfield, Chavey Down
SL5 . . . . 28 B8
Winkfield SL4 . . . . 8 C5
Woking, Horsell GU21 . . . . 69 E4
Woking, St John's GU21 . . 89 A8
Woldingham CR3 . . . . 101 E4
Church Rd E
Crowthorne RG45 . . . . 45 B5
Farnborough GU14 . . . . . . 85 D2
Church Rd W
Crowthorne RG45 . . . . 45 B4
Farnborough GU14 . . . . . . 85 C1
Church Rise
Chessington KT9 . . . . 56 F4
Forest Hill SE23. . . . . 23 D6
Church Row GU23 . . . . . . 91 C6
Church St E GU21. . . . . . . 69 F2
Church St W GU21 . . . . . . 69 E2
Church Side
Epsom KT18. . . . . 76 B6
Gatton RH2 . . . . 118 F6
Churchside RH1 TN16. . . . 83 C2
Church Sq TW17 . . . . 34 B2
Church St
Aldershot GU11. . . . . 104 F2
Betchworth RH3 . . . . 137 E8
Chiswick W4 . . . . 7 F8
Cobham KT11. . . . . 73 B4
Crawley RH11 . . . . 201 C6
Crowthorne RG45 . . . . 45 B4
Croydon CR0, CR9 . . . . . . 61 C8
Dorking RH4 . . . . 136 A7
Effingham KT24 . . . . 113 D8
Epsom KT17, KT18. . . . . . . 76 E6
Esher KT10 . . . . 55 B6
Ewell KT17. . . . . 58 A2
Godalming GU7 . . . . 150 D4
Hampton TW12 . . . . 36 C8
Isleworth TW7 . . . . 6 B5
Kingston u T KT1 . . . . 37 D7
Leatherhead KT22 . . . . 95 B5
Old Woking GU22 . . . . 90 C6
Reigate RH2. . . . . 118 B1
Rudgwick, Cox Green
RH12. . . . . 195 E1
Rudgwick RH12 . . . . 214 E8
Staines TW18 . . . . 12 E4
Sunbury TW16 . . . . 35 B6
Twickenham TW1. . . . . 17 A7
Walton-on-T KT12 . . . . 35 A2
Warnham RH12 . . . . 216 F8
Weybridge KT13 . . . . 53 A6
Church Stretton Rd
TW3 . . . . 5 C2
Church Terr
22 Richmond TW10 . . . . 6 D2
South Holmwood RH5 . . . 157 C6
Church Vale SE23 . . . . 23 D6
Church View GU12 . . . . . . 106 A2
Church View Cl RH6 . . . . 160 F2
Churchview Rd TW2 . . . . . 16 D6
Church Villa TW16 . . . . . . 35 B6
Church Way
Oxted RH8 . . . . 122 F3
South Croydon CR2 . . . . . . 81 A8
Church Wlk
Bletchingley RH1 . . . . 120 D2
Brentford TW8 . . . . 6 C8
Caterham CR3 . . . . 101 A3
Chertsey KT16 . . . . 33 A3
Crawley RH10 . . . . 201 D6
Horley RH6 . . . . 160 F2
Leatherhead KT22 . . . . 95 B5
Mitcham SW16 . . . . 41 C7
Reigate RH2. . . . . 118 C1
14 Richmond TW10 . . . . 6 D2
Thames Ditton KT7 . . . . . . 36 F3
Walton-on-T KT12 . . . . 35 A1
West Barnes SW20 . . . . . . 39 C6
Weybridge KT13 . . . . 53 A7
Churston Cl **17** SW2. . . . . 22 A7
Churston Dr SM4 . . . . 39 E4
Churstonville Ct BR3 . . . . 44 B6
CHURT 167 F1
Churton Pl W4 . . . . 7 B8
Churt Rd
Beacon Hill GU26. . . . . . . 188 C6
Headley Down GU10,
GU35. . . . . 187 C8
Churt Wynde GU26 . . . . . 188 D7
Chuters Cl KT14 . . . . 71 F7
Chuters Gr KT17 . . . . 76 F7
Cibber Rd SE23 . . . . 23 D6
Cidermill Rd RH5 . . . . 158 E3
Cinderford Way BR1 . . . . 24 E4
Cinder Path GU22 . . . . 89 C8
Cinnamon Cl CR0 . . . . 41 E2
Cinnamon Gdns GU2 . . . . 109 A6
Cinque Cotts SW19 . . . . . 19 C2
Cintra Ct SE19 . . . . 22 F2
Cintra Pk SE19. . . . . 22 F1
Circle Gdns
Byfleet KT14 . . . . 71 E6
Merton SW19 . . . . 40 A7
Circle Hill Rd RG45 . . . . . 45 C5
Circle Rd KT12. . . . . 53 E2
Circle The GU7 . . . . 150 F6

Circuit Ctr KT13 . . . . 71 E8
Circus The KT22 . . . . 95 B7
Cirrus Cl SM6 . . . . 60 E3
Cissbury Cl RH12 . . . . 218 A6
Cissbury Hill RH11 . . . . . . 201 C4
Cissbury Ho **6** SE26 . . . . 23 A5
City Bsns Ctr RH13. . . . . . 217 D1
City of London Freemen's
Sch KT21 . . . . 96 A8
City Prospect **6** SE19 . . . 22 E2
City Wharf Ho KT7 . . . . . . 37 B3
Clacket La TN16 . . . . 103 E2
Claire Ct
Beckenham BR3 . . . . 44 B6
Walton-on-T KT12 . . . . 54 C7
Clairvale Rd TW5 . . . . 4 E6
Clairview Rd SW16,
SW17 . . . . 21 B4
Clairville Ct **1** RH2 . . . . . 118 D1
Clairville Point **12**
SE23 . . . . 23 D5
Clammer Hill GU27 . . . . . 189 F1
Clandon Ave TW20 . . . . . 12 C1
Clandon CE Inf Sch
GU4. . . . . 111 A4
Clandon Cl KT17 . . . . 58 A4
Clandon Ct
Farnborough GU14 . . . . . . 85 D3
Sutton SM2 . . . . 59 D4
Clandon Ho
Guildford GU1 . . . . 130 F7
12 Kingston u T KT2 . . . 18 B2
Clandon Mews RH4 . . . . . 136 B6
Clandon Pk★ GU4 . . . . . . 111 A3
Clandon Rd
Guildford GU1 . . . . 130 E8
Send Marsh GU4, GU23. . . 91 A1
West Clandon GU4,
GU23. . . . . 111 A8
Clandon Regis GU4 . . . . . 111 B4
Clanfield Ho **12** SW15 . . . 19 A7
Clanfield Ride GU17. . . . . 64 D5
Clappers Gate RH10. . . . . 201 C4
Clappers La GU24 . . . . 68 D8
Clappers Mdw GU6 . . . . . 194 A3
Clare Ave RG40 . . . . 25 C7
Clare Cl
Crawley RH10 . . . . 182 C1
West Byfleet KT14. . . . . . . 71 A6
Clare Cotts RH1 . . . . 120 B3
Clare Cres KT22 . . . . 75 B1
Clare Ct
Wimbledon SW19 . . . . 19 E2
Wokingham RG40 . . . . 25 C7
Woldingham CR3 . . . . 102 A4
Claredale GU22 . . . . 89 E8
Claredale Ct SM2 . . . . 59 C3
Clarefield Ct SL5 . . . . 30 A3
Clare Gdns TW20 . . . . 12 A3
Clare Hill KT10 . . . . 55 B5
Clare Hill (No 1) KT10. . . . 55 B5
Clare Hill (No 2) KT10. . . . 55 B5
Clare House Prim Sch
BR3 . . . . 44 C7
Clare Lawn Ave SW14 . . . . 7 D2
Clare Mead GU10 . . . . 145 F4
Claremont TW17 . . . . 34 B3
Claremont Ave
Camberley GU15 . . . . 65 F5
Esher KT10 . . . . 54 E4
Hersham KT12 . . . . 54 D6
Sunbury TW16 . . . . 35 B8
West Barnes KT3. . . . . 39 B4
Woking GU22. . . . . 89 E8
Claremont Cl
Hamsey Green CR2 . . . . . . 81 B4
Hersham KT12 . . . . 54 D5
4 Streatham SW2 . . . . . 21 F7
Claremont Ct
Dorking RH4 . . . . 136 B6
11 Kingston u T KT6 . . . 37 E3
Claremont Dr
Esher KT10 . . . . 55 B4
Shepperton TW17 . . . . 34 B3
Woking GU22. . . . . 89 E8
Claremont End KT10 . . . . 55 B4
Claremont Fan Court Sch
KT10 . . . . 55 A3
Claremont Gdns KT6 . . . . 37 E4
Claremont Gr **10** W4 . . . . 7 E7
Claremont Ho **7** SM2 . . . 59 A3
Claremont La KT10. . . . . . 55 B4
Claremont Landscape
Gdn★ KT10. . . . . 54 F3
Claremont Lo **16** SW20 . . 19 D1
CLAREMONT PARK 55 A4
Claremont Park Rd
KT10 . . . . 55 B4
Claremont Pl
Blackwater GU17 . . . . 64 F3
Claygate KT10 . . . . 55 F4
Claremont Rd
Claygate KT10 . . . . 55 E3
Croydon CR0 . . . . 43 A1
Egham TW18 . . . . 12 D3
Kingston u T KT6 . . . . 37 E4
Redhill RH1 . . . . 119 A4
Teddington TW11 . . . . 16 F4
Twickenham TW1. . . . . 6 C1
West Byfleet KT14. . . . . . . 71 A7
Claremont Terr KT7. . . . . . 37 B2
Claremount Cl KT18. . . . . 77 C2
Claremount Gdns
KT18 . . . . 77 D2

Clarence Ave
Kingston u T KT3 . . . . **38** D7
Streatham SW4 . . . . **21** D8
Clarence Cl
Aldershot GU12 . . . . **105** D2
Hersham KT12 . . . . **54** B6
Clarence Ct
Egham TW20 . . . . **11** F2
Horley RH6 . . . . **161** D4
Clarence Dr
Camberley GU15 . . . . **66** B7
2 East Grinstead
RH19 . . . . **205** F7
Englefield Green TW20 . . . **11** C4
Clarence Ho KT12 . . . . . **54** B5
Clarence La SW5 . . . .**7** F1
Clarence Mews 1
SW12 . . . . **21** B8
Clarence Rd
Biggin Hill TN16 . . . . **83** F1
Hersham KT12 . . . . **54** B6
Horsham RH13 . . . . **217** E1
Reigate RH1 . . . . **139** D6
Richmond TW9 . . . .**7** A6
Sutton SM1 . . . . **59** B5
Teddington TW11 . . . . **17** A2
Thornton Heath CR0 . . . . . . **42** D2
Wallington SM6 . . . . **60** B5
Wimbledon SW19 . . . . **20** B2
Clarence St
Egham TW20 . . . . **11** F2
Kingston u T KT1, KT2 . . . . **37** E7
9 Richmond TW9 . . . .**6** E3
Staines TW18 . . . . **12** E4
Clarence Terr TW3. . . . .**5** B3
Clarence Way RH6 . . . . . **161** D4
Clarence Wlk RH1 . . . . . . **139** D6
Clarendon Cres TW2 . . . . . **16** D5
Clarendon Ct
Beckenham BR3. . . . . **44** B8
Blackwater GU17. . . . . **64** D3
Morden SM4 . . . . **40** E4
1 Richmond TW9 . . . .**7** A6
Clarendon Gate KT16 . . . **51** D4
Clarendon Gr 10 CR4 . . . . **40** F6
Clarendon Mews KT21 . . . **95** F8
Clarendon Prim Sch
TW15 . . . . **13** F4
Clarendon Rd
Ashford TW15 . . . . **13** F4
Croydon CR0, CR9 . . . . **61** B8
Mitcham SW19 . . . . **20** E1
Redhill RH1 . . . . **118** F2
Wallington SM6 . . . . **60** C4
Clarendon Sch TW12. . . . . **16** B2
Clarens St SE6. . . . . **23** F6
Clare Park Hospl (Private)
GU10. . . . . **124** B4
Clare Rd
Hounslow TW4. . . . .**4** F4
Stanwell TW19 . . . . **13** E8
Clares The CR3 . . . . **101** A3
Claret Gdns SE25 . . . . **42** E5
Clareville Rd CR3 . . . . . . **101** A3
Clareways SL5. . . . . **29** F2
Clare Wood KT22 . . . . **75** B1
Clarewood Dr GU15 . . . . . **65** E6
Clarice Way SM6 . . . . **60** E2
Claridge Gdns RH7. . . . . **165** A2
Claridges Mead RH7 . . . . **165** A2
Clarke Cres GU15 . . . . **64** E7
Clarke Ho 5 TW10 . . . . . . **17** C5
Clarke Pl GU6 . . . . **173** E7
Clarke's Ave KT4, SM3 . . . **58** D8
Clark Rd RH11 . . . . **201** A1
CLARK'S GREEN **178** C4
Clarks Hill GU10 . . . . **124** D1
Clarks La CR6, RH8,
TN16 . . . . **103** C4
Clark Way TW5 . . . .**4** D7
Claudia Pl SW19 . . . . **19** E7
Claverdale Rd SW2 . . . . . . **22** A8
Claverdon RG12 . . . . **27** A2
Claver Dr SL5. . . . . **29** D5
Clavering Cl TW1 . . . . **17** A4
Claverton KT21 . . . . **75** E2
Clay Ave CR4 . . . . **41** B7
Claycart Rd
Aldershot GU11. . . . . **104** D4
Aldershot GU11. . . . . **104** E3
Clay Cnr KT15 . . . . **33** B1
Claydon Ct 5 TW18. . . . . . **13** A4
Claydon Dr CR0. . . . . **60** E6
Claydon Gdns GU17. . . . . . **65** A1
Claydon Rd GU21 . . . . **69** A3
Clayford RH7. . . . . **165** B2
CLAYGATE **55** F3
Claygate Cl SM1 . . . . **59** C7
Claygate Cres CR0 . . . . . . **63** D4
Claygate La
Hinchley Wood KT10 . . . . . . **56** A8
Thames Ditton KT7 . . . . **37** A1
Claygate Lodge Cl
KT10. . . . . **55** E3
Claygate Prim Sch
KT10. . . . . **55** E3
Claygate Rd RH4. . . . . . . **136** B5
Claygate Sta KT10 . . . . . . **55** E4
Clayhall Ho 8 RH2. . . . . . **118** A2
Clayhall La RH2. . . . . **138** E6
Clay Hall La RH10 . . . . . . **183** C4
Clayhanger GU4 . . . . **110** C3
Clayhill Cl
Bracknell RG12 . . . . **28** A6
Leigh RH2. . . . . **138** A2

Clay Hill Ho GU27 . . . . . . **208** A6
Clayhill Rd RH2. . . . . **137** F1
Clay La
Guildford, Burpham
GU4. . . . . **110** A5
Guildford, Jacobswell
GU4. . . . . **109** E7
Headley KT18 . . . . **96** B3
Horne RH7. . . . . **163** D3
South Nutfield RH1 . . . . . . **140** D7
Stanwell TW19. . . . . **13** F8
Wokingham RG40 . . . . **25** F5
Claylands Ct SE19 . . . . . . **22** D3
Claymore Cl SM3, SM4 . . . **40** A2
Claypole Dr TW5. . . . .**4** E6
Clays Cl RH19. . . . . **205** E8
Clayton Dr GU2 . . . . **108** F4
Clayton Gr RG12 . . . . **27** E8
Clayton Hill RH11 . . . . . . **201** C4
Clayton Ho KT7 . . . . **37** B1
Clayton Mead RH9 . . . . . **121** B4
Clayton Rd
Chessington KT10, KT9 . . . **56** D6
Ewell KT17 . . . . **76** E6
Farnborough GU14 . . . . **64** F1
Isleworth TW7 . . . .**5** E4
Cleardene RH4 . . . . **136** B7
Cleardown GU22. . . . . **70** B1
Clearmount GU24. . . . . . . **49** E4
Clears Cotts RH2 . . . . **117** E3
Clearsprings GU18. . . . . . **67** A8
Clears The RH2. . . . . **117** E3
Clearwater Ho BR3 . . . . . . **44** B4
Clear Water Ho 12
TW10 . . . .**6** E2
Clear Water Pl KT6 . . . . . . **37** C3
Cleaveland Rd KT6. . . . . . **37** D4
Cleave Prior CR5 . . . . **98** E8
Cleaverholme Cl SE25. . . . **43** B3
Cleave's Almshouses 1
KT2 . . . . **37** E7
Cleeve Ct TW14. . . . . **14** E7
Cleeve Hill SE23 . . . . **23** B7
Cleeve Ho RG12. . . . . **27** E5
Cleeve Rd KT22 . . . . **95** A7
Cleeves Ct 6 RH1 . . . . . . **119** A2
Cleeve The GU1 . . . . **110** A1
Cleeve Way
Cheam SM1. . . . . **40** B1
Roehampton SW15 . . . . **18** F8
Clement Cl CR8. . . . . **80** B3
Clement Rd
Penge BR3. . . . . **43** D7
Wimbledon SW19 . . . . **19** E3
Clements Ct TW4 . . . .**4** D3
Clements Ho KT22 . . . . **95** A8
Clements Mead KT22. . . . . **95** A8
Clements Rd KT12 . . . . . . **54** B8
Clensham Ct SM3. . . . . . . **59** A8
Clensham La SM1. . . . . . . **59** A8
Clerics Wlk TW17 . . . . **34** D3
Clerks Croft RH1. . . . . . . **120** D2
Cleve Ct 3 GU21. . . . . **68** D2
Clevedon KT13 . . . . **53** D5
Clevedon Ct
2 Croydon CR0 . . . . **61** E5
Farnborough GU14 . . . . **85** D3
Frimley GU16. . . . . **86** A8
West Norwood SE21 . . . . . . **22** D5
Clevedon Gdns TW5 . . . .**4** B6
Clevedon Ho 7 SM1 . . . . . **59** C6
Clevedon Mans 2 TW1 . . . .**6** D1
Clevedon Rd
Kingston u T KT1 . . . . **38** A7
Penge SE20 . . . . **43** D8
Twickenham TW1 . . . .**6** D1
Clevehurst KT13 . . . . **53** D5
Cleveland Ave
Hampton TW12 . . . . **15** F1
Merton SW20 . . . . **39** F7
Cleveland Cl KT12 . . . . **54** B7
Cleveland Ct TW10. . . . .**6** F2
Cleveland Dr TW18 . . . . . . **33** B8
Cleveland Gdns
Barnes SW13. . . . .**7** F5
Worcester Park KT4 . . . . . . **57** F8
Cleveland Pk TW19 . . . .**2** E1
Cleveland Pl GU7 . . . . . . **150** E7
Cleveland Rd
Barnes SW13. . . . .**7** F5
Isleworth TW7. . . . .**6** A3
New Malden KT3 . . . . **38** E5
Worcester Park KT4 . . . . . . **57** E8
Cleveland Rise SM4 . . . . . **39** D2
Cleve Pl KT13. . . . . **53** D5
Cleves Ave KT17 . . . . **58** B2
Cleves Cl KT11. . . . . **73** B5
Cleves Cres CR0 . . . . **82** C8
Cleves Ct
Epsom KT17. . . . . **76** F7
Kingston u T KT6 . . . . **37** E3
Cleves Sch KT13 . . . . **53** F6
Cleves Way
Ashford TW16 . . . . **14** F2
Hampton TW12 . . . . **15** F1
Cleves Wood KT13 . . . . . . **53** E6
Clewborough Dr GU15 . . . **66** B6
Clewborough House Sch
GU16. . . . . **65** F1
Clews La GU24. . . . . **68** B3
Clifden Centre (Richmond
Adult & Community Coll)
TW1 . . . . **16** F7
Clifden Ct 8 TW8. . . . .**6** D8
Clifden Ho 7 TW8 . . . .**6** D8
Clifden Rd
Brentford TW8. . . . .**6** D8

Clifden Rd continued
Twickenham TW1 . . . . **16** F7
Cliff End CR8. . . . . **80** B7
Cliffe Rd
Croydon CR2 . . . . **61** D5
Godalming GU7 . . . . **150** C2
Cliffe Rise GU7 . . . . **150** C3
Cliffe Wlk 2 SM1 . . . . **59** C5
Clifford Ave
Mortlake SW14, TW10,
TW9 . . . .**7** B4
Wallington SM6 . . . . **60** C6
Clifford Ct SW18 . . . . **20** D8
Clifford Gr TW15 . . . . **14** A4
Clifford Ho BR3. . . . . **24** B2
Clifford Manor Rd
GU4 . . . . **130** E5
Clifford Rd
Croydon SE25 . . . . **43** A5
Hounslow TW4. . . . .**4** D4
Richmond TW10. . . . . **17** D6
Clifton Ave
Feltham TW13 . . . . **15** C5
Sutton SM2 . . . . **78** B8
Clifton Cl
Caterham CR3 . . . . **100** D4
Chertsey KT15. . . . . **52** B8
Horley RH6 . . . . **161** D3
Rowledge GU10. . . . . **146** A4
Clifton Ct
Beckenham BR3. . . . . **44** B8
South Norwood SE25 . . . . . **42** E4
9 Wimbledon SW19 . . . .**2** E1
Clifton Gdns GU16 . . . . . . **85** F6
Clifton Hill Sch CR3. . . . . **100** D4
Clifton Mews SE25 . . . . . . **42** E5
Clifton Par TW13 . . . . **15** C4
Clifton Park Ave SW20 . . . **39** C7
Clifton Pl SM7. . . . . **78** A4
Clifton Rd
Coulsdon CR5 . . . . **79** C4
Crawley RH10 . . . . **202** C5
Harlington TW6 . . . .**3** B4
Hounslow TW7. . . . .**5** C5
Kingston u T KT3 . . . . **37** F8
South Norwood SE25 . . . . . **42** E5
Teddington TW11 . . . . **16** E4
Wallington SM6 . . . . **60** B5
Wimbledon SW19 . . . . **19** D2
Wokingham RG41 . . . . **25** A8
Cliftons La RH2 . . . . **117** D2
Clifton Terr RH4 . . . . **136** B6
Clifton The KT6. . . . . **56** E8
Cliftonville RH4. . . . . **136** B6
Clifton Way GU21. . . . . . . **68** F2
Climping Rd RH11 . . . . . . **201** B8
Cline Rd GU1 . . . . **130** F7
Clinton Ave KT8 . . . . **36** C5
Clinton Cl
Knaphill GU21 . . . . **68** D1
Weybridge KT13 . . . . **53** B8
Clinton Hill RH7. . . . . **186** A8
Clinton Ho
New Malden KT3 . . . . **38** D1
6 Surbiton KT6 . . . . **37** D2
Clinton Rd KT22 . . . . **95** C4
Clintons Gn RG42 . . . . **27** A8
Clinton Terr SM1 . . . . **59** C6
Clippesby Cl KT9. . . . . **56** F4
Clipstone Rd 1 TW3. . . . . . .**5** A4
Clitherow Gdns RH10 . . . **201** E5
Clive Ct
Streatham SW16 . . . . **21** D3
Tolworth KT6 . . . . **57** A8
Cliveden Pl TW17. . . . . **34** C3
Cliveden Rd SW19 . . . . **39** F8
Clivedon Ho KT4. . . . . **58** A8
Clive Gn RG12 . . . . **27** B4
Clive Ho
3 Croydon CR0 . . . . **42** F1
Redhill RH1 . . . . **118** E3
Clive Pl KT10 . . . . **55** B5
Clive Rd
Aldershot GU12 . . . . **105** D1
Esher KT10 . . . . **55** B6
Feltham TW14 . . . .**4** A1
Mitcham SW19 . . . . **20** E2
Teddington TW11 . . . . **17** A4
West Norwood SE21,
SE27. . . . . **22** D5
Clive Way RH10 . . . . **202** C6
Clock Barn La GU8. . . . . . **171** F6
CLOCK HOUSE **79** A5
Clock House Apartments
GU8 . . . . **171** B3
Clockhouse Cl SW19 . . . . **19** C6
Clock House Cl KT14 . . . . . **71** F7
Clock House Cotts
Capel RH5 . . . . **178** C2
Enton Green GU8. . . . . **171** B3
Clock House Ct GU1 . . . . . **109** C5
Clock House Ct BR3. . . . . . **43** E7
Clockhouse La
Ashford TW14, TW15. . . . . . **14** B5
Bramley GU5. . . . . **151** F7
East Bedfont TW14,
TW15 . . . . **14** B5
Clockhouse La E TW20 . . . **12** B1
Clockhouse La W
TW20. . . . . **12** A1
Clock House Mead
KT11 . . . . **74** B5
Clockhouse Rd GU14. . . . . **85** B4
Clock House Rd BR3 . . . . . **43** E7
Clock House Sta BR3 . . . . **43** E8
Clock Tower Rd TW7. . . . . . .**5** F4
Clock Twr The 10
GU21 . . . . **70** A3

Clodhouse Hill GU22 . . . . **88** D5
Cloister Cl TW11. . . . . **17** B3
Cloister Gdns SE25. . . . . . **43** B3
Cloisters Ho 8 SW19 . . . . . **20** A1
Cloisters The
Frimley GU16. . . . . **65** D1
Old Woking GU22. . . . . **90** B6
Clone The 5 KT2 . . . . **18** B1
Clonmel Rd TW11 . . . . **16** D4
Clonmore St SW18 . . . . . . **19** F7
Close The
Beckenham BR3. . . . . **43** B5
Bracknell RG12 . . . . **27** C5
Brockham RH3. . . . . **137** B5
Cheam SM3. . . . . **39** F2
Croydon SE25 . . . . **43** A3
East Grinstead RH19 . . . . . **205** D8
Esher KT10 . . . . **55** B3
Farnham GU9. . . . . **125** C1
Frimley GU16. . . . . **85** C8
Godalming GU7 . . . . **150** F3
Horley RH6 . . . . **161** C1
Lightwater GU18 . . . . **48** A1
Mitcham CR4 . . . . **40** F5
Mortlake TW9 . . . .**7** B4
North Ascot SL5. . . . . **28** D7
Purley CR8. . . . . **61** B1
Purley, Russell Hill CR8. . . . **60** F1
Reigate RH2. . . . . **139** B8
Sandhurst GU47 . . . . **64** E8
Surbiton KT6 . . . . **37** E3
Virginia Water GU25 . . . . . . **31** D4
Wallington SM5 . . . . **59** E2
West Byfleet KT14. . . . . **71** A6
Woking GU22. . . . . **70** B2
Wonersh GU5 . . . . **152** B2
Closeworth Rd GU14 . . . . **105** E8
Cloudesdale Rd SW17. . . . **21** B6
Clouston Cl SM6. . . . . **60** E5
Clouston Rd GU14 . . . . **84** F5
Clovelly Ave CR6. . . . . . . **101** B8
Clovelly Ct KT17 . . . . **76** F6
Clovelly Dr GU26. . . . . . . **188** D7
Clovelly Gdns SE19 . . . . . . **42** F8
Clovelly Pk GU26 . . . . . . **188** C7
Clovelly Rd
Beacon Hill GU26. . . . . . . **188** C7
Hounslow TW3. . . . .**5** B5
Clover Cl RG40 . . . . **25** C4
Clover Ct
New Malden KT4 . . . . **39** A2
Sutton SM2 . . . . **59** B4
Woking GU22. . . . . **89** D8
Cloverdale Ct 16 SM6 . . . . **60** B4
Clover Field RH13. . . . . . . **215** D3
Cloverfields RH6. . . . . **161** B4
Clover Hill CR5 . . . . **99** B6
Clover Ho TW3 . . . .**5** C6
Cloverlands RH10 . . . . . . **201** F8
Clover Lea GU7 . . . . **150** E8
Clover Rd GU2 . . . . **108** E2
Clovers Cotts RH12 . . . . . **199** F1
Clovers End RH12 . . . . . . **218** A5
Clovers Way RH12 . . . . . . **218** D7
Clover Way
Carshalton CR4 . . . . **41** A1
Smallfield RH6. . . . . **162** C3
Clowders Rd SE6 . . . . **23** F5
Clowser Cl 6 SM1 . . . . **59** C5
Clubhouse Rd GU11. . . . . **104** F5
Club La RG45 . . . . **45** D5
Club Row GU24 . . . . **87** D8
Clump Ave KT20 . . . . **116** C4
Clumps Rd GU10. . . . . . . **146** E4
Clumps The TW15 . . . . **14** D4
Clyde Ave CR2 . . . . **81** B4
Clyde Cl RH1 . . . . **119** A2
Clyde Ct
Aldershot GU12 . . . . **126** E8
17 Redhill RH1 . . . . **119** A2
Clyde Ho 8 KT2 . . . . **37** D8
Clyde Rd
Croydon CR0 . . . . **61** F8
Stanwell TW19. . . . . **13** E7
Sutton SM1 . . . . **59** A5
Wallington SM6 . . . . **60** C4
Clydesdale Cl TW7. . . . .**5** F4
Clydesdale Gdns TW10 . . . .**7** B3
Clyde Terr SE23 . . . . **23** C6
Clyde Vale SE23 . . . . **23** C6
Clyde Works 10 SM6 . . . . . **60** C4
Clymping Dene TW14 . . . . . **15** B8
Clytha Ct SE27. . . . . **22** C4
Clyve Way TW18 . . . . **32** E8
Coach Ho The KT4 . . . . . . **57** D8
Coach House Cl GU16. . . . . **65** E3
Coach House La SW19 . . . . **19** D5
Coach House Mews
RH1 . . . . **139** F8
Coachlads Ave 3
GU2 . . . . **108** F1
Coachmans Dr
Crawley RH11 . . . . **201** B2
Sandhurst GU47 . . . . **64** B7
Coach Rd
Brockham RH3. . . . . **137** A7
Crawley, North Terminal
RH6. . . . . **181** F6
Crawley, South Terminal
RH6. . . . . **182** B7
Dorking RH4 . . . . **115** A1
North Ascot SL5. . . . .**8** E1
Ottershaw KT16. . . . . **51** C4
Coalbrook Mans 4
SW12 . . . . **21** B7

Coaldale Wlk SE21 . . . . . . **22** C8
Coast Hill RH4, RH5. . . . . **134** F4
Coast Hill La RH4 . . . . . . **135** A5
Coates Cl CR7. . . . . **42** C6
Coates Wlk 15 TW8 . . . .**6** E8
Coatham Pl GU6 . . . . **174** F3
Cobalt Cl BR3 . . . . **43** D5
Cobbets Ridge GU10 . . . . **147** D5
Cobbett Cl RH10 . . . . **202** C8
Cobbett Hill Rd GU3 . . . . **107** E7
Cobbett Rd
Guildford GU2 . . . . **108** F2
Twickenham TW2 . . . . **16** A7
Cobbetts Cl
Woking GU21. . . . . **69** B2
Wood St V GU3 . . . . **107** F6
Cobbetts Farm GU24 . . . . . **68** A4
Cobbetts Hill KT13 . . . . . . **53** B3
Cobbetts Mews 11
GU9 . . . . **125** B2
Cobbetts Way GU9 . . . . . . **145** F6
Cobbetts Wlk GU24 . . . . . . **68** A4
Cobblers The RH13 . . . . . **215** D3
Cobbler's Wlk TW11 . . . . . **16** F1
Cobbles Cres RH10. . . . . **201** E7
Cobb's Rd TW4 . . . .**4** F3
Cobbsthorpe Villas
SE26. . . . . **23** D4
Cob Cl RH10 . . . . **204** C8
Cobden La GU27 . . . . **208** D7
Cobden Mews SE26 . . . . . . **23** B3
Cobden Rd SE25 . . . . **43** A4
COBHAM **73** B5
Cobham Ave KT3 . . . . **39** A4
Cobham Bus Mus★
KT11. . . . . **72** B7
Cobham Cl
Lingfield RH7. . . . . **164** C6
Wallington SM6 . . . . **60** E4
Cobham Cottage Hospl
KT11. . . . . **73** B6
Cobham Ct CR4. . . . . **40** D7
Cobham Gate KT11 . . . . . . **73** B5
Cobham Park Rd KT11 . . . **73** C2
Cobham Rd
Fetcham KT11, KT22 . . . . . . **94** C6
Heston TW5. . . . .**4** C7
Kingston u T KT1, KT2 . . . . **38** A7
Cobham & Stoke
D'Abernon Sta KT11 . . . . **73** E2
Cobham Way
Crawley RH10 . . . . **182** B4
East Horsley KT24 . . . . **92** C6
Cobnor Cl RH11. . . . . **200** F4
Cobs Way KT15 . . . . **52** C1
Coburg Cres SW2 . . . . **22** A7
Cob Wlk RH11 . . . . **201** A6
Cochrane Ct KT23. . . . . . . **94** A2
Cochrane Pl GU20 . . . . **48** D5
Cochrane Rd SW19 . . . . . . **19** F1
Cock-A-Dobby GU47. . . . . **45** A1
Cock La KT22 . . . . **94** C6
Cocks Cres KT3. . . . . **38** F5
Cockshot Hill RH2 . . . . . . **139** B7
Cockshot Rd RH2 . . . . . . **139** C8
Cock's La RG42 . . . .**8** A6
Codrington Ct GU21. . . . . . **68** F1
Codrington Hill SE23,
SE4. . . . . **23** E8
Cody Cl
Ash Vale GU12. . . . . **105** F5
Wallington SM6 . . . . **60** D3
Cody Rd GU14 . . . . **84** F3
Cody Tech Pk GU14 . . . . . **84** C1
Coe Ave SE25 . . . . **43** A3
Coe Cl GU11. . . . . **105** A1
Cogman's La RH6. . . . . . . **162** D4
Cokenor Wood GU10. . . . . **145** F6
Cokers La SE21 . . . . **22** C7
Colborne Ct 8 SW19 . . . . . **40** B8
Colborne Way KT4. . . . . . . **58** C8
Colburn Ave CR3. . . . . **100** F3
Colburn Cres GU4 . . . . . . **110** A4
Colburn Way SM1. . . . . . . **59** D7
Colby Rd
Dulwich SE19 . . . . **22** E3
Walton-on-T KT12 . . . . **35** A1
Colchester Vale RH18 . . . **206** C4
Colchester Villas CR7 . . . . **42** A3
Colcokes Rd SM7. . . . . **78** A3
COLDHARBOUR **156** E4
Coldharbour Cl TW20 . . . . **32** C6
Coldharbour La
Bletchingley RH1. . . . . **120** F1
Dorking RH4, RH5. . . . . . . **135** F3
Egham TW20 . . . . **32** D6
Purley CR8. . . . . **61** A1
Pyrford GU22. . . . . **70** F4
South Holmwood RH4,
RH5. . . . . **156** F6
West End GU24 . . . . **67** F8
Cold Harbour La GU14 . . . **84** F4
Coldharbour Rd
Croydon CR0 . . . . **61** A5
Pyrford GU22, KT14. . . . . . . **70** F4
Coldharbour Way CR0. . . . **61** A5
Coldshott RH8. . . . . **123** A2
Coldstream Rd CR3 . . . . . **100** C5
Cole Ave GU11. . . . . **104** F3
Colebrook KT16 . . . . **51** D4
Colebrook Cl SW19 . . . . . . **19** D8
Colebrooke Pl KT16. . . . . . **51** C3
Colebrooke Rd RH1. . . . . **118** E3
Colebrook Rd SW16. . . . . . **41** E8
Colebrook Rise BR2. . . . . . **44** E7
Cole Cl RH11 . . . . **201** B1
Cole Court Lo 11 TW1 . . . . **17** A8

Coleford Bridge Rd GU16 85 E4
Coleford Cl GU16 85 F3
Coleford Paddocks GU16 85 F4
Cole Gdns TW5 4 A7
Colekitchen La GU5 133 D6
Coleman Cl SE25 43 A7
Coleman Ct SW18 20 A8
Coleman Rd GU12 105 D1
Cole Park Gdns TW1 6 A1
Cole Park Rd TW1 6 A1
Cole Park View 2 TW1 6 A1
Cole Rd TW1 6 A1
Coleridge Ave SM1 59 E6
Coleridge Cl
Crowthorne RG45 45 C4
Horsham RH12 217 E6
Coleridge Cres SL3 1 E6
Coleridge Ct 2 TW10 17 D4
Coleridge Rd
Ashford TW15 13 F4
Croydon CR0 43 C2
Colesburg Rd BR3 43 F7
Colescroft Hill CR8 80 A4
Coleshill Rd TW11 16 E2
Coles La RH5 178 C5
Cole's La RH5 178 B5
Colesmead Rd RH1 118 F4
COLES MEADS 118 F4
Coleson Hill Rd GU10 145 F5
Colet Rd RH10 201 D3
Coleville Rd GU14 84 F5
Coley Ave GU22 70 A2
Colfe Rd SE23 23 E7
Colgate Cl RH11 201 B8
Colin Cl
Coney Hall BR4 63 F7
Croydon CR0 62 F7
Colin Ct
Forest Hill SE6 23 F8
Streatham SW16 21 D6
Colin Rd CR3 101 A4
Coliston Pas SW18 20 A8
Coliston Rd SW18 20 A8
Collamore Ave SW18 20 E7
Collard Cl CR3 100 E7
Collards Gate GU27 208 D6
Collards La GU27 208 D6
College Ave
Egham TW20 12 B2
Epsom KT17 76 F5
College Cl
Addlestone KT15 52 D7
Camberley GU15 65 D7
East Grinstead RH19 185 F1
Lingfield RH7 164 D4
Twickenham TW2 16 D7
College Cres
Redhill RH1 119 A4
Sandhurst GU47 64 E8
College Ct CR0 62 A8
College Dr KT7 36 E2
College Fields Bsns Ctr SW19 40 E8
College Gdns
Dulwich SE21 22 E7
Farnham GU9 125 B2
New Malden KT3 38 F4
Upper Tooting SW17 20 E6
College Gn SE19 22 E1
College Hill
Godalming GU7 150 C2
Haslemere GU27 208 C6
College Hill Terr GU27 208 C6
College La
East Grinstead RH19 185 F1
Woking GU22 89 C8
College Pl GU9 125 C1
College Rd
Ash GU12 106 B3
Bracknell RG12 27 D5
Crawley RH10 201 E6
Croydon CR0, CR9 61 D8
Dulwich SE19, SE21 22 E6
Epsom KT17 76 F5
Ewell KT17 77 B5
Guildford GU1 130 D8
Hounslow TW7 5 F6
Mitcham SW19 20 D2
Sandhurst GU47 64 E8
Woking GU22 70 B3
College Rdbt 1 KT1 37 E6
College Ride
Bagshot GU19 47 C2
Camberley GU15 65 D7
COLLEGE TOWN 64 E8
College Town Inf Sch GU47 64 E8
College Town Jun Sch GU47 64 E8
College Way TW15 13 F4
College Wlk 10 KT1 37 E6
Collendean La RH6 159 F4
Collens Field GU24 87 F4
Collette Ct SE25 42 E4
Colley La RH2 117 E3
Colley Manor Dr RH2 117 D2
Colley Way RH2 117 E4
Collier Cl
Farnborough GU14 84 D5
West Ewell KT19 57 B4
Collier Ct 1 CR0 61 D6
Collier Row RH10 201 D4
Colliers CR3 101 A2
Colliers Cl GU21 69 B2
Colliers Water La CR7 42 A4
COLLIER'S WOOD 20 E2
Collier's Wood Sta SW19 20 D1
Collier Way GU4 110 D3
Collingdon GU6 174 F1
Collingsbourne KT15 52 B6
Collingtree Rd SE26 23 C4
Collingwood GU14 85 E2
Collingwood Ave KT5 38 C1
Collingwood Cl
4 East Grinstead RH19 205 F7
Horley RH6 161 B4
Horsham RH12 217 C4
3 Penge SE20 43 B8
Twickenham TW2 16 A8
Collingwood Coll GU15 66 A8
Collingwood Cres GU1 110 A2
Collingwood Ct SM1 59 B6
Collingwood Grange Cl GU15 66 B8
Collingwood Mount GU15 66 A7
Collingwood Pl
Camberley GU15 66 B8
Walton-on-T KT12 54 B7
Collingwood Rd
Crawley RH10 202 D5
Horsham RH12 217 B4
Mitcham CR4 40 E6
Sutton SM1 59 A6
Collingwood Rise GU15 66 A7
Collingwood Sch SM6 60 B5
Collins Gdns GU12 106 B2
Collins Rd RH11 200 E4
Collis Prim Sch TW11 17 B2
Coll of Richard Collyer The RH12 217 D4
Coll of St Barnabas RH7 185 F8
Collyer Ave CR0 60 E6
Collyer Rd CR0 60 E6
Colman Cl KT18 77 C2
Colman Ho RH1 118 F3
Colmans Hill GU5 154 E7
Colman Way RH1 118 E4
Colmer Rd SW16 21 E1
COLNBROOK 1 D7
Colnbrook By-Pass
Colnbrook SL3 1 D7
Harmondsworth UB7 2 C7
Colnbrook CE Prim Sch SL3 1 D7
Colnbrook Ct
Poyle SL3 1 F6
Upper Tooting SW17 20 D4
Colndale Rd SL3 1 E5
Colne Bank SL3, TW19 1 C4
Colnebridge Cl TW18 12 E3
Colne Ct KT19 57 C6
Colne Dr KT12 54 D7
Colne Ho 2 RH1 118 F2
Colne Lo KT12 54 D7
Colne Rd TW2 16 E7
Colne Reach TW19 1 F2
Colne Way
Ash GU12 106 A1
Wraysbury TW19 12 B6
Colne Wlk RH11 200 F4
Coln Trad Est SL3 1 F6
Coloma Convent Girls' Sch CR9 62 D7
Colonel's La KT16 33 A3
Colonial Ave TW2 5 C1
Colonial Rd TW14 14 E8
Colonnades The CR0 61 A4
Colonsay Rd RH11 201 B3
Colony Gate GU16 66 D2
Colson Rd CR0, CR9 61 E8
Colson Way SW16 21 C4
Colston Ave SM5 59 E6
Colston Ct SM5 59 F6
Colston Rd SW14 7 C3
Coltash Rd RH10 202 A5
Coltsfoot Dr
Guildford GU1 110 B4
Horsham RH12 217 E5
Coltsfoot La RH8 123 A2
Columbia Ave KT4 38 F2
Columbia Ct KT3 38 F2
Columbine Ave CR2 61 B3
Columbus Dr GU14 84 C4
Colvill Ct CR2 61 B2
Colville Gdns GU18 67 C8
Colvin Cl SE26 23 C3
Colvin Rd CR7 42 A4
Colwood Gdns SW19 20 D1
Colworth Rd CR0 43 A1
Colwyn Cl
Crawley RH11 200 F4
Streatham SW16 21 C3
Colwyn Cres TW3 5 C6
Colyton Cl GU21 69 C1
Colyton La 2 SW16 22 A3
Combe Ho SW14 7 C5
Combe La
Bramley GU5 151 D2
Chiddingfold GU8 191 A7
Farnborough GU14 85 A6
Shere KT24, GU4 133 B8
Whiteley Village KT12 53 F2
Wormley GU8 170 F1
Combemartin Rd SW18 19 E7
Combe Rd GU7 150 E8
Combe Rise GU10 146 D5
Combermere Rd SM4 40 B4
Combe View GU8 191 A5
Comeragh Cl GU22 89 A7
Comet Cl GU12 105 F5
Comet Rd
Farnborough GU14 84 C1
Stanwell TW19 13 D8
Comforts Farm Ave RH8 123 A3
Comfrey Cl
Farnborough GU14 84 C5
Wokingham RG40 25 E8
Commerce Pk CR0 60 F8
Commerce Rd TW8 6 C7
Commerce Way CR0 60 F8
Commercial Rd
Aldershot GU12 126 C8
Guildford GU1 130 D8
Staines TW18 13 A2
Commercial Way GU21 69 F2
Commodore Ct GU14 105 B8
Common Cl GU21 69 D5
Commonfield Rd SM7 78 B6
Commonfields GU24 67 F6
Common La
Claygate KT10 56 A3
New Haw KT15 52 C2
Common Rd
Claygate KT10 56 A3
Redhill RH1 139 F7
Commonside
Great Bookham KT23 94 A5
Redhill RH1 139 F7
Common Side KT18 76 A4
Commonside Cl
Coulsdon CR5 100 B7
Sutton SM2 78 B8
Commonside Ct SW16 21 E2
Commonside E CR4 41 B6
Commonside W CR4 40 F6
Common The
Ashtead KT21 75 D3
Cranleigh GU6 174 C3
Wonersh GU5 152 B8
Commonwealth Rd CR3 101 A4
Community Cl TW5 4 B6
Como Rd SE23 23 E6
Compass Cl TW15 14 C1
Compasses Mobile Home Pk GU6 193 F5
Compass Hill TW10 6 D1
Compassion Cl RH11 200 E5
Comper Cl RH11 200 E4
Comport Gn CR0 82 E7
COMPTON
Farnham 125 F1
Guildford 129 B3
Compton Cl
Bracknell RG12 26 E3
Esher KT10 55 D5
Sandhurst GU47 45 C1
Compton Cres
Chessington KT9 56 E4
Chiswick W4 7 C8
Compton Ct
7 Guildford GU1 130 F8
Sutton SM1 59 C6
9 West Norwood SE19 22 E3
Compton Gdns KT15 52 B5
Compton Hts GU3 129 D6
Compton Place Bsns Ctr GU15 65 A4
Compton Rd
Croydon CR0 43 B1
Wimbledon SW19 19 F2
Comptons Brow La RH13 218 A3
Comptons Ct 4 RH13 217 F3
Comptons La RH13 217 F3
Comptons The RH13 218 A3
Compton Way GU10 126 B1
Comsaye Wlk RG12 27 C4
Conal Ct SW16 21 D3
Conaways Cl KT17 58 A1
Concord Ct KT1 37 F6
Concorde Bsns Pk TN16 83 D4
Concorde Cl TW3 5 B5
Concorde Ho
Addlestone KT15 52 B6
Crawley RH6 182 B7
Concorde Rd GU14 84 C1
Concord Ho 4 KT3 38 E6
Condor Ct GU2 130 C7
Condor Rd TW18 33 C6
Conduit La CR0 62 A5
Conduit The RH1 120 D6
Coney Acre SE21 22 C7
Coneyberry RH2 139 D5
Coneybury RH1 120 E1
Coneybury Cl CR6 101 B8
Coney Cl RH11 201 B8
Coney Croft RH12 218 B5
CONEY HALL 63 F7
Coney Hall Par BR4 63 E7
Coney Hill Rd BR4 63 F8
Coneyhurst La GU6 175 D7
Conford Dr GU4 130 E2
Coniers Way GU4 110 B4
Conifer Cl RH2 118 A3
Conifer Ct
Ashford TW15 13 F3
23 Putney SW19 19 D7
Sutton SM2 59 D4
Conifer Dr GU15 66 A6
Conifer Gdns
Streatham SW16 21 F5
Sutton SM1 59 B8
Conifer La TW20 12 C3
Conifer Park Cvn Site RH4 135 F8
Conifer Pk KT17 76 E8
Conifers KT13 53 F6
Conifers Cl
Horsham RH12 218 B6
Teddington TW11 17 C1
Conifers The RG45 45 A7
Coningsby RG12 27 C5
Coningsby Ct CR4 41 A7
Coningsby Rd CR2 61 C2
Conisborough Cres SE6 24 C5
Conista Ct GU21 68 F3
Coniston Cl
Barnes SW13 7 F7
Chiswick W4 7 C7
Crawley RH11 200 D4
Farnborough GU14 84 E3
Frimley GU15 66 C3
Horsham RH12 218 B6
West Barnes SM4 39 D3
Coniston Ct
Ashford TW15 13 D5
Beckenham BR3 44 C8
Chessington KT9 56 E7
Lightwater GU18 48 B1
Penge SE26 23 B2
3 Wallington SM6 60 B6
Weybridge KT13 53 B4
Coniston Dr GU9 125 A6
Coniston Gdns SM2 59 D4
Coniston Rd
Catford BR1 24 E2
Coulsdon CR5 79 C3
Croydon CR0 43 A2
Old Woking GU22 90 B7
Twickenham TW2 5 B1
Coniston Way
Chessington KT9 56 E7
Redhill RH2 118 E2
2 Thorpe Lea TW20 12 B1
Connaught Ave
Ashford TW15 13 E4
Hounslow TW4 4 E3
Mortlake SW14 7 C3
Connaught Bsns Ctr
Mitcham CR4 40 F4
Wallington CR9 60 F4
Connaught Cl SM1 59 D8
Connaught Cres GU24 87 F7
Connaught Dr KT13 72 A8
Connaught Gdns
Crawley RH10 201 D8
Morden SM4 40 C5
Connaught Ho KT6 37 D4
Connaught Jun Sch GU19 47 E2
Connaught Rd
Aldershot GU12 105 D2
Bagshot GU19 47 C3
Brookwood GU24 87 F7
Camberley GU15 65 F5
Carshalton SM1 59 D8
New Malden KT3 38 E5
5 Richmond TW10 6 F2
Teddington TW11 16 D3
Connaught Sch The GU12 126 E7
Connell Ho 6 SM6 60 C4
Connington 2 KT1 38 A7
Connolly Ct GU25 31 E5
Connolly Ho
Epsom KT19 57 B2
Wimbledon SW19 20 C2
Connop Way GU16 65 F3
Conquest Rd KT15 52 A5
Conrad Dr KT4 39 D1
Consero Ct 8 RH1 119 A3
Conservatory Ct SE19 22 E1
Consfield Ave KT3 39 A4
Consort Ct 1 GU22 69 E1
Consort Dr GU15 66 C7
Consort Mews TW7 5 D2
Consort Way RH6 161 A3
Consort Way E RH6 161 B2
Constable Gdns TW7 5 D2
Constable Rd RH10 201 F2
Constable Way GU47 64 E6
Constable Wlk SE21 22 E5
Constance Cres BR2 44 F1
Constance Rd
Sutton SM1 59 C6
Thornton Heath CR0 42 B2
Twickenham TW2 16 B8
Constantine Ho SW2 22 B7
Constant Rd GU14 84 A2
Constitution Hill GU22 89 E8
Control Tower Rd
Crawley RH6 181 D6
Harlington TW6 3 B4
Convent Cl BR3 24 C1
Convent Hill SE19 22 C2
Convent La KT11 72 F7
Convent Lo TW15 14 B3
Convent of the Sacred Heart Digby-Stuart Coll SW15 7 F2
Convent Rd TW15 14 B3
Conway Cl GU16 65 F1
Conway Dr
Ashford TW15 14 C2
Farnborough GU14 84 D4
Sutton SM2 59 B4
Conway Gdns CR4 41 E5
Conway Ho
Reigate RH2 139 A4
6 Streatham SW2 21 E7
Conway Rd
Feltham TW13 15 D3
Harlington TW6 3 B4
Twickenham TW4 16 A8
Wimbledon SW20 39 C8
Conway Wlk TW12 15 F2
Conyers Cl KT12 54 D5
Conyer's Rd SW16 21 D3
Cookes La SM3 58 E4
Cookham Cl GU47 45 C1
Cookham Rd RG12 26 E7
Cook Rd
Crawley RH10 201 F4
Horsham RH12 217 D6
Cooks Hill RH12 214 A8
Cooks Mdw RH12 199 D7
Cooks Mead RH12 199 D7
Cook Way GU2 108 D2
Coolarne Rise GU15 66 A6
Coolgardie Rd TW15 14 C3
Coolham Ct RH11 200 F6
Coolhurst La RH13 218 A1
COOMBE 18 D1
Coombe Ave CR0 61 E6
Coombe Bank KT2, KT3 38 E8
Coombe Boys' Sch KT3 39 A4
Coombe Cl
Crawley RH11 181 D1
Frimley GU16 85 D8
Hounslow TW3 5 A3
Coombe Cotts RH3 116 D4
Coombe Cres TW12 15 E1
Coombe Ct
2 Beckenham BR3 43 F8
2 Croydon CR0 61 D6
Tadworth KT20 97 C4
Coombe Dene 8 BR2 44 F5
Coombe Dr KT15 51 F4
Coombe End KT2 18 D1
Coombefield Cl KT3 38 E4
Coombe Gdns
New Malden KT3 38 F5
Wimbledon SW20 39 A8
Coombe Girls Sch KT3 38 D7
Coombe Hall Pk RH19 205 D6
Coombe Hill Glade KT2 18 E1
Coombe Hill Inf Sch KT3 38 D8
Coombe Hill Jun Sch KT3 38 D8
Coombe Hill Rd
East Grinstead RH19 205 D6
Kingston u T KT2 18 E1
Coombe Hill Stables KT2 18 E1
Coombe House Chase KT3 38 D8
Coombehurst (Kingston University) KT2 18 C3
Coombe La
South Croydon CR0 62 B5
Wimbledon SW20 39 B7
Worplesdon GU3 108 D7
Coombelands La KT15 52 A4
Coombe Lane Flyover SW20 38 F8
Coombe Lane Sta CR0 62 C5
Coombe La W KT2 18 E1
Coombe Manor GU24 68 B4
Coombe Neville KT2 18 D1
Coombe Pine RG12 27 D3
Coombe Pk KT2 18 D3
Coombe Pl KT2 18 C3
Coombe Rd
Croydon CR0 61 E6
Forest Hill SE26 23 B4
Hampton TW12 15 F2
Kingston u T KT3 38 E6
Kingston u T, Norbiton KT2 38 A8
South Croydon CR0, CR2 61 E6
Coombe Ridings KT2 18 C3
Coombe Rise KT2 38 C8
Coomber Way CR0, CR4 41 D2
Coombes The GU5 152 A5
Coombe The RH3 116 D4
Coombe Way KT14 71 F7
Coombe Wlk SM1 59 B7
Coombe Wood Hill CR8 80 C6
Coombe Wood Rd KT2 18 C3
Cooper Cl RH6 162 A3
Cooper Cres SM5 59 F7
Cooper Ct GU14 85 C4
Cooper Ho
Hounslow TW4 4 F4
Upper Tooting SW17 20 D4
7 West Norwood SW27 22 B3
Cooper Lo RH6 160 F2
Cooper Rd
Croydon CR0, CR9 61 B6
Guildford GU1 130 F8
Windlesham GU20 48 D4
Cooper Row RH10 201 D3
Coopers Cl TW18 12 E3
Coopers Hill Dr GU24 87 C7
Cooper's Hill La TW20 11 D4

Cooper's Hill Rd
Nutfield RH1 120 A1
South Nutfield RH1 141 B5
Coopers Mews BR3 44 A7
Coopers Place Bsns Pk GU8 190 F8
Coopers Rise GU7 150 C3
Cooper's Terr GU9 125 C3
Cooper's Yd SE19 22 E2
Cootes Ave RH12 217 A3
Copeland Ho SW17 20 D4
Copelands BR3 23 F1
Copelands Cl GU15 66 D4
Copeman Cl SE26 23 C3
Copenhagen Way KT12 54 B7
Copenhagen Wlk RG45 45 B4
Copers Cope Rd BR3 23 F1
Copgate Path SW16 22 A2
Copleigh Dr KT20 97 E7
Copley Cl
Knaphill GU21 88 E8
Redhill RH1 118 E3
Copley Pk SW16 21 F2
Copley Way KT20 97 D7
Copnall Way 12 RH12 217 C2
Coppard Gdns KT9 56 C4
Coppedhall 2 SE21 22 D6
Copped Hall Dr GU15 66 C6
Copped Hall Way GU15 66 C6
Copper Beech RG42 28 A8
Copper Beech Cl GU22 89 B6
Copper Beeches TW7 5 D6
Copper Beech Ho 17 GU22 69 F2
Copper Cl SE19 22 F1
Copperfield Ave GU47 45 E2
Copperfield Cl CR2 80 C8
Copperfield Ct KT22 95 A6
Copperfield Pl RH12 217 B4
Copperfield Rise KT15 51 F4
Copperfields
Beckenham BR3 44 C8
Fetcham KT22 94 C5
Copper Mill Dr TW7 5 F5
Copper Mill La SW17 20 C4
Coppermill Rd TW19 1 B2
Coppice Cl
Beckenham BR3 44 B5
Guildford GU2 108 D2
Heath End GU9 125 E6
West Barnes SW20 39 C6
Coppice Dr TW19 11 D8
Coppice End GU22 70 E3
Coppice La RH2 117 F3
Coppice Pl GU8 190 F8
Coppice Rd RH12 218 A5
Coppice The
Ashford TW15 14 B2
Crawley Down RH10 204 B8
Coppice Wlk RH10 202 A7
Copping Cl CR0 61 E6
Coppin Ho SW2 22 B7
Coppins The CR0 63 B4
Coppsfield KT8 36 A6
Copse Ave
Heath End GU9 125 E8
West Wickham BR4 63 B7
Copse Cl
Camberley GU15 66 A6
Chilworth GU4 131 C3
Crawley Down RH10 204 B8
East Grinstead RH19 186 A3
Horsham RH12 217 F6
Copse Cres RH11 201 C7
Copse Dr RG41 25 A7
Copse Edge
Cranleigh GU6 174 F4
Elstead GU8 148 C3
Copse Edge Ave KT17 76 F6
Copse End GU15 66 A6
Copse Glade KT6 37 D1
COPSE HILL 19 B1
Copse Hill
Belmont SM2 59 B3
Purley CR8 79 E6
Wimbledon SW20 19 B1
Copse Ho RG41 25 A5
Copse La RH6 161 C4
Copsem Dr KT10 55 B4
Copsem La
Esher KT10 55 C3
Oxshott KT22 55 C1
Copsem Way KT10 55 C4
Copsen Wood KT22 74 C8
Copse Rd
Cobham KT11 73 B6
Haslemere GU27 207 D5
Knaphill GU21 68 F1
Reigate RH1 139 D7
Copse Side GU7 129 D1
Copse The
Caterham CR3 101 A1
Cranleigh GU6 175 A3
Crawley RH10 202 A6
Farnborough GU14 84 D3
Fetcham KT22 94 B4
Rowledge GU10 145 F4
South Nutfield RH1 140 E7
Copse View CR2 62 E2
Copse Way GU10 145 F6
Copse Wood Ct RH1 118 E3
Copsleigh Ave RH1 140 A3
Copsleigh Cl RH1 140 A3
Copsleigh Way RH1 140 A3
Copthall Gdns TW1 16 F7
Copthall Way KT15 52 A1
Copt Hill La KT20 97 F7
COPTHORNE 183 C3
Copthorne Ave SW12 21 D8
Copthorne Bank RH10, RH6 183 C4
Copthorne CE Jun Sch RH10 183 B3
Copthorne Chase TW15 13 F4
Copthorne Cl TW17 34 C3
Copthorne Common Rd RH10 183 C3
Copthorne Ct
Crawley RH10 182 A1
Sutton SM1 59 C7
Copthorne Dr GU18 48 B1
Copthorne Ho KT20 97 E7
Copthorne Prep Sch RH10 183 E3
Copthorne Rd
Copthorne RH10 182 F1
Crawley RH10 202 E8
Domewood RH19 184 D4
Leatherhead KT22 95 B7
Copthorne Rise CR8 80 D6
Copthorne Way RH10 182 F2
Copyhold Rd RH19 205 D8
Corban Rd TW3 5 A4
Corbet Cl SM6 60 A8
Corbet Rd KT17 57 E1
Corbett Cl CR0 82 D7
Corbett Ct 3 SE6 23 F4
Corbett Dr GU18 66 F7
Corbiere Ct SW19 19 D2
Corby Cl
Crawley RH11 200 E3
Englefield Green TW20 11 C2
Corby Dr TW20 11 C2
Cordelia Croft RG42 27 E8
Cordelia Gdns
Ash Vale GU12 85 F1
Stanwell TW19 13 E8
Cordelia Rd TW19 13 E8
Corderoy Pl KT16 32 F3
Cordrey Gdns CR5 79 E4
Cordrey Ho KT15 52 B8
Cordwalles Cres GU15 65 F8
Cordwalles Jun Sch GU15 65 F8
Coresbrook Way GU21 88 B8
Corfe Cl
Ashtead KT21 75 C1
Feltham TW4 15 E7
Corfe Gdns GU16 65 F1
Corfe Lo 15 SE21 22 D6
Corfe Way GU14 85 E1
Coriander Cl GU14 84 C4
Coriander Cres GU2 109 A6
Coriander Ct SL5 29 E3
Corium Ho GU7 150 F5
Cork Ho BR1 24 D3
Corkran Rd KT6 37 E2
Corkscrew Hill BR4 63 D7
Cork Tree Ho 3 SW27 22 B3
Cormongers La RH1 119 D2
Cormorant Ct 13 SE21 22 D6
Cormorant Pl
Cheam SM1 58 F5
Sandhurst GU47 64 E7
Cornbunting Cl GU47 64 D8
Cornelia Cl GU14 84 D3
Cornelia Ho 19 TW1 6 D1
Cornelian Cotts 1 SM6 60 B5
Cornercroft SM3 58 D5
Corner Farm Cl KT20 97 C5
Corner Fielde SW2 21 F7
Corner House Par 3 KT17 57 F1
Cornerside TW15 14 C1
Cornerstone Sch The KT19 76 C6
Corney Rd W4 7 E8
Corney Reach Way W4 7 E7
Cornfield Rd RH2 139 C8
Cornfields GU7 151 A8
Cornfield Sch RH1 139 F4
Cornflower La CR0 43 D1
Cornford Gr SW12 21 B6
Cornhill Cl KT15 52 B8
Cornish Gr SE20 43 B8
Cornwall Ave
Byfleet KT14 71 F5
Claygate KT10 55 F3
Cornwall Cl GU15 65 F7
Cornwall Ct SW17 20 E4
Cornwall Gdns 6 RH19 205 F8
Cornwallis Cl CR3 100 C5
Cornwall Rd
Belmont SM2 59 A2
Thornton Heath CR0, CR9 61 B8
Twickenham TW1 17 A7
Cornwall Way TW18 12 E2
Coronation Cotts GU8 191 C5
Coronation Rd
Aldershot GU11 126 B7
Ascot SL5 29 A2
East Grinstead RH19 205 E7
Coronation Sq RG40 25 D7
Coronet Cl RH10 202 E7
Coronet The RH6 161 C1
Corporation Ave TW4 4 E3
Corpus Christi RC Prim Sch KT3 38 C6
Corrib Dr SM1 59 E5
Corrie Gdns GU25 31 C2
Corrie Rd
Addlestone KT15 52 D6
Old Woking GU22 90 C7
Corrigan Ave CR5 79 A5
Corry Rd GU26 188 C6
Corsair Cl TW19 13 E8
Corsair Rd TW19 13 E8
Corscombe Cl KT2 18 C3
Corsehill St SW16 21 C2
Corsell Ho 5 TW8 6 C7
Corsham Way RG45 45 B5
Corsletts Ave RH12 216 D3
Corsten Hollow 7 RH1 139 F8
Cortayne Cl 4 TW2 16 E6
Corunna Dr RH13 217 F2
Cosdach Ave SM6 60 D3
Cosedge Cres CR0, CR9 61 B5
Cosford Rd GU8 169 E4
Coteford St SW17 21 A4
Cotelands CR0 61 E7
Cotford Rd CR7 42 C5
Cotherstone KT19 57 D2
Cotherstone Rd SW2 21 F7
Cotland Acres RH1 139 D7
COTMANDENE 136 B7
Cotsford Ave KT3 38 D4
Cotswold Cl
Crawley RH11 201 B6
Farnborough GU14 84 E7
Hinchley Wood KT10 55 F8
Kingston u T KT2 18 C2
Staines TW18 13 A3
Cotswold Ct RH13 217 E2
Cotswold Rd
Belmont SM2 59 B1
Hampton TW12 16 A2
Cotswold St SE27 22 B4
Cotswold Way KT4 58 C8
Cottage Cl
Horsham RH12 218 B6
Ottershaw KT16 51 C4
Cottage Farm Way TW20 32 C6
Cottage Gdns GU14 84 F4
Cottage Gr KT6 37 D3
Cottage Pl RH10 183 E3
Cottage Rd KT19 57 D3
Cottage The KT15 52 D7
Cottenham Cl SW20 39 B8
Cottenham Dr SW20 19 B1
Cottenham Par SW20 39 B7
COTTENHAM PARK 39 B8
Cottenham Park Rd
Wimbledon, Copse Hill SW20 19 C1
Wimbledon, Cottenham Park SW20 39 B8
Cottenham Pl SW20 19 B1
Cottenhams RH7 163 E8
Cotterill Rd KT6 37 F1
Cottesbrooke Cl SL3 1 D6
Cottesloe Cl GU24 67 F3
Cottesmore RG12 27 A2
Cottimore Ave KT12 35 B1
Cottimore Cres KT12 35 B2
Cottimore La
Walton-on-T KT12 35 B2
Walton-on-T KT12 35 D1
Cottimore Terr KT12 35 B2
Cottingham Ave RH12 217 D7
Cottingham Rd SE20 23 D1
Cottington Rd TW13 15 D4
Cotton Cl GU11 104 F3
Cottongrass Cl CR0 43 D1
Cotton Hill BR1 24 D4
Cotton Ho 17 SW12 21 E8
Cotton Row RH5 176 C8
Cotton Wlk RH11 201 A1
Cottrell Flats GU14 105 D8
Cotts Wood Dr GU4 110 A6
Couchmore Ave KT10 55 E8
COULSDON 79 C3
Coulsdon CE Prim Sch CR5 79 F1
Coulsdon Coll CR5 100 A8
Coulsdon Court Rd CR5 79 F3
Coulsdon High Sch CR5 100 B7
Coulsdon Ho 5 SW2 21 E7
Coulsdon La CR5 99 A8
Coulsdon Pl CR3 100 D5
Coulsdon Rd CR3, CR5 100 B7
Coulsdon Rise CR5 79 E2
Coulsdon South Sta CR5 79 D3
Coulthurst Ct SW16 21 E1
Council Cotts
Betchworth RH3 116 D1
Loxwood RH14 213 A2
Plaistow RH14 211 D3
West End GU24 67 F7
Countisbury Gdns KT15 52 B5
Countisbury Ho SE26 23 A5
Country Way TW13, TW16 15 C3
County Bsns Ctr RH11 181 D2
County Mall RH10 201 E5
COUNTY OAK 181 D2
County Oak Ind Est RH10 181 D2
County Oak La RH11 181 D3
County Oak Ret Pk RH11 181 D2
County Oak Way RH10, RH11 181 D2
County Par TW8 6 D7
County Rd CR7 42 B7
Courier Ho 17 SW2 22 A8
Courland Rd KT15 52 B7
Course Rd SL5 29 A6
Court Ave CR5 100 A8
Court Bushes Rd CR3 101 B7
Court Cl
East Grinstead RH19 185 F1
Twickenham TW2 16 B5
Wallington SM6 60 D3
Court Close Ave TW2 16 B5
Court Cres
Chessington KT9 56 D4
East Grinstead RH19 185 F1
Court Downs Rd BR3 44 B7
Court Dr
Carshalton SM1 59 E6
Croydon CR0 60 F6
Courtenay Ave SM2 59 A2
Courtenay Dr BR3 44 D7
Courtenay Mews GU21 70 A3
Courtenay Rd
Heath End GU9 125 E7
North Cheam KT4, SM3 58 C7
Penge BR3, SE20 23 D2
Woking GU21 70 A3
Court Farm Ave KT19 57 D5
Court Farm Gdns KT19 76 C8
Court Farm Ind Est TW19 2 F1
Court Farm Pk CR6 81 A3
Court Farm Rd CR6 81 A2
Courtfield Rd TW15 14 B2
Courtfield Rise BR4 63 D7
Court Gdns GU15 65 D5
Court Green Hts GU22 89 C7
Court Haw SM7 78 E4
Court Hill
Sanderstead CR2 80 E7
Woodmansterne CR5 78 F2
Courthope Rd SW19 19 E3
Courthope Villas SW19 19 E1
Court House Mans KT19 76 D7
Court La
Dulwich SE21 22 F8
Epsom KT19 76 C6
Courtland Ave SW16 21 F1
Courtlands
11 Beckenham BR3 44 B7
10 Belmont SM2 59 B3
Richmond TW10 7 A2
2 Walton-on-T KT12 35 A2
Courtlands Ave
Esher KT10 55 A4
Hampton TW12 15 F2
Richmond TW9 7 B5
West Wickham BR2 44 F1
Courtlands Cl CR2 62 A1
Courtlands Cres SM7 78 A3
Courtlands Dr KT19 57 F4
Courtlands Rd KT5 38 A2
Court Lane Gdns SE21 22 E8
Courtleas KT11 74 A6
Courtleigh Manor SL5 30 A2
Court Lodge Rd RH6 160 F3
Courtney Cl SE19 22 E2
Courtney Cres SM5 59 F2
Courtney Pl
Cobham KT11 73 F7
Croydon CR0 61 A7
Dorking RH4 115 D1
Courtney Rd
Croydon CR0, CR9 61 A7
Mitcham SW19 20 E1
Courtney Way TW6 3 A5
Court One TW15 14 C5
Court Rd
10 Aldershot GU11 105 A2
Banstead SM7 78 A4
Caterham CR3 100 E4
South Norwood SE25 42 F6
Tyler's Green RH9 121 C4
Courts Hill Rd GU27 208 B6
Courtside SE23 23 C5
Courts Mount Rd GU27 208 B6
Court The
Guildford GU2 130 C7
Warlingham CR6 81 E1
Court Three TW15 14 C5
Court Two TW15 14 C5
Court Way TW2 16 F8
Court Wood La CR0 62 F1
Courtwood Prim Sch CR0 62 F1
Courtyard Apartments TW11 16 D3
Courtyard The
Addlestone KT15 52 C6
Cranleigh GU6 153 E1
1 Crawley RH10 201 D5
East Grinstead RH19 186 B1
Faygate RH12 218 E4
1 Guildford GU1 130 D8
Kingswood KT20 98 C4
Oxted RH8 122 E6
Staines TW18 12 F4
Thornton Heath CR0 41 F3
West Byfleet KT14 71 A7
Courtyard The *continued*
Whyteleafe CR3 80 F1
Coutts Ave KT9 56 E5
Coval Gdns SW14 7 B3
Coval La SW14 7 B3
Coval Pas SW14 7 C3
Coval Rd SW14 7 C3
COVE 84 D5
Coveham Cres KT11 73 A6
Cove Inf Sch GU14 84 E6
Cove Jun Sch GU14 84 E5
Coventry Hall SW16 21 E3
Coventry Rd SE25 43 A5
Coverack Cl CR0 43 E2
Cove Rd GU14 84 F4
Coverdale Ct RH19 185 C3
Coverdale Gdns CR0 61 F7
Covers La GU27 207 C6
Covert Cl RH10 201 E7
Covert La RG12 27 C5
Coverton Rd SW17 20 E3
Coverts Cl GU9 125 E4
Coverts Rd KT10 55 F3
Covert The
Ascot SL5 29 B2
Farnborough GU14 84 E8
South Norwood SE19 22 F1
Cove Sch GU14 84 E5
Coves Farm Wood RG42 26 D7
Covey Cl
Farnborough GU14 85 A8
Merton SW19 40 B7
Covey The RH10 202 E8
Covington Gdns SW16 22 B1
Covington Way
South Norwood SW16 22 A1
South Norwood SW16 22 B1
Streatham SW16 21 F2
Cowbridge Mdw GU24 87 F4
Cowden St SE6 24 A4
Cowdray Cl RH10 202 C5
Cowdrey Rd SW19 20 C3
Cowfold Cl RH11 200 F3
Cowick Rd SW17 20 F4
Cow La GU7 150 D4
Cowleaze Rd KT2 37 E8
Cowley Ave KT16 32 F2
Cowley Cl CR2 62 C2
Cowley Cres KT12 54 C6
Cowley La KT16 32 F2
Cowley Rd SW14 7 E4
Coworth Cl SL5 30 B4
Coworth Park Sch GU24 49 B6
Coworth Rd SL5 30 A4
Cowper Ave SM1 59 D6
Cowper Cl KT16 32 F3
Cowper Gdns SM6 60 C4
Cowper Rd
Richmond TW10 17 F3
Wimbledon SW19 20 C2
Cowshot Cres GU24 87 D7
Cowslip La RH5 115 B7
Coxbridge GU9 124 F1
Coxbridge Bsns Pk GU10 145 E8
Coxbridge Mdws GU9 124 F1
Coxbridge Rdbt GU9 145 F8
Cox Cnr RH5 177 A7
Coxcombe La GU8 191 B4
Coxcomb Wlk RH11 201 A4
Coxdean KT18 97 C8
Coxgreen GU47 64 D6
COX GREEN 195 E2
Cox Green Rd RH12 195 C2
Cox Ho RH12 217 B2
Cox La
Chessington KT9 56 F6
West Ewell KT19 57 C5
Coxley Rise CR8 80 C6
Coxs Ave TW17 34 E6
Coxwell Rd SE19 22 E1
Coxwold Path KT9 56 E3
Crabbet Rd RH10 202 B7
Crab Hill BR3 24 D1
Crab Hill La RH1 140 F4
Crabtree Cl KT23 94 C1
Crabtree Cnr TW20 32 B8
Crabtree Dr KT22 95 C2
Crabtree La
Churt GU10 168 A2
Great Bookham KT23 94 C1
Headley KT18 96 C1
Westhumble RH5 115 A5
Crabtree Office Village TW20 32 C7
Crabtree Rd
Camberley GU15 65 B2
Crawley RH11 201 C7
Thorpe TW20 32 C7
Crabwood RH8 122 E7
Craddocks Ave KT21 75 F3
Craddocks Cl KT21 76 A3
Craddocks Par KT21 75 E2
Cradhurst Cl RH4 135 C6
Cradle La GU35 166 C4
Crafnant Ct TW15 13 F3
Craigans RH11 201 A5
Craigen Ave CR0 43 B1
Craigmore Twr 11 GU22 89 E8
Craignair Rd SW2 22 A8
Craignish Ave SW16 41 F7
Craig Rd TW10 17 C4
Craigside
Kingston u T KT2 38 B8
Purley CR8 79 F5

Craigwell Ave TW13 15 A5
Craigwell Cl TW18 32 E8
Crail Cl RG41 25 A3
Crakell Rd RH2 139 C8
Crake Pl GU47 64 D8
Cramer Ct KT3 38 C6
CRAMHURST 170 E6
Cramhurst Ho 3 SM1 59 D5
Cramhurst La GU8 170 E6
Cramond Ct TW14 14 E7
Crampshaw La KT21 95 F7
Crampton Rd SE20 23 C2
Cranberry Wlk GU17 64 F3
Cranborne Ave KT6 57 A7
Cranborne Wlk RH10 201 F4
CRANBOURNE 9 B6
Cranbourne Cl
Hersham KT12 54 C4
Horley RH6 161 B5
Thornton Heath SW16 41 E6
Cranbourne Cotts SL4 9 B5
Cranbourne Ct KT12 35 B2
Cranbourne Hall SL4 9 B7
Cranbourne Hall Cvn Site SL4 9 B7
Cranbourne Prim Sch SL4 9 A4
Cranbourne Twrs SL5 28 D8
Cranbrook Ct
10 Brentford TW8 6 D8
Croydon CR2 61 E5
Cranbrook Dr
Thames Ditton KT10 36 C1
Twickenham TW2 16 B7
Cranbrook Ho SE19 42 D8
Cranbrook Rd
Hounslow TW4 4 F3
South Norwood CR7 42 C7
Wimbledon SW19 19 E1
Cranbrook Terr GU6 174 F3
Crane Ave TW7 6 A2
Cranebank TW4 4 A4
Cranebank Mews TW7 6 A3
Cranebrook TW2 16 C6
Crane Ct
Sandhurst GU47 64 D8
West Ewell KT19 57 C6
Craneford Cl TW2 16 F8
Craneford Way TW2 16 F8
Crane Ho
Catford BR1 24 D3
Feltham TW13 16 A5
Crane Lodge Rd TW5 4 B8
Crane Mead Ct TW1 16 F8
Crane Park Prim Sch TW13 15 F6
Crane Park Rd TW2 16 B6
Crane Rd
Stanwell TW19 3 A1
Twickenham TW2 16 E7
Cranes Dr KT5 37 F5
Cranes Park Ave KT5, KT6 37 F5
Cranes Park Cres KT5 37 F5
Cranes Pk KT5, KT6 37 E4
Craneswater TW6 3 F7
Crane Way TW2 16 C8
Cranfield Ct 6 GU21 68 F1
Cranfield Rd E SM5 60 A2
Cranfield Rd W SM5 60 A2
CRANFORD 4 C6
Cranford Ave TW19 13 F8
Cranford Cl
Purley CR8 80 C6
Stanwell TW19 13 E8
Wimbledon SW20 19 B1
Cranford Com Coll TW5 4 B8
Cranford Ct SM1 59 C6
Cranford Jun & Inf Schs TW4 4 B5
Cranford La
Harlington TW6 3 F6
Harlington UB3 3 E7
Hatton TW6 3 F4
Heston TW5 4 D7
Cranford Lo SW19 19 E6
Cranford Rise KT10 55 C5
CRANLEIGH 174 D2
Cranleigh Cl
Penge SE20 43 B7
Sanderstead CR2 81 A7
Cranleigh Ct
Farnborough GU14 84 F4
Mitcham CR4 40 D6
Richmond TW9 7 A4
Cranleigh Gdns
Kingston u T KT2 17 F2
Sanderstead CR2 81 A7
South Norwood SE25 42 E6
Sutton SM1 59 B8
Cranleigh Ho SW20 39 B7
Cranleigh Inf Sch GU6 174 E3
Cranleigh Mead GU6 174 F2
Cranleigh Rd
Ewhurst GU6 175 D4
Feltham TW13 14 F4
Merton SW19 40 A6
Thames Ditton KT10 36 C1
Wonersh GU5 152 C7
Cranleigh Sch GU6 174 C5
Cranleigh Village Hospl GU6 174 D3
Cranley Cl GU1 110 A1
Cranley Ct BR2 44 D7
Cranley Dene GU1 110 A1
Cranley Gdns SM6 60 C3
Cranley Manor 4 GU1 110 A1
Cranley Pl GU21 68 D1
Cranley Rd
Guildford GU1 109 F1
Hersham KT12 53 F5
Cranmer Cl
Warlingham CR6 81 E2
West Barnes SM4 39 E3
Weybridge KT13 53 A3
Cranmer Ct
Hampton TW12 16 B3
Kingston u T KT2 17 D4
2 Knaphill GU21 68 C1
Cranmere Prim Sch KT10 36 C1
Cranmer Farm Cl CR4 40 F5
Cranmer Gdns CR6 81 E2
Cranmer Prim Sch CR4 40 F5
Cranmer Rd
Croydon CR0, CR9 61 C7
Hampton TW12 16 B3
Kingston u T KT2 17 E3
Mitcham CR4 40 F5
Cranmer Terr SW17 20 D3
Cranmer Wlk RH10 202 C5
Cranmore Ave TW7 5 C7
Cranmore Cl GU11 104 E1
Cranmore Ct GU16 85 F4
Cranmore Gdns GU11 104 E1
Cranmore La
Aldershot GU11 104 E1
West Horsley KT24 112 C6
Cranmore Prep Sch KT24 112 C6
Cranmore Rd
Catford BR1 24 F5
Mytchett GU16 86 A4
Cranston Cl
Hounslow TW3, TW4 4 E5
Reigate RH2 139 B8
Cranston Rd
East Grinstead RH19 185 F2
Forest Hill SE23 23 E6
Cranston Way RH10 204 C8
Cranstoun Cl GU3 108 F5
Crantock Rd SE6 24 C6
Cranwell Ct CR0 62 D8
Cranwell Gr
Lightwater GU18 66 F8
Littleton TW17 33 F5
Cranwell Rd TW6 3 B5
Craster Rd SW2 21 F8
Cravan Ave TW13 15 A6
Craven Cl GU10 146 C6
Craven Ct GU15 64 F4
Craven Gdns SW19 20 B3
Craven Ho 2 SW14 7 D4
Craven Rd
Crawley RH10 202 B5
Croydon CR0 43 B1
Kingston u T KT2 37 F8
Cravens The RH6 162 A3
Crawford Cl TW7 5 E5
Crawford Gdns
Camberley GU15 65 B5
Horsham RH13 217 E4
Crawfurd Way RH19 185 F3
CRAWLEY 201 F5
Crawley Ave
Crawley, Ifield RH10, RH11 201 A6
Crawley RH10 182 C1
Crawley Bsns Ctr RH10 181 E2
Crawley Chase RG42 8 B2
Crawley Coll RH10 201 E6
Crawley Coll (West Green Annexe) RH11 201 C7
CRAWLEY DOWN 204 C7
Crawley Down Rd RH19 184 F4
Crawley Down Village CE Prim Sch RH10 204 B8
Crawley Dr GU15 65 F6
Crawley Foyer The RH11 201 C6
CRAWLEY HILL 65 E5
Crawley Hill GU15 65 F5
Crawley Hospl RH11 201 C6
Crawley La RH10 202 C7
Crawley Mus Ctr* RH11 201 C5
Crawley Rd
Crawley RH12 200 B1
Faygate RH12 218 D7
Horsham RH12 218 B5
Crawley Ridge GU15 65 F6
Crawley Ridge Inf Sch GU15 65 F6
Crawley Ridge Jun Sch GU15 65 F7
Crawley Rise GU15 66 A7
Crawley Sta RH10 201 E5
Crawley Wood Cl GU15 65 F5
Crawshaw Rd KT16 51 D4
Crawters Cl RH10 201 F7
Cray Ave KT21 75 F2
Crayke Hill KT9 56 E3
Crayonne Cl TW16 34 E8
Crealock St SW18 20 B8
Creasys Dr RH11 201 A1
Credenhill St SW16 21 C2
Crediton Way KT10 56 A5
Credon Cl GU14 84 F5
Creed Ct CR0 61 F8
Creek Rd KT8 36 E5
Creek The TW16 35 A4
Creeland Gr SE6 23 F7
Cree's Mdw GU20 48 D3
Creg Malin 7 TW10 6 E2
Cremorne Gdns KT19 57 D2
Crendon Ct TW13 15 B7
Crerar Cl GU14 84 D3
Crescent Ct
Beckenham BR3 44 B7
Kingston u T KT6 37 D4
Crescent Gdns SW19 20 A5
Crescent Gr CR4 40 E5
Crescent Ho 8 SW20 39 D8
Crescent La GU12 106 B5
Crescent Rd
Beckenham BR3 44 B7
Bletchingley RH1 120 C2
Caterham CR3 101 A3
East Grinstead RH19 185 D1
Kingston u T KT2 18 B1
Reigate RH2 139 A7
Shepperton TW17 34 C4
Wimbledon SW20 39 D8
Wokingham RG40 25 C5
Crescent Resource Ctr CR0 63 C1
Crescent The
Ashford TW15 13 F3
Barnes SW13 7 F5
Beckenham BR3 44 A8
Belmont SM2 78 A8
Bracknell RG12 27 C5
Carshalton SM1 59 D5
Chertsey KT16 33 A6
East Molesey KT8 36 A5
Egham TW20 11 F2
Epsom KT18 76 A4
Farnborough GU14 85 C3
Felcourt RH19 185 C8
Guildford GU2 109 A3
Harlington UB7 3 D7
Heath End GU9 125 D8
Horley RH6 182 B8
Horsham RH12 217 A2
Kingston u T KT6 37 E4
Kingston u T, Norbiton KT3 38 C7
Leatherhead KT22 95 B5
Lower Halliford TW17 34 F2
Reigate, Mead Vale RH1 139 D6
Reigate RH2 118 B1
Thornton Heath CR0, SE25 42 D3
West Wickham BR4 44 E3
Weybridge KT13 53 A7
Wimbledon SW19 20 A5
Woldingham CR3 102 A4
Crescent Way
Horley RH6 161 A1
South Norwood SW16 22 A1
Crescent Wood Rd SE21, SE26 23 A5
Cressage Ho 9 TW8 6 E8
Cressall Cl KT22 95 B7
Cressall Mead KT22 95 B7
Cressingham Gr SM1 59 C6
Cressinghams The KT18 76 D6
Cresswell Ct TW19 2 D1
Cresswell Rd
Croydon SE25 43 A5
Feltham TW13 15 E4
Twickenham TW1 6 D1
Cresta Dr KT15 51 F1
Crest Hill GU5 133 E1
Crest Ho 5 TW15 14 A3
Creston Ave GU21 68 E3
Creston Way KT4 39 D1
Crest Rd
South Croydon CR2 62 B3
West Wickham BR2 44 F2
Crest The
Surbiton KT5 38 A4
10 West Norwood SW27 22 B3
Crestwood Way TW4 4 E2
Creswell GU21 68 D2
Creswell Cnr GU21 68 D2
Creswell Dr BR3 44 B4
Crewdson Rd RH6 161 B3
Crewe's Ave CR6 81 C3
Crewe's Cl CR6 81 C2
Crewe's Farm La CR6 81 E2
Crewe's La CR6 81 D3
Crichton Ave SM6 60 D6
Crichton Rd SM5 59 F3
Cricket Cl GU26 188 D6
Cricket Ct RH19 185 E3
Cricketers Cl
Chessington KT9 56 D6
Ockley RH5 177 C4
Cricketers La
Englefield Green TW20 11 C4
Windlesham GU20 48 D4
Winkfield RG42 8 A3
Cricketers Terr 2 SM5 59 E7
Cricketers Wlk SE26 23 C3
Cricket Field Gr RG45 45 D4
Cricket Field Rd RH12 217 B1
Cricket Gn CR4 40 F5
Cricket Green Sch CR4 40 E6
Cricket Hill RH1 140 F7
Cricket La
Farnham GU10 146 D6
Penge BR3 23 E3
Cricketts Hill GU5 133 A4
Cricket View KT13 53 B5
Cricket Way KT13 53 E8
Cricklade Ave SW2 21 F6
Crieff Ct 3 TW11 17 C1
Criffel Ave SW2 21 E7
Crimea Rd GU11 105 B2
Crimp Hill SL4, TW20 11 A6
Cripley Rd GU14 84 D6
Cripplecrutch Hill GU27 209 F5
Cripps Ho RH11 201 B2
Crispen Rd TW13 15 E4
Crispin Cl
Ashtead KT21 75 F1
Wallington SM6 60 E8
Crispin Cres CR0 60 D8
CRITCHMERE 207 E7
Critchmere Hill GU27 207 E7
Critchmere La GU27 207 E6
Critchmere Vale GU27 207 E6
Criterion Bldgs KT7 37 B2
Crittenden Lo BR4 44 A1
Critten La KT24, RH5 113 D2
Crocker Cl SL5 28 F8
Crockers La RH7 163 D4
Crockerton Rd SW17 20 F6
Crockford Cl KT15 52 C6
Crockford Park Rd KT15 52 C5
Crockham Cl RH11 201 C4
Crocknorth Rd KT24 113 A2
Crocus Cl CR0 43 D1
Croffets KT20 97 D6
Croft Ave
Dorking RH4 115 B1
West Wickham BR4 44 C1
Croft Cl
Harlington UB7 3 C7
Wokingham RG41 25 A2
Croft Ct SM1 59 D8
Croft End Cl KT9 56 F7
Crofters Cl
Frimley GU16 86 D8
Isleworth TW7 5 D2
Redhill RH1 140 B7
Crofter's Cl GU47 64 A8
Crofters Mead CR0 62 F2
Croftleigh Ave CR8 80 B3
Crofton
Ashtead KT21 75 E1
Haslemere GU27 207 F7
Crofton Ave
Chiswick W4 7 D7
Walton-on-T KT12 54 C7
Crofton Cl
Bracknell RG12 27 E4
Ottershaw KT16 51 C3
Crofton Terr TW9 6 F3
Croft Rd
Aldershot GU11 126 B8
Carshalton SM1 59 E5
Godalming GU7 150 E4
Merton SW19 20 C1
South Norwood SW16 22 A1
Witley GU8 170 E5
Wokingham RG40 25 A1
Woldingham CR3 102 A5
Crofts Cl GU8 191 B5
Croftside The SE25 43 A6
Crofts The TW17 34 E5
Croft The
Crawley RH11 201 A6
Croydon CR9 61 F6
Elstead GU8 148 E3
Epsom KT17 76 F5
Heston TW5 4 E7
New Malden KT3 38 E4
Wokingham RG40 25 D5
Croft Way
Frimley GU16 65 F2
Horsham RH12 217 A3
Richmond TW10 17 B5
Croham Cl CR2 61 E4
Croham Hurst Sch CR2 61 F5
Croham Manor Rd CR2 61 E4
Croham Mount CR2 61 E3
Croham Park Ave CR0, CR2 61 F5
Croham Rd
Croydon CR0, CR2 61 E5
South Croydon CR2 61 E5
Croham Valley Rd CR2 62 B3
Croindene Rd SW16 41 E8
Cromar Ct GU21 69 C3
Cromer Ct SW16 21 E5
Cromer Mans 6 SM1 59 B5
Cromer Rd
Croydon SE25 43 B6
Harlington TW6 3 A5
Mitcham SW17 21 A2
Cromford Way KT3 38 D8
Crompton Fields RH10 181 E1
Crompton Way RH10 181 E1
Cromwell Ave KT3 38 F4
Cromwell Cl KT12 35 B1
Cromwell Ct
15 Kingston u T KT2 18 A1
Knaphill GU21 88 C8
Cromwell Gr CR3 100 C6
Cromwell Ho CR0 61 B7
Cromwell Lo TW13 14 F5
Cromwell Pl
Cranleigh GU6 174 F1
1 East Grinstead RH19 205 F7
Mortlake SW14 7 C4
15 Redhill RH1 118 F2
Cromwell Rd
Ascot SL5 29 B4
Beckenham BR3 43 E6
Camberley GU15 65 D7
Caterham CR3 100 C6
Feltham TW13 15 B7
Hounslow TW3 5 A3
Kingston u T KT2 37 E8
Redhill RH1 118 F1
Teddington TW11 17 A2
Thornton Heath CR0 42 D2
Walton-on-T KT12 35 C1
Wimbledon SW19 20 B3
Worcester Park KT4 57 E7
Cromwell St TW3 5 A3
Cromwell Way GU14 85 C7
Cromwell Wlk 3 RH1 118 F1
Crondall Ct GU15 65 B4
Crondall Ho SW15 19 A7
Crondall La GU10, GU9 124 D2
Crondall Rd GU10 145 A6
Cronks Hill RH1, RH2 139 D7
Cronks Hill Cl RH1 139 D7
Cronks Hill Rd RH1 139 D7
CROOKED BILLET 19 C2
Crooked Billet SW19 19 C2
Crooksbury Rd
Farnham GU10 126 C2
Tilford GU10 147 D8
Crosby Cl TW13 15 E4
Crosby Hill Dr GU15 65 F7
Crosby Way
Farnham GU9 125 A1
Streatham SW2 22 A8
Crosby Wlk SW2 22 A8
Crossacres GU22 70 E4
Cross Deep TW1 17 A6
Cross Deep Gdns TW1 16 F6
Cross Farm Inf Sch GU16 85 E6
Cross Fell RG12 27 A5
Crossfield Pl KT13 53 B3
Cross Gates Cl RG12 27 F6
Cross Gdns GU16 85 F6
Cross Keys RH10 201 D6
Cross La
Burstow RH6 162 C1
Frimley GU16 85 F6
Ottershaw KT16 51 C4
Cross Lances Rd TW3 5 B3
Crossland Rd
Redhill RH1 119 A1
Thornton Heath CR7 42 B3
Crosslands KT16 51 E6
Crosslands Rd KT19 57 D4
Cross Lanes GU1 130 F8
Crossleigh Ct SW16 21 C4
Crossley Cl TN16 83 D4
Crossman Ct RH11 201 B1
Crossman Hos 18 SW12 21 E8
Crossness Ho KT19 57 A1
Cross Oak La RH1 161 C7
Crosspath RH10 201 E7
Cross Rd
Ash GU12 106 B3
Belmont SM2 59 A1
Carshalton SM1 59 D5
Croydon CR0 42 D1
Farnborough GU14 84 E1
Feltham TW13 15 E4
Kingston u T KT2 17 F1
Merton SW19 20 A1
Oatlands Park KT13 53 D7
Purley CR8 80 B6
Tadworth KT20 97 C5
Wentworth SL5 30 A1
Crossroads The KT24 113 D7
Cross St
6 Aldershot GU11 105 A2
Farnborough GU14 105 C8
Hampton TW12 16 C3
Mortlake SW13 7 E4
Wokingham RG40 25 C6
CROSSWATER 167 E4
Crosswater La GU10 167 F4
Crossway
Bracknell RG12 27 C7
Crawley RH6 181 F8
Walton-on-T KT12 54 B8
West Barnes KT3, SW20 39 C5
CROSSWAYS 170 F5
Crossways
Aldershot GU12 105 C1
Charlton TW16 14 F1
Churt GU10 167 F1
Crawley RH10 202 A7
Effingham KT24 113 D8
Egham TW20 12 D2
South Croydon CR0, CR2 62 F3
Sutton SM2 59 D2
Tatsfield TN16 103 C7
Crossways Ave RH19 185 C1
Crossways Cl
Churt GU10 167 F1
Crawley RH10 201 F7
Crossways Cotts GU6 194 A3
Crossways Ct TN16 103 C7
Crossways La RH2 118 D7
Crossways Par CR0 62 F3
Crossways Rd
Beckenham BR3 44 A5
Grayshott GU26 188 D3
Mitcham CR4 41 B6

Crossways The
Abinger Hammer RH5 134 B3
Coulsdon CR5 100 A8
Guildford GU2 129 F7
Heston TW5 4 F7
Lower Kingswood RH2 118 C7
Merstham RH1 119 C6
Crosswell Cl TW17 34 C7
Crouch Cl BR3 24 A2
Crouchfield RH4 136 C4
Crouch Ind Est KT22 95 B8
Crouch La SL4 8 F7
Crouchmans Cl SE21, SE26 23 A5
Crouch Oak La KT15 52 C6
Crowberry Cl 1 RH11 201 A2
Crowborough Cl CR6 81 E1
Crowborough Dr CR6 81 E1
Crowborough Rd SW17 21 A3
Crowcroft Cl GU2 109 B5
Crowholt GU10 145 F5
CROWHURST 143 E3
Crowhurst SE25 43 A6
Crowhurst Cl RH10 202 E6
Crowhurst Keep RH10 202 E6
Crowhurst La RH7, RH8 143 D4
CROWHURST LANE END 143 B5
Crowhurst Mead RH9 121 C5
Crowhurst Rd RH7 164 D7
Crowhurst Village Rd RH7 143 E2
Crowland Rd CR7 42 D5
Crowland Wlk SM4 40 C3
Crowley Cres CR0 61 A5
Crowmarsh Gdns SE23 23 C8
Crown Arc KT1 37 D7
Crownbourne Ct SM1 59 B6
Crown Cl
Colnbrook SL3 1 C7
Walton-on-T KT12 35 C2
Crown Cotts
Bracknell SL5 28 C4
Oxshott KT22 74 B5
Crown Ct
Godalming GU7 150 E4
4 Twickenham TW1 17 B8
Crown Dale SE19, SE27 22 C3
Crown Dr GU9 126 A5
Crown Hill Ct SL5 29 B4
Crown Ho CR0 61 C8
Crown Hts GU1 130 E6
Crown La
Badshot Lea GU9 126 A5
Merton SM4, SW19 40 A6
South Norwood SW16 22 A3
Virginia Water GU25 31 D3
Crown Lane Gdns SE27 22 A3
Crown Lane Prim Sch SW16 22 B3
Crown Mdw SL3 1 B7
Crown Mill CR4 40 E4
Crown Par SM4 40 A5
Crown Pas KT1 37 D7
Crownpits La GU7 150 E3
Crown Pl GU47 45 E1
Crown Point Par SE19 22 B2
Crown Rd
Kingston u T KT3 38 C8
Morden SM4, SW19 40 B5
Sutton SM1 59 B6
Twickenham TW1 6 B1
Virginia Water GU25 31 C3
Crown Rise KT16 32 F1
Crown Row RG12 27 D3
Crown St TW20 12 A4
Crown Terr TW9 6 F3
Crowntree Cl TW7 5 F8
CROWN WOOD 27 D3
Crown Wood Prim Sch RG12 27 E3
Crown Yd TW3 5 C4
Crowther Rd SE25 43 A5
CROWTHORNE 45 D5
Crowthorne Bsns Est The RG45 45 D7
Crowthorne CE Prim Sch RG45 45 C5
Crowthorne Cl SW18 19 F7
Crowthorne Lo RG12 27 B5
Crowthorne Rd
Bracknell, Easthampstead RG12 27 A5
Bracknell RG40, RG12 26 F2
Sandhurst GU47 45 B2
Crowthorne Rd N RG12 27 B6
Croxall Ho KT12 35 C3
Croxden Wlk SM4 40 C3
Croxted Cl SE21 22 C8
Croyde Cl GU14 85 A7
CROYDON 61 D7
Croydon Airport Ind Est CR9 60 F4
Croydonbarn La RH6, RH9 163 B4
Croydon Coll CR9 61 D8
Croydon Coll Annexe CR0 42 D1
Croydon Coll (Selhurst Tertiary Ctr) SE25 42 D4
Croydon Flyover The CR0, CR9 61 C7
Croydon Gr CR0 42 B1
Croydon High Sch CR2 62 C1
Croydon Ho CR0 41 F3
Croydon La SM7 78 D6
Croydon La S SM7 78 B5
Croydon Rd
Beckenham BR3 43 E6
Caterham CR3 101 A5
Coney Hall BR2, BR4 63 F7
Croydon CR0, SM6 60 D7
Harlington TW6 3 B4
Mitcham CR0, CR4, CR9 41 C4
Penge SE20 43 C8
Reigate RH2 118 C2
Tatsfield TN16 103 F3
Titsey CR6 102 D5
Croydon Rd Ind Est BR3 43 D5
Croydon Valley Trad Pk CR0 41 E2
Croylands Dr KT6 37 E2
Croysdale Ave TW16 35 A6
Crozier Dr CR2 62 B1
Cruikshank Lea GU47 64 E6
Crunden Rd CR2 61 D3
Crundwell Ct GU9 125 D3
Crusader Gdns CR0 61 E7
Crusoe Rd CR4 20 F1
Crutchfield La
Sidlow RH6 160 B5
Walton-on-T KT12 54 B8
Crutchley Rd
Catford SE6 24 E6
Wokingham RG40 25 D7
Crystal Ct SE19 22 F3
CRYSTAL PALACE 23 A3
Crystal Palace Mus* SE19 22 F2
Crystal Palace National Sports Ctr SE19 23 A2
Crystal Palace Par SE19 22 F3
Crystal Palace Park Rd SE19, SE26 23 B3
Crystal Palace Sta SE19 23 A2
Crystal Palace Station Rd SE19 23 A2
Crystal Terr SE19 22 D2
Crystal View Ct BR1 24 D4
Cubitt Way GU21 68 D1
Cuckfield Cl RH11 200 F3
Cuckmere Cres RH11 200 F5
Cuckoo La GU24 67 D6
Cuckoo Vale GU24 67 D6
Cuda's Cl KT19 57 F6
Cuddington Ave KT4 57 F7
Cuddington Cl KT20 97 D7
Cuddington Com Prim Sch KT4 57 F7
Cuddington Croft Prim Sch SM2 58 D2
Cuddington Glade KT19 76 A7
Cuddington Park Cl SM7 77 F6
Cuddington Way SM2, SM7 77 D8
Cudham Cl SM2 59 A1
Cudham Dr CR0 82 C8
Cudham Rd TN16 103 E8
Cudham St SE6 24 C8
CUDWORTH 179 F8
Cudworth La
Cudworth RH5 179 E8
Newdigate RH5 158 C1
Cudworth Pk RH5 179 F8
Cuffs Hill RH10 202 E2
Culham Ho RG12 27 E5
Cullens Mews 5 GU11 105 A1
Cullerne Cl KT17 57 F1
Cullesden Rd CR8 80 B4
Cull's Rd GU3 107 C1
CULMER 170 F3
Culmer Hill GU8 170 F2
Culmer La GU8 171 A2
Culmington Rd CR2 61 C2
Culsac Rd 1 KT6 56 E8
Culverden Ct KT13 53 D7
Culverden Rd SW12 21 C6
Culverden Terr 5 KT13 53 D7
Culver Dr RH8 122 E5
Culverhay KT21 75 E3
Culver Ho GU1 110 A1
Culverhouse Gdns SW16 21 F5
Culverlands Cres GU12 106 A3
Culverley Rd SE6 24 C7
Culver Rd GU47 45 D1
Culvers Ave SM5 59 F8
Culvers House Prim Sch CR4 41 A1
Culvers Retreat SM5 59 F8
Culverstone Cl BR2 44 F4
Culvers Way SM5 59 F8
Culworth Ho GU1 130 E8
Cumber Ho SW18 20 A7
Cumberland Ave GU2, GU3 109 A6
Cumberland Cl
Epsom KT19 57 E1
Cumberland Cl *continued*
2 Twickenham TW1 6 B1
13 Wimbledon SW20 19 D1
Cumberland Ct
4 Croydon CR0 42 D1
North Cheam KT4 39 B1
Cumberland Dr
Bracknell RG12 27 E8
Chessington KT9 56 F7
Hinchley Wood KT10 56 A8
Cumberland Ho KT2 18 B1
Cumberland Lo SL4 10 D3
Cumberland Pl
Catford SE6 24 F7
Sunbury TW16 35 A5
Cumberland Rd
Ashford TW15 13 D5
Barnes SW13 7 F6
Beckenham BR2 44 F6
Croydon SE25 43 B3
Frimley GU15 66 C4
Richmond TW9 7 A7
Cumberlands CR8 80 D4
Cumberland St TW18 12 D3
Cumberlow Ave SE25 43 A6
Cumbernauld Gdns TW16 14 F3
Cumbernauld Wlk RH11 200 E2
Cumbrae Gdns KT6 56 D8
Cumbria Ct
Farnborough GU14 85 E1
Reigate RH2 118 D2
Cumnor Gdns KT17 58 A4
Cumnor House Sch CR2 61 B2
Cumnor Rd SM2 59 C4
Cumnor Rise CR8 80 C2
Cumnor Way RG12 27 E5
Cunard Mews GU6 193 E2
Cunliffe Cl KT18 96 B3
Cunliffe Rd KT19 57 F6
Cunliffe St SW16 21 C2
Cunningham Ave GU1 110 B2
Cunningham Cl BR4 63 B8
Cunningham Rd SM7 78 D4
Cunnington Rd GU14 85 E2
Cunworth Ct RG12 26 F3
Curfew Bell Rd KT16 32 F2
Curlew Cl CR2 81 D8
Curlew Ct
Aldershot GU11 126 A7
Tolworth KT6 57 A7
Curlew Gdns GU4 110 D3
Curley Hill Rd GU18 66 F7
Curling Cl CR5 100 A7
Curling Vale GU2 130 A7
Curl Way RG41 25 A5
Curly Bridge Cl GU14 84 F8
Curnick's La SE27 22 C4
Curran Ave SM6 60 A7
Currie Hill Cl SW19 19 F4
Currie Ho 11 SW12 21 D8
Curteys Wlk RH11 201 A3
Curtis Cl GU15 66 C7
Curtis Field Rd SW16 22 A4
Curtis Gdns 2 RH4 136 A8
Curtis Rd
Dorking RH4 136 A8
Twickenham TW4 15 F8
West Ewell KT19 57 C6
Curvan Cl KT17 57 F1
Curzon Ave RH12 217 B3
Curzon Cl KT13 53 A6
Curzon Ct BR2 44 D7
Curzon Rd
Thornton Heath CR7 42 A3
Weybridge KT13 53 A5
Cusack Cl TW1 16 F4
Cuthbert Gdns SE25 42 E6
Cuthbert Rd
Ash GU12 106 B6
Thornton Heath CR0, CR9 61 B8
Cuttinglye La RH10 184 A1
Cuttinglye Rd RH10 184 C2
Cutts Rd GU11 105 D7
Cyclamen Cl 4 TW12 16 A2
Cyclamen Way KT19 57 C5
Cygnet Ave TW14 15 D8
Cygnet Cl GU21 69 B3
Cygnets Cl RH1 119 A3
Cygnets The
Feltham TW13 15 E4
6 Staines TW18 12 F3
Cypress Ave TW2 16 C8
Cypress Ct
Charlton TW16 34 E8
Sutton SM1 59 A4
Thorpe GU25 31 F5
8 West Norwood SW16 22 A3
Cypress Gr GU12 105 F7
Cypress Hill Ct GU14 64 F1
Cypress Inf Sch SE25 42 E7
Cypress Jun Sch SE25 42 E7
Cypress Lo SE25 42 E7
Cypress Rd
Guildford GU1 109 C4
South Norwood SE25 42 E7
Cypress Way
Banstead KT17 77 D5
Blackwater GU17 64 B5
Grayshott GU26 188 D2
Cypress Wlk TW20 11 B2
Cyprians Ave GU24 88 B6
Cyprus Rd GU16 86 D8
Cyrillian Ho 3 SM2 59 B4

D

D'abernon Cl KT10 55 A6
D'Abernon Dr KT11 73 E3
Dacre Rd CR0 41 E2
Dacres Rd SE23 23 D5
Daffodil Cl
Croydon CR0 43 D1
7 Hampton TW12 16 A2
Daffodil Dr GU24 68 A3
Dafforne Rd SW17 21 A5
Dagden Rd GU4 130 E3
Dagley La GU4 130 D3
Dagmar Rd
4 Kingston u T KT2 18 A1
South Norwood SE25 42 E4
Dagnall Pk CR0, SE25 42 E4
Dagnall Rd SE25 42 E4
Dagnan Rd SW12 21 C8
Dahlia Gdns CR4 41 D5
Dahomey Rd SW16 21 C2
Daimler Way SM6 60 E3
Dainford Cl BR1 24 D3
Dairy Cl CR7 42 C7
Dairyfields RH11 201 A5
Dairy Gate Rd GU14 105 B8
Dairymans Wlk GU4 110 B6
Daisy Cl CR0 43 D1
Daisy Mdw TW20 12 A3
Dakin Cl RH10 202 C2
Dakins The RH19 205 E8
Dakota Cl SM6 60 F3
Dalcross RG12 27 E3
Dalcross Rd TW4, TW5 4 E5
Dale Ave TW4 4 E4
Dalebury Rd SW17 20 F6
Dale Cl
Addlestone KT15 52 B5
Horsham RH12 217 F5
Sunningdale SL5 30 A4
Wrecclesham GU10 145 F7
Dale Ct 3 KT2 17 F1
Daledene RH19 205 F8
Dalegarth Gdns CR8 80 D6
Dale Gdns GU47 64 A8
Daleham Ave TW20 12 A2
Dale Lodge Rd SL5 30 A4
Dale Park Ave SM5 59 F8
Dale Park Rd SE19 42 D8
Dale Rd
Ashford TW16 14 F1
Cheam SM1 58 F6
Forest Row RH18 206 F1
Purley CR8 80 B7
Walton-on-T KT12 34 F2
Daleside Rd
Streatham SW17 21 B3
West Ewell KT19 57 D4
Dale View
Haslemere GU27 207 F5
Headley KT18 96 B4
Woking GU21 69 B1
Dalewood Gdns
Crawley RH10 201 F8
North Cheam KT4 58 B8
Dalkeith Rd SE21 22 C8
Dallas Ct SM3 58 E4
Dallas Rd
Cheam SM3 58 E4
Forest Hill SE26 23 B5
Dallaway Gdns RH19 185 E1
Dalley Ct GU47 64 D7
Dallington Cl KT12 54 C4
Dalmain Prim Sch SE23 23 E7
Dalmain Rd SE23 23 D7
Dalmally Pas CR0 42 F2
Dalmally Rd CR0 43 A2
Dalmeny Ave SW16 42 A7
Dalmeny Cres TW3 5 D3
Dalmeny Rd
North Cheam KT4 58 B7
Wallington SM5 60 A3
Dalmore Ave KT10 55 F4
Dalmore Rd SE21 22 C6
Dalston Cl GU15 66 D3
Dalton Ave CR4 40 E7
Dalton Cl
Crawley RH11 201 B1
Purley CR8 80 C7
Dalton Ct GU16 86 D8
Dalton Ho
8 Balham SW12 21 B8
Merton SW19 40 C8
Dalton St SE27 22 B5
Damascene Wlk SE21 22 C7
Damask Cl GU24 67 E6
Damask Ct SM1 40 B1
Damer Ho 10 TW10 6 F1
Dampier Wlk RH11 201 B1
Damson Way SM5 59 F2
Danbrook Rd SW16 21 E1
Dan Bryant Ho 5 SW12 21 C8
Danbury Mews SM6 60 B6
Danby Ct RH6 161 B5
Dancer Rd TW9 7 A4
Danebury CR0 63 B4
Danebury Ave SW15 7 E1
Danebury Wlk GU16 85 F8
Daneby Rd SE6 24 C6
Danecourt Gdns CR0 61 F7
Dane Ct GU22 70 F4
Dane Ho SW17 20 C4
Danehurst TW8 6 C7
Danehurst Cl TW20 11 E2
Danehurst Cres RH13 217 F2
Danehurst Ct KT17 76 F6
Danemore La RH9 142 E2
Dane Rd
Ashford TW15 14 D2
Merton SW19 40 C8
Warlingham CR6 81 D2
Danesbury Rd TW13 15 B7
Danes Cl KT22 74 C5
Danescourt Cres SM1 59 C8
Danesfield
Send Marsh GU23 90 F4
Wokingham RG40 25 D6
Danesfield Cl KT12 54 B8
Danesfield Manor Sch KT12 54 C8
Daneshill RH1 118 E2
Danes Hill GU22 70 B1
Daneshill Cl RH1 118 E2
Danes Hill Prep Sch KT22 74 D6
Danesmead KT11 74 A8
Danesrood GU1 130 F8
Danes Way KT22 74 D5
Daneswood Ave SE6 24 C5
Daneswood Cl KT13 53 C5
Danetree Cl KT19 57 C3
Danetree Jun Sch KT19 57 C4
Danetree Rd KT19 57 D3
Daniel Cl
Mitcham SW17, SW19 20 E2
Twickenham TW4 15 F8
Daniel Ct 3 BR3 24 A1
Daniell Way CR0, CR9 41 F1
Daniels La CR6 81 F4
Daniel Way SM7 78 B5
Danley La GU27 207 A3
Danses Cl GU4 110 D3
Danvers Way CR3 100 C4
Dapdune Ct GU1 109 C1
Dapdune Rd GU1 109 D1
Dapdune Wharf* GU1 109 C1
Daphne Ct KT4 57 E8
Daphne Jackson Rd GU2 129 E8
Daphne St SW18 20 C8
Darby Cl CR3 100 C5
Darby Cres TW16 35 C7
Darby Gdns TW16 35 C7
DARBY GREEN 64 B6
Darby Green La
Blackwater GU17 64 B5
Blackwater GU46 64 A5
Darby Green Rd GU17 64 B5
Darcy Ave SM6 60 C6
Darcy Cl CR5 100 B8
Darcy Pl KT21 75 F2
Darcy Rd
Ashtead KT21 75 F2
Isleworth TW7 6 A6
Thornton Heath SW16 41 E7
D'arcy Rd SM3 58 D6
Darell Prim Sch TW9 7 A4
Darell Rd TW9 7 A4
Darent Ho BR1 24 D3
Darenth Way RH6 160 F6
Darfield Rd GU4 110 A4
Dargate Cl SE19 22 F1
Dark La GU3 128 B4
Darlaston Rd SW19 19 E1
Darley Cl
Addlestone KT15 52 C5
Croydon CR0 43 E3
Darleydale RH11 201 C3
Darleydale Cl GU47 45 D2
Darley Dene Ct KT15 52 C6
Darley Dene Inf Sch KT15 52 C5
Darley Dr KT3 38 D7
Darley Gdns SM4 40 B3
Darling Ho 24 TW1 6 D1
Darlington Ct SE6 24 F7
Darlington Ho 2 KT6 37 D2
Darlington Rd SE27 22 B3
Darmaine Cl CR2 61 C3
Darnley Pk KT13 53 B7
Darracott Cl GU15 66 B8
Darrell Ct BR2 44 E6
Darsena Ho 6 SM2 59 C3
Dart Cl SL3 1 B8
Dart Ct RH19 186 A3
Dartmouth Ave GU21 70 D5
Dartmouth Cl RG12 27 E6
Dartmouth Gn GU21 70 D5
Dartmouth Ho
17 Kingston u T KT2 37 E8
Thornton Heath CR0 42 B2
Dartmouth Path GU21 70 D5
Dartmouth Pl
Chiswick W4 7 E8
Forest Hill SE23 23 C6
Dartmouth Rd SE23, SE26 23 C5
Dartnell Ave KT14 71 B7
Dartnell Cl KT14 71 B7
Dartnell Cres KT14 71 B7
Dartnell Ct KT14 71 C7
DARTNELL PARK 71 C7
Dartnell Park Rd KT14 71 C8
Dartnell Pl KT14 71 B7
Dartnell Rd CR0 42 F2
Dart Rd GU14 84 D6
Darvel Cl GU21 69 A3
Darvills La GU9 125 C2
Darwall Dr SL5 28 D7
Darwin Cl RH12 217 F4

Darwin Ct
Camberley GU15 . . . . 65 B3
Guildford GU1 . . . . .109 D5
Darwin Gr GU11 . . . . 105 C3
Darwin Pl RG12. . . . . 27 C5
Daryngton Dr GU1 . . . . . . 110 B1
Dashwood Cl
Bracknell RG12 . . . . 27 D8
West Byfleet KT14. . . . . 71 C7
Dashwood Ct TW3 . . . . 5 C3
Dashwood Ho SE21 . . . . . . 22 F5
Dashwood Lang Rd
KT15 . . . . 52 E6
Dassett Rd SE27 . . . . 22 B3
Datchet Rd
Forest Hill SE6. . . . . 23 F6
Horton SL3. . . . . 1 A4
Daubeney Pl TW12. . . . . . . 36 C8
Davenant Rd CR0, CR9 . . . . 61 B6
Davenport Cl TW11 . . . . . . 17 A2
Davenport Lo
Heston TW5. . . . . 4 E7
Heston TW5. . . . . 4 E7
Davenport Rd RG12 . . . . . . 27 E8
Daventry Cl SL3 . . . . .1 F6
Daventry Ct RG42 . . . . 27 B8
Dave Porter Hts SW18. . . . 19 E8
David Cl UB3 . . . . .3 E7
David Ct 1 TW18 . . . . 13 A4
David Henry Waring Ct
TW14. . . . . 14 C7
David Ho SE25. . . . . 43 A6
David Livingstone Prim
Sch CR7. . . . . 42 C8
David Rd SL3 . . . . .1 F5
Davids Ct SE6 . . . . 24 A3
Davidson Lo CR0. . . . . 42 E2
Davidson Prim Sch
CR0. . . . . 42 F2
Davidson Rd CR0, SE25 . . . 42 F3
David's Rd SE23 . . . . 23 C7
David Twigg Cl 7 KT2 . . . 37 E8
Davies Cl
Croydon CR0, SE25 . . . . 43 A3
Farncombe GU7. . . . . .150 D7
Davies Wlk TW7 . . . . 5 D6
Davington Ct 16 SM2. . . . . 59 A3
Davis Cl RH11 . . . . 201 A1
Davis Gdns GU47 . . . . 64 E7
Davison Cl KT19 . . . . 76 B8
Davis Rd
Chessington KT9 . . . . 57 A6
Weybridge KT13 . . . . 52 F1
Davos Cl GU22. . . . . 89 E8
Davy Cl RG40 . . . . 25 C5
Dawell Dr TN16. . . . . 83 C2
Dawes Ave TW7 . . . . 6 A3
Dawes Ct KT10 . . . . 55 B6
DAWESGREEN 137 F3
Dawes Green Cotts
RH2 . . . . 138 A3
Dawley Ride SL3. . . . . 1 E6
Dawlish Ave SW18 . . . . 20 B6
Dawnay Cl SL5. . . . . 28 F8
Dawnay Gdns SW18. . . . . . . 20 D6
Dawnay Prim Sch The
KT23. . . . . 94 A1
Dawnay Rd
Camberley GU15 . . . . 65 B7
Great Bookham KT23. . . . . . 94 C1
Wandsworth SW17,
SW18 . . . . 20 D6
Dawn Cl TW4. . . . . .4 E4
Dawn Ct GU15 . . . . 65 F7
Dawney Hill GU24. . . . . 87 F5
Dawneys Rd GU24 . . . . 87 E5
Dawn Redwood Cl SL3 . . . . 1 A4
Dawn Rise RH10 . . . . 183 A3
Dawn Wlk BR2. . . . . 44 D7
Dawsmere Cl GU15 . . . . . . 66 C5
Dawson Rd
Byfleet KT14 . . . . 71 E8
Kingston u T KT1 . . . . 37 F6
Dax Ct TW16. . . . . 35 C6
Daybrook Rd SW19 . . . . . . 40 B6
Day Ct GU6. . . . . 173 F2
Daymerslea Ridge
KT22 . . . . 95 C6
Day's Acre CR2 . . . . 61 F1
Daysbrook Rd SW2 . . . . . . 21 F7
Dayseys Hill RH1. . . . . 162 A8
Dayspring GU2 . . . . 109 B5
Daytone Ho SW20. . . . . 39 D8
Deacon Cl
Downside KT11 . . . . 93 B8
Wallington CR8 . . . . 60 E2
Wokingham RG40 . . . . 25 C8
Deacon Ct RH7 . . . . 164 C4
Deacon Field GU2 . . . . 109 A2
Deacon Ho SM2 . . . . 59 A1
Deacon Rd KT2. . . . . 37 F8
Deacons Wlk TW12 . . . . . . 16 A4
Deadbrook La GU12. . . . . . 105 E3
Deal Rd SW17 . . . . 21 A2
Dean Cl GU22. . . . . 70 E3
Dean Ct
6 Chertsey KT16 . . . . 33 A3
Farncombe GU7. . . . . 150 D6
10 Kingston u T KT2 . . . . . . 18 A1
Deanery Pl 1 GU7 . . . . . . 150 D4
Deanery Rd GU7 . . . . 150 E6
Deanfield Gdns CR0. . . . . . 61 D6
Dean Gr RG40 . . . . 25 C7
Deanhill Ct SW14 . . . . .7 B3
Deanhill Rd SW14. . . . . .7 B3
Dean La RH1 . . . . 99 C3
Deanoak La RH2. . . . . 159 D8
Dean Par GU15 . . . . 65 F8
Dean Rd
Croydon CR0 . . . . 61 D6
Farncombe GU7. . . . . .150 D6
Hampton TW12 . . . . 16 A3
Isleworth TW3. . . . . 5 B2
Deans Cl
Chiswick W4 . . . . 7 B8
South Croydon CR0 . . . . 61 F7
Walton on t H KT20. . . . . . . 97 B3
Deans Ct GU20. . . . . 48 D4
Deansfield CR3 . . . . 100 F2
Deansgate RG12 . . . . 27 B2
Deans Gate Cl SE23 . . . . . . 23 D5
Dean Shaw Cotts
RH8 . . . . 122 A2
Deanside GU15 . . . . 65 F8
Deans La
Nutfield RH1 . . . . .120 A2
Walton on t H KT20. . . . . . . 97 B2
Deans Rd
Merstham RH1. . . . . .119 C5
Sutton SM1 . . . . 59 B7
Deans Wlk CR5 . . . . 80 A1
Dean Wlk KT23 . . . . 94 B1
Dearmer Ho 2 SW2 . . . . . 22 A8
De'arn Gdns CR4 . . . . 40 E6
Debden Cl KT2 . . . . 17 D3
Deborah Cl TW7 . . . . .5 E6
De Broome Rd TW13 . . . . . 15 C7
De Burgh Gdns KT20 . . . . . 97 D8
De Burgh Ho 10 SW19. . . . 20 C1
De Burgh Pk SM7. . . . . 78 B4
Deburgh Rd SW19 . . . . 20 C1
Decimus Cl 1 CR7. . . . . . . 42 D5
Decon Pl CR3. . . . . 100 C4
Dedham Ho SE6 . . . . 24 C4
Dedisham Cl RH10 . . . . . . 202 A5
Dedswell Dr GU4 . . . . 111 A6
Deedman Cl GU12 . . . . . . 106 A2
DEEPCUT 86 C6
Deepcut Bridge Rd
GU16 . . . . 86 C7
Deepdale
Bracknell RG12 . . . . 27 A5
Horley RH6 . . . . 161 B2
Wimbledon SW19 . . . . 19 D4
Deepdale Ave BR2 . . . . 44 F5
Deepdale Ct CR0. . . . . 61 D6
DEEPDENE 136 C8
Deepdene
Farnham GU10. . . . . .146 D7
Haslemere GU27 . . . . 207 E6
Deepdene Ave
Dorking RH4, RH5 . . . . 136 C6
South Croydon CR0 . . . . 61 F7
Deepdene Avenue Rd
RH4 . . . . 115 C1
Deepdene Ct BR2. . . . . 44 E6
Deepdene Dr RH4. . . . . . . 136 C7
Deepdene Gdns
Dorking RH4 . . . . .136 C8
Streatham SW2 . . . . 21 F8
Deepdene Lo 8 SW2 . . . . 21 F8
Deepdene Park Rd
RH5 . . . . 136 D8
Deepdene Point 9
SE26. . . . . 23 D5
Deepdene Rdbt RH4 . . . . 136 C8
Deepdene Vale RH4. . . . . 115 C1
Deepdene Wood RH5 . . . 136 D7
Deepfield Rd RG12. . . . . . . 27 D7
Deepfields RH6. . . . . 160 F5
Deepfield Way CR5 . . . . . . 79 E3
Deep Pool La GU24 . . . . . . 69 B6
Deeprose Cl GU3 . . . . 109 B5
Deepwell Cl TW7 . . . . 6 A6
Deep Well Dr GU15 . . . . . . 65 E5
Deerbarn Rd GU2. . . . . . . 109 B2
Deerbrook Rd SE24 . . . . . . 22 B7
Dee Rd TW9. . . . . .6 F3
Deerhurst
Kingston u T KT2 . . . . 38 B8
Streatham SW16 . . . . 21 E3
Deerhurst Cl TW13. . . . . . . 15 B4
Deerhurst Cres TW12 . . . . 16 C3
Deerhurst Ct CR0 . . . . 42 B1
Deerhurst Rd SW16 . . . . . . 21 F3
Deerings Rd RH2 . . . . 118 C1
Deerleap GU35 . . . . 187 C4
Deer Leap GU18 . . . . 67 A8
Deerleap Cotts RH5. . . . . 134 C4
Deerleap Rd RH4 . . . . 135 B6
Deer Park Cl KT2 . . . . 18 B1
Deer Park Gdns CR4 . . . . . 40 D5
Deer Park Rd SW19 . . . . . . 40 C7
Deer Park Way BR4 . . . . . . 63 F8
Deer Rock Hill RG12 . . . . . 27 C3
Deer Rock Rd GU15 . . . . . . 65 F8
Deers Farm Cl GU23 . . . . . 71 E3
Deerstead Ho GU22 . . . . . . 89 B8
Deerswood Cl
Caterham CR3 . . . . .101 A3
Crawley RH11 . . . . 201 B7
Deerswood Ct RH11. . . . . 201 A7
Deerswood Rd RH11 . . . . 201 B7
Deer Way RH12. . . . . 217 A1
Deeside Rd SW17 . . . . 20 D5
Dee Way KT19. . . . . 57 E1
Defence Evaluation &
Research Agency
GU14. . . . . 84 C1
Defiant Rd GU14. . . . . 104 F8
Defiant Way SM6 . . . . 60 E3
Defoe Ave TW9 . . . . .7 A7
Defoe Cl SW17, SW19. . . . . 20 E2
Defoe Pl SW17. . . . . 20 F4
De Frene Rd SE23, SE26. . . 23 E5
De Havilland Dr KT13 . . . . 71 E8
De Havilland Rd TW5 . . . . . 4 C7
De Havilland Way TW19. . . .2 E1
Delabole Rd RH1 . . . . 119 E6
Delacy Ct SM2. . . . . 78 A8
Delamare Cres CR0 . . . . . . 43 C3
Delamere Rd
Reigate RH2. . . . . .139 C5
Wimbledon SW20 . . . . 39 D8
Delancey Ct RH12. . . . . . . 217 C4
Delaporte Cl KT17 . . . . 76 E7
De Lara Way GU21 . . . . 69 D1
De La Warr Rd RH19 . . . . 185 F1
Delcombe Ave KT4. . . . . . . 39 C1
Delderfield KT21. . . . . 95 D6
Delfont Cl RH10 . . . . 202 D4
Delft Ho KT2 . . . . 37 F8
Delia St SW18 . . . . 20 B8
Delius Gdns RH12. . . . . . . 218 B4
Dellbow Rd TW14. . . . . .4 B2
Dell Cl
Fetcham KT22 . . . . 94 E4
Haslemere GU27 . . . . 208 A7
Mickleham RH5 . . . . 115 C8
Wallington SM6. . . . . 60 D6
Dell Close Cotts RH5. . . . 115 C8
Dellfield Cl BR3. . . . . 44 C8
Dell Gr GU16 . . . . 65 F2
Dell Ho CR2 . . . . 61 C2
Dell La KT17. . . . . 58 A5
Dell Rd KT17 . . . . 58 A4
Dells Cl TW11 . . . . 16 F2
Dell The
Brentford TW8. . . . . 6 C8
Burgh Heath KT20. . . . . 97 C6
East Grinstead RH19. . . . . 186 B1
Englefield Green SL4. . . . . . 11 A5
Feltham TW14 . . . . 15 B8
Heath End GU9 . . . . 125 D7
Horley RH6 . . . . 161 B4
Reigate RH2. . . . . .118 A2
Sidlow RH6 . . . . .160 C5
South Norwood SE19. . . . . . 42 F8
Woking GU21. . . . . 69 C1
Dell Wlk KT3 . . . . 38 E7
Delmey Cl CR0. . . . . 61 F7
Delphian Ct 5 SW16. . . . . 22 A4
Delta Bglws RH6. . . . . 161 A1
Delta Cl
Chobham GU24 . . . . 49 F1
Worcester Park KT4 . . . . . . 57 F7
Delta Dr RH6 . . . . 161 A1
Delta Ho RH6. . . . . 161 A1
Delta Rd
Chobham GU24 . . . . 49 F1
Woking GU21. . . . . 70 A3
Worcester Park KT4 . . . . . . 57 E7
Delta Way TW20. . . . . 32 C8
Delves KT20 . . . . 97 D6
Delville Cl GU14 . . . . 84 D3
De Mel Cl KT19 . . . . 76 B7
Demesne Rd SM6. . . . . 60 D6
De Montfort Par 1
SW16. . . . . 21 E5
De Montfort Rd SW16 . . . . 21 E6
Dempsey Wlk RH11 . . . . . 201 A8
Dempster Cl KT6. . . . . 37 C1
Dempster Ho GU9 . . . . . . 125 D8
Denbies Wine Est*
RH5. . . . . 115 B3
Denbigh Cl SM1 . . . . 58 F5
Denbigh Gdns TW10 . . . . . . .6 F2
Denbigh Rd
Haslemere GU27 . . . . .208 D5
Hounslow TW3. . . . . 5 B5
Denby Ct GU14 . . . . 85 C1
Denby Dene GU12 . . . . . . 106 B2
Denby Rd KT11 . . . . 73 C7
Denchers Plat RH11. . . . . 181 D1
Den Cl BR3. . . . . 44 D6
Dencliffe 3 TW15 . . . . 14 A3
Dendy St SW12 . . . . 21 A7
Dene Ave TW3. . . . . .4 F4
Dene Cl
Ash GU12. . . . . 106 C3
Camberley GU15 . . . . 66 A8
Chipstead CR5. . . . . 98 E8
Farnham GU10. . . . . 146 E6
Haslemere GU27 . . . . 208 C6
Hayes BR2. . . . . 44 F1
Horley RH6 . . . . 160 E5
Worcester Park KT4 . . . . . . 57 F8
Dene Ct
12 Croydon CR2 . . . . 61 C5
Guildford GU1 . . . . 110 B3
Denefield Dr CR8 . . . . 80 D4
Dene Gdns KT7. . . . . 56 A8
Denehurst Gdns
Mortlake TW10 . . . . 7 A3
Twickenham TW2. . . . . 16 D8
Denehyrst Ct 2 GU1 . . . . 130 E8
Dene La GU10 . . . . 146 E6
Dene La W GU10. . . . . 146 E5
Dene Pl GU21. . . . . 69 C1
Dene Rd
Ashtead KT21 . . . . 95 F8
Farnborough GU14 . . . . 84 F3
Guildford GU1 . . . . 130 E8
Dene St RH4. . . . . 136 B7
Dene Street Gdns
RH4 . . . . 136 B7
Dene The
Abinger Hammer RH5 . . . . 134 B3
Belmont SM2. . . . . 77 F8
East Molesey KT12, KT8 . . . 35 F4
South Croydon CR0 . . . . 62 D6
Dene Tye RH10 . . . . 202 D7
Dene Wlk GU10. . . . . 146 E6
Denewood 8 KT17. . . . . . . 76 E6
Denewood Ho 11 SM1. . . . 59 C6
Denfield RH4. . . . . 136 C5
Denham Cres CR4 . . . . 40 F5
Denham Ct SE26. . . . . 23 B5
Denham Gr RG12 . . . . 27 C3
Denham Rd
Egham TW20 . . . . 12 A4
Ewell KT17. . . . . 76 F7
Feltham TW14 . . . . 15 C8
Denholm Gdns GU4 . . . . . 110 A4
Deniel Lo TW1. . . . . 6 C2
Denison Rd
Feltham, Lower Feltham
TW13 . . . . 14 F4
Mitcham SW19 . . . . 20 D2
Denleigh Gdns KT7 . . . . . . 36 E3
Denly Way GU18 . . . . 48 C1
Denman Dr
Ashford TW15 . . . . 14 B2
Claygate KT10. . . . . 56 A5
Denmans RH10 . . . . 202 D7
Denmark Ave SW19. . . . . . 19 E1
Denmark Ct
Morden SM4 . . . . 40 A4
2 Weybridge KT13. . . . . . . 53 B7
Denmark Gdns SM5. . . . . . 59 F7
Denmark Rd
Carshalton SM5. . . . . 59 F7
Croydon SE25 . . . . 43 B4
Guildford GU1 . . . . 130 E8
Kingston u T KT1 . . . . 37 E6
Twickenham TW2. . . . . 16 D5
Wimbledon SW19 . . . . 19 D2
Denmark Sq GU12 . . . . . . 105 E2
Denmark St
Aldershot GU12. . . . . .105 D2
Wokingham RG40 . . . . 25 C5
Denmead Ct RG12 . . . . 27 E3
Denmead Ho SW15 . . . . .7 F1
Denmead Rd CR0 . . . . 42 B1
Denmead Sch TW12 . . . . . 16 B1
Denmore Ct SM6 . . . . 60 B5
Dennan Rd KT6. . . . . 37 F1
Denne Par RH12,
RH13 . . . . 217 C1
Denne Pl RH12 . . . . 217 C1
Denne Rd
Crawley RH11 . . . . .201 D5
Horsham RH12 . . . . .217 C1
Dennett Rd CR0 . . . . 42 A2
Denning Ave CR0 . . . . 61 A5
Denning Cl TW12 . . . . 15 F3
Dennington The KT4. . . . 57 E8
Dennis Cl
Ashford TW15 . . . . 14 D1
Redhill RH1 . . . . 118 E3
Dennis Ho SM1 . . . . 59 A6
Dennis Park Cres
SW20. . . . . 39 E8
Dennis Pilcher Ho
RG12 . . . . 27 E6
Dennis Rd KT8. . . . . 36 C5
Dennis Reeve Cl CR4. . . . . 40 F8
Dennistoun Cl GU15. . . . . . 65 D5
DENNISVILLE 129 F8
Dennis Way GU1 . . . . 109 E6
Denny Ho 2 TW12. . . . . . . 36 B8
Den Rd BR2 . . . . 44 D6
Densham Dr CR8 . . . . 80 A5
Densole Cl BR3. . . . . 43 E8
Denton Cl RH1. . . . . 140 A4
Denton Gr KT12. . . . . 54 E8
Denton Rd
Twickenham TW1. . . . . 6 D1
Wokingham RG40 . . . . 25 C6
Denton Way
Frimley GU16. . . . . 65 D2
Woking GU21. . . . . 69 A2
Dents Gr KT20 . . . . 117 F7
Denvale Trad Pk
Crawley RH10 . . . . 201 E5
Mitcham CR4 . . . . 40 D5
Denvale Wlk GU21 . . . . 69 A1
Denvegan Ho 7 SM2. . . . . 59 C3
Denwood SE23 . . . . 23 D5
Denzil Rd GU2. . . . . 130 B8
Departures Rd RH6 . . . . . 181 F8
Depot Rd
Crawley RH11 . . . . .181 D1
Epsom KT17. . . . . 76 E6
Horsham RH13 . . . . 217 E2
Hounslow TW3, TW7 . . . . 5 D4
Derby Arms Rd KT18 . . . . . 76 F2
Derby Cl KT18 . . . . 97 B8
Derby Ct SW14 . . . . .7 B3
Derby Hill SE23. . . . . 23 C6
Derby Hill Cres SE23 . . . . . 23 C6
Derby Ho 4 SM6 . . . . 60 B5
Derby Rd
Cheam SM1 . . . . 58 F4
Guildford GU2 . . . . 108 F1
Haslemere GU27. . . . . 208 B7
Hounslow TW3. . . . . 5 B3
Merton SW19 . . . . 20 A1
Mortlake SW14 . . . . 7 B3
Surbiton KT5, KT6 . . . . 38 A1
Thornton Heath CR0 . . . . . . 42 B1
Derby Sq The 10 KT19. . . . 76 D6
Derby Stables Rd KT18. . . 76 F2
Derek Ave
Hackbridge SM6 . . . . 60 B6
West Ewell KT19 . . . . 57 B5
Derek Cl KT19 . . . . 57 B5
Derek Horn Ct GU15 . . . . . 65 B6
Deri Dene Cl 2 TW19 . . . . . .2 E1
Dering Pl CR0 . . . . 61 C6
Dering Rd CR0, CR9. . . . . . . 61 C6
Derinton Rd SW17 . . . . 21 A4
Deronda Rd SE24, SW2 . . . 22 B7
De Ros Pl TW20. . . . . 12 A2
Deroy Cl SM5. . . . . 59 F4
Derrick Ave CR2 . . . . 61 C1
Derrick Ho 18 SW2. . . . . . . 22 A7
Derrick Rd BR3 . . . . 43 F5
Derry Cl GU12 . . . . 105 F5
Derrydown GU22 . . . . 89 C6
Derry Rd
Farnborough GU14 . . . . 84 F8
Wallington CR0 . . . . 60 E7
Derryswood Ho GU5 . . . . 152 E7
Derwent Ave
Ash Vale GU12. . . . . 105 F4
Kingston u T SW15 . . . . 18 E4
Derwent Cl
Addlestone KT15 . . . . 52 D5
Claygate KT10. . . . . 55 F4
Crawley RH11 . . . . 200 F5
East Bedfont TW14 . . . . 14 F7
Farnborough GU14 . . . . 84 E4
Hale GU9. . . . . .125 A6
Horsham RH12 . . . . 218 B6
Derwent Dr CR8 . . . . 80 E6
Derwent Ho
Penge SE20 . . . . 43 B7
Reigate RH2. . . . . .139 A7
Derwent Lo KT4 . . . . 58 B8
Derwent Rd
Lightwater GU18 . . . . 67 B8
Penge SE20 . . . . 43 B7
Thorpe Lea TW20. . . . . 12 B1
Twickenham TW2. . . . . 5 B1
West Barnes SM4 . . . . 39 D3
Derwent Wlk SM6. . . . . 60 B3
Desborough Cl TW17. . . . . 34 A2
Desborough Ct SE25 . . . . . 43 B5
Deseret Ho 7 CR4. . . . . . . 40 F6
Desford Way TW15. . . . . . . 13 F6
Desmond Anderson Prim
Sch RH10 . . . . .201 D2
Desmond Tutu Dr
SE23. . . . . 23 E7
Despard Ho SW2 . . . . 22 A6
de Stafford Coll CR3 . . . . 100 F6
Detherick Ct TW3. . . . . 5 C3
Detillens La RH8. . . . . 123 A6
Detling Rd RH11. . . . . 201 C1
Dettingen Cres GU16. . . . . 86 D8
Dettingen Rd GU16 . . . . . . 86 E8
Devana End SM5. . . . . 59 F7
Devas Rd SW20. . . . . 39 C8
Devenish La GU20, SL5. . . . 29 D1
Devenish Rd SL5. . . . . 29 D2
Deveraux Cl BR3. . . . . 44 C4
De Vere Cl SM6. . . . . 60 E3
Deverill Ct SE20 . . . . 43 C8
Devey Cl KT2 . . . . 18 D3
Devil's La TW20. . . . . 12 C2
De-Vitre Gn RG40. . . . . 25 F7
Devitt Cl KT21 . . . . 76 A3
Devoil Cl GU4 . . . . 110 B5
Devoke Way KT12. . . . . 54 D8
Devon Ave TW2. . . . . 16 C7
Devon Bank GU2. . . . . 130 C6
Devon Cl
Kenley CR8 . . . . 80 E3
Sandhurst GU47 . . . . 64 D7
Devon Cres RH1, RH2. . . . 118 D1
Devoncroft Gdns TW1. . . . 17 A8
Devon Ct 2 TW12 . . . . 16 A1
Devon Ho
Caterham CR3 . . . . 100 F3
2 Knaphill GU21 . . . . 68 D2
Penge SE20 . . . . 23 B1
Devon Rd
Belmont SM2. . . . . 58 E2
Hersham KT12. . . . . 54 C6
Merstham RH1. . . . . .119 C5
Devonshire Ave
Box Hill KT20. . . . . .116 C4
Sheerwater GU21 . . . . 70 D6
Sutton SM2 . . . . 59 C3
Devonshire Ct
16 Balham SW12. . . . . 21 B8
Croydon CR0 . . . . 44 A1
Feltham TW13 . . . . 15 B6
6 Richmond TW9. . . . . .6 F6
Devonshire Dr
Camberley GU15 . . . . 65 F7
Long Ditton KT6. . . . . 56 D8
Devonshire Gdns W4 . . . . . 7 C7
Devonshire Ho
Hounslow TW3. . . . . 5 C4
14 Sutton SM2. . . . . 59 C3
Devonshire Pl GU11. . . . . 104 F1
Devonshire Prim Sch
SM2 . . . . 59 C3
Devonshire Rd
6 Chiswick W4. . . . . 7 E8
Feltham TW13 . . . . 15 E4
Forest Hill SE23. . . . . 23 C8
Hackbridge SM5, SM6. . . . . 60 A6
Horsham RH13 . . . . .217 D2
Mitcham SW17, SW19. . . . . 20 E1
Sutton SM2 . . . . 59 C3
Thornton Heath CR0 . . . . . . 42 D2
Weybridge KT13 . . . . 53 A6
Devonshire St 1 W4. . . . . . .7 E8
Devonshires The KT18 . . . 76 F5
Devonshire Way CR0,
CR9 . . . . 62 F8
Devon Way
Chessington KT9 . . . . 56 C6
West Ewell KT19 . . . . 57 B5

Devon Waye TW5 . . . . .4 F7
Dewar Cl 2 RH11 . . . . .200 E5
Dewar Ho SW17 . . . . 20 E3
Dewey St SW17 . . . . 20 F3
Dewlands RH9 . . . . .121 C4
Dewlands Cl GU6 . . . . . . .174 E5
Dewlands La GU6 . . . . . . .174 E3
Dew Pond Cl RH13 . . . . . .217 F3
Dewsbury Gdns KT4 . . . . . 58 A7
Dexter Dr RH19 . . . . .205 E8
Diamedes Ave TW19 . . . . . 13 D7
Diamond Cotts GU5 . . . . .152 B7
Diamond Ct 4 RH1 . . . . . .119 A2
Diamond Est SW17 . . . . . . 20 E5
Diamond Hill GU15 . . . . . . 65 E7
Diamond Pl RH2 . . . . .118 C2
Diamond Ridge GU15 . . . . 65 E7
Diana Ct SM5 . . . . 60 A3
Diana Gdns KT6 . . . . 56 F8
Diana Ho SW13 . . . . .7 F6
Dianthus Cl KT16 . . . . 32 E2
Dianthus Ct GU22 . . . . 69 D1
Dianthus Pl RG42 . . . . .8 B2
Dibdin Cl SM1 . . . . 59 A7
Dibdin Ho SW1 . . . . 59 A8
Diceland Lo SM7 . . . . 77 F3
Diceland Rd SM7 . . . . 77 F3
Dickens Cl
  East Grinstead RH19 . . . . .185 C1
  Richmond TW10 . . . . 17 E6
Dickens Ct RG40 . . . . 25 B6
Dickens Dr KT15 . . . . 51 F4
Dickenson Rd TW13 . . . . . 15 D3
Dickenson's La SE25 . . . . 43 A3
Dickenson's Pl SE25 . . . . . 43 A3
Dickens Pl SL3 . . . . .1 E6
Dickens Rd RH10 . . . . . . .201 E3
Dickenswood Cl SE19 . . . . 22 B1
Dickerage Hill KT3 . . . . . . 38 C7
Dickerage La KT3 . . . . 38 C6
Dickerage Rd KT1, KT2,
  KT3 . . . . 38 C7
Dickins Way RH13 . . . . . .217 F1
Dickson Ho 9 TW10 . . . . . .6 F1
Dick Turpin Way TW14 . . . .3 F3
Digby Pl CR0 . . . . 61 F7
Digby Way KT14 . . . . 71 F7
Digdens Rise KT18 . . . . . . 76 C4
Dillwyn Cl SE26 . . . . 23 E4
Dilston Rd KT22 . . . . 95 A8
Dilton Gdns SW15 . . . . . . 19 B7
Dingle Cl RH11 . . . . .201 B7
Dingle Rd TW15 . . . . 14 B3
Dingle The RH11 . . . . . . .201 B6
Dingley La SW16 . . . . 21 D6
Dingley Way GU14 . . . . . .105 A8
Dingwall Ave CR0, CR9 . . . 61 C8
Dingwall Rd
  Croydon CR0, CR9 . . . . . . 61 D8
  Wallington SM6 . . . . 59 F2
  Wandsworth SW18 . . . . . . 20 C8
Dinorben 3 SM6 . . . . 60 C3
Dinsdale Cl GU22 . . . . 70 A1
Dinsdale Gdns SE25 . . . . . 42 E4
Dinsmore Rd SW12 . . . . . 21 B8
Dinton Rd
  Kingston u T KT2 . . . . 17 F1
  Mitcham SW17, SW19 . . . . 20 D2
Dione Wlk RH11 . . . . . . .200 E4
DIPPENHALL 124 D2
Dippenhall Rd GU10 . . . . .124 C2
Dippenhall St GU10 . . . . .124 A5
Diprose Lo SW17 . . . . 20 D4
Dirdene Cl KT17 . . . . 76 F7
Dirdene Gdns KT17 . . . . . 76 F7
Dirdene Gr KT17 . . . . 76 F7
Dirtham La KT24 . . . . . . .113 B6
Dirty La RH19 . . . . .206 E7
Discovery Pk RH10 . . . . . .182 A2
Disraeli Ct SL3 . . . . .1 B8
Distillery Wlk 14 TW8 . . . .6 E8
Distin Ct 3 SM1 . . . . 59 B5
Ditches La CR3, CR5 . . . . . 99 E6
Ditchling RG12 . . . . 27 A2
Ditchling Hill RH11 . . . . . .201 C4
Ditton Cl KT7 . . . . 37 A2
Dittoncroft Cl CR0 . . . . . . 61 E6
Ditton Grange Cl KT6 . . . . 37 D1
Ditton Grange Dr KT6 . . . . 37 D1
Ditton Hill KT6 . . . . 56 D8
Ditton Hill Rd KT6 . . . . . . 37 C1
Ditton Lawn KT7 . . . . 37 A1
Ditton Pl 7 SE20 . . . . 43 B8
Ditton Rd KT6 . . . . 37 E1
Ditton Reach KT7 . . . . 37 B3
Dixon Dr KT13 . . . . 52 F1
Dixon Pl BR4 . . . . 44 B1
Dixon Rd SE25 . . . . 42 F6
Dobbins Pl RH11 . . . . . . .200 E5
Doble Ct CR2 . . . . 81 A8
Dobson Rd RH11 . . . . . . .181 D1
DOCKENFIELD 166 E6
Dockenfield St GU10 . . . . .166 C6
Dockett Eddy La TW17 . . . 33 F1
Dockett Moorings
  KT16 . . . . 33 F1
Dock Rd 2 TW8 . . . . .6 D7
Dockwell Cl TW14 . . . . . . .4 A3
Dockwell's Ind Est TW14 . . .4 B2
Doctors St SE26 . . . . 23 C3
Doctors La CR3 . . . . .100 A3
Dodbrooke Rd SE27 . . . . . 22 A5
Dodds Cres KT14 . . . . 71 B5
Dodd's La KT14 . . . . 71 A5
Dodds Pk RH3 . . . . .137 B7

Doel Cl SW19 . . . . 20 C1
Dogflud Way GU9 . . . . . . .125 C3
Doggett Rd SE6 . . . . 24 A8
Doghurst Ave UB3 . . . . . . .3 B7
Doghurst Dr UB7 . . . . .3 B7
Doghurst La CR5 . . . . 98 F7
DOGKENNEL GREEN 113 D1
Doland Ct SW17 . . . . 20 F2
Dolby Terr RH6 . . . . .180 E6
Dolliffe Cl CR4 . . . . 40 E7
Dollis Cl RH10 . . . . .202 C5
Dollis Cl GU9 . . . . .125 D3
Dollis Dr GU9 . . . . .125 D3
Dolphin Cl
  Haslemere GU27 . . . . . . .207 E6
  Kingston u T KT6 . . . . 37 D4
Dolphin Ct
  Bracknell RG12 . . . . 27 C5
  Merton SW19 . . . . 20 A1
  Stanwell TW19 . . . . 13 A5
  2 Wallington SM6 . . . . . 60 B4
Dolphin Ct N TW19 . . . . . 13 A5
Dolphin Rd TW16 . . . . 34 E8
Dolphin Rd N TW16 . . . . . 34 E8
Dolphin Rd S TW16 . . . . . 34 E8
Dolphin Rd W TW16 . . . . . 34 E8
Dolphin Sq 2 W4 . . . . . . .7 E7
Dolphin St KT2 . . . . 37 E8
Doman Rd GU15 . . . . 65 A4
Dome Hill CR3 . . . . .120 E8
Dome Hill Peak CR3 . . . . .100 E1
Dome Hill Pk SE26 . . . . . . 22 F4
Dome The RH1 . . . . .118 F2
Dome Way RH1 . . . . .118 F2
DOMEWOOD 184 A5
Dominion Cl TW3 . . . . 5 D5
Dominion Rd CR0 . . . . 42 F2
Donald Ct CR2 . . . . 61 E4
Donald Lynch Ho CR4 . . . . 40 F7
Donald Rd CR0, CR9 . . . . . 41 F2
Donald Woods Gdns
  KT5 . . . . 57 C8
Doncaster Wlk RH10 . . . . .202 A4
Doncastle Rd RG12 . . . . . 26 E6
Donkey La
  Abinger Common
  RH5 . . . . .155 D8
  Crawley RH6 . . . . .182 D7
DONKEY TOWN 67 D6
Donnafields GU24 . . . . . . 68 A3
Donne Cl RH10 . . . . .202 B8
Donne Gdns GU22 . . . . . . 70 E4
Donne Pl CR4 . . . . 41 B5
Donnington Cl GU15 . . . . . 65 B4
Donnington Ct 2
  RH11 . . . . .200 F3
Donnington Rd KT4 . . . . . 58 A8
Donnybrook RG12 . . . . . . 27 A2
Donnybrook Rd SW16 . . . . 21 D1
Donovan Cl KT19 . . . . 57 D1
Donyngs Place Recn Ctr
  RH1 . . . . .118 E2
Doods Park Rd RH2 . . . . .118 C1
Doods Pl RH2 . . . . .118 D2
Doods Rd RH2 . . . . .118 C2
Doods Way RH2 . . . . .118 D2
Doomsday Gdn RH13 . . . .218 A1
Doone Cl TW11 . . . . 17 A2
Doradus Ct 20 SW19 . . . . 19 D7
Doral Way SM5 . . . . 59 F5
Doran Dr RH2 . . . . .118 D1
Doran Gdns RH2 . . . . . . .118 D1
Dora Rd SW19 . . . . 20 A4
DORA'S GREEN 124 C5
Dora's Green La
  GU10 . . . . .124 C5
Dorcas Ct GU15 . . . . 65 B3
Dorchester Ct
  Camberley GU15 . . . . 65 B6
  Reigate RH2 . . . . .118 C2
  Staines TW18 . . . . 13 A4
  5 Streatham SW16 . . . . 21 E6
  Woking GU22 . . . . 70 A3
Dorchester Dr TW14 . . . . .3 E1
Dorchester Gr 8 W4 . . . . .7 E8
Dorchester Ho
  Richmond TW9 . . . . .7 B7
  Wallington SM5 . . . . 59 F5
Dorchester Mews
  New Malden KT3 . . . . 38 D5
  Twickenham TW1 . . . . 6 C1
Dorchester Par SW16 . . . . 21 E6
Dorchester Prim Sch
  KT4 . . . . 39 C1
Dorchester Rd
  Morden CR4 . . . . 40 C2
  North Cheam KT4 . . . . . . 39 C1
  Weybridge KT13 . . . . 53 B7
Doreen Cl GU14 . . . . 84 E7
Dore Gdns SM4 . . . . 40 B2
Dorey Ho 7 TW8 . . . . .6 C7
Dorian Dr SL5 . . . . 29 E8
Doric Dr KT20 . . . . 97 F7
Dorien Rd SW20 . . . . 39 D7
Dorin Ct
  Pyrford GU22 . . . . 70 E4
  Warlingham CR6 . . . . . . .101 B7
Doris Rd TW15 . . . . 14 D2
DORKING 136 C6
Dorking Bsns Pk RH4 . . . .136 A8
Dorking Cl KT4 . . . . 58 D8
Dorking (Deepdene) Sta
  RH4 . . . . .115 C1
Dorking General Hospl
  RH4 . . . . .136 A6
Dorking Mus★ RH4 . . . . . .136 A7

Dorking Rd
  Chilworth GU4 . . . . .131 E3
  Epsom KT18 . . . . 76 B4
  Gomshall GU5 . . . . .133 D4
  Great Bookham KT23 . . . .114 C8
  Kingsfold RH12, RH5 . . . .198 B4
  Leatherhead KT22 . . . . . . 95 B3
  Lower Kingswood KT20 . . .116 F7
  Walton on t H KT20 . . . . . 97 C3
  Warnham RH12 . . . . .217 B6
Dorking Sta RH4 . . . . .115 C1
Dorking West Sta
  RH4 . . . . .136 A8
Dorlcote GU8 . . . . .170 E5
Dorlcote Rd SW18 . . . . . . 20 E8
Dorling Dr KT17 . . . . 76 F7
Dorly Cl TW17 . . . . 34 E4
Dormans RH11 . . . . .201 A5
Dormans Ave RH7 . . . . . .165 A2
Dorman's Cl RH7 . . . . . . .186 A8
Dormans Gdns RH19 . . . .185 E6
Dormans High St
  RH7 . . . . .186 A8
DORMANSLAND 165 B1
Dormansland Prim Sch
  RH7 . . . . .165 B1
DORMANS PARK 185 E6
Dormans Park Rd
  Dormans Park RH19 . . . . .185 E6
  East Grinstead RH19 . . . .185 D3
Dormans Rd RH7 . . . . . . .165 A2
Dormans Sta RH7 . . . . . . .185 F8
Dormans Station Rd
  RH7 . . . . .185 F7
Dormer Cl RG45 . . . . 45 A5
Dormers Cl GU7 . . . . .150 D7
Dormy Ho The GU25 . . . . 30 F3
Dorney Gr KT13 . . . . 53 B8
Dorney Way TW4 . . . . .4 E2
Dornford Gdns CR5 . . . . .100 C8
Dornton Rd
  South Croydon CR2 . . . . . 61 D5
  Upper Tooting SW12,
  SW17 . . . . 21 C6
Dorothy Pettingel Ho 5
  SM1 . . . . 59 B7
Dorrien Wlk SW16 . . . . . . 21 D6
Dorrington Ct SE25 . . . . . 42 E7
Dorrington Way BR3 . . . . . 44 C4
Dorrit Cres GU3 . . . . .108 E3
Dorryn Ct SE26 . . . . 23 D3
Dorset Ave RH19 . . . . . . .185 C3
Dorset Ct
  Camberley GU15 . . . . 65 F8
  Epsom KT17 . . . . 76 F7
  3 Horsham RH12 . . . . . .217 D2
Dorset Dr GU22 . . . . 70 B2
Dorset Gdns
  East Grinstead RH19 . . . .185 C3
  Thornton Heath SW16 . . . 41 F5
Dorset Hall SW19 . . . . 40 A8
Dorset Ho 2 SE20 . . . . . . 43 B8
Dorset Rd
  Ashford TW15 . . . . 13 D5
  Ash GU12 . . . . .106 B5
  Belmont SM2 . . . . 59 A1
  Merton SW19 . . . . 40 A7
  Mitcham CR4 . . . . 40 E7
  Penge BR3 . . . . 43 D6
Dorset Sq KT19 . . . . 57 D1
Dorset Way
  Byfleet KT14 . . . . 52 D1
  Twickenham TW2 . . . . 16 D7
Dorset Waye TW5 . . . . . . .4 F7
Dorsten Sq RH11 . . . . . . .200 F3
Dorton Villas UB7 . . . . . . .3 A6
Dorton Way GU23 . . . . . . 91 B6
Douai Cl GU14 . . . . 85 C4
Douai Gr TW12 . . . . 36 C8
Douglas Ave KT3 . . . . 39 B5
Douglas Cl
  Guildford GU4 . . . . .109 D6
  Wallington SM6 . . . . 60 E4
Douglas Ct
  Biggin Hill TN16 . . . . 83 E2
  Caterham CR3 . . . . .100 D5
  1 Upper Tooting SW17 . . 20 E2
Douglas Dr
  Croydon CR0 . . . . 63 A7
  Godalming GU7 . . . . .150 F5
Douglas Gr GU10 . . . . . . .146 C5
Douglas Gracey Ho
  SW18 . . . . 19 E8
Douglas Ho
  Little Bookham KT23 . . . . 94 A3
  Twickenham TW1 . . . . 6 B2
Douglas Houghton Ho 11
  RH1 . . . . .118 F2
Douglas Mews SM7 . . . . . 77 F3
Douglas Pl GU14 . . . . 85 A5
Douglas Rd
  Addlestone KT15 . . . . 52 B7
  Hounslow TW3 . . . . .5 B4
  Kingston u T KT1 . . . . 38 B7
  Reigate RH2 . . . . .118 B2
  Stanwell TW19 . . . . .2 D1
  Surbiton KT6 . . . . 37 F1
  Thames Ditton KT10 . . . . . 55 B8
Douglas Robinson Ct
  SW16 . . . . 21 E1
Douglas Sq SM4 . . . . 40 A3
Doultons The TW18 . . . . . 13 A1
Dounesforth Gdns
  SW18 . . . . 20 B7
Dove Cl
  Crawley RH11 . . . . .201 D8
  Selsdon CR2 . . . . 81 D8
  Wallington SM6 . . . . 60 F3

Dovecote Cl KT13 . . . . . . 53 B7
Dovecote Gdns 9 SW14 . . .7 D4
Dove Ct TW19 . . . . 13 E8
Dovedale Cl
  Guildford GU4 . . . . .110 A4
  Sandhurst GU47 . . . . 45 D2
Dovedale Cres RH11 . . . . .201 B4
Dovedale Rise CR4 . . . . . . 20 F1
Dovehouse Gn 1 KT13 . . . 53 D6
Dovercourt Ave CR7 . . . . . 42 A5
Dovercourt La SM1 . . . . . 59 C7
Dovercourt Rd SE21,
  SE22 . . . . 22 E8
Dover Ct
  Carshalton SM1 . . . . 59 D6
  Cranleigh GU6 . . . . .175 A3
Doverfield Rd
  Guildford GU4 . . . . .110 A4
  Streatham SW2 . . . . 21 E8
Dover Gdns SM5 . . . . 59 F7
Dover Ho
  7 Beckenham BR3 . . . . . 24 A1
  15 Penge SE20 . . . . 43 B8
Dover House Rd SW15 . . . 19 B8
Dover Rd SE19 . . . . 22 D2
DOVERSGREEN 139 B5
Dovers Green Sch
  RH2 . . . . .139 C5
Dovers Green Rd RH2 . . . .139 B4
Doversmead GU21 . . . . . . 68 E3
Dover Terr TW9 . . . . .7 A5
Doveton Rd CR2 . . . . 61 D5
Dowanhill Rd SE6 . . . . . . 24 D7
Dowdeswell Cl SW15 . . . . .7 E3
Dowding Ct RG45 . . . . 45 C6
Dowding Rd TN16 . . . . 83 D4
Dowell Ho SE21 . . . . 22 F5
Dower Ave SM6 . . . . 60 B2
Dower Cotts GU8 . . . . . . .170 F8
Dower Ho The SL5 . . . . . . 29 C4
Dower Wlk RH11 . . . . . . .201 A5
Dowes Ho 13 SW16 . . . . . 21 E5
Dowgate Ho KT13 . . . . . . 53 A7
Dowlands La RH10,
  RH6 . . . . .183 D7
Dowlans Cl KT23 . . . . . . .114 A8
Dowlans Rd KT23 . . . . . . .114 B8
Dowler Ct 2 KT2 . . . . 37 F8
Dowles Gn RG40 . . . . 25 E8
DOWLESGREEN 25 E8
Dowman Cl 3 SW19 . . . . . 20 B1
Downderry Prim Sch
  BR1 . . . . 24 E4
Downderry Rd BR1 . . . . . . 24 E4
Downe Cl RH6 . . . . .160 E5
Downe Rd CR4 . . . . 40 F7
Downer Mdw GU7 . . . . . .150 E8
Downes Cl TW1 . . . . .6 B1
Downes Ho CR0 . . . . 61 B6
Downey Lo RH10 . . . . . . .201 E4
Downfield 7 KT4 . . . . 39 A1
Downfield Ho KT3 . . . . . . 38 D1
Down Hall Rd KT2 . . . . . . 37 D8
DOWNHAM 24 F3
Downham Ent Ctr SE6 . . . 24 F6
Downham La BR1 . . . . 24 D3
Downham Way BR1 . . . . . 24 E4
Downhurst Rd GU6 . . . . . .175 E6
Downing Ave GU2 . . . . . .129 F8
Downing Ho 9 SW19 . . . . 20 A1
Downing St GU9 . . . . .125 B2
Down La GU3 . . . . .129 B4
Downland Cl
  Burgh Heath KT18 . . . . . . 77 B1
  Wallington CR5 . . . . 79 B5
Downland Ct RH11 . . . . . .201 C4
Downland Dr RH11 . . . . . .201 C3
Downland Gdns KT18 . . . . 77 B1
Downland Pl RH11 . . . . . .201 C4
Downlands Circular Walk
  Start A★ KT18 . . . . 99 E7
Downlands Rd CR8 . . . . . . 79 F6
Downland Way KT18 . . . . . 77 B1
Downmill Rd RG12 . . . . . . 26 F7
Down Rd
  Guildford GU1 . . . . .110 B1
  Teddington TW11 . . . . 17 B2
Downs Ave KT18 . . . . 76 F4
Downs Bridge Rd BR3 . . . . 44 D8
Downs Cl GU14 . . . . 84 E7
Downs Court Rd CR8 . . . . 80 B6
Downs Ct
  Purley CR8 . . . . 61 B1
  2 Redhill RH1 . . . . .119 A4
  17 Wimbledon SW20 . . . 19 D1
Downsend Sch
  Ashtead KT22 . . . . 95 C6
  Leatherhead KT22 . . . . . . 95 C6
Downsend Sch (Epsom
  Lodge) KT17 . . . . 76 F7
Downs Hill BR2, BR3 . . . . . 44 D8
Downs Hill Rd KT18 . . . . . 76 E5
Downshire Way
  Bracknell, Priestwood GU21,
  RG42 . . . . 27 A7
  Bracknell RG12 . . . . 27 B6
DOWNSIDE 93 B8
Downside
  Beacon Hill GU26 . . . . . .188 D7
  Epsom KT18 . . . . 76 E5
  Twickenham TW1 . . . . 16 F5
Downside Bridge Rd
  KT11 . . . . 73 B4
Downside Cl SW19 . . . . . . 20 C2
Downside Common Rd
  KT11 . . . . 73 C1
Downside Ct RH1 . . . . . . .119 C6

Downside Orch GU22 . . . . 70 A2
Downside Rd
  Carshalton SM2 . . . . 59 E4
  Downside KT11 . . . . 73 B2
  Guildford GU4 . . . . .131 B8
Downside Wlk TW8 . . . . . .6 C8
Downs La KT22 . . . . 95 B3
Downs Lodge Ct KT17 . . . 76 E5
Downsman Ct RH10 . . . . .201 D3
Downs Rd
  Ashtead KT18 . . . . 96 C7
  Beckenham BR3 . . . . 44 B7
  Coulsdon CR5 . . . . 79 D1
  Epsom KT17, KT18 . . . . . 76 E3
  Mickleham RH5 . . . . .115 C7
  Purley CR8 . . . . 80 B8
  South Norwood CR7 . . . . 42 C8
  Sutton SM2 . . . . 78 C8
Downs Side SM2 . . . . 77 F8
Down St KT8 . . . . 36 A4
Downs The
  Leatherhead KT22 . . . . . . 95 C2
  Wimbledon SW20 . . . . . . 19 D1
Downs View
  Dorking RH4 . . . . .115 D1
  Hounslow TW7 . . . . .6 A6
  Tadworth KT20 . . . . 97 B6
Downsview Ave GU22 . . . . 89 F6
Downsview Cl KT11 . . . . . 73 B8
Downsview Ct GU1 . . . . . .109 C5
Downsview Gdns
  Dorking RH4 . . . . .136 B6
  South Norwood SE19 . . . . 22 C1
Downs View Lo 9 KT6 . . . 37 E3
Downsview Prim Sch
  SE19 . . . . 22 C1
Downsview Rd
  Headley Down GU35 . . . . .187 C5
  Horsham RH12 . . . . .218 B6
  South Norwood SE19 . . . . 22 C1
Downs View Rd KT23 . . . .114 C8
Downsway
  Guildford GU1 . . . . .110 E1
  South Croydon CR2 . . . . . 80 E8
  Whyteleafe CR3 . . . . 80 F2
Downs Way
  Epsom KT18 . . . . 76 F3
  Great Bookham KT23 . . . . 94 C1
  Oxted RH8 . . . . .122 E8
  Tadworth KT20 . . . . 97 B6
Downsway Cl KT20 . . . . . . 97 A6
Downs Way Sch RH8 . . . . .122 E2
Downsway The SM2 . . . . . 59 C2
Downswood RH2 . . . . . . .118 D4
Downs Wood KT18 . . . . . . 77 B2
Downton Ave SW2 . . . . . . 21 F6
Downview Ct GU26 . . . . . .188 D6
Down Yhonda GU8 . . . . . .148 C3
Doyle Ct GU27 . . . . .208 A6
Doyle Rd SE25 . . . . 43 A5
Dragon La KT13 . . . . 53 A1
Dragoon Ct GU11 . . . . . . .104 E2
Drake Ave
  Caterham CR3 . . . . .100 C5
  Mytchett GU16 . . . . 86 A1
  Staines TW18 . . . . 12 F3
Drake Cl
  Bracknell RG12 . . . . 27 B4
  Horsham RH12 . . . . .217 E6
Drake Ct
  Dulwich SE19 . . . . 22 F3
  Kingston u T KT5 . . . . 37 F5
Drakefield Rd SW17 . . . . . 21 A5
Drake Rd
  Chessington KT9 . . . . 57 A5
  Crawley RH10 . . . . .201 E3
  Horley RH6 . . . . .160 E3
  Mitcham CR4 . . . . 41 A3
  Thornton Heath CR0,
  CR9 . . . . 41 F2
Drakes Cl GU6 . . . . .174 A6
Drake's Cl KT10 . . . . 55 A6
Drakes Ct SE23 . . . . 23 C7
Drakes Way GU22 . . . . . . 89 D5
Drakewood Rd SW16 . . . . 21 D1
Draper Cl TW7 . . . . 5 D5
Drapers Cres KT12 . . . . . . 53 F1
Draven Cl BR2 . . . . 44 F2
Drax Ave SW20 . . . . 19 A1
Draxmont SW19 . . . . 19 E2
Draycot Rd KT6 . . . . 38 A1
Draycott RG12 . . . . 27 E4
Dray Ct GU2 . . . . .130 B8
Drayhorse Dr GU19 . . . . . 47 E2
Draymans Way TW7 . . . . . .5 F4
Drayton Cl
  Bracknell RG12 . . . . 27 D7
  Fetcham KT22 . . . . 94 E3
  Hounslow TW4 . . . . .4 F2
Drayton Ct
  Tolworth KT5 . . . . 57 B8
  West Byfleet KT14 . . . . . . 71 A6
Drayton Rd CR0, CR9 . . . . 61 B8
Dreadnought Cl SW19 . . . 40 D7
Dresden Way KT13 . . . . . . 53 C5
Drew Ho 12 SW16 . . . . . . 21 E5
Drew Pl CR3 . . . . .100 D4
Drewstead La SW16 . . . . . 21 D6
Drewstead Rd SW16 . . . . 21 D6
Dreycourt 4 KT4 . . . . 58 A8
Driftbridge The KT17 . . . . 77 C5
Drifters Dr GU16 . . . . 66 D1
Drift La SL4 . . . . .9 B8
Drift The KT24 . . . . 92 C3
Drift Way SL3 . . . . .1 C7
Driftway The
  Banstead SM7 . . . . 77 C4
  Leatherhead KT22 . . . . . . 95 C4

Driftway The *continued*
Mitcham CR4 41 A8
Driftway (Worple Road)
The KT22 95 B4
Driftwood Dr CR8 80 C2
Drill Hall Rd KT16 33 A2
Drive Ho CR4 40 E5
Drive Mead CR5 79 E5
Drive Rd CR5 99 F7
Drivers Mead RH7 164 D3
Drive Spur KT20 98 B6
Drive The
Artington GU3 130 B5
Ashford TW15 14 D1
Banstead SM7 77 E3
Beckenham BR3 44 A8
Belmont SM2 77 F7
Cobham KT11 73 F5
Copthorne RH10 183 C3
Coulsdon CR5, CR8 79 E5
Cranleigh GU6 174 F2
Farnham GU9 146 B7
Feltham TW14 15 C8
Fetcham KT22 94 E5
Godalming GU7 150 F2
Guildford GU2 130 A7
Guildford, Park Barn
GU2 108 F1
Headley KT18, KT22 96 A3
Horley RH6 161 B1
Hounslow TW3, TW7 5 D5
Ifold RH14 212 D2
Kingston u T KT2 18 C1
Leatherhead KT22, KT18 95 F4
Morden SM4 40 D4
Shackleford GU7, GU8 149 E4
South Norwood CR7 42 D5
Thames Ditton KT10 36 C1
Thorpe GU25 31 F4
Wallington CR8, SM6 60 D1
West Ewell KT19 57 F4
West Wickham BR4 44 D2
Wimbledon SW19, SW20 19 C1
Woking GU22 89 B7
Wonersh GU5 152 B6
Dr Johnson Ave SW17 21 B5
Dr Johnson Ho SW16 21 D4
Drodges Cl GU5 151 F8
Droitwich Cl
Bracknell RG12 27 E6
Forest Hill SE26 23 A5
Drove Rd GU4 132 A7
Drovers Ct 3 KT1 37 E7
Drovers Rd CR2 61 D5
Drovers Way
Ash GU12 106 C1
Bracknell RG12 27 F6
Hale GU9 125 A6
Druce Wood SL5 28 E8
Druid's Cl KT21 95 F7
Druids Way BR2 44 D5
Drumaline Ridge KT4 57 E8
Drummond Cl RG12 27 F8
Drummond Ct 4
GU1 109 D1
Drummond Ctr CR9 61 C8
Drummond Gdns KT19 76 B8
Drummond Rd
Crawley RH11 200 E5
Croydon CR0, CR9 61 C8
Guildford GU1 109 D1
Drummonds Pl TW9 6 E3
Drungewick La RH14 213 D2
Drury Cl RH10 202 D4
Drury Cres CR0, CR9 61 A8
Drury Lo 6 RH19 185 F2
Dry Arch Rd SL5 29 F3
Dryden RG12 27 A2
Dryden Ct 11 TW10 17 D4
Dryden Rd
Farnborough GU14 84 F6
Wimbledon SW19 20 C2
Drynham Pk KT13 53 E7
Du Cane Ct SW12 21 A7
Ducavel Ho SW2 21 F7
Duchess Cl
Crowthorne RG45 45 B7
Sutton SM1 59 C6
Duchess Ct KT13 53 D7
Duchess of Kent Cl
GU2 109 B5
Duck's Wlk TW1 6 C2
Dudley Cl KT15 52 C7
Dudley Dr SM4 39 E2
Dudley Gr KT18 76 C5
Dudley Ho RG12 27 C7
Dudley Rd
Ashford TW15 13 F4
East Bedfont TW14 14 D7
Kingston u T KT1 37 F6
Richmond TW9 7 A5
Walton-on-T KT12 35 A2
Wimbledon SW19 20 A2
Dudset La TW5 4 A6
Duett Ct TW5 4 E7
Duffield Rd KT20 97 B3
Duffins Orch KT16 51 C3
Duke Cl RH10 202 C2
Duke Of Cambridge Cl
TW2 5 D1
Duke of Connaughts Rd
GU11 105 D5
Duke Of Cornwall Ave
GU15 46 D1
Duke Of Edinburgh Rd
SM1 59 D8
Duke of Kent Sch
GU6 154 D2
Dukes Ave
Hounslow TW4 4 E3
New Malden KT3 38 F6
Richmond KT2, TW10 17 D4
Duke's Ave W4 7 D8
Dukes Cl
Ashford TW15 14 C4
Cranleigh GU6 175 A2
Hale GU9 125 A6
Hampton TW12 15 F3
Dukes Covert GU19 47 E6
Dukes Ct
Addlestone KT15 52 C6
Beckenham BR3 43 E6
Dulwich SE22 23 A7
4 Epsom KT19 57 E2
Farnborough GU14 85 B3
Duke's Dr GU7 150 B7
Dukes Green Ave TW14 4 A2
Dukes Hill CR3 101 E7
Duke's Hill GU19 47 E5
Dukeshill Rd RG42 27 B8
Duke's La
Cranbourne SL5 9 F1
Old Windsor SL4, SL5 10 B3
Dukes Pk GU11 105 D6
Dukes Rd KT12 54 D5
Duke's Rd RH5 179 D6
Dukes Ride RH5 136 D4
Duke's Ride RG45 45 B5
Dukes Sq RH12 217 C1
Duke St
Carshalton SM1 59 D6
Richmond TW10, TW9 6 D2
Woking GU21 69 F2
Dukesthorpe Rd SE26 23 D4
Dukes Way BR4 63 E7
Dukes Wlk GU9 125 A6
Dukes Wood RG45 45 B5
Dulcima Ho 13 RH12 217 C2
Dulverton Ct 12 KT6 37 E4
Dulverton Rd CR2 62 C1
DULWICH 22 E5
Dulwich Bsns Ctr SE23 23 D7
Dulwich Coll SE21 22 E6
Dulwich Coll Picture
Gall* SE21 22 E8
Dulwich Coll Prep Sch
SE21 22 E5
Dulwich Comm SE21 22 E7
Dulwich Ct SE22 23 B7
Dulwich Oaks The
SE21 22 F5
DULWICH VILLAGE 22 E8
Dulwich Village SE21 22 E8
Dulwich Wood Ave
SE19 22 E3
Dulwich Wood Pk SE19,
SE21 22 E4
Dumbleton Cl KT2 38 B8
Dump Rd GU14 84 E1
Dumville Dr RH9 121 B4
Dunally Pk TW17 34 D2
Dunbar Ave
Beckenham BR3 43 E5
Thornton Heath CR7,
SW16 42 A7
Dunbar Ct
3 Bromley BR2 44 F5
Carshalton SM1 59 D5
6 Walton-on-T KT12 35 C1
Dunbar Ho 1 RH1 118 F1
Dunbar Rd
Frimley GU16 85 F7
Kingston u T KT3 38 C5
Dunbar St SE27 22 C5
Dunboe Pl TW17 34 C2
Dunbridge Ho SW15 7 F1
Duncan Dr
Guildford GU1 110 A2
Wokingham RG40 25 E5
Duncan Gate 10 BR1 24 F1
Duncan Gdns TW18 13 A2
Duncan Rd
Burgh Heath KT20 97 E8
Richmond TW9 6 E3
Duncombe Ct TW18 12 F1
Duncombe Hill SE23 23 E8
Duncombe Ho 7
SW19 19 D7
Duncombe Rd GU7 150 D2
Duncroft Cl RH2 117 F1
Duncroft Manor TW18 12 E4
Duncton Cl RH11 201 B8
Dundaff Cl GU15 66 A5
Dundas Cl RG12 27 B5
Dundas Gdns KT8 36 B6
Dundee Rd SE25 43 B4
Dundela Gdns KT17,
KT4 58 B6
Dundonald Prim Sch
SW19 19 F1
Dundonald Rd SW19 19 F1
Dundrey Cres RH1 119 E6
Dundry Ho 8 SE26 23 A5
Dunedin Dr CR3 100 E2
Duneevan KT13 53 E8
Dunelm Gr SE27 22 C5
Dunfee Way KT14 71 E7
Dunfield Gdns SE6 24 B3
Dunfield Rd SE6 24 B3
Dungates La RH3 117 A2
Dunheved Cl CR7 42 A3
Dunheved Ct 2 CR7 42 A3
Dunheved Rd N CR7 42 A3
Dunheved Rd S CR7 42 A3
Dunheved Rd W CR7 42 A3
Dunhill Point 12 SW15 19 B7
Dunkeld Rd SE25 42 D5
Dunkirk St 12 SE27 22 C4
Dunleary Cl TW4 15 F8
Dunley Dr CR0 63 C4
Dunlin Cl RH1 139 F4
Dunlin Ct 12 SE21 22 D6
Dunlin Rise GU4 110 D3
Dunmail Dr CR2, CR8 80 E6
Dunmore GU2 108 D2
Dunmore Rd SW20 39 D8
Dunmow Cl TW13 15 E4
Dunnets GU21 68 E2
Dunnings Mill L Complex
RH19 205 E6
Dunning's Rd RH19 205 E7
Dunnock Ct 11 SE21 22 D6
Dunnymans Rd SM7 77 F4
Dunoon Gdns SE23 23 D8
Dunoon Rd SE23 23 C8
Dunottar Cl RH1 139 D7
Dunottar Day Sch for Girls
RH2 139 D8
Dunraven Ave RH1 140 B2
Dunraven Ho 12 TW9 6 F6
Dunraven Lower Sch
SW16 21 F5
Dunraven Upper Sch
SW16 21 F5
Dunsborough Cotts
GU23 91 C7
Dunsbury Cl SM2 59 B2
Dunsdon Ave GU2 130 B8
DUNSFOLD 192 F5
Dunsfold Cl RH11 201 A5
Dunsfold Common Rd
GU8 192 F6
Dunsfold Ct 8 SM2 59 B3
DUNSFOLD GREEN 192 F6
Dunsfold Ho
10 Kingston u T KT2 18 B2
7 Streatham SW2 21 F8
Dunsfold Rd
Alfold GU6 193 E3
Bramley GU6 173 C1
Dunsfold GU8 193 B8
Plaistow GU8, RH14 211 D4
Dunsfold Rise CR5 79 D6
Dunsfold Way CR0 63 C3
Dunsmore Rd KT12 35 B3
Dunstable Rd
East Molesey KT8 35 F5
Richmond TW10, TW9 6 E3
Dunstall Pk GU14 85 A7
Dunstall Rd SW20 19 C2
Dunstall Way KT8 36 B6
Dunstan Ct
Staines TW18 13 A4
1 Whyteleafe CR3 101 A8
Dunstan Rd CR5 79 D2
Dunstan's Rd SE22 23 A8
Dunster Ave SM4 39 D1
Dunster Ct 6 SW20 39 D8
Dunster Ho SE6 24 B5
Dunster Way SM6 41 A1
Dunton Cl KT6 37 E1
Dunton Ct SE26 23 B6
Dunton Ho 14 SW16 21 E5
Dunthill Rd SW18 20 B7
Dunvegan Cl KT8 36 B5
Dunvegan Ho 14 RH1 118 F1
Dupont Rd SW20 39 D7
Duppas Ave CR0 61 B6
Duppas Cl TW17 34 D4
Duppas Ct CR0 61 B7
Duppas Hill La CR0 61 B6
Duppas Hill Rd CR0 61 B6
Duppas Hill Terr CR0,
CR9 61 B7
Duppas Jun Sch CR0 61 B5
Duppas Rd CR0, CR9 61 B7
Dura Den Cl BR3 24 B1
Durand Cl SM5 40 F1
Durban Rd
Beckenham BR3 43 F7
West Norwood SE27 22 D4
Durbin Rd KT9 56 F6
Durfold Dr RH2 118 C1
Durfold Rd RH12 217 D7
Durfold Wood RH14 211 D5
Durfold Wood Woodlands
Wlks* GU8 211 C6
Durford Cres SW15 19 B7
Durham Ave BR2 44 F5
Durham Cl
Crawley RH10 201 E2
Guildford GU2 108 F3
Wimbledon SW20 39 B7
Durham Ct
2 Leatherhead KT22 95 A5
Teddington TW11 16 E4
Durham Dr GU16 66 D1
Durham Hill BR1 24 F4
Durham Ho BR2 44 E5
Durham Lo SW20 39 B8
Durham Rd
Beckenham BR2 44 F6
Feltham TW14 15 C8
Sandhurst GU47 45 E2
Wimbledon SW20 39 B8
Durham Wharf Dr TW8 6 C7
Durkins Rd RH19 185 D3
Durleston Park Dr
KT23 94 C2
Durley Mead RG12 27 F4
Durlston Rd KT2 17 E2
Durnford Ho SE6 24 B5
Durning Rd SE19 22 D3
Durnsford Ave SW18,
SW19 20 A6
Durnsford Rd SW18,
SW19 20 B5
Durnsford Way GU6 175 A2
Durnston Ct SM1 59 B4
Durrell Way TW17 34 D3
Durrington Ave SW20 19 C1
Durrington Park Rd
SW20 39 C8
Dutch Barn Cl TW19 2 D1
Dutchells Copse
RH12 217 E7
Dutch Gdns KT2 18 B2
Dutton Ho SW2 22 B7
Duval Pl GU19 47 E3
Duxford 10 KT1 38 A7
Duxhurst La RH2 160 B7
Dwelly La
Haxted TN8 165 D8
Oxted TN8 144 D3
Dyehouse Rd GU8 169 C4
Dyer Ho TW12 36 B8
Dyer Rd RG40 25 E7
Dyers Almshouses
RH10 201 D7
Dyer's Field RH6 162 B3
Dykes Ct 11 SW2 21 F7
Dykes Path GU22 70 C4
Dykes Way BR2 44 F6
Dymes Path SW19 19 D6
Dymock Ho SM6 60 C6
Dynevor Pl GU3 108 C5
Dynevor Rd TW10 6 E2
Dysart Ave KT2, TW10 17 C4
Dysart Sch KT6 37 F2
Dyson Ct 8 RH4 136 A7
Dyson Wlk RH11 201 B1

E

Eady Cl RH13 217 F2
Eagle Cl
Crowthorne RG45 45 A7
Wallington SM6 60 E4
Eagle Ct 10 SE21 22 D6
Eagle Hill SE19 22 D2
Eagle House Sch
Mitcham CR4 40 F7
Sandhurst GU47 45 B2
Eagle Rd GU1 109 D1
Eagles Dr TN16 83 D1
Eagles Nest GU47 45 A1
Eagle Star Ho SM1 59 B6
Eagle Trad Est CR4 40 F3
Ealing Rd TW8 6 E8
Eardley Rd SW16 21 C2
Eardley Sch SW16 21 C2
Earle Gdns KT2 17 E1
Earle Ho 2 RH19 185 F2
Earles Mdw RH12 218 B6
Earleswood KT11 73 E7
Earleydene SL5 29 B1
Earl Of Chester Dr
GU16 86 D8
Earl Rd SW14 7 C3
Earlsbrook Rd RH1 139 F7
EARLSFIELD 20 C7
Earlsfield Ho 13 KT2 37 D8
Earlsfield Prim Sch
SW18 20 C6
Earlsfield Rd SW18 20 C8
Earlsfield Sta SW18 20 C7
Earls Gr GU15 65 E6
Earlsthorpe Rd SE26 23 D4
EARLSWOOD 139 F7
Earlswood RG12 27 B2
Earlswood Ave CR7 42 A4
Earlswood Cl RH13 218 A4
Earlswood Ct RH1 139 F7
Earlswood Ho 2 SW2 21 F7
Earlswood Inf Sch
RH1 140 A8
Earlswood Rd RH1 139 F7
Earlswood Sta RH1 139 F7
Early Commons RH10 201 F7
Easby Cres SM4 40 B3
Easedale Ho TW7 5 F2
Eashing La
Godalming GU7, GU8 150 A3
Shackleford GU7, GU8 149 F3
Eashing Point 5 SW15 19 B7
Easington Pl GU1 130 F8
East Ave
Heath End GU9 125 D6
Wallington SM6 60 F5
Whiteley Village KT12 53 F1
Eastbank Rd TW12 16 C3
EAST BEDFONT 14 E7
Eastbourne Gdns SW14 7 C4
Eastbourne Rd
Chiswick W4 7 C8
Felbridge RH7 184 E8
Feltham TW13 15 D6
Godstone RH9 121 D2
Mitcham SW17 21 A2
Newchapel RH7 163 F5
South Godstone RH9 142 E4
Eastbrook Cl GU21 70 A3
Eastbury Gr 7 W4 7 E8
Eastbury La GU3 129 A3
Eastbury Rd KT2 17 E1
Eastchurch Rd TW6 3 E4
Eastchurch Road Rdbt
TW6 3 E5
EAST CLANDON 111 E4
Eastcote Ave KT8 36 A4
Eastcour t TW16 35 C7
Eastcourt Villas 3
RH19 185 F2
Eastcroft Ct GU1 131 A8
Eastcroft Mews RH12 216 F1
Eastcroft Rd KT19 57 E3
East Croydon Sta CR0 61 D8
Eastdean Ave KT18 76 B6
East Dr
Wallington SM5 59 F2
Wentworth GU25 31 B3
Eastern Ave
Brookwood GU24 88 B6
Chertsey KT16 33 A6
Eastern Bsns Pk TW6 3 F5
Eastern Ind Area RG12 27 D7
Eastern La RG45 45 F4
Eastern Perimeter Rd
TW14 3 F5
Eastern Rd
Aldershot GU12 105 E2
Bracknell RG12 27 D7
Eastern View TN16 83 C2
Easter Way RH9 142 F5
EAST EWELL 58 D1
Eastfield Rd RH1 140 C8
Eastfields GU8 170 F5
Eastfields Rd CR4 41 A7
East Flexford La GU3 128 F6
Eastgate
Banstead SM7 77 F5
12 Woking GU22 69 F2
Eastgate Gdns GU1 130 E8
Eastgate Ho 3 GU1 130 E8
Eastgate Mews 4
RH13 217 D1
East Gdns
Mitcham SW17, SW19 20 E2
Woking GU22 70 C2
East Gn GU17 64 C4
EAST GRINSTEAD 185 E2
East Grinstead Rd
RH7 164 D3
East Grinstead Sta
RH19 185 D1
East Grinstead Town
Mus* RH19 185 F1
EASTHAMPSTEAD 27 B5
East Hampstead Mobile
Home Pk RG40 45 C8
Easthampstead Park Sch
RG12 26 D3
Easthampstead Rd
Bracknell RG12 27 A7
Wokingham RG40 25 E4
EASTHEATH 25 B3
Eastheath Ave RG41 25 A4
Eastheath Gdns RG41 25 B3
East Hill
Biggin Hill TN16 83 B1
Dormans Park RH19 185 E6
Oxted RH8 122 F6
South Croydon CR2 61 E1
Woking GU22 70 C2
East Hill Ct RH8 122 E5
East Hill La RH10 183 D5
East Hill Rd RH8 122 E6
EAST HORSLEY 92 E1
East India Way CR0 42 F1
East La
Kingston u T KT1 37 D6
West Horsley KT24 92 D2
Eastlands Cl RH8 122 D8
Eastlands Way RH8 122 D8
Eastleigh Cl SM2 59 B3
Eastleigh Rd TW6 3 F4
Eastleigh Way TW14 15 A7
Eastleigh Wlk 10 SW15 19 A8
East Lo 8 KT22 95 C6
Eastman Way KT19 57 B1
Eastmead
Farnborough GU14 85 B3
Woking GU21 69 B2
East Meads GU2 130 A8
Eastmearn Rd SE21,
SE27 22 C6
EAST MOLESEY 36 C4
Eastmont Rd KT10 55 F8
Eastney Rd CR0 42 B1
Eastnor Cl RH2 138 F6
Eastnor Rd RH2 139 A6
Easton Ho 4 SE27 22 B5
East Park La RH7 163 C1
East Parkside CR6 82 B4
East Pk RH10 201 D5
East Pl SE27 22 C4
East Ramp TW6 3 B6
East Rd
East Bedfont TW14 14 D8
Kingston u T KT2 37 E8
Merton SW19 20 C2
Reigate RH2 117 F2
Weybridge KT13 53 D3
East Ring GU10 127 A7
Eastry Ave BR2 44 F3
EAST SHALFORD 131 A3
East Shalford La GU4 131 A3
EAST SHEEN 7 D3
East Sheen Ave SW14 7 D3
East Sheen Prim Sch
SW14 7 E3
East St
Brentford TW8 6 C7
Ewell KT17 76 E7
Farnham GU9 125 C3

East St *continued*
Great Bookham KT23 94 B2
Horsham RH12 217 C1
Rusper RH12 199 E7
Turners Hill RH10, RH19 204 C4
East Station Rd GU12 105 B1
East Stratton Cl RG12 27 F4
East Surrey Coll RH1 119 A5
East Surrey Hospl The RH1 140 A5
East Surrey Mus★ CR3 101 A3
East View Cotts GU6 174 C3
East View La GU6 174 C3
Eastway
Crawley RH6 182 B7
Epsom KT19 76 D8
Guildford GU2 108 F1
Merton SM4, SW20 39 E5
Wallington SM6 60 C6
East Way CR0 62 E7
Eastway E RH6 182 C7
Eastwell Cl BR3 23 E1
East Whipley La GU5 173 F7
Eastwick Ct 2 SW19 19 D7
Eastwick Dr KT23 94 B4
Eastwick Inf Sch KT23 94 B3
Eastwick Jun Sch KT23 94 B3
Eastwick Park Ave KT23 94 B3
Eastwick Rd
Great Bookham KT23 94 B2
Hersham KT12 54 B5
East Wlk RH2 118 B1
Eastwood
Crawley RH10 201 F6
3 Weybridge KT13 53 D4
Eastwood Lo GU5 151 F7
Eastwood Rd GU5 151 F7
Eastwood St SW16 21 C2
Eastworth Rd KT15, KT16 33 A1
Eaton Ct
Guildford GU1 110 A3
Sutton SM2 59 D4
West Norwood SE27 22 D4
Eaton Dr KT2 18 A1
Eaton Ho GU1 130 F7
Eaton Lo SM2 59 D4
Eaton Park Rd KT11 73 F5
Eaton Pk KT11 73 E5
Eaton Rd
Camberley GU15 65 B4
Isleworth TW3, TW7 5 D3
Sutton SM2 59 D4
Eatonville Rd SW17 20 F6
Eatonville Villas SW17 20 F6
Eaves Cl KT15 52 C4
Ebba's Way KT18 76 B4
Ebbisham Cl RH4 136 A7
Ebbisham Ct
Epsom KT18 76 C4
Felbridge RH19 185 A4
Ebbisham La KT20 97 A4
Ebbisham Rd
Epsom KT18 76 B5
North Cheam KT4 58 C8
Ebenezer Wlk CR4 41 C8
Ebor Cotts SW15 18 E5
Ebsworth St SE23 23 D8
Ebury Mews SE27 22 B5
Ecclesbourne Inf Sch CR7 42 C4
Ecclesbourne Jun Sch CR7 42 C4
Ecclesbourne Rd CR7 42 C4
Eccleshill 6 BR2 44 F5
Eccles Hill RH5 136 C3
Echelforde Dr TW15 14 A4
Echelford Prim Sch The TW15 14 B3
Echo Barn La GU10 145 F5
Echo Pit Rd GU1, GU4 130 E6
Eclipse Est KT19 76 C6
Ecob Cl GU3 108 F5
Ecton Rd KT15 52 B6
Ector Rd SE6 24 E6
Eddeys Cl GU35 187 B6
Eddeys La GU35 187 B6
Eddington Hill RH11 201 B1
Eddington Rd RG12 26 E3
Eddisbury Ho 7 SE26 23 A5
Eddy Rd GU12 105 C1
Eddystone Ct GU10 167 F1
Eddystone Wlk TW19 13 E8
Ede Cl TW4 4 F4
Ede Ct KT17 76 F7
Edenbrook RH7 164 E4
Eden Cl KT15 52 B1
Edencourt Rd SW16 21 B2
Edencroft GU5 151 F7
Edenfield Gdns KT4 57 F7
Eden Grove Rd KT14 71 E6
Edenhall 1 KT12 35 A2
Edenham High Sch CR0 43 F2
Eden Mews SW17 20 C5
Eden Park Ave BR3 44 A4
Eden Park Sta BR3 44 A4
Eden Pl SL5 30 A2
Eden Rd
Crawley RH11 200 F4
Croydon CR0 61 D6
Penge BR3 43 E8
Eden Rd *continued*
West Norwood SE27 22 B3
Edenside Rd KT23 93 F3
Edensor Gdns W4 7 E7
Edensor Rd W4 7 E7
Eden St KT1, KT2 37 E7
Eden Vale
Dormans Park RH19 185 F5
East Grinstead RH19 185 D4
Edenvale Cl CR4 21 A1
Edenvale Rd CR4 21 A1
Eden Way
Beckenham BR3 44 A3
Warlingham CR6 81 E1
Eden Wlk 5 KT1 37 E7
Ederline Ave SW16 42 A7
Ede's Cotts KT21 95 D8
Edgar Cl RH10 202 E5
Edgar Ct KT3 38 E6
Edgar Rd
South Croydon CR2 61 D2
Tatsfield TN16 103 D6
Twickenham TW4 15 F8
Edgbarrowhill Star RG45 45 A3
Edgbarrow Rise GU47 45 A2
Edgbarrow Sch RG45 45 C3
Edgcumbe Park Dr RG45 45 A5
Edgeborough Ct 6 GU1 130 F8
Edgeborough Sch GU10 146 C3
Edge Cl KT13 53 A3
Edgecombe Ho SW19 19 E8
Edgecoombe CR2 62 D2
Edgecoombe Cl KT2 18 D1
Edgecumbe Ct
2 Croydon CR0 43 A1
Egham TW18 12 F2
Edgedale Cl RG45 45 B4
Edgefield Cl
Cranleigh GU6 174 C4
Redhill RH1 140 A4
Edge Hill SW19 19 D1
Edgehill Ct 4 KT12 35 C1
Edge Hill Ct SW19 19 D1
Edgehill Ho 4 RH1 118 F1
Edgehill Rd
Mitcham CR4 41 B8
Purley CR2, CR8 61 B1
Edgeley KT23 93 E3
Edgeley Cvn Pk GU5 153 E8
Edgell Cl GU25 31 F6
Edgell Rd TW18 12 F3
Edgemoor Rd GU16 66 C3
Edge Point Cl SE27 22 B3
Edgewood Cl RG45 45 A7
Edgewood Gn CR0 43 D1
Edgeworth Cl CR3 81 A1
Edgington Rd SW16 21 D2
Edinburgh Cl GU12 106 A5
Edinburgh Ct
Catford SE6 24 F7
2 Kingston u T KT1 37 E6
West Barnes SM4 39 D4
Edinburgh Dr TW15, TW18 13 D2
Edinburgh Ho SM1 59 D8
Edinburgh Rd SM1 59 D8
Edinburgh Way RH19 205 F7
Edith Ct TW14 3 D1
Edith Gdns KT5 38 B2
Edith Rd
Thornton Heath SE25 42 D4
Wimbledon SW19 20 B2
Edmonds Ct RG12 27 C8
Edmund Gr TW13 15 F6
Edmund Rd CR4 40 E6
Edmunds Gate 7 GU7 150 D4
Edna Rd SW20 39 D7
Edrich Rd RH11 201 A1
Edridge Ho 9 SE27 22 B5
Edridge Rd CR0, CR9 61 D7
Edward Alleyn Ho SE21 22 E8
Edward Ave
Camberley GU15 65 A5
Morden CR4, SM4 40 D4
Edward Cl TW12 16 C3
Edward Ct
10 Aldershot GU11 105 A1
Farnborough GU14 85 B4
Staines TW18 13 C2
Edward Ho
East Molesey KT8 36 A4
Epsom KT19 57 B1
12 Guildford GU1 109 D1
Redhill RH1 140 A6
Edward II Ave KT14 71 F5
Edward Pauling Ho TW14 14 F8
Edward Pauling Prim Sch TW13 14 E6
Edward Pinner Ct 5 KT6 56 E8
Edward Rd
Biggin Hill TN16 83 E1
Coulsdon CR5 79 D4
Croydon CR0 42 E2
Farnham GU9 146 C7
Hampton TW12 16 C3
Hatton TW14 3 E2
Penge SE20 23 D2
Windlesham GU20 48 D4
Edwards Cl KT4 58 D8
Edwards Ct 6 CR2 61 E6
Edwards Ho 7 TW10 17 C5
Edward St 2 GU11 105 A2
Edward Way TW15 13 F6
Edwina Ct SM1 59 B6
Edwin Cl KT24 92 D2
Edwin Rd
Twickenham TW2 16 E7
West Horsley KT24 92 D2
Edwins Ct GU14 85 C7
Edwin Stray Ho TW13 16 A5
Eelmoor Plain Rd GU11 104 D5
Eelmoor Rd
Aldershot GU11 104 D5
Farnborough GU14 84 F2
Eelmoor Road Trad Est GU14 84 F2
EFFINGHAM 113 E8
Effingham Cl SM2 59 B3
Effingham Common Rd KT24 93 C2
Effingham Ct
Mitcham SW19 20 E1
13 Woking GU22 89 E8
Effingham Ho 9 KT2 18 B2
Effingham Junction Sta KT24 93 A4
Effingham La RH10 183 E4
Effingham Lo 1 KT6 37 E4
Effingham Pl KT24 113 D8
Effingham Rd
Copthorne RH10, RH6 183 D6
Reigate RH2 139 B8
Thames Ditton KT6, KT7 37 C2
Thornton Heath CR0 41 F2
Effort St SW17 20 E3
Effra Cl SW19 20 B2
Effra Ct SE19 22 E1
Effra Rd SW19 20 B2
Egan Cl CR3 100 D7
Egbury Ho SW15 7 F1
Egerton Ct
7 Guildford GU2 108 E1
5 Richmond TW10 6 E2
Egerton Ho W4 7 C8
Egerton Pl KT13 53 C4
Egerton Rd
Guildford GU2 129 F8
New Malden KT3 38 F5
Sandhurst GU15 64 F7
Sandhurst GU15 65 A7
South Norwood SE25 42 E6
Twickenham TW2 16 E8
Weybridge KT13 53 C4
Egerton Way UB3 3 B7
Eggar's Ct GU12 105 B1
Eggar's Hill GU11 126 A8
EGHAM 12 A4
Egham Bsns Village TW20 32 C7
Egham By-Pass TW20 12 A4
Egham Cl
Cheam SM3 58 E8
Putney SW19 19 E6
Egham Cres SM3 58 D8
Egham Ct KT6 37 D4
Egham Hill TW20 11 D2
Egham Hill Rdbt TW20 11 F3
EGHAM HYTHE 12 E2
Egham Mus★ TW20 12 A3
Egham Sta TW20 12 A3
EGHAM WICK 11 A1
Egleston Rd SM4 40 B3
Egley Dr GU22 89 D5
Egley Rd GU22 89 D6
Eglinton Rd GU10 168 B7
Eglise Rd CR6 81 E2
Egmont Ave KT6 37 F1
Egmont Ct KT12 35 B2
Egmont Ho
18 Sutton SM2 59 C3
Walton-on-T KT12 35 B1
Egmont Park Rd KT20 97 A2
Egmont Rd
New Malden KT3 38 F5
Surbiton KT6 38 A1
Sutton SM2 59 C3
Walton-on-T KT12 35 B2
Egmont Way KT20 97 E8
Egremont Rd SE27 22 A5
Egret Gdns GU11 126 A7
Eight Acres GU26 188 C7
Eighteenth Rd CR4 41 E5
Eileen Rd SE25 42 D4
Eisenhower Ho KT8 37 C8
Eland Pl CR9 61 B7
Eland Rd
Aldershot GU12 105 D1
Croydon CR0, CR9 61 B7
Elberon Ave CR0 41 C3
Elborough Rd SE25 43 A4
Elborough St SW18 20 A7
Elbourne Ho 3 RH6 161 B3
Elbow Mdw SL3 1 F6
Elcho Rd GU24 87 D8
Elderberry Gr 10 SE27 22 C4
Elder Cl GU4 110 A4
Elderfield Pl SW17 21 B4
Elder Gdns 9 SE27 22 C4
Eldergrove GU14 85 E2
Elder Oak Cl SE20 43 B8
Elder Rd
Bisley GU24 68 A4
West Norwood SE27 22 C3
Eldersley Cl RH1 118 F3
Eldersley Gdns RH1 118 F3
Elderslie Cl BR3 44 B3
Elderton Rd SE26 23 E4
Eldertree Pl CR4 41 C8
Eldertree Way CR4 41 C8
Elder Way RH5 136 C3
Elderwood Pl SE27 22 C3
Eldon Ave
Croydon CR0 62 C8
Heston TW5 5 A7
Eldon Ct KT13 53 C5
Eldon Dr GU10 146 D5
Eldon Pk SE25 43 B5
Eldon Rd CR3 100 D6
Eldrick Ct TW14 14 D7
Eldridge Cl TW14 15 A7
Eleanor Ave KT19 57 D1
Eleanor Ct GU1 130 D7
Eleanor Gr SW13, SW14 7 E4
Eleanor Ho
Ewell KT17 76 E7
6 Merton SW19 40 B8
Electric Par KT6 37 D3
Elenora Terr 5 SM1 59 C5
Elfin Gr TW11 16 F3
Elfin Lo 11 TW11 16 F3
Elfrida Cres SE6 24 A4
Elfrida Prim Sch SE6 24 A4
Elgar Ave
Crowthorne RG45 45 B7
Thornton Heath SW16 41 E6
Tolworth KT5, KT6 38 B2
Elgar Ho
Kenley CR8 80 C5
Twickenham TW2 5 D1
Elgar Way RH13 218 B4
Elger Way RH10 183 A4
Elgin Ave TW15 14 C2
Elgin Cl RH13 217 F3
Elgin Cres
Caterham CR3 101 A5
Harlington TW6 3 E5
Elgin Ct
6 Croydon CR0 61 C6
Purley CR8 80 B8
Elgin Gdns GU1 110 A2
Elgin Pl KT13 53 C4
Elgin Rd
Croydon CR0 61 F8
Sutton SM1 59 C7
Wallington SM6 60 C4
Weybridge KT13 53 B5
Elgin Way GU16 85 F8
Eliot Bank SE23, SE26 23 B6
Eliot Bank Prim Sch SE26 23 B6
Eliot Cl GU15 66 B7
Eliot Dr GU27 207 E6
Eliot Ho 11 TW10 6 F1
Elis David Almshouses CR0 61 B6
Elixwood Cotts RH5 134 D1
Elizabethan Cl TW19 13 D8
Elizabethan Way
Crawley RH10 202 C5
Stanwell TW19 13 D8
Elizabeth Ave
Bagshot GU19 47 F2
Staines TW18 13 D2
Elizabeth Cl
Bracknell RG12 27 C5
Cheam SM1 58 F6
Elizabeth Cotts 5 TW9 7 A6
Elizabeth Cres RH19 185 F3
Elizabeth Ct
Croydon CR0 61 E7
Ewell KT17 57 F2
Farncombe GU7 150 E7
Horley RH6 161 A3
Kingston u T KT2 37 E8
2 Oatlands Park KT13 53 D6
Streatham SW17 21 A3
Sunbury TW16 35 C6
3 Teddington TW11 16 E3
West Barnes SM4 39 E2
Whyteleafe CR3 80 F1
Elizabeth Gdns
Ascot SL5 29 B4
Isleworth TW7 6 A3
Sunbury TW16 35 C6
Elizabeth Hart Ct KT13 52 F5
Elizabeth Ho
1 Ashford TW15 13 F4
Caterham CR3 101 A3
Cheam SM3 58 E4
Elizabeth Rd
Farncombe GU7 150 E7
Wokingham RG40 25 D6
Elizabeth Way
Feltham TW13 15 C4
South Norwood SE19 22 D1
Elkins Gdns GU4 110 A4
Elkins Gr GU9 124 F2
Ella Cl BR3 44 A7
Ellacombe Ho 1 SW2 22 A8
Elland Rd KT12 54 D8
Ellenborough Cl RG12 27 D8
Ellenbridge Way CR2 61 E2
Ellens Ct BR4 63 D8
ELLEN'S GREEN 196 A4
Elleray 2 GU22 70 B2
Elleray Ct GU12 106 A5
Elleray Rd TW11 16 F2
Ellerdine Rd TW3 5 D3
Ellerker Gdns TW10 6 E1
Ellerman Ave TW2 15 F7
Ellerslie Ct 6 SM6 60 B4
Ellerton Rd
Surbiton KT6 37 F1
Ellerton Rd *continued*
Wandsworth SW17, SW18 20 D7
Wimbledon SW20 19 A1
Ellery Cl GU6 174 E1
Ellery Rd SE19 22 D1
Elles Ave GU1 110 C1
Elles Cl GU14 85 B3
Ellesfield Ave RG12 26 E5
Ellesmere Ave BR3 44 B7
Ellesmere Ct
Chiswick W4 7 D8
Penge SE20 43 B7
Weybridge KT12 53 E4
Ellesmere Dr CR2 81 B5
Ellesmere Pl KT12 53 E5
Ellesmere Rd
Twickenham TW1 6 C1
Weybridge KT13 53 E4
Elles Rd GU14 84 F2
Ellice Rd RH8 122 F6
Ellies Mews TW15 13 E6
Ellingham GU22 89 E8
Ellingham Prim Sch KT9 56 D3
Ellingham Rd KT9 56 D4
Ellington Rd
Feltham TW13 14 F4
Hounslow TW3 5 B5
Ellington Way KT18 77 B2
Elliot Cl RH10 202 C4
Elliott Ct GU21 70 A3
Elliott Gdns TW17 34 A5
Elliott Ho 3 CR7 42 B5
Elliott Pk GU12 105 E2
Elliott Rd CR7 42 B5
Elliott Rise SL5 28 D7
Ellis Ave GU2 129 F7
Ellis Cl CR5 99 F7
Ellis Farm Cl GU22 89 D5
Ellisfield Dr SW15 19 A8
Ellison Rd
Barnes SW13 7 F5
Streatham SW16 21 E1
Ellison Way
Tongham GU10 126 F7
Wokingham RG40 25 B6
Ellis Rd
Coulsdon CR5 99 F7
Crowthorne RG45 45 B6
Mitcham CR4 40 F3
Ellman Rd RH11 200 F4
Ellora Rd SW16 21 D3
Ellson Cl RH10 202 C4
Ellswood Ct 18 KT6 37 D2
Elmbank Ave
Englefield Green TW20 11 B2
Guildford GU2 130 A8
Elm Bank Gdns SW13 7 E5
Elm Bank Mans SW13 7 E5
Elmbourne Rd SW17 21 B5
Elmbridge Ave KT5 38 C3
Elmbridge Cotts GU6 174 B3
Elmbridge La GU22 89 F8
Elmbridge Mus★ KT13 53 A6
Elmbridge Rd GU6 173 F2
ELMBRIDGE VILLAGE 173 F2
Elmbrook Cl TW16 35 B8
Elmbrook Rd SM1 58 F6
Elm Cl
Box Hill KT20 116 C5
Carshalton SM5 40 F1
Leatherhead KT22 95 B5
Send Marsh GU23 91 A3
South Croydon CR2 61 E4
Stanwell TW19 13 D7
Tolworth KT5 38 C2
Twickenham TW2 16 B6
Warlingham CR6 81 D2
West Barnes SW20 39 C5
Woking GU21 69 D4
ELM CORNER 92 B8
Elm Cotts RH5 115 C8
Elmcourt Rd SE21, SE27 22 B6
Elm Court Sch SE27 22 C6
Elm Cres
Heath End GU9 125 D7
Kingston u T KT2 37 E8
Elmcroft
2 Ashford TW15 14 A3
Little Bookham KT23 94 A3
12 Woking GU22 69 E1
Elmcroft Cl
Chessington KT9 56 E7
Feltham TW14 3 F1
Frimley GU16 85 F7
Elm Croft Ct RH10 201 E6
Elmcroft Dr
Ashford TW15 14 A3
Chessington KT9 56 E7
Elm Ct
Catford SE6 24 B7
5 Charlton TW16 14 F1
3 East Grinstead RH19 185 D2
East Grinstead, Sunnyside RH19 205 E8
Knaphill GU21 68 D2
Mitcham CR4 40 F7
Sandhurst GU47 45 E2
Walton-on-T KT12 54 C8
Elmdene KT5 38 C1
Elmdene Cl BR3 43 F4
Elmdene Ct 15 GU22 89 E8
Elmdon Rd
Hatton TW6 3 F4
Hounslow TW5 4 E5

Elm Dr
Chobham GU24 .... 49 F1
Cranbourne SL4 .... 9 B7
East Grinstead RH19 ..... 186 A1
Leatherhead KT22 .... 95 B4
Sunbury TW16 .... 35 C7
Elmer Cotts KT22 .... 95 A4
Elmer Gdns TW7 .... 5 D4
Elmer Mews KT22 .... 95 A5
Elmer Rd SE6 .... 24 C8
Elmer's Dr TW11 .... 17 B2
ELMERS END 43 D6
Elmers End Rd
Beckenham BR3 .... 43 D5
Penge BR3, SE20 .... 43 C6
Elmers End Sta BR3 ...... 43 D5
Elmerside Rd BR3 .... 43 E5
Elmers Rd
Croydon CR0, SE25 .... 43 A2
Ockley RH5 .... 177 C4
Elm Farm Cvn Pk KT16 ... 32 C3
Elmfield KT23 .... 94 A4
Elmfield Ave
Mitcham CR4 .... 41 A8
Teddington TW11 .... 16 F3
Elm Field Cotts GU3 .... 108 A2
Elmfield Ho GU4 .... 110 C3
Elmfield Mans 5
SW17 .... 21 A6
Elmfield Rd SW17 .... 21 B6
Elmfield Way CR2 .... 61 F2
Elmgate Ave TW13 .... 15 C5
Elm Gdns
Burgh Heath KT18 .... 97 C8
Claygate KT10 .... 55 F4
Mitcham CR4 .... 41 D5
Elm Gr
Bisley GU24 .... 68 A3
Caterham CR3 .... 100 E5
Cranleigh GU6 .... 174 A3
Epsom KT18 .... 76 C5
Heath End GU9 .... 125 C7
Horsham RH13 .... 217 E1
Kingston u T KT2 .... 37 E8
Sutton SM1 .... 59 B6
Wimbledon SW19 .... 19 E1
Elmgrove Cl GU21 .... 88 D8
Elm Grove Par SM6 ...... 60 A7
Elmgrove Rd
Croydon CR0 .... 43 B2
Weybridge KT13 .... 53 A7
Elm Grove Rd
Cobham KT11 .... 73 D3
Farnborough GU14 .... 85 B4
Elm Hill Bglws GU3 ..... 106 E3
Elm Ho
2 Kingston u T KT2 ...... 17 F1
Teddington TW11 .... 17 C1
Weybridge KT13 .... 53 B6
Elmhurst SM1 .... 59 D8
Elmhurst Ave CR4 .... 21 B1
Elmhurst Ct
Camberley GU15 .... 65 D5
Croydon CR0 .... 61 D5
Guildford GU1 .... 130 F8
Elmhurst Dr RH4 .... 136 B5
Elmhurst Lo 5 SM2 ...... 59 C3
Elmhurst Sch CR2 .... 61 D5
Elm La
Ash GU10 .... 126 F8
Forest Hill SE6 .... 23 F6
Ockham GU23 .... 92 A8
Elmore Rd CR5 .... 99 A6
Elmpark Gdns CR2 .... 62 C1
Elm Park Rd SE25 .... 42 F6
Elm Pk
Streatham SW2 .... 21 F8
Sunningdale SL5 .... 29 E1
Elm Pl GU11 .... 126 C8
Elm Rd
Beckenham BR3 .... 43 F7
Carshalton CR4, SM6 ...... 41 A1
Chessington KT9 .... 56 E6
Claygate KT10 .... 55 F4
East Bedfont TW14 .... 14 D8
Ewell KT17 .... 57 F4
Farncombe GU7 .... 150 F8
Heath End GU9 .... 125 D7
Kingston u T KT2 .... 37 F8
Leatherhead KT22 .... 95 B5
Mortlake SW14 .... 7 C3
New Malden KT3 .... 38 D6
Purley CR8 .... 80 B6
Redhill RH1 .... 118 E1
South Norwood CR7 ...... 42 D5
Warlingham CR6 .... 81 D2
Woking GU21 .... 69 D1
Woking, Horsell GU21 ..... 69 F4
Elm Rd W SM3, SM4 ...... 39 F2
Elmscott Rd BR1 .... 24 F3
Elms Cotts CR4 .... 40 F7
Elms Ct SW19 .... 20 B1
Elmshorn KT17 .... 77 C3
Elmside
Guildford GU2 .... 130 A8
Milford GU8 .... 149 F1
New Addington CR0 .... 63 B4
Elmsleigh Ct
Farnborough GU14 .... 84 F4
1 Sutton SM1 .... 59 B7
Elmsleigh Ctr The
TW18 .... 12 F4
Elmsleigh Ho TW2 .... 16 D6
Elmsleigh Rd
Farnborough GU14 .... 84 F4
Staines TW18 .... 12 F3
Twickenham TW2 .... 16 D6
Elmslie Cl KT18 .... 76 C5
Elms Rd
Aldershot GU11 .... 105 A2
Wokingham RG40 .... 25 B5
Elmstead RH19 .... 205 E8
Elmstead Cl KT19 .... 57 E5
Elmstead Gdns KT4 ...... 58 A7
Elmstead Rd KT14 .... 71 A5
Elms The
7 Ashford TW15 .... 14 A3
Ash GU10 .... 126 F8
Blackwater GU17 .... 64 D4
Claygate KT10 .... 55 F3
Croydon CR0 .... 42 C1
Farnham GU9 .... 125 C2
Hamsey Green CR6 .... 81 C4
Mortlake SW13 .... 7 F4
Newell Green RG42 .... 8 A2
Twickenham TW1 .... 6 C2
Wallington SM6 .... 60 C6
Elmsway TW15 .... 14 A3
Elmswood KT23 .... 93 F3
Elmsworth Ave TW3 .... 5 B5
Elm Tree Ave KT10 .... 36 E2
Elmtree Cl KT14 .... 71 E6
Elm Tree Cl
Addlestone KT16 .... 51 E8
Ashford TW15 .... 14 B3
Elmtree Rd TW11 .... 16 E3
Elm Tree Wlk GU14 ...... 84 F8
Elm View GU12 .... 106 B3
Elm Way
North Cheam KT4 .... 58 C7
West Ewell KT19 .... 57 D5
Elm Wlk SW20 .... 39 D5
Elmwood Ave TW13 ...... 15 B5
Elmwood Cl
Ashtead KT21 .... 75 D2
Hackbridge SM6 .... 60 B8
Stoneleigh KT17 .... 58 A3
Elmwood Ct KT21 .... 75 D2
Elmwood Dr KT17 .... 58 A3
Elmwood Ho TW13 .... 15 B5
Elmwood Inf Sch CR0 .... 42 B3
Elmwood Jun Sch CR0 ... 42 B2
Elmwood Rd
Chiswick W4 .... 7 C8
Knaphill GU21 .... 88 D8
Mitcham CR4 .... 40 F6
Redhill RH1 .... 119 B5
Thornton Heath CR0 ...... 42 B2
Elm Wood Sch SE27 ..... 22 D5
Elmworth Gr SE21 .... 22 D6
Elphinstone Cl
Brookwood GU24 .... 88 A6
Pirbright GU24 .... 87 F6
Elphinstone Ct SW16 ..... 21 E2
Elsa Ct 6 BR3 .... 43 F8
Elsdon Rd GU21 .... 69 A1
Elsenham St SW18,
SW19 .... 19 F6
Elsenwood Cres GU15 .... 66 A6
Elsenwood Dr GU15 ...... 66 A7
Elsinore Ave TW19 .... 13 E8
Elsinore Rd SE23 .... 23 E7
Elsinore Way TW9 .... 7 B4
Elsley Cl GU16 .... 85 F6
Elsrick Ave SM4 .... 40 A4
Elstan Way CR0 .... 43 E2
ELSTEAD 148 D3
Elstead Ct SM4 .... 39 E1
Elstead Gn GU8 .... 148 D4
Elstead Ho 12 SW2 ...... 21 F8
Elstead Rd
Milford GU8 .... 149 C3
Seale GU10 .... 127 B2
Shackleford GU8 .... 149 E6
Elsted Cl RH11 .... 201 B8
Elston Pl GU12 .... 126 C8
Elston Rd GU12 .... 126 C8
Elstree Hill BR1 .... 24 E1
Elsworth Cl TW14 .... 14 E7
Elsworthy KT7 .... 36 E3
Elthorne Ct TW13 .... 15 C7
Elton Cl KT1 .... 17 C1
Elton Rd
Kingston u T KT2 .... 38 A8
Purley CR8 .... 79 C7
Elveden Cl GU22 .... 71 B2
Elveden Ct 9 KT22 .... 95 C6
Elveden Rd KT11 .... 73 C8
Elvedon Rd TW13 .... 14 F5
Elvington Gn BR2 .... 44 F4
Elvington Lo 5 RH2 ..... 118 A2
Elvino Rd SE26 .... 23 E3
Elwell Cl TW20 .... 12 A2
Elwill Way BR3 .... 44 D5
Ely Cl
Crawley RH10 .... 201 F2
Frimley GU16 .... 86 A7
Kingston u T SW20 .... 38 F7
Ely Ho 9 RH1 .... 118 F1
Ely Rd
Hatton TW6 .... 3 F5
Hounslow TW4 .... 4 C4
Thornton Heath CR0 ...... 42 D4
Elystan Cl SM6 .... 60 C2
Emanuel Dr TW12 .... 15 F3
Emarc Ho 3 GU11 ...... 105 B2
Embankment The
Twickenham TW1 .... 17 A7
Wraysbury TW19 .... 11 C7
Embassy Ct
Kingston u T KT6 .... 37 D4
7 Wallington SM6 .... 60 B4
Embassy Gdns BR3 .... 43 F8
Ember Cl KT15 .... 52 D5
Embercourt Rd KT10, KT7,
KT8 .... 36 E3
Ember Ctr KT12 .... 54 E8
Ember Farm Ave KT8 ..... 36 D3
Ember Farm Way KT8 .... 36 D4
Ember Gdns KT10, KT8 .... 36 E2
Ember Ho BR1 .... 24 D3
Ember La KT10, KT8 ...... 36 D2
Emberwood RH11 .... 201 D8
Embleton Rd GU35 ...... 187 B6
Embleton Wlk TW12 ...... 15 F3
Emerald Ct CR5 .... 79 D4
Emerald Ho 9 CR0 .... 61 D8
Emerson Ct
Crowthorne RG45 .... 45 B5
7 Wimbledon SW19 .... 19 E2
Emerton Rd KT22 .... 94 C6
Emery Down Cl RG12 ..... 28 A6
Emily Davison Dr
Banstead KT18 .... 77 B1
Burgh Heath KT18 .... 97 B8
Emley Rd KT15 .... 52 B6
Emlyn La KT22 .... 95 A5
Emlyn Rd
Horley RH6 .... 160 E4
Redhill RH1 .... 140 A7
Emmanuel Cl GU2 ...... 109 A4
Emmanuel Ho SE21 ...... 22 D5
Emmanuel Rd SW12 ...... 21 C7
Emmbrook Rd RG41 ...... 25 A8
Emmbrook Sch The
RG41 .... 25 A8
Emmeline Ct KT12 .... 35 C2
Emmetts Cl GU21 .... 69 D2
Emmott Ho RH2 .... 118 B1
Empire Villas RH1 ...... 161 A7
Empress Ave GU14 .... 85 B5
Emsworth Cl RH10 ...... 202 C3
Emsworth Ct SW16 ...... 21 E5
Emsworth St SW2 .... 21 F6
Ena Rd SW16 .... 41 E6
Endale Cl SM5 .... 59 F8
Endeavour Pl GU10 ..... 145 E8
Endeavour Way
Wallington CR0 .... 41 E2
Wimbledon SW19 .... 20 B4
Enderley Ho SE19 .... 42 F8
Endlesham Ct 4 SW12 ... 21 A8
Endlesham Rd SW12 ..... 21 A8
Endsleigh Cl CR2 .... 62 C1
Endsleigh Gdns
Hersham KT12 .... 54 C5
Kingston u T KT6 .... 37 C3
Endsleigh Mans 4
SW16 .... 21 E5
Endsleigh Rd RH1 ...... 119 C6
Endway KT5 .... 38 B2
Enfield Rd
Ash GU12 .... 106 B5
Crawley RH11 .... 201 C2
Harlington TW6 .... 3 E5
Enfield Road Rdbt TW6 .... 3 E5
Engadine Cl CR0 .... 61 F7
Engadine St SW18 .... 20 A7
Engalee RH19 .... 185 C2
England Way KT3 .... 38 B5
Englefield RH12 .... 216 F2
Englefield Cl
Englefield Green TW20 .... 11 C2
Thornton Heath CR0 ...... 42 C3
ENGLEFIELD GREEN 11 B1
Englefield Green Inf Sch
TW20 .... 11 C3
Englefield Rd GU21 .... 68 D2
Engleheart Dr TW14 .... 3 F1
Engleheart Rd SE6 .... 24 C8
Englehurst TW20 .... 11 C2
Englemere Pk
Ascot SL5 .... 28 D5
Oxshott KT22 .... 74 B6
Englemere Pond Nature
Trail★ SL5 .... 28 C6
Englesfield GU15 .... 66 D5
Engliff La GU22 .... 71 A3
English Cotts RH1 ...... 120 A6
Enid Wood Ho RG12 ...... 27 C7
Enmore Ave SE25 .... 43 A4
Enmore Gdns SW14 .... 7 D2
Enmore Rd SE25 .... 43 A4
Ennerdale RG12 .... 27 A5
Ennerdale Cl
Cheam SM1 .... 58 F6
Crawley RH11 .... 201 B4
East Bedfont TW14 .... 14 F7
Ennerdale Gr GU9 ...... 125 A6
Ennerdale Rd TW9 .... 6 F5
Ennismore Ave GU1 ..... 109 F1
Ennismore Gdns KT7 ..... 36 E3
Ennor Ct KT4 .... 58 C6
Ensign Cl
Purley CR8 .... 61 A1
Stanwell TW19 .... 13 D7
Ensign Way
Stanwell TW19 .... 13 D7
Wallington SM6 .... 60 E3
Enterdent Cotts RH9 .... 121 D2
Enterdent Rd RH9 ...... 121 D2
Enterdent The RH9 ..... 121 D2
Enterprise Cl CR0 .... 42 A1
Enterprise Ct RG12 ...... 26 F7
Enterprise Ct RH10 ..... 181 D2
Enterprise Ctr The
RH10 .... 181 F2
Enterprise Est GU1 ..... 109 E5
Enterprise Ho
2 Aldershot GU11 ...... 105 B2
Walton-on-T KT12 .... 35 B2
Enterprise Ind Est
GU12 .... 105 F7
Enterprise Way TW11 .... 16 F2
ENTON GREEN 171 B5
Enton Hall GU8 .... 171 B3
Enton La GU8 .... 171 B3
Enton Pl TW3 .... 5 B3
Eversham Ct SE23 ...... 23 E5
Envis Way GU3 .... 108 C4
Eothen Cl CR3 .... 101 A3
Epping Way RG12 .... 27 F5
Epping Wlk RH10 ...... 201 F4
EPSOM 76 C5
Epsom Bsns Pk KT17 ..... 76 E8
Epsom Cl GU15 .... 65 C8
Epsom Coll KT17 .... 77 A5
Epsom Downs Metro Ctr
KT20 .... 97 B7
Epsom Downs Sta
KT17 .... 77 B4
Epsom & Ewell High Sch
KT19 .... 57 C5
Epsom General Hospl
KT18 .... 76 C4
Epsom Ho SM1 .... 59 B6
Epsom Lane N KT18,
KT20 .... 97 B7
Epsom Lane S KT20 ...... 97 C5
Epsom Pl GU6 .... 174 F3
Epsom Prim Sch KT19 ... 76 D8
Epsom Rd
Ashtead KT18, KT21 ...... 76 A2
Crawley RH10 .... 202 A4
Croydon CR0 .... 61 A6
East Clandon GU4 .... 111 D3
Ewell KT17 .... 76 F8
Guildford GU4 .... 110 F2
Guildford, Merrow GU1,
GU4 .... 110 C1
Leatherhead KT22 .... 95 C6
Morden SM3, SM4 .... 39 F2
West Horsley GU4,
KT24 .... 112 C5
Epsom Sq TW6 .... 3 F5
Epsom Sta KT19 .... 76 D6
Epworth Rd TW7, TW8 ..... 6 B7
Eresby Dr BR3 .... 44 A1
Erica Cl GU24 .... 67 E6
Erica Cotts GU26 .... 188 C6
Erica Ct GU22 .... 69 D1
Erica Dr RG40 .... 25 D5
Erica Gdns CR0 .... 63 B7
Erica Ho 6 SW19 .... 19 E1
Erica Way
Copthorne RH10 .... 183 A2
Horsham RH12 .... 217 D5
Eridge Cl RH10 .... 202 C6
Erin Cl BR1 .... 24 E1
Erindale Ct 1 BR3 .... 44 A8
Eriswell Cres KT12 .... 53 F4
Eriswell Rd KT12 .... 53 F5
Erkenwald Cl KT16 .... 32 E3
Ermine Cl TW4 .... 4 C5
Ermyn Cl KT21 .... 95 D6
Ermyn Cotts RH6 .... 163 A6
Ermyn Way KT22 .... 95 D6
Erncroft Way TW1 .... 5 F1
Ernest Ave SE27 .... 22 B4
Ernest Bevin Coll
SW17 .... 20 E6
Ernest Cl
Beckenham BR3 .... 44 A4
Farnham GU10, GU9 ..... 146 B6
Ernest Cotts KT17 .... 57 F3
Ernest Gdns W4 .... 7 B8
Ernest Gr BR3 .... 43 F4
Ernest Rd KT1 .... 38 B7
Ernest Sq KT1 .... 38 B7
Ernle Rd SW20 .... 19 C1
Ernst Chain Rd GU2 ..... 129 D8
Eros Ho SE6 .... 24 B8
Erridge Rd SW19 .... 40 A7
Errington Manor SM5 .... 59 F7
Errol Gdns KT3 .... 39 A5
Erskine Cl
Carshalton SM1 .... 59 E7
Crawley RH11 .... 200 E2
Erskine Rd SM1 .... 59 D7
Esam Way SE27, SW16 .... 22 A3
Escombe Ct 5 CR3 ..... 101 A8
Escombe Dr GU2, GU3 ... 109 B6
Escot Rd TW16 .... 14 E1
Escott Pl KT16 .... 51 D4
ESHER 55 C6
Esher Ave
Cheam SM3 .... 58 D7
Walton-on-T KT12 .... 35 A1
Esher CE High Sch
KT10 .... 55 A7
Esher CE Prim Sch
KT10 .... 55 C5
Esher Cl KT10 .... 55 B5
Esher Coll KT7 .... 36 E2
Esher Cres TW6 .... 3 F5
Esher Gdns SW19 .... 19 D6
Esher Gn KT10 .... 55 B6
Esher Green Dr KT10 ..... 55 B7
Esher Mews 3 CR4 .... 40 F6
Esher Park Ave KT10 ..... 55 C5
Esher Place Ave KT10 .... 55 B6
Esher Rd
Camberley GU15 .... 47 A1
East Molesey KT8 .... 36 D4
Hersham KT10, KT12 ...... 54 E6
Esher Sta KT10 .... 55 D8
Eskdale Gdns CR8 .... 80 D5
Eskdale Way GU15 .... 66 D4
Eskmont Ridge SE19 ..... 22 E1
Esme Ho SW15 .... 7 F3
Esparto St SW18 .... 20 B8
Essame Cl RG40 .... 25 D6
Essendene Cl CR3 ...... 100 E4
Essendene Lodge Sch
CR3 .... 100 E4
Essendene Rd CR3 ...... 100 E5
Essenden Rd CR2 .... 61 E3
Essex Ave TW7 .... 5 E4
Essex Cl
Addlestone KT15 .... 52 C6
Frimley GU16 .... 86 A7
West Barnes SM4 .... 39 D2
Essex Ct
Barnes SW13 .... 7 F5
South Norwood SE19 ...... 22 D2
Essex Dr GU6 .... 173 F2
Essex Gr SE19 .... 22 D2
Essex Ho
5 Croydon CR0 .... 61 D8
Thames Ditton KT7 .... 37 A2
Essex Twr 5 SE20 .... 43 B8
Estcots Dr RH19 .... 186 A1
Estcots Prim Sch
RH19 .... 186 A1
Estcourt Rd CR0, SE25 .... 43 B3
Estella Ave KT3 .... 39 B5
Estoria Cl SW2 .... 22 A8
Estreham Rd SW16 .... 21 D2
Estridge Cl TW3 .... 5 A3
Eswyn Rd SW17 .... 20 F3
Ethel Bailey Cl KT19 ..... 76 A7
Ethelbert Rd SW20 .... 39 D8
Ethelbert St SW12 .... 21 B7
Ethel Rd TW15 .... 13 E3
Ethelred Ct 4 CR3 ...... 101 A8
Ethelworth Ct 4 SW2 .... 22 A7
Etherley Hill RH5 .... 177 A7
Etherow St SE22 .... 23 A8
Etherstone Gn SW16 ..... 22 A4
Etherstone Rd SW16 ..... 22 A4
Eton Ave
Heston TW5 .... 5 A8
New Malden KT3 .... 38 D5
Eton Cl SW18 .... 20 B8
Eton Ct
Staines TW18 .... 12 F3
Teddington TW11 .... 16 D3
Eton Ho 7 TW20 .... 12 A3
Eton Pl GU9 .... 125 B7
Eton Rd UB3 .... 3 F7
Eton St TW10 .... 6 E2
Etps Rd GU14 .... 105 A8
Ettrick Ct GU14 .... 105 B8
Etwell Pl KT5 .... 37 F3
Eureka Rd KT1 .... 38 A7
Europa Park Rd GU1 .... 109 C2
Eurythmy Sch RH19 ..... 205 E6
Eustace Cres RG40 .... 25 D8
Eustace Rd GU4 .... 110 D3
Euston Rd CR0 .... 42 A1
Evans Cl RH10 .... 202 D5
Evans Gr TW13 .... 16 A6
Evans Rd SE6 .... 24 E6
Eve Ct CR4 .... 41 A7
Evedon RG12 .... 27 B2
Evelina Rd SE20 .... 23 D1
Eveline Rd CR4 .... 40 F8
Evelyn Ave
Aldershot GU11 .... 126 B8
Titsey RH8 .... 103 C3
Evelyn Cl
Felbridge RH19 .... 184 F4
Twickenham TW2 .... 16 B8
Woking GU22 .... 89 D7
Evelyn Clark Ho RH18 ... 206 F2
Evelyn Cotts
Abinger Common
RH5 .... 155 D8
South Godstone RH9 ..... 142 E6
Evelyn Cres TW16 .... 34 F8
Evelyn Ct CR0 .... 43 A2
Evelyn Gdns
Richmond TW9 .... 6 E3
Tyler's Green RH9 .... 121 C5
Evelyn Lancaster Ho
RH12 .... 217 E6
Evelyn Rd
Richmond, Ham TW10 ..... 17 C5
Richmond TW9 .... 6 E4
Wimbledon SW19 .... 20 B2
Evelyn Terr TW9 .... 6 E4
Evelyn Way
Epsom KT19 .... 76 A8
Stoke D'Abernon KT11 .... 73 F3
Sunbury TW16 .... 34 F8
Wallington SM6 .... 60 D6
Evelyn Wlk RH10 .... 201 E3
Evelyn Woods Rd
GU11 .... 105 C7
Evendon's Cl RG41 .... 25 A3
Evendon's La RG41 .... 25 A3
Evening Hill BR3 .... 24 C1
Evenlode Way GU47 ...... 64 D8
Everard La CR3 .... 101 B5
Eve Rd
Isleworth TW7 .... 6 A3
Sheerwater GU21 .... 70 B4
Everest Ct
South Norwood SE19 ...... 42 E8
Woking GU21 .... 68 E3
Everest Rd
Camberley GU15 .... 65 D8
Crowthorne RG45 .... 45 B6
Stanwell TW19 .... 13 E8
Everglade TN16 .... 83 D1
Everglades BR2 .... 44 E6
Evergreen Cl SE20 .... 23 C1

Evergreen Ct TW19 13 D8
Evergreen Rd GU16 66 A3
Evergreens The GU8 171 B1
Evergreen Way TW19 13 D8
Everlands Cl 6 GU22 69 E1
Eversfield Ct 2 RH2 118 C1
Eversfield Rd
Horsham RH13 217 E1
Reigate RH2 118 B1
Richmond TW9 6 F5
Eversley Cres TW7 5 D6
Eversley Pk SW19 19 B3
Eversley Rd
Kingston u T KT5 37 F4
South Norwood SE19 22 D1
Eversley Way
Croydon CR0 63 A7
Thorpe TW20 32 C7
Everton Rd CR0 43 A1
Evesham Cl
Belmont SM2 59 A3
Reigate RH2 117 F2
Evesham Ct GU1 131 A8
Evesham Gn SM4 40 B3
Evesham Rd
Morden SM4 40 B3
Reigate RH2 117 F2
Evesham Rd N RH3 117 F2
Evesham Wlk GU47 45 D1
Ewart Rd SE23 23 D8
Ewelands RH6 161 C4
EWELL 58 A1
Ewell By-Pass KT17 58 A2
Ewell Castle Sch KT17 58 A2
Ewell Court Ave KT19 57 E5
Ewell Downs Rd KT17 77 A7
Ewell East Sta KT17 58 B1
Ewell Grove Ct 4 KT17 57 F2
Ewell Grove Inf Sch
KT17 57 F1
Ewell Ho KT17 57 F1
Ewell House Gr KT17 57 F1
Ewell Park Gdns KT17 58 A3
Ewell Park Way KT17 58 A3
Ewell Rd
Cheam SM2, SM3 58 D4
Surbiton KT5, KT6 37 F2
Thames Ditton KT6, KT7 37 B2
Tolworth KT6 38 B1
Ewell West Sta KT19 57 E2
Ewelme Rd SE23 23 C7
Ewen Cres SW2 22 A8
EWHURST 175 F5
Ewhurst Ave CR2 61 F2
Ewhurst CE Inf Sch
GU6 175 E5
Ewhurst Cl
Crawley RH11 201 C6
East Ewell SM2 58 C2
Ewhurst Ct CR4 40 D6
EWHURST GREEN 175 E4
Ewhurst Rd
Cranleigh GU6 174 E3
Crawley RH11 201 C7
Peaslake GU6 154 D5
Ewins Cl GU12 106 A2
Ewood La RH5 158 C6
EWSHOT 124 D8
Ewshot Hill Cross
GU10 124 D7
Exbury Rd SE6 24 A6
Excalibur Cl RH11 200 E5
Excelsior Cl KT1 38 A7
Exchange Rd
Ascot SL5 29 C4
Crawley RH10 201 E6
Exchange The
8 Purley CR8 80 A8
14 Woking GU22 69 F2
Exeforde Ave TW15 14 A4
Exeter Cl RH10 201 E2
Exeter Ct
Kingston u T KT6 37 E4
Mitcham SW19 20 E1
Exeter Ho
Feltham TW13 16 A6
Woking GU21 69 F3
Exeter Rd
Ash GU12 106 A3
Croydon CR0 42 F2
Feltham TW13 15 F5
Harlington TW6 3 E4
Exeter Way TW6 3 E5
Exhibition Rd GU14 105 B8
Explorer Ave TW19 13 E7
Eyebright Cl CR0 43 D1
Eyhurst Cl KT20 97 F3
Eyhurst Spur KT20 97 F3
Eyles Cl RH12 217 B4
Eylewood Rd SE27 22 C3
Eyot Lo 9 TW1 17 A7
Eyre Ct RG40 25 B4
Eyston Dr KT13 53 A1

F

Fabyc Ho TW9 7 A7
Factory Cotts GU10 124 D2
Factory La CR0, CR9 61 B8
Fagg's Rd TW14 4 A2
Fairacre
Hounslow TW7 5 D6
Kingston u T KT3 38 E6
Fairacres
Burgh Heath KT20 97 C6
Cobham KT11 73 E7
New Addington CR0 62 F2
Salfords RH1 140 C1
Fairbairn Cl CR8 80 A6
Fairborne Way GU2 109 A4
Fairbourne KT11 73 D6
Fairbourne Cl GU21 69 A1
Fairbourne La CR3 100 C4
Fairbriar Ct 9 KT18 76 E6
Fairchildes Ave CR0 82 D7
Fairchildes Cotts CR6 82 F6
Fairchildes Prim Sch
CR9 82 E7
Fairchildes Rd CR6 82 E4
Faircroft SE26 23 C4
Faircross RG12 27 B6
Fairdene Rd CR5 79 D2
Fairfax RG42 27 A8
Fairfax Ave
Ewell KT17 58 B2
Redhill RH1 118 F2
Fairfax Cl
Oxted RH8 122 E5
Walton-on-T KT12 35 B1
Fairfax Ind Est GU12 105 E2
Fairfax Mews GU14 85 D2
Fairfax Rd
Farnborough GU14 85 C7
Old Woking GU22 90 B7
Teddington TW11 17 B1
FAIRFIELD 95 B6
Fairfield App TW19 11 D8
Fairfield Ave
Horley RH6 161 A1
Staines TW18 12 F4
Twickenham TW2 16 B7
Fairfield Cl
Dorking RH4 115 C1
Great Bookham KT23 94 B1
Guildford GU2 109 A2
Mitcham CR4 20 E1
West Ewell KT19 57 E5
Fairfield Cotts GU8 191 C3
Fairfield Ct
Dorking RH4 115 B1
Leatherhead KT22 95 B6
Fairfield Dr
Dorking RH4 136 B8
Frimley GU16 65 E3
Fairfield E KT1 37 E7
Fairfield Ind Est KT1 37 F6
Fairfield La GU24 68 A7
Fairfield Lo GU2 109 A2
Fairfield N KT1, KT2 37 E7
Fairfield Path CR0, CR9 61 D7
Fairfield Pk KT11 73 D5
Fairfield Pl KT1 37 E6
Fairfield Rd
Beckenham BR3 44 A7
East Grinstead RH19 205 F8
Kingston u T KT1 37 E7
Leatherhead KT22 95 B6
South Croydon CR0, CR9 61 E7
Fairfield Rise GU2 108 F2
Fairfields
Chertsey KT15 33 B1
Lewisham SE6 24 B8
Fairfield S KT1 37 F7
Fairfields Rd TW3 5 C4
Fairfield The GU9 125 C2
Fairfield W KT1 37 E7
Fairfield Way
Coulsdon CR5 79 D5
West Ewell KT19 57 E5
Fairfield Wlk KT22 95 B6
Fairford SE6 24 A7
Fairford Ave CR0 43 D4
Fairford Cl
Croydon CR0 43 E4
Pyrford KT14 70 F5
Reigate RH2 118 C3
Fairford Ct SM2 59 B3
Fairford Gdns KT4 57 F7
Fair Green Ct 1 CR4 40 F6
Fairgreen Rd CR7 42 B4
Fairhall RH2 117 E2
Fairhaven TW20 11 F3
Fairhaven Ave CR0 43 D3
Fairhaven Ct
7 Croydon CR2 61 C5
1 Egham TW20 11 F3
Fairhaven Rd RH1 119 A5
Fairhill GU7 150 D6
Fairholme TW14 14 E8
Fairholme Cres KT21 75 C2
Fairholme Gdns GU9 125 C1
Fairholme Ho 4 KT3 38 E5
Fairholme Prim Sch
TW14 14 D7
Fairholme Rd
Ashford TW15 13 F3
Cheam SM1 58 F4
Thornton Heath CR0 42 A2
Fairings The KT12 54 B6
Fair La CR5, RH2 98 D1
FAIRLANDS 108 C4
Fairlands GU35 187 D5
Fairlands Ave
Fairlands GU3 108 C5
Sutton SM1 59 A8
Thornton Heath CR7 42 A4
Fairlands Ct GU3 108 C5
Fairlands Rd GU3 108 D5
Fairlawn
Little Bookham KT23 93 F3
Weybridge KT13 53 E5
Fairlawn Cl
Claygate KT10 55 F4
Feltham TW13 15 F4
Kingston u T KT2 18 C2
Fairlawn Cres RH19 185 B2
Fairlawn Ct 1 SE26 23 E3
Fairlawn Dr
East Grinstead RH19 185 B2
Reigate RH1 139 E7
Fairlawnes SM6 60 B5
Fairlawn Gr SM7 78 D6
Fairlawn Ho RH10 202 A6
Fairlawn Pk
Forest Hill SE26 23 E3
Woking GU21 69 E4
Fairlawn Prim Sch
SE23 23 C8
Fairlawn Prim Sch Annexe
SE23 23 C7
Fairlawn Rd
Merton SW19 19 F1
Sutton SM2, SM5 78 C8
Fairlawns
Addlestone KT15 52 B5
Guildford GU1 110 C1
Horley RH6 161 B2
Sunbury TW16 35 A6
Twickenham TW1 6 C1
Woodham KT15 70 F8
Fairlawns Cl TW18 13 B2
Fairleas 12 BR3 44 B7
Fairlie Gdns SE23 23 C8
Fairlight
Hampton TW12 16 B3
Sheerwater GU21 70 B7
Fairlight Cl KT4 58 C6
Fairlight Rd SW17 20 D4
Fairline Ct BR3 44 C7
Fairlop Wlk GU6 173 F2
Fairmead
Tolworth KT5, KT6 38 B1
Woking GU21 69 C1
Fairmead Cl
Heston TW5 4 D7
Kingston u T KT3 38 D6
Sandhurst GU47 64 E7
Fairmead Ct
Camberley GU15 65 C4
Richmond TW9 7 B5
Fairmead Rd CR0 42 A2
Fairmeads KT11 73 F6
FAIRMILE 73 F7
Fairmile Ave
Cobham KT11 73 F6
Streatham SW16 21 D3
Fairmile Ct KT11 73 E7
Fairmile Ho TW11 17 A4
Fairmile Hts KT11 74 A6
Fairmile La
Cobham KT11 73 E6
Stoke D'Abernon KT11 73 E4
Fairmile Park Copse
KT11 73 F6
Fairmile Park Rd KT11 73 F6
Fairoak Cl CR8 80 B4
Fair Oak Cl KT22 74 D7
Fairoak La
Chessington KT9, KT22,
KT10 75 B8
Oxshott KT22 74 E8
Fairoaks Airport GU24 50 E1
Fairoaks Ct KT15 52 B5
Fairoaks Residential Pk
GU3 108 A6
Fairs Rd KT22 95 A8
Fair St TW3 5 C4
Fairstone Ct RH6 161 B4
Fairview KT17 77 C8
Fair View RH12 217 A3
Fairview Ave GU22 69 F1
Fairview Cl
Forest Hill SE26 23 E3
Woking GU22 69 F1
Fairview Cotts GU25 31 D3
Fairview Ct
Ashford TW15 14 A3
13 East Grinstead
RH19 205 F8
Kingston u T KT2 38 B8
Fairview Dr TW17 33 F4
Fairview Gdns GU9 125 D6
Fairview Ho 17 SW2 21 F8
Fairview Pl SW2 21 F8
Fairview Rd
Ash GU12 106 B3
Carshalton SM1 59 E5
Ewell KT17 76 F8
Headley Down GU35 187 C5
Thornton Heath SW16 41 F8
Wokingham RG40 25 C5
Fairview Terr GU35 187 A6
Fairwater Dr KT15 52 D2
Fairwater Ho TW11 17 A4
Fairway
Chertsey KT16 33 B1
Copthorne RH10 183 B2
Crawley RH11 200 D4
Guildford GU1 110 D1
Sutton SM5 78 C8
West Barnes SW20 39 C6
Fairway Cl
Copthorne RH10 183 A2
Croydon BR3, CR0 43 E4
Heston TW4 4 C2
Hounslow TW4 4 D2
West Ewell KT19 57 C6
Woking GU23 89 B7
Fairway Est TW4 4 C2
Fairway Gdns BR3 44 D3
Fairway Hts GU15 66 B6
Fairway Inf Sch RH10 183 B3
Fairways
Ashford TW15 14 B2
Beacon Hill GU26 188 B6
Hounslow TW7 5 E6
Kenley CR8 80 C2
Teddington TW11 17 D1
Fairways The RH1 139 D6
Fairway The
East Molesey KT8 36 B6
Farnborough GU14 84 A1
Farnborough GU14 104 B8
Frimley GU15 66 A3
Godalming GU7 150 F2
Heath End GU9 125 D7
Kingston u T KT3 38 D8
Leatherhead KT22 75 A1
Pirbright GU3 88 C3
Weybridge KT13 72 A8
Fairwell La KT24 112 B7
Fairwood Ho KT13 52 F6
Fairwyn Rd SE26 23 E4
Fakenham Way GU47 45 D2
Falaise TW20 11 F3
Falaise Cl GU11 105 B3
Falcon Cl
Chiswick W4 7 C8
Crawley RH11 201 D8
Lightwater GU18 66 F8
Falcon Ct
Frimley GU16 65 D1
Sheerwater GU21 70 C6
9 West Norwood SE21 22 D6
Falcon Dr TW19 2 E1
Falcon Ho 9 SW19 40 B8
Falconhurst
4 Kingston u T KT6 37 E4
Oxshott KT22 74 D4
Falcon Rd
Guildford GU1 109 D1
Hampton TW12 15 F1
Falconry Ct KT1 37 E6
Falcons Cl TN16 83 D2
Falcon Way
Feltham TW14 4 B2
Sunbury TW16 34 E7
Falconwood
East Horsley KT24 92 F3
Englefield Green TW20 11 E3
Falcon Wood KT22 94 F7
Falconwood Rd CR0 63 A3
Falcourt Cl SM1 59 B5
Falkland Ct GU14 105 E8
Falkland Gdns RH4 136 A6
Falkland Gr RH4 136 A6
Falkland Ho SE6 24 C4
Falkland Park Ave
SE25 42 E7
Falkland Rd RH4 136 A6
Falklands Dr RH13 218 B4
Falkner Ct GU9 125 C2
Falkner Rd GU9 125 B2
Fallow Deer Cl RH13 218 B4
Fallowfield Way RH6 161 B4
Fallsbrook Rd SW16 21 C2
Falmer Cl RH11 201 D4
Falmouth Cl GU15 66 A4
Falmouth Ho 12 KT2 37 D8
Falmouth Rd KT12 54 C6
Falstaff Mews TW12 16 D3
Falstone GU21 69 B1
Fambridge Cl SE26 23 F4
Famet Ave CR8 80 C6
Famet Cl CR8 80 C6
Famet Ct RH19 185 C3
Famet Gdns CR8 80 C5
Famet Wlk CR8 80 C6
Fanchford Rd RH2 117 E1
Fanes Cl RG42 26 F8
Fanfare The GU21 70 C4
Fangrove Cvn Pk KT16 32 B1
Fanshawe Rd TW10 17 C4
Faraday Ave RH19 205 F6
Faraday Ct RH10 181 F2
Faraday Ctr The RH10 181 F1
Faraday Ho
7 Balham SW12 21 B8
5 Hampton TW12 16 B2
Faraday Pl KT8 36 A5
Faraday Rd
Crawley RH10 181 F2
East Molesey KT8 36 A5
Farnborough GU14 85 C6
Guildford GU1 109 C2
Wimbledon SW19 20 B2
Faraday Way CR0, CR9 41 F1
Farcrosse Cl GU47 64 C8
Farebrothers RH12 216 F8
Fareham Ho 13 SW15 19 A7
Fareham Rd TW14 15 C8
Farendon Ho 18 SM2 59 C4
Farewell Pl CR4 40 E8
Farhalls Cres RH12 217 F6
Faringdon Cl GU47 45 C1
Faringdon Dr RG12 27 D4
Farington Acres KT13 53 D7
Faris Barn Dr KT15 70 F8
Faris La KT15 70 F8
FARLEIGH 81 F5
Farleigh Ave BR2 44 F2
Farleigh Court Rd CR6 82 B5
Farleigh Ct
Croydon CR2 61 C5
3 Guildford GU2 108 E1
Farleigh Dean Cres
CR0 82 B8
Farleigh Ho 7 KT2 18 B2
Farleigh Prim Sch CR6 81 E2
Farleigh Rd
Warlingham CR6 81 E2
Woodham KT15 71 A8
Farleton Cl KT13 53 D4
Farley Copse RG42 26 E8
Farleycroft 1 CR0 43 A1
Farley Croft BR2 44 E7
Farley Ct GU14 85 D2
FARLEY GREEN 153 E7
Farley Heath Rd GU5 153 C6
Farley Ho SE26 23 B5
Farley Mews SE6 24 C8
Farley Moor RG42 26 D8
Farley Pk RH8 122 D5
Farley Pl SE25 43 A5
Farley Rd
Lewisham SE6 24 C8
South Croydon CR2 62 B2
Farleys Cl KT24 92 C1
Farlington Pl SW15 19 B8
Farlington Sch RH12 216 B6
Farlton Rd SW18 20 B8
Farm App RH9 163 C5
Farm Ave
Horsham RH12 217 B3
Streatham SW16 21 E4
Farm Cl
Ascot SL5 29 C4
Bracknell RG42 26 F8
Byfleet KT14 71 F7
Chertsey KT16 32 A3
Chipstead CR5 98 F7
Coney Hall BR4 63 F7
Crawley RH10 202 A7
Crowthorne RG45 45 C7
East Grinstead RH19 206 B8
East Horsley KT24 112 F7
Egham TW18 12 E3
Fairlands GU3 108 C6
Fetcham KT22 94 E3
Guildford GU1 109 D4
Lower Halliford TW17 34 A2
Loxwood RH14 213 A3
Sutton SM2 59 D3
Wallington SM6 60 C1
Warnham RH12 216 F7
Farmdale Rd SM5 59 E3
Farm Dr
Croydon CR0 62 F8
Purley CR8 79 D8
Farmer's Rd TW18 12 E3
Farmfield Dr RH6 181 B8
Farmfield Hospl (private)
RH6 160 B1
Farmfield Rd BR1 24 E3
Farm Fields CR2 80 F8
Farmhouse Cl GU22 70 D4
Farmhouse Rd SW16 21 C1
Farmington Ave SM1 59 D7
Farm La
Addlestone KT15 52 A3
Ashtead KT21, KT18 76 B2
Croydon CR0 62 F8
East Horsley KT24 112 F7
Purley CR8 60 C1
Send GU23 90 C3
Farmleigh Cl RH10 202 C8
Farmleigh Gr KT12 53 F5
Farm Pk★ RH5 198 A8
Farm Rd
Aldershot GU12 105 E3
Frimley GU16 65 F2
Morden SM4 40 B4
Old Woking GU22 90 B7
Staines TW18 13 B2
Sutton SM2 59 D3
Thames Ditton KT10 55 B8
Twickenham TW4 15 E7
Warlingham CR6 101 E8
Farmstead KT19 57 A2
Farmstead Ct 3 SM6 60 B5
Farmstead Rd SE6 24 B4
Farmview KT11 73 D3
Farm View KT20 117 F8
Farm Way
North Cheam KT4 58 C7
Stanwell TW19 1 F1
Farm Wlk
Ash GU12 127 C8
Guildford GU2 129 F7
Farnaby Rd BR1 44 E8
Farnan Hall SW16 21 E3
Farnan Rd SW16 21 E3
FARNBOROUGH 85 C3
Farnborough Airport
GU14 84 E1
Farnborough Air Sciences
Trust★ GU14 85 C1
Farnborough Ave CR2 62 E3
Farnborough Bsns Ctr
GU14 84 F2
Farnborough Bsns Pk
GU14 85 B2
Farnborough Coll of Tech
GU14 85 C2
Farnborough Cres
3 Coney Hall BR2 44 F1
South Croydon CR2 62 E2
Farnborough Gate Ret Pk
GU14 85 C7
Farnborough Grange Inf
Sch GU14 85 A8
FARNBOROUGH GREEN
85 C6
Farnborough Hill Sch
GU14 85 C5

Farnborough Ho 1 SW15 . . . 19 A7
Farnborough Ind Est GU14 . . . 85 A3
Farnborough North Sta GU14 . . . 85 D6
FARNBOROUGH PARK . . . 85 D4
Farnborough Rd
Aldershot GU11 . . . 104 E3
Farnborough GU14 . . . 85 C5
Heath End GU11, GU9 . . . 125 D7
Farnborough St GU14 . . . 85 D6
Farnborough Sta GU14 . . . 85 B5
FARNBOROUGH STREET . . . 85 D5
FARNCOMBE . . . 150 E8
Farncombe CE Inf sch GU7 . . . 150 E7
Farncombe Hill GU7 . . . 150 E7
Farncombe St GU7 . . . 150 E7
Farncombe Sta GU7 . . . 150 F7
Farnell Mews KT13 . . . 53 B7
Farnell Rd
Isleworth TW7 . . . 5 D4
Stanwell TW18 . . . 13 A5
Farnell's Almshouses TW7 . . . 5 F5
FARNHAM . . . 125 B1
Farnham Bsns Ctr GU9 . . . 125 C3
Farnham Bsns Pk GU9 . . . 146 A8
Farnham By-Pass GU9 . . . 125 C2
Farnham Castle★ GU9 . . . 125 B3
Farnham Cl RG12 . . . 27 D7
Farnham Cloisters GU9 . . . 146 A6
Farnham Coll GU9 . . . 125 C1
Farnham Com Hospl GU9 . . . 125 E4
Farnham Ct SM3 . . . 58 E4
Farnham Gdns SW20 . . . 39 B7
Farnham Heath End Sch GU9 . . . 125 E6
Farnham La GU27 . . . 208 A7
Farnham Mus★ GU9 . . . 125 B2
Farnham Park Cl GU9 . . . 125 B6
Farnham Park Dr GU9 . . . 125 B6
Farnham Rd
Churt GU10 . . . 167 D3
Elstead GU8 . . . 148 C4
Guildford, Guildford Park GU1, GU2, GU3 . . . 130 B7
Guildford, Onslow Village GU2, GU3 . . . 129 E6
Farnham Rd Hospl GU2 . . . 130 B7
Farnham Sta GU9 . . . 125 C2
Farnham Trad Est GU9 . . . 125 F4
Farnhurst La GU6 . . . 193 F4
Farningham RG12 . . . 27 E3
Farningham Cres CR3 . . . 101 A4
Farningham Ct SW16 . . . 21 D1
Farningham Ho RG12 . . . 27 E3
Farningham Rd CR3 . . . 101 A4
Farnley GU21 . . . 68 F2
Farnley Rd CR7, SE25 . . . 42 D5
Farnsworth Ho 8 SW27 . . . 22 B3
Farquhar Rd
Dulwich SE19 . . . 22 F3
Wimbledon SW19 . . . 20 A5
Farquharson Rd CR0 . . . 42 C1
Farrell Cl GU15 . . . 65 C3
Farren Ho GU14 . . . 85 C1
Farren Rd SE23 . . . 23 E6
Farrer Ct TW1 . . . 17 D8
Farrer's Pl CR0 . . . 62 D6
Farrier Cl TW16 . . . 35 A5
Farrier Pl
Sandhurst GU47 . . . 64 B7
Sutton SM1 . . . 59 B8
Farriers KT18 . . . 96 C3
Farriers Cl KT17 . . . 76 E7
Farriers Ct
Belmont SM2 . . . 58 E3
Wimbledon SW19 . . . 19 E1
Farriers Rd KT17 . . . 76 E8
Farriers The GU5 . . . 152 A5
Farthing Ct 3 SL5 . . . 30 B2
Farthingfield Ho GU9 . . . 125 C3
Farthingham La GU6 . . . 175 E6
Farthings GU21 . . . 68 E3
Farthings The 1 KT2 . . . 38 A8
Farthings Wlk RH12 . . . 216 F3
Farwig La BR1 . . . 44 F8
Fassett Rd KT1 . . . 37 E5
Fauconberg Ct W4 . . . 7 C8
Fauconberg Rd W4 . . . 7 C8
Faulkner Pl GU19 . . . 47 F4
Faulkner's Rd KT12 . . . 54 C5
Faversham Ct SE6 . . . 23 F7
Faversham Rd
Beckenham BR3 . . . 43 F7
Forest Hill SE6 . . . 23 F7
Morden SM4 . . . 40 B3
Sandhurst GU47 . . . 45 D1
Fawcett Cl SW16 . . . 22 A4
Fawcett Rd CR0, CR9 . . . 61 C7
Fawcus Cl KT10 . . . 55 E4
Fawler Mead RG12 . . . 27 F5
Fawley Cl GU6 . . . 174 F2
Fawley Ct SE27 . . . 22 B6
Fawn Dr GU12 . . . 105 E3
Fawns Manor Cl TW14 . . . 14 C7
Fawns Manor Rd TW14 . . . 14 D7
Fawsley Cl SL3 . . . 1 E7
FAYGATE . . . 199 F1
Faygate Bsns Ctr RH12 . . . 199 F1
Faygate Ct CR2 . . . 61 B3
Faygate La
Blindley Heath RH9 . . . 142 E3
Faygate RH12 . . . 199 F4
Faygate Rd SW2 . . . 21 F6
Faygate Sta RH12 . . . 199 F1
Fayland Ave SW16 . . . 21 C3
Fay Rd RH12 . . . 217 C5
Fays Pas 12 GU1 . . . 130 C8
Fearn Cl KT24 . . . 112 E6
Fearnley Cres TW12 . . . 15 F2
Featherbed La CR0, CR6 . . . 82 C7
Feathercombe La GU8 . . . 171 E4
Feathers La TW19 . . . 12 A6
Featherstone RH7 . . . 142 D1
Featherstone Ave SE23 . . . 23 C6
Fee Farm Rd KT10 . . . 55 F3
FELBRIDGE . . . 184 F4
Felbridge Ave RH10 . . . 202 D7
Felbridge Cl
Belmont SM2 . . . 59 B2
East Grinstead RH19 . . . 185 C3
Frimley GU16 . . . 65 F1
Streatham SW16 . . . 22 A4
Felbridge Ct
East Grinstead RH19 . . . 185 A4
Feltham TW13 . . . 15 B7
Harlington UB3 . . . 3 D8
South Croydon CR2 . . . 61 C3
Felbridge Ctr The RH19 . . . 185 A3
Felbridge Prim Sch RH19 . . . 184 F4
Felbridge Rd RH19 . . . 184 D3
Felcote Ho RH2 . . . 138 F7
Felcot Rd RH19 . . . 184 C4
Felcott Cl KT12 . . . 54 C7
Felcott Rd KT12 . . . 54 C7
FELCOURT . . . 185 C8
Felcourt Cotts RH19 . . . 185 C8
Felcourt La RH19 . . . 164 C1
Felcourt Rd RH19, RH7 . . . 185 C7
Felday Glade RH5 . . . 155 B5
Felday Hos RH5 . . . 155 C7
Felday Rd RH5 . . . 133 F3
Feldemore Cotts RH5 . . . 155 C6
Feld The RH19 . . . 185 A4
Felicia Ct GU7 . . . 150 E4
Felix Dr GU4 . . . 111 A7
Felix La TW17 . . . 34 F3
Felix Rd KT12 . . . 35 A3
Felland Way RH2 . . . 139 D5
Fellbrook TW10 . . . 17 B5
Fellcott Way RH12 . . . 216 F1
Fellmongers Yd 4 CR0 . . . 61 C7
Fellowes Ct UB3 . . . 3 D8
Fellowes Rd SM1, SM5 . . . 59 E8
Fellow Gn GU24 . . . 67 F6
Fellow Green Rd GU24 . . . 67 F6
Fellows Rd GU14 . . . 85 D1
Fell Rd CR0, CR9 . . . 61 C7
Felmingham Rd SE20 . . . 43 C7
Felnex Trad Est SM6 . . . 60 A8
Felsberg Rd SW2 . . . 21 E8
Felside Ct KT13 . . . 53 A5
Felstead Rd KT19 . . . 76 D8
FELTHAM . . . 15 B6
Feltham Arena TW14 . . . 15 A8
Feltham Ave KT8 . . . 36 E5
Felthambrook Ind Est TW13 . . . 15 B5
Felthambrook Way TW13 . . . 15 B3
Feltham Bsns Complex TW13 . . . 15 B6
Feltham Com Coll TW13 . . . 15 C6
Feltham Corporate Ctr TW13 . . . 15 B5
FELTHAMHILL . . . 14 F3
Feltham Hill Jun & Inf Schs TW13 . . . 14 F5
Feltham Hill Rd
Ashford TW15 . . . 14 C2
Feltham TW13 . . . 15 C3
Feltham Rd
Ashford TW15 . . . 14 C4
Mitcham CR4 . . . 41 A7
Redhill RH1 . . . 139 F4
Feltham Sta TW13 . . . 15 B7
Feltham Wlk RH1 . . . 139 F4
Feltonfleet Sch KT11 . . . 72 E6
Felwater Ct RH19 . . . 185 A3
Fenby Cl RH13 . . . 218 C4
Fenchurch Rd RH10 . . . 202 B4
Fencote RG12 . . . 27 D3
Fendall Rd KT19 . . . 57 C5
Fender Ho RH12 . . . 217 B2
Fenemore Rd CR3 . . . 100 D7
Fengates Rd RH1 . . . 118 E1
Fenhurst Cl RH12 . . . 216 F1
Fennel Cl
Ascot SL5 . . . 29 A5
Croydon CR0 . . . 43 D1
Fennel Cl *continued*
Farnborough GU14 . . . 84 B4
Guildford GU1 . . . 110 B4
Fennel Cres RH11 . . . 201 B2
Fennells Mead KT17 . . . 57 F2
Fenner Ho KT12 . . . 54 A6
Fenn Ho TW7 . . . 6 B6
Fenning Ct CR4 . . . 40 E5
Fennscombe Ct GU24 . . . 67 F6
Fenns La GU24 . . . 67 E5
Fenn's Way GU21 . . . 69 E4
Fenns Yd GU9 . . . 125 B2
Fenstanton Prim Sch SW2 . . . 22 A7
Fenton Ave TW18 . . . 13 C3
Fenton Cl RH1 . . . 119 A1
Fenton Ct TW5 . . . 4 E7
Fenton Ho TW5 . . . 5 A8
Fenton Lo GU15 . . . 65 E6
Fenton Rd RH1 . . . 119 A1
Fentum Rd GU2 . . . 109 A3
Fenwick Cl GU21 . . . 69 B1
Fenwick Pl CR2 . . . 61 B3
Ferguson Ave KT5 . . . 37 F4
Ferguson Cl BR2 . . . 44 D6
Fermandy La RH10 . . . 184 A1
Fermor Dr GU11 . . . 104 F3
Fermor Rd SE23 . . . 23 E7
Fern Ave CR4 . . . 41 D5
Fernbank Ave KT12 . . . 35 E2
Fernbank Cres SL5 . . . 28 D8
Fernbank Pl SL5 . . . 28 D7
Fernbank Rd
Addlestone KT15 . . . 52 A5
North Ascot SL5 . . . 28 D8
Fernbrae Cl GU10 . . . 146 B3
Fern Cl
Crowthorne RG45 . . . 45 A7
Frimley GU16 . . . 66 C3
Warlingham CR6 . . . 81 E1
Fern Cotts RH5 . . . 133 E4
Fern Ct GU12 . . . 105 F1
Ferndale GU3 . . . 108 E3
Ferndale Ave
Addlestone KT16 . . . 51 E7
Hounslow TW4 . . . 4 E4
Ferndale Rd
Ashford TW15 . . . 13 E3
Banstead SM7 . . . 77 F3
Croydon SE25 . . . 43 B4
Woking GU21 . . . 69 F3
Fernden Hts GU27 . . . 208 B2
Fernden La GU27 . . . 208 C2
Fernden Rise GU7 . . . 150 E7
Ferndown
Crawley RH10 . . . 182 D2
Horley RH6 . . . 161 A5
5 Kingston u T KT6 . . . 37 E4
Ferndown Cl
Guildford GU1 . . . 131 A8
Sutton SM2 . . . 59 D4
Ferndown Ct GU10 . . . 146 D5
Ferndown Gdns
Cobham KT11 . . . 73 C6
Farnborough GU14 . . . 84 E4
Fernery The TW18 . . . 12 E3
Ferney Ct KT14 . . . 71 D8
Ferney Meade Way TW7 . . . 6 A5
Ferney Rd KT14 . . . 71 D7
Fern Gr TW14 . . . 15 B8
Ferngrove Cl KT22 . . . 94 E4
Fernham Rd CR7 . . . 42 C6
Fernhead 18 SM1 . . . 59 C6
FERNHILL . . . 182 E7
Fernhill KT22 . . . 74 D5
Fernhill Cl
Crawley Down RH10 . . . 184 B1
Farnborough GU17 . . . 64 F1
Hale GU9 . . . 125 B6
Woking GU22 . . . 89 D7
Fernhill Ct KT2 . . . 17 D3
Fernhill Dr GU9 . . . 125 B6
Fernhill Gdns KT2 . . . 17 E3
Fernhill Ho GU14 . . . 85 D2
Fernhill La
Farnborough GU17 . . . 64 F1
Hale GU9 . . . 125 B6
Woking GU22 . . . 89 C7
Fernhill Pk GU22 . . . 89 D7
Fernhill Prim Sch GU14 . . . 64 F1
Fern Hill Prim Sch KT2 . . . 17 E2
Fernhill Rd
Blackwater GU14, GU17 . . . 64 E2
Crawley RH6 . . . 182 D7
Farnborough, West Heath GU14 . . . 84 E6
Fernhill Sch GU14 . . . 64 F1
Fernhill Wlk GU17 . . . 64 F1
Fernhurst Cl RH11 . . . 201 B8
Fernhurst Rd
Ashford TW15 . . . 14 C4
Croydon CR0 . . . 43 B1
Ferniehurst GU15 . . . 65 F4
Fernihough Cl KT13 . . . 72 A8
Fernlands Cl KT16 . . . 51 E7
Fernlea KT23 . . . 94 B3
Fern Lea GU9 . . . 126 B6
Fernlea Pl KT11 . . . 73 D7
Fernlea Rd
Balham SW12 . . . 21 B7
Mitcham CR4 . . . 41 A8
Fernleigh Cl
Croydon CR0 . . . 61 A6
Walton-on-T KT12 . . . 54 B7
Fernleigh Ct GU14 . . . 85 B4
Fernleigh Rise GU16 . . . 86 C7
Fernley Ho GU7 . . . 150 E8
Fern Lo 14 SW16 . . . 22 A3
Fern Rd GU7 . . . 150 F6
Ferns Cl CR2 . . . 62 B1
Fernside Ave TW13 . . . 15 B4
Fernside Rd SW12 . . . 21 A8
Ferns Mead GU9 . . . 125 B1
Ferns The 4 GU14 . . . 105 D8
Fernthorpe Rd SW16 . . . 21 C2
Fern Twrs CR3 . . . 101 A2
Fern Way RH12 . . . 217 D5
Fern Wlk TW15 . . . 13 D3
Fernwood
New Addington CR0, CR2 . . . 62 E2
Putney SW19 . . . 19 F7
Fernwood Ave SW16 . . . 21 D4
Feroners Cl RH10 . . . 202 A4
Feroners Ct RH10 . . . 202 A4
Ferrard Cl SL5 . . . 28 D8
Ferraro Cl TW5 . . . 5 A8
Ferrers Ave SM6 . . . 60 D6
Ferrers Rd SW16 . . . 21 D3
Ferriby Ct RG12 . . . 27 C7
Ferriers Ct RH12 . . . 217 C2
Ferring Cl RH11 . . . 201 B8
Ferrings SE21 . . . 22 E5
Ferris Ave CR0 . . . 62 F7
Ferry Ave TW18 . . . 12 E1
Ferry La
Barnes SW13 . . . 7 F8
Brentford TW8 . . . 6 E8
Chertsey KT16 . . . 33 A3
Guildford GU2, GU3 . . . 130 C5
Laleham TW18 . . . 33 C6
Lower Halliford TW17 . . . 34 A1
Richmond TW9 . . . 6 F8
Wraysbury TW19 . . . 12 B5
Ferrymoor TW10 . . . 17 B5
Ferry Quays Ctyd 15 TW8 . . . 6 D8
Ferry Rd
East Molesey KT8 . . . 36 A6
Richmond TW11 . . . 17 B3
Thames Ditton KT7 . . . 37 B3
Twickenham TW1 . . . 17 B7
Ferry Sq
1 Brentford TW8 . . . 6 E8
Lower Halliford TW17 . . . 34 B2
Ferry Wks TW17 . . . 34 A1
Festival Cotts SL3 . . . 1 C7
Festival Ct
Cheam SM1 . . . 40 B1
Crawley RH10 . . . 202 C4
FETCHAM . . . 94 C4
Fetcham Common La KT22 . . . 94 B6
Fetcham Grove Cotts KT22 . . . 95 A5
Fetcham Lo KT22 . . . 94 D5
Fetcham Park Dr KT22 . . . 94 E4
Fetcham Village Inf Sch KT22 . . . 94 D5
Fettes Rd GU6 . . . 175 A3
FICKLESHOLE . . . 82 E5
Fiddicroft Ave SM7 . . . 78 C5
Field Cl
Chessington KT9 . . . 56 C5
Cranford TW4 . . . 4 B6
East Molesey KT8 . . . 36 B4
Guildford GU4 . . . 110 D3
Hamsey Green CR2 . . . 81 B5
Harlington UB7 . . . 3 C7
Fieldcommon La KT12 . . . 35 F1
Field Ct
Oxted RH8 . . . 122 E8
Wimbledon SW19 . . . 20 A5
Fieldend
Horsham RH12 . . . 218 B5
Teddington TW1 . . . 16 F4
Field End
Coulsdon CR5 . . . 79 D5
Farnham GU9 . . . 125 F4
West End GU24 . . . 67 F6
Fieldend Rd SW16 . . . 41 C8
Fielden Pl RG12 . . . 27 D7
Fielders Gn 3 GU1 . . . 110 A1
Fieldgate Ct KT11 . . . 73 A5
Field Ho 8 TW10 . . . 17 C5
Field House Cl SL5 . . . 29 A1
Fieldhouse Rd SW12 . . . 21 C7
Fieldhouse Villas SM7 . . . 78 E4
Fieldhurst Cl KT15 . . . 52 B5
Fielding Ave TW2 . . . 16 C5
Fielding Gdns RG45 . . . 45 B4
Fielding Ho 3 W4 . . . 7 E8
Fielding Rd GU47 . . . 64 E6
Fieldings The
Banstead SM7 . . . 77 F2
Forest Hill SE23 . . . 23 C7
Horley RH6 . . . 161 C4
Woking GU21 . . . 68 F3
Field La
Brentford TW8 . . . 6 C7
Farncombe GU7 . . . 150 F7
Frimley GU16 . . . 65 E1
Teddington TW11 . . . 17 A3
Fieldpark Gdns CR0 . . . 43 E1
Field Path GU14 . . . 64 F1
Field Pk RG12 . . . 27 D8
Field Pl KT3 . . . 38 F3
Field Rd
Farnborough GU14 . . . 64 F1
Feltham TW14 . . . 4 B1
Fieldsend Rd SM3 . . . 58 E5
Fieldside Rd BR1 . . . 24 D3
Field Stores App GU11 . . . 105 C3
Fieldview
Horley RH6 . . . 161 B4
Wandsworth SW17, SW18 . . . 20 D7
Field View
Egham TW20 . . . 12 C3
Feltham TW13 . . . 14 D5
Field View Cotts GU7 . . . 150 B4
Fieldview Ct TW18 . . . 13 A2
Fieldway GU27 . . . 208 C7
Field Way
Aldershot GU12 . . . 105 E3
New Addington CR0 . . . 63 B4
Send Marsh GU23 . . . 90 F2
Tongham GU10 . . . 126 F7
Field Wlk RH6 . . . 162 C4
Fiennes Ct RH12 . . . 217 D6
Fifehead Cl TW15 . . . 13 E2
Fife Rd
Kingston u T KT2 . . . 37 E7
Mortlake SW14 . . . 7 C2
Fife Way KT23 . . . 94 A2
Fifield La GU10 . . . 146 C2
Fifield Path SE23 . . . 23 D5
Fifth Cross Rd TW2 . . . 16 D6
Figge's Rd CR4 . . . 21 A1
Figgs Wood CR5 . . . 99 C5
Filbert Cres RH11 . . . 201 A6
Filby Rd KT9 . . . 56 F4
Filey Cl
Biggin Hill TN16 . . . 103 B8
Crawley RH11 . . . 200 F4
Sutton SM2 . . . 59 C3
Filmer Gr GU7 . . . 150 E5
Finborough Rd SW17 . . . 20 F2
Finchampstead Rd RG41, RG40 . . . 25 B3
Finch Ave SE27 . . . 22 D4
Finch Cl GU21 . . . 68 C2
Finch Cres RH10 . . . 204 C5
Finchdean Ho SW15 . . . 18 F8
Finch Dr TW14 . . . 15 D8
Finches Rise GU1 . . . 110 C3
Finch Rd 9 GU1 . . . 109 D1
Finch's Cross RH8 . . . 144 A8
Findhorn Cl GU47 . . . 64 D7
Findings The GU14 . . . 84 E8
Findlay Dr GU3 . . . 108 F5
Findon Ct KT15 . . . 51 F5
Findon Rd RH11 . . . 201 B8
Findon Way RH12 . . . 216 D3
Finlay Gdns KT15 . . . 52 C6
Finlays Cl KT9 . . . 57 A5
Finmere RG12 . . . 27 C2
Finnart Cl KT13 . . . 53 C6
Finney Dr GU20 . . . 48 D4
Finney La TW7 . . . 6 A6
Finsbury Cl RH11 . . . 201 C2
Finstock Gn RG12 . . . 27 F5
Finton House Sch SW17 . . . 20 F6
Fintry Pl GU14 . . . 84 E7
Fintry Wlk GU14 . . . 84 E7
Finucane Ct TW9 . . . 6 F4
Fiona Cl KT23 . . . 94 A3
Fir Acre Rd GU12 . . . 106 A6
Firbank 3 BR3 . . . 43 F7
Firbank Ct BR2 . . . 44 D6
Firbank Dr GU21 . . . 89 B8
Firbank La GU21 . . . 89 B8
Firbank Pl TW20 . . . 11 B2
Firbank Way RH19 . . . 185 D1
Fir Cl KT12 . . . 35 A2
Fircroft 2 KT22 . . . 95 C6
Fircroft Cl GU22 . . . 69 F1
Fircroft Ct 10 GU22 . . . 69 F1
Fircroft Prim Sch SW17 . . . 20 F5
Fircroft Rd
Chessington KT9 . . . 56 F6
Englefield Green TW20 . . . 11 C1
Upper Tooting SW17 . . . 20 F5
Firdene KT5 . . . 38 C1
Fir Dr GU17 . . . 64 D3
Fireball Hill SL5 . . . 29 D2
Fire Bell Alley KT6 . . . 37 E3
Fire Station Flats TW7 . . . 5 E5
Fire Station Mews BR3 . . . 44 B8
Fire Station Rd GU11 . . . 105 B3
Firfield Rd
Addlestone KT15 . . . 52 A6
Farnham GU9 . . . 146 A7
Firfields KT13 . . . 53 B4
Fir Gr KT3 . . . 38 F3
Fir Grange Ave KT13 . . . 53 B5
Firgrove GU21 . . . 89 B8
Firgrove Ct
7 Farnborough GU14 . . . 85 B4
Farnham GU9 . . . 125 C1
Firgrove Hill GU9 . . . 125 C1
Firgrove Par 5 GU14 . . . 85 B4
Firgrove Rd 6 GU14 . . . 85 B4
Firhill Rd SE6 . . . 24 A5
Firlands
Bracknell RG12 . . . 27 C4
Horley RH6 . . . 161 B4
North Ascot SL5 . . . 28 D6
Weybridge KT13 . . . 53 E4
Firlands Ave GU15 . . . 65 D5
Firle Cl RH10 . . . 201 E8
Firmston Ho 10 SW14 . . . 7 D4
Fir Rd
Cheam SM3 . . . 39 F1

Fir Rd *continued*
Feltham TW13 15 D3
Firs Ave
Bramley GU5 152 A6
Mortlake SW14 7 C3
Firsby Ave CR0 43 E1
Firs Cl
Claygate KT10 55 E4
Dorking RH4 136 A5
Farnborough GU14 85 C2
Forest Hill SE23 23 E8
Mitcham CR4 41 B8
Firsdene Cl KT16 51 D4
Firs Dr TW5 4 B7
Firs La GU5 152 D4
Firs Rd CR8 80 B4
First Ave
East Molesey KT8 36 A5
Mortlake SW14 7 E4
Walton-on-T KT12 35 B3
West Ewell KT19 57 E2
Woodham KT15 52 B2
First Cl KT8 36 C6
First Cross Rd TW2 16 E6
Firs The
Artington GU3 130 B5
Belmont SM2 59 B3
Bisley GU24 68 A3
[6] Bracknell RG12 27 F5
[2] Caterham CR3 100 D5
Claygate KT10 55 E4
East Molesey KT7 36 E5
Ewell KT17 77 A5
Forest Hill SE26 23 C3
[2] Forest Hill, Upper Sydenham SE26 23 B3
Great Bookham KT23 94 C3
Lower Kingswood KT20 97 F1
Wimbledon SW20 19 A1
First Quarter Bsns Pk KT19 76 E8
Firstway SW20 39 C7
Firsway GU2 109 A2
Firswood Ave KT19 57 F5
Fir Tree Alley [14] GU11 105 A2
Firtree Ave CR4 41 A7
Fir Tree Ave GU27 207 D6
Fir Tree Cl
Ascot SL5 29 A2
Banstead KT17 77 C4
Crawley RH11 181 B1
Esher KT10 55 C5
Leatherhead KT22 95 C4
Streatham SW16 21 C3
Worcester Park KT19 57 F6
Firtree Ct BR2 44 F6
Fir Tree Gdns CR0 63 A6
Fir Tree Gr SM5 59 F3
Firtree Ho SE13 24 D8
Fir Tree Rd
Banstead KT17, SM7 77 D5
Guildford GU1 109 D4
Hounslow TW4 4 E3
Leatherhead KT22 95 C4
Fir Tree Wlk RH2 118 D1
Firway GU26 187 E5
Fir Wlk KT17, SM3 58 D4
Firwood Cl GU21 88 E8
Firwood Ct GU15 65 C5
Firwood Dr GU15 65 C5
Firwood Rd GU25 30 E3
Fisher Cl
Crawley RH10 201 E4
Croydon CR0 42 F1
Hersham KT12 54 B6
Fisherdene KT10 56 A3
Fisher La
Chiddingfold GU8 210 E7
Dunsfold GU8 211 B7
Fisherman Cl TW10 17 C4
Fisherman Ho KT16 33 C1
Fishermen's Cl GU11 105 E5
Fisher Rowe Cl GU5 152 A6
Fishers Cl SW16 21 D5
Fishers Ct
Horsham RH12 217 C4
[7] Teddington TW11 16 F3
FISHER'S HILL 88 F6
FISHERSTREET 209 F3
Fishers Wood SL5 30 C1
Fishing Temple Park Homes TW18 32 F8
Fishponds Cl RG41 25 A4
Fishponds Est RG41 25 A4
Fishponds Rd
Upper Tooting SW17 20 F4
Wokingham RG41 25 A4
Fisk Cl TW16 14 F2
Fiske Ct
[1] Merton SW19 20 C1
Sutton SM2 59 C3
Fitch Ct CR4 41 A7
Fitchet Cl RH11 201 B8
Fitzalan Rd
Claygate KT10 55 E3
Horsham RH12, RH13 218 A4
Fitzgeorge Ave KT2, KT3 38 D8
Fitzgerald Ave SW14 7 E4
Fitzgerald Rd
Mortlake SW14 7 D4
Thames Ditton KT7 37 A3
Fitzhardinge Ho BR3 44 B7
Fitzherbert Ho [12] TW10 6 F1
Fitzjames Ave CR0 62 A8
Fitzjohn Cl GU4 110 C4
Fitzrobert Pl TW20 12 A2
Fitzroy Cl RG12 27 A3
Fitzroy Cres W4 7 D7
Fitzroy Gdns SE19 22 E1
Fitzroy Pl RH2 118 D1
Fitzwilliam Ave TW9 6 F5
Fitzwilliam Ho TW9 6 D3
Fitzwilliam Hts SE23 23 C6
Fitz Wygram Cl TW12 16 C3
Fiveacre Cl CR7 42 A3
Five Acres RH10 201 E8
Five Oaks Cl GU21 88 E8
Five Oaks Rd RH12, RH13 216 B2
Flag Cl CR0 43 D1
Flambard Way GU7 150 E4
Flamborough Cl TN16 103 B8
Flamsteed Hts RH11 201 B1
Flanchford Ho [2] RH2 118 A2
Flanchford Rd RH2 138 D5
Flanders Cotts GU5 152 D5
Flanders Cres SW17, SW19 20 F2
Flanders Ct TW20 12 C3
Flatford Ho SE6 24 C4
Flather Cl [12] SW16 21 C3
Flats The GU17 64 C4
Flat The [3] GU7 150 D4
Flaxley Rd SM4 40 B2
Flaxmore Ct CR7 42 D7
Fleece Rd KT6 37 C1
Fleet Cl KT8 35 F4
Fleet Rd
Aldershot GU11 104 D6
Blackwater GU51 84 A4
Farnborough GU14 84 C4
Fleet GU11, GU14 104 D6
Fleetside KT8 36 A4
Fleet Terr SE6 24 C8
Fleetway TW20 32 C6
Fleetwood Cl
Chessington KT9 56 D3
South Croydon CR0 61 F7
Tadworth KT20 97 D7
Fleetwood Ct
[8] Stanwell TW19 2 E1
[3] West Byfleet KT14 71 A6
Fleetwood Rd KT3 38 B6
Fleetwood Sq KT3 38 B6
Fleming Cl GU14 85 D6
Fleming Ct CR0 61 A5
Fleming Ctr The RH10 181 E2
Fleming Mead CR4, SW19 20 F1
Fleming Way
Crawley RH10, RH11 181 F2
Isleworth TW7 5 F3
Fleming Wlk RH19 205 F6
Flemish Fields KT16 33 A2
Flemming Ho KT19 57 B2
Fletcher Cl
Crawley RH10 201 E4
Ottershaw KT16 51 E4
Fletcher Gdns RG42 26 D8
Fletcher Rd KT16 51 D4
Fletchers Cl RH13 217 E1
Fleur Gates [7] SW19 19 D8
FLEXFORD 107 C1
Flexford Gn RG12 26 E3
Flexford Rd GU3 107 C1
Flexlands Sch GU24 68 F8
Flimwell Cl BR1 24 E3
Flint Cl
Banstead SM7 78 B5
Crawley RH10 202 B3
Great Bookham KT23 94 C1
Redhill RH1 118 F2
Flint Ct CR0 41 F3
Flintgrove RG12 27 D8
Flint Hill RH4, RH5 136 B5
Flint Hill Cl RH4 136 B4
Flintlock Cl TW19 2 A3
Flitwick Grange GU8 149 F1
Flock Mill Pl SW18 20 B7
Flockton Ho KT13 53 A8
Flood La [5] TW1 17 A7
Flora Gdns CR0 82 C8
Floral Ct KT21 75 C1
Floral Ho KT16 32 F1
Florence Ave
Morden SM4 40 C4
Woodham KT15 71 A8
Florence Cl KT12 35 B2
Florence Cotts
Kingston u T SW15 18 E5
Winkfield SL4 8 C7
Florence Ct
Knaphill GU21 68 C1
[5] Wimbledon SW19 19 E2
Florence Gdns
Chiswick W4 7 C8
Staines TW18 13 B1
Florence Ho [5] KT2 17 F1
Florence Rd
Feltham TW13 15 B7
[6] Kingston u T KT2 17 F1
Penge BR3 43 E7
Sandhurst GU47 64 E7
South Croydon CR2 61 D2
Walton-on-T KT12 35 B2
Wimbledon SW19 20 B2
Florence Terr SW15 18 E5
Florence Villas GU18 48 B1
Florence Way
Knaphill GU21 68 C1
Upper Tooting SW12 20 F7
Florian Ave SM1 59 D6
Florida Ct
Beckenham BR2 44 F5
Staines TW18 13 A3
Florida Rd
Shalford GU4 130 E3
South Norwood CR7 42 B8
Florys Ct [7] SW19 19 E7
Flower Cres KT16 51 C4
Flower La RH9 121 D6
Flowersmead SW17 21 A6
Flower Wlk GU2 130 C6
Floyd's La GU22 71 A3
Foden Rd GU11 105 A1
Foley Cotts KT10 55 F4
Foley Mews KT10 55 E4
Foley Rd
Biggin Hill TN16 83 D1
Claygate KT10 55 E3
Follyfield Rd SM7 78 A5
Folly Hill GU9 125 A5
Folly Hill Inf Sch GU9 125 A6
Folly La RH5 157 B7
Folly La N GU9 125 B6
Folly La S GU9 125 A6
Fontaine Ct [3] BR3 43 F8
Fontaine Rd SW16 21 F1
Fontana Cl RH10 202 E5
Fontenoy Rd SW12, SW17 21 C6
Fonthill Cl SE20 43 A7
Fonthill Ct SE23 23 C8
Fonthill Lodge Sch RH19 205 C6
Fontigarry Farm Bsns Pk RH2 160 C8
Fontley Way SW15 19 A8
Fontmell Cl TW15 14 A3
Fontmell Pk TW15 14 A3
Fontwell Cl GU12 105 D2
Fontwell Rd RH10 202 A3
Forbench Cl GU23 91 B5
Forbes Chase GU47 64 D7
Forbes Cl RH10 202 B2
Forbes Ct SE19 22 E3
Forburys GU9 146 B8
Fordbridge Cl KT16 33 B1
Fordbridge Ct TW15 13 E2
Fordbridge Rd
Ashford TW15 13 F3
Sunbury TW16 35 A5
Upper Halliford TW16, TW17 34 F3
Ford Cl
Ashford TW15 13 E2
Littleton TW17 34 A4
Thornton Heath CR7 42 B4
Fordel Rd SE6 24 D7
Ford Ho TW20 11 C1
Fordingbridge Cl RH12 217 C1
Fordington Ho SE26 23 B5
Ford La GU10 146 B6
Ford Manor Cotts RH7 165 B1
Ford Manor Rd RH7 165 B2
Fordmill Rd SE6 24 A6
Ford Rd
Ashford TW15 13 F4
Bisley GU24 67 F4
Chertsey KT16 33 B1
Chobham GU24 49 C1
Old Woking GU22 90 B7
Fordwater Rd KT15, KT16 33 B1
Fordwater Trad Est KT16 33 C1
Fordwells Dr RG12 27 F5
Fordyce Ho [3] SW16 21 C4
Foreman Pk GU12 106 B2
Foreman Rd GU12 106 B1
Forest Cl
Bracknell SL5 28 C6
Crawley Down RH10 204 B8
East Horsley KT24 92 F2
Horsham RH12 218 B4
Woking GU22 70 D4
Forest Cres KT21 76 A3
Forest Croft SE23 23 B6
Forest Ct RG41 25 A4
FORESTDALE 62 F2
Forestdale GU26 188 E3
Forestdale Ctr The CR0 62 F3
Forestdale Prim Sch CR0 62 F2
Forest Dene Ct [10] SM2 59 C4
Forest Dr
Charlton TW16 14 F1
Farnham GU10 146 C4
Kingswood KT20 98 A6
Forest End Rd GU47 64 A8
Forester Rd RH10 201 E4
Foresters Cl
Knaphill GU21 68 F1
Wallington SM6 60 D3
Foresters Dr CR8, SM6 60 D2
Foresters Prim Sch SM6 60 D4
Foresters Sq RG12 27 E6
Foresters The RH13 217 F1
Foresters Way RG45 45 F1
FOREST ESTATE 11 A2
Forestfield
Crawley RH10 202 B3
Forestfield *continued*
Horsham RH13 218 A3
Forest Gate RH11 201 D1
Forest Glade GU10 145 D3
Forest Gn RG12 27 D7
FOREST GREEN 176 E7
FOREST HILL 23 D7
Forest Hill Bsns Ctr SE23 23 C6
Forest Hill Ct SE26 23 B5
Forest Hill Ind Est SE23 23 C6
Forest Hill Rd SE23 23 C8
Forest Hills GU15 65 B4
Forest Hill Sec Sch SE23 23 D5
Forest Hill Sta SE23 23 C6
Forestholme Cl SE23 23 C6
Forest Ho The SE23 23 E7
Forest La KT24 92 F3
Forest Lo
[2] East Grinstead RH19 205 F8
Forest Hill SE23 23 C5
Forest Mews RH12 218 B5
Forest Oaks RH13 218 B4
Forest Rd
Cheam SM3, SM4 40 A2
Crowthorne RG45 45 C5
East Horsley KT24 92 F2
Faygate RH12, RH13 218 D5
Feltham TW13 15 C5
Richmond TW9 7 A7
Windsor SL4 9 E7
Winkfield RG42, SL5 8 D2
Woking GU22 70 D4
Forest Ridge BR3 44 A6
FOREST ROW 206 F3
Forest Row Bsns Pk RH18 206 F3
Forest Row CE Prim Sch RH18 206 F2
Forest Sch The RH13 217 F1
Forest Side KT4 38 F1
Forest View RH10 202 A3
Forest View Rd RH19 205 E6
FOREST WALK 27 E3
Forest Way
Ashtead KT21 76 A3
Newell Green RG42 8 A2
Forest Wlk GU6 173 F2
Forge Ave CR5 100 B7
Forge Bridge La CR5 99 B5
Forge Cl
Broadbridge Heath RH12 216 D4
Farnham GU9 125 D3
Harlington UB3 3 D8
Forge Cotts KT23 93 F4
Forge Dr KT10 56 A3
Forge End GU21 69 E2
Forgefield TN16 83 D3
Forge La
Broadbridge Heath RH12 216 D4
Cheam SM3 58 E3
Crawley RH10 202 A7
Farnborough GU11 105 A6
Feltham TW13 15 E3
Richmond TW10 17 E7
Sunbury TW16 35 A6
Forge Lane Prim Sch TW13 15 E3
Forge Lo [2] TW7 6 A4
Forge Mews
Addington CR0 63 A5
Sunbury TW16 35 A6
Forge Pl RH6 160 E1
Forge Rd
Crawley RH10 202 A7
Sleaford GU35 166 A1
Forge Steading SM7 78 B4
Forge The RH12 216 E7
Forge Wood RH10 182 D3
Forge Wood Ind Est RH10 182 B2
Forman Ct TW1 16 F7
Forrester Path SE26 23 C4
Forrest Gdns SW16 41 F6
Forster Ho SE6 24 D5
Forster Park Prim Sch SE6 24 E5
Forster Rd
Beckenham BR3 43 E6
Guildford GU2 109 A5
Streatham SW2 21 E8
Thornton Heath CR0 42 C2
Forsyte Cres SE19 42 E8
Forsyte Ct KT2 38 B8
Forsyth Ct KT3 38 E7
Forsythe Shades BR3 44 C8
Forsythia Pl GU1 109 C3
Forsyth Path GU21 70 D6
Forsyth Rd GU21 70 C5
Fortescue Ave TW2 16 C5
Fortescue Rd
Mitcham SW19 20 D1
Weybridge KT13 52 F6
Forth Cl GU14 84 D6
Fort La RH2 118 B5
Fort Narrien GU15 64 F7
Fort Rd
Box Hill KT20 116 B4
Guildford GU1 130 E6
Fortrose Cl GU47 64 D7
Fortrose Gdns SW12, SW2 21 E7
Fortune Dr GU6 174 E1
Fortyfoot Rd KT22 95 C6
Forum The
Chertsey KT16 32 F1
East Molesey KT8 36 B5
[3] Horsham RH12 217 C2
Forval Cl CR4 40 F4
Foss Ave CR0, CR9 61 A5
Fosseway RG45 45 A5
Fosse Way KT14 70 F6
Fossewood Dr GU15 65 D7
Foss Rd SW17 20 D4
Fosterdown RH9 121 B6
Fosters Gr GU20 48 B6
Fosters La GU21 68 C2
Foulser Rd SW17 21 A5
Foulsham Rd CR7 42 D6
Foundation Units GU1 109 E5
Founders Gdns SE19 22 C1
Foundry Cl RH13 217 E4
Foundry Ct KT16 33 A2
Foundry Ct RH13 217 E3
Foundry La
Haslemere GU27 208 A6
Horsham RH13 217 E3
Horton SL3 1 B4
Foundry Mews [1] KT16 33 A2
Foundry Pl SW18 20 B8
Fountain Ct
New Malden KT3 38 C5
Penge SE26 23 C2
Fountain Dr
Dulwich SE19 22 F4
Wallington SM5 59 F2
Fountain Ho [3] CR4 40 F7
Fountain Rd
Redhill RH1 139 E7
South Norwood CR7 42 C7
Upper Tooting SW17 20 D4
Fountains Ave TW13 15 F5
Fountain Sch SM5 59 F1
Fountains Cl
Crawley RH11 201 A4
Feltham TW13 15 F5
Fountains Garth RG12 27 A6
Four Acres
Cobham KT11 73 E6
Guildford GU1 110 C3
Four Seasons Cres SM3 58 F8
Four Square Ct TW4 5 A1
Fourth Cross Rd TW2 16 D6
Fourth Dr CR5 79 D3
Fourways [2] CR0 61 F8
Four Wents KT11 73 C5
Fowler Ave GU14 85 B2
Fowler Cl RH10 202 C4
Fowler Rd
Farnborough GU14 84 F3
Mitcham CR4 41 A7
Fowlerscroft GU3 129 B2
Fowlers La RG42 27 B8
Fowlers Mead GU24 49 E2
Fowler's Rd GU11 105 D6
Foxacre CR3 100 E5
Foxborough Hill Rd GU5 151 D6
Foxbourne Rd SW17 21 A6
Foxbridge La RH14 212 C1
Foxburrow Hill GU5 151 D6
Foxburrows Ave GU2 108 F2
Foxburrows Ct GU2 108 F2
Fox Cl
Crawley RH11 181 B1
Weybridge KT13 53 D5
Woking GU22 70 D4
Foxcombe CR0 63 B4
Foxcombe Rd [6] SW15 19 A7
FOX CORNER 88 C2
Fox Covert
Fetcham KT22 94 D3
Lightwater GU18 67 A8
Fox Covert Cl SL5 29 C4
Fox Ct
Aldershot GU12 105 E3
Sandhurst GU47 64 C8
Fox Dene GU7 150 C2
Foxdown Cl GU15 65 C5
Foxearth Cl TN16 83 E1
Foxearth Rd CR2 62 C2
Foxearth Spur CR2 62 C2
Foxenden Rd GU1 109 E1
Foxes Dale BR2 44 D6
Foxes Path GU4 89 F1
Foxglove Ave RH12 217 E6
Foxglove Cl
Stanwell TW19 13 D7
Winkfield RG42 8 A2
Foxglove Gdns
Guildford GU4 110 C3
Purley CR8 79 F8
Foxglove La KT9 57 A6
Foxglove Way CR4 41 B1
Foxglove Wlk RH11 201 B3
Fox Gr KT12 35 B2
Foxgrove Ave BR3 24 B1
Foxgrove Dr GU21 70 A4
Foxgrove Rd BR3 24 C1
Foxhanger Gdns GU22 70 A3
Foxhaven Ct SL5 29 C4
Foxheath RG12 27 E4
Fox Heath GU14 84 C3
Fox Hill SE19 22 F1
Foxhill Cres GU15 66 B8
Fox Hill Gdns SE19 22 F1
Fox Hill Prim Sch RG12 27 B4

Foxhills GU21 69 C2
Foxhills Cl KT16 51 C4
Fox Hills La GU12 106 C3
Foxhills Mews KT16 51 B7
Fox Hills Rd KT16 51 B5
Fox Ho KT16 32 F1
Foxholes
Rudgwick RH12 214 D8
Weybridge KT13 53 D5
Foxhurst Rd GU12 106 A4
Fox La
Little Bookham KT23 93 F3
Reigate RH2 118 B4
Foxlake Rd KT14 71 F7
Fox La N KT16 32 F1
FOX LANE 84 F8
Fox La S KT16 32 F1
Foxleigh Chase RH12 217 F5
Foxley Cl
Blackwater GU17 64 C5
Redhill RH1 140 A4
Foxley Ct SM2 59 C3
Foxley Gdns CR8 80 B6
Foxley Hall CR8 80 A6
Foxley Hill Rd CR8 80 A7
Foxley La CR8 60 E1
Foxley Lo 5 CR8 80 A7
Foxley Rd
Purley CR8 80 B5
Thornton Heath CR7 42 B5
Foxoak Hill KT12 53 E1
Foxon Cl CR3 100 E6
Foxon La CR3 100 E6
Foxon Lane Gdns CR3 100 E6
Fox Path CR4 40 E7
Fox Rd
Bracknell RG12 27 C5
Farnham GU10 146 C7
Haslemere GU27 207 E6
Foxtail Ho TW3 5 C6
Foxton KT1 38 A6
Foxton Gr CR4 40 D7
Foxwarren KT10 55 F2
Fox Way GU10 124 D8
Foxwood Cl
Feltham TW13 15 B5
Wormley GU8 190 F8
Fox Yd GU9 125 B2
Frailey Cl GU22 70 B3
Frailey Hill GU22 70 B3
Framfield Cl RH11 201 A8
Framfield Rd CR4 21 A1
Frampton Cl SM2 59 A3
Frampton Rd TW4 4 E2
France Hill Dr GU15 65 C5
Frances Ct
Ascot SL5 29 D5
South Norwood SE25 42 F7
Franche Court Rd
SW17 20 C5
Francis Ave TW13 15 A5
Francis Barber Cl
SW16 21 F4
Franciscan Prim Sch
SW17 21 A3
Franciscan Rd SW17 21 A4
Francis Chichester Cl
SL5 29 B4
Francis Cl
Littleton TW17 34 A5
West Ewell KT19 57 D6
Francis Cnr KT24 133 B8
Francis Crick Rd GU2 129 D8
Francis Ct
Farnborough GU14 84 F4
Guildford GU2 109 B3
Kingston u T KT5 37 E5
Francis Edwards Way
RH11 200 E2
Francis Gr SW19 19 F2
Francis Rd
Caterham CR3 100 D5
Hounslow TW4 4 D5
Thornton Heath CR0 42 B2
Wallington SM6 60 C4
Francis Way GU15 66 C4
Frangate KT24 112 E8
Frank Dixon Cl SE21 22 E7
Frank Dixon Way SE21 22 E7
Frankland Ho 4 SW12 21 B8
Franklands Dr KT15 51 F3
Franklin Cl
Kingston u T KT1 38 A6
West Norwood SE27 22 B5
Franklin Cres CR4 41 C5
Franklin Ct
Farnborough GU14 84 C4
2 Guildford GU2 108 F1
Wormley GU8 170 F1
Franklin Ho BR2 44 E7
Franklin Ind Est SE20 43 C8
Franklin Rd
Crawley RH10 202 C5
Penge SE20 43 C8
Walton-on-T KT12 35 A3
Franklin Way CR0, CR9 41 E2
Franklyn Rd
Godalming GU7 150 B3
Walton-on-T KT12 35 B3
Franks Ave KT3 38 C5
Franksfield GU5 154 E7
Franks Ho TW7 6 B3
Franks Rd GU2 109 A3
Frank Towell Ct TW14 15 A7
Fransfield Gr SE26 23 B5
Frant Cl SE20 23 C1
Franthorne Way SE6 24 B5
Frant Rd CR0, CR7 42 B4
Fraser Ct TW5 4 E7
Fraser Gdns RH4 136 A8
Fraser Mead GU47 64 E6
Fraser Rd RG42 27 B8
Frederick Cl SM1 58 F5
Frederick Gdns
Cheam SM1 58 F5
Thornton Heath CR0 42 B3
Frederick Ho TW15 13 E4
Frederick Pl RG41 25 A6
Frederick Rd SM1 58 F5
Frederick Sanger Rd
GU2 129 D8
Frederick St GU11 105 A2
Freeborn Way RG12 27 E7
Freedown La SM2 78 C6
Freehold Ind Ctr TW4 4 C2
Freelands Ave CR2 62 D2
Freelands Rd KT11 73 B5
Freeman Cl TW17 34 E5
Freeman Ct SW16 41 E7
Freeman Dr KT8 35 F5
Freeman Ho 13 SW2 21 E8
Freeman Rd
Morden CR4, SM4 40 D4
Warnham RH12 216 F8
Freemantle Rd GU19 47 F4
Freemantles Sch KT16 32 E2
Freemason's Rd CR0 42 E1
Free Prae Rd KT16 33 A1
Freesia Dr GU24 68 A3
Freethorpe Cl SE19 42 E8
French Apartments The
CR8 80 A7
Frenchaye KT15 52 C5
Frenches Ct 4 RH1 119 A3
Frenches Rd RH1 119 B4
Frenches The RH1 119 A3
French Gdns
Blackwater GU17 64 D4
Cobham KT11 73 C5
Walton-on-T KT12 35 F1
French La GU8 169 E3
Frenchlands Hatch
KT24 112 E8
French St TW16 35 C7
FRENSHAM 167 D7
Frensham RG12 27 D3
Frensham Ct
Mitcham CR4 40 D6
Rowledge GU10 146 B4
Frensham Ctry Pk*
GU10 167 E5
Frensham Dr
New Addington CR0 63 C3
Roehampton SW15 19 A6
Frensham Heights Fst Sch
GU10 146 A2
Frensham Heights Rd
GU10 146 A2
Frensham Ho 7 KT6 37 E4
Frensham La GU35,
GU10 166 F1
Frensham Rd
Crowthorne RG45 45 B7
Farnham GU10, GU9 146 D6
Purley CR8 80 B5
Frensham Vale GU10 146 C4
Frensham Way KT17 77 C3
Frere Cotts KT23 94 C1
Fresham Ho BR2 44 F6
Freshborough Ct 1
GU1 130 F8
Freshfield KT20 117 F8
Freshfield Bank RH18 206 E2
Freshfield Cl RH10 202 A5
Freshfields CR0 43 F1
Freshford Ct 16 BR2 44 F5
Freshford St SW17,
SW18 20 C5
Freshmount Gdns
KT19 76 B8
Freshwater Cl SW17 21 A2
Freshwater Rd SW17 21 A2
Freshwood Cl BR3 44 B8
Freshwoods RH12 214 D8
Freshwood Way SM6 60 C2
Frewin Rd SW18 20 D7
Friar Mews SE27 22 B5
Friars Ave SW15 18 F5
Friars Croft GU4 110 C4
Friars Ct
Farnham GU9 125 D7
5 Wallington SM6 60 B6
Friars Field GU9 125 B3
Friar's Gate GU2 130 A7
Friars Keep RG12 27 B5
Friars La TW9 6 D2
Friars Orch KT22 94 D6
Friars Rd GU25 31 D5
Friars Rise GU22 70 A1
Friars Rookery RH10 201 F6
Friars Stile Pl 10 TW10 6 E1
Friars Stile Rd TW10 6 E1
Friars Way KT16 33 A3
Friars Wood CR0 62 E2
Friary Bridge GU1 130 C7
Friary Ct GU21 68 F1
Friary Ho 4 GU1 130 C8
Friary Island SL4 11 C8
Friary Rd
Ascot SL5 29 B3
Wraysbury TW19 11 C8
Friary St GU1 130 C7
Friary The 5 GU1 130 C8
Friary Way RH10 201 E5
Friday Grove Mews
SW12 21 C8
Friday Rd CR4 20 F1
Friday St
Abinger Common RH5 155 F8
Faygate RH12 198 E6
Ockley RH5 177 E4
Warnham RH12 216 E7
Friend Ave GU12 105 D1
Friends Cl RH11 181 D1
Friendship Way RG12 27 B6
Friends Rd CR8 80 B7
Friends' Rd CR0, CR9 61 D7
Friends Wlk 1 TW18 12 F3
Friern Rd SE22 23 A8
FRIMLEY 65 F2
Frimley Ave SM6 60 F5
Frimley Bsns Pk GU16 85 B8
Frimley CE Jun Sch
GU16 85 E7
Frimley Cl
New Addington CR0 63 C3
Putney SW19 19 E6
Frimley Cres CR0 63 C3
Frimley Gdns CR4 40 E6
FRIMLEY GREEN 85 F6
Frimley Green Rd
GU16 85 E7
Frimley Grove Gdns
GU16 65 E1
Frimley Hall Dr GU15 65 F6
Frimley High St GU16 85 D8
Frimley Ho CR4 40 E6
Frimley Park Hospl
GU16 65 D2
Frimley Rd
Ash Vale GU12 106 A8
Camberley GU15, GU16 65 B3
Chessington KT9 56 E5
FRIMLEY RIDGE 66 B3
Frimley Sq GU16 65 E1
Frimley Sta GU16 85 C8
Frinton Rd SW17 21 A2
Friston Wlk RH11 201 A7
Fritham Cl KT3 38 E3
FRITHEND 166 C4
Frith End Rd GU34,
GU35 166 A6
FRITH HILL 150 E6
Frith Hill Rd
Farncombe GU7 150 D6
Frimley GU16 66 B1
Frith Knowle KT12 54 B5
Frith Pk RH19 185 E3
Frith Rd CR0, CR9 61 C8
Friths Dr RH2 118 B4
Frithwald Rd KT16 32 F2
Frobisher RG12 27 C2
Frobisher Cl CR8 80 C2
Frobisher Cres TW19 13 E8
Frobisher Ct
Belmont SM2 58 F3
Forest Hill SE23 23 B6
Frobisher Gdns
Guildford GU1 110 A2
Stanwell TW19 13 E8
Frodsham Way GU47 45 E2
Froggetts La RH5 176 C1
Frog Grove La GU3 107 F4
Frog Hall RG40 25 F5
Frog Hall Dr RG40 25 E5
Frog La
Bracknell RG12 27 A6
Woking GU4 89 E2
FROGMORE 64 C6
Frogmore Cl SM3 58 E7
Frogmore Comm Coll
GU46 64 A5
Frogmore Ct GU17 64 C4
Frogmore Gdns SM3 58 E6
Frogmore Gr GU17 64 C4
Frogmore Inf Sch
GU17 64 B5
Frogmore Jun Sch
GU17 64 B5
Frogmore Park Dr
GU17 64 D4
Frogmore Rd GU17 64 C5
Frome Cl GU14 84 D6
Fromondes Rd SM3 58 E5
Fromow Gdns GU20 48 D4
Froxfield Down 6
RG12 27 F4
Fruen Rd TW14 14 F8
Fry Cl RH11 201 B1
Fryern Wood CR3 100 C3
Fry La GU19 47 D2
Frylands Ct CR0 82 C8
Fry's Cross GU8 193 A2
Fryston Ave
Croydon CR0 62 A8
Wallington CR5 79 B5
Fuchsia Way GU24 67 E6
Fuel Farm Rd
Crawley RH6 181 E8
Hookwood RH6 160 E1
Fulbourn 4 KT1 38 A7
Fulbourne Cl RH1 118 E3
Fulbrook La GU8 148 C5
Fulford Rd
Caterham CR3 100 D6
West Ewell KT19 57 D3
Fulham Cl RH11 201 B2
Fullbrook Ave KT15 71 A8
Fullbrooks Ave KT4 38 F1
Fullbrook Sch KT15 71 A8
Fullers Ave KT6 56 F8
Fullers Farm Rd KT24 112 B1
Fullers Rd GU10 145 D3
Fullers Vale GU35 187 A5
Fullers Way N KT6 56 F7
Fullers Way S KT9 56 E7
Fuller's Wood CR0 63 A6
Fullers Wood La RH1 119 C1
Fullerton Cl KT14 71 F5
Fullerton Ct 9 TW11 17 A3
Fullerton Dr KT14 71 E5
Fullerton Rd
Byfleet KT14 71 F5
Croydon CR0 42 F2
Wallington SM5 59 E2
Fullerton Way KT14 71 E5
Fullmer Way KT15 51 F1
Fulmar Cl 1 RH11 200 D5
Fulmar Ct
Surbiton KT5 37 F3
6 West Norwood SE21 22 D6
Fulmar Dr RH19 186 B3
Fulmer Cl TW12 15 E3
Fulstone Cl TW4 4 F3
Fulvens GU5 133 E1
Fulwell Ct TW11 16 E4
Fulwell Park Ave TW2 16 C6
Fulwell Rd TW11 16 D4
Fulwell Sta TW11 16 D4
Fulwood Ct TW19 2 F1
Fulwood Gdns TW1 6 A1
Fulwood Wlk SW19 19 F7
Furlong Cl CR4 41 B1
Furlong Rd RH4 135 C6
Furlong Way RH6 181 F8
Furlough The GU22 70 A2
Furmage St SW18 20 B8
Furnace Dr RH10 201 F4
Furnace Farm Rd
RH10 202 A4
FURNACE GREEN 202 A5
Furnace Par RH10 202 A4
Furnace Pl RH10 202 A4
Furnance Farm Rd
RH19 184 C3
Furneaux Ave SE27 22 B3
Furness Lo SW14 7 B3
Furness Rd SM4 40 B3
Furniss Ct GU6 173 F2
Furnival Cl GU25 31 D3
Furrows Pl CR3 100 F4
Furrows The KT12 54 C8
Furse Cl GU15 66 C4
Furtherfield GU6 174 E4
Furtherfield Cl CR0 42 A3
Further Green Rd SE6 24 E7
Furzebank SL5 29 D5
Furze Cl
Ash Vale GU12 106 A7
Horley RH6 161 D3
Redhill RH1 118 F2
Furzecroft 4 TW15 14 A3
Furze Ct CR0 62 A8
FURZEDOWN 21 B4
Furzedown Cl TW20 11 E2
Furzedown Dr SW17 21 B3
Furzedown Prim Sch
SW17 21 A2
Furzedown Rd
Streatham SW17 21 B3
Sutton SM2 78 C8
Furzefield RH11 201 C7
Furze Field KT22 74 E6
Furzefield Chase
RH19 185 E6
Furzefield Cres RH2 139 C7
Furzefield Prim Sch
RH1 119 D7
Furzefield Rd
East Grinstead RH19 185 D4
Horsham RH12 218 B5
Reigate RH2 139 C7
Furze Gr KT20 97 F6
Furze Hall KT20 97 F6
Furzehill RH1 118 E2
Furze Hill
Kingswood KT20 97 F6
Purley CR8 79 F8
Furze Hill Cres RG45 45 C4
Furze Hill Rd GU35 187 C4
Furze La
East Grinstead RH19 185 B4
Farncombe GU7, GU3 150 F8
Purley CR8 79 F8
Furzeland Ho 2 KT3 38 E2
Furzemoors RG12 27 B4
Furzen Cotts RH12 196 A3
Furzen La RH12, RH5 196 B4
Furze Rd
Addlestone KT15 51 F4
Rudgwick RH12 214 D8
South Norwood CR7 42 C6
Furze Vale Rd GU35 187 B4
Furzewood TW16 35 A8
Furzey Hill Camping Gd
GU24 87 B5
Fuscia Ct TW13 14 F5
Fusion Ct SW15 18 E5
Fydlers Cl SL4 9 B2
Fyfield Cl
Beckenham BR2 44 D5
Blackwater GU17 64 D5

G

Gable Ct
Forest Hill SE26 23 B4
9 Redhill RH1 119 A2
Gable End
6 Aldershot GU11 105 B2
Farnborough GU14 85 B4
Gable Lo BR4 44 C1
Gables Ave TW15 13 F3
Gables Cl
Ash Vale GU12 106 A5
Farnborough GU14 85 A4
Old Woking GU22 89 F7
Gables Ct
Cheam SM3 58 D6
Old Woking GU22 89 F7
Gables The
Banstead SM7 77 F2
Copthorne RH10 183 B3
Elstead GU8 148 C3
Grayshott GU26 188 D3
Horsham RH12 217 D4
Hounslow TW5 5 A8
Mitcham CR4 41 B6
Oxshott KT22 74 C7
Weybridge KT13 53 C5
Gables Way SM7 77 F3
Gabriel Cl TW13 15 D4
Gabriel Dr GU15 66 B4
Gabriel Rd RH10 202 C2
Gabriel St SE23 23 E8
Gadbridge La GU6 175 E4
Gadbrook Rd RH3 137 D4
Gadd Cl RG40 25 F7
Gadesden Rd KT19 57 C4
Gaffney Cl GU11 105 D7
Gage Cl RH10 184 C1
Gage Ridge RH18 206 E2
Gainsborough RG12 27 C3
Gainsborough Cl
Beckenham BR3 24 A1
Camberley GU15 65 F7
Farnborough GU14 85 D2
Thames Ditton KT10 36 E1
Gainsborough Ct
Dulwich SE21 22 E6
Farnborough GU12 105 C8
Walton-on-T KT12 54 A6
Worcester Park KT19 57 F4
Gainsborough Dr
North Ascot SL5 28 D7
Sanderstead CR2 81 A6
Gainsborough Gdns
TW7 5 D2
Gainsborough Ho
RH10 201 D6
Gainsborough Mews
SE26 23 B5
Gainsborough Rd
Crawley RH10 201 F3
Epsom KT19 57 C1
New Malden KT3 38 D2
Richmond TW9 6 F4
Gaist Ave CR3 101 B5
Galahad Ho 20 RH1 119 A2
Galahad Rd RH11 200 E6
Galba Ct 1 TW8 6 D7
Gale Cl
Hampton TW12 15 E2
Mitcham CR4 40 D6
Gale Cres SM7 78 A2
Gale Dr GU18 48 A1
Gale Ho SM5 59 E5
Galen Cl KT19 76 A8
Gales Cl
Guildford GU4 110 D3
Haslemere GU27 207 E5
Gales Dr RH10 201 F6
Gales Pl RH10 201 F6
Galgate Cl 4 SW19 19 E7
Galileo Ct RG12 27 E7
Gallery Ct 14 TW20 12 A3
Gallery Rd
Dulwich SE21 22 D7
Pirbright GU24 87 D8
Galleymead Rd SL3 1 F6
Gallica Ct SM1 40 B1
Gallop The
South Croydon CR2 62 B3
Sutton SM2 59 D2
Galloway Path CR0 61 D6
Gallwey Rd GU11 105 C3
Galpin's Rd CR4, CR7 41 F5
Galsworthy Rd
6 Chertsey KT16 33 A2
Kingston u T KT2 38 B8
Galton Rd SL5 29 F3
Galvani Way CR0, CR9 41 F1
Galvins Cl GU2 109 A4
Gambles La GU23 91 C2
Gambole Rd SW17 20 E4
Gamma Ct 8 CR0 42 D1
Gander Green Cres
TW12 36 A8
Gander Green La KT4, SM1,
SM3 58 F7
Gangers Hill RH9 121 F7
Ganghill GU1 110 A3
Gannet Ct 5 SE21 22 D6
Ganymede Ct RH11 200 E3
Gapemouth Rd GU16,
GU24 86 E5
Gap Rd SW19 20 B3
Garbetts Way GU10 126 F6
Garbrand Wlk KT17 57 F2
Garden Ave CR4 21 B1
Garden Cl
Addlestone KT15 52 D6
Ashford TW15 14 C2
Banstead SM7 78 A4
East Grinstead RH19 205 F7
Farnborough GU14 84 E3

Garden Cl *continued*
Hampton TW12 . . . 15 F3
Leatherhead KT22 . . . 95 C3
Putney SW15 . . . 19 B8
Shamley Green GU5 . . . 152 D4
Wallington SM6 . . . 60 E5
Garden Cotts SL3 . . . 1 D7
Garden Ct
10 Belmont SM2 . . . 59 A3
Bromley BR1 . . . 24 F1
Hampton TW12 . . . 15 F3
4 Richmond TW9 . . . 6 F6
South Croydon CR0 . . . 61 F7
Wimbledon SW20 . . . 39 D8
Gardeners Cl RH12 . . . 216 E8
Gardeners Ct 2 RH13 . . . 217 D1
Gardeners Gn RH12 . . . 199 C6
GARDENERS GREEN . . . 25 F2
Gardener's Hill Rd GU10 . . . 146 B4
Gardeners Rd
Thornton Heath CR0 . . . 42 B1
Winkfield RG42 . . . 8 A2
Gardener's Wlk KT23 . . . 94 B1
Gardenfields KT20 . . . 97 E8
Garden Flats SW16 . . . 21 E5
Garden Ho The SL5 . . . 30 C4
Garden House La RH19 . . . 205 F7
Gardenia Ct 1 BR3 . . . 24 A1
Gardenia Dr GU24 . . . 67 F6
Garden La SW2 . . . 21 F7
Garden Pl 2 RH12 . . . 217 C4
Garden Prim Sch CR4 . . . 41 D6
Garden Rd
Mortlake TW9 . . . 7 A4
Penge SE20 . . . 43 C8
Walton-on-T KT12 . . . 35 B2
Gardens The
Beckenham BR3 . . . 44 D7
Esher KT10 . . . 55 A6
Hatton TW14 . . . 3 D1
Pirbright GU24 . . . 87 F5
Tongham GU10 . . . 126 F7
Garden Wlk
Beckenham BR3 . . . 43 F8
Crawley RH11 . . . 201 C6
Hooley CR5 . . . 99 B4
3 Horsham RH12 . . . 217 C4
Garden Wood Rd RH19 . . . 205 C8
Gardiner Ct CR2 . . . 61 D4
Gardner Ct TW3 . . . 5 A4
Gardner Ho TW13 . . . 15 F6
Gardner Ind Est SE26 . . . 23 F3
Gardner La RH10 . . . 204 A8
Gardner Pl TW14 . . . 4 B1
Gardner Rd GU1 . . . 109 D1
Garendon Gdns SM4 . . . 40 B2
Garendon Rd SM4 . . . 40 B2
Gareth Cl KT4 . . . 58 D8
Gareth Ct SW16 . . . 21 D5
Garfield Prim Sch SW19 . . . 20 C2
Garfield Rd
Addlestone KT15 . . . 52 C6
Camberley GU15 . . . 65 C5
3 Twickenham TW1 . . . 17 A7
Wimbledon SW19 . . . 20 C2
Garibaldi Rd RH1 . . . 139 F8
Garland Dr TW3 . . . 5 C5
Garland Ho 18 KT2 . . . 37 E8
Garland Rd RH19 . . . 185 D2
Garlands Ct CR0 . . . 61 D6
Garlands Rd
Leatherhead KT22 . . . 95 C6
Redhill RH1 . . . 118 F1
Garland Way CR3 . . . 100 D5
Garlichill Rd KT17, KT18 . . . 77 B2
Garlies Rd SE23 . . . 23 E5
Garner Ct 13 TW19 . . . 2 E1
Garnet Ct TW13 . . . 14 E5
Garnet Ho KT4 . . . 38 D1
Garnet Rd CR7 . . . 42 D5
Garrad's Rd SW16 . . . 21 D4
Garrard Rd SM7 . . . 78 A3
Garrat La SW17, SW18 . . . 20 C5
Garratt Cl CR0 . . . 60 E6
Garratt La SW17, SW18 . . . 20 C5
Garratt Park Sec Sch SW18 . . . 20 C5
Garratts La SM7 . . . 78 A3
Garratt Terr SW17 . . . 20 E4
Garraway Ho SE21 . . . 22 F5
Garrett Cl RH10 . . . 202 C4
Garrett Mews 9 GU11 . . . 105 A1
Garrick Cl
Hersham KT12 . . . 54 B6
1 Richmond TW9 . . . 6 D2
Staines TW18 . . . 13 A1
Garrick Cres CR0 . . . 61 E8
Garrick Gdns KT8 . . . 36 A6
Garrick Ho
4 Chiswick W4 . . . 7 E8
2 Kingston u T KT1 . . . 37 E5
7 Streatham SW16 . . . 21 C3
Garrick Rd TW9 . . . 7 A5
Garrick's Ait KT8 . . . 36 C7
Garricks ho KT1 . . . 37 D7
Garrick's Villa TW12 . . . 36 C7
Garrick Way GU16 . . . 85 E7
Garrick Wlk RH10 . . . 201 E3
Garrison Cl TW4 . . . 4 F2
Garrison La KT9 . . . 56 E3
Garrones The RH10 . . . 202 E7
Garside Cl TW12 . . . 16 B2
Garson Cl KT10 . . . 54 F4
Garson La TW19 . . . 11 D8
Garson Rd KT10 . . . 54 F4
Garson's La SL4 . . . 8 A7
Garston Gdns CR8 . . . 80 D4
Garston La CR8 . . . 80 D4
Garstons The KT23 . . . 94 A2
Garswood RG12 . . . 27 D3
Garth Cl
Farnham GU9 . . . 146 A7
Kingston u T KT2 . . . 17 F3
West Barnes SM4 . . . 39 D2
Garth Ct W4 . . . 7 D8
Garth Hill Coll RG12 . . . 27 C8
Garthorne Rd SE23 . . . 23 D8
Garth Rd
Chiswick W4 . . . 7 D8
Kingston u T KT2 . . . 17 F3
West Barnes SM4 . . . 39 D2
Garth Road Ind Ctr The SM4 . . . 39 D1
Garthside TW10 . . . 17 E3
Garth The
Ash GU12 . . . 105 F1
Cobham KT11 . . . 73 E6
Farnborough GU14 . . . 85 D4
Hampton TW12 . . . 16 B2
Gartmoor Gdns SW19 . . . 19 F7
Garton Cl RH11 . . . 200 E5
Garvens SE19 . . . 22 E3
Gascoigne Rd
New Addington CR0 . . . 63 C2
Weybridge KT13 . . . 53 B7
Gasden Copse GU8 . . . 170 D5
Gasden Dr GU8 . . . 170 D6
Gasden La GU8 . . . 170 D6
Gaskyns Cl RH12 . . . 214 D7
Gassiot Rd SW17 . . . 20 F4
Gassiot Way SM1 . . . 59 D7
Gasson Wood Rd RH11 . . . 200 E4
Gaston Bell Cl TW9 . . . 6 F4
Gaston Bridge Rd
Shepperton TW17 . . . 34 D3
Upper Halliford TW17 . . . 34 E4
Gaston Rd CR4 . . . 41 A6
Gaston Way TW17 . . . 34 D4
Gatcombe Cres 2 SL5 . . . 28 F8
Gatcombe Ct BR3 . . . 24 A1
Gate Ct 4 KT13 . . . 53 B7
Gateford Dr RH12 . . . 217 F6
Gate Ho 4 KT6 . . . 37 E1
Gatehouse Cl KT2 . . . 18 C1
Gatehouse Lo RH1 . . . 140 A6
Gates Cl RH10 . . . 202 C2
Gatesden Cl KT22 . . . 94 C4
Gatesden Rd KT22 . . . 94 C4
Gates Green Rd BR4 . . . 63 F7
Gateside Rd SW17 . . . 20 F5
Gatestone Ct 11 SE19 . . . 22 E2
Gatestone Rd SE19 . . . 22 E2
Gate Way 7 KT13 . . . 53 B7
Gateway 3 KT9 . . . 57 A6
Gateway Ho
11 Guildford GU1 . . . 130 C8
3 Upper Tooting SW17 . . . 20 E2
Gateways
Guildford GU1 . . . 131 B8
Kingston u T KT6 . . . 37 E4
Gateways Ct SM6 . . . 60 B5
Gateways The TW9 . . . 6 D3
Gateway The GU21 . . . 70 C5
Gatfield Gr TW13 . . . 16 A6
Gatfield Ho TW13 . . . 16 A6
Gatley Ave KT19 . . . 57 B5
Gatley Dr GU1 . . . 109 F4
GATTON . . . 118 F7
Gatton Bottom
Gatton RH2, RH1 . . . 118 E7
Merstham RH1, RH2 . . . 119 B8
Gatton Cl
Belmont SM2 . . . 59 B2
Reigate RH2 . . . 118 C4
Gatton Park Ct RH1 . . . 118 F4
Gatton Park Rd RH1, RH2 . . . 118 E4
Gatton Point RH1 . . . 119 A5
Gatton Prim Sch SW17 . . . 20 E4
Gatton Rd
Reigate RH2 . . . 118 C4
Upper Tooting SW17 . . . 20 E4
Gatwick Airport Beehive Area RH6 . . . 182 B5
Gatwick Airport-London RH6 . . . 181 F7
Gatwick Airport Sta RH6 . . . 182 B7
Gatwick Aviation Mus★ RH6 . . . 180 F5
Gatwick Gate Est RH11 . . . 181 E5
Gatwick Ho RH6 . . . 182 E7
Gatwick Metro Ctr RH6 . . . 161 B3
Gatwick Park Hospl (private) RH6 . . . 160 E2
Gatwick Rd
Crawley RH6, RH10 . . . 182 A3
Wandsworth SW18 . . . 19 F8
Gatwick Way RH6 . . . 181 F8
Gauntlett Rd SM1 . . . 59 D5
Gavell Rd KT11 . . . 73 A6
Gaveston Cl KT14 . . . 71 F6
Gaveston Rd KT22 . . . 95 A7
Gavina Cl SM4 . . . 40 E4
Gawton Cres CR5 . . . 99 C5
Gayfere Rd KT17 . . . 58 A5
Gayhouse La RH1 . . . 162 E8
Gayler Cl RH1 . . . 120 F2
Gaynesford Rd
Forest Hill SE23 . . . 23 D6
Wallington SM5 . . . 59 F3
Gays Cotts RH7 . . . 143 A2
Gayton Cl KT21 . . . 75 E1
Gayton Ct
New Malden KT3 . . . 38 F4
Reigate RH2 . . . 118 A2
Gaywood Cl SW2 . . . 22 A7
Gaywood Rd KT21 . . . 75 F1
Gearing Cl SW17 . . . 21 A4
Geary Cl RH6 . . . 162 B1
Gedge Ct CR4 . . . 40 E5
Geffers Ride SL5 . . . 28 E7
Gemima Ct SM1 . . . 59 A5
Gemini Cl RH11 . . . 200 E4
Gemini Ct 11 CR8 . . . 80 A8
Gemma Ct BR3 . . . 43 F7
Gemmell Cl CR8 . . . 79 F5
Genesis Bsns Ctr RH13 . . . 217 F3
Genesis Bsns Pk GU21 . . . 70 C4
Genesis Cl TW19 . . . 13 F7
Genesis Ho KT6 . . . 37 D1
Geneva Cl TW17 . . . 34 E7
Geneva Rd
Kingston u T KT1 . . . 37 E5
Thornton Heath CR7 . . . 42 C4
Genoa Rd SE20 . . . 43 C8
Gentles La GU30, GU35 . . . 187 A3
Genyn Rd GU2 . . . 130 B8
Geoffrey Ct TW18 . . . 13 A1
George Abbot Sch GU1 . . . 110 A3
George Denyer Cl GU27 . . . 208 C7
George Eliot Cl GU8 . . . 170 F4
George Gdns GU11 . . . 126 C7
George Groves Rd SE20 . . . 43 A8
Georgeham Rd GU47 . . . 45 D2
George Ho
8 Penge SE26 . . . 23 B3
16 Richmond TW9 . . . 6 D2
George Horley Pl RH5 . . . 158 B1
Georgelands GU23 . . . 91 B6
George Pinion Ct RH12 . . . 217 B3
George Rd
Farncombe GU7 . . . 150 F7
Guildford GU1 . . . 109 D1
Kingston u T KT2 . . . 18 C1
Milford GU8 . . . 149 F2
New Malden KT3 . . . 38 F4
George Sq SW19 . . . 40 A6
George's Rd TN16 . . . 103 D7
George St
Croydon CR0, CR9 . . . 61 D8
Hounslow TW3, TW5 . . . 4 F5
Pirbright GU24 . . . 87 A6
Richmond TW10 . . . 6 D2
Staines TW18 . . . 12 F4
Georges Terr CR3 . . . 100 D5
Georgetown Cl 4 SE19 . . . 22 E3
George Wyver Cl SW18 . . . 19 E8
Georgian Cl
Camberley GU15 . . . 65 E7
Crawley RH10 . . . 202 D5
Staines TW18 . . . 13 B4
Georgian Ct CR0, CR9 . . . 42 D1
Georgia Rd
Kingston u T KT3 . . . 38 C5
South Norwood CR7 . . . 42 B8
Georgina Ct 5 TW1 . . . 6 C1
Gerald Ct RH13 . . . 217 E2
Geraldine Rd W4 . . . 7 A8
Gerald's Gr SM7 . . . 77 D5
Geranium Cl RG45 . . . 45 B8
Gerard Ave TW4 . . . 16 A8
Gerardes Lo GU27 . . . 208 D8
Gerard Rd SW13 . . . 7 F6
Germander Dr GU24 . . . 68 A4
German Sch The TW10 . . . 17 D7
Gerrards Mead SM7 . . . 77 F3
Ghent St SE6 . . . 24 A6
Ghyll Cres RH13 . . . 217 F1
Gibbet La GU15 . . . 66 A7
Gibbon Rd KT2 . . . 17 F1
Gibbons Cl
Crawley RH10 . . . 202 C3
Sandhurst GU47 . . . 64 C8
Gibb's Acre GU24 . . . 87 F4
Gibbs Ave SE19 . . . 22 D3
Gibbs Brook La RH8 . . . 143 D6
Gibbs Cl SE19 . . . 22 D3
Gibbs Ho
6 Balham SW12 . . . 21 B8
2 Bromley BR1 . . . 44 F8
Gibbs Sq SE19 . . . 22 D3
Giblets La RH12 . . . 217 F7
Giblets Way RH12 . . . 217 E7
Gibraltar Cres KT19 . . . 57 E1
Gibson Cl
Chessington KT9 . . . 56 C5
Isleworth TW7 . . . 5 D4
Gibson Ct KT10 . . . 55 F7
Gibson Ho
South Croydon CR2 . . . 61 C4
Sutton SM1 . . . 59 A6
Gibson Mews 14 TW1 . . . 6 C1
Gibson Pl TW19 . . . 2 C1
Gibson Rd SM1 . . . 59 B5
Gibson's Hill
South Norwood SW16 . . . 22 A1
South Norwood SW16 . . . 22 A2
Gidd Hill CR5 . . . 79 A3
Giffard Dr GU14 . . . 84 F5
Giffards Cl RH19 . . . 185 F1
Giffards Mdw GU9 . . . 125 E1
Giffard Way GU2 . . . 109 A4
Giggshill Gdns KT7 . . . 37 A1
Giggs Hill Rd KT7 . . . 37 A2
Gilbert Cl 1 SW19 . . . 40 B8
Gilbert Ct CR5 . . . 79 D3
Gilbert Rd
Frimley GU15 . . . 65 C2
Merton SW19 . . . 20 C1
Gilbert Scott Jun & Inf Com Sch CR2 . . . 62 E3
Gilberts Lo KT17 . . . 76 E8
Gilbert St TW3 . . . 5 C4
Gilbey Rd SW17 . . . 20 E3
Gilders Rd KT9 . . . 56 F4
Giles Coppice SE19 . . . 22 F4
Gilesmead KT18 . . . 76 E5
Giles Travers Cl TW20 . . . 32 C6
Gilham La RH18 . . . 206 E2
Gilham's Ave SM7 . . . 77 E7
Gill Ave GU2 . . . 129 E8
Gillespie Ho GU25 . . . 31 E5
Gillett Ct RH13 . . . 218 B4
Gillette Cnr TW7 . . . 6 A7
Gillett Ho RH13 . . . 218 B4
Gillett Rd CR7 . . . 42 D5
Gillham's La GU27 . . . 207 A5
Gilliam Gr CR8 . . . 61 A1
Gilliams Ho 12 RH4 . . . 136 A7
Gillian Ave GU11, GU12 . . . 126 D8
Gillian Cl GU12 . . . 126 D8
Gillian Park Rd SM3 . . . 39 F1
Gilliat Dr GU4 . . . 110 D3
Gilligan Cl RH12 . . . 217 B2
Gillman Lo TN16 . . . 83 C7
Gillray Ho 2 SM1 . . . 59 D5
Gilmais KT23 . . . 94 C2
Gilmore Cres TW15 . . . 14 A2
Gilpin Ave SW14 . . . 7 D3
Gilpin Cl CR4 . . . 40 E7
Gilpin Cres TW2 . . . 16 B8
Gilpin Ho KT3 . . . 38 E4
Gilpin Way UB3 . . . 3 D7
Gilsland Rd CR7 . . . 42 D5
Gilson Ct SL4 . . . 11 C8
Gilton Rd SE6 . . . 24 E5
Gimcrack Hill KT22 . . . 95 B5
Gingell Ho TW20 . . . 11 D3
Gingers Cl GU6 . . . 174 F2
Ginhams Rd RH11 . . . 201 B6
Gipsy Hill SE19 . . . 22 E3
Gipsy Hill Sta SE19 . . . 22 E3
Gipsy La
Bracknell RG12 . . . 27 D7
Wokingham RG40 . . . 25 C4
Gipsy Rd SE21, SE27 . . . 22 D4
Gipsy Road Gdns SE27 . . . 22 C4
Girdwood Rd SW18, SW19 . . . 19 E8
Girling Way TW14 . . . 4 A4
Girtin Ho 12 SM2 . . . 59 B3
Girton Cl GU47 . . . 45 E1
Girton Gdns CR0 . . . 63 A7
Girton Rd SE26 . . . 23 D3
Gisbourne Cl SM6 . . . 60 D7
Gittens Cl BR1 . . . 24 F4
GIVONS GROVE . . . 95 C2
Gladebury Ct 2 SW19 . . . 19 F2
Glade Cl KT6 . . . 56 D8
Glade Gdns CR0 . . . 43 E2
Glade Ho SL5 . . . 29 C4
Glade Mews GU1 . . . 130 F8
Gladeside CR0 . . . 43 D3
Gladeside Cl KT9 . . . 56 D3
Gladeside Ct CR6 . . . 101 B7
Glade Spur KT20 . . . 98 B6
Glades The RH19 . . . 186 B1
Glade The
Ascot SL5 . . . 29 C4
Belmont SM2 . . . 58 E2
Coulsdon CR5, CR8 . . . 100 A8
Crawley RH10 . . . 202 A4
Croydon CR0 . . . 43 D3
Fetcham KT22 . . . 94 B5
Heath End GU9 . . . 125 D7
Horsham RH13 . . . 218 A3
Kingswood KT20 . . . 98 B6
Mytchett GU16 . . . 86 A2
Rowledge GU10 . . . 145 B1
Sheerwater KT14 . . . 70 E6
Staines TW18 . . . 13 B2
Stoneleigh KT17 . . . 58 A4
West Wickham BR4 . . . 63 B7
Gladiator St SE23 . . . 23 E8
Gladiator Way GU14 . . . 105 A8
Gladioli Cl 6 TW12 . . . 16 A2
Gladsmuir Cl KT12 . . . 54 C8
Gladstone Ave
Feltham TW14 . . . 4 B1
Twickenham TW2 . . . 16 D8
Gladstone Ct 12 SW19 . . . 20 A1
Gladstone Gdns TW3 . . . 5 C6
Gladstone Ho
Epsom KT19 . . . 76 B8
2 Mitcham CR4 . . . 40 F7
Gladstone Mews 5 SE20 . . . 23 C1
Gladstone Pl KT8 . . . 36 E4
Gladstone Rd
Ashtead KT21 . . . 75 D1
Croydon CR0 . . . 42 D2
Horsham RH12 . . . 217 D3
Kingston u T KT1 . . . 38 A6
Merton SW19 . . . 20 A1
Surbiton KT6 . . . 56 E8
Glaisdale Sch SM2 . . . 58 F3
Glamis Cl GU16 . . . 85 F7
Glamis Ho 12 RH2 . . . 118 F1
Glamorgan Cl CR4, SW16 . . . 41 E6
Glamorgan Rd KT1 . . . 17 C1
Glanfield Rd BR3 . . . 43 F5
Glanty The TW20 . . . 12 B4
Glanville Ho 4 SW12 . . . 21 C8
Glanville Wlk 7 RH11 . . . 201 A3
Glasbrook Ave TW2 . . . 15 F7
Glasford St SW17 . . . 20 F2
Glassmill La BR2 . . . 44 F7
Glassonby Wlk GU15 . . . 66 C5
Glastonbury Rd SM4 . . . 40 A2
Glayshers Hill GU35 . . . 187 B6
Glazebrook Cl SE21 . . . 22 D6
Glazebrook Rd TW11 . . . 16 F1
Glaziers La GU3 . . . 107 C2
Gleave Cl RH19 . . . 186 A2
Glebe Ave CR4 . . . 40 E7
Glebe Cl
Aldershot GU11 . . . 126 A7
Crawley RH10 . . . 201 E7
Great Bookham KT23 . . . 94 A1
Lightwater GU18 . . . 48 C1
Sanderstead CR2 . . . 80 F8
Glebe Cotts
Feltham TW13 . . . 16 A5
Sutton SM1 . . . 59 B6
West Clandon GU4 . . . 111 B3
Glebe Ct
Coulsdon CR5 . . . 79 B4
Guildford GU1 . . . 109 F1
Mitcham CR4 . . . 40 F6
Glebe Gdns
Byfleet KT14 . . . 71 E5
New Malden KT3 . . . 38 E2
Glebe Ho TW13 . . . 16 A5
Glebehyrst 18 SE19 . . . 22 E4
Glebe Hyrst CR2 . . . 80 F7
Glebe La
Abinger Common RH5 . . . 155 D8
Rushmoor GU10 . . . 168 C5
Glebeland Ctr 1 RH4 . . . 136 A7
Glebeland Gdns TW17 . . . 34 C3
Glebeland Rd GU15 . . . 64 F4
Glebelands
Claygate KT10 . . . 55 F2
Crawley Down RH10 . . . 204 A7
East Molesey KT8 . . . 36 B5
Loxwood RH14 . . . 212 F4
Mitcham CR4 . . . 40 E6
Glebelands Rd
East Bedfont TW14 . . . 15 A8
Wokingham RG40 . . . 25 C7
Glebelands Sch GU6 . . . 174 D3
Glebe Path CR4 . . . 40 F6
Glebe Rd
Ashtead KT21 . . . 75 D1
Belmont SM2 . . . 58 E2
Cranleigh GU6 . . . 174 E4
Dorking RH4 . . . 135 F7
Egham TW20 . . . 12 C2
Farnborough GU14 . . . 84 F5
Merstham CR5 . . . 99 B3
Staines TW18 . . . 13 B3
Wallington SM5 . . . 59 F4
Warlingham CR6 . . . 81 D2
Glebe Sch BR4 . . . 63 D8
Glebe Side TW1 . . . 5 F1
Glebe Sq CR4 . . . 40 F6
Glebe The
Blackwater GU17 . . . 64 E4
Copthorne RH10 . . . 183 B3
Ewhurst GU6 . . . 175 E6
Felbridge RH19 . . . 185 A4
Horley RH6 . . . 160 F3
Leigh RH2 . . . 138 A2
New Malden KT4 . . . 38 F1
Streatham SW16 . . . 21 D4
Glebe Way
Feltham TW13 . . . 16 A5
Sanderstead CR2 . . . 80 F8
West Wickham BR4 . . . 63 D8
Glebewood RG12 . . . 27 C4
Gledhow Wood KT20 . . . 98 B5
Gleeson Mews KT15 . . . 52 C6
Glen Albyn Rd SW19 . . . 19 D6
Glenalmond Ho TW15 . . . 13 E5
Glena Mount SM1 . . . 59 C6
Glen Ave TW15 . . . 14 A4
Glenavon Cl KT10 . . . 56 A4
Glenavon Ct KT4 . . . 58 B8
Glenbow Rd BR1 . . . 24 E3
Glenbuck Ct 6 KT6 . . . 37 E3
Glenbuck Rd KT6 . . . 37 E3
Glenburnie Rd SW17 . . . 20 F5
Glencairn Rd SW16 . . . 21 E1
Glen Cl
Beacon Hill GU26 . . . 188 C6
Kingswood KT20 . . . 97 E4
Littleton TW17 . . . 34 A5
Glencoe Cl GU16 . . . 86 A8
Glencoe Rd KT13 . . . 53 A7
Glencroft Ct SM1 . . . 59 A5
Glen Ct
Addlestone KT15 . . . 51 F5
Beacon Hill GU26 . . . 188 C6

Gle–Gra 255

Glen Ct *continued*
9 Bromley BR1 24 F1
Glen Ct KT14 71 D8
Glen Ct
10 Penge SE20 43 B8
Staines TW18 12 F1
Woking GU21 89 A8
Glendale Cl
Horsham RH12 218 A6
Woking GU21 69 C1
Wokingham RG41 25 A3
Glendale Dr
Guildford GU4 110 C5
Wimbledon SW19 19 F3
Glendale Ho 5 TW10 6 E1
Glen Dale Mews BR3 44 B8
Glendale Rise CR8 80 B4
Glendene Ave KT24 92 E1
Glendon Ho 9 RH10 201 D5
Glendower Gdns 11 SW14 7 D4
Glendower Rd SW14 7 D4
Glendyne Cl RH19 206 A8
Glendyne Way RH19 206 A8
Gleneagle Lo BR3 44 A8
Gleneagle Mews SW16 21 D3
Gleneagle Rd SW16 21 D3
Glen Eagles RH6 161 B2
Gleneagles Cl TW19 2 D1
Gleneagles Ct
Crawley RH10 201 D5
3 Teddington TW11 17 A3
Gleneagles Dr GU14 84 C3
Gleneagles Ho RG12 26 E3
Gleneldon Mews SW16 21 E4
Gleneldon Rd SW16 21 E4
Glenelg Ho TW14 15 A8
Glenesk Sch KT24 92 D2
Glenfarg Rd SE6 24 D7
Glenfield Cl RH3 137 B5
Glenfield Cotts RH6 180 D7
Glenfield Ho RG12 27 C5
Glenfield Rd
Ashford TW15 14 C2
Banstead SM7 78 B4
Brockham RH3 137 B6
Streatham SW12 21 C7
Glengall Ct SE23 23 E8
Glen Gdns CR0, CR9 61 A6
Glenheadon Cl KT22 95 D4
Glenheadon Rise KT22 95 D4
Glen Ho SM6 60 C6
Glenhurst BR3 44 C8
Glenhurst Cl GU17 64 E4
Glenhurst Ct SE19 22 F3
Glenhurst Rd TW8 6 C8
Glenhurst Rise SE19 22 C1
Glen Innes GU47 45 E1
Glenister Park Rd SW16 21 D1
Glenlea GU26 188 E1
Glenlea Hollow GU26 207 E8
Glenlee GU22 89 D8
Glenlion Ct 2 KT13 53 D7
Glenmill TW12 15 F3
Glenmore Cl KT15 52 B7
Glenmore Ho 4 TW10 6 E1
Glenmount Rd GU16 86 A2
Glenn Ave CR8 80 B8
Glennie Ct SE21 23 A7
Glennie Rd SE27, SW16 22 A5
Glen Rd
Beacon Hill GU26 188 C6
Chessington KT9 56 E7
Grayshott GU26 188 D3
Glen Road End SM6 60 B2
Glenrose Ho 13 SM1 59 C6
Glenside 1 RH19 185 E1
Glentanner Way SW17 20 D5
Glen The
Addlestone KT15 51 F5
Ascot SL5 29 D5
Beckenham BR2 44 E7
Croydon CR0 62 D7
Heath End GU9 125 C6
8 Redhill RH1 139 F8
Glenthorne Ave CR0, CR9 43 C1
Glenthorne Cl SM3 40 A1
Glenthorne Gdns SM3 40 A1
Glenthorne High Sch SM3 40 A1
Glenthorne Rd KT1 37 F5
Glenthorpe Rd SM4 39 D4
Glenview Cl RH10 201 F8
Glenville Gdns GU26 188 F4
Glenville Mews SW18 20 A8
Glenville Rd KT2 38 A8
Glen Vue RH19 185 E1
Glen Wlk TW7 5 D2
Glenwood
Bracknell RG12 27 D5
Dorking RH5 136 C5
Heath End GU9 125 C6
Virginia Water GU25 31 C8
Glenwood Ct GU14 85 A4
Glenwood Rd
Forest Hill SE6 24 A7
Hounslow TW3 5 D4
Stoneleigh KT17 58 A4
Glenwood Way CR0 43 D3
Globe Farm La GU17 64 B5
Glorney Mead GU9 126 A6
Glory Mead RH4 136 C4
Glossop Ho TW7 6 A3
Glossop Rd CR2 61 D2
Gloster Cl GU12 105 F5
Gloster Ct GU21 69 F3
Gloster Rd
New Malden KT3 38 E5
Old Woking GU22 90 A7
Gloucester Cl
East Grinstead RH19 206 A8
Frimley GU16 85 E6
Thames Ditton KT7 37 A1
Gloucester Cres TW18 13 D2
Gloucester Ct
Dulwich SE22 23 A7
Richmond TW9 7 A7
8 Surbiton KT6 37 D2
Gloucester Dr TW18, TW19 12 D5
Gloucester Gdns
Bagshot GU19 47 E3
Sutton SM1 59 B8
Gloucester Ho TW10 7 A2
Gloucester Lo 9 CR0 61 F8
Gloucester Rd
Aldershot GU11 126 C7
Bagshot GU19 47 E3
Crawley RH10 201 E2
Croydon CR0 42 E2
Feltham TW13 15 C7
Guildford GU2 108 F3
Hampton TW12 16 B1
Hounslow TW4 4 E3
Kingston u T KT1, KT2 38 B7
Redhill RH1 118 F2
Richmond TW9 7 A7
Teddington TW11 16 E3
Twickenham TW2 16 C7
Glovers Cl TN16 83 B3
Glovers Field GU27 207 F6
Glovers Ho GU27 207 F6
Glovers Lo 25 TW9 6 D2
Glover's Rd
Charlwood RH6 180 D7
Reigate RH2 139 B8
Gloxinia Wlk TW12 16 A2
Glyn Cl
Ewell KT17 58 A2
South Norwood SE19, SE25 42 E8
Glyn Ct SE27 22 A5
Glyndale Grange SM2 59 B4
Glynde Ho RH10 201 E8
Glynde Pl 8 RH12 217 C2
Glyn Rd KT4, SM3 58 D8
Glynswood
Frimley GU15 65 F3
Rowledge GU10 146 A4
Glyn Tech Sch KT17 76 F8
Glynwood Ct SE23 23 C6
Goaters Rd SL5 28 C7
Goat Rd CR4 40 F2
Goatsfield Rd TN16 103 C7
Goat Wharf TW8 6 E8
GODALMING 150 F3
Godalming Ave SM6 60 F5
Godalming Bsns Ctr GU7 150 F4
Godalming Coll GU7 150 D2
Godalming Jun Sch GU7 150 F5
Godalming Mus★ GU7 150 D4
Godalming Rd
Dunsfold GU8 193 A8
Hascombe GU8 172 E3
Godalming Sta GU7 150 D4
Goddard Cl
Crawley RH10 202 B3
Guildford GU2 109 A5
Littleton TW17 33 F6
Goddard Ho SW19 19 D6
Goddard Rd BR3 43 E5
Goddards Ho SM7 78 B5
Goddards La GU15 65 B3
Goddens The RH19 205 E7
Godfrey Ave TW2 16 D8
Godfrey Cl GU47 64 D7
Godfrey Way TW4 15 F8
Godley Rd
Byfleet KT14 71 F6
Wandsworth SW18 20 D7
Godolphin Cl SM2 77 F8
Godolphin Ct RH10 201 D5
Godolphin Ho 7 SW2 22 A7
Godolphin Rd KT13 53 D4
Godric Cres CR0 63 D1
Godson Rd CR0, CR9 61 A7
GODSTONE 121 B3
Godstone Farm★ RH9 121 C3
Godstone Green Rd RH9 121 B4
Godstone Hill RH9 121 C5
Godstone Ho 1 KT2 18 B2
Godstone Mount 3 CR8 80 B7
Godstone Rd
Bletchingley RH1 120 F2
Caterham CR3 101 A3
Lingfield RH7 164 C4
Oxted RH8, RH9 122 C5
Purley CR8 80 D4
Sutton SM1 59 C6
Twickenham TW1 6 B1
Godstone Sta RH9 142 E5
Godstone Village Sch RH9 121 B3
Godstone Vineyards★ RH9 121 C7
Godwin Cl KT19 57 C4
Godwin Ct
3 Horsham RH12 217 A1
Godwin Ct *continued*
South Croydon CR2 61 C4
Godwin Way RH13 218 A4
Goepel Ct RH10 202 A7
Goffs Cl RH11 201 C5
Goffs La RH11 201 B6
Goffs Park Rd RH11 201 C4
Goffs Rd TW15 14 D2
Gogmore Farm Cl KT16 32 F2
Gogmore La KT16 33 A2
Goidel Cl SM6 60 D6
Goldcliff Cl SM4 40 A2
Goldcrest Cl RH6 160 E4
Goldcrest Way
New Addington CR0 63 D3
Wallington CR8 60 D1
Gold Cup La SL5 28 D8
Golden Ct
Hounslow TW7 5 D5
9 Richmond TW9 6 D2
Golden Mews SE20 43 C8
Golden Orb Wood RG42 26 D8
Goldfinch Cl
Aldershot GU11 125 F8
Crawley RH11 201 D8
Horsham RH12 217 C7
Goldfinch Gdns GU4 110 D2
Goldfinch Rd CR0, CR2 62 E1
Goldfort Wlk GU21 68 E3
Goldhill GU10 146 C6
Golding Cl
Chessington KT9 56 C4
Crawley RH10 202 C5
Goldings The GU21 68 F3
Gold La GU11 105 E4
Goldney Rd GU15 66 C4
Goldrings Rd KT22 74 C6
Goldsmiths Cl GU21 69 C1
Goldsmith Way RG45 45 B4
Goldstone Farm View KT23 114 A8
Goldsworth Orch 6 GU21 69 A1
GOLDSWORTH PARK 69 A3
Goldsworth Park Ctr GU21 69 A2
Goldsworth Park Trad Est GU21 69 B3
Goldsworth Prim Sch GU21 69 C1
Goldsworth Rd GU21 69 D2
Goldsworth Road Ind Est GU21 69 D2
Goldwell Rd CR7 41 F5
Gole Rd GU24 87 D6
Golf Cl
Pyrford GU22 70 E5
South Norwood SW16 42 A8
Golf Club Dr KT2 18 D1
Golf Club Rd
Weybridge KT13 53 C1
Woking GU22 89 B7
Golf Course Cotts KT20 98 A3
Golf Dr GU15 65 F4
Golf Links Ave GU26 188 B6
Golf Rd CR8 80 D1
Golf Side
Belmont SM2 77 E8
Twickenham TW2 16 D5
Golf Side Cl KT3 38 E7
Gomer Gdns TW11 17 A2
Gomer Pl TW11 17 A2
GOMSHALL 133 D4
Gomshall Ave SM6 60 E5
Gomshall Gdns CR8 80 E4
Gomshall La GU5 133 B4
Gomshall Rd KT17, SM2 58 C1
Gomshall Sta GU5 133 D4
Gong Hill Dr GU10 146 D4
Gong Hill Frensham Rd GU10 146 D4
Gonston Cl SW19 19 E6
Gonville Prim Sch CR7 41 F4
Gonville Rd CR7 41 F4
Goodbehere Ho 7 SE27 22 C4
Goodchild Rd RG40 25 D6
Goodden Cres GU14 84 F3
Goodenough Cl CR5 100 A7
Goodenough Rd SW19 19 F1
Goodenough Way CR5 99 F7
Goodhart Way BR4 44 E3
Goodhew Rd CR0, SE25 43 A3
Gooding Cl KT3 38 C4
Goodings Gn RG40 25 F6
Goodland Ho 1 KT3 38 E2
Goodman Cres SW2 21 D6
Goodman Pl TW18 12 F4
Good Shepherd RC Prim Sch
Catford BR1 24 F4
New Addington CR0 63 B3
Goodson Ho SM4 40 C2
Goodways Dr RG12 27 D7
Goodwin Cl
Crawley RH11 200 F3
Mitcham CR4 40 D6
Goodwin Ct SW19 20 E1
Goodwin Gdns CR0, CR2 61 B4
Goodwin Rd CR0 61 B5
Goodwins Cl RH19 185 D3
Goodwood Cl
Camberley GU15 65 C8
Crawley RH10 202 A3
Goodwood Cl *continued*
Morden SM4 40 A5
Goodwood Ct SE27 22 C5
Goodwood Ho SE26 23 B2
Goodwood Lo SM6 60 D7
Goodwood Par BR3 43 E5
Goodwood Pl GU14 85 E3
Goodwood Rd RH1 118 F3
Goodwyns Pl RH4 136 B5
Goodwyns Rd RH4 136 C4
Goose Gn GU5 133 C4
Goose Green Cl RH12 217 D5
Goose La GU22 89 B5
Goose Rye Rd
Woking GU3 89 A2
Worplesdon GU3 88 E1
Goossens Cl 1 SM1 59 C5
Gordon Ave
Camberley GU15 65 C4
Isleworth TW1 6 B2
Mortlake SW14 7 E3
South Croydon CR2, CR8 61 C1
Gordon Cl
Addlestone KT16 51 E7
Staines TW18 13 B2
Gordon Clifford Ct 3 RG42 27 B8
Gordon Cres
Camberley GU15 65 C4
Croydon CR0 42 F1
Gordon Ct
Chiswick W4 7 B8
Hampton TW12 16 C3
6 Wimbledon SW20 19 D1
Gordondale Rd SW18, SW19 20 A6
Gordon Dr
Addlestone KT16 51 E7
Shepperton TW17 34 D2
Gordon Rd
Aldershot GU11 105 A1
Ashford TW15 13 E5
Beckenham BR3 43 F6
Camberley GU15 65 C5
Caterham CR3 100 D6
Chiswick W4 7 B8
Claygate KT10 55 E3
Crowthorne RG45 45 D3
Farnborough GU14 105 D8
Horsham RH12 217 D4
Hounslow TW3 5 C3
Kingston u T KT2 37 F8
Redhill RH1 119 A4
Richmond TW9 6 F5
Shepperton TW17 34 D3
Surbiton KT5 37 F2
Wallington SM5 59 F4
Gordon's Sch GU24 67 E7
Gordons Way RH8 122 D7
Gore Rd SW20 39 C7
Goring Rd TW18 12 E3
Goring's Mead RH13 217 D1
Goring's Sq TW18 12 E4
Gorling Cl RH11 200 E5
Gorrick Sq RG41 25 B3
Gorringe Park Ave CR4, SW17 21 A1
Gorringe Park Prim Sch CR4 41 A8
Gorringes Brook RH12 217 D6
Gorse Bank GU18 67 A8
Gorse Cl
Burgh Heath KT20 97 B7
Copthorne RH10 183 B2
Crawley RH11 201 B1
Wrecclesham GU10 146 B6
Gorse Cotts GU26 207 C8
Gorse Ct GU4 110 C3
Gorse Dr RH6 162 C3
Gorse End RH12 217 D5
Gorse Hill La GU25 31 D5
Gorse Hill Rd GU25 31 D5
Gorse La
Chobham GU24 49 E3
Wrecclesham GU10 146 B6
Gorselands GU9 125 C7
Gorselands Cl
Ash GU12 106 A5
Headley Down GU35 187 C4
West Byfleet KT14 71 C8
Gorse Pl RG42 8 B1
Gorse Rd
Croydon CR0 63 A7
Frimley GU16 65 E2
Gorse Rise SW17 21 A3
Gorsewood Rd GU21 88 E7
Gort Cl GU11 105 E7
Gosberton Rd SW12 21 A7
Gosbury Hill KT9 56 E6
Gosden Cl
Crawley RH10 202 A5
Shalford GU5 151 F8
GOSDEN COMMON 151 E8
Gosden Cotts GU5 151 F7
Gosden Hill Rd GU4 110 C5
Gosden Ho 17 GU22 89 E8
Gosden House Sch GU5 151 E8
Gosden Rd GU24 67 F6
Gosfield Rd KT19 76 D7
Gosnell Cl GU16 66 D3
Gospatric Home Ho 3 SW14 7 E4
GOSPEL GREEN 209 E4
Gosport Ho 9 SW15 19 A7
Gossops Dr RH11 201 A5
GOSSOPS GREEN 201 A5
Gossops Green La RH11 201 A5
Gossops Green Prim Sch RH11 201 A5
Gossops Par RH11 200 F5
Gostling Rd TW2 16 A7
Goston Gdns CR7 42 A6
Gostrode La GU8 210 A6
Gothic Ct
Harlington UB3 3 D8
Sandhurst GU47 64 B7
Gothic Ho 2 KT12 35 A1
Gothic Rd TW2 16 D6
Goudhurst Cl RH10 202 E6
Goudhurst Ho 9 SE20 23 C1
Goudhurst Keep RH10 202 E6
Goudhurst Rd BR1 24 F3
Gough Ho 4 KT1 37 E7
Gough's La RG12 27 D8
Gough's Mdw GU47 64 B7
Gould Ct
Dulwich SE19 22 E3
Guildford GU4 110 D3
Goulding Gdns CR7 42 C7
Gould Rd
East Bedfont TW14 14 E8
Twickenham TW2 16 E7
Government House Rd GU11, GU14 105 B7
Government Rd GU11 105 E4
Governor's Rd GU15 64 F6
Govett Ave TW17 34 C4
Govett Gr GU20 48 D5
Gower Ho SW19 20 D3
Gower Lo KT13 53 D4
Gower Pk GU47 64 D7
Gower Rd
Horley RH6 160 E3
Hounslow TW7 5 F8
Weybridge KT13 53 D4
Gower The TW20 32 C6
Gowland Pl BR3 43 F7
Gowlland Cl CR0 43 A2
Gowrie Pl CR3 100 C5
Graburn Way KT8 36 D6
Grace Bennett Cl GU14 85 A7
Grace Bsns Ctr CR4 40 F3
Grace Ct
Belmont SM2 59 B2
Croydon CR0 61 B7
2 Twickenham TW2 16 E6
Gracedale Rd SW16, SW17 21 B3
Gracefield Gdns SW16 21 E5
Grace Ho SE26 23 B3
Grace Path SE26 23 C4
Grace Rd
Crawley RH11 201 A1
Thornton Heath CR0 42 C3
Grace Reynolds Wlk GU15 65 C6
Gracious Pond Rd GU24 50 B4
Gradient The SE26 23 A4
Graemesdyke Ave SW14 7 B3
Graffham Cl RH11 201 B8
Grafton Cl
Twickenham TW4 15 F7
West Byfleet KT14 70 F6
Worcester Park KT4 57 E7
Grafton Ct TW14 14 D7
Grafton Park Rd KT4 57 E8
Grafton Rd
Kingston u T KT3 38 E6
Thornton Heath CR0 42 A1
Worcester Park KT4 57 E7
Grafton Way KT8 35 F5
Graham Ave CR4 41 A8
Graham Cl CR0 63 A8
Graham Gdns KT6 37 E1
Graham Ho
5 Balham SW12 21 B8
Little Bookham KT23 94 A3
Redhill RH1 118 E3
Graham Rd
Hampton TW12 16 A4
Merton SW19 19 F1
Mitcham CR4 41 A8
Purley CR8 80 A6
Windlesham GU20 48 C4
Grainford Ct RG40 25 C5
Grainger Rd TW7 5 F5
Grampian Cl
Harlington UB3 3 D7
Sutton SM2 59 C3
Grampian Rd GU47 45 A2
Gramsci Way SE6 24 B5
Granada St SW17 20 F3
Granard Rd SW11, SW12 20 F8
Granary Cl
Horley RH6 161 A5
Horsham RH12 216 F1
Granary Way RH12 217 A1
Grand Ave
Camberley GU15 65 C6
Tolworth KT5 38 B3
Grand Avenue Prim Sch KT5 38 C3
Grand Dr KT3, SM4, SW20 39 C5
Granden Rd SW16 41 E7
Grandfield Ct W4 7 D8
Grandis Cotts GU23 91 B5

Grandison Rd KT4 .... 58 C7
Grand Par
Crawley RH10 .... 201 D6
Mortlake SW14 .... 7 C3
Tolworth KT6 .... 38 A1
Grand Regency Hts
SL5 .... 28 E6
Grand Stand Rd KT17,
KT18 .... 77 A2
Grand View Ave TN16 .... 83 C3
Grange Ave
Crowthorne RG45 .... 45 B6
South Norwood SE25 ...... 42 E7
Twickenham TW2 .... 16 E6
Grange Cl
Ashtead KT22 .... 95 D7
Bletchingley RH1 .... 120 D2
Crawley RH10 .... 202 A8
East Molesey KT8 .... 36 B5
Godalming GU7 .... 151 A5
Guildford GU2 .... 109 B5
Heston TW5 .... 4 F8
Merstham RH1 .... 119 B7
Grangecliffe Gdns
SE25 .... 42 E7
Grange Com Inf Sch The
KT15 .... 52 A1
Grange Com Jun Sch
GU14 .... 85 A7
Grange Cres RH10 ...... 204 B7
Grange Ct
Belmont SM2 .... 59 B3
Egham TW20 .... 11 F3
Hackbridge SM6 .... 60 B7
Littleton TW17 .... 34 A5
Merstham RH2 .... 119 B7
South Godstone RH9 ..... 142 E5
5 Staines TW18 .... 13 A3
Walton-on-T KT12 .... 54 A8
Grange Dr
Merstham RH1 .... 119 B7
Woking GU21 .... 69 E4
Grange End RH6 .... 162 A3
Grange Farm Est TW17 ... 34 E6
Grange Farm Rd
GU12 .... 106 A3
Grangefields Rd GU4 .... 109 D6
Grange Gdns
Banstead SM7 .... 78 B6
South Norwood SE25 ...... 42 E7
Grange Hill SE25 .... 42 E7
Grange La SE21 .... 22 F6
Grange Lo SW19 .... 19 D2
Grange Mans KT17 .... 57 F3
Grange Mdw SM7 .... 78 B6
Grangemill Rd SE6 .... 24 A6
Grange Mills SW12 .... 21 C7
Grangemill Way SE6 ..... 24 A6
Grangemount KT22 ...... 95 D7
Grange Park Pl SW20 .... 19 B1
Grange Park Rd CR7 ..... 42 D6
Grange Pk
Cranleigh GU6 .... 174 F3
Woking GU21 .... 69 F5
Grange Pl
Laleham TW18 .... 33 C7
Walton-on-T KT12 .... 54 A8
Grange Rd
Ash GU12 .... 106 B1
Ashtead KT21 .... 95 D7
Belmont SM2 .... 59 A3
Bracknell RG12 .... 27 C8
Camberley GU15 .... 65 E5
Caterham CR3 .... 101 A2
Chessington KT9 .... 56 E6
Crawley Down RH10 ..... 204 A7
East Molesey KT8 .... 36 B5
Egham TW20 .... 11 F3
Farnborough GU14 .... 85 B7
Guildford GU2, GU3 ...... 109 B5
Hersham KT12 .... 54 E6
Kingston u T KT1 .... 37 E6
Pirbright GU24 .... 87 D5
Rushmoor GU10 .... 168 C7
South Croydon CR2 .... 61 C2
South Norwood SE19,
SE25 .... 42 D7
Tongham GU10 .... 126 E6
Woking GU21 .... 69 E5
Woodham KT15 .... 52 B1
Grange The
Bletchingley RH1 .... 120 D2
Chobham GU24 .... 49 E1
Croydon CR0 .... 62 F8
Frensham GU10 .... 167 D7
Horley RH6 .... 161 A6
New Malden KT3 .... 39 A4
Virginia Water GU25 ...... 31 E5
Walton on t H KT20 .... 97 A2
Walton-on-T KT12 .... 54 B8
Wimbledon SW19 .... 19 D2
Worcester Park KT4 ...... 57 D6
Grange Vale SM2 .... 59 B3
Grangeway RH6 .... 162 A3
Grangewood La BR3 ...... 23 F2
Gransden Cl GU6 .... 175 E5
Grantchester 3 KT1 ...... 38 A7
Grant Cl TW17 .... 34 B3
Grantham Cl GU47 .... 45 E1
Grantham Ct KT2 .... 17 D3
Grantham Dr GU14 .... 84 D5
Grantham Ho 5 TW16 ... 14 E1
Grantham Rd W4 .... 7 E7
Grantley Ave GU5 .... 152 B6
Grantley Cl GU4 .... 130 E2
Grantley Ct GU9 .... 145 F6
Grantley Gdns GU2 ...... 109 A2
Grantley Ho SW19 .... 19 D7
Grantley Pl KT10 .... 55 C5
Grantley Rd
Cranford TW4, TW5 .... 4 C5
Guildford GU2 .... 109 A2
Granton Prim Sch
SW16 .... 21 C1
Granton Rd SW16 .... 41 C8
Grant Pl 2 CR0 .... 42 F1
Grant Rd
Crowthorne RG45 .... 45 C3
Croydon CR0 .... 42 F1
Grants Cotts KT10 .... 55 D8
Grants La TN8, RH8 ..... 144 C6
Grant Way TW7, TW8 ...... 6 A8
Grant Wlk SL5 .... 29 E1
Grantwood Cl RH1 ...... 140 B4
Granville Ave
Feltham TW13 .... 15 A6
Hounslow TW3, TW4 .... 5 A2
Granville Cl
Byfleet KT14 .... 71 F6
South Croydon CR0 .... 61 E8
Weybridge KT13 .... 53 C4
Granville Gdns SW16 ..... 21 F1
Granville Rd
Limpsfield RH8 .... 123 A7
Merton SW19 .... 20 A1
Wandsworth SW18 .... 19 F8
Weybridge KT13 .... 53 C4
Woking GU22 .... 89 F7
Granwood Ct TW7 .... 5 E6
Grapsome Cl KT9 .... 56 C3
Grasmere GU15 .... 65 E7
Grasmere Ave
Kingston u T SW15 .... 18 E4
Merton SW19 .... 40 A6
Twickenham TW3 .... 5 B1
Grasmere Cl
East Bedfont TW14 .... 14 F7
Guildford GU1 .... 110 B2
5 Thorpe Lea TW20 ...... 12 B1
Grasmere Ct
Forest Hill SE26 .... 23 A3
13 Sutton SM2 .... 59 C4
Grasmere Gdns RH12 ... 218 B6
Grasmere Rd
Bromley BR1 .... 24 F1
Croydon SE25 .... 43 B4
Farnborough GU14 .... 84 E4
Hale GU9 .... 125 A6
Lightwater GU18 .... 48 B1
Purley CR8 .... 80 B8
Streatham SW16 .... 21 F3
Grasmere Way KT14 ..... 71 F7
Grassfield Cl CR5 .... 99 C8
Grasslands RH6 .... 162 A3
Grassmere RH6 .... 161 C4
Grassmount
Forest Hill SE23 .... 23 B6
Wallington CR8 .... 60 C1
Grassway SM6 .... 60 C6
Grateley Ho 10 SW15 ..... 19 B7
Grattons Dr RH10 .... 182 C1
Grattons The RH13 ...... 215 E3
Graveley 7 KT1 .... 38 A7
Gravel Hill
Leatherhead KT22 .... 95 B6
South Croydon CR0, CR2 ... 62 E4
Gravel Hill Rd GU10 ..... 145 A3
Gravel Hill Sta CR0 .... 62 E4
Gravelly Hill CR3 .... 120 F7
Gravelpits Cotts GU5 .... 133 C4
Gravel Pits La GU5 ...... 133 C4
Gravel Rd
Farnborough GU14 ...... 105 D8
Hale GU9 .... 125 B7
Twickenham TW2 .... 16 E7
Gravenel Gdns SW17 ..... 20 E3
Graveney Gr SE20 .... 23 C1
Graveney Rd
Crawley RH10 .... 202 C5
Upper Tooting SW17 ...... 20 E4
Graveney Sch SW17 ...... 21 B3
Gravetts La GU3 .... 108 E5
Gravetye Cl RH10 .... 202 A4
Gray Cl
Addlestone KT15 .... 52 B5
Lingfield RH7 .... 164 E4
Gray Ct 8 KT2 .... 17 D4
Grayham Cres KT3 .... 38 D5
Grayham Rd KT3 .... 38 D5
Graylands GU21 .... 69 E3
Graylands Cl GU21 .... 69 E3
Graylands Ct 5 GU1 .... 130 F8
Graylings Ho KT16 .... 33 C1
Gray Pl
Bracknell RG42 .... 26 E8
Ottershaw KT16 .... 51 D4
Grays Cl GU27 .... 208 E8
Grayscroft Rd SW16 ...... 21 D1
Grayshot Dr GU17 .... 64 C5
GRAYSHOTT 188 C3
Grayshott CE Prim Sch
GU26 .... 188 B3
Grayshott Ct 15 SM2 ..... 59 B3
Grayshott Rd GU26,
GU35 .... 187 C5
Grays La TW15 .... 14 B4
Gray's La KT21 .... 95 F8
Grays Rd GU7 .... 150 F7
GRAYSWOOD 189 F1
Grays Wood RH6 .... 161 C3
Grayswood CE Inf Sch
GU27 .... 189 F2
Grayswood Dr GU16 ...... 86 A2
Grayswood Gdns SW20 ... 39 B7
Grayswood Pl GU27 ..... 208 E8
Grayswood Point 14
SW15 .... 19 A7
Grayswood Rd GU27 .... 189 F1
Grazeley Ct SE19 .... 22 E3
Great Austins GU9 ...... 146 D8
Great Austins Ho
GU9 .... 146 D8
GREAT BOOKHAM 94 B1
Great Brownings SE21 ... 22 F4
GREAT BURGH 77 C2
Great Chertsey Rd
Chiswick SW14, W4 .... 7 D6
Feltham TW13, TW2 .... 16 A5
Great Ellshams SM7 ...... 78 A3
GREAT ENTON 171 A4
Greatfield Cl GU14 .... 85 B8
Great Field Pl RH19 ..... 186 B3
Greatfield Rd GU14 ...... 85 B8
Greatford Dr GU1 .... 110 D1
Great Gatton Cl CR0 ..... 43 E2
Great George St GU7 .... 150 E4
Great Goodwin Dr
GU1 .... 110 B3
Greatham Rd RH10 ...... 202 C3
Greatham Wlk 8
SW15 .... 19 A7
Greathed Manor*
RH7 .... 165 C1
GREAT HOLLANDS 26 F3
Great Hollands Prim Sch
RG12 .... 26 E4
Great Hollands Rd
RG12 .... 26 F3
Great Hollands Sq
RG12 .... 26 F3
Great House Ct 4
RH19 .... 205 F8
Greathurst End KT23 ..... 93 F3
Greatlake Ct RH6 .... 161 B4
Great Oaks Pk GU4 ..... 110 C5
Great Quarry GU1 .... 130 D6
Great South-West Rd
East Bedfont TW14, TW6,
TW4, TW5 .... 3 D2
Hounslow TW5 .... 4 B4
Greatstone Ho 12 SE20 ... 23 C1
Great Tattenhams
KT18 .... 77 C1
Great West Ho TW8 .... 6 C8
Great West Rd
Brentford TW8 .... 6 B8
Cranford, Heston TW5 ...... 4 F6
Hounslow TW5, TW7 .... 5 C6
**Great West Road Cedars
Rd** W4 .... 7 C8
Great West Road Chiswick
1 W4 .... 7 F8
**Great West Road
Ellesmere Rd** W4 .... 7 D8
**Great West Road Hogarth
La** W4 .... 7 E8
Great West Trad Est
TW8 .... 6 B8
Greatwood Cl KT16 ...... 51 C2
Great Woodcote Dr
CR8 .... 60 D1
Great Woodcote Pk CR8,
SM6 .... 60 E1
Greaves Pl SW17 .... 20 E4
Grebe Cres RH13 .... 218 A1
Grebe Ct
Cheam SM1 .... 58 F5
Staines TW18 .... 13 B4
Grebe Terr 4 KT1 .... 37 E6
Grecian Cres SE19 .... 22 B2
Greenacre
Knaphill GU21 .... 68 E3
Whyteleafe CR3 .... 101 B7
Green Acre GU11 .... 104 F1
Greenacre Ct TW20 ...... 11 C2
Greenacre Pl SM6 .... 60 B8
Greenacres
Crawley RH10 .... 202 A5
Farnham GU10 .... 126 C2
Great Bookham KT23 ...... 94 A3
Horsham RH12 .... 217 C4
Lower Kingswood KT20 ... 117 F7
Oxted RH8 .... 122 E8
Green Acres CR0 .... 61 F7
Greenacre Sch for Girls
SM7 .... 78 B6
Greenaway Terr TW19 ... 13 E7
Greenbank Way GU15 .... 65 D2
Green Bsns Ctr The
TW20 .... 12 C4
Greenbush La GU6 ...... 174 F1
Green Cl
Beckenham BR2 .... 44 E6
Carshalton SM5 .... 59 F8
Feltham TW13 .... 15 E3
Green Cotts The GU6 .... 175 E4
Green Court Ave CR0 .... 62 B8
Green Court Gdns CR0 ... 62 B8
Greencroft
2 Farnborough GU14 ..... 85 B4
Guildford GU1 .... 110 B1
Green Croft
Badshot Lea GU9 .... 126 B6
Wokingham RG40 .... 25 E8
Greencroft Rd TW5 .... 4 F6
GREEN CROSS 168 B1
Green Cross La GU10 ... 168 A1
Green Ct TW16 .... 14 F2
Green Curve SM7 .... 77 F4
Greendale Ct CR2 .... 61 C4
Green Dene KT24 .... 112 E3
Green Dr
Send Marsh GU23 .... 90 F4
Wokingham RG40 .... 25 E4
Green Dragon Prim Sch
TW8 .... 6 E8
Greene Fielde End
TW18 .... 13 D1
Green End KT9 .... 56 E6
Greener Ct 10 SW20 ...... 39 D8
Green Farm Rd GU19 ..... 47 F3
Greenfield Ave KT5 ...... 38 B3
Greenfield Ho
Englefield Green TW20 .... 11 B2
28 Putney SW19 .... 19 D7
Greenfield Link CR5 ..... 79 E4
Greenfield Rd
Farnham GU9, GU10 ..... 146 A7
Slinfold RH13 .... 215 D3
Wrecclesham GU9 .... 145 F7
Greenfield Sch GU22 ..... 89 E8
Greenfields Cl
Horley RH6 .... 160 E5
Horsham RH12 .... 218 A6
Greenfields Pl RH5 ..... 157 D4
Greenfields Rd
Horley RH6 .... 160 F5
Horsham RH12 .... 218 A5
Greenfields Sch
RH18 .... 206 C1
Greenfields Way
RH12 .... 218 A6
Greenfield Way RG45 .... 45 A7
Greenfinch Cl GU47 ...... 64 D8
Green Finch Cl RG45 ..... 45 A6
Greenfinch Way
RH12 .... 217 D7
Greenford Rd SM1 .... 59 B6
Greenham Ho TW7 .... 5 D4
Greenham Lo CR2 .... 61 D1
Greenham Wlk GU21 ..... 69 C1
Greenham Wood RG12 ... 27 C3
Greenhanger GU10 ..... 188 A8
Greenhayes Ave SM7 ..... 78 A4
Greenhayes Cl RH2 ..... 118 C1
Greenhayes Gdns SM7 ... 78 A4
Green Hedges 8 TW1 ..... 6 C1
Green Hedges Ave
RH19 .... 185 D2
Green Hedges Cl
RH19 .... 185 D2
Greenheys Pl GU22 ...... 69 F1
Greenhill SM1 .... 59 C8
Green Hill BR6 .... 83 F7
Greenhill Ave CR3 ...... 101 B6
Greenhill Cl
Godalming GU7 .... 150 D3
Wrecclesham GU9 .... 146 A7
Green Hill Cl GU15 ...... 66 C6
Greenhill Gdns GU4 ..... 110 C3
Greenhill La CR6 .... 81 F2
Greenhill Rd GU9 .... 146 D8
Green Hill Rd GU15 ...... 66 C6
Greenhills GU9 .... 146 E8
Greenhill Way GU9 ...... 146 A7
Greenholme GU15 .... 66 D5
Green House The 5
SW19 .... 19 E7
Greenhow RG12 .... 27 A6
Greenhurst La RH8 ..... 123 A3
Greenhurst Rd SE27 ..... 22 A3
Green La
Addlestone KT15, KT16 .... 51 E7
Alfold Crossways GU6 .... 193 F4
Ascot SL5 .... 29 E8
Ashford TW16 .... 14 F2
Ashtead KT22 .... 95 D6
Ashtead, Lower Ashtead
KT21 .... 75 D1
Bagshot GU19 .... 47 F2
Blackwater GU17 .... 64 B4
Blackwater, Hawley
GU17 .... 64 E4
Burstow RH6 .... 182 F6
Byfleet KT14 .... 71 F7
Caterham CR3 .... 100 C5
Chessington KT9 .... 56 E3
Chobham GU24 .... 49 F1
Churt GU10 .... 168 A1
Cobham KT11 .... 73 E7
Copthorne RH10 .... 183 F4
Crawley, Northgate
RH10 .... 201 E8
Crawley, Worth RH10 ..... 202 D6
Cudworth RH5 .... 179 D8
Dockenfield GU10 .... 166 E6
East Molesey KT8 .... 36 B4
Egham TW20 .... 12 B3
Farncombe GU7 .... 150 E8
Farnham GU9 .... 146 A7
Farnham, Weybourne
GU9 .... 125 F5
Faygate RH12 .... 198 F4
Feltham TW13 .... 15 E3
Guildford GU1 .... 110 B1
Hersham KT12 .... 54 B5
Hounslow TW4 .... 4 C3
Kingsley Green GU27 ..... 208 B4
Leigh RH2 .... 158 E8
Lingfield RH7 .... 164 C4
Lower Kingswood KT20 .... 97 F1
Milford GU8 .... 170 E8
Morden SM4 .... 40 B3
New Malden KT3 .... 38 C4
North Cheam KT4 .... 39 A1
Penge SE20 .... 23 D1
Purley CR8 .... 60 D1
Redhill RH1 .... 118 E3
Green La *continued*
Redhill, Whitebushes
RH1 .... 140 A4
Reigate RH2 .... 117 F1
Sandhurst GU47 .... 64 C7
Shamley Green GU5 ..... 153 A7
Shepperton TW17 .... 34 C4
South Norwood CR7,
SW16 .... 42 B8
South Nutfield RH1 ...... 140 F1
Streatham SW16 .... 21 F1
Thorpe TW18 .... 32 E8
Tilford GU10 .... 147 E6
West Clandon GU4 ...... 111 B8
West Horsley GU23 .... 92 B3
Wood St V GU3 .... 108 A3
Green La E GU3 .... 128 B8
Greenlake Terr TW18 .... 13 A1
Green La Mews SM4 ..... 40 B3
Greenlands
Addlestone KT16 .... 51 C7
Selsdon CR2 .... 62 C2
West Ewell KT19 .... 57 B5
Greenlands Ct 6
TW18 .... 13 A4
Greenlands Rd
Camberley GU15 .... 65 B1
Staines TW18 .... 13 A4
Weybridge KT13 .... 53 C7
Green Lane Ave KT12 .... 54 C5
Green Lane Cl
Addlestone KT16 .... 51 E8
Byfleet KT14 .... 71 F7
Camberley GU15 .... 65 C7
Green Lane Cotts
GU10 .... 167 F1
Green Lane E GU12 ..... 127 F8
Green Lane Gdns CR7 .... 42 C7
Green Lane Prim Sch
KT4 .... 39 B2
Green Lanes KT19 .... 57 E2
Green Lane W GU12 .... 127 E8
Green La W KT24 .... 92 A2
Greenlaw Gdns KT3 ...... 38 F2
Green Leaf Ave SM6 ..... 60 D6
Greenleaf Cl 6 SW2 ...... 22 A8
Greenlea Pk SW19 .... 40 E8
Greenleas GU16 .... 65 E2
Green Leas
Ashford TW16 .... 14 F2
Kingston u T KT1 .... 37 E6
Green Leas Cl TW16 ...... 14 F2
Greenleaves Ct TW15 .... 14 B2
Green Link Wlk TW9 ...... 7 B6
Green Man La TW14 .... 4 A3
Green Mead KT10 .... 54 F4
Greenmead Cl SE25 ...... 43 A4
Greenmeads GU22 .... 89 E5
Greenoak Rise TN16 ..... 83 C1
Greenoak Way SW19 ..... 19 D4
Greenock Rd SW16 ...... 41 D8
Greeno Cres TW17 .... 34 A4
Green Pk TW18 .... 12 E5
Green Rd TW20 .... 32 B5
Greensand Cl RH1 ...... 119 D7
Greensand Rd RH1 ...... 119 A2
Green Sch (Girls) The
TW7 .... 6 A6
Greenshaw High Sch
SM1 .... 59 D8
Greenside Cl
Catford SE6 .... 24 D6
Guildford GU4 .... 110 C3
Greenside Cotts GU23 .... 91 C6
Greenside Dr KT21 .... 75 B1
Greenside Rd CR0 .... 42 A2
Greenside Wlk TN16 ..... 83 B1
Greensleeves Manor
SM1 .... 59 B4
Green's School La
GU14 .... 85 A4
Green St TW16 .... 35 A7
Greenstede Ave RH19 ... 185 F2
Green The
Badshot Lea GU9 .... 126 A6
Bracknell RG12 .... 27 B5
Burgh Heath KT20 .... 97 E8
Carshalton SM6 .... 60 A8
Chiddingfold GU8 .... 191 C3
Claygate KT10 .... 55 F4
Copthorne RH10 .... 183 B3
Crawley RH11 .... 201 C7
Ewell KT17 .... 77 A7
Ewhurst GU6 .... 175 E4
Feltham TW13 .... 15 B6
Fetcham KT22 .... 94 D3
Frimley GU16 .... 85 F6
Hale GU9 .... 125 C6
Heston TW5 .... 5 A8
Kingston u T KT3 .... 38 C7
Merton SM4 .... 39 E5
New Addington CR0 .... 62 F2
Richmond TW9 .... 6 D3
Ripley GU23 .... 91 C6
Staines TW18 .... 13 D3
Sutton SM1 .... 59 B7
The Sands GU10 .... 126 E1
Twickenham TW2 .... 16 E6
Tyler's Green RH9 .... 121 C4
Upper Halliford TW17 ..... 34 E5
Wallington SM5 .... 60 A6
Warlingham CR6 .... 81 D1
Whiteley Village KT12 ..... 53 E1
Wimbledon SW19 .... 19 D3
Woldingham CR3 .... 102 A4
Greenvale Prim Sch
CR2 .... 81 D8
Greenvale Rd GU21 ...... 68 D1

Greenvale Sch SE23 23 E5
Green View
Chessington KT9 56 F3
Godstone RH9 121 B4
Greenview Ave CR0 43 E3
Greenview Ct
Ashford TW15 13 F4
Wandsworth SW18 20 E8
Greenway
Great Bookham KT23 94 B4
Horsham RH12 217 B3
Tatsfield TN16 103 C7
Wallington SM6 60 C6
West Barnes SW20 39 C5
Green Way
Aldershot GU12 105 E3
Redhill RH1 118 E3
Sunbury TW16 35 A5
Greenway Cl KT14 71 A6
Greenway Dr TW18 33 D8
Greenway Gdns CR0 62 F7
Greenways
Beckenham BR3 44 A7
Egham TW20 11 E3
Forest Hill SE26 23 C4
Hinchley Wood KT10 55 E6
Sandhurst GU47 45 B1
Walton on t H KT20 97 B2
Greenway Sch RH12 217 B3
Greenways Dr SL5 29 E1
Greenways The [1] TW1 6 A1
Greenways Wlk RH11 201 C1
Greenway The
Epsom KT18 76 A5
Hounslow TW4 4 F3
Oxted RH8 123 B2
Greenwell Cl RH9 121 B5
Greenwich Cl RH11 201 C2
Green Wlk
Crawley RH10 201 E8
Hampton TW12 15 F2
Greenwood
[4] Bracknell RG12 27 F5
North Ascot SL5 28 C8
[8] Putney SW19 19 D8
Greenwood Cl
Hinchley Wood KT7 37 A1
Merton SM4 39 E5
Woodham KT15 70 F8
Greenwood Cotts SL5 30 C3
Greenwood Ct
[2] Crawley RH11 201 B1
[10] Epsom KT18 76 E6
Greenwood Dr RH1 140 A4
Greenwood Flats RH6 182 F6
Greenwood Gdns
Caterham CR3 101 A2
Oxted RH8 123 A1
Greenwood La TW12 16 B3
Greenwood Pk KT2 18 E1
Greenwood Rd
Crowthorne RG45 45 B6
Hinchley Wood KT7 56 A8
Isleworth TW7 5 F4
Knaphill GU21 88 E7
Mitcham CR4 41 D6
Pirbright GU24 87 C7
Thornton Heath CR0, CR9 42 C2
Greenwood The GU1 110 A1
Green Wrythe Cres
SM5 40 E1
Green Wrythe La SM4, SM5 40 E2
Green Wrythe Prim Sch
SM5 40 D3
Gregan Ct GU11 104 F1
Gregory Cl
Crawley RH10 202 C2
Woking GU21 69 C2
Gregory Ct
[2] East Grinstead RH19 185 E1
Purley CR8 80 B6
Gregsons RH12 216 E8
Greig Ho [9] TW10 17 C5
Grenaby Ave CR0 42 D2
Grenaby Rd CR0 42 D2
Grenadier Pl CR3 100 C5
Grenadier Rd GU12 106 B4
Grenadiers Way GU14 84 C3
Grena Gdns TW9 6 F3
Grena Rd TW10, TW9 6 F3
Grendon Cl RH6 160 F5
Grenehurst Pk RH5 178 B4
Grenfell Rd CR4, SW17 20 F2
Grennell Cl SM1 59 D8
Grennell Rd SM1 59 C8
Grenside Rd KT13 53 B7
Grenville Cl
Cobham KT11 73 E6
Tolworth KT5 38 C1
Grenville Ct SE19 22 F3
Grenville Gdns GU16 85 E6
Grenville Mews TW12 16 B3
Grenville Pl
Ashtead KT21 75 F1
Bracknell RG12 27 C7
Grenville Rd
New Addington CR0 63 C2
Shackleford GU8 149 D7
Gresham Ave CR6 81 E1
Gresham Cl RH8 122 F7
Gresham Ct
Farnborough GU14 105 C8
Frimley GU15 65 F4
Hounslow TW3 5 C6
[3] Purley CR8 80 A8
Gresham Ct *continued*
[3] Staines TW18 13 A3
Gresham Ho
[5] Teddington TW11 16 F3
[3] Thames Ditton KT7 37 A2
West Barnes KT3 39 B5
Gresham Ind Est
GU12 105 E2
Gresham Prim Sch
CR2 81 A7
Gresham Rd
Croydon SE25 43 A5
Hampton TW12 16 A2
Hounslow TW3, TW5 5 C6
Limpsfield RH8 122 F6
Penge BR3 43 E7
Staines TW18 13 A3
Gresham Way
Frimley GU16 85 E6
Wimbledon SW19 20 A5
Gresham Way Est
SW19 20 B5
Gresham Wlk RH10 201 E3
Gressenhall Rd SW18 19 F8
Greta Bank KT24 92 C1
Greville Ave CR2 62 D1
Greville Cl
Aldershot GU11 104 F3
Ashtead KT21 95 E8
Guildford GU2 108 E1
Twickenham TW1 17 B8
Greville Ct
Ashtead KT21 75 E1
Fetcham KT23 94 C2
Greville Park Ave KT21 75 E1
Greville Park Rd KT21 75 E1
Greville Prim Sch The
KT21 75 F2
Greville Rd TW10 6 F1
Grey Alders KT17 77 C5
Greycot Rd BR3 24 A3
Grey Court Sch TW10 17 C5
Greyfields Cl CR8 80 B6
Greyfriars [16] SE26 23 A5
Greyfriars Dr
Ascot SL5 29 B3
Bisley GU24 68 A4
Greyfriars Rd GU23 91 A3
Greyhound Cl GU12 105 F1
Greyhound La SW16 21 D2
Greyhound Rd SM1 59 C5
Greyhound Slip RH10 202 D7
Greyhound Terr SW16 41 C8
Greylees GU7 150 E5
Greys Ct GU11 104 E2
Greystead Pk GU10 145 E5
Greystead Rd SE23 23 C8
Greystoke Ct RG45 45 A4
Greystone Cl CR2 81 C8
Greystones Cl RH1 139 D7
Greystones Ct TW2 16 C6
Greystones Dr RH2 118 C3
Greyswood St SW16 21 B2
Greythorne Rd GU21 69 A1
Greytiles TW11 16 F2
Greywaters GU5 152 A6
Grice Ave TN16 83 C6
Grier Cl RH11 200 E5
Grierson Ho SW16 21 C4
Grierson Rd SE23 23 D8
Grieve Cl GU10 126 E7
Griffin Ct
Ashtead KT21 95 E8
[8] Brentford TW8 6 E8
Great Bookham KT23 94 B1
Griffin Ctr TW14 4 B1
Griffin Ctr The KT1 37 D7
Griffin Pk (Brentford FC)
TW8 6 D8
Griffin Way
Great Bookham KT23 94 A1
Sunbury TW16 35 A7
Griffiths Cl KT4 58 B8
Griffiths Rd SW19 20 B1
Griffon Cl GU14 84 D3
Griggs Mdw GU8 192 F7
Grimwade Ave CR0 62 A7
Grimwood Rd TW1 16 F8
Grindall Cl CR0 61 B6
Grindley Gdns CR0 42 F3
Grindstone Cres GU21 68 B1
Grindstone Handle Cnr
GU21 68 B1
Grinstead La RH19 205 B1
Grisedale Cl
Crawley RH11 201 C4
Sanderstead CR8 80 E5
Grisedale Gdns CR8 80 E5
Grizedale Terr SE23 23 B6
Grobars Ave GU21 69 C4
Grogan Cl TW12 15 F2
Groombridge Cl KT12 54 B5
Groombridge Ho SE20 23 D1
Groombridge Way
RH12 216 F1
Groom Cres SW18 20 D8
Groomfield Cl SW17 21 A4
Grooms The RH10 202 D8
Groom Wlk GU1 109 E4
Grosslea SM4 40 D4
Grosvenor Ave
Mortlake SW14 7 E4
Richmond TW10 6 E2
Wallington SM5 60 A4
Grosvenor Cl RH6 161 A1
Grosvenor Ct
Blackwater GU17 64 D3
Guildford GU4 110 B4
Grosvenor Ct *continued*
[11] Leatherhead KT22 95 C6
Morden SM4 40 A5
Penge SE19 22 F2
[2] Richmond TW10 6 F1
[7] Sutton SM2 59 C4
Teddington TW11 17 A2
[2] Wimbledon SW19 19 E2
Grosvenor Gdns
Kingston u T KT2 17 D2
Mortlake SW14 7 E4
Wallington SM6 60 C3
Grosvenor Hill SW19 19 E2
Grosvenor Ho RH19 185 E3
Grosvenor Ho
[2] Farnborough GU14 105 D8
[8] Guildford GU1 130 F8
[5] Sutton SM1 59 B5
Grosvenor Mews RH2 139 B6
Grosvenor Pl
[1] Oatlands Park KT13 53 D7
[1] Woking GU21 69 F2
Grosvenor Rd
Aldershot GU11 105 A1
Brentford TW8 6 D8
Castle Green GU24 68 D6
Croydon SE25 43 A5
East Grinstead RH19 185 D1
Godalming GU7 150 E3
Hounslow TW3, TW4 4 F4
Langley Vale KT18 96 E8
Richmond TW10 6 E2
Staines TW18 13 A1
Twickenham TW1 17 A7
Wallington SM6 60 B5
West Wickham BR4 63 B8
Groton Rd SW18 20 B6
Grotto Rd
Twickenham TW1 16 F6
Weybridge KT13 53 B7
Grove Ave
Epsom KT17 76 E6
Sutton SM1 59 A4
Twickenham TW1 16 F7
Grovebarns TW18 13 A2
Grovebell Ind Est
GU9 145 F7
Grove Cl
Cranleigh GU6 174 F1
Epsom KT19 57 B1
Forest Hill SE23 23 E7
[8] Kingston u T KT1 37 F5
Old Windsor SL4 11 B8
Grove Cnr [1] KT23 94 B1
Grove Cres
Feltham TW13 15 E4
Kingston u T KT1 37 E6
Walton-on-T KT12 35 B2
Grove Cross Rd GU16 65 D1
Grove Ct
Dorking RH4 136 A6
East Molesey KT8 36 D4
Egham TW20 12 A3
[3] Forest Hill SE26 23 E4
Hounslow TW3 5 A3
[8] Kingston u T KT1 37 E6
New Malden KT3 38 E6
Penge SE20 23 B1
[1] Sutton SM1 59 B4
Grove End GU19 47 F5
Grove End La KT10 36 D1
Grove End Rd GU9 146 B8
Grove Farm Ct CR4 40 F4
Grove Farm Pk GU12 85 F1
Grovefields Ave GU16 65 D1
Grove Gdns TW11 17 A4
Grove Heath Ct GU23 91 C3
Grove Heath La GU23 91 D4
Grove Heath N GU23 91 B5
Grove Heath Rd GU23 91 B4
Grovehill Ct BR1 24 F2
Grovehill Rd RH1 118 F1
Grove Ho
[7] Epsom KT17 76 E6
Old Windsor SL4 11 C8
[8] Redhill RH1 118 F1
Grove La
Kingston u T KT1 37 E5
Wallington CR5 79 B5
Winkfield RG42 8 B4
Groveland Ave SW16 21 F1
Groveland Rd BR3 43 F6
Grovelands
East Molesey KT8 36 A5
Farnham GU10 146 E7
Horley RH6 161 B2
Kingston u T KT1 37 D5
Grovelands Inf Sch
KT12 35 B3
Grovelands Rd CR8 79 F7
Groveland Way KT3 38 D4
Groveley Rd TW13, TW16 14 F3
Grove Lo [8] TW1 17 A7
Grove Mill CR4 40 E4
Grove Mill Pl SM5 60 A7
GROVE PARK 7 C6
Grove Park Bridge W4 7 C7
Grove Park Gdns W4 7 C7
Grove Park Prim Sch
W4 7 C8
Grove Park Rd W4 7 B7
Grove Park Terr W4 7 B8
Grove Pl KT13 53 C5
Grove Pl Cvn Pk SM7 78 F7
Grove Prim Sch The
GU16 65 E2
Grove Rd
Ash GU12 106 A3
Ashtead KT21 95 F8
Barnes SW13 7 F5
Beacon Hill GU26 188 C6
Camberley GU15 65 F5
Chertsey KT16 32 F3
Cranleigh GU6 174 F1
East Molesey KT8 36 D5
Epsom KT17, KT18 76 E6
Godalming GU7 150 C3
Guildford GU1 110 C1
Horley RH6 160 F4
Hounslow, Spring Grove TW7 5 E6
Hounslow TW3 5 A3
Kingston u T KT6 37 D4
Lingfield RH7 164 E5
Merton SW19 20 C1
Mitcham CR4 41 B7
Richmond TW10 6 F1
Shepperton TW17 34 C3
Sutton SM1 59 A4
Tandridge RH8 122 C2
Tatsfield TN16 103 C7
Thornton Heath CR7 42 A5
Twickenham TW2 16 D5
Woking GU21 69 F3
Grove Rd Prim Sch TW3 5 A3
Grovers Manor GU26 188 D6
Grove Shaw KT20 97 E3
Groveside KT23 114 A8
Groveside Cl
Carshalton SM5 59 E8
Great Bookham KT23 114 A8
Grovestile Waye TW14 14 D8
Grove Terr TW11 17 A4
Grove The
Addlestone KT15 52 B5
Aldershot GU11 105 A1
Biggin Hill TN16 83 E1
Caterham CR3 100 C6
Coulsdon CR5 79 D5
Crawley RH11 201 C6
Egham TW20 12 A3
Epsom KT17 76 E6
Farnborough GU14 85 D1
Frimley GU16 65 D1
Horley RH6 161 B2
Hounslow TW7 5 E6
North Ascot SL5 28 C8
Teddington TW11 17 A4
[1] Twickenham TW1 6 B1
Walton-on-T KT12 35 B2
West Wickham BR4 63 C7
Woking GU21 69 F3
Grove Villas GU12 106 A3
Grove Way KT10 36 C1
Grovewood [9] TW9 7 A6
Grovewood Ct TW7 5 E6
Grove Wood Hill CR5 79 D5
Grub St RH8 123 C7
Guardian Ct GU8 148 C3
Guards Ave CR3 100 C5
Guards Ct SL5 30 B2
Guerdon Pl RG12 27 D2
Guernsey Cl
Crawley RH11 201 A2
Guildford GU4 110 A6
Heston TW5 5 A7
Guernsey Farm Dr
GU21 69 D4
Guernsey Gr SE24 22 C8
Guildables La TN8 144 E7
Guildcroft GU1 110 A1
Guildersfield Rd SW16 21 E1
GUILDFORD 130 A7
Guildford Ave TW13 15 A6
Guildford Business Park Rd GU2 109 B2
Guildford Castle* GU1 130 D7
Guildford Cath* GU2 109 B1
Guildford Coll Merrist Wood Campus GU3 108 C7
Guildford Coll of F Ed & H Ed GU1 109 E2
Guildford Cty Sch
GU2 130 B7
Guildford & Godalming By-Pass Rd
Guildford GU2, GU3 129 E6
Shackleford GU7, GU8 149 F6
Guildford Grove Prim Sch
GU2 108 E1
Guildford High Sch
GU1 109 E1
Guildford Ind Est
GU2 109 A2
Guildford La GU22 89 E8
Guildford Lodge Dr
KT24 112 F6
Guildford Mus* GU1 130 D7
Guildford Nuffield Hospl The GU2 108 E1
GUILDFORD PARK 130 B8
Guildford Park Ave
GU2 130 B8
Guildford Park Rd
GU2 130 C8
Guildford Rd
Aldershot GU11, GU12 126 D7
Ash GU12, GU3 106 D3
Bagshot GU19 47 E3
Broadbridge Heath RH12 216 B6
Guildford Rd *continued*
Castle Green GU21, GU24 68 D6
Chertsey KT16 32 F1
East Horsley KT24 112 F5
Farncombe GU7 151 B7
Farnham GU10, GU9 125 F4
Fetcham KT22 94 F3
Frimley GU16 85 F6
Great Bookham KT23, KT22 94 A1
Horsham RH12 217 A2
Lightwater GU18, GU19 48 B1
Loxwood RH14 212 F4
Mytchett GU16 86 B5
Normandy GU3 107 B4
Ottershaw KT16 51 C5
Pirbright GU3 88 A2
Pirbright GU24 87 F4
Rowhook RH12, RH13 215 C7
Rowly GU6 174 B6
Rudgwick RH12 214 C6
Runfold GU10 126 B4
Shamley Green GU5 152 D5
Shamley Green GU5 153 A1
Thornton Heath CR0 42 D3
Westcott RH4 135 C6
West End GU24 67 F7
Windlesham GU19 47 F2
Woking GU22 89 E8
Woking, Westfield GU22, GU4 89 D4
Wotton RH5 134 C3
Guildford Rd E GU14 85 C1
Guildford Rd W GU14 85 C1
Guildford Road Ind Est
GU9 125 D3
Guildford Sch of Acting
GU2 130 C7
Guildford St
Chertsey KT16 33 A2
Staines TW18 13 A2
Guildford Sta GU1 130 C8
Guildford Way SM6 60 E5
Guildown Ave GU2 130 B6
Guildown Rd GU2 130 C6
Guildway Hos GU7 150 D7
Guileshill La GU23 91 F5
Guilford Ave KT5 37 F4
Guillemont Fields
GU14 84 D5
Guillemont Jun Sch
GU14 84 D6
Guillemont Pk GU14 84 C6
Guillemot Path [2]
RH11 200 D5
Guinevere Ct SE6 24 C4
Guinevere Ho [19] RH1 119 A2
Guinevere Rd RH11 200 E6
Guinness Ct
Crawley RH11 201 C2
[6] Croydon CR0 61 F8
[4] Knaphill GU21 68 F1
Gulley Rd GU14 105 A8
Gulliver Ct CR2 61 B3
Gumbrells Cl GU3 108 C5
Gumley Gdns TW7 6 A4
Gumley House RC Convent Sch (Girls) TW7 6 A4
Gun Hill GU11 105 B3
Gunnell Cl
Croydon SE25 43 A3
Penge SE26 23 A3
Gunnell Ct [8] CR4 40 E8
Gunners Rd SW18 20 D6
Gunning Cl RH11 201 A3
Gun Pit Rd RH7 164 D4
Gunters Mead KT22 74 C8
Gunton Rd SW17 21 A2
Gurdon's La GU8 170 F2
Gurney Cres CR0 41 F1
Gurney Rd SM5 60 A6
Gurney's Cl [4] RH1 139 F8
Guyatt Gdns CR4 41 A7
Guy Rd SM6 60 D7
Gwendolen Ho TW19 13 E7
Gwendoline Ct TW15 13 E4
Gwydor Rd BR3 43 D6
Gwydyr Rd BR2 44 F6
Gwynne Ave CR0 43 D2
Gwynne Cl [4] W4 7 F8
Gwynne Ct
Guildford GU2 109 B5
Wimbledon SW20 39 C8
Gwynne Gdns RH19 185 C2
Gwynne Ho [6] SW2 21 F7
Gwynne Rd CR3 100 D4

H

Habershon Dr GU16 66 D2
Haccombe Rd SW19 20 C2
HACKBRIDGE 60 B8
Hackbridge Park Gdns
SM5 59 F8
Hackbridge Prim Sch
SM6 41 A1
Hackbridge Rd SM6 60 A8
Hackbridge Sta SM6 60 B8
Hackenden Cl RH19 185 E3
Hackenden La RH19 185 E3
Hacketts La GU22 70 F4
Hackhurst La RH5 133 F4
Hackington Cres BR3 24 A2

Haddenham Ct SW17 20 D4
Haddington Rd BR1 24 D4
Haddon Cl
New Malden KT3 38 F4
Oatlands Park KT13 53 D6
Haddon Rd SM1 59 B6
Hadfield Rd TW19 2 D1
Hadleigh Cl SW20 39 F7
Hadleigh Dr SM2 59 B2
Hadleigh Gdns GU16 85 E6
Hadley Ct SL3 1 E6
Hadley Pl KT13 53 A3
Hadley Rd CR4 41 D5
Hadleys GU10 145 E3
Hadley Wood Rise CR8 80 B5
Hadlow Pl SE19 23 A1
Hadmans Cl RH12 217 C1
Hadrian Cl TW19 13 E8
Hadrian Ct 1 SM2 59 B3
Hadrians GU9 125 E4
Hadrian Way
Stanwell TW19 13 D8
Stanwell TW19 13 E8
Hafton Rd SE6 24 E6
Haggard Rd TW1 17 B8
Haigh Cres RH1 140 B7
HAIG HOMES 40 A3
Haig Pl SM4 40 A3
Haig Rd
Aldershot GU12 105 C1
Biggin Hill TN16 83 E2
Sandhurst GU15 64 F6
Hailes Cl SW19 20 C2
Hailey Pl GU6 174 F4
Hailsham Ave SW2 21 F6
Hailsham Cl
Sandhurst GU47 45 D1
Surbiton KT6 37 D2
Hailsham Rd SW17 21 A2
Haines Ct KT13 53 D5
Haines Wlk SM4 40 B2
Haining Gdns GU16 86 A3
Hainthorpe Rd SE27 22 B4
Halcroft Ct SM1 59 D6
Halcyon Ct TW18 33 B7
Haldane Pl SW18 20 B7
HALE 125 C6
Halebourne La GU24 49 A2
Hale End RG12 27 F5
Hale Ends GU22 89 B6
Hale House La GU10 168 B2
Hale Pit Rd KT23 94 C1
Hale Pl GU9 125 E5
Hale Rd GU9 125 D5
Hale Rdbt GU9 125 E5
Hale Reeds GU9 125 E6
Hale Sch GU9 125 B7
Hales Ct 6 TW11 17 A3
Hales Field GU27 208 C6
Hales Ho 3 SW12 21 B8
Hales Oak KT23 94 C1
Halesowen Rd SM4 40 B2
Hale St TW18 12 E4
Haleswood KT11 73 C5
Hale Way GU16 85 D8
Halewood RG12 26 F3
Half Acre TW8 6 D8
Half Acre Mews TW8 6 D8
Halfacres RH10 201 E7
Half Moon Hill GU27 208 C6
Half Moon St GU19 47 E3
Halford Ct KT9 56 E3
Halford Rd TW10 6 E2
Halfpenny Cl GU4 131 D3
Halfpenny Cross KT11 73 A2
Halfpenny Ct 2 SL5 30 B2
Halfpenny La
Guildford GU4 131 C5
Sunningdale SL5 30 A2
Half Way Cotts GU10 124 C3
Halfway Gn KT12 54 B7
Halfway La GU7 150 B4
Haliburton Rd TW1, TW7 6 A3
Halifax Cl
Crawley RH10 182 E1
Farnborough GU14 84 F3
Teddington TW11 16 E2
Halifax St SE26 23 B5
Halimote Rd GU11 105 A1
Haling Down Pas CR8 61 C1
Haling Gr CR2 61 C3
Haling Manor High Sch
CR2 61 B3
Haling Park Gdns CR2 61 B4
Haling Park Rd CR2 61 C4
Haling Rd CR2 61 D4
Hallam Rd GU7 150 F5
Halland Cl RH10 202 A7
Hallane Ho SE27 22 C3
Hall Cl
Camberley GU15 65 E6
Farncombe GU7 150 E7
Hall Ct TW11 16 F3
Hall Dene Cl GU1 110 C2
Hall Dr SE26 23 C3
Halley Cl RH11 201 B1
Halley Dr SL5 28 D7
Halley's App GU21 69 A1
Halley's Ct 1 GU21 69 A1
Halley's Wlk KT15 52 C3
Hall Farm Dr TW2 16 D8
Hallgrove Bottom
GU19 47 F5
Hall Grove Farm GU19 47 F5
Hall Grove Sch GU19 48 A5
Hall Hill RH8 122 D4
Halliards The KT12 35 A3
Halliford Cl TW17 34 E6
Halliford Rd
Sunbury TW16 35 A5
Upper Halliford TW16,
TW17 34 F5
Halliford Sch TW17 34 C2
Hallington Cl GU21 69 B2
Hall La UB3 3 D7
Hallmark Cl GU47 64 E8
Hallmead Rd SM1 59 B7
Hallowell Ave CR0 60 E6
Hallowell Cl CR4 41 A6
Hallowes Cl GU2 109 B6
Hallowfield Way CR4 40 E6
Hallows Gr TW16 14 F3
Hall Pl
Dunsfold GU6 193 D7
Woking GU21 70 A3
Hall Place Dr KT13 53 E5
Hall Rd
Bramley GU5 151 F6
Isleworth TW7 5 D2
Wallington SM6 60 B2
Hall Sch SW20 39 D8
Hall Sch Wimbledon
SW15 19 A5
Halls Dr RH12 199 F1
Halls Farm Cl GU21 68 D2
Hallsland RH10 204 C8
Hallsland Way RH8 122 F3
Hall Way CR8 80 B6
Halnaker Wlk 8
RH11 200 F3
Halsford Croft RH19 185 B3
Halsford Gn RH19 185 B3
Halsford La RH19 185 C3
Halsford Park Prim Sch
RH19 185 C2
Halsford Park Rd
RH19 185 C2
Halstead Cl CR0, CR9 61 C7
Halstead Sch GU21 70 A4
Halters End GU26 188 A3
Halton Rd CR3 100 E7
HAM 17 C5
Hamble Ave GU17 64 D5
Hamble Cl GU21 69 A2
Hamble Ct KT1 17 D1
Hambleden Ct RG12 27 E5
HAMBLEDON 171 D2
Hambledon Ct 9 SM6 60 B4
Hambledon Gdns SE25 42 F6
Hambledon Hill KT18 76 C3
Hambledon Ho 2 KT2 18 B2
Hambledon Pk GU8 171 B1
Hambledon Pl
Dulwich SE21 22 F7
Little Bookham KT23 94 A4
Hambledon Rd
Caterham CR3 100 D4
Hydestile GU8, GU7 171 D5
Wandsworth SW18 19 F8
Hambledon Vale KT18 76 C3
Hambleton Cl
Frimley GU16 66 B3
North Cheam KT4 58 C8
Hambleton Ct RH11 201 C4
Hambleton Hill RH11 201 C4
Hamble Wlk GU21 69 A2
Hambly Mans SW16 21 E2
Hambridge Way SW2 22 A8
Hambrook Rd SE25 43 B6
Hambro Rd SW16 21 D3
Ham Cl TW10 17 C5
Ham Comm TW10 17 D5
Ham Croft Cl TW13 15 A5
Hamers Ho 10 SW2 22 A8
Hamesmoor Rd GU16 85 F4
Hamesmoor Way GU16 85 F4
Ham Farm Rd KT2,
TW10 17 E4
Hamfield Cl RH8 122 C8
Ham Gate Ave
Richmond, Richmond Park
TW10 18 A4
Richmond TW10 17 E4
Hamhaugh Island
TW17 53 A8
Ham Ho* TW10 17 C6
Hamilton Ave
Cheam SM3 58 E8
Cobham KT11 73 A6
Pyrford GU22 70 E3
Tolworth KT6 57 A8
Hamilton Cl
Ashford TW13 14 F3
Bagshot GU19 47 E3
Chertsey KT16 32 F1
Epsom KT19 76 C7
Guildford GU2 109 A6
Purley CR8 80 B7
Hamilton Cres TW3 5 B2
Hamilton Ct
Catford SE6 24 F7
Cobham KT11 73 A6
Croydon CR0 43 A1
Farnborough GU17 64 E1
Great Bookham KT23 94 B2
Hamilton Dr
Guildford GU2 109 A6
Sunningdale SL5 29 E2
Hamilton Gdns GU14 84 D5
Hamilton Gordon Ct
GU1 109 C2
Hamilton Ho
5 Chiswick W4 7 E8
Hamilton Ho *continued*
10 Richmond TW9 7 A6
Hamilton Mews
Wandsworth SW18 20 A7
Weybridge KT13 53 A6
Hamilton Par TW13 15 A4
Hamilton Pl
Aldershot GU11 104 F1
Guildford GU2 109 A6
Kingswood KT20 97 F4
Sunbury TW16 15 B1
Hamilton Rd
Brentford TW8 6 D8
Feltham TW13 14 F4
Horsham RH12 217 B3
Merton SW19 20 B1
South Norwood CR7 42 D6
Twickenham TW2 16 E7
West Norwood SE27 22 D4
Hamilton Road Ind Est
SE27 22 D4
Hamilton Road Mews 1
SW19 20 B1
Hamilton Way SM6 60 D2
Ham La
Elstead GU8 148 E4
Englefield Green TW20 11 B4
Hamlash Cotts GU10 146 C2
Hamlash La GU10 146 C1
Hamlet Rd SE19 23 A1
Hamlet St RG42 27 E8
Hamlyn Gdns SE19 22 E1
Hamlyn Ho TW13 15 B7
Hamm Court Est KT13 52 F8
Hammelton Ct 4 BR1 44 F8
Hammelton Rd 5 BR1 44 F8
HAMMER 207 D5
Hammerfield Dr RH5 133 F3
Hammer Hill GU27 207 C4
Hammer La
Grayshott GU10,
GU26 187 E6
Haslemere GU27,
GU30 207 A6
Haslemere, Hammer
GU27 207 C5
Haslemere, Nutcombe GU26,
GU27 207 C8
Hammerpond Rd
RH13 217 F1
Hammersley Rd GU11 105 C7
Hammer Vale GU27 207 B6
Hammerwood Copse
GU27 207 D5
Hammerwood Rd
RH19 206 E6
HAMM MOOR 52 E6
Hamm Moor La KT15 52 E6
Hammond Ave CR4 41 B7
Hammond Cl
Hampton TW12 36 A8
Woking GU21 69 C4
Hammond Com Jun Sch
GU18 48 A1
Hammond Rd GU21 69 C4
Hammonds Ho TW19 13 F7
Hammond Way GU18 48 B1
Hamond Cl CR2 61 B2
Hampden Ave BR3 43 E7
Hampden Cl RH10 182 E1
Hampden Rd
Beckenham BR3 43 E7
Kingston u T KT1 38 A6
Hampers Ct 2 RH13 217 D2
Hamper's La RH13 218 A2
Hampshire Cl GU12 126 D7
Hampshire Ct
Addlestone KT15 52 C5
Barnes SW13 7 F5
6 Horsham RH12 217 D2
Hampshire Rd GU15 65 F8
Hampstead La RH4 135 F6
Hampstead Rd RH4 136 A6
HAMPTON 36 A7
Hampton Cl
1 Knaphill GU21 68 C1
Wimbledon SW20 19 C1
Hampton Com Coll
TW12 16 A3
Hampton Court Ave
KT8 36 E3
Hampton Court Cres
KT8 36 D6
Hampton Court Pal*
KT8 36 F6
Hampton Court Par
KT8 36 E5
Hampton Court Rd KT1,
KT8 37 B6
Hampton Court Sta
KT8 36 E5
Hampton Court Way KT10,
KT7, KT8 36 E3
Hampton Farm Ind Est
TW13 15 E5
Hampton Gr KT17 76 F8
HAMPTON HILL 16 C3
Hampton Hill Bsns Pk
TW12 16 C3
Hampton Hill Jun Sch
TW12 16 C3
Hampton Inf Sch
TW12 16 A1
Hampton Jun Sch
TW12 36 A8
Hampton La TW13 15 E4
Hampton Lo RH6 161 A2
Hampton Rd
Hale GU9 125 B6
North Cheam KT4 58 B8
Redhill RH1 139 F4
Teddington TW11, TW12 16 D3
Thornton Heath CR0 42 C3
Twickenham TW2 16 D5
Hampton Rd E TW13 15 F5
Hampton Rd W TW13 15 E5
Hampton Road Ind Pk
CR0 42 C3
Hampton Sch TW12 16 A3
Hampton Sta TW12 36 A8
Hampton Terr GU26 188 C6
Hampton Way RH19 205 F7
HAMPTON WICK 37 D8
Hampton Wick Inf Sch
KT1 17 D1
Hampton Wick Sta
KT1 37 C8
Ham Ridings TW10 17 F3
HAMSEY GREEN 81 C4
Hamsey Green Gdns
CR6 81 C3
Hamsey Green Inf Sch
CR6 81 B3
Hamsey Green Jun Sch
CR6 81 B3
Hamsey Way CR2 81 B4
Ham St TW10 17 C5
Ham The TW8 6 C7
Ham View CR0 43 E3
Hanbury Ct GU23 71 E3
Hanbury Dr TN16 83 B6
Hanbury Path GU21 70 D5
Hanbury Rd RH11 200 E5
Hanbury Way GU15 65 C3
Hancock Rd SE19 22 D2
Hancocks Mount SL5 29 D3
Hancombe Rd GU47 45 A1
Handcroft Rd CR0 42 B1
Handel Ho TW2 5 D1
Handley Page Rd SM6 60 F3
Handpost Cnr RG40 25 A1
Handside Cl KT4 39 D1
Handsworth Ho 8
RH10 201 D5
Hanford Cl SW18 20 A7
Hanford Row SW19 19 C2
Hanger Ct GU21 68 E2
Hanger Hill KT13 53 B5
Hanley Pl BR3 24 A1
Hannah Cl BR3 44 C6
Hannah Ct
14 Sutton SM1 59 B4
Wimbledon SW19 19 D1
4 Woking GU21 70 A3
Hannah Mews SM6 60 C3
Hannah Peschar Gall &
Gdn* RH5 177 A2
Hannay Wlk SW16 21 D6
Hannen Rd SE27 22 B5
Hannibal Rd TW19 13 E8
Hannibal Way CR0 60 F4
Hanning Lo TW3 5 C3
Hanover Ave TW13 15 A6
Hanover Cl
Cheam SM3 58 F6
Crawley RH10 201 F3
Englefield Green TW20 11 B2
Frimley GU16 65 E1
Merstham RH1 119 C7
Richmond TW9 7 A7
Hanover Ct
Dorking RH4 135 F7
Guildford GU1 109 D3
1 Horsham RH13 217 F3
1 Penge SE19 23 A1
2 Teddington TW11 16 F3
4 Woking GU22 89 E8
Hanover Gdns
Bracknell RG12 26 F2
Farnborough GU14 84 E6
Hanover Ho
9 New Malden KT3 38 E5
Tolworth KT6 38 A1
Hanover Pk 1 SL5 28 F8
Hanover Rd SW19 20 C1
Hanover St CR0, CR9 61 B7
Hanover Terr TW7 6 A6
Hanover Wlk KT13 53 E7
Hansard KT18 97 D8
Hansler Ct 14 SW19 19 E7
Hansler Gr KT8 36 D5
Hanson Cl
Balham SW12 21 B8
Beckenham BR3 24 B2
Camberley GU15 66 B7
Guildford GU1 109 F4
Mortlake SW14 7 C4
HANWORTH
Feltham 15 D4
Bracknell 27 A2
Hanworth Cl RG12 27 C3
Hanworth La KT16 32 F1
Hanworth Park Ct
TW13 15 C7
Hanworth Rd
Bracknell RG12 27 A2
Feltham TW13 15 B7
Hampton TW12 16 A3
Hounslow TW3, TW4 5 A2
Redhill RH1 139 F4
Sunbury TW16 15 A1
Twickenham TW4 15 F8
Hanworth Terr TW3 5 B3
Hanworth Trad Est
Chertsey KT16 32 F1
Hanworth Trad Est
continued
Feltham TW13 15 E5
Harberson Rd SW12 21 B7
Harbie Brow KT4 57 E7
Harbin Ho 5 SW2 22 A7
Harbledown Rd CR2 81 A8
Harborough Rd SW16 21 F4
Harbour Cl GU14 85 A8
Harbourfield Rd SM7 78 B4
Harbridge Ave SW15 19 A8
Harbury Rd SM5 59 E3
Harcourt Ave SM6 60 B6
Harcourt Cl
Egham TW20 12 C2
Isleworth TW7 6 A4
Harcourt Field SM6 60 B6
Harcourt Lo 2 SM6 60 B6
Harcourt Rd
Bracknell RG12 27 B4
Camberley GU15 65 B5
Merton SW19 20 A1
Thornton Heath CR7 42 A3
Wallington SM6 60 B6
Harcourt Way RH9 142 E6
Hardcastle Cl SE25 43 A3
Hardcourts Cl BR4 63 B7
Hardell Cl TW20 12 A3
Hardel Rise SW2 22 B7
Hardel Wlk SW2 22 A8
Harden Farm Cl CR5 99 C6
Hardham Cl RH11 201 A8
Hardie Ho TW13 15 E4
Harding Cl
Kingston u T KT2 37 F8
South Croydon CR0 61 F7
Harding Ct SE25 42 F7
Harding Ho SM6 60 C2
Harding Pl SE23 23 E8
Harding Rd KT18 96 E8
Hardings La SE20 23 D2
Hardman Rd KT2 37 E7
Hardwell Way RG12 27 E5
Hardwick Cl KT22 74 C4
Hardwicke Ave TW5 5 A6
Hardwicke Rd
Reigate RH2 118 A2
Richmond TW10 17 C4
Hardwick La KT16 32 D1
Hardwick Rd RH1 139 D7
Hardy Cl
Crawley RH10 202 C7
Dorking RH5 136 B3
Horley RH6 160 E3
Horsham RH12 217 B4
Hardy Gn RG45 45 B4
Hardy Ho KT19 57 B1
Hardy Rd SW19 20 B1
Hardys Mews KT8 36 E5
Harebell Hill KT11 73 E5
Harecroft
Dorking RH4 136 C4
Fetcham KT23 94 C3
Haredon Cl SE23 23 D8
Harefield KT10 55 E7
Harefield Ave SM2 58 E2
Harefield Ct 4 SW19 20 A1
Harefield Rd SW16 21 F1
Hare Hill KT15 51 F4
Hare Hill Cl GU22 71 A4
Hare La
Claygate KT10 55 E4
Crawley RH11 201 B8
Farncombe GU7 150 F6
Horne RH7 163 D5
Harelands Cl GU21 69 C2
Harelands La GU21 69 C2
Harendon KT20 97 D6
Hares Bank CR0 63 D1
Harestone Ct CR2 61 E4
Harestone Dr CR3 100 F2
Harestone Hill CR3 100 F2
Harestone La CR3 100 E2
Harestone Valley Rd
CR3 100 F2
Hareward Rd GU4 110 C4
Harewood SW15 18 D4
Harewood Cl
Crawley RH10 182 A1
Reigate RH2 118 C4
Harewood Gdns CR2 81 C4
Harewood Rd
Hounslow TW7 5 F6
Mitcham SW19 20 E2
South Croydon CR2 61 E4
Harfield Rd TW16 35 D7
Harkness Cl KT17 77 C3
Harkness Ct SM1 40 B1
Harland Ave CR0 62 A7
Harland Cl SW19 40 B6
Harlech Ct 1 SE23 23 C7
Harlech Gdns TW5 4 C7
Harlech Rd GU17 64 D4
Harlequin Ave TW8 6 A8
Harlequin Cl TW7 5 E2
Harlequin Ct CR2 61 C3
Harlequin Rd TW11 17 B1
Harlequins RFC TW2 16 E8
HARLINGTON 3 C8
Harlington Cl UB7 3 C7
Harlington Cnr UB3 3 D6
Harlington Rd E TW13,
TW14 15 C7
Harlington Rd W TW14 4 B1
Harlow Ct 4 RH2 118 D1
Harman Pl CR8 80 B8
Harmans Dr RH19 186 B1
Harmans Mead RH19 186 B1

HARMANS WATER 27 D5
Harmans Water Prim Sch RG12 27 E4
Harmans Water Rd RG12 27 D4
Harmar Cl RG40 25 E6
Harmes Way GU14 105 D7
HARMONDSWORTH 2 E8
Harmondsworth La UB7 2 E8
Harmondsworth Moor Ctry Pk* UB7 2 B7
Harmondsworth Prim Sch UB7 2 D8
Harmony Cl
- Crawley RH11 200 E4
- Wallington SM6 60 E2
Harms Gr GU4 110 C4
Harold Ct 6 TW11 16 E3
Harold Rd
- Carshalton SM1 59 D6
- Crawley RH10 202 E5
- South Norwood SE19 22 D1
Haroldslea RH6 161 E2
Haroldslea Cl RH6 161 C1
Haroldslea Dr RH6 161 D1
Harpenden Rd SE27 22 B6
Harper Dr RH10 202 C2
Harper Mews SW17 20 C5
Harper's Rd GU12 106 D2
HARPESFORD 31 C3
Harpesford Ave GU25 31 C4
Harps Oak La RH1 99 A2
Harpswood Cl CR5 99 C5
Harpurs KT20 97 D5
Harrier Cl GU6 174 E4
Harrier Ct RH10 182 D1
Harrier Ho 10 KT2 37 E8
Harrier Rd GU14 84 C1
Harriet Ct 7 GU11, GU12 105 B1
Harriet Gdns CR0 62 A8
Harriet Tubman Cl SW2 22 A8
Harrington Cl
- Leigh RH2 138 A2
- Wallington CR0 60 E8
Harrington Ct 7 CR0 61 D8
Harrington Rd SE25 43 B5
Harriotts Cl KT22 95 C7
Harriotts La KT21, KT22 95 C8
Harris Academy Merton CR4 41 D6
Harris City Tech Coll SE19 42 F8
Harris Cl
- Crawley RH11 201 B3
- Hounslow TW5 5 A6
Harris Lo SE6 24 C7
Harrison Cl RH2 139 B8
Harrison's Rise CR0, CR9 61 B7
Harrison Way TW17 34 B4
Harris Path RH11 201 B3
Harris Way TW16 34 E8
Harrodian Sch SW13 7 F7
Harrogate Ct 2 SE26 23 A5
Harrow Bottom Rd GU25 31 F3
Harrow Cl
- Chertsey KT15 52 B8
- Chessington KT9 56 D3
- Dorking RH4 136 A6
Harrowdene GU6 174 E4
Harrowdene Ct SW19 19 E3
Harrowdene Gdns TW11 17 A1
Harrow Gate Gdns RH4 136 A5
Harrow Gdns CR6 81 F3
Harrow La GU7 150 E7
Harrowlands Pk RH4 136 B6
Harrow Lo SM2 59 D4
Harrow Rd
- Ashford TW15 14 A6
- Carshalton SM5 59 E4
- Warlingham CR6 81 F3
Harrow Rd E RH4 136 B6
Harrow Rd W RH4 136 A6
Harrowsley Ct RH6 161 B4
Harrow Way TW17 34 C7
Hart Cl
- Bletchingley RH1 120 E2
- Farnborough GU14 84 E8
Hart Dene Ct GU19 47 E3
Hart Dyke Cl RG40, RG41 25 B2
Harte Rd TW3 4 F5
Hartfield Cres SW19 19 F1
Hartfield Ct CR2 61 B3
Hartfield Gr SE20 43 C8
Hartfield Rd
- Chessington KT9 56 D5
- Forest Row RH18 206 F2
- Merton SW19 20 A1
Hartford Rd KT19 57 B4
Hartford Rise GU15 65 D6
Hart Gdns RH4 136 B8
Hartham Cl TW7 6 A6
Hartham Rd TW7 6 A6
Hart Ho SW2 22 A7
Harting Ct RH11 200 F3
Hartington Cl RH2 118 A3
Hartington Ct W4 7 B7
Hartington Rd
- Chiswick W4 7 C6
- Twickenham TW1 6 B1
Hartland Cl KT15 52 C2
Hartland Pl GU14 85 A7
Hartland Rd
- Addlestone KT15 52 A3
- Cheam SM4 40 B2
- Hampton TW12 16 B4
- Isleworth TW7 6 A4
Hartlands The TW5 4 B8
Hartland Way
- Croydon CR0 62 E8
- Morden SM4 39 F2
Hartley Cl GU17 64 B5
Hartley Ct 2 CR4 40 E8
Hartley Down CR8 79 F5
Hartley Farm CR8 79 F4
Hartley Hill CR8 79 F4
Hartley Old Rd CR8 79 F5
Hartley Rd CR0 42 C2
Hartley Way CR8 79 F4
Hart Rd
- Byfleet KT14 71 E6
- Dorking RH4 136 B8
Hartscroft CR0 62 E2
Harts Gdns GU2 109 B4
Harts Gr GU8 191 B5
Hartshill GU2 108 D2
Hartshill Wlk GU21 69 B3
Hart's La RH9 142 D7
Harts Leap Cl GU47 45 B1
Harts Leap Rd GU47 64 A8
Hartspiece Rd RH1 140 B7
Hart Sq SM4 40 A3
Hartswood RH5 136 D4
Hartswood Ave RH2 139 A5
Hartswood Ho 10 SW2 21 E7
Harts Yd
- 15 Farnham GU9 125 B2
- Godalming GU7 150 E4
Hart The GU9 125 B2
Harvard Hill W4 7 B8
Harvard Rd
- Hounslow TW7 5 E6
- Sandhurst GU47 45 E1
Harven Sch GU22 70 A2
Harvest Bank Rd BR4 63 F7
Harvest Ct
- Beckenham BR3 24 A1
- Hamsey Green CR2 81 B5
- Littleton TW17 34 A5
- Thames Ditton KT10 55 A8
Harvester Rd KT19 57 D1
Harvesters RH12 217 D5
Harvesters Cl TW7 5 D2
Harvest Hill
- East Grinstead RH19 205 E8
- Godalming GU7 150 D4
Harvest La KT7 37 A3
Harvest Lea RG42 28 A8
Harvest Rd
- Crawley RH10 202 C4
- Englefield Green TW20 11 D2
- Feltham TW13 15 A5
Harvest Ride RG12, RG42, SL5 28 A8
Harvestside RH6 161 C4
Harvey Cl RH11 201 A1
Harvey Ct KT19 57 B2
Harvey Dr TW12 36 A8
Harvey Lo 8 GU1 130 E8
Harvey Rd
- Farnborough GU14 84 C5
- Guildford GU1 130 E8
- Twickenham TW4 15 F8
- Walton-on-T KT12 35 A2
Harwarden Cl RH10 204 C8
Harwood Ave CR4 40 E6
Harwood Ct SE24 22 B7
Harwood Gdns SL4 11 B8
Harwood Pk RH1 161 A8
Harwood Rd RH12, RH13 218 A3
Harwoods Cl 3 RH19 205 F7
Harwoods La RH19 205 F7
HASCOMBE 172 D4
Hascombe Ct RH11 201 A5
Hascombe Ho 11 SW15 19 B7
Haseley End SE23 23 C8
Haseltine Prim Sch SE6 23 F4
Haseltine Rd SE26 23 F4
Haslam Ave SM3, SM4 39 E1
Hasle Dr GU27 208 B6
HASLEMERE 208 D6
Haslemere Ave
- Cranford TW5 4 C5
- Mitcham CR4, SW19 40 D7
- Wimbledon SW18 20 B6
Haslemere Cl
- Frimley GU16 66 C3
- Hampton TW12 15 F3
- Wallington SM6 60 E5
Haslemere & District Hospl GU27 208 D7
Haslemere Educational Mus* GU27 208 D7
Haslemere & Heathrow Est The TW4 4 B5
Haslemere Ind Est
- Feltham TW14 4 A2
- Haslemere GU27 208 C7
- Wimbledon SW18 20 B6
Haslemere Prep Sch GU27 208 D5
Haslemere Prim Sch CR4 40 D7
Haslemere Rd
- Brook GU8 170 C5
- Kingsley Green GU27 208 B1
- Thornton Heath CR7 42 B4
Haslemere Sta GU27 208 B6
Haslett Ave E RH10 202 A6
Haslett Ave W RH10 201 D5
Haslett Rd TW17 34 E7
Hassall Ct GU22 90 A6
Hassocks Cl SE23, SE26 23 B5
Hassocks Ct 3 RH11 200 F3
Hassocks Rd SW16 41 D8
Haste Hill GU27 208 D5
Hastings Cl GU16 86 A7
Hastings Ct
- Carshalton SM1 59 D6
- Teddington TW11 16 D3
Hastings Dr KT6 37 C3
Hastings Pl 1 CR0 42 F1
Hastings Rd
- Crawley RH10 202 C6
- Croydon CR0 42 F1
Hasty Cl CR4 41 A8
Hatch Cl
- Addlestone KT15 52 B7
- Alfold Crossways GU6 194 A3
Hatch End
- Forest Row RH18 206 F2
- Windlesham GU20 48 C4
Hatches The
- Farnham GU9 145 F8
- Frimley GU16 85 F6
Hatchet La SL4, SL5 9 B5
Hatchett Rd TW14 14 C7
Hatchetts Dr GU27 207 D7
Hatch Farm Mews KT15 52 C7
HATCHFORD END 92 C8
Hatchford Manor KT11 72 E1
Hatchgate RH6 160 F2
Hatchgate Copse RG12 26 E3
Hatch Gdns KT20 97 D7
Hatch Hill GU27 208 B1
Hatch Ho 14 TW10 17 C5
Hatchingtan The GU3 89 C1
Hatch La
- Harmondsworth UB7 2 D7
- Kingsley Green GU27 208 B2
- Ockham GU23 72 B1
- Ockham GU23 92 B7
- South Nutfield RH1 140 F3
- Wormley GU8 190 D8
Hatchlands
- Capel RH5 178 C5
- Horsham RH12 218 A7
Hatchlands Pk* GU4 111 F5
Hatchlands Rd RH1 118 E1
Hatch Pl TW10 17 F3
Hatch Rd SW16 41 E7
Hatch Ride RG45 45 B7
Hatch Ride Prim Sch RG45 45 B7
Hatfield Cl
- Belmont SM2 59 B2
- Mitcham CR4 40 D5
- West Byfleet KT14 71 B7
Hatfield Ct GU15 65 B5
Hatfield Fst Sch SM4 39 E3
Hatfield Gdns GU14 85 E3
Hatfield Ho
- 4 Ash Vale GU12 105 F5
- 16 Kingston u T KT6 37 E4
Hatfield Mead SM4 40 A4
Hatfield Rd KT21 95 F8
Hatfield Wlk RH11 200 E2
Hathaway Ct 10 RH1 119 A2
Hathaway Rd CR0 42 B2
Hatherleigh Cl
- Chessington KT9 56 D5
- Morden SM4 40 A5
Hatherleigh Ho SM4 40 A5
Hatherley Rd TW9 6 F6
Hatherop Rd TW12 15 F1
Hathersham Cl RH6 162 A4
Hathersham La RH1, RH6 161 F6
Hatherwood KT21 95 E6
HATTON 3 F2
Hatton Cross Rdbt TW6 3 F4
Hatton Cross Sta TW6 3 F3
Hatton Gdns CR4 40 F4
Hatton Gn TW14 4 A3
HATTON HILL 48 C5
Hatton Hill GU20 48 C5
Hatton Rd
- East Bedfont TW14 14 D8
- Hatton TW14, TW6 3 E2
- Thornton Heath CR0 42 A1
Hatton Rd N TW6 3 D6
Haughton Ho GU27 208 B6
Havana Rd SW18, SW19 20 A6
Havelock Cotts GU22 89 D5
Havelock Hall 8 CR0 42 F1
Havelock Ho
- 4 Croydon CR0 42 F1
- Farnborough GU14 105 C8
- Forest Hill SE23 23 C7
Havelock Rd
- Croydon CR0 61 F8
- Wimbledon SW19 20 C3
- Wokingham RG41 25 A6
Havelock St RG41 25 A6
Havelock Wlk SE23 23 C6
Havenbury Ind Est 1 RH4 136 A8
Haven Cl
- Hinchley Wood KT10 55 E8
- Wimbledon SW19 19 D5
Haven Ct
- Beckenham BR3 44 C7
- Hinchley Wood KT10 55 E8
Havengate RH12 217 F5
Haven Gdns RH10 184 B1
Haven Pl KT10 55 E8
Haven Rd
- Ashford TW15 14 B5
- Rudgwick RH12, RH14 214 D3
Haven The
- Ashford TW16 15 A1
- Richmond TW9 7 A4
- Thornton Heath CR7 42 A6
Haven Way GU9 125 D4
Haverfield Gdns TW9 7 A7
Haverhill Rd SW12 21 C7
Haverley 19 SW19 19 D1
Havers Ave KT12 54 D5
Haversham Cl
- Crawley RH10 201 F6
- Twickenham TW1 6 D1
Haversham Dr RG12 27 B3
Haversham Ho RH6 161 B5
Havisham Pl SW16 22 B1
Hawarden Gr SE24 22 C8
Hawarden Rd CR3 100 C6
Hawes Down Schs BR4 44 D1
Hawes La
- West Wickham BR4 44 D1
- West Wickham BR4 63 E8
Hawes Rd KT20 97 D7
Haweswater Ho TW1 5 F2
Hawkedale Inf Sch TW16 34 F6
Hawker Ct 14 KT2 18 A1
Hawke Rd SE19 22 E2
Hawker Rd GU12 105 F5
Hawkesbourne Rd RH12 217 F5
Hawkes Cl RG41 25 A7
Hawkesfield Rd SE23, SE6 23 F6
Hawkes Leap GU20 48 B6
Hawkesley Cl TW1 17 A4
Hawkesmoor Rd RH11 200 E4
Hawkes Rd
- East Bedfont TW14 15 A8
- Mitcham CR4 40 F8
Hawkesworth Dr GU19 47 E1
Hawkewood Rd TW16 35 A6
Hawkfield Ct TW7 5 E5
Hawkhirst Rd CR8 80 E3
Hawk Ho TW13 15 A6
Hawkhurst KT11 74 A5
Hawkhurst Gdns KT9 56 E6
Hawkhurst Rd SW16 41 D8
Hawkhurst Way
- New Malden KT3 38 D4
- West Wickham BR4 63 B8
Hawkhurst Wlk RH10 202 B4
Hawkins Cl RG12 28 A7
Hawkins Ho 10 TW10 17 C5
Hawkins Rd
- Crawley RH10 201 E4
- Teddington TW11 17 B2
Hawkins Way
- Catford SE6 24 A3
- Wokingham RG40 25 E6
Hawk La RG12 27 D5
Hawkley Gdns SE27 22 B6
Hawkridge RH12 195 E1
Hawkridge Ct RG12 27 E6
Hawksbrook La BR3 44 C3
Hawkshead Cl BR1 24 E1
HAWK'S HILL 94 F4
Hawk's Hill KT22 94 F4
Hawkshill Cl KT10 55 A4
Hawks Hill Cl KT22 94 F4
Hawks Hill Ct KT22 95 A4
Hawks Hill Ho KT22 94 F3
Hawkshill Way KT10 55 A4
Hawksmoor Dr RH5 157 C4
Hawks Rd KT1 37 F7
Hawksview KT11 73 F6
Hawksway TW18 12 F5
Hawkswell Cl GU21 68 F2
Hawkswell Wlk GU21 68 F3
Hawkswood Ave GU16 65 F2
Hawkswood Ho RG42 26 E8
Hawkwood Dell KT23 94 A1
Hawkwood Ho 8 KT23 94 A1
Hawkwood Rise KT23 94 A1
HAWLEY 64 E3
Hawley Cl TW12 15 F2
Hawley Ct GU14 84 E8
Hawley Garden Cotts GU17 64 D4
Hawley Gn GU17 64 E3
Hawley Gr GU17 64 E2
Hawley La GU14 85 B8
HAWLEY LANE 85 B7
Hawley Lo GU14 64 F2
Hawley Place Sch GU17 64 E1
Hawley Prim Sch GU17 64 E3
Hawley Rd GU14, GU17 64 F3
Hawley Way TW15 14 B3
Hawmead RH10 204 C8
Haworth Rd RH10 202 C5
Hawth Ave RH10 201 F4
Hawth Cl RH10 201 E4
Hawthorn Ave CR7 42 B8
Hawthorn Cl
- Banstead SM7 77 E5
- Bracknell RG42 27 A8
- Cranford TW5 4 B7
- Crawley RH11 181 C1
- Hampton TW12 16 A3
- Horsham RH12 217 C4
- Redhill RH1 140 A4
- Woking GU22 89 E7
Hawthorn Cotts CR2 61 C6
Hawthorn Cres
- Selsdon CR2 81 C8
- Upper Tooting SW17 21 A3
Hawthorn Ct
- 1 Farnborough GU14 105 C8
- Littleton Common TW15 14 C1
- Richmond TW9 7 B6
- Sutton SM1 59 A6
- 9 West Norwood SW16 22 A3
Hawthorndene Cl BR2 63 F8
Hawthorndene Rd BR2 63 F8
Hawthorn Dr BR4 63 E6
Hawthorne Ave
- Biggin Hill TN16 83 D4
- Cranbourne SL4 9 B6
- Mitcham CR4 40 D7
- Wallington SM5 60 A3
Hawthorne Cl
- Aldershot GU12 126 E7
- Sutton SM1 59 C8
Hawthorne Cres GU17 64 E4
Hawthorne Ct TW19 13 D8
Hawthorne Dr SL4 9 B7
Hawthorne Pl KT17 76 E7
Hawthorne Rd TW20 12 C4
Hawthorne Way
- Cranbourne SL4 9 B7
- Guildford GU4 110 B5
- Stanwell TW19 13 D8
Hawthorn Gr SE20 43 B8
Hawthorn Hatch TW8 6 B7
Hawthorn La
- Newell Green SL4 8 A7
- Rowledge GU10 145 F3
Hawthorn Lo 4 KT12 35 A1
Hawthorn Pl GU4 110 D3
Hawthorn Rd
- Brentford TW8 6 B7
- Carshalton SM1 59 E4
- Feltham TW13 15 A7
- Frimley GU16 65 F2
- Godalming GU7 150 B2
- Send Marsh GU23 91 A3
- Wallington SM5, SM6 60 B3
- Woking GU22 89 D7
Hawthorns Sch The RH1 120 B4
Hawthorns The
- 1 Belmont SM2 59 A4
- Ewell KT17 58 A3
- Oxted RH8 123 A2
- Poyle SL3 1 F6
Hawthorn Trad Est RH13 217 E4
Hawthorn Way
- Bisley GU24 68 A3
- Redhill RH1 140 B8
- Upper Halliford TW17 34 D5
- Woodham KT15 52 C1
HAXTED 165 F8
Haxted Rd RH7, TN8 165 C7
Haxted Watermill Mus* TN8 165 D8
Haybarn Dr RH12 217 E7
Haycroft Cl CR8 80 B1
Haycroft Rd KT6 56 E7
Hayden Ct KT15 71 B8
Haydn Ave CR8 80 A4
Haydock Lo SM6 60 D7
Haydon Ct
- 3 Leatherhead KT22 95 A5
- West Barnes SM4 39 D1
Haydon Park Rd SW19 20 B3
Haydon Pl
- Farnborough GU14 85 A8
- Guildford GU1 130 D8
Haydon's Rd SW19 20 C2
Haydons Road Sta SW19 20 C3
HAYES 44 F3
Hayes Barton GU22 70 D3
Hayes Chase BR4 44 E3
Hayes Cres SM3 58 D6
Hayes Ct
- Streatham SW12 21 E7
- Wimbledon SW19 19 E2
Hayesend Ho SW17 20 C4
Hayesford Park Dr BR2 44 F4
Hayes Hill BR2 44 E1
Hayes Hill Rd BR2 44 F1
Hayes La
- Beckenham BR2, BR3 44 D5
- Purley CR8 80 B3
- Slinfold RH13 215 D2
Hayes Mead Rd BR2 44 E1
Hayes Prim Sch The CR8 80 B3
Hayes Sta BR2 44 F1
Hayes The KT18 96 E8
Hayes Way BR3 44 D5
Hayes Wlk RH6 162 A4
Hayfields RH6 161 C4
Haygarth Pl SW19 19 D3
Haygreen Cl KT2 18 B2
Haylett Gdns KT1 37 D5
Hayling Ave TW13 15 A5
Hayling Ct
- Cheam SM3 58 C6
- Crawley RH11 201 C3
Haymeads Dr KT10 55 C4
Haymer Gdns KT4 58 A7
Hayne Rd BR3 43 F8
Haynes Cl GU23 91 B5

Haynes La SE19 22 E2
Haynt Wlk SW20 39 E6
Hays Bridge Bsns Ctr
RH9 163 C6
Haysbridge Cotts
RH9 163 C7
Haysleigh Gdns SE20 43 A7
Haysleigh Ho SE20 43 B7
Hays Wlk SM2 58 D1
Haywain RH8 122 D5
Hayward Cl SW19 40 B8
Hayward Ct CR4 40 D7
Haywardens RH7 164 D5
Hayward Rd KT7 36 F1
Haywards RH10 182 D1
Haywood RG12 27 C2
Hazel Ave
Farnborough GU14 84 F3
Guildford GU1 109 C5
Hazelbank KT5 38 C1
Hazel Bank SE25 42 E7
Hazel Bank Cotts
GU6 175 E5
Hazelbank Ct
Chertsey KT16 33 C1
Chessington KT9 56 F4
Hazelbank Rd
Catford SE6 24 E6
Chertsey KT16 33 C2
Hazelbury Cl SW19 40 A7
Hazel Cl
Brentford TW8 6 B7
Crawley Down RH10 204 C8
Crawley RH11 181 C1
Croydon CR0 43 D1
Englefield Green TW20 11 B2
Mitcham CR4 41 D5
Reigate RH2 139 C7
Twickenham TW2 16 C8
Hazel Ct
Cobham KT11 73 A6
Guildford GU1 109 D5
4 Horsham RH12 217 F4
Warlingham CR6 81 E1
10 West Norwood SW16 22 A3
Hazeldene KT15 52 C5
Hazeldene Ct
Kenley CR8 80 D4
Woking GU21 69 C4
Hazel Dr GU23 90 F2
Hazel Gr
Feltham TW13 15 A7
Forest Hill SE26 23 D4
Haslemere GU26 188 E2
Staines TW18 13 C2
Hazelhurst
Beckenham BR3 44 D8
Horley RH6 161 C4
Hazelhurst Cl GU4 110 B6
Hazelhurst Cres RH12 216 F1
Hazelhurst Ct SE6 24 C3
Hazelhurst Dr RH10 202 E6
Hazelhurst Rd SW17 20 D4
Hazell Hill RG12 27 C6
Hazel Lo TW20 12 A4
Hazell Rd GU9 124 F1
Hazel Mead KT17 58 A1
Hazelmere Cl
Hatton TW14 3 E1
Leatherhead KT22 95 B8
Hazelmere Ct 10 SW2 21 F7
Hazel Par KT22 94 C5
Hazel Rd
Ash GU12 127 C8
Mytchett GU16 86 A2
Reigate RH2 139 C7
West Byfleet KT14 71 A5
Hazel Way
Chipstead CR5 78 F1
Crawley Down RH10 204 C8
Fetcham KT22 94 C4
Hazelway Cl KT22 94 C4
Hazelwick Ave RH10 202 B8
Hazelwick Mill La
RH10 202 A8
Hazelwick Rd RH10 202 A7
Hazelwick Sch RH10 202 A8
Hazel Wlk RH5 136 C4
Hazelwood RH11 201 A5
Hazelwood Ave SM4 40 B5
Hazelwood Cl RH10 203 F8
Hazelwood Cotts
Cranleigh GU6 194 D4
8 Godalming GU7 150 D4
Hazelwood Ct
Farnborough GU14 84 E8
Surbiton KT6 37 E3
Hazelwood Gr CR2 81 B6
Hazelwood Ho
Beckenham BR2 44 E6
9 Sutton SM1 59 C6
Hazelwood Hts RH8 123 A4
Hazelwood La CR5 98 F8
Hazelwood Lo BR4 44 C2
Hazelwood Rd
Knaphill GU21 68 E1
Oxted RH8 123 B3
Hazelwood Sch RH8 123 A4
Hazledean Rd CR0, CR9 61 D8
Hazleden Cross RH19 205 B6
Hazledene Rd W4 7 C8
Hazlemere KT12 54 C8
Hazlemere Gdns KT4 39 A1
Hazlewood GU8 148 E4
Hazlitt Cl TW13 15 E4
Hazon Way KT19 76 C7
Headcorn Pl CR7 41 F5
Headcorn Rd
Bromley BR1 24 F3
Thornton Heath CR7 41 F5
Headington Cl RG40 25 D8
Headington Dr RG40 25 D8
Headington Rd SW18 20 C6
Headlam Rd SW4 21 D8
Headland Way RH7 164 D4
HEADLEY 96 C2
Headley Ave SM6 60 F5
Headley Cl
Chessington KT19 57 A4
Crawley RH10 182 D1
Headley Common Rd KT18,
KT20 116 D7
Headley Ct SE26 23 C3
HEADLEY DOWN 187 B4
Headley Dr
Burgh Heath KT18 97 B8
New Addington CR0 63 C3
Headley Gr
Burgh Heath KT20 97 C7
Headley KT20 116 D7
Headley Heath App
KT20 116 B4
Headley Hill Rd GU35 187 A5
Headley Rd
Ashtead KT18 96 C6
Grayshott GU26 188 C3
Headley KT18, KT22 96 A4
Leatherhead KT18, KT22 95 E4
Mickleham RH5 115 E7
Headon Ct GU9 125 D1
Headstart Montessori Sch
SW17 20 C4
Headway Cl TW10 17 C4
Headway The KT17 57 F2
HEARN 187 B7
Hearne Rd W4 7 A8
Hearn Vale GU35 187 A7
Hearnville Rd SW12 21 A7
Hearn Wlk RG12 27 E8
Hearsey Gdns GU17 64 C6
Heart The KT12 34 F1
Heathacre SL3 1 E6
Heatham Pk TW2 16 F8
Heathbridge KT13 53 A4
Heath Bsns Ctr RH1 161 B8
Heath Bsns Ctr The
TW3 5 C3
Heath Cl
Banstead SM7 78 B5
Beacon Hill GU26 188 C7
Broadbridge Heath
RH12 216 E3
Croydon CR2 61 B4
Harlington UB3 3 D7
Heath End GU9 125 C7
Stanwell TW19 2 C1
Virginia Water GU25 31 D5
Wokingham RG41 25 B4
Heath Cnr GU15 66 A3
Heathcote KT20 97 D5
Heathcote Cl GU12 106 A3
Heathcote Dr RH19 185 C2
Heathcote Rd
Ash GU12 106 B3
Camberley GU15 65 D5
Epsom KT18 76 E6
Twickenham TW1 6 B2
Heath Cotts GU26 188 C6
Heathcroft Ave TW16 14 F1
Heath Ct
Carshalton SM1 59 D8
4 Croydon CR0 61 D6
Heathdale Ave TW4 4 E4
Heathdene
Burgh Heath KT20 77 E1
Weybridge KT13 53 A5
Heathdene Rd
Streatham SW16 21 F1
Wallington SM5, SM6 60 B3
Heathdown Rd GU22 70 D4
Heath Dr
Brookwood GU24 88 A7
Send GU23 90 B5
Sutton SM2 59 C2
Walton on t H KT18 97 A2
West Barnes SW20 39 C5
Heathedge SE23, SE26 23 B6
HEATH END 125 D6
Heath End Cotts GU8 170 E7
Heatherbank GU26 188 E4
Heatherbank Cl KT11 73 D8
Heather Cl
Aldershot GU11 104 E1
Ash GU12 106 B5
Copthorne RH10 183 B2
Guildford GU2 109 B3
Hampton TW12 35 F8
Horsham RH12 217 D5
Isleworth TW7 5 D2
Kingswood KT20 97 E5
2 Lewisham SE13 24 D8
Redhill RH1 119 B5
Woking GU21 69 C4
Woodham KT15 52 B1
Wrecclesham GU9 145 F6
Heather Cotts GU12 106 A8
Heather Ct
12 Aldershot GU11 105 A1
Hindhead GU26 188 F4
West Norwood SW16 22 A4
Heatherdale Cl KT2 18 B1
Heatherdale Rd GU15 65 D4
Heatherdene KT24 92 D2
Heatherdene Cl CR4 40 E5
Heatherdene Ct CR4 40 D5
Heatherdene Mans 8
TW1 6 D1
Heather Dr SL5 30 B2
Heatherfield La KT13 53 E5
Heatherfields KT15 52 B1
Heather Gdns
Belmont SM2 59 A4
Farnborough GU14 84 E2
Heatherlands
Ashford TW16 15 A2
Horley RH6 161 B4
Heatherleigh Ct RH12 217 C4
Heatherley Cl GU15 65 B5
Heatherley Rd GU15 65 B5
Heather Mead GU16 65 F2
Heather Mead Ct GU16 65 F2
Heathermount RG12 27 E5
Heather Mount GU3 108 E3
Heathermount Dr
RG45 45 A6
Heathermount, The
Learning Ctr SL5 29 D3
Heather Pl KT10 55 B6
Heather Ridge Arc
GU15 66 C4
Heather Ridge Inf Sch
GU15 66 D4
Heatherset Cl KT10 55 C5
Heatherset Gdns SW16 21 F1
HEATHERSIDE 66 B4
Heatherside Cl KT23 93 F2
Heatherside Cnr GU15 66 D6
Heatherside Dr GU25 31 A3
Heatherside Rd KT19 57 D3
Heathers Land RH4 136 C4
Heathers The TW19 13 F8
Heathervale Cvn Pk
KT15 52 C1
Heathervale Rd KT15 52 B1
Heathervale Way
West Byfleet KT15 71 C8
Weybridge KT15 52 C1
Heatherway
Crowthorne RG45 45 A5
Felbridge RH19 184 F7
Heather Way
Chobham GU24 49 E3
Hindhead GU26 188 F4
South Croydon CR2 62 D2
Heather Wlk
Crawley RH11 201 B3
Pirbright GU24 87 D7
Smallfield RH6 162 C3
Twickenham TW2 16 A8
Whiteley Village KT12 53 F1
Heatherwood Hospl
SL5 28 E6
HEATHFIELD 62 D4
Heathfield
Cobham KT11 74 A5
Crawley RH10 202 D8
Reigate RH2 138 D8
Heathfield Ave
Ascot SL5 29 E4
Wandsworth SW18 20 D8
Heathfield Cl
Ashtead KT21 95 C8
Godalming GU7 150 E2
Woking GU22 70 A1
Heathfield Ct
Ashford TW15 13 E5
Penge SE20 23 C1
Wandsworth SW18 20 D8
Heathfield Dr
Mitcham CR4 20 E1
Redhill RH1 139 E4
Heathfield Gdns CR0 61 D6
Heathfield Inf Sch
TW2 16 A7
Heathfield Jun Sch
TW2 16 A7
Heathfield N TW2 16 F8
Heathfield Rd
Bromley BR1 24 F1
Croydon CR0 61 D6
Hersham KT12 54 E6
Wandsworth SW18 20 D8
Woking GU22 70 A1
Heathfield S TW2 16 F8
Heathfield St Mary's Sch
SL5 28 B7
Heathfield Sq SW18 20 D8
Heathfield Vale CR2 62 E2
Heath Gdns TW1 16 F6
Heath Gr
Ashford TW16 14 F1
Penge SE20 23 C1
Heath Hill
Dockenfield GU10 166 E3
Dorking RH4 136 B7
Heath Hill Rd N RG45 45 B5
Heath Hill Rd S RG45 45 B4
Heath Ho
Frimley GU16 85 F6
Thornton Heath CR7 42 A4
Weybridge KT13 53 A6
Heath House Rd GU22 88 D5
Heathhurst Rd CR2 61 E2
Heath La
Albury GU5 132 E2
Crondall GU10 124 B7
Godalming GU7 151 A2
Heath End GU9 125 C7
Heathlands
Chobham GU24 49 E1
Tadworth KT20 97 D5
Heathlands *continued*
Weybridge KT13 53 C5
Heathland Sch The TW4 4 F1
Heathlands Cl
Sunbury TW16 35 A7
Twickenham TW1 16 F7
Woking GU21 69 E5
Heathlands Ct
Hounslow TW4 4 E2
Mitcham CR4 41 A6
Heathlands Rd RG40 25 E2
Heathland St GU11 105 A2
Heathlands Way TW4 4 E2
Heath Mead SW19 19 D5
Heathmere Prim Sch
SW15 19 A7
Heath Mews GU23 91 B4
Heath Mill La GU3 88 C2
Heathmoors RG12 27 C4
Heathpark Dr GU20 48 E4
Heath Rd
Bagshot GU19 47 E3
Caterham CR3 100 D3
Haslemere GU27 207 D5
Isleworth TW3, TW7 5 C3
Oxshott KT22 74 C7
South Norwood CR7 42 C6
Twickenham TW1 16 F7
Weybridge KT13 53 A5
Woking GU21 69 F4
Heath Ridge Gn KT11 74 A6
Heathrise GU23 91 B4
Heath Rise
Camberley GU15 65 D5
Hayes BR2 44 F3
Virginia Water GU25 31 D5
Westcott RH4 135 C5
Heathrow GU5 133 C4
Heathrow Airport London
TW6 3 A5
Heathrow Airport Visitor
Ctr* TW6 3 C6
Heathrow Bvd UB7 2 F7
Heathrow Causeway Est
TW4 4 B4
Heathrow Central Sta
TW6 3 B4
Heathrow Cl TW6 2 B6
Heathrow International
Trad Est TW4 4 B4
Heathrow Prim Sch UB7 2 F8
Heathrow Terminal 4 Sta
TW6 3 C1
Heathshott 9 TW10 6 E1
Heathside
Hinchley Wood KT10 55 E7
Twickenham TW4 15 F8
Weybridge KT13 53 B5
Heathside Cl KT10 55 E7
Heathside Cres GU22 69 F2
Heathside Ct KT20 97 C4
Heathside Gdns GU22 70 A2
Heathside La GU26 188 D6
Heathside Park Rd
GU22 70 A1
Heathside Pk GU15 66 C7
Heathside Pl KT18 77 D1
Heathside Rd GU22 69 F1
Heathside Sch KT13 52 F4
Heath The CR3 100 C3
Heathvale Bridge Rd
GU12 106 A6
Heathview GU21 69 E3
Heath View KT24 92 F2
Heathview Ct SW19 19 D6
Heathview Gdns SW15 19 C8
Heathview Rd
Thornton Heath CR7 42 A5
Witley GU8 170 E7
Heathway
Camberley GU15 65 D5
Caterham CR3 100 D2
Croydon CR0 62 F7
East Horsley KT24 93 A3
North Ascot SL5 28 E8
Heath Way RH12 217 D5
Heathway Cl GU15 65 D5
Heathwood KT20 97 C4
Heathwood Ct
Hounslow TW3 5 B3
Streatham SW12 21 C7
Heathwood Point 7
SE23 23 D5
Heathyfields Rd GU9 125 A6
Heaton Rd CR4 21 A1
Heavers Farm Prim Sch
SE25 42 F4
Hebdon Rd SW17 20 F5
Hebe Ct SM1 59 C6
Hectors La RH19 206 C7
Heddon Cl TW7 6 A3
Heddon Wlk 1 GU14 85 A7
Hedge Cnr KT20 97 C4
Hedgecourt Pl RH19 184 E4
Hedge Croft Cotts
GU23 91 B6
Hedgehog La GU27 208 B5
Hedgerley Ct GU21 69 C2
Hedgers Almshouses
GU1 110 D2
Hedgeside RH11 201 C1
Hedgeway GU2 130 A7
Hedge Wlk SE6 24 B4
Hedingham Cl RH6 161 C4
Hedingham Ho 13 KT2 37 E8
Hedley Rd TW2 16 A8
Heelas Rd RG41 25 A5
Heenan Cl GU16 85 E7
Heighton Gdns CR0 61 B5
Heights Cl
Banstead SM7 77 E3
Wimbledon SW20 19 B1
Heights The
Beckenham BR3 24 C1
Forest Hill SE23 23 C8
Helder Gr SE12 24 F8
Helder St CR2 61 D4
Heldmann Cl TW7 5 D3
Helena Ho RH1 140 A6
Helen Ave TW14 15 B8
Helen Cl KT8 36 B5
Helen Ct GU14 85 B4
Helford Wlk 8 GU21 69 A1
Helgiford Gdns TW16 14 E1
Helicon Ho RH11 201 C5
Helios Rd SM6 41 A1
Helix Bsns Pk GU15 65 B3
Helix Ho TW7 6 B5
Helix The SW19 19 D6
Helm Cl KT19 76 A7
Helme Cl SW19 19 F3
Helmsdale
Bracknell RG12 27 E4
3 Woking GU21 69 B1
Helmsdale Rd SW16 21 D1
Helston Cl GU16 86 A7
Helvellyn Cl TW20 12 C1
Helvetia St SE6 23 F6
Hemingford Rd SM3 58 C6
Hemlock Cl KT20 97 E4
Hemming Cl 9 TW12 36 A8
Hemmings Mead KT19 57 C4
Hempshaw Ave SM7 78 F3
Hemsby Rd KT9 56 F4
Hemsby Wlk RH10 202 B4
Henage Cnr GU24 49 E2
Henbane Ct 2 RH11 201 B2
Henbit Cl KT20 97 B8
Henchley Dene GU4 110 D4
Henderson Ave GU2 109 B5
Henderson Ct SW18 20 E8
Henderson Dr TN16 83 C7
Henderson Hospl SM2 59 B2
Henderson Rd
Crawley RH11 201 B1
Thornton Heath CR0 42 D3
Wandsworth SW18 20 E8
Henderson Way RH12 216 F1
Hendfield Ct 5 SM6 60 B4
Hendham Rd SW17 20 F6
Hendon Gr KT19 57 A2
Hendon Terr TW15 14 D2
Hendon Way TW19 2 D1
Hendrick Ave SW12 20 F8
Heneage Cres CR0 63 C1
Henfield Rd SW19 39 F8
Henfold Cotts RH5 158 A2
Henfold Dr RH5 157 E3
Henfold La RH5 157 F5
Hengelo Gdns CR4 40 D5
Hengist Cl RH12 217 A1
Hengist Way BR2 44 E5
Hengrave Rd SE23 23 D8
Hengrove Cres TW15 13 D5
Henhurst Cross La
RH5 157 A2
Henley Ave SM3 58 E7
Henley Bank GU2 130 A7
Henley Cl
Crawley RH10 202 D3
Farnborough GU14 84 E8
Hounslow TW7 5 F6
Henley Ct
11 Egham TW20 12 A3
Kingston u T KT3 38 D6
Mitcham CR4 41 A6
Old Woking GU22 90 A7
Henley Dr
Frimley GU16 85 E7
Kingston u T KT2 18 F1
Henley Gate GU24 107 C8
Henley Lo SE25 42 F5
Henley Way TW13 15 D3
Henley Wood CR6 82 A2
Henlow Pl TW10 17 D6
Hennel Cl SE23 23 C5
Hennessy Ct GU21 70 C6
Henrietta Ct TW1 17 C8
Henry Cavendish Prim Sch
SW12 21 C7
Henry Ct GU12 86 A1
Henry Doulton Dr
SW17 21 B4
Henry Hatch Ct SM2 59 C3
Henry Macaulay Ave 11
KT2 37 D8
Henry Marshall Ho 5
GU7 150 D4
Henry Peters Dr TW11 16 E3
Henry Randell's
Almshouses GU17 64 E3
Henry Tate Mews
SW16 22 A3
Henry Tyndale Sch
GU14 85 D6
Hensford Gdns SE26 23 B4
Henshaw Cl RH11 200 F4
Henslow Way GU21 70 D5
Henson Rd RH10 202 B7
Hensworth Rd TW15 13 D3
Henty Cl RH11 200 E3
Hepburn Gdns BR2 44 F1
Hepple Cl TW7 6 B5
Hepplewhite Cl RH11 201 B1
Hepworth Croft GU47 64 E6
Hepworth Ct SM3 40 A1

Hepworth Rd SW16 . . . . . . **21** E1
Hepworth Way KT12 . . . . . **34** F1
Herald Ct
5 Aldershot GU12 . . . . . . **105** B1
South Norwood SE19. . . . . . **22** B2
Herald Gdns SM6 . . . . **60** B7
Herbert Cl RG12 . . . . **27** B4
Herbert Cres GU21 . . . . **68** E1
Herbert Ct KT5 . . . . **37** F3
Herbert Gdns W4. . . . . **7** B8
Herbert Pl TW7. . . . . **5** D5
Herbert Rd
Kingston u T KT1 . . . . **37** F6
Merton SW19 . . . . **19** F1
Herbs End GU14 . . . . **84** C5
Hercules Way GU14 . . . . . **104** F8
Hereford Cl
Crawley RH10 . . . . **201** E2
Epsom KT18. . . . . **76** D6
Guildford GU2 . . . . **108** F3
Staines TW18. . . . . **33** B8
Hereford Copse GU22 . . . . **89** B8
Hereford Ct
Belmont SM2. . . . . **59** A3
6 Croydon CR0 . . . . **42** F1
Hereford Gdns TW2. . . . . . **16** C7
Hereford Ho 11 GU11. . . . **105** A1
Hereford La GU9. . . . . **125** B7
Hereford Rd TW13 . . . . **15** C7
Hereford Way KT9 . . . . **56** D5
Hereward Ave CR8. . . . . . . **61** A1
Hereward Rd SW17 . . . . . . **20** F4
Heriot Ct KT16. . . . . **32** F2
Heriot Rd KT16 . . . . **33** A2
Heritage Cl TW16 . . . . **35** A8
Heritage Cotts GU3 . . . . . **107** B4
Heritage Ct 2 TW20 . . . . . **12** A3
Heritage Ho
22 Putney SW19 . . . . **19** D7
4 Twickenham TW1 . . . . . . **17** A8
Heritage Lawn RH6 . . . . . **161** C4
Herlwyn Gdns SW17 . . . . . **20** F4
Herm Cl
Crawley RH11 . . . . **201** A2
Hounslow TW7. . . . . **5** C7
Hermes Ho BR3. . . . . **43** E8
Hermes Way SM6 . . . . **60** D3
Hermitage Cl
Claygate KT10 . . . . **56** A4
Farnborough GU14 . . . . **85** D1
Frimley GU16. . . . . **65** F1
Littleton TW17 . . . . **34** A5
Hermitage Ct TW18 . . . . . . **12** F3
Hermitage Dr SL5. . . . . **28** E7
Hermitage Gdns SE19 . . . . **22** C1
Hermitage Jun Sch The
GU21. . . . . **88** E8
Hermitage La
Croydon CR0 . . . . **43** A3
East Grinstead RH19. . . . . **205** F8
Streatham SW16 . . . . **21** F1
Hermitage Par SL5. . . . . . . **29** A6
Hermitage Rd
East Grinstead RH19. . . . . **185** D3
Kenley CR8 . . . . **80** C3
Knaphill GU21 . . . . **88** D8
South Norwood SE19. . . . . . **22** D2
Hermitage Rdbt GU21. . . . **88** D8
Hermitage The
Barnes SW13. . . . . **7** F6
Feltham TW13 . . . . **14** F5
Forest Hill SE23. . . . . **23** C7
Kingston u T KT1 . . . . **37** D5
Richmond TW10. . . . . **6** E2
Hermitage Woods Cres
GU21 . . . . **88** E7
Hermitage Woods Est
GU21 . . . . **88** E8
Hermits Rd RH10 . . . . **201** F7
Hermonger La RH12 . . . . **195** F2
Herndon Cl TW20. . . . . **12** A4
Herne Rd KT6 . . . . **56** E8
Hernes Cl TW18 . . . . **33** B8
Heron Cl
Cheam SM1 . . . . **58** F5
Crawley RH11 . . . . **201** C8
Farnham GU9. . . . . **145** F8
Guildford GU2 . . . . **109** B4
Mytchett GU16. . . . . **85** F4
North Ascot SL5. . . . . **28** D8
Heron Ct
8 Dorking RH4. . . . . **136** A8
6 Hampton TW12. . . . . **36** B8
5 Kingston u T KT1 . . . . . . **37** E6
Merton SW20 . . . . **39** C7
3 Mitcham CR4 . . . . **40** E8
Sandhurst GU47 . . . . **64** C7
Staines TW18. . . . . **13** B4
Stanwell TW19. . . . . **13** E7
7 West Norwood SE21 . . . **22** D6
Herondale
Bracknell RG12 . . . . **27** C2
Haslemere GU27 . . . . **207** E6
Selsdon CR2 . . . . **62** D2
Heron Dale KT15. . . . . **52** D5
Herondale Ave SW18. . . . . **20** E7
Heronfield TW20. . . . . **11** C2
Heron Ho KT1 . . . . **37** C8
Heron Pl RH19. . . . . **205** F8
Heron Rd
Croydon CR0 . . . . **61** E8
Isleworth TW1. . . . . **6** B3
Heronry The KT12 . . . . **54** A4
Heronsbrook SL5 . . . . **29** F7
Herons Cl RH10. . . . . **184** B5
Heronscourt GU18 . . . . **67** C8
Herons Crest GU1. . . . . . . **109** F1
Herons Croft KT13 . . . . **53** D4
Heron Shaw GU6 . . . . **174** E1
Herons L Ctr The
GU27. . . . . **207** F6
Herons Lea RH10 . . . . **184** A4
Herons Pl TW7 . . . . **6** B4
Heron Sq 28 TW10 . . . . **6** D2
Herons Way GU24. . . . . **87** D6
Heron's Way RG40 . . . . **25** E7
Heronswood Ct RH6 . . . . **161** B4
Herontye Dr RH19 . . . . . . **206** A8
Herontye Ho RH19 . . . . . . **205** F7
Heron Way
Hatton TW14 . . . . **4** A3
Horsham RH13 . . . . **218** A1
Heron Way Prim Sch
RH13. . . . . **218** A1
Heron Wlk GU21 . . . . **70** C5
Heron Wood Rd
GU12 . . . . **126** D7
Herretts Gdns GU12. . . . . **105** D1
Herrett St GU12. . . . . **126** D8
Herrick Cl
Crawley RH10 . . . . **202** C8
Frimley GU16. . . . . **66** C3
Herrick Ct 4 TW10 . . . . . . **17** D4
Herrings La
Chertsey KT16. . . . . **33** A3
Windlesham GU20. . . . . **48** D4
Herron Ct 15 BR2 . . . . **44** F5
Herschell Rd SE23 . . . . **23** E8
Herschel Wlk 9
RH11 . . . . **201** B1
HERSHAM **54** D5
Hersham Cl SW15. . . . . **19** A8
Hersham Ctr KT12 . . . . **54** D5
Hersham Gdns KT12 . . . . . **54** C6
Hersham Rd
Hersham KT12. . . . . **54** D6
Walton-on-T KT12 . . . . **54** B7
Hersham Sta KT12 . . . . **54** E7
Hersham Trad Est
KT12 . . . . **54** E8
Hershell Ct SW14 . . . . **7** B3
Hertford Ave SW14 . . . . **7** E3
Hertford Lo 10 SW19 . . . . . **19** E7
Hertford Way CR4 . . . . **41** E5
Hesiers Hill CR6 . . . . **82** E2
Hesiers Rd CR6. . . . . **82** F3
Hesketh Cl GU6. . . . . **174** E3
Heslop Ct 1 SW12. . . . . . . **21** A7
Heslop Rd SW12 . . . . **20** F7
Hessle Gr KT17 . . . . **76** F8
Hester Ct SW16. . . . . **21** C3
Hesterman Way CR0,
CR9 . . . . **41** F1
Hester Terr TW9. . . . . **7** A4
HESTON **4** F7
Heston Ave TW5. . . . . **4** E7
Heston Com Sch TW5. . . . . **5** A7
Heston Grange TW5 . . . . . . **4** F8
Heston Grange La TW5. . . . **4** F8
Heston Ind Mall TW5 . . . . . . **4** F7
Heston Inf Sch TW5. . . . . . . **5** A7
Heston Jun Sch TW5. . . . . . **5** A7
Heston Phoenix
Distribution Pk TW5 . . . . . **4** C8
Heston Rd
Heston TW5. . . . . **5** A7
Redhill RH1 . . . . **139** F4
Heston Wlk RH1 . . . . **139** F4
Hetherington Rd TW17. . . **34** C7
Hethersett Cl RH2 . . . . . . **118** C4
Hetley Gdns 1 SE19 . . . . . **22** F1
Heverfield Ct CR4. . . . . **20** F1
Hevers Ave RH6 . . . . **161** A4
Hevers Cnr RH6. . . . . **160** F4
Hewells Ct 4 RH12 . . . . . . **217** C2
Hewers Way KT20. . . . . **97** C7
Hewitt Cl CR0 . . . . **63** A7
Hewitts Ind Est GU6 . . . . **174** B3
Hewlett Pl GU19 . . . . **47** F3
Hewshott La GU30 . . . . . . **207** A5
Hexal Rd SE6 . . . . **24** E5
Hexham Cl
Crawley RH10 . . . . **202** E6
Sandhurst GU47 . . . . **45** D2
Hexham Gdns TW7. . . . . **6** A7
Hexham Rd
Cheam SM4 . . . . **40** B1
West Norwood SE27 . . . . . . **22** C6
Hextalls La RH1. . . . . **120** E6
Heybridge Ave SW16. . . . . **21** F2
Heydon Ct BR4 . . . . **63** E8
Heyford Ave SW20 . . . . **39** F6
Heyford Rd CR4. . . . . **40** E7
Heymede KT22 . . . . **95** C4
Hey The CR2. . . . . **61** E1
Heythorp Cl GU21. . . . . **68** F2
Heythorp St SW18 . . . . **19** F6
Heyward Ct SM2. . . . . **59** A4
Heywood Dr GU19 . . . . **47** D3
Hibernia Gdns TW3 . . . . **5** A2
Hibernia Rd TW3 . . . . **5** A3
Hickey's Almshouses 10
TW9. **6** F3
Hickling Wlk RH10 . . . . . . **202** B4
Hickmans Cl RH9 . . . . **121** C3
Hicks La GU17 . . . . **64** B5
Hidaburn Ct 7 SW16. . . . . **21** C4
Hidcote Cl GU22 . . . . **70** B3
Hidcote Gdns SW20. . . . . . **39** B6
Hidcote Ho 15 SM2. . . . . . . **59** C3
Hieover SE21 . . . . **22** C6
Higgins Wlk TW12 . . . . **15** E2
Higgs La GU19. . . . . **47** D3
Highacre RH4 . . . . **136** B4
Highams Hill RH11 . . . . . . **200** F5
Highams La GU20,
GU24 . . . . **49** A5
High Ashton 11 KT2. . . . . . **18** B1
High Barn Rd KT24,
RH5 . . . . **113** E3
Highbarrow Cl CR8 . . . . . . **60** F1
Highbarrow Rd CR0. . . . . . **43** A1
High Beech
Bracknell RG12 . . . . **27** F5
South Croydon CR2 . . . . **61** E3
High Beeches
Banstead KT17, SM7. . . . . . **77** D5
Frimley GU16. . . . . **65** D2
Weybridge KT13 . . . . **53** E4
High Beeches Cl CR8. . . . . **60** D1
Highbirch Cl RH12 . . . . . . **218** B5
High Broom Cres BR4. . . . **44** B2
Highbury Ave CR7 . . . . **42** B7
Highbury Cl
New Malden KT3. . . . . **38** C4
West Wickham BR4 . . . . **63** B8
Highbury Cres GU15 . . . . . **66** A8
Highbury Gr GU27 . . . . . . **208** C8
Highbury Rd SW19. . . . . . . **19** E3
High Cedar Dr SW20 . . . . . **19** B1
Highclere
Ascot SL5. . . . . **29** D4
Guildford GU1 . . . . **110** A4
Highclere Cl
Bracknell RG12 . . . . **27** E7
Kenley CR8 . . . . **80** C4
Highclere Ct GU21 . . . . **68** C2
Highclere Dr GU15. . . . . . . **66** A7
Highclere Gdns GU21 . . . . **68** D2
Highclere Rd
Aldershot GU12. . . . . **126** D8
Kingston u T KT3 . . . . **38** D6
Knaphill GU21 . . . . **68** C2
Highclere St SE26. . . . . **23** E4
Highcliffe BR3. . . . . **44** B8
Highcliffe Dr SW15 . . . . **7** F1
High Close Sch RG40 . . . . **25** C7
High Coombe Pl KT2. . . . . **18** D1
High Copse GU9 . . . . **125** A6
Highcotts La GU4,
GU23 . . . . **91** A1
Highcroft
Beacon Hill GU26. . . . . **188** D6
Milford GU8. . . . . **170** F8
Purley CR8. . . . . **79** F5
2 Surbiton KT5 . . . . **37** F4
High Croft GU5 . . . . **152** E4
Highcroft Ct KT23. . . . . **94** A4
Highcroft Dr RH12 . . . . . . **195** E1
Highcross Way 4
SW15 . . . . **19** A7
Highdaun Dr SW16. . . . . . . **41** F5
Highdene
Guildford GU1 . . . . **131** A8
6 Woking GU22 . . . . **69** F1
Highdown KT4. . . . . **57** F8
Highdown Cl SM7. . . . . **77** F3
Highdown Ct RH10. . . . . . **202** B3
High Down Rd SM2 . . . . . . **78** B8
Highdown Way RH12. . . . **217** F6
High Dr
Kingston u T KT2, KT3 . . . . . **38** C7
Oxshott KT22. . . . . **74** D5
Woldingham CR3 . . . . **102** A5
Higher Alham RG12 . . . . . . **27** E2
Highercombe Rd
GU27 . . . . **208** E8
Higher Dr
Belmont KT17, SM7. . . . . . . **77** D6
East Horsley KT24. . . . . . . **112** E8
Kenley CR8 . . . . **80** B5
Purley CR8. . . . . **80** A6
Higher Gn KT17. . . . . **77** A6
Highfield
Bracknell RG12 . . . . **26** F3
Shalford GU4 . . . . **130** F1
Woodmansterne SM7 . . . . . **78** E2
Highfield Ave GU11 . . . . . **126** A8
Highfield Cl
Aldershot GU11. . . . . **126** B8
Englefield Green TW20 . . . . **11** C2
Farnborough GU14 . . . . **84** F4
Farnham GU9. . . . . **146** B7
Long Ditton KT6. . . . . **37** C1
Oxshott KT22. . . . . **74** D8
West Byfleet KT14. . . . . **71** A6
Wokingham RG40 . . . . **25** B6
Highfield Cres GU26 . . . . **188** F4
Highfield Ct
Englefield Green TW20 . . . . **11** D2
Mitcham CR4 . . . . **40** E5
Highfield Dr
Beckenham BR2. . . . . **44** F5
West Ewell KT19 . . . . **57** F4
West Wickham BR4 . . . . **63** C7
Highfield Gdns GU11. . . . **126** B8
Highfield Hill SE19. . . . . . . **22** E1
Highfield Ho RH11 . . . . . . **201** D7
Highfield Inf Sch BR2 . . . . **44** E5
Highfield Jun Sch BR2 . . . **44** E5
Highfield La
Puttenham GU3 . . . . **128** A3
Thursley GU8. . . . . **169** B2
Highfield Path GU14 . . . . . **84** F4
Highfield Rd
Biggin Hill TN16. . . . . **83** C3
Carshalton SM1. . . . . **59** E5
Caterham CR3 . . . . **101** A5
Chertsey KT16. . . . . **33** A1
East Grinstead RH19. . . . . **185** D3
Farnborough GU14 . . . . **84** F4
Feltham TW13 . . . . **15** A6
Hounslow TW7. . . . . **5** F6
Highfield Rd *continued*
Purley CR8. . . . . **61** A1
Tolworth KT5. . . . . **38** C2
Upper Halliford TW16 . . . . . **34** F4
Walton-on-T KT12 . . . . **35** A1
West Byfleet KT14. . . . . **71** A6
Highfields
Ashtead KT21 . . . . **95** D8
East Horsley KT24. . . . . . . **112** F7
Fetcham KT22 . . . . **94** D3
Forest Row RH18. . . . . **206** F2
Sutton SM1 . . . . **59** A8
High Fields SL5. . . . . **29** F4
Highfield Sch SW18. . . . . . **20** E8
High Foleys KT10 . . . . **56** B3
High Gables BR2. . . . . **44** E7
High Garth KT10. . . . . **55** C4
HIGHGATE **206** F1
Highgate Ct
Crawley RH11 . . . . **201** C2
Farnborough GU14 . . . . **85** C5
Highgate Ho 11 SE26. . . . . **23** A5
Highgate La GU14. . . . . **85** C5
Highgate Rd RH18 . . . . . . **206** F1
Highgate Wlk SE23 . . . . . . **23** C6
High Gdns GU22 . . . . **89** B8
Highgrove 2 GU14 . . . . . . **85** B7
Highgrove Ave SL5. . . . . . . **28** F8
Highgrove Ct BR3. . . . . **24** A1
Highgrove Ho GU4 . . . . . . **110** C3
Highgrove Mews SM5. . . . **59** E7
High Hill Rd CR6. . . . . **82** C5
High La
Haslemere GU27 . . . . **208** C8
Warlingham CR3, CR6 . . . . **101** F8
Highland Cotts SM6. . . . . . **60** C6
Highland Croft BR3 . . . . . . **24** B2
Highland Lo 2 SE19 . . . . . **22** F1
Highland Pk TW13 . . . . **14** F4
Highland Rd
Aldershot GU12. . . . . **105** D2
Beare Green RH5 . . . . **157** D3
Bromley BR1 . . . . **44** F8
Camberley GU15 . . . . **65** E8
Purley CR8. . . . . **80** A5
West Norwood SE19 . . . . . . **22** E2
Highlands KT21. . . . . **95** C8
Highlands Ave
Horsham RH13 . . . . **217** E2
Leatherhead KT22 . . . . **95** C5
Highlands Cl
Farnham GU9. . . . . **146** B7
Hounslow TW3. . . . . **5** B6
Leatherhead KT22 . . . . **95** B5
Highlands Cres RH13. . . . **217** E2
Highlands Ct SE19 . . . . **22** E2
Highlands Heath SW15 . . . **19** C8
Highlands La GU22. . . . . . . **89** E5
Highlands Pk KT22. . . . . . . **95** D4
Highlands Rd
Heath End GU9 . . . . **125** C7
Horsham RH13 . . . . **217** F2
Leatherhead KT22 . . . . **95** C5
Reigate RH2. . . . . **118** D2
Highlands The KT24. . . . . . **92** E2
Highland View GU6 . . . . . . **174** C7
High Level Dr SE26 . . . . . . **23** A4
High Limes 2 SE19 . . . . . . **22** E2
High Loxley Rd GU8. . . . . **193** B7
Highmead GU7 . . . . **150** F6
High Mead
Farncombe GU7. . . . . **150** F6
West Wickham BR4 . . . . **63** E8
High Meadow Cl RH4 . . . **136** B6
High Meadow Ho
RH4 . . . . **136** B6
High Meadow Pl KT16. . . . **32** F3
High Oaks RH11 . . . . **201** B4
High Park Ave
East Horsley KT24. . . . . **92** F1
Richmond TW9. . . . . **7** A6
High Park Rd
Farnham GU9. . . . . **125** C3
Richmond TW9. . . . . **7** A6
High Par The SW16 . . . . . . **21** E5
High Path SW19 . . . . **40** C8
High Path Rd GU1 . . . . . . **110** C1
High Pewley GU1 . . . . **130** E7
High Pine Cl KT13 . . . . **53** C5
High Pines CR6. . . . . **101** C8
High Pines The RG42. . . . . . . **8** B5
High Pitfold GU26. . . . . . . **188** D1
Highpoint KT13. . . . . **53** A5
High Range SW20. . . . . **19** C1
High Rd
Byfleet KT14 . . . . **71** E6
Chipstead CR5, RH2 . . . . . . **98** F4
High Ridge GU7 . . . . **150** D2
Highridge Cl KT18 . . . . **76** E5
Highridge Ct KT18 . . . . **76** E5
High St Mews SW19. . . . . . **19** E3
High St
Addlestone KT15 . . . . **52** B6
Aldershot GU11. . . . . **105** A2
Aldershot GU11, GU12 . . . **105** B1
Ascot SL5. . . . . **29** A6
Ascot, Sunninghill SL5. . . . . **29** D4
Bagshot GU19 . . . . **47** E3
Banstead SM7 . . . . **78** B4
Beckenham BR3. . . . . **44** A7
Bletchingley RH1. . . . . **120** D2
Bracknell RG12 . . . . **27** B7
Bracknell RG12 . . . . **27** C7
Bramley GU5 . . . . **151** F6
Brentford TW8. . . . . **6** D8
Camberley GU15 . . . . **65** D6
Carshalton SM5. . . . . **60** A6
Caterham CR3 . . . . **100** E4
High St *continued*
Cheam SM1, KT17 . . . . **58** E4
Chobham GU24 . . . . **68** E8
Claygate KT10 . . . . **55** F4
Cobham KT11. . . . . **73** B4
Colnbrook SL3 . . . . **1** C7
Cranford, Heston TW5. . . . . . **4** B7
Cranleigh GU6 . . . . **174** D3
Crawley RH10 . . . . **201** D6
Crowthorne RG45 . . . . **45** C4
Croydon CR0, CR9 . . . . **61** C7
Croydon, Woodside SE25. . . **43** A5
Dorking RH4 . . . . **136** B8
East Grinstead RH19. . . . . **205** F8
East Molesey KT8 . . . . **36** A5
4 Egham TW20 . . . . **11** F3
Epsom KT17, KT18. . . . . **76** D6
Esher KT10 . . . . **55** B6
Ewell KT17. . . . . **58** A2
Farnborough GU14 . . . . . . **105** D8
Feltham TW13 . . . . **15** A6
Godalming GU7 . . . . **150** D4
Godstone RH9 . . . . **121** C4
Great Bookham KT23. . . . . . **94** B2
Guildford GU1, GU2. . . . . . **130** D7
Harlington UB3 . . . . **3** D8
Harmondsworth UB7. . . . . . . **2** D8
Haslemere GU27 . . . . **208** D7
Horley RH6 . . . . **161** B3
Hounslow TW3. . . . . **5** B4
Kingston u T KT1 . . . . **37** D6
Knaphill GU21 . . . . **68** C2
Leatherhead KT22 . . . . **95** B5
Limpsfield RH8 . . . . **123** B7
Lingfield RH7. . . . . **164** D4
Loxwood RH14. . . . . **212** F3
Merstham RH1. . . . . **119** B7
New Malden KT3 . . . . **38** E5
Nutfield RH1 . . . . **119** F2
Old Woking GU22. . . . . **90** B6
Oxshott KT22. . . . . **74** D5
Oxted RH8 . . . . **122** D5
Penge SE19, SE20, BR3. . . . **23** C1
Purley CR8. . . . . **80** A8
Purley CR8. . . . . **80** B8
Redhill RH1 . . . . **118** F2
Reigate RH2. . . . . **118** A1
Ripley GU23. . . . . **91** C6
Rowledge GU10. . . . . **145** E4
Rusper RH12 . . . . **199** D7
Sandhurst GU47 . . . . **64** A8
Sandhurst, Little Sandhurst
GU47. . . . . **45** A1
Shepperton TW17 . . . . **34** C3
South Norwood CR7,
SE25 . . . . **42** D5
South Norwood, Woodside
SE25 . . . . **43** A6
Staines TW18. . . . . **12** F4
Stanwell TW19. . . . . **2** D1
Sunningdale SL5 . . . . **30** A4
Sutton SM1 . . . . **59** B5
Tadworth KT20 . . . . **97** C4
Teddington, Hampton Hill
TW12 . . . . **16** C2
Teddington, Hampton Wick
KT1 . . . . **37** D8
Teddington TW11. . . . . **17** A3
Thames Ditton KT7 . . . . **37** A3
Twickenham TW2. . . . . **16** C8
Walton-on-T KT12 . . . . **35** A1
West End GU24 . . . . **67** F7
West Wickham BR4 . . . . **44** B1
Weybridge KT13 . . . . **53** A6
Wimbledon SW19 . . . . **19** D3
Woking GU21. . . . . **69** F2
Woking, Horsell GU21. . . . . **69** C3
High Standing CR3. . . . . . **100** C2
High Street Collier's Wood
SW17, SW19 . . . . **20** D2
High Street Gn GU8 . . . . . **191** F2
HIGHSTREET GREEN
. . . . **192** A3
High Street Harlington
TW6. **3** D7
High Thicket Rd
GU10 . . . . **166** D5
High Tree Cl KT15 . . . . **52** A5
High Trees
Cheam SM3 . . . . **39** F2
Croydon CR0 . . . . **43** E1
Streatham SW2 . . . . **22** A7
High Trees Cl CR3 . . . . . . **100** F5
High Trees Ct
Caterham CR3 . . . . **100** F4
Sidlow RH6 . . . . **160** A4
High Trees Rd RH2. . . . . . **139** D8
Highview CR3 . . . . **100** E2
High View
Belmont SM2. . . . . **77** F8
Godalming GU7 . . . . **150** E4
Gomshall GU5 . . . . **133** C4
Knaphill GU21 . . . . **68** E2
5 Penge SE19 . . . . **22** F1
High View Ave SM6 . . . . . . **60** F5
High View Cl
Farnborough GU14 . . . . **85** A4
South Norwood SE19,
SE25 . . . . **42** F7
Highview Cres GU15 . . . . . **46** F1
Highview Ct
2 Putney SW19 . . . . **19** E7
2 Reigate RH2. . . . . **118** D1
High View Ct SW16 . . . . . . **22** A5

High View Lo 18 GU11 105 A2
High View Prim Sch SM6 60 E5
High View Rd
Farnborough GU14 85 A4
Guildford GU2 129 E6
Lightwater GU18 66 F8
South Norwood SE19 22 D2
Highway RG45 45 A5
Highwayman's Ridge GU20 48 B6
Highway The SM2 59 C2
Highwold CR5 79 A1
Highwood BR2 44 D6
Highwood Cl
Dulwich SE22 23 A7
Kenley CR8 80 C2
Highwood Pk RH11 201 C2
Highwoods
Caterham CR3 100 E2
Leatherhead KT22 95 C6
Highwoods Ct RH12 216 D3
Hilary Ave CR4 41 A6
Hilbert Rd SM3 58 D7
Hilborough Cl SW19 20 C1
Hildenborough Gdns BR1 24 F2
Hildenbrough Ho BR3 23 F1
Hildenlea Pl BR2 44 E7
Hildenley Cl RH1 119 D7
Hildens The RH4 135 C5
Hilder Gdns GU14 85 D3
Hilders La TN8 144 F4
Hilders The KT21 76 B2
Hilditch Ho 7 TW10 6 F1
Hildreth St SW12 21 B7
Hildreth Street Mews 3 SW12 21 B7
Hilgay GU1 109 F1
Hilgay Cl GU1 109 F1
Hilgay Ct GU1 109 F1
Hillacre CR3 100 E2
Hillars Heath Rd CR5 79 E4
Hillary Cl
East Grinstead RH19 186 A3
Farnham GU9 146 B7
Hillary Cres KT12 35 C1
Hillary Ct TW19 13 E7
Hillary Dr
Crowthorne RG45 45 B6
Isleworth TW7 5 F2
Hillary Ho 10 RH1 118 F2
Hillary Rd GU9 146 B7
Hillbarn CR2 80 E8
Hillberry RG12 27 C2
Hillbrook Gdns KT13 53 A3
Hillbrook Rd SW17 21 A4
Hillbrook Rise GU9 125 B6
Hillbrook Sch SW17 21 A4
Hillbrow
New Malden KT3 38 F6
3 Reigate RH2 118 C1
Richmond TW10 6 E1
Hillbrow Cl GU3 108 B2
Hillbrow Cotts RH9 121 C3
Hillbrow Ct
Esher KT10 55 C6
Godstone RH9 121 C3
Hillbrow Rd
Catford BR1 24 E2
Esher KT10 55 C6
Hillbury Cl CR6 81 C1
Hillbury Gdns CR6 81 C1
Hillbury Rd
Upper Tooting SW17 21 B5
Warlingham CR3, CR6 81 B1
Hill Cl
Cobham KT11 74 A7
Purley CR8 80 C6
Woking GU21 69 D3
Wonersh GU5 152 B6
Hill Copse View RG12 27 E8
Hill Corner Farm Est GU14 84 D7
Hillcote Ave SW16 22 A1
Hill Cres
Kingston u T KT5 37 F4
North Cheam KT4 58 C8
Hillcrest
Heath End GU9 125 D8
Oxted RH8 122 E6
Weybridge KT13 53 B6
Hill Crest
Dormans Park RH19 185 E6
Elstead GU8 148 D4
Hillcrest Ave KT16 51 E6
Hillcrest Cl
Beckenham BR3 43 F3
Crawley RH10 202 D6
Epsom KT18 76 F4
Forest Hill SE26 23 A4
Hillcrest Ct
3 Lewisham SE6 24 D8
Sutton SM2 59 D4
4 Weybridge KT13 53 B6
Hillcrest Gdns KT10 55 F7
Hillcrest Ho GU4 110 C3
Hillcrest (Mobile Home Pk) KT20 116 B4
Hillcrest Par CR5 79 B5
Hillcrest Rd
Biggin Hill TN16 83 D3
Camberley GU15 66 B7
Guildford GU2 108 F2
Hillcrest Rd *continued*
Kenley CR3 80 F2
Wallington CR8 60 F1
Hillcrest View BR3 43 F3
Hillcroft GU27 208 C6
Hillcroft Ave CR5, CR8 79 D6
Hillcroft Coll KT6 37 E3
Hillcroft Ct CR3 100 E4
Hillcroft Prim Sch CR3 100 E4
Hillcroome Rd SM2 59 D4
Hillcross Ave SM4 39 E4
Hillcross Prim Sch SM4 39 F5
Hill Ct
Farncombe GU7 150 E6
Haslemere GU27 208 B6
3 Kingston u T KT2 18 B1
14 Surbiton KT6 37 E4
3 Wimbledon SW19 19 E2
Hilldale Rd SM1 58 F6
Hilldeane Rd CR8 61 A1
Hilldown Ct SW16 21 E1
Hilldown Rd
Streatham SW16 21 F1
West Wickham BR2 44 F1
Hill Dr SW16 41 F6
Hillers KT20 97 B6
Hilley Field La KT22 94 C6
Hill Farm Cl GU27 207 F5
Hillfield Ave SM4 40 E4
Hillfield Cl
Guildford GU1 110 C3
Redhill RH1 119 A1
Hillfield Ct KT10 55 B5
Hillfield Lo SW17 20 F3
Hillfield Par SM4 40 D3
Hillfield Rd RH1 119 A1
Hill Field Rd TW12 35 F8
Hillford Pl RH1 140 A3
Hillgarth GU26 188 D5
Hillgate Pl SW12 21 B8
Hill Gr TW13 15 F6
Hillhampton SL5 29 F2
Hill Ho
Beacon Hill GU26 188 C6
Bromley BR2 44 F7
Hill House Cl RH10 204 A5
Hill House Dr
Hampton TW12 36 A8
Reigate RH2 139 B7
Weybridge KT13 72 A8
Hillhouse La RH12 194 F1
Hill House Rd SW16 21 F3
Hillhurst Gdns CR3 100 E7
Hilliard Ct SM6 60 D4
Hilliards View GU6 174 E4
Hillier Gdns CR0 61 A5
Hillier Ho
Guildford GU1 110 A1
Guildford, Guildford Park GU2 130 B7
Hillier Lo TW11 16 D3
Hillier Mews GU1 110 A1
Hillier Pl KT9 56 C4
Hillier Rd GU1 110 A1
Hillier's La CR0, SM6 60 E7
Hillingdale
Biggin Hill TN16 83 B1
Crawley RH11 201 C1
Hillingdon Ave TW19 13 E7
Hill La KT20 97 E6
Hillmead RH11 200 F6
Hill Mead RH12 217 B3
Hillmont Rd KT10 55 E7
Hillmore Gr SE26 23 E3
Hillmount 13 GU22 69 E1
Hill Park Dr KT22 94 F8
Hill Pl RH11 201 C5
Hill Rd
Beacon Hill GU26 188 C6
Carshalton SM5 59 E4
Fetcham KT23 94 B5
Grayshott GU26 188 C3
Haslemere GU27 208 C6
Heath End GU9 125 D7
Mitcham CR4 21 B1
Purley CR8 79 F7
Sutton SM1 59 B5
Hillrise
Brands Hill SL3 1 A8
Walton-on-T KT12 34 F2
Hill Rise
Dorking RH4 115 A1
Forest Hill SE23 23 B7
Hinchley Wood KT10 56 B8
Richmond TW10 6 D2
Hill Rise Ct KT22 95 B6
Hillsborough Ct GU14 84 E8
Hillsborough Pk GU15 66 C5
Hills Farm La RH12 216 F1
Hillside
Ascot SL5 29 C4
Banstead SM7 77 E4
10 Carshalton SM1 59 D5
Crawley Down RH10 204 B8
Esher KT10 55 B5
Forest Row RH18 206 F3
Horsham RH12 217 A2
Sandhurst GU15 64 F7
Wentworth GU25 31 C3
Wimbledon SW19 19 D2
Woking GU22 89 D7
Hillside Ave CR8 80 B6
Hillside Cl
Banstead SM7 77 E3
Brockham RH3 137 A8
Crawley RH11 201 B4
Hillside Cl *continued*
East Grinstead RH19 185 E3
Headley Down GU35 187 A6
Knaphill GU21 68 D2
Merton SM4 39 E5
Hillside Cres GU16 85 F7
Hillside Ct
6 Guildford GU1 130 E8
7 Kingston u T KT2 18 B1
Hillside Flats GU26 188 D6
Hillside Gdns
Addlestone KT15 51 F5
Brockham RH3 116 A1
Streatham SW2 22 A6
Wallington SM6 60 C3
Hillside Glen CR0 61 B6
Hillside Ho CR0 61 B6
Hillside La
Coney Hall BR2 63 F8
Heath End GU9 125 D8
Hillside Pk SL5 29 F1
Hillside Rd
Aldershot GU11 126 A8
Ash GU12 106 B3
Ashtead KT21 75 F2
Beckenham BR2 44 F6
Belmont SM2 58 F3
Coulsdon CR5 79 F1
Croydon CR0 61 B6
East Ewell KT17 58 C1
Farnham GU10 146 C3
Haslemere GU27 207 F5
Heath End GU9 125 E7
Kingston u T KT5 38 A4
Streatham SW2 22 A6
Tatsfield TN16 103 E8
Whyteleafe CR3 81 A1
Hillside Way GU7 150 D7
Hills Manor RH12 217 A2
Hillsmead Way CR2 81 B6
Hills Pl RH12 217 A2
Hillspur Cl GU2 108 F2
Hillspur Rd GU2 108 F2
Hill St TW10 6 D2
Hillswood Dr KT16 51 C6
Hill The CR3 100 F3
Hillthorpe Cl CR8 60 F1
Hill Top SM3 39 F2
Hilltop Cl
Ascot SL5 29 E7
Guildford GU3 108 F5
Leatherhead KT22 95 C4
Hilltop Cotts RH6 160 D2
Hilltop Ct SE19 42 D8
Hilltop La CR3, RH1 100 A1
Hilltop Prim Sch RH11 201 C4
Hilltop Rd
Kenley CR3 80 F2
Reigate RH2 139 B7
Hilltop Rise KT23 94 C1
Hilltop Wlk CR3 101 E6
Hillview
Whyteleafe CR3 80 F2
Wimbledon SW20 19 B1
Hill View
Dorking RH4 136 C8
Mitcham CR4 41 E5
Hill View Cl
Purley CR8 80 B8
Tadworth KT20 97 C6
Hill View Cres GU2 108 F3
Hillview Ct SE19 22 E4
Hill View Ct 15 GU22 69 E1
Hillview Dr RH1 140 A8
Hillview Rd SM1 59 D7
Hill View Rd
Claygate KT10 56 A3
Farnham GU9 124 F2
Twickenham TW1 6 A1
Woking GU22 69 F1
Hillworth 7 BR3 44 B7
Hillworth Rd SW2 22 A8
Hillybarn Rd RH11 180 C1
Hilly Mead SW19 19 E1
Hilsea Point 7 SW15 19 B7
Hilton Ct RH6 161 C4
Hilton Way CR2 81 B4
Himley Rd SW17 20 F2
Hinaidi Way GU14 105 A8
Hinchley Cl KT10 55 F7
Hinchley Dr KT10 55 F7
Hinchley Manor KT10 55 F7
Hinchley Way KT10 56 A7
HINCHLEY WOOD 55 F8
Hinchley Wood Prim Sch KT10 56 A8
Hinchley Wood Sch & Sixth Form Ctr KT10 56 A8
Hinchley Wood Sta KT10 55 F7
Hindell Cl GU14 85 A8
HINDHEAD 188 F4
Hindhead Cl RH11 201 C4
Hindhead Comm* GU8 189 A5
Hindhead Ho GU26 188 F4
Hindhead Point 6 SW15 19 B7
Hindhead Rd GU26, GU27 188 F2
Hindhead Way SM6 60 E5
Hindhead YH* GU8 189 A6
Hindsley's Pl SE23 23 C6
Hine Cl
Epsom KT19 76 B8
Hooley CR5 99 C5
Hinstock Cl GU14 85 A3
Hinton Ave TW4 4 D3
Hinton Cl RG45 45 B7
Hinton Dr RG45 45 B7
Hinton Rd SM6 60 C4
Hipley Ct GU1 131 A8
Hipley St GU22 90 B7
Hippisley Ct TW7 5 F4
Hitchcock Cl TW17 33 F6
Hitchings Way RH2 139 A5
Hitherbury Cl GU2 130 C6
Hitherfield Prim Sch SW2 22 A6
Hitherfield Rd SE27, SW16 22 A5
Hither Green La SE13 24 E8
Hitherhooks Hill RG42 26 E8
Hitherlands SW12 21 B6
Hithermoor Rd TW19 2 A2
Hitherwood GU6 174 E2
Hitherwood Cl RH2 118 E3
Hitherwood Ct SE19 22 F4
Hitherwood Dr SE19 22 F4
H Jones Cres GU11 105 C3
Hoadly Rd SW16 21 D6
Hobart Ct CR2 61 D5
Hobart Gdns CR7 42 D6
Hobart Ho 23 KT6 37 E4
Hobart Pl 15 TW10 6 F1
Hobart Rd KT4 58 B7
Hobbs Cl KT14 71 B6
Hobbs Ind Est RH7 184 D7
Hobbs Rd
Crawley RH11 201 A2
5 West Norwood SE27 22 C4
Hobill Wlk KT5 37 F3
Hocken Mead RH10 202 D8
HOCKERING ESTATE 70 B1
Hockering Gdns GU22 70 B1
Hockering Rd GU22 70 B1
Hockford Cl GU24 88 B1
Hockley Ind Ctr RH1 139 F8
Hodge La SL4 9 A3
Hodges Cl GU19 47 E1
Hodgkin Cl RH10 202 C5
Hodgson Gdns GU4 110 A4
HOE 154 E8
Hoe Bridge Sch GU22 90 B8
Hoebrook Cl GU22 89 E6
Hoe Cotts GU5 154 E8
Hoe La
Hascombe GU8 172 D4
Peaslake GU5, RH5 154 F8
Hoffmann Gdns CR2 62 B3
Hogarth Ave TW15 14 C2
Hogarth Bsns Pk W4 7 E8
Hogarth Cl GU47 64 E6
Hogarth Cres
Mitcham CR4, SW19 40 D8
Thornton Heath CR0 42 C2
Hogarth Ct
Dulwich SE19 22 F4
Heston TW5 4 E7
Hogarth Gdns TW5 5 A7
Hogarth Ho
1 Carshalton SM1 59 D5
6 West Norwood SE27 22 C4
Hogarth La W4 7 E8
Hogarth Rd RH10 201 F3
Hogarth Rdbt 9 W4 7 E8
Hogarth's Ho* W4 7 E8
Hogarth Way TW12 36 C8
Hogden La RH5 113 E3
HOG HATCH 125 A6
Hoghatch La GU9 125 A6
Hogoak La SL4 8 A8
Hogscross La CR5 98 F5
Hogshill La KT11 73 C5
Hogsmill Way KT19 57 C6
Hogspudding La RH5 158 C2
Hogtrough La
Nutfield RH1 140 D8
Oxted RH8 122 B6
Hogwood Rd RH14 212 C3
Holbeach Mews 2 SW12 21 B7
Holbeach Prim Sch SE6 24 A8
Holbeach Rd SE6 24 B8
Holbeck RG12 26 F3
Holbein Rd RH10 201 F3
Holberry Ho 5 SE21 22 E4
Holborn Way CR4 40 F7
Holbreck Pl GU22 69 F1
HOLBROOK 217 E8
Holbrook Cl
Heath End GU9 125 F8
Shalford GU4 130 E2
Holbrook Ct TW20 12 C3
Holbrooke Pl 26 TW9 6 D2
Holbrook Ho 5 SW2 21 F7
Holbrook Mdw TW20 12 C2
Holbrook Pk RH12 217 E8
Holbrook Prim Sch RH12 217 E7
Holbrook School La RH12 217 E7
Holbrook Way GU11 126 B7
Holcon Ct RH1 119 A4
Holden Pl KT11 73 B5
Holdernesse Rd
Isleworth TW7 6 A6
7 Upper Tooting SW17 21 A6
Holderness Way SE27 22 B3
Holder Rd
Aldershot GU12 105 E1
Crawley RH10 202 B3
Holdfast La GU27 208 F7
Holdsworth Ho 4 SW2 22 A8
Hole Hill RH4 135 B7
Hole La TN8 144 F7
Holford Rd GU1 110 C1
HOLLAND 123 A1
Holland Ave
Belmont SM2 59 A2
Wimbledon SW20 38 F8
Holland Cl
Coney Hall BR2 63 F8
Farnham GU9 146 E8
Redhill RH1 118 F1
Holland Cres RH8 123 A2
Holland Ct TW15 13 F2
Holland Dr SE23 23 E5
Holland Gdns
Brentford TW8 6 E8
Egham TW20 32 F7
Holland Jun Sch RH8 123 A1
Holland La RH8 123 A2
Holland Pines RG12 26 F2
Holland Rd
Croydon SE25 43 A4
Oxted RH8 123 A1
Hollands Field RH13 216 E4
Hollands The
Feltham TW13 15 D4
New Malden KT4 38 F1
3 Woking GU22 69 E1
Hollands Way
East Grinstead RH19 186 A4
Warnham RH12 216 F8
Holland Way BR2 63 F8
Hollerith Rise RG12 27 B3
Holles Cl TW12 16 A3
Hollies Ave KT14 70 F6
Hollies Cl
South Norwood SW16 22 A2
Twickenham TW1 16 F6
Hollies Ct KT15 52 C5
Hollies The
Oxted RH8 123 B2
14 Redhill RH1 118 F2
Streatham SW12 21 C6
Hollies Way 3 SW12 21 A8
Hollin Ct RH10 181 E1
Hollingbourne Cres RH11 201 C1
Hollingsworth Ct 7 KT6 37 D2
Hollingsworth Rd CR0, CR2 62 B4
Hollington Cres KT3 39 A3
Hollingworth Cl KT8 35 F5
Hollis Row RH1 139 F7
Hollis Wood Dr GU10 145 E5
Hollman Gdns SW16 22 B2
Holloway Dr GU25 31 E5
HOLLOWAY HILL 150 E2
Holloway Hill
Godalming GU7 150 D4
Lyne KT16 51 D8
Holloway La UB7 2 E8
Holloway St TW3 5 B4
Hollow Cl GU2 130 B8
Hollow Combe SE26 23 B4
Hollow La
Dormansland RH19, RH7 186 D6
Virginia Water GU25 31 C6
Wotton RH5 134 D2
Hollow The
Crawley RH11 200 F5
Shackleford GU7 149 F4
Holly Acre GU22 89 C4
Holly Ave
Frimley GU16 66 B3
Walton-on-T KT12 35 D1
Woodham KT15 52 A1
Hollybank GU24 67 F6
Hollybank Cl TW12 16 A3
Hollybank Rd KT14 71 A5
Holly Bank Rd GU22 89 B7
Hollybush Bsns Ctr RH6 182 F4
Hollybush Cl RH10 201 E8
Holly Bush Ind Pk GU11 105 E5
Hollybush La GU11 105 E6
Holly Bush La TW12 15 F1
Hollybush Rd
Crawley RH10 201 E8
Kingston u T KT2 17 E2
Hollybush Tk GU19, GU20 47 F6
Holly Cl
Aldershot GU12 105 C2
Beckenham BR3 44 C5
Crawley RH10 202 A8
Englefield Green TW20 11 B2
Farnborough GU14 85 A4
Feltham TW13 15 E3
Headley Down GU35 187 C5
Horsham RH12 218 B5
Longcross KT16 50 A7
Wallington SM6 60 B3
Woking GU21 89 B8
Hollycombe TW20 11 C4
Holly Cott KT7 37 A1
Holly Cres BR3 43 F4
Hollycroft Cl
Harmondsworth UB7 3 A8
South Croydon CR2 61 E5
Hollycroft Gdns UB7 3 A8
Holly Ct
4 Belmont SM2 59 A3
Catford SE6 24 C5

Holly Ct *continued*
Leatherhead KT22 . . . . 95 A5
Hollydene BR1 . . . . 44 F8
Hollyfield Rd KT5 . . . . 37 F2
Hollyfield Sch The KT6 . . . 37 E4
Hollyfields Cl GU15 . . . . . . 65 B5
Holly Gate KT15 . . . . 52 B6
Holly Gn KT13 . . . . 53 D6
Holly Grove Cl TW3 . . . . 4 F3
Holly Hedge Cl GU16 . . . . . 65 E2
Hollyhedge Rd KT11 . . . . . 73 B5
Holly Hedge Rd GU16 . . . . 65 E2
Holly Hill Dr SM7 . . . . 78 A3
Holly Hill Pk SM7 . . . . 78 A2
Holly Ho
Bracknell RG12 . . . . 27 B3
Brentford TW8 . . . . 6 C8
Dorking RH4 . . . . 136 B7
Whyteleafe CR3 . . . . 80 F2
Hollyhock Dr GU24 . . . . 68 A4
Hollyhook Cl RG45 . . . . 45 A6
Holly Hough KT20 . . . . 116 B5
Holly La
Banstead SM7 . . . . 78 C2
Godalming GU7 . . . . 150 C4
Worplesdon GU3 . . . . 108 D7
Holly La E SM7 . . . . 78 B3
Holly La W SM7 . . . . 78 B2
Holly Lea GU4 . . . . 109 D7
Holly Lo
Oatlands Park KT13 . . . . 53 E7
4 Wimbledon SW19 . . . . 19 E2
Wimbledon SW20 . . . . 39 B7
16 Woking GU22 . . . . 69 F2
Holly Lodge (Mobile Home Pk) KT20 . . . . 97 E1
Holly Lodge Prim Sch
GU12 . . . . 105 F8
Hollymead SM5 . . . . 59 F7
Hollymead Rd CR5 . . . . 79 A1
Hollymeoak Rd CR5 . . . . . . 79 B1
Hollymoor La KT19 . . . . 57 D1
Hollymount Sch SW20 . . . 39 C8
Holly Rd
Aldershot GU12 . . . . 105 D1
Farnborough GU14 . . . . 85 A4
Hampton TW12 . . . . 16 C2
Hounslow TW3 . . . . 5 B3
Reigate RH2 . . . . 139 B7
Twickenham TW1 . . . . 17 A7
Hollyridge GU27 . . . . 208 B6
Holly Ridge GU24 . . . . 67 E6
Holly Spring Inf Sch
RG12 . . . . 27 E7
Holly Spring Jun Sch
RG12 . . . . 27 E7
Holly Spring La RG12 . . . . . 27 D8
Hollytree Cl SW19 . . . . 19 D7
Hollytree Gdns GU16 . . . . . 85 D8
Holly Tree Rd CR3 . . . . . . 100 E5
Holly Way
Blackwater GU17 . . . . 64 D4
Mitcham CR4 . . . . 41 D6
Holly Wlk SL4 . . . . 9 E4
Hollywoods CR0 . . . . 62 F2
Holman Ct KT17 . . . . 58 A2
Holman Rd KT19 . . . . 57 C5
Holmbank Dr TW17 . . . . 34 E5
Holmbrook Gdns GU14 . . . 84 C4
Holmbury Ave RG45 . . . . . . 45 A7
Holmbury Cl RH11 . . . . . . 201 C4
Holmbury Ct
6 Croydon CR0 . . . . 61 E5
Mitcham SW19 . . . . 20 E1
Upper Tooting SW17 . . . . . . 20 F5
Holmbury Dr RH5 . . . . 136 C4
Holmbury Gr CR0 . . . . 62 F3
Holmbury Hill Rd
RH5 . . . . 155 B3
Holmbury Keep RH6 . . . . 161 C4
Holmbury Rd RH5 . . . . 155 D1
HOLMBURY ST MARY
. . . . 155 B5
Holmbush Cl RH12 . . . . . . 217 D6
Holmbush Farm World*
RH12 . . . . 200 B1
Holm Cl KT15 . . . . 70 E7
Holmcroft
Crawley RH10 . . . . 201 E5
Walton on t H KT20 . . . . 97 B2
Holm Ct
6 Caterham CR3 . . . . 100 D5
Dorking RH4 . . . . 136 B4
Farncombe GU7 . . . . 150 D7
Holmdene Cl BR3 . . . . 44 C7
Holme Chase KT13 . . . . 53 C4
Holme Cl RG45 . . . . 45 A7
Holme Ct 10 TW7 . . . . 6 A4
Holme Grange Craft Village RG40 . . . . 25 E2
Holme Grange Sch
RG40 . . . . 25 F3
HOLME GREEN 25 F3
Holme Lo GU7 . . . . 150 E6
Holmes Cl
Ascot SL5 . . . . 29 C3
Purley CR8 . . . . 79 F6
Woking GU23 . . . . 89 F6
Wokingham RG41 . . . . 25 A4
Holmes Cres RG41 . . . . 25 A4
Holmes Ct GU26 . . . . 188 D3
Holmesdale 2 KT13 . . . . . 53 D4
Holmesdale Ave SW14 . . . . . 7 B3
Holmesdale Cl
Guildford GU1 . . . . 110 B2
South Norwood SE25 . . . . . . 42 F6
Holmesdale Com Inf Sch
RH2 . . . . 118 B3
Holmesdale Pk RH1 . . . . . 119 F1
Holmesdale Rd
Dorking RH5 . . . . 136 C3
Reigate RH2 . . . . 118 B2
Richmond TW9 . . . . 6 F6
South Norwood SE25 . . . . . . 42 E5
South Nutfield RH1 . . . . . . 140 F7
Teddington TW11 . . . . 17 C2
Thornton Heath CR0 . . . . . . 42 D4
Holmesdale Villas
RH5 . . . . 136 B1
Holmes Rd
Merton SW19 . . . . 20 C1
Twickenham TW1 . . . . 16 F6
Holmeswood 18 SM2 . . . . . 59 B3
HOLMETHORPE 119 B4
Holmethorpe Ave
RH1 . . . . 119 B4
Holmethorpe Ind Est
RH1 . . . . 119 B4
Holmewood Cl RG41 . . . . . 25 A2
Holmewood Gdns SW2 . . . 21 F8
Holmewood Ho SM7 . . . . . 77 F2
Holmewood Rd
South Norwood SE25 . . . . . . 42 E6
Streatham SW2 . . . . 21 F8
Holmgrove Ho CR8 . . . . . . 80 A7
Holmhurst SW20 . . . . 19 C1
Holming End RH12 . . . . . . 218 B5
Holmlea Ct CR0 . . . . 61 D6
Holmoaks Ho BR3 . . . . 44 C7
Holmshaw Cl SE26, SE6 . . . 23 E4
Holmsley Cl KT3 . . . . 38 F2
Holmsley Ho SW15 . . . . 18 F8
Holmstead Ct CR2 . . . . 61 D5
Holmstoun KT15 . . . . 70 E7
Holmwood 2 KT5 . . . . 37 F3
Holmwood Ave CR2 . . . . . . 80 F6
Holmwood Cl
Addlestone KT15 . . . . 52 A5
Cheam SM2 . . . . 58 D3
East Horsley KT24 . . . . 112 E6
HOLMWOOD CORNER
. . . . 157 D5
Holmwood Ct KT3 . . . . 38 D6
Holmwood Gdns SM6 . . . . 60 B4
Holmwood Rd
Chessington KT9 . . . . 56 E5
East Ewell KT17, SM2 . . . . . 58 C2
Holmwood Sta RH5 . . . . . 157 C4
Holmwood View Rd
RH5 . . . . 136 B1
Holne Chase SM4 . . . . 40 A3
Holroyd Rd KT10 . . . . 55 F2
Holsart Cl KT20 . . . . 97 B5
Holstein Ave KT13 . . . . 53 A6
Holsworthy Way KT9 . . . . . 56 C5
Holt Barns GU35 . . . . 166 A5
Holt Cl GU14 . . . . 85 C7
Holt La RG41 . . . . 25 B7
Holton Heath 8 RG12 . . . . 27 F5
HOLT POUND 145 D4
Holt Pound La GU10 . . . . 145 C5
Holt Sch The RG41 . . . . 25 B7
Holt The
Morden SM4 . . . . 40 A5
Wallington SM6 . . . . 60 C6
Holt Wood CR6 . . . . 82 A3
Holtwood Rd KT22 . . . . 74 C6
Holtye Ave RH19 . . . . 186 A3
Holtye Pl RH19 . . . . 186 B3
Holtye Rd RH19 . . . . 186 B3
Holtye Wlk RH10 . . . . 202 A4
Holwood Cl KT12 . . . . 54 C8
Holybourne Ave SW15 . . . . 19 A8
Holy Cross Hospl
GU27 . . . . 207 F7
Holy Cross Prep Sch
KT2 . . . . 18 C1
Holy Cross RC Prim Sch
SE6 . . . . 24 C7
Holy Cross Sch The
KT3 . . . . 38 E4
Holy Family RC Prim Sch
KT15 . . . . 52 A5
Holy Ghost RC Prim Sch
SW12 . . . . 21 A8
Holyhead Ct KT1 . . . . 37 D5
Holyoake Ave GU21 . . . . . . 69 C2
Holyoake Cres GU21 . . . . . 69 C2
Holyrood RH19 . . . . 206 A8
Holy Trinity CE Jun Sch
Guildford GU1 . . . . 130 F7
Wallington SM6 . . . . 60 C6
Holy Trinity CE Prim Sch
Forest Hill SE26 . . . . 23 C6
Mortlake TW10 . . . . 7 A3
Streatham SW2 . . . . 21 F8
Sunningdale SL5 . . . . 30 A3
West End GU24 . . . . 68 A7
Wimbledon SW19 . . . . 20 B2
Holy Trinity Sch The
RH11 . . . . 201 A4
Holywell GU22 . . . . 89 B6
Holywell Cl
Farnborough GU14 . . . . 85 A7
Stanwell TW19 . . . . 13 E7
Holywell Way TW19 . . . . . . 13 E7
Homan Ho 4 SW4 . . . . 21 D8
Hombrook Dr RG42 . . . . . . 26 E8
Hombrook Ho RG42 . . . . . . 26 E8
Homebeech Ho 7
GU22 . . . . 69 E1
Home Cl
Carshalton SM5 . . . . 59 F8
Crawley RH10 . . . . 202 C8
Fetcham KT22 . . . . 94 D6
Virginia Water GU25 . . . . . . 31 D3
Homecoppice Ho 1
BR1 . . . . 24 F1
Homecroft Rd SE26 . . . . . . 23 C3
Home Ct KT6 . . . . 37 D4
Homedale Ho SM1 . . . . 59 B6
Home Farm RH2 . . . . 118 F6
Home Farm Cl
Betchworth RH3 . . . . 137 E8
Burgh Heath KT18 . . . . 77 D2
Esher KT10 . . . . 55 B4
Farnborough GU14 . . . . 85 D6
Ottershaw KT16 . . . . 51 A3
Thames Ditton KT7 . . . . 36 F2
Upper Halliford TW17 . . . . . 34 E5
Home Farm Cotts
GU8 . . . . 149 C5
Home Farm Gdns KT12 . . . 54 C8
Home Farm Ho 1
RH12 . . . . 217 C2
Home Farm Rd GU7 . . . . . 150 F2
Homefield
Hersham KT12 . . . . 54 D6
Leatherhead KT22 . . . . 95 C6
Morden SM4 . . . . 40 A5
Thursley GU8 . . . . 169 C3
Homefield Cl
Horley RH6 . . . . 161 B4
Leatherhead KT22 . . . . 95 C6
Woodham KT15 . . . . 70 E7
Homefield Gdns
Burgh Heath KT20 . . . . 97 C7
Mitcham CR4, SW19 . . . . . . 40 D7
Homefield Ho SE23 . . . . . . 23 D5
Homefield Pk SM1 . . . . 59 B4
Homefield Pl SW19 . . . . . . 19 D3
Homefield Prep Sch
SM1 . . . . 59 A5
Homefield Rd
Coulsdon CR5 . . . . 100 B7
Walton-on-T KT12 . . . . 35 E2
Warlingham CR6 . . . . 101 C8
Wimbledon SW19 . . . . 19 E3
Homegreen Ho GU27 . . . . 208 A6
Homeland Dr SM2 . . . . 59 B2
Homelands
Kingsley Green GU27 . . . . . 208 B1
Leatherhead KT22 . . . . 95 C6
Homelands Dr SE19 . . . . . . 22 E1
Homelea Cl GU14 . . . . 85 B8
Homeleigh Cres
GU12 . . . . 106 A8
Homeleigh Ct 8 SW16 . . . 21 E5
Home Mdw SM7 . . . . 78 A3
Homemead SW12 . . . . 21 B6
Homemead Rd CR0 . . . . . . 41 C3
Home Park Cl GU5 . . . . . . 151 F6
Homepark Ho GU9 . . . . . . 125 C2
Home Park Rd SW19 . . . . . 19 F4
Home Park Wlk KT1 . . . . . 37 D5
Home Pk RH8 . . . . 123 A4
Homer Rd CR0 . . . . 43 D3
Homersham Rd KT1 . . . . . . 38 B7
Homesdale Rd CR3 . . . . . 100 D4
Homestall GU2 . . . . 108 D2
Homestall Rd RH19 . . . . . 206 E8
Homestead GU6 . . . . 174 F4
Homestead Dr GU3 . . . . . 107 D4
Homestead Gdns KT10 . . . 55 E5
Homestead Rd
Caterham CR3 . . . . 100 D4
Staines TW18 . . . . 13 B2
Homesteads The BR3 . . . . 24 B2
Homestead The GU1 . . . . 130 F7
Homestead Way CR0 . . . . . 82 D7
Homestream Ho
RH12 . . . . 217 B1
Homethorne Ho
RH11 . . . . 201 C5
Homewalk Ho SE26 . . . . . . 23 C4
Homewater Ho 1
KT17 . . . . 76 E6
Homewaters Ave TW16 . . . 34 F8
Homewood GU6 . . . . 175 A3
Homewood Cl TW12 . . . . . 15 F2
Homewood Gdns SE25 . . . 42 E4
Homewoods 2 SW12 . . . . 21 C8
Homeworth 8 GU22 . . . . . 69 E1
Homildon Ho 10 SE26 . . . . 23 A5
Homington Ct KT2 . . . . 17 E1
Hone Hill GU47 . . . . 64 B8
Hones Yard Bsns Pk
GU9 . . . . 125 D2
Honeybrook Rd SW12, SW4 . . . . 21 C8
Honeycrock Ct RH1 . . . . . 140 A2
Honeycrock La RH1 . . . . . 140 B2
Honey Hill RG40 . . . . 26 A1
Honeyhill Rd RG42 . . . . 27 A8
Honeypot La TN8 . . . . 144 D4
Honeypots Rd GU22 . . . . . 89 D5
Honeysuckle Bottom
KT24 . . . . 112 E2
Honeysuckle Cl
Crowthorne RG45 . . . . 45 A7
Horley RH6 . . . . 161 C4
Honeysuckle Ct
Colnbrook SL3 . . . . 1 C7
15 Sutton SM1 . . . . 59 B4
Honeysuckle Gdns
CR0 . . . . 43 D1
Honeysuckle La
Crawley RH11 . . . . 181 C1
Dorking RH5 . . . . 136 C4
Headley Down GU35 . . . . . 187 B5
Honeysuckle Wlk
RH12 . . . . 218 A5
Honeywood Heritage Ctr*
SM5 . . . . 59 F6
Honeywood La RH5 . . . . . 196 F5
Honeywood Rd
Horsham RH13 . . . . 218 A4
Isleworth TW7 . . . . 6 A3
Honeywood Wlk SM5 . . . . 59 F6
Honister Hts CR8 . . . . 80 E5
Honister Wlk GU15 . . . . . . 66 D4
Honley Rd SE6 . . . . 24 B8
Honnor Gdns TW7 . . . . 5 D5
Honnor Rd TW18 . . . . 13 D1
Honor Oak Rd SE23 . . . . . . 23 C8
Hood Ave SW14 . . . . 7 C2
Hood Cl CR0, CR9 . . . . 42 B1
Hood Rd SW20 . . . . 18 F1
HOOK 56 E6
Hooke Rd KT24 . . . . 92 F2
Hookfield KT18, KT19 . . . . . 76 C6
Hookfield Mews KT19 . . . . 76 C6
HOOK HEATH 89 B7
Hook Heath Ave GU22 . . . . 89 C8
Hook Heath Farm
GU22 . . . . 89 A7
Hook Heath Gdns
GU22 . . . . 88 F6
Hook Heath Rd GU22 . . . . 89 B6
Hook Hill CR2 . . . . 61 E1
Hook Hill La GU22 . . . . 89 C6
Hook Hill Pk GU22 . . . . 89 B6
Hook Ho 9 SW27 . . . . 22 B3
Hookhouse Rd GU8 . . . . . 192 D6
Hook La
Gomshall GU5 . . . . 133 C2
Puttenham GU3 . . . . 128 D3
West End GU24 . . . . 67 C6
Hookley Cl GU8 . . . . 148 E3
Hookley La GU8 . . . . 148 E3
Hook Mill La GU18 . . . . 48 D2
Hook Rd
Chessington KT6 . . . . 56 E7
Epsom KT19, KT17 . . . . 57 C2
Ewell KT19 . . . . 76 D8
Surbiton KT6, KT9 . . . . 56 E7
Hook Rise N
Surbiton KT6 . . . . 56 E7
Tolworth KT6 . . . . 57 B8
Hook Rise S
Chessington KT6 . . . . 56 E7
Tolworth KT5, KT6 . . . . 57 B8
Hook Rise South Ind Pk
KT6 . . . . 57 A7
Hookstile La GU9 . . . . 125 C1
Hookstone La GU24 . . . . . . 67 F8
Hook Underpass KT6 . . . . . 56 E7
HOOKWOOD 160 D2
Hookwood Bglws
RH8 . . . . 123 B7
Hookwood Cnr RH8 . . . . . 123 B7
Hookwood Cotts KT18 . . . . 96 C3
HOOLEY 99 B5
Hooley La RH1 . . . . 139 F8
Hoover Ho SE6 . . . . 24 C4
Hope Ave RG12 . . . . 27 E2
Hope Cl SM1 . . . . 59 C5
Hope Ct RH11 . . . . 201 B1
Hope Fountain GU15 . . . . . 65 F4
Hope Grant's Rd
GU11 . . . . 105 A4
Hope La GU9 . . . . 125 B6
Hopeman Cl GU47 . . . . 64 D7
Hope Pk BR1 . . . . 24 F1
Hopes Cl TW5 . . . . 5 A8
Hope St GU8 . . . . 148 D4
Hope Way GU11 . . . . 104 F3
Hopfield GU21 . . . . 69 E3
Hopfield Ave KT14 . . . . 71 E6
Hophurst Cl RH10 . . . . . . 204 B8
Hophurst Dr RH10 . . . . . . 204 B8
Hophurst Hill RH19 . . . . . 184 D2
Hophurst La RH10 . . . . . . 184 B1
Hop Kiln The GU9 . . . . . . 146 B8
Hop Kiln Villas GU12 . . . . 105 C1
Hopkin Cl GU2 . . . . 109 B5
Hopkins Ct RH11 . . . . 201 B1
Hopper Vale RG12 . . . . 27 A3
Hoppety The KT20 . . . . 97 D5
Hoppingwood Ave KT3 . . . 38 E6
Hopton Ct 1 GU2 . . . . 108 E1
Hopton Gdns KT3 . . . . 39 A3
Hopton Par SW16 . . . . 21 E3
Hopton Rd SW16 . . . . 21 E3
Hopwood Cl SW17 . . . . 20 C5
Horace Rd KT1 . . . . 37 F6
Horatio Ave RG42 . . . . 27 E8
Horatio Ho 4 SW19 . . . . . . 20 B1
Horatio Pl SW19 . . . . 40 A8
Horatius Way CR0 . . . . 60 F4
Horbury Lo TW12 . . . . 16 A1
Hordern Ct RH12 . . . . 217 A1
Horewood Rd RG12 . . . . . . 27 B3
Horizon Bsns Village
KT13 . . . . 72 A7
HORLEY 161 C3
Horley Inf Sch RH6 . . . . . 161 A3
Horley Lodge La RH1 . . . . 161 A8
Horley Rd
Hookwood RH6 . . . . 181 B7
Redhill RH1 . . . . 139 F5
Horley Row RH6 . . . . 161 A4
Horley Sta RH6 . . . . 161 B2
Hormer Cl GU47 . . . . 45 D1
Hornbeam Cl
Farnborough GU14 . . . . 84 C5
Horsham RH13 . . . . 217 F1
Sandhurst GU47 . . . . 45 D1
Hornbeam Copse
RG42 . . . . 28 A8
Hornbeam Cres TW8 . . . . . . 6 B7
Hornbeam Gdns KT3 . . . . . 39 A3
Hornbeam Ho SE26 . . . . . . 23 D1
Hornbeam Rd
Guildford GU1 . . . . 109 C3
Reigate RH2 . . . . 139 C6
Hornbeam Terr SM5 . . . . . 40 E1
Hornbeam Wlk KT12 . . . . . 53 F2
Hornby Ave RG12 . . . . 27 D2
Hornby Ho 13 TW10 . . . . . . 17 C5
Hornchurch Cl KT2 . . . . . . 17 D3
Hornchurch Hill CR3 . . . . . 80 F1
Horndean Cl
Crawley RH10 . . . . 182 D2
3 Roehampton SW15 . . . . . 19 A7
Horndean Rd RG12 . . . . . . 27 F3
HORNE 162 F5
Hornecourt Hill RH6 . . . . 162 F7
Horne Rd TW17 . . . . 34 A5
Horner La CR4 . . . . 40 D7
Hornhatch GU4 . . . . 131 B3
Hornhatch Cl GU4 . . . . . . 131 B3
Hornhatch La GU4 . . . . . . 131 B2
Horniman Dr SE23 . . . . 23 C8
Horniman Grange 7
SE23 . . . . 23 C7
Horniman Mus & Gdns*
SE23 . . . . 23 B7
Horniman Prim Sch
SE23 . . . . 23 B7
Horn Rd GU14 . . . . 84 E5
Hornsby House Sch
SW12 . . . . 21 A7
Hornshill La RH12 . . . . 213 F7
Horsebrass Dr GU19 . . . . . 47 E2
Horsecroft SM7 . . . . 77 F2
Horsecroft Mdws SM7 . . . . 77 F3
Horse Fair KT1 . . . . 37 D7
Horse Gate Ride SL5 . . . . . 29 A3
Horse Hill RH6 . . . . 160 B4
HORSELL 69 D3
Horsell Birch
Woking GU21 . . . . 69 A4
Woking GU21 . . . . 69 B4
Horsell CE Jun Sch
GU21 . . . . 69 C3
HORSELL COMMON 69 E6
Horsell Common Rd
GU21 . . . . 69 C5
Horsell Ct KT16 . . . . 33 B2
Horsell Moor GU21 . . . . 69 D2
Horsell Park Cl GU21 . . . . . 69 D3
Horsell Pk GU21 . . . . 69 E3
Horsell Rise GU21 . . . . 69 E4
Horsell Rise Cl GU21 . . . . . 69 D4
Horsell Vale GU21 . . . . 69 E3
Horsell Village Sch
GU21 . . . . 69 D3
Horsell Way GU21 . . . . 69 C3
Horseshoe Bend
GU26 . . . . 188 B3
Horseshoe Cl
Camberley GU15 . . . . 65 F8
Crawley RH10 . . . . 202 D7
Horseshoe Cres GU15 . . . . 65 F8
Horse Shoe Gn SM1 . . . . . . 59 B8
Horseshoe La
Ash Vale GU12 . . . . 106 A7
Cranleigh GU6 . . . . 174 D4
Horseshoe La E GU1 . . . . 110 C2
Horseshoe La W GU1 . . . . 110 B1
Horseshoe Ridge KT13 . . . 72 C8
Horseshoe The
Banstead SM7 . . . . 77 F4
Coulsdon CR5, CR8 . . . . 79 D6
Godalming GU7 . . . . 150 C3
HORSHAM 217 C3
Horsham Hospl RH12 . . . 217 C3
Horsham Mus* RH12 . . . 217 C1
Horsham Rd
Alfold Crossways GU6, RH12 . . . . 194 C1
Alfold GU6 . . . . 193 F8
Bramley GU5 . . . . 151 E7
Capel RH5 . . . . 178 D8
Cranleigh GU6 . . . . 174 E1
Crawley RH11 . . . . 201 B4
Dorking, Mid Holmwood RH5 . . . . 136 B2
Dorking RH4 . . . . 136 A6
East Bedfont TW14 . . . . 3 C1
Ellen's Green RH12, RH5 . . . . 196 D5
Ewhurst GU6 . . . . 175 F3
Holmbury St M RH5 . . . . . . 155 C5
Kingsfold RH5 . . . . 178 C2
Palmers Cross GU5, GU6 . . . . 173 D5
Rusper RH12 . . . . 199 B5
Sandhurst GU47 . . . . 45 D1
Shalford GU4 . . . . 130 E3
South Holmwood RH5 . . . . 157 C6
Wallis Wood RH5, GU6 . . . 176 E4
Horsham Sta RH13 . . . . . . 217 D2
Horsham Trad Est
RH13 . . . . 217 E4
Horsley Cl KT19 . . . . 76 D6
Horsley Ct KT24 . . . . 92 E1
Horsley Dr
Kingston u T KT2 . . . . 17 D3
New Addington CR0 . . . . . . 63 C3
Horsley Rd KT11, KT24 . . . . 93 B7
Horsley Sta KT24 . . . . 92 E2
Horsneile La RG42 . . . . 27 B8
HORTON 1 B4
Horton Cres KT19 . . . . 57 B1
Horton Ctry Pk* KT19 . . . 57 A3

Horton Gdns KT19 76 C8
Horton Hill KT19 76 C8
Horton La KT19, KT18 57 B2
Horton Park Children's Farm★ KT19 57 A1
Horton Rd
Horton SL3 1 A6
Poyle SL3, TW19 1 E4
Stanwell TW19 2 A2
Horton Trad Est SL3 1 C4
Horton Way CR0 43 D4
Horvath Cl KT13 53 D6
Hosack Rd SW12, SW17 21 A6
Hoskins Pl RH19 186 A4
Hoskins Place Ind Est GU15 65 B3
Hoskins Rd RH8 122 E6
Hoskins The RH8 122 E6
Hoskins Wlk RH8 122 E6
Hospital Bridge Rd TW2 16 B7
Hospital Hill GU11 105 A3
Hospital of the Holy Trinity (Almshouses) 5 CR9 61 C8
Hospital Rd
Aldershot GU11 105 B3
Hounslow TW3 5 A4
Hospital Way 1 SE13 24 D8
Hostel Rd GU14 105 B8
Hotham Cl KT8 36 A6
Hotham Rd SW19 20 C1
Hotham Road Mews 12 SW19 20 C1
Houblon Almshouses 15 TW10 6 E2
Houblon Rd TW10 6 E2
Houghton Cl TW12 15 E2
Houghton Rd RH10 202 C3
Houlder Cres CR0 61 B4
Houlton Ct GU19 47 F2
Hound House Rd GU5 154 A5
HOUNSLOW 5 A5
Hounslow Ave TW3 5 B2
Hounslow Bsns Pk TW3 5 B3
Hounslow Central Sta TW3 5 B4
Hounslow Ctr The TW3 5 B4
Hounslow East Sta TW3 5 C5
Hounslow Gdns TW3 5 B2
Hounslow Heath Jun & Inf Schs TW4 4 E4
Hounslow Heath Nature Reserve★ TW4, TW14 4 E1
Hounslow Manor Sch TW3 5 C4
Hounslow Rd
Feltham, Hanworth TW13 15 D4
Feltham, North Feltham TW14 4 B1
Twickenham TW2, TW3 5 C1
Hounslow Sta TW3 5 B2
Hounslow Town Prim Sch TW3 5 D4
HOUNSLOW WEST 4 D4
Hounslow West Sta TW3 4 E5
Houseman Rd GU14 84 F6
Houston Ct 3 CR0 42 E1
Houston Pl KT10 36 E1
Houston Rd
Forest Hill SE23, SE6 23 E5
Thames Ditton KT7 37 B3
Houstoun Ct TW5 4 F7
Hove Gdns SM1 40 B1
Hovenden Ho 6 SE21 22 E4
Howard Ave KT17 58 A1
Howard Bldgs GU4 110 A5
Howard Cl
Ashford TW16 14 F2
Ashtead KT21 75 F1
Bracknell RG12 27 A4
Hampton TW12 16 C2
Leatherhead KT22 95 C4
Walton on t H KT20 97 A2
West Horsley KT24 92 D2
Howard Cole Way GU11 104 E2
Howard Ct
Beckenham BR3 44 C7
Knaphill GU21 88 C8
Reigate RH2 118 B2
Howard Dr GU14 84 B4
Howard Gdns GU1 110 A2
Howard Ho
Penge SE20 43 C8
Reigate RH2 118 B2
Howard of Effingham Sch KT24 113 E8
Howard Pl RH2 118 A3
Howard Prim Sch CR0 61 C6
Howard Rd
Coulsdon CR5 79 D5
Crawley RH11 200 D2
Croydon SE25 43 A3
Dorking, North Holmwood RH5 136 C3
Dorking RH4 136 A7
East Horsley KT24 93 A4
Great Bookham KT23 114 C8
Horsham RH13 218 A4
Isleworth TW7 5 F4
New Malden KT3 38 F5
Penge SE20 43 C8
Howard Rd continued
Reigate RH2 139 B8
Surbiton KT5 37 F3
Wokingham RG40 25 C5
Howard Ridge GU4 110 A5
Howards Cl GU22 90 A7
Howards Crest Cl BR3 44 C7
Howards La KT15 51 F3
Howards Rd GU22 89 F7
Howard St KT7 37 B3
Howberry Chase GU27 208 B6
Howberry Rd CR7 42 D7
Howden Ct SE25 42 F7
Howden Rd SE25 42 F7
Howe Dr CR3 100 D5
Howell Hill Cl KT17 77 C8
Howell Hill Gr KT17 58 C1
Howe Lo TW1 17 A8
Howe The GU14 84 B1
Howgate Rd SW14 7 D4
Howitts Cl KT10 55 A5
How La CR5 79 A1
Howland Ho 9 SW16 21 E5
Howley Rd CR0, CR9 61 C7
Howmic Ct 1 TW1 6 C1
Howorth Ct RG12 27 E5
Howson Terr TW10 6 E1
Hoylake Cl RH11 200 D5
Hoylake Gdns CR4 41 C6
Hoyle Hill RH5 157 D1
Hoyle Rd SW17 20 D3
Hubbard Dr KT9 56 C4
Hubbard Rd SE27 22 C4
Hubberholme RG12 27 A6
Hub Bldgs The 1 SW12 21 B7
Huddleston Cres RH1 119 D7
Hudson Ct
Croydon SE25 43 A5
Guildford GU2 108 F1
4 Merton SW19 40 B8
Hudson Rd
Crawley RH10 201 E4
Harlington UB7 3 D8
Hudsons KT20 97 D6
Huggins Pl SW2 21 F7
Hughenden Rd KT4 39 A2
Hughes Ct CR0 42 A1
Hughes Rd
Ashford TW15 14 C2
Wokingham RG40 25 E7
Hughes Wlk CR0 42 C2
Hugh Herland KT1 37 E6
Hulbert Gate RG40 25 B6
Hullbrook La GU5 152 D4
Hullmead GU5 152 E4
Hulton Cl KT22 95 C4
Hulverston Cl SM2 59 B2
Humberstone Ct 1 GU22 70 B3
Humber Way GU47 64 D8
Humbolt Cl GU2 108 F1
Hummer Rd TW20 12 A4
Humphrey Cl KT22 94 C5
Humphries Ind Est RG12 27 C5
Humphries Yd RG12 27 C5
Hungerford Cl GU47 64 C8
Hungerford Sq 4 KT13 53 D6
Hungry Hill La GU23 91 D3
Hunstanton Cl
Colnbrook SL3 1 C7
8 Crawley RH11 200 D5
Hunston Rd SM4 40 B1
Hunter Cl
Upper Tooting SW12 21 A7
Wallington SM6 60 E3
Huntercombe Roehampton Hospl The SW15 19 A8
Hunter Ct KT19 57 A1
Hunter Ho
Crawley RH10 201 D3
Feltham TW13 15 A7
Hunter Rd
Crawley RH10 201 D4
Farnborough GU14 84 F3
Guildford GU1 130 E8
South Norwood CR7 42 D6
Wimbledon SW20 39 C8
Hunters Chase RH9 142 F6
Hunters Cl KT19 76 C6
Hunters Ct 5 TW9 6 D2
Huntersfield Cl RH2 118 B4
Hunters Gate RH1 119 F2
Hunters Lo 8 RH11 200 E5
Hunters Mdw SE19 22 E4
Hunters Mews GU11 104 F2
Hunters Rd KT9 56 E6
Hunters The BR3 44 C8
Hunters Way CR0 61 E6
Hunting Cl KT10 55 A6
Huntingdon Cl CR4, SW16 41 E5
Huntingdon Ct SW14 7 C4
Huntingdon Gdns
Chiswick W4 7 C7
North Cheam KT4 58 C7
Huntingdon House Dr GU26 188 E3
Huntingdon Rd
Redhill RH1 118 F1
Woking GU21 68 F2
Huntingfield CR0 62 F3
Huntingfield Way TW20 12 D2
Huntingford Cl GU26 188 C7
Hunting Gate Dr KT9 56 E3
Hunting Gate Mews
Sutton SM1 59 B7
Twickenham TW2 16 E7
Huntley Cl TW19 13 E8
Huntley Ho
7 Dulwich SE21 22 E4
Whiteley Village KT12 53 F2
Huntley Way SW20 39 A7
Huntly Rd SE25 42 E5
Hunts Cl GU2 108 D2
Huntsgreen Ct RG12 27 C7
Hunts Hill Rd GU3 107 A4
Huntsmans Cl
Feltham TW13 15 B4
Fetcham KT22 94 D3
Warlingham CR6 101 C8
Huntsmans Ct 2 CR3 100 C6
Huntsmans Mdw SL5 28 F8
Huntsman's Mews GU16 85 F3
Huntsmoor Rd KT19 57 D5
Huntspill St SW17 20 C5
Hunts Slip Rd SE21 22 E6
Huntsworth Ct SE6 24 A7
Hurland La GU30, GU35 187 A3
Hurlands Bsns Ctr GU9 125 F4
Hurlands Cl GU9 125 F4
Hurlands La GU8 192 F2
Hurlands Pl GU9 125 F4
Hurley Cl KT12 54 B8
Hurley Ct RG12 27 E5
Hurley Gdns GU4 110 A4
Hurlford GU21 69 A2
Hurlstone Rd SE25 42 E4
Hurn Court Rd TW5 4 D5
Hurn Ct TW5 4 D5
Hurnford Cl CR2 61 E1
Huron Rd SW17 21 A5
Hurricane Rd SM6 60 E3
Hursley Ct 11 KT6 37 D2
Hurst Ave RH12 217 D3
Hurstbourne KT10 55 F4
Hurstbourne Ho SW15 7 F1
Hurstbourne Priors CR2 61 E4
Hurstbourne Rd SE23 23 E7
Hurst Cl
Chessington KT9 57 A5
Crawley RH11 200 F4
Hayes BR2 44 F1
Headley KT18 96 C3
Woking GU22 89 C7
Hurstcourt Rd SM1 59 B8
Hurst Croft GU1 130 E6
Hurst Ct
Beckenham BR3 24 A1
Horsham RH12 217 D3
South Norwood SE25 42 F5
Hurstdene Ave
Hayes BR2 44 F1
Staines TW18 13 B2
Hurst Dr KT20 97 A1
Hurst Farm Cl GU8 149 F2
Hurst Farm Rd RH19 205 D7
Hurstfield Rd KT8 36 A6
Hurst Gr KT12 34 F1
HURST GREEN 123 B3
Hurst Green Cl RH8 123 A3
Hurst Green Inf Sch RH8 123 A3
Hurst Green Rd RH8 122 F3
Hurst Green Sta RH8 122 F3
Hurst Hill Cotts GU5 152 A4
Hurst Ho 7 SE26 23 B3
Hurst La
East Molesey KT8 36 C6
Headley KT18 96 D4
Thorpe TW20 32 A7
Hurstlands RH8 123 A3
Hurstleigh Cl RH1 118 F3
Hurstleigh Dr RH1 118 F3
Hurst Lo 4 KT13 53 D4
Hurst Lodge Sch SL5 29 B1
Hurstmere Cl GU26 188 D3
Hurstmere Ho GU26 188 D3
HURST PARK 36 C7
Hurst Park Prim Sch KT8 36 A6
Hurst Pk RH12 217 D3
Hurst Rd
Aldershot GU11 105 C4
Croydon CR0 61 D5
East Molesey KT8, KT12 36 C6
Epsom KT19 76 D8
Farnborough GU14 85 B8
Headley KT18, KT20 96 E4
Horley RH6 160 E4
Horsham RH12 217 D3
Walton-on-T KT8, KT12 35 D5
Hurst View Grange CR2 61 B3
Hurst View Rd CR2 61 E3
Hurst Way
Pyrford GU22 70 E5
South Croydon CR2 61 E4
Hurstwood SL5 29 A3
Hurtbank Cotts RH5 155 C6
HURTMORE 150 A7
Hurtmore Chase GU7 150 B7
Hurtmore Rd GU7 150 B7
Hurtwood House Sch (International Sixth Form Coll) RH5 155 A2
Hurtwood Rd KT12 35 F2
Hussar Ct GU11 104 E2
Hussars Cl TW4 4 E4
Hutchingson's Rd CR0 82 C8
Hutchins Ho 6 SW4 21 D8
Hutchins Way RH6 160 F5
Hutsons Cl RG40 25 D8
Hutton Cl
Hersham KT12 54 B5
Windlesham GU20 48 D3
Hutton Rd GU12 106 A6
Huxley Cl GU7 150 D7
Huxley Rd GU2 129 D8
Hyacinth Cl 3 TW12 16 A2
Hyacinth Rd SW15 19 A7
Hyde Cl TW16 14 E2
Hyde Ct
Forest Hill SE23 23 E6
Hounslow TW3 5 A2
Hyde Dr RH11 200 E5
Hyde Farm Mews SW12 21 D7
Hyde Heath Ct RH10 202 D8
Hyde Ho 8 SM7 77 F5
Hyde La
Beacon Hill GU10, GU8 168 E1
Thursley GU8 169 A2
Hyde Rd
Richmond TW10 6 F2
Sanderstead CR2 80 E6
HYDESTILE 171 E6
Hydestile Cotts GU8 171 D5
Hyde Terr TW15, TW16 14 E2
Hydethorpe Rd SW12 21 C7
Hyde Wlk SM4 40 A2
Hydons The GU8 171 E5
Hydro Ho KT16 33 C1
Hylands Cl
Crawley RH10 202 A5
Epsom KT18 76 C4
Hylands Mews KT18 76 C4
Hylands Rd KT18 76 C4
Hylton Lo KT12 54 C5
Hyndewood 14 SE23 23 D5
Hyperion Ct RH11 200 E4
Hyperion Ho 1 SW2 21 F8
Hyperion Pl KT19 57 D2
Hyperion Wlk RH6 161 B1
Hyrstdene CR0 61 B6
Hyrst The CR0 43 E1
Hythe Cl RG12 27 E4
HYTHE END 12 B6
Hythe End Rd TW19 12 A5
Hythe Field Ave TW20 12 D2
Hythe Park Rd TW20 12 D2
Hythe Prim Sch TW18 12 D3
Hythe Rd
Egham TW18 12 D3
South Norwood CR7, SE25 42 D7
Hythe The TW18 12 E3

I

Ian Ct SE23 23 C6
Iberian Ave SM6 60 E6
Iberian Way GU15 66 B6
Ibis La W4 7 C6
Ibotson Ct SL3 1 E6
Ibsley Gdns SW15 19 A7
Ibstock Place Sch SW15 7 E1
Icehouse Wood RH8 122 F4
Icklesham Ho 9 RH11 200 F3
Icklingham Gate KT11 73 C7
Icklingham Rd KT11 73 D6
Iden Cl BR2 44 E6
Idlecombe Rd SW17 21 A2
Idmiston Ho KT4 38 F2
Idmiston Rd
New Malden KT4 38 F2
West Norwood SE21, SE27 22 C6
Idmiston Sq KT4 38 F2
IFIELD 201 A7
Ifield Ave RH11 201 C7
Ifield Cl RH1 139 E7
Ifield Com Coll RH11 201 A6
Ifield Dr RH11 201 A7
Ifield Gn RH11 181 A1
IFIELD GREEN 181 A1
Ifield Rd
Charlwood RH6 180 E5
Crawley, West Green RH11 201 C6
Ifield St RH11 200 F8
Ifield Sta RH11 201 A6
Ifield Watermill★ RH11 200 E5
IFIELDWOOD 180 D1
Ifield Wood RH11 180 E1
IFOLD 212 D3
Ifold Bridge La RH14 212 D4
Ifoldhurst RH14 212 C2
Ifold Rd RH1 140 A7
Ightham Ho BR3 23 F1
Ikona Ct KT13 53 C5
Ildersly Gr SE21 22 D6
Ilex Cl
Englefield Green TW20 11 B1
Sunbury TW16 35 C7
Ilex Ho KT15 52 A1
Ilex Way SW16 22 A3
Ilford Ct GU6 173 F2
Ilfracombe Rd BR1 24 F5
Ilkley Cl SE19 22 D2
Illingworth Cl CR4 40 D6
Illingworth Gr RG12 27 F8
Imber Cl KT7 36 D1
Imber Court Trad Est KT8 36 D3
Imber Cross KT7 36 F3
Imber Gr KT10 36 D2
Imberhorne Bsns Ctr RH19 185 B3
Imberhorne La RH19 185 B2
Imberhorne Lower Sch RH19 185 D3
Imberhorne Sch RH19 185 B3
Imberhorne Way RH19 185 B3
Imber Park Rd KT10 36 D1
Imjin Cl GU11 105 B3
Immanuel & St Andrew CE Prim Sch SW16 21 E2
Impact Ct SE20 43 B7
Imperial Ctr RH10 182 A3
Imperial Gdns CR4 41 B6
Imperial Ho GU25 31 E4
Imperial Pk KT22 95 A7
Imperial Rd TW14 14 E8
Imperial Way CR0, CR9 61 A4
Impington 8 KT1 38 A7
Imran Ct GU12 126 C8
Ince Rd KT12 53 E4
Inchmery Rd SE6 24 C7
Inchwood
Bracknell RG12 27 C1
Croydon BR4, CR0 63 B6
Independence Ho 4 SW19 40 D8
Independent Bsns Pk The RH19 185 A3
Indigo Ct TW13 14 F5
Ingatestone Rd SE25 43 B5
Ingham Cl CR2 62 D2
Ingham Rd CR2 62 D2
Ingleboro Dr CR8 80 D6
Ingleby Way SM6 60 D3
Ingle Dell GU15 65 D4
Ingle Ho SW12 21 D7
Inglehurst KT15 52 B1
Inglemere Ct CR4, SW17 20 F1
Inglemere Rd
Forest Hill SE23 23 D5
Mitcham CR4, SW17 20 F1
Inglenook Yd RH5 158 B1
Ingleside
Poyle SL3 1 F6
Surbiton KT6 37 E2
Ingleside Cl BR3 24 A1
Ingleside Ct CR2 61 C4
Ingleton RG12 27 A6
Ingleton Rd SM5 59 E2
Inglewood
Addlestone KT16 51 F7
New Addington CR0 62 E2
Woking GU21 69 B1
Inglewood Ave GU15 66 D5
Inglewood Ct 5 BR1 24 F1
Inglis Rd CR0 42 F1
Ingram Cl RH12 217 A2
Ingram Ho KT8 37 C8
Ingram Rd CR7 42 C8
Ingrams Cl KT12 54 C5
Ingrebourne Ho BR1 24 D3
Inholms La RH5 136 C3
Inkerman Rd GU21 68 E1
Inkerman Way GU21 68 E1
Inkpen La RH18 206 F1
Inman Rd SW18 20 C8
Inner Park Rd SW19 19 D6
Inner Ring E TW6 3 B4
Inner Ring W TW6 3 A4
Innes Cl SW20 39 E7
Innes Lo SE23 23 D5
Innes Rd RH12 217 F4
Innes Yd CR0, CR9 61 C7
Innings La RG12 27 E8
Innisfail Gdns GU11 125 F8
Institute Rd
Aldershot GU12 105 D1
Westcott RH4 135 C6
Institute Wlk 6 RH19 185 E1
Instow Gdns GU14 85 A7
Int Coll of Accountancy The SW17 20 F5
Interchange The 1 CR0 42 B2
International Way TW16 34 E8
Inval Hill GU27 208 C8
Inveresk Gdns KT4 58 A7
Inverness Ct SE6 24 F7
Inverness Rd
Hounslow TW3 5 A3
North Cheam KT4 39 D1
Inverness Way GU47 64 D7
Invicta Cl TW14 14 F7
Invicta Ct KT9 56 F5
Invincible Rd GU14 85 A3
Inwood Ave
Coulsdon CR5 100 A7
Hounslow TW3 5 C4
Inwood Bsns Pk TW3 5 B3
Inwood Cl CR0 62 E8
Inwood Ct 1 KT12 54 C8
Inwood Rd TW3 5 C3
Iona Cl
Crawley RH11 201 B3
Forest Hill SE13, SE4, SE6 24 A8
Morden SM4 40 B2

Iona Ho 20 GU11 105 A2
Ipsley Lo GU10 126 E5
Ipswich Rd SW17 21 A2
Irene Rd KT11 74 B5
Ireton Ave KT13 53 F8
Iris Cl
Croydon CR0 43 D1
Surbiton KT6 37 F2
Iris Rd
Bisley GU24 68 A4
West Ewell KT19 57 B5
Iron La GU5 151 D5
Ironsbottom RH2 159 F8
IRONS BOTTOM 139 A1
Irvine Ct CR7 42 A3
Irvine Dr GU14 84 E8
Irvine Pl GU25 31 E4
Irving Wlk RH10 201 E3
Irwin Ct TW15 13 D5
Irwin Dr RH12 217 A2
Irwin Rd GU2 130 A7
Isabel Cotts KT18 76 B5
Isabel Hill Cl 3 TW12 36 B8
Isabella Ct 8 TW10 6 F1
Isabella Pl KT2 17 F3
Isbells Dr RH2 139 B7
Isham Rd SW16 41 E7
Isis Ct W4 7 B7
Isis Ho KT16 33 C2
Isis St SW18 20 C6
Isis Way GU47 64 D8
Island Cl TW18 12 E4
Island Cotts GU23 91 D6
Island Farm Ave KT8 35 F4
Island Farm Rd KT8 36 A4
Island Ho SW19 40 C5
Island Rd CR4, SW19 20 F1
Island The
Downside KT11 73 B1
Wraysbury TW19 12 A5
Islay Gdns TW4 4 D2
ISLEWORTH 6 B4
Isleworth Bsns Complex TW7 5 F5
Isleworth Sta TW7 5 F5
Isleworth & Syon Sch for Boys TW7 5 E7
Isleworth Town Prim Sch TW7 6 A5
Islington Ho 7 RH11 201 B2
Itchingwood Common Rd RH8 123 E2
Ivanhoe Cl RH11 181 D1
Ivanhoe Ho 12 SW12 21 B8
Ivanhoe Rd TW4 4 D4
Iveagh Cl RH11 201 C1
Iveagh Ct
Beckenham BR3 44 B6
Bracknell RG12 27 C4
Iveagh Rd GU2 130 B7
Ively Rd GU14 84 D1
Ively Rdbt GU14 84 E2
Iverna Gdns TW14 3 D2
Ivers Way CR0 63 B3
Ivestor Terr SE23 23 C8
Ivies The 2 RH1 139 F8
Ivor Cl GU1 131 A8
Ivory Ct TW13 15 A7
Ivory Wlk RH11 200 E3
Ivybank GU7 150 E6
Ivybridge Cl 3 TW1 17 A8
Ivybridge Prim Sch TW1 5 F1
Ivychurch Cl SE20 23 C1
Ivy Cl TW16 35 C7
Ivydale Rd SM5 59 F8
Ivyday Gr SW16 21 F5
Ivydene
East Molesey KT12, KT8 35 F4
Knaphill GU21 68 B1
Ivydene Cl
Redhill RH1 140 B4
Sutton SM1 59 C6
Ivydene Ind Est RH19 206 D7
Ivy Dene La RH19 206 D6
Ivy Dr GU18 67 A7
Ivy Gdns CR4 41 D6
Ivy Hall Bglw GU6 174 D3
Ivy Hatch Ct 3 BR3 24 F1
Ivy Ho CR0 43 D1
Ivy La
Farnham GU9 125 B2
Hounslow TW4 4 F3
Woking GU22 70 B1
Ivy Lo KT15 52 B6
Ivy Mill Cl RH9 121 B3
Ivy Mill La RH1, RH9 121 B3
Ivymount Rd SE27 22 A5
Ivy Rd
Aldershot GU12 105 E2
Hounslow TW3 5 B3
Tolworth KT6 38 A1
Upper Tooting SW17 20 E3

J

Jacaranda Cl KT3 38 E6
Jacaranda Ho KT15 52 D8
Jackass La RH9 121 F4
Jack Ct GU17 64 E4
Jackdaw Cl RH11 201 C8
Jackdaw La RH12 217 E6
Jack Goodchild Way KT1 38 B6
Jack & Jill Sch TW12 16 A2
Jackman's La GU21 89 B8
Jackson Cl
Bracknell RG12 27 B4
Elmbridge Village GU6 173 F2
Epsom KT18 76 D5
Jackson's Pl CR0 42 E1
Jackson's Way CR0 63 B7
Jackson Way KT19 57 A2
Jacob Cl RG42 26 D7
Jacobean Cl RH10 202 C5
Jacob Rd GU15 65 A7
Jacobs Ct RH10 202 C7
JACOBSWELL 109 D7
Jacobs Well Rd GU4 109 D6
Jaggard Way SW12 20 F8
Jail La TN16 83 E3
Jamaica Rd CR7 42 B3
James Black Rd GU2 129 D8
James Boswell 1 SW16 22 A4
James Dixon Prim Sch SE20 43 A8
James Est CR4 40 F7
James Pl RH10 201 D5
James Rd
Camberley GU15 65 B2
Shalford GU3 130 C1
James's Cotts TW9 7 A7
James Searle Ind Est RH12 217 E4
James St TW3 5 D4
Jameston RG12 27 C1
James Watt Way RH10 182 A4
James Way GU15 65 B2
Jamieson Ho TW4 4 F1
Jamnagar Cl TW18 12 F2
Janoway Hill GU21 89 C8
Japonica Cl GU21 69 C1
Japonica Ct GU12 105 F1
Japonica Ho KT15 52 D8
Jarman Ct 6 GU21 70 A3
Jarrett Cl SW2 22 B7
Jarrow Cl SM4 40 B4
Jarvis Rd CR2 61 D4
Jasmine Cl
Redhill RH1 140 A4
Woking GU21 68 F3
Jasmine Ct
Horsham RH12 217 C2
11 Wallington SM6 60 B4
Wimbledon SW19 20 A3
Jasmine Gdns CR0 63 B7
Jasmine Gr SE20 43 B8
Jasmine Ho KT15 52 D8
Jasmine Way KT7 36 E5
Jasmin Rd KT19 57 B5
Jason Cl
Redhill RH1 139 E4
Weybridge KT13 53 C5
Jasons Dr GU4 110 C4
Jasper Ho KT4 38 D1
Jasper Rd SE19 22 F2
Javelin Ct RH10 182 D1
Jawahar Bagh SW16 22 B2
Jay Ave KT15 52 E7
Jays Ct SL5 29 D5
Jay's La GU27 209 C3
Jays Nest Cl GU17 64 D4
Jayson Ct 7 CR0 43 A1
Jay Wlk RH10 204 C5
Jeal Oakwood Ct KT18 76 E5
Jean Batten Cl SM6 60 F3
Jeanette Ct 5 TW15 13 F4
Jean Ho SW17 20 E3
Jean Humbert Ho 2 SE27 22 D4
Jeans Ct 10 RH11 201 B1
Jeddere Cotts RH7 165 A2
Jefferies Rd KT24 112 C5
Jefferson Rd GU24 87 C7
Jeffries Pas GU1 130 D8
Jeffs Cl TW12 16 B2
Jeffs Rd SM1 58 F6
Jefton Ct SM6 60 C4
Jemma Cl 16 SW2 22 A7
Jemmett Cl KT2 38 B8
Jengar Cl SM1 59 B6
Jenkins Ct GU19 47 D2
Jenkins' Hill London Rd GU19 47 D2
Jenkins Pl GU11 105 D8
Jenner Dr GU24 68 A6
Jenner Rd
Crawley RH10 181 F3
Guildford GU1 130 E8
Jenners Cl RH7 164 D4
Jenner Way KT19 57 A2
Jennett Rd CR0, CR9 61 A7
Jennifer Rd BR1 24 F5
Jennings Cl
Long Ditton KT6 37 C2
New Haw KT15 52 C2
Jennings Way RH6 161 D3
Jenny La RH7 164 C4
Jennys Way CR5 99 C5
Jenson Way SE19 22 F1
Jeppo's La CR4 40 F5
Jerome Cnr RG45 45 C3
Jerome Ho KT1 37 D7
Jersey Cl
Addlestone KT16 51 F7
Guildford GU4 110 B6
Jersey Pl SL5 29 D3
Jersey Rd
Crawley RH11 201 A2
Hounslow TW5, TW7 5 D7
Mitcham SW17 21 B2
Jerviston Gdns SW16 22 A2
Jesmond Cl CR4 41 B6
Jesmond Rd CR0 42 F2
Jessamy Rd KT13 53 B8
Jesses La GU5 154 C8
Jessie's Hollow GU5 133 C1
Jessiman Terr TW17 34 A4
Jessop Ho GU27 208 A6
Jessop Pl CR4 40 E5
Jessops Way CR0, CR4 41 C3
Jessops Wharf 4 TW8 6 C7
Jeston Ho 10 SE27 22 B5
Jetty Ho KT16 33 C2
Jevington RG12 27 C1
Jewell Ho 3 SW12 21 C8
Jewels Hill TN16 83 A6
Jewel Wlk RH11 201 A3
Jews Wlk SE26 23 B4
Jeypore Rd SW18 20 C8
Jigsaw Sch The GU16 85 E3
Jig's La S RG42 27 E8
Jillian Cl TW12 16 A1
Joanne Ct 4 TW1 6 A1
Jobson's La GU27 209 D2
Jocelyn Rd TW9 6 E4
Jockey Mead RH12 217 A1
Jock's La RG42 26 E8
Jodie Ct BR3 24 A2
Jodrell Cl TW7 6 A6
Joe Hunte Ct 2 SW27 22 B3
John Austin Cl KT2 37 F8
John Baird Ct SE26 23 D4
John Baird Ho 13 SE20 23 C1
John Barter Ho TW3 4 F5
John Burns Cotts RH8 123 E5
John Cl GU11 125 E8
John Cobb Rd KT13 53 A3
John Day Ho TW7 6 B4
John Dee Ho 3 SW14 7 D4
John Fisher Sch The CR8 60 E1
John F Kennedy Meml★ TW20 11 D6
John Gale Ct KT17 57 F2
John Kaye Ct TW17 34 A4
John Kirk Ho
Kenley CR8 80 B5
5 Streatham SW16 21 E5
John Nike Way RG12 26 C7
John Paul II Sch SW19 19 D8
John Pounds Ho RH11 201 D4
John Ruskin Coll CR2 62 E3
John Russell Cl GU2 109 A4
John's Ct 2 SM2 59 B4
Johnsdale RH8 122 F6
Johns La SM4 40 C4
Johnson Rd
Heston TW5 4 C7
Thornton Heath CR0 42 D2
Johnson's Cl SM5 59 F7
Johnsons Dr TW12 36 C8
Johnson Wlk RH10 201 E3
John's Rd TN16 103 D7
John St
Croydon SE25 43 A5
Hounslow TW3, TW5 4 E5
John's Terr CR0 42 E1
Johnstone Ct CR0 61 D7
Johnston Gn GU2 109 A5
Johnston Wlk GU2 109 A5
Johns Wlk CR3 101 A8
John Watkin Cl KT19 57 B2
John Wesley Ct 6 TW1 17 A7
John William Cl 10 KT2 37 D8
John Wiskar Dr GU6 174 D2
Joinville Pl KT15 52 D6
Jolesfield Ct RH11 200 F3
Jolliffe Rd RH1 99 C1
Jones Cnr SL5 28 E8
Jones Wlk 6 TW10 6 F1
Jonquil Gdns 5 TW12 16 A2
Jonson Cl CR4 41 B6
Jordan Cl CR2 80 F8
Jordan Lo SW17 20 E3
Jordans Cl
Crawley RH11 201 D8
Guildford GU1 110 A2
Redhill RH1 140 A4
Stanwell TW19 13 C8
Jordans Cres RH11 181 D1
Jordans The RH19 205 E8
Josef Perrin Ho 1 SE27 22 D4
Joseph Hood Fst Sch SW20 39 E6
Josephine Ave KT20 117 F8
Josephine Cl KT20 117 F8
Joseph Locke Way KT10 55 A8
Joseph's Rd GU1 109 D2
Joshua Cl CR2 61 B3
Joshua Oldfield Ho SW17 20 F3
Joviel Ho TW18 13 A1
Jubilee Ave
North Ascot SL5 28 E8
Twickenham TW2 16 C7
Wokingham RG41 25 B7
Jubilee Cl
Farnborough GU14 84 D4
North Ascot SL5 28 E8
Stanwell TW19 13 C8
Teddington KT1 37 C8
Jubilee Cres KT15 52 D5
Jubilee Ct
Bracknell RG12 27 C6
Hounslow TW3 5 B4
Staines TW18 13 A4
20 Sutton SM2 59 C4
Thornton Heath CR7 42 A5
Jubilee Dr GU12 106 A6
Jubilee Hall Rd GU14 85 C4
Jubilee High Sch KT15 52 A5
Jubilee Ho 5 TW12 36 A8
Jubilee La
Grayshott GU26 188 C3
Rowledge GU10 146 A5
Jubilee Rd
Aldershot GU11 126 B7
Cheam SM3 58 D3
Mytchett GU16 86 A2
Rudgwick RH12 214 D8
Jubilee Terr
Brockham RH3 137 C5
Dorking RH4 136 B8
Jubilee Villas KT10 36 E1
Jubilee Way
East Bedfont TW14 15 A7
Merton SW19 40 B8
Tolworth KT5, KT6, KT9 57 B7
Jubilee Wks SW19 40 C7
Jubilee Wlk
Crawley RH10 202 A6
14 Horsham RH12 217 C2
Judges Cl RH19 205 E8
Judge's Terr RH19 205 E8
Judge Wlk KT10 55 E4
Julian Cl GU21 69 C1
Julian Hill KT13 53 B3
Julian Ho
Dulwich SE21 22 E4
Wallington SM6 60 C5
Julian's Sch SW16 22 A4
Julian Taylor Path SE23 23 B6
Julien Rd CR5 79 D4
Juliet Gdns RG42 27 F8
Julius Ct TW8 6 E7
Julius Hill RG42 27 F8
Jumps Rd GU10 168 B3
Junction Pl GU27 207 F6
Junction Rd
Ashford TW15 14 D3
Croydon CR2 61 D5
Dorking RH4 136 A7
Lightwater GU18 48 B1
June Cl CR5 79 B5
June La RH1 140 B2
Junewood Cl KT15 70 F8
Juniper RG12 27 C1
Juniper Cl
Biggin Hill TN16 83 E2
Chessington KT9 56 F5
Guildford GU1 109 C6
Oxted RH8 123 B2
Reigate RH2 139 C7
Juniper Ct
East Molesey KT8 36 B5
Hounslow TW3 5 B3
6 Thornton Heath CR0 42 A3
Juniper Dr GU24 68 A4
Juniper Gdns
Ashford TW16 14 F2
Mitcham CR4 41 C8
Juniper Hall (Field Study Ctr) RH5 115 C6
Juniper Ho 9 TW9 7 B6
Juniper Pl GU4 130 D2
Juniper Rd
Crawley RH11 181 C1
Farnborough GU14 84 C5
Reigate RH2 139 C7
Juniper Terr GU4 130 D2
Juniper Wlk RH3 137 C7
Jura Cl RH11 201 B3
Justin Cl TW8 6 D7
Justin Ct 3 CR7 42 A4
Justin Plaza CR4 40 E5
Jutland Gdns CR5 99 F7
Jutland Pl TW20 12 C3
Jutland Rd SE6 24 C8
Juxon Cl RH11 200 F4

K

Kaithewood Ho RH12 218 B5
Kangley Bridge Ctr SE26 23 F3
Kangley Bridge Rd SE26 23 F3
Karen Ct BR1 44 F8
Kashmir Cl KT15 52 D2
Kashmir Ct 3 GU14 85 C1
Katana 8 GU22 89 E8
Katharine Rd 1 TW1 17 A7
Katharine St CR0, CR9 61 C7
Katherine Cl KT15 52 A4
Katherine Ct
2 Camberley GU15 65 D5
Forest Hill SE23 23 C7
Knaphill GU21 88 C8
Katherine Ho
3 Croydon CR0 61 C7
West Norwood SE19 22 E2
Kathleen Godfree Ct SW19 20 A3
Kathleen Moore Ct BR4 63 C8
Kavanagh Ct 1 KT3 38 E6
Kay Ave KT15 52 E7
Kay Cres GU35 187 B6
Kaye Ct GU1 109 C5
Kaye Don Way KT13 53 A1
Kayemoor Rd SM2 59 E4
Kaynes Pk SL5 28 E8
Keable Rd GU10 145 E7
Kean Ho 14 TW1 6 D1
Kearton Cl CR8 80 C2
Kearton Pl CR3 101 A5
Keates Gn RG42 27 B8
Keats Ave RH1 119 B3
Keats Cl
Horsham RH12 217 F7
Mitcham SW17, SW19 20 D2
Keats Ho BR3 24 B2
Keats Pl RH19 185 D1
Keats Way
Crowthorne RG45 45 B6
Croydon CR0 43 C3
Keble Cl
Crawley RH10 182 D1
New Malden KT4 38 F1
Keble Ct 7 SW19 20 A2
Keble St SW17 20 C4
Keble Way GU47 45 E2
Kedeston Ct SM3 40 B1
Keeble Ho RG41 25 A6
Keedonwood Rd BR1 24 F3
Keel KT16 33 C2
Keeley Rd CR0, CR9 61 C8
Keeling 2 TW11 16 E3
Keeling Ct CR0 61 B6
Keens Cl SW16 21 D3
Keens La GU2, GU3 108 F5
Keens Park Rd GU3 108 F5
Keen's Rd CR0 61 C6
Keepers Cl GU4 110 D4
Keepers Combe RG12 27 D3
Keepers Ct 4 CR2 61 C5
Keepers Mews TW11 17 C2
Keepers Terr GU25 31 B4
Keepers Wlk GU25 31 D4
Keephatch Ho RG40 25 F7
Keep Hatch Prim Sch RG40 25 D7
Keephatch Rd RG40 25 E7
Keep The
Catford SE6 24 B7
Kingston u T KT2 17 F1
Keevil Dr SW19 19 E8
Keir Hardie Ho 7 RH11 201 B1
Keir The SW19 19 C3
Keith Lucas Rd GU14 84 F2
Keith Park Cres TN16 83 C7
Keldholme RG12 27 A6
Kellie Ho SL5 30 A1
Kelling Gdns CR0 42 B2
Kellino St SW17 20 F4
Kelly Cl TW17 34 E7
Kelmscott 5 SE23 23 D5
Kelsall Mews TW9 7 B6
Kelsey Cl RH6 160 F3
Kelsey Ct BR3 44 B6
Kelsey Gate 8 BR3 44 B7
Kelsey La BR3 44 A6
Kelsey Park Ave BR3 44 B7
Kelsey Park Mans BR3 44 B6
Kelsey Park Rd BR3 44 A7
Kelsey Park Sports Coll BR3 44 A6
Kelsey Sq BR3 44 A7
Kelsey Way BR3 44 A6
Kelso Cl RH10 202 E7
Kelso Ct SE20 23 B1
Kelso Rd SM5 40 C2
Kelvedon Ave KT12 53 F3
Kelvedon Cl KT2 18 A2
Kelvin Ave KT22 94 F8
Kelvinbrook KT8 36 B6
Kelvin Bsns Ctr RH10 181 F1
Kelvin Cl KT19 57 A4
Kelvin Ct
Chiswick W4 7 C7
Isleworth TW7 5 E5
8 Penge SE20 43 B8
8 Twickenham TW1 6 B1
Kelvin Dr TW1 6 B1
Kelvin Gdns CR0 41 E2
Kelvin Gr
Chessington KT6 56 E7
Forest Hill SE26 23 B5
Kelvin Grove Prim Sch SE26 23 B5
Kelvington Cl CR0 43 E2
Kelvin Ho RH10 181 F2
Kelvin La RH10 181 F2
Kelvin Way RH10 181 F2
Kelyway Ho 20 SW2 22 A8
Kemble Cl KT13 53 D6
Kemble Cotts KT15 52 A6
Kemble Rd
Croydon CR0, CR9 61 B7
Forest Hill SE23 23 D7
Kembleside Rd TN16 83 C1
Kemerton Rd
Beckenham BR3 44 B7
Croydon CR0 42 F2
Kemishford GU22 89 A4
Kemnal Pk GU27 208 D7
Kemp Ct GU19 47 F2
Kemp Gdns CR0 42 C3
Kempshott Rd
Horsham RH12 217 B4
Streatham SW16 21 E1
Kempston Ho SM2 59 B2

Kempton Ave TW16 . . . . 35 B8
Kempton Ct
　Farnborough GU14 . . . . . . 84 F2
　Sunbury TW16 . . . . 35 B8
Kempton Ho KT20 . . . . . . 97 C4
Kempton Lo SM6 . . . . 60 D7
Kempton Park Race
　Course TW16 . . . . 15 C1
Kempton Park Sta
　TW16 . . . . 15 B1
Kempton Wlk CR0 . . . . 43 E3
Kemsing Cl
　Coney Hall BR2 . . . . 63 F8
　Thornton Heath CR7 . . . . . 42 C5
Kemsley Rd TN16 . . . . . . 103 D8
Kendal Cl
　East Bedfont TW14 . . . . . . 14 F7
　Farnborough GU14 . . . . . . 84 E4
　Redhill RH2 . . . . 118 D2
Kendal Ct
　7 Croydon CR0 . . . . 42 E1
　Kenley CR8 . . . . 80 D5
Kendale Cl RH10 . . . . 202 C2
Kendale Rd BR1 . . . . 24 E3
Kendal Gdns SM1 . . . . 59 C8
Kendal Gr GU15 . . . . 66 D4
Kendal Ho
　5 Croydon CR0 . . . . 42 E1
　Forest Hill SE23 . . . . 23 F7
　Penge SE20 . . . . 43 B7
Kendall Ave
　Penge BR3 . . . . 43 E7
　South Croydon CR2 . . . . . 61 D2
Kendall Ave S CR2 . . . . . . 61 D1
Kendall Ct
　Mitcham SW17 . . . . 20 D2
　4 Penge SE19 . . . . 22 F1
Kendall Ct Bsns Pk
　GU17 . . . . 64 F4
Kendall Ho **3** SE12 . . . . 24 F8
Kendall Rd
　Isleworth TW7 . . . . 6 A5
　Penge BR3 . . . . 43 E7
Kendor Ave KT19 . . . . 76 C8
Kendra Ct CR2 . . . . 61 B3
Kendra Hall Rd CR2 . . . . . 61 B3
Kendrey Gdns TW2 . . . . . . 16 E8
Kendrick Cl RG40 . . . . 25 C5
Kenilford Rd SW12 . . . . . . 21 B8
Kenilworth Ave
　Bracknell RG12 . . . . 27 D8
　Oxshott KT11 . . . . 74 B5
　Wimbledon SW19 . . . . 20 A4
Kenilworth Cl
　Banstead SM7 . . . . 78 B3
　Crawley RH11 . . . . 201 B2
Kenilworth Ct TW2 . . . . . . 16 E6
Kenilworth Dr KT12 . . . . . 54 D7
Kenilworth Gdns TW18 . . . 13 C3
Kenilworth Rd
　Ashford TW15, TW19 . . . . . 13 D5
　Farnborough GU14 . . . . . . 84 C5
　Penge SE20 . . . . 43 D8
　Stoneleigh KT17 . . . . 58 A5
Kenilworth Terr **5**
　SM2 . . . . 59 A3
KENLEY 80 D3
Kenley Gdns CR7 . . . . 42 B5
Kenley Ho **5** CR0 . . . . . . 43 A1
Kenley La CR8 . . . . 80 D3
Kenley Prim Sch CR3 . . . . 80 E3
Kenley Rd
　Headley Down GU35 . . . . 187 C5
　Kingston u T KT1, KT3 . . . 38 B7
　Merton SW19 . . . . 40 A6
　Twickenham TW1 . . . . 6 B1
Kenley Sta CR8 . . . . 80 C5
Kenley Wlk SM3 . . . . 58 D6
Kenlor Rd SW17 . . . . 20 D3
Kenmara Cl RH10 . . . . . . 182 A1
Kenmara Ct RH10 . . . . . . 182 A2
Kenmare Dr CR4 . . . . 20 F1
Kenmare Rd CR7 . . . . 42 A3
Kenmore Cl
　Frimley GU16 . . . . 85 D8
　Richmond TW9 . . . . 7 A7
Kenmore Rd CR8 . . . . 80 B5
Kennard Ct RH18 . . . . . . 206 E3
Kennedy Ave RH19 . . . . . 185 D3
Kennedy Cl CR4 . . . . 41 A7
Kennedy Ct TW15 . . . . 14 C3
Kennedy Rd RH13 . . . . . . 217 D2
Kennel Ave SL5 . . . . 28 F8
Kennel Cl
　Fetcham KT22 . . . . 94 C3
　North Ascot SL5 . . . . 8 F2
Kennel Gn SL5 . . . . 28 E8
Kennel La
　Fetcham KT22 . . . . 94 C4
　Frensham GU10 . . . . 146 C2
　Hookwood RH6 . . . . 160 C4
　Windlesham GU20 . . . . . . 48 C5
Kennel Ride SL5 . . . . 8 F1
Kennels La GU14 . . . . 84 C2
Kennel Wood SL5 . . . . 28 F8
Kennelwood Cres CR0 . . . 82 D8
Kennet Cl
　Ash GU12 . . . . 106 A1
　Crawley RH11 . . . . 200 F5
　Farnborough GU14 . . . . . . 84 E6
Kennet Ct GU21 . . . . 69 F3
Kennet Ho **6** RH1 . . . . . 118 F2
Kenneth Rd SM7 . . . . 78 D4
Kennet Rd TW7 . . . . 5 F4
Kennet Sq CR4 . . . . 40 E8

Kennett Ct W4 . . . . 7 B7
Kennoldes SE21 . . . . 22 D6
Kenny Dr SM5 . . . . 60 A2
Kenrick Sq RH1 . . . . 120 E1
Kensington Ave CR7 . . . . . 42 A8
Kensington Avenue Prim
　Sch CR7 . . . . 42 A8
Kensington Gdns KT1 . . . . 37 D6
Kensington Rd RH11 . . . . 201 C2
Kensington Terr CR2 . . . . . 61 D3
Kent Cl
　Mitcham SW4, SW16 . . . . . 41 E5
　Staines TW18 . . . . 13 D2
Kent Ct **4** RH12 . . . . . . 217 D2
Kent Dr TW11 . . . . 16 E3
Kent Gate Way
　Addington CR0 . . . . 63 B5
　New Addington CR0 . . . . . 62 F4
Kent Hatch Rd RH8,
　TN8 . . . . 123 D4
Kent Ho TW10 . . . . 7 A2
Kent House La BR3 . . . . . . 23 E3
Kent House Rd SE26,
　BR3 . . . . 23 E2
Kent House Sta BR3 . . . . . 43 E8
Kent House Station App
　BR3 . . . . 43 D8
Kentigern Dr RG45 . . . . . . 45 E5
Kent Lo **9** TW9 . . . . 7 A6
Kenton Cl
　Bracknell RG12 . . . . 27 D7
　Frimley GU16 . . . . 65 F1
Kenton Ct
　2 Forest Hill SE26 . . . . . 23 E4
　8 Twickenham TW1 . . . . . 6 D1
Kenton Way GU21 . . . . 68 F2
Kent Rd
　East Molesey KT8 . . . . 36 C5
　Kingston u T KT1 . . . . 37 D6
　Richmond TW9 . . . . 7 A7
　West Wickham BR4 . . . . . . 44 B1
　Windlesham GU20 . . . . . . 48 D5
　Woking GU22 . . . . 70 C3
Kent Way KT6 . . . . 56 F4
Kentwood Farm RG40 . . . . 25 D8
Kentwyns Rise RH1 . . . . . 140 F8
Kenward Ct RH3 . . . . 137 C5
Kenwood Cl UB7 . . . . 3 A8
Kenwood Dr
　Beckenham BR3 . . . . 44 C6
　Hersham KT12 . . . . 54 B5
Kenwood Pk KT13 . . . . 53 D4
Kenwood Ridge CR8 . . . . . 80 B2
Kenworth Gr GU18 . . . . . . 48 A1
Kenwyn Rd SW20 . . . . 39 C8
Kenya Ct RH6 . . . . 160 F4
Kenyngton Dr TW16 . . . . . 15 A3
Kenyngton Manor Prim
　Sch TW16 . . . . 15 A2
Kenyons KT24 . . . . 112 B7
Keogh Barracks GU16 . . . . 86 B1
Keogh Cl GU12 . . . . 86 B2
Keppel Rd RH4 . . . . 115 B1
Keppel Spur SL4 . . . . 11 B8
Kepple Pl GU19 . . . . 47 F3
Kerria Way GU24 . . . . 67 F6
Kerrill Ave CR5 . . . . 100 A8
Kerrsland Cotts GU7 . . . . 149 F7
Kerry Terr GU21 . . . . 70 B3
Kersey Dr CR2 . . . . 81 D7
Kershaw Ho **7** SE27 . . . . 22 B5
Keston Ave
　Coulsdon CR5, CR8 . . . . . 100 B8
　Woodham KT15 . . . . 71 A8
Keston Prim Sch CR5 . . . 100 A8
Keston Rd CR7 . . . . 42 A3
Kestral Ct SM6 . . . . 60 C5
Kestrel Ave TW18 . . . . 12 F5
Kestrel Cl
　Ash Vale GU12 . . . . 106 A7
　Crawley RH11 . . . . 201 C8
　Crondall GU10 . . . . 124 D7
　Epsom KT19 . . . . 76 B8
　Guildford GU4 . . . . 110 D3
　Horsham RH12 . . . . 217 E5
　Kingston u T KT2 . . . . 17 D4
Kestrel Ct CR2 . . . . 61 C4
Kestrel Ho GU9 . . . . 146 A8
Kestrel Rd GU14 . . . . 85 B2
Kestrel Way
　New Addington CR0 . . . . . 63 D2
　Woking GU21 . . . . 69 B3
Kestrel Wlk RH10 . . . . . . 204 C5
Keswick Ave
　Kingston u T SW15 . . . . . . 18 E3
　Merton SW19 . . . . 40 A7
　Upper Halliford TW17 . . . . 34 E6
Keswick Cl
　Crawley RH11 . . . . 200 D4
　Frimley GU15 . . . . 66 D4
　Sutton SM1 . . . . 59 C6
Keswick Ct
　17 Bromley BR2 . . . . 44 F5
　Catford SE6 . . . . 24 F7
　Woking GU18 . . . . 67 B8
Keswick Rd
　Fetcham KT22, KT23 . . . . . 94 C2
　Thorpe Lea TW20 . . . . 12 B1
　Twickenham TW2 . . . . 5 C1
　West Wickham BR4 . . . . . . 63 E8
　Witley GU8 . . . . 170 D6
Kettering Ct CR7 . . . . 42 C5
Kettering St SW16 . . . . 21 C2
Kettlewell Cl GU21 . . . . . . 69 E4
Kettlewell Dr GU21 . . . . . . 69 E5
Kettlewell Hill GU21 . . . . . 69 E4
Ketton Gn RH1 . . . . 119 D7

Kevan Dr GU23 . . . . 90 E2
Kevin Cl TW4 . . . . 4 D5
KEW 7 A8
Kew Bridge Rd TW8 . . . . 6 F8
Kew Coll TW9 . . . . 7 A7
Kew Cres SM3 . . . . 58 F7
Kew Ct KT2 . . . . 37 E8
Kew Foot Rd TW9 . . . . 6 E4
Kew Gardens Rd TW9 . . . . . 7 A6
Kew Gardens Sta TW9 . . . . . 7 A6
Kew Gn TW9 . . . . 6 F8
Kew Green Prep Sch
　TW8 . . . . 6 F8
Kew Lo **11** TW9 . . . . 6 F6
Kew Montessori Sch
　TW9 . . . . 7 A6
Kew Obsy★ TW9 . . . . 6 C4
Kew Pal★ TW9 . . . . 6 E7
Kew Rd TW9, W4 . . . . 6 F5
Kew Ret Pk TW9 . . . . 7 B6
Kew Riverside Prim Sch
　. . . . . 7 B5
Key Cross GU10 . . . . 147 D5
Keymer Cl TN16 . . . . 83 D3
Keymer Rd
　Crawley RH11 . . . . 201 D4
　Streatham SW2 . . . . 21 F6
Keynsham Rd SM4 . . . . . . 40 B1
Keynsham Way GU47 . . . . 45 D2
Keynsham Wlk SM4 . . . . . 40 B1
Keys Ct GU21 . . . . 61 D7
Keysham Ave TW5 . . . . 4 A6
Keywood Dr TW16 . . . . 15 A2
Khama Rd SW17 . . . . 20 E4
Khartoum Rd
　Upper Tooting SW17 . . . . . 20 D4
　Witley GU8 . . . . 170 E6
Kibble Gn RG12 . . . . 27 C3
Kidborough Down
　KT23 . . . . 114 A8
Kidborough Rd RH11 . . . . 200 F5
Kidbrooke Rise RH18 . . . . 206 E2
Kidderminster Pl CR0 . . . . 42 B1
Kidderminster Rd CR0 . . . 42 C2
Kidmans Cl RH12 . . . . 217 F5
Kidworth Cl RH6 . . . . 160 F5
Kielder Wlk GU15 . . . . 66 C4
Kier Pk SL5 . . . . 29 C6
Kilberry Cl TW7 . . . . 5 D6
Kilcorral Cl KT17 . . . . 77 A5
Killasser Ct KT20 . . . . 97 C4
Killburns Mill Cl SM6 . . . . 60 B8
Killearn Rd SE6 . . . . 24 D7
Killester Gdns KT17,
　KT4 . . . . 58 B6
Killick Ho SM1 . . . . 59 B6
Killicks GU6 . . . . 174 F4
Killieser Ave SW2 . . . . 21 E6
Killigrew Ho **4** TW16 . . . . 14 E1
Killinghurst La GU27,
　GU8 . . . . 209 D8
Killy Hill GU24 . . . . 49 E3
Kilmarnock Pk RH2 . . . . . 118 B2
Kilmartin Ave SW16 . . . . . 42 A6
Kilmartin Gdns GU16 . . . . 65 F1
Kilmington Cl RG12 . . . . . 27 E2
Kilmiston Ave TW17 . . . . . 34 C3
Kilmiston Ho TW17 . . . . . . 34 C3
Kilmore Dr GU15 . . . . 66 B4
Kilmorey Gdns TW1 . . . . . . 6 B3
Kilmorey Rd TW1 . . . . 6 B3
Kilmorie Prim Sch
　SE23 . . . . 23 E6
Kilmorie Rd SE23 . . . . 23 E6
Kilmuir Cl GU47 . . . . 64 D7
Kiln Ave GU27 . . . . 208 C8
Kilnbridge Ho GU21 . . . . . 88 F8
Kiln Cl
　Crawley Down RH10 . . . . 204 B7
　Harlington UB3 . . . . 3 D8
Kiln Copse GU6 . . . . 174 E4
Kilnfield Rd RH12 . . . . . . 214 D8
Kiln La
　Bracknell RG12 . . . . 27 A7
　Brockham RH3 . . . . 116 C1
　Cranbourne SL4 . . . . 9 B2
　Ewell KT17 . . . . 76 E8
　Farnham GU10, GU9 . . . . 146 C6
　Horley RH6 . . . . 161 A5
　Ripley GU23 . . . . 91 B3
　Sunningdale SL5 . . . . 30 A4
Kiln Mdws GU3 . . . . 108 C5
Kilnmead RH10 . . . . 201 E7
Kilnmead Cl RH10 . . . . . . 201 E7
Kiln Mews SW17 . . . . 20 D3
Kiln Rd RH10 . . . . 204 B7
Kilnside KT10 . . . . 56 A3
Kilns The
　Farnham GU10 . . . . 125 F3
　Frithend GU35 . . . . 166 A5
Kiln Way
　Aldershot GU11 . . . . 126 B7
　Grayshott GU26 . . . . 187 E5
Kiln Wlk RH1 . . . . 140 A4
Kilnwood La
　Crawley RH12 . . . . 200 B3
　Faygate RH12 . . . . 199 F3
Kilravock Ho SE25 . . . . . . 42 D6
Kilross Rd TW14 . . . . 14 E7
Kilrue La KT12 . . . . 53 F6
Kilrush Terr GU21 . . . . 70 A3
Kilsha Rd KT12 . . . . 35 C3
Kimber Gr GU4 . . . . 110 D3
Kimber Ctr The SW18 . . . . 20 A8
Kimberley RG12 . . . . 27 C1
Kimberley Cl RH6 . . . . 160 E3
Kimberley Pl **7** CR8 . . . . 80 A8

Kimberley Rd
　Crawley RH10 . . . . 202 B7
　Penge BR3 . . . . 43 D7
　Thornton Heath CR0,
　CR7 . . . . 42 B3
Kimberley Ride KT11 . . . . . 74 B6
Kimberley Wlk KT12 . . . . . 35 B2
Kimber Rd SW18 . . . . 20 B8
Kimble Ho SW17 . . . . 20 D2
Kimble Rd SW19 . . . . 20 D2
Kimbolton Cl **1** SE12 . . . 24 F8
Kimmeridge RG12 . . . . 27 E3
Kimpton Ho SW15 . . . . 19 A8
Kimpton Link Bsns Ctr
　SM3 . . . . 58 F8
Kimpton Park Way
　SM3 . . . . 58 F8
Kimpton Rd SM3 . . . . 58 F8
Kimpton Trad & Bsns Ctr
　SM3 . . . . 58 F8
Kinburn Dr TW20 . . . . 11 E3
Kindell Ho **4** SW14 . . . . . . 7 D4
Kindersley Cl RH19 . . . . . 186 B3
Kinfauns Rd SW2 . . . . 22 A6
King Acre Ct TW18 . . . . . . 12 E5
King Alfred Ave
　Catford SE6 . . . . 24 A4
　Catford SE6 . . . . 24 A5
Kingates Ct SB3 . . . . 44 B6
King Athelstan Prim Sch
　KT1 . . . . 37 F6
King Charles Cres KT5 . . . 37 F2
King Charles' Rd KT5,
　KT6 . . . . 37 F3
King Charles Wlk **6**
　SW19 . . . . 19 E7
Kingcup Cl CR0 . . . . 43 D1
Kingcup Dr GU24 . . . . 68 A4
Kingdom Ho **5** GU14 . . . 105 D8
King Edward Dr KT6 . . . . . 56 E7
King Edwards Cl SL5 . . . . 28 E8
King Edward's Gr
　TW11 . . . . 17 C2
King Edwards Rd SL5 . . . . 28 E8
King Edwards Rise SL5 . . . 28 E8
King Edward's Sch
　GU8 . . . . 170 F1
KINGFIELD 89 F7
Kingfield Cl GU22 . . . . 89 F7
Kingfield Dr GU22 . . . . 89 F7
Kingfield Gdns GU22 . . . . 89 F7
Kingfield Rd GU22 . . . . . . 89 F7
Kingfield Sch GU22 . . . . . 90 A7
Kingfisher Cl
　Crawley RH10 . . . . 182 A1
　Farnborough GU14 . . . . . . 84 D6
　Hersham KT12 . . . . 54 E5
Kingfisher Ct
　Cheam SM1 . . . . 58 F5
　4 Dorking RH4 . . . . 136 A8
　East Molesey KT8 . . . . 36 E5
　Guildford GU4 . . . . 110 D3
　Hounslow TW7 . . . . 5 D5
　Isleworth TW3 . . . . 5 B2
　Putney SW19 . . . . 19 E6
　Sheerwater GU21 . . . . 70 C5
　Woking GU21 . . . . 69 E2
Kingfisher Dr
　Guildford GU4 . . . . 110 C3
　Redhill RH1 . . . . 119 A3
　Staines TW18 . . . . 12 F4
　Teddington TW10 . . . . 17 B4
Kingfisher Gdns CR2 . . . . 62 D1
Kingfisher La RH10 . . . . . 204 C5
Kingfisher Lo TW11 . . . . . . 17 A4
Kingfisher Rd GU9 . . . . . . 145 F8
Kingfisher Rise RH19 . . . . 205 F8
Kingfisher Way
　Beckenham CR0 . . . . 43 D4
　Horsham RH12 . . . . 217 C5
Kingfisher Wlk GU12 . . . . 105 F2
King Garth Mews SE23 . . . 23 C6
King Gdns CR0 . . . . 61 B5
King George Ave
　East Grinstead RH19 . . . . 185 C3
　Walton-on-T KT12 . . . . . . 35 D1
King George Cl
　Ashford TW16 . . . . 14 E3
　Farnborough GU14 . . . . . . 85 D2
King George's Cotts
　GU8 . . . . 192 F6
King George's Dr KT15 . . . 52 A1
King George's Lo
　GU2 . . . . 109 A4
King George Sq TW10 . . . . 6 F1
King George's Trad Est
　KT9 . . . . 57 A6
King George V1 Ave
　TN16 . . . . 83 D3
King George VI Ave
　CR4 . . . . 40 F5
Kingham Cl SW18 . . . . 20 C8
Kingham Pl GU9 . . . . 125 B2
King Henry's Dr CR0 . . . . . 82 E8
King Henry's Rd KT1,
　KT3 . . . . 38 B6
Kinglake Ct **2** GU21 . . . . 68 E1
Kings Acre RH1 . . . . 140 F6
Kings Apartments
　GU15 . . . . 65 C4
Kings Ave
　Ash GU10 . . . . 126 F8
　Bromley BR1 . . . . 24 F2
　Byfleet KT14 . . . . 71 D7
　New Malden KT3 . . . . 38 F5
　Redhill RH1 . . . . 139 D7
　Streatham SW12, SW4 . . . 21 D8
　Wallington SM5 . . . . 59 F3

King's Ave
　Ashford TW16 . . . . 14 F2
　Hounslow TW3, TW5 . . . . . 5 B6
Kingsbridge Ho **11**
　SE20 . . . . 43 B8
Kingsbridge Rd
　Walton-on-T KT12 . . . . . . 35 B2
　West Barnes SM4 . . . . 39 D2
Kingsbrook KT22 . . . . 75 A1
Kingsbury Cres TW18 . . . . 12 D4
Kingsbury Dr SL4 . . . . 11 B8
Kings Chase KT8 . . . . 36 C6
Kings Cl KT12 . . . . 35 B1
King's Cl
　Staines TW18 . . . . 13 D1
　Thames Ditton KT7 . . . . . . 37 A2
Kingsclear Pk GU15 . . . . . 65 D4
Kingsclere Cl SW15 . . . . . 19 A8
Kingscliffe Gdns SW19 . . . 19 F7
Kings' Coll for the Arts &
　Technology GU2 . . . . 108 E1
Kings' Coll Sch SW19 . . . . 19 D2
Kings Copse **9** RH19 . . . 205 F8
Kingscote Hill RH11 . . . . . 201 B4
Kingscote Rd
　Croydon CR0, CR9 . . . . . . 43 B2
　Kingston u T KT3 . . . . 38 D6
Kingscote Sta RH19 . . . . . 204 F4
King's Court Fst Sch
　SL4 . . . . 11 B8
Kings Court Mews KT8 . . . 36 D4
Kingscourt Rd SW16 . . . . . 21 D5
Kings Cres GU15 . . . . 65 C8
Kingscroft Jun Sch
　TW18 . . . . 13 A2
Kingscroft La RG42 . . . . . . 8 A6
Kingscroft Rd
　Leatherhead KT22 . . . . . . 95 B7
　Woodmansterne SM7 . . . . 78 E4
Kings Cross La RH1 . . . . . 140 E6
Kings Ct
　Horsham RH13 . . . . 217 E3
　16 Kingston u T KT2 . . . . 18 A1
　Leatherhead KT22 . . . . . . 95 A6
　11 Roehampton SW15 . . . 19 A8
　Tadworth KT20 . . . . 97 C5
　3 Wallington SM6 . . . . . 60 B4
King's Ct
　Aldershot GU10,
　GU12 . . . . 126 E8
　Beckenham BR3 . . . . 44 B6
　Wimbledon SW19 . . . . 20 A2
Kingsdale Rd SE20 . . . . . . 23 D1
Kingsdale Sec Sch
　SE21 . . . . 22 E5
Kingsdene KT20 . . . . 97 B5
Kingsdown SW19 . . . . 19 D1
Kingsdown Ave CR2,
　CR8 . . . . 61 C2
Kingsdowne Rd KT6 . . . . . 37 F2
Kingsdown Rd
　Cheam SM3 . . . . 58 E5
　Ewell KT17 . . . . 77 A6
Kings Dr KT5 . . . . 38 A3
King's Dr KT7 . . . . 37 B2
Kings Dr The KT12 . . . . . . 53 F2
Kings Farm Ave TW10 . . . . . 7 A3
Kingsfield GU5 . . . . 153 E7
Kingsfield Bsns Pk
　RH1 . . . . 140 A8
Kingsfield Ct GU12 . . . . . 106 A7
Kingsfield Way RH1 . . . . . 140 A8
KINGSFOLD 198 B5
Kingsfold Ct RH12 . . . . . . 198 B5
Kings Gate
　Addlestone KT15 . . . . 52 B6
　Farncombe GU7 . . . . 150 F6
　Horsham RH12 . . . . 217 B2
　8 Knaphill GU21 . . . . . . 68 D2
　Woking GU21 . . . . 69 D1
Kingsgate Bsns Ctr
　KT2 . . . . 37 E8
Kingsgate Rd KT2 . . . . 37 E8
Kingsgrove Ind Est
　GU14 . . . . 85 A3
Kings Hall Rd BR3 . . . . . . 43 E8
King's Head La KT14 . . . . . 71 D8
Kingshill Ave KT4 . . . . 39 B2
Kings Ho **12** KT2 . . . . 37 E8
King's House Sch TW10 . . . . 6 F2
King's House Sch (Jun)
　TW10 . . . . 6 F2
Kings International Coll
　GU15 . . . . 65 C2
Kings Keep KT6 . . . . 37 E5
King's Keep
　Beckenham BR2 . . . . 44 E6
　Sandhurst GU47 . . . . 45 B1
Kings La
　Englefield Green TW20 . . . 11 A2
　Windlesham GU20 . . . . . . 48 E5
　Wrecclesham GU10 . . . . . 145 F6
King's La SM1 . . . . 59 D5
Kingsland RH5 . . . . 158 A1
Kingsland Ct RH10 . . . . . . 202 A6
Kingslea
　Horsham RH13 . . . . 217 E3
　Leatherhead KT22 . . . . . . 95 A7
Kingslea Prim Sch
　RH13 . . . . 217 E3
Kingslee Ct **13** SM2 . . . . 59 B3
Kingsleigh Cl TW8 . . . . 6 D8
Kingsleigh Pl CR4 . . . . 40 F6
Kingsleigh Wlk BR2 . . . . . 44 F5
Kingsley Ave
　Banstead SM7 . . . . 78 A4
　Camberley GU15 . . . . 65 D3
　Carshalton SM1 . . . . 59 D6

Kingsley Ave *continued*
Englefield Green TW20 . . . . 11 B2
Hounslow TW3. . . . . 5 C5
Kingsley Cl
Crowthorne RG45 . . . . 45 B3
Horley RH6 . . . . 160 F5
Kingsley Ct
Aldershot GU11. . . . . 105 B2
Walton-on-T KT12 . . . . 54 A7
Worcester Park KT4 . . . . . . 57 F8
Kingsley Dr KT4 . . . . 57 F8
Kingsley Gr RH2 . . . . 139 B5
KINGSLEY GREEN 208 B2
Kingsley Ho 8 KT6 . . . . . . 37 E4
Kingsley Prim Sch CR0 . . . 42 A1
Kingsley Rd
Crawley RH11 . . . . 201 A3
Farnborough GU14 . . . . 84 F6
Horley RH6 . . . . 160 F5
Hounslow TW3. . . . . 5 C5
Thornton Heath CR0 . . . . . . 42 A1
Wimbledon SW19 . . . . 20 B3
Kingslyn Cres SE19 . . . . . . 42 E8
Kingsmead
Biggin Hill TN16. . . . . 83 D3
Cranleigh GU6 . . . . 174 E3
Farnborough GU14 . . . . 85 B4
Frimley GU16. . . . . 85 E7
Richmond TW10. . . . . 6 F1
Weybridge KT13 . . . . 53 D4
11 Woking GU21 . . . . 70 A3
Kings Mead
Smallfield RH6. . . . . 162 B3
South Nutfield RH1 . . . . . . 140 E7
Kingsmead Ave
Mitcham CR4 . . . . 41 C6
North Cheam KT4 . . . . 58 B7
Sunbury TW16 . . . . 35 C7
Tolworth KT6 . . . . 57 A8
Kingsmead Cl
Horsham RH12 . . . . 218 B6
Teddington TW11. . . . . 17 B2
West Ewell KT19 . . . . 57 D3
Kingsmead Ct BR1 . . . . 24 F1
Kingsmead Lo SM2 . . . . . . 59 D4
Kings Mead Pk KT10 . . . . . 55 E3
Kingsmead Pk Cvn Pk
GU8 . . . . 148 C2
Kingsmead Pl RH12 . . . . . 216 C3
Kingsmead Rd
Broadbridge Heath
RH12. . . . . 216 D3
Streatham SW2 . . . . 22 A6
Kingsmead Sh Ctr
GU14. . . . . 85 B3
Kingsmere SE6 . . . . 24 B7
Kingsmere Rd
Bracknell RG42 . . . . 26 F8
Putney SW19. . . . . 19 D6
Kings Mews
Frimley GU16. . . . . 85 F6
Horsham RH12 . . . . 217 B2
Kingsmill Bsns Pk KT1 . . . 37 F6
Kings Mill La RH1. . . . . . . 140 D5
Kingsmount Ct SM1. . . . . . 59 B6
Kingsnympton Pk KT2. . . . . 18 B2
Kingsoak Ho 2 GU21 . . . . 70 A3
King's Paddock TW12 . . . . 36 C8
Kings Par 3 SM5 . . . . 59 E7
Kingspark Bsns Ctr
KT3 . . . . 38 C6
King's Pas KT2 . . . . 37 D8
Kings Peace The
GU26 . . . . 188 C3
Kings Penny Ho 4
KT2 . . . . 17 E1
Kings Pl RH13 . . . . 217 E3
Kings Rd
Belmont SM2. . . . . 59 A1
Biggin Hill TN16. . . . . 83 C2
Feltham TW13 . . . . 15 C7
Horley RH6 . . . . 161 A3
Mitcham CR4 . . . . 41 A6
Richmond TW10, TW9 . . . . . . 6 F2
Rudgwick RH12 . . . . 214 D7
Shalford GU4 . . . . 130 E2
Walton-on-T KT12 . . . . 35 B1
West End GU24 . . . . 68 A6
Woking GU21. . . . . 70 A3
Wonersh GU5 . . . . 152 B8
Woodham KT15 . . . . 71 B8
King's Rd
Aldershot GU11. . . . . 104 F1
Ascot SL5. . . . . 29 D4
Cranleigh GU6 . . . . 174 F2
Crowthorne RG45 . . . . 45 C5
Croydon SE25 . . . . 43 A6
Egham TW20 . . . . 12 A4
Farncombe GU7. . . . . 150 F6
Haslemere GU27 . . . . 208 A6
Horsham RH13 . . . . 217 E3
Long Ditton KT6. . . . . 37 C1
Mortlake SW14 . . . . 7 D4
Teddington TW11. . . . . 16 D3
Twickenham TW1. . . . . 6 B1
Wimbledon SW19 . . . . 20 A2
Kings Rd Ind Est
GU27. . . . . 208 A6
King's Ride
Bracknell SL5. . . . . 28 D5
Camberley GU15 . . . . 65 D7
Kings Ride Gate TW10. . . . . 7 A3
King's Ride Ho SL5 . . . . . . 28 E5
Kingsridge SW19 . . . . 19 E6
King's Shade Wlk 1
KT18 . . . . 76 D6
Kings's Rd 2 GU1 . . . . . . 109 D1

King St
Chertsey KT16. . . . . 33 A1
East Grinstead RH19. . . . . 185 E1
Richmond TW10, TW9 . . . . . . 6 D2
Twickenham TW1. . . . . 17 A7
King's Terr
Brands Hill SL3 . . . . 1 B8
9 Isleworth TW7 . . . . 6 A4
Kingsthorpe Rd SE26. . . . . 23 D4
Kingston Ave
Cheam SM3 . . . . 58 E7
East Horsley KT24. . . . . 92 E1
Feltham TW14 . . . . 3 F1
Leatherhead KT22. . . . . 95 B6
Kingston Bsns Ctr KT9 . . . 56 F7
Kingston By-Pass KT6, KT7,
KT9 . . . . 56 C7
Kingston By - Pass
KT6 . . . . 57 B8
Kingston Cl TW11. . . . . 17 B2
Kingston Coll KT1 . . . . 37 D6
Kingston Coll of F Ed
KT2 . . . . 37 E8
Kingston Cres
Beckenham BR3. . . . . 43 F8
Staines TW15. . . . . 13 D2
Kingston Gdns CR0 . . . . . . 60 E7
Kingston Gram Sch
KT2 . . . . 37 F7
Kingston Hall Rd KT1 . . . . 37 D6
Kingston Hill KT2 . . . . 18 C2
Kingston Hill Pl KT2 . . . . . 18 C4
Kingston Hospl KT2. . . . . . 38 B8
Kingston House Est
KT6 . . . . 37 B3
Kingston House Gdns
KT22 . . . . 95 B6
Kingston La
Teddington TW11. . . . . 17 B2
West Horsley KT24 . . . . . . 112 A8
Kingston Lo 2 KT3 . . . . . . 38 E5
Kingston Mus* KT1. . . . . . . 37 E7
Kingston Par KT19 . . . . 57 F4
Kingston Rd
Ashford TW15, TW17. . . . . . 13 F2
Ashtead KT22, KT9 . . . . 75 A3
Camberley GU15 . . . . 47 A1
Kingston u T KT1, KT3 . . . . . 38 C5
Leatherhead KT22. . . . . 75 A1
Merton SW19, SW20. . . . . . 39 E7
Putney SW15, SW19 . . . . . . 19 B7
Staines TW15, TW18 . . . . . . 13 B2
Teddington TW11. . . . . 17 B2
Worcester Park KT17, KT19,
KT4, KT5, KT6. . . . . 57 D6
Kingston Rise KT15 . . . . . . 52 A1
Kingstons Ind Est
GU12. . . . . 105 E2
Kingston Sq
Leatherhead KT22. . . . . 95 A8
West Norwood SE19 . . . . . . 22 D3
Kingston Sta KT2 . . . . 37 E8
Kingston Univ
Kingston u T, Kingston Vale
KT2. . . . . 18 D3
Kingston u T KT1 . . . . 37 E6
Kingston Univ Annex
KT1 . . . . 37 F7
Kingston Univ
Roehampton Vale Ctr
SW15 . . . . 18 F5
KINGSTON UPON THAMES
. . . . 37 C6
KINGSTON VALE 18 D4
Kingston Vale SW15 . . . . . 18 E5
King Street Par 7
TW1. . . . . 17 A7
Kings View Ct 1
SW20. . . . . 19 D1
Kings Warren KT22 . . . . . . 74 D8
Kingsway
Aldershot GU11. . . . . 104 E1
Blackwater GU17. . . . . 64 E5
Coney Hall BR4 . . . . 63 F7
Mortlake SW14, TW9. . . . . . . 7 B4
Stanwell TW19. . . . . 13 E7
West Barnes KT3. . . . . 39 C4
Woking GU21. . . . . 69 D1
Kings Way CR0 . . . . 60 F5
King's Way GU24 . . . . 87 D8
Kingsway Ave
Selsdon CR2 . . . . 62 D2
Woking GU21. . . . . 69 D1
Kingsway Bsns Pk
GU21. . . . . 70 C5
Kingsway Bsns Pk The
TW12 . . . . 35 F8
Kingsway Rd SM3. . . . . 58 E3
Kingsway Terr KT13. . . . . . 53 A2
Kingsway The KT17 . . . . . . 57 F1
Kingswear Ho SE23 . . . . . . 23 C6
Kingswick Cl SL5 . . . . 29 D5
Kingswick Dr SL5. . . . . 29 D5
Kings Wlk CR2. . . . . 81 B5
King's Wlk GU15. . . . . 64 F6
KINGSWOOD 97 F6
Kingswood GU26 . . . . 188 D2
Kingswood Ave
Beckenham BR2. . . . . 44 E5
Hampton TW12 . . . . 16 B2
Hamsey Green CR2 . . . . 81 C4
Hounslow TW3, TW5 . . . . 4 F5
Thornton Heath CR7 . . . . . . 42 A4
Kingswood Cl
Ashford TW15 . . . . 14 D3
Camberley GU15 . . . . 66 A8
Englefield Green TW20 . . . . 11 D4
Guildford GU1 . . . . 110 C2

Kingswood Cl *continued*
New Malden KT3. . . . . 38 F3
Surbiton KT6 . . . . 37 E2
Weybridge KT13 . . . . 53 B3
Kingswood Ct
7 Richmond TW10 . . . . 6 F2
Woking GU21. . . . . 69 E3
Kingswood Dr
Belmont SM2. . . . . 59 B2
Carshalton SM5. . . . . 40 F1
Dulwich SE19, SE21. . . . . . . 22 F4
Kingswood Firs GU26 . . . 188 C2
Kingswood Grange
KT20 . . . . 118 A8
Kingswood Hall of
Residence TW20 . . . . 11 D4
Kingswood Ho 3 KT2 . . . . 18 B2
Kingswood House Sch
KT19. . . . . 76 C6
Kingswood La
Grayshott GU26. . . . . 188 C2
Warlingham CR6 . . . . 81 C4
Kingswood Mans 3
SM2. . . . . 59 A3
Kingswood Pk KT20. . . . . . 97 E6
Kingswood Pl CR3 . . . . . . 101 A4
Kingswood Prim Sch
Lower Kingswood
KT20. . . . . 117 F7
West Norwood SE27 . . . . . . 22 D3
Kingswood Rd
Beckenham BR2. . . . . 44 E6
Merton SW19 . . . . 39 F8
Penge SE20 . . . . 23 C2
Streatham SW2 . . . . 21 E8
Tadworth KT20 . . . . 97 B6
Kingswood Rise TW20. . . . 11 D4
Kingswood Sta KT20 . . . . . 97 F6
Kingswood Way
Hamsey Green CR2 . . . . 81 C6
Selsdon CR2 . . . . 81 D7
Wallington SM6 . . . . 60 E5
Kingsworth Cl BR3. . . . . . . 43 E4
Kingsworthy Cl KT1. . . . . . 37 F6
King's Yd SL5. . . . . 28 E5
King William IV Gdns
SE20. . . . . 23 C2
Kinloss Rd SM5. . . . . 40 C2
Kinnaird Ave
Bromley BR1 . . . . 24 F2
Chiswick W4 . . . . 7 C7
Kinnaird Cl BR1. . . . . 24 F2
Kinnear Ct 7 SW20 . . . . . . 39 D8
Kinnersley Wlk RH2. . . . . 139 B4
Kinnibrugh Dr RH7. . . . . . 165 A1
Kinross Ave
Ascot SL5. . . . . 28 F4
Worcester Park KT4 . . . . . . 58 A8
Kinross Cl TW16 . . . . 14 F3
Kinross Ct
Ascot SL5. . . . . 28 F4
Catford SE6 . . . . 24 F6
Kinross Dr TW16. . . . . 14 F3
Kinsella Gdns SW19. . . . . . 19 B3
Kinsey Ho SE21 . . . . 22 E4
Kintyre Cl SW16 . . . . 41 F6
Kintyre Ct 16 SW2. . . . . 21 E8
Kinver Rd SE26 . . . . 23 C4
Kipings KT20 . . . . 97 D5
Kipling Cl RH10. . . . . 202 C8
Kipling Ct RH13. . . . . 218 A4
Kipling Dr SW17. . . . . 20 D2
Kipling Hall RG45. . . . . 45 B5
Kipling Way RH19. . . . . . . 185 C1
Kirby Cl KT19. . . . . 57 F5
Kirby Rd GU21. . . . . 69 D2
Kirby Way KT12. . . . . 35 C3
Kirdford Cl RH11. . . . . 201 A8
Kirkby Ct GU16 . . . . 65 E1
Kirkdale SE26 . . . . 23 B5
Kirkefields GU2. . . . . 109 A4
Kirkgate The 2 KT17 . . . . 76 E6
Kirkham Cl GU47 . . . . 45 D2
Kirkland Ave GU21. . . . . . . 68 F3
Kirkland Terr BR3 . . . . 24 A2
Kirkleas Rd KT6 . . . . 37 E1
Kirklees Rd CR7 . . . . 42 A4
Kirkley Rd SW19. . . . . 40 A8
Kirkly Cl CR2 . . . . 61 E2
Kirk Rise SM1 . . . . 59 B7
Kirkstall RH4 . . . . 136 A6
Kirkstall Gdns SW2 . . . . . . 21 E7
Kirkstall Rd SW2. . . . . 21 E7
Kirksted Rd SM4. . . . . 40 B1
Kirkstone Cl GU15 . . . . 66 D4
Kirkstone Way BR1 . . . . . . 24 E1
Kirrane Cl KT3. . . . . 38 F4
Kirriemuir Gdns
GU12 . . . . 106 D3
Kirtley Rd SE26 . . . . 23 E4
Kitchener Rd CR7. . . . . 42 D6
Kitchenride Cnr KT16 . . . . 51 A6
Kites Cl RH11. . . . . 201 C6
Kithurst Cl RH11 . . . . 201 D4
Kitley Gdns SE19. . . . . 42 F8
Kitsbridge Ho RH10 . . . . . 183 A2
Kitsmead RH10 . . . . 183 A2
Kitsmead La KT16. . . . . 50 D8
Kittiwake Cl
Crawley RH11 . . . . 200 D4
Selsdon CR0, CR2 . . . . 62 E1
Kittiwake Pl SM1 . . . . 58 F5
Klondyke Villas GU27 . . . 190 A1
Knaggs Ho 1 TW11. . . . . . 16 E3
Knap Ct 5 GU21 . . . . 68 D2
Knapdale Cl SE23 . . . . 23 B6
KNAPHILL 68 D1

Knaphill Lower Sch The
GU21. . . . . 68 B1
Knaphill Sch GU21. . . . . . . 68 C1
Knapmill Rd SE6. . . . . 24 B6
Knapmill Way SE6 . . . . 24 B6
Knapp Rd TW15. . . . . 13 F4
Knapton Mews SW17. . . . . 21 A2
Knaresborough Dr
SW18. . . . . 20 B7
Kneller Gdns TW7 . . . . 5 D1
Kneller Rd
New Malden KT3. . . . . 38 E2
Twickenham TW2. . . . . 5 D1
Knepp Cl RH10 . . . . 202 C6
Knevett Terr TW3. . . . . 5 A3
Knight Ho KT4. . . . . 58 A8
Knighton Cl
Crawley RH10 . . . . 182 D2
Croydon CR2 . . . . 61 B2
Knighton Lo KT12. . . . . 54 C8
Knighton Park Rd
SE26. . . . . 23 D3
Knighton Rd RH1 . . . . 140 A7
Knightons La GU8. . . . . . . 193 A2
Knightsbridge Cres
TW18 . . . . 13 B2
Knightsbridge Ho 10
GU1 . . . . 130 F8
Knightsbridge Rd
GU15 . . . . 65 E7
Knights Cl
East Molesey KT8 . . . . 35 F4
Egham TW20 . . . . 12 D2
Knights Ct
Kingston u T KT1 . . . . 37 E6
Penge BR3. . . . . 43 E8
Reigate RH2. . . . . 118 C1
South Croydon CR2 . . . . 61 D4
Knight's Ct BR1. . . . . 24 F5
KNIGHT'S HILL 22 C7
Knight's Hill SE27. . . . . 22 B4
Knight's Hill Sq SE27. . . . . 22 B4
Knight's Pk KT1 . . . . 37 E6
Knights Pl 21 RH1. . . . . . . 119 A2
Knight's Pl TW2 . . . . 16 E7
Knights Rd GU9. . . . . 125 E7
Knights Way GU15 . . . . 66 C4
Knightswood
Bracknell RG12 . . . . 27 B1
Woking GU21. . . . . 68 F1
Knightwood Cl
Farnborough GU14 . . . . 85 E2
Reigate RH2. . . . . 139 A7
Knightwood Cres KT3 . . . . 38 E3
Knipp Hill KT11 . . . . 73 F6
Knobfield RH5. . . . . 154 F8
Knob Hill RH12 . . . . 198 A1
Knockholt Cl SM2. . . . . 59 B1
Knockhundred La
GU26 . . . . 207 C8
Knock The GU47 . . . . 64 D7
Knole Cl
Crawley RH10 . . . . 202 D7
Croydon CR0 . . . . 43 C3
Knole Gr RH19. . . . . 185 C3
Knole Wood SL5. . . . . 29 E1
Knoll Ct SE19. . . . . 22 F3
Knoll Ho BR3 . . . . 44 B8
Knollmead KT4, KT5 . . . . . . 38 C1
Knollmead Prim Sch
KT5. . . . . 57 C8
Knoll Park Rd KT16 . . . . . . 32 F1
Knoll Quarry GU7 . . . . 150 E6
Knoll Rd
Camberley GU15 . . . . 65 D6
Dorking RH4 . . . . 136 A5
Farncombe GU7. . . . . 150 E6
Knolls Cl KT4. . . . . 58 B7
Knolls The KT17 . . . . 77 C3
Knoll The
Beckenham BR3. . . . . 44 B8
Chertsey KT16. . . . . 32 F1
Cobham KT11. . . . . 74 A6
Leatherhead KT22. . . . . 95 C6
Knoll Wood GU7 . . . . 150 D6
Knolly's Cl SW16. . . . . 22 A5
Knollys Rd GU11 . . . . 104 F3
Knolly's Rd SW16 . . . . 22 A5
Knott Park Ho KT22 . . . . . . 74 C4
Knowle Cl RH10 . . . . 183 C3
Knowle Dr RH10 . . . . 183 B3
Knowle Gdns KT14. . . . . . . 70 F6
Knowle Gn TW18 . . . . 13 A3
Knowle Gr GU25 . . . . 31 C2
KNOWLE GREEN 13 A3
Knowle Grove Cl GU25 . . . 31 C2
KNOWLE HILL 31 C2
Knowle Hill GU25 . . . . 31 C2
Knowle La GU6, RH12 . . . . 194 D4
Knowle Lo CR3 . . . . 101 A4
Knowle Park Ave
TW18. . . . . 13 B3
Knowle Park Inf Sch
TW18 . . . . 13 A3
Knowle Pk KT11 . . . . 73 E4
Knowle Rd TW2 . . . . 16 E7
Knowle The GU35. . . . . . . 187 B5
Knowl Hill GU22 . . . . 70 B1
Knowl Hill Sch GU24. . . . . 87 E5
Knowlton Gn 2 BR2 . . . . . 44 F4
Knox Rd GU2 . . . . 109 A6
Kohat Ct GU11. . . . . 104 F2
Kohat Rd SW19. . . . . 20 B3
Kohima Cl GU11 . . . . 105 B3
Koonowla Cl TN16 . . . . 83 D4
Kooringa CR6 . . . . 101 B8
Korda Cl TW17. . . . . 33 F6
Korea Cotts KT11 . . . . 73 D3

Kreisel Wlk TW9. . . . . 6 F8
Kristina Ct 4 SM2 . . . . 59 A4
Krooner Rd GU15 . . . . 65 B3
Kuala Gdns SW16. . . . . 41 F8
Kurnool Mortar Cross
Roads GU15. . . . . 65 A6
Kyle Cl RG12. . . . . 27 B6
Kyle Ho TW12 . . . . 36 C8
Kynaston Ave CR7 . . . . 42 C4
Kynaston Cres CR0,
CR7 . . . . 42 C4
Kynaston Ct CR3. . . . . 100 E2
Kynaston Ho 7 SW2 . . . . . 21 F7
Kynaston Rd CR0, CR7 . . . . 42 C4
Kynersley Cl SM5 . . . . 59 F7
Kyngeshene Gdns
GU1 . . . . 131 B8

L

Laburnam Ct 13 SW16. . . . 22 A3
Laburnham Ct SM1 . . . . . . 59 A5
Laburnum Ave 6 SM1 . . . 59 E7
Laburnum Cl
1 Aldershot GU11 . . . . . . 105 A1
Guildford GU1 . . . . 109 C4
Laburnum Cres TW16 . . . . 35 B8
Laburnum Ct
Chertsey KT16. . . . . 33 A1
Mitcham CR4 . . . . 41 A7
3 Twickenham TW1 . . . . 6 A1
Laburnum Gdns CR0 . . . . . 43 D1
Laburnum Gr
Brands Hill SL3 . . . . 1 B8
Hounslow TW3. . . . . 4 F3
Kingston u T KT3 . . . . 38 D7
Laburnum Pas 2
GU11 . . . . 105 A1
Laburnum Pl TW20. . . . . . . 11 B2
Laburnum Rd
Aldershot GU11. . . . . 105 A2
Chertsey KT16. . . . . 33 A1
Epsom KT18. . . . . 76 E6
Heath End GU9 . . . . 125 E7
Merton SW19 . . . . 20 C1
Mitcham CR4 . . . . 41 A7
Woking GU22. . . . . 89 D7
Laburnums The GU17 . . . . 64 B5
Laburnum Villas KT18. . . . 76 E6
Laburnum Way TW19 . . . . 13 F7
Lacey Ave CR5. . . . . 100 A7
Lacey Cl TW20. . . . . 12 D1
Lacey Dr
Coulsdon CR5 . . . . 100 B7
Hampton TW12 . . . . 35 F8
Lackford Rd CR5. . . . . 78 F1
Lacock Cl SW19 . . . . 20 C2
Lacrosse Way SW16. . . . . . 41 D8
Lacy Gn CR5. . . . . 100 A7
Ladas Rd SE27. . . . . 22 C3
Ladbroke Cotts 2
RH1. . . . . 119 A2
Ladbroke Ct 7 RH1. . . . . . 119 A3
Ladbroke Gr RH1 . . . . 119 A2
Ladbroke Hurst RH7 . . . . 165 A1
Ladbroke Rd
Epsom KT18. . . . . 76 D5
Horley RH6 . . . . 161 B5
Redhill RH1 . . . . 119 A3
Ladbrook Rd SE25 . . . . 42 D5
Ladderstile Ride KT2. . . . . 18 B3
Ladlands SE22. . . . . 23 A8
Ladybank RG12 . . . . 27 B1
Lady Booth Rd 7 KT1. . . . 37 E7
Ladycross GU8 . . . . 170 E8
Ladyegate Cl RH5. . . . . . . 136 D8
Ladyegate Rd RH5 . . . . . . 136 D8
Lady Eleanor Holles Sch
The (Jun Girls) TW12 . . . 16 B3
Lady Eleanor Holles Sch
The (Senior Girls)
TW12 . . . . 16 B3
Lady Elizabeth Ho SW14. . . 7 C4
Lady Forsdyke Way
KT19 . . . . 57 A2
Ladygate Dr GU26. . . . . . . 188 A3
Ladygrove CR2 . . . . 62 D2
Ladygrove Dr GU4 . . . . . . 110 B6
Lady Harewood Way
KT19 . . . . 57 A2
Lady Hay KT4. . . . . 57 F8
Lady Jane Ct 1 KT2 . . . . . 37 F7
Lady Margaret Rd
Crawley RH11 . . . . 201 A7
Sunningdale SL5 . . . . 29 F2
Lady Margaret Wlk
RH11 . . . . 201 A7
Ladymead GU1 . . . . 109 C2
Ladymead Cl RH10. . . . . . 202 C3
Ladymead Ret Ctr
GU1. . . . . 109 C2
Ladymere Pl GU7 . . . . 150 D4
Ladythorpe Cl KT15 . . . . . . 52 B6
Ladywood Ave GU14 . . . . . 84 C4
Ladywood Grange SL5 . . . 29 F1
Ladywood Rd KT6. . . . . 57 A8
Laffan's Rd GU11 . . . . 104 E6
Lafone Ave TW13 . . . . 15 C6
Lafone Ho 11 SW2 . . . . 21 E8
Lagham Pk RH9 . . . . 142 E6
Lagham Rd RH9 . . . . 142 F5
Laglands Cl RH2. . . . . 118 C3
Laings Ave CR4. . . . . 40 F7
Laings Cnr CR4. . . . . 40 F8

Lainlock Pl TW3 5 B6
Lainson St SW18 20 A8
Lairdale Cl SE21 22 C8
Laird Ct GU19 47 E1
Lait Ho BR3 44 B8
Laitwood Rd SW12 21 B7
Lake Cl
Byfleet KT14 71 D7
[6] Wimbledon SW19 19 F3
Lake Cotts GU8 169 F4
Lake End Way RG45 45 A4
Lakefield Cl SE20 23 B1
Lake Gdns
Hackbridge SM6 60 B7
Richmond TW10 17 B6
Lakehall Gdns CR7 42 B4
Lakehall Rd CR7 42 B4
Lake Ho [4] SW27 22 B3
Lakehurst Rd KT19 57 E5
Lake La
Dockenfield GU10 166 E6
Horley RH1, RH6 161 C6
Lakeland Dr GU16 65 E1
Lakeman Ct CR7 42 C7
Laker Ct RH10 202 A6
Lake Rd
Croydon CR0 62 F8
Frimley GU16 86 B6
Ockley RH5 177 D6
Virginia Water GU25 31 B5
Wimbledon SW19 19 F3
Lakers Lea RH14 212 F1
Lakers Rise SM7 78 E3
Lakes Cl GU4 131 B3
Lakeside
Beckenham BR3 44 B6
Hackbridge SM6 60 B6
Horsham RH12 217 C5
[10] Kingston u T KT2 18 B1
Knaphill GU21 88 E8
Oatlands Park KT13 53 E8
Redhill RH1 119 A3
West Ewell KT19 57 E4
Lakeside Bsns Pk GU47 64 A7
Lakeside Cl
Ash Vale GU12 105 F4
Knaphill GU21 88 E8
South Norwood SE25 43 A7
Lakeside Dr KT10 55 C4
Lakeside Est SL3 2 A8
Lakeside Gdns GU14 84 D7
Lakeside Grange KT13 53 C7
Lakeside Pk KT16 33 C1
Lakeside Prim Sch GU16 65 F1
Lakeside Rd
Ash Vale GU11, GU12 105 F4
Colnbrook SL3 1 F7
Farnborough GU14 105 A7
Lake Side The GU17 64 D4
Lakeview SL5 28 D6
Lake View RH5 136 C4
Lake View Cotts RH4 135 A6
Lakeview Rd SE27 22 B3
Lake View Rd
Copthorne RH19 184 C4
Dormans Park RH19 185 F5
LALEHAM 33 C6
Laleham Abbey TW18 33 C5
Laleham CE Prim Sch TW18 33 C7
Laleham Cl TW18 33 B8
Laleham Ct GU21 69 E3
Laleham Lea Prep Sch CR8 60 E1
Laleham Rd
Catford SE6 24 C8
Littleton TW17 34 A4
Staines TW18 12 F2
Laleham Reach KT16 33 B6
Lamberhurst Rd SE27 22 A3
Lamberhurst Wlk RH10 202 A5
Lambert Ave TW9 7 B4
Lambert Cl TN16 83 D3
Lambert Cotts RH1 120 E2
Lambert Cres GU17 64 C4
Lambert Ho SM7 78 B5
Lambert Rd SM7 78 B5
Lambert's Pl CR0 42 D1
Lambert's Rd KT6 37 F4
Lambeth Cl RH11 201 B2
Lambeth Prospect SE19 22 D2
Lambeth Rd CR0 42 B1
Lambeth Wlk RH11 201 B2
Lambly Hill GU25 31 E6
Lamborne Cl GU47 45 A1
Lambourn Cl
Croydon CR2 61 B2
East Grinstead RH19 185 E3
Lambourne Ave SW19 19 F4
Lambourne Cl RH10 201 F4
Lambourne Cres GU21 70 D6
Lambourne Dr
Bagshot GU19 47 D2
Cobham KT11 73 D4
Lambourne Gr
Bracknell RG12 27 E7
Kingston u T KT1 38 B7
Lambourne Way GU10 126 F7
Lambrook Haileybury Sch RG42 8 A3
Lamb's Bsns Pk RH9 142 C5
Lambs Cres RH12 217 F5
Lambs Farm Cl RH12 218 A5
Lambs Farm Rd RH12 218 A6
LAMBS GREEN 199 F6
Lambs Green Rd RH12 199 F6
Lambton Rd SW20 39 C8
Lambyn Croft RH6 161 C4
Lamerock Rd BR1 24 F4
Lamerton Lo [10] TW9 6 F6
Lammas Ave CR4 41 A7
Lammas Cl
Godalming GU7 151 A6
Staines TW18 12 E5
Lammas Ct
Farncombe GU7 150 E5
Stanwell TW19 12 D5
Lammas Dr TW18 12 D4
Lammas Gate GU7 150 F6
Lammas Gn SE26 23 B5
Lammas Hill KT10 55 A5
Lammas La KT10 55 A6
Lammas Rd
Godalming GU7 151 A5
Richmond TW10 17 C4
Lammermoor Rd SW12 21 B8
Lampard La GU10 167 E2
Lampeter Cl GU22 69 E1
Lampeter Ho [4] GU22 69 E1
Lampson Ct RH10 183 B3
LAMPTON 5 B6
Lampton Ave TW5 5 B6
Lampton Ct TW5 5 B6
Lampton House Cl SW19 19 D4
Lampton Park Rd TW3 5 B5
Lampton Rd TW3, TW5 5 B5
Lampton Sch TW3 5 A6
Lanain Ct SE12 24 F8
Lanark Cl
Frimley GU16 65 E2
Horsham RH13 217 E2
Lancaster Ave
Farnham GU9 146 D8
Guildford GU1 130 F7
Mitcham CR4 41 E4
West Norwood SE21, SE27 22 C6
Wimbledon SW19 19 D3
Lancaster Cl
Ashford TW15 13 E4
Ash Vale GU12 105 F5
Beckenham BR2 44 F5
Crawley RH10 182 D1
Englefield Green TW20 11 D3
Kingston u T KT2 17 D3
New Malden KT4 39 B2
Stanwell TW19 2 E1
Woking GU21 70 A3
Lancaster Cotts [1] TW10 6 E1
Lancaster Ct
Banstead SM7 77 F5
[1] Belmont SM2 59 A3
Crawley RH10 201 F5
Epsom KT19 57 D1
Stanwell TW19 13 E7
Walton-on-T KT12 35 B2
West Norwood SE27 22 B6
Lancaster Dr
Camberley GU15 65 D6
East Grinstead RH19 186 A3
Lancaster Gdns
Blindley Heath RH7 163 E8
Kingston u T KT2 17 D3
Wimbledon SW19 19 E3
Lancaster Ho
Bracknell RG12 27 B4
Redhill RH1 139 E6
Wandsworth SW18 20 B8
Lancaster Mews [2] TW10 6 E1
Lancaster Pk TW10 6 E2
Lancaster Pl
Hounslow TW5 4 D5
Twickenham TW1 17 A8
Wimbledon SW19 19 D3
Lancaster Rd
Farnborough GU14 85 B1
South Norwood SE25 43 A6
Wimbledon SW19 19 E3
Lancaster Way GU14 85 C7
Lancastrian Rd SM6 60 F3
Lancelot Cl RH11 200 E6
Lancelot Ho
Carshalton SM5 40 E1
[18] Redhill RH1 119 A2
Lancer Ct GU11 104 E2
Lanchester Dr RG45 45 C7
Lancing Cl RH11 201 A8
Lancing Ct RH12 218 A4
Lancing Ho [7] CR0 61 D6
Lancing Rd
Feltham TW13 14 F6
Thornton Heath CR0 41 F2
Landau Ct [11] CR2 61 C5
Landen Ct RG40 25 B4
Landen Pk RH6 160 E5
Landgrove Rd SW19 20 A3
Landon Way TW15 14 B2
Landscape Rd CR6 101 B8
Landsdowne Cl KT5 57 B8
Landseer Cl
[8] Mitcham SW19 40 D8
Sandhurst GU47 64 E6
Landseer Rd
Cheam SM1 59 A4
Landseer Rd *continued*
New Malden KT3 38 D2
Lane Cl KT15 52 B5
Lane Ct SW11 20 F8
LANE END 167 D8
Lane End
Dormansland RH7 165 B1
Epsom KT18 76 B5
Hambledon GU8 191 B8
Lane End Dr GU21 68 C2
Lane Gdns KT10 55 F3
Lane Ho [1] RH13 217 D2
Lanehurst Gdns RH10 202 C8
Lanercost Cl SW2 22 A6
Lanercost Rd
Crawley RH11 201 C5
Streatham SW2 22 A6
Lanesborough Sch GU1 109 F1
Laneside Cotts KT22 74 B5
Lane The
Chertsey KT16 33 A6
Ifold RH14 212 C4
Thursley GU8 169 C4
Virginia Water GU25 31 E6
Langaller La KT22 94 B6
Langborough Rd RG40 25 C5
Langbourne Prim Sch SE21 22 E5
Langbourne Way KT10 56 A4
Lang Cl KT23 94 B4
Langcroft Cl SM5 59 F7
Lang Ct KT6 37 E2
Langdale Ave CR4 40 F6
Langdale Cl
Farnborough GU14 84 E4
Mortlake SW14 7 B3
Woking GU21 69 C3
Langdale Dr SL5 28 E7
Langdale Par [9] CR4 40 F6
Langdale Rd
Crawley RH11 200 D4
Thornton Heath CR7 42 A5
Langdon Cl GU15 66 C4
Langdon Pk TW11 17 C1
Langdon Pl SW14 7 C4
Langdon Rd SM4 40 C4
Langdon Wlk SM4 40 C4
Langham Cl GU7 150 F4
Langham Ct
Farnham GU9 146 C7
Merton SW20 39 C7
[12] Twickenham TW1 6 C1
Langham Dene CR8 80 B4
Langham Gdns TW10 17 C4
Langham Ho KT4 38 F2
Langham House Cl TW10 17 D4
Langham Park Pl BR2 44 F5
Langham Pk GU7 150 F4
Langham Pl
Chiswick W4 7 E8
Egham TW20 11 F3
Langham Rd
Teddington TW11 17 B2
Wimbledon SW20 39 C8
Lang Ho TW19 13 E7
Langholm Cl SW12 21 D8
Langhorn Dr TW2 16 E8
LANGHURST 144 E7
Langhurst Cl RH12 198 E4
Langhurst La RH12 200 A8
Langhurstwood Rd RH12 198 D3
Langland Gdns CR0 62 F8
Langland Ho SW19 20 D3
Langlands Rise KT19 76 C6
Langley Ave
North Cheam KT4, SM3 58 D8
Surbiton KT6 37 E1
Langley Cl
Guildford GU1 109 D2
Langley Vale KT18 96 D8
Langley Cres UB3 3 F7
Langley Ct
Crawley RH10 202 A8
Reigate RH2 118 B2
[21] Sutton SM2 59 C4
Langley Dr
Aldershot GU11 126 A8
Camberley GU15 65 D6
Crawley RH11 201 D8
Langley Gr KT3 38 E7
LANGLEY GREEN 181 C2
Langley Green Prim Sch RH11 201 C8
Langley Ho GU21 89 A8
Langley La RH11 201 A8
Langley Lawns SM2 59 D3
Langley Manor BR3 44 C4
Langley Oaks Ave CR2 62 A1
Langley Par RH11 181 C1
Langley Park Rd SM1, SM2 59 C3
Langley Park Sch for Boys BR3 44 B3
Langley Park Sch for Girls BR3 44 C3
Langley Pl RH11 181 C1
Langley Rd
Beckenham BR3 43 E5
Isleworth TW7 5 F5
Merton SW19 40 A8
Selsdon CR2 62 D2
Staines TW18 12 F2
Surbiton KT6 37 E2
LANGLEY VALE 96 D8
Langley Vale Rd KT18, KT21 76 E1
Langley Way BR4 44 E2
Langley Wlk
Crawley RH11 181 B1
Woking GU22 89 E8
Langmans Way GU21 68 E3
Langmead St SE27 22 C4
Langport Ct KT12 35 C1
Langridge Dr RH19 205 E8
Langridge Ho [2] RH12 217 B2
Langridge Mews TW12 15 F2
Langroyd Rd SW17 20 F6
Langshott RH6 161 C5
Langshott Cl KT15 70 F8
Langshott Inf Sch The RH6 161 C3
Langshott La RH6 161 C4
Langsmead RH7 163 E8
Langstone Cl RH10 202 C3
Langthorne Ct SE6 24 C4
Langton Ave KT17 76 F8
Langton Cl
Addlestone KT15 52 B7
Woking GU21 68 F2
Langton Dr GU35 187 A7
Langton Ho [5] SW16 21 C4
Langton Pl SW18 20 A7
Langton Rd KT8 36 C5
Langton Rise SE22, SE23 23 B8
Langton Way
Egham TW20 12 C2
South Croydon CR0 61 E6
Langwood Chase TW11 17 C2
Langwood Cl KT21 76 A2
Lanherne Ho [11] SW20 19 D1
Lanigan Dr TW3 5 B2
Lankester Sq RH8 122 D7
Lankton Cl BR3 44 C8
Lannock Ct [2] SW17 20 E2
Lansbury Ave TW14 4 B1
Lansbury Est GU21 68 D1
Lansbury Rd RH11 201 B1
Lansdell Rd CR4 41 A7
Lansdown GU1 110 A1
Lansdown Cl
Horsham RH12 218 B6
Knaphill GU21 88 F8
Walton-on-T KT12 35 C1
Lansdowne Cl
Twickenham TW1 16 F7
Wimbledon SW20 19 D1
Lansdowne Copse [1] KT4 58 A8
Lansdowne Ct
Purley CR8 61 B1
[2] Worcester Park KT4 58 A8
Lansdowne Hill SE27 22 B5
Lansdowne Ho [19] SM2 59 B3
Lansdowne Pl SE19 22 F1
Lansdowne Rd
Aldershot GU11 105 A1
Croydon CR0 42 D1
Frimley GU16 86 A8
Hounslow TW3 5 B4
Purley CR8 80 A7
Staines TW18 13 B1
West Ewell KT19 57 D3
Wimbledon SW19, SW20 19 C1
Lansdowne Wood Cl [11] SE27 22 B5
Lantern Ct [4] SW20 39 D8
Lanyon Cl RH12 218 A6
Lanyon Mews RH12 218 A6
Lapse Wood Wlk SE22 23 B7
Lapwing Cl
Horsham RH13 217 F3
Selsdon CR0, CR2 62 E1
Lapwing Ct KT6 57 A7
Lapwing Gr GU4 110 D3
Lara Cl KT9 56 E3
Lara Lo SM1 59 A5
Larbert Rd SW16 21 C1
Larby Pl KT17 57 E1
Larch Ave
Ascot SL5 29 E4
Guildford GU1 109 C4
Wokingham RG41 25 A7
Larch Cl
Camberley GU15 65 E8
Kingswood KT20 98 C6
Reigate RH1 139 C7
Upper Tooting SW12 21 B6
Warlingham CR6 101 E8
Larch Cres KT19 57 B4
Larch End RH12 217 B4
Larches Ave SW14 7 D3
Larches Ho RH19 186 B4
Larches The
East Grinstead RH19 186 B4
Horsham RH12 218 C6
Newell Green RG42 8 A1
Woking GU21 69 E3
Larches Way
Blackwater GU17 64 B5
Crawley Down RH10 204 C8
Larch Rd GU35 187 B6
Larch Tree Way CR0 63 A7
Larchvale Ct SM2 59 B3
Larch Way GU14 84 C3
Larchwood [5] RG12 27 F5
Larchwood Cl SM7 77 E4
Larchwood Dr TW20 11 B2
Larchwood Glade GU15 66 A7
Larchwood Rd GU21 88 D8
Larcombe Cl CR0 61 F6
La Retraite RC Girls Sch SW12 21 C8
Larges Bridge Dr RG12 27 D6
Larges La RG12 27 C7
Largewood Ave KT6 57 A8
Lark Ave TW18 12 F5
Larkbere Rd SE26 23 E4
Larkfield
Cobham KT11 73 A6
Ewhurst GU6 175 E4
Larkfield Cl
Coney Hall BR2 63 F8
Farnham GU9 124 F2
Larkfield Ct RH6 162 A3
Larkfield Rd
Farnham GU9 124 F2
Richmond TW9 6 E3
Larkhall Cl KT12 54 C4
Larkham Cl TW13 14 E5
Larkin Cl CR5 79 F2
Larkins Rd RH6 181 D7
Lark Rise
Crawley RH11 201 C8
East Horsley KT24 112 E4
Turners Hill RH10 204 C5
Larksfield
Englefield Green TW20 11 C1
Horley RH6 161 B4
Larkspur Cl GU11 126 A7
Larkspur Ct SM6 60 B3
Larkspur Way
Dorking RH5 136 D4
West Ewell KT19 57 C5
Larks Way GU21 68 C3
Larkswood Cl GU47 45 A1
Larkswood Dr RG45 45 B5
Lark Way SM5 40 E2
Lascombe La GU3 128 B4
Lashmere
Copthorne RH10 183 D3
Cranleigh GU6 174 B3
Laski Ct RH11 201 B1
Lasswade Ct KT16 32 F2
Lasswade Rd KT16 32 F2
Lastingham Ct TW18 13 A2
Latchmere Cl KT2, TW10 17 E3
Latchmere Jun & Inf Schs KT2 17 F2
Latchmere La KT2, TW10 17 F3
Latchmere Rd KT2 17 F2
Latchwood La GU10 146 D5
Lateward Rd TW8 6 D8
Latham Ave GU16 65 E2
Latham Cl
Biggin Hill TN16 83 C3
[6] Twickenham TW1 17 A8
Latham Ct GU21 68 C2
Latham Rd TW1 16 F8
Latham's Way CR0 60 F8
Lathkill Ct [5] BR3 43 F8
Lathwood Ho [6] SE26 23 B3
Latimer RG12 27 B1
Latimer Cl
Crawley RH11 181 D1
North Cheam KT4 58 B6
Woking GU22 70 B3
Latimer Ct
[4] Bromley BR2 44 F5
Redhill RH1 139 F7
Latimer Ho GU7 150 E3
Latimer Rd
Croydon CR0, CR9 61 B7
Godalming GU7 150 E4
Teddington TW11 16 F3
Wimbledon SW19 20 B2
Wokingham RG41 25 B5
Latitude KT16 33 C1
Lattimer Pl W4 7 E7
Latton Cl
Esher KT10 55 B6
Walton-on-T KT12 35 E2
Latymer Cl KT13 53 C6
Laubin Cl TW1 6 B3
Laud Dr RH10 202 D5
Lauder Cl GU16 65 E2
Lauderdale GU14 84 D3
Lauderdale Dr TW10 17 D5
Lauderdale Ho [4] TW18 12 F3
Laud St CR0, CR9 61 C7
Laud Way RG40 25 E6
Laughton Rd RH12 217 F5
Launceston Ct CR7 42 A3
Laundry La GU47 64 E5
Laundry Mews SE23 23 E8
Laundry Rd GU1 130 C8
Laundry Way RH5 178 C5
Lauradale RG12 27 A5
Laurel Ave
Englefield Green TW20 11 B3
Twickenham TW1 16 F7
Laurel Cl
Camberley GU15 65 D4
Crawley RH10 202 A3
Farnborough GU14 84 C3
Poyle SL3 1 E7
Upper Tooting SW17 20 E3
Laurel Cres
Croydon CR0 63 A7
Sheerwater GU21 70 D6
Laurel Ct
[2] Croydon CR2 61 E6
South Norwood SE25 42 E4
Laureldene GU3 107 B1

Laurel Dene RH19 . . . . . . 185 F1
Laurel Dr RH8 . . . . 122 F4
Laurel Gdns
  Aldershot GU11 . . . . . . 126 A7
  Hounslow TW4 . . . . 4 E3
  Woodham KT15 . . . . 52 B1
Laurel Gr
  Forest Hill SE26 . . . . . . 23 E4
  Penge SE20 . . . . 23 C1
  Rowledge GU10 . . . . . . 145 F5
Laurel Grange KT14 . . . 71 E7
Laurel Ho SM4 . . . . 40 B4
Laurel Manor SM2 . . . . . 59 C3
Laurel Rd
  Teddington TW12 . . . . . 16 D3
  Wimbledon SW20 . . . . . 39 B8
Laurels The
  Banstead SM7 . . . . 77 F2
  Beckenham BR3 . . . . . . 44 C7
  Camberley GU15 . . . . . . 66 A7
  Crawley RH10 . . . . 182 A1
  Effingham KT24 . . . . . . 113 D8
  Heath End GU9 . . . . . . 125 F7
  [6] Oatlands Park KT13 . . 53 D7
  Penge BR3 . . . . 23 F1
  Stoke D'Abernon KT11 . . 73 E4
Laurel Wlk RH13 . . . . . 217 F1
Laurier Rd CR0 . . . . 42 F2
Lauriston Cl GU21 . . . . . 68 D2
Lauriston Rd SW19 . . . . 19 D2
Lauser Rd TW19 . . . . . . 13 C8
Laustan Cl GU1 . . . . . . 110 C2
Lavant Cl RH11 . . . . . . 200 F5
Lavender Ave
  Mitcham CR4 . . . . 40 F8
  North Cheam KT4, SM3 . . 58 C7
Lavender Cl
  Caterham CR3 . . . . 100 C2
  Coulsdon CR5 . . . . 99 C8
  Leatherhead KT22 . . . . . 95 C5
  Redhill RH1 . . . . 140 B4
  Wallington SM5 . . . . . . 60 B6
Lavender Cotts KT22 . . . 95 C5
Lavender Ct
  East Molesey KT8 . . . . . 36 B6
  Feltham TW14 . . . . 4 B1
  Leatherhead KT22 . . . . . 95 C5
  Sutton SM2 . . . . 59 C3
Lavender Gate KT22 . . . 74 B5
Lavender Gr CR4 . . . . . . 40 E8
Lavender Ho [8] TW9 . . . . 7 B6
Lavender La GU10 . . . . 145 F4
Lavender Lo [1] KT17 . . . 57 F2
Lavender Park Rd [5]
  KT14 . . . . 71 A6
Lavender Pk SL5 . . . . . . 28 C6
Lavender Rd
  Carshalton SM1 . . . . . . 59 D6
  Thornton Heath CR0 . . . 41 F3
  Wallington SM5 . . . . . . 60 A6
  West Ewell KT19 . . . . . . 57 B4
  Woking GU22 . . . . 70 B3
Lavender Vale SM6 . . . . 60 D4
Lavender Way CR0 . . . . . 43 D3
Lavengro Rd SE27 . . . . . 22 C6
Laverock Sch RH8 . . . . 122 E7
Laverstoke Gdns SW15 . 19 A8
Lavington Cl RH11 . . . . 201 A8
Lavington Rd CR0 . . . . . 60 F6
Lavinia Ct BR1 . . . . 24 E1
Lawbrook La GU5 . . . . . 154 C7
Lawday Link GU9 . . . . . 125 A7
Lawday Pl GU9 . . . . 125 A7
Lawday Place La GU9 . . 125 A7
Lawdons Gdns CR0 . . . . 61 B6
Lawford Gdns CR8 . . . . 80 C3
Lawford Rd W4 . . . . 7 C7
Lawford's Hill Cl GU3 . . 88 C3
Lawford's Hill Rd GU3 . . 88 C3
Lawley Ho [23] TW1 . . . . . 6 D1
Lawman Ct [2] TW9 . . . . . 6 F6
Lawn Cl KT3 . . . . 38 E7
Lawn Cres TW9 . . . . 7 A5
Lawn Ho BR3 . . . . 23 F1
Lawn Rd
  Beckenham BR3 . . . . . . 23 F1
  Guildford GU2 . . . . 130 C6
Lawns Cotts RH12 . . . . 195 A3
Lawnsmead GU5 . . . . . . 152 B7
Lawns Rd RH12 . . . . . . 195 A3
Lawns The
  Belmont SM2 . . . . 58 E3
  Farnborough GU14 . . . . 84 E3
  Milford GU8 . . . . 149 F1
  North Ascot SL5 . . . . . . 28 D6
  Purley CR8 . . . . 61 B1
  South Norwood SE19 . . . 42 D8
  [1] Wimbledon SW19 . . . 19 F3
Lawnwood Ct GU7 . . . . 151 A5
Lawrence Ave KT3 . . . . . 38 E7
Lawrence Cl
  Crawley RH10 . . . . 202 D4
  Guildford GU2 . . . . 110 B6
  Wokingham RG40 . . . . . 25 D6
Lawrence Ctr RG41 . . . . 25 A4
Lawrence Ct TW4 . . . . . . 4 C3
Lawrence Gr RG42 . . . . . 26 D8
Lawrence La RH3 . . . . . 117 B3
Lawrence Lo GU15 . . . . 65 D7
Lawrence Rd
  Hampton TW12 . . . . . . 15 F1
  Hounslow TW4 . . . . 4 C3
  Richmond TW10 . . . . . . 17 C4
  South Norwood SE25 . . . 42 F5
Lawrence Way GU15 . . . 64 F4
Lawrence Weaver Cl
  SM4 . . . . 40 A3

Lawrie Park Ave SE26 . . 23 B3
Lawrie Park Cres SE26 . . 23 B3
Lawrie Park Gdns
  SE26 . . . . 23 B3
Lawrie Park Rd SE19,
  SE26 . . . . 23 C3
Laws Cl
  Crawley RH11 . . . . 200 E5
  South Norwood SE25 . . . 42 D5
Lawson Cl SW19 . . . . . . 19 D5
Lawson Ct [13] KT6 . . . . . 37 D2
Lawson-Hunt Ind Pk
  RH12 . . . . 216 D4
Lawson Way SL5 . . . . . . 30 B3
Lawson Wlk SM5 . . . . . . 60 A2
Laws Terr GU11 . . . . . . 105 C3
Laxton Ct CR7 . . . . 42 C5
Laxton Gdns RH1 . . . . . 119 D7
Layard Ct CR7 . . . . 42 D7
Layburn Cres SL3 . . . . . . .1 B8
Layhams Rd
  Coney Hall BR2, BR4 . . . 63 E5
  West Wickham BR2 . . . . 63 F1
Layton Cres CR0 . . . . . . 61 B5
Layton Ct KT13 . . . . 53 B6
Layton [1] TW9 . . . . 7 A6
Layton Rd TW3 . . . . .5 B3
Layton's La TW16 . . . . . . 34 F7
Lazare Ct [2] TW18 . . . . 12 F3
Lazell Gdns RH3 . . . . . 137 C3
Leach Gr KT22 . . . . 95 C5
Lea Cl
  Ash GU12 . . . . 106 A1
  Badshot Lea GU9 . . . . . 126 A6
  Crawley RH11 . . . . 200 F5
  Twickenham TW2 . . . . . 15 F8
Lea Cotts CR4 . . . . 41 A7
Leacroft
  East Grinstead RH19 . . . 185 D2
  Staines TW18 . . . . 13 B4
  Sunningdale SL5 . . . . . . 30 A4
Lea Croft RG45 . . . . 45 B6
Leacroft Ave SW12 . . . . 20 F8
Leacroft Cl
  Kenley CR8 . . . . 80 C3
  Staines TW18 . . . . 13 B4
Leaf Cl KT7, KT8 . . . . . . 36 E4
Leaf Gr SE27 . . . . 22 A3
Leafield Cl
  South Norwood SW16 . . . 22 B2
  Woking GU21 . . . . 69 B1
Leafield Copse RG12 . . . 27 F5
Leafield Rd
  Merton SW19, SW20 . . . 39 F6
  Sutton SM1 . . . . 59 A8
Leafy Way CR0 . . . . 61 B8
Leamington Ave SM4 . . . 39 F5
Leamington Cl TW3 . . . . . 5 C2
Leamington Ct [4]
  SE26 . . . . 23 A5
Leander Ct [5] KT6 . . . . . 37 D2
Leander Rd
  [4] Streatham SW2 . . . . 21 F8
  Thornton Heath CR7 . . . 41 F5
Leapale La GU1 . . . . . . 130 D8
Leapale Rd GU1 . . . . . . 130 D8
Lea Rd
  Beckenham BR3 . . . . . . 44 A7
  Camberley GU15 . . . . . . 65 B2
Leas Cl KT9 . . . . 56 F3
Leaside KT23 . . . . 94 A4
Leas La CR6 . . . . 81 D1
Leas Rd
  Guildford GU1 . . . . 130 C8
  Warlingham CR6 . . . . . . 81 D1
Lea The TW20 . . . . 12 C1
Leather Cl CR4 . . . . 41 A7
LEATHERHEAD 95 C5
Leatherhead Bsns Pk
  KT22 . . . . 94 F8
Leatherhead By-Pass Rd
  KT22 . . . . 95 D5
Leatherhead General
  Hospl KT22 . . . . 95 C5
Leatherhead Ind Est
  KT22 . . . . 95 A6
Leatherhead Mus of Local
  History ★ KT22 . . . . 95 B5
Leatherhead Rd
  Ashtead KT21, KT22 . . . 95 E7
  Chessington KT9 . . . . . . 75 C6
  Great Bookham KT23 . . . 94 C2
  Oxshott KT22 . . . . 74 D4
Leatherhead Sta KT22 . . 95 A6
Leatherhead Trinity Sch
  Leatherhead KT22 . . . . . 95 A8
  Leatherhead KT22 . . . . . 95 B7
  Leatherhead KT22 . . . . . 95 C5
Leather La GU5 . . . . . . 133 C4
Leaveland Cl BR3 . . . . . 44 A5
Leavesden Rd KT13 . . . . 53 B5
Leaves Gn RG12 . . . . . . 27 D3
LEAVES GREEN 83 D8
Leaves Green Cres
  BR2 . . . . 83 C8
Leaves Green Rd BR2 . . 83 D8
Lea Way GU12 . . . . 105 F3
Leazes Ave CR3 . . . . . . 100 A4
Lebanon Ave TW13 . . . . 15 D3
Lebanon Ct [11] TW1 . . . 17 B8
Lebanon Dr KT11 . . . . . . 74 A6
Lebanon Gdns TN16 . . . 83 C7
Lebanon Park Mans [12]
  TW1 . . . . 17 B8
Lebanon Pk TW1 . . . . . . 17 B8
Lebanon Rd CR0 . . . . . . 42 E1
Le Chateau CR0 . . . . . . 61 D7

Lechford Rd RH6 . . . . . 161 A1
Leckford Rd SW18 . . . . . 20 C7
Leckhampton Pl SW2 . . . 22 A8
Leconfield Ave SW13,
  SW15 . . . . .7 F4
Ledbury Pl CR0 . . . . 61 C6
Ledbury Rd
  Croydon CR0, CR9 . . . . . 61 D6
  Reigate RH2 . . . . 118 A2
Ledger Cl GU1 . . . . 110 B3
Ledger Dr KT15 . . . . 51 F4
Ledgers Rd CR6 . . . . 82 B2
Ledrington Rd SE19 . . . . 23 A2
Leechcroft Rd SM6 . . . . . 60 A7
Leechpool La RH12,
  RH13 . . . . 218 A4
Leechpool & Owlbeech
  Woods Nature Reserve ★
  RH13 . . . . 218 C4
Leechpool Prim Sch
  RH13 . . . . 218 A4
Lee Ct GU11 . . . . 126 C8
Leeds Ct
  Carshalton SM5 . . . . . . 59 F7
  Catford SE6 . . . . 24 B5
Leegate Cl GU21 . . . . . . 69 B3
Lee Ho SW16 . . . . 20 B2
Lee Hollow GU5 . . . . . . 133 C1
Leehurst GU8 . . . . 148 E1
Lee Mews BR3 . . . . 43 E6
Lee Rd
  Aldershot GU11 . . . . . . 104 E2
  Merton SW19 . . . . 40 B8
Lee's Ct GU20 . . . . 48 D4
Lees Farm Barn GU22 . . 71 B4
Leeside RH12 . . . . 199 C6
Leeson Ho [8] TW1 . . . . 17 B8
Lee St RH6 . . . . 160 E4
Lees The GU6 . . . . 62 F8
Leeward Gdns SW19 . . . 19 F2
Leewood Way KT24 . . . 113 D8
Legge Cres GU11 . . . . . 104 E1
Leggyfield Ct RH12 . . . 217 B5
Legion Ct SM4 . . . . 40 A3
Legion Ho BR1 . . . . 24 D3
Legrace Ave TW4, TW5 . . .4 D5
Legsheath La RH19 . . . . 205 D1
Leicester RG12 . . . . 27 E2
Leicester Ave CR4 . . . . . 41 E5
Leicester Cl KT4 . . . . 58 C6
Leicester Ct
  [6] Bromley BR1 . . . . . . 24 F1
  Crawley RH10 . . . . 202 D6
  [10] Twickenham TW1 . . . 6 D1
Leicester Ho
  [7] Carshalton SM1 . . . . 59 E7
  [2] Thames Ditton KT7 . . 37 A2
Leicester Rd CR0 . . . . . . 42 E2
LEIGH 138 B2
Leigham Ave SW16 . . . . 21 E5
Leigham Ct [9] SM6 . . . . 60 C4
  Dorking RH4 . . . . 115 D1
Leigham Ct Rd [7] TW7 . . .5 E7
Leigham Hall [3] SW16 . . 21 E5
Leigham Hall Par [2]
  SW16 . . . . 21 E5
Leigham Vale SW2,
  SW16 . . . . 22 A6
Leigh Cl
  Addlestone KT15 . . . . . . 51 F3
  New Malden KT3 . . . . . . 38 D5
Leigh Close Ind Est
  KT3 . . . . 38 D5
Leigh Court Cl KT11 . . . 73 D5
Leigh Cres CR0 . . . . 63 C3
Leigh Ct CR0 . . . . 82 E8
Leigh Hill Rd KT11 . . . . 73 D5
Leigh Ho [4] KT2 . . . . . . 18 B2
Leigh Jenkins Way
  RH6 . . . . 182 B7
Leigh La GU9 . . . . 146 E8
Leighlands RH10 . . . . . 202 C8
Leigh Orchard Cl
  SW16 . . . . 21 F5
Leigh Pl
  Cobham KT11 . . . . 73 C5
  Feltham TW13 . . . . 15 C7
Leigh Place La RH9 . . . 121 E3
Leigh Rd
  Betchworth RH3 . . . . . . 137 C2
  Cobham KT11 . . . . 73 B5
  Isleworth TW3 . . . . .5 D3
Leigh The KT2 . . . . 18 E1
Leighton Gdns
  Sanderstead CR2 . . . . . . 81 B6
  Thornton Heath CR0 . . . 42 B1
Leighton Ho [7] KT6 . . . 37 E3
Leighton St CR0 . . . . 42 B1
Leighton Way KT18 . . . . 76 D5
Leinster Ave SW14 . . . . . .7 C3
Leisure La KT14 . . . . 71 B7
Leith Cl RG45 . . . . 45 A7
Leithcote Gdns SW16 . . . 21 F4
Leithcote Path SW16 . . . 21 F5
Leith Dr GU11 . . . . 104 F3
Leith Gr RH5 . . . . 157 D4
Leith Hill Rd
  Abinger Common RH5 . . . 155 F5
  Wotton RH5 . . . . 156 A3
Leith Hill Twr ★ RH5 . . . 156 B3
Leith Ho
  Leatherhead KT22 . . . . . 95 A6
  Reigate RH2 . . . . 139 A4
  [18] Streatham SW2 . . . . 21 F8
Leith Lea RH5 . . . . 157 D4

Leith Rd
  Beare Green RH5 . . . . . 157 D4
  Ewell KT17 . . . . 76 F7
Leith Twrs SM2 . . . . 59 B3
Leith Vale Cotts RH5 . . . 177 A2
Leith View RH5 . . . . 136 C3
Leith View Cotts
  RH12 . . . . 198 B6
Leith View Rd RH12 . . . 218 A5
Lela Ave TW4, TW5 . . . . . .4 C5
Le Marchant Rd GU15,
  GU16 . . . . 65 F3
Le May Cl RH6 . . . . 161 A4
Lemington Gr RG12 . . . . 27 B3
Lemmington Way
  RH12 . . . . 218 A7
Lemon Gr TW13 . . . . 15 A7
Lemon's Farm Rd
  RH5 . . . . 155 F6
Lendore Rd GU16 . . . . . . 85 D8
Lenelby Rd KT6 . . . . 38 A1
Leney Cl RG40 . . . . 25 D8
Lenham Rd
  South Norwood CR7 . . . . 42 D7
  Sutton SM1 . . . . 59 C5
Lennard Ave BR4 . . . . . . 63 E8
Lennard Cl BR4 . . . . 63 E8
Lennard Rd
  Penge BR3, SE20, SE26 . . 23 E2
  Thornton Heath CR0 . . . 42 C1
Lennox Ct [13] RH1 . . . . 119 A2
Lennox Gdns CR0 . . . . . 61 B6
Lennox Ho [9] SW1 . . . . . 6 D1
Lenten Cl GU5 . . . . 133 D1
Lentmead Rd BR1 . . . . . 24 F5
Lenton Rise TW9 . . . . . . .6 E4
Leo Ct [4] TW8 . . . . .6 D7
Leof Cres SE6 . . . . 24 B3
Leominster Rd SM4 . . . . 40 C3
Leominster Wlk SM4 . . . 40 C3
Leonard Ave SM4 . . . . . 40 C4
Leonard Cl GU16 . . . . . . 85 D8
Leonard Rd CR4, SW16 . . 41 C8
Leonardslee Ct RH10 . . . 202 B3
Leonard Way RH13 . . . . 217 F2
Leopardstown Ho
  RH7 . . . . 142 E1
Leopold Ave
  Farnborough GU14 . . . . 85 B5
  Wimbledon SW19 . . . . . 19 F3
Leopold Ct [13] SW19 . . 19 F3
Leopold Rd
  Crawley RH11 . . . . 201 C6
  Wimbledon SW19 . . . . . 19 F4
Leopold Terr SW19 . . . . 20 A3
Le Personne Homes [1]
  CR3 . . . . 100 D5
Leppington RG12 . . . . . . 27 B2
Leret Way KT22 . . . . 95 B6
Lesbourne Rd RH2 . . . . 139 B8
Lescombe Cl SE23 . . . . . 23 E5
Lescombe Rd SE23, SE6 . . 23 E5
Lesley Ct [8] SM6 . . . . . 60 B6
Leslie Gdns SM2 . . . . . . 59 A3
Leslie Gr CR0 . . . . 42 E1
Leslie Grove Pl CR0 . . . . 42 E1
Leslie Park Rd CR0 . . . . . 42 E1
Leslie Rd
  Chobham GU24 . . . . 49 E1
  Dorking RH4 . . . . 115 D1
Lessingham Ave SW17 . . 21 A4
Lessing St SE23 . . . . 23 E8
Lessness Rd SM4 . . . . . . 40 C4
Lestock Cl SE25 . . . . 43 A6
Lestor Ct TW7 . . . . .5 F4
Letchworth Ave TW14 . . 14 F8
Letchworth Ct RH11 . . . 200 E3
Letchworth St SW17 . . . 20 F4
Letcombe Sq RG12 . . . . 27 F5
Levana Cl SW19 . . . . 19 E7
Levehurst Ho SE27 . . . . . 22 C3
Levendale Rd SE23, SE6 . . 23 F6
Leveret Cl CR0 . . . . 82 D8
Leveret La RH11 . . . . . . 201 B8
Leverette Cl GU12 . . . . . 105 D3
Leverkusen Rd RG12 . . . 27 B6
Levern Dr GU9 . . . . 125 C6
Leverson St SW16 . . . . . 21 C2
Levett Ho [8] SW16 . . . . 21 C3
Levett Rd KT22 . . . . 95 B7
Levylsdene Ct GU1 . . . . 110 D1
Levylsdene GU1 . . . . . . 110 D1
Lewes Cl RH10 . . . . 202 C6
Lewes Ct [5] CR4 . . . . . . 40 F6
Lewesdon Cl [18] SW19 . . 19 D7
Lewes Ho RH12 . . . . . . 139 B5
Lewes Rd
  Ashurst Wood RH19 . . . . 206 C6
  Forest Row RH18 . . . . . 206 E2
Lewin Cl SW16 . . . . 21 C2
Lewin Rd
  Mortlake SW14 . . . . .7 D4
  Streatham SW16 . . . . . . 21 D2
Lewins Rd KT18 . . . . 76 B5
Lewin Terr TW14 . . . . . . 14 D8
Lewis Cl KT15 . . . . 52 C6
LEWISHAM 24 C8
Lewisham Cl RH11 . . . . 201 C2
Lewisham Way GU47 . . . 45 D2
Lewis Rd
  Mitcham CR4 . . . . 40 E7
  [20] Richmond TW10 . . . . 6 D2
  Sutton SM1 . . . . 59 B6
Lewiston Cl KT4 . . . . 39 B2
Lexden Rd CR4 . . . . 41 D5
Lexington Ct CR8 . . . . . . 80 C8
Lexington Pl KT1 . . . . . . 37 D8
Lexton Gdns SW12 . . . . 21 D7

Leyborne Pk TW9 . . . . . . .7 A6
Leybourne Ave KT14 . . . 71 F6
Leybourne Cl
  Byfleet KT14 . . . . 71 F6
  Crawley RH11 . . . . 201 C1
Leybourne Ct SE25 . . . . 43 A6
Leybourne Gdns CR0 . . . 61 E8
Leybourne Pl RH19 . . . . 184 F1
Leyburn Gdns CR0 . . . . . 61 E8
Leycester Cl GU20 . . . . . 48 B6
Leyfield KT4 . . . . 38 F1
Leyland Ho [12] TW10 . . . 17 C5
Leylands La TW19 . . . . . .2 A2
Ley Rd GU14 . . . . 85 A8
Leyside RG45 . . . . 45 A5
Leys Rd KT22 . . . . 74 D7
Leys The KT12 . . . . 54 E6
Leyton Rd SW19 . . . . . . 20 C1
Liberty Ave SW19 . . . . . 40 D8
Liberty Ct RH2 . . . . 139 B8
Liberty Hall Rd KT15 . . . 52 A5
Liberty Ho KT16 . . . . 32 F1
Liberty La KT15 . . . . 52 B5
Liberty Rise KT15 . . . . . . 52 A4
Liberty Sch CR4 . . . . 40 E7
Licensed Victuallers Sch
  SL5 . . . . 28 C7
Lichfield Ct
  Kingston u T KT6 . . . . . . 37 E4
  Richmond TW9 . . . . .6 E3
Lichfield Gdns TW10,
  TW9 . . . . .6 E2
Lichfield Rd
  Hounslow TW4 . . . . .4 C4
  Richmond TW9 . . . . .6 F6
Lichfields RG12 . . . . 27 E7
Lichfield Terr [1] TW9 . . . .6 E2
Lichfield Way CR2 . . . . . 62 D2
Lickfolds Rd GU10 . . . . 145 E3
Liddell Ct [2] CR8 . . . . . 80 A7
Liddell Way SL5 . . . . 29 A4
Liddesdale Ho E KT2 . . . 38 B8
Liddesdale Ho W KT2 . . . 38 B8
Liddington Hall Dr
  GU3 . . . . 108 E4
Liddington Hall Est
  GU3 . . . . 108 E4
Liddington New Rd
  GU3 . . . . 108 E4
Lidiard Rd SW18 . . . . . . 20 C6
Lido Rd GU1 . . . . 109 D2
Lidsey Cl RH10 . . . . 202 C4
Lidstone Cl GU21 . . . . . . 69 B2
LIGHTWATER 66 F8
Lightwater Ctry Pk ★
  GU18 . . . . 47 F1
Lightwater Mdw GU18 . . 67 B8
Lightwater Rd GU18 . . . . 67 C8
Lightwater Village Sch
  GU18 . . . . 48 A1
Lightwood RG12 . . . . . . 27 D3
Lilac Ave GU22 . . . . 89 D7
Lilac Cl GU1 . . . . 109 C5
Lilac Ct TW11 . . . . 16 F4
Lilac Gdns CR0 . . . . 63 A7
Lilah Mews BR2 . . . . 44 F7
Lilian Rd CR4, SW16 . . . 41 C8
Lilian Rolfe Ho [5]
  SE27 . . . . 22 D4
Lilleshall Rd SM4 . . . . . . 40 D3
Lilley Dr KT20 . . . . 98 B5
Lillie Rd TN16 . . . . 83 D1
Lilycourt RG41 . . . . 25 A6
Lilyfields Chase GU6 . . . 175 E4
Lily Hill Dr RG12 . . . . . . 27 E7
Lily Hill Rd RG12 . . . . . . 27 E7
Lime Ave
  Camberley GU15 . . . . . . 66 A6
  Cranbourne SL4 . . . . .9 F5
  Horsham RH12 . . . . 218 A4
Limebush Cl KT15 . . . . . 52 C2
Lime Cl
  Carshalton SM5 . . . . . . 59 F8
  Copthorne RH10 . . . . . . 183 B3
  Crawley RH11 . . . . 181 C1
  Reigate RH2 . . . . 139 B6
  West Clandon GU4 . . . . 111 B3
Lime Cres
  Ash GU12 . . . . 106 B2
  Sunbury TW16 . . . . 35 C7
Limecroft Cl KT19 . . . . . 57 D3
Limecroft Rd GU21 . . . . 68 B2
Lime Ct
  Chipstead CR5 . . . . 78 F1
  [3] Kingston u T KT3 . . . 38 E6
  Kingston u T, Norbiton
    KT1 . . . . 38 B6
  Mitcham CR4 . . . . 40 D7
Lime Gr
  Addlestone KT15 . . . . . . 52 A6
  Guildford GU1 . . . . 109 B5
  Kingston u T KT3 . . . . . . 38 E6
  Twickenham TW1 . . . . . . 6 A1
  Warlingham CR6 . . . . . . 81 E1
  West Clandon GU4 . . . . 111 B7
  Woking GU22 . . . . 89 E6
Lime Ho [7] TW9 . . . . .7 B6
Limekiln Pl SE19 . . . . . . 22 F1
Lime Lo [3] TW16 . . . . . . 14 F1
Lime Meadow Ave CR2 . . 81 B6
Lime Mews TW3 . . . . 11 F3
Limerick Cl
  Bracknell RG42 . . . . 27 A8
  Streatham SW12 . . . . . . 21 C8
Limerick Ct [1] SW12 . . . 21 C8
Limerick Ho GU22 . . . . . 70 A1

Lime St Rdbt GU11 104 F2
Limes Ave
Barnes SW13 7 F5
Carshalton SM5 40 F1
Croydon CR0, CR9 61 A7
Horley RH6 161 B1
Penge SE20 23 B1
Limes Cl TW15 14 A3
Limes Ct BR3 44 B7
Limes Field Rd SW14 7 E4
Limes Rd
Beckenham BR3 44 B7
Egham TW20 11 F3
Farnborough GU14 84 C5
Thornton Heath CR0 42 D2
Weybridge KT13 53 A6
Lime St GU11 104 F2
Limes The
2 Belmont SM2 59 A4
Dormans Park RH19 185 A5
East Molesey KT8 36 B5
Epsom KT19 57 B1
Haslemere GU27 208 A6
Leatherhead KT22 95 B4
9 Woking GU21 70 A3
Woking, Horsell GU21 69 D4
Lime Tree Ave KT10, KT7 36 E1
Limetree Cl SW2 21 F7
Lime Tree Cl KT23 94 A3
Lime Tree Copse RG42 8 A1
Lime Tree Ct
Ashtead KT21 75 E1
Old Windsor SL4 11 C8
South Croydon CR2 61 C4
Lime Tree Gr CR0 62 F7
Limetree Pl CR4 41 B8
Lime Tree Rd TW5 5 B6
Limetree Wlk
2 Upper Tooting SW17 21 A3
Virginia Water GU25 31 E5
Lime Tree Wlk
Coney Hall BR4 63 F6
Farnborough GU14 105 E8
Lime Villas KT3 38 E6
Limeway Terr RH4 115 A1
Lime Wlk RG12 27 C5
Limewood Cl
Beckenham BR3 44 C4
Knaphill GU21 88 D7
LIMPSFIELD 123 A6
Limpsfield Ave
Putney SW19 19 D6
Thornton Heath CR7 41 F4
Limpsfield CE Inf Sch RH8 123 C6
Limpsfield Grange Sch RH8 123 A8
Limpsfield Rd
Chelsham CR6 102 B8
Hamsey Green CR2, CR6 81 C3
Linacre Dr GU6, RH12 195 C4
Lince La RH4 135 D6
LINCHMERE 207 B2
Linchmere Pl RH11 201 A7
Linchmere Rd
Haslemere GU27 207 D5
Lewisham SE12 24 F8
Linchmere GU27 207 C4
Lincoln Ave
Twickenham TW2 16 C6
Wimbledon SW19 19 D5
Lincoln Cl
Ash Vale GU12 105 F5
Crawley RH10 201 E3
Croydon SE25 43 B3
Frimley GU15 66 B4
Horley RH6 161 A2
Lincoln Ct
5 Croydon CR2 61 C5
Hampton TW12 15 F3
Mitcham CR4 41 E4
Weybridge KT13 53 D4
Lincoln Dr GU22 70 E3
Lincoln Hall KT4 39 B2
Lincoln Lo 10 BR3 44 B7
Lincoln Rd
Croydon SE25 43 B6
Dorking RH4 115 C1
Farnborough GU14 105 B8
Feltham TW13 15 F5
Guildford GU2 108 F3
Kingston u T KT3 38 C6
Mitcham CR4 41 E4
North Cheam KT4 39 B1
Lincolns Mead RH7 164 C3
Lincoln Terr 6 SM2 59 A3
Lincoln Way TW16 34 E8
Lincoln Wlk KT19 57 D1
Lincombe Ct KT15 52 B5
Lincombe Rd BR1 24 F5
Linda Ct KT9 56 D6
Lindale SW19 19 E6
Lindale Cl GU25 30 F5
Lindbergh Rd SM6 60 E3
Linden 3 RG12 27 F4
Linden Ave
Coulsdon CR5 79 B3
East Grinstead RH19 185 C2
Hounslow TW3 5 B2
Thornton Heath CR7 42 B5
Linden Bridge Specl Sch KT4 57 E7
Linden Cl
Crawley RH10 202 A3
Horsham RH12 217 E4
Tadworth KT20 97 D7
Thames Ditton KT7 37 A2
Woodham KT15 71 A8
Linden Cotts 6 SW19 19 E2
Linden Cres KT1 37 F7
Linden Ct
Beckenham BR3 44 B6
2 Bromley BR1 24 F1
Camberley GU15 65 F7
Englefield Green TW20 11 B2
Leatherhead KT22 95 B6
Penge SE20 23 B1
Linden Dr CR3 100 C3
Linden Gate SW20 39 C6
Linden Gdns KT22 95 C6
Linden Gr
Kingston u T KT3 38 E6
Penge SE20 23 C2
Teddington TW11 16 F3
Walton-on-T KT12 53 F8
Warlingham CR6 81 E1
Lindenhill Rd RG42 26 F8
Linden Ho TW12 16 B2
Linden Lea RH4 136 C5
Linden Leas BR4 63 D8
Linden Lodge Sch SW19 19 E7
Linden Pit Path KT22 95 B6
Linden Pl
Ewell KT17 76 E7
Mitcham CR4 40 E5
Staines TW18 13 A4
Linden Rd
Guildford GU1 109 D1
Hampton TW12 36 A8
Headley Down GU35 187 C5
Leatherhead KT22 95 B6
Weybridge KT13 53 C2
Lindens Cl KT24 113 E7
Lindens The
Chiswick W4 7 D6
Copthorne RH10 183 B3
Farnham GU9 125 D1
New Addington CR0 63 C4
Linden Way
Send Marsh GU23 90 F3
Shepperton TW17 34 C4
Wallington CR8 60 C1
Woking GU22 89 F6
Lindfield Gdns GU1 109 F2
Lindfield Rd CR0 42 F3
Lindgren Wlk RH11 201 B1
Lindisfarne Rd SW20 19 A1
Lindley Ct KT1 37 C8
Lindley Ho KT14 71 B7
Lindley Pl TW9 7 A6
Lindley Rd
Tyler's Green RH9 121 C5
Walton-on-T KT12 54 D7
Lindon Bennett Sch TW13 15 D3
Lindon Ct SL5 28 E6
Lindores Rd SM5 40 C1
Lind Rd SM1 59 C5
Lindsay Cl
Chessington KT9 56 E3
Epsom KT18 76 C6
Stanwell TW19 2 D2
Lindsay Ct
6 Croydon CR0 61 D6
Sutton SM1 59 A5
Lindsay Dr TW17 34 D3
Lindsay Rd
Hampton TW12 16 B4
North Cheam KT4 58 B8
Woodham KT15 71 B8
Lindsey Cl CR4, SW16 41 E5
Lindsey Gdns TW14 14 D8
Lindum Cl GU11 105 A1
Lindum Dene GU11 105 A1
Lindum Rd TW11 17 C1
Lindums The BR3 23 F2
Lindvale GU21 69 E4
Lindway SE27 22 B3
Linersh Dr GU5 152 A6
Linersh Wood Cl GU5 152 B5
Linershwood Rd GU5 152 A6
Lines Rd GU11 105 D7
Linfield Cl KT12 54 B5
Linford Ct 6 CR4 40 E8
Ling Cres GU35 187 B6
Ling Dr GU18 66 F7
LINGFIELD 164 D5
Lingfield Ave KT1, KT5 37 F5
LINGFIELD COMMON 164 D6
Lingfield Common Rd RH7 164 C6
Lingfield Ct
Croydon CR0 61 F8
Wimbledon SW19 19 D2
Lingfield Dr RH10 202 E7
Lingfield Gdns CR5 100 B8
Lingfield Ho
Kingston u T KT1 37 E5
Penge SE26 23 B2
Tadworth KT20 97 B4
Lingfield Notre Dame Sch RH7 164 F3
Lingfield Park Race Course RH7 164 E2
Lingfield Pl 1 RH1 118 E2
Lingfield Prim Sch RH7 164 D4
Lingfield Rd
East Grinstead RH19 185 D3
Edenbridge TN8 165 F8
Haxted TN8 165 F8
North Cheam KT4 58 C7
Wimbledon SW19 19 D2
Lingfield Sta RH7 164 E4
Ling's Coppice SE21 22 D6
Lingwell Rd SW17 20 E5
Lingwood RG12 27 C3
Lingwood Gdns TW7 5 E7
Linkfield KT8 36 B6
Linkfield Cnr RH1 118 E2
Linkfield Gdns RH1 118 E1
Linkfield La RH1 118 F3
Linkfield Rd TW7 5 F5
Linkfield St RH1 118 E1
Link La SM6 60 E4
Linklater's Cotts GU14 84 B6
Link Prim Sch CR0 60 E6
Link Rd
Addlestone KT15 52 E6
Carshalton CR4, SM6 41 A1
East Bedfont TW14 14 F8
Farnborough GU14 84 D1
Links Ave SM4 40 A5
Links Brow KT22 94 E4
Links Bsns Ctr GU22 90 C8
Links Cl
Ashtead KT21 75 C2
Ewhurst GU6 175 E6
Linkscroft Ave TW15 14 B2
Link Sec Sch CR0 60 F6
Links Gdns SW16 22 A1
Links Green Way KT11 74 A5
LINKSIDE 188 B6
Linkside KT3 38 E7
Linkside E GU26 188 C7
Linkside N GU26 188 B7
Linkside S GU26 188 C6
Linkside W GU26 188 B6
Links Ind Est TW13 15 E5
Links Pl KT21 75 D2
Links Prim Sch SW17 21 A2
Links Rd
Ashford TW15 13 E3
Ashtead KT21 75 C2
Bramley GU5 151 E7
Mitcham SW16, SW17 21 A2
West Wickham BR4 44 C1
Link's Rd KT17 77 A5
Links The
North Ascot SL5 28 E7
Walton-on-T KT12 54 A8
Links View Ave RH3 116 A1
Links View Rd
Croydon CR0 63 A7
Hampton TW12 16 C4
Links Way
Beckenham BR3 44 A3
Effingham KT24 113 E7
Farnborough GU14 84 C3
Mitcham SW17 21 A2
Link The
Crawley RH11 201 D6
Teddington TW11 16 F2
Linkway
Camberley GU15 65 C4
Crawley RH6 182 C7
Crowthorne RG45 45 A5
Guildford GU2 108 F2
West Barnes SW20 39 B5
Woking GU22 70 C2
Link Way
Richmond TW10 17 B6
Staines TW18 13 B2
Linkway The SM2 59 C2
Linley Ct
1 Dulwich SE21 22 E4
Sutton SM1 59 C6
Linnell Rd RH1 140 B8
Linnet Cl
Selsdon CR2 62 D1
Turners Hill RH10 204 C6
Linnet Ct
1 Croydon CR0 61 E7
5 Mitcham CR4 40 E8
Linnet Gr GU4 110 D3
Linnet Mews SW12 21 A8
Linsford Bsns Pk GU16 85 F3
Linsford La GU16 85 F3
Linslade Cl TW4 4 E2
Linstead Rd GU14 84 E8
Linstead Way SW18, SW19 19 E8
Linton Cl CR4, SM5 40 F2
Linton Glade CR0 62 E1
Linton Gr SE27 22 C3
Linton's La KT17 76 E7
Lintott Ct TW19 2 D1
Lintott Gdns RH13 217 E3
Lion Ave TW1 16 F7
Lion Cl
Haslemere GU27 207 F7
Littleton TW17 33 E6
Lion Ctr The TW13 15 E5
Lion Gate Gdns TW9 6 F4
Lion Gate Mews SW18 20 A8
Lion Gn GU27 207 F6
Lion Green Rd CR5 79 D3
Lion Ho 18 TW10 6 D2
Lion La
Haslemere GU27 207 F7
Turners Hill RH10 204 A4
Lion & Lamb Way 12 GU9 125 B2
Lion & Lamb Yd 14 GU9 125 B2
Lion Mead GU27 207 F6
Lion Park Ave KT9 57 A6
Lion Rd
Thornton Heath CR0 42 C4
Twickenham TW1 16 F7
Lion Ret Pk GU22 70 B3
Lion Way TW8 6 D7
Lion Wharf Rd TW7 6 B4
Liphook Cres SE23 23 C8
Liphook Rd
Haslemere GU27 207 F6
Linchmere GU27 207 B4
Lipsham Cl SM7 78 D6
Lisbon Ave TW2 16 C6
Liscombe RG12 27 B2
Liscombe Ho RG12 27 B2
Liskeard Dr 2 GU14 85 A6
Liskeard Lo CR3 101 A1
Lisle Cl SW17 21 B4
Lismore 9 SW19 19 F3
Lismore Cl TW7 6 A5
Lismore Cres RH11 201 B3
Lismore Rd CR2 61 E4
Lissant Cl KT6 37 D2
Lissoms Rd CR5 79 A1
Lister Ave RH19 205 F6
Lister Cl SW19 40 E8
Lister Ct 1 CR8 80 B7
Litchfield Ave SM4 39 F2
Litchfield Gdns KT11 73 B5
Litchfield Rd SM1 59 C6
Litchfield Way GU2 129 F7
Lithgow's Rd TW14, TW6 3 F3
Little Acre
Beckenham BR3 44 A6
Little Bookham KT23 93 F3
Little Austins Rd GU9 146 D8
Little Birch Cl KT15 52 D2
LITTLE BIRKETTS 155 D1
LITTLE BOOKHAM 93 E3
Little Bookham St KT23 93 F2
Little Bornes SE21 22 E4
Little Borough RH3 137 A8
Littlebourne 2 SE13 24 E8
Littlebrook Cl CR0 43 D3
Little Brownings SE23 23 B6
Little Browns La TN8 144 F4
Little Collins RH1 162 B7
Little Common La RH1 120 C3
Little Comptons RH13 217 F2
Littlecote Cl SW19 19 E8
Little Crabtree RH11 201 C7
Little Cranmore La KT24 112 C6
Littlecroft Rd 2 TW20 11 F3
Little Ct BR4 63 E8
Littledale Cl RG12 27 E6
Little Dimocks SW12 21 B6
Little East Field CR5 99 D6
Little Elms UB3 3 D7
Little Ferry Rd TW1 17 B7
Littlefield Cl
Ash GU12 106 A1
Fairlands GU3 108 D5
9 Kingston u T KT1 37 E7
Littlefield Cotts GU3 108 B6
Littlefield Ct UB7 2 D7
Littlefield Gdns GU12 106 A1
Littlefield Way GU3 108 D5
Littleford La GU4, GU5 152 F7
Little Gn
Elstead GU8 148 D4
Richmond TW9 6 D3
Little Grebe RH12 217 C5
Little Green La
Addlestone KT16 51 E7
Wrecclesham GU9 146 A6
Little Halliards KT12 35 A3
Little Hatch RH12 217 F5
LITTLE HAVEN 217 E4
Littlehaven Inf Sch RH12 217 F5
Littlehaven La RH12 217 F5
Littlehaven Sta RH12 217 F5
Little Heath La KT11 74 A5
Littleheath Rd CR2 62 B2
Little Heath Rd GU24 49 E2
Little Hide GU1 110 B3
Little Kiln GU7 150 E8
Little King St RH19 185 E1
Little Lascombe Cotts GU3 128 A4
LITTLE LONDON 132 F2
Little London
Shere GU5 132 F2
Witley GU8 170 E5
Little Lullenden RH7 164 E5
Little Manor Gdns GU6 174 E2
Littlemead KT10 55 D6
Little Mead GU21 68 F3
Little Mead Ind Est GU6 174 B3
Little Moor GU47 45 C1
Little Moreton Cl KT14 71 B7
Little Oak Cl TW17 33 F5
Little Orch
Woking GU21 70 A5
Woodham KT15 71 A8
Little Orchards KT18 76 E5
Little Orchard Way GU4 130 E1
Little Paddock GU15 66 A8
Little Park Dr TW13 15 E6
Little Park Enterprises RH6 180 E3
Little Platt GU2 108 D2
Little Queens Rd TW11 16 F2
Littleriding GU22 70 B3
Little Ringdale RG12 27 E5
Little Roke Ave CR8 80 B5
Little Roke Rd CR8 80 C5
Littlers Cl SW19 40 D8
Little St Leonards SW14 7 C4
LITTLE SANDHURST 45 B1
Little St GU2 109 B5
Littlestone Cl BR3 24 A2
Little Tangley Flats GU5 131 C1
Little Thatch GU7 150 F6
Little Thurbans Cl GU9 146 A6
LITTLETON
Chertsey 34 A6
Guildford 130 A3
Littleton CE Inf Sch TW17 34 A6
LITTLETON COMMON 14 D1
Littleton Cross GU3 130 A4
Littleton Grange RH2 138 C7
Littleton Ho
Littleton Common TW15 14 C1
4 Reigate RH2 118 A2
Littleton La
Artington GU3 130 A3
Littleton TW17, TW18 33 E4
Reigate RH2 138 E7
Littleton Rd TW15, TW17 14 C1
Littleton St SW18 20 C6
Little Tumners Ct GU7 150 E6
Little Warren Cl GU4 131 B7
Little Wellington St 9 GU11 105 A2
Littlewick Cotts GU21 68 F4
Littlewick Rd GU21 68 E3
Littlewood GU6 174 F3
Little Woodcote Est SM5 79 A8
Little Woodcote La CR8, SM5, SM6 79 B8
Littlewood Ho CR2 81 B5
Littleworth Ave KT10 55 D5
Littleworth Common Rd KT10 55 D7
Littleworth La KT10 55 D6
Littleworth Pl KT10 55 D6
Littleworth Rd
Hinchley Wood KT10 55 E6
Puttenham GU10 148 C8
The Sands GU10 126 F1
Liverpool Rd
Kingston u T KT2 18 A1
South Norwood CR7 42 C6
Livesey Cl KT1 37 F6
Livingstone Ct TW19 13 E7
Livingstone Rd
Caterham CR3 100 D5
Crawley RH10 201 E4
Horsham RH13 217 D1
Hounslow TW3 5 C3
South Norwood CR7 42 D7
Llanaway Cl GU7 150 F6
Llanaway Ho GU7 150 F6
Llanaway Rd GU7 150 F6
Llangar Gr RG45 45 A5
Llanthony Rd SM4 40 D4
Llanvair Cl SL5 29 A3
Llanvair Dr SL5 28 F3
Llewellyn Ct SE20 43 C8
Lloyd Ave
Thornton Heath SW16 41 E8
Wallington CR5 79 B5
Lloyd Ct 6 SE27 22 B5
Lloyd Ho BR3 24 B2
Lloyd Park Ave CR0 61 F6
Lloyd Rd KT4, SM3 58 D7
Lloyds Ct RH10 181 E1
Lloyds Way BR3 43 F4
Lobelia Rd GU24 68 A4
Locarno Ct 15 SW16 21 C3
Lochinvar St SW12 21 B8
Lochinver RG12 27 B2
Lock Cl KT15 70 E7
Locke King Cl KT13 53 A3
Locke King Rd KT13 53 A3
Lockesley Sq KT6 37 D3
Lockestone KT13 52 F4
Lockestone Cl KT13 52 F4
Locke Way GU21 69 F2
Lockfield Cotts GU21 69 A1
Lockfield Dr GU21 68 F2
Lockhart Rd KT11 73 C6
Lockhursthatch La GU5 153 E6
Lock La GU22, GU23 71 C3
Lock Rd
Farnborough GU11 105 D5
Guildford GU1 109 D4
Richmond TW10 17 C4
Lock's La CR4 41 A7
Locksley Dr GU21 68 F2
Locks Mdw RH7 165 A1
Locksmeade Rd TW10 17 C4
Locks Ride SL5 8 C2
Lockswood GU24 88 B7
Lockton Chase SL5 28 D6
Lockton Ho RG40 25 C6
Lockwood Cl
Farnborough GU14 84 E8
Forest Hill SE26 23 D4
Horsham RH12 218 A5

Lockwood Ct
Crawley RH10 201 F8
Kingston u T KT3 38 C5
Lockwood Path GU21 70 E6
Lockwood Way KT9 57 A5
Locomotive Dr TW14 15 A7
Lodden Lo 17 SM2 59 C3
Loddon Cl GU15 66 A6
Loddon Rd GU14 84 D6
Loddon Way GU12 106 A1
Loder Cl GU21 70 D6
Lodge Ave
Croydon CR0, CR9 61 A7
Mortlake SW14 7 E4
Lodgebottom Rd KT18, RH5 116 A8
Lodge Cl
Aldershot GU11 126 C8
Brentford TW7 6 B6
Carshalton CR4 41 A1
Crawley RH11 201 C6
Dorking RH5 136 C3
East Ewell KT17 58 C1
East Grinstead RH19 185 D1
Englefield Green TW20 11 D3
Fetcham KT22 94 D5
Stoke D'Abernon KT11 73 F3
Lodge Gdns BR3 43 F4
Lodge Hill CR8 80 A4
Lodge Hill Cl GU10 146 D6
Lodge Hill Rd GU10 146 E7
Lodge La
New Addington CR0 63 B3
Salfords RH1 139 F1
South Croydon CR0 63 A4
South Holmwood RH5 157 F8
Lodge Pl SM1 59 B5
Lodge Rd
Fetcham KT22 94 D5
Sutton SM1 59 B5
Thornton Heath CR0 42 B2
Wallington SM6 60 B5
Lodge Sch CR8 79 D7
Lodge The
Englefield Green TW20 11 C3
Farnham GU9 125 E4
Guildford GU1 130 F8
Newchapel RH7 163 E1
8 Sutton SM1 59 C6
Lodge Way
Ashford TW15 13 E6
Charlton TW17 34 C7
Lodge Wlk CR6 82 A3
Lodsworth GU14 84 D3
Lofthouse Pl KT9 56 C4
Lofts The GU8 190 F8
Logan Cl TW4 4 F4
Loggetts SE21 22 E5
LOGMORE GREEN 135 C2
Logmore La RH4 135 D3
Lois Dr TW17 34 B4
Lollesworth La KT24 112 C8
Loman Rd GU16 86 A4
Lomas Cl CR0 63 C3
Lombard Bsns Pk
Merton SW19 40 B7
Thornton Heath CR0 41 F2
Lombard Rd SW19 40 B7
Lombard St GU8 149 B7
Lombardy Cl GU21 68 F2
Lomond Gdns CR2 62 E3
Loncin Mead Ave KT15 52 C2
Lond Meadow Villas RH6 180 E5
London Acad of Computing & Electronics SW17 20 F5
London Acad The CR0 61 D8
London Aerial Photo Liby GU24 50 E1
London Butterfly Ho* TW8 6 B6
London Cross KT24 112 F4
London Fields Ho RH11 201 C2
London Ho 5 GU11 105 B2
London Ho TW9 6 F4
London Inst The SW17 21 B3
London La
Bromley BR1 24 F1
Shere GU5 133 A5
London Rd
Ascot SL5 29 D5
Ashford TW15, TW18, TW19, TW14 13 D5
Bagshot GU15, GU19 47 D2
Blackwater GU15, GU17 64 E4
Bracknell RG12, SL5 28 C6
Brands Hill SL3 1 B8
Brentford TW7, TW8 6 B6
Bromley BR1 24 F1
Camberley GU15 65 C6
Caterham CR3 100 D4
Crawley RH10 181 E3
Dorking RH4RH5 115 C3
East Grinstead RH19 185 C3
Englefield Green TW20 11 C1
Forest Hill SE22, SE23 23 C7
Forest Row RH18 206 E4
Guildford, Burpham GU1, GU4 110 B4
Guildford GU1 109 F1
Hackbridge SM6 60 B7
Hindhead GU26 188 F4
Horsham RH12 217 C2
Hounslow TW3, TW7, TW1, TW8 5 D5
Kingston u T KT1, KT2 37 F7
London Rd *continued*
Mitcham CR4, SW17 40 F6
Morden SM4 40 A5
Redhill RH1 119 A3
Reigate RH2 118 A2
Send Marsh GU23 90 E1
Stoneleigh KT17, KT4, SM3 58 B5
Sunningdale, Blacknest SL5 30 B6
Thornton Heath CR0, CR7, SW16 42 A3
Twickenham TW1 17 A7
Virginia Water GU25, TW20 31 B7
Wentworth SL5, GU25 30 C4
Windlesham GU19, GU20, SL5 48 C7
Wokingham RG40 25 E6
London Rd N RH1 99 B2
London Rd S
Merstham RH1 119 B6
Redhill RH1 119 B6
London Road Sta (Guildford) GU1 109 E1
London Sq GU1 109 E1
London St KT16 33 A2
Loneacre GU20 48 E4
Lone Oak RH6 162 B1
Lonesome Fst Sch CR4 41 B7
Lonesome La RH1, RH2 139 D3
Lonesome Way CR4 41 C8
Longacre GU12 106 A2
Long Acre RH10 204 A8
Longacre Pl SM5 60 A4
Longacre Sch GU5 152 D4
Long Acres Cvn & Camping Site RH7 163 F2
Long Ave GU24 88 A6
Long Beech Dr GU14 84 C3
Longbourne Gn GU7 150 E8
Longbourne Way KT16 32 F3
Longboyds KT11 73 B4
Long Bridge GU9 125 C2
Longbridge Gate RH6 181 E8
Longbridge Rd
Crawley RH6 181 F8
Horley RH6 160 F1
Longbridge Rdbt RH6 160 E2
Longbridge Wlk RH6 160 F1
Longbrook Ct GU20 48 D4
Longchamp Cl RH6 161 C3
Long Cl RH10 202 D6
Long Copse Cl KT23 94 B4
Longcroft Ave SM7 78 C5
LONGCROSS 50 A7
Longcross Rd
Addlestone KT16 51 B7
Longcross KT16 50 C7
Longcross Sta GU25 30 F1
Longdale Mans SW12 21 D7
Longdene Rd GU27 208 B6
LONG DITTON 37 C1
Long Ditton Inf Sch KT6 37 C1
Longdown Cl GU10 146 C6
Longdown La N KT17 77 A6
Longdown La S KT17, KT18 77 A4
Longdown Lo GU47 64 B8
Longdown Rd
Catford SE6 24 A4
Ewell KT17 77 A6
Farnham GU10 146 C5
Guildford GU4 131 B6
Sandhurst GU47 45 B1
Long Dyke GU1 110 B3
Longfellow Cl RH12 217 E7
Longfellow Rd KT4 39 B1
Longfield 3 BR1 44 F8
Longfield Ave CR4, SM6 41 A1
Longfield Cl GU14 85 B8
Longfield Cres
Burgh Heath KT20 97 C7
Forest Hill SE23, SE26 23 C5
Longfield Dr
Mitcham SW19 40 E8
Mortlake SW14 7 B2
Longfield Ho SW14 7 B2
Longfield Rd
Ash GU12 106 A2
Dorking RH4 135 F6
Horsham RH12 217 A1
Longfield St SW18 20 A8
LONGFORD 2 C6
Longford Ave
Feltham TW14 3 F1
Stanwell TW19 13 E7
Longford Cl
Camberley GU15 65 D4
Feltham TW13 15 E5
Hampton TW12 16 A4
Longford Com Sch TW14 14 F8
Longford Ct
Hampton TW12 16 B2
West Ewell KT19 57 C6
Longford Gdns SM1 59 C8
Longford Ho
Catford BR1 24 D3
Hampton TW12 16 A4
Longford Ind Est TW12 16 B2
LONGFORDMOOR 2 A6
Longford Rd TW2 16 B7
Longford Rdbt UB7 2 B6
Longford Way TW19 13 E7
Longford Wlk 10 SW2 22 A8
Long Garden Mews 3 GU9 125 B2
Long Garden Way GU9 125 B2
Long Garden Wlk 4 GU9 125 B2
Long Garden Wlk E 2 GU9 125 B2
Long Garden Wlk W 1 GU9 125 B2
Long Gdn Pl GU9 125 B3
Long Gore GU7 150 E8
Longheath Dr KT23 93 E3
Longheath Gdns CR0 43 C4
Longhedge Ho SE26 23 A4
Long Hill
The Sands GU10 126 E1
Woldingham CR3 101 F6
Longhill Rd SE6 24 D5
Long Hill Rd RG12, SL5 28 A7
Long Ho SM5 59 E8
Longhope Dr GU10 146 A6
Long Houses GU24 87 D3
Longhurst Rd
Crawley RH11 201 A1
Croydon CR0 43 B3
East Horsley KT24 112 E6
Long La
Croydon CR0 43 C3
Stanwell TW15, TW19 13 F7
Longlands Ave CR5 79 A5
Longlands Ct CR4 41 A8
Longlands Way GU15 66 D5
Longleat Sq GU14 85 E3
Longleat Way TW14 14 D8
Longley Rd
Farnham GU9 125 D1
Thornton Heath CR0 42 B2
Upper Tooting SW17 20 F2
Long Lodge Dr KT12 54 C7
Longmead GU1 110 C1
Longmead Bsns Ctr KT19 76 D8
Longmead Cl CR3 100 E5
Longmead Ho SE27 22 C3
Longmeadow
Frimley GU15, GU16 65 F3
Little Bookham KT23 93 F2
Long Meadow Cl BR4 44 C2
Longmead Rd
Epsom KT19 57 E1
Thames Ditton KT7 36 F2
Upper Tooting SW17 20 F3
Longmere Gdns KT20 97 C8
Longmere Rd RH10 201 D8
Long Mickle GU47 45 B1
Longmoors RG42 26 E8
Longmore Rd KT12 54 E6
Long Orchards KT20 97 E7
Longpoles Rd GU6 174 F2
Long Rd The GU10 146 A2
Long Reach GU23, KT24 92 B3
Longridge Gr GU22 70 E5
Longs Cl GU22 71 A3
Longs Ct 2 TW9 6 F3
Longsdon Way CR3 101 A3
Longshaw CR5 98 F7
Long Shaw KT22 95 A7
Longshot Ind Est RG12 26 E7
Longshot La RG12 26 E7
Longside Cl TW20 32 C8
Longstaff Cres SW18 20 A8
Longstaff Rd SW18 20 A8
Longstone Rd SW17 21 B3
Long's Way RG40 25 E7
Longthorne Lo 7 SW2 22 A8
Longthornton Rd SW16 41 D7
Longton Ave SE26 23 A4
Longton Gr SE26 23 B4
Longwater Rd RG12 27 C3
Long Wlk
Burgh Heath KT18 97 D8
Kingston u T KT3 38 C6
Longwood Bsns Pk TW16 34 F4
Longwood Ct 3 KT4 58 A8
Longwood Dr SW15 19 B8
Longwood Rd CR8 80 D3
Longwood View RH10 202 A3
Longyard Ho RH6 161 B5
Lonsdale Gdns CR7, SW16 41 F5
Lonsdale Mews 4 TW9 7 A6
Lonsdale Pl 1 RH4 136 B8
Lonsdale Rd
Barnes SW13 7 F7
Croydon SE25 43 B5
Dorking RH4 136 B8
Weybridge KT13 53 A3
Look Out Discovery Ctr The* RG12 27 D1
Loop Rd
Epsom KT18 76 C3
Old Woking GU22 89 F7
Loppets Rd RH10 201 F3
Lorac Ct SM2 59 A3
Loraine Gdns KT21 75 E2
Loraine Ho 1 SM5 60 B6
Loraine Rd W4 7 B8
Lord Chancellor Wlk KT2 38 C8
Lordell Pl SW19 19 C2
Lord Knyvett Cl TW19 2 D1
Lord Knyvetts Ct 3 TW19 2 E1
Lordsbury Field SM6 60 C1
Lords Cl
Feltham TW13 15 E6
West Norwood SE21 22 C6
Lordsgrove Cl KT20 97 B7
Lords Hill Cotts GU5 152 C4
Lordshill Rd GU5 152 C5
Lordship La SE21, SE22 23 A8
Lords Wood Ho CR5 99 D5
Loretto Cl GU6 175 A3
Lorian Dr RH2 118 C2
Loriners RH10 201 D3
Loriners Cl KT11 73 A5
Loring Rd TW7 5 F5
Lorne Ave CR0 43 D2
Lorne Gdns
Croydon CR0 43 D2
Knaphill GU21 88 D8
Lorne Rd 3 TW10 6 F2
Lorne The KT23 94 A1
Lorraine Ct BR3 44 C8
Lorraine Sch GU15 65 E8
Lory Ridge GU19 47 E4
Loseberry Rd KT10 55 D5
Loseley Fields Prim Sch GU7 129 E1
Loseley Ho* GU3 129 E3
Loseley Rd GU7 150 E8
Lothian Rd GU24 87 A6
Lothian Wood KT20 97 B5
Lotus Rd TN16 83 F1
Loubet St SW17 20 F2
Loudwater Cl TW16 35 A5
Loudwater Rd TW16 35 A5
Loughborough RG12 27 E3
Louie Black Ho 4 SW19 19 E1
Louisa Ct TW2 16 E6
Louisa Ho SW15 7 F3
Louise Margaret Rd GU11 105 C3
Louis Fields GU3 108 C5
Louisville Rd SW17 21 A5
Lovatt Ct SW12 21 B7
Lovat Wlk TW5 4 E7
Loveday Ho 2 SW2 22 A7
Lovedean Ct RG12 27 E3
Lovekyn Cl KT2 37 F7
Love La
Cheam SM3 58 E4
Croydon SE25 43 B6
Godstone RH9 121 C3
Long Ditton KT6 56 D8
Mitcham CR4 40 E6
Morden SM4 40 B2
Walton on t H KT20 97 A1
Lovelace Cl KT24 93 A4
Lovelace Ct GU23 91 B6
Lovelace Dr GU22 70 F3
Lovelace Gdns
Hersham KT12 54 C5
Surbiton KT6 37 D2
Lovelace Prim Sch KT9 56 C5
Lovelace Rd
Bracknell RG12 26 E5
Surbiton KT6 37 D2
West Norwood SE21 22 C7
Lovelands La
Castle Green GU24 68 C6
Lower Kingswood KT20 118 B8
Loveletts RH11 201 A5
Lovel La SL4 9 B3
Lovell Ho 4 SW19 40 C8
Lovell Path 1 RH11 200 E5
Lovell Rd TW10 17 C5
Lovells Cl GU18 48 B1
Lovelock Cl CR8 80 C2
Lovel Rd SL4 9 A4
Lovers La GU10 167 C7
Lovett Dr SM5 40 D2
Lovett Ho 8 GU9 125 B2
Lovett Rd TW20 12 C4
Lowbury RG12 27 E5
Lowburys RH4 136 B4
Lowdells Cl RH19 185 C4
Lowdells Dr RH19 185 D4
Lowdells La RH19 185 C3
Lowe Cl GU11 104 F3
Lower Addiscombe Rd CR0 42 E1
LOWER ASHTEAD 75 D1
Lower Barn Cl RH12 217 F5
Lower Barn Rd CR8 80 D6
LOWER BOURNE 146 D5
Lower Breache Rd GU6 176 B4
Lower Bridge Rd RH1 118 F1
Lower Broadmoor Rd RG45 45 D4
Lower Charles St GU15 65 C6
Lower Church La 21 GU9 125 B2
Lower Church St CR0, CR9 61 B8
Lower Coombe St CR0, CR9 61 C6
Lower Court Rd KT19 76 C8
Lower Ct
Epsom KT19 76 D8
Sutton SM1 59 C6
Lower Dene RH19 186 A1
Lower Downs Rd SW20 39 D8
Lower Dunnymans 4 SM7 77 F5
LOWER EASHING 149 E4
Lower Eashing GU7 149 F4
Lower Edgeborough Rd GU1 130 F8
Lower Farm Rd KT24 93 C3
Lower Farnham Rd GU11, GU12 126 C7
LOWER FELTHAM 14 F5
Lower Forecourt RH6 182 B7
Lower George St 12 TW10 6 D2
Lower Gn KT12 54 D5
Lower Gn W CR4 40 E6
LOWER GREEN 55 A8
Lower Green Gdns 8 KT4 39 A1
Lower Green Rd KT10 55 C8
Lower Grove Rd TW10 6 F2
Lower Guildford Rd GU21 68 D1
LOWER HALLIFORD 34 D2
Lower Ham La GU8 148 E4
Lower Hampton Rd TW12, TW16 35 D7
Lower Ham Rd KT2 17 D2
Lower Hanger GU27 207 D6
Lower Hill Rd KT19 76 B7
Lower House Rd GU8 169 F2
Lower Kings Rd KT2 17 E1
LOWER KINGSWOOD 117 F8
Lower Manor Rd
Farncombe GU7 150 F6
Milford GU8 149 E1
Lower Marsh La KT1, KT5 38 A5
Lowermead RH1 118 F3
Lower Mere RH19 205 F8
Lower Mill Field GU19 47 D2
Lower Morden La SM4 39 E3
Lower Mortlake Rd TW9 6 F4
Lower Moushill La GU8 149 D1
Lower Nelson St 4 GU11 105 A2
Lower Northfield 5 SM7 77 F5
Lower Nursery SL5 30 A4
Lower Park Rd CR5 78 E1
Lower Peryers KT24 112 E7
Lower Pillory Down SM5 79 B7
Lower Rd
Effingham KT24 113 D8
Forest Row RH18 206 F3
Grayswood GU27 189 F2
Great Bookham KT22, KT23 94 C3
Purley CR8 80 B6
Reigate RH1 139 D7
Sutton SM1 59 C6
Lower Richmond Rd SW14, TW9 7 B4
Lower Sandfields GU23 90 D3
Lower Sand Hills KT6 37 C2
Lower Sawleywood 2 SM7 77 F5
Lower Shott KT23 94 B1
LOWER SOUTH PARK 142 B3
Lower South St 4 GU7 150 D4
Lower South View GU9 125 C3
Lower Sq
Forest Row RH18 206 F3
Isleworth TW7 6 B4
Lower St
Haslemere GU27 208 C6
Shere GU5 133 A4
Lower Sunbury Rd TW12 36 A7
LOWER SYDENHAM 23 E4
Lower Sydenham Sta SE26 23 F3
Lower Tanbridge Way 11 RH12 217 B2
Lower Teddington Rd KT1 37 D8
Lower Terrace Rd GU14 105 A8
Lower Village Rd SL5 29 C4
Lower Weybourne La
Badshot Lea GU9 126 A6
Heath End GU9 125 F6
Lower Wood Rd KT10 56 B4
Lowestoft Wlk RH10 202 B4
Loweswater Wlk GU15 66 D4
Lowfield Cl GU18 67 A8
LOWFIELD HEATH 181 E4
Lowfield Heath Ind Est RH11 181 E5
Lowfield Heath Rd RH6 180 F5
Lowfield Heath Windmill* RH6 180 C6
Lowfield Rd RH13 215 D3
Lowfield Way RH11 181 E5
Lowicks Rd GU10 168 C6
Low La GU9 126 B6
Lowlands Dr TW19 2 D2
Lowlands Rd GU17 64 C4
Lowndes Bldgs GU9 125 B3
Lowood Ct SE19 22 F3
Lowry Cl GU47 64 D6

Lowry Cres CR4 40 E7
Lowry Ct 3 W4 7 E7
Lowther Hill SE23 23 E8
Lowther Rd
Barnes SW13 7 F6
Kingston u T KT2 37 F8
Lowthorpe 5 GU21 69 A1
Loxford Ct GU6 173 F2
Loxford Rd CR3 100 F2
Loxford Way CR3 100 F2
LOXHILL 172 E1
Loxley Cl SE26 23 D3
Loxley Rd
Hampton TW12 15 F4
Wandsworth SW18 20 D7
Loxmeadows RH14 212 D3
Loxton Rd SE23 23 E7
LOXWOOD 212 F4
Loxwood Cl TW14 14 E7
Loxwood Ct CR0 60 E7
Loxwood Place Farm RH14 212 F3
Loxwood Prim Sch RH14 213 A4
Loxwood Rd
Alfold GU6 193 F2
Loxwood, Alfold Bars GU6, RH14 212 F8
Loxwood RH12, RH14 213 D4
Plaistow RH14 212 A2
Rudgwick RH12 214 A6
Loxwood Wlk RH11 201 A8
Lucan Dr TW18 13 D1
Lucas Cl
Crawley RH10 202 C3
East Grinstead RH19 186 A1
Lucas Ct SE26 23 E3
Lucas Field GU27 207 E6
LUCAS GREEN 67 E5
Lucas Green Rd GU24 67 E5
Lucas Rd
Penge SE20 23 C2
Warnham RH12 216 F8
Lucerne Cl GU22 89 E8
Lucerne Ct 8 BR3 24 A1
Lucerne Dr RH10 202 D4
Lucerne Rd CR7 42 C5
Lucie Ave TW15 14 B2
Lucien Rd
Upper Tooting SW17 21 A4
Wimbledon SW18 20 B6
Lucille Ho SE26 23 B2
Luckley Oakfield Sch RG40 25 B3
Luckley Path RG40 25 C6
Luckley Rd RG41 25 B3
Luckley Wood RG41 25 B3
Lucraft Ho 12 SW2 21 E8
Luddington Ave GU25 31 F7
Ludford Cl CR0 61 B6
Ludgrove Sch RG40 25 D3
Lud Lo TW15 13 E6
Ludlow RG12 27 B2
Ludlow Cl GU16 86 A7
Ludlow Rd
Feltham TW13 15 A4
Guildford GU2 130 B8
Ludovick Wlk SW15 7 E3
Ludshott Gr GU35 187 B5
Ludshott Manor GU30 187 C1
Luke Rd GU11 125 E8
Luke Rd E GU11 125 F8
Lukes Ct SE6 24 A3
Lullarook Cl TN16 83 C3
Lullington Garth 2 BR1 24 E1
Lullington Rd SE20 23 A1
Lulworth Ave TW5, TW7 5 C7
Lulworth Cl
Crawley RH11 201 B3
Farnborough GU14 85 A7
Lulworth Cres CR4 40 E7
Lumiere Ct 6 SW17 21 A6
Lumley Ct RH6 161 A4
Lumley Gdns SM3 58 E5
Lumley Ho KT3 38 D1
Lumley Rd
Cheam SM3 58 E5
Horley RH6 161 A3
Lunar Cl TN16 83 D3
Luna Rd CR7 42 C6
Lundy Cl RH11 201 C3
Lunghurst Rd CR3 102 A5
Lunham Rd SE19 22 E2
Lunn Cotts GU26 188 F4
Lupin Cl
Bagshot GU19 47 C1
Croydon CR0 43 D1
Streatham SW2 22 B6
Lupin Ride RG45 45 B7
Lupus Ct SE19 42 D8
Luscombe Ct BR2 44 E7
Lushington Dr KT11 73 B5
Lushington Ho KT12 35 C3
Lushington Rd SE6 24 B3
Lusted Hall La TN16 103 C7
Lusteds Cl RH4 136 C4
Lutea Ho SM2 59 C3
Luther Mews 3 TW11 16 F3
Luther Rd TW11 16 F3
Lutwyche Rd SE23, SE6 23 F6
Lutyens Cl RH11 200 E4
Luxford Cl RH12 217 F5
Luxford's La RH19 206 B6
Lyall Ave SE21 22 F4
Lyall Pl GU9 125 B7
Lycett Ho 10 SW2 21 E8
Lych Way GU21 69 D3
Lyconby Gdns CR0 43 E2
Lydbury RG12 27 F6
Lydden Gr SW18 20 B8
Lydden Rd SW18 20 B8
Lydele Cl GU21 69 F4
Lydford Cl
2 Farnborough GU14 85 A7
Frimley GU16 86 A7
Lydger Cl GU22 90 C7
Lydhurst Ave SW2 21 F6
Lydia Park Cvn Pk GU6 193 C8
Lydney RG12 27 B2
Lydney Cl SW19 19 E6
Lydon Ho RH11 181 D1
Lye Copse Ave GU14 85 B8
Lyefield La GU6, RH5 176 C5
Lye The KT20 97 C5
Lye View Cotts GU21 89 A8
Lyfield KT22 74 B5
Lyford Rd SW18 20 E7
Lygon Ct SW19 19 F1
Lyham Rd SW2 21 E8
Lyle Cl CR4 41 A2
Lyle Ct SM4 40 D3
Lymbourne Cl SM2 59 A1
Lymden Gdns RH2 139 B7
Lymer Ave SE19 22 F3
Lyme Regis Ct SM7 77 F2
Lyme Regis Rd SM7 77 F2
Lymescote Gdns SM1 59 A8
Lyminge Gdns SW17, SW18 20 E7
Lymington Cl SW16 41 D7
Lymington Ct SM1 59 C7
Lymington Gdns KT19 57 F5
Lynchen Cl TW5 4 B6
Lynchford La GU11, GU14 105 E8
Lynchford Rd GU14 105 D8
Lynchmere Pl GU2 109 A4
Lynch Rd GU9 125 E2
Lyncroft Gdns
Ewell KT17 57 F2
Isleworth TW3 5 C2
Lyn Ct GU1 131 A8
Lyndale Ct
3 Redhill RH1 119 A4
6 West Byfleet KT14 71 A6
Lyndale Rd RH1 119 A4
Lynde Ho KT12 35 C3
Lynden Gate SW15 19 B8
Lynden Hurst CR0 61 F8
Lyndhurst Ave
Aldershot GU11 126 C6
Blackwater GU17 64 C6
Mitcham SW16 41 D7
Sunbury TW16 35 A6
Tolworth KT5 38 B1
Twickenham TW2 16 A7
Lyndhurst Cl
Bracknell RG12 28 A6
Crawley RH11 201 D5
South Croydon CR0 61 F7
Woking GU21 69 D4
Lyndhurst Ct 12 SM2 59 A3
Lyndhurst Dr KT3 38 F2
Lyndhurst Farm Cl RH19 184 D4
Lyndhurst Ho 2 SW15 19 A8
Lyndhurst Rd
Ascot SL5 29 A5
Coulsdon CR5 79 A3
Reigate RH2 139 A6
Thornton Heath CR7 42 A5
Lyndhurst Sch GU15 65 B5
Lyndhurst Way
Addlestone KT16 51 E8
Belmont SM2 59 A2
Lyndon Ave SM6 60 A7
Lyndon Yd SW17 20 B4
Lyndsey Cl GU14 84 B4
LYNE 32 B1
Lyne Cl GU25 31 F3
Lyne Crossing Rd KT16, GU25 32 B3
Lyne Ct GU25 31 F2
Lynegrove Ave TW15 14 C3
Lyneham Rd RG45 45 B5
Lyne Ho RH5 179 A1
Lyne La
Chertsey KT16, TW20, GU25 32 A3
Lyne KT16 32 A2
Lyne & Longcross CE Inf Sch KT16 51 B8
Lyne Place Manor GU25 31 F2
Lyne Rd GU25 31 E3
Lynfield Ct SE23 23 D8
Lynford Ct 5 CR2 61 E6
Lynmouth Ave SM4 39 D2
Lynmouth Gdns TW5 4 D6
Lynn Cl TW15 14 D3
Lynn Ct
Streatham SW16 21 D3
Whyteleafe CR3 80 F1
Lynne Cl CR2 81 C8
Lynne Ct
Forest Hill SE23 23 F8
13 Guildford GU1 130 F8
South Croydon CR2 61 E6
Wimbledon SW20 39 B8
Lynne Wlk KT10 55 C5
Lynn Rd SW12 21 B8
Lynn Way GU14 84 F7
Lynn Wlk RH2 139 B6
Lynscott Way CR2 61 B2
Lynsted Ct BR3 43 E7
Lynton KT7 37 A2
Lynton Cl
Chessington KT9 56 E6
East Grinstead RH19 186 A2
Farnham GU9 146 A7
Isleworth TW7 5 F3
Lynton Ct
Ewell KT17 76 F8
Sutton SM2 59 C4
Lynton Park Ave RH19 186 A2
Lynton Rd
New Malden KT3 38 D4
Thornton Heath CR0, CR7 42 A3
Lynwick St
Rudgwick, Cox Green RH12 195 D1
Rudgwick RH12 214 C8
Lynwood GU2 130 B8
Lynwood Ave
Egham TW20 11 E2
Epsom KT17 76 F5
Wallington CR5 79 B4
Lynwood Cl GU21 70 D6
Lynwood Cres SL5 29 E3
Lynwood Ct
Ashford TW15 13 F3
Horsham RH12 217 C3
Kingston u T KT1 38 B7
Lynwood Dr
Mytchett GU16 86 A3
North Cheam KT4 58 A8
Lynwood Flats SL5 29 E4
Lynwood Gdns CR0 60 F6
Lynwood Rd
Epsom KT17 76 F5
Hinchley Wood KT7 55 F8
Redhill RH1 119 A3
Thames Ditton KT7 36 F1
Upper Tooting SW17 20 F4
Lynx Hill KT24 112 F8
Lynx Terr SW17 20 A5
Lyon Cl RH10 202 C2
Lyon Ct RH13 217 E2
Lyon Rd
Crowthorne RG45 45 C6
Merton SW19 40 C8
Walton-on-T KT12 54 E8
Lyons Cl RH13 215 D3
Lyons Ct RH4 136 B7
Lyonsdene KT20 117 F8
Lyons Dr GU2 109 A6
Lyons Rd RH13 215 E3
Lyon Way GU16 65 C1
Lyon Way Ind Est GU16 65 C1
Lyric Cl RH10 202 D4
Lyric Mews SE26 23 D4
Lyric Rd SW13 7 F6
Lysander Rd CR0 60 F4
Lysander Way GU14 85 B1
Lysias Rd SW12 21 B8
Lysons Ave GU12 105 F8
Lysons Rd GU11 105 A1
Lysons Way GU12 106 A7
Lyster Mews KT11 73 C6
Lytchet Minster Cl 4 RG12 27 F4
Lytchgate Cl CR2 61 E3
Lytcott Dr KT8 35 F6
Lytham
Bracknell RG12 26 E3
Horley RH6 161 B2
Lytham Ct SL5 29 C4
Lytton Dr RH10 202 D7
Lytton Gdns SM6 60 D6
Lytton Ho 3 TW12 16 B2
Lytton Pk KT11 73 F7
Lytton Rd GU22 70 B3
Lyveden Rd SW17, SW19 20 F2
Lywood Cl KT20 97 C5

M

Mabbotts KT20 97 D6
Mabel St GU21 69 D2
Maberley Cres SE19 23 A1
Maberley Ct SE19 23 A1
Maberley Rd
Penge, Elmers End BR3 43 D6
Penge SE19 23 A1
Mabley Ct RG12 27 A3
MacAdam Ave RG45 45 C7
McAlmont Ridge GU7 150 D7
McArdle Way SL3 1 D7
Mac Arthur Ho 4 SW2 21 E8
MacAulay Ave KT10 55 E8
MacAulay Ct CR3 100 E6
MacAulay Rd CR3 100 E6
Macbeth Ct RG42 27 E8
McCarthy Rd TW13 15 D3
McClaren Tech Ctr GU21 70 A8
Macclesfield Rd CR0, SE25 43 C4
McCormick Ho 9 SW2 22 A7
MacDonald Ct TW3 5 C3
McDonald Ho 1 KT2 17 F1
MacDonald Rd
Heath End GU9 125 B7
Lightwater GU18 67 A8
McDonald's Almshouses GU9 125 A1
McDonough Cl KT9 56 E6
McDougall Ct TW9 7 A5
MacDowall Rd GU2 109 B5
Macfarlane La TW7 6 A8
McGechie Ho RH19 185 D3
MacGregor Ho SW12 21 D7
McIndoe Rd RH19 185 D3
McIntosh Cl SM6 60 E3
McIver Cl RH19 184 F4
McKay Cl GU11 105 C3
McKay Rd SW20 19 C2
McKay Trad Est SL3 1 E5
Mackenzie Ho RH19 185 A4
Mackenzie Rd BR3 43 D7
McKenzie Way KT19 57 A1
Mackie Ho 18 SW2 22 A8
Mackie Rd SW2 22 A8
Mackies Hill GU5 154 D7
McKinlay Ct BR3 43 F7
Macklin Ho SE23 23 B6
Mackrells RH1 139 C6
MacLaren Dr
Bracknell RG42 27 F8
Newell Green RG42 8 A1
Winkfield RG42 28 A8
McLeod Ct SE21 23 A7
McLeod Ho SE23 23 C6
MacLeod Rd RH13 217 F1
Macmahon Cl GU24 49 E1
McMillan Ct
Catford SE6 24 F7
Whyteleafe CR3 80 F1
Macmillan Ho SM7 77 F4
Macmillan Way SW17 21 B4
Macnaghten Woods GU15 65 E6
McNaughton Cl GU14 84 D3
MacPhail Cl RG40 25 E8
McRae La CR4 40 F2
Maddison Cl TW11 16 F2
Maddox Dr RH10 202 E5
Maddox La KT23 93 E3
Maddox Pk KT23 93 E4
Madehurst Ct RH11 200 F3
Madeira Ave
Bromley BR1 24 E1
Horsham RH12 217 C2
Madeira Cl KT14 71 A6
Madeira Cres KT14 70 F6
Madeira Rd
Mitcham CR4 40 F5
Streatham SW16 21 E3
West Byfleet KT14 71 A6
Madeira Wlk RH2 118 D2
Madeline Rd SE20 23 A1
Maderia Ct GU14 84 E5
Madgehole La GU5 153 B3
Madingley RG12 27 B1
Madingley Ct TW1 6 C2
Madison Gdns BR2 44 F6
Madox Brown End GU47 64 E6
Madrid Rd GU2 130 B8
Maesmaur Rd TN16 103 D6
Mafeking Ave TW8 6 E8
Mafeking Rd TW19 12 B6
Magazine Cotts GU4 131 C3
Magazine Pl KT22 95 B5
Magazine Rd
Caterham CR3 100 B5
Farnborough GU14 104 D8
Magdala Rd
Isleworth TW7 6 A4
South Croydon CR2 61 D3
Magdalen Cl KT14 71 E5
Magdalen Cres KT14 71 E5
Magdalen Ct SE25 43 A4
Magdalene Cl RH10 182 C1
Magdalene Rd
Littleton TW17 33 F6
Sandhurst GU47 45 F2
Magdalen Rd SW18 20 D7
Magellan Terr RH10 182 A2
Magna Carta La TW19 11 E7
Magna Carta Sch The TW18 12 D2
Magna Rd TW20 11 B2
Magnolia Cl
Kingston u T KT2 18 B2
Sandhurst GU47 45 D1
Winkfield RG42 28 A8
Magnolia Ct
3 Belmont SM2 59 B3
Feltham TW13 15 A7
Horley RH6 161 A3
Penge SE26 23 C3
Richmond TW9 7 B6
Wallington SM6 60 B5
Magnolia Dr TN16 83 E3
Magnolia Pl GU1 109 C4
Magnolia Rd W4 7 B8
Magnolia Way
Dorking RH5 136 D4
West Ewell KT19 57 C5
Magnolia Wharf W4 7 B8
Magpie Cl
Coulsdon CR5 79 C1
Crondall GU10 124 D8
Magpie Wlk RH10 201 F8
Maguire Dr
Frimley GU16 66 C3
Richmond TW10 17 C4
Mahonia Cl GU24 67 F6
Maida Rd GU11 105 B4
MAIDENBOWER 202 C4
Maidenbower Bsns Pk RH10 202 E4
Maidenbower Dr RH10 202 D4
Maidenbower Jun & Inf Schs RH10 202 C4
Maidenbower La RH10 202 C4
Maidenbower Pl RH10 202 C4
Maidenbower Sq RH10 202 C4
Maiden La RH11 201 C8
Maiden's Gn SL4 8 B6
MAIDEN'S GREEN 8 B5
Maidenshaw Rd KT19 76 D7
Maids of Honour Row 4 TW9 6 D2
Main Dr
Newell Green, Chavey Down RG42, SL5 28 B8
Newell Green RG42 8 A1
Main Gate Lodges SL4 10 F5
Mainprize Rd RG12 27 E7
Main Rd TN16 83 C5
Main St
Chertsey KT15 52 E7
Feltham TW13 15 D3
Mainstone Cl GU16 86 C7
Mainstone Cres GU24 87 D6
Mainstone Rd GU24 67 F3
Mainwaring Ct CR4 41 A7
Mais Ho SE26 23 B6
Maisie Webster Cl TW19 13 D8
Maisonettes The SM1 58 F5
Maitland Cl
Hounslow TW4 4 F4
Walton-on-T KT12 54 E8
West Byfleet KT14 71 A6
Maitland Rd
Farnborough GU14 105 B8
Penge SE26 23 D2
Maitlands Cl GU10 126 F6
Maizecroft RH6 161 C4
Majestic Way CR4 40 F7
Major's Farm Rd SL3 1 A8
Major's Hill RH10 203 C5
Malacca Farm GU4 111 B7
Malan Cl TN16 83 E2
Malatia CR2 61 C4
Malcolm Cl SE20 23 C1
Malcolm Dr KT6 37 E1
Malcolm Gdns RH6 160 D1
Malcolm Prim Sch SE20 23 C1
Malcolm Rd
Coulsdon CR5 79 D4
Croydon CR0, SE25 43 A3
Penge SE20 23 C1
Wimbledon SW19 19 E2
Malden Ave SE25 43 B6
Malden CE Prim Sch KT4 38 E1
Malden Ct KT3 39 B6
Malden Green Ave KT4 39 A1
Malden Hill KT3 38 F6
Malden Hill Gdns KT3 38 F6
Malden Manor Prim Sch KT3 38 E2
Malden Manor Sta KT3 38 E2
Malden Pk KT3 38 F3
Malden Rd
Cheam KT4, SM3 58 D5
New Malden KT3, KT4 38 F2
MALDEN RUSHETT 75 C7
Malden Way KT3 39 A5
Malden Way (Kingston By Pass) KT3, KT5 38 E4
Maldon Ct SM6 60 C5
Maldon Rd SM6 60 B5
Malet Cl TW20 12 D2
Maley Ave SE27 22 B6
Malham Cl RH10 202 C3
Malham Fell RG12 27 A5
Malham Rd SE23 23 D7
Malham Road Ind Est SE23 23 D7
Mallard Cl
Ash GU12 105 F2
Haslemere GU27 207 E6
Horley RH6 161 A5
Horsham RH12 217 C5
Redhill RH1 119 A4
Twickenham TW2 16 A8
Mallard Ct
Aldershot GU11 126 A7
7 Dorking RH4 136 A8
28 Richmond TW10 6 D1
Mallard Pl
East Grinstead RH19 205 F8
Twickenham TW1 17 A5
Mallard Rd CR2 62 D1
Mallard's Reach KT13 53 D8
Mallards The
Frimley GU16 65 F2
Laleham TW18 33 B7
Mallards Way GU18 67 A8
Mallard Way SM6 60 C2
Mallard Wlk BR3, CR0 43 D4
Malling Cl CR0 43 C3
Malling Gdns SM4 40 C3
Malling Ho 9 BR3 24 A1
Malling Way BR2 44 F2
Mallinson Rd CR0 60 D7

Mal–Mar 273

Mallow Cl
Burgh Heath KT20 97 B8
Croydon CR0 43 D1
Horsham RH12 217 E6
Mallow Cres GU4 110 C4
Mallowdale Rd RG12 27 E2
Mall The
Brentford TW8 6 D8
6 Guildford GU1 130 C8
Hersham KT12 54 D5
Kingston u T KT6 37 D4
Mortlake SW14 7 C2
Mall The (Prep Sch)
TW2 16 D5
Malmains Cl BR3 44 D5
Malmains Way BR3 44 D5
Malmesbury Prim Sch
SM4 40 C3
Malmesbury Rd SM4 40 C3
Malmstone Ave RH1 119 D6
Malory Cl BR3 43 E7
Malta Rd GU16 86 E8
Maltby Rd KT9 57 A4
Malt Hill TW20 11 E3
Malt Ho SL4 11 B8
Malt House Cl SL4 11 B8
Malthouse Ct GU4 130 E4
Malthouse Dr
Chiswick W4 7 F8
Feltham TW13 15 D3
Malthouse La
Hambledon GU8 171 C1
Pirbright GU3 88 C2
West End GU24 67 F7
Malthouse Mead GU8 170 F5
Malthouse Rd RH10 201 D4
Malthouses The GU6 174 E3
Maltings Cl SW13 7 E5
Maltings Lo 5 W4 7 E7
Maltings The
Byfleet KT14 71 F6
Oxted RH8 122 F4
Staines TW18 12 E4
Malting Way TW7 5 F4
Malton Ho SE25 42 E5
Malus Cl KT15 51 F3
Malus Dr KT15 51 F3
Malvern Cl
Mitcham CR4 41 C6
Ottershaw KT16 51 C4
Penge SE20 43 A7
Surbiton KT6 37 E1
Malvern Ct
Belmont SM2 59 A3
Brands Hill SL3 1 A8
Epsom KT18 76 D5
3 Surbiton KT6 37 E1
Malvern Dr TW13 15 D3
Malvern Rd
Crawley RH11 201 C5
Farnborough GU14 84 D7
Hampton TW12 16 A1
Harlington UB3 3 E7
Surbiton KT6 37 E1
Thornton Heath CR7 42 A5
Malyons The TW17 34 D3
Manatee Pl SM6 60 D7
Manby Lodge Inf Sch
KT13 53 C5
Manchester Rd CR7 42 C6
Mandeville Cl
Guildford GU2 109 A4
Merton SW19 39 E8
Mandeville Ct TW20 12 A4
Mandeville Dr KT6 37 D1
Mandeville Rd
Isleworth TW7 6 A5
Littleton TW17 34 A4
Mandora Rd GU11 105 B4
Mandrake Rd SW17 20 F5
Manfield Pk GU6 174 B5
Manfield Rd GU12 106 A2
Mangles Ct 1 GU1 130 C8
Mangles Rd GU1 109 D3
Manley Bridge Rd
GU10 145 E4
Mannamead KT18 96 E8
Mannamead Cl KT18 96 E8
Mann Cl CR0, CR9 61 C7
Manning Cl RH19 185 D2
Manning Pl TW10 6 F1
Mannings Cl RH10 182 D1
Manningtree Cl SW19 19 E7
Mann's Cl TW7 5 F2
Manoel Rd TW2 16 C6
Manor Ave
Caterham CR3 100 E3
Hounslow TW4 4 D5
Manor Chase KT13 53 B5
Manor Cl
East Horsley KT24 112 E7
Haslemere GU27 207 E6
Horley RH6 160 F3
New Malden KT4 38 E1
Pyrford GU22 70 F3
South Godstone RH9 142 F5
Tongham GU10 126 F7
Warlingham CR6 81 E2
Manor Cotts GU21 68 E5
Manor Cres
Byfleet KT14 71 F6
Epsom KT19 76 A7
Guildford GU2 109 B3
Haslemere GU27 207 E6
Pirbright GU24 87 D7
Surbiton KT5 38 A3
Manorcroft Prim Sch
TW20 12 A2
Manorcrofts Rd TW20 12 A2
Manor Ct
Horsham RH12 218 A5
Kingston u T KT2 38 A8
Streatham SW16 21 E5
14 Sutton SM1 59 C6
Twickenham TW2 16 C6
Wallington SM6 60 A7
Weybridge KT13 53 B6
Manordene Cl KT7 37 A1
Manor Dr
Feltham TW13 15 D3
Hinchley Wood KT10 56 A7
Horley RH6 160 F3
Sunbury TW16 35 A7
Surbiton KT5 38 A3
West Ewell KT19 57 E4
Woodham KT15 52 A1
Manor Dr N KT3, KT4 38 D2
Manor Dr The KT4 38 F1
Manor Farm
9 Egham TW20 12 A3
Wanborough GU3 128 C6
Manor Farm Ave TW17 34 B3
Manor Farm Bsns Ctr
GU10 126 F5
Manor Farm Cl
Ash GU12 105 F1
New Malden KT4 38 E1
Normandy GU3 107 B3
Manor Farm Cotts
GU3 128 C6
Manor Farm Ct TW20 12 A3
Manor Farm La TW20 12 A3
Manor Farm Rd CR7,
SW16 42 A7
Manorfield Prim Sch
RH6 160 F3
Manorfields RH11 200 D2
Manor Fields
Horsham RH12, RH13 218 A4
Milford GU8 149 E2
Seale GU10 127 B4
Manorgate Rd KT2 38 A8
Manor Gdns
Effingham KT24 113 D7
Farncombe GU7 150 E7
Farnham GU10 146 D5
Guildford GU2 109 B3
Hampton TW12 16 C1
Merton SW19, SW20 39 F7
Richmond TW10, TW9 6 F3
South Croydon CR2 61 F4
Sunbury TW16 35 A7
Manor Gn GU8 149 E1
Manor Gr
Beckenham BR3 44 B7
Richmond TW9 7 A4
Manor Green Coll
RH11 201 A7
Manor Green Prim Sch
RH11 201 A7
Manor Green Rd KT19 76 C7
Manor Hill SM7 78 F4
Manor Ho
Horsham RH12 217 C1
5 Twickenham TW2 16 E6
Wallington SM6 60 B5
Manor Ho The
Kingswood KT20 98 C4
Limpsfield RH8 123 B7
Manor House Ct
Epsom KT18 76 C6
Lower Halliford TW17 34 B2
Manor House Dr
Ascot SL5 9 A1
Hersham KT13 53 F5
Manor House Flats
GU10 126 F6
Manorhouse La KT23 113 E8
Manor House Sch
KT23 113 E8
Manor House The
GU15 65 D6
Manor House Way TW7 6 B4
Manor Inf Sch GU14 84 E6
Manor Jun Sch GU14 84 F6
Manor La
Feltham TW13 15 A6
Harlington UB3 3 D8
Lewisham SE12 24 F8
Lower Kingswood KT20 118 A6
Shamley Green GU5 152 E3
Sunbury TW16 35 B7
Sutton SM1 59 C5
Manor Lea GU27 207 E6
Manor Lea Cl GU8 149 E2
Manor Lea Rd GU8 149 E2
Manor Leaze TW20 12 B3
Manor Lo GU2 109 B3
Manor Mead Sch
TW17 34 B4
Manor Mews GU22 90 B6
Manor Mount SE23 23 C7
Manor Park Cl BR4 44 B1
Manor Park Ind Est 2
GU12 105 C1
Manor Park Prim Sch
SM1 59 C5
Manor Park Rd
Sutton SM1 59 C5
West Wickham BR4 44 B1
Manor Pk
Richmond TW9 6 F3
Staines TW18 12 D5
Manor Pl
East Bedfont TW14 15 A7
Great Bookham KT23 94 A1
Manor Pl *continued*
Mitcham CR4 41 C6
Staines TW18 13 B3
Sutton SM1 59 B6
4 Walton-on-T KT12 35 A2
Manor Rd
Aldershot GU11,
GU12 126 A8
Ashford TW15 14 A3
Ash GU10, GU12 126 F8
Beckenham BR3 44 B7
Belmont SM2 58 F2
Croydon SE25 43 A6
East Grinstead RH19 185 C2
East Molesey KT8 36 D5
Farnborough GU14 85 D3
Farnham GU9 125 E4
Guildford GU2 109 B3
Horsham RH12 218 A5
Merstham RH1 119 C6
Merton SW20 39 F7
Mitcham CR4, SW16 41 C6
Reigate RH2 117 F3
Richmond TW10, TW9 6 F3
Send Marsh GU23 90 F4
Tatsfield TN16 103 E7
Teddington TW11 17 B3
Twickenham TW2 16 D6
Wallington SM5, SM6 60 B5
Walton-on-T KT12 34 F2
West Wickham BR4 63 B8
Woking GU21 69 C3
Wokingham RG41 25 A2
Manor Rd N
Hackbridge SM6 60 B6
Hinchley Wood KT7 56 A8
Manor Rd S KT10 55 E6
MANOR ROYAL 181 F2
Manor Royal RH10 181 E1
Manor Royal Ind Est
RH10 181 E2
Manor The
Forest Hill SE23 23 C8
Milford GU8 149 F1
Manor Way
Bagshot GU19 47 F3
Beckenham BR3 44 A6
Egham TW20 11 F2
Guildford GU2 129 F6
Mitcham CR4, SW16 41 C6
New Malden KT4 38 F1
Old Woking GU22 90 B6
Oxshott KT22 74 C3
Purley CR8 79 E7
South Croydon CR2 61 F4
Woodmansterne SM7 78 F3
Manor Way The SM6 60 B6
Manor Wlk
1 Aldershot GU12 105 B1
Weybridge KT13 53 B5
Manor Wood Rd CR8 79 E6
Mansard Beeches
SW17 21 A3
Mansard Manor 8
SM2 59 C3
Manse Cl UB3 3 D8
Mansel Cl GU2 109 B6
Mansell Way CR3 100 D5
Mansel Rd SW19 19 F2
Mansfield Cl SL5 28 D7
Mansfield Cres RG12 27 B3
Mansfield Dr RH1 119 D6
Mansfield Ho CR2 61 D4
Mansfield Pl SL5 28 D8
Mansfield Rd
Chessington KT9 56 D5
South Croydon CR2 61 D4
Wokingham RG41 25 A5
Manship Rd CR4 41 A8
Mansion Apartments The
BR3 44 C5
Manston Cl SE20 43 C8
Manston Dr RG12 27 C3
Manston Gr KT2 17 D3
Manston Rd GU4 110 A5
Mantelmas Cotts
RH10 204 A4
Mantilla Rd SW17 21 A4
Mantlet Cl SW16 21 C1
Manton Ct SW20 39 B8
Manville Ct GU4 130 E1
Manville Gdns SW17 21 B5
Manville Rd SW17 21 B5
Manygate La TW17 34 C3
Many Gates SW12 21 B6
Maori Rd GU1 130 F8
Mapel Ct 8 RG12 27 F5
Maple Ave GU14 84 D5
Maple Cl
Ash Vale GU12 106 A7
Blackwater GU17 64 C5
Crawley RH11 181 C1
Hampton TW12 15 F2
Horsham RH12 218 A5
Mitcham CR4 41 B8
Whyteleafe CR3 80 F2
Maple Ct
Ashford TW15 14 D1
Carshalton SM1 59 D6
Catford SE6 24 B7
2 Croydon CR0 61 C6
Englefield Green TW20 11 B2
Kingston u T KT3 38 D6
12 West Norwood SW16 22 A3
Woking GU21 69 C3
Mapledale Ave CR0 62 B7
Maple Dr
Crowthorne RG45 45 C7
Maple Dr *continued*
East Grinstead RH19 186 A1
Great Bookham KT23 94 B2
Lightwater GU18 66 F8
Mapledrakes Cl GU6 175 E5
Mapledrakes Rd GU6 175 E5
Maple Gdns
Epsom KT17 76 E6
Stanwell TW15, TW19 13 E6
Maple Gr
Brentford TW8 6 B7
Guildford GU1 109 D3
Woking GU22 89 E6
Maple Gr Bsns Ctr TW4 4 C3
Maplegreen RH11 201 C5
Maplehatch Cl GU7 150 E2
Maple Ho
2 Kingston u T KT6 37 E4
10 Reigate RH2 118 F1
4 Richmond TW9 7 B6
Teddington KT1 17 C1
Maplehurst
2 Beckenham BR2 44 E7
Fetcham KT22 94 D4
Maplehurst Cl KT1 37 E5
Maple Ind Est TW13 15 A5
Maple Inf Sch KT6 37 D4
Mapleleaf Cl CR2 81 D8
Maple Leaf Cl
Biggin Hill TN16 83 D3
Farnborough GU14 84 F3
Maple Mews SW16 21 F3
Maple Pl KT17 77 D5
Maple Rd
Ashtead KT21 95 D8
Kingston u T KT6 37 D4
Penge SE20 43 C8
Redhill RH1 139 F5
Send Marsh GU23 91 A3
Whyteleafe CR3 80 F2
Maplestead Rd SW2 21 F8
Maples The
Banstead SM7 78 B5
Ottershaw KT16 51 C4
4 Teddington KT1 17 C1
Maplethorpe Rd CR7 42 B5
Maple Way
Feltham TW13 15 B5
Headley Down GU35 187 B6
Hooley CR5 99 B6
Maple Wlk
Aldershot GU12 126 D8
Belmont SM2 59 B1
Marble Hill Cl TW1 17 B8
Marble Hill Gdns TW1 17 B8
Marble Hill Ho* TW1 17 C8
Marbles Way KT20 97 D8
Marcheria Cl RG12 27 B3
Marches Rd RH12 197 E4
Marches The RH12 198 B5
Marchmont Ho 10
SW16 21 C3
Marchmont Rd
Richmond TW10 6 F2
Wallington SM6 60 C3
March Rd
9 Twickenham TW1 17 A8
Weybridge KT13 53 A5
Marchside Cl TW5 4 D6
Marcus Ct
Brentford TW8 6 E7
Woking GU22 69 F1
Marcuse Rd CR3 100 D4
Mardale GU15 66 C4
Mardell Rd CR0 43 D4
Marden Ave BR2 44 F3
Marden Cres CR0 41 F3
Marden Lodge Prim Sch
CR3 101 B6
Marden Rd CR0 41 F3
Mardens The RH11 201 B7
Mare Hill GU8 170 E5
Mare La GU8 172 C4
Marenello Ho KT24 92 E1
Mareschal Rd GU2 130 C7
Maresfield CR0 61 E7
Maresfield Ho GU4 110 D2
Mareth Cl GU11 105 B2
Marfleet Cl SM5 59 E8
Margaret Cl TW18 13 D2
Margaret Ho 6 SM1 59 B7
Margaret Lockwood Cl
KT1 37 F5
Margaret Rd GU1 130 C8
Margaret Roper RC Prim
Sch CR8 61 A1
Margaret Way CR8 100 B8
MARGERY 118 A6
Margery Gr KT20 117 E6
Margery Hall RH2 118 B5
Margery La KT20, RH2 118 A6
Margin Dr SW19 19 D4
Marham Gdns
Morden SM4 40 C3
Wandsworth SW17,
SW18 20 E7
Marian Ct 1 SM1 59 B5
Marian Lo 9 SW20 19 D1
Marian Rd CR4, SW16 41 C8
Marian Vian Prim Sch
BR3 43 E4
Maria Theresa Cl KT3 38 D4
Marie Carlile 2 GU22 70 A2
Mariette Way SM6 60 E2
Marigold Cl RG45 45 A6
Marigold Ct GU1 109 E4
Marigold Dr GU24 68 A4
Marigold Way CR0 43 D1
Marina Ave KT3 39 B4
Marina Cl KT16 33 C1
Marina Pl 9 KT1 37 D8
Marina Way TW11 17 D1
Mariner Gdns TW10 17 C5
Mariners Dr
Farnborough GU14 85 C6
Normandy GU3 107 B4
Marion Ave TW17 34 B4
Marion Ct SW17 20 E3
Marion Rd
Crawley RH10 202 B3
Thornton Heath CR0 42 D4
Marist Catholic Prim Sch
The KT14 70 F6
Marist Schs The SL5 29 D5
Maritime Ct KT19 76 D8
Marius Mans 3 SW17 21 A6
Marius Rd SW17 21 A6
Marjoram Cl
Farnborough GU14 84 B4
Guildford GU2 109 A5
Marjorie Fosters Way
GU24 87 D8
Marjory Kinnon Sch
TW14 3 E2
Marjory Pease Cotts
RH8 123 E5
Markedge La CR5, RH1,
RH2 98 F2
Markenfield Rd GU1 109 D1
Markenhorn GU7 150 D7
Market Field Rd 16
RH2 118 F1
Marketfield Way RH1 119 A1
Market Par
Croydon SE25 43 A5
3 Ewell KT17 57 F2
Feltham TW13 15 E6
Market Pl
Bracknell RG12 27 B7
Brentford TW8 6 C7
Kingston u T KT1 37 D7
Wokingham RG40 25 C5
Market Rd TW9 7 A4
Market Sq
9 Horsham RH12 217 C2
Reigate RH2 118 A1
Staines TW18 12 E4
Market St
Bracknell RG12 27 B7
Guildford GU1 130 D8
Market The SM1, SM5 40 C1
Markfield CR0 81 F8
Markfield Rd CR3 101 B2
Markham Ct
Beckenham BR3 44 B6
Camberley GU15 65 D6
Markham Ho 9 SE21 22 E4
Markham Rd RH5 178 C5
Markhole Cl TW12 15 F1
Mark Oak La KT22 94 A6
Marksbury Ave TW9 7 A4
Marks Ct SE6 24 A3
Marks Rd
Warlingham CR6 81 E1
Wokingham RG41 25 A8
Mark St RH2 118 B2
Markville Gdns CR3 101 A2
Mark Way GU7 150 B8
Markway The TW16 35 C7
Markwell Cl SE26 23 B4
Markwick La GU8 172 C2
Marlang Ct BR3 44 D8
Marlborough Rd TW7,
TW8 6 B7
Marlborough 11 SW19 19 D7
Marlborough Cl
Crawley RH11 201 C2
Hersham KT12 54 D7
Horsham RH12 217 D5
Mitcham SW19 20 E2
Marlborough Cres UB3 3 D7
Marlborough Ct
Ashtead KT21 75 F1
6 Beckenham BR3 44 A8
7 Bromley BR1 24 F1
3 Croydon CR2 61 E6
Dorking RH4 136 B7
1 Wallington SM6 60 C3
Wokingham RG40 25 D7
Marlborough Dr KT13 53 C7
Marlborough Gdns
KT6 37 D2
Marlborough Hill
RH4 136 B7
Marlborough Ho
Richmond TW10 7 A2
Wimbledon SW19 19 D5
Marlborough Inf Sch
GU11 105 C7
Marlborough Mews
SM7 78 A4
Marlborough Pl RH12 217 C3
Marlborough Prim Sch
TW7 6 A6
Marlborough Rd
Ashford TW15 13 E3
Dorking RH4 136 B7
Feltham TW13 15 D6
Hampton TW12 16 A2
Mitcham SW19 20 E2
Richmond TW10 6 F1
South Croydon CR2 61 C3
Sutton SM1 59 A8

Marlborough Rd *continued*
Woking GU21 70 A3
Marlborough Rise GU15 65 E6
Marlborough Trad Est TW9 7 B6
Marlborough View GU14 84 C5
Marld The KT21 75 F1
Marler Rd SE23 23 F7
Marlesford Ct SM6 60 C6
Marles La RH14 214 C1
Marley Cl KT15 51 F4
Marley Combe Rd GU27 207 F4
Marley Croft TW18 12 E5
Marley Hanger GU27 208 A3
MARLEY HEIGHTS 208 A1
Marley La GU27 207 E4
Marley Rise RH4 136 A4
Marl Field Cl KT4 39 A1
Marlfield Ct KT3 38 F2
Marlin Cl TW16 14 E2
Marling Ct TW12 15 F2
Marlingdene Cl TW12 16 A2
Marlings Cl CR3 80 E2
Marlins Cl 3 SM1 59 C5
Marlow Cl SE20 43 B6
Marlow Cres TW1 5 F1
Marlow Ct RH10 201 D7
Marlow Dr SM3 58 D7
Marlowe Ct
Dulwich SE19 22 F3
6 Kingston u T KT2 17 D4
Marlowe Ho
Kingston u T KT1 37 D5
Wimbledon SW20 39 B8
Marlowe Lo CR0 62 E8
Marlowe Sq CR4 41 C5
Marlowe Way CR0 60 E8
Marlow Ho
Teddington TW11 17 A4
Wallington SM6 60 E7
Marlow Rd SE20, SE25 43 B7
Marlpit Ave CR5 79 E2
Marlpit Cl RH19 185 E4
Marlpit La CR5 79 E2
Marlyns Cl GU4 110 A4
Marlyns Dr GU4 110 A5
Marmion Ho 14 SW12 21 B8
Marmot Rd TW4 4 D4
Marncrest Ct
Hersham KT12 54 B5
Surbiton KT5 37 F4
Marnell Way TW4 4 D4
Marneys Cl KT18 76 A4
Marnfield Cres SW2 21 F7
Marnham Pl KT15 52 C6
Maroons Way SE6 24 A3
Marqueen Twrs SW16 21 F1
Marquis Ct
1 Kingston u T KT1 37 E5
Stanwell TW19 13 E7
Marriott Cl TW14 3 D1
Marriott Ho SE6 24 C4
Marriott Lodge Cl KT15 52 C6
Marrowbrook Cl GU14 85 A4
Marrowbrook La GU14 85 A3
Marrowells KT13 53 F7
Marryat Cl 8 TW3 4 F3
Marryat Pl SW19 19 E4
Marryat Rd SW19 19 E3
Marsault Ct 2 TW9 6 E3
Marshall Cl
Farnborough GU14 84 F7
Frimley GU16 66 D2
Hounslow TW4 4 F2
Sanderstead CR2 81 A6
Marshall Ho 5 KT3 38 E5
Marshall Par GU22 70 F4
Marshall Pl KT15 52 C2
Marshall Rd
Crawley RH10 202 C4
Farncombe GU7 150 E6
Sandhurst GU47 64 D6
Marshalls GU9 146 B8
Marshalls Cl KT19 76 C6
Marshall's Rd SM1 59 B6
Marsham Ct 19 SW19 19 D7
Marsh Ave
Epsom KT19 57 E1
Mitcham CR4 41 A7
Marsh Ct
Crawley RH11 201 B1
3 Merton SW19 40 C8
Marsh Farm Rd TW2 16 F7
Marshfields CE Inf Sch KT16 51 E4
Marshgate Prim Sch TW10 6 F2
Marsh La KT15 52 B6
Marsh View RH5 133 F4
Marshwood Rd GU18 67 D8
Marston KT19 76 C8
Marston Ave KT9 56 E4
Marston Ct KT12 35 C1
Marston Dr
Farnborough GU14 85 B7
Warlingham CR6 81 E1
Marston Ho 2 RH1 118 F1
Marston Rd
Farnham GU9 124 F2
Richmond TW11 17 B3
Woking GU21 69 B2
Marston Way
North Ascot SL5 28 E7
South Norwood SE19 22 C1
Martel Cl GU15 66 C7
Martell Rd SE21 22 D5
Martens Pl GU7 150 E6
Martin Cl
Crawley RH11 201 D8
Selsdon CR2 62 D1
Warlingham CR6 81 B3
Martin Cres CR0 42 A1
Martin Ct
Croydon CR0 61 E5
Lewisham SE12 24 F8
Merton SW19 20 A1
Martindale SW14 7 C2
Martindale Ave GU15 66 C4
Martindale Cl GU4 110 D3
Martindale Rd
Balham SW12 21 B8
Hounslow TW4 4 E4
Woking GU21 69 A1
Martineau Cl KT10 55 D6
Martineau Dr
Dorking RH4 136 B5
Isleworth TW1 6 B3
Martingale Cl TW16 35 A5
Martingale Ct GU11 104 E2
Martingales Cl TW10 17 D5
Martin Gr SM4, SW19 40 A6
Martin Ho 7 KT3 38 E5
Martin Rd GU2 109 A3
Martins Cl
Blackwater GU17 64 D4
Guildford GU1 110 C2
West Wickham BR4 63 D8
Martins Dr RG41 25 B7
MARTIN'S HERON 27 F6
Martin's Heron Sta RG12 27 F5
Martins La RG12 27 E6
Martins Pk GU14 84 D7
Martin's Rd BR2 44 F7
Martins The
Crawley Down RH10 204 C8
Forest Hill SE26 23 B3
Martins Wood GU8 170 E7
Martinsyde GU22 70 C2
Martin Way
Frimley GU16 65 E2
Merton SW19 , SW20, SM4 39 E6
Woking GU21 69 A1
Martlands Ind Est GU22 89 A4
Martlet Cnr RH12 214 D7
Martlets Cl RH12 217 C5
Martlets The RH10 201 E6
Marton Cl SE6 24 A5
Marts The RH12 214 D7
Martyns Pl RH19 206 A8
Martyr Rd GU1 130 D8
Martyrs Ave RH11 181 D1
MARTYR'S GREEN 92 E7
Martyrs La GU21 70 B7
Marvell Cl RH10 202 C8
Marwell Cl BR4 63 F8
Mary Adelaide Cl SW15 18 E5
Mary Ct 20 SM2 59 C3
Marydene Ct RG12 26 C7
Mary Drew Almshouses The TW20 11 D2
Marygold Ho TW3 5 C6
Maryhill Cl CR8 80 C2
Maryland Ct KT1 38 B7
Maryland Rd CR7 42 B8
Maryland Way TW16 35 A7
Marylebone Ho 16 RH1 118 F2
Marymount International Sch KT2 18 C1
Mary Rd GU1 130 C8
Mary Rose Cl TW12 36 A8
Mary's Terr TW1 17 A8
Mary Tates Cotts CR4 40 F5
Mary Vale GU7 150 D2
Marzena Ct TW3 5 C2
Masefield Ct 19 KT6 37 D2
Masefield Gdns RG45 45 B3
Masefield Rd
Crawley RH11 200 E3
Hampton TW13 15 F4
Masefield Way TW19 13 F7
Maskall Cl SW2 22 A7
Maskani Wlk 2 SW16 21 C1
Maskell Rd SW17 20 C5
Maskell Way GU14 84 D3
Mason Cl
East Grinstead RH19 185 E2
Hampton TW12 35 F8
Wimbledon SW20 39 D8
Mason Ct 3 SE19 22 F1
Masonic Hall Rd KT16 32 F3
Mason Rd
Crawley RH10 201 E4
Farnborough GU14 84 E6
Sutton SM1 59 B5
Mason's Ave CR0, CR9 61 C7
Mason's Bridge Rd RH1 140 C3
Masons Paddock RH4 115 A1
Mason's Pl CR4 40 F8
Mason's Yd SW19 19 D3
Mason Way GU11 126 B7
Massetts Rd RH6 161 A2
Massingberd Way SW17 21 B4
Master Cl RH8 122 E6
Masters Cl SW16 21 C2
Mastin Ho SW18 20 A7
Maswell Park Cres TW3 5 C2
Maswell Park Rd TW3 5 C3
Matcham Ct 15 TW1 6 D1
Matham Rd KT8 36 D4
Mathews Cl GU14 105 E8
Mathew Terr GU11 105 C2
Mathias Cl KT18 76 C6
Mathisen Way SL3 1 E6
Mathon Ct GU1 109 F1
Matilda Cl SE19 22 D1
Matlock Cres SM3 58 E6
Matlock Gdns SM3 58 E6
Matlock Pl SM3 58 E6
Matlock Rd CR3 100 E6
Matlock Way KT3 38 D8
Mattew Ct TW15 13 E5
Matthew Arnold Cl
Cobham KT11 73 A5
Staines TW18 13 C2
Matthew Arnold Sch The TW18 13 C2
Matthew Ct CR4 41 D4
Matthew Rd GU11 125 E8
Matthews Ct SL5 29 D5
Matthews Dr RH10 202 C3
Matthew's Gdns CR0 82 D8
MATTHEWSGREEN 25 A8
Matthewsgreen Rd RG41 25 A8
Matthews La TW18 12 F4
Matthews Rd GU15 65 C8
Matthew's St RH2 139 A5
Matthey Pl RH10 182 D1
Matthias Ct 13 TW10 6 E1
Maultway Cl GU15 66 B8
Maultway Cres GU15 66 B8
Maultway Ct KT19 57 D5
Maultway N GU15 47 B1
Maultway The GU15, GU16 66 D6
Maunsell Pk RH10 202 B6
Maureen Campbell Ct TW17 34 B4
Maurice Ave CR3 100 D5
Maurice Ct 3 TW8 6 D7
Mauveine Gdns TW3 5 A3
Mavery Ct 8 BR1 24 F1
Mavins Rd GU9 146 D8
Mavis Ave KT19 57 E5
Mavis Cl KT19 57 E5
Mawbey Rd KT16 51 D4
Mawson Cl SW20 39 E7
Mawson La W4 7 F8
Maxdata Ctr The RG12 27 A7
Maxine Cl GU47 45 B1
Maxton Wlk RH11 201 B2
Maxwell Cl CR0 41 E1
Maxwell Ct SE21 23 A7
Maxwell Dr KT14 71 C8
Maxwell Rd TW15 14 C2
Maxwell Way RH10 182 A1
Maybelle Cl RH5 157 D3
Mayberry Pl KT5 37 F2
Maybourne Cl SE26 23 B3
Maybourne Grange CR0 61 E8
Maybourne Rise GU22 89 D3
MAYBURY 70 C2
Maybury Bsns Ctr GU22 70 A2
Maybury Cl
Burgh Heath KT20 97 E8
Frimley GU16 85 D8
Maybury Ct
Beckenham BR3 23 F1
South Croydon CR2 61 B5
Woking GU22 70 B2
MAYBURY ESTATE 70 C3
Maybury Hill GU21, GU22 70 B2
Maybury Ho GU22 70 B2
Maybury Inf Sch GU21 70 A3
Maybury Rd GU21 70 A3
Maybury Rough GU22 70 B2
Maybury St SW17 20 E3
May Cl
Chessington KT9 56 F4
Godalming GU7 150 B2
2 Sandhurst GU47 64 D8
May Cotts CR5 98 B2
May Cres GU12 105 E1
Maycroft
2 Coney Hall BR2 44 F1
Reigate RH2 139 C7
Maycross Ave SM4 40 A5
May Ct 2 SW19 40 C8
Mayday Rd CR0, CR7 42 B3
Mayday University Hospl CR7 42 B3
Maydwell Ave RH13 215 C2
Mayefield Rd CR7 41 F4
Mayell Cl KT22 95 C4
Mayes Cl
Crawley RH10 202 C5
Warlingham CR6 81 D1
MAYES GREEN 176 E3
Mayes La RH12 197 F3
Mayfair Ave
New Malden KT4 39 A1
Twickenham TW2 16 C8
Mayfair Cl
Beckenham BR3 44 B8
Surbiton KT6 37 E1
Mayfair Ct
Beckenham BR3 44 B8
7 Croydon CR0 61 F8
13 Merton SW19 19 E1
Mayfield
Crawley RH10 202 D6
Dormansland RH7 165 A1
Hersham KT12 54 C6
6 Leatherhead KT22 95 C6
Rowledge GU10 145 F3
Mayfield Ave KT15 52 C1
Mayfield Cl
Ashford TW15 14 B2
Badshot Lea GU9 126 B6
Hersham KT12 54 A6
Hinchley Wood KT7 37 B1
Penge SE20 43 B8
Redhill RH1 140 A3
Weybridge KT15 52 C1
Mayfield Cres CR7 41 F5
Mayfield Ct
11 Bromley BR2 44 F5
Redhill RH1 139 F4
Sutton SM2 59 C3
Mayfield Gdns
Egham TW18 12 F2
New Haw KT15 52 B1
Walton-on-T KT12 54 A6
Mayfield Gn KT23 114 A8
Mayfield Ho KT13 53 A5
Mayfield Light Ind Est SL4 9 B5
Mayfield Rd
Camberley GU15 65 B1
Farnborough GU14 84 F7
Hersham KT12 54 A6
Merton SW19 39 F8
South Croydon CR2 61 D2
Sutton SM2 59 D4
Weybridge KT13 52 F5
Mayflower Cl RH10 202 D5
MAYFORD 89 D5
Mayford Cl
Balham SW12 20 F8
Penge BR3 43 D6
Woking GU22 89 D5
Mayford Ctr The GU22 89 C5
Mayford Gn GU22 89 C5
Mayford Rd SW12 21 A8
May Gate Ave KT2 37 D8
Mayhurst Ave GU22 70 C3
Mayhurst Cl GU22 70 C3
Mayhurst Cres GU22 70 C3
Mayhurst Mews GU22 70 C3
Maynard Cl RH10 183 C4
Maynard Ct TW18 13 A4
Maynooth Gdns CR4 40 F2
Mayo Rd
Thornton Heath CR0 42 D4
Walton-on-T KT12 35 A2
Mayow Rd SE23, SE26 23 D4
Maypole Rd
Ashurst Wood RH19 206 E6
East Grinstead RH19 185 D2
May Rd TW2 16 E7
Mayroyd Ave KT6 57 A8
Mays Cl KT13 52 F1
Mays Cnr GU23 90 D3
Maysfield Rd GU23 90 D4
Mays Gr GU23 90 D4
MAY'S GREEN 92 F7
May's Hill Rd BR2 44 E6
Mays Rd
Teddington TW11 16 D3
Wokingham RG40 25 E6
Maytree Cl GU1 109 C5
Maytree Ct CR4 41 A6
Maytrees GU21 68 C2
Maytree Wlk SW2 22 A6
Maywater Cl CR2 80 D8
Maywood Cl BR3 24 B1
Maywood Dr GU15 66 A7
Maze Rd TW9 7 A7
Meachen Ct RG40 25 C6
Mead Ave RH1 140 A1
Mead Cl
Cranleigh GU6 174 E2
Egham TW20 12 B2
Redhill RH1 119 A4
Mead Cotts GU7 151 A6
Mead Cres
Carshalton SM1 59 E6
Little Bookham KT23 94 A2
Meadcroft Ho 5 KT3 38 E2
Mead Ct
Addlestone KT15 52 D7
Egham TW20 12 C2
Woking GU21 68 E3
Meade Cl W4 7 A8
Meade Ct
Bagshot GU19 47 F3
Walton on t H KT20 97 A3
Mead End KT21 75 F3
Meades Cl RH7 165 B1
Meades The RH7 165 A1
Meadfoot Rd SW16 41 C8
Mead Ho TN16 83 D3
Meadhurst Pk TW16 14 E2
Meadhurst Rd KT16 33 B1
Mead Inf Sch The KT19 57 F6
Mead La
Chertsey KT16 33 C1
Farnham GU9 125 B2
Meadlands Dr TW10 17 D6
Meadlands Prim Sch TW10 17 C4
Meadow App RH10 183 A3
Meadow Ave CR0 43 D3
Meadowbank KT5 37 F3
Meadow Bank
East Horsley KT24 112 E8
Farnham GU9 125 B1
Guildford GU1 109 C3
Meadowbank Gdns TW4, TW5 4 B6
Meadowbank Rd GU18 48 C1
Meadow Bglws GU4 131 B3
Meadowbrook RH8 122 D5
Meadowbrook Cl SL3 1 F6
Meadowbrook Ct TW7 5 F3
Meadow Brook Ind Ctr RH10 182 A1
Meadowbrook Rd RH4 136 A7
Meadow Cl
Ash Vale GU12 85 F1
Blackwater GU17 64 D4
Catford SE6 24 A3
Copthorne RH10 183 A3
Farncombe GU7 150 E7
Hersham KT12 54 F6
Hinchley Wood KT10 55 F7
Horsham RH12 218 A5
Milford GU8 150 A1
Purley CR8 79 D6
Richmond TW10 17 E7
Sutton SM1 59 C8
Twickenham TW4 16 A8
West Barnes SW20 39 C5
Meadow Cotts GU24 67 F7
Meadowcroft Cl
Crawley RH11 200 F5
East Grinstead RH19 185 C2
Meadow Croft Cl RH6 182 C8
Meadowcroft Com Inf Sch KT16 51 F7
Meadow Ct
East Grinstead RH19 185 E2
Epsom KT18 76 C6
Farnborough GU14 84 F4
Staines TW18 12 E5
Meadow Dr GU23 90 F4
Meadow Farm La RH12 217 F7
Meadow Gate KT21 75 E2
Meadow Gate Ave GU14 84 F1
Meadow Gdns TW18 12 D3
Meadow Hill
New Malden KT3 38 E3
Purley CR5, CR8 79 C6
Meadow Ho
Blackwater GU17 64 E4
Guildford GU4 110 D2
Meadow La KT22 94 C5
Meadowlands
Cobham KT11 73 A6
Crawley RH11 201 C6
Oxted RH8 123 A1
West Clandon GU4 111 B5
Meadowlea Cl UB7 2 D8
Meadow Pl 1 W4 7 E7
Meadow Rd
Ashford TW15 14 D3
Ashtead KT21 75 E2
Beckenham BR2 44 E7
Carshalton SM1 59 E5
Claygate KT10 55 E4
Farnborough GU14 85 B7
Feltham TW13 15 E6
Guildford GU4 110 A5
Merton SW19 20 C1
Wentworth GU25 30 E4
Wokingham RG41 25 A5
Meadow Rise
Coulsdon CR5 79 D6
Knaphill GU21 68 C2
Meadows Bsns Pk The GU17 64 E4
Meadows End TW16 35 A8
Meadowside
Great Bookham KT23 94 A4
Horley RH6 161 B4
Twickenham TW1 17 D8
Walton-on-T KT12 54 C8
Meadowside Pk (Mobile Homes) RH7 164 C6
Meadowside Rd SM2 58 E2
Meadows Leigh Cl KT13 53 C7
Meadows The
Ash GU12 106 B2
Churt GU10 167 F1
Guildford GU2 130 C6
Meadows The GU47 64 E5
Meadows The CR6 81 E2
Meadow Stile CR0, CR9 61 C7
Meadowsweet Cl KT3 39 C5
Meadow The RH10 183 A3
Meadow Vale GU27 208 A6
Meadow Vale Prim Sch RG42 26 F8
Meadowview
Shepperton TW17 34 C2
Stanwell TW19 1 F2
Meadow View
Chertsey KT16 33 C1
Smallfield RH6 162 C3
Meadow View Cotts TW17 34 B3
Meadowview Rd
Catford SE6 24 A3
West Ewell KT19 57 E2
Meadow View Rd CR7 42 B4
Meadow Way
Addlestone KT15 52 B6

Meadow Way *continued*
Aldershot GU12 105 F3
Blackwater GU17 64 C5
Bracknell RG42 27 A8
Burgh Heath KT20 77 E2
Chessington KT9 56 E5
Great Bookham KT23 94 B4
Reigate RH2 139 B5
Rowledge GU10 145 F3
West End GU24 67 F6
West Horsley KT24 92 D2
Wokingham RG41 25 A5
Meadow Waye TW5 4 E7
Meadow Wlk
Hackbridge SM6 60 B7
Walton on t H KT20 97 B3
West Ewell KT17, KT19 57 F3
Wokingham RG41 25 A6
Mead Pl
Smallfield RH6 162 C3
Thornton Heath CR0 42 C1
Mead Rd
Caterham CR3 100 F4
Cranleigh GU6 174 E3
Crawley RH10 201 F7
Hersham KT12 54 E6
Hindhead GU26 188 F4
Richmond TW10 17 C5
Meadrow GU7 150 F6
Meadrow Ct GU7 151 A6
Meadside
4 Epsom KT18 76 D6
7 Woking GU22 69 F1
Meadside Cl BR3 43 E8
Meads Prim Sch RH19 205 E7
Meads Rd GU1 110 B1
Meads The
Cheam SM3 58 E7
East Grinstead RH19 205 E7
Haslemere GU27 207 F6
Weybridge KT13 53 D4
Meadsview Ct 3 GU14 85 B4
Mead The
Ashtead KT21 95 E8
Beckenham BR3 44 C8
Dorking RH4 136 C4
Farnborough GU14 85 B3
Wallington SM6 60 D4
West Wickham BR4 44 D1
Meadvale RH12 216 F2
MEAD VALE 139 D6
Meadvale Hts RH1 139 D7
Meadvale Rd CR0 43 A3
Meadway
Ashford TW15 14 A4
Beckenham BR3 44 C8
Effingham KT24 113 E7
Epsom KT19 76 C7
Esher KT10 55 B2
Frimley GU16 65 F2
Haslemere GU27 207 F6
Oxshott KT22 74 E5
Staines TW18 13 A1
Tolworth KT5 38 C1
Twickenham TW2 16 D7
Warlingham CR6 81 C3
West Barnes SW20 39 C5
Mead Way
Coulsdon CR5 79 F1
Croydon CR0 62 E8
Guildford GU4 110 C6
Hayes BR2 44 F3
Meadway Cl TW18 13 A1
Meadway Dr
New Haw KT15 52 C3
Woking GU21 69 D4
Meadway The RH6 161 C3
Meaford Way SE20 23 B1
Meare Cl KT20 97 D4
MEATH GREEN 160 F5
Meath Green Ave RH6 160 F5
Meath Green Inf Sch RH6 160 F5
Meath Green Jun Sch RH6 160 F5
Meath Green La RH1, RH6 160 E6
Meath Sch KT16 51 D3
Medawar Rd GU2 129 D8
Medcroft Gdns SW14 7 C3
Mede Cl TW19 11 D7
Mede Ct TW18 12 E5
Medefield KT22 94 D3
Medfield St SW15 19 B8
Medhurst Cl GU24 49 F2
Medina Ave KT10 55 E7
Medina Sq KT19 57 A2
Medlake Rd TW20 12 C2
Medland Cl CR4 41 A1
Medlar Cl
Crawley RH11 181 C1
Guildford GU1 109 C3
Medlar Dr GU17 64 F3
Medlars Ct RH5 158 B1
Medora Rd SW2 21 F8
Medway RH10 204 A5
Medway Cl CR0 43 C3
Medway Ct
Horsham RH12 218 B5
South Norwood SE25 42 E4
Medway Dr
East Grinstead RH19 205 D6
Farnborough GU14 84 E7
Medway Ho 6 KT2 37 D8
Medway Rd RH11 200 F5
Medwin Wlk 5 RH12 217 C2
Meers Ct SW20 39 C8
Melbourne Cl SM6 60 C5
Melbourne Ct
Penge SE20 23 A1
Twickenham TW2 16 D7
Melbourne Ho SE25 42 F5
Melbourne Mews SE6 24 C8
Melbourne Rd
Merton SW19 40 A8
Teddington TW11 17 C2
Wallington SM6 60 C5
Melbourne Way RH12 217 F5
Melbury Cl
Chertsey KT16 33 A2
Claygate KT10 56 B4
West Byfleet KT14 71 A5
Melbury Gdns SW20 39 B8
Melbury Ho TW2 16 D6
Meldone KT3 38 D1
Meldone Cl KT5 38 B3
Meldrum Cl RH8 123 A3
Melfield Gdns SE6 24 C3
Melford Cl KT9 56 F5
Melford Ct
Dulwich SE22 23 A8
2 Sutton SM2 59 C3
Melford Rd SE21, SE22 23 A7
Melfort Ave CR7 42 B6
Melfort Rd CR7, SW16 42 B6
Meliot Rd SE6 24 D6
Melksham Cl
Horsham RH13 217 E1
Sandhurst GU47 45 D1
Meller Cl CR0 60 E7
Mellersh Hill Rd GU5 152 C6
Mellish Ct KT6 37 E3
Mellison Rd SW17 20 E3
Melliss Ave TW9 7 B6
Mellor Cl KT12 35 F2
Mellor Ct 2 SW19 20 C1
Mellor Ho 2 SE21 22 E4
Mellow Cl SM7 78 C5
Mellows Rd SM6 60 D5
Melody Rd TN16 83 C1
Melrose RG12 27 B1
Melrose Ave
Farnborough GU14 84 C5
Mitcham CR4 21 B1
Thornton Heath SW16 42 A6
Twickenham TW2 16 B8
Wimbledon SW19 20 A5
Melrose Cl GU14 84 C5
Melrose Gdns
Hersham KT12 54 C5
Kingston u T KT3 38 D6
Melrose Rd
Barnes SW13 7 F5
Biggin Hill TN16 83 C3
Coulsdon CR5 79 B4
Merton SW19 40 A8
Weybridge KT13 53 A5
Melrose Sch CR4 40 E6
Melrose Tudor SM6 60 E5
Melsa Rd SM4 40 C3
Melton Ct
11 Croydon CR0 61 F8
Sutton SM2 59 C3
2 Twickenham TW1 17 B8
Melton Fields KT19 57 D2
Melton Pl KT19 57 D2
Melton Rd RH1 119 C5
Melville Ave
Frimley GU16 65 F1
South Croydon CR0, CR2 61 F5
Wimbledon SW20 19 A1
Melville Ct
Guildford GU2 130 C6
West Byfleet KT14 71 E7
Melvin Ct 11 TW9 7 A6
Melvin Rd SE20 43 C8
Melvinshaw KT22 95 C6
Membury Cl GU16 86 A7
Membury Wlk RG12 27 F5
Memorial Cl
Heston TW5 4 F8
Oxted RH8 122 D8
Memory Cotts KT20 97 E8
Mendip Cl
Forest Hill SE26 23 C4
Harlington UB3 3 D7
North Cheam KT4 58 C8
Mendip Ct CR0 61 E5
Mendip Rd
Bracknell RG12 27 E4
Farnborough GU14 84 E7
Mendip Wlk RH11 201 B6
Menin Way GU9 125 D1
Menin Wks CR4 40 F7
Menlo Gdns SE19 22 D1
Mennis Ho SM5 59 E8
Meon Cl
Farnborough GU14 84 D6
Tadworth KT20 97 B5
Meon Ct TW7 5 E5
Meopham Rd CR4, SW16 41 C8
Merantun Way SW19 40 C8
Mercer Cl
Crawley RH10 202 C3
Thames Ditton KT7 36 F2
Mercer Rd RH12 217 C8
Mercers Park Ctry Pk* RH1 119 E4
Merchants Cl
Croydon SE25 43 A5
Knaphill GU21 68 C2
Merchiston Rd SE6 24 D6
Mercia Ct SE22 23 A7
Mercia Ho TW15 34 C8
Mercia Wlk 8 GU21 69 F2
Mercury Cl RH11 200 E3
Mercury Ctr TW14 4 A2
Merebank RH5 157 D4
Merebank La CR0 60 F5
Mere Cl SW15, SW19 19 D8
Meredith Ct KT1 37 F7
Mere End CR0 43 D2
Merefield KT18 97 D8
Merefield Gdns KT20 97 D8
Mere Rd
Oatlands Park KT13 53 D7
Shepperton TW17 34 B3
Walton on t H KT20 97 B4
Mereside Pk TW15 14 C4
Meretune Ct SM4 39 F6
Merevale Cres SM4 40 C3
Mereway Industry TW2 16 E7
Mereway Rd TW2 16 E7
Merewood Gdns CR0 43 D2
Mereworth Cl BR2 44 F4
Mereworth Dr RH10 202 D8
Meridian Cl RH11 200 F3
Meridian Ct
Catford SE6 24 F7
Croydon CR0 61 A6
Sunningdale SL5 29 B1
Meridian Ctr CR0 63 E1
Meridian Gr RH6 161 C4
Meridian Way RH19 185 F3
Merland Cl KT20 97 C7
Merland Gn KT20 97 C7
Merland Rise KT18, KT20 97 C8
Merle Common Rd RH8 144 B7
Merlewood RG12 27 D4
Merlewood Cl CR3 100 D7
Merlin Cl
Brands Hill SL3 1 B8
Crawley RH11 200 E6
Mitcham CR4 40 E6
South Croydon CR0 61 E6
Wallington SM6 60 F4
Merlin Clove RG42 8 B2
Merlin Ct
Beckenham BR2 44 F5
Frimley GU16 65 D1
4 Mitcham CR4 40 E8
Sheerwater GU21 70 C5
Merlin Ctr RH11 181 D2
Merling Cl KT9 56 D5
Merlin Gr BR3 44 A4
Merlin Rd GU14 85 B2
Merlins Cl GU9 125 C1
Merlin Way
East Grinstead RH19 186 A3
Farnborough GU14 84 D3
Merrick Ho RH2 118 C1
Merricks Ct SW14 7 B3
Merrilands Rd KT4 39 C1
Merrilyn Cl KT10 56 A4
Merrin Hill CR2 80 E8
Merritt Gdns KT9 56 C4
Merrivale Gdns GU21 69 C2
MERROW 110 C2
Merrow Bsns Pk GU4 110 D4
Merrow CE Inf Sch GU4 110 D3
Merrow Chase GU1 110 D1
Merrow Common Rd GU4 110 D4
Merrow Copse GU1 110 B2
Merrow Croft GU1 110 C2
Merrow Ct
Guildford GU1 110 D1
Mitcham CR4 40 D7
Merrow Grange GU1 110 C1
Merrow Ho GU4 110 D2
Merrow La GU4 110 C5
Merrow Pl GU4 110 D3
Merrow Rd SM2 58 D2
Merrow St GU4 110 D2
Merrow Way CR0 63 C4
Merrow Woods GU1 110 B3
Merryacres GU8 170 E6
Merryfield Dr RH12 217 A3
Merryhill Rd RG42 27 B8
Merryhills Cl TN16 83 D3
Merry Hills La RH14 213 A5
Merrylands KT16 51 E7
Merrylands Ct KT23 93 F4
Merrylands Farm
Great Bookham KT23 94 A3
Little Bookham KT23 93 F3
Merrylands Rd KT23 93 F3
Merryman Dr RG45 45 A7
Merrymeet SM7 78 F5
Merryweather Ct 1 KT3 38 E4
Merrywood 7 KT22 95 C6
Merrywood Gr KT20 117 E5
Merrywood Pk
Frimley GU15 65 F4
Reigate RH2 118 B3
Merrywood Pk (Mobile Home Pk) KT20 116 B5
Merryworth Cl GU12 105 F1
Mersham Pl
Penge SE20 43 B8
South Norwood CR7 42 D7
Mersham Rd CR7 42 D7
MERSTHAM 119 D7
Merstham Prim Sch RH1 119 C6
Merstham Rd RH1 120 A5
Merstham Sta RH1 119 C7
MERTON 40 B8
Merton KT18 97 D8
Merton Abbey Mills SW19 40 C8
Merton Abbey Prim Sch SW19 40 B8
Merton Cl GU47 45 F2
Merton Coll SM4 39 F4
Mertonford RG40 25 D5
Merton Gdns KT20 97 D8
Merton Hall Gdns SW20 39 E8
Merton Hall Rd SW19, SW20 39 E8
Merton High St SW19 20 C1
Merton Ho
2 New Malden KT3 38 F4
Wandsworth SW18 20 A7
Merton Ind Pk SW19 40 C8
Merton Lo SW16 21 E3
Merton Mans SW20 39 D7
MERTON PARK 40 A7
Merton Park Par SW19 39 F8
Merton Park Prim Sch SW19 40 A7
Merton Pl 9 SW19 20 C1
Merton Rd
Croydon SE25 43 A4
Merton SW19 20 B1
Wandsworth SW18 20 A7
Merton Road Ind Est SW18 20 A8
Merton Way
East Molesey KT8 36 C6
Leatherhead KT22 95 A8
Merton Wlk KT22 75 A1
Mervyn Rd TW17 34 C2
Messenger Cl RH11 201 A8
Messer Ct CR0 61 B6
Metana Ho RH10 182 A3
Metcalfe Wlk TW13 15 E4
Metcalf Rd TW15 14 B3
Metcalf Way RH11 181 D2
Meteor Way
Farnborough GU14 85 B1
Wallington SM6 60 E3
Metro Bsns Ctr The SE26 23 F3
Metro Ind Ctr TW7 5 E5
Metropolis Apartments 5 SW12 21 B7
Metro The 4 GU21 69 E2
Meudon Ave GU14 85 B3
Meudon Ct KT6 37 D4
Mews Ct RH19 205 F6
Mewsend TN16 83 D1
Mews The
Banstead SM7 78 B4
11 Beckenham BR3 44 A8
Broadbridge Heath RH12 216 D4
Dunsfold GU8 192 F5
6 Farnham GU9 125 B2
Guildford GU1 130 C8
Hampton TW12 16 C2
Meyer Ho 2 SW12 21 B8
Meyrick Cl GU21 68 E3
Meyrick Ct 4 CR7 42 A3
Mezel Hill Cotts SL4 10 C3
Miall Wlk SE26 23 E4
Michael Cres RH6 161 A1
Michael Fields RH18 206 E2
Michael Hall Sch RH18 206 D1
Michael La GU2 109 B6
Michaelmas Cl SW20 39 C6
Michael Rd SE25 42 E6
Michaelson Ho 4 SE21 22 E4
Micheldever Way RG12 27 F4
Michelet Cl GU18 48 B1
Michelham Gdns
Burgh Heath KT20 97 C7
Twickenham TW1 16 F5
Michell Cl RH12 217 A2
Michels Almshouses 9 TW10 6 E2
Michelsdale Dr 4 TW9 6 E3
Michel's Row 3 TW9 6 E3
Micklefield Ct 2 CR0 42 B3
Micklefield Sch RH2 118 A2
MICKLEHAM 115 C7
Mickleham Downs RH5 95 D1
Mickleham Dr KT22 95 C1
Mickleham Gdns SM3 58 E4
Mickleham Hall RH5 115 C7
Mickleham Way CR0 63 D3
Mickle Hill GU47 45 A1
Midas Metro Ctr SM4 39 D2
Middle Ave GU9 146 D8
MIDDLE BOURNE 146 C7
Middle Bourne La GU10 146 C7
Middle Church La 20 GU9 125 B2
Middle Cl
Coulsdon CR5 100 A7
Ewell KT17 76 E7
Frimley GU15 66 C6
Middle Farm Cl KT24 113 D8
Middle Farm Pl KT24 113 D8
Middlefield
Farnham GU9 146 A7
Horley RH6 161 C4
Middlefield Cl GU9 146 A8
Middlefields CR0 62 E2
Middle Gn
Brockham RH3 137 B7
Staines TW18 13 D1
Middle Gordon Rd GU15 65 D5
Middle Green Cl 3 KT5 37 F3
Middle Hill
Aldershot GU11 105 A3
Englefield Green TW20 11 D3
Middle La
Ewell KT17 76 E7
Teddington TW11 16 F2
Middlemarch GU8 170 E5
Middlemead Cl KT23 94 A2
Middlemead Rd KT23 93 F2
Middle Mill KT5 37 F6
Middlemoor Rd GU16 85 E8
Middle Old Pk GU9 124 F4
Middle Rd
Leatherhead KT22 95 B6
Mitcham SW16 41 D7
Middle Row 1 RH19 205 F8
Middlesex Ct KT15 52 C6
Middlesex Ho 4 SE20 23 C1
Middlesex Rd CR4 41 E4
Middle St
Brockham RH3 137 C5
Croydon CR0, CR9 61 C7
7 Horsham RH12 217 C2
Shere GU5 133 A4
Middleton Gdns GU14 84 E6
Middleton Rd
Camberley GU15 65 F7
Downside KT11 93 C8
Epsom KT19 57 D1
Horsham RH12 217 A2
Morden SM4, SM5 40 D2
Middleton Way RH11 200 E5
Middleview Dr GU3 107 D4
Middle Way SW16 41 D7
Midgarth Cl KT22 74 D6
Midgley Rd RH10 201 F8
Midholm Rd CR0 62 E8
MID HOLMWOOD 136 B1
Mid Holmwood La RH5 136 B1
Midhope Cl GU22 89 E8
Midhope Gdns 5 GU22 89 E8
Midhope Rd GU22 89 E8
Midhurst SE26 23 C2
Midhurst Ave CR0 42 A2
Midhurst Cl RH11 201 A7
Midhurst Rd GU27 208 B5
Midleton Cl GU8 149 F2
Midleton Industrial Estate Rd GU2 109 B2
Midleton Rd
Guildford GU2 109 A2
Guildford GU2 109 B2
Kingston u T KT3 38 C7
Midmoor Rd
Streatham SW12 21 C7
Wimbledon SW19 39 E8
Mid St
Nutfield RH1 119 F1
South Nutfield RH1 140 F7
Midsummer Apartments 14 SM2 59 A3
Midsummer Ave TW4 4 F3
Midsummer Wlk GU21 69 D3
Midway
Cheam SM3 39 F2
Walton-on-T KT12 54 B8
Midway Ave
Chertsey KT16 33 A6
Thorpe TW20 32 B6
Midway Cl TW19 13 B5
Miena Way KT21 75 D2
Mike Hawthorn Dr GU9 125 C3
Milbanke Ct RG12 26 F7
Milbanke Way RG12 26 F7
Milborne Rd RH10 202 C2
Milborough Cres SE12 24 E8
Milbourne La KT10 55 C5
Milbourne Lodge Jun Sch KT10 55 C4
Milbourne Lodge Senior Sch KT10 55 D4
Milbrook KT10 55 C4
Milburn Ho SW20 39 B7
Milburn Wlk KT18 76 E4
Milcombe Cl 5 GU21 69 B1
Milden Cl GU16 86 A6
Milden Gdns GU16 85 F6
Mile Path GU22 89 B7
Mile Rd
Carshalton CR4, SM6 41 A1
Wallington CR0, CR4, CR9, SM6 41 C1
Miles Ct CR9 61 B8
MILES GREEN 68 A2
Miles La
Cobham KT11 73 E6
South Godstone RH9 142 F7
Tandridge RH8 143 A7
Miles Pl GU18 66 F7
Miles Rd
Ash GU12 106 B3
Epsom KT19 76 D7
Mitcham CR4 40 E6
Miles's Hill RH5 155 C3

Milestone Cl
Ripley GU23 . . . . **91** B5
Sutton SM2 . . . . **59** D3
Milestone Ct TW7 . . . . **6** A6
Milestone Dr CR8 . . . . **79** F5
Milestone Rd SE19 . . . . . . **22** F2
MILFORD **149** E1
Milford By Pass Rd
GU8 . . . . **149** D2
Milford Ct RH5 . . . . **157** C6
Milford Gdns CR0 . . . . . . **43** D4
Milford Gr SM1 . . . . **59** C6
Milford Heath Rd
GU8 . . . . **170** E8
Milford Ho
Milford GU8 . . . . **150** A1
1 Woking GU22 . . . . **70** B2
Milford Hospl GU7 . . . . **171** C8
Milford Lo TW1 . . . . **170** F8
Milford Mews SW16 . . . . . **21** F5
Milford Rd GU8 . . . . **148** E4
Milford Sta GU8 . . . . . . **171** A7
Milkhouse Gate 2
GU1 . . . . **130** D7
Milking La
Biggin Hill BR6 . . . . **83** E7
Biggin Hill, Leaves Green
BR2 . . . . **83** D8
Millais RH13 . . . . **218** A3
Millais Cl RH11 . . . . **200** F2
Millais Cres KT19 . . . . . . **57** E5
Millais Ct RH13 . . . . **218** A4
Millais Rd KT3 . . . . **38** E2
Millais Sch RH13 . . . . . . **217** F2
Millais Way KT19 . . . . . . **57** C6
Millan Cl KT15 . . . . **52** B1
Milland Ho 11 SW15 . . . . . **19** A7
Millbank SM6 . . . . **60** D5
Millbank The RH11 . . . . . **200** F6
Mill Bay La RH12 . . . . . . **217** B1
Millbottom La RH5 . . . . . **157** D7
Millbourne Rd TW13 . . . . . **15** E4
MILLBRIDGE **146** D1
Millbrook
Guildford GU1 . . . . **130** D7
Oatlands Park KT13 . . . . . **53** E6
Millbrook Way SL3 . . . . . .**1** E5
Mill Cl
Bagshot GU19 . . . . **47** D3
Carshalton SM5 . . . . **60** A8
East Grinstead RH19 . . . . **205** E4
Great Bookham KT23 . . . . **94** A3
Haslemere GU27 . . . . . . **207** E6
Horley RH6 . . . . **160** E4
Mill Cleave 11 KT14 . . . . . **71** A7
Mill Copse Rd GU27 . . . . **208** B4
Mill Cotts
East Grinstead RH19 . . . . **205** E7
Rudgwick RH12 . . . . **214** D5
Millcroft Ho SE6 . . . . **24** B4
Mill Ct SE19 . . . . **22** E1
Millennium Cotts
GU5 . . . . **132** C4
Millennium Ctr GU9 . . . . **125** A1
Millennium Ho RH11 . . . . **200** F3
Millennium Way RG12 . . . . **27** C8
Miller Cl CR4 . . . . **40** F2
Miller Ho
5 Penge SE20 . . . . **23** A1
9 Streatham SW2 . . . . . . **21** E8
Miller Rd
Guildford GU4 . . . . **110** C4
Mitcham SW19 . . . . **20** D2
Thornton Heath CR0 . . . . **42** A1
Millers Bsns Ctr RG41 . . . **25** A5
Millers Cl TW18 . . . . **13** B3
Millers Copse
Langley Vale KT18 . . . . . . **96** D8
Outwood RH1 . . . . **162** B7
Miller's Ct TW20 . . . . **12** D2
Millers Gate RH12 . . . . . **217** D6
Miller's La RH1 . . . . **162** C1
Millers Mead Ct SW19 . . . **20** D1
Millers Thumb RG12 . . . . **27** E8
Mill Farm Ave TW16 . . . . . **14** E1
Millfarm Bsns Pk TW4 . . . **15** E8
Mill Farm Cres TW4 . . . . . **15** E7
Mill Farm Rd RH13 . . . . . **218** A4
Millfield
Charlton TW16 . . . . **34** D8
Kingston u T KT1 . . . . . . **37** F6
Worcester Park KT4 . . . . . **57** F8
Mill Field GU19 . . . . **47** D3
Millfield La KT20 . . . . **98** A2
Millfield Rd TW4 . . . . **15** F7
Millfields Cres RH6 . . . . **180** D6
Millford GU21 . . . . **69** B2
Millford Ho 5 GU8 . . . . . **149** F1
Millgate Ct GU9 . . . . **125** D3
Mill Gdns SE26 . . . . **23** B5
Mill Gn CR4 . . . . **41** A2
Mill Green Bsns Pk
CR4 . . . . **41** A2
Mill Green Rd CR4 . . . . . . **41** A2
Millhedge Cl KT11 . . . . . . **73** E3
Mill Hill RH3 . . . . **137** B8
Mill Hill La RH3 . . . . **116** B1
Mill Ho SW19 . . . . **40** C5
Millholme Wlk GU15 . . . . . **66** C4
Mill House La KT16 . . . . . **32** B5
Millhouse Pl SE27 . . . . . . **22** B4
Milligan Ho SE23 . . . . **23** F7
Millins Cl GU47 . . . . **45** E1
Mill La
Ascot SL5 . . . . **30** A7

Mill La *continued*
Bracknell RG12 . . . . **26** F5
Bramley GU5 . . . . **151** F6
Byfleet KT14 . . . . **71** F6
Carshalton SM5 . . . . **60** A7
Chiddingfold GU8 . . . . . . **191** B3
Chilworth GU4, GU5 . . . . **131** F4
Copthorne RH10 . . . . . . **183** E3
Crawley RH11 . . . . **201** A8
Croydon CR0 . . . . **61** A7
Dorking RH4 . . . . **136** B8
Dunsfold GU8 . . . . **192** F4
Ewell KT17 . . . . **57** F2
Felbridge RH19 . . . . **184** E5
Felcourt RH7 . . . . **164** F2
Fetcham KT22 . . . . **95** A5
Forest Green RH5 . . . . . . **176** D7
Frensham GU10 . . . . **167** B7
Godalming GU7 . . . . **150** D4
Guildford GU1 . . . . **130** D7
Hookwood RH6 . . . . **160** D3
Horton SL3 . . . .**1** C4
Kingsley Green GU27 . . . . **208** C3
Merstham RH1 . . . . **119** D4
Ockham GU23 . . . . **91** D8
Oxted RH8 . . . . **122** F2
Parkgate RH5 . . . . **158** D5
Pirbright GU24 . . . . **87** E3
Shalford GU3 . . . . **130** C1
The Chart RH8 . . . . **123** F4
Thorpe TW20 . . . . **32** C5
Witley GU8 . . . . **170** F5
Mill Lane Trad Est CR0 . . . **60** F7
Millmead
Byfleet KT14 . . . . **71** F7
Guildford GU2 . . . . **130** C7
Wokingham RG41 . . . . . . **25** A7
Mill Mead TW18 . . . . **12** F4
Millmead Terr GU2 . . . . . **130** C7
Mill Pl KT1 . . . . **37** F6
Mill Plat TW7 . . . . **6** A5
Mill Plat Ave TW7 . . . . **6** A5
Millpond Cotts GU8 . . . . **172** D4
Millpond Ct KT15 . . . . . . **52** E5
Millpond Pl SM6 . . . . **60** A7
Mill Pond Rd GU20 . . . . . **48** B6
Mill Pool Ho GU7 . . . . . . **150** D4
Mill Prim Sch The
RH1 . . . . **201** A6
Mill Rd
Cobham KT11 . . . . **73** C4
Crawley RH10 . . . . **202** B7
Epsom KT17 . . . . **76** F7
Kingswood KT20 . . . . **97** D4
Merton SW19 . . . . **20** C1
South Holmwood RH5 . . . **157** D7
Thames Ditton KT10 . . . . . **55** A8
Twickenham TW2 . . . . **16** C6
Mill Reach GU4 . . . . **131** F5
Mill Ride SL5 . . . . **28** D8
Mills Cl RH13 . . . . **217** F1
Mills Ho GU12 . . . . **105** D3
Millside SM5 . . . . **59** F8
Millside Ct KT23 . . . . **94** A2
Millside Pl TW7 . . . .**6** B5
Mills Rd KT12 . . . . **54** C5
Mills Spur SL4 . . . . **11** B8
Mill St
Colnbrook SL3 . . . .**1** D7
Kingston u T KT1 . . . . . . **37** E6
Redhill RH1 . . . . **139** F8
Millstead Cl KT20 . . . . **97** B5
Mill Stream GU9 . . . . **125** E6
Millstream The GU27 . . . . **207** E5
Mill The KT13 . . . . **53** A7
Millthorpe Rd RH12 . . . . **217** F4
Mill Vale BR2 . . . . **44** F7
Millview Cl RH2 . . . . **118** D3
Mill View Cl KT17 . . . . **57** F3
Mill View Gdns CR0 . . . . . **62** D7
Millway RH2 . . . . **118** D1
Mill Way
East Grinstead RH19 . . . . **205** E7
Feltham TW14 . . . .**4** B2
Headley KT22, KT18 . . . . . **96** A2
Millwood RH10 . . . . **204** E5
Millwood Rd TW3, TW7 . . . . **5** C2
Milman Cl RG12 . . . . **28** A7
Milne Cl RH11 . . . . **200** E3
Milne Pk E CR0 . . . . **82** D8
Milne Pk W CR0 . . . . **82** D8
Milner App CR3 . . . . **101** A6
Milner Cl CR3 . . . . **101** A5
Milner Dr
Cobham KT11 . . . . **73** F7
Twickenham TW2 . . . . . . **16** D8
Milner Rd
Caterham CR3 . . . . **101** A6
Kingston u T KT1 . . . . . . **37** D6
Merton SW19 . . . . **40** B8
Morden CR4, SM4 . . . . . . **40** D4
South Norwood CR7 . . . . . **42** D6
Milnthorpe Rd W4 . . . . **7** D8
Milnwood Rd RH12 . . . . . **217** C3
Milton Ave
Carshalton SM1 . . . . **59** E6
Croydon CR0 . . . . **42** D7
Westcott RH4 . . . . **135** D6
Milton Cl
Bracknell RG12 . . . . **27** B3
Carshalton SM1 . . . . **59** D7
Horton SL3 . . . .**1** A4
Normandy GU3 . . . . **107** B3
Miltoncourt La RH4 . . . . . **135** E7
Milton Cres RH19 . . . . . . **205** C8
Milton Ct
Richmond KT2 . . . . **17** E4

Milton Ct *continued*
Twickenham TW2 . . . . **16** E5
Wokingham RG40 . . . . . . **25** B7
Milton Dr
Littleton TW17 . . . . **33** E5
Wokingham RG40 . . . . . . **25** B7
Milton Gdns
Epsom KT18 . . . . **76** E5
Stanwell TW19 . . . . **13** F7
Wokingham RG40 . . . . . . **25** B6
Milton Grange GU12 . . . . **106** A5
Milton Ho
12 Beckenham BR3 . . . . . . **24** A1
5 Kingston u T KT2 . . . . . **18** B2
Sutton SM1 . . . . **59** A7
Milton Lo TW1 . . . . **16** F8
Milton Mount RH10 . . . . . **182** D1
Milton Mount Ave
RH10 . . . . **202** D8
Milton Mount Prim Sch
RH10 . . . . **202** C8
Milton Rd
Addlestone KT15 . . . . **52** A4
Caterham CR3 . . . . **100** D6
Crawley RH10 . . . . **202** D7
Croydon CR0 . . . . **42** D2
Egham TW20 . . . . **11** F3
Hampton TW12 . . . . **36** B8
Horsham RH12 . . . . **217** C3
Mitcham CR4 . . . . **21** A1
Mortlake SW14 . . . .**7** D4
Sutton SM1 . . . . **59** A6
Wallington SM6 . . . . **60** D4
Walton-on-T KT12 . . . . . . **54** D7
Wimbledon SW19 . . . . . . **20** C2
Wokingham RG40, RG41 . . **25** B6
Miltons Cotts GU8 . . . . . **170** F5
Miltons Cres GU7 . . . . . . **150** B2
Milton St RH4 . . . . **135** D6
Milton Way KT13 . . . . **94** C2
Milverton Ho SE23 . . . . . . **23** E5
Milward Gdns RG12 . . . . . **26** C7
MIMBRIDGE **69** A7
Mina Rd SW19 . . . . **40** A8
Minard Rd SE6 . . . . **24** E7
Minchin Cl KT22 . . . . **95** A5
Mincing La GU24 . . . . **49** F2
Mindelheim Ave
RH19 . . . . **186** B2
Minden Rd
Cheam SM3 . . . . **58** F8
Penge SE20 . . . . **43** B8
Minehead Rd SW16 . . . . . . **21** F3
Minehurst Rd GU16 . . . . . . **85** F4
Minerva Cl TW19 . . . .**2** A2
Minerva Rd KT1 . . . . **37** F7
Minimax Cl TW14 . . . .**4** A1
Mink Ct TW4 . . . .**4** C5
Minley Cl GU14 . . . . **84** E4
Minley Ct RH2 . . . . **118** A2
Minley Rd
Blackwater GU17,
GU14 . . . . **84** A7
Farnborough GU14 . . . . . **84** D5
Minniedale KT5 . . . . **37** F4
Minorca Ave GU16 . . . . . . **66** E2
Minorca Rd
Frimley GU16 . . . . **66** E1
Weybridge KT13 . . . . **53** A6
Minshull Pl 24 BR3 . . . . . . **24** A1
Minstead Cl RG12 . . . . **27** F6
Minstead Gdns SW15 . . . . **18** F8
Minstead Way KT3 . . . . . . **38** E3
Minster Ave SM1 . . . . **59** A8
Minster Ct GU14 . . . . **85** D1
Minster Ct
Camberley GU15 . . . . **65** D7
Camberley, York Town
GU15 . . . . **64** F4
Minster Dr CR0 . . . . **61** E6
Minster Gdns KT8 . . . . . . **35** F5
Minsterley Ave TW16,
TW17 . . . . **34** E5
Minster Rd GU7 . . . . **150** E1
Minstrel Gdns KT5 . . . . . . **37** F5
Mint Gdns RH4 . . . . **136** A8
Mint La KT20 . . . . **118** A6
Mint Rd
Wallington SM6 . . . . **60** B6
Woodmansterne SM7 . . . . **78** C3
Mint St GU7 . . . . **150** D4
Mint The GU7 . . . . **150** D4
Mintwater Cl KT17 . . . . . . **58** A1
Mint Wlk
Croydon CR0, CR9 . . . . . . **61** C7
Knaphill GU21 . . . . **68** E2
Warlingham CR6 . . . . **81** D2
Miranda Wlk RH11 . . . . . . **200** E4
Mirfield Ct SE20 . . . . **43** A7
Misbrooks Green Rd
RH5 . . . . **178** E8
Missenden Cl TW14 . . . . . **14** F7
Missenden Gdns SM4 . . . . **40** C3
Mission Sq 13 TW8 . . . .**6** E8
Mistletoe Cl CR0 . . . . **43** D1
Mistley Ct 6 KT18 . . . . . . **76** D6
Mistley Gdns RH6 . . . . . . **160** D2
Misty's Field KT12 . . . . . . **35** C1
MITCHAM **40** F7
Mitcham Ct SW19 . . . . **47** B1
Mitcham Garden Village
CR4 . . . . **41** A4
Mitcham Ind Est CR4 . . . . **41** A8
Mitcham Junc CR4 . . . . . . **41** A4
Mitcham La SW16 . . . . **21** C3
Mitcham Pk CR4 . . . . **40** F5
Mitcham Rd
Camberley GU15 . . . . **47** A1

Mitcham Rd *continued*
Thornton Heath CR0,
CR9 . . . . **41** F3
Upper Tooting SW17 . . . . . **20** F3
Mitchell Ct
Horley RH6 . . . . **161** A2
Mortlake SW14 . . . .**7** E3
Mitchell Gdns RH13 . . . . **215** E3
Mitchells Cl GU4 . . . . **130** E3
Mitchells Cotts GU4 . . . . **131** E1
Mitchell's Pl SE21 . . . . . . **22** E8
Mitchells Rd RH10 . . . . . **201** F6
Mitchell's Row GU4 . . . . . **130** E2
Mitchley Ave CR2, CR8 . . . **80** D6
Mitchley Gr CR2 . . . . **81** A6
Mitchley Hill CR2 . . . . . . **80** F6
Mitchley View CR2 . . . . . . **81** A6
Mitford Cl KT9 . . . . **56** C4
Mitford Wlk 10 RH11 . . . . **201** A3
Mitre Cl
Shepperton TW17 . . . . . . **34** D3
Sutton SM2 . . . . **59** D3
Mitre Ct
10 Horsham RH12 . . . . . . **217** B2
Weybridge KT13 . . . . **53** A5
Mixbury Gr KT13 . . . . **53** D4
Mixnams La KT16 . . . . **33** A6
Mizen Cl KT11 . . . . **73** D5
Mizen Way KT11 . . . . **73** D4
Moat Ct
Ashtead KT21 . . . . **75** E2
Ottershaw KT16 . . . . **51** C4
Moated Farm Dr KT15 . . . . **52** C3
Moat Lo GU6 . . . . **174** D3
Moat Rd RH19 . . . . **185** E2
Moat Side TW13 . . . . **15** C4
Moats La RH1 . . . . **140** F3
Moat The KT3 . . . . **38** E8
Moat Wlk RH10 . . . . **202** C7
Moberly Rd SW4 . . . . **21** D8
Model Cotts
Mortlake SW14 . . . .**7** C4
Pirbright GU24 . . . . **87** D6
Moffat Ct
Upper Tooting SW17 . . . . . **20** E4
Wimbledon SW19 . . . . . . **20** A3
Moffat Rd
South Norwood CR7 . . . . . **42** D7
Upper Tooting SW17 . . . . . **20** F4
Moffatts Cl GU47 . . . . **64** A8
MOGADOR **117** D6
Mogador Cotts KT20 . . . . **117** D7
Mogador Rd KT20 . . . . . . **117** E7
Mogden La TW7 . . . .**5** F2
Moira Ct SW17 . . . . **21** A6
Moir Cl CR2 . . . . **62** A2
Mole Abbey Gdns KT8 . . . **36** B6
Mole Bsns Pk
Leatherhead KT22 . . . . . . **95** A6
Thames Ditton KT10 . . . . . **55** A8
Mole Cl
Crawley RH11 . . . . **201** B8
Farnborough GU14 . . . . . **84** D6
Mole Ct KT19 . . . . **57** C6
Mole Ho KT12 . . . . **54** E5
Molember Ct KT7 . . . . **36** E5
Molember Rd KT8 . . . . . . **36** E4
Mole Rd
Fetcham KT22 . . . . **94** D6
Hersham KT12 . . . . **54** D5
Moles Cl RG40 . . . . **25** D5
Molesey Ave KT12, KT8 . . . **35** F4
Molesey Bsns Ctr KT8 . . . **35** F4
Molesey Cl KT12 . . . . **54** E6
Molesey Dr SM3 . . . . **58** E7
Molesey Hospl KT8 . . . . . . **36** A4
Molesey Park Ave KT8 . . . **36** A4
Molesey Park Cl KT8 . . . . **36** A4
Molesey Park Rd KT8 . . . . **36** C4
Molesey Rd
East Molesey KT12 . . . . . . **35** E2
Hersham KT12 . . . . **54** D5
Molesham Cl KT8 . . . . **36** B6
Molesham Way KT8 . . . . . **36** B6
Moles Hill KT22 . . . . **74** D8
Molesley Rd
Hersham KT12 . . . . **54** E8
Walton-on-T KT12 . . . . . . **54** E8
Mole St RH5 . . . . **177** B5
Molesworth Rd KT11 . . . . **73** A6
Mole Valley Pl KT21 . . . . . **95** D8
Mole Valley Visitor
Information Ctr★
RH4 . . . . **136** B8
Moliner Ct 4 BR3 . . . . . . **24** A1
Molins Ct 4 RH11 . . . . . . **201** A3
Mollie Davis Ct SE19 . . . . **22** F2
Mollison Dr SM6 . . . . **60** E3
Mollison Sq SM6 . . . . **60** E3
Molloy Ct GU21 . . . . **70** A3
Molly Huggins Cl
SW12 . . . . **21** C8
Molly Millar Bridge
RG41 . . . . **25** B4
Molly Millars Cl RG41 . . . . **25** B4
Molly Millar's La RG41 . . . **25** A4
Molvic Ct 2 BR3 . . . . **43** F7
Molyneux Dr SW17 . . . . . . **21** B4
Molyneux Rd
Farncombe GU7 . . . . **150** F7
Weybridge KT13 . . . . **53** A5
Windlesham GU20 . . . . . . **48** D4
Monahan Ave CR8 . . . . . . **79** F8
Monarch Cl
Coney Hall BR4 . . . . **63** F6
Crawley RH11 . . . . **201** A3
East Bedfont TW14 . . . . . . **14** E8
Monarch Mews SW16 . . . . **22** A3

Monarch Par CR4 . . . . **40** F7
Monarch Pl SM1 . . . . **59** D5
Monaveen Gdns KT8 . . . . . **36** B6
Mondial Way UB7 . . . .**3** C7
Monet Ho 4 W4 . . . .**7** E7
Money Ave CR3 . . . . **100** E5
Money Rd CR3 . . . . **100** C5
Mongers La 11 KT17 . . . . . **57** F1
Monica Ct SW16 . . . . **21** D2
Monivea Rd BR3 . . . . **23** F1
Monkey Puzzle Rdbt
GU14 . . . . **84** E3
Monkleigh Rd SM4,
SW20 . . . . **39** E5
Monks Ave KT8 . . . . **35** F4
Monks Cl
Ascot SL5 . . . . **29** B3
Farnborough GU14 . . . . . **85** C4
Monks Cres
Addlestone KT15 . . . . **52** B5
Walton-on-T KT12 . . . . . . **35** B1
Monks Ct RH2 . . . . **118** B1
Monksdene Gdns SM1 . . . **59** B7
Monks Dr SL5 . . . . **29** B3
Monksfield RH10 . . . . **201** F7
Monks Gn KT22 . . . . **94** D6
Monkshanger GU9 . . . . . **125** E2
Monkshood Ct RG40 . . . . . **25** D7
Monks La
Oxted TN8 . . . . **144** E6
Rowhook RH5 . . . . **196** F5
Monks Manor RH5 . . . . . **196** F5
MONKS ORCHARD **43** E2
Monks Orchard Rd BR3,
CR0 . . . . **44** A2
Monks Orchard Sch
CR0 . . . . **43** D4
Monks Pl CR3 . . . . **101** B5
Monks Rd
Banstead SM7 . . . . **78** A3
Virginia Water GU25 . . . . . **31** D5
Monks Way
Beckenham BR3 . . . . **44** A3
Harmondsworth UB7 . . . . .**2** E8
Staines TW18 . . . . **13** D1
Monks' Well GU10 . . . . . . **147** C8
Monkswell La CR5 . . . . **98** B2
Monks Wlk SL5 . . . . **29** B3
Monk's Wlk
Farnham GU10, GU9 . . . . **146** F8
Reigate RH2 . . . . **118** B1
Monk Terr SE23 . . . . **23** F6
Monkton La GU9 . . . . **125** E5
Monkton Pk GU9 . . . . **125** F4
Monmouth Ave KT1 . . . . . . **17** C1
Monmouth Cl CR4,
SW16 . . . . **41** E5
Mono La TW13 . . . . **15** B6
Monro Dr GU2 . . . . **109** B4
Monroe Dr SW14 . . . .**7** B2
Monro Pl KT19 . . . . **57** A2
Mons Cl GU11 . . . . **105** E7
Monsell Gdns TW18 . . . . . **12** E3
Monson Rd RH1 . . . . **118** F4
Mons Wlk TW20 . . . . **12** C3
Montacute Cl GU14 . . . . . . **85** C4
Montacute Rd
Forest Hill SE23, SE6 . . . . **23** F8
Morden SM4 . . . . **40** D3
New Addington CR0 . . . . . **63** C2
Montague Ave CR2 . . . . . . **80** E7
Montague Cl
Camberley GU15 . . . . **65** B5
Lightwater GU18 . . . . **48** A1
Walton-on-T KT12 . . . . . . **35** A2
Wokingham RG40 . . . . . . **25** B7
Montague Dr CR3 . . . . . . **100** C5
Montague House Coll
RG40 . . . . **25** C6
Montague Rd
Hounslow TW3 . . . .**5** B4
Merton SW19 . . . . **20** B1
Richmond TW10 . . . .**6** E1
Thornton Heath CR0 . . . . . **42** B1
Montague Terr 7 BR2 . . . . **44** F5
Montagu Gdns SM6 . . . . . **60** C6
Montana Cl CR2 . . . . **61** D1
Montana Gdns
2 Beckenham SE6 . . . . . . **23** F3
7 Sutton SM1 . . . . **59** C5
Montana Rd
Upper Tooting SW17 . . . . . **21** A5
Wimbledon SW20 . . . . . . **39** C4
Montem Rd
Forest Hill SE23 . . . . **23** F8
New Malden KT3 . . . . **38** E5
Montford Rd TW16 . . . . . . **35** A5
Montfort Pl SW19 . . . . **19** D7
Montfort Rise RH1 . . . . . **139** F1
Montgomerie Ct 2
BR3 . . . . **44** A8
Montgomerie Dr GU2 . . . **109** A6
Montgomery Ave KT10 . . . **55** E8
Montgomery Cl
Mitcham CR4 . . . . **41** E5
Sandhurst GU47 . . . . **64** B8
Montgomery Ct
Chiswick W4 . . . .**7** C8
Leatherhead KT22 . . . . . . **95** C7
Montgomery Gdns
SM2 . . . . **59** D3
Montgomery Ho 5
SW14 . . . .**7** D4
Montgomery Of Alamein
Ct RG12 . . . . **27** D8
Montgomery Rd
Farnborough GU14 . . . . . **84** F3
2 Woking GU22 . . . . **69** E2

Montpelier Ct [10] BR2 44 F5
Montpelier Rd
Purley CR2, CR8 61 B1
Sutton SM1 59 C6
Montpelier Row TW1 17 C8
Montpellier Ct KT12 35 B3
Montrave Rd SE20 23 C1
Montreal Ho SE6 24 B7
Montrell Rd SW2 21 E7
Montreux Ct RH11 201 B6
Montrose Ave TW2 16 B8
Montrose Cl
Ashford TW15 14 C3
Frimley GU16 65 E2
Montrose Ct SE6 24 F6
Montrose Gdns
Mitcham CR4 40 F7
Oxshott KT22 74 D7
Sutton SM1 59 B8
Montrose Rd TW14 3 D1
Montrose Way SE23 23 D7
Montrose Wlk KT13 53 B7
Montrouge Cres KT17 77 C3
Montserrat Cl SE19 22 D3
Montway Hts SW19 20 B1
Monument Bridge Ind Est E GU21 70 B4
Monument Bridge Ind Est W GU21 70 A4
Monument Bsns Ctr GU21 70 B4
Monument Gn KT13 53 B6
Monument Hill KT13 53 B6
Monument Rd
Sheerwater GU21 70 B4
Weybridge KT13 53 B7
Monument Way E GU21 70 B4
Monument Way W GU21 70 A4
Moon Ct KT22 94 D6
Moon Hall Rd GU6 154 C1
Moon Hall Sch RH5 155 D6
Moonsgate RH13 217 E1
Moons Hill GU10 146 C2
Moons La RH13 217 E1
Moon's La RH7 186 E8
Moor Cl GU47 45 E1
Moorcroft RH9 121 C3
Moorcroft Cl RH11 201 B7
Moorcroft Rd SW16 21 E5
Moordale Ave RG42 26 E8
Moore Cl
Addlestone KT15 52 B5
Ash GU10 126 F8
Mitcham CR4 41 B7
Mortlake SW14 7 C4
Moore Ct RH12 217 A1
Moore Grove Cres TW20 11 F1
Moore Ho
Wandsworth SW17 20 D5
[1] West Norwood SE27 22 C4
Mooreland Rd [15] BR1 24 F1
Moore Rd
Pirbright GU24 87 B6
South Norwood SE19 22 C2
Moores Gn RG40 25 E8
Moore's Rd RH4, RH5 136 B8
Moore Way SM2 59 A2
Moorfield
Haslemere GU27 207 F5
South Holmwood RH5 157 D7
Moorfield Ctr The GU1 109 D5
Moorfield Point GU1 109 E5
Moorfield Rd
Chessington KT9 56 E5
Guildford GU1 109 E5
Moorfields Cl TW18 32 E8
Moorfields Ct [6] SW16 21 C4
Moorhayes Dr TW18 33 C6
Moorhead Rd RH12 218 B5
Moorholme GU22 89 E8
Moorhouse Rd RH8 123 F5
Moor House Sch RH8 122 F3
Moorhurst La RH5 157 B4
Moorings Ho [3] TW8 6 C7
Moorings The
East Grinstead RH19 185 A3
Great Bookham KT23 94 A2
Hindhead GU26 188 E3
Old Windsor SL4 11 C8
West Byfleet KT14 71 C7
Moor La
Bracknell RG12 26 C6
Chessington KT9 56 E5
Harmondsworth UB7 2 C8
Lingfield RH7, TN8 165 D3
Staines TW18 12 D6
Woking GU22 89 F5
Moorland Cl TW2 16 A8
Moorland Ct KT4 58 A6
Moorland Rd
Crawley RH10 202 C3
Harmondsworth UB7 2 C8
Moorlands
[18] Wallington SM6 60 B4
Walton-on-T KT12 54 A7
Moorlands Cl GU26 188 E4
Moorlands Pl GU15 65 B5
Moorlands Rd GU15 65 B4
Moorlands The GU22 89 F6
Moor Lane Jun Sch KT9 56 F5
Moormead Dr KT19 57 E5
Moor Mead Rd TW1 6 A1
Moormede Cres TW18 12 F4
Moor Park Cres RH11 200 D5
Moor Park Gdns KT2 18 E1
Moor Park Ho RG12 26 E3
Moor Park La GU10, GU9 126 A2
Moor Park Way GU9 125 F2
Moor Pk RH6 161 B2
Moor Pl
East Grinstead RH19 185 D2
Windlesham GU20 48 B5
Moor Rd
Farnborough GU14 85 A8
Frimley GU16 85 F8
Haslemere GU27 207 C5
Moorside Cl GU14 65 A1
Moorside Rd BR1 24 F4
Moors La GU8 148 C3
Moorsom Way CR5 79 D2
Moors The GU10 126 F7
Moray Ave GU47 64 D7
Moray Ho [11] KT6 37 E4
Mordaunt Dr RG45 45 B3
MORDEN 40 B3
Morden BR2 44 D7
Morden Cl
Bracknell RG12 27 F5
Burgh Heath KT20 97 D7
Morden Court Par SM4 40 A5
Morden Ct SM4 40 B5
Morden Gdns CR4 40 D5
Morden Hall Park* SW19 40 C6
Morden Hall Rd SM4, SW19 40 C5
Morden Ho SM4 40 A5
MORDEN PARK 39 E3
Morden Park Sch Sports Ctr SM4 39 F4
Morden Prim Sch SM4 40 A4
Morden Rd
Merton SW19 40 B7
Mitcham CR4, SM4, SW19 40 D5
Morden South Sta SM4 40 A4
Morden Sta SW19 40 B6
Morden Way SM3 40 A2
Mordred Rd SE6 24 E6
Morecambe Cl RH11 200 F4
More Circ GU7 150 E7
More Cl CR8 80 A8
Morecoombe Cl KT2 18 B1
Morecote Cl GU4 130 E2
Morecroft TW2 16 D6
More House Sch GU10 146 C2
More La KT10 55 B7
Moreland Ave SL3 1 C7
Moreland Cl SL3 1 C7
Morella Cl GU25 31 D5
Morella Rd SW11, SW12 20 F8
Moremead Rd SE6 24 A4
Morena St SE6 24 B8
More Rd GU7 150 E7
Moresby Ave KT5 38 B2
Moretaine Rd TW15 13 D5
Moreton Ave TW7 5 E6
Moreton Cl GU10 167 E1
Moreton Ho SW17 20 D4
Moreton Rd
North Cheam KT4 58 B8
South Croydon CR2 61 D5
Morey Ct [10] CR2 61 C5
Morgan Ct
Ashford TW15 14 B3
Carshalton SM5 59 F6
Farnborough GU14 84 C4
Moring Rd SW17 21 A4
Morkyns Wlk SE21 22 E5
Morland Ave CR0 42 E1
Morland Cl
Hampton TW12 15 F3
Mitcham CR4 40 E6
Morland Rd
Aldershot GU11 126 C6
Croydon CR0 42 F2
Penge SE20 23 D2
Sutton SM1 59 C5
Morland's Rd GU11 105 D5
Morley Ct
Bromley BR3 44 D8
Fetcham KT22 94 D6
Hayes BR2 44 F5
Sunningdale SL5 29 F3
Morley Ho SW2 21 E8
Morley Rd
Cheam SM3 39 F1
Farnham GU9 125 D1
South Croydon CR2 61 F1
Twickenham TW1 6 D1
Morningside Rd KT4 58 C8
Mornington Cl TN16 83 D2
Mornington Cres TW5 4 B6
Mornington Rd TW15 14 C3
Mornington Wlk TW10 17 C4
Morrell Ave RH12 217 F6
Morris Cl BR3, CR0 43 E4
Morris Ct CR0 61 B6
Morris Gdns SW18 20 A8
Morrish Rd SW2 21 E8
Morrison Ct [5] RH11 201 B1
Morrison Ho
Feltham TW13 15 A5
Streatham SW2 22 A7
Morris Rd
Farnborough GU14 105 D8
Isleworth TW7 5 F4
Morris Rd *continued*
South Nutfield RH1 140 E7
Morriss Ct [5] RH2 118 F1
Morris Stephany Ho [4] SE27 22 B4
Morston Cl KT20 97 B7
Morth Gdns [3] RH12 217 C1
Mortimer Cl SW16 21 D6
Mortimer Cres KT4 57 D7
Mortimer Dr TN16 83 C7
Mortimer Lo [11] SW19 19 E7
Mortimer Rd
Capel RH5 178 D6
Mitcham CR4 40 F8
MORTLAKE 7 C4
Mortlake Cl CR0 60 E7
Mortlake Dr CR4 40 E8
Mortlake High St SW14 7 D4
Mortlake Rd SW14, TW9 7 A6
Mortlake Sta SW14 7 C4
Mortlake Terr TW9 7 A7
Morton KT20 97 D6
Morton Cl
Frimley GU16 85 F7
Wallington SM6 60 F3
Woking GU21 69 D4
Morton Gdns SM6 60 C5
Morton Ho SE27 22 D3
Morton Rd
East Grinstead RH19 205 E7
Morden CR4, SM4 40 D4
Woking GU21 69 D4
Morval Cl GU14 84 E4
Morven Rd SW17 20 F5
Moselle Cl GU14 84 D5
Moselle Rd TN16 83 F1
Mosford Cl RH6 160 F5
Mospey Cres KT17 76 F4
Mosquito Way GU14 84 F2
Mossfield KT11 73 A6
Moss Gdns
Feltham TW13 15 A6
South Croydon CR2 62 D3
Moss La GU7 150 D4
Moss Lane Sch GU7 150 D4
Mosslea Rd
Kenley CR3 80 F2
Penge SE20 23 C2
Mossville Gdns SM4, SW20 39 F5
Mostyn Rd SW19 39 F7
Mostyn Terr RH1 140 A8
Moth Cl SM6 60 E3
MOTSPUR PARK 39 A3
Motspur Park Sta KT3 39 B4
Motspur Pk KT3 39 A3
Mott Ho KT19 57 B1
Motts Hill La KT20 97 A4
Mouchotte Cl TN16 83 C7
Moulton Ave TW3, TW5 4 F5
Mountacre Cl SE26 23 A4
Mount Adon Pk SE21, SE22 23 A8
Mountain Ash Ct [1] RH12 217 F4
Mount Alvernia Hospl GU1 130 E7
Mount Angelus Rd SW15 18 F8
Mount Ararat Rd TW10 6 E2
Mount Arlington [3] BR2 44 E7
Mount Ash Rd SE26 23 B5
Mount Ave CR3 100 C3
Mountbatten Cl
Crawley RH11 201 C2
[6] West Norwood SE19 22 E3
Mountbatten Ct [15] GU11 105 A2
Mountbatten Gdns BR3 43 E5
Mountbatten Lo [9] GU9 125 B2
Mountbatten Mews GU15 65 D7
Mountbatten Rise GU47 45 A1
Mount Cl
Crawley RH10 202 D7
Ewhurst GU6 175 E5
Fetcham KT22 94 F4
Kenley CR8 80 D3
Wallington SM5 60 A2
Woking GU22 89 C6
Mount Cl The GU25 31 D3
Mountcombe Cl KT6 37 E2
Mountcombe Ho SW19 20 D3
Mount Ct
Guildford GU2 130 C7
[6] Kingston u T KT2 18 B1
West Norwood SE27 22 B5
West Wickham BR4 63 E8
Mount Dr The RH2 118 D3
Mountearl Gdns SW16, SW2 21 F5
Mount Ephraim La SW16 21 D5
Mount Ephraim Rd SW16 21 D5
Mount Felix KT12 34 F2
Mountfield Cl SE6 24 D8
Mount Gdns SE26 23 B5
MOUNT HERMON 89 D8
Mount Hermon Cl GU22 69 E1
Mount Hermon Rd GU22 69 E1
Mounthurst Rd BR2 44 F2
Mount La
Bracknell RG12 27 C7
Turners Hill RH10 204 A4
Mount Lee TW20 11 F3
Mount Mews TW12 36 B8
Mount Noddy RH10 203 C2
Mount Nod Rd SW16, SW2 21 F5
Mount Park Ave CR2 61 B2
Mount Pk SM5 60 A2
Mount Pl GU1 130 C7
Mount Pleasant
Biggin Hill TN16 83 D2
Bracknell RG12 27 C6
Effingham KT24 113 E7
Ewell KT17 57 F1
Farnham GU9 125 A1
Guildford GU2 130 C7
Sandhurst GU47 45 A1
West Horsley KT24 112 B6
West Norwood SE27 22 C4
Weybridge KT13 53 A7
Wokingham RG41 25 A6
Mount Pleasant Cl GU18 48 A1
Mount Pleasant Cotts TW20 11 D2
Mount Pleasant Rd
Aldershot GU12 105 C2
Caterham CR3 101 A4
Kingston u T KT3 38 C6
Lingfield RH7 164 C4
Mount Prim Sch The KT3 38 C6
Mount Rd
Chessington KT9 56 F5
Chobham GU24 69 B7
Cranleigh GU6 174 E2
Feltham TW13 15 E5
Kingston u T KT3 38 D6
Mitcham CR4 40 E7
South Norwood SE19 22 D2
Wimbledon SW18, SW19 20 B6
Woking GU22 89 B6
Mount Rise
Forest Hill SE23 23 C6
Reigate RH1 139 D7
Mountsfield Cl TW19 2 A2
Mounts Hill SL4 9 C3
Mountside
Caterham CR3 100 F3
Guildford GU2 130 B7
Mountside Pl [1] GU22 69 F1
Mount St RH4 136 A7
Mount The
Belmont SM1 59 A4
Cranleigh GU6 174 E2
[6] Croydon CR2 61 C5
Esher KT10 55 A4
Ewell KT17 57 F1
Ewhurst GU6 175 E5
Fetcham KT22 94 E4
Grayswood GU27 189 F1
Guildford GU2 130 C7
Headley Down GU35 187 A6
Lower Kingswood KT20 97 F1
New Malden KT3 38 F6
North Cheam KT4 58 B6
Oatlands Park KT13 53 E8
Rusper RH1, RH12 180 B1
Rusper RH12 200 B8
Virginia Water GU25 31 D3
Wallington CR5 79 B5
Warlingham CR6 101 A8
Witley GU8 170 F3
Woking GU21, GU22 69 D1
Mountview [5] SW16 21 F5
Mount View GU11 105 A1
Mountview Dr RH1 139 E7
Mount View Rd KT10 56 B3
Mount Villas SE27 22 B5
Mount Way SM5 60 A2
Mountwood KT8 36 B6
Mountwood Cl CR2 62 B1
MOUSEHILL 170 E8
Moushill La GU8 170 E8
Mowat Ct KT4 57 F8
Mowatt Rd GU26 188 D2
Mowbray Ave KT14 71 E6
Mowbray Cres TW20 12 A3
Mowbray Ct SE19 42 F8
Mowbray Dr RH11 200 F4
Mowbray Gdns RH4 115 B1
Mowbray Rd
Richmond TW10 17 C5
South Norwood SE19 42 F8
Mower Cl RG40 25 F7
Mower Pl GU6 174 E4
Moyne Ct [3] GU21 68 F1
Moyne Rd RH11 201 C2
Moys Cl CR0 41 E3
Moyser Rd SW16, SW17 21 B3
Moys Ho RH1 118 F3
Muchelney Rd SM4 40 C3
Muckhatch La TW20 32 B7
Mudie Ho [8] SW2 21 E8
Muggeridge Cl CR2 61 D5
Muggeridge's Hill RH12, RH5 198 E8
MUGSWELL 98 B2
Muirdown Ave SW14 7 D3
Muirfield Cl RH11 200 D5
Muirfield Ho
Bracknell RG12 26 E3
Sunningdale SL5 30 A1
Muirfield Rd GU21 69 A1
Muirkirk Rd SE6 24 C7
Mulberries The GU9 125 F4
Mulberry Ave TW19 13 E7
Mulberry Bsns Pk RG41 25 A4
Mulberry Cl
Ash GU12 106 A4
Crowthorne RG45 45 C4
Horsham RH12 217 C5
[1] Sandhurst GU47 64 D8
Streatham SW16 21 C4
Weybridge KT13 53 B7
Woking GU21 69 E5
Mulberry Cres TW8 6 C7
Mulberry Ct
Ashtead KT21 75 D1
[1] Bracknell RG12 27 F4
Guildford GU4 110 D3
[4] Surbiton KT6 37 D2
Twickenham TW1 16 F5
Wokingham RG40 25 C6
Mulberry Gate SM7 77 F3
Mulberry La CR0 42 F1
Mulberry Mews [2] SM6 60 C4
Mulberry Rd RH11 181 B1
Mulberry The CR3 80 F2
Mulberry Trees TW17 34 D2
Mulgrave Ct [7] SM2 59 B4
Mulgrave Hall [8] SM2 59 B4
Mulgrave Manor SM2 59 B4
Mulgrave Rd
Croydon CR0, CR9 61 D7
Frimley GU16 65 F2
Sutton SM2 59 B4
Mulgrave Way GU21 68 E1
Mulholland Cl CR4 41 B7
Mullards Cl CR4 40 F1
Mullberry Pl RH5 158 C2
Mullein Wlk RH11 201 A2
Mullens Rd TW20 12 C3
Mullins Path SW14 7 D4
Mulroy Dr GU15 66 A6
Multon Rd SW18 20 D8
Muncaster Cl TW15 14 A4
Muncaster Rd TW15 14 B3
Muncies Mews SE6 24 C6
Munday's Boro GU3 128 A4
Munday's Boro Rd GU3 128 B4
Munnings Dr GU47 64 E6
Munnings Gdns TW7 5 D2
Munroe Ho RH2 139 A6
Munro Way GU14 105 D8
Munslow Gdns SM1 59 D6
Munstead Ct [16] SM2 59 C3
Munstead Heath Rd GU8 151 C3
Munstead Pk GU8 151 C2
Munstead View GU3 130 C4
Munstead View Rd GU5 151 D5
Munster Ave TW4 4 E2
Munster Ct TW11 17 C2
Munster Rd TW11 17 C2
Murdoch Cl TW18 13 A3
Murdoch Rd RG40 25 D5
Murdock Ct RG40 25 D5
Murfett Cl SW19 19 E6
Murray Ave TW3 5 B2
Murray Ct
Ascot SL5 29 C3
Crawley RH11 201 A1
Horsham RH13 218 B4
Twickenham TW2 16 D6
Murray Gn GU21 70 C5
Murray Ho
Ottershaw KT16 51 D4
Wokingham RG41 25 A6
Murray Rd
Farnborough GU14 84 F3
Ottershaw KT15, KT16 51 D5
Richmond TW10 17 C6
Wimbledon SW19 19 D2
Wokingham RG41 25 A6
Murray's La KT14 71 E5
Murrays Rd GU11 105 D6
Murrellhill La RG42 26 C8
Murrell Rd GU12 106 A3
Murrells La GU15 65 B3
Murrells Wlk KT23 94 A3
Murreys The KT21 75 D1
Murthead La GU3 128 A2
Muschamp Prim Sch SM5 59 E8
Muschamp Rd SM1, SM5 59 E8
Museum Hill GU27 208 D6
Museum of Richmond* TW10 6 D2
Museum of Rugby* TW1 5 E1
Musgrave Ave RH19 205 E8
Musgrave Rd TW7 5 F6
Mushroom Castle La RG42 8 B2
Musical Mus The* TW8 6 E8
Musquash Way TW4 4 C5
Mustard Mill Rd TW18 12 F4
Mutton Hill RH7 186 F7
Mutton Oaks RG12 26 D8
Muybridge Rd KT3 38 C7
Mychell Ho [8] SW19 20 C1
Mychett Prim Sch GU16 85 F4
Myers Way GU16 66 D2
Myherin Ct SE23 23 F6

Mylis Cl SE26 23 B4
Mylne Sq RG40 25 D6
Mylor Cl GU21 69 E5
Mynn's Cl KT18 76 B5
Mynterne Ct 16 SW19 19 D7
Mynthurst Farm Cotts RH2 159 B7
Myrna Cl SW19 20 E1
Myrtle Ave TW14 3 E2
Myrtle Cl
Lightwater GU18 67 B8
Poyle SL3 1 E6
Myrtle Dr GU17 64 D5
Myrtle Gr KT3 38 C7
Myrtle Rd
Croydon CR0 63 A7
Dorking RH4 136 A8
Hampton TW12 16 C2
Hounslow TW3 5 C5
Sutton SM1 59 C5
MYTCHETT 85 F3
Mytchett Farm Crvn Pk GU16 85 F2
Mytchett Heath GU16 86 A3
Mytchett Lake Rd GU16 86 A1
Mytchett Place Rd GU12, GU16 86 C1
Mytchett Rd GU12, GU16 85 F3
Myton Rd SE21 22 D5

N

Naafi Rdbt GU11 105 B2
Nadine Ct SM6 60 C2
Nailsworth Cres RH1 119 D6
Nairn Cl GU16 65 E2
Nairn Ct
3 Wallington SM6 60 C4
Wimbledon SW19 20 B2
Naish Ho SW19 40 B6
NALDERSWOOD 159 C7
Naldrett Cl RH12 217 F4
Naldretts La RH12 214 D5
Nallhead Rd TW13 15 C3
Namba Roy Cl SW16 21 F4
Namton Dr CR7, SW16 41 F5
Nanhurst Park Ho GU6 173 E2
Naomi Watts Ho 11 SW19 19 E1
Napier Cl
Crowthorne RG45 45 D5
Farnborough GU11 105 E7
Napier Ct
Caterham CR3 100 E5
13 Croydon CR0 61 F8
1 Surbiton KT6 37 D2
12 Wallington SM6 60 B4
Woking GU21 69 E3
Napier Dr GU15 66 A8
Napier Gdns GU1 110 B2
Napier La GU12 106 A4
Napier Lo TW15 14 D2
Napier Rd
Ashford TW15 14 D1
Crowthorne RG45 45 C4
Croydon SE25 43 B5
Isleworth TW7 6 A3
South Croydon CR2 61 D3
Napier Way RH10 182 A1
Napier Wlk TW15 14 D1
Napoleon Ave GU14 85 B6
Napoleon Rd TW1 17 B8
Napper Cl SL5 28 D7
Napper Pl GU6 174 E1
Narrow La CR6 101 B8
Naseby RG12 27 B1
Naseby Cl TW7 5 E6
Naseby Ct KT12 54 C8
Naseby Rd SE19 22 D2
Nash Cl
Carshalton SM1 59 D7
Farnborough GU14 84 F4
Nash Dr 6 RH1 119 A3
Nash Gdns
North Ascot SL5 28 E7
Redhill RH1 118 F3
Nash Rd RH10 201 E3
Nassau Rd SW13 7 F6
Nasturtium Dr GU24 68 A4
Natalie Cl TW14 14 D8
Natalie Mews TW2 16 D5
Natal Rd
South Norwood CR7 42 D6
Streatham SW16 21 D2
National Archives The TW9 7 B7
National Physical Laboratory TW11 16 E2
National Wks TW4 4 F4
Nayland Ho SE6 24 C4
Neald Ct 6 SW19 20 A2
Neale Cl RH19 185 B3
Neath Gdns SM4 40 C3
Neb La RH8 122 D4
Needles Bank RH9 121 B4
Needles Cl RH12 217 B1
Neelem Ct 4 GU14 85 C1
Neil Cl TW15 14 C3
Neil Wates Cres 18 SW2 22 A7
Nelgarde Rd SE6 24 A8
Nell Ball RH14 211 E2
Nell Gwynn Ave TW17 34 D3
Nell Gwynne Ave SL5 29 D5
Nell Gwynne Cl
Ascot SL5 29 D5
Epsom KT19 76 A8
Nello James Gdns SE27 22 D4
Nelson Cl
Aldershot GU12 105 D1
Biggin Hill TN16 83 E2
Bracknell RG12 27 E7
Crawley RH10 202 C5
East Bedfont TW14 14 F7
Heath End GU9 125 D8
Thornton Heath CR0 42 B1
Walton-on-T KT12 35 B1
Nelson Ct
Carshalton SM5 59 F7
Chertsey KT16 33 A1
Nelson Gdns
Guildford GU1 110 A2
Twickenham TW3, TW4 5 A1
Nelson Grove Rd SW19 40 C8
Nelson Ho
19 Aldershot GU11 105 A2
Epsom KT19 57 B1
Nelson Hospl SW20 39 F7
Nelson Prim Sch TW2 5 B1
Nelson Rd
Ashford TW15 13 E3
Caterham CR3 100 D4
Harmondsworth TW6 2 F6
Heath End GU9 125 D8
Horsham RH12 217 C3
Merton SW19 20 C1
New Malden KT3 38 D4
Twickenham TW2 16 B8
Nelson St 3 GU11 105 A2
Nelson Trad Est SW19 40 B8
Nelson Way GU15 64 F4
Nelson Wlk KT19 57 A2
Nene Gdns TW13 15 F6
Nene Rd TW6, UB7 3 B6
Nepean St 4 SW15 19 A8
Neptune Cl RH11 200 E4
Neptune Ct RH12 217 B4
Neptune Rd TW6 3 C6
Nero Ct TW8 6 D7
Nesbit Ct RH11 200 E3
Nesbitt Sq SE19 22 E1
Netheravon Rd S 2 W4 7 F8
Netherby Pk KT13 53 E5
Netherby Rd SE23 23 C8
Nethercote Ave GU21 68 F2
Netherfield BR2 44 D6
Netherfield Rd SW17 21 A5
Netherlands Ct 14 SM2 59 C4
Netherlands The CR5 99 C8
Netherleigh Pk RH1 140 E6
Nether Mount GU2 130 B7
Nethern Court Rd CR3 102 A4
Netherne Dr CR5 99 C5
Netherne La
Netherne-on-t-H CR5 99 C6
Netherne-on-t-H CR5, RH1 99 C4
NETHERNE-ON-THE-HILL 99 D5
Netherton RG12 27 A5
Netherton Rd TW1 6 B2
Netherwood RH11 201 B4
Netherwood Ct GU7 150 E5
Netley Cl
Cheam SM3 58 D5
Gomshall GU5 133 C5
New Addington CR0 63 C3
Netley Dr KT12 35 F2
Netley Gdns SM4 40 C2
Netley Rd
Brentford TW8 6 E8
Morden SM4 40 C2
Netley St GU14 105 C8
Nettlecombe RG12 27 D3
Nettlecombe Cl SM2 59 B2
Nettlefold Pl SE27 22 B5
Nettlestead Cl BR3 23 F1
Nettles Terr 3 GU1 109 D1
Nettleton Rd TW6 3 B6
Nettlewood Rd SW16 21 D1
Neuchatel Rd SE6 23 F6
Neuman Cres RG12 27 A3
Nevada Cl
Farnborough GU14 84 D3
Kingston u T KT3 38 C5
Nevelle Cl RG42 26 D8
Nevile Cl RH11 201 A3
Neville Ave KT3 38 D8
Neville Cl
Banstead SM7 78 B5
Esher KT10 54 F4
Hounslow TW3 5 B5
Neville Ct 10 SW12 21 C8
Neville Duke Rd GU14 84 F8
Neville Ho 8 TW1 17 A8
Neville Rd
Croydon CR0 42 D2
Kingston u T KT1 38 A7
Richmond TW10 17 C6
Neville Wlk SM5 40 E2
Nevis Rd SW17 21 A6
New Acres Cvn Pk GU6 193 C8
NEW ADDINGTON 63 D3
Newall Rd TW6 3 C6
Newark Cl
Guildford GU4 110 B6
Newark Cl *continued*
Ripley GU23 91 A6
Newark Ct KT12 35 C1
Newark La
Ripley GU23 91 B6
Woking GU22 90 F8
Newark Rd
Crawley RH10 201 F8
South Croydon CR2 61 D4
Windlesham GU20 48 B6
New Barn Cl SM6 60 F4
New Barn La
Kenley CR3 80 E3
Wallis Wood RH5 177 A3
New Barns Ave CR4 41 D5
New Battlebridge La RH1 119 B5
NEW BECKENHAM 23 F2
New Beckenham Sta BR3 23 F1
New Belmont Ho 4 SE23 23 C7
New Berry La KT12 54 D5
Newbolt Ave SM3 58 D5
Newborough Gn KT3 38 D5
Newborough Ho SW19 20 D1
Newbridge Cl RH12 216 C3
Newbridge Ct
Cranleigh GU6 174 B3
Upper Tooting SW17 20 C4
Newbridge Point 3 SE23 23 D5
Newbury Gdns KT19 57 F6
Newbury Rd
Crawley RH10 202 D6
Harmondsworth TW6 2 F6
NEWCHAPEL 163 F1
Newchapel Rd
Lingfield RH7 164 B3
Newchapel RH7 163 F2
New Chapel Sq TW13 15 B7
New Church Ct 4 SE19 23 A1
New Cl
Feltham TW13 15 E3
Mitcham SW19 40 C6
New Colebrooke Ct SM5 60 A3
Newcombe Gdns 7 TW3 4 F3
Newcombe Rd GU9 125 E6
Newcome Gdns SW16 21 E4
Newcome Pl GU12 126 D7
New Coppice GU21 88 E8
New Cotts
Betchworth RH3 116 D4
Pirbright GU24 87 D5
Sidlow RH2 138 F1
Turners Hill RH10 204 A4
New Cross Rd GU2 109 B3
New Cswy RH2 139 C6
New Ct KT15 52 C7
New Dawn Cl GU14 84 D3
NEWDIGATE 158 B1
Newdigate CE Inf Sch RH5 158 B1
Newdigate Ho
6 Kingston u T KT2 18 B2
West Norwood SW16 22 A4
Newdigate Rd
Beare Green RH5 157 E2
Leigh RH2 137 F2
Rusper RH12 199 C8
NEWELL GREEN 8 A1
NEW ENGLAND 67 D7
New England Trad Est RH8 123 A2
Newenham Rd KT23 94 A1
Newent Cl SM5 40 F1
New Epsom & Ewell Cottage Hospl The KT19 75 E8
New Farm Cl TW18 33 C8
New Farthingdale RH7 186 B8
Newfield Ave GU14 84 E6
Newfield Cl TW12 36 A8
Newfield Rd GU12 106 A6
New Forest Cotts GU22 89 F7
New Forest Ride RG12 27 F4
Newfoundland Rd GU16 86 D8
Newgate CR0 42 C1
Newgate Cl TW13 15 E5
New Green Pl SE19 22 E2
Newhache RH7 165 A1
Newhall Gdns KT12 54 C8
Newhaven Cres TW15 14 D3
Newhaven Rd SE25 42 D4
NEW HAW 52 C3
New Haw Com Jun Sch KT15 52 A1
New Haw Rd KT15 52 C4
New Heston Rd TW5 4 F7
Newholme Ct 2 KT13 53 E7
New Horizons Ct TW8 6 A8
New Horton Manor SL3 1 A4
Newhouse 6 KT3 38 E2
Newhouse Bsns Ctr RH12 218 C7
Newhouse Cl KT3 38 E2
New House Farm La GU3 108 C2
New House La RH1 161 E8
Newhouse Wlk SM4 40 C2
New Inn Ct The KT8 36 D4
New Inn La GU4 110 B4
New Kelvin Ave TW11 16 E2
New La GU22, GU4 89 F3
Newland House Sch TW1 16 F4
Newland House Sch Annex TW1 16 F4
Newlands Ave
Thames Ditton KT7 36 E1
Woking GU22 89 F6
Newlands Cl
Hersham KT12 54 E6
Horley RH6 160 F5
Newlands Cres
East Grinstead RH19 185 D2
Guildford GU1 130 F7
Newlands Croft SE20 23 D2
Newlands Ct
Addlestone KT15 52 B5
1 Caterham CR3 100 C6
Penge SE26 23 C2
Streatham SW16 21 E3
Newlands Dr
Ash GU12 106 B4
Poyle SL3 1 E4
Newlands Est GU8 170 F5
Newlands Flats GU1 109 F2
Newlands Pk
Copthorne RH10 183 E3
Penge SE26 23 D3
Newlands Pl RH18 206 F3
Newlands Rd
Camberley GU15 65 B1
Crawley RH11 201 C5
Horsham RH12 217 C4
Thornton Heath SW16 41 E7
Newlands The
Thames Ditton KT7 36 E1
Wallington SM6 60 D3
Newlands Way KT9 56 C5
Newlands Woods CR0 62 F2
New Lodge Dr RH8 122 F7
Newlyn KT13 53 F6
Newlyn Ho 12 SM1 59 C6
NEW MALDEN 38 F5
New Malden Sta KT3 38 E6
Newman Cl RH10 202 C4
Newman Ho 11 TW10 17 C5
Newman Rd CR0 41 F1
Newmans Ct GU9 125 A7
Newmans Pl SL5 30 B2
Newman Terr 11 CR4 40 F6
Newmarket Rd RH10 202 A4
New Mdw SL5 28 D8
New Mile Rd SL5 29 C7
Newminster Rd SM4 40 C3
New Monument Sch GU22 70 C4
New Moorhead Dr RH12 218 C6
Newnham Cl CR7 42 C7
Newnham Ho SE6 24 C5
New North Rd RH2 138 F6
New Par TW15 13 F4
New Park Ct 25 SW2 21 E8
New Park Par 16 SW2 21 E8
New Park Rd
Ashford TW15 14 C3
Cranleigh GU6 174 F2
Streatham, Streatham Hill SW12, SW2 21 E7
Streatham SW2 21 E8
New Pl CR0 63 A4
New Place Gdns RH7 164 E4
New Pond Rd GU3, GU7 129 E1
New Poplars Ct GU12 106 A1
Newport Jun Sch GU12 105 D1
Newport Rd
Aldershot GU12 105 D1
Harmondsworth TW6 3 A6
Newquay Rd SE6 24 C6
New Rd
Albury GU5 132 D3
Bagshot GU19 47 F3
Blackwater GU17 64 E4
Bracknell RG12 27 D7
Brentford TW8 6 D8
Carshalton CR4 41 A1
Chilworth GU4 131 B3
Crowthorne RG45 45 C5
East Bedfont TW14 3 D1
East Clandon GU4 111 E4
East Molesey KT8 36 A6
Egham TW18 12 C3
Esher KT10 55 C6
Feltham, Hanworth TW13 15 E3
Feltham TW14 15 B7
Forest Green RH5 176 E6
Gomshall GU5 133 C4
Harlington TW6, UB7 3 C7
Haslemere GU27 207 F5
Hounslow TW3 5 B3
Hydestile GU8 171 F5
Kingston u T KT2 18 A1
Limpsfield RH8 123 B5
Littleton TW17 34 B6
Milford GU8 170 E8
North Ascot SL5 8 F1
Oxshott KT22 74 F8
Richmond TW10 17 C4
Sandhurst GU47 64 A8
Smallfield RH6 162 B3
Tadworth KT20 97 C4
Tandridge RH8 143 A7
Tongham GU10 126 F6
Weybridge KT13 53 C5
New Rd *continued*
Windlesham GU19, GU20 48 A4
Wonersh GU5 152 B8
Wormley GU8 191 A8
New Rd Units TW3 5 B3
New Residences KT16 51 C7
Newry Rd TW1 6 A2
New Scotland Hill Prim Sch GU47 45 A2
Newsham Rd 1 GU21 68 F2
New Site KT15 52 E7
New Sq TW14 14 C7
New St
Crawley RH10 202 A7
Horsham RH13 217 D2
Staines TW18 13 A4
Newstead Cl GU7 150 D6
Newstead Hall RH6 161 D1
Newstead Ho
Caterham CR3 101 B1
Thames Ditton KT8 36 D3
Newstead Rd SE12 24 F8
Newstead Rise CR3 101 B1
Newstead Way SW19 19 E4
Newstead Wlk SM4, SM5 40 C2
Newton Ave RH19 205 F6
Newton Ct 2 KT19 57 E2
Newton Rd
Crawley RH10 181 F2
Farnborough GU14 85 D6
Isleworth TW7 5 F5
Merton SW19 19 E1
Purley CR8 79 C7
Newton Way GU10 126 F7
Newton Wood Rd KT21 75 F3
New Town RH10 183 B3
Newtown Ct RH13 217 E1
Newtown Rd GU47 64 B8
New Victoria Hospl KT3 38 E8
New Way GU7 150 C4
New Wickham La TW20 12 B1
New Wokingham Rd RG45 45 A6
New Woodlands Sch BR1 24 E4
New Zealand Ave KT12 34 F1
Nexus Pk GU12 105 F8
Nicholas Ct 7 W4 7 E7
Nicholas Gdns GU22 70 F3
Nicholas Ho SE26 23 B2
Nicholas Lo KT10 55 A8
Nicholas Rd CR0 60 E6
Nicholass Ct 2 CR8 80 B7
Nicholes Rd TW3 5 A3
Nicholls Cl CR3 100 C5
Nichols Cl KT9 56 C4
Nicholsfield RH14 212 F4
Nicholson Mews 4 KT1 37 E5
Nicholson Rd CR0 42 F1
Nicholson Wlk 3 TW20 12 A3
Nicola Cl CR2 61 C4
Nicola Ct GU12 105 D2
Nicol Cl 6 TW1 6 B1
Nicosia Rd SW18 20 E8
Niederwald Rd SE26 23 E6
Nigel Fisher Way KT9 56 D3
Nightingale Ave KT24 92 D2
Nightingale Cl
Biggin Hill TN16 83 C4
Carshalton SM5 60 A8
Chiswick W4 7 C8
Cobham KT11 73 D8
Crawley RH11 201 C8
East Grinstead RH19 205 D7
Epsom KT19 76 A8
Farnborough GU14 84 C6
Nightingale Cres
Bracknell RG12 27 D4
West Horsley KT24 92 C2
Nightingale Ct
2 Knaphill GU21 68 F1
Penge SE19 22 F2
8 Redhill RH1 119 A2
Sutton SM1 59 C5
Nightingale Dr
Mytchett GU16 86 A3
West Ewell KT19 57 B4
Nightingale Gdns GU47 64 B8
Nightingale Ind Est RH12 217 D3
Nightingale La
Balham SW11, SW12 20 F8
Richmond TW10 17 E8
Turners Hill RH10 204 C5
Nightingale Pl GU27 208 D7
Nightingale Rd
Ash GU12 106 C3
Carshalton SM5 60 A8
East Horsley KT24 92 F2
East Molesey KT8 36 B4
Esher KT10 54 F4
Farncombe GU7 150 E6
Guildford GU1 109 E1
Hampton TW12 16 A2
Horsham RH12 217 D3
Selsdon CR2 62 D1
Walton-on-T KT12 35 B2
Nightingales GU6 174 E1
Nightingale Sch SW17 20 E6
Nightingales Cl RH13 217 F2

Nightingale Shott TW20 . . . 11 F2
Nightingale Sq SW12 . . . 21 A8
Nightingales The TW19 . . . 13 F7
Nightingale Way RH1 . . . 120 E2
Nightjar Cl GU10 . . . 124 D8
Nimbus Rd KT19 . . . 57 D1
Nimrod Ct RH10 . . . 182 D1
Nimrod Rd SW16, SW17 . . . 21 B3
Nineacres Way CR5 . . . 79 E3
Nine Elms Cl TW14 . . . 14 F7
Ninehams Cl CR3 . . . 100 D7
Ninehams Gdns CR3 . . . 100 D7
Ninehams Rd
Caterham CR3 . . . 100 D6
Tatsfield TN16 . . . 103 D6
Nine Mile Ride RG12, RG40 . . . 26 F1
Nineteenth Rd CR4 . . . 41 E5
Ninfield Ct RH11 . . . 200 F2
Niton Rd TW9 . . . 7 A4
Niven Cl RH10 . . . 202 D5
Noahs Ct RH10 . . . 204 A4
Nobel Dr UB3 . . . 3 E7
Noble Cnr TW5 . . . 5 A6
Noble Ct CR4 . . . 40 D7
Noble St KT12 . . . 54 C7
Nobles Way TW20 . . . 11 E2
Noel Ct TW4 . . . 4 F4
Noel Terr SE23 . . . 23 C6
Noke Dr RH1 . . . 119 A2
Nonsuch Court Ave KT17 . . . 58 B1
Nonsuch Ct SM3 . . . 58 E4
Nonsuch High Sch for Girls SM3 . . . 58 D3
Nonsuch Ho 5 SW19 . . . 40 D8
Nonsuch Ind Est KT17 . . . 76 E8
Nonsuch Prim Sch KT17 . . . 58 B5
Nonsuch Wlk SM2 . . . 58 D1
Nook The SW19 . . . 40 C7
Noons Corner Rd RH5 . . . 156 A8
NORBITON . . . 38 A7
Norbiton Ave KT1, KT2 . . . 38 A7
Norbiton Common Rd KT1, KT3 . . . 38 B6
Norbiton Hall KT2 . . . 37 F7
Norbiton Sta KT1 . . . 38 A8
Norbury Ave
Isleworth TW3 . . . 5 D3
South Norwood CR7, SW16 . . . 42 B7
Norbury Cl SW16 . . . 42 B8
Norbury Court Rd SW16 . . . 41 E7
Norbury Cres SW16 . . . 42 A7
Norbury Cross SW16 . . . 41 E6
Norbury Hill SW16 . . . 22 B1
Norbury Manor Bsns & Ent Coll for Girls CR7 . . . 42 A8
Norbury Manor Prim Sch SW16 . . . 41 E8
Norbury Rd
Feltham TW13 . . . 14 F5
Reigate RH2 . . . 117 F1
South Norwood CR7 . . . 42 C6
Norbury Rise SW16 . . . 41 E6
Norbury Sta SW16 . . . 41 F8
Norbury Trad Est SW16 . . . 41 F7
Norbury Way KT23 . . . 94 C2
Norcroft Gdns SE22 . . . 23 A8
Norcutt Rd TW2 . . . 16 E7
Norfolk Ave CR2 . . . 62 A1
Norfolk Cl
Crawley RH11 . . . 200 E2
Horley RH6 . . . 161 A2
5 Twickenham TW1 . . . 6 B1
Norfolk Cotts RH1 . . . 140 E7
Norfolk Ct
Dorking RH5 . . . 136 D3
Horsham RH12 . . . 218 B5
Surbiton KT5 . . . 37 F3
Norfolk Farm Cl GU22 . . . 70 D3
Norfolk Farm Rd GU22 . . . 70 D3
Norfolk Gdns GU21 . . . 88 F8
Norfolk Ho
13 Bromley BR2 . . . 44 F5
2 Croydon CR0 . . . 61 D8
11 Merton SW19 . . . 20 C1
Penge SE20 . . . 43 C8
Richmond TW10 . . . 7 A2
Norfolk House Rd SW16 . . . 21 D5
Norfolk La RH5 . . . 136 B1
Norfolk Mews 9 RH4 . . . 136 A7
Norfolk Rd
Claygate KT10 . . . 55 E5
Dorking RH4 . . . 136 A7
Feltham TW13 . . . 15 C7
Horsham RH12 . . . 217 D2
Mitcham SW19 . . . 20 E2
South Holmwood RH5 . . . 157 C6
South Norwood CR7 . . . 42 C6
Norfolk Terr 7 RH12 . . . 217 D2
Norgrove St SW12 . . . 21 A8
Norheads La TN16 . . . 83 B2
Norhyrst Ave SE25 . . . 42 F6
NORK . . . 77 D4
Nork Gdns SM7 . . . 77 E5
Nork Rise SM7 . . . 77 D3
Nork Way KT17, SM7 . . . 77 D4
Norlands La TW18, TW20 . . . 32 E7
Norley Vale SW15 . . . 19 A7
Norman Ave
Ewell KT17 . . . 76 F7
Feltham TW13 . . . 15 F6
South Croydon CR2, CR8 . . . 61 C1
Twickenham TW1 . . . 17 C8
Norman Cl KT18 . . . 97 B8
Norman Colyer Ct KT19 . . . 57 D1
Norman Cres TW5 . . . 4 D7
Norman Ct
Dulwich SE22 . . . 23 A8
Farnham GU9 . . . 125 C1
11 Hampton TW12 . . . 36 A8
4 Staines TW18 . . . 13 A4
Streatham SW16 . . . 22 A3
Normande Ct SE21 . . . 22 D7
NORMANDY . . . 107 A3
Normandy RH12 . . . 217 C1
Normandy Cl
Crawley RH10 . . . 202 C4
7 East Grinstead RH19 . . . 205 F8
Forest Hill SE26 . . . 23 E5
Frimley GU16 . . . 86 E8
Normandy Common La GU3 . . . 107 B4
Normandy Gdns 4 RH12 . . . 217 C1
Normandy Wlk TW20 . . . 12 C3
Norman Ho
Belmont SM1 . . . 59 A4
Feltham TW13 . . . 15 F6
Lower Halliford TW17 . . . 34 A2
Reigate RH2 . . . 138 F6
Normanhurst TW15 . . . 14 A3
Normanhurst Cl RH10 . . . 201 F6
Normanhurst Dr TW1 . . . 6 B2
Normanhurst Rd
Streatham SW2 . . . 21 F6
Walton-on-T KT12 . . . 54 D8
Norman Keep RG42 . . . 27 F8
Norman Rd
Ashford TW15 . . . 14 D2
Merton SW19 . . . 20 C1
Sutton SM1 . . . 59 A5
Thornton Heath CR7 . . . 42 B4
Normansfield Ave KT1, TW11 . . . 17 C1
Normans La TN8 . . . 165 E7
Norman's Rd RH1, RH6 . . . 162 C5
Normanton RH2 . . . 117 D2
Normanton Ave SW18, SW19 . . . 20 A6
Normanton Ct 4 CR0 . . . 61 E5
Normanton Rd CR2 . . . 61 E4
Normanton St SE23 . . . 23 D6
Normington Cl SW16 . . . 22 A3
NORNEY . . . 149 E6
Norrels Dr KT24 . . . 92 F1
Norrels Ride KT24 . . . 92 F2
Norreys Ave RG40 . . . 25 D7
Norris Cl KT19 . . . 76 B8
Norris Hill Rd GU51, GU14 . . . 104 A8
Norris Rd TW18 . . . 12 F4
Norstead Pl SW15 . . . 19 A6
North Acre SM7 . . . 77 F3
Northampton Cl RG12 . . . 27 E6
Northampton Rd CR0, CR9 . . . 62 A8
Northanger Rd SW16 . . . 21 E2
NORTH ASCOT . . . 28 F8
North Ash 1 RH12 . . . 217 C4
North Ave
Heath End GU9 . . . 125 D7
8 Richmond TW9 . . . 7 A6
Wallington SM5 . . . 60 A3
Whiteley Village KT12 . . . 53 E2
Northborough Rd SW16 . . . 41 E7
Northbourne GU7 . . . 150 F8
North Breache Rd GU6 . . . 176 A5
Northbrook Coll of Design & Tech RH12 . . . 217 C4
Northbrook Copse RG12 . . . 27 F3
Northbrook Rd
Aldershot GU11 . . . 126 B8
Thornton Heath CR0 . . . 42 D4
Northbury Ho 1 GU22 . . . 70 A2
NORTH CAMP . . . 105 C7
North Camp Sta GU12 . . . 105 F8
NORTH CHEAM . . . 58 C8
North Cl
Ash GU12 . . . 105 E1
Crawley RH10 . . . 201 F7
Dorking RH5 . . . 136 C3
East Bedfont TW14 . . . 3 D1
Farnborough GU14 . . . 85 A8
Merton SM4 . . . 39 E5
Northcliffe Cl KT4 . . . 57 E7
North Comm KT13 . . . 53 C6
Northcote KT15 . . . 52 D6
Northcote Ave
Isleworth TW7 . . . 6 A2
Tolworth KT5 . . . 38 B2
Northcote Cl KT24 . . . 92 C2
Northcote Cres KT24 . . . 92 C2
Northcote La GU5 . . . 152 E6
Northcote Pk KT22 . . . 74 C4
Northcote Rd
Ash Vale GU12 . . . 106 A7
Farnborough GU14 . . . 84 F6
Isleworth TW1, TW7 . . . 6 A2
Kingston u T KT3 . . . 38 D6
Thornton Heath CR0 . . . 42 D3
Northcote Rd *continued*
West Horsley KT24 . . . 92 C2
Northcott RG12 . . . 27 A1
Northcott Gdns GU14 . . . 84 D5
Northcroft Cl TW20 . . . 11 B3
Northcroft Gdns TW20 . . . 11 B3
Northcroft Rd
Englefield Green TW20 . . . 11 B3
West Ewell KT19 . . . 57 E3
North Crofts SE21 . . . 23 B7
Northcroft Villas TW20 . . . 11 B3
North Ct 6 TW1 . . . 6 D1
North Dene TW5 . . . 5 B6
North Down CR2 . . . 80 E7
Northdown Cl RH12 . . . 217 F4
Northdown Ct RH9 . . . 121 C5
Northdown La GU1 . . . 130 E6
Northdown Rd
Belmont SM2 . . . 59 A1
Woldingham CR3 . . . 102 A2
Northdowns GU6 . . . 174 E1
North Downs Cres CR0 . . . 63 B1
North Downs Hospl CR3 . . . 100 F2
North Downs Private Hospl CR3 . . . 101 A2
North Downs Rd CR0 . . . 63 C1
Northdown Terr RH19 . . . 185 D3
North Dr
Beckenham BR3 . . . 44 B5
Dormansland RH19 . . . 186 B6
Hounslow TW3, TW7 . . . 5 C5
Pirbright GU24 . . . 87 C6
Streatham SW16 . . . 21 C4
Wentworth GU25 . . . 30 E4
North East Surrey Coll of Tech KT17 . . . 77 A8
NORTH END . . . 185 B3
North End CR0, CR9 . . . 61 C8
Northend Ct KT23 . . . 94 C1
North End La SL5 . . . 30 B2
Northernhay Wlk SM4 . . . 39 E5
Northern Perimeter Rd TW6 . . . 3 E6
Northern Perimeter Rd W TW6 . . . 2 E6
Northey Ave SM2 . . . 58 E1
North Farm Cl GU14 . . . 84 F8
North Farm Rd GU14 . . . 84 F8
North Farnborough Inf Sch GU14 . . . 85 D5
NORTH FELTHAM . . . 4 B2
North Feltham Trad Est TW14 . . . 4 B3
Northfield
Lightwater GU18 . . . 67 B8
Shalford GU4 . . . 130 E1
Witley GU8 . . . 170 F4
Northfield Cl GU12 . . . 105 D1
Northfield Cres SM3 . . . 58 E6
Northfield Ct TW18 . . . 33 B8
Northfield Farm Mews KT11 . . . 73 A5
Northfield Pl KT13 . . . 53 B3
Northfield Rd
Cobham KT11 . . . 73 B6
Heston TW5 . . . 4 D7
Staines TW18 . . . 33 B8
Northfields
Ashtead KT21 . . . 95 E8
Ewell KT17 . . . 76 E8
Northfleet Lo 16 GU22 . . . 89 E8
NORTHGATE . . . 201 F7
Northgate Ave RH10 . . . 201 F7
Northgate Dr GU15 . . . 66 A7
Northgate Pl RH10 . . . 201 E7
Northgate Prim Sch RH10 . . . 201 E7
Northgate Rd
Crawley, North Terminal RH6 . . . 181 F8
Crawley RH10 . . . 201 D6
North Gdns SW19 . . . 20 D1
North Gn RG12 . . . 27 D8
North Gr KT16 . . . 32 F3
North Heath Cl RH12 . . . 217 D5
North Heath Com Prim Sch RH12 . . . 217 D5
North Heath La RH12 . . . 217 E6
North Heath Lane Ind Est RH12 . . . 217 D6
North Holmes Cl RH12 . . . 218 B5
NORTH HOLMWOOD . . . 136 A3
North Hyde La TW5 . . . 4 F8
Northington Cl RG12 . . . 27 F3
North La
Aldershot GU11, GU12 . . . 105 D2
Teddington TW11 . . . 16 F2
Northlands Bglws RH5 . . . 158 B1
Northlands Bsns Pk RH12 . . . 197 C4
Northlands Cotts RH12 . . . 197 D4
Northlands Rd
Horsham RH12 . . . 217 E7
Warnham RH12 . . . 197 D2
North Lodge Dr SL5 . . . 28 C7
NORTH LOOE . . . 77 C6
Northmead GU14 . . . 85 B4
North Mead
Crawley RH10 . . . 201 E8
Redhill RH1 . . . 118 F4
Northmead Jun Sch GU2 . . . 109 B4
North Minden Ho GU16 . . . 86 D7
Northmoor 4 SE23 . . . 23 D5
North Moors GU1 . . . 109 E6
North Munstead La GU8 . . . 151 A1
Northolmes Jun Sch RH12 . . . 218 A4
Northolt Rd UB7 . . . 2 D6
Northover BR1 . . . 24 F5
North Par
Chessington KT9 . . . 56 F5
Horsham RH12 . . . 217 C3
North Park La RH9 . . . 121 A5
North Pl
Mitcham SW19 . . . 20 F1
Teddington TW11 . . . 16 F2
Northpoint Cl SM1 . . . 59 C7
North Pole La BR2 . . . 63 F4
North Rd
Ash Vale GU12 . . . 105 F4
Brentford TW8 . . . 6 E8
Crawley RH10 . . . 202 A7
East Bedfont TW14 . . . 3 D1
Guildford GU2 . . . 109 B4
Hersham KT12 . . . 54 C5
Heston TW5 . . . 4 C8
Kingston u T KT6 . . . 37 D3
Mitcham SW17, SW19 . . . 20 C2
Reigate RH2 . . . 138 F6
Richmond TW9 . . . 7 A5
1 West Wickham BR4 . . . 44 B1
Winkfield SL5 . . . 28 B8
Woking GU21 . . . 70 A3
Northrop Rd TW6 . . . 3 E6
NORTH SHEEN . . . 7 A5
North Sheen Sta TW10 . . . 7 A3
North Side GU10 . . . 126 F7
Northspur Rd SM1 . . . 59 A7
North St
Carshalton SM5 . . . 59 F6
Cranbourne SL4 . . . 9 A6
Dorking RH4 . . . 136 A7
Egham TW20 . . . 11 F2
Farncombe GU7 . . . 150 E7
Guildford GU1 . . . 130 D8
Horsham RH12, RH13 . . . 217 D3
Isleworth TW7 . . . 6 A4
Leatherhead KT22 . . . 95 A6
Redhill RH1 . . . 118 F2
Turners Hill RH10 . . . 204 A4
Westcott RH4 . . . 135 C6
North Station App RH1 . . . 140 F7
Northstead Rd SW2 . . . 22 A6
North Terminal App RH6 . . . 181 F8
NORTH TOWN . . . 105 D2
Northtown Trad Est GU12 . . . 105 E1
Northumberland Ave TW7 . . . 6 A7
Northumberland Cl TW19 . . . 2 E1
Northumberland Cres TW14 . . . 3 E1
Northumberland Ct 1 CR0 . . . 61 E5
Northumberland Gdns
Hounslow TW7 . . . 6 A7
Mitcham CR4 . . . 41 D4
Northumberland Pl 27 TW10 . . . 6 D2
Northumbria Ct 12 TW9 . . . 6 E3
North View
Bracknell RG12 . . . 26 C6
Wimbledon SW19 . . . 19 C3
North View Cres KT18 . . . 77 C2
Northway
Crawley RH6 . . . 181 F8
Farncombe GU7 . . . 150 B7
Guildford GU2 . . . 109 A3
Merton SM4, SW20 . . . 39 E5
Wallington SM6 . . . 60 C6
Northway Rd CR0 . . . 42 F2
North Weald La KT2 . . . 17 D3
North Weylands Ind Est KT12 . . . 54 E8
North Wlk CR0 . . . 63 C5
Northwood Ave
Knaphill GU21 . . . 68 D1
Purley CR8 . . . 80 B6
Northwood Pk RH10 . . . 182 A2
Northwood Rd
Forest Hill SE23 . . . 23 F7
Harmondsworth TW6 . . . 2 D6
South Norwood CR7 . . . 42 C7
Wallington SM5 . . . 60 A4
Northwood Way 1 SE19 . . . 22 E2
North Worple Way SW14 . . . 7 D4
Norton Ave KT5 . . . 38 B2
Norton Cl GU3 . . . 88 D1
Norton Ct BR3 . . . 43 F8
Norton Gdns SW16 . . . 41 E7
Norton Ho 6 KT3 . . . 38 E5
Norton Pk SL5 . . . 29 C4
Norton Rd
Frimley GU15 . . . 66 C4
Wokingham RG40 . . . 25 C5
Norwegian Sch The SW20 . . . 19 C1
Norwich Ave GU15 . . . 65 E3
Norwich Rd
Crawley RH10 . . . 202 B5
Norwich Rd *continued*
South Norwood CR7 . . . 42 C6
Norwood Cl
Effingham KT24 . . . 113 E7
Twickenham TW2 . . . 16 D6
Norwood Cres TW6 . . . 3 C6
Norwood Farm La KT11 . . . 73 B8
Norwood Heights Sh Ctr SE19 . . . 22 E2
Norwood High St SE27 . . . 22 C4
NORWOOD HILL . . . 159 E3
Norwood Hill RH6 . . . 159 D3
Norwoodhill Rd RH6 . . . 159 F2
Norwood Junction Sta SE25 . . . 43 A5
Norwood Lo KT13 . . . 53 C5
NORWOOD NEW TOWN . . . 22 C2
Norwood Park Rd SE27 . . . 22 C3
Norwood Rd
Effingham KT24 . . . 113 E7
Streatham SE24, SE27 . . . 22 B7
Norwood Sch SE27 . . . 22 C3
Notley End TW20 . . . 11 C1
Notre Dame Sch KT11 . . . 72 F8
Notson Rd SE25 . . . 43 B5
Nottingham Cl GU21 . . . 68 F1
Nottingham Ct 5 GU21 . . . 68 F1
Nottingham Rd
Croydon CR2 . . . 61 C5
Isleworth TW7 . . . 5 F5
Upper Tooting SW17 . . . 20 F7
Nova Mews SM4 . . . 39 E2
Nova Rd CR0 . . . 42 C2
Nower Cl E RH4 . . . 135 F6
Nower Cl W RH4 . . . 135 F6
Nower Lodge Sch RH4 . . . 136 A6
Nower Rd RH4 . . . 136 A6
Nowhurst La RH12 . . . 216 A5
Noyna Rd SW17 . . . 20 F5
Nubia Way SE6 . . . 24 E5
Nuffield Ct TW5 . . . 4 F7
Nuffield Dr GU47 . . . 45 F1
Nugee Ct RG45 . . . 45 B5
Nugent Cl GU8 . . . 192 F6
Nugent Ct
Guildford GU2 . . . 109 B4
Streatham SW16 . . . 21 C4
Nugent Rd
Guildford GU2 . . . 129 D8
South Norwood SE25 . . . 42 F6
Numa Ct TW8 . . . 6 D7
Nunappleton Way RH8 . . . 123 A3
Nuneaton RG12 . . . 27 E3
Nuneham SW16 . . . 21 D4
Nunns Field RH5 . . . 178 D6
Nuns Wlk GU25 . . . 31 D4
Nuptown La SL4 . . . 8 A8
Nursery Ave CR0 . . . 62 D8
Nursery Cl
Capel RH5 . . . 178 C5
Croydon CR0 . . . 62 D8
Ewell KT17 . . . 57 E1
Feltham TW14 . . . 15 B8
Frimley GU16 . . . 85 F7
Walton on t H KT20 . . . 97 B2
Woking GU21 . . . 69 C3
Woodham KT15 . . . 51 F1
Nursery Cotts GU21 . . . 88 F8
Nursery Gdns
Chilworth GU4 . . . 131 B3
Feltham TW12 . . . 15 F4
Hounslow TW4 . . . 4 F2
Staines TW18 . . . 13 B1
Sunbury TW16 . . . 34 F7
Nursery Hill GU5 . . . 152 D5
Nursery La
Hookwood RH6 . . . 160 D2
North Ascot SL5 . . . 28 E8
Nurserylands RH11 . . . 201 A6
Nursery Rd
Farncombe GU7 . . . 150 F7
Knaphill GU21 . . . 68 D2
Merton SW19 . . . 40 B7
Mitcham CR4 . . . 40 E6
South Norwood CR7, SE25 . . . 42 D5
Sunbury TW16 . . . 34 F7
Sutton SM1 . . . 59 C6
Walton on t H KT20 . . . 97 B2
Wimbledon SW19 . . . 19 E1
Nutborn Ho SW19 . . . 19 D2
Nutbourne GU9 . . . 125 E7
Nutbourne Cotts GU8 . . . 191 E7
Nutbourne Ct
2 Horsham RH12 . . . 217 D5
Staines TW18 . . . 12 F1
NUTCOMBE . . . 188 E1
Nutcombe Height GU26 . . . 188 F4
Nutcombe La
Dorking RH4 . . . 135 F7
Haslemere GU26, GU27 . . . 188 E1
Nutcroft Gr KT22 . . . 94 E6
NUTFIELD . . . 119 F2
Nutfield Church CE Prim Sch RH1 . . . 140 F8
Nutfield Cl SM5 . . . 59 E7
Nutfield Ct
Camberley GU15 . . . 65 D7

Nutfield Ct continued
Nutfield RH1 . . . . **119** F2
Nutfield Marsh Rd
RH1 . . . . **119** E4
Nutfield Pl 1 CR7 . . . . . **42** B5
Nutfield Rd
Coulsdon CR5 . . . . **79** A3
Merstham RH1 . . . . **119** C5
Nutfield RH1 . . . . **119** C1
Redhill RH1 . . . . **119** C1
Thornton Heath CR7 . . . . . **42** B5
Nutfield Sta RH1 . . . . **140** E7
Nuthatch Cl GU10 . . . . . . **124** D7
Nuthatch Gdns RH2 . . . . **139** C5
Nuthatch Way
Horsham RH12 . . . . **217** D2
Turners Hill RH10 . . . . . . **204** C5
Nuthurst RG12 . . . . **27** E4
Nuthurst Ave
Cranleigh GU6 . . . . **174** E3
Streatham SW2 . . . . **21** F6
Nuthurst Cl RH11 . . . . . . **201** A7
Nutley RG12 . . . . **27** A1
Nutley Ct 1 RH2 . . . . . . **118** A1
Nutley Dean Bsns Pk
RH6 . . . . **159** E6
Nutley La RH2 . . . . **117** F2
Nutmeg Ct GU14 . . . . **84** C5
Nutshell La GU9 . . . . **125** C6
Nuttall Gdns GU6 . . . . . . **174** E4
Nutty La TW17 . . . . **34** C6
Nutwell St SW17 . . . . **20** E3
Nutwood SW7 . . . . **150** D6
Nutwood Ave RH3 . . . . . **137** C8
Nutwood Cl RH3 . . . . **137** C8
Nyefield Pk KT20 . . . . **97** A1
Nylands Ave TW9 . . . . **7** A5
Nymans Cl RH12 . . . . . . **218** A7
Nymans Ct RH10 . . . . . . **202** B3
Nymans Gdns SW20 . . . . . **39** B6
Nyon Gr SE23, SE6 . . . . . . **23** F6

O

Oakapple Cl
Crawley RH11 . . . . **201** B1
Hamsey Green CR2 . . . . . . **81** B5
Oak Ave
Brookwood GU24 . . . . **88** A6
Croydon CR0 . . . . **63** B8
Egham TW20 . . . . **12** D1
Hampton TW12 . . . . **15** E2
Heston TW5 . . . . **4** E7
Sandhurst GU47 . . . . **45** D1
Oakbank
Fetcham KT22 . . . . **94** D4
Woking GU22 . . . . **89** E8
Oak Bank CR0 . . . . **63** C4
Oakbank Ave KT12 . . . . . **35** F2
Oakbark Ho 10 TW8 . . . . . . **6** C7
Oakbraes GU7 . . . . **150** D6
Oakbrook 3 BR3 . . . . . . **44** B7
Oak Cl
Box Hill KT20 . . . . **116** B5
Chiddingfold GU8 . . . . . . **191** A4
Copthorne RH10 . . . . **183** A3
Ewhurst GU6 . . . . **175** E6
Farncombe GU7 . . . . **150** E8
Sutton SM1 . . . . **59** C8
Oak Cnr RH5 . . . . **157** C4
Oakcombe Cl KT3 . . . . **38** E8
Oak Cottage Cl
Catford SE6 . . . . **24** F7
Wood St V GU3 . . . . **108** C2
Oak Cotts
Compton GU3 . . . . **129** C2
Haslemere GU27 . . . . **207** E6
Oak Croft RH19 . . . . **206** A8
Oakcroft Bsns Ctr KT9 . . **56** F6
Oakcroft Cl KT14 . . . . **70** F5
Oakcroft Ho 4 KT3 . . . . . **38** E2
Oakcroft Rd
Chessington KT9 . . . . **56** F6
Pyrford KT14 . . . . **70** F5
Oakcroft Villas KT9 . . . . **56** F6
Oak Ct CR5 . . . . **78** F1
Oak Ct RH10 . . . . **181** D2
Oak Ct
Farnborough GU14 . . . . . **85** E1
Farnham GU9 . . . . **125** B1
Oakdale
Beckenham BR3 . . . . **44** C7
Bracknell RG12 . . . . **27** D3
Windlesham GU20 . . . . . . **48** D4
Oakdale Rd
Epsom KT19 . . . . **57** D2
Streatham SW16 . . . . **21** E3
Weybridge KT13 . . . . **53** A7
Oakdale Way CR4 . . . . . . **41** A2
Oak Dell RH10 . . . . **202** C7
Oakdene
Beckenham BR3 . . . . **44** C7
Chobham GU24 . . . . **49** F1
Kingswood KT20 . . . . **97** E7
Sunningdale SL5 . . . . **29** F3
1 West Norwood SE19 . . . **22** E3
Oakdene Ave KT7 . . . . . . **37** A1
Oakdene Cl
Brockham RH3 . . . . **137** C7
Great Bookham KT23 . . . . **114** C8
Oakdene Ct
Hampton TW12 . . . . **15** F4
Streatham SW16 . . . . **21** E3
Walton-on-T KT12 . . . . . . **54** B7

Weybridge KT13 . . . . **53** A6
Oakdene Dr KT5 . . . . **38** C1
Oakdene Ho KT15 . . . . . . **52** C5
Oakdene Lo SE20 . . . . **23** B1
Oakdene Mews SM3 . . . . . **39** F1
Oakdene Par KT11 . . . . . . **73** B5
Oakdene Pl GU3 . . . . **130** C1
Oakdene Rd
Brockham RH3 . . . . **137** C7
Cobham KT11 . . . . **73** B5
Godalming GU7 . . . . **150** D3
Little Bookham KT23 . . . . . **93** F3
Redhill RH1 . . . . **118** F1
Shalford GU3 . . . . **130** C1
Oaken Coppice KT21 . . . . **96** A8
Oaken Copse GU15 . . . . . **66** C7
Oaken Copse Cres
GU14 . . . . **85** B7
Oak End RH5 . . . . **157** C3
Oaken Dr KT10 . . . . **55** F4
Oak End Way KT15 . . . . . **70** F7
Oakengates RG12 . . . . **27** A1
Oaken La KT10 . . . . **55** E5
Oakenshaw Cl KT6 . . . . . . **37** E2
Oakey Dr RG40 . . . . **25** B5
Oak Farm Cl GU17 . . . . . . **64** C5
Oak Farm Com Sch
GU14 . . . . **84** F6
Oakfield
Plaistow RH14 . . . . **211** A8
Woking GU21 . . . . **68** E3
Oakfield Cl
New Malden KT3 . . . . **38** F4
Weybridge KT13 . . . . **53** C6
Oakfield Ct
Croydon CR2 . . . . **61** C4
5 Weybridge KT13 . . . . . **53** C5
Wokingham RG41 . . . . **25** A5
Oakfield Dr RH2 . . . . **118** B3
Oakfield Gdns
Beckenham BR3 . . . . **44** A4
Carshalton SM5 . . . . **40** F1
3 Dulwich SE19 . . . . **22** E3
Oakfield Glade KT13 . . . . **53** C6
Oakfield Jun Sch KT22 . . **94** D4
Oakfield Pl GU14 . . . . **84** C4
Oakfield Prep Sch
SE21 . . . . **22** D7
Oakfield Rd
Ashford TW15 . . . . **14** B3
Ashtead KT21 . . . . **75** E1
Blackwater GU17 . . . . **64** F3
Cobham KT11 . . . . **73** B5
Penge SE20 . . . . **23** B1
Thornton Heath CR0 . . . . . **42** C1
Wimbledon SW19 . . . . **19** D5
Oakfield Road Ind Est
SE20 . . . . **23** B1
Oakfields
Camberley GU15 . . . . **65** B5
Crawley RH10 . . . . **202** D7
Guildford GU3 . . . . **108** F3
Wallis Wood RH5 . . . . **196** D8
Walton-on-T KT12 . . . . **35** A1
West Byfleet KT14 . . . . **71** B5
Oakfield Sch GU22 . . . . . . **70** F4
Oakfield Way RH19 . . . . **185** D9
Oak Gdns CR0 . . . . **63** A8
Oak Glade KT19 . . . . **76** A7
Oak Gr
Cranleigh GU6 . . . . **174** F1
Loxwood RH14 . . . . **213** A4
Sunbury TW16 . . . . **15** B1
West Wickham BR4 . . . . . . **44** C1
Oak Grange Rd GU4 . . . . **111** B6
Oak Grove Cres GU15 . . . **64** F6
Oak Grove Rd SE20 . . . . . **43** C7
Oakhall Ct TW16 . . . . **14** F3
Oakhall Dr TW16 . . . . **14** F3
Oakham Cl SE6 . . . . **23** F6
Oakham Dr BR2 . . . . **44** F5
Oakhaven RH10 . . . . **201** D4
OAKHILL **217** E2
Oakhill KT10 . . . . **56** A4
Oak Hill
Epsom KT18 . . . . **76** D3
Guildford GU4 . . . . **110** C6
Surbiton KT6 . . . . **37** E2
Wood St V GU3 . . . . **108** B3
Oakhill Chase RH10 . . . . **202** D7
Oakhill Cl KT21 . . . . **75** C1
Oak Hill Cres KT6 . . . . . . **37** E2
Oakhill Ct
8 Surbiton KT6 . . . . **37** E3
Wimbledon SW19 . . . . **19** D1
Oakhill Gdns KT13 . . . . . . **53** E8
Oak Hill Gr KT6 . . . . **37** E3
Oakhill Lo
Purley CR8 . . . . **80** A6
3 Sutton SM1 . . . . **59** B7
Oakhill Rd
Addlestone KT15 . . . . **51** F4
Ashtead KT21 . . . . **75** C1
Beckenham BR3 . . . . **44** C7
Headley Down GU35 . . . . **187** B5
Horsham RH13 . . . . **217** E2
Reigate RH2 . . . . **139** B8
Sutton SM1 . . . . **59** C7
Thornton Heath SW16 . . . . **41** F8
Oak Hill Rd KT6 . . . . **37** E3
Oak Ho
Enton Green GU8 . . . . . . **171** B3
Farnborough GU14 . . . . . **85** A7
Grayshott GU26 . . . . **188** D3
Penge SE20 . . . . **43** B7
2 Richmond TW9 . . . . **7** B6

Teddington TW11 . . . . **17** C2
18 Woking GU22 . . . . **69** F2
Oakhurst
Chobham GU24 . . . . **49** E2
Grayshott GU26 . . . . **188** D3
Kenley CR8 . . . . **80** C5
Woking GU21 . . . . **69** D3
Oakhurst Cl 4 TW11 . . . . **16** E3
Oakhurst Cottage ★
GU8 . . . . **191** C8
Oakhurst Gdns RH19 . . . **185** C2
Oakhurst La RH14 . . . . . **212** E7
Oakhurst Mews RH12 . . . **218** A4
Oakhurst Rd KT19 . . . . . . **57** D4
Oakhurst Rise SM5 . . . . . **59** E1
Oakhyrst Grange Sch
CR3 . . . . **100** D1
Oakies Ho SW16 . . . . **188** D3
Oakington 6 KT1 . . . . **38** A7
Oakington Cl TW16 . . . . . . **35** C7
Oakington Dr TW16 . . . . . **35** C7
Oak La
Broadbridge Heath
RH12 . . . . **216** E3
Englefield Green TW20 . . . **11** C5
Isleworth TW7 . . . . **5** E3
Twickenham TW1 . . . . **17** A8
Woking GU22 . . . . **70** B3
Oakland Ave GU9 . . . . . . **125** E7
Oaklands
Croydon CR0 . . . . **61** B5
Fetcham KT22 . . . . **94** D3
Haslemere GU27 . . . . **208** C5
Horley RH6 . . . . **161** C3
Horsham RH13 . . . . **217** E2
Purley CR8 . . . . **80** C5
South Godstone RH9 . . . . **142** E5
Twickenham TW2 . . . . **16** C8
Oaklands Ave
Hounslow TW7 . . . . **5** F8
Thames Ditton KT10 . . . . . **36** D1
Thornton Heath CR7 . . . . . **42** A5
West Wickham BR4 . . . . . . **63** B7
Oaklands Cl
Chessington KT9 . . . . **56** C6
North Ascot SL5 . . . . **8** F1
Shalford GU4 . . . . **130** C1
Oaklands Ct
Addlestone KT15 . . . . **52** B7
Beckenham BR3 . . . . **44** C7
Oaklands Dr
North Ascot SL5 . . . . **8** F1
Redhill RH1 . . . . **140** B7
Twickenham TW2 . . . . **16** C8
Wokingham RG41 . . . . **25** A5
Oaklands Gdns CR8 . . . . . **80** C5
Oaklands Inf Sch
Biggin Hill TN16 . . . . **83** C3
Crowthorne RG45 . . . . **45** A6
Oaklands Jun Sch
Biggin Hill TN16 . . . . **83** C3
Crowthorne RG45 . . . . **45** A6
Oaklands La
Biggin Hill TN16 . . . . **83** C5
Crowthorne RG45 . . . . **45** B7
Oaklands Pk RG41 . . . . . . **25** A4
Oaklands Rd
Bromley BR1 . . . . **24** E1
Mortlake SW14 . . . . **7** D4
Oaklands Sch TW3 . . . . **5** D4
Oaklands Way
Tadworth KT20 . . . . **97** C5
Wallington SM6 . . . . **60** D3
Oakland Way KT19 . . . . . . **57** E4
Oaklawn GU21 . . . . **70** A4
Oaklawn Rd KT22 . . . . **74** E2
Oaklea GU12 . . . . **106** A5
Oaklea Ct CR2 . . . . **61** D2
Oak Leaf Cl
Epsom KT19 . . . . **76** C7
Guildford GU2 . . . . **108** D2
Oak Leaf Ct SL5 . . . . **28** D8
Oakleigh
Epsom KT18 . . . . **76** E5
Lightwater GU18 . . . . **67** C8
Oakleigh Ave KT6 . . . . **57** B8
Oakleigh Ct
Oxted RH8 . . . . **122** E6
Penge SE20 . . . . **23** B1
Oakleigh Rd RH12 . . . . . **217** F4
Oakleigh Way
Mitcham CR4 . . . . **41** B8
1 Tolworth KT6 . . . . **38** B1
Oakley Ave CR0 . . . . **60** E6
Oakley Cl
Addlestone KT15 . . . . **52** D6
East Grinstead RH19 . . . . **206** B7
Hounslow TW7 . . . . **5** D6
Oakley Cotts RH19 . . . . . **206** C7
Oakley Ct
Carshalton CR4 . . . . **41** A2
Harlington UB3 . . . . **3** C7
15 Redhill RH1 . . . . **119** A2
Oakley Dell GU4 . . . . **110** C3
Oakley Gdns
Banstead SM7 . . . . **78** B4
Brockham RH3 . . . . **137** C3
Oakley Ho GU7 . . . . **150** E8
Oakley Rd
Camberley GU15 . . . . **65** B4
Croydon SE25 . . . . **43** B4
Whyteleafe CR6 . . . . **81** A1
Oak Lo
4 Charlton TW16 . . . . . . **14** F1
Cobham KT11 . . . . **73** C4
Crowthorne RG45 . . . . **45** C5
18 Sutton SM1 . . . . **59** C6

14 West Norwood SE21 . . . **22** D6
Oak Lodge Cl KT12 . . . . . **54** C5
Oak Lodge Dr
Salfords RH1 . . . . **140** A1
West Wickham BR4 . . . . . . **44** B2
Oak Lodge Prim Sch
BR4 . . . . **44** B2
Oak Lodge Sch SW12 . . . . **21** A8
Oakman Ho 29 SW19 . . . . **19** D7
Oak Mead GU7 . . . . **150** E8
Oakmead Gn KT18 . . . . . . **76** C4
Oakmead Pl CR4 . . . . **40** E8
Oakmead Rd
Upper Tooting SW12 . . . . . **21** B7
Wallington CR0 . . . . **41** D3
Oak Park Gdns SW19 . . . . **19** D7
Oak Pk KT14 . . . . **70** E6
Oak Rd
Caterham CR3 . . . . **100** E5
Crawley RH10 . . . . **201** C5
Farnborough GU14 . . . . . **85** C3
Kingston u T KT3 . . . . **38** D7
Leatherhead KT22 . . . . . . **95** A8
Reigate RH2 . . . . **118** B2
Stoke D'Abernon KT11 . . . . **73** E4
Oakridge GU24 . . . . **67** F6
Oak Ridge RH4 . . . . **136** B4
Oakridge La BR1 . . . . **24** D3
Oakridge Rd BR1 . . . . **24** E3
Oak Row CR4 . . . . **41** C7
Oaks Ave
Feltham TW13 . . . . **15** E6
North Cheam KT4 . . . . **58** B6
West Norwood SE19,
SE27 . . . . **22** E3
Oaks Cl
Horsham RH12 . . . . **218** B6
Leatherhead KT22 . . . . . . **95** A6
Oaks Ct KT22 . . . . **95** A6
Oaksford Ave SE26 . . . . . . **23** B5
Oakshade Rd
Catford BR1 . . . . **24** D4
Oxshott KT22 . . . . **74** C5
Oakshaw RH8 . . . . **122** D8
Oakshaw Rd SW18 . . . . . . **20** B8
Oakside Ct RH6 . . . . **161** C4
Oakside La RH6 . . . . **161** C4
Oaks La
South Croydon CR0 . . . . . . **62** C7
South Holmwood RH5 . . . . **157** B8
Oaks Prim Sch The
RH10 . . . . **201** F3
Oaks Rd
Purley CR8 . . . . **80** B5
Reigate RH2 . . . . **118** D2
South Croydon CR0 . . . . . . **62** C6
Stanwell TW19 . . . . **2** D1
Oak's Rd GU21 . . . . **69** E2
Oaks Sports Ctr SM5 . . . . **78** E8
Oaks Sq The 9 KT19 . . . . **76** D6
Oaks The
Bracknell RG12 . . . . **27** D7
Chiddingfold GU8 . . . . . . **191** B4
Claygate KT9 . . . . **56** C7
Dorking RH4 . . . . **136** B4
East Grinstead RH19 . . . . **206** B8
Epsom KT18 . . . . **76** F5
Farnborough GU14 . . . . . **84** D3
Smallfield RH6 . . . . **162** B3
Staines TW18 . . . . **12** F4
Sutton SM1 . . . . **59** A5
Tadworth KT20 . . . . **97** C4
Wallington SM6 . . . . **60** C6
West Byfleet KT14 . . . . **71** A5
Wimbledon SW19 . . . . **19** E2
Oaks Tk SM5, SM6 . . . . . . **60** B1
Oaks Way
Burgh Heath KT18 . . . . . . **97** B8
Long Ditton KT6 . . . . **37** D1
Purley CR8 . . . . **80** C5
Send Marsh GU23 . . . . . . **91** A3
Wallington SM5 . . . . **59** F3
Oak Tree Cl
Aldershot GU12 . . . . **126** E8
Ash Vale GU12 . . . . **85** F1
East Grinstead RH19 . . . . **185** C3
Guildford, Burpham
GU4 . . . . **110** C6
Guildford, Jacobswell
GU4 . . . . **109** D6
Knaphill GU21 . . . . **68** B1
Virginia Water GU25 . . . . . **31** D3
Oak Tree Dr
Englefield Green TW20 . . . **11** C3
Guildford GU1 . . . . **109** C5
Oak Tree La
Dunsfold GU8 . . . . **192** F5
Haslemere GU27 . . . . **207** D6
Oak Tree Rd
Knaphill GU21 . . . . **68** B1
Milford GU8 . . . . **149** F1
Oaktrees
Ash GU12 . . . . **105** F5
Hale GU9 . . . . **125** B6
Oaktree Sch The GU22 . . . **88** E8
Oaktrees Ct 1 GU12 . . . . **105** F5
Oak Tree View GU9 . . . . . **125** E6
Oaktree Way GU47 . . . . . . **45** A1
Oak Tree Way RH13 . . . . **217** F4
Oaktree Wlk CR3 . . . . . . **100** E5
Oakview Gr CR0 . . . . **43** E1
Oakview Gr CR0 . . . . **43** E1
Oakview Rd SE6 . . . . **24** B3
Oakway
Aldershot GU12 . . . . **126** E8
Beckenham BR2 . . . . **44** D7
Knaphill GU21 . . . . **88** B8

West Barnes SW20 . . . . . **39** C5
Oak Way
Ashtead KT21 . . . . **76** A3
Crawley RH10 . . . . **201** E8
Croydon CR0 . . . . **43** D3
East Bedfont TW14 . . . . . . **14** E7
Ifold RH14 . . . . **212** D2
Reigate RH2 . . . . **139** D8
Oakway Dr GU16 . . . . **65** E1
Oak Wlk SM6 . . . . **41** A1
Oakwood
Epsom KT18 . . . . **76** E5
Guildford GU2 . . . . **109** A6
Wallington SM6 . . . . **60** B2
Oakwood Ave
Beckenham BR3 . . . . **44** C7
Epsom KT19 . . . . **57** B2
Mitcham CR4 . . . . **40** D7
Purley CR8 . . . . **80** C7
Oakwood Cl
East Horsley KT24 . . . . . . **112** E8
Redhill RH1 . . . . **119** A1
South Nutfield RH1 . . . . . **140** F7
Oakwood Ct
Beckenham BR3 . . . . **44** C7
Bisley GU24 . . . . **68** A3
1 Sutton SM1 . . . . **59** C6
Oakwood Dr
East Horsley KT24 . . . . . . **112** E8
West Norwood SE19 . . . . . **22** E2
Oakwood Gdns
Knaphill GU21 . . . . **68** B1
Sutton SM1 . . . . **59** A8
Oakwood Grange KT13 . . **53** E7
Oakwood Hall KT20 . . . . . **98** C4
OAKWOOD HILL **197** A7
Oakwood Ho GU23 . . . . . . **71** E3
Oakwood Ind Pk
RH10 . . . . **182** A2
Oakwood Pk RH18 . . . . . **206** F2
Oakwood Pl
Crowthorne RG45 . . . . **45** A4
Thornton Heath CR0 . . . . . **42** A3
Oakwood Rd
Bletchingley RH1 . . . . **120** A6
Bracknell RG12 . . . . **27** E7
Horley RH6 . . . . **161** B4
Knaphill GU21 . . . . **88** E8
Thornton Heath CR0,
CR7 . . . . **42** A3
Thorpe GU25 . . . . **31** C4
Wimbledon SW20 . . . . **39** A8
Windlesham GU20 . . . . . . **48** E4
Oakwood Rise CR3 . . . . . **100** E2
Oakwood Sch
Horley RH6 . . . . **161** C3
Purley CR8 . . . . **80** B5
Oareborough RG12 . . . . . . **27** E4
Oarsman Pl KT8 . . . . **36** E5
Oast House Cl TW19 . . . . . **11** E8
Oast House Cres GU9 . . . **125** D6
Oast House La GU9 . . . . . **125** D6
Oast La GU11 . . . . **126** B7
Oast Lo 6 W4 . . . . **7** E7
Oast Rd RH8 . . . . **122** F4
Oates Cl BR2 . . . . **44** D6
Oates Wlk RH10 . . . . **201** F3
Oatfield Rd KT20 . . . . **97** B6
Oatlands
Crawley RH11 . . . . **201** A5
Horley RH6 . . . . **161** C1
Horley RH6 . . . . **161** C4
Oatlands Ave KT13 . . . . . . **53** E6
Oatlands Chase KT12,
KT13 . . . . **53** E7
Oatlands Cl KT13 . . . . **53** D6
Oatlands Ct 3 SW19 . . . . **19** D7
Oatlands Dr KT13, KT12 . . **53** D7
Oatlands Gn KT13 . . . . **53** D7
Oatlands Mere KT13 . . . . . **53** E6
OATLANDS PARK **53** E6
Oatlands Rd KT20 . . . . **97** E8
Oatlands Sch KT13 . . . . . . **53** D6
Oban Rd SE25 . . . . **42** D5
Oberon Way
Crawley RH11 . . . . **200** E3
Littleton TW17 . . . . **33** E6
Oberursel Way GU11 . . . **104** F2
Observatory Rd SW14 . . . . **7** C3
Observatory Wlk 6
RH1 . . . . **118** F1
Observer St RH12 . . . . . . **217** C1
Occam Rd GU2 . . . . **129** D8
Ochre Ct TW13 . . . . **14** F5
Ockenden Cl 16 GU22 . . . . **69** F1
Ockenden Gdns GU22 . . . . **69** F1
Ockenden Rd GU22 . . . . . . **69** F1
Ockfields GU8 . . . . **149** F1
Ockford Ct GU7 . . . . **150** D4
Ockford Dr GU7 . . . . **150** D4
Ockford Rd GU7 . . . . **150** D4
OCKFORD RIDGE **150** B3
Ockford Ridge GU7 . . . . **150** B2
OCKHAM **92** B6
Ockham Dr KT24 . . . . **92** D3
Ockham La GU23, KT11 . . **92** D7
Ockham Rd N GU23,
KT24 . . . . **92** C3
Ockham Rd S KT24 . . . . . **112** E7
OCKLEY **177** D5
Ockley Ct
Guildford GU4 . . . . **110** B6
2 Sutton SM1 . . . . **59** C6
Ockley Ho 8 KT2 . . . . **18** B2
Ockley Rd
Beare Green RH5 . . . . . . **157** C2

Ockley Rd *continued*
Ewhurst GU6 . . . . 175 F6
Forest Green GU6, RH5 . . . 176 C7
Ockley RH5 . . . . 177 B7
Streatham SW16 . . . . 21 E4
Thornton Heath CR0, CR9 . . . . 41 F2
Ockleys Mead RH9 . . . . 121 C5
Ockley Sta RH5 . . . . 178 A5
O'Connor Rd GU11 . . . . 105 E7
Octagon Rd KT12 . . . . 53 E1
Octavia RG12 . . . . 27 A1
Octavia Cl CR4 . . . . 40 E4
Octavia Ho SE6 . . . . 24 B8
Octavia Rd TW7 . . . . 5 F4
Octavia Way TW18 . . . . 13 A2
October Ct BR2 . . . . 44 F6
Odard Rd KT8 . . . . 36 A5
Odette Ho 6 SE27 . . . . 22 D4
Odiham Rd GU9, GU10 . . . 124 D7
Offley Pl TW7 . . . . 5 D5
Off Upper Manor Rd GU7 . . . . 150 E7
Ogden Ho TW13 . . . . 15 E4
Ogden Pk RG12 . . . . 27 E6
Okeburn Rd SW17 . . . . 21 A3
Okehurst Rd RH14 . . . . 214 C1
Okingham Cl GU47 . . . . 45 D1
Olaf Palme Ho TW13 . . . . 15 B5
Oldacre GU24 . . . . 67 F7
Old Acre KT14 . . . . 71 A5
Old Ave
Sheerwater KT14 . . . . 70 E6
Weybridge KT13 . . . . 53 C3
Old Avenue Cl KT14 . . . . 70 E6
Old Bakehouse Ct RG45 . . . . 45 B4
Old Bakery Ct GU6 . . . . 175 E5
Old Bakery Mews GU5 . . . . 132 B4
Old Barn Cl SM2 . . . . 58 E3
Old Barn Dr RH5 . . . . 178 D6
Old Barn La
Churt GU10 . . . . 168 B1
Kenley CR3 . . . . 80 F3
Old Barn Rd KT18 . . . . 76 C2
Old Barn View GU7 . . . . 150 C2
Old Bisley Rd GU16 . . . . 66 C3
Old Bracknell Cl RG12 . . . . 27 B6
Old Bracknell La E RG12 . . . . 27 B6
Old Bracknell La W RG12 . . . . 27 B6
Old Brewery Ct RH4 . . . . 136 B7
Old Brickfield Rd GU11 . . . . 126 B7
Old Bridge Rd GU10 . . . . 126 B4
Old Bridge St KT1 . . . . 37 D7
Old Brighton Rd S RH11 . . . . 181 E5
Old Bromley Rd BR1 . . . . 24 D3
Oldbury RG12 . . . . 26 F6
Oldbury Cl
Frimley GU16 . . . . 85 F8
Horsham RH12 . . . . 218 A7
Old Bury Hill Ho RH4 . . . . 135 E5
Oldbury Rd KT16 . . . . 32 E2
Old Chapel La GU12 . . . . 106 A1
Old Charlton Rd TW17 . . . 34 C4
Old Char Wharf RH4 . . . . 135 F8
Old Chertsey Rd GU24 . . . . 50 C1
Old Chestnut Ave KT10 . . . . 55 B4
Old Chiswick Yd 12 W4 . . . . 7 E8
Old Church La GU9 . . . . 146 D7
Old Church Path KT10 . . . . 55 B6
Old Claygate La KT10 . . . . 56 A5
Old Coalyard The TW20 . . . . 11 F2
Old Common Rd KT11 . . . . 73 B7
Old Compton La GU9 . . . . 125 F2
Old Control Tower Rd RH6 . . . . 181 D6
Old Convent The
Dockenfield GU10 . . . . 166 D3
East Grinstead RH19 . . . . 185 E2
Old Corn Mews GU7 . . . . 150 F6
Old Cote Dr TW5 . . . . 5 A8
Old Cotts GU3 . . . . 130 C2
OLD COULSDON 100 B7
Old Court Rd GU2 . . . . 130 A8
Old Crawley Rd RH12 . . . 218 C7
Old Cross Tree Way GU12 . . . . 127 C8
Old Ct KT21 . . . . 95 E8
Old Dairy Mews SW12 . . . . 21 A7
Old Dairy The
5 Dorking RH4 . . . . 136 B8
Woking GU21 . . . . 69 D2
Old Dean Rd GU15 . . . . 65 D7
Old Deer Park Gdns TW9 . . . . 6 E4
Old Denne Gdns 6 RH12 . . . . 217 C1
Old Devonshire Rd SW12 . . . . 21 B8
Old Dock Cl TW9 . . . . 7 A8
Old Dr GU5 . . . . 133 C5
Olde Farm Dr GU17 . . . . 64 B5
Old Elstead Rd GU8 . . . . 149 E2
Olden La CR8 . . . . 80 A7
Old Esher Cl KT12 . . . . 54 D5
Old Esher Rd KT12 . . . . 54 E5
Old Farleigh Rd CR6, CR22 . . . . 81 E6
Old Farm Cl TW4 . . . . 4 F3
Old Farm Ct KT10 . . . . 55 A8
Old Farmhouse Dr KT22 . . . . 74 D4
Old Farm Pl GU12 . . . . 105 F5
Old Farm Rd
Guildford GU1 . . . . 109 D4
Hampton TW12 . . . . 15 F2
Old Farnham La
Bentley GU10 . . . . 124 A1
Farnham GU9 . . . . 146 C8
Oldfield Cl RH6 . . . . 160 F1
Oldfield Gdns KT21 . . . . 95 D8
Oldfield Ho SW16 . . . . 21 B4
Oldfield Rd
Hampton TW12 . . . . 35 F8
Horley RH6 . . . . 160 F1
Wimbledon SW19 . . . . 19 E2
Oldfields Rd SM1, SM3 . . . . 59 A8
Oldfields Trad Est SM1 . . . 59 A7
Oldfieldwood GU22 . . . . 70 B2
Old Ford Ho CR0 . . . . 60 E7
Old Forge Cl RH12 . . . . 199 F1
Old Forge Cres TW17 . . . . 34 B3
Old Forge End GU47 . . . . 64 B7
Old Fox Cl CR3 . . . . 100 B6
Old Frensham Rd GU10 . . . . 146 E4
Old Green La GU15 . . . . 65 C7
Old Guildford Rd
Mytchett GU16 . . . . 86 C4
Warnham RH12 . . . . 216 E4
Old Hall Cotts GU3 . . . . 107 B4
Oldham Ho 10 SE21 . . . . 22 E4
Old Haslemere Rd GU27 . . . . 208 C5
Old Heath Way GU9 . . . . 125 C7
Old Hill GU22 . . . . 89 D7
Old Hollow RH10 . . . . 202 F7
Old Horsham Rd
Beare Green RH5 . . . . 157 C4
Crawley RH11 . . . . 201 B4
Old Hospital Cl SW12, SW17 . . . . 20 F7
Old House Cl
Ewell KT17 . . . . 57 F1
Wimbledon SW19 . . . . 19 E3
Old House Gdns 9 TW1 . . . 6 C1
Oldhouse La
Bisley GU24 . . . . 68 A5
Windlesham GU18, GU20 . . . . 48 C2
Old House Unit (Clarendon Sch) TW12 . . . . 35 F8
Olding Ho 6 SW12 . . . . 21 C8
Old Ively Rd GU14 . . . . 104 B8
Old Kiln GU9 . . . . 125 A2
Old Kiln Cl GU10 . . . . 167 F2
Old Kiln Ctyd 16 GU9 . . . . 125 B2
Old Kiln La
Brockham RH3 . . . . 137 C8
Churt GU10 . . . . 167 F2
Old Kiln Mus* GU10 . . . . 146 F3
Old Kingston Rd KT4 . . . . 57 C7
Old La
Aldershot GU11 . . . . 126 A7
Aldershot, North Town GU12 . . . . 105 E3
Dockenfield GU10 . . . . 166 F4
East Horsley KT11 . . . . 93 A5
Martyr's Green KT11 . . . . 92 E7
Ockham GU23, KT11 . . . . 72 B1
Oxted RH8 . . . . 122 F5
Tatsfield TN16 . . . . 103 D6
Old Lands Hill RG12 . . . . 27 D8
Old Lane Gdns KT11 . . . . 93 A5
Old Lane The GU10 . . . . 187 F8
Old Lodge Cl GU7 . . . . 150 B3
Old Lodge La CR8 . . . . 80 A3
Old Lodge Pl 7 TW1 . . . . 6 B1
Old London Rd
Epsom KT17, KT18 . . . . 77 A2
Kingston u T KT2 . . . . 37 E7
Mickleham RH5 . . . . 115 C8
OLD MALDEN 38 E1
Old Malden La KT4 . . . . 57 E8
Old Malt Way GU21 . . . . 69 D2
Old Manor Cl RH11 . . . . 201 A8
Old Manor Ct RH11 . . . . 201 A8
Old Manor Dr TW7 . . . . 5 C1
Old Manor Gdns GU4 . . . . 131 C3
Old Manor House Mews TW17 . . . . 34 A6
Old Market Ct SM1 . . . . 59 B6
Old Martyrs RH11 . . . . 181 D1
Oldmeadow Ho RH11 . . . . 201 D6
Old Merrow St GU4 . . . . 110 D3
Old Mill La RH1 . . . . 119 B7
Old Millmeads RH12 . . . . 217 C5
Old Mill Pl
Haslemere GU27 . . . . 207 F7
Horton TW19 . . . . 1 B1
Old Mus Ct GU27 . . . . 208 D6
Old Nursery Pl TW15 . . . . 14 B3
Old Oak Ave CR5 . . . . 98 E8
Old Oak Cl
Chessington KT9 . . . . 56 F6
Cobham KT11 . . . . 73 B6
Old Orch
Byfleet KT14 . . . . 71 F7
Sunbury TW16 . . . . 35 C7
Old Orchards RH10 . . . . 202 E6
Old Orchard The GU9 . . . 146 A7
Old Palace La TW9 . . . . 6 C2
Old Palace Rd
Croydon CR0, CR9 . . . . 61 C7
Guildford GU2 . . . . 130 A8
Weybridge KT13 . . . . 53 B7
Old Palace Sch of John Whitgift CR0 . . . . 61 B7
Old Palace Terr 7 TW9 . . . 6 D2
Old Palace Yd 2 TW9 . . . . 6 D2
Old Park Cl GU9 . . . . 125 A6
Old Park La
Farnham GU9 . . . . 125 A4
Hale GU9 . . . . 124 F6
Old Park Mews TW5 . . . . 4 F7
Old Parvis Rd KT14 . . . . 71 C7
Old Pasture Rd GU16, GU15 . . . . 65 F3
Old Pharmacy Ct RG45 . . . 45 C4
Old Pond Cl GU15 . . . . 65 C1
Old Portsmouth Rd
Artington GU2, GU3, GU7 . . . . 130 C3
Frimley GU15 . . . . 66 A5
Thursley GU8 . . . . 169 D4
Old Pottery Cl RH2 . . . . 139 B7
Old Pound Cl TW7 . . . . 6 A6
Old Quarry The GU27 . . . . 207 F4
Old Rd
Addlestone KT15 . . . . 51 F3
Buckland RH3 . . . . 116 F1
East Grinstead RH19 . . . . 185 F1
Old Rectory Cl
Bramley GU5 . . . . 151 F6
Walton on t H KT20 . . . . 97 A3
Old Rectory Cvn Site The SM7 . . . . 78 F4
Old Rectory Dr GU12 . . . . 106 B2
Old Rectory Gdns
Farnborough GU14 . . . . 85 D4
Godalming GU7 . . . . 150 F2
Old Rectory La KT24 . . . . 92 E1
Old Rectory The KT23 . . . 113 F8
Old Redstone Dr RH1 . . . 140 A8
Old Reigate Rd
Brockham RH3 . . . . 116 C1
Dorking RH4 . . . . 115 F2
Oldridge Rd SW12 . . . . 21 B8
Old St Mary's KT24 . . . . 112 B6
Old Sawmill La RG45 . . . . 45 C6
Old School Cl
Ash GU12 . . . . 106 A3
10 Guildford GU1 . . . . 109 D1
Merton SW19 . . . . 40 A7
Penge BR3 . . . . 43 E7
Old School Ct
Leatherhead KT22 . . . . 95 B5
Wraysbury TW19 . . . . 11 E8
Old School Ho CR4 . . . . 40 E6
Old School La RH3 . . . . 137 A7
Old School Mews
Egham TW20 . . . . 12 D3
Oatlands Park KT13 . . . . 53 D6
Old School Pl
Croydon CR0 . . . . 61 A6
Lingfield RH7 . . . . 164 D4
Woking GU22 . . . . 89 F6
Old Schools La KT17 . . . . 57 F2
Old School Sq KT7 . . . . 36 F3
Old School Terr SM3 . . . . 58 D3
Old School The SW19 . . . . 40 A7
Old Stables The GU1 . . . . 110 D2
Old Station App KT22 . . . . 95 A6
Old Station Cl RH10 . . . . 204 B7
Old Station Rd GU7 . . . . 150 E6
Old Station Way GU7 . . . . 150 E5
Old Station Works TW9 . . . 7 A5
Oldstead RG12 . . . . 27 D4
Oldstead Rd BR1 . . . . 24 D4
Old Stede Cl KT21 . . . . 75 F2
Old Studio Cl CR0 . . . . 42 D2
Old Surgery The 4 RH19 . . . . 185 F2
Old Surrey Mews The RH9 . . . . 121 C5
Old Swan Yd SM5 . . . . 59 F6
Old Town CR0, CR9 . . . . 61 B7
Old Tye Ave TN16 . . . . 83 E3
Old Vicarage Sch TW10 . . . . 6 E1
Old Vicarage The
Mitcham CR4 . . . . 40 E6
Wrecclesham GU10 . . . . 145 F7
Old Village Stores The GU23 . . . . 71 E3
Old Water Yd RH4 . . . . 136 A8
Old Westhall Cl CR6 . . . . 101 C8
Old Wharf Way KT13 . . . . 52 F6
Old Wickhurst La RH12 . . . . 216 D2
OLD WINDSOR 11 A8
OLD WOKING 90 A7
Old Wokingham Rd RG45 . . . . 45 C7
Old Woking Rd
Pyrford GU22, KT14 . . . . 70 D3
West Byfleet KT14 . . . . 71 A6
Woking GU22 . . . . 90 C8
Oldwood Chase GU14 . . . . 84 C3
Oleander Cl RG45 . . . . 45 A7
Oliver Ave SE25 . . . . 42 F6
Oliver Cl
Addlestone KT15 . . . . 52 B6
Brentford W4 . . . . 7 B8
Oliver Ct
Isleworth TW7 . . . . 5 F4
Penge SE26 . . . . 23 C2
Olive Rd 3 SW19 . . . . 20 C1
Oliver Gr SE25 . . . . 42 F5
Oliver Ho GU22 . . . . 69 E1
Oliver Rd
Ascot SL5 . . . . 29 B5
Carshalton SM1 . . . . 59 D6
Horsham RH12 . . . . 217 A1
Kingston u T KT3 . . . . 38 C7
Olivier Rd RH10 . . . . 202 D5
Ollerton RG12 . . . . 27 A1
Olley Cl SM6 . . . . 60 E4
Olveston Wlk SM4, SM5 . . . 40 D3
Olyffe Dr BR3 . . . . 44 C8
Omega Rd GU21 . . . . 70 A3
Omega Way TW20 . . . . 32 C8
One Tree Cnr GU1 . . . . 131 B8
One Tree Hill Rd GU4 . . . 131 B7
Ongar Cl KT15 . . . . 51 F4
Ongar Hill KT15 . . . . 52 A4
Ongar Par KT15 . . . . 52 A4
Ongar Pl KT15 . . . . 52 A4
Ongar Place Inf Sch KT15 . . . . 52 A4
Ongar Rd KT15 . . . . 52 A5
Onslow Ave
Belmont SM2 . . . . 77 F8
Richmond TW10 . . . . 6 E2
Onslow Avenue Mans 13 TW10 . . . . 6 E2
Onslow Cl
Thames Ditton KT7 . . . . 36 E1
Woking GU22 . . . . 70 A2
Onslow Cres GU22 . . . . 70 A2
Onslow Ct RH10 . . . . 182 A1
Onslow Dr SL5 . . . . 9 A1
Onslow Gdns
Sanderstead CR2 . . . . 81 A7
Thames Ditton KT7 . . . . 36 E1
Wallington SM6 . . . . 60 C3
Onslow Ho 1 KT2 . . . . 37 F8
Onslow Inf Sch GU2 . . . . 129 F7
Onslow Lo
Staines TW18 . . . . 12 F1
Streatham SW2 . . . . 22 A8
Onslow Mews 1 KT16 . . . . 33 A3
Onslow Rd
Guildford GU1 . . . . 109 D1
Hersham KT12 . . . . 54 A5
New Malden KT3 . . . . 39 A5
Richmond TW10 . . . . 6 E1
Sunningdale SL5 . . . . 30 B2
Thornton Heath CR0 . . . . 42 A1
Onslow St GU1 . . . . 130 C8
ONSLOW VILLAGE 129 E7
Onslow Way
Pyrford GU22 . . . . 70 F4
Thames Ditton KT7 . . . . 36 E1
Ontario Cl RH6 . . . . 162 A2
Onyx Ho KT4 . . . . 38 D1
Onyz The RG12 . . . . 27 E6
Opal Ho KT4 . . . . 38 D1
Openview SW17, SW18 . . . . 20 D6
Opladen Way RG12 . . . . 27 E4
Opossum Dr TW4 . . . . 4 C4
Opus Pk GU4 . . . . 109 D6
Orangery The TW10 . . . . 17 C6
Orchard Ave
Ashford TW15 . . . . 14 C2
Carshalton CR4 . . . . 41 A1
Croydon CR0 . . . . 43 E1
Hatton TW14 . . . . 3 D2
Heston TW5 . . . . 4 E7
Hinchley Wood KT7 . . . . 56 A8
Kingston u T KT3 . . . . 38 E6
Woodham KT15 . . . . 70 F8
Orchard Bsns Ctr SE26 . . . 23 F3
Orchard Bsns Ctr The RH1 . . . . 161 A8
Orchard Cl
Ashford TW15 . . . . 14 C2
Ash Vale GU12 . . . . 106 A5
Badshot Lea GU9 . . . . 126 A6
Banstead SM7 . . . . 78 B5
East Horsley KT24 . . . . 92 F3
Egham TW20 . . . . 12 B3
Elstead GU8 . . . . 148 E4
Farnborough GU17 . . . . 64 F1
Fetcham KT22 . . . . 94 D5
Flexford GU3 . . . . 107 B1
Guildford GU1 . . . . 110 B1
Haslemere GU27 . . . . 207 F5
Horley RH6 . . . . 160 F4
Leatherhead KT22 . . . . 94 F8
Thames Ditton KT6 . . . . 37 B2
Walton-on-T KT12 . . . . 35 B2
West Barnes SW20 . . . . 39 C5
West End GU24 . . . . 67 D6
West Ewell KT19 . . . . 57 B4
Woking GU22 . . . . 70 B3
Wokingham RG40 . . . . 25 D6
Orchard Cotts
Charlwood RH6 . . . . 180 F7
Lingfield RH7 . . . . 165 B3
Woking GU21 . . . . 69 A1
Orchard Ct
Barnes SW13 . . . . 7 F4
Beckenham BR2 . . . . 44 E6
Bracknell RG12 . . . . 27 C7
Camberley GU15 . . . . 65 B2
Caterham CR3 . . . . 100 F3
Croydon CR0 . . . . 44 A1
Forest Hill SE26 . . . . 23 E3
Harmondsworth UB7 . . . . 2 C7
Hounslow TW7 . . . . 5 D7
9 New Malden KT4 . . . . 39 A1
Penge SE26 . . . . 23 D3
Wallington SM6 . . . . 60 B5
Walton-on-T KT12 . . . . 34 F1
Orchard Dene 4 KT14 . . . 71 A6
Orchard Dr
Ashtead KT21 . . . . 95 D7
Upper Halliford TW17 . . . . 34 E6
Woking GU21 . . . . 69 F4
Orchard End
Caterham CR3 . . . . 100 E5
Fetcham KT22 . . . . 94 C3
Oatlands Park KT13 . . . . 53 E8
Rowledge GU10 . . . . 145 F3
Orchard Farm Pk RH1 . . . . 161 F8
Orchardfield Rd GU7 . . . . 150 F7
Orchard Gate
Sandhurst GU47 . . . . 64 B8
Thames Ditton KT10 . . . . 36 D1
Orchard Gdns
Aldershot GU11 . . . . 126 C8
Chessington KT9 . . . . 56 E6
Cranleigh GU6 . . . . 174 F2
Effingham KT24 . . . . 113 E7
Epsom KT18 . . . . 76 C4
Sutton SM1 . . . . 59 A5
Orchard Gr
Croydon CR0 . . . . 43 E2
Penge SE20 . . . . 23 A1
Orchard Hill
Rudgwick RH12 . . . . 214 C7
Wallington SM5 . . . . 59 F5
Windlesham GU20 . . . . 48 D3
Orchard Hill Coll SM6 . . . . 60 B4
Orchard Ho
Crawley RH10 . . . . 181 D1
Guildford GU4 . . . . 110 D2
Tongham GU10 . . . . 126 F7
Orchard Inf Sch The KT8 . . . . 36 D5
Orchard Jun & Inf Sch The TW3 . . . . 5 A3
Orchard La
Thames Ditton KT8 . . . . 36 D3
Wimbledon SW20 . . . . 39 B8
Orchard Lea Cl GU22 . . . . 70 E4
Orchardleigh KT22 . . . . 95 B5
Orchard Mains GU22 . . . . 89 C8
Orchard Mew GU21 . . . . 68 B1
Orchard (Mobile Home Pk) The KT20 . . . . 116 B5
Orchard Pl RG40 . . . . 25 C6
Orchard Rd
Badshot Lea GU9 . . . . 126 A6
Brentford TW8 . . . . 6 C8
Chessington KT9 . . . . 56 E6
Dorking RH4 . . . . 136 B6
Farnborough GU14 . . . . 85 A4
Feltham TW13 . . . . 15 A7
Guildford, Burpham GU4 . . . . 110 B5
Guildford, Onslow Village GU2 . . . . 129 F7
Hampton TW12 . . . . 15 F1
Hamsey Green CR2 . . . . 81 B5
Horsham RH13 . . . . 217 E2
Hounslow TW4 . . . . 5 A2
Kingston u T KT1 . . . . 37 E7
Mortlake TW9 . . . . 7 A4
Reigate RH2 . . . . 118 B1
Shalford GU4 . . . . 130 E3
Shere GU5 . . . . 133 A4
Smallfield RH6 . . . . 162 C3
Sunbury TW16 . . . . 15 B1
Sutton SM1 . . . . 59 A6
Twickenham TW1 . . . . 6 B2
Orchard Rise
Croydon CR0 . . . . 43 F1
Kingston u T KT2 . . . . 38 C8
Mortlake TW10 . . . . 7 B3
Orchard School Sports Ctr SE20 . . . . 43 A8
Orchard Sch The SW2 . . . . 21 F8
Orchards Cl KT14 . . . . 71 A5
Orchards Sch RH2 . . . . 139 A6
Orchard St RH10, RH11 . . . . 201 D6
Orchards The
4 Crawley RH11 . . . . 200 D5
Horsham RH12 . . . . 217 F5
14 Woking GU22 . . . . 69 F1
Orchard The
Banstead SM7 . . . . 78 A4
Dorking RH5 . . . . 136 C3
Ewell KT17 . . . . 57 F1
Horley RH6 . . . . 161 A3
Horsham RH12 . . . . 218 B4
Hounslow TW3 . . . . 5 C5
Lightwater GU18 . . . . 67 B8
Virginia Water GU25 . . . . 31 E4
West Ewell KT17 . . . . 57 F3
Weybridge KT13 . . . . 53 B6
Woking, Horsell GU21 . . . . 69 B3
Woking, Westfield GU22 . . . 89 E5
Orchard View KT16 . . . . 33 A3
Orchard Way
Addlestone KT15 . . . . 52 B4
Aldershot GU11, GU12 . . . 126 C8
Ashford TW15 . . . . 13 F6
Beckenham BR3, CR0 . . . . 43 E3
Camberley GU15 . . . . 65 B2
Carshalton SM1 . . . . 59 D6
Croydon BR3, CR0 . . . . 43 E3
Dorking RH4 . . . . 136 B6
East Grinstead RH19 . . . . 185 E1
Esher KT10 . . . . 55 C4
Flexford GU3 . . . . 107 B1
Lower Kingswood KT20 . . . . 97 F1
Oxted RH8 . . . . 123 A2
Reigate RH2 . . . . 139 B6
Send GU23 . . . . 90 C2
Orchard Way Prim Sch CR0 . . . . 43 E2
Orchid Cl KT9 . . . . 56 C3
Orchid Ct BR1 . . . . 24 D5
Orchid Dr GU24 . . . . 68 A4
Orchid Gdns TW4 . . . . 4 F3
Orchid Mead SM7 . . . . 78 B5

Orde Cl RH10 . . . . 182 D1
Ordnance Cl TW13 . . . . 15 A6
Ordnance Rd GU11 . . . . . . 105 C3
Ordnance Rdbt GU11 . . . . 105 B2
Oregano Way GU2 . . . . . . 109 A6
Oregon Cl KT3 . . . . 38 C5
Orestan La KT24 . . . . 113 C8
Orewell Gdns RH2 . . . . . . 139 B7
Orford Ct
  Wallington SM6 . . . . 60 C5
  West Norwood SE27 . . . . 22 B6
Orford Gdns TW1 . . . . 16 F6
Orford Rd SE6 . . . . 24 B5
Organ Crossroads
  KT17 . . . . 58 A3
Oriana Ct CR2 . . . . 61 D3
Oriel Cl
  Crawley RH10 . . . . 182 C1
  Mitcham CR4 . . . . 41 D6
Oriel Ct 6 CR0 . . . . 42 D1
Oriel High Sch RH10 . . . . 202 C4
Oriel Hill GU15 . . . . 65 D4
Oriel Prim Sch TW13 . . . . 15 E5
Oriental Cl GU22 . . . . 70 A2
Oriental Rd
  Ascot SL5 . . . . 29 D5
  Woking GU22 . . . . 70 A3
Orion RG12 . . . . 27 A1
Orion Ct
  Crawley RH11 . . . . 200 D4
  Horsham RH12 . . . . 217 B3
Orion Ctr The CR0 . . . . . . 60 E8
Orion Mews SM4 . . . . 40 A5
Orlando Gdns KT19 . . . . . 57 D1
Orleans Cl KT10 . . . . 55 D8
Orleans Ct 10 TW1 . . . . . 17 B8
Orleans House Gallery★
  TW1 . . . . 17 B7
Orleans Inf Sch TW1 . . . . 17 B8
Orleans Park Sch TW1 . . 17 B8
Orleans Rd
  South Norwood SE19 . . . . 22 D2
  Twickenham TW1 . . . . 17 C8
Orltons La RH12 . . . . 179 F2
Ormanton Rd SE26 . . . . . . 23 A4
Orme Ho RH9 . . . . 142 D8
Ormeley Rd SW12 . . . . . . 21 B7
Orme Rd
  Kingston u T KT1, KT3 . . . 38 B7
  Sutton SM1 . . . . 59 B4
Ormerod Gdns CR4 . . . . . 41 A8
Ormesby Wlk RH10 . . . . . 202 B4
Ormond Ave
  Hampton TW12 . . . . 36 B8
  24 Richmond TW10 . . . . . 6 D2
Ormond Cres TW12 . . . . . 36 B8
Ormond Dr TW12 . . . . 16 B1
Ormonde Ave KT19 . . . . . 57 D1
Ormonde Pl KT13 . . . . 53 D4
Ormonde Rd
  Farncombe GU7 . . . . 150 E6
  Mortlake SW14 . . . . 7 C4
  Woking GU21 . . . . 69 C3
  Wokingham RG41 . . . . 25 A5
Ormond Rd TW10 . . . . 6 D2
Ormsby SM2 . . . . 59 B3
Ormside Way RH1 . . . . . . 119 B5
Ormuz Cotts RH7 . . . . . . 164 C4
Orpin Rd RH1 . . . . 119 C5
Orpwood Cl KT12 . . . . 15 F2
Orwell Cl GU14 . . . . 84 E6
Orwell Ho 7 RH1 . . . . 118 F2
Osborne Ave TW19 . . . . . . 13 F7
Osborne Cl
  Beckenham BR3 . . . . 43 E5
  Feltham TW13 . . . . 15 D3
  Frimley GU16 . . . . 85 F8
Osborne Ct
  Crawley RH11 . . . . 201 B2
  Farnborough GU14 . . . . . 105 C8
  10 Surbiton KT6 . . . . 37 E3
Osborne Dr GU18 . . . . 67 A8
Osborne Gdns CR7 . . . . . 42 C7
Osborne Pl SM1 . . . . 59 D5
Osborne Rd
  Egham TW20 . . . . 11 F2
  Farnborough GU14 . . . . . 105 C8
  Hounslow TW3, TW4 . . . . . 4 F4
  Kingston u T KT2 . . . . 17 E1
  Redhill RH1 . . . . 119 A4
  South Norwood CR7 . . . . . 42 C7
  Walton-on-T KT12 . . . . . . 35 A1
  Wokingham RG40 . . . . 25 C6
Osborne Way KT9 . . . . . . 56 F5
Osborn La SE23 . . . . 23 E8
Osborn Rd GU9 . . . . 125 D4
Osbourne Ho
  Richmond TW10 . . . . 7 A2
  Twickenham TW2 . . . . 16 D6
Osbourne Terr 1
  SW17 . . . . 21 A3
Osgood Ct GU10 . . . . 126 E8
Osier Mews 6 W4 . . . . 7 F8
Osier Pl TW20 . . . . 12 C2
Osier Way
  Banstead KT17, SM7 . . . . 77 F8
  Mitcham CR4 . . . . 40 F4
Oslac Rd SE6 . . . . 24 B3
Oslo Ct SW19 . . . . 20 D1
Osman's Cl RG42 . . . . 8 B1
Osmond Gdns SM6 . . . . . 60 C5
Osmunda Bank RH19 . . . 185 E6
Osmund Cl RH10 . . . . 202 E6
Osnaburgh Hill GU15 . . . . 65 B5
Osney Cl RH11 . . . . 201 C5

Osney Wlk SM4, SM5 . . . . 40 D3
Osprey Cl
  Cheam SM1 . . . . 58 F5
  Fetcham KT22 . . . . 94 C5
Osprey Ct SW16 . . . . 41 F7
Osprey Gdns
  Aldershot GU11 . . . . 126 A7
  Selsdon CR0, CR2 . . . . . . 62 E1
Osprey Ho TW7 . . . . 6 B4
Ospringe Cl 8 SE20 . . . . 23 C1
Ostade Rd SW2 . . . . 21 F8
OSTERLEY 5 D7
Osterley Ave TW7 . . . . 5 D7
Osterley Cl RG40 . . . . 25 F5
Osterley Cres TW7 . . . . . . 5 F6
Osterley Ct TW7 . . . . 5 D6
Osterley Lo TW7 . . . . 5 E6
Osterley Rd TW7 . . . . 5 E6
Osterley Sta TW7 . . . . 5 D7
Osterly dens CR7 . . . . . . 42 C7
Ostlers Dr TW15 . . . . 14 C3
Oswald Cl KT22 . . . . 94 C5
Oswald Rd KT22 . . . . 94 C5
Osward CR0 . . . . 62 F1
Osward Rd SW12, SW17 . . 20 F6
Otford Cl SE20 . . . . 43 C8
Othello Gr RG42 . . . . 27 E8
Otho Ct 5 TW8 . . . . 6 D7
Otterbourne Pl RH19 . . . 185 B1
Otterbourne Rd 1 CR0,
  CR9 . . . . 61 C8
Otterburn Gdns TW7 . . . . . 6 A7
Otterburn St SW17 . . . . . 20 F2
Otter Cl
  Aldershot GU12 . . . . 105 D3
  Crowthorne RG45 . . . . . . 45 A7
  Ottershaw KT16 . . . . 51 B4
Otterden St SE6 . . . . 24 A4
Otter Mdw KT22 . . . . 94 F8
Ottermead La KT16 . . . . . 51 C4
OTTERSHAW 51 D5
Ottershaw Pk KT16 . . . . . 51 A3
Otto Cl SE26 . . . . 23 B5
Ottways Ave KT21 . . . . . . 95 D8
Ottways La KT22 . . . . 95 D8
Otway Cl RH11 . . . . 200 F4
Oulton Wlk RH10 . . . . . . 202 B4
Our Lady of the Rosary RC
  Sch TW18 . . . . 13 A2
Our Lady Queen of Heaven
  RC Sch
  Crawley RH11 . . . . 201 B8
  Putney SW19 . . . . 19 D8
Our Lady & St Philip Neri
  RC Sch SE26 . . . . 23 E4
Our Lady's Prep Sch
  RG45 . . . . 45 B5
Ouseley Rd
  Upper Tooting SW12 . . . . 20 F7
  Wraysbury TW19 . . . . 11 D8
Outdowns KT24 . . . . 113 B5
Outram Pl KT13 . . . . 53 C5
Outram Rd CR0 . . . . 61 F8
OUTWOOD 162 B7
Outwood Ct CR2 . . . . 61 C3
Outwood Ho 6 SW2 . . . . 21 F8
Outwood La
  Bletchingley RH1 . . . . . . 141 D7
  Chipstead CR5, KT20 . . . . 98 C6
  Outwood RH1 . . . . 141 D1
Outwood Post Mill★
  RH1 . . . . 162 D8
Oval Ct 9 TW1 . . . . 16 F3
Oval Prim Sch CR0 . . . . . . 42 E1
Oval Rd CR0 . . . . 42 E1
Oval The
  Banstead SM7 . . . . 78 A5
  Farncombe GU7 . . . . 150 F7
  Guildford GU2 . . . . 130 A8
  Wood St V GU3 . . . . 108 B2
Overbrae BR3 . . . . 24 A3
Overbrook
  Godalming GU7 . . . . 151 A5
  West Horsley KT24 . . . . . 112 B6
Overbury Ave BR3 . . . . . . 44 C6
Overbury Cres CR0 . . . . . 63 C1
Overdale
  Ashtead KT21 . . . . 75 E3
  Bletchingley RH1 . . . . . . 120 C2
  Dorking RH5 . . . . 136 D8
Overdale Ave KT3 . . . . . . 38 D7
Overdale Rise GU16 . . . . . 65 E3
Overdene Dr RH11 . . . . . 201 A6
Overdown Rd SE6 . . . . . . 24 B4
Overford Cl GU6 . . . . 174 E2
Overford Dr GU6 . . . . 174 E2
Overhill CR6 . . . . 101 C8
Overhill Rd
  Dulwich SE21, SE22 . . . . 23 A8
  Wallington CR8 . . . . 61 A1
Overhill Way BR3 . . . . . . 44 D4
Overlord Cl GU15 . . . . . . 65 C8
Overlord Ct KT22 . . . . 94 D6
Overslea Lo 10 KT22 . . . . 95 C6
Overstand Cl BR3 . . . . . . 44 A4
Overstone Gdns CR0 . . . . 43 F2
Overthorpe Cl GU21 . . . . 68 E2
Overton Cl
  Aldershot GU11 . . . . 126 C6
  Hounslow TW7 . . . . 5 F6
Overton Ct
  Belmont SM2 . . . . 59 A3
  4 East Grinstead
  RH19 . . . . 185 E1
Overton Grange Sch
  SM2 . . . . 59 B2
Overton Ho SW15 . . . . . . 18 F8

Overton Rd SM2 . . . . 59 A3
Overton Shaw RH19 . . . . 185 E4
Overton's Yd CR0, CR9 . . . 61 C7
Overton Toft SM2 . . . . . . 59 A4
Oveton Way KT23 . . . . . . 94 B1
Ovett Cl SE19 . . . . 22 E2
Ovington Ct GU21 . . . . . . 68 F3
Owen Cl CR0 . . . . 42 D3
Owen Ho
  Feltham TW14 . . . . 15 A8
  6 Twickenham TW1 . . . . 17 B8
Owen Pl KT22 . . . . 95 B5
Owen Rd
  Farncombe GU7 . . . . 150 F6
  Windlesham GU20 . . . . . . 48 D5
Owens Way SE23 . . . . 23 E8
Owen Wlk 10 SE20 . . . . . 23 A1
Owers Cl RH13 . . . . 217 E2
Owlbeech Ct RH13 . . . . . 218 B4
Owlbeech Lo RH13 . . . . . 218 B4
Owlbeech Pl RH13 . . . . . 218 B4
Owlbeech Way RH13 . . . 218 B4
Owl Cl CR2 . . . . 62 D1
Owletts RH10 . . . . 202 D7
Owlscastle Cl RH12 . . . . 217 D5
OWLSMOOR 45 E1
Owlsmoor Prim Sch
  GU47 . . . . 45 E1
Owlsmoor Rd GU47 . . . . . 45 D1
Ownstead Gdns CR2 . . . . 80 F8
Ownsted Hill CR0 . . . . . . 63 D1
Oxdowne Cl KT11 . . . . . . 74 B5
Oxenden Cl GU10 . . . . . . 126 E8
Oxenden Rd GU10,
  GU12 . . . . 126 F8
Oxenhope RG12 . . . . 27 A5
Oxford Ave
  Harlington TW6 . . . . 3 F7
  Merton SW20 . . . . 39 E7
Oxford Cl
  Littleton Common TW15,
  TW17 . . . . 14 C1
  Mitcham CR4 . . . . 41 C6
Oxford Cres KT3 . . . . 38 D3
Oxford Ct
  Epsom KT18 . . . . 76 E5
  17 Kingston u T KT6 . . . . 37 E4
Oxford Gdns W4 . . . . 7 A8
Oxford Ho
  8 New Malden KT3 . . . . . 38 F4
  Wokingham RG41 . . . . 25 A6
Oxford Rd
  Carshalton SM5 . . . . 59 E5
  Crawley RH10 . . . . 201 F2
  Farnborough GU14 . . . . . 85 C1
  Guildford GU1 . . . . 130 C7
  Horsham RH13 . . . . 217 E2
  Redhill RH1 . . . . 118 E2
  Sandhurst GU47 . . . . 45 E2
  South Norwood SE19 . . . . 22 D2
  Teddington TW11 . . . . 16 D3
  Wallington SM6 . . . . 60 C5
  Wokingham RG41 . . . . 25 A6
Oxford Terr GU1 . . . . 130 D7
Oxford Way TW13 . . . . . . 15 D4
Oxleigh Cl KT3 . . . . 38 E4
Oxlip Cl CR0 . . . . 43 D1
OXSHOTT 74 C6
Oxshott Rd
  Ashtead KT22 . . . . 74 F3
  Leatherhead KT22 . . . . . . 75 A2
Oxshott Rise KT11 . . . . . . 73 E5
Oxshott Sta KT22 . . . . . . 74 C6
Oxshott Way KT11 . . . . . . 73 E4
OXTED 122 E5
Oxted Cl CR4 . . . . 40 D6
Oxted Gn GU8 . . . . 170 E7
Oxted Rd RH9 . . . . 121 D4
Oxted Sch RH8 . . . . 122 F7
Oxted Sta RH8 . . . . 122 E6
Oxtoby Way SW16 . . . . . . 41 D8
Oyster La KT14 . . . . 71 E7

P

Pacific Cl TW14 . . . . 14 F7
Pacific Hts BR3 . . . . 24 A1
Packer Cl RH19 . . . . 186 A3
Packham Ct KT4 . . . . 58 C7
Packway GU9 . . . . 146 E7
Padbrook RH8 . . . . 123 A6
Padbrook Cl RH8 . . . . 123 B6
Padbury Cl TW14 . . . . 14 D7
Padbury Oaks UB7 . . . . 2 B1
Paddock Cl
  Beare Green RH5 . . . . . . 157 D4
  Camberley GU15 . . . . 66 A6
  Forest Hill SE26 . . . . 23 D4
  Hambledon GU8 . . . . 171 C1
  Lingfield RH7 . . . . 164 C4
  New Malden KT4 . . . . 38 E1
  Oxted RH8 . . . . 122 F4
Paddock Ct SW20 . . . . . . 39 C5
Paddock Gdns
  East Grinstead RH19 . . . 205 E7
  South Norwood SE19 . . . . 22 D2
Paddock Gr RH5 . . . . 157 D4
Paddock Ho
  Ascot SL5 . . . . 28 E6
  Guildford GU4 . . . . 110 D2
Paddockhurst Rd
  Crawley, Gossops Green
  RH11 . . . . 201 A5
  Crawley RH10 . . . . 203 C2
Paddock Sch SW15 . . . . . . 7 F3
Paddocks Cl
  Ashtead KT21 . . . . 75 E1

Paddocks Cl continued
  Cobham KT11 . . . . 73 C5
Paddocks Mead GU21 . . . 68 F3
Paddocks Rd GU4 . . . . . . 110 A5
Paddocks The
  Addington CR0 . . . . 63 A4
  Flexford GU3 . . . . 107 C1
  Great Bookham KT23 . . . 94 B1
  Oatlands Park KT13 . . . . 53 E7
  Virginia Water GU25 . . . . 31 E3
  Woodham KT15 . . . . 52 B1
Paddocks Way
  Ashtead KT21 . . . . 75 E1
  Chertsey KT16 . . . . 33 B1
Paddock The
  Bracknell RG12 . . . . 27 C6
  Cranleigh GU6 . . . . 174 D3
  Crawley RH10 . . . . 202 D7
  Crowthorne RG45 . . . . . . 45 A6
  Ewhurst GU6 . . . . 175 E4
  Godalming GU7 . . . . 150 F3
  Grayshott GU26 . . . . 188 A4
  Guildford GU1 . . . . 110 D2
  Haslemere GU27 . . . . . . 208 A8
  Westcott RH4 . . . . 135 C6
Paddock Way
  Grayswood GU27 . . . . . . 190 A2
  Oxted RH8 . . . . 122 F4
  Putney SW15 . . . . 19 C8
  Sheerwater GU21 . . . . . . 70 B5
Paddock Wlk CR6 . . . . . 101 B8
Padley Cl KT9 . . . . 56 F6
Padstow Wlk
  Crawley RH11 . . . . 200 F4
  East Bedfont TW14 . . . . . 14 F7
Padua Rd SE20 . . . . 43 C8
Padwick Rd RH13 . . . . . . 218 A4
Pageant Wlk CR0 . . . . . . 61 E7
Page Cl TW12 . . . . 15 E2
Page Cres CR0 . . . . 61 B5
Page Croft KT15 . . . . 52 B8
Page Ct RH13 . . . . 217 D1
Pagehurst Rd CR0 . . . . . . 43 B2
Page Rd TW14 . . . . 3 D1
Page's Croft RG40 . . . . . . 25 D5
Page's Yd 11 W4 . . . . 7 E8
Paget Ave SM1 . . . . 59 D7
Paget Cl
  Camberley GU15 . . . . 66 B7
  Hampton TW12 . . . . 16 D4
Paget La TW7 . . . . 5 E4
Paget Pl
  Kingston u T KT2 . . . . 18 C2
  Thames Ditton KT7 . . . . . 36 F1
PAGEWOOD 180 D7
Pagewood Cl RH10 . . . . . 202 D4
Pagoda Ave TW9 . . . . 6 F4
Pagoda Gr SE21, SE27 . . . 22 C6
Paice Gn RG40 . . . . 25 D7
Painesfield Dr KT16 . . . . . 33 A1
Pain's Cl CR4 . . . . 41 B7
Pains Hill RH8 . . . . 123 C4
Pain's Hill Ho KT11 . . . . . 72 F5
Painshill Landscape Gdn★
  KT11 . . . . 72 E5
Paisley Rd SM5 . . . . 40 D1
Paisley Terr SM5 . . . . 40 D2
Pakenham Cl SW12 . . . . . 21 A7
Pakenham Dr GU11 . . . . 104 F3
Pakenham Rd RG12 . . . . 27 D2
Palace Cl
  2 South Norwood
  CR7 . . . . 42 D5
  Streatham SW2 . . . . 22 A6
  8 Woking GU21 . . . . 70 A3
Palace Dr KT13 . . . . 53 B7
Palace Gate KT8 . . . . 36 E6
Palace Gn CR0 . . . . 62 F3
Palace Gr SE19 . . . . 22 F1
Palace Rd
  East Molesey KT8 . . . . . . 36 D6
  Kingston u T KT1 . . . . 37 D5
  Penge SE19 . . . . 22 F1
  Streatham SW2 . . . . 22 A6
  Woodham KT15 . . . . 52 B2
Palace Sq SE19 . . . . 22 F1
Palace View CR0 . . . . 62 F6
Palace Way
  Old Woking GU22 . . . . . . 90 B7
  6 Weybridge KT13 . . . . . 53 B7
Palestine Gr SW19 . . . . . 40 D8
Palewell Common Dr
  SW14 . . . . 7 D2
Palewell Pk SW14 . . . . . . 7 D3
Palgrave Ho TW2 . . . . . . 16 C8
Palisade Ct 5 BR1 . . . . . . 24 E1
Palladino Ho SW17 . . . . . 20 E3
Pallingham Dr RH10 . . . . 202 C3
Palliser Ct GU26 . . . . 188 C6
Palm Ct BR3 . . . . 43 F6
Palmer Ave KT4, SM3 . . . 58 C6
Palmer CE Jun Sch The
  RG40 . . . . 25 D7
Palmer Cl
  Crowthorne RG40 . . . . . . 45 A8
  Heston TW5 . . . . 5 A6
  Horley RH6 . . . . 160 F5
  Redhill RH1 . . . . 140 A8
  West Wickham BR4 . . . . . 63 D8
Palmer Cres
  Kingston u T KT1 . . . . 37 E6
  Ottershaw KT16 . . . . 51 D4
  Woodham KT15 . . . . 202 C3
Palmer School Rd
  RG40 . . . . 25 C6
PALMERS CROSS 173 C6
Palmersfield Rd SM7 . . . . 78 B5
Palmers Gr KT8 . . . . 36 A5

Palmer's Lo GU2 . . . . 130 B8
Palmers Rd
  Mortlake SW14 . . . . 7 C4
  Thornton Heath SW16 . . . 41 F7
Palmerston Cl
  Farnborough GU14 . . . . . 84 D3
  Redhill RH1 . . . . 140 A6
  Woking GU21 . . . . 70 A5
Palmerston Ct
  8 Richmond TW10 . . . . . . 6 E1
  9 Surbiton KT6 . . . . 37 D2
  8 Sutton SM1 . . . . 59 C5
Palmerstone Ct GU25 . . . 31 E4
Palmerston Gr 11
  SW19 . . . . 20 A1
Palmerston Ho SM7 . . . . 77 F4
Palmerston Rd
  Carshalton SM5 . . . . 60 A6
  Hounslow TW3 . . . . 5 C6
  Merton SW19 . . . . 20 A1
  Mortlake SW14 . . . . 7 C3
  Sutton SM1 . . . . 59 C5
  Thornton Heath CR0 . . . . 42 D4
  Twickenham TW2 . . . . 5 E1
Palm Gr GU1 . . . . 109 C5
Pamela Ct 13 BR1 . . . . . . 24 F1
Pamir Ct 10 SM2 . . . . 59 B4
Pampisford Rd
  Croydon CR2, CR8 . . . . . . 61 B2
  Purley CR2, CR8 . . . . 61 B2
Pams Way KT19 . . . . 57 D5
Pandora Ct 4 KT6 . . . . . . 37 E3
Pangbourne Ct SW17 . . . 20 C4
Pankhurst Cl TW7 . . . . 5 F4
Pankhurst Ct 11 RH11 . . 201 B1
Pankhurst Dr RG12 . . . . . 27 D4
Pankhurst Farm GU24 . . . 68 A8
Pankhurst Ho 5 SW16 . . 21 D3
Pankhurst Rd KT12 . . . . . 35 C2
Panmuir Rd SW20 . . . . . . 39 B8
Panmure Rd SE26 . . . . . . 23 B5
Pannell Cl RH19 . . . . 185 D1
Pannells GU10 . . . . 146 D5
Pannells Ash RH14 . . . . . 212 C3
Pannells Ct KT16 . . . . 32 F1
Pannells Ct
  Guildford GU1 . . . . 130 D8
  Hounslow TW5 . . . . 5 A8
Pan's Gdns GU15 . . . . . . 65 F4
Pantile Rd KT13 . . . . 53 D6
Pantiles Cl GU21 . . . . 69 B1
Panton Cl CR0 . . . . 42 B1
Papercourt La GU23 . . . . 90 F6
Paper Mews RH4 . . . . . . 136 B8
Papermill Cl SM5 . . . . . . 60 A6
Papplewick Sch SL5 . . . . 29 A8
Papworth Way SW2 . . . . . 22 A8
Parade Mews SE27,
  SW2 . . . . 22 B6
Parade The
  Ashford TW16 . . . . 14 F1
  Ash GU12 . . . . 106 A4
  Burgh Heath, Great Burgh
  KT20 . . . . 77 E2
  Burgh Heath KT20 . . . . . . 97 E8
  Claygate KT10 . . . . 55 E4
  Coulsdon CR5 . . . . 80 A1
  Crawley RH10 . . . . 201 E7
  Epsom KT18 . . . . 76 D6
  Epsom, The Wells KT18 . . 76 A5
  Leatherhead KT22 . . . . . . 95 B7
  Loxwood RH14 . . . . 212 C4
  Thornton Heath CR0 . . . . 41 E3
  Thornton Heath, Norbury
  CR7 . . . . 42 A6
  Virginia Water GU25 . . . . 31 D3
  Wallington CR0 . . . . 60 F5
  Worcester Park KT4 . . . . 57 F6
Paradise Rd TW10 . . . . 6 E2
Paragon Gr KT5 . . . . 37 F3
Parbury Rise KT9 . . . . . . 56 E4
Parchmore Rd CR7 . . . . . 42 C6
Parchmore Way CR7 . . . . 42 B7
Parc Ho 11 KT2 . . . . 37 E8
Pares Cl GU21 . . . . 69 D3
Parfew Ct SE22 . . . . 23 B6
Parfitts Cl GU9 . . . . 125 A2
Parfour Dr CR8 . . . . 80 C3
Parham Rd RH11 . . . . . . 200 F7
Parish Church CE Inf &
  Jun Schs CR0 . . . . 61 B7
Parish Cl
  Ash GU12 . . . . 106 B1
  Hale GU9 . . . . 125 A6
Parish Ct KT6 . . . . 37 E3
Parish Ho 6 RH11 . . . . . 201 D5
Parish La SE20, SE26 . . . . 23 D1
Parish Rd GU14 . . . . 105 B8
Park Ave
  Bromley BR1 . . . . 24 F2
  Camberley GU15 . . . . 65 D4
  Caterham CR3 . . . . 100 E3
  Egham TW20 . . . . 12 C1
  Isleworth TW3 . . . . 5 B1
  Mitcham CR4 . . . . 21 B1
  Mortlake SW14 . . . . 7 D3
  Peper Harow GU8 . . . . . 149 C5
  Salfords RH1 . . . . 139 F1
  Staines TW18 . . . . 13 A2
  Upper Halliford TW17 . . . 34 E6
  Wallington SM5 . . . . 60 A4
  West Wickham BR4 . . . . . 63 C8
  Wokingham RG40 . . . . . . 25 B6
Park Ave E KT17 . . . . 58 A4
Park Avenue Mews
  CR4 . . . . 21 B1
Park Ave W KT17 . . . . 58 A4
PARK BARN 108 E2

Park Barn Dr GU2 . . . . 108 E2
Park Barn E GU2 . . . . 108 F2
Park Chase
  Godalming GU7 . . . . 150 E2
  Guildford GU1 . . . . 109 E1
Park Cl
  Brockham RH3 . . . . 137 B4
  Esher KT10 . . . . 55 A4
  Fetcham KT22 . . . . 94 D3
  Grayswood GU27 . . . . 190 A1
  Hampton TW12 . . . . 36 C8
  Isleworth TW3, TW7 . . . . . . 5 C2
  Kingston u T KT2 . . . . 38 A8
  Limpsfield RH8 . . . . 122 F7
  Oatlands Park KT13 . . . . . . 53 F8
  Rowledge GU10 . . . . 145 A2
  Wallington SM5 . . . . 59 F4
  Woodham KT15 . . . . 52 C1
Park Close Cotts TW20 . . . 10 F3
Park Copse RH5 . . . . 136 D7
Park Corner Dr KT24 . . . . 112 E7
Park Cotts 10 TW1 . . . . .6 B1
Park Cres
  Sunningdale SL5 . . . . 29 F3
  Twickenham TW2 . . . . 16 D7
Parkcroft Rd SE12 . . . . 24 F8
Park Ct
  Beckenham BR3 . . . . 44 B6
  16 Croydon CR2 . . . . 61 C5
  Farnham GU9 . . . . 125 D3
  Great Bookham KT23 . . . . . 94 A2
  Hounslow TW3 . . . . 5 B2
  New Malden KT3 . . . . 38 D5
  Teddington KT1 . . . . 37 C8
  Upper Tooting SW12 . . . . . 21 A7
  Wallington SM6 . . . . 60 E5
  West Norwood SE21 . . . . . 22 D5
  Woking GU22 . . . . 69 F1
Parkdale Cres KT4 . . . . 57 D7
Park Dr
  Bramley GU5 . . . . 151 F6
  Cranleigh GU6 . . . . 174 F3
  Mortlake SW14 . . . . 7 D3
  Sunningdale SL5 . . . . 29 F3
  Weybridge KT13 . . . . 53 B5
  Woking GU22 . . . . 69 F1
Park End BR1 . . . . 44 F8
Parker Cl
  Crawley RH10 . . . . 202 D5
  Wallington SM5 . . . . 59 F4
Parker Ct SW19 . . . . 19 E1
Parke Rd TW16 . . . . 35 A5
Parker Rd CR0, CR9 . . . . . . 61 C6
Parker's Cl KT21 . . . . 95 E8
Parkers Ct GU19 . . . . 47 E3
Parker's Hill KT21 . . . . 95 E8
Parker's La
  Ashtead KT21 . . . . 95 E8
  Winkfield RG42 . . . . .8 B5
Park Farm GU9 . . . . 126 A5
Park Farm Cl RH12 . . . . . . 217 D7
Park Farm Ct BR3 . . . . 44 B6
Park Farm Ind Est
  GU15 . . . . 65 C1
Park Farm Rd
  Horsham RH12 . . . . 217 D7
  Kingston u T KT2 . . . . 17 E1
Parkfield
  Godalming GU7 . . . . 150 F2
  Horsham RH12 . . . . 217 A1
  Hounslow TW7 . . . . 5 E6
  15 Wimbledon SW19 . . . . . 19 D1
Parkfield Ave
  Feltham TW13 . . . . 15 A5
  Mortlake SW14 . . . . 7 E3
Parkfield Cl RH11 . . . . 200 F6
Parkfield Cres TW13 . . . . . 15 A5
Parkfield Ho RG45 . . . . 45 C4
Parkfield Par TW13 . . . . . . 15 A5
Parkfield Rd TW13 . . . . 15 A5
Parkfields
  Croydon CR0 . . . . 43 F1
  Oxshott KT22 . . . . 74 D8
Parkfields Ave SW20 . . . . . 39 B7
Parkfields Cl SM5 . . . . 60 A6
Parkfields Rd TW10 . . . . . . 17 F3
PARKGATE 158 D4
Parkgate Cl KT2 . . . . 18 B2
Park Gate Cotts GU6 . . . . 174 C3
Park Gate Ct
  Teddington TW12 . . . . 16 C3
  11 Woking GU22 . . . . 69 E1
Parkgate Gdns SW14 . . . . . .7 A3
Parkgate Rd
  Newdigate RH5 . . . . 158 C3
  Reigate RH2 . . . . 139 B8
  Wallington SM5, SM6 . . . . . 60 B5
Park Gdns KT2 . . . . 17 F3
Park Gn KT23 . . . . 94 A3
Park Hall Rd
  Reigate RH2 . . . . 118 A3
  West Norwood SE21 . . . . . 22 D5
Park Hall Road Trad Est
  SE21 . . . . 22 D5
Parkham Ct BR2 . . . . 44 E7
Park Hill
  Forest Hill SE23 . . . . 23 C7
  Richmond TW10 . . . . .6 F1
  Wallington SM5 . . . . 59 F4
Parkhill Cl SM5 . . . . 59 E5
Park Hill Ct
  South Croydon CR0 . . . . . . 61 E8
  Upper Tooting SW17 . . . . . 20 F5
Parkhill Ho SW16 . . . . 22 A3
Park Hill Inf Sch CR0 . . . . . 61 E7
Park Hill Jun Sch CR0 . . . . 61 E7
Park Hill Mans 1 CR0 . . . . 61 E8

Parkhill Rd GU17 . . . . 64 D4
Park Hill Rd
  Beckenham BR2 . . . . 44 E7
  Ewell KT17 . . . . 76 F8
  South Croydon CR0, CR2 . . 61 E7
  Wallington SM6 . . . . 60 B3
Park Hill Rise CR0 . . . . 61 F7
Park Hill Sch KT2 . . . . 18 A1
Park Ho
  3 Aldershot GU11 . . . . . . 105 A1
  Penge SE26 . . . . 23 A3
  Reigate RH2 . . . . 138 F7
  Richmond TW10 . . . . .6 E1
Park Horsley KT24 . . . . . 113 A6
Park House Cotts
  GU6 . . . . 174 F3
Park House Dr RH2 . . . . . 138 F7
Park House Gdns TW1 . . . . .6 C2
Park Hts
  Epsom KT18 . . . . 76 D5
  17 Woking GU22 . . . . 69 E1
Parkhurst KT19 . . . . 57 C1
Parkhurst Cotts GU10 . . . 187 F8
Parkhurst Fields
  GU10 . . . . 167 F1
Parkhurst Gr RH6 . . . . 160 F4
Parkhurst Rd
  Carshalton SM1 . . . . 59 D6
  Guildford GU2 . . . . 109 B2
  Horley RH6 . . . . 160 E4
Parkin Ho SE20 . . . . 23 D1
Park La
  Ashtead KT21 . . . . 96 A8
  Ashurst Wood RH19 . . . . 206 D6
  Brook GU8 . . . . 190 A8
  Camberley GU15 . . . . 65 C5
  Cheam SM3 . . . . 58 E4
  Cranbourne SL4 . . . . 9 B7
  Cranford TW5 . . . . 4 A7
  Croydon CR0, CR9 . . . . 61 D7
  Guildford GU4 . . . . 110 D3
  Hooley CR5 . . . . 99 D6
  Horton SL3 . . . . 1 A4
  Lingfield RH7 . . . . 164 F5
  Ockley RH5 . . . . 177 F7
  Reigate RH2 . . . . 138 E8
  Richmond TW9 . . . . 6 D3
  Teddington TW11 . . . . 16 F2
  Wallington SM5, SM6 . . . . . 60 A5
Park La E RH2 . . . . 139 A7
Parkland Dr RG12 . . . . 27 E8
Parkland Gdns 12
  SW19 . . . . 19 D7
Parkland Gr
  Ashford TW15 . . . . 14 A4
  Heath End GU9 . . . . 125 F8
  Hounslow TW7 . . . . .5 F6
Parkland Rd TW15 . . . . 14 A4
Parklands
  Addlestone KT15 . . . . 52 C5
  Dorking RH5 . . . . 136 B3
  Gomshall GU5 . . . . 133 A2
  Great Bookham KT23 . . . . . 94 A4
  Guildford GU2 . . . . 109 A5
  Haslemere GU26 . . . . 188 E1
  Kingston u T KT5 . . . . 37 F4
  Oxted RH8 . . . . 122 E4
  Redhill RH1 . . . . 119 A3
Parklands Cl SW14 . . . . .7 C2
Parklands Ct TW5 . . . . 4 D5
Parklands Par TW5 . . . . 4 D5
Parklands Pl GU1 . . . . 110 B1
Parklands Rd SW16,
  SW17 . . . . 21 B3
Parklands Way KT4 . . . . . . 57 E8
Park Lane Mans CR0 . . . . . 61 D7
PARK LANGLEY 44 D4
Park Lawn CR7 . . . . 42 C7
Parklawn Ave
  Epsom KT18 . . . . 76 B6
  Horley RH6 . . . . 160 F5
Park Lawn Rd KT13 . . . . . . 53 C6
Parkleigh Ct SW19 . . . . 40 B7
Parkleigh Rd SW19 . . . . . . 40 B7
Park Ley Rd CR3 . . . . 101 D6
Parkleys KT2, TW10 . . . . . . 17 D4
Park Lo KT23 . . . . 94 A2
Park Manor 3 SM2 . . . . . . 59 C3
Park Mans
  Forest Hill SE26 . . . . 23 C5
  Hampton TW12 . . . . 16 B3
Park Mead Prim Sch
  GU6 . . . . 175 A3
Park Mews
  East Molesey KT8 . . . . 36 C5
  Stanwell TW19 . . . . 13 F8
Parkpale La RH3 . . . . 137 A4
Park Pl
  Blackwater GU17 . . . . 64 F3
  Hampton TW12 . . . . 16 C2
  1 Horsham RH12 . . . . . . 217 C1
  4 Woking GU22 . . . . 69 F1
Park Prim Sch GU11 . . . . 126 C7
Park Rd
  Albury GU5 . . . . 132 C2
  Aldershot GU11 . . . . 126 B8
  Ashford TW15 . . . . 14 B3
  Ashtead KT21 . . . . 75 E1
  Banstead SM7 . . . . 78 C3
  Beckenham BR3 . . . . 23 F1
  Bracknell RG12 . . . . 27 D8
  Burstow RH6 . . . . 162 C1
  Camberley GU15 . . . . 65 C5
  Caterham CR3 . . . . 100 E4
  Cheam SM3 . . . . 58 E4
  Chiswick W4 . . . . 7 D8
  Crowhurst RH7 . . . . 143 E2
  Dormans Park RH19 . . . . 185 F6

Park Rd *continued*
  East Grinstead RH19 . . . . 185 D1
  East Molesey KT8 . . . . 36 C5
  Egham TW20 . . . . 12 A4
  Esher KT10 . . . . 55 B6
  Farnborough GU14 . . . . . 105 E8
  Farnham GU9 . . . . 125 D4
  Faygate RH12 . . . . 199 F1
  Feltham TW13 . . . . 15 D4
  Fickleshole CR6 . . . . 82 E5
  Forest Row RH18 . . . . 206 F2
  Godalming GU7 . . . . 150 E2
  Guildford GU1 . . . . 109 D1
  Hackbridge SM6 . . . . 60 B8
  Hampton TW12 . . . . 16 C3
  Haslemere GU27 . . . . 208 C5
  Hounslow TW3, TW7 . . . . . . 5 C2
  Isleworth TW7 . . . . 6 B5
  Kenley CR8 . . . . 80 C4
  Kingston u T KT2 . . . . 18 A1
  Limpsfield RH8 . . . . 122 F7
  Lower Halliford TW17 . . . . 34 A1
  Mitcham SW19 . . . . 20 E2
  New Malden KT3 . . . . 38 D5
  Redhill RH1 . . . . 118 F3
  Richmond TW10 . . . . .6 F1
  Sandhurst GU47 . . . . 64 C8
  Slinfold RH13 . . . . 215 D3
  South Norwood SE25 . . . . . 42 E5
  Stanwell TW19 . . . . 2 C1
  Sunbury TW16 . . . . 15 B1
  Surbiton KT5 . . . . 37 C8
  Teddington, Hampton Wick
    KT1 . . . . 37 C8
  Teddington TW11 . . . . 16 F2
  Twickenham TW1 . . . . 6 C1
  Wallington SM6 . . . . 60 B5
  Woking GU22 . . . . 70 A2
  Wokingham RG40 . . . . 25 B6
Park Rise
  Forest Hill SE23 . . . . 23 E7
  Horsham RH12 . . . . 217 B4
  Leatherhead KT22 . . . . 95 B6
Parkrise Cl KT22 . . . . 95 B6
Park Rise Rd SE23 . . . . 23 E7
Park Road Ho 3 KT2 . . . . . 18 A1
Park Row GU9 . . . . 125 B3
Park Sch The GU22 . . . . . . 70 A2
Park Sheen SW14 . . . . .7 B3
Parkshot TW9 . . . . .6 E3
Parkside
  1 Beckenham BR3 . . . . . . 44 B7
  Cheam SM3 . . . . 58 E4
  Crawley RH10 . . . . 201 E6
  East Grinstead RH19 . . . . 185 C1
  Hale GU9 . . . . 125 C6
  Teddington TW11 . . . . 16 D3
  Wimbledon SW19 . . . . 19 D4
  Woodham KT15 . . . . 52 C1
Parkside Ave SW19 . . . . . . 19 D3
Parkside Cl
  East Horsley KT24 . . . . 92 F2
  Penge SE20 . . . . 23 C1
Parkside Cotts
  Tatsfield TN16 . . . . 103 E6
  West Clandon GU4 . . . . . . 111 A3
Parkside Cres KT5 . . . . 38 C3
Parkside Ct
  Epsom KT18 . . . . 76 F6
  Redhill RH1 . . . . 119 A5
  Weybridge KT13 . . . . 53 A6
Parkside Gdns
  Coulsdon CR5 . . . . 79 B2
  Wimbledon SW19 . . . . 19 D4
Parkside Ho
  Guildford GU4 . . . . 110 A5
  2 West Byfleet KT14 . . . . . 71 A7
  Wimbledon SW19 . . . . 19 D3
Parkside Hospl SW19 . . . . 19 D5
Parkside Mews
  Chelsham CR6 . . . . 82 A3
  Horsham RH12 . . . . 217 D2
Parkside Pl
  East Horsley KT24 . . . . 92 F2
  Staines TW18 . . . . 13 A2
Parkside Rd
  Hounslow TW3 . . . . 5 B2
  Sunningdale SL5 . . . . 30 A4
Parkside Sch KT11 . . . . 74 A1
Park Sq KT10 . . . . 55 B6
Park St
  Bagshot GU19 . . . . 47 E3
  Camberley GU15 . . . . 65 C5
  Croydon CR0, CR9 . . . . 61 C8
  Guildford GU1, GU2 . . . . . 130 C7
  Horsham RH12 . . . . 217 D2
  Poyle SL3 . . . . 1 D6
  Slinfold RH13 . . . . 215 C3
  Teddington TW11 . . . . 16 E2
Parkstone Dr GU15 . . . . . . 65 C4
PARK STREET 215 C4
Park Terr
  1 Carshalton SM5 . . . . . . 59 E7
  New Malden KT4 . . . . 39 A1
Park Terr E RH13 . . . . 217 D1
Park Terr W RH13 . . . . 217 D1
Park The
  Forest Hill SE23 . . . . 23 C7
  Great Bookham KT23 . . . . . 94 A3
  Wallington SM5 . . . . 59 F5
Parkthorne Rd SW12 . . . . . 21 D8
Park View
  Addlestone KT15 . . . . 52 C5
  Ascot SL5 . . . . 29 E8
  Bagshot GU19 . . . . 47 D3
  Banstead SM7 . . . . 78 B4
  Caterham CR3 . . . . 101 A2
  Crawley RH11 . . . . 201 C5

Park View *continued*
  Great Bookham KT23 . . . . . 94 A2
  Horley RH6 . . . . 161 A3
  Morden CR4 . . . . 40 D4
  New Malden KT3 . . . . 38 F6
  Purley CR8 . . . . 80 B8
  Tandridge RH8 . . . . 143 B5
Parkview Ct
  Sunbury TW16 . . . . 35 A6
  Twickenham TW1 . . . . 17 C8
Park View Ct
  Croydon SE20 . . . . 43 B8
  Woking GU22 . . . . 89 F8
Park View Dr CR4 . . . . 40 D7
Park View Ho TW16 . . . . . . 15 C3
Parkview Lo BR3 . . . . 44 B6
Parkview Lo CR0, CR9 . . . . 43 A1
Park View Rd
  Salfords RH1 . . . . 140 A1
  Woldingham CR3 . . . . 101 F5
Parkview Vale GU4 . . . . . . 110 C3
Parkway
  Camberley GU15 . . . . 65 C3
  Crawley RH10 . . . . 202 C7
  Crowthorne RG45 . . . . 45 A5
  Dorking RH4 . . . . 136 A8
  Guildford GU1 . . . . 109 E2
  Horley RH6 . . . . 161 A3
  New Addington CR0 . . . . . . 63 C1
  Oatlands Park KT13 . . . . . . 53 D6
  West Barnes SW20 . . . . . . 39 D5
Park Way
  East Molesey KT8 . . . . 36 B6
  Feltham TW13 . . . . 15 B8
  Great Bookham KT23 . . . . . 94 A4
  Horsham RH12 . . . . 217 C2
Parkway Ho
  2 Horsham RH12 . . . . . . 217 C1
  Mortlake SW14 . . . . 7 D3
Parkway The TW5 . . . . .4 B7
Parkway Trad Est TW5 . . . . 4 C8
Park Wlk KT21 . . . . 95 F8
Parkwood BR3 . . . . 24 A1
Parkwood Ave KT10 . . . . . . 36 C5
Park Wood Cl SM7 . . . . 77 D4
Parkwood Gr TW16 . . . . . . 35 A6
Parkwood Rd
  Biggin Hill TN16 . . . . 103 F6
  Hounslow TW7 . . . . .5 F6
  Nutfield RH1 . . . . 119 C2
  Wimbledon SW19 . . . . 19 F3
Park Wood Rd SM7 . . . . . . 77 D4
Park Wood View SM7 . . . . 77 D4
Park Works Rd RH1 . . . . . 119 C2
Parley Dr GU21 . . . . 69 C1
Parliamentary Rd
  GU24 . . . . 87 A6
Parliament Mews SW14 . . . .7 A5
Parnall Ho 11 SE19 . . . . . . 22 E4
Parnell Cl RH10 . . . . 202 D4
Parnell Gdns KT13 . . . . . . 72 A8
Parnham Ave GU18 . . . . . . 67 D8
Parr Ave KT17 . . . . 58 B2
Parr Cl KT22 . . . . 94 F7
Parr Ct
  1 Epsom KT19 . . . . 57 E2
  Feltham TW13 . . . . 15 C4
  Knaphill GU21 . . . . 88 C8
Parris Croft RH4 . . . . 136 C4
Parrs Cl CR2 . . . . 61 D2
Parr's Pl TW12 . . . . 16 A1
Parry Cl
  Horsham RH12 . . . . 218 C4
  Stoneleigh KT17 . . . . 58 A3
Parry Dr KT13 . . . . 53 A1
Parry Rd SE25 . . . . 42 E6
Parsley Gdns CR0 . . . . 43 D1
Parsonage Bsns Pk
  RH12 . . . . 217 E4
Parsonage Cl
  Warlingham CR6 . . . . 81 F3
  Westcott RH4 . . . . 135 C5
Parsonage Farm Inf Sch
  GU14 . . . . 84 C5
Parsonage La RH4 . . . . . . 135 C6
Parsonage Rd
  Cranleigh GU6 . . . . 174 D3
  Englefield Green TW20 . . . 11 D3
  Horsham RH12 . . . . 217 E4
Parsonage Sq 3 RH4 . . . . 136 A7
Parsonage Way
  Frimley GU16 . . . . 65 E1
  Horsham RH12 . . . . 217 E1
Parsons Cl
  Aldershot GU11 . . . . 105 B2
  Haslemere GU27 . . . . 208 C8
  Horley RH6 . . . . 160 E4
  Sutton SM1 . . . . 59 B7
Parsons Field GU47 . . . . . . 64 B8
Parsonsfield Cl SM7 . . . . . 77 D4
Parsonsfield Rd SM7 . . . . . 77 D4
Parsons Gn
  Guildford GU1 . . . . 109 D3
  Haslemere GU27 . . . . 208 C8
Parsons Ho 20 SW12 . . . . . 21 E8
Parsons La GU26 . . . . 188 D6
Parsons Mead KT8 . . . . . . 36 C6
Parson's Mead CR0 . . . . . . 42 B1
Parson's Mead Sch
  KT21 . . . . 95 E8
Parson's Pightle CR5 . . . . 100 A7
Parthia Cl KT20 . . . . 97 B8
Partridge Cl
  Crondall GU10 . . . . 124 D8
  Frimley GU16 . . . . 65 E1
Partridge Knoll CR8 . . . . . . 80 B6

Partridge La
  Newdigate RH5,
    RH12 . . . . 179 F3
  Parkgate RH5 . . . . 158 E2
Partridge Mead SM7 . . . . . 77 C4
Partridge Pl RH10 . . . . 204 C6
Partridge Rd 3 TW12 . . . . 16 A2
Partridge Way GU4 . . . . . . 110 D3
Parvis Rd KT14 . . . . 71 D7
Paschal Rd GU15 . . . . 65 F8
Passfield Lo GU18 . . . . 48 C1
Passfields SE6 . . . . 24 C5
Passingham Ho TW5 . . . . . . 5 A8
Pastens Rd RH8 . . . . 123 C4
Paston Cl SM6 . . . . 60 C7
Pasture Rd SE6 . . . . 24 F7
Pasture The RH10 . . . . 202 C6
Pasturewood Rd RH5 . . . . 155 D6
Patcham Ct SM2 . . . . 59 C2
Patching Cl RH11 . . . . 200 F5
Patchings RH13 . . . . 217 F3
Paterson Cl GU16 . . . . 66 C3
Pates Manor Dr TW14 . . . . 14 D8
Pathfield GU8 . . . . 191 B4
Pathfield Cl
  Chiddingfold GU8 . . . . . . 191 B4
  Rudgwick RH12 . . . . 214 D7
Pathfield Rd
  Rudgwick RH12 . . . . 214 D7
  Streatham SW16 . . . . 21 D2
Pathfields
  Haslemere GU27 . . . . 208 C7
  Shere GU5 . . . . 133 A4
Pathfields Cl GU27 . . . . . . 208 D7
Pathfinders The GU14 . . . . 84 C3
Path Link RH10 . . . . 201 E7
Path The SW19 . . . . 40 B8
Pathway Ho SW17 . . . . 20 F2
Pathway Lo CR4 . . . . 40 F8
Pathway The GU22 . . . . 90 F2
Patmore La KT12 . . . . 53 F4
Patricia Gdns SM2 . . . . 78 A8
Patrington Cl RH11 . . . . . . 201 A3
Patten Ash Dr RG40 . . . . . 25 E7
Patten Ct SE23, SE6 . . . . . . 23 F7
Patten Rd SW18 . . . . 20 E8
Patterdale Cl
  Catford BR1 . . . . 24 E2
  Crawley RH11 . . . . 201 C4
Patterson Ct SE19 . . . . 22 F2
Patterson Rd SE19 . . . . . . 22 F2
Pat Williams Ho SE27 . . . . 22 C5
Paul Cl GU11 . . . . 125 E8
Paul Gdns CR0 . . . . 61 F8
Pauline Cres TW2 . . . . 16 C7
Pauls Mead RH7 . . . . 164 E5
Paul's Pl KT21 . . . . 96 B8
Paul Vanson Ct KT12 . . . . . 54 D4
Paved Ct 8 TW9 . . . . 6 D2
Pavement The
  Crawley RH10 . . . . 201 E6
  11 Isleworth TW7 . . . . 6 A4
  11 West Norwood SE27 . . . 22 C4
Pavilion Ct
  3 Merton SW19 . . . . 19 E1
  Streatham SW16 . . . . 21 F1
Pavilion Gdns TW18 . . . . . 13 B1
Pavilion Rd GU14 . . . . 104 E1
Pavilions End The
  GU15 . . . . 65 D3
Pavilion Sq SW17 . . . . 20 F5
Pavilions The BR3 . . . . 24 A2
Pavilion The KT20 . . . . 98 C4
Pavilion Way RH19 . . . . . . 205 E8
Pavillion Ct GU6 . . . . 174 C3
Paviors GU9 . . . . 125 C3
Pawley Cl GU10 . . . . 126 F7
Pawleyne Cl SE20 . . . . 23 C1
Pawson's Rd CR0 . . . . 42 C4
Pax Cl RH11 . . . . 200 E4
Paxton Cl
  Richmond TW9 . . . . .6 F5
  Walton-on-T KT12 . . . . 35 C2
Paxton Ct
  1 Forest Hill SE26 . . . . . . 23 E4
  Mitcham CR4 . . . . 40 F7
Paxton Gdns GU21 . . . . . . 70 E7
Paxton Pl SE27 . . . . 22 E4
Paxton Prim Sch SE19 . . . . 22 E2
Paxton Rd
  Chiswick W4 . . . . 7 E8
  Forest Hill SE23 . . . . 23 E5
Payley Dr RG40 . . . . 25 E8
Payne Cl RH10 . . . . 202 D8
Paynesfield Ave SW14 . . . . 7 D4
Paynesfield Rd
  Tatsfield TN16 . . . . 103 D7
  Tatsfield TN16 . . . . 103 D8
PAYNES GREEN 197 D8
Paynetts Ct KT13 . . . . 53 D5
Peabody Cl CR0 . . . . 43 C1
Peabody Est SE24 . . . . 22 C8
Peabody Hill SE21 . . . . 22 C7
Peabody Rd GU14 . . . . 105 D8
Peacemaker Ct RH11 . . . . 200 E4
Peaches Cl SM2 . . . . 58 E3
Peach Rd TW13 . . . . 15 A7
Peach St RG40 . . . . 25 C6
Peach Tree Cl GU14 . . . . . . 85 A7
Peacock Ave TW14 . . . . 14 D7
Peacock Cotts RG40 . . . . . 26 C5
Peacock Gdns CR0,
  CR2 . . . . 62 E1
Peacock La RG12 . . . . 26 D6

Peacocks Sh Ctr The 1 GU21 . . . . 69 E2
Peacock Wlk 8 RH11 . . . 201 A3
Peakfield GU10 . . . . 167 C7
Peak Hill SE26 . . . . 23 C4
Peak Hill Ave SE26 . . . . 23 C4
Peak Hill Gdns SE26 . . . . 23 C4
Peak Rd GU2 . . . . 109 A4
Peaks Hill CR8 . . . . 60 E1
Peaks Hill Rise CR8 . . . . 60 E1
Peak The SE26 . . . . 23 C5
Peall Rd CR0 . . . . 41 F3
Peall Rd Ind Est CR0 . . . . 41 F3
Pear Ave TW17 . . . . 34 E6
Pearce Cl CR4 . . . . 41 A7
Pearcefield Ave 5 SE23 . . . . 23 C7
Pearce Ho 7 SW2 . . . . 21 E8
Pearfield Rd SE23 . . . . 23 E5
Pearl Ct GU21 . . . . 68 E3
Pearmain Cl TW17 . . . . 34 B4
Pearson Cl CR8 . . . . 80 B8
Pearson Ct SM4 . . . . 40 B4
Pearson Rd RH10 . . . . 202 C6
Pearson Way CR4 . . . . 41 A8
Pears Rd TW3 . . . . 5 C4
Peartree Ave SW17 . . . . 20 C5
Peartree Cl CR2 . . . . 81 B5
Pear Tree Cl
Addlestone KT15 . . . . 52 A5
Chessington KT9 . . . . 57 A5
Mitcham CR4 . . . . 40 E7
Pear Tree Ct GU15 . . . . 66 B8
PEARTREE GREEN 192 D7
Pear Tree Hill RH1 . . . . 161 A8
Pear Tree Ho 4 SE19 . . . . 22 E2
Pear Tree La GU10 . . . . 145 F3
Pear Tree Rd
Addlestone KT15 . . . . 52 A5
Ashford TW15 . . . . 14 C3
Peary Cl RH12 . . . . 217 D6
Pease Pottage Hill RH11 . . . . 201 D1
PEASLAKE 154 D6
Peaslake Ct SM2 . . . . 59 C3
Peaslake La GU5 . . . . 154 D6
Peaslake Rd GU6 . . . . 154 D2
Peaslake Sch GU5 . . . . 154 E7
PEASMARSH 130 C1
Peat Comm GU8 . . . . 148 C2
Peatmore Ave GU22 . . . . 71 A3
Peatmore Cl GU22 . . . . 71 A3
Peatmore Dr GU24 . . . . 87 C6
Pebble Cl KT20 . . . . 116 E6
Pebble Hill KT24 . . . . 112 C2
Pebble Hill Cotts RH8 . . . 123 B6
Pebblehill Rd KT20, RH3 . . . . 116 E5
Pebble La KT18, KT22 . . . . 96 A5
Pebworth Ct 10 RH1 . . . . 119 A3
Pebworth Lo
17 Belmont SM2 . . . . 59 B3
South Norwood SE25 . . . . 42 F5
Peckarmans Wood SE21, SE26 . . . . 23 A5
Peek Cres SW19 . . . . 19 D3
Peeks Brook La
Crawley RH6 . . . . 182 E7
Horley RH6 . . . . 161 F2
Peel Ave GU16 . . . . 86 A7
Peel Ct GU14 . . . . 105 C8
Peel Ctr The RG12 . . . . 27 B7
Peel Ho TW20 . . . . 11 F2
Pegasus Ave GU12 . . . . 105 E2
Pegasus Cl GU27 . . . . 207 D5
Pegasus Ct GU12 . . . . 105 E1
Pegasus Ct
Banstead SM7 . . . . 78 A4
Caterham CR3 . . . . 101 A4
Crawley RH11 . . . . 200 E4
Farnborough GU14 . . . . 85 E1
Kingston u T KT1 . . . . 37 D6
12 Leatherhead KT22 . . . . 95 C6
Sutton SM1 . . . . 59 B8
Pegasus Pl RH10 . . . . 182 A1
Pegasus Rd
Croydon CR0, CR9 . . . . 61 A4
Farnborough GU14 . . . . 84 F7
Pegasus Way RH19 . . . . 186 B3
Peggotty Pl GU47 . . . . 45 E2
Pegg Rd TW5 . . . . 4 D7
Pegler Way RH11 . . . . 201 D6
Pegwell Cl RH11 . . . . 200 F4
Peket Cl TW18 . . . . 32 E8
Pelabon Ho 20 TW1 . . . . 6 D1
Peldon Ct TW10 . . . . 6 F2
Pelham Ct
Great Bookham KT23 . . . . 94 C1
5 Horsham RH12 . . . . 217 B2
Staines TW18 . . . . 13 B3
Pelham Ct Bsns Ctr RH11 . . . . 201 B2
Pelham Dr RH11 . . . . 201 A2
Pelham Ho CR3 . . . . 100 F3
Pelham Pl
Crawley RH11 . . . . 201 B2
Rowledge GU10 . . . . 146 A4
Pelham Prim Sch SW19 . . . . 20 A1
Pelham Rd
Merton SW19 . . . . 20 A1
Penge BR3, SE20 . . . . 43 C7
Pelhams Cl KT10 . . . . 55 A6
Pelhams Wlk KT10 . . . . 55 A6
Pelham Way KT23 . . . . 94 C1
Pelinore Rd SE6 . . . . 24 E6
Pelling Hill SL4 . . . . 11 B7
Pellings Cl BR2 . . . . 44 E6
Pelton Ave SM2 . . . . 59 B1
Pelton Ct CR2 . . . . 61 C4
Pemberley Chase KT19 . . . . 57 B5
Pemberley Cl KT19 . . . . 57 B5
Pemberton Ho SE26 . . . . 23 A4
Pemberton Pl KT10 . . . . 55 C7
Pemberton Rd KT8 . . . . 36 C5
Pemberton Terr KT8 . . . . 36 C5
Pembley Gn RH10 . . . . 183 E3
Pembridge Ave TW4 . . . . 15 F7
Pembroke RG12 . . . . 27 A1
Pembroke Ave
Hersham KT12 . . . . 54 D6
Surbiton KT5 . . . . 38 B4
Pembroke Broadway GU15 . . . . 65 C5
Pembroke Cl
Ascot SL5 . . . . 29 D4
Banstead SM7 . . . . 78 B2
Pembroke Ct
Beckenham BR3 . . . . 44 B6
Woking GU22 . . . . 70 B3
Pembroke Gdns GU22 . . . . 70 A1
Pembroke Ho SW19 . . . . 20 D3
Pembroke Mews SL5 . . . . 29 D4
Pembroke Pl TW7 . . . . 5 E5
Pembroke Rd
Crawley RH10 . . . . 182 C1
Mitcham CR4 . . . . 41 A7
South Norwood SE25 . . . . 42 E5
Woking GU22 . . . . 70 A2
Pembroke Villas TW9 . . . . 6 D3
Pembrook Lo 2 SW16 . . . 21 F5
Pembury Ave KT4 . . . . 39 A2
Pembury Cl
Hayes BR2 . . . . 44 F2
Wallington CR5 . . . . 79 A5
Pembury Ct UB3 . . . . 3 D8
Pembury Pl 5 GU12 . . . . 105 C1
Pembury Rd SE25 . . . . 43 A5
Pemdevon Rd CR0 . . . . 42 A2
Penarth Ct SM2 . . . . 59 C3
Penates KT10 . . . . 55 D6
Penberth Rd SE6 . . . . 24 C7
Penceat Ct SE20 . . . . 43 C7
Pendarves Rd SW20 . . . . 39 C8
Pendell Ave UB3 . . . . 3 F7
Pendell Ct RH1 . . . . 120 B4
Pendell Rd RH1 . . . . 120 B4
Pendennis Cl KT14 . . . . 71 A5
Pendennis Rd SW16 . . . . 21 E4
Pendenza KT11 . . . . 73 E3
Penderel Rd TW3 . . . . 5 A2
Penderry Rise SE6 . . . . 24 D6
Pendine Pl RG12 . . . . 27 B4
Pendlebury RG12 . . . . 27 A2
Pendle Ho 13 SE26 . . . . 23 A5
Pendle Rd SW16 . . . . 21 B3
Pendleton Cl RH1 . . . . 139 F7
Pendleton Rd RH1 . . . . 139 E6
Pendragon Rd BR1 . . . . 24 F5
Pendragon Way GU15 . . . . 66 D3
Penerley Rd SE6 . . . . 24 B7
Penfold Cl CR0, CR9 . . . . 61 A7
Penfold Croft GU9 . . . . 125 F4
Penfold Ct CR4 . . . . 41 A7
Penfold Manor GU27 . . . . 208 D6
Penfold Rd RH10 . . . . 202 B2
PENGE 23 D2
Penge East Sta SE20 . . . . 23 C2
Penge La SE20 . . . . 23 D1
Penge Rd SE20, SE25 . . . . 43 A6
Penge West Sta SE20 . . . . 23 B2
Pengilly Ho GU1 . . . . 110 C1
Pengilly Rd GU9 . . . . 125 B1
Penhurst GU21 . . . . 69 F5
Peninsula Pl RG45 . . . . 45 C4
Peninsular Cl
Camberley GU15 . . . . 66 B7
Feltham TW14 . . . . 3 E1
Penistone Rd SW16 . . . . 21 E1
Penlee Ho 10 GU22 . . . . 89 E8
Pennards The TW16 . . . . 35 C6
Penn Cl RH11 . . . . 181 D1
Pennefather's Rd GU11 . . . . 104 F3
Penner Cl SW19 . . . . 19 E6
Penners Gdns KT6 . . . . 37 E2
Pennine Cl RH11 . . . . 201 B6
Pennine Way
Farnborough GU14 . . . . 84 E7
Harlington UB7 . . . . 3 D7
Pennings Ave GU3 . . . . 108 F3
Pennington Cl 10 SE27 . . . 22 D4
Pennington Dr KT13 . . . . 53 E7
Pennington Lo 18 KT5 . . . . 37 E4
Penns Wood GU14 . . . . 85 D1
Pennthorpe Sch RH12 . . . . 214 D7
Pennycroft CR0 . . . . 62 E2
Penny Dr GU3 . . . . 108 B2
Pennyfield KT11 . . . . 73 A6
Penny La TW17 . . . . 34 E2
Pennymead Dr KT24 . . . . 112 F8
Pennymead Rise KT24 . . . . 112 F8
Penny Mews SW12 . . . . 21 B8
PENNY POT 68 C7
Pennypot La GU24 . . . . 68 C7
Penny Royal SM6 . . . . 60 D4
Penrhyn Cl
Aldershot GU11 . . . . 105 B1
Caterham CR3 . . . . 100 D7
Penrhyn Cres SW14 . . . . 7 C3
Penrhyn Gdns KT1 . . . . 37 D5
Penrhyn Rd KT1 . . . . 37 E6
Penrith Cl
Beckenham BR3 . . . . 44 B8
Redhill RH2 . . . . 118 E2
Penrith Pl SE27 . . . . 22 B6
Penrith Rd
New Malden KT3 . . . . 38 D5
South Norwood CR7 . . . . 42 C7
Penrith St SW16 . . . . 21 C2
Penrose Ct TW20 . . . . 11 C2
Penrose Dr KT19 . . . . 76 A8
Penrose Gdns GU12 . . . . 106 A6
Penrose Rd KT22 . . . . 94 C5
Penryn Dr GU35 . . . . 187 C5
Penryn Ho 5 RH1 . . . . 119 A3
Pensfold La RH12 . . . . 214 E5
Pensford Ave TW9 . . . . 7 A5
Pensford Cl RG45 . . . . 45 B7
Penshurst Cl RH10 . . . . 202 D7
Penshurst Ct CR2 . . . . 61 B3
Penshurst Gn BR2 . . . . 44 F4
Penshurst Rd CR7 . . . . 42 B4
Penshurst Rise GU16 . . . . 85 F8
Penshurst Way SM2 . . . . 59 A3
Penshurst Wlk 6 BR2 . . . . 44 F4
Penstock Mews GU7 . . . . 151 A5
Pentelow Gdns TW14 . . . . 4 A1
Pentire Cl GU21 . . . . 69 E5
Pentland Ave TW17 . . . . 34 A4
Pentland Pl GU14 . . . . 84 E7
Pentlands BR3 . . . . 44 C8
Pentlands Cl CR4 . . . . 41 B6
Pentney Rd
Streatham SW12 . . . . 21 C7
Wimbledon SW19, SW20 . . . . 39 E8
Penton Ave TW18 . . . . 32 F8
Penton Ct TW18 . . . . 12 F2
Penton Hall TW18 . . . . 33 A8
Penton Hall Dr TW18 . . . . 33 A8
Penton Ho SM2 . . . . 59 C3
Penton Hook Marina KT16 . . . . 33 A6
Penton Hook Rd TW18 . . . 33 A8
Penton Rd TW18 . . . . 12 F1
Pentreath Ave GU2 . . . . 129 F8
Penwerris Ave TW5, TW7 . . . . 5 C7
Penwerris Ct TW7 . . . . 5 C7
Penwith Dr GU27 . . . . 207 E5
Penwith Rd SW18 . . . . 20 B6
Penwith Wlk GU22 . . . . 89 D8
Penwood End GU22 . . . . 89 B6
Penwood Gdns RG12 . . . . 26 D3
Penwood Ho SW15 . . . . 7 F1
Penwortham Prim Sch SW17 . . . . 21 B2
Penwortham Rd
South Croydon CR2 . . . . 61 D1
Streatham SW16 . . . . 21 C2
Peperham Cotts GU27 . . . . 208 C7
Peperham Ho GU27 . . . . 208 C7
Peperham Rd GU27 . . . . 208 C8
PEPER HAROW 149 C5
Peper Harow Ho GU8 . . . 149 D4
Peper Harow La GU8 . . . . 149 C6
Peperharow Rd GU7 . . . . 150 C6
Peppard Rd RH10 . . . . 202 D3
Pepperbox La GU5 . . . . 173 E4
Pepper Cl CR3 . . . . 100 E2
Peppercorn Cl CR7 . . . . 42 D7
Peppermint Cl CR0 . . . . 41 E2
Peppin Ct 2 KT12 . . . . 35 C1
Pepys Cl
Ashtead KT21 . . . . 76 A2
Brands Hill SL3 . . . . 1 B8
Pepys Ct SW20 . . . . 39 C7
Pepys Rd SW20 . . . . 39 C8
Perak Ct KT5 . . . . 38 C2
Peralta Terr CR4 . . . . 41 E5
Percheron Cl TW7 . . . . 5 F4
Percheron Dr GU21 . . . . 88 C8
Percival Cl KT22 . . . . 74 B8
Percival Rd
Feltham TW13 . . . . 14 F6
Mortlake SW14 . . . . 7 C3
Percival Way KT19 . . . . 57 D6
Percy Ave TW15 . . . . 14 A3
Percy Bilton Ct TW5 . . . . 5 B6
Percy Bryant Rd TW16 . . . . 14 E1
Percy Ct 1 KT5 . . . . 37 F3
Percy Gdns
4 Isleworth TW7 . . . . 6 A4
New Malden KT4 . . . . 38 E1
Percy Ho 4 SW16 . . . . 21 C4
Percy Rd
Carshalton CR4 . . . . 41 A2
Croydon SE25 . . . . 43 A4
Guildford GU2 . . . . 109 B3
Hampton TW12 . . . . 16 A1
Horsham RH12 . . . . 217 B3
Isleworth TW7 . . . . 6 A3
Penge SE20 . . . . 43 D8
Twickenham TW2 . . . . 16 C7
Percy Way TW2 . . . . 16 C7
Peregrin Ct SW16 . . . . 21 F4
Peregrine Cl
Bracknell RG12 . . . . 27 B4
Cranleigh GU6 . . . . 174 E4
Peregrine Gdns CR0 . . . . 62 E8
Peregrine Rd TW16 . . . . 34 F7
Peregrine Way SW19, SW20 . . . . 19 C1
Performing Arts & Tech Sch SE25 . . . . 42 D3
Perifield SE21 . . . . 22 C7
Perimeter Rd E RH6 . . . . 182 B6
Perimeter Rd N RH6 . . . . 181 D8
Perimeter Rd S RH6, RH11 . . . . 181 E5
Perkin Cl TW3 . . . . 5 B3
Perkins Ct TW15 . . . . 13 F3
Perkins Way RG41 . . . . 25 A5
Perkstead Ct 6 RH11 . . . 201 A3
Perleybrooke La GU21 . . . 69 A2
Perowne St GU11 . . . . 104 F2
Perram Works GU4 . . . . 110 C4
Perran Rd SE24, SW2 . . . . 22 B6
Perran Wlk 16 TW8 . . . . 6 E8
Perrin Cl TW15 . . . . 13 F3
Perrin Ct
Ashford TW15 . . . . 14 A4
Sheerwater GU21 . . . . 70 B4
Perring Ave GU14 . . . . 84 F8
Perring Rd GU14 . . . . 85 A1
Perrior Rd GU7 . . . . 150 E7
Perry Ave RH19 . . . . 185 E3
Perry Cl GU7 . . . . 151 B5
Perry Ct
2 Kingston u T KT2 . . . . 37 E7
Sutton SM1 . . . . 59 A5
Perryfield Ho 7 RH10 . . . . 201 D5
Perryfield Rd RH11 . . . . 201 D5
Perryfield Way TW10 . . . . 17 B6
Perry Hill SE6 . . . . 23 F5
Perry Ho 23 SW2 . . . . 21 E8
Perry How KT4 . . . . 38 F1
Perrylands RH6 . . . . 180 F7
Perrylands La RH6 . . . . 162 A2
Perrymount Prim Sch SE23 . . . . 23 D6
Perryn Ct 2 TW1 . . . . 17 A8
Perry Oaks RG12 . . . . 27 E7
Perry Rise SE23, SE6 . . . . 23 E5
Perry Vale SE23 . . . . 23 D6
Perry Way
Bracknell RG12 . . . . 27 E7
Farnham GU9 . . . . 125 B7
Lightwater GU18 . . . . 66 F7
Perrywood Bsns Pk RH1 . . . . 140 B1
Persant Rd SE6 . . . . 24 E6
Perseverance Cotts GU23 . . . . 91 C6
Persfield Cl KT17 . . . . 58 A1
Persfield Mews 2 KT17 . . . . 57 F1
Pershore Gr SM5 . . . . 40 D3
Perth Cl
Crawley RH11 . . . . 181 D1
Wimbledon SW20 . . . . 39 A7
Perth Rd BR3 . . . . 44 C7
Perth Way RH12 . . . . 217 F4
Perystreete SE23 . . . . 23 C6
Petavel Rd TW11 . . . . 16 E2
Peter Ave RH8 . . . . 122 D6
Peterborough Rd
Carshalton CR4, SM4, SM5 . . . . 40 E3
Crawley RH10 . . . . 201 E2
Guildford GU2 . . . . 108 F3
Peterhouse Cl GU47 . . . . 45 F2
Peterhouse Par RH10 . . . 182 C1
Peter Kennedy Ct CR0 . . . . 43 F3
Peterlee Wlk RH11 . . . . 200 E2
Peters Ct KT18 . . . . 76 E5
Petersfield Ave TW15, TW18 . . . . 13 C2
Petersfield Cres CR5 . . . . 79 E4
Petersfield Rd TW18 . . . . 13 C3
Petersfield Rise SW15 . . . . 19 B7
PETERSHAM 17 E7
Petersham Ave KT14 . . . . 71 E7
Petersham Cl
Byfleet KT14 . . . . 71 E7
Cheam SM1 . . . . 59 A5
Richmond TW10 . . . . 17 D6
Petersham Rd TW10 . . . . 17 E7
Petersham Terr CR0 . . . . 60 E7
Peters Ho SM3 . . . . 58 D5
Petersmead Cl KT20 . . . . 97 B4
Peter's Path SE26 . . . . 23 B4
Peterstow Cl SW19 . . . . 19 E6
Peters Wood RH5 . . . . 178 C5
Peterwood Pk CR9 . . . . 60 F8
Peterwood Way CR0 . . . . 60 F8
Petrel Ct 8 SE21 . . . . 22 D6
Petridge Rd RH1 . . . . 139 F4
Petters Rd KT21 . . . . 75 F3
Petts La TW17 . . . . 34 A5
Petworth Cl
Coulsdon CR5 . . . . 99 C8
Frimley GU16 . . . . 85 F8
Petworth Ct
Crawley RH11 . . . . 200 F3
Frimley GU15 . . . . 65 F4
Haslemere GU27 . . . . 208 D6
2 Woking GU22 . . . . 70 B3
Petworth Dr RH12 . . . . 217 F7
Petworth Gdns SW20 . . . . 39 B6
Petworth Rd
Chiddingfold, Ansteadbrook GU27 . . . . 209 B6
Chiddingfold GU8 . . . . 191 C4
Witley GU8 . . . . 170 F5
Wormley GU8 . . . . 171 A1
Pevensey Cl
Crawley RH10 . . . . 202 C5
Hounslow TW7 . . . . 5 C7
Pevensey Ct SW16 . . . . 22 A5
Pevensey Ho RH2 . . . . 139 B5
Pevensey Rd
Feltham TW13 . . . . 15 E7
Upper Tooting SW17 . . . . 20 D4
Pevensey Way GU16 . . . . 86 A8
Peverel Rd RH11 . . . . 200 E5
Peveril Dr TW11 . . . . 16 D3
Pewley Bank GU1 . . . . 130 E7
Pewley Down Inf Sch GU1 . . . . 130 E7
Pewley Hill GU1 . . . . 130 E7
Pewley Point GU1 . . . . 130 E7
Pewley Way GU1 . . . . 130 F7
Pewsey Vale RG12 . . . . 27 F4
Peyton's Cotts RH1 . . . . 119 F3
Pharaoh Cl CR4 . . . . 40 F2
Pheasant Cl CR8 . . . . 80 B6
Philanthropic Rd RH1 . . . 140 B8
Philip Gdns CR0 . . . . 62 F8
Philip Morris Ho TW13 . . . 15 B7
Philip Rd TW18 . . . . 13 D2
Philips Ho GU26 . . . . 188 B3
Philip Southcote Sch KT15 . . . . 52 C8
Phillip Copse RG12 . . . . 27 D2
Phillips Cl
Aldershot GU10 . . . . 126 E8
Crawley RH10 . . . . 202 C2
Godalming GU7 . . . . 150 D2
Phillips Cotts GU7 . . . . 150 B4
Phillips Hatch GU5 . . . . 152 C8
Philpot La GU24 . . . . 69 C7
Phipp's Bridge Rd CR4, SW19 . . . . 40 D6
Phoenix Bsns Pk RG12 . . . 26 C7
Phoenix Cl
Epsom KT19 . . . . 76 A7
West Wickham BR4 . . . . 63 E8
Phoenix Ct
13 Aldershot GU11 . . . . 105 A2
Croydon SE25 . . . . 43 A4
3 Epsom KT17 . . . . 76 E6
Feltham TW13 . . . . 14 E4
Guildford GU1 . . . . 130 D7
South Croydon CR2 . . . . 61 F5
Phoenix Ctr SM6 . . . . 60 E3
Phoenix Ctr The KT20 . . . . 97 C7
Phoenix Ho KT3 . . . . 38 F6
Phoenix La RH19 . . . . 206 E6
Phoenix Pl TW18 . . . . 13 A3
Phoenix Rd SE20 . . . . 23 C2
Phoenix Terr RH19 . . . . 206 E6
Phoenix Way TW5 . . . . 4 D8
Phyllis Ave KT3 . . . . 39 B4
Phyllis Ho CR0 . . . . 61 B6
Piccards The GU2 . . . . 130 C5
Pickering RG12 . . . . 27 A5
Pickering Gdns SE25 . . . . 42 F3
Pickering Pl GU2 . . . . 109 A3
Picket Post Cl RG12 . . . . 27 F6
Pickets St SW12 . . . . 21 B8
Picketts Hill GU35 . . . . 166 C1
Picketts La RH1 . . . . 161 C8
Pickford St GU11 . . . . 105 B2
Pickhurst Gn BR2 . . . . 44 F2
Pickhurst Inf Sch BR4 . . . . 44 F3
Pickhurst Jun Sch BR4 . . . 44 F3
Pickhurst La BR2, BR3, BR4 . . . . 44 E2
Pickhurst Mead BR2 . . . . 44 F2
Pickhurst Pk BR2 . . . . 44 F4
Pickhurst Rd GU8 . . . . 191 D2
Pickhurst Rise BR4 . . . . 44 D1
Pickins Piece SL3 . . . . 1 A5
Pickwick Cl TW4 . . . . 4 E2
Pickwick Gdns GU15 . . . . 66 B4
Pickwick Rd SE21 . . . . 22 E8
Picquets Way KT20, SM7 . . . . 77 F2
Picton Cl GU15 . . . . 66 B7
Picton Ho 1 SW4 . . . . 21 E8
Picton Mount CR3 . . . . 101 A8
Picture Ho SW16 . . . . 21 E6
Pier Five Rd E RH6 . . . . 181 E8
Pier Four Rd N RH6 . . . . 181 F8
Pier Rd TW14 . . . . 4 B2
Pierrefondes Ave GU14 . . . . 85 B5
Pierrepoint SE25 . . . . 42 E6
Pierson Ho 12 SE19 . . . . 22 E4
Pigbush La RH14 . . . . 213 A7
Pigeonhouse La
Lower Kingswood CR5 . . . . 98 C3
Winkfield SL5 . . . . 8 E4
Pigeon La TW12 . . . . 16 A4
Pigeon Pass RH10 . . . . 204 C5
Pigott Ct RG40 . . . . 25 D6
Pigott Rd RG40 . . . . 25 E8
Pike Cl GU11 . . . . 105 C2
Pikes Hill KT17 . . . . 76 E6
Pikes La RH7 . . . . 143 E2
Pikethorne SE23 . . . . 23 D6
Pilgrim Cl SM4 . . . . 40 B2
Pilgrim Ct GU8 . . . . 170 F8
Pilgrim Hill SE27 . . . . 22 C4
Pilgrim Ho GU1 . . . . 130 D7
Pilgrims Cl
Farnham GU9 . . . . 146 A8
Shere GU5 . . . . 133 A4
Westhumble RH5 . . . . 115 B4
Pilgrims La
Caterham CR3 . . . . 100 B1
Titsey RH8, TN16 . . . . 103 D3
Pilgrims Pl RH2 . . . . 118 A3
Pilgrims View GU12 . . . . 127 C8
Pilgrims Way
Bisley GU24 . . . . 68 A3
Shere GU5 . . . . 133 A4
Westhumble RH5 . . . . 115 B4
Pilgrims' Way
Guildford GU4 . . . . 130 E5
Reigate RH2 . . . . 118 A3
Pilgrim's Way CR2 . . . . 61 F5

Pilgrims Way Cotts RH3 116 C2
Pilgrims Way Prim Sch The GU9 146 B8
Pilsden Cl SW19 19 D7
Pilton Est The CR0 61 B8
Pimms Cl GU4 110 A5
Pinckards GU8 191 B5
Pincott La KT24 112 B6
Pincott Rd SW19 40 C8
Pineacre Ct GU22 70 B2
Pine Ave
Brookwood GU24 88 A6
Camberley GU15 65 D3
West Wickham BR4 44 B1
Pine Bank GU26 188 E4
Pine Cl
Ash Vale GU12 106 A6
Crawley RH11 181 C1
Kenley CR8 80 D2
Penge SE20 43 C8
Sandhurst GU15 64 E7
Woking GU21 69 C3
Woodham KT15 71 B8
Pine Coombe CR0 62 D6
Pinecote Dr SL5 29 F2
Pine Cres SM5 78 D8
Pinecrest GU17 64 E1
Pine Croft KT13 53 D4
Pine Croft Rd RG41 25 A2
Pine Ct
Bracknell RG12 27 E5
Farnborough GU14 85 C1
1 Guildford GU1 110 A1
3 Weybridge KT13 53 C5
Pine Dean KT23 94 B2
Pine Dr GU17 64 E3
Pinefields KT15 52 B6
Pinefields Cl RG45 45 B4
Pine Gdns
Horley RH6 161 A2
Surbiton KT5 38 A3
Pine Gr
East Grinstead RH19 185 B3
Farnham GU10 146 E6
Weybridge KT13 53 C5
Wimbledon SW19 19 F3
Windlesham GU20 48 D4
Pine Grove Mews 2 KT13 53 C5
Pine Hill KT18 76 D4
Pinehill Rd RG45 45 C3
Pinehill Rise GU47 64 C8
Pinehurst
Ascot SL5 29 D4
Horsham RH12 217 C4
8 Woking GU22 69 F1
Pinehurst Ave GU14 85 B2
Pinehurst Cl KT20 98 A5
Pinehurst Cotts GU14 85 B2
Pinehurst Rd GU14 85 A2
Pinel Cl GU25 31 E5
Pine Lo KT11 73 C4
Pine Mount Rd GU15 65 D4
Pine Pk GU3 108 A6
Pine Pl KT17 77 D5
Pine Rd GU22 89 C7
Pine Ridge SM5 60 A2
Pineridge Cl KT13 53 E6
Pine Ridge Dr GU10 146 C5
Pine Ridge Inf Sch GU15 47 A1
Pines Ct 14 SW19 19 D7
Pine Shaw RH10 202 D7
Pines Jun Sch The RG12 27 A2
Pines Prim Sch The RG12 27 A2
Pines The
Camberley GU15 65 F7
Chessington KT9 56 E7
Crawley RH10 202 D6
Dorking RH4 136 B6
Horsham RH12 218 C5
Purley CR8 80 C6
South Norwood SE19 22 B2
Sunbury TW16 35 A6
Woking GU21 69 F5
Pines Trad Est The GU3 108 E3
Pine Tree Cl TW5 4 B6
Pine Tree Hill GU22 70 D3
Pine Tree Lo BR2 44 F5
Pine Trees Bsns Pk TW18 12 E3
Pinetrees Cl RH10 183 B3
Pineview GU14 85 A4
Pine View GU35 187 C6
Pine View Cl
Badshot Lea GU9 126 A5
Chilworth GU4 131 F3
Haslemere GU27 208 C8
Pine Way TW20 11 B2
Pine Way Cl RH19 205 E7
Pine Wlk
Caterham CR3 100 F5
Cobham KT11 73 D5
East Horsley KT24 112 F7
Great Bookham KT23 94 B2
Surbiton KT5 38 A3
Sutton SM5, SM2 59 D1
Woodmansterne CR5, SM7 78 F2
Pinewood 3 BR1 24 E1
Pine Wood TW16 35 A8
Pinewood Ave
Crowthorne RG45 45 C6
Woodham KT15 52 C1
Pinewood Cl
Broadbridge Heath RH12 216 D3
South Croydon CR0 62 E7
Woking GU21 70 A4
Pinewood Cotts GU21 70 B7
Pinewood Cres GU14 84 C5
Pinewood Ct
Addlestone KT15 52 D6
Wimbledon SW19 20 B1
1 Woking GU21 70 A3
Pinewood Dr TW18 13 A3
Pinewood Gdns GU19 47 C3
Pinewood Gr KT15 52 B1
Pinewood Inf Sch GU14 84 D7
Pinewood Mews TW19 2 D1
Pinewood Pk
Bracknell RG40 45 C8
Farnborough GU14 84 C7
Woodham KT15 71 B8
Pinewood Pl KT19 57 D6
Pinewood Rd
Feltham TW13 15 B5
Normandy GU12 106 D3
Wentworth GU25 31 A5
Pinfold Rd SW16 21 E4
Pinglestone Cl UB7 2 E7
Pinkcoat Cl TW13 15 B5
Pinkerton Pl SW16 21 D4
Pinkhurst La RH13 216 A2
Pinks Mews GU8 170 F8
Pioneer Pl CR0 63 A2
Pioneers Ind Pk CR0 41 E1
Piper Rd KT1 38 A6
Pipers Cl KT11 73 D3
Pipers End RH13 215 E3
Piper's End GU25 31 D6
Pipers Gdns CR0 43 E2
Pipers Patch 1 GU14 85 B4
Pipewell Rd SM5 40 E3
Pippbrook Gdns RH4 136 B8
Pippin Cl CR0 43 F1
Pippins Ct TW15 14 B2
Pippins Sch SL3 1 F6
Piquet Rd BR3, SE20 43 C7
PIRBRIGHT 87 F4
Pirbright Cres CR0 63 C4
Pirbright Ho 11 KT2 18 B2
Pirbright Rd
Farnborough GU14 85 C3
Normandy GU3 107 B6
Wandsworth SW18 20 A7
Pirbright Terr GU24 87 F4
Pirbright Village Prim Sch GU24 87 E5
Piries Pl RH12 217 C2
Pisley La RH5 177 A4
Pitcairn Ct CR4 20 F1
Pitcairn Rd CR4 20 F1
Pitchfont La CR6, RH8 102 F2
PITCH PLACE
Guildford 108 F6
Beacon Hill 169 A3
Pit Farm Rd GU1 110 A1
Pitfold Ave GU27 207 D6
Pitfold Cl GU27 207 E6
Pitlake CR0, CR9 61 B8
Pitland St RH5 155 C5
Pitson Cl KT15 52 D6
Pitt Cres SW19 20 B4
Pitt La GU10 167 A6
Pitt Pl KT17 76 E5
Pitt Rd
Epsom KT17 76 E5
Thornton Heath CR0, CR7 42 C4
Pitts Rd GU11 105 B4
Pittville Gdns SE25 43 A6
Pitt Way GU14 84 F5
Pit Wood Gn KT20 97 C7
Pitwood Park Ind Est KT20 97 B7
Pixfield Ct BR2 44 F7
PIXHAM 115 D1
Pixham Ct 14 SW19 19 F3
Pixham Firs RH4 115 C2
Pixham La RH4 115 C2
Pixholme Ct RH4 115 C2
Pixholme Gr RH4 115 C1
Pixton Way CR0, CR2 62 E2
Place Ct GU11 126 C7
Place Farm Rd RH1 120 D4
Placehouse La CR5 80 A1
PLAISTOW 211 F2
Plaistow & Kirdford Prim Sch RH14 211 F3
Plaistow Rd
Chiddingfold GU8 210 D6
Dunsfold GU8 192 D2
Ifold RH14 212 D1
Plaistow St RH7 164 D4
Plane St SE26 23 B5
Planes The KT16 33 C2
Plane Tree Cres TW13 15 B5
Plane Tree Wlk 5 SE19 22 E2
Plantagenet Cl KT4 57 D6
Plantagenet Pk RG42 27 F8
Plantain Cres RH11 201 A2
Plantation La CR6 101 E8
Plantation Row GU15 65 B5
Plantation The RH7 184 C7
Plassy Rd SE6 24 B8
Plateau The
Newell Green RG42 8 A1
Winkfield RG42 28 A8
Plat The RH12 217 A3
Platt Mdw GU4 110 D3
Platt's Eyot TW12 36 A7
Platt The RH7 186 A8
Plaws Hill GU5 154 D6
Playden Ct 3 RH11 201 A3
Playgreen Way SE6 24 A4
Playground Cl BR3 43 D7
Playing Field Cl GU27 208 C8
Pleasant Gr CR0 62 F7
Pleasant Pl KT12 54 D4
Pleasure Pit Rd KT21 76 B1
Plesman Way SM6 60 E2
Plevna Rd TW12 36 B8
Pleydell Ave SE19 22 F1
Plough Cl RH11 200 F8
Plough Ind Est KT22 95 A7
Plough La
Downside KT11 73 A2
Horsham RH12 217 E5
Purley CR8 60 F1
7 Teddington TW11 17 A3
Wallington, Bandonhill SM6 60 E5
Wimbledon SW17, SW19 20 C4
Wokingham RG40 25 F6
Ploughlands RG42 26 F8
Plough Lane Cl SM6 60 E5
Ploughmans End TW7 5 D2
Plough Rd
Dormansland RH7 165 A2
Smallfield RH6 162 C3
West Ewell KT19 57 D3
Plover Cl
Crawley RH11 201 C8
Staines TW18 12 F5
Plovers Rd RH13 217 F3
Plovers Rise GU24 87 E7
Plowman Ho SW19 19 D6
Plum Cl TW13 15 A7
Plummer La CR4 40 F7
Plummer Rd SW4 21 D8
Plumpton Ct SE23 23 E8
Plumpton Way SM5 59 E7
Plumtree Cl SM6 60 D3
Plymen Ho KT8 36 A4
Plynlimmon Cotts GU6 174 A3
Pocket Cl RG42 26 D7
Pockford Rd GU8 191 D4
Pocklington Ct SW15 19 A7
Poels Ct RH19 185 E2
Pointers Cotts TW10 17 C6
Pointers Hill RH4 135 C5
Pointers Rd KT11 72 E2
Pointers The KT21 95 E7
Point Royal RG12 27 B4
Point Wharf La TW8 6 E7
Polden Cl GU14 84 E7
Polecat Hill GU26 188 F1
Polecat Valley GU26 188 F1
Polecroft La SE6 23 F6
Polesden Gdns SW20 39 B7
Polesden La
Ripley GU23 91 A6
Send Marsh GU23 90 F5
Polesden Lacey* KT23 114 B5
Polesden Rd KT23, RH5 114 B6
Polesden View KT23 114 B8
Poles La RH11 181 C3
Polesteeple Hill TN16 83 D2
Police Station Rd KT12 54 C4
Pollard Ct SM4 40 E4
Pollard Gr GU15 66 C4
Pollard Ho KT4 58 C6
Pollard Rd
Morden SM4 40 D4
Woking GU22 70 B3
Pollardrow Ave RG42 26 F8
Pollards RH11 201 A5
Pollards Cres SW16 41 E6
Pollards Dr RH13 217 F2
Pollards Hill E SW16 41 F6
Pollards Hill N SW16 41 F6
Pollards Hill S SW16 41 F6
Pollards Hill W SW16 41 F6
Pollards Oak Cres RH8 123 A3
Pollards Oak Rd RH8 123 A3
Pollards Wood Hill RH8 123 B5
Pollards Wood Rd
Limpsfield RH8 123 B4
Thornton Heath SW16 41 E6
POLLINGFOLD 195 F5
Polo Ctr The SL5 30 C5
Polsted La GU3 129 C3
Polsted Rd SE6 23 F8
Poltimore Rd GU2 130 B7
Polworth Rd SW16 21 E3
Polyanthus Way RG45 45 B8
Polygon Bsns Ctr SL3 1 F5
Pomeroy Cl TW1 6 B3
Pond Cl
Hersham KT12 54 A4
Loxwood RH14 212 F4
Pond Copse La RH14 212 F5
Pond Cottage La BR3, BR4 44 A1
Pond Cotts SE21 22 E7
Pond Farm RH7 164 B5
Pond Farm Cl KT20 97 B3
Pondfield Ho SE27 22 C3
Pondfield Rd
Farncombe GU7 150 F7
Kenley CR8 80 B3
Rudgwick RH12 214 E8
Pondfield Rd *continued*
West Wickham BR2 44 E1
Pond Head La
Forest Green RH5 176 E5
Wallis Wood RH5 176 D3
Pond Hill Gdns SM3 58 E4
Pond Ho
Chertsey KT16 33 B2
Guildford GU4 110 D2
Pond La
Frensham GU10 167 C5
Peaslake GU5 154 D7
Pond Mdw GU2 108 E2
Pond Meadow Sch GU2 108 E2
Pond Moor Rd RG12 27 B4
Pondpenny La GU14 84 A1
Pond Piece KT22 74 B6
Pond Rd
Egham TW20 12 C2
Headley Down GU35 187 B4
Woking GU22 89 B7
Pondside Cl UB3 3 D7
Ponds La GU5 153 F7
Ponds The KT13 53 E4
Pondtail Cl RH12 217 D6
Pondtail Copse RH12 217 D6
Pondtail Dr RH12 217 D7
Pondtail Pk RH12 217 D6
Pondtail Rd RH12 217 D6
Pond Way
East Grinstead RH19 186 B1
Teddington TW11 17 C2
Pond Wood Rd RH10 202 A8
Ponsonby Rd SW15 19 B8
Pontefract Rd BR1 24 F3
Ponton Ho SW2 22 A7
Pony Chase KT11 73 F6
Pook Hill GU8 190 F3
Pool Cl
Beckenham BR3 24 A3
East Molesey KT8 35 F4
Pool Ct SE6 24 A6
Poole Court Rd TW5 4 E5
Poole Ct TW5 4 E5
Pool End Cl TW17 34 A4
Poole Rd
West Ewell KT19 57 D4
Woking GU21 69 E1
Pooley Ave TW20 12 B3
POOLEY GREEN 12 C2
Pooley Green Cl TW20 12 C3
Pooley Green Rd TW20 12 C3
Pool Rd
Aldershot GU11 126 C7
East Molesey KT12, KT8 35 F4
Pope Cl
East Bedfont TW14 14 F7
Mitcham SW17, SW19 20 D2
Pope Ct 10 KT2 17 D4
Pope's Ave TW2 16 E6
Popes Cl SL3 1 C7
Popes Ct 3 TW2 16 E6
Popes Gr CR0 62 F7
Pope's Gr TW1, TW2 16 F6
Popes La RH8 143 F8
Popes Mead GU27 208 C7
POPESWOOD 26 D8
Popeswood Rd RG42 26 D8
Popham Cl
Bracknell RG12 27 F4
Feltham TW13 15 F5
Popham Gdns TW9 7 B4
Poplar Ave
Leatherhead KT22 95 C5
Mitcham CR4 40 F8
Windlesham GU20 48 B6
Poplar Cl
Bracknell RG12 27 D6
Crawley RH11 181 C1
Mytchett GU16 86 A3
Poyle SL3 1 E6
Poplar Cotts GU16 85 F6
Poplar Cres KT19 57 C4
Poplar Ct
4 Streatham SW16 21 F5
13 Twickenham TW1 6 C1
Wimbledon SW19 20 A3
Poplar Dr KT17, SM7 77 D5
Poplar Farm Cl KT19 57 C4
Poplar Gdns KT3 38 D7
Poplar Gr
Kingston u T KT3 38 D6
Woking GU22 89 E8
Poplar La BR3 44 B4
Poplar Prim Sch SW19 40 A6
Poplar Rd
Ashford TW15 14 C3
Cheam SM3 39 F1
Leatherhead KT22 95 C5
Merton SW19 40 A7
Shalford GU4 130 E2
Poplar Rd S SM4, SW19 40 A6
Poplars Cl GU14 84 C5
Poplars The
Ascot SL5 29 A4
Cudworth RH5 179 E8
Horsham RH13 217 E3
Poplar Way TW13 15 B5
Poplar Wlk
Caterham CR3 100 E4
Croydon CR0 42 C1
Heath End GU9 125 D7
Poppy Cl SM6 41 A1
Poppyhills Rd GU15 65 F8
Poppy La CR0, CR9 43 C1
Poppy Pl RG40 25 B6
Porchester SL5 29 A5
Porchester Mead BR3 24 B2
Porchester Rd KT1 38 B7
Porchfield Cl SM2 59 B1
Porlock Ho 5 SE26 23 A5
Porridge Pot Alley GU2 130 C7
Portal Cl SE27 22 A5
Porteridges RH4 136 C4
Portesbery Hill Dr GU15 65 E6
Portesbery Rd GU15 65 E6
Portesbery Sch GU15 65 D6
Porthcawe Rd SE26 23 F4
Portia Gr RG42 27 E8
Portland Ave KT3 38 F2
Portland Cl KT4 39 B2
Portland Cotts
11 Dorking RH4 136 A8
Feltham TW13 15 E3
Wallington CR0 41 D2
Portland Cres TW13, TW15 14 D4
Portland Ct SM1 59 B4
Portland Dr RH1 119 D6
Portland Ho
5 East Grinstead RH19 205 F8
Merstham RH1 119 D6
20 Streatham SW2 22 A7
Portland House Mews KT18 76 D5
Portland Pl
Croydon SE25 43 A5
Ewell KT17 76 E7
Portland Rd
Ashford TW15 13 E5
Croydon SE25 43 B4
Dorking RH4 136 A8
East Grinstead RH19 205 F8
Kingston u T KT1 37 F6
Mitcham CR4 40 E7
Portland Terr TW9 6 D3
Portley La CR3 100 E6
Portley Wood Rd CR3 101 A7
Portman Ave SW14 7 D4
Portman Cl 5 RG42 27 A8
Portman Rd KT1 37 F7
Portmore Park Rd KT13 53 A7
Portmore Pl 7 KT13 53 D7
Portmore Quays KT13 52 F6
Portmore Way KT13 53 A7
Portnall Dr GU25 30 F4
Portnall Rd GU25 30 F4
Portnall Rise GU25 30 F3
Portnalls Cl CR5 79 B3
Portnalls Rd CR5 79 B2
Portnalls Rise CR5 79 C3
Portobello Ho 6 SW27 22 B3
Porton Ct KT6 37 C3
Portsea Ho 3 SW15 19 B7
Portsmouth Ave KT7 37 A2
Portsmouth Rd
Camberley GU15 66 A7
Cobham KT10, KT11 73 C7
Downside KT11 72 F6
Esher KT10 55 D7
Godalming GU7, GU8 150 B2
Guildford GU2 130 C6
Hindhead GU26 188 E2
Milford GU8 149 E1
Putney SW15 19 C8
Ripley GU23 91 B4
Thames Ditton KT1, KT6, KT7 37 C3
Thursley GU8 169 D3
Wisley GU23, KT11 72 C3
Witley GU8 170 B6
Portswood Pl SW15 7 F1
Portugal Gdns TW2 16 C6
Portugal Rd GU21 69 F3
Portway KT17 58 A2
Port Way GU24 68 A3
Portway Cres KT17 58 A2
Post Boys Row KT11 73 A5
Postford Mill Cotts GU4 131 F5
Post House La KT23 94 A2
Post La TW2 16 D7
Postmill Cl CR0, CR9 62 D7
Post Office Row RH8 123 E4
Potbury Cl SL4 9 B2
POT COMMON 148 C2
Potley Hill Prim Sch GU46 64 A5
Potley Hill Rd GU46 64 A5
Potter Cl CR4 41 B7
Potterhill Ct TW11 17 B1
Potteries La GU16 85 F4
Potteries The
Farnborough GU14 84 D6
Ottershaw KT16 51 E4
Potterne Cl 5 SW15, SW19 19 D8
Potters Cl
Croydon CR0 43 E1
Milford GU8 149 F2
Potters Cres GU12 106 B2
Potters Croft RH13 217 E2
Pottersfield RH10 201 D7
Potters Gate GU9 125 B2
Potters Gate CE Prim Sch GU9 125 A2
Potters Gr KT3 38 C5

Potters Hill GU8 . . . . .171 D4
Potters La GU23 . . . . .90 B2
Potter's La SW16 . . . . . . .21 D2
Potters Pl RH2 . . . . .217 C2
Potters Way RH2 . . . . . . .139 C5
Pottery Ct GU10 . . . . .145 F6
Pottery La GU10 . . . . .145 F6
Pottery Rd TW8 . . . . .6 E8
Poulett Gdns TW1 . . . . . . .17 A7
Poullett Ho SW2 . . . . .22 B7
Poulton Ave SM1 . . . . .59 D7
Pound Cl
  Epsom KT19 . . . . .76 D8
  Godalming GU7 . . . . .150 E4
  Long Ditton KT6 . . . . .37 C1
  Loxwood RH14 . . . . .212 F5
Pound Cnr RH12 . . . . .197 E2
Pound Cres KT22 . . . . .94 D6
Pound Ct
  Ashtead KT21 . . . . .75 F1
  Wood St V GU3 . . . . .108 B2
Pound Farm Cl KT10 . . . . . .36 D1
Pound Farm La GU12 . . . . .106 D1
Pound Field GU1 . . . . .109 D1
Poundfield Ct GU22 . . . . . . .90 C7
Poundfield Gdns GU22 . . . . .90 C7
Poundfield La RH14 . . . . . .212 B3
POUND HILL 202 C8
Pound Hill GU3 . . . . .108 B2
Pound Hill Jun & Inf Schs
  RH10 . . . . .202 C7
Pound Hill Par RH10 . . . . . .202 C7
Pound Hill Pl RH10 . . . . . . .202 C6
Pound La
  Epsom KT19 . . . . .76 D8
  Godalming GU7 . . . . .150 E4
  Windlesham GU20 . . . . . . .48 C4
  Wood St V GU3 . . . . .108 B2
Pound Lane Cvn Site
  GU3 . . . . .108 B2
Pound Pl GU4 . . . . .130 F3
Pound Place Cl GU4 . . . . . .130 F3
Pound Rd
  Aldershot GU12 . . . . .105 C1
  Banstead SM7 . . . . .78 A2
  Chertsey KT16 . . . . .33 B2
Pound St SM5 . . . . .59 F5
POVEY CROSS 160 D1
Povey Cross Rd RH6 . . . . . .160 E1
Powderham Ct GU21 . . . . . .68 D1
Powder Mill La TW2 . . . . . . .16 A7
Powell Cl
  Chessington KT9 . . . . .56 D5
  Guildford GU2 . . . . .129 F7
  Horley RH6 . . . . .160 E4
  Wallington SM6 . . . . .60 E3
Powell Corderoy Prim Sch
  RH4 . . . . .135 F6
Powell Ct CR0 . . . . .61 C6
Powell Ho SW19 . . . . .19 E2
Powells Cl RH4 . . . . .136 C4
Powell's Wlk W4 . . . . .7 F8
Powell Terr CR4 . . . . .41 E5
Power Cl GU1 . . . . .109 C2
Power Ho TW9 . . . . .7 A6
Powers Ct TW1 . . . . .17 D8
Pownall Gdns TW3 . . . . .5 B3
Pownall Rd TW3 . . . . .5 B3
POYLE 1 E6
Poyle 14 Trad Est SL3 . . . . . .1 E4
Poyle Gdns RG12 . . . . .27 D8
Poyle Ho GU4 . . . . .110 D2
Poyle New Cotts SL3 . . . . . . .1 F5
Poyle Pk SL3 . . . . .1 E4
Poyle Rd
  Guildford GU1 . . . . .130 E7
  Poyle SL3 . . . . .1 E5
  Tongham GU10 . . . . .127 B7
Poyle Tech Ctr The SL3 . . . . .1 E5
Poynder Lo TW7 . . . . .6 A6
Poynders Gdns SW12 . . . . . .21 C8
Poynders Rd SW12,
  SW4 . . . . .21 D8
Poynes Rd RH6 . . . . .160 E5
Poynings Rd RH11 . . . . . . .200 E5
Prairie Cl KT15 . . . . .52 B7
Prairie Rd KT15 . . . . .52 B7
Pratts Cnr GU8 . . . . .193 A8
Pratts La KT12 . . . . .54 D6
Precincts The SM4 . . . . .40 A3
Precinct The
  Cranleigh GU6 . . . . .174 E4
  Egham TW20 . . . . .12 A3
Prendergast Ho **5**
  SW4 . . . . .21 D8
Prentice Cl GU14 . . . . .85 B8
Prentice Ct **2** SW19 . . . . . .19 F3
Prentis Rd SW16 . . . . .21 D4
Presburg Rd KT3 . . . . .38 E4
Prescott RG12 . . . . .26 F2
Prescott Ho CR0 . . . . .61 A7
Prescott Pl SW16 . . . . .21 E1
Prescott Rd SL3 . . . . .1 E5
Presentation Mews
  SW2 . . . . .21 F7
Preshaw Cres CR4 . . . . .40 E6
Prestbury Cres SM7 . . . . . . .78 F3
Prestbury Ct GU21 . . . . .69 A1
Preston Cl TW2 . . . . .16 E5
Preston Cross KT23 . . . . . . .93 F1
Preston Ct SM1 . . . . .35 C1
Preston Dr KT19 . . . . .57 F4
Preston Gr KT21 . . . . .75 C2
Preston La KT20 . . . . .97 C2
Preston Pl TW10 . . . . .6 E2

Preston Rd
  Littleton TW17 . . . . .34 A4
  South Norwood SE19 . . . . .22 B2
  Wimbledon SW20 . . . . . . .18 F1
Prestwick Cl RH11 . . . . . . .200 D5
Prestwick La GU8,
  GU27 . . . . .190 C3
Prestwood Cl RH11 . . . . . . .181 B1
Prestwood Gdns CR0 . . . . . .42 C2
Prestwood Rd RH11 . . . . . .180 C3
Pretoria Rd
  Chertsey KT16 . . . . .32 F1
  Streatham SW16 . . . . .21 C3
Pretty La CR5 . . . . .99 C6
Prey Heath Cl GU22 . . . . . . .89 C3
Prey Heath Rd GU22 . . . . . .89 B3
Preymead Ind Est
  GU9 . . . . .126 B7
Price Cl SW17 . . . . .20 F5
Price Rd CR0 . . . . .61 B5
Prices La RH2 . . . . .139 B6
Price Way TW12 . . . . .15 E2
Prickley Wood BR2 . . . . . . .44 F1
Priddy's Yd **4** CR9 . . . . . .61 C8
Prideaux Gdns RH5 . . . . . .177 D4
Prides Crossing SL5 . . . . . . .9 A1
Pridham Rd CR7 . . . . .42 D5
Priest Ave RG40 . . . . .25 F5
Priest Croft Cl RH11 . . . . . .201 A6
Priestfield Rd SE23 . . . . . . .23 E5
PRIEST HILL 77 B8
Priest Hill
  Englefield Green TW19,
  TW20 . . . . .11 C6
  Limpsfield RH8 . . . . .123 B6
Priest Hill Sch Sports Ctr
  KT17 . . . . .77 B8
Priest La GU24 . . . . .67 C5
Priestlands Cl RH6 . . . . . . .160 F4
Priestley Gdns GU22 . . . . . .90 A7
Priestley Rd
  Guildford GU2 . . . . .129 D8
  Mitcham CR4 . . . . .41 A7
Priestley Way RH10 . . . . . .182 A3
Priests Bridge SW14,
  SW15 . . . . .7 E4
PRIESTWOOD 27 A8
Priestwood Ave RG42 . . . . . .26 F8
Priestwood Court Rd
  RG42 . . . . .27 A8
Priestwood Sq **1**
  RG42 . . . . .27 A8
Primrose Ave RH6 . . . . . . .161 B1
Primrose Cl
  Carshalton CR4 . . . . .41 A8
  Catford SE6 . . . . .24 C3
  Crawley RH11 . . . . .201 B3
Primrose Copse RH12 . . . . .217 E7
Primrose Ct
  Guildford GU4 . . . . .110 C4
  New Malden KT4 . . . . .39 A2
  9 Streatham SW12 . . . .21 D8
Primrose Dr GU24 . . . . .68 A4
Primrose Gdns GU14 . . . . . .84 E3
Primrose Ho **1** TW9 . . . . . .6 F6
Primrose La GU6 . . . . .43 D1
Primrose Pl TW7 . . . . .5 F5
Primrose Rd KT12 . . . . .54 C5
Primrose Ridge GU7 . . . . . .150 B2
Primrose Way
  Bramley GU5 . . . . .151 D5
  Sandhurst GU47 . . . . .45 B1
Primrose Wlk
  Bracknell RG12 . . . . .27 C4
  Ewell KT17 . . . . .57 F3
Prim Sch of Our Lady
  Immaculate KT6 . . . . .38 B1
Prince Albert Ct **6**
  TW16 . . . . .14 E1
Prince Albert Dr SL5 . . . . . .28 D5
Prince Albert Sq RH1 . . . . .140 A4
Prince Andrew Way
  SL5 . . . . .28 D7
Prince Charles Cres
  GU14 . . . . .85 C8
Prince Charles Way
  SM6 . . . . .60 B7
Prince Consort Dr SL5 . . . . .28 D5
Prince Consort's Dr
  SL4 . . . . .10 A6
Prince Dr GU47 . . . . .45 A1
Prince George's Ave
  SW20 . . . . .39 C7
Prince Georges Rd
  SW19 . . . . .40 D8
Prince Of Wales Rd
  RH1 . . . . .141 A4
Prince Of Wales' Rd
  SM1 . . . . .59 D8
Prince of Wales Wlk
  GU15 . . . . .65 C6
Prince Rd SE25 . . . . .42 E4
Prince Regent Rd TW3 . . . . . .5 C4
Princes Ave
  Hamsey Green CR2 . . . . . .81 B4
  Tolworth KT6 . . . . .57 A8
  Wallington SM5 . . . . .59 F2
Prince's Ave
  Farnborough GU11 . . . . . .105 C5
  Farncombe GU7 . . . . .150 C7
Princes Cl
  Bagshot GU19 . . . . .47 E1
  Hamsey Green CR2 . . . . . .81 B4
Prince's Cl TW11 . . . . .16 D4
Princes Ct
  Englefield Green TW20 . . . .11 C3
  11 Guildford GU1 . . . . .109 D1
  New Malden KT3 . . . . .38 F6

Princes Ct continued
  Weybridge KT13 . . . . .53 B5
Prince's Dr KT22 . . . . .74 E7
Princes Gdns GU3 . . . . . . .108 E8
Princes Mead GU14 . . . . . . .85 B4
Princes Mews TW3 . . . . .5 A3
Princes Rd
  Ashford TW15 . . . . .13 F3
  Egham TW20 . . . . .11 F2
  Feltham TW13 . . . . .14 F5
  Kingston u T KT2 . . . . .18 A1
  Penge SE20 . . . . .23 D2
  Richmond, Kew TW9 . . . . . .6 F4
  Richmond TW10 . . . . .6 F2
Prince's Rd
  Mortlake SW14 . . . . .7 D4
  Redhill RH1 . . . . .139 F7
  Teddington TW11 . . . . . . .16 D4
  Weybridge KT13 . . . . .53 C5
  Wimbledon SW19 . . . . . . .20 A2
Princess Anne Rd
  RH12 . . . . .214 D6
Princess Ct
  Beckenham BR3 . . . . .44 B7
  3 Croydon CR0 . . . . . . .61 F8
  3 Farnborough GU14 . . .105 C8
  Hounslow TW4 . . . . .4 C4
  7 Wimbledon SW20 . . . .19 D1
Princess Gdns GU22 . . . . . .70 B3
Princess Ho **1** RH1 . . . . .119 A2
Princess Margaret Rd
  RH12 . . . . .214 D7
Princess Mary Cl
  GU2 . . . . .109 A5
Princess Mary's Rd
  KT15 . . . . .52 C6
Princess Rd
  Crawley RH11 . . . . .201 C6
  Thornton Heath CR0 . . . . .42 C3
  Woking GU22 . . . . .70 C3
Princess Sq RG12 . . . . .27 B7
Princes St SM1 . . . . .59 D6
Prince's St TW10, TW9 . . . . . .6 E2
Princess Way
  Camberley GU15 . . . . .65 C5
  Redhill RH1 . . . . .119 A2
Princes Way
  Aldershot GU11 . . . . .105 A2
  Coney Hall BR4 . . . . .63 F7
  Croydon CR0 . . . . .60 F5
  Putney SW19, SW19 . . . . .19 E7
Princethorpe Rd SE26 . . . . .23 D4
Princeton Mews **3**
  KT2 . . . . .38 A8
Prince William Ct
  TW15 . . . . .13 F3
Pringle Gdns
  Purley CR8 . . . . .60 F1
  Streatham SW16 . . . . .21 C4
Prins Willem-Alexander
  Sch GU27 . . . . .70 C2
Prior Ave SM2 . . . . .59 E3
Prior Croft Cl GU15 . . . . . . .66 A4
Prior End GU15 . . . . .66 A5
Prioress Rd SE27 . . . . .22 B5
Prior Heath Inf Sch
  GU15 . . . . .66 A5
Prior Place Cross Roads
  GU15 . . . . .66 B4
Prior Rd GU15 . . . . .66 A5
Priors Cl
  Compton GU7 . . . . .129 A1
  Farnborough GU14 . . . . . .85 B8
Priors Croft GU22 . . . . .90 A7
Priors Ct
  Ash GU12 . . . . .105 E1
  Woking GU21 . . . . .69 A1
Priorsfield Rd GU7 . . . . . . .129 A1
Priors Field Sch GU7 . . . . . .129 A1
Priors Hatch La GU7 . . . . . .128 F1
Prior's La GU17 . . . . .64 A5
Priors Lo **1** TW10 . . . . . . .6 E1
Priors Mead KT23 . . . . .94 C2
Priors The KT21 . . . . .95 D8
Priors Wlk RH10 . . . . .201 F6
Priorswood GU3 . . . . .128 F2
Priors Wood
  Haslemere GU27 . . . . . . .207 F6
  Hinchley Wood KT10 . . . . .55 F8
  Kingsfold RH12 . . . . .198 B6
Priory Ave SM3 . . . . .58 D6
Priory CE Prim Sch
  SW19 . . . . .20 B3
Priory CE Sch The
  RH4 . . . . .135 F6
Priory Cl
  Beckenham BR3 . . . . .43 E6
  Dorking RH4 . . . . .136 A5
  Hampton TW12 . . . . .35 F8
  Horley RH6 . . . . .160 F4
  3 Merton SW19 . . . . . . .40 B8
  Sheerwater GU21 . . . . . . .70 D6
  Sunbury TW16 . . . . .15 A1
  Sunningdale SL5 . . . . .30 A2
  Walton-on-T KT12 . . . . . . .54 A7
Priory Ct
  Camberley GU15 . . . . .64 F5
  Cheam SM3 . . . . .58 E6
  Dorking RH4 . . . . .136 B5
  Egham TW20 . . . . .12 C2
  Farnham GU9 . . . . .146 C8
  3 Hampton TW12 . . . . . .16 A1
  Hounslow TW3 . . . . .5 B4
  Reigate RH2 . . . . .117 F1
  Roehampton SW15 . . . . . . .7 F3

Priory Dr RH2 . . . . .139 A7
Priory Gdns
  Ashford TW15 . . . . .14 D3
  Hampton TW12 . . . . .35 F8
  Mortlake SW13 . . . . .7 F4
  South Norwood SE25 . . . . .42 F5
Priory Gn TW18 . . . . .13 B3
Priory Ho Ct SE6 . . . . .24 B7
Priory Hospl The
  Knaphill GU21 . . . . .68 C3
  Roehampton SW15 . . . . . . .7 F3
Priory La
  East Molesey KT8 . . . . . . .36 B5
  Frensham GU10 . . . . .167 E8
  Roehampton SW15 . . . . . . .7 F2
Priory Lo BR4 . . . . .63 E7
Priory Mews TW18 . . . . .13 B3
Priory Pl KT12 . . . . .54 A7
Priory Rd
  Cheam SM3 . . . . .58 D6
  Chessington KT9 . . . . .56 E7
  Forest Row RH18 . . . . . . .206 D2
  Hampton TW12 . . . . .16 A1
  Isleworth TW3 . . . . .5 C2
  Mitcham SW19 . . . . .20 D1
  Reigate RH2 . . . . .139 A6
  Richmond TW9 . . . . .7 A7
  Sunningdale SL5 . . . . .30 A2
  Thornton Heath CR0 . . . . .42 A2
  Winkfield SL5 . . . . .28 B7
Priory Ret Pk SW19 . . . . . . .20 D1
Priory Sch
  Banstead SM7 . . . . .78 A4
  South Norwood SE25 . . . . .42 F5
Priory St GU14 . . . . .85 D4
Priory The
  Croydon CR0 . . . . .61 A7
  Godstone RH9 . . . . .121 B3
  21 Kingston u T KT6 . . . .37 E4
Priory Way UB7 . . . . .2 E8
Priory Wlk
  Bracknell RG12 . . . . .27 F5
  Sunbury TW16 . . . . .15 A1
Priscilla Ho **8** TW16 . . . . .14 F1
Probyn Rd SW2 . . . . .22 B6
Proctor Cl
  Crawley RH10 . . . . .202 C4
  Mitcham CR4 . . . . .41 A8
Proctor Gdns KT23 . . . . . . .94 B2
Proctors Cl TW14 . . . . .15 A7
Proctors Rd RG40 . . . . .25 F6
Proffits Cotts RH10 . . . . . . .201 D5
Profumo Rd KT12 . . . . .54 D5
Progress Bsns Pk CR9 . . . . .60 F8
Progress Way CR0 . . . . .60 F8
Prologis Pk
  Hounslow TW4 . . . . .4 C4
  Wallington CR0 . . . . .41 D2
Promenade Approach Rd
  W4 . . . . .7 E7
Promenade De Verdun
  CR8 . . . . .79 D8
Promenade The W4 . . . . .7 F7
Prospect Ave GU14 . . . . . . .85 B6
Prospect Cl
  Forest Hill SE26 . . . . .23 B4
  Hounslow TW5 . . . . .4 F6
Prospect Cott GU12 . . . . . .106 A4
Prospect Cotts RG42 . . . . . .26 D8
Prospect Cres TW2 . . . . .5 C1
Prospect Ct **4** GU1 . . . . .130 E8
Prospect Ho
  Epsom KT19 . . . . .57 B1
  3 Mitcham SW19 . . . . . .40 D8
  Old Woking GU22 . . . . . . .90 B7
Prospect House Sch
  SW15 . . . . .19 D8
Prospect La TW20 . . . . .11 A3
Prospect Pl
  Crawley RH11 . . . . .201 C6
  Ewell KT17 . . . . .76 E6
  Staines TW18 . . . . .12 F3
  Wimbledon SW20 . . . . . . .19 B1
Prospect Rd
  Ash GU12 . . . . .106 A5
  Farnborough GU14 . . . . . .85 A5
  Rowledge GU10 . . . . .145 E3
  Thames Ditton KT6 . . . . . .37 C3
Prossers KT20 . . . . .97 D6
Providence Cotts
  RH3 . . . . .137 B8
Providence Ct UB3 . . . . .3 D7
Providence Ho GU19 . . . . . .47 E3
Providence La UB3 . . . . .3 D7
Providence Pl
  Ewell KT17 . . . . .76 E7
  Farnham GU9 . . . . .125 C2
  West Byfleet GU22 . . . . . . .71 A5
Provincial Terr SE20 . . . . . .23 D1
Prune Hill TW20 . . . . .11 E1
Prunus Cl GU24 . . . . .67 E6
Puccinia Ct TW19 . . . . .13 E7
Puckridge Gate Rd
  GU11 . . . . .104 E6
Puckridge Hill Rd
  GU11 . . . . .104 E6
Puckshill GU21 . . . . .68 D2
Puckshott Way GU27 . . . . . .208 D8
Puddenhole Cotts
  RH4 . . . . .116 A2
Pudding La RH6 . . . . .180 E7
Puffin Cl BR3, CR0 . . . . . . .43 D4
Puffin Hill RH10 . . . . .204 C5
Puffin Rd RH11 . . . . .200 D5
Pulborough Rd SW18 . . . . . .19 F8
Pulborough Way TW4 . . . . . . .4 C3
Pullman Ct SW2 . . . . .21 F7
Pullman La GU7 . . . . .150 C2

Pullman Pl RH1 . . . . .119 C7
Pullmans Pl **4** TW18 . . . . .13 A3
Pulteney Cl TW7 . . . . .6 A4
Puma Trade Pk CR4 . . . . . . .40 D5
Pump Alley **7** TW8 . . . . . . .6 D7
Pump House Cl BR2 . . . . . . .44 F7
Pumping Station Rd W4 . . . . .7 E8
Pump La SL5 . . . . .29 E8
Pump Pail N CR0, CR9 . . . . .61 C7
Pump Pail S CR0, CR9 . . . . .61 C7
Punchbowl La RH4,
  RH5 . . . . .136 D6
Punch Copse Rd
  RH10 . . . . .201 F7
Punnetts Ct RH11 . . . . .200 F3
Purbeck Ave KT3 . . . . .38 F3
Purbeck Cl RH1 . . . . .119 D7
Purbeck Ct **6** GU2 . . . . . .108 E1
Purbeck Dr GU21 . . . . .69 F5
Purberry Gr KT17 . . . . .57 F1
Purberry Shot KT17 . . . . . . .57 F1
Purbrook RH4 . . . . .115 C2
Purbrook Ct RG12 . . . . .27 E3
Purbrook Ho **2** SW15 . . . .19 B7
Purcell Cl CR8 . . . . .80 C5
Purcell Ho TW2 . . . . .5 D1
Purcell Rd
  Crawley RH11 . . . . .200 F3
  Crowthorne RG45 . . . . . . .45 B7
Purcell's Cl KT21 . . . . .75 F1
Purdey Ct **3** KT4 . . . . . . .39 A1
PURLEY 80 B7
Purley Bury Ave CR8 . . . . . .80 C8
Purley Bury Cl CR8 . . . . . . .80 C8
Purley Cl RH10 . . . . .202 D3
Purley Ct CR8 . . . . .61 B1
Purley & District War
  Meml Hospl CR8 . . . . . . .80 A8
Purley Downs Rd CR2 . . . . .80 E8
Purley Grange CR2 . . . . . . .61 C1
Purley Hill CR8 . . . . .80 B7
Purley Knoll CR8 . . . . .80 A8
Purley Oaks Prim Sch
  CR2 . . . . .61 D3
Purley Oaks Rd CR2 . . . . . .61 D1
Purley Oaks Sta CR2 . . . . . .61 D2
Purley Par **9** CR8 . . . . . . .80 A8
Purley Park Rd CR8 . . . . . . .61 B1
Purley Rd
  Purley CR8 . . . . .80 A8
  South Croydon CR2 . . . . . .61 D3
Purley Rise CR8 . . . . .79 F7
Purley Sta CR8 . . . . .80 A7
Purley Vale CR8 . . . . .80 B6
Purley View Terr CR2 . . . . . .61 D3
Purley Way
  Croydon CR0, CR9 . . . . . .61 A4
  Frimley GU16 . . . . .85 E3
  Purley CR8 . . . . .80 A8
  Thornton Heath CR0,
  CR9 . . . . .41 F1
Purley Way Cres CR0 . . . . . .41 F2
Purmerend Cl GU14 . . . . . . .84 C5
Pursers Hollow GU5 . . . . . .154 D8
Pursers La GU5 . . . . .154 D7
Pursers Lea GU5 . . . . .154 D7
Purslane RG40 . . . . .25 D5
Purton Rd RH12 . . . . .217 B4
Purvis Ho CR0 . . . . .42 D2
PUTNEY 19 C7
Putney Heath SW15 . . . . . . .19 C8
Putney Heath SW15 . . . . . . .19 B8
Putney Hill SW15 . . . . .19 D8
PUTNEY VALE 19 A5
PUTTENHAM 128 C4
Puttenham CE Inf Sch
  GU3 . . . . .128 C4
Puttenham Common
  Nature Trails★ GU3 . . . . .148 D3
Puttenham Heath Rd
  GU3 . . . . .128 E3
Puttenham Hill GU3 . . . . . .128 C5
Puttenham La GU3,
  GU8 . . . . .128 C1
Puttenham Rd GU10 . . . . . .127 C4
Puttocks Cl GU27 . . . . .207 D5
Pye Cl CR3 . . . . .100 D4
Pyecombe Ct **4** RH11 . . .200 F3
Pyegrove Chase RG12 . . . . .27 E2
PYESTOCK 84 B2
Pyestock Cres GU14 . . . . . .84 C4
Pyke Cl RG40 . . . . .25 D6
Pylbrook Rd SM1 . . . . .59 B7
Pyle Hill GU22 . . . . .89 D3
Pylon Way CR0 . . . . .41 E1
Pymers Mead SE21 . . . . . . .22 C7
Pyne Rd KT6 . . . . .38 A1
Pyrcroft CE Inf Sch 32 F2
Pyrcroft Grange Prim Sch
  KT16 . . . . .32 E3
Pyrcroft La KT13 . . . . .53 B5
Pyrcroft Rd KT16 . . . . .32 E2
PYRFORD 70 E4
Pyrford CE Prim Sch
  GU22 . . . . .71 A3
Pyrford Common Rd
  GU22 . . . . .70 E2
PYRFORD GREEN 71 B2
Pyrford Heath GU22 . . . . . .70 F3
Pyrford Pl GU22 . . . . .71 C1
Pyrford Rd GU22, KT14 . . . .71 A4
PYRFORD VILLAGE 71 A1
Pyrford Woods Cl
  GU22 . . . . .70 F4
PYRFORD WOODS ESTATE
  . . . . .70 F4
Pyrford Woods Rd
  GU22 . . . . .70 F4

Pyrian Cl GU22 . . . . . 70 D2
Pyrland Rd TW10 . . . . 6 F1
Pyrmont Gr SE27 . . . . 22 B5
Pyrmont Rd W4 . . . . 7 A8
Pytchley Cres SE19 . . . . . 22 C2

Q

Quadrangle Lo SW19 . . . . . 20 A2
Quadrangle The
  Guildford GU2 . . . . 130 A8
  2 Horley RH6 . . . . 161 B3
Quadrant Ct RG12 . . . . . 27 E6
Quadrant Ctyd KT13 . . . 53 A6
Quadrant Rd
  Richmond TW9 . . . . 6 D3
  Thornton Heath CR7 . . . 42 B5
Quadrant The
  Addlestone KT15 . . . . 52 C5
  Ash Vale GU12 . . . . 106 A4
  Epsom KT17 . . . . 76 E6
  Merton SW20 . . . . 39 E8
  Richmond TW9 . . . . 6 E3
  Sutton SM2 . . . . 59 C4
Quadrant Way KT13 . . . . 53 A6
Quadrum Pk GU3 . . . . . . 130 B2
Quail Cl RH12 . . . . 217 D7
Quail Gdns CR0 . . . . 62 E1
QUAKER'S PLATT . . . 186 A8
Quakers Way GU3 . . . . . 108 C5
Qualitas RG12 . . . . 26 F1
Quality St RH1 . . . . 119 B7
Quantock Cl
  Crawley RH11 . . . . 201 B6
  Harlington UB3 . . . . 3 D7
Quantock Dr KT4 . . . . . . 58 C8
Quarr Rd SM5 . . . . 40 E3
Quarry Bank GU18 . . . . . 67 A8
Quarry Cl
  Horsham RH12 . . . . 217 F6
  Leatherhead KT22 . . . . . 95 D6
  Oxted RH8 . . . . 122 E5
Quarry Cotts RH1 . . . . . . 99 C1
Quarry Gdns KT22 . . . . . 95 D6
Quarry Hill GU7 . . . . 150 B3
Quarry Hill Pk RH1 . . . . 118 C4
Quarry Park Rd SM1 . . . 58 F4
Quarry Rd
  Oxted RH8 . . . . 122 E5
  Shackleford GU7 . . . . . . 150 A7
  Woldingham RH9 . . . . . . 121 C7
Quarry Rise
  Cheam SM1 . . . . 58 F4
  East Grinstead RH19 . . . . 186 A3
Quarry St GU1 . . . . 130 D7
Quarry The RH3 . . . . . . 116 D3
Quarterbrass Farm Rd
  RH12 . . . . 217 D7
Quartermaine Ave
  GU22 . . . . 89 F5
Quartermaine Ho GU22 . . 89 F5
Quartermain Ho SM4 . . . . 40 C4
Quarter Mile Rd GU7 . . . 150 E2
Quayside Wlk KT1 . . . . . 37 D7
Quay W TW11 . . . . 17 B3
Quebec Cl RH6 . . . . 162 A3
Quebec Gdns GU17 . . . . 64 D4
Queen Adelaide Ct
  SE20 . . . . 23 C2
Queen Adelaide Rd
  SE20 . . . . 23 C1
Queen Alexandra's Ct **5**
  SW19 . . . . 19 F3
Queen Alexandra's Way
  KT19 . . . . 76 A7
Queen Anne Ave BR2 . . . 44 F6
Queen Anne Dr KT10 . . . 55 E3
Queen Annes Cl TW2 . . . 16 D5
Queen Anne's Cl SL4 . . . 10 B5
Queen Annes Ct KT22 . . . 95 B6
Queen Annes Gate
  GU9 . . . . 125 D7
Queen Anne's Gdns
  Leatherhead KT22 . . . . . 95 B6
  4 Mitcham CR4 . . . . . . 40 F6
Queen Anne's Terr
  KT22 . . . . 95 B6
Queenborough Ho N **3**
  KT13 . . . . 53 E7
Queenborough Ho S **4**
  KT13 . . . . 53 E7
Queendale Ct GU21 . . . . 68 F3
Queen Eleanor's CE Jun
  Sch GU2 . . . . 130 A8
Queen Eleanor's Rd
  GU2 . . . . 129 F8
Queen Elizabeth Cl
  GU12 . . . . 106 A2
Queen Elizabeth Dr
  GU11 . . . . 104 F2
Queen Elizabeth Gdns
  SM4 . . . . 40 A5
Queen Elizabeth Ho
  2 Balham SW12 . . . . . 21 A8
  Weybridge KT13 . . . . . . 53 D5
Queen Elizabeth II Jubilee
  Sch The RH13 . . . . . . 217 F1
Queen Elizabeth Rd
  Camberley GU15 . . . . . . 46 D1
  Kingston u T KT2 . . . . . . 37 F7
  Rudgwick RH12 . . . . . . 214 D7
Queen Elizabeth's Dr
  CR0 . . . . 63 D1
Queen Elizabeth's
  Foundation Training Coll
  KT22 . . . . 74 D2

Queen Elizabeth's Gdns
  CR0 . . . . 63 D1
Queen Elizabeth's Wlk
  SM6 . . . . 60 D6
Queen Elizabeth Way
  GU22 . . . . 90 A8
Queenhill Rd CR2 . . . . . . 62 B1
Queenhythe Cres
  GU4 . . . . 109 D7
Queenhythe Rd GU4 . . . 109 D7
Queen Mary Ave
  Camberley GU15 . . . . . . 65 A5
  West Barnes SM4,
  SW20 . . . . 39 D4
Queen Mary Cl
  Tolworth KT9 . . . . 57 A8
  Woking GU22 . . . . 70 C3
Queen Mary Ct TW19 . . . 13 E7
Queen Mary Rd
  Charlton TW17 . . . . 34 C7
  South Norwood SE19 . . . . 22 B2
Queen Mary's Ave SM5 . . 59 F3
Queen Mary's Dr KT15 . . 52 A1
Queen Mary's Hospital Sch
  SM5 . . . . 59 F2
Queens Acre SM3 . . . . . . 58 E3
Queens Ave
  Byfleet KT14 . . . . 71 D7
  Feltham TW13 . . . . 15 C4
Queen's Ave GU11 . . . . 105 B5
Queens Bench **4** 36 B8
Queensberry Ho **6**
  TW9 . . . . 6 D2
Queensberry Pl **33**
  TW10 . . . . 6 D2
Queensbridge Pk TW7 . . . 5 E2
Queensbury Ct RH2 . . . . 42 C7
Queensbury Pl GU17 . . . 64 C3
Queen's CE Prim Sch The
  TW7 . . . . 7 A7
Queens Cl
  Bisley GU24 . . . . 68 A3
  Walton on t H KT20 . . . . 97 A3
Queen's Cl
  Esher KT10 . . . . 55 B6
  Farnborough GU14 . . . . . 105 B8
  North Ascot SL5 . . . . . . 28 E8
  Wallington SM6 . . . . 60 B5
Queens Court Ride
  KT11 . . . . 73 A6
Queens Cres TW10 . . . . . 6 F1
Queen's Cres RH4 . . . . 136 A6
Queens Ct
  Beckenham BR3 . . . . 24 B1
  Belmont SM2 . . . . 78 A8
  Epsom KT19 . . . . 57 E1
  Hale GU9 . . . . 125 B7
  Horsham RH13 . . . . 217 D1
  3 Redhill RH1 . . . . . . 119 A2
  Weybridge KT13 . . . . . . 53 E4
  9 Woking GU22 . . . . . . 69 F1
Queen's Ct
  Beckenham BR3 . . . . 44 A8
  Croydon CR2 . . . . 61 C5
  Farnborough GU14 . . . . . 105 C8
  Horley RH6 . . . . 161 B4
  1 Kingston u T KT2 . . . . 18 A1
  3 Richmond TW10 . . . . . 6 F1
  Staines TW18 . . . . 13 D2
  Thornton Heath CR7 . . . . 42 A4
Queens Dr
  Oxshott KT22 . . . . 74 C8
  Surbiton KT5 . . . . 38 A3
Queen's Dr
  Farncombe GU7 . . . . . . 150 C7
  Guildford GU2 . . . . 109 A4
  Thames Ditton KT7 . . . . . 37 A3
Queensfield Ct SM3 . . . . 58 C6
Queensgate KT11 . . . . . . 73 D7
Queens Gate RH6 . . . . . 182 A8
Queen's Gate Rd
  GU14 . . . . 105 B8
Queen's Gdns TW5 . . . . . 4 E6
Queenshill Lo SL5 . . . . . . 29 B6
Queens Hill Rise SL5 . . . . 29 C6
Queen's Ho TW11 . . . . . . 16 F2
Queens Keep
  Camberley GU15 . . . . . . 65 D5
  10 Twickenham TW1 . . . . 6 C1
Queens La GU9 . . . . 125 B7
Queensland Ave SW19 . . . 40 B8
Queensmead
  Ashford TW15 . . . . 13 F3
  Farnborough GU14 . . . . . 85 B3
Queen's Mead GU8 . . . . 191 B4
Queensmead Ave KT17 . . 58 B1
Queen's Mead Rd BR2 . . . 44 F7
Queensmere **4** SM1 . . . . 59 B5
Queensmere Cl SW19 . . . 19 D6
Queensmere Rd SW19 . . . 19 D6
Queens Park Gdns
  TW13 . . . . 14 F5
Queen's Park Rd CR3 . . . 100 E4
Queens Pine RG12 . . . . . 27 E3
Queen's Pl
  Ascot SL5 . . . . 29 A6
  Morden SM4 . . . . 40 A5
Queens Rd
  Aldershot GU11 . . . . . . 104 F2
  Belmont SM2 . . . . 78 A8
  Bisley GU24 . . . . 67 F1
  Camberley GU15 . . . . . . 65 B4
  Farnborough GU14 . . . . . 105 D8
  Hale GU9 . . . . 125 C6
  Hersham KT12 . . . . 54 A6
  Morden SM4 . . . . 40 A5
  Twickenham TW1 . . . . . . 17 A7

Queens Rd continued
  Weybridge KT13 . . . . . . 53 C5
Queen's Rd
  Ascot SL5 . . . . 29 D4
  Beckenham BR3 . . . . 43 E7
  East Grinstead RH19 . . . . 185 E1
  Egham TW20 . . . . 11 F2
  Feltham TW13 . . . . 15 B7
  Guildford GU1 . . . . 109 D1
  Hampton TW12 . . . . 16 B4
  Horley RH6 . . . . 161 A3
  Hounslow TW3 . . . . 5 B4
  Kingston u T KT2 . . . . . . 18 A1
  Knaphill GU21 . . . . 68 D1
  Mitcham CR4 . . . . 40 D6
  Mortlake SW14 . . . . 7 D4
  New Malden KT3 . . . . . . 38 F4
  Richmond, Petersham KT2,
  TW10 . . . . 17 E7
  Richmond TW10 . . . . 6 F1
  Teddington TW11 . . . . . . 16 F2
  Thames Ditton KT7 . . . . . 36 F4
  Thornton Heath CR0 . . . . 42 C3
  Wallington SM6 . . . . 60 B5
  Wimbledon SW19 . . . . . . 20 A2
Queen's Rdbt GU11 . . . . 105 B7
Queens Reach KT8 . . . . . 36 E5
Queens Ride RG45 . . . . . 45 B7
Queen's Rise 6 F1
Queens Sq RH10 . . . . . 201 D6
Queens St **3** TW15 . . . . 13 F4
Queen St
  Aldershot GU12 . . . . . . 105 D2
  Chertsey KT16 . . . . 33 A1
  Croydon CR0, CR9 . . . . . 61 C6
  Godalming GU7 . . . . . . 150 E4
  Gomshall GU5 . . . . 133 C4
  Horsham RH13 . . . . 217 D1
Queen's Terr TW7 . . . . . . 6 A3
Queensthorpe Rd
  SE26 . . . . 23 D4
Queensville Rd SW12,
  SW4 . . . . 21 D8
Queensway
  Coney Hall BR4 . . . . 63 F6
  Cranleigh GU6 . . . . 174 F2
  Crawley RH10 . . . . 201 E6
  East Grinstead RH19 . . . . 185 E1
  Frimley GU16 . . . . 86 A7
  Hersham KT12 . . . . 54 C6
  Horsham RH13 . . . . 217 C1
  Redhill RH1 . . . . 118 F2
  Sunbury TW16 . . . . 35 B7
Queens Way
  Croydon CR0 . . . . 60 F5
  Feltham TW13 . . . . 15 C4
Queen's Way GU24 . . . . . 87 D8
Queensway N KT12 . . . . . 54 C5
Queensway S KT12 . . . . . 54 C5
Queen's Wlk TW15 . . . . . 13 D4
Queen's Wlk RH19 . . . . 185 E1
Queenswood Ave
  Hampton TW12 . . . . 16 B2
  Hounslow TW3, TW5 . . . . . 4 F5
  Thornton Heath CR7 . . . . 42 A4
  Wallington CR0, SM6 . . . . 60 D6
Queenswood Ct **11**
  SE27 . . . . 22 D4
Queenswood Rd
  Forest Hill SE23 . . . . . . 23 E5
  Knaphill GU21 . . . . 88 D3
Queen Victoria Cross
  Roads GU15 . . . . 65 A6
Queen Victoria Ct
  GU14 . . . . 85 B5
Queen Victoria Ho
  RG40 . . . . 25 D6
Queen Victoria Hospl The
  RH19 . . . . 185 F3
Queen Victoria Way
  GU24 . . . . 87 D8
Quennel Ho **7** SW12 . . . . 21 C8
Quennell Cl KT21 . . . . . . 95 F8
Quennells Hill GU10 . . . 145 A6
Quentin Way GU25 . . . . . 31 B5
Quicks Rd SW19 . . . . . . 20 B1
Quiet Cl KT15 . . . . 52 A6
Quillot The KT12 . . . . . . 53 F5
Quince Cl SL5 . . . . 29 D5
Quince Dr GU24 . . . . 68 B4
Quince Ho TW13 . . . . . . 15 A7
Quincy Rd TW20 . . . . . . 12 A3
Quinnettes GU10 . . . . . 167 F1
Quinneys SW14 . . . . 85 C1
Quintet The KT12 . . . . . . 35 A1
Quintilis RG12 . . . . 26 F1
Quintin Ave SW20 . . . . . 39 F8
Quintin Ct W4 . . . . 7 C7
Quintock Ho **2** TW9 . . . . 7 A6
Quinton Cl
  Beckenham BR3 . . . . 44 C6
  Hackbridge SM6 . . . . 60 B6
  Heston TW5 . . . . 4 B7
Quinton Rd KT7 . . . . 37 A1
Quinton St SW18 . . . . . . 20 C6
Quintrell Cl GU21 . . . . . . 69 B2

R

Rabbit La KT12 . . . . 54 B3
Rabies Heath Rd
  Bletchingley RH1 . . . . . . 120 F2
  Godstone RH1, RH9 . . . . . 121 B1
Raby Rd KT3 . . . . 38 D5
Raccoon Way TW4 . . . . . . 4 C5
Racecourse Rd
  Crawley RH6 . . . . 182 A8

Racecourse Rd continued
  Dormansland RH7 . . . . . 165 A2
  Lingfield RH7 . . . . 164 F3
Racecourse Way RH6 . . . 181 F8
Rachel Ct SM2 . . . . 59 D3
Rackfield GU27 . . . . 207 D7
Rackham Mews SW16 . . . 21 C2
Racks GU1 . . . . 130 D7
Rackstraw Rd GU47 . . . . 45 D2
Racquets Court Hill
  GU7 . . . . 150 C6
Radar Rd GU14 . . . . 84 D1
Radbourne Rd SW12 . . . . 21 D7
Radcliffe Cl GU16 . . . . . . 86 A7
Radcliffe Gdns SM5 . . . . 59 E3
Radcliffe Rd CR0 . . . . . . 61 F7
Radcliffe Way RG42 . . . . 26 E8
Radcliff Mews SW17 . . . . 21 B7
Radcot Point **2** SE23 . . . 23 D5
Radford Cl GU9 . . . . 125 E5
Radford Rd RH6, RH10 . . 182 C4
Radius Pk TW6 . . . . 3 F3
Rad La GU5 . . . . 133 D1
Radlet Ave SE23 . . . . . . 23 B6
Radley Cl TW14 . . . . 14 F7
Radley Ct BR1 . . . . 24 C4
Radley Lo **30** SW19 . . . . 19 D7
Radnor Ct CR4 . . . . 41 E5
Radnor Ct
  6 Forest Hill SE23 . . . . 23 D5
  Redhill RH1 . . . . 118 E1
Radnor Gdns TW1 . . . . . 16 F6
Radnor Ho
  East Molesey KT8 . . . . . . 36 D5
  4 New Malden KT3 . . . . 38 F4
  Thornton Heath SW16 . . . 41 F7
Radnor La
  Abinger Common RH5 . . . 155 B7
  Ewhurst RH5 . . . . 155 A2
Radnor Rd
  Bracknell RG12 . . . . 27 F6
  Peaslake GU5, GU6 . . . . . 154 E4
  Twickenham TW1 . . . . . . 16 F6
  Weybridge KT13 . . . . . . 53 A7
Radnor Wlk CR0 . . . . 43 E3
Radolphs KT20 . . . . 97 D5
Radstock Way RH1 . . . . . 119 D7
Radstone Ct **11** GU22 . . . 69 F1
Raeburn Ct **6** SW16 . . . . 21 E5
Raeburn Ave KT5 . . . . . . 38 B3
Raeburn Cl KT1 . . . . 17 D1
Raeburn Gr GU21 . . . . . . 89 A8
Raeburn Ho **11** SM2 . . . . 59 B3
Raeburn Way GU47 . . . . . 64 D6
Rae Rd GU14 . . . . 85 B1
RAFBOROUGH 84 F3
Rafdene Copse GU22 . . . 89 C8
RAF Gate Rd GU14 . . . . . 85 B1
RAF Staff Coll RG12 . . . . 27 D5
RAG HILL 103 E6
Rag Hill Cl TN16 . . . . . . 103 E6
Rag Hill Rd TN16 . . . . . . 103 E6
Raglan Cl
  Aldershot GU12 . . . . . . 105 C1
  Frimley GU16 . . . . 86 A8
  Hounslow TW4 . . . . 4 F2
  Reigate RH2 . . . . 118 D3
Raglan Ct CR0, CR2 . . . . 61 B5
Raglan Prec The CR3 . . . 100 E5
Raglan Rd
  Knaphill GU21 . . . . 68 E1
  Reigate RH2 . . . . 118 C3
Raglans Bglws RH2 . . . . 118 B4
Ragwort Ct **1** SE26 . . . . 23 B3
Raikes La RH5 . . . . 134 B2
Railey Rd RH10 . . . . 201 E7
Railshead Rd TW1, TW7 . . . 6 B3
Railton Rd GU2 . . . . 109 B5
Railway App
  East Grinstead RH19 . . . . 185 E1
  13 Twickenham TW1 . . . . 17 A8
  Wallington SM6 . . . . 60 B5
Railway Cotts
  East Grinstead RH19 . . . . 204 F3
  Purley CR8 . . . . 79 F6
Railway Rd TW11 . . . . . . 16 F4
Railway Side SW13,
  SW14 . . . . 7 E4
Railway Terr
  Egham TW18 . . . . 12 D3
  Feltham TW13 . . . . 15 A7
Rainbow Ct GU21 . . . . . . 68 E3
Rainbow Ctr The KT17 . . . 76 E7
Rainbow Ind Est SW20 . . . 39 B7
Rainbow Sch The
  SW17 . . . . 20 C6
Rainforest Wlk RG12 . . . . 27 B4
Rake La
  Milford GU8 . . . . 171 A7
  Witley GU8 . . . . 170 F7
Rakers Ridge RH12 . . . . 217 D5
Raleigh Ave SM6 . . . . . . 60 D6
Raleigh Ct SM3 . . . . 44 B8
Raleigh Ct RH10 . . . . . . 182 A3
Raleigh Ct
  Dulwich SE19 . . . . 22 F3
  Staines TW18 . . . . 13 A4
  Wallington SM6 . . . . 60 B4
Raleigh Dr
  Esher KT10 . . . . 55 D5
  Smallfield RH6 . . . . 162 A3
  Tolworth KT5 . . . . 38 C1
Raleigh Gdns CR4 . . . . . 40 F6
Raleigh Ho **1** KT7 . . . . . 37 A2
Raleigh Rd
  Feltham TW13 . . . . 14 F6

Raleigh Rd continued
  Penge SE20 . . . . 23 D1
  Richmond TW9 . . . . 6 F4
Raleigh Sch The KT24 . . . 92 C2
Raleigh Way
  Feltham TW13 . . . . 15 C3
  Frimley GU16 . . . . 65 F3
Raleigh Wlk RH10 . . . . . 201 E4
Ralliwood Rd KT21 . . . . . 96 A8
Ralph Perring Ct BR3 . . . 44 A5
Ralphs Ride RG12 . . . . . 27 E6
Rama Cl SW16 . . . . 21 E1
Rama La SE19 . . . . 22 F1
Rambler Cl SW16 . . . . . . 21 C4
Ramblers Ct RH12 . . . . . 216 E3
Ramblers Way **12**
  RH11 . . . . 201 B1
Rame Cl SW17 . . . . 21 A3
Ramillies Cl GU11 . . . . . 105 E7
Ramillies Rd GU11 . . . . . 105 D5
Ramin Ct GU1 . . . . 109 C4
Ramornie Cl KT12 . . . . . 54 F6
Ramsay Cl GU15 . . . . . . 66 B8
Ramsay Rd GU20 . . . . . . 48 E5
Ramsbury Cl RG12 . . . . . 26 E3
Ramsdale Rd SW17 . . . . 21 A3
Ramsdean Ho **1** SW15 . . 19 B7
Ramsden Rd
  Balham SW12 . . . . 21 A8
  Godalming GU7 . . . . . . 150 D3
Ramsey Cl
  Horley RH6 . . . . 160 F3
  Horsham RH12 . . . . 217 D5
Ramsey Ct **18** RH11 . . . 201 B1
Ramsey Ho **7** SW19 . . . . 40 B8
Ramsey Pl CR3 . . . . 100 C5
Ramsey Rd CR7 . . . . 41 F3
Rams La GU8 . . . . 193 B3
Ramslade Cotts RG12 . . . 27 C6
Ramslade Rd RG12 . . . . . 27 D5
RAMSNEST COMMON
  . . . . 210 A6
Rances La RG40 . . . . 25 E5
Randal Cres RH2 . . . . . . 139 A7
Randall Scofield Ct
  RH10 . . . . 202 A7
Randalls Cotts KT11 . . . . 73 B7
Randalls Cres KT22 . . . . . 95 A7
Randalls Park Ave
  KT22 . . . . 95 A7
Randalls Park Dr KT22 . . . 95 A6
Randalls Rd KT22 . . . . . . 94 E7
Randalls Way KT22 . . . . . 95 A7
Randell Cl GU17 . . . . 64 E1
Randisbourne Gdns
  SE6 . . . . 24 B5
Randle Rd TW10 . . . . 17 C4
Randlesdown Rd SE6 . . . . 24 B5
Randmore Ct **6** BR3 . . . . 24 A1
Randolph Cl
  Kingston u T KT2 . . . . . . 18 C3
  Knaphill GU21 . . . . 68 E2
  Oxshott KT11 . . . . 74 A4
Randolph Dr GU14 . . . . . 84 C3
Randolph Rd KT17 . . . . . 76 F5
Ranelagh CE Sch RG12 . . 27 C6
Ranelagh Cres SL5 . . . . . 28 D8
Ranelagh Dr
  Bracknell RG12 . . . . 27 C6
  Isleworth TW1 . . . . 6 B2
Ranelagh Gdns W4 . . . . . . 7 C7
Ranelagh Pl KT3 . . . . . . 38 E4
Ranelagh Rd RH1 . . . . . . 118 E1
Ranfurly Rd SM1 . . . . . . 59 A8
Rangefield Prim Sch
  BR1 . . . . 24 E3
Rangefield Rd BR1 . . . . . 24 E3
Range Rd GU14 . . . . 84 D1
Range Ride GU15 . . . . . . 64 F7
Ranger Mans SE19 . . . . . 22 F2
Ranger Wlk KT15 . . . . . . 52 B5
Range The GU5 . . . . 152 A4
Range View GU47 . . . . . . 64 E8
Range Villas TW17 . . . . . 33 E2
Range Way TW17 . . . . . . 34 A2
Rankine Cl GU9 . . . . 126 A6
Ranmere St SW12 . . . . . 21 B7
Ranmore Ave CR0 . . . . . 61 F7
Ranmore Cl RH1 . . . . . . 119 A4
Ranmore Common Rd
  RH5 . . . . 114 D2
Ranmore Ct
  Kingston u T KT6 . . . . . . 37 D4
  5 Wimbledon SW20 . . . . 39 D8
Ranmore Pl KT13 . . . . . . 53 C5
Ranmore Rd
  Dorking RH4, RH5 . . . . . 114 C2
  East Ewell SM2 . . . . 58 D2
Ranmore View **10**
  RH4 . . . . 136 A7
Rann Ho **1** SW14 . . . . . . 7 D4
Rannoch Ct **9** KT6 . . . . . 37 E4
Ransford Ho **16** SE21 . . . 22 E4
Ransome Cl RH11 . . . . . 200 E3
Ranyard Cl KT9 . . . . 56 F7
Rapallo Cl GU14 . . . . 85 C4
Raphael Dr KT7 . . . . 36 F1
Raphel Dr KT7 . . . . 37 A2
Rapley Cl GU15 . . . . 65 F8
Rapley Gn RG12 . . . . 27 C3
Rapley's Field GU24 . . . . 87 E4
Rapsley La GU21 . . . . . . 68 B1
Rastell Ave SW12 . . . . . . 21 D7
Ratcliffe Rd GU14 . . . . . . 85 A8

Rathbone Ho
Crawley RH11 . . . . 201 B1
4 Wimbledon SW20. . . . . . 19 D1
Rathbone Sq CR0 . . . . 61 C6
Rathfern Prim Sch SE6. . . 23 F7
Rathfern Rd SE23, SE6 . . . . 23 F7
Rathgar Cl RH1. . . . . 140 A4
Rathlin Rd RH11 . . . . 201 B3
Rattray Ct SE6. . . . . 24 F6
Raven Cl
Horsham RH12 . . . . 217 E6
Turners Hill RH10 . . . . 204 C5
Ravendale Rd TW16. . . . . . 34 F7
Ravendene Ct 3
RH10 . . . . 201 D5
Ravenfield Rd SW17 . . . . . 20 F5
Raven La RH11. . . . . 201 C8
Ravensbourne Ave
Bromley BR2 . . . . 44 E8
Catford BR2. . . . . 24 D1
Stanwell TW19. . . . . 13 E7
Ravensbourne Ct SE6 . . . . 24 A8
Ravensbourne Ho
Catford BR1. . . . . 24 D3
3 Twickenham TW1 . . . . 6 C1
Ravensbourne Park Cres
SE6. 23 F8
Ravensbourne Pk SE4,
SE6. 24 A8
Ravensbourne Rd
Forest Hill SE23. . . . . 23 F7
Twickenham TW1. . . . . 6 C1
Ravensbourne Sta BR3. . . 24 D1
Ravensbury Ave SM4. . . . . 40 C4
Ravensbury Ct
5 Carshalton SM1 . . . . 59 D5
Mitcham CR4 . . . . 40 D5
Ravensbury Gr CR4 . . . . . . 40 D5
Ravensbury La CR4 . . . . . . 40 D5
Ravensbury Rd SW18. . . . . 20 B6
Ravensbury Terr SW18 . . . 20 B6
Ravenscar Lo 18 SW20 . . . 19 D1
Ravenscar Rd
Catford BR1. . . . . 24 E4
Surbiton KT6 . . . . 56 F8
Ravens Cl
Bromley BR2 . . . . 44 F7
Kingston u T KT6 . . . . 37 D3
Knaphill GU21 . . . . 68 C3
Redhill RH1 . . . . 118 F2
Ravenscote Com Jun Sch
GU16. . . . . 66 A3
Ravenscourt TW16. . . . . . . 34 F8
Ravenscroft Cl GU12 . . . . 106 C3
Ravenscroft Ct RH12 . . . . 217 C3
Ravenscroft Rd
Penge BR3. . . . . 43 D7
Weybridge KT13 . . . . 72 C8
Ravensdale Gdns
Hounslow TW4. . . . . 4 E4
South Norwood SE19. . . . . . 22 D1
Ravensdale Mews
TW18. . . . . 13 B2
Ravensdale Rd
Ascot SL5. . . . . 29 A4
Hounslow TW4. . . . . 4 E4
Ravensfield TW20. . . . . 11 C2
Ravensfield Gdns KT19. . . 57 E6
Ravenshead Cl CR2 . . . . . . 81 C8
Ravens Ho KT1 . . . . 37 D7
Ravenside KT6. . . . . 37 D4
Ravenslea Rd SW11,
SW12. . . . . 20 F8
Ravensmead Rd BR2 . . . . . 24 D1
Ravensroost SE19. . . . . 42 D8
Ravenstone Prim Sch
SW12 . . . . 21 A6
Ravenstone Rd GU15. . . . . 66 D5
Ravenstone St SW12 . . . . . 21 A7
Ravensview Ct KT6. . . . . . . 37 D4
Ravenswold CR8. . . . . 80 C4
Ravenswood Ave
Tolworth KT6. . . . . 57 A8
West Wickham BR4 . . . . 44 C1
Ravenswood Cl KT11. . . . . 73 D4
Ravenswood Cres BR4 . . . 44 C1
Ravenswood Ct
Dorking RH4 . . . . 136 B6
Kingston u T KT2 . . . . 18 B2
Woking GU22. . . . . 69 F1
Ravenswood Dr GU15 . . . . 66 A5
Ravenswood Gdns TW7 . . . .5 E6
Ravenswood Rd
Balham SW12 . . . . 21 B8
Croydon CR0, CR9 . . . . 61 B7
Rawdon Rise GU15. . . . . . . 66 B5
Rawlings Cl BR3 . . . . 44 C4
Rawlins Cl CR2 . . . . 62 F3
Rawlinson Rd
Farnborough GU11 . . . . . . 105 C5
Sandhurst GU15 . . . . 64 F6
Rawnsley Ave CR4 . . . . 40 E4
Raworth Cl RH10. . . . . 202 C4
Raybell Ct TW7 . . . . .5 F5
Ray Cl
Chessington KT9 . . . . 56 C4
Lingfield RH7. . . . . 164 C5
Ray Cnr RH7. . . . . 164 B6
Rayford Ave SE12 . . . . 24 F8
Ray La
Blindley Heath RH7 . . . . . . 163 F7
Lingfield RH7. . . . . 164 B6
Rayleigh Ave TW11 . . . . . . 16 E2
Rayleigh Ct 3 KT1. . . . . . . 37 F7
Rayleigh Rd SW19 . . . . 39 F8
Rayleigh Rise CR2 . . . . 61 E4
Raymead Ave CR7 . . . . 42 A4
Raymead Cl KT22 . . . . 94 F5
Raymead Way KT22 . . . . . . 94 F5
Raymer Wlk RH6. . . . . 161 C4
Raymond Cl
Forest Hill SE26. . . . . 23 C3
Poyle SL3. . . . . 1 E6
Raymond Cres GU2 . . . . . 129 F8
Raymond Ct SM2 . . . . 59 B4
Raymond Rd
Beckenham BR3. . . . . 43 E5
Wimbledon SW19 . . . . 19 E2
Raymond Way KT10. . . . . . 56 A4
Raynald Ho 15 SW16 . . . . . 21 E5
Rayners Cl SL3 . . . . 1 C7
Raynesfield SW20. . . . . 39 C6
RAYNES PARK 39 C6
Raynes Park High Sch
SW20 . . . . 39 B6
Raynes Park Sta SW20 . . . 39 C7
Ray Rd KT8. . . . . 36 B4
Rays Rd BR4. . . . . 44 C2
Raywood Cl UB7. . . . . 3 C7
Read Cl KT7 . . . . 37 A2
Readens The SM7. . . . . 78 F3
Reading Arch Rd RH1 . . . 118 F1
Reading Rd
Blackwater GU17. . . . . 64 B4
Farnborough GU14 . . . . 85 D1
Sutton SM1 . . . . 59 C5
Wokingham RG41 . . . . 25 A7
Readman Ct 9 SE20 . . . . . 43 B8
Read Rd KT21 . . . . 75 D2
Reads Rest La KT20. . . . . . 98 A7
Reapers Cl RH12. . . . . 217 D5
Reapers Way TW7 . . . . 5 D2
Rebecca Ct 3 BR3. . . . . . . 44 A8
Recovery St SW17 . . . . 20 E3
Recreation Cl GU14 . . . . . . 64 F1
Recreation Rd
Bromley BR2 . . . . 44 F7
Forest Hill SE26. . . . . 23 D4
Guildford GU1 . . . . 109 D1
Rowledge GU10. . . . . 145 E3
Recreation Way CR4,
SW16. . . . . 41 E6
Rectory Cl
Ashtead KT21 . . . . 95 F8
Bracknell RG12 . . . . 27 C5
Byfleet KT14 . . . . 71 E6
Ewhurst GU6 . . . . 175 E5
Godalming GU7 . . . . 150 F2
Guildford GU4 . . . . 110 D3
Littleton TW17. . . . . 34 A6
Long Ditton KT6. . . . . 37 C1
Ockley RH5 . . . . 177 C3
West Barnes SW20 . . . . 39 C6
Wokingham RG40 . . . . 25 C6
Rectory Ct
1 Beckenham BR3. . . . . . . 43 F7
Cranford TW5 . . . . 4 C5
Feltham TW13 . . . . 15 C4
8 Guildford GU1 . . . . 130 C8
Sanderstead CR2. . . . . 80 F7
Wallington SM6 . . . . 60 C6
Rectory Gdns BR3 . . . . 44 A8
Rectory Gn BR3. . . . . 43 F8
Rectory Gr
Croydon CR0, CR9 . . . . 61 B8
Hampton TW12 . . . . 15 F4
Rectory La
Ashtead KT21 . . . . 95 F8
Bracknell RG12 . . . . 27 B5
Buckland RH3 . . . . 116 F3
Byfleet KT14 . . . . 71 E6
Charlwood RH6 . . . . 180 D7
Crawley RH11 . . . . 200 F8
Great Bookham KT23. . . . . 113 F8
Long Ditton KT6. . . . . 37 C1
Shere GU5 . . . . 133 A4
Streatham SW17 . . . . 21 A3
Titsey TN16 . . . . 103 E4
Wallington SM6 . . . . 60 C6
Windlesham GU20. . . . . 48 C4
Woodmansterne CR5,
SM7 . . . . 78 F3
Rectory Orch SW19 . . . . . . 19 E4
Rectory Pk CR2. . . . . 80 F7
Rectory Rd
Beckenham BR3. . . . . 44 A8
Cranford TW5 . . . . 4 C5
Farnborough GU14 . . . . 85 D4
Lower Kingswood CR5. . . . . 98 C2
Sutton SM1 . . . . 59 B7
Wokingham RG40 . . . . 25 C6
Rectory Row RG12 . . . . 27 B5
Red Admiral St RH12. . . . 217 E5
Redan Gdns GU12. . . . . . . 105 C2
Redan Hill Est GU12 . . . . 105 C2
Redan Rd GU12 . . . . 105 C2
Redbarn Cl CR8. . . . . 80 B8
Redberry Gr SE23, SE26 . . . 23 C5
Redcar Ho SE26 . . . . 23 B2
Redcliffe Gdns W4. . . . . .7 B7
Redclose Ave SM4 . . . . 40 A4
Redclyffe Terr 2 SM2. . . . . 59 A3
Redcote Pl RH4. . . . . 115 D1
Redcourt
Pyrford GU22. . . . . 70 E4
Woking GU22. . . . . 70 D4
Redcrest Gdns GU15 . . . . . 65 F5
Redcroft Wlk GU6 . . . . . . 174 E2
Red Deer Cl RH13. . . . . . . 218 B4
Reddington Cl CR2. . . . . . . 61 D2
Redding Way GU21 . . . . . . 68 C1
Redditch RG12. . . . . 27 D2
Redditch Cl RH11 . . . . 200 E2
Reddons Rd BR3. . . . . 23 E1
Reddown Rd CR5 . . . . 79 D2
Rede Ct
Farnborough GU14 . . . . 85 C1
Weybridge KT13 . . . . 53 B7
Redehall Ind Pk RH6. . . . 183 C7
Redehall Prep Sch
RH6. . . . . 162 B2
Redehall Rd
Burstow RH6 . . . . 183 C8
Smallfield RH6. . . . . 162 B2
Redesdale Gdns TW7 . . . . . 6 A7
Redfern Ave TW4 . . . . 16 A8
Redfern Rd SE6. . . . . 24 C8
Redford Ave
Horsham RH12 . . . . 217 B4
Thornton Heath CR7 . . . . . . 41 F5
Wallington, Clock House
CR5. . . . . 79 B4
Wallington, Roundshaw
SM6 . . . . 60 E4
Redford Cl TW13. . . . . 14 F6
Redgarth Ct RH19. . . . . . . 185 B3
Red Gates Sch CR0 . . . . . . 61 A5
Redgrave Cl SE25. . . . . 42 F3
Redgrave Ct GU12 . . . . . . 105 F2
Redgrave Dr RH10 . . . . . . 202 D5
Redhall Ct CR3 . . . . 100 D4
Redhearne Fields
GU10 . . . . 167 E2
REDHILL 118 E2
Redhill Aerodrome
RH1. . . . . 140 D4
Redhill Coll RH1. . . . . 140 B8
Redhill Ct SW2 . . . . 22 A6
Redhill Distribution Ctr
RH1. . . . . 161 A8
Redhill Rd KT11. . . . . 72 B5
Redhill Sta RH1. . . . . 119 A2
Red Ho The RH8 . . . . 123 C5
Red House La
Elstead GU8. . . . . 148 C2
Walton-on-T KT12 . . . . 54 A8
Redhouse Rd TN16. . . . . . 103 C6
Red House Rd CR0,
CR9 . . . . 41 D3
Redkiln Cl RH13 . . . . 217 F4
Redkiln Close Trad Est
RH13. . . . . 217 F3
Redkiln Way RH13 . . . . . . 217 F3
Redknap Ho TW10 . . . . 17 C5
Red La
Claygate KT10 . . . . 56 A4
Headley Down GU35 . . . . . 187 B7
Oxted RH8 . . . . 144 B7
South Holmwood RH5,
RH3. . . . . 136 F1
Redlake La RG40. . . . . 25 F2
Redland Gdns KT8 . . . . 35 F5
Redlands
Coulsdon CR5 . . . . 79 E3
Teddington TW11. . . . . 17 A2
Redlands Cotts RH5. . . . . 136 B1
Redlands Ct BR1. . . . . 24 F1
Redlands Ctr CR5. . . . . 79 E4
Redlands La
Crondall GU10. . . . . 124 B7
Dorking RH5 . . . . 136 A1
Redlands The 5 BR3. . . . . 44 B7
Redlands Way SW2 . . . . . . 21 F8
Redlane Cotts RH8. . . . . . 123 B2
Redleaf Cl KT22. . . . . 94 E3
Redleaves Ave TW15 . . . . . 14 B2
Redlees Cl TW7. . . . . 6 A3
Redlin Ct RH1 . . . . 118 F3
Red Lion Bsns Ctr KT6 . . . 56 F7
Red Lion Cotts GU5 . . . . . 152 E4
Red Lion Ct TW3. . . . . .5 B4
Red Lion La
Chobham GU24 . . . . 49 E2
Farnham GU9. . . . . 125 B1
Red Lion Rd
Chobham GU24 . . . . 49 E2
Surbiton KT6 . . . . 57 A8
Red Lion St TW10. . . . . 6 D2
Red Lo BR4. . . . . 44 C2
Red Lodge Rd BR3,
BR4 . . . . 44 D2
Redmayne GU15 . . . . 66 C4
Red Rd GU18, GU24,
GU15 . . . . 67 C7
Red River Ct RH12 . . . . . . 217 B5
Redroofs Cl BR3 . . . . 44 B8
Redruth Gdns KT10 . . . . . . 55 F3
Redruth Ho SM2. . . . . 59 B3
Redshank Ct 5 RH11 . . . 200 D5
Redstart Cl CR0. . . . . 63 D1
Redstone Hill RH1 . . . . . . 119 A1
Redstone Hollow
RH1 . . . . 140 A8
Redstone Manor RH1 . . . 119 A1
Redstone Pk RH1 . . . . 119 B1
Redstone Rd RH1 . . . . 140 A8
Redvers Buller Rd
GU11 . . . . 105 D7
Redvers Ct CR6 . . . . 81 C1
Redvers Rd
Bracknell RG12 . . . . 27 B4
Warlingham CR6 . . . . 81 D1
Redway Cotts GU21 . . . . . . 88 F8
Redway Dr TW2 . . . . 16 C8
Redwing Ave GU7. . . . . . . 150 E8
Redwing Cl
Horsham RH13 . . . . 217 F3
Selsdon CR2 . . . . 81 D8
Redwing Ct 4 CR8. . . . . . . 80 B7
Redwing Gdns KT14. . . . . . 71 B7
Redwing Rd SM6 . . . . 60 E3
Redwing Rise GU4 . . . . . . 110 D3
Redwood TW20. . . . . 32 E7
Redwood Cl
Crawley RH10 . . . . 201 E8
Kenley CR8 . . . . 80 C5
Redwood Ct
Ewell KT17. . . . . 76 F8
10 Surbiton KT6 . . . . 37 D2
Redwood Dr
Frimley GU15. . . . . 66 D4
Sunningdale SL5 . . . . 30 B3
Redwood Est TW5 . . . . .4 B8
Redwood Gr GU4 . . . . 131 C3
Redwood Lo RH2 . . . . 118 C2
Redwood Manor
GU27 . . . . 208 C7
Redwood Mews TW15. . . . 14 D1
Redwood Mount RH2 . . . 118 A4
Redwoods
Addlestone KT15 . . . . 52 A4
Roehampton SW15 . . . . 19 A7
Redwood Wlk KT6 . . . . 37 D1
Reed Cl GU11. . . . . 105 D5
Reed Dr RH1 . . . . 140 A6
Reedham Dr CR8 . . . . 80 A6
Reedham Park Ave
CR8 . . . . 80 A3
Reedham Park Sch Ltd
CR8. 80 A5
Reedham Sta CR8 . . . . 79 F6
Reedings RH11 . . . . 200 D4
Reed Pl
Lower Halliford TW17 . . . . . 33 F1
Sheerwater GU21, KT14 . . . 70 E6
Reedsfield Cl TW15 . . . . . . 14 B5
Reedsfield Rd TW15 . . . . . 14 B4
Reed's Hill RG12. . . . . 27 B4
Reeds Rd The
Frensham GU10. . . . . 146 E2
Tilford GU10 . . . . 147 A3
Reeds Sch KT11 . . . . 74 A7
Rees Gdns CR0 . . . . 42 F3
Reeve Ct GU2. . . . . 109 A5
Reeve Rd RH2 . . . . 139 C5
Reeves Cnr CR0, CR9 . . . . . 61 B8
Reeves Rd GU12 . . . . 105 C1
Reeves Way RG41. . . . . 25 A4
Regal Cres SM6. . . . . 60 B7
Regal Ct
1 Guildford GU1 . . . . 109 D1
2 Mitcham CR4 . . . . 40 F6
Regal Dr 10 RH19 . . . . 205 F8
Regalfield Cl GU2. . . . . . . 109 A5
Regan Cl GU2 . . . . 109 B6
Regatta Ho TW11 . . . . 17 A4
Regatta Point TW8. . . . . .6 F8
Regency Cl TW12 . . . . 15 F3
Regency Ct
6 Penge SE19 . . . . 23 A1
4 Surbiton KT5 . . . . 37 F4
Sutton SM1 . . . . 59 B6
Wimbledon SW19 . . . . 19 F1
Regency Dr KT14 . . . . 70 F6
Regency Gdns KT12. . . . . . 35 D1
Regency Ho KT16 . . . . 32 F1
Regency Lo KT13 . . . . 53 E7
Regency Mews
Beckenham BR3. . . . . 44 C8
Isleworth TW7. . . . . 5 E2
Regency Pl KT16. . . . . 33 A1
Regency Wlk
Croydon CR0 . . . . 43 F3
11 Richmond TW10. . . . . 6 E2
Regent Cl
Cranford TW5 . . . . 4 B6
New Haw KT15 . . . . 52 D2
Redhill RH1 . . . . 119 C6
Regent Cres RH1 . . . . 118 F3
Regent Ct
Bagshot GU19. . . . . 47 F2
Guildford GU2 . . . . 109 B3
South Norwood SE19. . . . . . 22 B2
Regent Ho 1 SM7 . . . . 77 F5
Regent Lo 9 SW2 . . . . 21 F7
Regent Par 8 SM2. . . . . . . 59 C4
Regent Pk KT22 . . . . 75 A1
Regent Pl
Croydon CR0 . . . . 42 F1
Wimbledon SW19 . . . . 20 C3
Regent Rd KT5 . . . . 38 A4
Regents Cl
Crawley RH11 . . . . 201 C2
South Croydon CR2 . . . . 61 E4
Whyteleafe CR3. . . . . 80 F1
Regents Ct
23 Beckenham BR3. . . . . . . 24 A1
Bromley BR1 . . . . 24 F1
1 Kingston u T KT2 . . . . . . 37 E8
Staines TW18. . . . . 13 B2
Weybridge KT13 . . . . 53 B4
Woking GU21. . . . . 69 F3
Regents Ho 4 TW20 . . . . . 12 A3
Regents Mews RH6 . . . . . 161 A3
Regents Pl GU47. . . . . 64 C8
Regent St W4 . . . . 7 A8
Regents Wlk SL5. . . . . 29 C2
Regent Way GU16. . . . . 66 A1
Regiment Cl GU14 . . . . 84 C3
Regina Coeli RC Prim Sch
CR2. 61 B3
Regina Ct TW11 . . . . 16 E3
Reginald Ct BR3 . . . . 44 C8
Regina Rd SE25. . . . . 43 A6
Regis Ct
East Bedfont TW14 . . . . 3 D1
Mitcham SW19 . . . . 40 E8
Regnolruf Ct KT12 . . . . 35 A2
Reid Ave CR3. . . . . 100 D6
Reid Cl CR5 . . . . 79 B3
Reid Ct SW14. . . . . 7 C5
Reidonhill Cotts GU21. . . . 68 B1
REIGATE 118 B2
Reigate Ave SM3, SM4 . . . . 40 B1
Reigate Cl RH10 . . . . 182 D1
Reigate Coll RH2 . . . . 118 B1
Reigate Gram Sch
RH2. . . . . 118 C1
Reigate Heath Cotts
RH2 . . . . 117 E1
Reigate Hill RH2. . . . . 118 B4
Reigate Hill Cl RH2 . . . . . 118 B4
Reigate Parish Church Inf
Sch RH2 . . . . 118 C1
Reigate Priory Com Jun
Sch RH2 . . . . 118 A1
Reigate Rd
Banstead KT17, KT18 . . . . . 77 C4
Betchworth RH3 . . . . 116 D2
Catford BR1. . . . . 24 F5
Dorking RH4 . . . . 115 E1
Hookwood RH2, RH6 . . . . 160 C4
Leatherhead KT22. . . . . 95 D4
Reigate RH2. . . . . 118 C1
Reigate St Mary's Prep
Sch RH2 . . . . 118 B1
Reigate Sch RH1. . . . . 139 C6
Reigate Sta RH2. . . . . 118 A2
Reigate Way SM6 . . . . 60 E5
Reindorp Cl GU2. . . . . 130 A8
Relko Ct KT19 . . . . 76 D8
Relko Gdns SM1 . . . . 59 D5
Rembrandt Ct KT19 . . . . . . 57 F4
Rembrandt Way KT12 . . . . 54 B8
Renaissance Ct SM1 . . . . . 40 C1
Rendle Cl CR0, SE25 . . . . . . 43 A4
Renfree Way TW17. . . . . . . 34 A2
Renfrew Ct TW5 . . . . .4 E5
Renfrew Rd
Hounslow TW5. . . . . 4 E5
Kingston u T KT2 . . . . 18 C1
Renmans The KT21 . . . . . . 75 F3
Renmuir St SW17 . . . . 20 F2
Rennie Cl TW15. . . . . 13 D5
Rennie Terr RH1. . . . . 140 A8
Renown Cl CR0 . . . . 42 B1
Renshaw Cnr CR4. . . . . 41 A8
Renshaw Ct SW19 . . . . 19 E4
Renshaw Ho 11 SW27 . . . . 22 B3
Replingham Rd SW18 . . . . 20 A7
Repton Cl SM5. . . . . 59 E5
Repton Ct BR3. . . . . 44 B8
Reservoir Cl CR7. . . . . 42 D6
Reservoir Rd GU14. . . . . . . 84 D1
Restmor Way SM5, SM6 . . . 60 A8
Restormel Cl TW3 . . . . 5 A2
Restwell Ave GU6. . . . . . . 174 B6
Retreat Rd TW9. . . . . 6 D2
Retreat The
Englefield Green TW20 . . . . 11 E3
Loxwood RH14. . . . . 212 F5
5 Mortlake SW14 . . . . 7 E4
North Cheam KT4 . . . . 58 B8
South Norwood CR7 . . . . . . 42 D5
Surbiton KT5 . . . . 37 F3
Revell Cl KT22 . . . . 94 B5
Revell Dr KT22. . . . . 94 B5
Revell Rd
Cheam SM1. . . . . 58 F4
Kingston u T KT1 . . . . 38 B8
Revelstoke Ave GU14. . . . . 85 B6
Revelstoke Rd SW18,
SW19. . . . . 20 A6
Revere Way KT19 . . . . 57 E2
Revesby Cl GU24. . . . . 67 D6
Revesby Rd SM5 . . . . 40 E3
Rewley Rd SM4 . . . . 40 D3
Rex Ave TW15 . . . . 14 A3
Rex Ct GU27 . . . . 207 F6
Rex Ho TW13 . . . . 15 E5
Reynard Cl RH12. . . . . 218 B5
Reynard Ct 12 CR8 . . . . 80 A8
Reynard Dr SE19. . . . . 22 F1
Reynolds Ave KT9. . . . . 56 E3
Reynolds Cl
Carshalton CR4, SM5. . . . . . 40 F1
Mitcham CR4, SW19 . . . . . . 40 D8
Reynolds Gn GU47 . . . . 64 D6
Reynolds Pl
Crawley RH11 . . . . 201 C7
13 Richmond TW10 . . . . 6 F1
Reynolds Rd
Crawley RH11 . . . . 201 C7
Farnborough GU14 . . . . . . 104 B8
New Malden KT3 . . . . 38 D2
Reynolds Way CR0 . . . . 61 E6
Rheingold Way SM6 . . . . . 60 E2
Rhine Banks GU14 . . . . 84 D5
Rhodes Cl TW20 . . . . 12 B3
Rhodes Ct TW20 . . . . 12 C3
Rhodes-Moorhouse Ct
SM4 . . . . 40 A3
Rhodes Way RH10 . . . . . . 201 F3
Rhododendron Cl SL5. . . . . .8 E1
Rhododendron Rd
GU16 . . . . 86 B8
Rhododendron Wlk SL5. . . .8 E1
Rhodrons Ave KT9 . . . . 56 E5
Rhyll Gdns GU11 . . . . 104 F1
Rialto Rd CR4. . . . . 41 A7
Ribble Pl GU14 . . . . 84 E7
Ribblesdale RH4. . . . . 136 B5
Ribblesdale Rd SW16 . . . . 21 B3
Ricardo Ct GU5 . . . . 151 F5
Ricards Lodge High Sch
SW19 . . . . 19 F3
Ricards Rd SW19 . . . . 19 F3

Rice's Cnr GU4 . . . . 131 A2
Rices Hill RH19 . . . . 185 E1
Richard Atkins Prim Sch
SW2 . . . . 21 E8
Richard Challoner Sch
KT3 . . . . 38 D2
Richard Ct TW15 . . . . 13 F3
Richard Meyjes Rd
GU2 . . . . 129 E8
Richards Cl
Ash GU12 . . . . 106 A5
Harlington UB3 . . . . 3 D8
Richards Ct BR3 . . . . 43 D8
Richards Field KT19 . . . . 57 D2
Richard Sharples Ct 21
SM2 . . . . 59 C3
Richardson Ct 17
RH11 . . . . 201 B1
Richardson Ho TW7 . . . . .5 F4
Richardson's Lawn Cotts
SL4 . . . . 10 B5
Richards Rd KT11 . . . . . . 74 B5
Richbell Cl KT21 . . . . 75 D7
Richborough Ct RH11 . . . 201 C6
Richens Cl TW3 . . . . 5 D5
Richfield Ct 4 BR3 . . . . . 43 F8
Richland Ave CR5 . . . . . . 79 A5
Richlands Ave KT17 . . . . . 58 A6
RICHMOND 6 D2
Richmond Adult Com Coll
TW9 . . . . 6 D3
Richmond Ave
Feltham TW14 . . . . 3 E1
Merton SW20 . . . . 39 E8
Richmond Bridge TW1 . . . 6 D1
Richmond Bridge Mans 1
TW1 . . . . 6 D1
Richmond Cl
Biggin Hill TN16 . . . . . . 103 B8
Epsom KT18 . . . . 76 E5
Farnborough GU14 . . . . 84 D3
Fetcham KT23 . . . . 94 C3
Frimley GU16 . . . . 65 F1
Richmond Coll TW10 . . . . 17 E8
Richmond Cres TW18 . . . 12 F3
Richmond Ct
Crawley RH10 . . . . 201 E5
12 Kingston u T KT2 . . . 18 A1
Mitcham CR4 . . . . 40 D6
Wimbledon SW20 . . . . . 39 B7
Richmond Dr TW17 . . . . . 34 D3
Richmond Gate TW10 . . . 17 F8
Richmond Gn CR0 . . . . . . 60 E7
Richmond Healthcare
Hamlet TW9 . . . . .6 E4
RICHMOND HILL 6 E1
Richmond Hill TW10 . . . . .6 E1
Richmond Hill Ct TW10. . . .6 E1
Richmond Ho
Caterham CR3 . . . . 100 F3
12 Forest Hill SE26 . . . . 23 A5
Sandhurst GU47 . . . . . . 64 E7
Richmond House Sch
(Hampton Com Coll)
TW12 . . . . 15 F3
Richmond Intnl Bsns Ctr
6 TW9. . . . . .6 F3
Richmond Mans 25 TW1. . . 6 D1
Richmond Park Rd
Kingston u T KT2 . . . . . 17 E1
Mortlake SW14 . . . . 7 D3
Richmond Rd
Coulsdon CR5 . . . . 79 B4
Farncombe GU7 . . . . . 150 E6
Horsham RH12 . . . . . . 217 D4
Isleworth TW7 . . . . 6 A4
Kingston u T KT2 . . . . . 17 E2
Sandhurst GU47 . . . . . . 64 E8
Staines TW18 . . . . 12 F3
Thornton Heath CR7 . . . 42 B5
Twickenham TW1 . . . . . 17 B8
Wallington CR0 . . . . . . 60 E7
Wimbledon SW20 . . . . . 39 B8
Richmond Sq RH19 . . . . 185 D2
Richmond Sta TW9 . . . . . .6 E3
Richmond Upon Thames
Coll TW2 . . . . 16 E8
Richmond Way
East Grinstead RH19 . . . 205 F8
Fetcham KT23 . . . . 94 C3
Richmondwood SL5 . . . . . 30 B1
Rickard Cl SW2 . . . . 22 A7
Rickards Ct KT6. . . . . 56 E8
Ricketts Hill Rd TN16 . . . 103 E7
Rickfield RH11 . . . . 201 A5
Rickford Hill GU3 . . . . 88 D1
Rickman Cl RG12 . . . . 27 C3
Rickman Cres KT15 . . . . . 52 B7
Rickman Ct KT15 . . . . 52 B7
Rickman Hill CR5 . . . . 79 B1
Rickman Hill Rd CR5 . . . . 79 B1
Rickman's La RH14 . . . . . 211 F2
Ricksons La KT24 . . . . . . 112 B8
Rickwood RH6. . . . . 161 B4
Rickyard GU2 . . . . 108 D1
Riddens The RH12 . . . . . . 214 A6
Riddings The CR3. . . . . . 100 F2
RIDDLESDOWN 80 C5
Riddlesdown Ave CR8. . . . 80 C7
Riddlesdown High Sch
CR2. . . . . 80 E5
Riddlesdown Rd CR8. . . . . 80 C8
Riddlesdown Sta CR8. . . . 80 C6
Ride La GU5 . . . . 153 D7
Riders Way RH9 . . . . 121 C4
Ride The RH14 . . . . 212 C2
Ride Way GU6 . . . . 154 C1
Rideway Cl GU15 . . . . 65 B4

Ridge Cl
Brockham RH3 . . . . 137 B5
Woking GU22. . . . . 89 B6
Ridge Ct CR6 . . . . 81 A1
Ridgedale RH10 . . . . 204 B8
Ridgegate Cl RH2 . . . . . . 118 D3
Ridge Gn RH1 . . . . 140 E6
RIDGE GREEN 140 E6
Ridge Green Cl RH1. . . . . 140 E6
Ridge Ho 4 KT2 . . . . 18 B1
Ridgehurst Dr RH12. . . . . 216 F1
Ridgelands GU22 . . . . 94 D3
Ridge Langley CR2. . . . . . 62 A2
Ridgemead Rd TW20 . . . . 11 B5
Ridge Moor Cl GU26 . . . . 188 E5
Ridgemount
Guildford GU2 . . . . 130 B8
Oatlands Park KT13. . . . . 53 E8
Ridgemount Ave
Coulsdon CR5 . . . . 79 B2
Croydon CR0 . . . . 62 D8
Ridgemount Cl SE20 . . . . 23 B1
Ridgemount Est GU16. . . . 86 C7
Ridge Mount Rd SL5 . . . . 30 A1
Ridgemount Way
RH1 . . . . 139 D7
Ridge Pk SM6 . . . . 60 D1
Ridge Rd
Cheam SM3, SM4 . . . . . 39 F1
Mitcham CR4 . . . . 21 B1
Ridgeside RH10. . . . . 201 F6
Ridges The GU3 . . . . 130 C4
Ridge The
Coulsdon CR5 . . . . 79 B3
Epsom KT18, KT21. . . . . 76 C1
Fetcham KT22 . . . . 94 D3
Rudgwick RH12 . . . . . . 214 E8
Sunningdale SL5 . . . . . . 30 A2
Surbiton KT5 . . . . 38 A4
Twickenham TW2. . . . . . 16 D8
Wallington CR8 . . . . 60 D1
Woking GU22. . . . . 70 B2
Woldingham CR3, CR6. . . 102 D2
Ridge View Cotts
GU7 . . . . 150 F4
Ridgeway
East Grinstead RH19 . . . 205 E7
Epsom KT19. . . . . 76 C7
12 Richmond TW10 . . . . . 6 E1
Walton-on-T KT12 . . . . . 34 F1
Woking GU21. . . . . 69 D4
Ridge Way
Feltham TW13 . . . . 15 E5
Virginia Water GU25 . . . . 31 E4
8 West Norwood SE19 . . 22 E2
Ridgeway Cl
Cranleigh GU6 . . . . 175 A3
Dorking RH4 . . . . 136 A5
Fetcham KT22 . . . . 94 D3
Lightwater GU18 . . . . . . 67 A8
Oxshott KT22. . . . . 74 C5
Woking GU21. . . . . 69 D4
Ridgeway Com Sch The
GU9. . . . . 146 C7
Ridgeway Ct RH1 . . . . . . 118 F1
Ridgeway Dr RH4 . . . . . . 136 A4
Ridgeway Gdns GU21 . . . 69 D4
Ridgeway Hill Rd
GU9. . . . . 146 C8
Ridgeway Ho RH6. . . . . . 161 A1
Ridge Way Ho 3 GU22 . . 70 B2
Ridgeway Prim Sch
CR2. . . . . 61 E1
Ridgeway Rd
Dorking RH4 . . . . 136 A5
Hounslow TW7. . . . . 5 E6
Redhill RH1 . . . . 118 F1
Ridgeway Rd N TW7 . . . . .5 E7
Ridgeway The
Bracknell RG12 . . . . 27 C6
Brookwood GU24. . . . . . 88 A7
Cranleigh GU6 . . . . 174 F3
Croydon CR0 . . . . 60 F7
Fetcham KT22 . . . . 94 D3
Guildford GU1 . . . . 131 A8
Horley RH6 . . . . 161 A1
Horsham RH12 . . . . . . 217 B4
Lightwater GU18 . . . . . . 48 B1
Oxshott KT22. . . . . 74 C5
Ridge Way The CR2. . . . . 61 E1
Ridgewell Cl SE26 . . . . . . 23 F4
Ridgewood Ctr (Hospl)
GU16. . . . . 66 C3
Ridgewood Dr GU16 . . . . 66 D3
Ridgley Rd GU8. . . . . 191 B4
Ridgway
Pyrford GU22. . . . . 71 A4
Wimbledon SW19, SW20. . 19 D2
Ridgway Ct SW19 . . . . . . 19 D2
Ridgway Gdns SW19 . . . . 19 D1
Ridgway Pl SW19 . . . . . . 19 E2
Ridgway Rd
Farnham GU9. . . . . 146 C8
Pyrford GU22. . . . . 70 F4
Ridgway The SM2. . . . . . . 59 D4
Riding Hill CR2 . . . . 81 A6
Ridings The
Addlestone KT15 . . . . . . 51 E4
Ashtead KT21 . . . . 75 D2
Biggin Hill TN16. . . . . . . 83 E2
Cobham KT11 . . . . 74 A7
Crawley RH10 . . . . 202 D7
East Horsley KT24 . . . . . 92 F2
Epsom KT18. . . . . 76 F4
Ewell KT17 . . . . 57 F2
Frimley GU16. . . . . 66 B3
Kingswood KT20 . . . . . . 97 F7
Redhill RH2 . . . . 118 D3

Ridings The continued
Send Marsh GU23 . . . . . . 91 A4
Sunbury TW16 . . . . 35 A8
Surbiton KT5 . . . . 38 A4
Riding The
Cranleigh GU6 . . . . 174 E4
Sheerwater GU21 . . . . . 70 B5
Ridlands Gr RH8 . . . . 123 C5
Ridlands La RH8 . . . . 123 E5
Ridlands Rise RH8 . . . . . 123 E4
Ridleigh Ct TW15 . . . . . . 14 B4
Ridley Ct
Crawley RH10 . . . . 202 D8
Streatham SW16 . . . . . . 21 E2
Ridley Rd
Bromley BR2 . . . . 44 F6
Merton SW19 . . . . 20 B1
Warlingham CR6 . . . . . . 81 D1
Ridsdale Rd
Penge SE20 . . . . 43 B8
Woking GU21. . . . . 69 B2
Riesco Dr CR0 . . . . 62 C4
Rifle Way GU14 . . . . 84 C3
Rigby Cl CR0, CR9 . . . . . 61 A7
Rigg Ho 2 SW4 . . . . 21 E8
Riggindale Rd SW16 . . . . 21 D4
Rikkyo Sch-in-England
RH14. . . . . 213 D8
Riley Cl KT19 . . . . 76 B8
Riley Ho 1 SW4 . . . . 21 D8
Rillside RH10. . . . . 202 A3
Rill Wlk RH19. . . . . 186 B1
Rimbault Cl GU11 . . . . . . 105 E7
Rimini Ct SW12 . . . . 20 F7
Rinaldo Rd SW12 . . . . . . 21 B8
Rindle Cl GU14 . . . . 84 C4
Ringley Ave RH6 . . . . 161 A2
Ringley Oak RH12. . . . . . . 217 F4
Ringley Park Ave
RH2 . . . . 139 D8
Ringley Park Rd RH2. . . . . 118 C1
Ringley Rd RH12. . . . . 217 E4
Ringmead
Bracknell, Great Hollands
RG12. . . . . 26 E3
Bracknell, Hanworth
RG12. . . . . 27 B2
Ringmore Dr GU4 . . . . . . 110 C4
Ringmore Rd KT12 . . . . . 54 C7
Ringmore Rise SE23 . . . . 23 B8
Ring Rd N RH6. . . . . 182 C8
Ring Rd S RH6 . . . . 182 C7
Ringstead Bldgs SE6 . . . . 24 B8
Ringstead Ct 4 SM1 . . . . 59 D5
Ringstead Rd
Carshalton SM1. . . . . . . 59 D5
Lewisham SE6 . . . . 24 B8
Ring The RG12. . . . . 27 C7
Ringwold Cl BR3. . . . . 23 E1
Ringwood RG12. . . . . 26 F2
Ringwood Ave
Redhill RH1 . . . . 118 F4
Thornton Heath CR0,
CR9 . . . . 41 E2
Ringwood Cl
Ascot SL5. . . . . 29 B5
Crawley RH10 . . . . 201 E4
Ringwood Gdns SW15. . . . 19 A7
Ringwood Lo 1 RH1 . . . . 119 A4
Ringwood Rd
Blackwater GU17. . . . . . . 64 C6
Farnborough GU14 . . . . 85 C7
Ringwood Way TW12. . . . . 16 A4
RIPLEY 91 C6
Ripley Ave TW20 . . . . 11 E2
Ripley By-Pass GU23. . . . . 91 C4
Ripley CE Inf Sch GU23. . . 91 B6
Ripley Cl CR0 . . . . 63 C4
Ripley Court Sch GU23 . . . 91 C6
Ripley Ct CR4 . . . . 40 D7
Ripley Gdns
Mortlake SW14 . . . . 7 D4
Sutton SM1 . . . . 59 C6
Ripley Ho
13 Kingston u T KT2 . . . 18 B2
2 Mortlake SW14 . . . . . 7 E4
5 Penge SE26 . . . . 23 B3
Ripley La
Ripley GU23 . . . . 91 F3
West Horsley KT24,
GU23. . . . . 112 A7
Ripley Rd
East Clandon GU23,
GU4. . . . . 111 D7
Hampton TW12 . . . . 16 A1
RIPLEY SPRINGS 11 E2
Ripley Way KT19 . . . . 76 A8
Riplington Ct SW15 . . . . . 19 B8
Ripon Cl
Frimley GU15. . . . . 66 D3
Guildford GU2 . . . . 108 F3
Ripon Gdns KT9 . . . . 56 D5
Ripon Rd GU14 . . . . 84 A7
Ripplesmere RG12 . . . . . 27 D5
Ripplesmere Cl GU47 . . . 64 B8
Ripston Rd TW15 . . . . . . 14 D3
Risborough Dr KT4 . . . . . 39 A2
Rise Rd SL5 . . . . 29 F3
Rise The
Crawley RH10 . . . . 202 D6
Crowthorne RG45 . . . . . 45 A5
East Grinstead RH19 . . . 205 F8
East Horsley KT24 . . . . . 92 E1
Ewell KT17 . . . . 57 F1
South Croydon CR2 . . . . 62 C2
Tadworth KT20 . . . . 97 C6
Winkfield RG42 . . . . 28 A8
Woking GU21. . . . . 69 D1

Rise The continued
Wokingham RG41 . . . . . . 25 A7
Ritchie Cl RH10 . . . . 202 C2
Ritchie Rd CR0 . . . . 43 B3
Ritherdon Rd SW17 . . . . . 21 B6
River Ave KT7 . . . . 37 A2
Riverbank
East Molesey KT8 . . . . . 36 E5
Staines TW18. . . . . 12 F2
Westcott RH4 . . . . 135 B7
River Bank KT7 . . . . 36 F4
Riverbank Way TW8 . . . . . 6 C8
River Cl GU1. . . . . 109 C3
River Crane Way TW13. . . 15 F6
River Ct
Kingston u T KT6 . . . . . 37 D4
Sheerwater GU21 . . . . . 70 C5
Shepperton TW17 . . . . . 34 C2
Riverdale
Dorking RH4 . . . . 115 C3
Wrecclesham GU10 . . . . 145 E7
Riverdale Dr
Wandsworth SW18 . . . . 20 B7
Woking GU22. . . . . 89 F6
Riverdale Gdns TW1 . . . . . 6 C2
Riverdale Rd
Feltham TW13 . . . . 15 F4
Twickenham TW1. . . . . . 6 C1
Riverdene Ct KT6 . . . . . . 37 D4
Riverdene Ind Est
KT12 . . . . 54 D5
Riverfield Rd TW18 . . . . . 12 F2
River Gdns
Carshalton SM5 . . . . . . 60 A7
Feltham TW14 . . . . 4 B2
River Gdns Bsns Ctr
TW14 . . . . 4 B3
River Grove Pk BR3 . . . . . 43 F8
Riverhead Dr SM2 . . . . . 59 B1
River Hill KT11 . . . . 73 B4
River Ho
Forest Hill SE26 . . . . . . 23 B5
Mortlake SW13 . . . . 7 E5
Riverholme SE6 . . . . 36 E6
Riverholme Dr KT19. . . . . 57 E2
River Island Cl KT22. . . . . 94 D7
River La
Cobham KT11 . . . . 73 E3
Fetcham KT22 . . . . 94 D6
Leatherhead KT22 . . . . . 94 D6
Richmond TW10. . . . . . . 17 D7
Wrecclesham GU10,
GU9. . . . . 145 E7
Rivermead
Byfleet KT14 . . . . 71 F6
East Molesey KT8 . . . . . 36 C6
Kingston u T KT6 . . . . . 37 D4
River Mead
Crawley RH11 . . . . 181 A1
Horsham RH12 . . . . . . 217 B1
Rivermead Cl
New Haw KT15 . . . . 52 C3
Richmond TW10. . . . . . . 17 B3
Rivermead Ho TW16 . . . . 35 C6
Rivermead Rd GU15. . . . . 65 B2
River Meads Ave TW2. . . . 16 B5
Rivermount TW16. . . . . . . 35 C6
River Mount KT12. . . . . . . 34 F2
River Mount Gdns
GU2 . . . . 130 C6
Rivernook Cl KT12. . . . . . 35 C4
River Park Ave TW18. . . . . 12 D4
River Park Gdns BR2. . . . . 24 D1
River Rd TW18. . . . . 32 F8
River Reach TW11 . . . . . 17 C3
River Row Cotts GU9 . . . . 145 F8
Rivers Cl GU14. . . . . 85 E1
Riversdale Prim Sch
SW18 . . . . 20 A7
Riversdale Rd KT7 . . . . . . 37 A3
Riversdell Cl KT16 . . . . . . 32 F2
Riverside
4 Catford SE6 . . . . 23 F4
Egham TW20 . . . . 12 A5
Forest Row RH18. . . . . . 206 E3
Guildford, Bellfields
GU1. . . . . 109 D3
Guildford GU1 . . . . 130 D7
Horley RH6 . . . . 161 A1
Horsham RH12 . . . . . . 217 A2
Oatlands Park KT17 . . . . 34 E2
Sunbury TW16 . . . . 35 D7
Twickenham TW1. . . . . . 16 B7
Wraysbury TW19 . . . . . . 11 C8
Riverside Ave
East Molesey KT8 . . . . . 36 D4
Lightwater GU18 . . . . . . 67 C8
Riverside Bsns Ctr
Guildford GU1 . . . . 109 C1
Wandsworth SW18 . . . . 20 B7
Riverside Bsns Pk
Farnham GU9. . . . . 125 D3
Merton SW19 . . . . 40 C8
Riverside Cl
Brookwood GU24. . . . . . 87 F7
Farnborough GU14 . . . . 84 F5
Hackbridge SM6 . . . . . . 60 B7
Kingston u T KT1 . . . . . 37 D5
Staines TW18. . . . . 32 F8
Riverside Ct
Dorking RH4 . . . . 115 D1
Farnham GU9. . . . . 125 D3
Teddington TW11. . . . . . 17 C3
Riverside Dr
Bramley GU5 . . . . 152 A7
Chiswick W4 . . . . 7 E6
Egham TW18 . . . . 12 E3
Esher KT10 . . . . 55 A6

Riverside Dr continued
Mitcham CR4. . . . . 40 E4
Richmond TW10. . . . . . . 17 B5
Staines TW18. . . . . 32 F8
Riverside Gdns
Cobham KT11. . . . . 73 A6
Old Woking GU22. . . . . . 90 B6
Riverside Ho
Morden SW19 . . . . 40 C5
31 Richmond TW9. . . . . . 6 D2
Riverside Ind Pk GU9 . . . 125 D3
Riverside Pk KT13 . . . . . . 52 E5
Riverside Pk SL3 . . . . . . .1 C5
Riverside Pl TW19 . . . . . . 2 D1
Riverside Rd
Hersham KT12. . . . . 54 E6
Staines TW18. . . . . 12 F1
Stanwell TW19 . . . . 2 E1
Wandsworth SW17,
SW19 . . . . 20 C5
Riverside The KT8 . . . . . . 36 D6
Riverside Way GU15. . . . . 65 A3
Riverside Wlk
Isleworth TW7. . . . . 5 E4
8 West Wickham BR4 . . 44 B1
Riversmeet GU10. . . . . . . 147 D4
Riverstone Ct KT2 . . . . . . 37 F8
Riverview
Guildford GU1 . . . . 109 C1
Shepperton TW17 . . . . . 34 D2
Riverview CE Prim Sch
KT19 . . . . 57 D6
Riverview Gdns KT11. . . . 72 F6
River View Gdns TW1 . . . 16 F6
Riverview Gr W4. . . . . . . .7 B8
Riverview Mans 4 TW1 . . 6 D1
Riverview Pk SE6 . . . . . . 24 A6
Riverview Rd
Chiswick W4 . . . . 7 B7
West Ewell KT19 . . . . . . 57 D6
Riverway TW18 . . . . 33 B8
River Way
Twickenham TW2. . . . . . 16 B6
West Ewell KT19 . . . . . . 57 E5
Riverway Est GU3 . . . . . . 151 C8
River Wlk KT12 . . . . 35 A3
Riverwood Ct GU1 . . . . . 109 C3
Rivett Drake Cl GU2. . . . . 109 B5
Rivey Cl KT14. . . . . 70 F5
Rix Ho RH8 . . . . 122 F2
Road House Est GU22. . . . 90 A7
Roakes Ave KT15 . . . . . . 52 B8
Robert Cl KT12 . . . . 54 B5
Robert Gerard Ho 7
SE27. . . . . 22 D4
Robertsbridge Rd SM5 . . . 40 D2
Roberts Cl
Cheam SM3 . . . . 58 D3
South Norwood CR7 . . . . 42 D6
Stanwell TW19 . . . . 2 C1
Roberts Ct SE20 . . . . 43 C8
Roberts Ho 5 SE27 . . . . 22 B5
Robertson Ct 5 GU21 . . . 68 E1
Robertson Ho SW17. . . . . 20 E3
Robertson Way GU12. . . . 105 F1
Roberts Rd
Aldershot GU12. . . . . . . 105 D1
Sandhurst GU15 . . . . . . 65 A6
Robert St CR0, CR9 . . . . . 61 C7
Roberts Way
Cranleigh GU6 . . . . 174 E4
Englefield Green TW20 . . 11 C1
Robert Way
Horsham RH12 . . . . . . 217 F7
Mytchett GU16. . . . . 85 F3
Robina Ho RG42 . . . . 26 F8
Robin Cl
Addlestone KT15 . . . . . . 52 D5
Ash Vale GU12. . . . . 106 A6
Crawley RH11 . . . . 201 C8
1 East Grinstead
RH19. . . . . 185 F2
Hampton TW12 . . . . 15 E3
Robin Ct SM6. . . . . 60 C4
Robin Gdns RH1 . . . . 119 A3
Robin Gr TW8 . . . . 6 C8
Robin Hill GU7 . . . . 150 D7
Robin Hill Dr GU15. . . . . . 66 A3
Robinhood Cl CR4 . . . . . . 41 C6
Robin Hood Cl
Farnborough GU14 . . . . 85 A7
Knaphill GU21 . . . . 68 F1
Robin Hood Cres GU21. . . 68 E2
Robin Hood Ct 2 SM1 . . . 59 B5
Robin Hood Inf Sch
SM1 . . . . 59 A5
Robin Hood Jun Sch
SM1 . . . . 59 B5
Robinhood La CR4 . . . . . . 41 C6
Robin Hood La
Kingston u T SW15 . . . . 18 E4
Sutton SM1 . . . . 59 B5
Warnham RH12 . . . . . . 216 F5
Woking GU4. . . . . 89 F3
Robin Hood Prim Sch
SW15 . . . . 18 E3
Robin Hood Rd
Knaphill GU21 . . . . 68 E2
Knaphill GU21 . . . . 68 F1
Robin Hood Rdbt
SW15 . . . . 18 E4
Robin Hood Way
(Kingston By Pass) KT2,
SW15, SW20 . . . . 18 E3

Robin Hood Works GU21 68 E2
Robinia Cl SE20 43 A8
Robin La GU47 45 C1
Robin Row RH10 204 C5
Robin's Bow GU15 65 B4
Robins Ct
Croydon CR2 61 E6
Richmond TW10 6 E1
Robin's Ct BR3 44 D7
Robins Dale GU21 68 C2
Robinson Cl GU22 90 C7
Robinson Ct
7 Richmond TW9 6 F3
1 Thornton Heath CR0 42 B3
Robinson Ho RH10 201 D5
Robinson Rd SW19 20 E2
Robinsway KT12 54 C6
Robinswood Ct RH12 217 F4
Robin Way
Guildford GU2 109 B5
Staines TW18 12 F5
Robinwood Pl SW15 18 D4
Robson Rd SE21, SE27 22 C5
Roby Dr RG12 27 D2
Rochdale 9 SE19 22 E2
Rochelle Ct BR3 24 B1
Roche Rd SW16 41 F8
Rochester Ave TW13 14 F6
Rochester Cl SW16 21 E1
Rochester Ct SE25 43 A7
Rochester Gdns
Caterham CR3 100 E5
South Croydon CR0 61 E7
Rochester Par TW13 15 A5
Rochester Rd
Carshalton SM5 59 F6
Egham TW20 12 D2
Rochester Wlk RH2 139 B5
Roche Wlk SM4, SM5 40 D3
Rochford Way CR0 41 E3
Rock Ave 14 SW14 7 D4
Rockbourne Rd SE23 23 D7
Rock Cl CR4 40 D7
Rockdale Dr GU26 188 D3
Rockdene Cl RH19 186 A1
Rockery The GU14 84 E3
Rocket Rd GU14 84 D1
Rockfield Cl RH8 122 F4
Rockfield Rd RH8 122 F5
Rockfield Way 7
GU47 64 D8
Rock Gdns GU11 104 F1
Rockhampton Cl 4
SE27 22 A4
Rockhampton Rd
South Croydon CR2 61 E4
West Norwood SE27,
SW16 22 A4
Rock Hill SE26 22 F4
Rockingham Cl SW15 7 F3
Rockingham Ct 20 BR3 24 A1
Rock La GU10 146 A5
Rockmount Prim Sch
SE19 22 D2
Rockmount Rd SE19 22 D2
Rockshaw Rd RH1 119 E8
Rocks The RH19 206 D6
Rockwell Gdns SE19 22 E4
Rockwood Pl RH1 119 B6
Rocky La RH1, RH2 119 A6
Rocombe Cres SE23 23 C8
Rodborough Tech Coll
GU8 170 F7
Rodd Est TW17 34 D4
Roden Gdns CR0, SE25 42 E3
Rodenhurst Rd SW4 21 C8
Rodgate La GU27 209 E5
Rodgers Ho 3 SW4 21 D8
Roding Cl GU6 173 F2
Rodmel Ct GU14 85 E1
Rodmill La SW2 21 E8
Rodney Cl
New Malden KT3 38 E4
Thornton Heath CR0 42 B1
3 Walton-on-T KT12 35 C1
Rodney Gn 3 KT12 54 C8
Rodney Pl SW19 40 C8
Rodney Rd
Mitcham CR4 40 E6
New Malden KT3 38 E4
Twickenham TW2 16 A8
Walton-on-T KT12 54 C8
Rodney Way
Guildford GU1 110 A2
Poyle SL3 1 E6
Rodona Rd KT13 72 D8
Rodway Rd SW15 19 A8
Rodwell Ct
Addlestone KT15 52 C6
Walton-on-T KT12 54 B7
Roebuck Cl
Ashtead KT21 95 E7
Feltham TW13 15 B4
Horsham RH13 218 B4
Reigate RH2 118 A1
Roebuck Ct 2 KT3 38 E4
Roebuck Rd KT9 57 A5
Roedean Cres SW15 7 E2
Roedeer Copse GU27 207 E6
ROEHAMPTON 7 F2
Roehampton CE Prim Sch
SW15 19 B8
Roehampton Gate SW15 7 E1
Roehampton High St
SW15 19 A8
Roehampton La SW15,
SW19 19 A8
Roehampton Univ Froebel
Coll SW15 7 F1
Roehampton Univ
(Whitelands Coll)
SW15 19 A8
Roehampton Vale
SW15 18 F5
Roe Way SM6 60 E4
Roffes La CR3 100 D2
ROFFEY 218 A5
Roffey Cl
Horley RH6 160 F3
Purley CR8 80 B3
Roffey Cnr RH12 218 B4
Roffey's Cl RH10 183 A4
Roffords GU21 69 B2
Roffye Ct RH12 218 A4
Rogers Cl
Caterham CR3 101 B5
Coulsdon CR5 80 B1
Roger Simmons Ct
KT23 94 A3
Rogers La CR6 81 F1
Rogers Mead RH9 121 B3
Rogers Rd SW17 20 E4
Rojack Rd SE23 23 D7
Rokeby Cl RG12 27 D8
Rokeby Ct GU21 68 F2
Rokeby Ho 10 SW12 21 B8
Rokeby Pl SW20 19 B1
Rokeby Sch KT2 18 C1
Roke Cl
Purley CR8 80 C5
Witley GU8 170 E5
Rokefield Ho RH4 135 B7
Roke Ho GU1 110 C1
Roke La GU8 170 F5
Roke Lane Cotts GU8 170 F5
Rokell Ho BR3 24 B3
Roke Lodge Rd CR8 80 B6
Roke Prim Sch CR8 80 C5
Roke Rd CR8 80 C5
Rokers La GU8 149 D7
Roland Ct SE19 42 F8
Roland Way KT4 57 F8
Rollesby Rd KT9 57 A4
Rolleston Rd CR2 61 D3
Rollit Cres TW3 5 A2
Rolls Royce Cl SM6 60 E3
Rolston Ho GU27 207 F6
Romana Ct TW18 13 A4
Romanby Ct 1 RH1 139 F8
Roman Cl TW14 4 C2
Roman Farm Rd GU2 108 D2
Romanfield Rd SW2 21 F8
Roman Ho RH2 138 F7
Romanhurst Ave BR2 44 E5
Romanhurst Gdns BR2 44 E5
Roman Ind Est CR0 42 E2
Roman Rd RH4 136 B5
Roman Rise SE19 22 D2
Romans Bsns Pk GU9 125 D3
Romans Ind Pk GU9 125 D3
Romans Way GU22 71 A4
Roman Way
Croydon CR9 61 B8
Farnham GU9 125 E4
Thornton Heath CR9 61 B8
Wallington SM5 59 F2
Winkfield RG42 27 F8
Romany Gdns SM3 40 A2
Romany Prospect
SE19 22 D2
Romany The GU14 84 A1
Roma Read Cl SW15 19 B8
Romayne Cl GU14 85 A5
Romberg Rd SW17 21 A5
Romeo Hill RG42 27 F8
Romeyn Rd SW16 21 F5
Romley Ct GU9 125 D1
Rommany Ct SE27 22 D4
Rommany Rd SE27 22 D4
Romney Cl
Ashford TW15 14 C3
Chessington KT9 56 E6
Romney Ho
Bracknell RG12 27 E5
Sutton SM2 59 B4
Romney Rd
Farnborough GU14 84 E1
New Malden KT3 38 D3
Romola Rd SE24 22 B7
Romsey Cl
Aldershot GU11 126 C6
Blackwater GU17 64 C6
Romulus Ct 6 TW8 6 D7
Rona Cl RH11 201 B3
Ronald Cl BR3 43 F4
Ronald Ho 8 SM1 59 D5
Ronald Ross Prim Sch
SW19 19 E8
Ronelean Rd KT6 56 F7
Ronneby Cl KT13 53 E7
Ronson Way KT22 95 A6
Ronver Rd SE12 24 F7
Roof Of The World (Park
Homes Est) KT20 116 B3
Rookeries Cl TW13 15 C5
Rookery Cl KT22 94 E3
Rookery Dr RH4 135 A5
Rookery Hill
Ashtead KT21 76 A1
Outwood RH1, RH6 162 B6
Rookery Mead CR5 99 D5
Rookery Rd TW18 13 B3
Rookery The RH4 135 A5
Rookery Way KT20 117 F8
Rook La CR3 100 B3
Rookley Cl SM2 59 B2
Rooks Hill GU5 152 C2
Rooksmead Rd TW16 35 A7
Rookstone Rd SW17 20 F3
Rook Way RH12 217 F6
Rookwood Ave
Sandhurst GU47 45 E2
Wallington SM6 60 D6
West Barnes KT3 39 A5
Rookwood Cl RH1 119 B6
Rookwood Ct GU2 130 C6
Rookwood Pk RH12 216 F3
Roosevelt Ct 15 SW19 19 E7
Roothill La RH3 137 A3
Ropeland Way RH12 217 E7
Roper Ho 13 SE21 22 E4
Ropers Wlk 13 SE24 22 A8
Roper Way CR4 41 A7
Rorkes Drift GU16 86 A4
Rosa Ave TW15 14 A4
Rosalind Franklin Cl
GU2 129 E8
Rosamond St SE26 23 B5
Rosamund Cl CR2 61 D6
Rosamund Rd RH10 202 B3
Rosary Cl TW3, TW5 4 E5
Rosary Gdns TW15 14 B4
Rosary RC Inf Sch The
TW5 5 A8
Rosary RC Jun Sch The
TW5 5 A8
Roseacre RH8 123 A1
Roseacre Cl TW17 34 A4
Roseacre Gdns GU4 131 F3
Rose Ave
Mitcham CR4 40 F8
Morden SM4 40 C4
Rosebank
Epsom KT18 76 C5
Penge SE20 23 B1
Rosebank Cl TW11 17 A2
Rose Bank Cotts GU22 89 E5
Rosebay RG40 25 E8
Rosebery Ave
Epsom KT17 76 E5
Kingston u T KT3 38 F6
South Norwood CR7 42 C7
Rosebery Cl SM4 39 D3
Rosebery Cres GU22 89 F7
Rosebery Ct KT9 56 F4
Rosebery Gdns SM1 59 B6
Rosebery Par KT17 57 F3
Rosebery Rd
Cheam SM1 58 F4
Isleworth TW3, TW7 5 C2
Kingston u T KT1 38 B7
Langley Vale KT18 96 E8
Rosebery Sch KT18 76 C5
Rosebery Sq KT1 38 B7
Rosebine Ave TW2 16 D8
Rosebriar Cl GU22 71 A3
Rosebriars
Caterham CR3 100 E7
Esher KT10 55 C5
Rosebury Ct SW16 41 F7
Rosebury Dr GU24 68 A4
Rose Bushes KT17 77 C3
Rose Cotts
Enton Green GU8 171 A2
Esher KT10 55 D5
Forest Row RH18 206 E3
Horsham RH12 218 D7
Rosecourt Rd CR0 41 F3
Rosecroft Cl TN16 83 F1
Rosecroft Gdns TW2 16 D7
Rose Ct
10 Wimbledon SW19 19 F3
Wokingham RG40 25 C6
Rosedale
Aldershot GU12 105 C2
Ashtead KT21 75 C1
Caterham CR3 100 E4
Rosedale Cl RH11 201 A4
Rosedale Gdns RG12 27 A4
Rosedale Ho 6 TW9 6 E3
Rosedale Pl CR0 43 D2
Rosedale Rd
Richmond TW9 6 E3
Stoneleigh KT17 58 A5
Rosedene Ave
Morden SM4 40 A4
Streatham SW16 21 F5
Thornton Heath CR0 41 E2
Rosedene La GU47 64 D7
Rose End KT4 39 D1
Rosefield Cl SM5 59 E5
Rosefield Gdns KT16 51 D4
Rosefield Rd TW18 13 A4
Rose Gdns
Farnborough GU14 84 E3
Feltham TW13 15 A6
Stanwell TW19 13 D8
Roseheath Rd TW4 4 F2
ROSEHILL 40 C1
Rosehill
Claygate KT10 56 A4
Hampton TW12 36 A8
Reigate RH2 118 D2
ROSE HILL 136 B7
Rose Hill
Dorking RH4 136 B7
Sutton SM1, SM4 40 B1
Rosehill Ave
Carshalton SM1, SM5 40 C1
Rosehill Ave *continued*
Woking GU21 69 C3
Rosehill Ct SM4 40 C2
Rosehill Farm Mdw
SM7 78 B4
Rosehill Gdns SM1 59 C8
Rose Hill Pk W SM1 59 C8
Rosehill Rd TN16 83 C2
Rose La GU23 91 D5
Roseleigh Cl 27 TW1 6 D1
Rose Lo TW20 12 A4
Rosemary Ave
Ash Vale GU12 106 A8
East Molesey KT8 36 A5
Hounslow TW4 4 D5
Rosemary Cl
Farnborough GU14 84 D4
Oxted RH8 123 A2
Thornton Heath CR0 41 E3
Rosemary Cotts SW19 19 C1
Rosemary Cres GU2 109 A5
Rosemary Ct
Haslemere GU27 208 C7
Horley RH6 160 E4
Rosemary Gdns
Blackwater GU17 64 D5
Chessington KT9 56 E6
Mortlake SW14 7 C4
Rosemary Ho RH10 182 A1
Rosemary La
Alfold GU6 212 E8
Blackwater GU17 64 D5
Charlwood RH6 180 E7
Horley RH6 161 B3
Mortlake SW14 7 C4
Rowledge GU10 145 E4
Thorpe TW20 32 B6
Rosemary Rd SW17 20 C5
Rosemead KT16 33 B2
Rosemead Ave
Feltham TW13 14 F6
Mitcham CR4, SW16 41 C7
Rosemead Cl RH1 139 D7
Rosemead Gdns
RH10 201 E5
Rosemead Prep Sch
SE27 22 C6
Rosemont Rd
Kingston u T KT3 38 C6
Richmond TW10 6 E1
Rosemount Ave KT14 71 A6
Rosemount Ct SE25 42 D6
Rosemount Ho 7
KT14 71 A6
Rosemount Par KT14 71 A6
Rosemount Point 10
SE23 23 D5
Rosemount Twrs 5
SM6 60 C4
Rosendale Prim Sch
SE21 22 C8
Rosendale Rd SE21,
SE24 22 C7
Roseneath Ct CR3 101 A2
Roseneath Dr GU8 191 B4
Roseneath Pl SW16 21 F4
Rose Pk KT16 51 E2
Rosery The CR0 43 D3
Roses Cotts RH4 136 A7
Rose St RG40 25 C6
Rosethorn Cl SW12 21 D8
Rosetrees GU1 131 A8
Rosetta Ct SE19 22 E1
Rose View KT15 52 C5
Roseville Ave TW3, TW4 5 A2
Rosevine Rd SW20 39 C8
Rosewall Ct SW19 20 B3
Rosewarne Cl GU21 69 A1
Rosewell Cl SE20 23 B1
Rose Wlk
Purley CR8 79 D8
Surbiton KT5 38 B4
West Wickham BR4 63 D8
Rosewood
Haslemere GU27 208 C5
Mytchett GU16 86 A4
Rose Wood GU22 90 A8
Rosewood Ct
Byfleet KT14 71 E7
Kingston u T KT2 18 A1
7 Woking GU21 70 A3
Rosewood Dr TW17 33 F4
Rosewood Gr SM1 59 C8
Rosewood Lo CR0 62 D8
Rosewood Way GU24 67 E6
Roshni Ho SW17 20 E2
Rosina Ct SW17 20 E3
Roskeen Ct SW19 19 C1
Roslan Ct RH6 161 B2
Roslyn Cl CR4 40 D7
Roslyn Ct 8 GU21 69 A1
Rossal Ct SE20 23 B1
Ross Cl RH10 201 F3
Ross Ct
Croydon CR2 61 C4
5 Horley RH6 161 B3
4 Putney SW15 19 D8
Rossdale SM1 59 E5
Rossendon Ct 1 SM6 60 C4
Rossenhallas RH1 119 B1
Rosset Cl RG12 27 B5
Rossetti Gdns CR5 79 F1
Ross Ho TW2 16 B6
Rossignol Gdns SM5 60 A8
Rossindel Rd TW3 5 A2
Rossiter Lo GU1 131 A8
Rossiter Rd SW12 21 B7
Rosslea GU20 48 A6
Rosslyn Ave
Feltham TW14 4 A1
Mortlake SW13, SW14 7 F4
Rosslyn Cl
Ashford TW16 14 E2
Coney Hall BR4 63 F7
Rosslyn Ho 8 TW9 6 F6
Rosslyn Pk KT13 53 D6
Rosslyn Rd TW1 6 C1
Rossmore Cl RH10 182 D2
Rossmore Gdns GU11 104 F1
Ross Par SM6 60 B4
Ross Rd
Cobham KT11 73 C6
South Norwood SE25 42 E6
Twickenham TW2 16 C7
Wallington SM6 60 C5
Rosswood Gdns SM6 60 C4
Rosswood Ho 13 SM6 60 B4
Rostella Rd SW17 20 D4
Rostrevor Rd SW19 20 A3
Rotary Ct KT8 36 E6
Rotary Lo SE27 22 B5
Rothbury Gdns TW7 6 A7
Rothbury Wlk GU15 66 C4
Rother Cl GU47 64 C8
Rother Cres RH11 200 F5
Rotherfield Ave RG41 25 A7
Rotherfield Rd SM5 60 A5
Rotherhill Ave SW16 21 D2
Rother Ho 4 RH1 118 F2
Rother Rd GU14 84 E7
Rothervale RH6 160 F5
Rotherwick Ct GU14 105 C8
Rotherwood Cl SW19,
SW20 39 E8
Rothesay Ave
Merton SW20 39 E7
Mortlake SW14, TW10 7 B3
Rothesay Ct SE6 24 F6
Rothesay Rd SE25 42 E5
Rothes Rd RH4 136 B8
Rothsay Ct KT13 53 D4
Rothschild St SE27 22 C4
Rothwell Ho
Crowthorne RG45 45 C4
Heston TW5 5 A8
Rotunda Est The
GU11 105 B2
Rougemont Ave SM4 40 A3
Roughets La RH1 120 E6
Rough Field RH19 185 D4
Roughlands GU22 70 E4
Rough Rd GU22 88 C5
Rough Rew RH4 136 B4
Rough Way RH12 217 F5
Rounce La GU24 67 D6
Roundabout Cotts
RH12 214 C5
Roundacre SW19 19 D6
Roundals La GU8 191 E8
Roundell Ho 14 SE21 22 E4
Round Gr CR0 43 D2
Roundhay Cl SE23 23 D6
Roundhill GU22 90 B8
Round Hill SE23 23 C5
Roundhill Dr GU22 70 B1
Roundhill Way
Guildford GU2 108 F1
Oxshott KT11 74 B7
Round Oak Rd KT13 52 F6
ROUNDSHAW 60 F3
Roundshead Dr RG42 27 D8
Roundtable Rd BR1 24 F5
Roundthorn Way GU21 68 F3
Roundway
Biggin Hill TN16 83 D4
Egham TW20 12 C3
Frimley GU15 66 C6
Roundway Cl GU15 66 C6
Roundway Ct RH10 201 D8
Roundway The KT10 55 F4
Roundwood View SM7 77 D4
Roundwood Way SM7 77 D4
Roupell Ho 7 KT2 17 F1
Roupell Rd SW2 21 F7
Rouse Gdns SE21 22 E4
Routh Ct TW14 14 D7
Routh Rd SW18 20 E8
Rowallan Ct SE6 24 F7
Rowan 2 RG12 27 F4
Rowan Ave TW20 12 C3
Rowan Chase GU10 146 A5
Rowan Cl
Ashford TW15 13 D4
Camberley GU15 65 F8
Crawley RH10 201 F6
Guildford GU1 109 C4
Horsham RH12 218 B5
Kingston u T KT3 38 E7
Mitcham SW16 41 C8
Reigate RH2 139 C7
Rowan Cres SW16 41 C8
Rowan Ct
Forest Hill SE26 23 C4
Hounslow TW3 5 B2
11 Kingston u T KT2 18 A1
Wimbledon SW20 39 B7
Rowan Dr RG45 45 C6
Rowan Gdns CR0 61 F7
Rowan Gn KT13 53 D6
Rowan Gr CR5 99 B6
Rowan Mead KT20 97 B8
Rowan Prep Sch KT10 55 F3
Rowan Rd
Brentford TW8 6 B7
Mitcham SW16 41 C7
Rowans Cl GU14 64 E1

Rowanside Cl GU35 187 C4
Rowans The
Ashford TW16 14 F3
Grayshott GU26 188 D2
12 Sutton SM2 59 B4
Woking GU22 69 E1
Rowan Way RH12 218 C5
Rowan Wlk RH10 204 C8
Rowbarns Way KT24 112 F5
Rowbury GU7 151 A7
Rowcliffe Springs GU8 172 E4
Rowcroft Cl GU12 106 A6
Rowden Rd
Penge BR3 43 F8
West Ewell KT19 57 C6
Rowdown Cres CR0 63 E2
Rowdown Prim Sch CR0 63 D1
Rowe La GU24 88 A3
Rowena Ct 4 RH12 217 A1
Rowfant Bsns Ctr RH10 203 E6
Rowfant Cl RH10 202 E6
Rowfant Rd SW12, SW17 21 A6
Row Hill KT15 51 F4
Rowhill Ave GU11 125 F8
Rowhill Cl GU14 84 C4
Rowhill Copse Nature Trail* GU9 125 D8
Rowhill Cres GU11 125 F8
Rowhills GU9 125 E8
Rowhills Cl GU9 125 F7
ROWHOOK 196 E1
Rowhook Hill RH12 215 F8
Rowhook Rd
Rowhook RH12 196 E1
Slinfold RH12 216 A8
Rowhurst Ave KT15 52 B4
Row La GU5 153 E5
Rowland Cl RH10 183 E5
Rowland Ct CR0 61 E8
Rowland Gr SE26 23 B5
Rowland Hill Almshouses 9 TW15 14 A3
Rowland Ho GU6 174 D3
Rowland Rd GU6 174 D3
Rowlands Rd RH12 218 A6
Rowland Way
Littleton Common TW15 14 D1
Merton SW19 40 B8
ROWLEDGE 145 F3
Rowledge CE Prim Sch GU10 145 E3
Rowley Cl
Bracknell RG12 27 E6
Pyrford GU22 71 B3
Rowley Ct CR3 100 C5
Rowlls Rd KT1 37 F6
ROWLY 174 B6
Rowly Dr GU6 174 A6
Rowly Edge GU6 174 A6
Rowntree Rd TW2 16 E7
Rowplatt Cl RH19 184 E4
Rowplatt La RH19 184 E4
Row The RH7 164 D4
ROW TOWN 51 F4
Row Town KT15 51 F3
Roxbee Cox Rd GU14, GU51 84 A1
Roxborough Ave TW7 5 F7
Roxburgh Cl GU15 66 C4
Roxburgh Rd SE27 22 B3
Roxeth Ct 8 TW15 14 A3
Roxford Cl TW17 34 E4
Roxton Gdns CR0 63 A5
Roxywood Ct CR2 61 C2
Royal Alexandra & Albert Sch RH2 118 E6
Royal Ave KT4 57 E8
Royal Botanic Gdns* TW9 6 E6
Royal Cir SE27 22 B5
Royal Cl
Putney SW19 19 D6
Worcester Park KT4 57 E8
Royal Crest Ho SM2 58 E3
Royal Ct
9 Kingston u T KT2 18 B1
Knaphill GU21 68 C1
Royal Dr KT18 97 B8
Royal Duchess Mews 15 SW12 21 B8
Royal Earlswood Pk RH1 140 A6
Royale Cl GU11 126 C8
Royal Fst Sch The SL4 10 C4
Royal Gram Sch GU1 130 D8
Royal Holloway Univ of London TW20 11 E1
Royal Horticultural Society Cotts GU23 71 E3
Royal Horticultural Society's Gdn* GU23 71 E1
Royal Hosp SW19 19 E8
Royal Hunt Ho SL5 28 D8
Royal Huts Ave GU26 188 F4
Royal Jun Sch The GU26 188 D1
Royal Kent CE Prim Sch The KT22 74 C5
Royal Logistic Corps Mus* GU16 86 D8
Royal Marsden Hospl (Surrey Branch) The SM2 59 C1
Royal Mews KT8 36 E6
Royal Military Acad GU15 64 F6
Royal Military Acad Hospl GU15 65 A8
Royal Military Sch of Music (Kneller Hall) TW2 5 D1
Royal Oak Ctr The CR2 61 C1
Royal Oak Dr RG45 45 B8
Royal Oak Ho RH10 204 B7
Royal Oak Mews 10 TW11 17 A3
Royal Oak Rd GU21 69 D1
Royal Orchard Cl SW18 19 E8
Royal Par
Hindhead GU26 188 F4
12 Richmond TW9 7 A6
Royal Rd TW11 16 D3
Royal Russell Sch CR9 62 B5
Royal Sch of Church Music RH5 115 B4
Royal Sch The GU27 189 A2
Royals The GU1 130 E8
Royal Surrey County Hospl GU2 108 E1
Royal Victoria Gdns SL5 29 A4
Royal Way The GU16 86 D7
Royal Wlk SM6 60 B7
Royce Rd RH10 182 A3
Roycroft Cl SW2 22 A7
Roydon Ct
Egham TW20 12 D2
Hersham KT12 54 A6
Roydon Lo KT15 52 D7
Roy Gr TW12 16 B2
Roy Ho TW12 16 B2
Roylon Ct BR3 43 E5
Roymount Ct TW2 16 E5
Royston Ave
Byfleet KT14 71 E7
Carshalton SM1 59 D7
Wallington SM6 60 D6
Royston Cl
Cranford TW5 4 B6
Crawley RH10 182 A2
Walton-on-T KT12 35 A1
Royston Ct
Hinchley Wood KT10 55 F8
3 Richmond TW9 6 F6
Tolworth KT6 57 A8
Royston Lo SW19 20 C2
Royston Prim Sch SE20 43 D8
Royston Rd
Byfleet KT14 71 E7
Penge BR3, SE20 43 D8
Richmond TW10 6 E2
Roystons The KT5 38 B4
Rozeldene GU26 188 E3
Rozelle Ct 1 CR7 42 A3
Rozel Terr CR0 61 C7
Rubens Gdns SE22 23 A8
Rubens St SE6 23 F6
Rubus Cl GU24 67 E6
Ruby Ct TW13 14 F5
Ruckmans La RH5 197 B7
Rudd Hall Rise GU15 65 E4
Ruden Way KT17 77 B4
Rudge Ho 2 RH19 185 F1
Rudge Rise KT15 51 F5
RUDGWICK 214 C7
Rudgwick Keep RH6 161 C4
Rudgwick Prim Sch RH12 214 D7
Rudgwick Rd RH11 200 F7
Rudloe Rd SW12 21 C8
Rudolph Ct SE22 23 B8
Rudsworth Cl SL3 1 D7
Ruffetts Cl CR2 62 B3
Ruffetts The CR2 62 B3
Ruffetts Way KT20 77 E1
Rufus Bsns Ctr SW18 20 B6
Rufwood RH10 204 A8
Rugby Cl GU47 45 E1
Rugby Ct TW9 6 E3
Rugby La SM2 58 D2
Rugby Rd TW1, TW2, TW7 5 E1
Ruggles-Brise Rd TW15 13 D3
Rugosa Rd GU24 67 E6
Ruislip St SW17 20 F4
Rumsey Cl TW12 15 F2
Runcorn Cl RH11 200 E2
Runes Cl CR4 40 E5
RUNFOLD 126 C4
Runfold - St George GU10 126 B5
Runnemede Rd TW20 12 A4
Running Horse Yd 12 TW8 6 E8
Runnymede* TW20 11 F5
Runnymede SW19 40 D8
Runnymede Cl TW2 16 B8
Runnymede Cotts TW19 12 D7
Runnymede Cres SW16 41 E8
Runnymede Ct
14 Croydon CR0 61 F8
Egham TW20 12 A4
Farnborough GU14 85 A7
Roehampton SW15 19 A7
1 Wallington SM6 60 B4
Runnymede Gdns TW2 16 B8
Runnymede Ho TW10 7 A2
Runnymede Hospl (private) The KT16 51 D7
Runnymede Rd TW2 5 B1
Runnymede Rdbt TW20 12 B4
Runshooke Ct 9 RH11 201 A3
Runtley Wood La GU4 89 F2
Runwick La GU10 124 C1
Rupert Rd GU2 130 C8
Rural Cl GU9 145 F6
Rural Life Ctr* GU10 146 F3
Rural Way
Mitcham SW16 21 B1
Redhill RH1 119 A1
Ruscoe Dr GU22 70 A2
Ruscoe Ho 12 SW27 22 B3
Ruscombe Way TW14 14 F8
Rusham Park Ave TW20 12 A2
Rusham Rd
Balham SW12 20 F8
Egham TW20 11 F2
Rushams Rd RH12 217 B3
Rusham Terr TW20 12 A2
Rushbury Ct 6 TW12 36 A8
Rush Common Mews SW2 21 F8
Rush Croft GU7 151 A8
Rushden Cl SE19 22 D1
Rushdene Wlk TN16 83 D2
Rushden Way GU9 125 D7
Rushen Wlk SM5 40 D1
Rushett Cl KT7 37 B1
Rushett Dr RH4 136 C4
Rushett La KT9, KT18 75 D7
Rushett Rd KT7 37 B2
RUSHETTS FARM 139 C6
Rushetts Pl RH11 181 C1
Rushetts Rd
Crawley RH11 181 B1
Reigate RH2 139 C5
Rushey Cl KT3 38 D5
Rushey Gn SE6 24 B8
Rushey Green Prim Sch SE6 24 B7
Rushfords RH7 164 E5
Rushmead TW10 17 B5
Rushmead Cl CR0 61 F6
Rushmere Ct KT4 58 A8
Rushmere Ho 2 SW15 19 A7
Rushmere Pl
Englefield Green TW20 11 E3
Wimbledon SW19 19 D3
Rushmon Ct KT16 32 F2
Rushmon Gdns KT12 54 B7
Rushmon Pl SM3 58 E4
Rushmon Villas KT3 38 F5
RUSHMOOR 168 C5
Rushmoor Cl GU2 108 F5
Rushmoor Ct GU14 105 C8
Rushmoor Ind Sch GU14 85 C1
Rushmoor Rd GU11 104 E4
Rusholme Gr SE19 22 E3
Rush The SW20 39 F8
Rushton Ave RH9 142 D5
Rushworth Rd RH2 118 B2
Rushy Ho RG12 27 E5
Rushy Meadow La SM5 59 E7
Rushy Meadow Prim Sch SM5 59 E7
Ruskin Ave
Feltham TW14 3 F1
Richmond TW9 7 A7
Ruskin Cl RH10 182 C1
Ruskin Dr KT4 58 C8
Ruskin Ho CR2 61 D5
Ruskin Par CR0 61 D5
Ruskin Rd
Croydon CR0, CR9 61 B8
Isleworth TW7 5 F4
Staines TW18 12 F2
Wallington SM5 60 A5
Ruskin Way SW19 40 D8
RUSPER 199 D7
Rusper Ct CR5 79 D3
Rusper Prim Sch RH12 199 C7
Rusper Rd
Capel RH5 178 D2
Crawley RH11 200 D7
Faygate RH12 199 A1
Horsham RH12 217 F6
Newdigate RH12, RH5 179 C4
Ruspers Keep RH11 200 F7
Russel Cl BR3 44 C6
Russell Cl
Bracknell RG12 27 D2
5 Chiswick W4 7 F8
Walton on t H KT20 97 A2
Woking GU21 69 C4
Russell Ct
Blackwater GU17 64 D5
Bromley BR1 24 F1
Croydon SE25 42 F5
Guildford GU1 109 C4
Hindhead GU26 188 F4
Leatherhead KT22 95 B5
Streatham SW16 21 F3
Surbiton KT6 37 E2
Wallington SM6 60 C5
Russell Dr TW19 2 D1
Russell Gdns
Harmondsworth UB7 3 A8
Richmond TW10 17 C6
Russell Green Cl CR8 61 A1
RUSSELL HILL 60 F1
Russell Hill CR8 60 F1
Russell Hill Par 6 CR8 80 A8
Russell Hill Pl CR8 80 A8
Russell Hill Rd CR8 80 A8
Russell Kerr Cl W4 7 C7
Russell Par 5 CR8 80 A8
Russell Rd
Lower Halliford TW17 34 C2
Merton SW19 20 A1
Mitcham CR4 40 E6
Twickenham TW1, TW2 5 F1
Walton-on-T KT12 35 A3
Woking GU21 69 C4
Russells KT20 97 D5
Russell Sch The TW10 17 D7
Russells Cres RH6 161 A2
Russell's Yd GU22 89 F7
Russell Way
Crawley RH10 202 A5
Sutton SM1 59 B5
Russell Wlk 4 TW10 6 F1
Russet Ave TW17 34 E6
Russet Cl
Hersham KT12 54 E7
Horley RH6 161 C3
Stanwell TW19 1 F1
Tongham GU10 126 E7
Russet Ct TW13 14 E5
Russet Dr CR0 43 E1
Russet Gdns GU15 65 D3
Russet Glade GU11 125 E8
Russet Ho 4 TW3 4 F3
Russets KT20 97 C4
Russett Ct
Caterham CR3 101 A2
Horsham RH12 218 A4
Russetts Cl GU21 69 F4
Russet Way RH5 136 D4
Russ Hill RH6 180 C5
Russ Hill Cotts RH6 180 C6
Russ Hill Rd RH6 180 D6
Russington Rd TW17 34 D3
Russley Gn RG40 25 A1
Rusthall Cl CR0 43 C3
Rustic Ave SW16 21 B1
Rustic Villas RH9 121 B5
Rustington Wlk SM4 39 F2
Ruston Ave KT5 38 B2
Ruston Cl RH10 202 C3
Ruston Way SL5 28 E7
Rutford Rd SW16 21 E3
Ruth Cl GU14 84 C5
Ruthen Cl KT18 76 B5
Rutherford Cl SM2 59 D4
Rutherford Ct SW19 20 D1
Rutherford Ho 14 TW11 16 F3
Rutherford Way RH10 182 A3
Rutherford Way Ind Est RH10 182 A3
Rutherwick Cl RH6 160 F3
Rutherwick Rise CR5 79 E3
Rutherwyke Cl KT17 58 A4
Rutherwyk Rd KT16 32 E2
Rutland Cl
Aldershot GU11 105 A3
Ashtead KT21 75 E2
Epsom KT19 57 D1
Mitcham SW19 20 E1
Mortlake SW14 7 C4
Redhill RH1 118 F2
Rutland Ct TW2 16 E5
Rutland Dr
Morden SM4 40 A2
Richmond TW10 17 E7
Rutland Gate BR2 44 F5
Rutland Gdns CR0 61 E6
Rutland Lo
Forest Hill SE6 23 F6
Teddington TW11 16 E3
Wimbledon SW19 19 D2
Rutland Pk SE6 23 F6
Rutland Rd
Mitcham SW19 20 E1
Twickenham TW2 16 D6
Rutland Terr GU11 105 A3
Rutland Wlk SE6 23 F6
Rutlish Rd SW19 40 A8
Rutlish Sch (Boys) SW20 39 F7
Rutson Rd KT14 71 F5
Rutter Gdns CR4, SW19 40 D5
Rutton Hill Rd GU8 189 E8
Ruxbury Ct TW15 13 E5
Ruxbury Rd KT16 32 D3
Ruxley Cl KT19 57 B5
Ruxley Cres KT10 56 B3
Ruxley Ct
West Ewell KT19 57 C5
Woking GU22 89 D8
Ruxley Gdns TW17 34 C4
Ruxley La KT19 57 C5
Ruxley Mews KT19 57 B5
Ruxley Ridge KT10 56 A3
Ruxton Cl CR5 79 C4
Ryan Ct SW16 21 E1
Ryan Dr TW8 6 A8
Ryan Mount GU47 64 A8
Rybrook Dr KT12 54 C8
Rycott Path SE22 23 A8
Rydal Cl
Crawley RH11 200 D4
Farnborough GU14 84 D3
Frimley GU15 66 D5
Sanderstead CR8 80 D6
Rydal Ct 1 SW20 39 D8
Rydal Dr BR4 63 E8
Rydal Gdns
Kingston u T SW15 18 E3
Twickenham TW2, TW3 5 B1
Rydal Mount 9 BR2 44 F5
Rydal Pl GU18 67 B8
Rydal Rd SW16 21 D4
Rydal Way TW20 12 B1
Ryde Cl GU23 91 C6
Ryde Ct GU12 105 C1
Ryde Heron GU21 68 E2
Ryde Lands GU6 174 F4
RYDENS 54 B8
Rydens Ave KT12 54 C8
Rydens Cl KT12 54 C8
Rydens Ct KT12 54 C7
Rydens Gr KT12 54 D6
Rydens Pk KT12 54 D8
Rydens Rd KT12 54 C8
Rydens Sch KT12 54 C6
Rydens Way GU22 90 A7
Ryde Pl TW1 6 D1
Ryder Ho 5 SW19 40 B8
Ryders Way RH12 217 F7
Rydes Ave GU2 108 F4
Rydes Cl GU22 90 C7
RYDESHILL 108 E4
Ryde's Hill Cres GU2 108 F5
Rydeshill Prep Sch GU2 108 F3
Ryde's Hill Rd GU2 108 F4
Ryde The TW18 33 B8
Ryde Vale Rd SW12 21 C6
Rydon Bsns Ctr KT22 95 B8
Rydon Mews SW19 19 C1
Rydon's La CR5 100 C7
Rydons Way RH1 140 A8
Rydon's Wood Cl CR5 100 C7
Rye Ash RH10 202 A7
Ryebridge Cl KT22 75 A1
Ryebrook Bsns Pk KT22 95 A7
Rye Brook Rd KT22 75 A1
Rye Cl
Farnborough GU14 84 E7
Guildford GU2 108 E3
Winkfield RG12 27 D8
Ryecotes Mead SE21 22 E7
Ryecroft Ave TW2 16 B7
Ryecroft Dr RH12 217 A3
Ryecroft Gdns GU17 64 E4
Ryecroft Ho SW19 20 B1
Ryecroft Rd SW16 22 A2
Rye Ct BR3 43 F8
Ryedale Ct 10 TW12 36 A8
Rye Field KT21 75 D3
Ryefield Path 7 SW15 19 A7
Ryefield Rd SE19 22 C2
Ryefield Terr SL3 1 D7
Rye Gr
Cranleigh GU6 174 A3
Windlesham GU20, GU18 48 F2
Ryehill Ct KT3 38 F2
Ryelands
Crawley RH11 201 A5
Horley RH6 161 C4
Ryelands Cl CR3 100 E6
Ryelands Ct KT22 75 A1
Ryelands Pl KT13 53 E7
Ryelands Prim Sch SE25 43 B4
Ryemead La SL4 8 C5
Ryersh La RH5 178 C8
Ryfold Rd SW19 20 A5
Rykens La RH3 137 C4
Ryland Cl TW13 14 F4
Rylandes Rd CR2 62 B1
Ryland Ho 11 SW16 21 C3
Ryle Rd GU9 146 B8
Rylton Ho 3 KT12 35 A1
Rymer Rd CR0 42 E2
Rythe Cl KT9 56 C3
Rythe Ct KT7 37 A2
Rythe Ho BR1 24 D3
Rythe Rd KT10 55 E5
Rythe The KT22 55 C1

S

Sabah Ct TW15 14 A4
Sabin Gates RG12 27 B6
Sable Cl TW4 4 C4
Sable Ct 3 KT3 38 E4
Sabre Ct GU11 104 E2
Sachel Court Dr GU6 193 F2
Sachel Court Rd GU6 193 D3
Sackville Cl RH19 185 C3
Sackville Coll* RH19 185 F1
Sackville Cotts RH1 120 D1
Sackville Ct 3 RH19 205 F8
Sackville Gdns RH19 185 C3
Sackville Ho 16 SW16 21 E5
Sackville La RH19 185 C3
Sackville Rd SM2 59 A3
Sackville Sch RH19 186 A1
Saco Ct 5 GU14 85 C1
Sacred Heart Catholic Prim Sch KT3 39 A5
Sacred Heart RC Prim Sch TW11 17 B1
Saddleback Rd GU15 65 E8
Saddlebrook Pk TW16 14 E1
Saddler Cnr GU47 64 B7
Saddler Row RH10 201 D3
Saddlers Ct KT19 76 D6

Saddlers Mews KT1 . . . . . . 37 C8
Saddlers Scarp GU26 . . . . 188 A4
Saddlers Way KT18 . . . . . . 96 D8
Saddlewood GU15 . . . . 65 C4
Sadler Cl CR4 . . . . 40 F7
Sadlers Cl GU4 . . . . 110 D2
Sadlers Ride KT8 . . . . 36 C7
Saffron Cl
Crawley RH11 . . . . 201 A3
Thornton Heath CR0 . . . . . . 41 E3
Saffron Ct
East Bedfont TW14 . . . . 14 C8
Farnborough GU14 . . . . 84 C4
Saffron Ho 6 TW9 . . . . 7 B6
Saffron Platt GU2 . . . . 109 A5
Saffron Rd RG12 . . . . 27 B5
Saffron Way KT6 . . . . 37 D1
Sage Ho RH10 . . . . 182 A1
Sailors La GU8 . . . . 169 A2
Sainfoin Rd SW17 . . . . 21 A6
Sainsbury Ctr The
KT16 . . . . 33 A2
Sainsbury Rd SE19 . . . . 22 E3
St Agatha's Dr KT2 . . . . 17 F2
St Agatha's Gr CR4,
SM5 . . . . 40 F1
St Agatha's RC Prim Sch
KT2 . . . . 17 F2
St Agnes Rd RH19 . . . . 185 E2
St Aidan's RC Prim Sch
CR5 . . . . 79 C3
St Albans Ave
Feltham TW13 . . . . 15 D3
Weybridge KT13 . . . . 53 A7
St Albans Cl GU3 . . . . 108 B2
St Alban's Gdns TW11 . . . . 17 A3
St Alban's Gr SM5 . . . . 40 E2
St Albans Ho 2 SW16 . . . . 22 A4
St Alban's RC Prim Sch
KT8 . . . . 36 C4
St Albans Rd
Cheam SM1 . . . . 58 F6
Kingston u T KT2 . . . . 17 E2
St Alban's Rd RH2 . . . . . . 118 A3
St Alban's Rdbt GU14 . . . . 105 C7
St Amunds Cl SE6 . . . . 24 A4
St Andrews
Bracknell RG12 . . . . 26 E3
Cranleigh GU6 . . . . 174 B4
Horley RH6 . . . . 161 B2
St Andrew's CE High Sch
CR0 . . . . 61 B6
St Andrew's CE Inf Sch
GU9 . . . . 125 B2
St Andrew's CE Prim Sch
Cobham KT11 . . . . 73 C6
Crawley RH10 . . . . 202 A4
St Andrews Cl
Hinchley Wood KT7 . . . . 37 B1
Wimbledon SW19 . . . . 20 B2
Woking GU21 . . . . 69 C2
St Andrew's Cl
Hounslow TW7 . . . . 5 E6
Reigate RH2 . . . . 139 B8
Upper Halliford TW17 . . . . . 34 D5
Wraysbury TW19 . . . . 11 E8
St Andrews Ct
Ascot SL5 . . . . 29 C4
4 Bromley BR1 . . . . 24 E1
Chiswick W4 . . . . 7 C6
St Andrew's Ct
5 Carshalton SM1 . . . . 59 E7
New Malden KT3 . . . . 38 F6
2 Wandsworth SW18 . . . . . 20 C6
St Andrews Gate 2
GU22 . . . . 69 F1
St Andrews Gdns KT11 . . . 73 C6
St Andrews Mews
SW12 . . . . 21 D7
St Andrew's RC Prim Sch
SW16 . . . . 21 E3
St Andrew's RC Sch
KT22 . . . . 95 D7
St Andrews Rd
Carshalton SM5 . . . . 59 E7
Crawley RH11 . . . . 200 D5
St Andrew's Rd
Coulsdon CR5 . . . . 79 B4
3 Croydon CR0, CR9 . . . . . 61 C6
Kingston u T KT6 . . . . 37 D3
St Andrew's & St Mark's
CE Jun Sch KT6 . . . . 37 D4
St Andrew's Sch GU21 . . . 69 D3
St Andrew's Sch, The
Grange KT22 . . . . 95 D7
St Andrew's Sq KT6 . . . . . . 37 D3
St Andrews Way RH8 . . . . 123 F4
St Andrew's Way GU16 . . . 85 F7
St Andrew's Wlk KT11 . . . . 73 B4
St Annes 13 SM2 . . . . 59 B4
St Anne's Ave TW19 . . . . . . 13 D8
St Annes Bvd RH1 . . . . 119 B3
St Annes Dr RG40 . . . . 26 A6
St Anne's Dr RH1 . . . . 119 A2
St Annes Dr N RH1 . . . . . . 119 A3
St Annes Glade GU19 . . . . . 47 D3
St Annes Mount 7
RH1 . . . . 119 A2
St Anne's RC Prim Sch
Banstead SM7 . . . . 78 A3
Chertsey KT16 . . . . 33 A1
St Anne's Rd
Crawley RH10 . . . . 182 C2
Godalming GU7 . . . . 151 A5
St Annes Rise RH1 . . . . . . 119 A2
St Annes Way 5 RH1 . . . 119 A2
St Ann's Cl KT16 . . . . 32 F3
ST ANN'S HEATH 31 F5
St Ann's Heath Jun Sch
GU25 . . . . 31 E4
St Ann's Hill SW18 . . . . 20 C8
St Ann's Hill Rd KT16 . . . . . 32 D3
St Anns Rd SW13 . . . . 7 F6
St Ann's Rd KT16 . . . . 32 F3
St Ann's Sch SM4 . . . . 40 B4
St Ann's Way CR2 . . . . 61 B4
St Anselm's Ct SW16 . . . . . 21 E3
St Anselm's RC Prim Sch
SW17 . . . . 21 A5
St Anthonys Cl
Bracknell RG42 . . . . 27 A8
Upper Tooting SW17 . . . . . . 20 E6
St Anthony's Ct
1 Balham SW12 . . . . 21 A8
Upper Tooting SW17 . . . . . . 21 A6
St Anthony's Hospl
KT4 . . . . 39 D1
St Anthony's RC Prim Sch
SE20 . . . . 43 B8
St Anthony's Way TW14 . . . . 3 F3
St Arvans Cl CR0 . . . . 61 E7
St Aubin Cl RH11 . . . . 200 F2
St Aubyn's Ave
Hounslow TW3, TW4 . . . . 5 A2
Wimbledon SW19 . . . . 19 F3
St Aubyn's Ct SW19 . . . . . . 19 E2
St Aubyn's Rd SE19 . . . . . . 22 F2
St Augustine's Ave
Croydon CR2 . . . . 61 C3
South Croydon CR2 . . . . 61 C3
St Augustine's Cl
GU12 . . . . 105 D1
St Augustines Ct BR3 . . . . 43 E7
St Augustine's Ho
SW17 . . . . 20 F4
St Augustine's RC Prim
Sch GU16 . . . . 65 F2
St Augustines's RC Prim
Sch SE6 . . . . 24 C3
St Austells Pl RH5 . . . . . . 157 C7
St Austins GU26 . . . . 188 D3
St Barnabas Cl BR3 . . . . . . 44 C7
St Barnabas Ct RH10 . . . . 202 C7
St Barnabas' Gdns KT8 . . . 36 A4
St Barnabas Ho CR4 . . . . . 21 A1
St Barnabas Rd
Carshalton SM1 . . . . 59 D5
Mitcham CR4 . . . . 21 A1
St Bartholomew's CE Prim
Sch
Forest Hill SE26 . . . . 23 C4
Haslemere GU27 . . . . 208 C7
St Bartholomew's Cl
SE26 . . . . 23 C4
St Bartholomew's Ct
GU1 . . . . 130 F7
St Bede's CE Jun Sch
GU23 . . . . 90 D3
St Bede's RC Inf Sch
SW12 . . . . 21 D7
St Bede's Sch RH1 . . . . . . 118 E4
St Benedict's Cl
Aldershot GU11 . . . . 105 A1
Upper Tooting SW17 . . . . . . 21 A3
St Benets Cl SW17 . . . . 20 E6
St Benet's Gr SM4, SM5 . . . 40 C2
St Bernadette RC Jun Sch
SW12 . . . . 21 C8
St Bernadette RC Prim
Sch GU14 . . . . 85 A5
St Bernards CR0 . . . . 61 E7
St Bernards Cl 8 SE27 . . . 22 D4
St Bernards Ho 7 KT6 . . . . 56 E8
St Boniface RC Prim Sch
SW17 . . . . 20 F3
St Brelades Cl RH4 . . . . . . 136 A5
St Brelades Rd RH11 . . . . 200 F2
St Catherines
Weybridge KT13 . . . . 53 B7
Woking GU22 . . . . 89 C8
St Catherines Cl
Chessington KT9 . . . . 56 D4
Upper Tooting SW17 . . . . . . 20 E6
St Catherine's Cross
RH1 . . . . 120 E2
St Catherines Ct
Feltham TW13 . . . . 15 A7
2 Staines TW18 . . . . 13 A4
St Catherine's Ct
RH19 . . . . 185 D2
St Catherine's Dr GU2 . . . 130 B5
St Catherine's Hill
GU2 . . . . 130 C5
St Catherine's Jun Sch
GU5 . . . . 151 F6
St Catherine's Pk
GU1 . . . . 130 F7
St Catherines Pl TW20 . . . 12 A3
St Catherines Rd
Crawley RH10 . . . . 182 D1
Frimley GU16 . . . . 86 A8
St Catherines Sch
RH1 . . . . 120 E2
St Catherine's Sch
Bramley GU5 . . . . 151 F7
Twickenham TW1 . . . . 17 A6
St Catherines Wood
GU15 . . . . 65 C4
St Cecilia's CE Sch
SW18 . . . . 19 F8
St Cecilias Cl SM3 . . . . 39 E1
St Cecilia's RC Prim Sch
SM3 . . . . 58 D8
St Chads Cl KT6 . . . . 37 C2
St Chad's RC Prim Sch
SE25 . . . . 42 E4
St Charles Borromeo RC
Prim Sch KT13 . . . . 53 A7
St Charles Ct KT13 . . . . 53 A5
St Charles Pl KT13 . . . . 53 A5
St Christopher's RH7 . . . . 164 D4
St Christophers Cl
Aldershot GU12 . . . . 105 D2
5 Horsham RH12 . . . . 217 C4
St Christopher's Cl
Haslemere GU27 . . . . 208 A6
Hounslow TW7 . . . . 5 E6
St Christophers Gdns
North Ascot SL5 . . . . 28 D8
Thornton Heath CR7 . . . . . . 42 A6
St Christopher's Gn
GU27 . . . . 208 A6
St Christopher's Hospice
SE26 . . . . 23 C3
St Christopher's Mews
SM6 . . . . 60 C5
St Christophers Pl 1
GU14 . . . . 85 A3
St Christopher's Rd
2 Farnborough GU14 . . . . . 85 A3
Haslemere GU27 . . . . 208 A6
St Christopher's Sch
Beckenham BR3 . . . . 44 C7
Epsom KT18 . . . . 76 E5
St Clair Cl
Oxted RH8 . . . . 122 D5
Reigate RH2 . . . . 118 C1
St Clair Cotts RH7 . . . . . . 165 B1
St Clair Dr KT4 . . . . 58 B6
St Clair's Rd CR0 . . . . 61 E8
St Clare Bsns Pk TW12 . . . 16 C2
St Clare Ct BR3 . . . . 24 B1
St Clement Rd RH11 . . . . 200 F2
St Clements Ct GU14 . . . . . 85 B7
St Clements Ho 3
KT12 . . . . 35 A2
St Clements RC Prim Sch
KT17 . . . . 57 F2
St Cloud Rd SE27 . . . . 22 D4
St Crispin Ho CR0 . . . . 61 D7
St Crispin's Sch RG40 . . . . 25 E6
St Crispins Way KT16 . . . . 51 C2
St Cross Rd
Farnham GU9 . . . . 125 C3
Frimley GU16 . . . . 86 B7
St Cuthbert Mayne RC
Prim Sch GU6 . . . . 174 E3
St Cuthbert's Cl TW20 . . . . 11 D2
St Cuthbert's RC Prim Sch
TW20 . . . . 11 C1
St Cyprian's Greek
Orthodox Prim Sch
CR7 . . . . 42 C8
St Cyprian's St SW17 . . . . . 20 F4
St David's CR5 . . . . 79 F2
St David's Cl
Farnborough GU14 . . . . 84 F8
Heath End GU9 . . . . 125 E7
Reigate RH2 . . . . 118 C2
West Wickham BR4 . . . . 44 B2
St David's Coll BR4 . . . . . . 44 B2
St Davids Ct
4 Aldershot GU12 . . . . . . 105 B1
Ashford TW15 . . . . 13 F6
St Davids Dr TW20 . . . . 11 C1
St David's Sch TW15 . . . . . 13 F5
St Denis Rd SE27 . . . . 22 D4
St Denys Cl CR8 . . . . 61 B1
St Deny's Cl GU21 . . . . 68 D1
St Dominic Cl GU14 . . . . . . 85 A8
St Dominic's Sch GU8 . . . . 171 C1
St Dunstan's Cheam CE
Prim Sch SM3 . . . . 58 E3
St Dunstan's Coll SE6 . . . . 24 A7
St Dunstan's Hill SM1,
SM3 . . . . 58 E5
St Dunstan's La BR3 . . . . . 44 C4
St Dunstan's RC Prim Sch
GU22 . . . . 70 A2
St Dunstan's Rd
Cranford TW5 . . . . 4 B5
Feltham TW13 . . . . 14 F5
South Norwood SE25 . . . . . . 42 F5
St Ebba's Hospl KT19 . . . . . 57 C2
St Edith Cl KT18 . . . . 76 C5
St Edmunds Cl
Crawley RH11 . . . . 181 D1
Upper Tooting SW17 . . . . . . 20 E6
St Edmund's La TW2 . . . . . 16 B8
St Edmund's RC Prim Sch
Godalming GU7 . . . . 150 F2
Twickenham TW2 . . . . 16 B8
St Edmunds Sch
GU26 . . . . 188 D3
St Edwards Cl CR0 . . . . 82 D8
St Edward's Cl RH19 . . . . 185 C1
St Elizabeth Dr KT18 . . . . . 76 C5
St Elizabeth's RC Prim Sch
TW10 . . . . 6 F1
St Elphege's RC Inf Sch
SM6 . . . . 60 E4
St Elphege's RC Jun Sch
SM6 . . . . 60 E4
SS Peter & Paul's RC Prim
Sch CR4 . . . . 40 F5
St Faith's Rd SE24 . . . . 22 B7
St Fillans GU22 . . . . 70 B3
St Fillans Rd SE6 . . . . 24 C8
St Francis Gdns RH10 . . . 183 C4
St Francis of Assisi RC
Prim Sch RH10 . . . . 201 E4
St Francis RC Prim Sch
Ascot SL5 . . . . 29 A3
Whyteleafe CR3 . . . . 100 F6
St Francis Wlk RH11 . . . . 200 E4
St Georges RH6 . . . . 161 B2
St George's Ave KT13 . . . . 53 C4
St George's Bsns Ctr
KT13 . . . . 53 A2
St Georges Cl RH6 . . . . . . 161 B3
St George's Cl
Badshot Lea GU9 . . . . 126 B6
Weybridge KT13 . . . . 53 C5
St George's Coll KT15 . . . . 52 D7
St Georges Coll Jun Sch
KT15 . . . . 52 D7
St George's Coll Jun Sch
KT13 . . . . 53 B7
St Georges Cotts KT13 . . . 53 C5
St George's Cotts
RH7 . . . . 143 E4
St Georges Ct
Addlestone KT15 . . . . 52 C6
Crawley RH10 . . . . 201 D8
East Grinstead RH19 . . . . . 185 C3
Penge SE20 . . . . 43 B8
Weybridge KT13 . . . . 53 C4
St George's Ct GU47 . . . . . 45 E2
St George's Gate KT15 . . . 52 D7
St George's Gdns
Epsom KT17 . . . . 76 F5
Horsham RH13 . . . . 217 E4
Tolworth KT6 . . . . 57 B8
St George's Gr SW17 . . . . . 20 D5
ST GEORGE'S HILL 53 C1
St George's Hospl
SW17 . . . . 20 D3
St Georges Ind Est
GU15 . . . . 65 B3
St George's Ind Est
KT2 . . . . 17 D3
St George's La SL5 . . . . 29 B5
St George's Lo KT13 . . . . . 53 D5
St Georges Mews
GU9 . . . . 125 C3
St Georges Rd
Addlestone KT15 . . . . 52 C6
Badshot Lea GU9 . . . . 126 B5
St George's Rd
Beckenham BR3 . . . . 44 B8
Camberley GU15 . . . . 65 D6
Farnham GU9 . . . . 125 D1
Feltham TW13 . . . . 15 D4
Isleworth TW1 . . . . 6 B2
2 Kingston u T KT2 . . . . . . 18 A1
Mitcham CR4 . . . . 41 B6
Richmond TW9 . . . . 6 F4
South Nutfield RH1 . . . . . . 140 E1
Wallington SM6 . . . . 60 B5
Weybridge KT13 . . . . 53 D4
Wimbledon SW19 . . . . 19 F2
St George's Rd E 6
GU12 . . . . 105 B1
St George's Sch SL5 . . . . . 29 B6
St George's Sq KT3 . . . . . . 38 E6
St George's Wlk CR0,
CR9 . . . . 61 C7
St Georges Wood
GU27 . . . . 208 D8
St Georges Yd 5
GU9 . . . . 125 B2
St German's Rd SE23 . . . . . 23 E7
St Giles CE Inf Sch
KT21 . . . . 75 F1
St Giles Cl TW5 . . . . 4 E7
St Giles Sch CR2 . . . . 61 B4
St Gothard Rd SE27 . . . . . . 22 D4
St Helena Terr 32 TW9 . . . . 6 D2
St Helens KT7 . . . . 36 F2
St Helens Cres GU47 . . . . . 64 B8
St Helen's Cres SW16 . . . . 41 F8
St Helen's Rd SW16 . . . . . . 41 F8
ST HELIER 40 D2
St Helier Ave SM4 . . . . 40 C3
St Helier Cl
Crawley RH11 . . . . 201 A2
Wokingham RG41 . . . . 25 B3
St Helier Hospl SM5 . . . . . 40 C1
St Heliers Ave TW3, TW4 . . . 5 A2
St Helier Sta SM4 . . . . 40 A3
St Hilary's Sch GU7 . . . . . 150 D3
St Hilda's Ave TW15 . . . . . . 13 E3
St Hildas Cl SW17 . . . . 20 E6
St Hilda's Cl
Crawley RH10 . . . . 182 C1
Horley RH6 . . . . 161 B3
Knaphill GU21 . . . . 68 D2
Saint Hill Gn RH19 . . . . . . 205 D4
Saint Hill Manor*
RH19 . . . . 205 C4
Saint Hill Rd RH19 . . . . . . 205 C5
St Hughes Cl SW17 . . . . 20 E6
St Hugh of Lincoln RC
Prim Sch GU21 . . . . 88 D8
St Hugh's Cl RH10 . . . . . . 182 C1
St Hugh's Rd SE20 . . . . 23 B1
St Ignatius RC Prim Sch
TW16 . . . . 35 A8
St Ives RH10 . . . . 202 C7
St Ives Sch GU27 . . . . 208 E8
St James Ave
Ewell KT17 . . . . 77 A8
Sutton SM1 . . . . 59 A5
St James' Ave GU9 . . . . . . 125 D3
St James CE Prim Sch
Elstead GU8 . . . . 148 C3
Weybridge KT13 . . . . 53 C7
St James Cl
Epsom KT18 . . . . 76 E5
St James Cl *continued*
Woking GU21 . . . . 69 A1
St James' Cl KT3 . . . . 38 F4
St James Ct
Ashtead KT21 . . . . 75 D2
East Grinstead RH19 . . . . . 185 E1
Farnham GU9 . . . . 125 C3
Forest Hill SE23 . . . . 23 E7
Thornton Heath CR0 . . . . . . 42 B2
St James' Ct
7 Kingston u T KT1 . . . . . . 37 E6
12 Surbiton KT6 . . . . 37 E3
St James Gate SL5 . . . . 30 A2
St James Ho
7 Banstead SM7 . . . . 77 F5
Woking GU21 . . . . 69 B1
St James Ind Sch for Boys
TW1 . . . . 17 A6
St James Mews KT13 . . . . . 53 B6
St James Rd
Carshalton SM5 . . . . 59 E7
East Grinstead RH19 . . . . . 185 D1
Sutton SM1 . . . . 59 A5
St James' Rd
Kingston u T KT6 . . . . 37 D3
Mitcham CR4 . . . . 21 A1
Purley CR8 . . . . 80 C6
St James's Ave
Beckenham BR3 . . . . 43 E6
Hampton TW12 . . . . 16 C3
St James's Cl SW17 . . . . . . 20 F6
St James's Cotts 13
TW10 . . . . 6 D2
St James's Dr
Balham SW12, SW17 . . . . . . 20 F8
Upper Tooting SW17 . . . . . . 20 F7
St James's Lo 4 CR0 . . . . . 42 E1
St James's Pk CR0 . . . . 42 C2
St James's Pl GU6 . . . . . . 174 C3
St James's RC Prim Sch
TW2 . . . . 16 E5
St James's Rd
Hampton TW12 . . . . 16 B3
Kingston u T KT1 . . . . 37 D7
Thornton Heath CR0 . . . . . . 42 D2
St James's Terr 2
SW12 . . . . 21 A7
St James' Terr GU9 . . . . . 125 C3
St James The Great RC
Prim Sch CR7 . . . . 42 B7
St James Wlk RH11 . . . . . 201 C2
St Joan Cl RH11 . . . . 181 D1
St John Baptist CE Prim
Sch BR1 . . . . 24 C4
St John Cl RH13 . . . . 217 E1
St John Fisher RC Prim
Sch SW20 . . . . 39 D4
ST JOHNS 139 E7
ST JOHN'S 89 B8
St John's RH5 . . . . 136 C3
St Johns Ave KT17 . . . . 77 A7
St John's Ave KT22 . . . . 95 B6
St John's Beaumont Sch
SL4 . . . . 11 B6
St John's CE Com Prim
Sch RH4 . . . . 136 B4
St John's CE Fst Sch
GU10 . . . . 167 E1
St John's CE Prim Sch
Caterham CR3 . . . . 101 B2
Croydon CR0 . . . . 62 D7
Kingston u T KT1 . . . . 37 E6
Penge SE20 . . . . 23 C1
St Johns Church Rd
RH5 . . . . 134 F4
St John's Cl
East Grinstead RH19 . . . . . 185 E2
Guildford GU2 . . . . 130 A8
Leatherhead KT22 . . . . 95 C7
St John's Cotts
2 Penge SE20 . . . . 23 C1
Richmond TW9 . . . . 6 E4
St John's Cres RH12 . . . . 216 E3
St Johns Ct
Egham TW20 . . . . 12 A3
South Godstone RH9 . . . . . 142 F5
Woking GU21 . . . . 89 A8
St John's Ct
Brookwood GU24 . . . . 87 F7
Farnborough GU14 . . . . 84 D5
Isleworth TW7 . . . . 5 F5
Kingston u T KT1 . . . . 37 E5
Westcott RH4 . . . . 135 C6
St Johns Dr KT12 . . . . 35 C1
St John's Dr SW18 . . . . 20 B7
St Johns Gdns GU21 . . . . . . 69 A1
St Johns Gr GU9 . . . . 146 B8
St John's Gr
Barnes SW13 . . . . 7 F5
1 Richmond TW9 . . . . 6 E3
St John's Hill CR8 . . . . 80 A2
St John's Hill Rd GU21 . . . 89 B8
St John's Ho SW16 . . . . 21 E2
St Johns Lo GU21 . . . . 89 A8
St John's Lye GU21 . . . . . . 88 F8
**St John's Lye (Festival
Path)** GU21 . . . . 88 F8
St John's Mdw RH7 . . . . . 163 E8
St Johns Mews GU21 . . . . . 89 A8
St John's Prim Sch
Knaphill GU21 . . . . 68 E1
Redhill RH1 . . . . 139 E7
St John's RC Prim Sch
RH12 . . . . 217 A1
St Johns Rd KT3 . . . . 38 C6
St John's Rd
Carshalton SM5 . . . . 59 E7
Crawley RH11 . . . . 201 C6

St John's Rd continued
Croydon CR0, CR9 . . . . **61** B7
East Grinstead RH19 . . . . . . **185** E2
East Molesey KT8 . . . . **36** D5
Farnborough GU14 . . . . **84** E5
Farnham GU9 . . . . **146** B8
Feltham TW13 . . . . **15** F4
Guildford GU2 . . . . **130** A8
Isleworth TW7 . . . . **5** F5
Leatherhead KT22 . . . . **95** C6
North Ascot SL5 . . . . **8** F1
Penge SE20 . . . . **23** C2
Redhill RH1 . . . . **139** F7
Richmond TW9 . . . . **6** E3
Sandhurst GU47 . . . . **64** C7
Sutton SM1 . . . . **59** B8
Teddington KT1 . . . . **37** C7
Westcott RH4 . . . . **135** C6
Wimbledon SW19 . . . . **19** E2
Woking GU21 . . . . **69** B2
St John's Rise GU21 . . . . . **89** B8
St John's Sch KT22 . . . . . . **95** B6
St Johns St RG45 . . . . **45** B5
St John's St GU7 . . . . **150** F6
St John's Terrace Rd
RH1 . . . . **139** F7
St Johns Waterside [7]
GU21 . . . . **68** F1
St Johns Way KT16 . . . . . . **33** A1
St John the Baptist CE Jun
Sch KT1 . . . . **17** D1
St John The Baptist RC
Comp Sch GU2 . . . . **90** A8
St Joseph's Coll SW16 . . . **22** B2
St Joseph's RC Inf Sch
SE19 . . . . **22** C2
St Joseph's RC Jun Sch
SE19 . . . . **22** C2
St Josephs RC Prim Sch
GU11 . . . . **126** A8
St Joseph's RC Prim Sch
Bracknell RG12 . . . . **27** D7
Dorking RH4 . . . . **136** A7
Epsom KT18 . . . . **76** C5
Guildford GU2 . . . . **108** F3
Kingston u T KT1 . . . . **37** F7
Redhill RH1 . . . . **118** E2
St Joseph's Rd GU12 . . . . **105** A1
St Joseph's Sch GU2 . . . . **174** F6
St Jude's CE Sch TW20 . . . **11** C2
St Jude's Cl TW20 . . . . . . **11** C3
St Jude's Cotts TW20 . . . . **11** C3
St Jude's Rd TW20 . . . . . . **11** C3
St Julian [5] RH19 . . . . . . **185** F2
St Julian's Cl SW16 . . . . . **22** A4
St Julian's Farm Rd SE27,
SW16 . . . . **22** B4
St Katharines Rd CR3 . . . **101** A2
St Kitts Terr SE19 . . . . . . **22** E3
St Lawrence CE Jun Sch
KT8 . . . . **36** D5
St Lawrence Ct GU24 . . . . **68** E8
St Lawrence Prim Sch
KT24 . . . . **113** D8
St Lawrence RC Prim Sch
TW13 . . . . **15** B6
St Lawrences Way
RH2 . . . . **118** A1
St Lawrence Way
CR3 . . . . **100** D4
St Leonards RH12 . . . . . . **217** F4
St Leonard's CE Prim Sch
SW16 . . . . **21** D3
St Leonards Ct SW14 . . . . . **7** C4
St Leonards Dr RH10 . . . . **202** A4
St Leonard's Gdns TW5 . . . **4** E6
St Leonard's Park Ho
RH13 . . . . **218** C3
St Leonards Pk RH19 . . . . **185** E1
St Leonards Rd
Burgh Heath KT18 . . . . **97** C8
Horsham RH13 . . . . **218** A1
Mortlake SW14 . . . . **7** C4
St Leonard's Rd
Claygate KT10 . . . . **55** F4
Croydon CR0, CR9 . . . . **61** B7
Kingston u T KT6 . . . . **37** D4
Thames Ditton KT7 . . . . **37** D4
Windsor SL4 . . . . **9** D8
St Leonard's Sq KT6 . . . . . **37** D4
St Leonard's Wlk SW16 . . . **21** F1
St Louis Ct SE27 . . . . **22** D4
St Louis Rd SE27 . . . . **22** D4
St Luke's CE Prim Sch
Kingston u T KT2 . . . . **37** F8
West Norwood SE27 . . . . . . **22** C3
St Luke's Cl SE25 . . . . . . **43** B3
St Lukes Ct GU21 . . . . **70** C5
St Lukes Mews CR3 . . . . . **80** F1
St Luke's Rd CR3 . . . . . . **80** F1
St Luke's Sq [9] GU1 . . . . **130** F8
St Margaret Clitherow RC
Prim Sch RG12 . . . . **26** F2
St Margaret Dr KT18 . . . . . **76** C5
ST MARGARETS **6** B1
St Margaret's GU1 . . . . . **109** F1
St Margarets Ave
TW15 . . . . **14** B3
St Margaret's Ave
Cheam SM3 . . . . **58** E7
Dormans Park RH19 . . . . . . **185** A4
St Margarets Bsns Ctr [11]
TW1 . . . . **6** B1
St Margaret's CE Prim Sch
RH11 . . . . **201** B7
St Margaret's Ct [9] TW1 . . **6** B1
St Margaret's Dr TW1 . . . . **6** B2

St Margaret's Gr TW1 . . . . . **6** A1
St Margaret's Rd
East Grinstead RH19 . . . . . **185** F3
Hooley CR5 . . . . **99** B6
Isleworth TW1 . . . . **6** B2
St Margaret's Sta TW1 . . . . **6** B1
St Mark's CE Acad CR4 . . . **41** B7
St Mark's CE Prim Sch
Bromley BR2 . . . . **44** F6
Croydon SE25 . . . . **43** A5
Farnborough GU14 . . . . . . **105** D8
Godalming GU7 . . . . **150** B3
St Marks Cl GU14 . . . . . . **85** C1
St Mark's Ct [9] GU22 . . . . **89** E8
St Mark's Hill KT6 . . . . . . **37** E3
St Mark's Hts [26] KT6 . . . **37** E4
St Mark's La RH12 . . . . . . **217** E6
St Mark's Pl GU9 . . . . . . **125** B7
St Mark's Pl SW19 . . . . . . **19** F2
St Mark's Prim Sch
CR4 . . . . **40** F7
St Mark's RC Sch TW3 . . . . **5** A4
St Marks Rd KT18, KT20 . . **77** C1
St Mark's Rd
Bracknell RG42 . . . . **26** C8
Croydon SE25 . . . . **43** A5
Teddington TW11 . . . . **17** B1
St Martha's Ave GU22 . . . . **89** F6
St Martha's Cotts
GU5 . . . . **154** E8
St Martha's Ct GU4 . . . . . **131** B3
St Martin in the Fields
High Sch for Girls
SW2 . . . . **22** A7
St Martin's Ave KT18 . . . . **76** E5
St Martin's CE Inf Sch
KT18 . . . . **76** D4
St Martin's CE Jun Sch
KT18 . . . . **76** D4
St Martin's CE Prim Sch
RH4 . . . . **136** A8
St Martin's CE Prim Sch
(Pixham) RH4 . . . . **115** C1
St Martins Cl KT24 . . . . . **112** E6
St Martin's Cl KT17 . . . . . **76** E6
St Martins Ct KT24 . . . . . **112** E6
St Martin's Ct
Staines TW15 . . . . **13** C3
West Norwood SE27 . . . . . . **22** B6
St Martins Dr KT12 . . . . . **54** C7
St Martin's La BR3 . . . . . **44** B4
St Martins Mews [4]
RH4 . . . . **136** A7
St Martin's Mews
GU22 . . . . **71** A3
St Martin's Sq RH4 . . . . **136** A8
St Martin's Way SW17 . . . **20** C5
St Martin's Wlk [4]
RH4 . . . . **136** B8
St Mary Ave SM6 . . . . . . **60** B7
St Mary Magdalen's RC
Prim Sch SW14 . . . . **7** D4
St Mary's [4] KT13 . . . . . . **53** D7
St Mary's Abbey
GU27 . . . . **207** D3
St Mary's Ave
Beckenham BR2 . . . . **44** E6
Stanwell TW19 . . . . **13** D8
Teddington TW11 . . . . **16** F2
St Mary's CE Inf Sch
Frensham GU10 . . . . **167** D7
Shackleford GU8 . . . . **149** E6
St Mary's CE Jun Sch
RH8 . . . . **122** E7
St Mary's CE Prim Sch
GU8 . . . . **191** C4
St Mary's CE Prim Sch
Byfleet KT14 . . . . **71** E6
Chessington KT9 . . . . **56** F4
Horsham RH12 . . . . **217** C1
Long Ditton KT7 . . . . **37** B1
Twickenham TW1 . . . . **17** A8
St Mary's CE Prim Sch
(Jun) TW1 . . . . **17** B8
St Mary's CE Sch
RH19 . . . . **185** D2
St Marys Cl GU47 . . . . . . **64** C8
St Mary's Cl
Chessington KT9 . . . . **56** F3
Ewell KT17 . . . . **57** F2
Fetcham KT22 . . . . **94** D4
Oxted RH8 . . . . **122** E6
Stanwell TW19 . . . . **13** D8
Sunbury TW16 . . . . **35** A5
St Mildred's Rd
SE12 . . . . **35** F8
St Marys Cotts GU10 . . . **167** C7
St Mary's Cres
Hounslow TW7 . . . . **5** E7
Stanwell TW19 . . . . **13** D8
St Mary's Ct
Kingston u T KT3 . . . . **38** E6
Wallington SM6 . . . . **60** C6
West Byfleet KT14 . . . . **71** E7
St Mary's Dr
Crawley RH10 . . . . **202** B8
East Bedfont TW14 . . . . . . **14** C8
St Mary's Gdns
Bagshot GU19 . . . . **47** E3
Horsham RH12 . . . . **217** C1
St Mary's Gn TN16 . . . . . **83** C1
St Mary's Gr
Biggin Hill TN16 . . . . **83** C1
Chiswick W4 . . . . **7** B8
Richmond TW10, TW9 . . . . . **6** F3
St Mary's High Sch
CR0 . . . . **42** C1
St Mary's Hill SL5 . . . . . . **29** C4

St Mary's Ho [5] RH12 . . . **217** C1
St Mary Homes RH9 . . . . **121** D3
St Marys La SL4 . . . . **8** D5
St Mary's Mews TW10 . . . **17** C6
St Mary's Mill GU8 . . . . . **191** C3
St Mary's Mt CR3 . . . . . . **100** F3
St Mary's Pl GU9 . . . . . . **125** C3
St Mary's RC Inf Sch
Carshalton SM5 . . . . **59** F6
Croydon CR0 . . . . **42** D1
St Mary's RC Jun Sch
Croydon CR0 . . . . **42** D1
Wallington SM5 . . . . **59** F7
St Marys Rd KT22 . . . . . . **95** B4
St Mary's Rd
Ascot SL5 . . . . **29** B3
Ash Vale GU12 . . . . **106** A5
Camberley GU15 . . . . **65** C6
East Molesey KT8 . . . . **36** D4
Kingston u T KT6 . . . . **37** D3
Long Ditton KT6 . . . . **37** C1
Oatlands Park KT13 . . . . . . **53** D6
Reigate RH2 . . . . **139** B8
South Croydon CR2 . . . . . . **61** D2
South Norwood SE25 . . . . . **42** E6
Wimbledon SW19 . . . . **19** F3
Woking GU21 . . . . **69** C2
Worcester Park KT4 . . . . . . **57** E8
St Mary's & St Peter's CE
Prim Sch TW11 . . . . **16** F3
St Mary's Jun Sch SL5 . . . **29** B2
St Mary's Univ Coll
TW1 . . . . **16** F5
St Marys Way GU2 . . . . . **108** E3
St Matthew's Ave KT6 . . . . **37** E1
St Matthew's CE Inf Sch
KT11 . . . . **73** B1
St Matthew's CE Prim Sch
Redhill RH1 . . . . **118** F3
Surbiton KT6 . . . . **37** E2
Wimbledon SW20 . . . . **39** A8
St Matthew's Ct [1]
TW15 . . . . **14** A3
St Matthew's Rd RH1 . . . **118** F2
St Merryn Ct BR3 . . . . . . **24** A1
St Michael RC Prim Sch
TW15 . . . . **14** A3
St Michaels RH8 . . . . **123** A5
St Michael's Ave GU3 . . . **108** C6
St Michael's CE Fst Sch
RH5 . . . . **115** C4
St Michaels CE Inf Sch
GU11 . . . . **126** B8
St Michael's CE Jun Sch
GU11 . . . . **126** C8
St Michael's CE Prim Sch
Forest Hill SE26 . . . . **23** E4
Wandsworth SW18 . . . . **19** F8
St Michaels Cl KT4 . . . . . . **57** F8
St Michael's Cl KT12 . . . . **54** C8
St Michaels Cotts
RG40 . . . . **45** C8
St Michaels Ct [4] KT13 . . **53** C5
St Michael's
Easthampstead CE Prim
Sch RG12 . . . . **27** A4
St Michael's Hall
GU11 . . . . **126** B8
St Michaels Ho [1]
SE26 . . . . **23** F4
St Michael's Pl GU15 . . . . **65** B5
St Michaels Rd
Ashford TW15 . . . . **14** A3
Camberley GU15 . . . . **65** B5
Caterham CR3 . . . . **100** D5
East Grinstead RH19 . . . . . **185** E2
St Michael's Rd
Aldershot GU11,
GU12 . . . . **105** B1
Croydon CR0 . . . . **42** C1
Farnborough GU14 . . . . . . **85** B6
Sheerwater GU21 . . . . **70** D5
Wallington SM6 . . . . **60** C4
St Michael's & St Martin's
RC Prim Sch TW4 . . . . **4** F4
St Micheal's CE Prim Sch
SL5 . . . . **29** D4
St Mildreds Rd SE12,
SE6 . . . . **24** F8
St Mildred's Rd GU1 . . . . **109** F2
St Monica's Rd KT20 . . . . **97** F6
St Nazaire Cl TW20 . . . . . **12** C3
St Nicholas Ave KT23 . . . . **94** B2
St Nicholas CE Prim
Federal Sch GU6 . . . . . . **174** D3
St Nicholas CE Prim Sch
TW17 . . . . **34** B3
St Nicholas Cres GU22 . . . **71** A3
St Nicholas Ct RH10 . . . . **202** C7
St Nicholas Ctr [7] SM1 . . **59** B5
St Nicholas Dr TW17 . . . . **34** A2
St Nicholas Glebe
SW17 . . . . **21** A2
St Nicholas Hill KT22 . . . . **95** B5
St Nicholas Ho [2] CR0 . . . **61** E8
St Nicholas Mans
SW17 . . . . **20** F6
St Nicholas Rd
Sutton SM1 . . . . **59** B5
Thames Ditton KT7 . . . . **36** F3
St Nicholas Sch
Merstham RH1 . . . . **119** D6

St Nicholas Sch continued
Purley CR8 . . . . **80** A6
St Nicholas Way SM1 . . . . **59** B5
St Nicolas Ave GU6 . . . . . **174** E3
St Nicolas CE Inf Sch
GU2 . . . . **130** C7
St Nicolas Cl GU6 . . . . . . **174** E3
St Normans Way KT17 . . . **58** A1
St Olave's Cl TW18 . . . . . **12** F1
St Olave's Wlk SW16 . . . . **41** D7
St Omer Rd GU1 . . . . **131** A8
St Omer Ridge GU1 . . . . . **131** A8
St Osmund's RC Prim Sch
SW13 . . . . **7** F6
St Oswald's Rd SW16 . . . . **42** B8
St Patrick's RC Prim Sch
GU14 . . . . **85** D4
St Paul's CE Inf Sch
TW8 . . . . **6** D8
St Paul's CE Prim Sch
Addlestone KT15 . . . . **52** A6
Chessington KT9 . . . . **56** E6
Dorking RH4 . . . . **136** B6
TW8 . . . . **6** D8
St Pauls Cl GU10 . . . . . . **126** F7
St Paul's Cl
Addlestone KT15 . . . . **52** A5
Ashford TW15 . . . . **14** C3
Carshalton SM5 . . . . **40** E1
Chessington KT9 . . . . **56** D6
Hounslow TW3, TW4 . . . . . . **4** E5
St Paul's Conversion
SE23 . . . . **23** C6
St Pauls Ct TW4 . . . . **4** E4
St Paul's Gate RG41 . . . . . **25** A6
St Pauls Mews RH4 . . . . **136** B6
St Paul's RC Coll TW16 . . . **35** A8
St Paul's RC Prim Sch
KT7 . . . . **36** E2
St Pauls Rd
Richmond TW9 . . . . **6** F4
Woking GU22 . . . . **70** B2
St Paul's Rd
Brentford TW8 . . . . **6** D8
Egham TW18 . . . . **12** D2
South Norwood CR7 . . . . . . **42** C6
St Paul's Rd E RH4,
RH5 . . . . **136** B7
St Paul's Rd W RH4 . . . . **136** B6
St Peter & St Paul CE Inf
Sch CR3 . . . . **100** A2
St Peter's CE Inf Sch
RH8 . . . . **122** A1
St Peter's CE Jun Sch
GU14 . . . . **85** C4
St Peters CE Prim Sch
GU9 . . . . **146** A6
St Peters Cl SW17 . . . . . . **20** E6
St Peter's Cl
Old Woking GU22 . . . . **90** C7
Staines TW18 . . . . **12** F2
St Peters Ct
East Molesey KT8 . . . . **36** A5
[5] Hampton TW12 . . . . **36** B8
St Peter's Gdns
West Norwood SE27 . . . . . . **22** A5
Wrecclesham GU10 . . . . . **145** F6
St Peter's Hospl KT16 . . . **51** D7
St Peters Mead GU12 . . . **106** B2
St Peters Pk GU11 . . . . . **125** E8
St Peter's Prim Sch
CR2 . . . . **61** E4
St Peter's RC Comp Sch
GU1 . . . . **110** C2
St Peter's RC Prim Sch
KT22 . . . . **95** C7
St Peter's RC Sch
RH19 . . . . **185** C1
St Peters Rd KT1 . . . . **38** A7
St Peter's Rd
Crawley RH11 . . . . **201** C6
Croydon CR0, CR2 . . . . **61** D6
East Molesey KT8 . . . . **36** A5
Isleworth TW1 . . . . **6** B2
Old Woking GU22 . . . . **90** B7
St Peter's St CR0, CR2 . . . **61** D5
St Peters Way UB3 . . . . **3** D8
St Peter's Way
Addlestone KT15, KT16 . . . **51** F6
Chertsey KT15 . . . . **52** B8
Frimley GU16 . . . . **85** F7
St Philip's Ave KT4 . . . . . **58** B8
St Philips Gate KT4 . . . . . **58** B8
St Philip's Rd KT6 . . . . . . **37** D3
St Philips Sch TW18 . . . . . **13** B4
St Philomena's Sch
SM5 . . . . **59** E5
St Piers Hospital Sch
RH7 . . . . **165** A4
St Pier's La RH7, TN8 . . . **165** B5
St Pinnock Ave TW18 . . . . **33** A8
St Polycarp's RC Prim Sch
GU9 . . . . **125** D1
St Richards Ct TW10 . . . . **17** B5
St Richard's with St
Andrew's CE Prim Sch
TW10 . . . . **17** B5
St Robert Southwell RC
Prim Sch RH12 . . . . **218** A6
St Sampson Rd RH11 . . . . **200** F2
St Saviour's Coll SE27 . . . **22** D4
St Saviour's Pl GU1 . . . . . **109** C1
St Saviour's Rd CR0 . . . . . **42** C3
Saints Cl SE27 . . . . **22** B4

Saints Mews CR4 . . . . **40** E6
St Stephen Cl RH11 . . . . . **181** D1
St Stephens Ave KT21 . . . . **75** E3
St Stephen's CE Jun Sch
TW1 . . . . **6** B1
St Stephen's CE Prim Sch
RH9 . . . . **142** F6
St Stephen's Cl GU27 . . . **207** F6
St Stephen's Cres CR7 . . . **42** A6
St Stephens Ct RH9 . . . . . **142** E5
St Stephen's Gdns TW1 . . . **6** C1
St Stephen's Rd TW3,
TW4 . . . . **5** A2
St Swithun's Cl RH19 . . . . **185** F1
St Teresa's Prep Sch
KT24 . . . . **113** D7
St Teresa's RC Prim Sch
SM4 . . . . **40** D3
St Theresa Cl KT18 . . . . . . **76** C5
St Theresa's RC Prim Sch
RG40 . . . . **25** D5
St Theresa's Rd TW14 . . . . . **3** F3
St Thomas Becket Prim
Sch SE25 . . . . **43** A3
St Thomas Cl
Chilworth GU4 . . . . **131** C3
Woking GU21 . . . . **69** C2
St Thomas' Cl KT6 . . . . . . **37** F1
St Thomas of Canterbury
RC Prim Sch
Guildford GU1 . . . . **110** B1
Mitcham CR4 . . . . **41** A6
St Thomas' Rd W4 . . . . **7** C8
St Thomas's Dr GU4 . . . . **111** E4
St Thomas's Mews
GU1 . . . . **130** F7
St Thomas Wlk SL3 . . . . . . **1** D7
St Vincent Cl
Crawley RH10 . . . . **202** D6
West Norwood SE27 . . . . . . **22** B3
St Vincent Rd
Twickenham TW2 . . . . **5** C1
Walton-on-T KT12 . . . . **54** B7
St Wilfrid's RC Comp Sch
RH11 . . . . **201** B5
St William of York RC
Prim Sch SE23 . . . . **23** E7
St Winifreds CR8 . . . . **80** C4
St Winifred's RC Jun Sch
SE12 . . . . **24** F8
St Winifred's Rd
Biggin Hill TN16 . . . . **83** F1
Teddington TW11 . . . . **17** B2
Salamander Cl KT2 . . . . . **17** C3
Salamander Quay KT1 . . . **37** D8
Salbrook Rd RH1 . . . . **140** A1
Salcombe Dr SM4 . . . . . . **39** D1
Salcombe Ho SE23 . . . . . **23** C6
Salcombe Rd TW15 . . . . . **13** E5
Salcombe Villas [10]
TW10 . . . . **6** E2
Salcot Cres CR0 . . . . **63** C1
Salcott Rd CR0 . . . . **60** F6
Saleem Ct CR2 . . . . **61** D5
Sale Garden Cotts
RG40 . . . . **25** C5
Salehurst Rd RH10 . . . . . **202** E6
Salem Pl CR0, CR9 . . . . . . **61** C7
Salerno Cl GU11 . . . . **105** A2
Sales Ct [6] GU11 . . . . . . **105** A1
Salesian Coll GU14 . . . . . **85** D1
Salesian Gdns SM4 . . . . . **33** A1
Salesian Sch KT16 . . . . . . **33** A1
Salesian Sch, Chertsey
KT16 . . . . **51** E8
Salesian View GU14 . . . . **105** E8
Salford Rd SW12, SW2 . . . **21** D7
SALFORDS **140** A3
Salfords Sta RH1 . . . . . . **140** B1
Salisbury Ave SM1 . . . . . . **58** F4
Salisbury Cl
Wokingham RG41 . . . . **25** A2
Worcester Park KT4 . . . . . . **57** F7
Salisbury Gdns SW19 . . . . **19** E1
Salisbury Gr GU16 . . . . . . **86** A3
Salisbury Ho
[5] Wallington SM6 . . . . . . **60** B5
Wimbledon SW19 . . . . **19** D5
Salisbury Pl KT14 . . . . . . **71** C8
Salisbury Rd
Ash GU12 . . . . **106** A3
Banstead SM7 . . . . **78** B5
Blackwater GU17 . . . . **64** C5
Crawley RH10 . . . . **201** F2
Croydon CR0, SE25 . . . . . . **43** A3
Farnborough GU14 . . . . . . **85** C3
Feltham TW13 . . . . **15** C7
Harlington TW6 . . . . **3** C1
Hounslow TW4 . . . . **4** C4
Kingston u T KT3 . . . . **38** D6
Richmond TW9 . . . . **6** E3
Tyler's Green RH9 . . . . **121** C4
Wallington SM5 . . . . **59** F4
Wimbledon SW19 . . . . **19** E1
Woking GU22 . . . . **89** E8
Worcester Park KT4 . . . . . . **57** E7
Salisbury Terr GU16 . . . . . **86** A3
Salix Cl
Fetcham KT22 . . . . **94** B4
Sunbury TW16 . . . . **15** B1
Salliesfield TW2 . . . . **5** D1
Salmon Rd GU11 . . . . . . **105** D5
Salmons La CR3 . . . . **100** F7

Salmons La W CR3 . . . . . . **100** E7
Salmons Rd
  Chessington KT9 . . . . **56** E4
  Effingham KT24 . . . . **113** C6
Saltash Cl SM1 . . . . **58** F6
Saltbox Hill TN16 . . . . **83** B6
Salt Box Rd GU3, GU4 . . . . **109** B6
Saltdean Cl RH10 . . . . **201** D3
Salterford Rd SW17 . . . . . . **21** A2
Salterns Rd RH10 . . . . **202** C3
Salter Ho 8 SW16 . . . . **21** C4
Salter's Hill SE19, SE27 . . . . **22** D3
Saltire Gdns 2 RG42 . . . . . **27** A8
Salt La GU8 . . . . **171** E5
Saltram Rd GU14 . . . . **85** E2
Salvador SW17 . . . . **20** F3
Salvation Pl KT22 . . . . **95** A3
Salvia Ct GU24 . . . . **68** A4
Salvington Rd RH11 . . . . . . **200** F3
Salwey Cl RG12 . . . . **27** B3
Samaritan Cl RH11 . . . . **200** E4
Samarkand Cl GU15 . . . . . . **66** B4
Sambrook Mews SE6 . . . . . **24** B7
Samos Rd SE20 . . . . **43** B7
Samphire Cl RH11 . . . . **201** A3
Sampleoak La GU4 . . . . . . **131** E2
Sampson Bsns Pk
  GU15 . . . . **65** B3
Sampson Ct TW17 . . . . **34** C4
Sampson Pk RG42 . . . . **26** D8
Sampson's Almshouses
  GU9 . . . . **125** A1
Samual Ho 3 SE27 . . . . **22** B4
Samuel Cody Ho
  GU12 . . . . **105** F7
Samuel Cody Sch The
  GU14 . . . . **105** B7
Samuel Ct BR3 . . . . **44** B6
Samuel Gray Gdns
  KT2 . . . . **37** D8
Samuel Johnson Cl
  SW16 . . . . **21** F4
San Carlos App GU11 . . . . **105** C2
Sanctuary Rd TW19,
  TW6 . . . . **3** A1
Sanctuary The SM4 . . . . . . **40** A3
Sandal Rd KT3 . . . . **38** E5
Sandalwood GU2 . . . . **130** B8
Sandalwood Ave KT16 . . . . **51** E7
Sandalwood Rd TW13 . . . . . **15** B5
Sandbourne Ave SW19 . . . . **40** B7
Sandcross La RH2 . . . . **139** A5
Sandcross Sch RH2 . . . . . . **138** F6
Sanders Cl TW12 . . . . **16** C3
Sandersfield Gdns
  SM7 . . . . **78** A4
Sandersfield Rd SM7 . . . . . **78** B5
Sanders Ho SW16 . . . . **21** E2
SANDERSTEAD **80** F6
Sanderstead Cl SW12 . . . . . **21** C8
Sanderstead Court Ave
  CR2 . . . . **81** A6
Sanderstead Ct CR2 . . . . . . **81** A7
Sanderstead Hill CR2 . . . . . **80** F8
Sanderstead Hts CR2 . . . . . **81** A8
Sanderstead Jun Sch
  CR2 . . . . **61** D2
Sanderstead Rd CR2 . . . . . . **61** D2
Sanderstead Sta CR2 . . . . . **61** D2
Sandes Pl KT22 . . . . **75** A1
Sandfield Ct GU1 . . . . **130** D8
Sandfield Gdns CR7 . . . . . . **42** B6
Sandfield Pl CR7 . . . . **42** C6
Sandfield Prim Sch
  GU1 . . . . **130** D8
Sandfield Rd CR7 . . . . **42** B6
Sandfields GU23 . . . . **90** D3
Sandfield Terr GU1 . . . . . . **130** D8
Sandford Ct GU11 . . . . **104** F1
Sandford Down RG12 . . . . . **27** F4
Sandford Rd
  Aldershot GU11 . . . . **104** F1
  Heath End GU9 . . . . **125** B7
Sandgate Ho 14 BR3 . . . . . . **24** A1
Sandgate La SW17,
  SW18 . . . . **20** E7
Sandgates KT16 . . . . **32** E1
Sandhawes Hill RH19 . . . . **186** A4
Sandheath Rd GU26 . . . . . **188** C7
Sand Hill GU14 . . . . **85** B7
Sand Hill Ct GU14 . . . . **85** B7
Sandhill La RH10 . . . . **204** B7
SANDHILLS **170** D1
Sandhills
  Wallington CR0, SM6 . . . . . **60** D6
  Walton on t H KT20 . . . . . . **97** A3
Sandhills Ct GU25 . . . . **31** E4
Sandhills La GU25,
  TW20 . . . . **31** F4
Sandhills Mdw TW17 . . . . . **34** C2
Sandhills Rd RH2 . . . . **139** A7
SANDHURST **64** C7
Sandhurst GU10 . . . . **126** C4
Sandhurst Ave KT5 . . . . **38** B2
Sandhurst Ct CR2 . . . . **61** E2
Sandhurst Jun & Inf Schs
  SE6 . . . . **24** E7
Sandhurst La GU17 . . . . **64** B6
Sandhurst Mkt SE6 . . . . **24** C7
Sandhurst Rd
  Catford SE6 . . . . **24** D7
  Crowthorne RG45 . . . . **45** B3
  Wokingham RG40 . . . . **25** A1
Sandhurst Sch GU47 . . . . . . **45** D1
Sandhurst Sta GU47 . . . . . . **64** A8

Sandhurst Way CR2 . . . . . . **61** E3
Sandiford Ho CR3 . . . . **100** E3
Sandiford Rd SM3 . . . . **58** F8
Sandiland Cres BR2 . . . . . . **63** F8
Sandilands CR0 . . . . **62** A7
Sandlands Gr KT20 . . . . **97** A4
Sandlands Rd KT20 . . . . **97** A3
Sandmartin Way SM6 . . . . . **41** A1
Sandmore GU23 . . . . **90** D3
Sandon Cl KT10 . . . . **36** D1
Sandon Ho 5 SW2 . . . . **21** E8
Sandown Ave KT10 . . . . **55** C5
Sandown Cl
  Blackwater GU17 . . . . **64** D5
  Cranford TW5 . . . . **4** A6
Sandown CresGU11 . . . . . **126** B7
Sandown Ct
  2 Belmont SM2 . . . . **59** B3
  Crawley RH10 . . . . **202** D6
  3 Redhill RH1 . . . . **118** E2
Sandown Dr
  Frimley GU16 . . . . **65** E2
  Wallington SM5 . . . . **60** A2
Sandown Gate KT10 . . . . . . **55** D7
Sandown Ho
  Esher KT10 . . . . **55** C6
  Penge SE26 . . . . **23** B2
Sandown Ind Est KT10 . . . . **55** A8
Sandown Lo KT18 . . . . **76** D5
Sandown Pk KT10 . . . . **55** C8
Sandown Rd
  Coulsdon CR5 . . . . **79** A3
  Croydon SE25 . . . . **43** B4
  Esher KT10 . . . . **55** C6
Sandpiper Cl RH11 . . . . . . **200** D4
Sandpiper Rd
  Cheam SM1 . . . . **58** F5
  Selsdon CR2 . . . . **81** D8
Sandpit Hall Rd GU24 . . . . . **69** A7
Sandpit Heath GU3 . . . . . . **108** D5
Sandpit Rd
  Catford BR1 . . . . **24** E3
  Redhill RH1 . . . . **139** F8
Sandpits Rd
  Richmond TW10 . . . . **17** D6
  South Croydon CR0 . . . . **62** D6
Sandra Cl TW3 . . . . **5** B2
Sandra Ho KT8 . . . . **36** D4
Sandringham Ave
  SW20 . . . . **39** E7
Sandringham Cl
  East Grinstead RH19 . . . . . **206** A8
  1 Putney SW19 . . . . **19** D7
  Pyrford GU22 . . . . **71** A3
Sandringham Ct
  Beckenham BR3 . . . . **44** C8
  Belmont SM2 . . . . **59** A2
  Kingston u T KT2 . . . . **37** E8
  2 Twickenham TW1 . . . . . . **17** A7
Sandringham Dr TW15 . . . . **13** D4
Sandringham Gdns
  Cranford TW5 . . . . **4** A6
  East Molesey KT8 . . . . **36** A5
Sandringham Ho TW10 . . . . . **7** A2
Sandringham Mews
  TW12 . . . . **35** F8
Sandringham Pk KT11 . . . . **74** A7
Sandringham Rd
  Crawley RH11 . . . . **201** B2
  North Cheam KT4 . . . . **58** A7
  Stanwell TW6 . . . . **2** E4
  Thornton Heath CR0 . . . . . . **42** C4
Sandringham Sch
  GU16 . . . . **85** F7
Sandringham Way
  GU16 . . . . **85** F8
Sandrock GU27 . . . . **208** C6
Sandrock Hill Rd
  GU10 . . . . **146** A5
Sandrock Ho GU7 . . . . **150** D6
Sandrock Pl CR0 . . . . **62** D6
Sandrock Rd RH4 . . . . **135** B5
Sandroyd Way KT11 . . . . . . **74** A4
Sands Cl GU10 . . . . **126** D2
Sands Rd GU10 . . . . **126** D2
Sandstone TW9 . . . . **7** A7
Sandways 6 TW9 . . . . **7** A6
Sandy Cl GU22 . . . . **70** C2
Sandycombe Ctr TW9 . . . . . . **7** A4
Sandycombe Rd
  East Bedfont TW14 . . . . **15** A7
  Richmond TW9 . . . . **7** A5
Sandycoombe Rd TW1 . . . . . **6** C1
Sandy Cotts RH10 . . . . **204** A8
Sandy Croft KT17 . . . . **58** C5
Sandy Cross GU10 . . . . . . **126** F4
Sandy Ct KT11 . . . . **73** F6
Sandy Dr
  Cobham KT11 . . . . **74** A8
  East Bedfont TW14 . . . . **14** E7
Sandy Hill Rd
  Heath End GU9 . . . . **125** B7
  Wallington SM6 . . . . **60** C2
Sandy Holt KT11 . . . . **73** F6
Sandy La
  Albury GU5 . . . . **132** D2
  Artington GU2, GU3 . . . . . **130** B5
  Belmont SM2 . . . . **58** E2
  Betchworth RH3 . . . . **116** E1
  Bletchingley RH1 . . . . **120** C3
  Bracknell RG12 . . . . **27** C8
  Camberley GU15 . . . . **65** E6
  Chobham GU24 . . . . **49** E2
  Cobham KT11, KT22 . . . . . . **74** B7
  Crawley Down RH10 . . . . . **204** A8
  East Grinstead RH19 . . . . . **185** F1
  Farnborough GU14 . . . . **84** D7
  Farncombe GU7 . . . . **150** D6

Sandy La continued
  Frensham GU10 . . . . **146** C1
  Grayswood GU27 . . . . **189** E1
  Haslemere GU26,
    GU27 . . . . **207** C7
  Kingswood KT20 . . . . **98** A4
  Limpsfield RH8 . . . . **123** B7
  Milford GU8 . . . . **170** E8
  Mitcham CR4 . . . . **41** A8
  North Ascot SL5 . . . . **28** C8
  Nutfield RH1 . . . . **119** E1
  Oxted RH8 . . . . **122** C6
  Pyrford GU22 . . . . **71** A3
  Reigate RH2 . . . . **138** B8
  Richmond TW10 . . . . **17** D6
  Rushmoor GU10 . . . . **168** B5
  Sandhurst GU47 . . . . **45** A2
  Send GU23 . . . . **90** C4
  Shere GU5 . . . . **133** A3
  Sunningdale SL5 . . . . **30** A4
  Teddington KT8, TW11 . . . . . **17** B1
  Virginia Water GU25 . . . . . . **31** E5
  Walton-on-T KT12 . . . . **35** C3
  Woking GU22 . . . . **70** C2
Sandy Lane N SM6 . . . . **60** D5
Sandy Lane Prim Sch
  RG12 . . . . **27** C8
Sandy Lane S SM6 . . . . **60** C3
Sandy Mead KT19 . . . . **57** A2
Sandy Rd KT15 . . . . **52** A4
Sandy Ride SL5 . . . . **29** E5
Sandy Way
  Cobham KT11 . . . . **74** A7
  Croydon CR0 . . . . **62** F7
  Walton-on-T KT12 . . . . **34** F1
  Woking GU22 . . . . **70** C2
San Feliu Ct RH19 . . . . **186** B2
Sanger Ave KT9 . . . . **56** F6
Sanger Dr GU23 . . . . **90** C4
Sangers Dr RH6 . . . . **160** F3
Sangley Rd
  Catford SE6 . . . . **24** C7
  South Norwood SE25 . . . . . . **42** E5
Santina Cl GU9 . . . . **125** D8
Sanway Cl KT14 . . . . **71** E5
Sanway Rd KT14 . . . . **71** E5
Sappho Cl GU21 . . . . **68** E3
Sapte Cl GU6 . . . . **175** A3
Saracen Cl CR0 . . . . **42** D3
Sarah Ho SW15 . . . . **7** F3
Sarah Way GU14 . . . . **85** B4
Sardeson Ho 13 SW27 . . . . **22** B3
Sarel Way RH6 . . . . **161** B5
Sargent Cl RH10 . . . . **201** F2
Sarjant Path SW19 . . . . **19** D6
Sark Cl
  Crawley RH11 . . . . **201** A2
  Heston TW5 . . . . **5** A7
Sarsby Dr TW19 . . . . **12** A6
Sarsen Ave TW3 . . . . **5** A5
Sarsfeld Rd SW12,
  SW17 . . . . **20** F7
Sarum RG12 . . . . **26** F1
Sarum Cres RG40 . . . . **25** D7
Sarum Gn KT13 . . . . **53** E7
Sassoons Cotts KT12 . . . . . **35** B2
Satellite Bsns Village The
  RH10 . . . . **181** E2
Satis Ct KT17 . . . . **76** F8
Saturn Cl RH11 . . . . **200** E4
Saturn Croft RG42 . . . . **8** B2
Saunders Cl RH10 . . . . **202** B7
Saunders Copse GU22 . . . . **89** B5
Saundersfield Ho SM7 . . . . **78** B5
Saunders Ho 11 SW2 . . . . . **22** A7
Saunders La GU22 . . . . **89** B5
Saunton Ave UB3 . . . . **3** F7
Saunton Gdns 1 GU14 . . . . **85** A6
Savernake Ct SE22 . . . . **23** A7
Savernake Way RG12 . . . . . **27** F4
Savernake Wlk RH10 . . . . . **201** F3
Savery Dr KT6 . . . . **37** C2
Savile Cl
  New Malden KT3 . . . . **38** E4
  Thames Ditton KT7 . . . . **37** A1
Savile Gdns CR0 . . . . **61** F8
Saville Cl KT19 . . . . **76** B8
Saville Cres TW15 . . . . **14** D2
Saville Gdns GU15 . . . . **66** B5
Saville Ho 6 TW20 . . . . **12** A3
Saville Row BR2 . . . . **44** F1
Savill Gardens The ★
  TW20 . . . . **10** E2
Savill Gdns SW20 . . . . **39** A6
Savill Mews TW20 . . . . **11** D2
Savin Lo 11 SM2 . . . . **59** C3
Savona Cl SW19 . . . . **19** D1
Savona Ct 2 SW20 . . . . **39** D8
Savoy Gr GU17 . . . . **64** D3
Sawkins Cl SW19 . . . . **19** E6
Sawtry Cl SM5 . . . . **40** E2
Sawyer Ho 15 SE21 . . . . . . **22** E4
Sawyer's Hill TW10 . . . . **17** F8
Saxby Rd SW2 . . . . **21** E8
Saxby's La RH7 . . . . **164** D5
Saxley RH6 . . . . **161** C4
Saxon Ave TW13 . . . . **15** F6
Saxon Bsns Ctr SW19 . . . . . **40** C8
Saxonbury Ave TW16 . . . . . **35** B7
Saxonbury Cl CR4 . . . . **40** D6
Saxonbury Gdns KT6 . . . . . **37** C1
Saxon Cl KT6 . . . . **37** D3
Saxon Cres RH12 . . . . **217** B4
Saxon Croft GU9 . . . . **125** C1
Saxon Ct 2 CR3 . . . . **101** A8
Saxon Dr RG42 . . . . **27** F8

Saxonfield Cl SW2 . . . . **21** F8
Saxon Ho
  Feltham TW13 . . . . **15** F6
  Reigate RH2 . . . . **138** F6
Saxon Prim Sch TW17 . . . . . **34** A4
Saxon Rd
  Ashford TW15 . . . . **14** D2
  Bromley BR1 . . . . **24** F1
  Crawley RH10 . . . . **202** E5
  Kingston u T KT2 . . . . **37** E8
  Thornton Heath CR0,
    SE25 . . . . **42** D4
  Walton-on-T KT12 . . . . **54** D7
Saxons KT20 . . . . **97** D6
Saxon Terr SE6 . . . . **23** F6
Saxon Way
  Harmondsworth UB7 . . . . . . **2** C8
  Reigate RH2 . . . . **117** F2
Sayers Cl
  Fetcham KT22 . . . . **94** C4
  Frimley GU16 . . . . **85** E7
  Horsham RH13 . . . . **217** E1
Sayers The 5 RH19 . . . . . . **185** C1
Sayer's Wlk TW10 . . . . **17** F8
Sayes Court Farm Dr
  KT15 . . . . **52** B5
Sayes Court Jun Sch
  KT15 . . . . **52** B5
Sayes Ct KT15 . . . . **52** C5
Sbac Tk GU11 . . . . **104** E6
Scallows Cl RH10 . . . . **202** A7
Scallows Rd RH10 . . . . **202** A7
Scania Wlk RG42 . . . . **8** B2
Scarborough Cl
  Belmont SM2 . . . . **77** F8
  Biggin Hill TN16 . . . . **83** C1
Scarborough Rd TW6 . . . . . . **3** C1
Scarbrook Rd CR0, CR9 . . . . **61** C7
Scarlet Oaks GU15 . . . . **65** E3
Scarlet Rd SE6 . . . . **24** E5
Scarlett Cl GU21 . . . . **68** F1
Scarlette Manor Wlk
  SW2 . . . . **22** A8
Scarlett's Rd GU11 . . . . **105** A3
Scarth Rd SW13 . . . . **7** F4
Scawen Cl SM5 . . . . **60** A6
Schaffer Ho RH10 . . . . **202** C4
Scholars Cl RH10 . . . . **204** A8
Scholars Rd SW12 . . . . **21** C7
Scholars Wlk
  Farnborough GU14 . . . . **85** B6
  Guildford GU2 . . . . **130** B8
School Cl
  Bisley GU24 . . . . **68** A4
  Guildford GU1 . . . . **109** D3
  Horsham RH12 . . . . **218** A6
School Cotts
  New Malden KT4 . . . . **38** E1
  Woking GU22 . . . . **89** C5
School Hill
  Crowthorne RG45 . . . . **45** D4
  Merstham RH1 . . . . **119** C7
  Sandhurst GU47 . . . . **45** A1
  Seale GU10 . . . . **127** B4
  Warnham RH12 . . . . **216** F8
  Wrecclesham GU10 . . . . . . **145** F6
School House La TW11 . . . . **17** C1
School Houses GU8 . . . . . . **172** E4
School La
  Addlestone KT15 . . . . **52** A6
  Ashurst Wood RH19 . . . . . **206** E6
  Bagshot GU19 . . . . **47** E2
  Caterham CR3 . . . . **100** F1
  Chiddingfold GU8 . . . . **191** C4
  Crondall GU10 . . . . **124** D8
  East Clandon GU4 . . . . **111** E4
  Egham TW20 . . . . **12** A3
  Farnham GU10 . . . . **146** D6
  Fetcham KT22 . . . . **94** D5
  Forest Row RH18 . . . . **206** F2
  Lower Halliford TW17 . . . . . **34** B3
  Mickleham RH5 . . . . **115** C8
  Normandy GU3 . . . . **106** A4
  Ockham GU23 . . . . **92** B5
  Pirbright GU24 . . . . **87** E5
  Puttenham GU3 . . . . **128** C3
  Shackleford GU8 . . . . **149** E6
  Surbiton KT6 . . . . **38** A1
  Teddington KT1 . . . . **37** C8
  Walton on t H KT20 . . . . **97** A2
  Westcott RH4 . . . . **135** D6
  West Horsley KT24 . . . . . . **112** B6
  Windlesham GU20 . . . . **48** D4
School Mdw GU2 . . . . **108** E2
School Pas 4 KT1 . . . . **37** F7
School Rd
  Ascot SL5 . . . . **29** D4
  Ashford TW15 . . . . **14** B2
  East Molesey KT8 . . . . **36** D5
  Grayshott GU26 . . . . **188** B4
  Hampton TW12 . . . . **16** C2
  Harmondsworth UB7 . . . . . . **2** D8
  Haslemere GU27 . . . . **207** F5
  Hounslow TW3 . . . . **5** C4
  Rowledge GU10 . . . . **145** E3
  Teddington KT1 . . . . **37** C8
  Windlesham GU20 . . . . **48** B5
  Wokingham RG40 . . . . **25** D6
School Road Ave
  TW12 . . . . **16** C2
School Wlk TW16 . . . . **35** A6
Schroder Ct TW20 . . . . **11** B3
Scillonian Rd GU2 . . . . **130** A7
Scilly Isles KT10 . . . . **55** D6
Scizdons Climb GU7 . . . . . **150** F4
Scoles Cres SW2 . . . . **22** A7
Scope Way 3 KT1 . . . . **37** E5
Scoresdale SE19 . . . . **42** E8

Scory Cl RH11 . . . . **201** A3
Scotia Rd SW2 . . . . **22** A8
Scotland Bridge Rd
  KT15 . . . . **71** A8
Scotland Cl GU12 . . . . **106** A5
Scotland Farm Rd
  GU12 . . . . **106** A5
Scotland Hill GU47 . . . . **64** A8
Scotland La GU27 . . . . **208** C5
Scotlands Cl GU27 . . . . **208** B5
Scotlands Dr GU27 . . . . . . **208** C5
Scotney Ho RH1 . . . . **139** F4
Scotsdale Cl SM2 . . . . **58** E3
Scotshall La CR6 . . . . **82** C4
*Scott-Broadwood CE Inf
  Sch*
  Capel RH5 . . . . **178** D6
  Ockley RH5 . . . . **177** D4
Scott Cl
  Guildford GU2 . . . . **109** A3
  Thornton Heath SW16 . . . . . **41** F8
  West Ewell KT19 . . . . **57** C5
Scott Farm Cl KT7 . . . . **37** B1
Scott Gdns TW5 . . . . **4** D7
Scott Ho TW10 . . . . **17** C6
Scott Rd RH10 . . . . **201** F3
Scott's Ave
  Ashford TW20 . . . . **14** E1
  Beckenham BR2 . . . . **44** D7
Scotts Cl TW19 . . . . **13** D7
Scott's Ct GU14 . . . . **85** B7
Scotts Dr TW12 . . . . **16** B1
Scotts Farm Rd KT19 . . . . . **57** C4
Scott's Grove Cl GU24 . . . . **68** D6
Scott's Grove Rd GU24 . . . . **68** C6
Scott's Hill RH1, RH6 . . . . . **162** D5
Scott's La BR2 . . . . **44** D7
Scotts Mews SL5 . . . . **28** B8
Scott's Way TW16 . . . . **14** E1
Scott Terr RG12 . . . . **27** E8
Scott Trimmer Way
  TW3 . . . . **4** E5
Scrooby St 3 SE6 . . . . **24** B8
Scrutton Cl SW12 . . . . **21** D8
Scylla Cres TW6, TW14 . . . . **14** B8
Scylla Pl GU21 . . . . **89** A8
Scylla Rd TW14, TW6 . . . . . . **3** B1
Seabrook Dr BR4 . . . . **63** E8
Seafire Way GU11 . . . . **104** E7
Seaford Rd
  Crawley RH11 . . . . **201** A2
  Stanwell TW6 . . . . **2** D2
  Wokingham RG40 . . . . **25** D6
Seaforth Ave KT3 . . . . **39** B5
Seaforth Gdns KT19 . . . . . . **57** F5
Seaforth Lo SW13 . . . . **7** F5
Sealand Rd TW6 . . . . **3** A1
SEALE **127** B4
Seale La
  Puttenham GU3,
    GU10 . . . . **127** F4
  The Sands GU10, GU3 . . . . **126** E4
Seale Rd GU8, GU10 . . . . . **148** B7
Seaman's Gn RH5 . . . . **178** D8
Searchwood Rd CR6 . . . . . . **81** B1
Searle Ct 7 CR4 . . . . **40** E8
Searle Hill RH2 . . . . **139** A7
Searle Rd GU9 . . . . **146** C8
Searle's View RH12 . . . . . . **217** E5
Searlewood Ct GU24 . . . . . . **67** F5
Seath Ho 4 SE26 . . . . **23** B3
Seaton Cl
  Putney SW15 . . . . **19** B8
  Twickenham TW2 . . . . **5** D1
Seaton Dr TW15 . . . . **13** E6
Seaton House Sch
  SM2 . . . . **59** D1
Seaton Rd
  Camberley GU15 . . . . **65** B5
  Mitcham CR4 . . . . **40** E7
  Twickenham TW2 . . . . **5** C1
Sebastopol Rd GU11 . . . . . **105** B2
Second Ave
  Mortlake SW14 . . . . **7** E4
  Walton-on-T KT12 . . . . **35** B3
  Woodham KT15 . . . . **52** B2
Second Cl KT8 . . . . **36** C5
Second Cross Rd TW2 . . . . . **16** E6
Secrett Ho 6 TW10 . . . . **17** C5
Seddon Ct RH11 . . . . **201** B1
Seddon Rd SM4 . . . . **40** D4
Sedgefield Cl RH10 . . . . . . **202** E2
Sedgehill Rd SE6 . . . . **24** B3
Sedgehill Sch SE6 . . . . **24** B3
Sedgemoor GU14 . . . . **85** B7
Sedgeway SE6 . . . . **24** F7
Sedgewick Cl RH10 . . . . . . **202** E6
Sedgewick Ho SW19 . . . . . . **19** D6
Sedgewood Cl BR2 . . . . **44** F2
Sedley Ct SE26 . . . . **23** B6
Seebys Oak GU47 . . . . **64** E6
Seeley Dr SE21 . . . . **22** E4
Seely Rd SW17 . . . . **21** A2
SEETHING WELLS **37** C3
*Seething Wells Halls Of
  Residence* KT6 . . . . **37** C3
Seething Wells La KT6 . . . . **37** C3
Sefton Cl GU24 . . . . **67** F6
Sefton Ct TW5 . . . . **5** B6
Sefton Ho 16 GU11 . . . . . . **105** A2
Sefton Lo
  Kingston u T KT2 . . . . **17** E2
  2 Twickenham TW1 . . . . . . **6** C1
Sefton Rd
  Croydon CR0 . . . . **43** A1
  Epsom KT19 . . . . **57** D1
Sefton Villas RH5 . . . . **136** B3
Segal Cl SE23 . . . . **23** E8

Segrave Cl KT13 53 A3
Segsbury Gr RG12 27 F5
Sekhon Terr TW13 16 A5
Selborne RG12 27 B6
Selborne Ave GU11 126 C6
Selborne Cl GU17 64 C6
Selborne Gdns GU9 146 A7
Selborne Rd
Kingston u T KT3 38 E7
South Croydon CR0 61 F7
Selbourne Ave KT15 52 B1
Selbourne Cl
Crawley RH10 182 D2
Woodham KT15 52 B1
Selbourne Rd GU4 110 A4
Selbourne Sq RH9 121 C5
Selbridge Ct 8 SW19 20 A2
Selby Cl KT9 56 E3
Selby Ct TW2 16 D6
Selby Gn SM5 40 E2
Selby Rd
Ashford TW15 14 C2
Carshalton SM5 40 E2
Penge SE20 43 A7
Selbys RH7 164 E5
Selby Wlk 1 GU21 69 B1
Selcroft Rd CR8 80 B7
Selham Cl RH11 201 A7
Selhurst Cl
Putney SW19 19 D7
Woking GU21 69 F4
Selhurst New Ct SE25 42 E3
Selhurst New Rd SE25 42 E3
Selhurst Park (Crystal Palace FC) SE25 42 E5
Selhurst Pl CR0, SE25 42 E3
Selhurst Rd CR0, SE25 42 E4
Selhurst Sta SE25 42 E4
Selkirk Rd
Twickenham TW2 16 C7
Upper Tooting SW17 20 E4
Sellar's Hill GU7 150 D7
Sellincourt Prim Sch SW17 20 E2
Sellincourt Rd SW17 20 E2
Sellindge Cl BR3 23 F1
Sells Cl GU1 130 F7
SELSDON 62 D1
Selsdon Ave CR2 61 D4
Selsdon Cl KT6 37 E4
Selsdon Cres CR2 62 C1
Selsdon High Sch CR2 62 D3
Selsdon Par CR2 62 C1
Selsdon Park Rd CR0, CR2 62 E2
Selsdon Prim Sch CR2 62 C2
Selsdon Rd
Croydon CR2 61 D4
West Norwood SE27 22 B4
Woodham KT15 71 A8
Selsdon Road Ind Est CR2 61 D4
Selsey Ct 3 RH11 201 B2
Selsey Rd RH11 201 A2
SELSFIELD COMMON 204 B1
Selsfield Rd RH10, RH19 204 A2
Seltops Cl GU6 174 F2
Selwood Cl TW19 2 C1
Selwood Gdns TW19 2 C1
Selwood Rd
Cheam SM3 39 F1
Chessington KT9 56 D6
Croydon CR0 43 B1
Old Woking GU22 90 B7
Selworthy Rd SE6 23 F5
Selwyn Ave TW9 6 F4
Selwyn Cl
Crawley RH10 182 C1
Hounslow TW4 4 E3
Selwyn Ct 8 TW10 6 F2
Selwyn Rd KT3 38 D4
Semaphore Rd GU1 130 E7
Semley Pl SW16 41 F7
Semley Rd SW16 41 E7
Semper Cl GU21 68 E2
SEND 90 C4
Send Barns La GU23 90 E2
Send CE Fst Sch GU23 90 E3
Send Cl GU23 90 C4
Send Hill GU23 90 C3
SEND MARSH 90 F3
Send Marsh Rd GU23 90 E4
Send Parade Cl GU23 90 C4
Send Rd GU23 90 C4
Seneca Rd CR7 42 C5
Senga Rd CR4 41 A1
Senhouse Rd SM3 58 D7
Sequoia Pk RH11 201 D4
Sergeants Pl CR3 100 C5
Serpentine Gn RH1 119 D6
Serrin Way RH12 217 E5
Service Rd RH6 181 F8
Servite Ho
Beckenham BR3 43 F8
Dorking RH4 136 A5
Knaphill GU21 68 D2
Worcester Park KT4 57 F8
Servius Ct 2 TW8 6 D7
Sessions Terr CR4 40 F8
Setley Way RG12 27 F6
Seven Acres SM5 59 E8
Seven Arches App KT13 53 A3
Seven Hills Cl KT12, KT13 53 E2
Seven Hills Rd
Weybridge KT12, KT13 53 E3
Whiteley Village KT11 72 E6
Seven Hills Road S KT11 72 E6
Seven Ho CR3 100 E5
Seven Kings Way KT2 37 E8
Sevenoaks Cl SM2 59 B1
Severn Cl GU47 64 C8
Severn Cres SL3 1 B8
Severn Dr
Hinchley Wood KT10 56 A8
Walton-on-T KT12 54 D8
Severn Rd
Crawley RH10 202 C5
Farnborough GU14 84 E6
Seward Rd BR3 43 D7
Sewell Ave RG41 25 A8
Sewer's Farm Rd RH5 155 F6
Sewill Cl RH6 180 F7
Seychelle Ct BR3 24 B1
Seymour Ave
Caterham CR3 100 C4
Ewell KT17 58 B2
West Barnes SM4 39 D2
Seymour Cl KT8 36 C4
Seymour Ct 3 KT19 57 E2
Seymour Dr GU15 66 B7
Seymour Gdns
Feltham TW13 15 C4
Kingston u T KT5 37 F4
Twickenham TW1 17 B8
Seymour Ho 6 SM2 59 B4
Seymour Mews KT17 58 A1
Seymour Pl
Croydon SE25 43 B5
Woking GU23 89 B7
Seymour Prim Sch RH11 201 B2
Seymour Rd
Carshalton CR4 41 A2
Crawley RH11 201 B2
East Molesey KT8 36 C4
Godalming GU7 150 B3
Hampton TW12 16 C3
Headley Down GU35 187 C4
Teddington KT1 37 D8
Wallington SM5 60 A5
Wandsworth SW18 19 F8
Wimbledon SW19 19 D5
Seymour Terr SE20 43 B8
Seymour Villas SE20 43 A8
Seymour Way TW16 14 E1
Shabden Cotts CR5 98 F6
Shabden Pk CR5 98 E5
SHACKLEFORD 149 D7
Shackleford Rd
Elstead GU8 148 F3
Old Woking GU22 90 A7
Shackleford GU8 149 E6
Shacklegate La TW11 16 E4
Shackleton Cl
Ash Vale GU12 105 F6
Forest Hill SE23 23 B6
Shackleton Ct
3 Dulwich SE21 22 D6
7 Stanwell TW19 2 E1
Shackleton Lo 7 SW16 21 D3
Shackleton Rd RH10 201 F3
Shackleton Wlk 4 GU2 108 E1
Shackstead La GU7 150 D3
Shackster La GU7 150 C3
Shadbolt Cl KT4 57 F8
Shadyhanger GU7 150 E6
Shady Nook GU9 125 B6
Shaef Way TW11 17 A1
Shaftesbury Ave TW14 4 A1
Shaftesbury Cl RG12 27 D4
Shaftesbury Cres TW18 13 D1
Shaftesbury Ct
2 Farnborough GU14 105 C8
Wokingham RG40 25 D7
Shaftesbury Ho
Croydon SE25 43 A3
Upper Tooting SW17 20 D4
Shaftesbury Mount GU17 64 D3
Shaftesbury Rd
Beckenham BR3 43 F7
Bisley GU24 67 F3
Carshalton SM5 40 E2
Crawley RH10 202 D4
Richmond TW9 6 E4
Woking GU22 70 B2
Shaftesbury Way TW2 16 D5
Shafteswood Ct SW17 20 F5
Shagbrook RH2 117 C2
Shakespeare Ave TW14 4 A1
Shakespeare Gdns GU14 84 D5
Shakespeare Rd KT15 52 D6
Shakespeare Way
Feltham TW13 15 C4
Winkfield RG42 27 E8
Shalbourne Rise GU15 65 D5
Shalden Ho SW15 7 F1
Shalden Rd GU12 126 D8
Shaldon Dr SM4 39 E4
Shaldon Way KT12 54 C7
Shale Gn RH1 119 D6
Shalesbrook La RH18 206 F1
SHALFORD 130 E2
Shalford Inf Sch GU4 130 E3
Shalford La GU4 130 E4
Shalford Mill★ GU4 130 E4
Shalford Rd GU1, GU4 130 D5
Shalford Sta GU4 130 E3
Shalstone Rd SW14, TW9 7 B4
Shalston Villas KT5, KT6 37 F3
Shambles The GU1 130 D7
SHAMLEY GREEN 152 E5
Shamrock Cl
Fetcham KT22 94 D6
Frimley GU16 85 D8
Shamrock Ho SE26 23 A4
Shamrock Rd CR0 41 F3
Shandys Cl RH12 217 A1
Shanklin Ct GU12 105 C1
Shannon Cnr KT3 39 A5
Shannon Cnr Ret Pk KT3 39 A5
Shannon Commercial Ctr KT3 39 A5
Shannon Ct CR0 42 C1
Shannon Way BR3 24 B2
Shanti Ct SW18 20 A7
Shap Cres SM5 40 F1
Sharland Cl CR7 42 A3
Sharon Cl
Crawley RH10 202 A4
Epsom KT19 76 C6
Great Bookham KT23 94 A3
Long Ditton KT6 37 C1
Sharon Ct 15 CR2 61 C5
Sharonelle Ct RG40 25 B6
Sharp Ho 17 TW1 6 D1
Sharpthorne Cl RH11 200 F6
Shaw Cl
Ewell KT17 76 F8
Ottershaw KT16 51 C4
Sanderstead CR2 80 F7
Shaw Cotts SE23, SE6 23 E5
Shaw Cres CR2 80 F7
Shaw Ct
Caterham CR3 100 D6
Morden SM4 40 C2
Shaw Dr KT12 35 C2
Shawfield La GU12 105 F2
Shawfield Prim Sch GU12 106 A3
Shawfield Rd GU12 106 A3
Shawfields 2 GU1 110 A1
Shawford Ct 9 SW15 19 A8
Shawford Rd KT19 57 D4
Shaw Ho CR3 101 B6
Shawley Com Prim Sch KT18 77 C1
Shawley Cres KT18 77 D1
Shawley Way KT18 77 C1
Shaw Path BR1 24 F5
Shaw Pk RG45 45 B3
Shaw Rd
Catford BR1 24 F5
Tatsfield TN16 103 C7
Shaws Cotts GU3 108 F6
Shaws Rd RH10 201 F7
Shaw Way SM6 60 E3
Shaxton Cres CR0 63 C2
Shearing Dr SM4 40 C2
Shears Ct TW16 14 E1
Shears Way TW16 34 E8
Shearwater Ct 6 RH11 200 D5
Shearwater Rd SM1 58 F5
Sheath La KT22 74 C6
Sheen Common Dr SW14, TW10 7 A2
Sheen Court Rd TW10 7 A3
Sheen Ct TW10 7 A3
Sheendale Rd TW9 6 F3
Sheenewood SE26 23 B4
Sheen Gate Gdns SW14 7 C3
Sheengate Mans SW14 7 D3
Sheen La SW14 7 C3
Sheen Mount Prim Sch SW14 7 B2
Sheen Pk TW10, TW9 6 E3
Sheen Rd TW10, TW9 6 F3
Sheen Way SM6 60 F5
Sheen Wood SW14 7 C2
Sheepbarn La CR6 82 F7
Sheepcote Cl TW5 4 A7
Sheepfold Rd GU2 108 F4
Sheephatch La GU10 147 C6
Sheephouse GU9 146 C8
Sheephouse Gn RH5 134 F3
Sheephouse La
Wotton RH5 135 A2
Wotton RH5 156 A6
Sheephouse Way KT3 38 E2
Sheeplands Ave GU1 110 C3
Sheep Leas (Forest Walk)★ KT24 112 E2
Sheepwalk
Littleton TW17 34 A3
Shepperton TW17 33 F3
Sheepwalk La RH5 113 A1
Sheep Walk Mews SW19 19 E2
Sheep Wlk
Langley Vale KT18 96 D6
Reigate RH2 117 E4
SHEERWATER 70 D6
Sheerwater Ave KT15 70 F7
Sheerwater Bsns Ctr GU21 70 C4
Sheerwater Cotts KT14 70 F6
Sheerwater Rd KT14, KT15 70 F6
Sheet's Heath La GU24 88 A7
Sheet Street Rd SL4 10 A7
Sheffield Cl
Crawley RH10 202 B4
Farnborough GU14 84 F4
Sheffield Rd TW14, TW6 3 C2
Sheffield Way TW14, TW6 3 D2
Shefford Cres RG40 25 D8
Shelburne Dr TW4 5 A1
Shelburne Ho 9 SW16 21 C3
Shelby Ct BR1 44 F8
Sheldon Cl
Crawley RH10 202 D5
Penge SE20 43 B8
Reigate RH2 139 B8
Sheldon Ct 3 GU1 130 F8
Sheldon Ho TW11 17 A2
Sheldon St CR0, CR9 61 C7
Sheldrick Cl CR4 40 D7
Shelford 9 KT1 38 A7
Shelford Rise SE19 22 F1
Shelley Ave RG12 27 E7
Shelley Cl
Banstead SM7 77 E4
Coulsdon CR5 79 F2
Crawley RH10 202 C8
Shelley Cres TW5 4 D6
Shelley Ct
Camberley GU15 65 C5
Horsham RH12 217 C1
9 Kingston u T KT2 17 D4
1 Walton-on-T KT12 35 C1
West Barnes KT3 39 A4
Shelley Dr RH12 216 C3
Shelley Ho 7 RH12 217 B2
Shelley Prim Sch RH12 216 E3
Shelley Rd
East Grinstead RH19 185 D1
Horsham RH12 217 B3
Shelley Rise GU14 84 F6
Shelley Way SW17 20 D2
Shellfield Cl TW19 2 A2
SHELLWOOD CROSS 158 D7
Shellwood Dr RH5 136 C3
Shellwood Rd RH2 137 D1
Shellys Ct RH13 218 A3
Shelson Ave TW13 14 F4
Shelton Ave CR6 81 C2
Shelton Cl
Guildford GU2 109 A6
Warlingham CR6 81 C2
Shelton Rd SW19 40 A8
Shelvers Gn KT20 97 C6
Shelvers Hill KT20 97 B6
Shelvers Spur KT20 97 C6
Shelvers Way KT20 97 D6
Shene Sch SW14 7 E3
Shenfield Cl CR5 99 C8
Shenley Cl CR2 61 F1
Shenley Ho SW16 21 F4
Shenley Rd TW5 4 E6
Shenstone Ho SW16 21 C3
Shenstone Pk SL5 29 E5
Shepherd Cl
Crawley RH10 201 E3
Feltham TW13 15 E4
Shepherd & Flock Rdbt GU9 125 E3
Shepherds Chase GU19 47 E2
Shepherds Cl TW17 34 B3
Shepherds Ct GU9 146 C8
Shepherdsgrove La RH19 186 F5
Shepherds Hill RG12 27 C8
SHEPHERD'S HILL 208 C6
Shepherd's Hill
Guildford GU2 109 A3
Haslemere GU27 208 C6
Merstham RH1 99 C1
Shepherd's Hill Bglws GU27 208 C6
Shepherds La GU20 49 A6
Shepherd's La GU2 108 F4
Shepherds Way
Horsham RH12 218 A5
South Croydon CR2 62 D3
Tilford GU10 147 D4
Shepherd's Way GU4 130 E4
Shepherds Wlk GU14 84 E7
Shepherds' Wlk KT18 96 B7
Shepley Cl SM5 60 A7
Shepley Ct SW16 21 C4
Shepley Dr SL5 30 D3
Shepley End SL5 30 D4
Sheppard Cl KT6 37 E5
Sheppard Ho 8 SW2 22 A7
SHEPPERTON 34 C3
Shepperton Bsns Pk TW17 34 C4
Shepperton Court Dr TW17 34 B4
Shepperton Ct TW17 34 B3
SHEPPERTON GREEN 34 B5
Shepperton Ho TW17 34 C3
Shepperton Rd TW17, TW18 33 D5
Shepperton Sta TW17 34 C4
Shepperton Studios TW17 33 F6
Sheppey Cl RH11 201 C3
Sheraton Cl GU17 64 E4
Sheraton Dr KT19 76 C6
Sheraton The 22 KT6 37 E4
Sheraton Wlk 13 RH11 201 B1
Sherborne Cl
Burgh Heath KT18 77 C2
Poyle SL3 1 E6
Sherborne Cres SM5 40 E2
Sherborne Ct
Guildford GU2 130 C7
Penge SE20 43 C7
Sherborne Rd
Cheam SM3 40 A1
Chessington KT9 56 E5
East Bedfont TW14 14 D7
Farnborough GU14 85 D1
Sherborne Wlk 1 KT22 95 C6
Sherbourne GU5 132 D5
Sherbourne Ct
2 Hampton TW12 36 A8
17 Sutton SM2 59 C4
Sherbourne Dr SL5 30 D4
Sherbourne Farm★ GU5 132 E6
Sherbourne Gdns TW17 34 E2
Sherbrooke Way KT4 39 B2
SHERE 133 B4
Shere Ave KT17, SM2 58 C1
Shere CE Inf Sch GU5 133 A4
Shere Cl
Chessington KT9 56 D5
Dorking RH5 136 C3
Shere Ct GU5 133 B2
Shere La GU5 133 A4
Shere Mus★ GU5 133 A4
Shere Rd
Albury GU4, GU5 132 C6
Ewhurst GU6 175 D7
Shere GU5 133 B5
West Clandon GU4, KT24 111 B1
West Horsley KT24 112 C4
Sherfield Cl KT3 38 B5
Sherfield Gdns SW15 7 F1
Sheridan Cl GU11 126 A8
Sheridan Ct
7 Croydon CR0 61 E6
Hounslow TW4 4 E2
Sheridan Dr RH2 118 B3
Sheridan Grange SL5 30 A3
Sheridan Pl
East Grinstead RH19 185 C1
Hampton TW12 36 C8
Mortlake SW13 7 F4
Sheridan Rd
Frimley GU16 85 D8
Merton SW19 39 F8
Richmond TW10 17 C5
Sheridans Rd KT23 94 C1
Sheridan Way BR3 43 F8
Sheridan Wlk SM5 59 F5
Sheringdale Prim Sch SW18 19 F7
Sheringham Ave
Feltham TW13 15 A5
Twickenham TW2 16 A7
Sheringham Ct SW18 20 C6
Sheringham Rd SE20 43 C6
Sherington Cl GU14 85 B6
Sheriton Ct SM1 59 A7
Sherland Rd TW1 16 F7
Shermanbury Ct RH12 217 D4
Sherriff Cl KT10 55 B8
Sherrydon GU6 174 F4
Sherwin Cres GU14 85 C7
Sherwood KT6 56 D8
Sherwood Ave SW16 41 D8
Sherwood Cl
Bracknell RG12 28 A7
Fetcham KT22 94 C4
Sherwood Cres RH2 139 B5
Sherwood Ct
Colnbrook SL3 1 D7
2 Croydon CR2 61 C5
Sutton SM1 59 A5
5 West Wickham BR4 44 B1
Sherwood Park Rd
Mitcham CR4 41 D5
Sutton SM1 59 A5
Sherwood Park Sch SM6 60 D7
Sherwood Rd
Coulsdon CR5 79 C3
Croydon CR0, CR9 43 B1
Hampton TW12 16 C3
Knaphill GU21 68 E2
Merton SW19 19 F1
Sherwood Sch The CR4 41 C5
Sherwood Way BR4 63 C8
Sherwood Wlk RH10 201 F3
Shetland Cl
Crawley RH10 202 E7
Guildford GU4 110 B6
Shetland Rd TW6 3 C1
Shewens Rd KT13 53 D6
Shey Copse GU22 70 C2
Shield Dr TW8 6 A8
Shield Rd TW15 14 D4
Shifford Path SE23 23 D5
Shilburn Way GU21 69 A1
Shildon Cl GU15 66 D3
Shillinglee Rd RH14 211 B4
Shimmings The GU1 110 A2
Shinners Cl SE25 43 A4
Shinwell Wlk 3 RH11 201 B1

Ship Alley GU14 . . . . **85** C6
Shipbourne Ho BR3 . . . . . . **23** F1
Ship Field Cl TN16 . . . . . . **103** C6
Ship Hill TN16 . . . . **103** D6
Shipka Rd SW12 . . . . **21** B7
Ship La
  Farnborough GU14 . . . . **85** C6
  Mortlake SW14 . . . . **7** C5
Shiplake Ct SW17 . . . . **20** D4
Shiplake Ho RG12 . . . . **27** F5
SHIPLEY BRIDGE **182** F6
Shipley Bridge La
  Burstow RH6, RH10 . . . . . . **182** F4
  Copthorne RH10 . . . . **183** A3
Shipley Ct SE20 . . . . **43** A7
Shipley Rd RH11 . . . . **201** A6
Shipman Rd SE23 . . . . **23** D6
Ship St RH19 . . . . **205** E8
Shirburn Cl SE23 . . . . **23** C8
Shire Cl GU19 . . . . **47** E2
Shire Ct
  Aldershot GU11 . . . . **104** E2
  Ewell KT17 . . . . **57** F3
Shire Horse Way TW7 . . . . **5** F4
Shire Mews TW2 . . . . **5** C1
Shire Par RH10 . . . . **202** D7
Shire Pl
  12 Brentford TW8 . . . . **6** C7
  Crawley RH1 . . . . **202** D7
  Redhill RH1 . . . . **140** A7
  Wandsworth SW18 . . . . **20** B8
Shires Cl KT21 . . . . **95** D8
Shires Ho KT14 . . . . **71** E6
Shires The TW10 . . . . **17** E4
SHIRLEY **62** C7
Shirley Ave
  Belmont SM2 . . . . **58** F1
  Carshalton SM1 . . . . **59** E6
  Coulsdon CR5 . . . . **100** B8
  Croydon CR0, CR9 . . . . **43** C1
  Redhill RH1 . . . . **139** F4
Shirley Church Rd CR0 . . . **62** E7
Shirley Cl
  Crawley RH11 . . . . **200** E2
  Isleworth TW3 . . . . **5** C2
Shirley Cott CR0 . . . . **62** D8
Shirley Cres BR3 . . . . **43** E5
Shirley Ct
  Guildford GU1 . . . . **130** D8
  Streatham SW16 . . . . **21** E1
  Thornton Heath SW16 . . . . . **41** F6
Shirley Dr TW3 . . . . **5** C2
Shirley High Sch CR0 . . . . **62** D7
Shirley Hills Rd CR0 . . . . **62** D5
Shirley Hts SM6 . . . . **60** C2
Shirley Hyrst KT13 . . . . . . **53** D4
Shirley Lo 4 SE26 . . . . **23** E4
SHIRLEY OAKS **43** E1
Shirley Oaks Hospl
  CR0 . . . . **43** C2
Shirley Oaks Rd CR0,
  CR9 . . . . **62** D8
Shirley Park Rd CR0 . . . . . **43** C1
Shirley Pl GU21 . . . . **68** C2
Shirley Rd
  Croydon CR0, CR9 . . . . **43** B1
  Wallington SM6 . . . . **60** C2
Shirley Way CR0 . . . . **62** F7
Shoe La GU11 . . . . **105** A6
Shophouse La GU5 . . . . . . **153** E7
Shord Hill CR8. . . . . **80** D3
Shore Cl
  Feltham TW14 . . . . **15** A8
  Hampton TW12 . . . . **15** E3
Shore Gr TW13 . . . . **16** A6
Shoreham Cl CR0 . . . . **43** C3
Shoreham Rd RH10 . . . . . . **202** C3
Shoreham Rd E TW6 . . . . . . **2** E2
Shoreham Rd W TW6 . . . . . . **2** E2
Shore's Rd GU21 . . . . **69** F5
Shorndean St SE6 . . . . **24** C7
Shortacres RH1 . . . . **119** F2
Short Cl RH11 . . . . **201** D8
Shortcroft Rd KT17 . . . . . . **57** F3
Shortdale Rd GU11 . . . . . . **126** C6
SHORTFIELD COMMON
  . . . . **146** C1
Shortfield Rd GU10 . . . . . . **146** C1
Short Gallop RH10 . . . . . . **202** D7
SHORTHEATH **146** A6
Shortheath Crest
  GU9 . . . . **145** F6
Shortheath Rd GU9,
  GU10 . . . . **146** A7
Short La
  Limpsfield RH8 . . . . **123** B3
  Stanwell TW15, TW19 . . . . . **13** F7
SHORTLANDS **44** E6
Shortlands UB3 . . . . **3** D8
Shortlands Gdns BR2 . . . . **44** E7
Shortlands Gr BR2 . . . . . . **44** D6
Shortlands Rd
  Beckenham BR2 . . . . **44** E6
  Kingston u T KT2 . . . . **17** F1
Shortlands Sta BR2 . . . . . . **44** E7
Short Rd
  Chiswick W4 . . . . **7** E8
  Stanwell TW19 . . . . **2** E1
Shortsfield Cl RH12 . . . . . **217** C5
Shorts Rd SM5 . . . . **59** E6
Short St GU11 . . . . **105** A2
Short Way TW2 . . . . **16** C8
Shortwood GU22. . . . . **89** D8
Shortwood Ave TW18 . . . . . **13** B5

Shortwood Comm
  TW18. . . . . **13** B5
Shortwood Inf Sch
  TW18 . . . . **13** B5
Shotfield SM6 . . . . **60** B4
Shott Cl 4 SM1 . . . . **59** C5
SHOTTERMILL **207** F6
Shottermill RH12 . . . . **218** A7
Shottermill Inf Sch
  GU27 . . . . **207** F7
Shottermill Jun sch
  GU27. . . . . **207** F7
Shottermill Pk GU27 . . . . **207** F7
Shottermill Rd GU27 . . . . **207** E5
Shottfield Ave SW14 . . . . . . **7** D3
Shovelstrode La
  RH19. . . . . **206** D8
Shrewsbury Ave SW14 . . . . . **7** D3
Shrewsbury Cl KT6. . . . . . . **56** E8
Shrewsbury House Sch
  KT6. . . . . **56** E8
Shrewsbury Rd
  Beckenham BR3. . . . . **43** C6
  Carshalton SM5 . . . . **40** E2
  Harlington TW14, TW6. . . . . . **3** D1
  Redhill RH1 . . . . **118** C1
Shrewsbury Wlk 8
  TW7 . . . . **6** A4
Shrewton Rd SW17 . . . . **20** F1
Shrivenham Cl 3
  GU47 . . . . **64** D8
Shroffold Rd BR1 . . . . **24** E4
Shropshire Cl CR4 . . . . **41** E5
Shrubbery Rd SW16 . . . . . . **21** E4
Shrubbery The
  Farnborough GU14 . . . . **84** D3
  2 Surbiton KT6 . . . . **37** E1
Shrubbs Hill GU24 . . . . . . **49** C2
Shrubbs Hill La SL5. . . . . . **30** C3
Shrubbs La GU10 . . . . **145** F4
Shrubland Ct SM7 . . . . **77** F3
Shrubland Gr KT4. . . . . **58** C7
Shrubland Rd SM7 . . . . **78** A3
Shrublands Ave CR0 . . . . . . **63** A6
Shrublands Cl SE26 . . . . . . **23** C5
Shrublands Dr GU18 . . . . . **67** B8
SHRUBS HILL **30** C3
Shuna KT15 . . . . **70** E7
Shute End RG40, RG41 . . . . **25** B6
Sibford Ct 6 CR4 . . . . **40** F4
Sibley Ct BR2 . . . . **44** E7
Sibthorp Rd 4 CR4 . . . . . . **40** F7
Sibton Rd SM5 . . . . **40** E2
Sickle Mill Ct GU27 . . . . . **207** F6
Sickle Rd GU27 . . . . **208** A5
Sidbury Cl SL5 . . . . **30** A4
Siddeley Dr TW4 . . . . **4** E5
Siddons Rd
  Croydon CR0, CR9 . . . . **61** B7
  Forest Hill SE23 . . . . **23** E6
Sidestrand Rd KT4 . . . . . . **104** E7
Sideways La RH6 . . . . **160** D2
Sidings The
  Aldershot GU11 . . . . **105** C3
  Rudgwick RH12 . . . . **214** D7
  Staines TW18. . . . . **13** B4
Sidlaws Rd GU14. . . . . **84** D6
SIDLOW **139** B2
Sidmouth Ave TW7 . . . . **5** E5
Sidmouth Ct SM3 . . . . **58** C6
Sidney Gdns TW8 . . . . **6** D8
Sidney Rd
  Croydon SE25 . . . . **43** A4
  Penge BR3. . . . . **43** E7
  Staines TW18. . . . . **13** A4
  Twickenham TW1. . . . . **6** B1
  Walton-on-T KT12 . . . . **35** B1
Sidney Wood Forest
  Wlks★ GU6. . . . . **193** C2
Sienna Ct TW13. . . . . **14** F5
Signal Ct RH7 . . . . **164** E5
Sigrist Sq 4 KT2 . . . . **37** E8
Silbury Ave CR4 . . . . **40** E8
Silbury Ho 9 SE26 . . . . **23** A5
Silchester Cl
  Ashford TW15 . . . . **13** E6
  Thornton Heath CR7 . . . . . . **42** A5
Silchester Dr RH11. . . . . . **201** B4
Silistria Cl GU21 . . . . **68** C1
Silkham Rd RH8 . . . . **122** E8
Silkin Wlk 8 RH11. . . . . . **201** B1
Silkmore La
  West Horsley KT24 . . . . **92** A2
  West Horsley KT24 . . . . . . **112** B7
Silk Pl RG40 . . . . **25** D7
Silo Cl GU7 . . . . **150** F8
Silo Dr GU7 . . . . **150** F8
Silo Rd GU7 . . . . **150** F8
Silver Birch Cl
  Forest Hill SE6. . . . . **23** F5
  Woodham KT15 . . . . **70** E7
Silver Birch Cotts
  GU10 . . . . **168** E1
Silver Birches Way
  GU8 . . . . **148** E3
Silver Birch Ho RH11. . . . **201** C6
Silver Cl KT20 . . . . **97** E3
Silver Ct
  East Grinstead RH19 . . . . . **185** B2
  Leatherhead KT22 . . . . **95** B7
Silverdale SE23, SE26 . . . . **23** C4
Silverdale Ave
  Oxshott KT22. . . . . **74** C5
  Walton-on-T KT12, KT13 . . . . **53** F7
Silverdale Cl
  Brockham RH3. . . . . **137** B5
  Cheam SM1 . . . . **58** F6
Silverdale Ct TW18. . . . . . . **13** B3

Silverdale Dr TW16 . . . . . . **35** B7
Silver Dr GU16. . . . . **66** C3
Silvergate KT19. . . . . **57** C5
Silverglade KT9. . . . . **75** C7
Silverglade Bsns Pk
  KT9. . . . . **75** C7
Silverhall St TW7 . . . . **6** A4
Silver Hill GU47. . . . . **64** E8
Silver Jubilee Way TW4 . . . **4** B5
Silver La
  Purley CR8. . . . . **79** E7
  West Wickham BR4 . . . . **63** D8
Silverlands Cl KT16 . . . . . . **51** D7
Silverlea Gdns RH6 . . . . . **161** C2
Silverleigh Rd CR7. . . . . . . **42** A4
Silvermere Ct
  Caterham CR3 . . . . **100** F3
  1 Purley CR8. . . . . **80** A7
Silvermere Rd 4 SE6 . . . . . **24** B8
Silversmiths Way
  GU21 . . . . **69** C1
Silverstone Cl RH1. . . . . . **118** F3
Silverton Lo SE19 . . . . **22** E1
Silver Tree Cl KT12 . . . . . . **54** A6
Silver Wing Ind Est
  CR0 . . . . **60** F4
Silverwood Cl
  Beckenham BR3. . . . . **24** A1
  New Addington CR0. . . . . . . **63** A2
Silverwood Dr GU15 . . . . . **66** A7
Silverwood Grange
  SL5. . . . . **29** F2
Silwood RG12 . . . . **26** E1
Silwood Cl SL5. . . . . **29** D7
Silwood Park (Imperial
  Coll) SL5. . . . . **29** F6
Silwood Rd SL5. . . . . **29** F5
Simkins Cl RG42 . . . . **8** B2
Simmil Rd KT10. . . . . **55** E5
Simmonds Cl RG42. . . . . . . **26** E8
Simmonds Cotts GU7 . . . . **150** B4
Simmonds Ct GU9 . . . . . . **125** C2
Simmondstone La
  GU10. . . . . **167** D2
Simmons Cl KT9 . . . . **56** C4
Simmons Gate KT10 . . . . . . **55** C5
Simmons Pl TW18 . . . . **12** E3
Simms Cl SM5 . . . . **59** E8
Simone Dr CR8 . . . . **80** C3
Simon Lo 31 SW19 . . . . . . **19** D7
Simons Cl KT16. . . . . **51** C4
Simons Wlk TW20 . . . . **11** C1
Simplemarsh Ct KT15 . . . . **52** B4
Simplemarsh Rd KT15. . . . **52** B6
Simpson Ho 1 KT12 . . . . . . **35** A1
Simpson Rd
  Richmond TW10. . . . . **17** C4
  Twickenham TW4 . . . . **4** F1
Simpson Way KT6 . . . . **37** C3
Sim's Cotts KT10. . . . . **55** F4
Sinclair Cl RH10 . . . . **202** C4
Sinclair Ct
  22 Beckenham BR3 . . . . . . **24** A1
  5 Croydon CR0 . . . . **61** F8
Sinclair Dr SM2. . . . . **59** B2
Sinclair Ho
  Streatham, Streatham Hill
  SW12 . . . . **21** D7
  Streatham SW16 . . . . **21** F1
Sincots Rd RH1 . . . . **118** F1
Sine Cl GU14 . . . . **85** B8
Singlegate Prim Sch
  SW19 . . . . **20** D1
Singleton Cl
  Mitcham SW17, SW19. . . . . **20** F1
  Thornton Heath CR0 . . . . . . **42** C2
Singleton Rd RH12. . . . . . **216** D3
Sinhurst Rd GU15 . . . . **65** B4
Sion Ct TW1 . . . . **17** B7
Sion Rd TW1 . . . . **17** B7
SIPSON **3** A8
Sipson Cl UB7 . . . . **3** A8
Sipson La UB7 . . . . **3** B8
Sipson Rd UB7. . . . . **3** A7
Sipson Way UB7 . . . . **3** A7
Sir Arthur Bliss Ct 6
  CR4 . . . . **40** F7
Sir Cyril Black Way 2
  SW19 . . . . **20** A1
Sirdar Rd CR4 . . . . **21** A2
Sirl Cotts SL5 . . . . **29** C5
Sir William Perkin's Sch
  KT16 . . . . **32** F1
Sisken Ct 2 CR0 . . . . **61** E7
Siskin Ave RH10 . . . . **204** C5
Siskin Cl RH12. . . . . **217** E5
Sissinghurst Cl
  Catford BR1. . . . . **24** E3
  Crawley RH10 . . . . **202** D7
Sissinghurst Rd CR0 . . . . . **43** A2
Sistova Rd SW12. . . . . **21** B7
Siward Rd SW17 . . . . **20** C5
Six Acres RH13 . . . . **215** D2
Six Cross-Roads GU21 . . . **70** A5
Sixth Cross Rd TW2 . . . . . . **16** C5
Sixth Form Coll
  Farnborough GU14 . . . . **85** B6
Skeat Ho KT22. . . . . **95** B5
Skeena Hill SW18,
  SW19. . . . . **19** E8
Skelbrook St SW18 . . . . **20** C6
Skelmersdale Wlk
  RH11 . . . . **200** E2
Skerne Rd KT2 . . . . **37** D8
Skerne Wlk KT2 . . . . **37** D8
Skid Hill La CR6 . . . . **82** F5
Skiffington Cl SW2. . . . . . . **22** A7
Skiff La RH14 . . . . **213** A1

SKIMMINGTON **138** D8
Skimmington Cotts
  RH2. . . . . **138** D8
Skinners La
  Ashtead KT21 . . . . **75** D1
  Chiddingfold GU8. . . . . **191** D5
  Heston TW5. . . . . **5** B6
Skipton Ct SE24 . . . . **22** B7
Skipton Way RH6 . . . . **161** B5
Skylark View RH12. . . . . . **217** D7
Skyline Ct CR0. . . . . **61** D7
Skyport Dr UB7 . . . . **2** D7
Skyview Appartments 8
  CR0 . . . . **61** D8
Skyway 14 Trad Est SL3 . . . **1** F4
Slade Ct KT16 . . . . **51** D4
Slade Ho TW4 . . . . **4** F1
Slade Rd
  Ottershaw KT16. . . . . **51** D4
  Pirbright GU24. . . . . **87** D7
Slade Way CR4 . . . . **41** A8
Slaidburn Gn RG12. . . . . . . **27** E2
Slattery Rd TW13 . . . . **15** C7
Slaugham Ct RH11. . . . . . . **200** F3
SLEAFORD **166** A1
Sledmere Ct SW14 . . . . **14** E7
Sleets Rd RH12 . . . . **216** E3
Slim Cl GU11 . . . . **105** E7
Slim Rd GU15 . . . . **65** C7
Slines New Rd CR3,
  CR6 . . . . **101** E7
Slines Oak Rd CR3,
  CR6 . . . . **102** B6
SLINFOLD **215** D3
Slinfold CE Prim Sch
  RH13. . . . . **215** D4
Slinfold Wlk RH11 . . . . . . **201** A6
Slip Of Wood GU6 . . . . . . **174** F4
Slipshatch Rd RH2. . . . . . . **138** E5
Slipshoe St 2 RH2. . . . . . . **118** A1
Sloane Hospl BR3 . . . . **44** D8
Sloane Wlk CR0 . . . . **43** F3
Slocock Hill GU21 . . . . **69** C2
Sloughbrook Cl RH12 . . . . **217** F6
Slough La
  Buckland RH3. . . . . **117** A3
  Headley KT18 . . . . **96** C2
SLYFIELD **109** D5
Slyfield Ct GU1 . . . . **109** E4
Slyfield Gn GU1. . . . . **109** E5
Slyfield Ind Est GU1. . . . . **109** E5
Smallberry Ave TW7 . . . . . . **5** F5
Smallberry Green Prim
  Sch The TW7 . . . . **6** A5
SMALLFIELD **162** B2
Smallfield Rd
  Horley RH6 . . . . **161** D3
  Horne RH6 . . . . **162** E3
Smallmead RH6 . . . . **161** B3
Smalls Hill Rd RH2,
  RH6 . . . . **159** C6
Small's La RH11 . . . . **201** C6
Smalls Mead RH11 . . . . . . **201** C6
Smallwood Prim Sch
  SW17 . . . . **20** D4
Smallwood Rd SW17 . . . . . . **20** D4
Smart's Heath La GU22. . . . **89** A4
Smart's Heath Rd
  GU22 . . . . **89** B5
Smeaton Cl KT9 . . . . **56** D4
Smeaton Rd SW18 . . . . **20** A8
Smeeds Cl RH19 . . . . **186** A3
Smitham Bottom La CR5,
  CR8 . . . . **79** D7
Smitham Downs Rd CR5,
  CR8 . . . . **79** E6
Smitham Prim Sch
  CR5. . . . . **79** C3
Smitham Sta CR5. . . . . **79** E4
Smithbarn RH13 . . . . **218** A2
Smithbarn Cl RH6. . . . . . . **161** B4
Smithbrook Cotts
  GU6 . . . . **173** D3
Smithbrook Gate
  GU6 . . . . **173** D3
Smith Cl RH10 . . . . **201** D3
Smith Ct GU21. . . . . **70** D6
Smithers Cotts RH12. . . . . **214** F7
Smithers Ho SE20. . . . . **23** D1
Smithers The RH3 . . . . **137** B7
Smithfield La GU35,
  GU10 . . . . **167** A1
Smith Rd RH2 . . . . **138** F6
Smith Sq RG12. . . . . **27** D7
Smith St KT5 . . . . **37** F3
Smith's Yd SW18 . . . . **20** C6
Smithwood Ave GU6 . . . . . **174** B7
Smithwood Cl SW19 . . . . . . **19** E6
Smithwood Common Rd
  GU6 . . . . **174** B7
Smithy Cl KT20 . . . . **97** F1
Smithy La
  Lower Kingswood KT20 . . . . **97** F1
  Sleaford GU10 . . . . **166** E2
Smithy's Gn GU20. . . . . **48** D4
Smock Wlk CR0. . . . . **42** C3
Smokejack Hill RH5. . . . . . **196** D7
Smoke La RH2 . . . . **139** B7
Smolletts RH19 . . . . **205** C8
Smoothfield TW3 . . . . **5** A3
Smugglers' La RH5 . . . . . . **197** E2
Smugglers' Way
  GU10 . . . . **126** E1
Snailslynch GU9 . . . . **125** D2
Snakey La TW13 . . . . **15** B4
Snatts Hill RH8 . . . . **122** F6

Snelgate Cotts GU4 . . . . . . **111** D4
Snell Hatch RH11 . . . . **201** B6
Snellings Rd KT12 . . . . **54** C5
Snera Lo SW19 . . . . **20** E1
Snipe La GU27 . . . . **208** A1
Snowdenham Hall
  GU5 . . . . **151** D5
Snowdenham La GU5 . . . . **151** E5
Snowdenham Links Rd
  GU5 . . . . **151** D6
Snowdon Rd
  Farnborough GU14 . . . . **84** E7
  Harlington TW6 . . . . **3** C1
Snowdown Cl SE20 . . . . **43** D8
Snowdrop Cl
  Crawley RH11 . . . . **201** A2
  2 Hampton TW12. . . . . **16** A2
Snowdrop Way GU24. . . . . . **68** A2
Snowe Ho SE27. . . . . **22** B5
Snowerhill Rd RH3. . . . . . . **137** F6
SNOW HILL **184** A4
Snow Hill
  Copthorne RH10 . . . . **183** F3
  Domewood RH10. . . . . **183** F5
Snow Hill Bsns Ctr
  RH10. . . . . **184** A4
Snowhill La RH10 . . . . **183** F5
Snows Paddock GU20 . . . . . **48** B7
Snows Ride GU20. . . . . **48** B6
Snowy Fielder Waye
  TW7 . . . . **6** B5
Soames Wlk KT3. . . . . **38** E8
Soane Cl RH11 . . . . **200** E4
Soaphouse La TW8 . . . . **6** E7
Sohomills Ind Est SM6 . . . **41** B1
Sola Ct 7 CR0. . . . . **42** D1
Solartron Rd GU14 . . . . **85** B3
Solartron Ret Pk GU14. . . . **85** A3
Solecote KT23. . . . . **94** A2
Sole Farm Ave KT23. . . . . . **93** F2
Sole Farm Cl KT23. . . . . . . **93** F2
Sole Farm Rd KT23. . . . . . . **93** F2
Solent Ct SW16 . . . . **41** F7
Soloms Court Rd CR5,
  SM7 . . . . **78** E2
Solway Cl TW4 . . . . **4** E4
Sol-y-vista GU7 . . . . **150** D6
Somborne Ho 12 SW15 . . . **19** A8
Somerfield Cl KT20 . . . . . . **97** E8
Somergate RH12. . . . . **216** F2
Somersbury La GU6,
  RH12 . . . . **195** F7
Somersby Est SE20 . . . . . . **23** C1
Somers Cl RH2 . . . . **118** A2
Somerset Ave
  Chessington KT9 . . . . **56** D6
  Wimbledon SW20 . . . . **39** B7
Somerset Cl
  Epsom KT19. . . . . **57** D2
  Hersham KT12. . . . . **54** B5
  New Malden KT3 . . . . **38** E3
Somerset Ct
  Farnborough GU14 . . . . **85** C1
  3 Hampton TW12. . . . . **36** A8
Somerset Gdns
  Teddington TW11. . . . . **16** E3
  Thornton Heath SW16. . . . . . **41** F6
Somerset Ho
  Wimbledon SW19 . . . . **19** E5
  15 Woking GU22 . . . . **69** F2
Somerset Lo 11 TW8 . . . . . . **6** D8
Somerset Rd
  Brentford TW8. . . . . **6** C8
  Farnborough GU14 . . . . **85** C1
  Kingston u T KT1 . . . . **37** F7
  Reigate RH1. . . . . **139** D7
  Teddington TW11. . . . . **16** E3
  Wimbledon SW19 . . . . **19** D5
Somerset Waye TW5. . . . . . . **4** F7
Somers Pl
  1 Reigate RH2 . . . . **118** A2
  Streatham SW2 . . . . **21** F8
Somers Rd
  Reigate RH2. . . . . **118** A2
  2 Streatham SW2 . . . . **21** F8
Somerswey GU4 . . . . **130** E1
Somerton Ave TW9 . . . . **7** B4
Somerton Cl CR8 . . . . **80** A3
Somertons Cl GU2 . . . . . . **109** A4
Somerville Ct SW16 . . . . . . **21** D2
Somerville Dr RH10. . . . . . **182** C1
Somerville Rd
  Cobham KT11. . . . . **74** A5
  Penge BR3, SE20. . . . . **23** D1
Somerville Rise RG12 . . . . . **27** B4
Sondes Farm RH4. . . . . **135** F7
Sondes Place Dr RH4 . . . . **135** F7
Songhurst Cl CR0. . . . . **41** F3
Sonia Gdns TW5. . . . . **5** A7
Sonic Ct GU1. . . . . **109** C2
Sonnet Wlk TN16 . . . . **83** C1
Sonning Ct CR0. . . . . **62** A8
Sonninge Cl GU47 . . . . **64** D8
Sonning Gdns TW12 . . . . . . **15** E2
Sonning Rd CR0 . . . . **43** A3
Soper Cl SE23 . . . . **23** D6
Soper Dr CR3 . . . . **100** D4
Sopwith Ave KT9 . . . . **56** E5
Sopwith Cl
  Biggin Hill TN16 . . . . **83** D3
  Richmond TW10. . . . . **17** F3
Sopwith Dr KT13 . . . . **71** E8
Sopwith Rd TW5. . . . . **4** C7
Sopwith Way KT2 . . . . **37** E8
Sorbie Cl KT13. . . . . **53** D6
Sorrel Bank CR0 . . . . **62** G2
Sorrel Cl
  Crawley RH11 . . . . **201** A2

Sorrel Cl *continued*
Farnborough GU14 . . . . 84 C5
Wokingham RG40 . . . . 25 E8
Sorrel Dr GU18 . . . . 66 F7
Sorrel Ho TW3. . . . . 5 C6
Sorrel Rd RH12 . . . . 217 E5
Sorrento Rd SM1 . . . . 59 B7
South Albert Rd RH2. . . . 117 F2
Southall La TW5 . . . . 4 B8
Southam Ho KT15. . . . . 52 B5
Southampton Cl GU17. . . . 64 C6
Southampton Gdns
CR4 . . . . 41 E4
Southampton Rd TW6. . . . . . 2 F1
Southampton St
GU14 . . . . 105 B8
South Atlantic Dr
GU11 . . . . 105 C3
South Ave
Egham TW20 . . . . 12 C2
Heath End GU9 . . . . 125 D6
Richmond TW9. . . . . 7 A5
Wallington SM5 . . . . 60 A3
Whiteley Village KT12 . . . . . 53 E1
Southbank KT7 . . . . 37 B2
South Bank KT6 . . . . 37 E3
South Bank Lo 2 KT6. . . . 37 E3
South Bank Terr KT6. . . . . 37 E3
SOUTH BEDDINGTON 60 C3
South Bookham Sch
KT23. . . . . 114 C8
South Border The CR8 . . . 79 E8
SOUTHBOROUGH 37 D1
Southborough Cl KT6 . . . . 37 D1
Southborough High Sch
KT6. . . . . 56 E7
Southborough Rd KT6 . . . 37 E1
Southbridge Pl CR0,
CR9 . . . . 61 C6
Southbridge Rd CR0,
CR9 . . . . 61 C6
Southbrook RH11. . . . . 201 C1
Southbrook Rd SW16 . . . . 41 E8
Southbury GU2 . . . . 130 C7
South Cl
Crawley RH10 . . . . 201 F7
Morden SM4 . . . . 40 A3
Twickenham TW2. . . . . 16 A5
Woking GU21. . . . . 69 C3
Wokingham RG40 . . . . 25 D4
South Close Gn RH1 . . . . 119 B6
Southcote GU21 . . . . 69 D3
Southcote Ave
Feltham TW13 . . . . 15 A6
Tolworth KT5. . . . . 38 B2
Southcote Dr GU15 . . . . . . 66 A5
Southcote Ho KT15 . . . . . . 52 D8
Southcote Rd
Croydon SE25 . . . . 43 B3
Merstham RH1. . . . . 119 C6
South Croydon CR2 . . . . 61 F1
Southcourt TW16 . . . . 35 C6
Southcroft
Carshalton SM1. . . . . 59 E5
Englefield Green TW20 . . . . 11 B3
Southcroft Ave BR4 . . . . . . 63 C8
Southcroft Rd SW17 . . . . . 21 A2
South Croxted Rd
SE21. . . . . 22 D4
SOUTH CROYDON 61 D3
South Croydon Sta
CR2. . . . . 61 D5
Southdean Gdns SW19 . . . 19 F6
Southdown Cl RH12 . . . . . 218 A5
Southdown Dr SW20 . . . . . 19 D1
Southdown Rd
Hersham KT12. . . . . 54 E6
Wallington SM5 . . . . 60 A2
Wimbledon SW20 . . . . 39 D8
Woldingham CR3 . . . . 101 F5
South Dr
Banstead SM7 . . . . 78 E6
Belmont SM2 . . . . 58 E2
Coulsdon CR5 . . . . 79 D4
Dorking RH4 . . . . 136 C7
Pirbright GU24. . . . . 87 C6
Wentworth GU25. . . . . 31 A2
Wokingham RG40 . . . . 25 C5
SOUTH EARLSWOOD
. . . . 139 F4
South Eden Park Rd
Beckenham BR3. . . . . 44 B4
West Wickham BR3 . . . . 44 B2
SOUTHEND 24 D4
South End
Croydon CR0, CR9 . . . . 61 C6
Great Bookham KT23. . . . . . 94 B1
Southend La
Catford SE6 . . . . 24 B4
Forest Hill SE26, SE6. . . . . . 23 F4
Southend Rd BR3 . . . . 44 A8
Southerland Cl KT13 . . . . . 53 C6
Southern Ave
East Bedfont TW14 . . . . 15 A7
Salfords RH1. . . . . 140 A1
South Norwood SE25. . . . . . 42 F6
Southern Bglws GU4. . . . 131 B2
Southern Cotts TW19 . . . . . 2 A2
Southern Ind Area
RG12. . . . . 26 F6
Southern Perimeter Rd
East Bedfont TW6 . . . . 3 B1
Harlington TW14, TW6. . . . . . 3 D2
Stanwell TW19, TW6 . . . . 2 D2
Southern Rd GU15 . . . . 65 C6
Southerns La CR5. . . . . 98 C3
Southern Way
Farnborough GU14 . . . . 84 E3
Southern Way *continued*
Farnham GU9. . . . . 125 C1
Southey Ct KT23 . . . . 94 B3
Southey Rd SW19. . . . . 20 A1
Southey St SE20 . . . . 23 D1
South Farm La GU19 . . . . . 48 A2
SOUTH FARNBOROUGH
. . . . 85 D1
South Farnborough Inf
Sch GU14 . . . . 105 D8
South Farnborough Jun
Sch GU14 . . . . 85 D2
South Farnham Com Jun
Sch GU9 . . . . 125 D1
Southfield Gdns TW1 . . . . 16 F4
Southfield Park Prim Sch
KT19. . . . . 76 C8
Southfield Pl KT13 . . . . 53 B3
SOUTHFIELDS 20 A7
Southfields KT8 . . . . 36 E3
Southfields Ave TW15. . . . 14 B2
Southfield Sch RG40 . . . . . 25 D5
Southfields Com Coll
SW18 . . . . 20 A7
Southfields Ct SM3 . . . . . . 59 A8
Southfields Rd CR3 . . . . . 102 B3
Southfields Sta SW18 . . . . 19 F7
SOUTHGATE 201 C4
Southgate Ave RH10 . . . . 201 E4
South Gate Ave TW13 . . . . 14 D4
Southgate Dr RH10 . . . . . 201 E4
Southgate Par RH10 . . . . 201 D4
Southgate Prim Sch
RH10. . . . . 201 D4
Southgate Rd RH10 . . . . . 201 D4
South Gdns SW19. . . . . 20 D1
SOUTH GODSTONE 142 F5
South Gr
Chertsey KT16. . . . . 32 F3
Horsham RH13 . . . . 217 D1
South Hill
Godalming GU7 . . . . 150 F4
Guildford GU1 . . . . 130 D7
South Hill Rd
Beckenham BR2. . . . . 44 E5
Bracknell RG12 . . . . 27 B3
Southholme Cl SE19 . . . . . 42 E8
South Holmes Rd
RH13 . . . . 218 B4
SOUTH HOLMWOOD 157 C7
South La
Ash GU12. . . . . 106 B1
Kingston u T KT1 . . . . 37 D6
New Malden KT3 . . . . 38 D4
New Malden, Old Malden
KT3 . . . . 38 E2
Southlands
East Grinstead RH19. . . . . 205 E7
Horley RH6 . . . . 160 F3
Tandridge RH8. . . . . 122 C2
Southlands Ave RH6 . . . . 161 A4
Southlands Cl
Ash GU12. . . . . 106 A1
Coulsdon CR5 . . . . 79 F2
Wokingham RG40 . . . . 25 D5
Southlands Dr SW19 . . . . . 19 D6
Southlands La RH8. . . . . . 122 C1
Southlands Rd
Ash GU12. . . . . 106 A1
Wokingham RG40 . . . . 25 D4
Southland Way TW7 . . . . . . 5 D2
South La W KT3 . . . . 38 D5
South Lawn Ct GU7 . . . . . 150 D6
South Lo TW2 . . . . 5 C1
South Lodge Ave CR4, CR7,
SW16. . . . . 41 E5
South Lodge Ct RH2 . . . . 159 F7
South Lodge Rd KT12 . . . . 54 B2
South Lynn Cres RG12. . . . 27 B4
South Mdw RG45 . . . . 45 D3
South Mead
Redhill RH1 . . . . 118 F4
West Ewell KT19 . . . . 57 F3
Southmead Prim Sch
SW19 . . . . 19 E7
Southmead Rd
Aldershot GU11. . . . . 126 B8
Putney SW19. . . . . 19 E7
SOUTH MERSTHAM 119 D5
South Merton Sta
SW20 . . . . 39 F6
Southmont Rd KT10. . . . . . 55 E7
South Munstead La
GU8 . . . . 172 B7
SOUTH NORWOOD 42 E5
South Norwood Ctry Pk*
SE25 . . . . 43 C5
South Norwood High Sch
SE25 . . . . 43 B4
South Norwood Hill SE19,
SE25. . . . . 42 F7
South Norwood Prim Sch
SE25 . . . . 43 A5
SOUTH NUTFIELD 140 E7
South Oak Rd SW16. . . . . . 21 F4
South Par
Horley RH6 . . . . 160 F4
Wallington SM6 . . . . 60 C4
SOUTH PARK
Reigate. 138 F6
South Godstone 142 A6
South Park Cres SE6 . . . . . 24 F7
Southpark Ct 4 SW19. . . . 20 A2
South Park Ct 25 BR3 . . . . 24 A1
South Park Gr KT3. . . . . . . 38 C5
South Park Hill Rd
CR2 . . . . 61 D6
South Park La RH1. . . . . . 142 A7
South Park Rd SW19. . . . . 20 B2
South Pier Rd RH6. . . . . . 182 B7
South Pl
Surbiton KT5 . . . . 37 F2
Wokingham RG40 . . . . 25 C6
South Rd
Ash Vale GU12. . . . . 106 A4
Bisley GU24. . . . . 67 F3
Bracknell RG40, RG12 . . . . . 26 E1
Cranford TW5 . . . . 4 D8
Crowthorne RG45 . . . . 45 E3
Englefield Green TW20 . . . . 11 D2
Feltham TW13 . . . . 15 D3
Forest Hill SE23. . . . . 23 D6
Guildford GU2 . . . . 109 B3
Hampton TW12 . . . . 15 F2
Mitcham SW19 . . . . 20 D2
Reigate RH2. . . . . 139 B8
Twickenham TW2. . . . . 16 D5
Weybridge KT13 . . . . 53 B2
Weybridge, St George's Hill
KT13 . . . . 53 C5
Woking GU21. . . . . 69 C4
South Ridge KT13. . . . . 72 B8
Southridge Pl SW20. . . . . . 19 D1
South Rise SM5. . . . . 59 E2
Southsea Rd KT1 . . . . 37 E5
South Side GU10. . . . . 126 F7
Southside Comm
SW19 . . . . 19 D2
South St
Dorking RH4 . . . . 136 A7
Epsom KT18. . . . . 76 D5
Farnborough GU14 . . . . 85 E1
Farnham GU9. . . . . 125 C2
Godalming GU7 . . . . 150 D4
Horsham RH12 . . . . 217 C2
Isleworth TW7. . . . . 6 A4
Staines TW18. . . . . 12 F3
South Station App
RH1 . . . . 140 F7
South Terr
Dorking RH4 . . . . 136 B6
Surbiton KT6 . . . . 37 E3
South Thames Coll
(Tooting Ctr) SW17 . . . . . 20 E3
South Vale SE19 . . . . 22 E2
South View
Bracknell RG12 . . . . 26 C6
Epsom KT19. . . . . 57 A1
Oxted RH8 . . . . 123 A2
Wimbledon SW19 . . . . 19 D2
Southview Cl SW17 . . . . . . 21 A3
South View Cl RH10. . . . . 183 E3
Southview Cotts
GU10 . . . . 146 D1
South View Cotts
GU5 . . . . 152 D4
Southview Ct 14 GU22. . . . 69 E1
South View Ct SE19. . . . . . 22 C1
Southview Gdns SM6. . . . . 60 C3
Southview Rd
Catford BR1. . . . . 24 D4
Headley Down GU35 . . . . . 187 B5
Woldingham CR3 . . . . 102 B3
South View Rd KT21 . . . . . 95 D8
Southviews CR2 . . . . 62 D2
Southville Cl
East Bedfont TW14 . . . . 14 E7
West Ewell KT19 . . . . 57 D2
Southville Cres TW14 . . . . 14 E7
Southville Jun & Inf Schs
TW14 . . . . 14 F7
Southville Rd
East Bedfont TW14 . . . . 14 E8
Thames Ditton KT7 . . . . 37 B2
Southwark KT18 . . . . 97 D8
Southwark Cl RH11 . . . . . 201 B2
Southwater Cl
Beckenham BR3. . . . . 24 B1
Crawley RH11 . . . . 201 A6
Southway
Camberley GU15 . . . . 65 B4
Guildford GU2 . . . . 108 F1
Wallington SM6. . . . . 60 C6
West Barnes SW20 . . . . 39 D5
South Way
Croydon CR0 . . . . 62 E7
Sutton SM5 . . . . 59 D1
Southway Ct GU2 . . . . 108 E1
Southway Pk GU2. . . . . . . 109 A2
Southways Pk RH10. . . . . 181 D3
Southwell Park Rd
GU15 . . . . 65 C5
Southwell Rd CR0, CR7 . . . 42 A3
South Western Rd TW1 . . . . 6 B1
Southwick GU19 . . . . 47 E1
Southwick Cl RH19. . . . . . 185 D2
Southwick Ct RG12 . . . . . . 27 E3
Southwick Ho RH19. . . . . 185 D2
SOUTH WIMBLEDON 20 B2
South Wimbledon Sta
SW19 . . . . 20 B1
South Wlk
Aldershot GU12. . . . . 105 D2
Coney Hall BR4 . . . . 63 E7
Southwold RG12. . . . . 26 E1
SOUTHWOOD 84 D3
Southwood RG40 . . . . 25 D4
Southwood Ave
Coulsdon CR5 . . . . 79 C4
Kingston u T KT2, KT3 . . . . . 38 C8
Knaphill GU21 . . . . 68 D1
Ottershaw KT16. . . . . 51 C3
Southwood Chase
GU6 . . . . 174 F1
Southwood Cl KT4 . . . . 39 D1
Southwood Cres GU14 . . . 84 D4
Southwood Ct
Knaphill GU21 . . . . 68 D1
Weybridge KT13 . . . . 53 B5
Southwood Dr KT5. . . . . . . 38 C1
Southwood Gdns KT10 . . . 56 A7
Southwood Inf Sch
GU14. . . . . 84 D3
Southwood La
Farnborough GU51 . . . . 84 A3
Farnborough, Southwood
GU14. . . . . 84 D3
Southwood Rd GU14 . . . . . 84 E4
South Worple Way
SW14. . . . . 7 D4
Sovereign Cl CR8 . . . . 60 F1
Sovereign Ct
14 Croydon CR2 . . . . 61 C5
East Molesey KT8 . . . . 35 F5
Harlington UB3 . . . . 3 B7
3 Richmond TW9. . . . . 6 F3
4 Sunningdale SL5. . . . . . . 30 B2
Sovereign Dr GU15. . . . . . . 66 B7
Sovereign Ho
Ashford TW15 . . . . 13 E4
3 Wimbledon SW19. . . . . . 19 E2
Sovereign Hts SL3 . . . . 1 A8
Soyer Ct 4 GU21 . . . . 68 E1
Spa Central SW16. . . . . 21 E1
Space Waye TW14 . . . . 4 B2
Spa Cl SE19 . . . . 42 E8
Spa Ct SW16. . . . . 21 F4
Spa Dr KT18 . . . . 76 A5
Spa Hill CR7, SE19 . . . . 42 D8
Spalding Rd SW17 . . . . 21 B3
Sparks Cl TW12. . . . . 15 E2
Sparrow Cl TW12 . . . . 15 E2
Sparrow Farm Com Jun
Sch KT17. . . . . 58 B6
Sparrow Farm Dr
TW14. . . . . 15 D8
Sparrow Farm Inf Sch
TW14 . . . . 15 C8
Sparrow Farm Jun Sch
TW14 . . . . 15 C8
Sparrow Farm Rd KT17,
KT4 . . . . 58 B6
Sparrowhawk Cl
GU10 . . . . 124 D8
Sparrow Row GU24 . . . . . . 49 B4
Sparrows Mead RH1 . . . . 119 A4
Spartan Cl SM6. . . . . 60 E3
Sparvell Rd GU21 . . . . 88 B8
Sparvell Way GU15. . . . . . . 65 C6
Spats La GU35 . . . . 187 A8
Spa View 6 SW16 . . . . 21 F5
Speaker's Ct 3 CR0. . . . . . 42 D1
Spean Ho GU14. . . . . 85 D2
Speart La TW5. . . . . 4 E7
Speedbird Way UB7. . . . . . . 2 C7
Speedwell Cl GU4. . . . . . . 110 C4
Speedwell Ho 5 RH1 . . . 119 A4
Speedwell Way RH12. . . . 217 E5
Speer Rd KT7. . . . . 36 F3
Speirs Cl KT3. . . . . 38 F3
Speke Rd CR7 . . . . 42 D7
Speldhurst Cl 4 BR2. . . . . 44 F4
Spelthorne Coll TW15. . . . 13 F4
Spelthorne Gr TW16 . . . . . 14 F1
Spelthorne Inf Sch
TW15 . . . . 14 E2
Spelthorne Jun Sch
TW15 . . . . 14 D2
Spelthorne La TW15,
TW17. . . . . 34 C8
Spelthorne Mus*
TW18 . . . . 12 F3
Spence Ave KT14 . . . . 71 F5
Spencer Cl
Frimley GU16. . . . . 85 E6
Langley Vale KT18. . . . . 96 E8
Sheerwater GU21 . . . . 70 D6
Spencer Ct
Leatherhead KT22. . . . . 95 C4
Wimbledon SW20 . . . . 39 B8
Spencer Gdns
Englefield Green TW20 . . . . 11 D3
Mortlake SW14 . . . . 7 C2
Spencer Hill SW19. . . . . 19 E1
Spencer Hill Rd SW19. . . . 19 E1
Spencer Ho
24 Putney SW19. . . . . 19 D7
Wimbledon SW19 . . . . 19 D5
Spencer Pk KT8 . . . . 36 C4
Spencer Pl CR0. . . . . 42 D2
Spencer Rd
Bracknell RG42 . . . . 26 F8
Bromley BR1 . . . . 24 F1
Carshalton CR4 . . . . 41 A2
Caterham CR3 . . . . 100 D6
Chiswick W4 . . . . 7 C7
Cobham KT11. . . . . 73 B4
East Molesey KT8 . . . . 36 C4
Hounslow TW3, TW5,
TW7 . . . . 5 C6
Mitcham CR4 . . . . 41 A6
South Croydon CR2 . . . . 61 E5
Twickenham TW2. . . . . 16 E6
Wimbledon SW20 . . . . 39 B8
Spencers La RH6 . . . . 159 F2
Spencers Pl RH12. . . . . . . 217 B4
Spencers Rd RH11 . . . . . . 201 D5
Spencer's Rd RH12 . . . . . 217 B3
Spencer Way RH1. . . . . . . 140 A4
Spenser Ave KT13. . . . . 53 A2
Spenser Ct 5 TW10. . . . . . 17 D4
Spenser Mews SE21. . . . . . 22 D7
Spiceall GU3 . . . . 129 B3
Spicer Cl KT12. . . . . 35 C3
Spicers Field KT22. . . . . . . 74 E6
Spices Yd CR0. . . . . 61 C6
Spiers Way RH6 . . . . 161 B1
Spindle Way RH10 . . . . . . 201 F5
Spindlewood Gdns CR0,
CR2 . . . . 61 E6
Spindlewoods KT20. . . . . . 97 B4
Spinis RG12 . . . . 26 F1
Spinnaker Ct 2 KT1 . . . . . 37 D8
Spinner Gn RG12 . . . . 27 B4
Spinney Cl
Beckenham BR3. . . . . 44 B5
Cobham KT11. . . . . 74 A8
Crawley Down RH10 . . . . . 204 C8
Horsham RH12 . . . . 218 B6
New Malden KT3 . . . . 38 E4
Worcester Park KT4 . . . . . . 57 F8
Spinneycroft KT22 . . . . 74 D4
Spinney Dr TW14 . . . . 14 C8
Spinney Gdns SE19 . . . . . . 22 F3
Spinney Hill KT15. . . . . 51 F5
Spinney La SL4 . . . . 9 B7
Spinney Oak KT16 . . . . 51 D4
Spinney The
Ascot SL5. . . . . 29 E4
Burgh Heath KT18. . . . . 97 B8
Cheam SM3 . . . . 58 C6
Crawley RH11 . . . . 201 B4
Frimley GU15. . . . . 66 C6
Grayshott GU26. . . . . 188 A4
Great Bookham KT23. . . . . . 94 B3
Haslemere GU27 . . . . 208 C8
Headley KT18 . . . . 96 C1
Horley RH6 . . . . 161 A5
Oxshott KT22. . . . . 74 C7
Purley CR8. . . . . 80 B8
Ripley GU23. . . . . 111 C8
Streatham SW16 . . . . 21 D5
Sunbury TW16. . . . . 35 A8
Spinning Wlk The
GU5 . . . . 133 A4
Spire Ct 11 TW10 . . . . 6 E1
Spire Pl CR6. . . . . 81 E1
Spires Ct 7 KT16 . . . . 33 A3
Spital Heath RH4 . . . . 136 C8
Spitfire Bsns Pk CR0. . . . . 61 A4
Spitfire Rd SM6. . . . . 60 E3
Spitfire Way GU14 . . . . . . 104 E7
Spoil La GU10 . . . . 126 F7
Spokane Cl GU11 . . . . 125 F8
Spook Hill RH5 . . . . 136 B3
Spooner Ho TW5 . . . . 5 A8
Spooners Rd RH12 . . . . . . 218 A4
Spooner Wlk SM6. . . . . 60 D5
Sportsbank St SE6 . . . . 24 C8
Spout Hill CR0. . . . . 63 A5
Spout La TW19 . . . . 2 A3
Spout La N TW19 . . . . 2 B3
Spratts La KT16. . . . . 51 E4
Spread Eagle Wlk 2
KT18 . . . . 76 D6
SPREAKLEY 167 B8
Spreighton Rd KT8. . . . . . . 36 B5
Spring Ave TW20 . . . . 11 F2
Springbank Rd SE13 . . . . . 24 E8
Springbok Farm GU6. . . . 193 E1
Spring Bottom La
RH1 . . . . 120 C8
Springbourne Ct BR3 . . . . 44 C8
Spring Cl 11 RH11. . . . . . . 201 D5
Springclose La SM3. . . . . . 58 E4
Spring Cnr TW13 . . . . 14 F5
Spring Copse
Copthorne RH10 . . . . 183 C3
East Grinstead RH19. . . . . 185 D3
Spring Copse Bsns Pk
RH13. . . . . 215 C3
Springcopse Rd RH2. . . . . 139 C7
Spring Cotts
Kingston u T KT6 . . . . 37 D4
South Holmwood RH5 . . . . 157 C6
Springcross Ave GU17. . . . 64 D4
Spring Ct
Ewell KT17. . . . . 57 F2
Guildford GU2 . . . . 109 B5
Springfarm Rd GU27 . . . . 207 E5
Springfield
East Grinstead RH19. . . . . 185 D4
Elstead GU8. . . . . 148 D3
Lightwater GU18 . . . . 67 D8
Oxted RH8 . . . . 122 D5
South Norwood SE25. . . . . . 43 A6
Springfield Ave
Hampton TW12 . . . . 16 B2
Merton SW20 . . . . 39 F6
Springfield Cl GU21. . . . . . 68 E1
Springfield Cres
RH12 . . . . 217 B2
Springfield Ct
Crawley RH11 . . . . 201 D5
2 Horsham RH12. . . . . . . 217 C2
9 Kingston u T KT1 . . . . . . 37 E6
Wallington SM6. . . . . 60 B5
Springfield Dr KT22. . . . . . 94 F8
Springfield Gdns BR4 . . . . 63 B8
Springfield Gr TW16 . . . . . 35 A8
Springfield Hospl
SW17 . . . . 20 E5
Springfield La KT13. . . . . . 53 B6
Springfield Mdws
KT13 . . . . 53 B6
Springfield Park Ho
RH12 . . . . 217 C3
Springfield Park Rd
RH12 . . . . 217 B2

Springfield Pl KT3 . . . . . . 38 C5
Springfield Prim Sch
 TW16 . . . . 34 F7
Springfield Rd
 Ashford TW15 . . . . 13 F3
 Ash GU12 . . . . 106 A5
 Bracknell RG12 . . . . 26 C8
 Brands Hill SL3 . . . . 1 B7
 Crawley RH11 . . . . 201 D5
 East Ewell KT17 . . . . . . 58 C1
 Frimley GU15 . . . . 66 B5
 Guildford GU1 . . . . 109 E1
 Horsham RH12 . . . . . . 217 C2
 Kingston u T KT1 . . . . . 37 E6
 Penge SE26 . . . . 23 B3
 South Norwood CR7 . . . . 42 C8
 8 Teddington TW11 . . . 17 A3
 Twickenham TW2 . . . . . 16 A7
 Wallington SM6 . . . . . . 60 B5
 Westcott RH4 . . . . 135 C6
 Wimbledon SW19 . . . . . 20 A3
Springfield Rise SE26 . . 23 B5
Springfields Cl KT16 . . 33 B1
Springfield Terr GU5 . . 151 F6
Springfield Way GU8 . . 148 E3
Spring Gdns
 Ascot SL5 . . . . 29 B5
 Biggin Hill TN16 . . . . . . 83 C1
 Copthorne RH10 . . . . . 183 C3
 Dorking RH4 . . . . 136 A8
 East Molesey KT8 . . . . . 36 C5
 Farnborough GU14 . . . . 85 A7
 Frimley GU15 . . . . 66 A5
 Horsham RH12 . . . . . . 217 C3
 Wallington SM6 . . . . . . 60 C5
Spring Gr
 Brentford W4 . . . . 7 A8
 Farncombe GU7 . . . . . . 150 E8
 Fetcham KT22 . . . . 94 B4
 Hampton TW12 . . . . . . 36 B8
 Mitcham CR4 . . . . 41 A8
SPRING GROVE 5 E5
Spring Grove Cres TW3,
 TW5 . . . . 5 C6
Spring Grove Prim Sch
 TW7 . . . . 5 D5
Spring Grove Rd
 Hounslow TW3, TW5,
  TW7 . . . . 5 C6
 Richmond TW10 . . . . . . 6 F2
Springhaven GU8 . . . . . 148 E3
Springhaven Cl GU1 . . 110 A1
SPRINGHEAD 207 E5
Springhill GU8 . . . . . . 148 E3
Spring Hill SE26 . . . . . 23 C4
Springhill Ct RG12 . . . 27 B5
Spring Ho SW19 . . . . . 39 F8
Springholm Cl
 Badshot Lea GU9 . . . . . 126 B6
 Biggin Hill TN16 . . . . . . 83 C1
Springhurst Cl CR0 . . . 62 F6
Spring La
 Croydon CR0, SE25 . . . . 43 B3
 Hale GU9 . . . . 125 A7
 Oxted RH8 . . . . 122 D4
 Slinfold RH13 . . . . 215 C3
Springlakes Est GU12 . . 105 E3
Spring La W GU9 . . . . . 125 A6
Spring Mdw
 Bracknell RG12 . . . . . . 27 D8
 Forest Row RH18 . . . . . 206 F1
Springmead Ct
 Haslemere GU27 . . . . . 207 D5
 Sandhurst GU47 . . . . . . 45 E1
SPRING PARK 62 F7
Spring Park Ave CR0 . . 62 D8
Springpark Dr BR3 . . . 44 C6
Spring Park Prim Sch
 CR0 . . . . 63 A7
Spring Park Rd CR0 . . . 62 D8
Spring Plat RH10 . . . . 202 C6
Spring Plat Ct RH10 . . 202 C6
Spring Rd TW13 . . . . . 14 F5
Spring Rise TW20 . . . . 11 E2
Spring Terr TW10 . . . . . 6 E2
Springvale Cl KT23 . . . 94 B1
Spring Way RH19 . . . . 186 A4
Springwell Cl SW16 . . . 21 F4
Springwell Ct TW5 . . . . 4 D5
Springwell Jun & Inf Schs
 TW5 . . . . 4 E7
Springwell Rd
 Beare Green RH5 . . . . . 157 D3
 Heston TW5 . . . . 4 D6
 Streatham SW16 . . . . . . 22 A3
Springwood GU8 . . . . . 150 A1
Springwood Ct CR2 . . . 61 E6
Spring Woods
 Sandhurst GU47 . . . . . . 45 C1
 Virginia Water GU25 . . . 31 B5
Sprint Ind Est KT14 . . . 71 D8
Spruce Cl RH1 . . . . . . 118 F2
Sprucedale Gdns
 South Croydon CR0 . . . . 62 D6
 Wallington SM6 . . . . . . 60 E2
Spruce Dr GU18 . . . . . 67 A7
Sprucefield Ct RH11 . . 201 B6
Spruce Ho 2 TW8 . . . . 6 C7
Spruce Pk BR2 . . . . . . 44 F5
Spruce Rd TN16 . . . . . 83 D3
Spurfield KT8 . . . . 36 B6
Spurgeon Ave SE19 . . . 42 D8
Spurgeon Cl RH11 . . . 201 C7

Spurgeon Rd SE19 . . . . 22 D1
Spurgeon's Coll SE25 . . 42 E7
Spur Ho 10 SW19 . . . . 40 B8
Spur Rd
 Brentford TW7 . . . . 6 B7
 Feltham TW14 . . . . 4 B3
Spurs Ct GU11 . . . . . . 104 E2
Spur The
 Knaphill GU21 . . . . 68 B1
 Walton-on-T KT12 . . . . . 54 C8
Spy La RH14 . . . . 213 A4
Sq The GU26 . . . . 188 D3
Square Dr GU27 . . . . . 208 B1
Square The
 Bagshot GU19 . . . . 47 E3
 Bracknell RG12 . . . . . . 27 E5
 Caterham CR3 . . . . 101 A3
 Crawley RH10 . . . . 201 D6
 Elstead GU8 . . . . 148 D4
 Guildford GU2 . . . . 129 F7
 Harmondsworth TW6 . . . 2 B6
 Lightwater GU18 . . . . . . 48 C1
 Lingfield RH7 . . . . 164 C4
 11 Richmond TW10 . . . 6 D2
 Rowledge GU10 . . . . . . 145 E3
 Shere GU5 . . . . 133 A4
 Tatsfield TN16 . . . . 103 C7
 Wallington SM5 . . . . . . 60 A5
 Weybridge KT13 . . . . . . 53 C5
 Wisley GU23 . . . . 71 E3
Squarey St SW17 . . . . 20 C5
Squash Court Gate Rd
 GU14 . . . . 85 B1
Squerryes The CR3 . . . 100 E6
Squire Ct 2 CR0 . . . . . 42 E1
Squires Bridge Rd
 KT17 . . . . 33 F5
Squire's Bridge Rd
 TW17 . . . . 34 A5
Squires Cl RH10 . . . . . 204 A8
Squires Ct
 Camberley GU15 . . . . . . 65 C3
 Chertsey KT16 . . . . 33 B1
 Wimbledon SW19 . . . . . 20 A4
Squires Rd TW17 . . . . . 34 A5
Squires Wlk TW15 . . . . 14 D1
Squirrel Cl
 Crawley RH11 . . . . 181 B1
 Hounslow TW4 . . . . 4 C4
 Sandhurst GU47 . . . . . . 64 B8
Squirrel Dr SL4 . . . . . . 9 B7
Squirrel La GU15 . . . . . 85 A5
Squirrels Cl GU7 . . . . . 129 D1
Squirrels Ct KT4 . . . . . 57 F8
Squirrels Gn
 Great Bookham KT23 . . . 94 A4
 12 Redhill RH1 . . . . . 118 F2
 Worcester Park KT4 . . . . 58 A8
Squirrel's Way KT18 . . . 76 D4
Squirrel Wood KT14 . . . 71 B7
Stable Cl
 Crawley RH10 . . . . 202 D3
 Kingston u T KT2 . . . . . 17 F2
 Langley Vale KT18 . . . . . 96 E8
 Stable Croft GU19 . . . . . 47 D2
Stable Ct
 Caterham CR3 . . . . 101 A5
 Wallington SM6 . . . . . . 60 A7
Stable Mews
 Reigate RH2 . . . . 118 A1
 Twickenham TW1 . . . . . 16 F7
 West Norwood SE27 . . . . 22 C3
Stables The
 Bletchingley RH1 . . . . . 120 D4
 Cobham KT11 . . . . 73 F5
 Guildford GU1 . . . . 109 D4
 Sunningdale SL5 . . . . . . 30 B1
Stace Way RH10 . . . . . 202 E8
Stacey Ct RH1 . . . . . . 119 C6
Stacey's Farm Rd
 GU8 . . . . 148 D4
Stacey's Mdw GU8 . . . 148 D4
Stackfield Rd RH11 . . . 200 E5
Stack Ho RH6 . . . . 122 E5
Staddon Cl BR3 . . . . . . 43 E5
Stadium House Bsns Ctr
 5 GU21 . . . . 70 A3
Staff College Rd GU15 . . 65 B6
Staffhurst Wood Rd TN8,
 RH8 . . . . 144 C6
Stafford Cl
 Caterham CR3 . . . . 100 F4
 Cheam SM3 . . . . 58 E4
Stafford Cross SM6 . . . 60 F5
Stafford Ct CR0 . . . . . . 61 A6
Stafford Gdns CR0 . . . . 60 F5
Stafford Lake GU21 . . . 68 A1
Stafford Pl TW10 . . . . . 17 F8
Stafford Rd
 Caterham CR3 . . . . 101 A6
 Crawley RH11 . . . . 181 B1
 Croydon CR0 . . . . 61 A6
 Kingston u T KT3 . . . . . 38 C6
 Wallington CR0, SM6 . . . 60 E4
Staffords Pl RH6 . . . . . 161 B2
Stafford Sq 3 KT13 . . . 53 D6
Staff Rd GU12 . . . . 105 C2
Stagbury Ave CR5 . . . . 78 E1
Stagbury Cl CR5 . . . . . 98 E8
Stagbury Ho CR5 . . . . . 98 E8
Stag Ct 15 SM6 . . . . . . 60 B4
Stagelands RH11 . . . . . 201 C8
Stagelands Ct RH11 . . . 201 C8
Stag Hill GU2 . . . . 130 A8
Stag Hill Ct GU2 . . . . . 109 B1
Stag La SW15 . . . . 18 F5
Stag Leys KT21 . . . . . . 95 E7

Stag Leys Cl SM7 . . . . . 78 E4
Stags Way TW7 . . . . . . 5 F8
Stainash Cres TW18 . . . 13 B3
Stainash Par TW18 . . . . 13 B3
Stainbank Rd CR4 . . . . 41 B6
STAINES 12 E6
Staines Ave SM3 . . . . . 58 D8
Staines By-Pass TW15,
 TW18 . . . . 13 C3
Staines La TW18 . . . . . 33 A3
Staines Lane Cl KT16 . . 32 F4
Staines Prep Sch
 TW18 . . . . 13 A3
Staines Rd
 Chertsey KT16 . . . . 33 A5
 East Bedfont TW14 . . . . 14 D8
 Feltham, Hounslow TW14,
  TW3, TW4 . . . . 4 D2
 Laleham TW18 . . . . 33 B7
 Twickenham TW2 . . . . . 16 C6
 Wraysbury TW19 . . . . . 11 F7
Staines Rd E TW12,
 TW16 . . . . 35 C8
Staines Rd W TW15 . . . 14 D1
Staines Sta TW18 . . . . . 13 A3
Stainford Cl TW15 . . . . 14 D3
Stainton Rd SE13 . . . . . 24 D8
Stainton Wlk GU21 . . . . 69 C1
Staiths Way KT20 . . . . . 97 B7
Stake La GU14 . . . . 85 A4
Stakescorner Rd GU3 . . 130 A2
Stambourne Way
 South Norwood SE19 . . . 22 F1
 West Wickham BR4 . . . . 63 C7
Stamford Ave GU16 . . . 65 F5
Stamford Dr BR2 . . . . . 44 F5
Stamford Green Prim Sch
 KT19 . . . . 76 B7
Stamford Green Rd
 KT18 . . . . 76 B6
Stamford Ho SW19 . . . . 19 C3
Stamford Rd KT12 . . . . 54 D7
Stammerham Bsns Ctr
 RH12 . . . . 198 E8
Stanacre KT20 . . . . 97 F6
Stanborough Cl TW12 . . 15 F2
Stanborough Rd TW3,
 TW7 . . . . 5 D4
Stanbridge Cl RH11 . . . 200 E6
Stancliffe Ho 10 SM1 . . 59 C6
Standard Rd TW4 . . . . . 4 E4
Standen Cl RH19 . . . . . 185 A4
Standen Ho ★ RH19 . . . 205 D4
Standen Pl RH12 . . . . . 218 A7
Standen Rd SW18 . . . . . 20 A8
Standinghall La RH10 . . 203 A3
Standlake Point 1
 SE23 . . . . 23 D5
Standon La RH5 . . . . . . 176 F2
Standor Ho 8 CR4 . . . . 40 F6
Stane Cl SW19 . . . . 20 B1
Stanedge Ct SW16 . . . . 21 E3
Stane St
 Ockley RH5 . . . . 177 D4
 Slinfold RH13 . . . . 215 C4
Stane Way KT17 . . . . . . 58 A1
Stanford Cotts GU24 . . . 87 E1
Stanford Ct RH10 . . . . . 202 C4
Stanford Orch RH12 . . . 216 F8
Stanford Prim Sch
 SW16 . . . . 41 D8
Stanford Rd SW16 . . . . 41 E7
Stanfords Pl RH7 . . . . . 164 D3
Stanfords The KT17 . . . 76 F7
Stanford Way
 Broadbridge Heath
  RH12 . . . . 216 D3
 Mitcham SW16 . . . . 41 D7
Stangate Mans TW1 . . . 16 F5
Stanger Rd SE25 . . . . . 43 A5
Stangrave Hall RH9 . . . 121 B3
Stan Hill RH6 . . . . 180 D8
Stanhope Ave BR2 . . . . 44 F1
Stanhope Cotts RH7 . . . 164 F3
Stanhope Gate GU15 . . . 65 A5
Stanhope Gr BR3 . . . . . 43 F5
Stanhope Heath TW19 . . 2 C1
Stanhope Rd
 Camberley GU15 . . . . . . 64 F4
 South Croydon CR0 . . . . 61 E7
 Wallington SM5 . . . . . . 60 A3
Stanhopes RH8 . . . . . . 123 B7
Stanhope Way TW19 . . . 2 C1
Stanier Cl RH10 . . . . . . 202 B5
Staniland Dr KT13 . . . . 52 F1
Stanley Ave
 Beckenham BR2, BR3 . . . 44 C6
 West Barnes KT3 . . . . . . 39 A4
Stanley Cl
 Coulsdon CR5 . . . . 79 F2
 Crawley RH10 . . . . 201 E4
Stanley Cotts 1 GU21 . . 68 D2
Stanleycroft Cl TW7 . . . 5 E6
Stanley Ct
 Belmont SM2 . . . . 59 B3
 Wallington SM5 . . . . . . 60 A3
 3 Wimbledon SW19 . . 20 A2
Stanley Ctr RH10 . . . . . 181 F2
Stanley Dr GU14 . . . . . 84 C3
Stanley Gardens Rd
 TW11 . . . . 16 E3
Stanley Gdns
 Hersham KT12 . . . . 54 C4
 Mitcham CR4 . . . . 21 A2
 Sanderstead CR2 . . . . . 81 A7
 Wallington SM6 . . . . . . 60 C4
Stanley Gr CR0, CR7 . . . 42 A3

Stanley Hill GU24 . . . . 87 C5
Stanley Inf Sch TW11 . . 16 E4
Stanley Jun Sch TW11 . . 16 E4
Stanley Mans SW17 . . . 20 F6
Stanley Park High Sch
 SM5 . . . . 60 A4
Stanley Park Inf Sch
 SM5 . . . . 59 F3
Stanley Park Jun Sch
 SM5 . . . . 59 F3
Stanley Park Rd SM5,
 SM6 . . . . 60 A3
Stanley Rd
 Ashford TW15 . . . . 13 E3
 Belmont SM2 . . . . 59 B3
 Hounslow TW3 . . . . 5 C3
 Mitcham CR4 . . . . 21 A1
 Morden SM4 . . . . 40 A5
 Mortlake SW14 . . . . 7 B3
 Teddington TW11 . . . . . 16 E3
 Thornton Heath CR0,
  CR7 . . . . 42 A3
 Twickenham TW2 . . . . . 16 D5
 Wallington SM5 . . . . . . 60 A3
 Wimbledon SW19 . . . . . 20 A2
 Woking GU21 . . . . 69 F2
 Wokingham RG40 . . . . . 25 E6
Stanley Sq SM5 . . . . . . 59 F2
Stanley St CR3 . . . . . . 100 C5
Stanley Tech High Sch for
 Boys SE25 . . . . 42 F6
Stanley Wlk
 Bracknell RG12 . . . . . . 27 C7
 8 Horsham RH13 . . . 217 D2
Stanmore Cl SL5 . . . . . 29 A5
Stanmore Gdns
 Richmond TW9 . . . . 6 F4
 Sutton SM1 . . . . 59 C7
Stanmore Rd TW9 . . . . 6 F4
Stanmore Terr BR3 . . . . 44 A7
Stannard Ct SE6 . . . . . 24 B7
Stannet Way SM6 . . . . . 60 C6
Stansfield Rd TW4, TW5 . . 4 B5
Stanstead Cl BR2 . . . . . 44 F3
Stanstead Gr SE23 . . . . 23 F7
Stanstead Manor SM1 . . 59 A4
Stanstead Rd
 Caterham CR3, RH1 . . . 100 E2
 Forest Hill SE23, SE6 . . . 23 E7
Stansted Rd TW6 . . . . . 2 F2
Stanthorpe Cl SW16 . . . 21 E3
Stanthorpe Rd SW16 . . . 21 E3
Stanton Ave TW11 . . . . 16 E2
Stanton Cl
 Cranleigh GU6 . . . . 174 A3
 North Cheam KT4 . . . . . 39 D1
 West Ewell KT19 . . . . . . 57 B5
Stanton Ct CR0 . . . . . . 61 E5
Stanton Rd
 Barnes SW13 . . . . 7 F5
 Thornton Heath CR0 . . . 42 C2
 Wimbledon SW20 . . . . . 39 D8
Stanton Sq 2 SE6 . . . . 23 F4
Stantons Wharf GU5 . . . 152 A7
Stanton Way SE26, SE6 . . 23 F4
Stanway Pl KT16 . . . . . 32 F2
Stanway Sch RH4 . . . . . 115 B1
STANWELL 13 C7
Stanwell Cl TW19 . . . . . 2 D1
Stanwell Fields CE Prim
 Sch TW19 . . . . 13 E8
Stanwell Gdns TW19 . . . 2 D1
STANWELL MOOR 2 A1
Stanwell Moor Rd
 Harmondsworth TW19, TW6,
  UB7 . . . . 2 B4
 Stanwell TW19 . . . . 2 B4
Stanwell New Rd TW18,
 TW19 . . . . 13 B5
STANWELL PLACE 2 C1
Stanwell Rd
 Ashford TW15 . . . . 13 E4
 East Bedfont TW14, TW19,
  TW6 . . . . 14 B8
 Horton SL3, TW19 . . . . . 1 C4
Stanworth Ct TW5 . . . . 5 A7
Stanyhurst SE23 . . . . . . 23 E7
Staplecross Ct 1
 RH11 . . . . 201 A3
Staplefield Cl 3 SW2 . . 21 E7
Stapleford Cl
 Kingston u T KT1 . . . . . 38 A6
 Putney SW19 . . . . 19 E8
Staple Hill GU24, KT16 . . 49 E6
Staplehurst RG12 . . . . . 26 E2
Staplehurst Cl RH2 . . . 139 C5
Staplehurst Rd
 Reigate RH2 . . . . 139 C5
 Sutton SM5 . . . . 59 E3
Staple La
 East Clandon GU4,
  GU5 . . . . 111 E2
 Shere GU4 . . . . 132 E3
Stapleton Gdns CR0 . . . 61 A5
Stapleton Rd SW17 . . . . 21 A5
Starborough Cotts
 RH7 . . . . 185 F7
Starborough Rd TN8 . . . 165 E5
Star Cl RH13 . . . . 218 A4
Star & Garter Hill
 TW10 . . . . 17 E8
Star Hill GU10 . . . . 167 D2
Star Hill Dr GU10 . . . . . 167 D2
Starhurst Sch RH5 . . . . 136 C5
Star La
 Ash GU12 . . . . 105 F2
 Hooley CR5 . . . . 99 A6

Star La continued
 Woking GU22 . . . . 89 C8
Starling Cl CR0 . . . . . . 43 E3
Starling Wlk TW12 . . . . 15 E3
Starmead Dr RG40 . . . . 25 E5
Star Post Rd GU15 . . . . 65 F8
Star Rd TW7 . . . . 5 D5
Starrett Ct KT12 . . . . . . 54 C8
Starrock La CR5 . . . . . . 99 A7
Starrock Rd CR5 . . . . . . 99 C8
Starwood Cl KT14 . . . . . 71 C8
Staten Gdns TW1 . . . . . 16 F7
Statham Ct RG42 . . . . . 26 E8
Station App
 Ashford TW15 . . . . 13 F4
 Ash Vale GU12 . . . . . . 106 A7
 Beckenham, Lower Sydenham
  SE6 . . . . 23 F3
 Belmont SM2 . . . . 59 B1
 Blackwater GU17 . . . . . 64 E4
 Cheam SM2 . . . . 58 E3
 Chipstead CR5 . . . . 78 F1
 Coulsdon CR5 . . . . 79 D4
 3 Croydon CR0 . . . . . 61 D8
 Dorking RH4 . . . . 115 C1
 East Horsley KT24 . . . . . 92 E1
 Epsom KT17, KT19 . . . . 76 D6
 Ewell KT17 . . . . 58 B1
 Faygate RH12 . . . . 199 F1
 Godalming GU7 . . . . . . 150 D4
 Guildford GU1 . . . . 130 E8
 Hampton TW12 . . . . . . 36 A8
 Haslemere GU27 . . . . . 208 B6
 Hinchley Wood KT10 . . . 55 F7
 Horley RH6 . . . . 161 B2
 4 Kingston u T KT1,
  KT2 . . . . 38 A8
 Leatherhead KT22 . . . . . 95 A6
 6 New Malden KT4 . . 39 A1
 Ockley RH5 . . . . 178 B5
 Oxted RH8 . . . . 122 E6
 Purley CR8 . . . . 80 A8
 Richmond TW9 . . . . 7 A6
 Shalford GU4 . . . . 130 E3
 Shepperton TW17 . . . . . 34 C4
 South Croydon CR2 . . . . 61 D2
 Staines TW18 . . . . 13 A3
 Streatham SW16 . . . . . . 21 D3
 Sunbury TW16 . . . . 35 A8
 1 Surbiton KT6 . . . . . 37 E3
 Tadworth KT20 . . . . 97 C5
 Virginia Water GU25 . . . 31 D5
 West Byfleet KT14 . . . . . 71 A7
 Weybridge KT13 . . . . . . 53 A4
 Whyteleafe CR3 . . . . . . 81 A1
 Woking GU22 . . . . 69 F2
 Worcester Park KT19 . . . 58 A5
 Wormley GU8 . . . . 190 F8
Station App E RH1 . . . . 139 F7
Station Approach Rd
 Chiswick W4 . . . . 7 C7
 Coulsdon CR5 . . . . 79 D4
 Crawley RH6 . . . . 182 B7
Station App W RH1 . . . . 139 F7
Station Ave
 Caterham CR3 . . . . 101 A3
 Kingston u T KT3 . . . . . 38 E6
 14 Richmond TW9 . . . 7 A6
 Walton-on-T KT12 . . . . . 54 A6
 West Ewell KT19 . . . . . . 57 E2
Station Bldgs
 Catford SE6 . . . . 24 A8
 Merton SW20 . . . . 39 C7
Station Cl
 Hampton TW12 . . . . . . 36 B8
 Horsham RH13 . . . . . . 217 D2
Station Cotts CR8 . . . . . 80 C5
Station Cres TW15 . . . . 13 E4
Station Cr CR4 . . . . 40 E5
Station Est BR3 . . . . . . 43 D5
Station Estate Rd
 TW14 . . . . 15 B7
Station Gdns W4 . . . . . 7 C7
Station Hill
 Ascot SL5 . . . . 29 A5
 Crawley RH10 . . . . 202 B7
 Farnham GU9 . . . . 125 C2
Station Ind Est RG40 . . . 25 B6
Station La
 Enton Green GU8 . . . . . 171 A7
 Wormley GU8 . . . . 170 F1
Station Par
 2 Ashford TW15 . . . . 13 F4
 East Horsley KT24 . . . . . 92 E1
 Feltham TW14 . . . . 15 B8
 Richmond TW9 . . . . 7 A6
 South Croydon CR2 . . . . 61 D2
 Sunningdale SL5 . . . . . . 30 A2
 6 Sutton SM2 . . . . . . 59 C4
 4 Upper Tooting SW12 . . 21 A7
 Virginia Water GU25 . . . 31 E4
Station Path TW18 . . . . 12 F4
Station Rd
 Addlestone KT15 . . . . . . 52 D6
 Aldershot GU11 . . . . . . 105 B2
 Ashford TW15 . . . . 13 F4
 Bagshot GU19 . . . . 47 E4
 Barnes SW13 . . . . 7 F5
 Beckenham BR2 . . . . . . 44 E7
 Belmont SM2 . . . . 59 A1
 Betchworth RH3 . . . . . . 116 E3
 Bracknell RG12 . . . . . . 27 B7
 Bramley GU5 . . . . 152 A7
 Carshalton SM5 . . . . . . 59 F6
 Chertsey KT16 . . . . 33 A1
 Chessington KT9 . . . . . . 56 E5
 Chobham GU24 . . . . . . 69 B6
 Claygate KT10 . . . . 55 E5

Station Rd *continued*
Cranleigh RH12 195 C3
Crawley Down RH10 204 B8
Crawley RH10, RH11 201 D5
Croydon CR0 42 C1
Dorking RH4 136 A8
East Grinstead RH19 185 D1
Egham TW20 12 A3
Farnborough GU14 85 B4
Farncombe GU7 150 F7
Forest Row RH18 206 F3
Godalming GU7 150 D4
Gomshall GU5 133 D4
Hampton TW12 36 B8
Horley RH6 161 B3
Horsham RH13 217 D2
Hounslow TW3 5 B3
Hydestile GU8 171 D6
Kenley CR8 80 C5
Kingston u T KT2 38 A8
Leatherhead KT22 95 A6
Lingfield RH7 164 E4
Loxwood RH14 213 A3
Merstham RH1 119 C7
Merton SW19 40 C8
Oxted RH8 122 E7
Penge SE20 23 C2
Redhill RH1 118 F2
Rudgwick RH12 214 D7
Shalford GU4 130 E3
Shepperton TW17 34 C4
South Godstone RH9 142 E5
South Norwood SE25 42 F5
Stoke D'Abernon KT11 73 E3
Sunbury TW16 15 A1
Sunningdale SL5 30 A4
Teddington, Hampton Wick KT1 37 D8
Teddington TW11 17 A2
Thames Ditton KT10 55 D8
Thames Ditton, Weston Green KT7 36 F2
Twickenham TW1 16 F8
Warnham RH12 217 B8
West Barnes KT3 39 B4
West Byfleet KT14 71 A7
West Wickham BR4 44 C1
Whyteleafe CR3 80 F1
Wokingham RG40 25 B6
Woldingham CR3 101 F5
Wraysbury TW19 1 A1
Station Rd E
Ash Vale GU12 106 A7
Oxted RH8 122 E6
Station Rd N
5 Egham TW20 11 F3
Merstham RH1 119 C7
Station Rd S RH1 119 C7
Station Rd W
Ash Vale GU12 105 F8
Oxted RH8 122 E6
Station Rise SE27 22 B6
Station Row GU4 130 E3
Station Terr RH4 136 A8
Station View
Ash Vale GU12 106 A8
Guildford GU1 130 C8
Station Way
Bracknell RG12 27 C7
Cheam SM2, SM3 58 E3
Claygate KT10 55 E4
Crawley RH10, RH11 201 D5
11 Epsom KT19 76 D6
Station Yd TW1 17 A8
Staunton Rd KT2 17 F1
Staveley Gdns W4 7 D6
Staveley Rd
Ashford TW15 14 D2
Chiswick W4 7 D7
Staveley Way GU21 68 E2
Staverton Cl RG40 25 F6
Stavordale Rd SM4, SM5 40 C2
Stayne End GU25 31 A5
Stayton Rd SM1 59 A7
Steadfast Rd KT1 37 D8
Steam Farm La TW14 3 F3
Steele Rd TW7 6 A3
Steele's Rd GU11 105 B4
Steel's La KT11, KT22 74 C5
Steep Hill
Chobham GU24 49 C3
South Croydon CR0 61 E6
Streatham SW16 21 D5
Steeple Cl SW19 19 E4
Steeple Ct
17 Egham TW20 12 A3
Wimbledon SW19 19 E3
Steeple Gdns KT15 52 B5
Steeple Heights Dr TN16 83 D2
Steeple Point SL5 29 B6
Steepways GU26 188 B6
Steeres Hill RH12 199 C6
Steerforth Copse GU47 45 E2
Steerforth St SW18 20 C6
Steers La RH10 182 C4
Steers Mead CR4 40 F8
Steetley Ct 19 SM2 59 C3
Steinman Ct TW7 5 F4
Stella Rd SW17 20 F2
Stembridge Rd SE20 43 B7
Stenning Ct KT22 95 B5
Stennings The RH19 185 C3
Stepgates KT16 33 B2
Stepgates Cl KT16 33 B2
Stepgates Com Sch KT16 33 B2
Stephanie Chase Ct RG40 25 D7
Stephen Cl TW20 12 C2
Stephen Ct 18 SW19 19 D7
Stephendale Rd GU9 125 D4
Stephen Gould Ho GU14 105 B8
Stephens Field GU8 191 A4
Stephenson Ct
Belmont SM2 58 F3
Farnham GU9 146 A8
Stephenson Dr RH19 205 F7
Stephenson Pl
Crawley RH10 202 B6
Merstham RH1 119 C7
Stephenson Rd
Guildford GU2 108 D1
Twickenham TW2 16 A8
Stephenson Way RH10 202 B6
Stepney Cl RH10 202 C4
Stepney Way CR4 41 A8
Sterling Bldgs 6 RH12 217 C2
Sterling Ctr The RG12 27 D6
Sterling Pk RH10 182 B3
Sterling Pl KT13 53 E6
Sternhold Ave SW12, SW2 21 D6
Sterry Dr
Thames Ditton KT7 36 E3
Worcester Park KT19 57 E6
Steucers La SE23 23 E7
Steve Biko La SE6 24 A4
Steve Biko Way TW3 5 A4
Stevenage Rd RH11 200 E3
Stevens Cl
Beckenham BR3 24 A2
Epsom KT17 76 E6
Hampton TW12 15 F2
Stevens Ct BR3 24 A2
Stevens Ho KT1 37 D7
Stevens' La KT10 56 A4
Stevens Pl CR8 80 B6
Stewards Rise GU10 145 F7
Stewart KT20 97 D6
Stewart Ave TW17 34 A5
Stewart Cl
Hampton TW12 15 E2
Woking GU21 68 F2
Stewart Fleming Prim Sch SE20 43 C6
Steyning Cl
Crawley RH10 201 E8
Purley CR8 80 B3
Steyning Way TW4 4 C3
Sthrathbrook Rd SW16 21 F1
Stickle Down GU16 86 D8
Stildon Mews RH19 185 C3
Stile Gdns GU27 207 F6
Stile Ho GU4 110 D2
Stile Path TW16 35 A6
Stillers GU8 191 B4
Stirling Ave
Upper Halliford TW17 34 E6
Wallington SM6 60 E3
Stirling Cl
1 Ash Vale GU12 105 F5
Banstead SM7 77 F2
Crawley RH10 202 C5
Farnborough GU14 85 A3
Frimley GU16 65 E2
Mitcham SW16 41 C8
Stirling Dr CR3 100 C6
Stirling Gr TW3 5 C5
Stirling Ho 15 RH1 118 F1
Stirling Rd
Guildford GU2 108 E1
Stanwell TW6 2 F1
Twickenham TW2 16 B8
Stirling Way
East Grinstead RH19 186 B3
Farnborough GU11 104 D7
Horsham RH13 217 E3
Thornton Heath CR0 41 E2
Stirrup Way RH10 202 D7
Stites Hill Rd CR3, CR5 100 C7
Stoatley Ho 10 SW15 19 A7
Stoatley Hollow GU27 208 A8
Stoatley Rise GU27 208 A8
Stoats Nest Rd CR5 79 E5
Stoats Nest Village CR5 79 E4
Stockbridge Dr GU11 126 C6
Stockbury Rd CR0 43 C3
Stockfield RH6 161 B4
Stockfield Rd
Claygate KT10 55 E5
Streatham SW16 21 F5
Stockhams Cl CR2 61 D1
Stock Hill TN16 83 D2
Stocklund Sq GU6 174 D3
Stocklund Sq Maisonettes GU6 174 D3
Stockport Rd SW16 41 D8
Stocks Cl RH6 161 B2
Stockton Ho RH2 139 A6
Stockton Rd RH2 139 A6
Stockwell Ctr RH10 202 A6
Stockwell Rd RH19 205 E6
Stockwood Rise GU15 65 F5
Stockwood Way GU9 125 F7
Stocton Cl GU1 109 C2
Stocton Rd GU1 109 D2
Stodart Rd SE20 43 C8
Stoford Cl SW19 19 E8
Stoke Brunswick Sch RH19 206 E7
Stoke Cl KT11 73 F3
Stoke Ct SE22 23 A7
STOKE D'ABERNON 73 F3
Stoke Fields 8 GU1 109 D1
Stokeford Cl 5 RG12 27 F4
Stoke Gr GU1 109 D1
Stoke Hills GU9 125 C3
Stoke Hosp (Almshouses) 6 GU1 109 D1
Stoke Mews GU1 130 D8
Stoke Mill Cl GU1 109 D3
Stoke Park Ct 5 GU1 109 D1
Stoke Rd
Guildford GU1 109 D1
Kingston u T KT2 18 C1
Stoke D'Abernon KT11 73 E3
Walton-on-T KT12 54 C7
Stoke Rd Cotts KT22 94 D6
Stokers Cl RH6 181 E7
Stokesby Rd KT9 56 F4
Stokes Cl RH10 202 C4
Stokesheath Rd KT22 74 C8
Stokes Rd CR0 43 D3
Stokes Ridings KT20 97 D4
Stompond La KT12 54 A8
Stoms Path SE6 24 A3
Stonards Brow GU5 152 D4
Stondon Pk SE23 23 E8
Stonebanks KT12 35 A2
STONEBRIDGE 136 D4
Stonebridge Ct
Crawley RH11 201 C2
Horsham RH12 217 A2
Stonebridge Fields GU4 130 D2
Stonebridge Wharf GU4 130 D2
Stonecot Cl SM3, SM4 39 E1
Stonecot Hill SM4 39 E1
Stone Cotts RH10 203 B1
Stonecourt Cl RH6 161 C3
Stone Cres TW14 14 F8
Stonecroft Way CR0 41 E2
Stonecrop Cl RH11 201 B3
Stonecrop Rd GU4 110 C3
Stonedene Cl GU35 187 B4
Stonefield Cl RH10, RH11 201 D5
Stonegate GU15 66 C6
Stone Hatch GU6 194 A3
Stonehaven BR3 44 B7
Stonehill Cl
Little Bookham KT23 94 A2
Mortlake SW14 7 D2
Stonehill Cres KT16 50 E4
Stonehill Pk GU35 187 C4
Stonehill Rd
Chobham GU24, KT16 50 D3
Headley Down GU35 187 C4
Lightwater GU18 48 A1
Mortlake SW14 7 D2
Stonehills Ct SE21 22 E5
Stonehill's Mans 3 SW16 21 E6
Stone House Gdns CR3 100 E2
Stonehouse Rise GU16 65 E1
STONELEIGH 58 A5
Stoneleigh Ave KT17, KT4 58 A7
Stoneleigh Broadway KT17 58 A5
Stoneleigh Cl RH19 185 F1
Stoneleigh Cres KT19 57 F5
Stoneleigh Ct
5 Croydon CR0 61 E5
Frimley GU16 65 F1
Kingston u T KT3 38 D6
Stoneleigh Fst Sch KT17 58 B6
Stoneleigh Lo 13 TW9 6 F6
Stoneleigh Par KT19 57 F4
Stoneleigh Park Ave CR0 43 D3
Stoneleigh Park Rd KT19, KT4 58 A5
Stoneleigh Pk KT13 53 C4
Stoneleigh Rd
Carshalton SM5 40 E2
The Chart RH8 123 E5
Stoneleigh Sta KT19 58 A5
Stone Park Ave BR3 44 B5
Stonepit Cl GU7 150 C4
Stone Pl KT4 58 A8
STONEQUARRY 186 A3
Stone Rd BR2 44 F4
Stones La RH4 135 C6
Stone's Rd KT17 76 E7
Stone St GU12 126 D8
Stoneswood Rd RH8 123 B5
Stoneworth Ct SE25 43 A3
Stoney Bottom GU26 188 C3
Stoneybrook RH12 216 F1
Stoney Brook GU2 108 E2
Stoney Castle Camping Gd GU24 87 A5
Stoneycroft GU11 104 F1
Stoney Croft CR5 99 C5
Stoneycroft Cl SE12 24 F8
Stoneycroft Wlk 3 RH11 200 D5
Stoney Deep TW11 17 A4
Stoneyfield Rd CR5 79 F2
Stoneyfields GU9 125 E1
Stoney La SE19 22 F2
Stoneyland Ct 6 TW20 11 F3
Stoneylands Rd TW20 11 F3
Stoney Rd RG42 27 A8
Stonny Croft KT21 75 F2
Stony Hill KT10 54 F3
Stoop Ct KT14 71 B7
Stoop Meml Ground TW2 16 E8
Stopham Rd RH10 202 C3
Storer Ho KT19 57 B1
Stormont Way KT9 56 C5
Storrington Ct RH11 201 A7
Storrington Rd CR0 42 F1
Storr's La GU3 88 C3
STOUGHTON 109 A4
Stoughton Ave SM3 58 E5
Stoughton Cl SW15 19 A7
Stoughton Inf Sch GU2 109 B4
Stoughton Rd GU1, GU2 109 B3
Stourhead Cl
Farnborough GU14 85 D4
6 Putney SW19 19 D8
Stourhead Gdns SW20 39 A6
Stourton Ave TW13 15 F4
Stovolds Hill GU6, GU8 193 D7
Stovold's Way GU11 125 F8
Stowell Ave CR0 63 D2
Stowford Coll SM2 59 C3
Strachan Pl SW19 19 C2
Strachey Ct 1 RH11 201 B1
Strafford Rd
Hounslow TW3 4 F4
Twickenham TW1 17 A8
Straight Rd SL4 11 C8
Strand Cl
Crawley RH10 202 D4
Langley Vale KT18 96 D8
Strand Dr TW9 7 B7
STRAND ON THE GREEN 7 A8
Strand-on-the-Green W4 7 A8
Strand-on-the-Green Inf Sch W4 7 A8
Strand-on-the-Green Jun Sch W4 7 A8
Stranraer Way 1 TW6 2 E1
Stratfield RG12 26 E1
Stratfield Ho 12 GU11 105 A2
Stratford Ct
Farnborough GU14 85 C4
Farnham GU9 125 C1
New Malden KT3 38 D5
Woking GU21 69 F3
Stratford Rd
Ash Vale GU12 85 F1
Harlington TW6 3 C2
Thornton Heath CR7 42 B6
Strathavon Cl GU6 174 B7
Strathcona Ave KT24 113 E7
Strathcona Gdns
Knaphill GU21 68 D1
Knaphill GU21 88 C8
Strathdale SW16 21 F3
Strathdon Dr SW17 20 D5
Strathearn Ave
Harlington UB3 3 F7
Twickenham TW2 16 C7
Strathearn Rd
Sutton SM1 59 A5
Wimbledon SW19 20 A4
Strathmore Cl CR3 100 E6
Strathmore Ct 3 GU15 65 D5
Strathmore Rd
Crawley RH11 181 A1
Teddington TW11 16 E4
Thornton Heath CR0 42 D2
Wimbledon SW19 20 A5
Strathmore Sch TW10 17 D6
Strathville Rd SW18 20 B6
Strathyre Ave CR7, SW16 42 A6
Stratton Ave SM6 60 D2
Stratton Cl
Heston TW5 5 A6
Merton SW19 40 A7
Walton-on-T KT12 35 C1
Stratton Ct
Guildford GU2 109 A3
10 Kingston u T KT6 37 E4
Stratton Rd
Merton SW19 40 A7
Sunbury TW16 34 F7
Stratton Wlk GU14 85 A7
Strawberry Cl GU24 87 D7
Strawberry Ct GU16 86 D8
Strawberry Fields GU24 68 A4
STRAWBERRY HILL 16 F5
Strawberry Hill Cl TW1 16 F5
Strawberry Hill Rd TW1 16 F5
Strawberry Hill Sta TW2 16 F5
Strawberry La SM5 60 A7
Strawberry Rise GU24 68 A4
Strawberry Vale TW1 17 A5
Straw Cl CR3 100 C4
Strawson Ct RH6 160 F4
Stream Cl KT14 71 E7
Stream Farm Cl GU10 146 D7
Streamline Ct SE22 23 A7
Streamline Mews SE22 23 A7
Stream Pk RH19 185 A3
Stream Valley Rd GU10 146 C6
STREATHAM 21 E2
Streatham Cl SW16 21 E6
Streatham & Clapham High Sch (Prep Dept) SW2 21 F7
Streatham & Clapham High Sch (Senior Sch) SW16 21 D5
Streatham Comm N SW16 21 F3
Streatham Common Sta SW16 21 D1
Streatham Comm S SW16 21 F2
Streatham Ct SW16 21 E5
Streatham High Rd SW16, SW2 21 E3
STREATHAM HILL 21 E7
Streatham Hill SW2 21 E7
Streatham Hill Sta SW2 21 E6
STREATHAM PARK 21 C4
Streatham Pl SW2 21 E8
Streatham Rd CR4 41 A8
Streatham Sta SW16 21 D3
STREATHAM VALE 21 D1
Streatham Vale SW16 21 D1
Streatham Wells Prim Sch SW2 22 A6
Streathbourne Rd SW17 21 A5
Streatleigh Par 4 SW16 21 E6
Streeters Cl GU7 151 A6
Streeters La SM6 60 D7
Streetfield GU8 169 C4
Streetfield Rd RH13 215 E3
Street Hill RH10 202 E5
Streets Heath GU24 67 F7
Street The
Albury GU5 132 C4
Ashtead KT21 75 F1
Betchworth RH3 116 E1
Capel RH5 178 D6
Charlwood RH6 180 E7
Compton GU3 129 B2
Dockenfield GU10 166 E6
East Clandon GU4 111 E4
Effingham KT24 113 D8
Ewhurst GU6 175 E5
Fetcham KT22 94 D5
Frensham GU10 167 C7
Plaistow RH14 211 E2
Puttenham GU3 128 C4
Shackleford GU8 149 C8
Shalford GU4 130 E3
Slinfold RH13 215 D4
Thursley GU8 169 C4
Tongham GU10 126 F6
West Clandon GU4 111 B5
West Horsley KT24 112 B7
Wonersh GU5 152 A7
Wrecclesham GU10 145 F6
Stretford Ct 1 SW19 19 E1
Stretton Ct KT13 52 F6
Stretton Rd
Croydon CR0 42 E2
Richmond TW10 17 C6
Strickland Cl 4 RH11 200 E5
Strickland Row SW18 20 D8
Strides Ct KT16 51 C4
Stringer's Ave GU4 109 D7
Stringhams Copse GU23 91 A3
Strode Ho 3 SW2 22 A7
Strode's Coll TW20 11 F3
Strodes College La TW20 11 F3
Strode's Cres TW18 13 C3
Strode St TW20 12 A4
STROOD GREEN
Dorking 137 C6
Horsham 216 A6
Strood Ho 11 SE20 23 C1
Strood La
Cranbourne SL4, SL5 9 C2
Warnham RH12 216 C7
Stroud Cres SW15 19 A5
STROUDE 31 F7
Stroude Rd
Egham TW20 12 A1
Virginia Water GU25, TW20 31 E6
Stroudes Cl KT4 38 F2
Stroud Green Gdns CR0 43 C2
Stroud Green Way CR0 43 C3
Stroud La
Shamley Green GU5 153 A3
Yateley GU17 64 A4
Stroudley Cl RH10 202 B5
Stroud Rd
Croydon SE25 43 A3
Wimbledon SW19 20 A5
Stroudwater Pk KT13 53 C4
Stroud Way TW15 14 B2
Struan Gdns GU21 69 E4
Strudgate Cl RH10 202 B4
Strudwicks Field GU6 174 F4
Stuart Ave KT12 35 C1
Stuart Cl
Crawley RH10 202 D5
Farnborough GU14 85 A5

Stuart Cres
Croydon CR0 62 F7
Reigate RH2 139 A6
Stuart Ct
Croydon CR0 61 B7
Godalming GU7 150 E4
16 Redhill RH1 119 A2
Stuart Gr TW11 16 E3
Stuart Ho
Bracknell RG42 26 F8
5 Horsham RH13 217 F3
Stuart Lo
7 Epsom KT18 76 D6
South Norwood SE25 42 E7
Stuart Pl CR4 40 F8
Stuart Rd
Reigate RH2 139 A6
Richmond TW10 17 B5
South Norwood CR7 42 C5
Warlingham CR3, CR6 101 C7
Wimbledon SW19 20 A5
Stuart Way
East Grinstead RH19 205 F7
Staines TW18 13 B2
Virginia Water GU25 31 A5
Stubbs Folly GU47 64 D7
Stubbs Ho SE19 22 D1
Stubbs La KT20 118 A7
Stubbs Moor Rd GU14 84 F5
Stubbs Way 9 SW19 40 D8
Stubfield RH12 217 A3
Stubpond La RH7 184 C8
Stubs Cl RH4 136 C5
Stubs Hill RH4 136 C4
Stubs Ind Site GU11 105 E5
Stucley Rd TW5, TW7 5 C7
Studios Rd TW17 33 F6
Studland Rd
Byfleet KT14 71 F6
Kingston u T KT2 17 E2
Penge SE26 23 D3
Study Prep Sch The SW19 19 C3
Study Sch The KT3 38 E4
Stumblets RH10 202 C7
Stumps Hill La BR3 24 A2
Sturdee Cl GU16 65 E1
Sturges Ct RG40 25 D5
Sturges Rd RG40 25 D5
Sturt Ave GU27 207 F5
Sturt Ct GU4 110 B3
Sturt Rd
Frimley GU16 85 F5
Haslemere GU27 207 F5
Heath End GU9 125 B7
Sturt's La KT20 117 A8
Stychens Cl RH1 120 C2
Stychens La RH1 120 C2
Styles End KT23 114 B8
Styles Way BR3 44 C5
Styventon Pl KT16 32 F2
Subrosa Dr RH1 119 B5
Succomb's Hill CR3, CR6 101 B7
Succombs Pl CR6 101 B8
Sudbrook Gdns TW10 17 E5
Sudbrook La TW10 17 E6
Sudbury Gdns CR0 61 E6
Sudell Ho KT6 37 E2
Suffield Cl CR2 81 D7
Suffield La GU3 128 B2
Suffield Rd SE20 43 C7
Suffolk Cl
Bagshot GU19 47 E2
Horley RH6 161 A2
Suffolk Ct
Frimley GU16 86 D8
3 West Norwood SW16 22 A4
Suffolk Dr GU4 110 B6
Suffolk Ho
12 Bromley BR2 44 F5
4 Croydon CR0 61 D8
Penge SE20 43 C8
Suffolk Rd
Barnes SW13 7 F7
South Norwood SE25 42 F5
Worcester Park KT4 57 F8
Sugden Rd KT7 37 B1
Sulina Rd SW2 21 E8
Sullington Hill RH11 201 D4
Sullington Mead RH12 216 E3
Sullivan Cl GU14 85 A4
Sullivan Ct 4 CR0 43 A1
Sullivan Dr RH11 200 E3
Sullivan Ho
Kenley CR8 80 C5
Twickenham TW2 5 D1
Sullivan Rd GU15 65 A5
Sullivans Reach KT12 35 A2
Sultan St BR3 43 D7
Sulzers Rdbt GU14 85 B3
Summer Ave KT8 36 E4
Summer Crossing KT7 36 F4
Summerene Cl 3 SW16 21 C1
Summerfield KT21 95 D8
Summerfield La
Long Ditton KT6 56 D8
Rowledge GU10 146 B2
Summerfield Pl KT16 51 D4
Summerfields Cl KT15 51 F5
Summerfield St SE12 24 F8
Summer Gdns
Frimley GU15 66 C5
Summer Gdns *continued*
Thames Ditton KT8 36 E4
Summerhayes Cl GU21 69 E5
Summerhays KT11 73 D6
Summerhill GU7 150 D6
Summerhill Way CR4 41 A8
Summer Ho RH11 201 C5
Summerhouse Ave TW5 4 E6
Summerhouse Cl GU7 150 D4
Summerhouse Ct GU26 188 D3
Summerhouse La UB7 2 D8
Summerhouse Rd GU7 150 D3
Summerlands GU6 174 E4
Summerlay Cl KT20 97 E7
Summerleigh 5 KT13 53 D4
Summerley St SW18 20 B6
Summerly Ave RH2 118 A2
Summer Pl RG12, RG42 27 A7
Summer Rd
East Molesey KT8 36 D4
Thames Ditton KT7, KT8 36 F4
Summersbury Dr GU4 130 E1
Summersbury Hall GU4 130 E1
Summersby Cl GU7 150 F7
Summers Cl
Belmont SM2 59 A3
Weybridge KT13 72 A8
Summersell Ho SE27 22 D3
Summers La GU7 150 A8
Summer's Rd GU7 151 A8
SUMMERSTOWN 20 C5
Summerstown SW17 20 C4
Summersvere Cl RH10 182 A1
Summerswood Cl CR8 80 D3
Summer Trees TW16 35 B8
Summerville Gdns SM1 58 F4
Summerwood Rd TW1, TW7 5 F1
Summit Ave GU14 84 C3
Summit Bsns Pk The TW16 15 A1
Summit Ctr
Farnborough GU14 84 D4
Harmondsworth UB7 2 D7
Summit Pl KT13 53 A3
Summit Way SE19 22 E1
Sumner Cl KT22 94 D3
Sumner Ct GU9 125 C3
Sumner Gdns CR0 42 A1
Sumner Pl KT15 52 A5
Sumner Rd
Farnham GU9 125 C3
Thornton Heath CR0 42 B1
Sumner Rd S CR0 42 A1
Sun Alley 10 TW9 6 E3
Sun Brow GU27 208 A5
SUNBURY 35 B6
Sunbury Ave SW14 7 D3
Sunbury Cl KT12 35 A3
SUNBURY COMMON 14 E1
Sunbury Court Island TW16 35 D6
Sunbury Court Mews TW16 35 D7
Sunbury Court Rd TW16 35 C7
Sunbury Cres TW13 14 F4
Sunbury Cross Ctr 9 TW16 14 F1
Sunbury Ct TW16 35 D7
Sunbury Ct (Conference Ctr) TW16 35 D7
Sunbury Int Bsns Ctr TW16 34 E8
Sunbury La KT12 35 A3
Sunbury Manor Sch TW16 34 F8
Sunbury Rd
Cheam SM3 58 E7
Feltham TW13 14 F4
Sunbury Sta TW16 35 A8
Sunbury Way TW13 15 C3
Suncroft Pl SE26 23 C5
Sundale Ave CR2 62 C1
Sunderland Ct
Dulwich SE22 23 A8
12 Stanwell TW19 2 E1
Sunderland Mount SE23 23 D6
Sunderland Rd SE23 23 D6
Sundew Cl
Crawley RH11 201 A2
Lightwater GU18 67 D8
Wokingham RG40 25 E7
Sundial Ave SE25 42 F6
Sundial Ct KT5 57 B8
Sundon Cres GU25 31 C4
Sundown Ave CR2 80 F8
Sundown Rd TW15 14 C3
Sundridge Rd
Croydon CR0, CR9 43 A1
Old Woking GU22 90 A7
Sun Hill GU22 89 A6
Sunhill Ho RH9 142 E2
Sun Inn Rd GU8 192 F5
Sunken Rd CR0 62 C5
Sunkist Way SM6 60 E2
Sun Life Trad Est TW14 4 A4
Sunlight Cl SW19 20 C2
Sunmead Cl KT22 94 F5
Sunmead Rd TW16 35 A6
Sunna Gdns TW16 35 B7
Sunna Lo TW16 14 F1
Sunniholme Ct CR2 61 C5
Sunning Ave SL5 29 E2
SUNNINGDALE 30 B4
Sunningdale RH6 161 B2
Sunningdale Ave TW13 15 E6
Sunningdale Cl 2 KT6 56 E8
Sunningdale Ct
Crawley RH10 201 D4
13 Kingston u T KT2 18 A1
Sunningdale Park (National Sch of Government) SL5 29 F4
Sunningdale Rd SM1 58 F6
Sunningdale Sch SL5 29 F3
Sunningdale Sta SL5 30 A2
SUNNINGHILL 29 C4
Sunninghill KT18 76 E4
Sunninghill Cl SL5 29 D5
Sunninghill Ct SL5 29 D5
Sunninghill Lo
Ascot SL5 29 C7
Sunninghill SL5 29 D5
Sunninghill Rd
Ascot SL5 29 D5
Cranbourne SL4, SL5 9 E2
Windlesham GU20 48 A7
Sunning Ho
Ascot SL5 29 C5
Windlesham SL5 48 F8
Sunningvale Ave TN16 83 D3
Sunningvale Cl TN16 83 D3
Sunny Ave RH10 204 A8
Sunnybank SL5 29 A5
Sunny Bank
Croydon SE25 43 A6
Epsom KT18 76 C3
Warlingham CR6 81 E2
Sunnybank Mews GU12 106 B3
Sunnybank Rd GU14 84 D6
Sunnybank Villas RH1 120 F3
Sunnycroft Rd
Croydon SE25 43 A6
Hounslow TW3 5 B5
Sunnydell La GU10 146 A6
Sunnydene Rd CR8 80 B6
Sunnydene St SE26 23 E4
Sunny Down GU8 170 E5
Sunnydown Sch CR3 100 F6
Sunnyhill GU8 170 E6
Sunnyhill Cl RH10 204 A8
Sunnyhill Prim Sch SW16 21 F4
Sunnyhill Rd SW16 21 E4
Sunny Hill Rd GU11 104 D2
Sunnyhurst Cl SM1 59 A7
Sunnymead RH11 201 D6
Sunnymead Ave CR4, SW16 41 D6
Sunnymede Ave
Sutton SM5 78 D8
West Ewell KT19 57 E3
Sunny Nook Gdns CR2 61 D4
Sunny Rise CR3 100 D3
SUNNYSIDE 205 E7
Sunnyside
Knaphill GU21 88 B8
Walton-on-T KT12 35 C4
Wimbledon SW19 19 E2
Sunnyside Pl SW19 19 E2
Sunnyside Rd
Headley Down GU35 187 C4
Teddington TW11 16 D4
Sunny View Cl GU12 105 C1
Sunray Ave KT5 57 B8
Sun Ray Est GU47 64 A8
Sunrise Cl TW13 15 F5
Sunset Gdns SE25 42 F7
Sunset Rd SW19 19 B3
Sunshine Way CR4 40 F7
Sunstone Gr RH1 119 E6
Sunvale Ave GU27 207 D6
Sunvale Cl GU27 207 D6
SURBITON 37 E2
Surbiton Boys Prep Sch KT6 37 E4
Surbiton Cres KT1, KT6 37 E5
Surbiton Ct KT6 37 D3
Surbiton Hall Cl KT1 37 E5
Surbiton High Sch For Girls KT1 37 E5
Surbiton Hill Pk KT5 38 A4
Surbiton Hill Rd KT6 37 E4
Surbiton Hospl KT6 37 E3
Surbiton Par KT6 37 E3
Surbiton Rd
Camberley GU15 47 A1
Kingston u T KT1 37 E5
Surbiton Sta KT6 37 E3
Surrey Ave GU15 65 A4
Surrey Bsns Pk KT17 76 E8
Surrey Cloisters GU7 150 F6
Surrey Countryside Scheme Visitor Ctr★ GU4 132 A7
Surrey Ct
Guildford GU2 109 B1
5 Horsham RH12 217 D2
Wallington SM6 60 C4
Surrey Gdns KT24 93 A4
Surrey Gr SM1 59 D7
Surrey Heath Mus★ GU15 65 D6
Surrey Hills Ave KT20 116 C4
Surrey Hills Pk GU3 107 E4
Surrey Hills Residential Pk KT20 116 C5
Surrey Hills Way KT20 116 C5
Surrey Ho GU4 131 C3
Surrey Inst of Art & Design The GU9 125 A2
Surrey Inst of Art & Design, Univ Coll
Epsom KT18 76 D5
Ewell KT17 76 E7
Surrey Lo
Claygate KT10 55 E4
Hersham KT12 54 B5
Merton SW20 39 C7
Surrey Mews SE27 22 E4
Surrey Mount SE23 23 B7
Surrey Rd BR4 44 B1
Surrey Research Pk The GU2 129 D8
Surrey St CR0, CR9 61 C7
Surrey Tech Ctr GU2 129 D8
Surrey Twrs KT15 52 C5
Surrey Way GU2 109 B2
Surridge Ct GU19 47 E2
Surridge Gdns SE19 22 D2
Sury Basin KT2 37 E8
Sussex Ave TW7 5 E4
Sussex Cl
Knaphill GU21 68 C1
New Malden KT3 38 E5
Reigate RH2 139 D8
4 Twickenham TW1 6 B1
Sussex Ct
Addlestone KT15 52 C5
Barnes SW13 7 F5
Horsham RH13 217 E1
Knaphill GU21 68 C2
Mitcham CR4 41 E4
Sussex Gdns KT9 56 D4
Sussex Ho TW9 6 F5
Sussex Lo RH12 217 C4
Sussex Manor Bsns Pk RH10 182 A2
Sussex Mews SE6 24 A7
Sussex Pl
Knaphill GU21 68 C1
New Malden KT3 38 E5
Sussex Rd
Croydon CR2 61 D4
Knaphill GU21 68 C1
Mitcham CR4 41 E4
New Malden KT3 38 E5
South Croydon CR2 61 D4
Wallington SM5 59 F4
2 West Wickham BR4 44 B1
Sussex Terr 3 SE20 23 C1
Sutherland Ave
Biggin Hill TN16 83 E1
Guildford GU4 109 E7
Sunbury TW16 34 F7
Sutherland Chase SL5 28 E7
Sutherland Dr
Guildford GU4 110 A4
Mitcham SW19 40 D8
Sutherland Gdns
Mortlake SW14 7 E4
North Cheam KT4 39 B1
Sunbury TW16 34 F7
Sutherland Gr
Putney SW18, SW19 19 F8
Teddington TW11 16 E3
Sutherland Ho
Guildford GU4 110 A5
Richmond TW10 17 C6
9 Sutton SM2 59 C4
Sutherland Rd
Chiswick W4 7 E8
Thornton Heath CR0 42 A2
SUTTON 59 C5
SUTTON ABINGER 155 B8
Sutton Ave GU21 88 E8
Sutton Cl BR3 44 B8
Sutton Coll of Liberal Arts SM1 59 B5
Sutton Common Rd
Cheam SM3 40 A1
Sutton SM1, SM3 59 B8
Sutton Common Sta SM1 59 B8
Sutton Courtenay Ho SW17 20 D4
Sutton Court Mans W4 7 C8
Sutton Court Rd
Chiswick W4 7 C8
Sutton SM1 59 C4
Sutton Ct
Chiswick W4 7 C8
East Molesey KT8 35 F4
Penge SE19 22 F1
Sutton SM2 59 C4
Sutton Dene TW3 5 B6
Sutton Gdns
Croydon CR0, SE25 42 F4
Merstham RH1 119 D6
Sutton Gr SM1 59 D5
Sutton Gram Sch For Boys SM1 59 C5
SUTTON GREEN 89 F2
Sutton Green Rd GU4 89 F1
Sutton Hall TW5 5 A7
Sutton High Sch SM1 59 B4
Sutton Hill GU4 110 C6
Sutton Hospl SM2 59 B1
Sutton Hts SM2 59 D3
Sutton La
Abinger Common RH5 155 C8
Sutton La *continued*
Banstead SM2, SM7 78 B6
Brands Hill SL3 1 B8
Hounslow TW3, TW4, TW5 4 F5
Sutton La S W4 7 C8
Sutton Lo GU1 109 E1
Sutton Park Rd SM1 59 B4
Sutton Pl
Brands Hill SL3 1 B8
Peaslake RH5 154 F8
Sutton Rd
Camberley GU15 47 A1
Heston TW5 5 A6
Sutton Sq TW5 4 F6
Sutton Sta SM2 59 C4
Sutton Way TW5 4 F6
Suva Ct RH19 185 C3
Swaby Rd SW17, SW18 20 C6
Swaffield Prim Sch SW18 20 C8
Swaffield Rd SW18 20 C8
Swail Ho 8 KT18 76 D6
Swain Cl SW16, SW17 21 B2
Swain Ho CR4 20 F1
Swain Rd CR7 42 C4
Swains Rd CR4, SW17, SW19 20 F1
Swaledale RG12 27 A4
Swaledale Cl RH11 201 C3
Swale Ho 2 RH1 119 A3
Swale Rd GU14 84 E6
Swallands Rd SE6 24 A5
Swallow Cl
Staines TW18 12 F4
Witley GU8 170 E7
Swallow Ct KT4 58 B8
Swallowdale CR2 62 D2
Swallowfield
Dormansland RH7 165 A2
Englefield Green TW20 11 B2
Swallow Gdns SW16 21 D3
Swallow La RH5 136 B1
Swallow Pk KT6 56 F7
Swallow Rd RH11 201 C8
Swallow Rise GU21 68 C2
Swallows Ct SE20 23 D1
Swallow St RH10 204 C5
Swallowtail Rd RH12 217 E6
Swan Barn Rd GU27 208 D6
Swan Cl
Croydon CR0 42 E2
Feltham TW13 15 E4
Swancote Gn RG12 27 B4
Swan Ct
Blackwater GU17 64 E4
Feltham TW13 15 E4
Guildford GU1 109 D3
Leatherhead KT22 95 B6
Swan Ctr SW17 20 C5
Swandrift TW18 12 F1
Swan Ho GU47 64 B7
Swan La
Charlwood RH6 180 F7
Guildford GU1 130 D7
Sandhurst GU47 64 B7
Swan Mill Gdns RH4 115 D1
Swann Ct 7 TW7 6 A4
Swanns Mdw KT23 94 A1
Swann Way RH12 216 E3
Swan Pl SW13 7 F5
Swan Rd TW13 15 E4
Swansea Rd TW14, TW6 3 D1
Swans Ghyll RH18 206 E3
Swan Sq RH12 217 C2
Swan St TW7 6 B4
Swanton Gdns SW19 19 D7
Swanwick Cl SW15 18 F8
Swan Wlk
Horsham RH12 217 C2
Oatlands Park TW17 34 E2
Swanworth La RH5 115 B7
Swayne's La GU1 110 E1
Swaynesland Rd RH8 123 F1
Swaythling Ho SW15 7 F1
Swedish Sch SW13 7 F8
Sweeps Ditch Cl TW18 13 B1
Sweeps La TW20 11 F3
Sweetbriar RG45 45 A7
Sweet La GU5 154 E8
Sweetwater Cl GU5 152 D4
Sweetwater La
Enton Green GU8 171 B2
Shamley Green GU5 152 D4
Swievelands Rd TN16 83 C1
Swift Ct SM2 59 B3
Swift Ctr CR0 60 F3
Swift La
Crawley RH11 201 C8
Windlesham GU19 47 F3
Swift Rd
Feltham TW13 15 E4
Heath End GU9 125 C7
Swift's Cl GU10 126 B1
Swiftsden Way BR1 24 E2
Swinburn Ct 3 SW20 39 D8
Swinburne Cres CR0 43 C3
Swindon Rd
Harlington TW6 3 C2
Horsham RH12 217 B4
Swinfield Cl TW13 15 E4
Swingate Rd GU9 146 D8
Swinley Prim Sch SL5 29 A4
Swinley Rd SL5 28 C4
Swiss Cl GU10 146 A4
Swissland Hill RH19, RH7 185 E7
Switchback La
Rowledge GU10 145 F4

Switchback La *continued*
Rowledge GU10 146 A3
Swordfish Way GU14 104 E7
Swordsman's Rd GU16 86 D8
Sycamore Ave RH12 218 C6
Sycamore Cl
Carshalton SM5 59 F6
Crawley RH11 181 C1
3 Croydon CR0 61 E5
Feltham TW13 15 A5
Fetcham KT22 94 F5
Frimley GU16 65 E1
Sandhurst GU47 64 B8
Sycamore Ct
4 Beckenham BR3 44 A8
Farncombe GU7 150 E8
Forest Hill SE26 23 C4
7 Guildford GU1 130 E8
Hounslow TW4 4 E3
Kingston u T KT3 38 E6
Ottershaw KT16 51 C5
Oxted RH8 122 E6
Walton-on-T KT13 53 F7
11 West Norwood SW16 22 A3
Sycamore Dr
Ash Vale GU12 106 A7
East Grinstead RH19 186 A1
Frimley GU16 65 E1
Wrecclesham GU10 146 A6
Sycamore Gdns CR4 40 D7
Sycamore Gr
Kingston u T KT3 38 E6
Penge SE20 43 A8
Sycamore Ho
Chelsham CR6 82 B4
Teddington TW11 17 C1
Twickenham TW2 16 F6
Sycamore Lo 7 TW16 14 F1
Sycamore Manor SM6 60 C3
Sycamore Rd
Farnborough GU14 85 D2
Guildford GU1 109 D1
Wimbledon SW19 19 C2
Sycamore Rise
Banstead KT17, SM7 77 D5
Bracknell RG12 27 D6
Sycamores The
Blackwater GU17 64 B5
Farnborough GU14 85 D3
Great Bookham KT23 94 C3
Hooley CR5 99 B5
Sycamore Way TW11 17 C2
Sycamore Wlk
Englefield Green TW20 11 B2
Reigate RH2 139 C6
Sydcote SE21 22 C7
Sydenham Ave SE26 23 B3
Sydenham High Sch SE26 23 B5
Sydenham High Sch For Girls SE26 23 B3
Sydenham Hill SE21, SE22, SE23, SE26, SE19 23 B5
Sydenham Hill Sta SE21 22 F5
Sydenham Ho 16 KT6 37 D2
Sydenham Ind Est SE26 23 F3
Sydenham Park Mans SE26 23 C5
Sydenham Park Rd SE23, SE26 23 C5
Sydenham Pk SE26 23 C5
Sydenham Rd
Forest Hill SE26, SE6 23 D3
Guildford GU1 130 E8
Thornton Heath CR0 42 D2
Sydenham Rise SE23 23 B6
Sydenham Sta SE26 23 C4
Sydenham Station App SE26 23 C4
Sydmons Ct SE23 23 C8
Sydney Ave CR8 79 F7
Sydney Cl RG45 45 C7
Sydney Cotts KT10 55 F4
Sydney Cres TW15 14 B2
Sydney Ct KT6 56 E8
Sydney Loader Pl GU46 64 A5
Sydney Pl GU1 130 F8
Sydney Rd
East Bedfont TW14 15 A7
Guildford GU1 130 F8
Merton SW20 39 D7
Richmond TW10, TW9 6 E3
Sutton SM1 59 A6
Teddington TW11 16 F3
Sydney Terr KT10 55 F4
Sydney Villas GU12 106 A8
Sykes Dr TW18 13 B3
Sylva Ct 3 SW15 19 D8
Sylvan Cl
Limpsfield RH8 123 B6
South Croydon CR2 62 B1
Woking GU22 70 B2
Sylvan Ct
1 Farnborough GU14 105 D8
South Croydon CR2 61 C4
Sylvan Gdns KT6 37 D2
Sylvan Hill SE19 42 E8
Sylvan Rd
Crawley RH10 202 A4
South Norwood SE19 42 F8
Sylvan Ridge GU47 45 A1
Sylvanus RG12 26 F2
Sylvan Way
Coney Hall BR4 63 E6
Sylvan Way *continued*
Redhill RH1 140 A8
Sylvaways Cl GU6 175 A3
Sylverdale Rd
Croydon CR0, CR9 61 B7
Purley CR8 80 B6
Syon Gate Way TW7, TW8 6 A7
Syon House & Pk* TW8 6 C6
Syon La
Brentford TW7 5 F8
Hounslow TW7 6 A7
Syon Lane Sta TW7 6 A7
Syon Park Cotts TW8 6 C6
Syon Park Gdns TW7 5 F7
Syon Park Sch TW7 6 B6
Syon Pl GU14 85 D4
Sythwood GU21 69 B2
Sythwood Prim Sch GU21 69 B3
Szabo Cres GU3 107 B1

T

Tabard Ho KT1 37 C8
Tabarin Way KT17 77 C3
Tabor Ct SM3 58 E4
Tabor Gdns SM3 58 F3
Tabor Gr SW19 19 F1
Tachbrook Rd TW14 14 F8
Tadcaster Ct 3 TW9 6 E3
Tadlow KT1 38 A6
Tadmor Cl TW16 34 F5
Tadorne Rd KT20 97 C5
TADWORTH 97 C5
Tadworth Ave KT3 38 F4
Tadworth Cl KT20 97 D5
Tadworth Prim Sch KT20 97 D5
Tadworth St KT20 97 C5
Tadworth Sta KT20 97 C5
Taffy's How CR4 40 E6
Taggs Ho KT1 37 D7
Tailors Ct 9 SW16 21 C4
Tait Rd CR0, SE25 42 E2
Talavera Inf Sch GU11 105 B3
Talavera Jun Sch GU11 105 A2
Talbot Cl
Mytchett GU16 86 A4
Reigate RH2 139 B8
Talbot La RH12 217 C1
Talbot Lo KT10 55 A5
Talbot Pl GU19 47 E4
Talbot Rd
Ashford TW15 13 E3
Farnham GU9 146 B8
Isleworth TW1, TW7 6 A3
Lingfield RH7 164 D4
South Norwood CR7 42 D5
Twickenham TW2 16 F7
Wallington SM5 60 A5
Talcott Path 12 SW2 22 A7
Taleworth Cl KT21 95 D7
Taleworth Pk KT21 95 D7
Taleworth Rd KT21 95 E7
Talfourd Way RH1 140 A6
Talgarth Dr GU14 85 D2
Taliesin Hts GU7 150 D6
Talisman Sq SE26 23 A4
Talisman Way KT17 77 C3
Tall Elms Cl BR2 44 F4
Tallis Cl RH11 200 F3
Tallow Rd TW8 6 C7
Tall Trees
Poyle SL3 1 E6
Thornton Heath SW16 41 F6
Tally Rd RH8 123 E4
Talma Gdns TW2 16 E8
Talmage Cl SE23 23 C8
Talman Cl RH11 200 E5
Tamar Cl RH10 202 C5
Tamarind Cl GU2 109 A6
Tamarind Ct 3 TW20 11 F3
Tamarisk Rise RG40 25 C7
Tamerton Sq 1 GU22 89 E8
Tamesa Ho TW17 34 A2
Tamesis Gdns KT4 57 E8
Tamian Ind Est TW4 4 C3
Tamian Way TW4 4 C3
Tamil Ho SE6 24 A6
Tamworth RG12 27 D2
Tamworth La CR4 41 B6
Tamworth Pk CR4 41 B6
Tamworth Pl 3 CR0, CR9 61 C8
Tamworth Rd CR0, CR9 61 C8
Tanbridge Ho RH12 217 B1
Tanbridge House Sch RH12 216 F2
Tanbridge Pk RH12 217 B1
Tanbridge Pl RH12 217 B1
Tanbridge Ret Pk RH12 217 B1
Tandem Ctr SW19 40 D8
TANDRIDGE 122 A2
Tandridge Ct
Caterham CR3 101 A5
Sutton SM2 59 B4
Tandridge Gdns CR2 81 A6
Tandridgehill La RH9 121 F6
Tandridge La RH7, RH8 143 B4
Tandridge Rd CR6 101 D8
Tanfield Ct 4 RH12 217 B2
Tanfield Rd CR0, CR9 61 C6
Tangier Ct GU11 104 F2
Tangier Rd
Guildford GU1 131 A8
Mortlake TW10 7 B4
Tangier Way KT20 77 E1
Tangier Wood KT20 77 E1
Tangle Oak RH19 184 E4
Tanglewood Cl
Longcross KT16 50 B7
South Croydon CR0 62 C7
Woking GU22 70 D3
Tanglewood Ride GU24 67 D7
Tanglewood Way TW13 15 B5
Tangley Dr RG41 25 B4
Tangley Gr SW15 18 F8
Tangley La GU3 108 F6
Tangley Park Rd TW12 15 F3
Tanglyn Ave TW17 34 B4
Tangmere Gr KT2 17 D3
Tangmere Rd RH11 200 F6
Tanhouse La RG41 25 A5
Tanhouse Rd RH8 122 E3
Tanhurst Ho 26 SW2 21 E8
Tanhurst La RH5 155 E2
Tanker Rd GU14 85 B1
Tankerton Rd KT6 56 F8
Tankerton Terr CR0 41 F3
Tankerville Rd SW16 21 E1
Tank Rd GU15 64 F5
Tanner Ho 1 SW19 40 C8
Tanners Cl KT12 35 B3
Tanners Ct GU27 208 C7
Tanner's Ct RH3 137 C5
Tanners Dean KT22 95 D5
Tannersfield GU4 130 E1
Tanner's Hill RH3 137 B8
Tanners La GU27 208 C7
Tanners Mdw RH3 137 B5
Tanners Yd GU19 47 E3
Tannery Cl
Beckenham BR3, CR0 43 D4
Slinfold RH13 215 D3
Tannery Ho GU23 90 D5
Tannery La
Send GU23 90 E5
Shalford GU5 151 F8
Tannery The RH1 118 F1
Tannsfeld Rd SE26 23 D3
Tansy Cl GU4 110 C3
Tantallon Rd SW12 21 A7
Tanyard Ave RH19 206 A8
Tanyard Cl
Crawley RH10 202 C3
Horsham RH13 217 E1
Tanyard Ho 3 TW8 6 C7
Tanyard Way RH6 161 B4
Tapestry Cl SM2 59 B3
Taplow Ct CR4 40 E5
Tapner's Rd RH2 137 F3
Tapping Cl 5 KT2 18 A1
Tara Ct 4 BR3 44 B7
Tarbat Ct 6 GU47 64 D8
Target Cl TW14 3 E1
Tarham Cl RH6 160 E5
Tarleton Gdns SE23 23 B7
Tarmac Way UB7 2 B7
Tarnbrook Way RG12 27 E2
Tarn Cl GU14 84 E2
Tarn Rd GU26 188 E3
Tarquin Ho SE26 23 A4
Tarragon Cl GU14 84 C4
Tarragon Ct GU2 109 A5
Tarragon Dr GU2 109 A5
Tarragon Gr SE26 23 D2
Tarrington Cl SW16 21 D5
Tartar Hill KT11 73 B6
Tartar Rd KT11 73 C6
Tasker Cl UB7 3 C7
Tasman Ct TW16 14 E1
Tatchbury Ho SW15 7 F1
Tate Cl KT22 95 C4
Tate Rd SM1 59 A5
Tate's Way RH12 214 D7
Tatham Ct RH11 201 B1
TATSFIELD 103 D7
TATSFIELD GREEN 103 E7
Tatsfield La TN16 103 F6
Tatsfield Prim Sch TN16 103 D6
Tattenham Corner Rd KT18 77 A1
Tattenham Corner Sta KT18 77 B1
Tattenham Cres KT18 77 B1
Tattenham Gr KT18 97 B8
Tattenham Way KT18, KT20 77 E2
Tattersall Cl RG40 25 E5
Taunton Ave
Caterham CR3 100 F4
Hounslow TW3 5 C5
Wimbledon SW20 39 B7
Taunton Cl
Cheam SM3 40 A1
Crawley RH10 202 E6
Taunton La CR5 100 B8
Tavern Cl SM5 40 E2
Tavistock Cl TW18 13 D1
Tavistock Cres CR4 41 E5
Tavistock Ct 1 CR0 42 D1
Tavistock Gdns GU14 85 B7
Tavistock Gr CR0 42 D2
Tavistock Rd
Carshalton SM5 40 D1
Croydon CR0 42 D1
Tavistock Wlk SM5 40 D1
Tavy Ho 3 RH1 118 F2
Tawfield RG12 26 E2
Tawny Cl TW13 15 A5
Tayben Ave TW2 5 E1
Tay Cl GU14 84 E6
Tayles Hill Dr KT17 57 F1
Tayles Hill Ho KT17 57 F1
Taylor Ave TW9 7 B5
Taylor Cl
Epsom KT19 76 A8
Hampton TW12 16 C3
Hounslow TW3 5 C6
Taylor Ct SE20 43 C7
Taylor Ho
Carshalton SM5 59 E8
10 Streatham SW2 22 A7
Taylor Rd
Ashtead KT21 75 D2
Farnborough GU11 105 D7
Mitcham CR4 20 E1
Wallington SM6 60 B5
Taylors Cres GU6 174 F3
Taylors Ct TW13 15 A6
Taylor's La SE26 23 B4
Taylor Wlk RH11 201 C6
Taymount Grange SE23 23 C6
Taymount Rise SE23 23 C6
Taynton Dr RH1 119 D6
Teal Cl
Horsham RH12 217 C5
Selsdon CR2 81 D8
Teal Ct
5 Dorking RH4 136 A8
Wallington SM6 60 C5
Tealing Dr KT19 57 D6
Teal Pl SM1 58 F5
Teasel Cl
Crawley RH11 201 B3
Croydon CR0 43 D1
Teazlewood Pk KT22 75 A1
Tebbit Cl RG12 27 D7
Tebbs Ho 14 SW2 22 A8
Teck Cl TW7 6 A5
Ted Adams Ho GU2 129 E8
Tedder Cl KT9 56 C5
Tedder Rd CR2 62 D2
TEDDINGTON 17 B3
Teddington Cl KT19 57 D1
Teddington Meml Hospl TW11 16 E2
Teddington Park Rd TW11 16 F4
Teddington Pk TW11 16 F3
Teddington Sch TW11 17 C2
Teddington Sta TW11 17 A2
Tedham La RH9 163 B7
Tees Cl GU14 84 E6
Teesdale RH11 201 C3
Teesdale Ave TW7 6 A6
Teesdale Ct TW7 6 A6
Teesdale Gdns
Isleworth TW7 6 A6
South Norwood SE25 42 E7
Teevan Cl CR0 43 A2
Teevan Rd CR0, CR9 43 A2
Tegg's La GU22 70 F3
Tekels Ave GU15 65 D4
Tekels Ct GU15 65 E4
Tekels Way GU15 65 F3
Telconia Cl GU35 187 C4
Telegraph La KT10 55 F5
Telegraph Rd SW15 19 C8
Telegraph Tk SM5, SM6 60 A1
Telfer Ho 8 SE21 22 E4
Telferscot Prim Sch SW12 21 D7
Telferscot Rd SW12 21 D7
Telford Ave
Crowthorne RG45 45 C8
Streatham SW12, SW2 21 E7
Telford Ave Mans 7 SW2 21 E7
Telford Cl SE19 22 F2
Telford Ct 2 GU1 130 F8
Telford Dr KT12 35 C2
Telford Par Mans 8 SW2 21 E7
Telford Pl RH10 201 E5
Telford Rd TW2 16 A8
Telham Ct 5 RH11 200 F3
Tellisford KT10 55 B6
Temperley Rd SW12 21 A8
Tempest Ho 9 KT2 37 E8
Tempest Rd TW20 12 C2
Templar Ave GU9 146 B8
Templar Cl GU47 64 A8
Templar Ct CR0 62 E2
Templar Pl TW12 16 A1
Templars Lo RG12 27 D3
Temple Ave CR0 62 F7
Temple Bar Rd GU21 88 F8
Temple Cl
Crawley RH10 202 D5
Epsom KT19 76 D7
Templecombe Mews GU22 70 B3
Templecombe Way SM4 39 E4
Templecroft TW15 14 D2
Temple Ct 6 KT13 53 B6
Templedene BR2 44 D7
Templedene Ave TW18 13 C2
Temple Field Cl KT15 52 B4
Temple Gdns TW18 32 F8
Temple La RH5 178 F5
Templeman Cl CR8 80 B3
Templemere KT13 53 D7
Temple Mkt KT13 53 B6
Templer Ave GU14 85 A2
Temple Rd
Biggin Hill TN16 83 D2
Croydon CR0 61 D6
Epsom KT19 76 D7
Hounslow TW3 5 C3
Richmond TW9 6 F4
Temple's Cl GU10 126 C1
Temple Sheen SW14 7 C2
Temple Sheen Rd SW14 7 C3
Templeton Cl CR7, SE19 42 D8
Temple Way
Bracknell RG42 26 E8
Carshalton SM1 59 D7
Temple Wood Dr RH1 118 F4
Templewood Ho RH1 118 F4
Ten Acre GU21 69 A1
Ten Acre La TW20 32 C7
Ten Acres KT22 94 D3
Ten Acres Cl KT22 94 D3
Tenbury Ct SW12 21 D7
Tenby Dr SL5 29 D4
Tenby Rd GU16 86 A8
Tenchley's La
Limpsfield RH8 123 D4
The Chart RH8 123 E2
Tenham Ave SW2 21 D6
Tenniel Cl GU2 109 B3
Tennison Cl CR5 100 B7
Tennison Rd SE25 42 F4
Tennyson Ave
Twickenham TW1 16 F7
West Barnes KT3 39 B4
Tennyson Cl
Crawley RH10 202 B8
Feltham TW14 4 A1
Horsham RH12 217 E6
Tennyson Ct 3 TW10 17 D4
Tennyson Ho KT3 39 A4
Tennyson Rd
Addlestone KT15 52 E6
Ashford TW15 13 E3
Hounslow TW3 5 C5
Penge SE20 23 D1
Wimbledon SW19 20 C2
Tennyson Rise RH19 205 C8
Tennyson's La
Haslemere GU27 208 E4
Lurgashall GU27 209 A2
Tennysons Ridge GU27 208 E5
Tensing Ct TW19 13 E7
Tenterden Gdns CR0 43 A2
Tenterden Rd CR0 43 A2
Tern Rd RH11 200 D5
Terrace Gdns SW13 7 F5
Terrace La TW10 6 E1
Terrace Rd KT12 35 B3
Terraces The 12 SW20 19 D1
Terrace The
Addlestone KT15 52 E5
Ascot SL5 29 D4
Barnes SW13, SW14 7 E5
Camberley GU15 65 A5
Crowthorne RG45 45 D5
Old Woking GU22 90 A6
Wokingham RG40 25 B6
Terracotta Rd RH9 142 C5
Terrano Ho 1 TW9 7 B6
Terrapin Ct SW17 21 B5
Terrapin Rd SW17 21 B5
Terrapins KT6 37 D2
Terry Ct 8 SM6 60 C4
Terry Ho SW2 22 A7
Terry Lo 2 CR7 42 A4
Terry Rd RH11 201 B1
Tersha St TW9 6 E3
Testard Rd GU2 130 C7
Testers Cl RH8 123 B3
Teviot Cl GU2 109 A4
Tewkesbury Ave SE23 23 B8
Tewkesbury Cl KT14 71 D8
Tewkesbury Rd SM5 40 D1
Teynham Ct BR3 44 B6
Thackeray Cl
Isleworth TW7 6 A5
Wimbledon SW19 19 D1
Thackeray Manor SM1 59 C5
Thackery Lo TW14 3 D1
Thakeham Cl SE26 23 B3
Thames Ave KT16 33 A6
Thames Bank SW14 7 C5
Thames Cl
Chertsey KT16 33 C2
East Molesey TW12 36 B7
Farnborough GU14 84 E6
Thames Cnr TW16 35 C6
Thames Cotts KT7 37 B3
Thames Cres W4 7 E7
Thames Ct KT8 36 B7
THAMES DITTON 37 B2
Thames Ditton Inf Sch KT7 36 F3
Thames Ditton Island KT7 37 A3
Thames Ditton Jun Sch KT7 36 F2
Thames Ditton Sta KT7 36 F2
Thames Edge Ct TW18 12 E4
Thames Eyot 10 TW1 17 A7
Thamesfield Ct TW17 34 C2
Thamesfield Ho TW17 34 C2

Thamesfield Mews TW17 . . . 34 C2
Thamesgate TW18 . . . 33 B8
Thamesgate Cl TW10 . . . 17 B4
Thames Haven KT6 . . . 37 D4
Thameside TW11 . . . 17 D1
Thameside Ctr TW8 . . . 6 F8
Thameside Pl KT1 . . . 37 D8
Thames Link Ho 11 TW9 . . . 6 E3
Thames Mdw
East Molesey KT8 . . . 36 A6
Lower Halliford KT12, TW17 . . . 34 E1
Thames Mead KT12 . . . 35 A2
Thamesmead Sec Sch TW17 . . . 34 D3
Thamespoint TW11 . . . 17 D1
Thames Rd W4 . . . 7 B8
Thames Row TW8 . . . 6 F8
Thames Side
Kingston u T KT1 . . . 37 D8
Laleham KT16, TW18 . . . 33 C4
Staines TW18 . . . 12 F2
Thames Ditton KT7 . . . 37 B3
Thames St
East Molesey TW12 . . . 36 B7
Kingston u T KT1, KT2 . . . 37 D7
Staines TW18 . . . 12 F3
Sunbury TW16 . . . 35 B6
Walton-on-T KT12 . . . 34 F2
Weybridge KT13 . . . 53 B7
Thamesvale Cl TW3 . . . 5 A5
Thames View Ho TW12 . . . 35 A3
Thames Village W4 . . . 7 C6
Thanescroft Ct CR0 . . . 61 F7
Thanescroft Gdns CR0 . . . 61 E7
Thanet Ho
10 Croydon CR0 . . . 61 C6
1 West Norwood SE27 . . . 22 B5
Thanet Pl CR0 . . . 61 C6
Tharp Rd SM6 . . . 60 D5
Thatcher Cl RH10 . . . 201 D3
Thatchers Cl
Horley RH6 . . . 161 B5
Horsham RH12 . . . 217 E4
Thatchers La GU3 . . . 108 E8
Thatchers Way TW7 . . . 5 D2
Thaxted Pl 14 SW20 . . . 19 D1
Thayers Farm Rd BR3 . . . 43 E8
Theal Cl GU47 . . . 64 D8
Theatre Rd GU14 . . . 105 B8
THE BOURNE . . . 146 D6
THE CHART . . . 123 E5
THE HAVEN . . . 214 D2
Thelma Gr TW11 . . . 17 A2
Thelton Ave RH12 . . . 216 D3
Theobald Rd CR0, CR9 . . . 61 B8
Theobalds Way GU16 . . . 66 C3
Thepps Cl RH1 . . . 140 F6
Therapia La
Thornton Heath CR0 . . . 41 E3
Wallington CR0 . . . 41 D2
Wallington CR0 . . . 41 E2
Theresa's Wlk CR2 . . . 61 D2
Therfield Sch KT22 . . . 95 A8
THE SANDS . . . 126 E2
Thesiger Rd BR3, SE20 . . . 23 D1
Thetford Ct
Dulwich SE21 . . . 23 B6
New Malden KT3 . . . 38 E4
Thetford Rd
Ashford TW15 . . . 13 E5
New Malden KT3 . . . 38 E4
Thetford Wlk RH11 . . . 200 E2
Thetis Terr TW9 . . . 7 A8
THE VILLAGE . . . 10 B5
THE WELLS . . . 76 A5
THE WRYTHE . . . 59 F8
Theydon Cl RH10 . . . 202 A4
Theydon Ct GU6 . . . 174 A2
Thibet Rd GU47 . . . 64 C8
Thicket Cres SM1 . . . 59 C6
Thicket Ct 5 SM1 . . . 59 C6
Thicket Gr SE20 . . . 23 A1
Thicket Rd
Penge SE19, SE20 . . . 23 B1
Sutton SM1 . . . 59 C6
Thickthorne La TW18 . . . 13 C1
Third Cl KT8 . . . 36 C5
Third Cross Rd TW2 . . . 16 D6
Thirlestane Ct GU26 . . . 188 F5
Thirlestane Ho TW12 . . . 16 B4
Thirlmere Cl
Farnborough GU14 . . . 84 E4
Thorpe Lea TW20 . . . 12 B1
Thirlmere Ho TW1 . . . 5 F2
Thirlmere Rd
Crawley RH11 . . . 200 D4
Streatham SW16 . . . 21 D4
Thirlmere Rise BR1 . . . 24 F2
Thirlmere Wlk GU15 . . . 66 D4
Thirsk Ct GU12 . . . 105 D2
Thirsk Rd
Mitcham CR4 . . . 21 A1
South Norwood SE25 . . . 42 D5
Thisledown Ct SE25 . . . 42 D6
Thistlecroft Rd KT12 . . . 54 C6
Thistledene
Thames Ditton KT7 . . . 36 E3
West Byfleet KT14 . . . 70 F6
Thistledown Vale RH14 . . . 212 D3
Thistles The KT22 . . . 95 C5
Thistle Way RH6 . . . 162 C3
Thistlewood Cres CR0 . . . 82 D7
Thistleworth Cl TW7 . . . 5 D7
Thistley Cl CR5 . . . 99 D5
Thistley La GU6 . . . 174 E4
Thomas Ave CR3 . . . 100 C6
Thomas Bennett Com Coll RH10 . . . 201 D2
Thomas Dean Rd SE26 . . . 23 F4
Thomas Ho 14 SM2 . . . 59 B3
Thomas' La SE6 . . . 24 A8
Thomas Moore Ho RH2 . . . 118 C1
Thomas More Catholic Sch CR8 . . . 61 A1
Thomas Pooley Ct KT6 . . . 37 E2
Thomas Rd GU11 . . . 105 D7
Thomas Wall Cl SM1 . . . 59 B5
Thompson Ave TW9 . . . 7 A4
Thompson Cl SM3 . . . 40 A1
Thompson Rd TW3 . . . 5 B3
Thompsons Cl GU24 . . . 87 D4
Thompson's La GU24 . . . 49 D2
Thomson Cres CR0 . . . 42 A1
Thomson Ct 16 RH11 . . . 201 B1
Thorburn Chase GU47 . . . 64 E6
Thorburn Way 7 SW19 . . . 40 D8
Thorfield GU8 . . . 169 C4
Thorkhill Gdns KT7 . . . 37 B1
Thorkhill Rd KT7 . . . 37 B2
Thorlands GU27 . . . 208 A7
Thorley Cl KT14 . . . 71 A5
Thorley Gdns KT14 . . . 71 A5
Thornash Cl GU21 . . . 69 C4
Thornash Rd GU21 . . . 69 C4
Thornash Way GU21 . . . 69 C4
Thorn Bank GU2 . . . 130 A7
Thornbank Cl TW19 . . . 2 A2
Thornberry Way GU1 . . . 109 F5
Thornbury Ave TW7 . . . 5 D7
Thornbury Cl RG45 . . . 45 B5
Thornbury Ct
Croydon CR2 . . . 61 D5
Hounslow TW7 . . . 5 E7
Whyteleafe CR3 . . . 100 F7
Thornbury Rd TW7 . . . 5 D6
Thornchace Sch GU1 . . . 110 C1
Thorn Cl GU10 . . . 145 F4
Thorncombe St GU5 . . . 151 E2
THORNCOMBE STREET . . . 151 E1
Thorncroft
Englefield Green TW20 . . . 11 C1
4 Leatherhead KT22 . . . 95 A5
Thorncroft Cl CR5 . . . 100 A8
Thorncroft Rd SM1 . . . 59 B6
Thorndean St SW18 . . . 20 C6
Thorndon Gdns KT19 . . . 57 E6
Thorndown La GU20 . . . 48 D3
Thorndyke Cl RH10 . . . 202 D5
Thorne Cl
Claygate KT10 . . . 56 A3
Crowthorne RG45 . . . 45 A7
Littleton Common TW15 . . . 14 C1
Thorneloe Gdns CR0, CR9 . . . 61 B5
Thorne's Cl BR3 . . . 44 C6
Thorne St SW13, SW14 . . . 7 E4
Thorneycroft Cl KT12 . . . 35 C3
Thornfield Gn GU17 . . . 64 F3
Thornfield Rd SM7 . . . 78 A2
Thornhill
Bracknell RG12 . . . 27 E5
Crawley RH11 . . . 201 B4
Thornhill Ave KT6 . . . 56 E8
Thornhill Cres GU11 . . . 105 C3
Thornhill Rd
Aldershot GU11 . . . 105 D4
Surbiton KT6 . . . 56 F8
Thornton Heath CR0 . . . 42 C2
Thornhill Way TW17 . . . 34 A4
Thornlaw Rd SE27 . . . 22 B4
Thornleas Pl KT24 . . . 92 E1
Thorn Rd GU10 . . . 146 A5
Thornsbeach Rd SE6 . . . 24 C6
Thornsett Pl SE20 . . . 43 B7
Thornsett Rd
Penge SE20 . . . 43 B7
Wandsworth SW18 . . . 20 B7
Thornsett Terr SE20 . . . 43 B7
Thornton Ave
Streatham SW2 . . . 21 D7
Thornton Heath CR0 . . . 41 F3
Thornton Cl
Guildford GU2 . . . 109 A4
Horley RH6 . . . 160 E3
Thornton Cres CR5 . . . 100 A8
Thornton Ct SW20 . . . 39 D4
Thornton Dene BR3 . . . 44 A7
Thornton Gdns SW12 . . . 21 D7
THORNTON HEATH . . . 42 B3
Thornton Heath Sta CR7 . . . 42 C5
Thornton Hill SW19 . . . 19 E1
Thornton Lo 8 SW19 . . . 19 E1
Thornton Pl RH6 . . . 160 F3
Thornton Rd
Carshalton SM5 . . . 40 D1
Mortlake SW14 . . . 7 D4
Streatham SW12, SW2 . . . 21 D7
Thornton Heath CR0, CR7, CR9 . . . 41 F3
Wimbledon SW19 . . . 19 D1
Thornton Rd E SW19 . . . 19 D2
Thornton Rd Ind Est CR0 . . . 41 F3
Thornton Row CR7 . . . 42 A4
Thornville Gr CR4 . . . 40 D7
Thornycroft Ct TW9 . . . 6 F5
Thornyhurst Rd GU16 . . . 86 A4
Thorold Cl CR0, CR2 . . . 62 D1
Thorold Ho 6 SW2 . . . 21 E8
Thorold Rd GU9 . . . 125 C3
Thoroughfare The KT20 . . . 97 A3
THORPE . . . 32 C6
Thorpe By-Pass TW20 . . . 32 B6
Thorpe CE Inf Sch TW20 . . . 32 B6
Thorpe Cl
Forest Hill SE26 . . . 23 D4
New Addington CR0 . . . 82 C8
Wokingham RG41 . . . 25 A3
Thorpe Ct SW17 . . . 20 E4
THORPE GREEN . . . 32 A5
Thorpe Ind Est TW20 . . . 32 C7
Thorpe Ind Pk TW20 . . . 32 C8
THORPE LEA . . . 12 B1
Thorpe Lea Prim Sch TW20 . . . 12 D2
Thorpe Lea Rd TW20 . . . 12 C2
Thorpe Pk★ TW20 . . . 32 E5
Thorpe Rd
Chertsey KT16 . . . 32 D4
Egham TW18, TW20 . . . 12 D3
Kingston u T KT2 . . . 17 E1
Thorpes Cl GU2 . . . 109 A4
Thorpeside Cl TW18, TW20 . . . 32 E7
Thorpewood Ave SE23, SE26 . . . 23 B6
Thorsden Cl GU22 . . . 89 E8
Thorsden Ct 10 GU22 . . . 69 E1
Thorsden Way 2 SE19 . . . 22 E3
Thrale Almhouses SW16 . . . 21 E3
Thrale Rd SW16 . . . 21 C3
Three Acres RH12 . . . 217 A1
Three Arch Bsns Pk RH1 . . . 140 A4
Three Arches Pk RH1 . . . 139 F5
Three Arch Rd RH1 . . . 140 A5
THREE BRIDGES . . . 202 A7
Three Bridges Inf Sch RH10 . . . 202 A7
Three Bridges Jun Sch RH10 . . . 201 F6
Three Bridges Rd RH10 . . . 202 A6
Three Bridges Sta RH10 . . . 202 B6
Three Gates GU1 . . . 110 C3
Three Gates La GU27 . . . 208 E8
Three Pears Rd GU1 . . . 110 E1
Threestile Cnr RH12 . . . 197 E1
Threestile Rd RH12 . . . 197 F1
Three Stiles Rd GU9 . . . 124 F3
Threeways TW1 . . . 16 F4
Three Ways GU10 . . . 166 D6
Threshfield RG12 . . . 27 A4
Threshold Way GU24 . . . 50 E1
Thriffwood SE23, SE26 . . . 23 D5
Thrift Vale GU4 . . . 110 D4
Thrigby Rd KT9 . . . 56 F4
Throwley Rd SM1 . . . 59 B5
Throwley Way SM1 . . . 59 B5
Thrupp Cl CR4 . . . 41 B7
Thrupps Ave KT12 . . . 54 D5
Thrupps La KT12 . . . 54 D5
Thundery Hill GU10 . . . 126 F4
Thurbans Rd GU9 . . . 146 A7
Thurbarn Rd SE6 . . . 24 B3
Thurbarns Hill RH5 . . . 157 E1
Thurlby Rd SE27 . . . 22 A4
Thurleigh Rd SW11, SW12 . . . 20 F8
Thurleston Ave SM4 . . . 39 E4
Thurlestone Cl TW17 . . . 34 C3
Thurlestone Par TW17 . . . 34 C3
Thurlestone Rd SE27 . . . 22 A4
Thurlow GU7 . . . 150 D3
Thurlow Hill SE21 . . . 22 C6
Thurlow Ho 17 SW16 . . . 21 E5
Thurlow Park Rd SE21, SE24 . . . 22 C6
Thurlow Twrs SE27 . . . 22 A5
Thurlow Wlk GU6 . . . 174 E1
Thurlton Ct GU21 . . . 69 E3
Thurnby Ct TW2 . . . 16 E5
Thurne Way RH12 . . . 214 D7
Thurnham Way KT20 . . . 97 D7
Thursby Rd GU21 . . . 69 A1
THURSLEY . . . 169 C4
Thursley Cres CR0 . . . 63 D3
Thursley Gdns SW19 . . . 19 D6
Thursley Ho
3 Kingston u T KT2 . . . 18 B1
13 Streatham SW2 . . . 21 F8
Thursley National Nature Reserve★ GU8 . . . 169 C5
Thursley Rd
Churt GU10, GU8 . . . 168 C3
Thursley GU8, GU10 . . . 169 B6
Thurso St SW17 . . . 20 D4
Thurstan Rd SW20 . . . 19 B1
Thurston Ho BR3 . . . 24 B2
Thurza Ct TW7 . . . 5 F5
Thyme Ct
Farnborough GU14 . . . 84 C5
Guildford GU4 . . . 110 B4
Thyme Ho RH10 . . . 182 A1
Tibbenham Pl SE6 . . . 24 A6
Tibbets Cl SW19 . . . 19 D7
Tibbet's Cnr SW19 . . . 19 D8
Tibbet's Ride SW19 . . . 19 D8
Ticehurst Cl RH10 . . . 202 E6
Ticehurst Rd SE23 . . . 23 E6
Tichborne Cl GU17 . . . 64 D5
Tichborne Pl GU12 . . . 126 D8
Tichbourne Cl GU16 . . . 65 F3
Tichmarsh KT19 . . . 57 C1
Tidenham Gdns CR0 . . . 61 E7
Tides End Ct GU15 . . . 65 F4
Tideswell Rd CR0 . . . 63 A7
Tideway Cl TW10 . . . 17 C4
Tideway Yd SW13 . . . 7 E5
Tidwells Lea RG12 . . . 27 E8
Tiepigs La BR2, BR4 . . . 44 F1
Tierney Ct 4 CR0 . . . 61 F8
Tierney Rd SW2 . . . 21 E7
Tierney Terr SW2 . . . 21 E7
Tiffin Girls' Sch The KT2 . . . 17 E2
Tiffin Sch KT2 . . . 37 F7
Tilburstow Cotts RH9 . . . 121 C3
Tilburstow Hill Rd RH9 . . . 142 D5
Tile Barn Cl GU14 . . . 85 A5
Tilehouse Rd GU4 . . . 130 E5
Tilehurst La RH3, RH5 . . . 136 F5
Tilehurst Rd
Cheam SM3 . . . 58 E5
Wandsworth SW17, SW18 . . . 20 D7
Tilers Cl RH1 . . . 119 C4
Tiler's Way RH2 . . . 139 C5
Tiler's Wlk RH2 . . . 139 C5
TILFORD . . . 147 D3
Tilford Ave CR0 . . . 63 C2
Tilford Gdns SW19 . . . 19 D7
Tilford Ho 11 SW2 . . . 21 F8
Tilford Rd
Beacon Hill GU10, GU26 . . . 188 D7
Farnham GU10, GU9 . . . 146 F7
Hindhead GU26 . . . 188 F4
Rushmoor GU10 . . . 168 C4
Tilford GU10 . . . 147 C4
Tilford St GU10 . . . 147 D5
TILGATE . . . 201 E2
Tilgate Comm RH1 . . . 120 C2
Tilgate Dr RH10, RH11 . . . 201 E2
Tilgate Forest Bsns Ctr RH11 . . . 201 D1
Tilgate Mans RH10 . . . 201 F1
Tilgate Par RH10 . . . 201 E3
Tilgate Park Ctry Pk★ RH10 . . . 201 F1
Tilgate Pl RH10 . . . 201 E3
Tilgates Cotts RH1 . . . 120 C3
Tilgate Way RH10 . . . 201 E3
Tilia Cl SM1 . . . 58 F5
Tilletts La RH12 . . . 216 E8
Tilley La KT18 . . . 96 C4
Tillingbourne Jun Sch GU4 . . . 131 B2
Tillingbourne Mews GU5 . . . 132 B4
Tillingbourne Rd GU4 . . . 130 E3
Tillingdown Hill CR3 . . . 101 A5
Tillingdown La
Caterham CR3 . . . 101 B2
Caterham CR3 . . . 101 B3
Tillman Ho 8 SW2 . . . 21 F7
Tillotson Cl RH10 . . . 202 D5
Tilly's La TW18 . . . 12 F4
Tilney Cl KT22 . . . 95 A7
Tilney Ct KT6 . . . 37 D4
Tilson Gdns SW2, SW4 . . . 21 E8
Tilson Ho SW2 . . . 21 E8
Tilt Cl KT11 . . . 73 E3
Tilthams Corner Rd GU5, GU7 . . . 151 C8
Tilthams Gn GU7 . . . 151 B8
Tilt Mdw KT11 . . . 73 E3
Tilt Rd KT11 . . . 73 D3
Tiltview KT11 . . . 73 C4
Tiltwood Dr RH10 . . . 204 C8
Timber Bank GU16 . . . 86 A6
Timber Cl
Farnham GU9 . . . 125 B2
Great Bookham KT23 . . . 114 C8
Pyrford GU22 . . . 70 F5
Timbercroft KT19 . . . 57 E6
Timber Ct RH12 . . . 217 C3
Timberham Farm Rd RH6 . . . 181 D8
Timberham Ho RH6 . . . 181 E8
Timberham Way RH6 . . . 181 E8
Timber Hill KT21 . . . 95 E8
Timber Hill Rd CR3 . . . 101 A3
Timber La CR3 . . . 101 A3
Timberlands 14 RH11 . . . 201 B1
Timberling Gdns CR2 . . . 61 D1
Timbermill Ct GU27 . . . 207 F6
Timberslip Dr SM6 . . . 60 D2
Timbertop Rd TN16 . . . 83 C1
Times Sq SM1 . . . 59 B5
Timline Gn RG12 . . . 27 F7
Timperley Ct
Putney SW19 . . . 19 E7
Redhill RH1 . . . 118 E3
Timperley Gdns RH1 . . . 118 E3
Timsbury Wlk 5 SW15 . . . 19 A7
Timsway TW18 . . . 12 F3
Tina Ct
Forest Hill SE6 . . . 23 F8
West Norwood SW16 . . . 22 A5
3 Wimbledon SW20 . . . 19 D1
Tindale Cl CR2 . . . 80 D8
Tinsey Cl TW20 . . . 12 B3
Tinsley Cl
Crawley RH10 . . . 182 A1
South Norwood SE25 . . . 43 B6
Tinsley Gn RH10 . . . 182 B4
TINSLEY GREEN . . . 182 C4
Tinsley La RH10 . . . 182 A1
Tinsley La N RH10 . . . 182 B3
Tinsley La S RH10 . . . 202 A8
Tintagel Cl KT17 . . . 76 F5
Tintagel Ct RH13 . . . 217 D1
Tintagel Dr GU16 . . . 65 F1
Tintagel Way GU22 . . . 70 A3
Tintells La KT24 . . . 112 B7
Tintern Cl SW19 . . . 20 C2
Tintern Rd
Carshalton SM5 . . . 40 D1
Crawley RH11 . . . 201 A4
Tippits Mead RG42 . . . 26 D8
Tipton Dr CR0 . . . 61 E6
Tiree Path RH11 . . . 201 B3
Tirlemont Rd CR2 . . . 61 C3
Tirrell Rd CR0 . . . 42 C3
Tisbury Rd SW16 . . . 41 E7
TISMAN'S COMMON . . . 214 A6
Titchfield Rd SM5 . . . 40 D1
Titchfield Wlk SM5 . . . 40 D2
Titchwell Rd SW18 . . . 20 D7
Tite Hill TW20 . . . 11 D3
Tithe Barn Cl KT2 . . . 37 F8
Tithebarns La GU23 . . . 91 B1
Tithe Barn The GU4 . . . 111 D4
Tithe Cl GU25 . . . 31 D3
Tithe Ct RG40 . . . 25 C7
Tithe La TW19 . . . 1 A1
Tithe Mdws GU25 . . . 31 D3
Tithe Orch RH19 . . . 184 E4
Tithepit Shaw La CR6 . . . 81 B3
Tithe The RH11 . . . 181 A1
Titlarks Hill Rd SL5 . . . 30 B1
Titmus Dr RH10 . . . 201 F2
TITSEY . . . 103 B2
Titsey Cnr RH8 . . . 123 A7
Titsey Hill CR6, RH8 . . . 103 B4
Titsey Pl★ RH8 . . . 103 B3
Titsey Rd
Limpsfield RH8 . . . 123 B8
Titsey RH8 . . . 103 B1
TITTENHURST . . . 30 A5
Tiverton Cl CR0 . . . 42 F2
Tiverton Rd TW3 . . . 5 C5
Tiverton Way
Chessington KT9 . . . 56 D5
Frimley GU16 . . . 65 F1
Tivoli Rd
Hounslow TW4 . . . 4 E3
West Norwood SE27 . . . 22 C3
Toad La GU17 . . . 64 E4
Tobias Sch of Art RH19 . . . 205 E6
Tobin Cl KT19 . . . 76 B8
Toby Way KT5 . . . 57 B8
Todds Cl RH6 . . . 160 E5
Toftwood Cl RH10 . . . 202 C5
Toldene Ct CR5 . . . 99 F8
Toll Bar Ct SM2 . . . 59 B2
Tolldene Cl GU21 . . . 68 E2
Tollers La CR5 . . . 99 F8
Tollgate GU1 . . . 110 D1
Tollgate Ave RH1 . . . 139 F4
Tollgate Ct RH1 . . . 139 F4
Tollgate Dr SE21 . . . 22 E6
Tollgate Hill RH11 . . . 201 C1
Tollgate Pl 12 RH19 . . . 205 F8
Tollgate Prim Sch CR0 . . . 43 C3
Tollgate Rd RH4 . . . 136 B4
Toll Gdns RG12 . . . 27 F6
Tollhouse La SM6 . . . 60 C2
Tolson Ho 3 TW7 . . . 6 A4
Tolson Rd TW7 . . . 6 A4
Tolvaddon GU21 . . . 69 A2
Tolverne Rd SW20 . . . 39 C8
TOLWORTH . . . 57 B7
Tolworth Cl KT6 . . . 38 B1
Tolworth Court Bridge KT19 . . . 57 C7
Tolworth Girls' Sch KT6 . . . 56 F7
Tolworth Hospl KT6 . . . 57 A8
Tolworth Inf Sch KT6 . . . 37 F1
Tolworth Jun Sch KT6 . . . 37 F1
Tolworth Park Rd KT6 . . . 56 F8
Tolworth Rd KT6 . . . 56 E8
Tolworth Rise N KT5 . . . 38 B1
Tolworth Rise S KT5 . . . 38 B1
Tolworth Sta KT5 . . . 57 B8
Tolworth Underpass KT5, KT6 . . . 57 B8
Tomlin Cl KT19 . . . 76 D8
Tomlin Ct KT19 . . . 76 D8
Tomlins Ave GU16 . . . 65 F2
Tomlinscote Sch & Sixth Form Coll GU16 . . . 66 A2
Tomlinscote Way GU16 . . . 66 A2
Tompset's Bank RH18 . . . 206 F1
Tomtit Cres RH10 . . . 204 C5
Tomtits La RH18 . . . 206 E1
Tonbridge Cl SM7 . . . 78 F5
Tonbridge Rd KT12, KT8 . . . 35 F5
Tonfield Rd SM3 . . . 39 F1
Tonge Cl BR3 . . . 44 A4
TONGHAM . . . 126 F6
Tongham Mdws GU10 . . . 126 F7
Tongham Rd
Aldershot GU12 . . . 126 D8
Runfold GU10 . . . 126 C4
Tonstall Rd
Epsom KT19 . . . 76 D8
Mitcham CR4 . . . 41 A7
Tooting Bec Gdns SW16 . . . 21 D4

Tooting Bec Rd SW16 21 B4
Tooting Bec Sta SW17 21 A5
Tooting Broadway SW17 20 F3
Tooting Broadway Sta SW17 20 E3
Tooting Gr SW17 20 E3
TOOTING GRAVENEY 20 D3
Tooting High St SW17, SW19 20 E3
Tooting Mkt SW17 20 F4
Tooting Sta SW17 20 F2
Tootswood Rd BR2 44 E5
Topaz Ct TW13 14 F5
Topaz Ho KT4 38 D1
Topiary Sq TW9 6 F4
Topiary The
Ashtead KT21 95 E7
Farnborough GU14 84 E3
Toplady Pl GU9 125 C7
Top Pk BR3 44 E4
Topsham Rd SW17 21 A4
Top Terrace Rd GU14 105 A8
Torcross Dr SE23 23 C6
Torin Ct TW20 11 C3
Tor La KT13 72 D8
Torland Dr KT22 74 D6
Tormead Cl SM1 59 A4
Tormead Rd GU1 109 F1
Tormead Sch GU1 109 F1
Toronto BR2 44 E6
Toronto Dr RH6 162 A3
Torquay Ho SM6 60 D5
Tor Rd GU9 124 F2
Torrens Cl GU2 109 A4
Torre Wlk SM5 40 E1
Torridge Rd
Brands Hill SL3 1 B8
Thornton Heath CR7 42 B4
Torridon Cl GU21 69 B2
Torridon Jun & Inf Schs SE6 24 D6
Torridon Rd SE13, SE6 24 D7
Torrington Cl KT10 55 E4
Torrington Ct SE26 23 A3
Torrington Rd KT10 55 E4
Torrington Sq CR0 42 D2
Torrington Way SM4 40 A3
Torr Rd SE20 23 D1
Torwood La CR3 100 F8
Totford La GU10 127 E4
Totham Lo SW20 39 B8
Totland Cl GU14 85 A6
Totnes Ho 18 TW1 6 D1
Tottenham Rd GU7 150 E6
Tottenham Wlk GU47 45 D1
Totterdown St SW17 20 F3
Totton Rd CR7 42 A6
Toulouse Cl GU15 66 B7
Tournai Cl GU11 105 E7
Toutley Rd RG41 25 A8
Tovil Cl SE20 43 B7
Tower Approach Rd RH6 181 E6
Tower Cl
East Grinstead RH19 185 E2
Hindhead GU26 188 E4
Horley RH6 160 F3
Penge SE20 23 B1
Woking GU21 69 D2
Tower Cotts KT10 54 F1
Tower Ct
East Grinstead RH19 185 E2
12 Egham TW20 12 A3
Tower Gate Bsns Ctr GU8 190 F7
Tower Gdns KT10 56 A3
Tower Gr KT13 53 E8
Towerhill GU5 133 C3
TOWER HILL 136 B5
Tower Hill
Dorking RH4 136 B5
Farnborough GU14 85 A3
Tower Hill Prim Sch GU14 84 F3
Tower Hill Rd RH4 136 B5
Tower Hill Rise GU5 133 C3
Tower Ho KT14 71 E7
Tower Pl CR6 82 A4
Tower Rd
Faygate RH12 218 F8
Hindhead GU26 188 E4
Tadworth KT20 97 C4
Twickenham TW1 16 F5
Tower Rise TW9 6 E4
Towers Dr RG45 45 B4
Towers Pl TW10 6 E2
Towers The
Kenley CR8 80 C4
1 Richmond TW9 6 F3
Towers Wlk KT13 53 B4
Tower View CR0 43 E2
Towfield Ct TW13 15 F6
Towfield Rd TW13 15 F6
Town Barn Rd RH11 201 C7
Townend CR3 100 E5
Town End Cl
Caterham CR3 100 E5
Godalming GU7 150 E4
Townend Ct 8 BR1 44 F8
Town End St GU7 150 E4
Town Farm Prim Sch TW19 13 D8
Town Farm Way TW19 13 D8
Townfield Ct RH4 136 A6
Townfield Rd RH4 136 A6
Town Field Way TW7 6 A5
Towngate KT11 73 E4
Town Hill RH7 164 E4
Town La TW19 13 D7
Town Mdw TW8 6 D7
Town Mead
Bletchingley RH1 120 D2
Crawley RH11 201 D7
Townmead Rd TW9 7 B5
Town Quay TW18 33 C6
Townsend Cl RG12 27 E4
Townsend Cotts GU22 90 B6
Townsend La GU22 90 B6
Townsend Mews 3 SW18 20 C6
Townsend Rd TW15 13 E3
Townshend Rd TW9 6 F3
Townshend Terr TW9 6 F3
Townshott Cl KT23 94 A1
Townside Pl GU15 65 D6
Town Sq
Bracknell RG12 27 C7
Camberley GU15 65 C6
6 Woking GU21 69 F2
Town Tree Rd TW15 14 A3
Towpath Way CR0, SE25 42 F4
Towton Rd SE27 22 C6
Toynbee Rd SW19, SW20 39 E8
Tracery The SM7 78 B4
Tracious Cl GU21 69 B3
Traemore Ct SW16 22 A5
Trafalgar Ave KT4, SM3, SM4 39 D1
Trafalgar Com Inf Sch RH12 217 B4
Trafalgar Ct
Cobham KT11 73 A6
Farnham GU9 125 C1
Hounslow TW3 4 F4
West Barnes KT3 39 B6
Trafalgar Dr KT12 54 B7
Trafalgar Inf Sch TW2 16 D6
Trafalgar Jun Sch TW2 16 D6
Trafalgar Rd
Horsham RH12 217 C4
Merton SW19 20 C1
Twickenham TW2 16 D6
Trafalgar Way
Camberley GU15 64 F4
Croydon CR0, CR9 61 A8
Trafalger Villas GU14 84 C4
Trafford Rd
Frimley GU16 85 D8
Thornton Heath CR7 41 F4
Trafford Villas CR7 41 F4
Traherne Lo 6 TW11 16 F3
Tramsheds Ind Est The CR0 41 D2
Tramway Cl SE20 43 C8
Tramway Path CR4 40 E5
Tranmere Ct 18 SM2 59 C3
Tranmere Rd
Twickenham TW2 16 B8
Wandsworth SW17, SW18 20 C6
Tranquil Dale RH3 116 F3
Transport Ave TW8 6 B8
Transport Police Training Ctr KT20 97 A4
Transport Rd GU14 85 B1
Trap La RH5 176 F2
Traps La KT2, KT3 38 E8
Trasher Mead RH4 136 C4
Travellers Way TW5 4 C5
Travis La GU47 64 C7
Treadcroft Dr RH12 217 E5
Treadwell Rd KT18 76 F4
Treasury Cl SM6 60 D5
Treaty Ctr TW3 5 B4
Trebor Ave GU9 146 D8
Tredenham Cl GU14 105 C8
Tredown Rd SE26 23 C3
Tredwell Cl SW2 21 F6
Tredwell Rd SE27 22 B4
Treebourne Rd TN16 83 C1
Treebys Ave GU4 109 D7
Tree Cl TW10 17 D7
Treelands RH5 136 C4
Treemount Ct KT17 76 E6
Treen Ave SW13, SW14 7 F4
Treeside Dr GU9 125 E7
Treetops RH9 142 E6
Tree Tops CR6 81 A1
Tree Tops Ave GU15 66 B8
Treetops Ct CR7 42 C4
Treeview RH11 201 C1
Tree View Cl SE19 42 E8
Treeview Ct 3 RH2 118 D1
Treeway RH2 118 B4
Trefoil Cl
Horsham RH12 217 E5
Wokingham RG40 25 E7
Trefoil Cres RH11 201 A2
Trefusis Ct TW5 4 B6
Tregaron Gdns KT3 38 E5
Tregarthen Pl KT22 95 C6
Tregarth Pl GU21 68 F2
Treglos Ct KT13 53 E8
Tregolls Dr GU14 85 D3
Trehaven Par RH2 139 B6
Treherne Ct SW17 21 A4
Trehern Rd 18 SW14 7 D4
Trelawn Cl KT16 51 C3
Trelawne Dr GU6 174 E2
Trelawney KT12 35 D1
Trelawney Gr KT13 53 A4
Trellis Ho SW19 20 C1
Treloar Gdns SE19 22 D2
Tremaine Rd SE20 43 B7
Trematon Pl TW11 17 C1
Tremayne Wlk GU15 66 C4
Trenance GU21 69 A2
Trenchard Cl KT12 54 C5
Trenchard Ct SM4 40 A3
Trenear Cl RH13 217 E2
Trenham Dr CR6 81 C3
Trenholme Cl SE20 23 B1
Trenholme Ct CR3 101 A4
Trenholme Rd SE20 23 B1
Trenholme Terr SE20 23 B1
Trent Cl
Crawley RH11 200 F4
Farnborough GU14 84 E6
Trent Ct 1 CR2 61 C5
Trentham Cres GU22 90 A6
Trentham Rd RH1 140 A7
Trentham St SW18 20 A7
Trent Ho 8 KT2 37 D8
Trenton Cl GU16 66 A1
Trent Rd SL3 1 B8
Trent Way KT4 58 C7
Treport St SW18 20 B8
Treryn Hts GU7 150 D6
Tresco Cl BR1 24 E2
Tresidder Ho 8 SW4 21 D8
Tresillian Way GU21 69 B2
Tresta Wlk GU21 69 A3
Trevanne Plat RH10 202 D7
Trevelyan RG12 26 E2
Trevelyan Ct KT3 38 F2
Trevelyan Ho 6 TW1 6 C1
Trevelyan Rd SW17 20 F2
Trevenna Ho 18 SE23 23 D5
Trevereux Hill RH8 123 F4
Treversh Ct 9 BR1 44 F8
Treville St SW15 19 B8
Treviso Rd SE23 23 D6
Trevithick Cl TW14 14 F7
Trevor Cl
Hayes BR2 44 F2
Isleworth TW7 5 F2
Trevor Rd SW19 19 E1
Trevose Ave KT14 70 F5
Trewenna Dr KT9 56 D5
Trewince Rd SW20 39 C8
Trewint St SW18 20 C6
Trewsbury Rd SE26 23 D3
Treyford Cl RH11 200 F6
Triangle The
Kingston u T KT3 38 C7
Woking GU21 69 C1
Trickett Ho SM2 59 B2
Trident Bsns Ctr SW17 20 F3
Trident Ho TW19 13 E8
Trident Ind Est SL3 1 E4
Trieste Ct SW12 20 F7
Trigg's Cl GU22 89 D8
Trigg's La GU21, GU22 89 D8
Trigo Ct KT19 76 D8
Trig St RH5 178 F8
Trilby Rd SE23 23 D6
Trimmer Ct TW7 5 F4
Trimmer's Almshouses GU9 125 A1
Trimmers Cl GU9 125 C7
Trimmers Field GU9 125 E1
Trimmers Wood GU26 188 E6
Trimmer Wlk 11 TW8 6 E8
Trinder Mews 11 TW11 17 A3
Trindles Rd RH1 140 F7
Tring Ct TW1 17 A4
Tringham Cl
Knaphill GU21 68 C1
Ottershaw KT16 51 C5
Tringham Cotts GU24 67 F7
Trinity GU47 45 E2
Trinity Churchyard 3 GU1 130 D7
Trinity Cl
Crawley RH10 202 C8
Hounslow TW4 4 E3
South Croydon CR2 61 E2
Stanwell TW19 2 C1
Trinity Cotts TW9 6 F4
Trinity Cres
Sunningdale SL5 30 A4
Upper Tooting SW17 21 A6
Trinity Ct
Addlestone KT15 52 B6
Bracknell RG12 26 F7
Forest Hill SE23 23 C5
Horsham RH12 217 C3
Thornton Heath SE25 42 E3
Twickenham TW2 16 E6
2 Wallington SM6 60 C3
1 Wimbledon SW19 20 A2
Trinity Fields GU9 125 A6
Trinity Gate 9 GU1 130 E8
Trinity Hill GU9 125 A6
Trinity Mews SE20 43 B8
Trinity Par TW3 5 B4
Trinity Rd
Knaphill GU21 68 B1
Richmond TW9 6 F4
Upper Tooting SW17, SW18 20 E7
Wimbledon SW19 20 A2
Trinity Rise SE24, SW2 22 B8
Trinity St Mary's CE Prim Sch SW12 21 A7
Trinity Sch CR9 62 C8
Trinity Sq RH12 217 D2
Tristram Rd BR1 24 F4
Trist Way RH11 201 A8
Tritton Ave CR0 60 E6
Tritton Rd SE21 22 D5
Trittons KT20 97 D6
Triumph Cl UB7 3 C6
Trodd's La
Albury GU4 132 A8
Guildford GU1, GU4 110 E1
Trojan Way CR0 60 F7
Troon RH6 161 B2
Troon Cl RH11 200 D5
Troon Ct SL5 29 C4
Troston Ct TW18 12 F3
Trotsford Mdw GU17 64 C4
Trotsworth Ave GU25 31 E5
Trotsworth Ct GU25 31 D5
Trotters La GU24 69 B7
Trotter Way KT19 76 A7
Trotton Cl RH10 202 C3
Trotwood Cl GU47 45 E2
Troutbeck Wlk GU15 66 D3
Trout Rd GU27 207 E6
Trowers Way RH1 119 B4
Trowlock Ave TW11 17 C2
Trowlock Way TW11 17 D2
Troy Cl KT20 97 B7
Troy La TN8 144 F4
Troy Rd SE19 22 D2
TROY TOWN 144 F5
Trumpeters Inn TW9 6 C2
Trumpetshill Rd RH2 138 B7
TRUMPS GREEN 31 D3
Trumps Green Ave GU25 31 D3
Trumps Green Cl GU25 31 E4
Trumps Green Inf Sch GU25 31 D3
Trumpsgreen Rd GU25 31 D3
Trumps Mill La GU25 31 F4
Trundle Mead RH12 217 C5
Trunk Rd GU14 84 C5
Trunley Heath Rd GU5 151 C8
Truscott Ho 3 CR0 42 A3
Truslove Rd SE27 22 B3
Truss Hill Rd SL5 29 C4
Trust Wlk SE21 22 B7
Trys Hill KT16 51 A8
Trystings Cl KT10 56 A4
Tucker Rd KT16 51 D4
Tuckers Dr GU6 174 B3
Tuckey Gr GU23 90 F3
Tudor Ave
Hampton TW12 16 A1
North Cheam KT4 58 B6
Tudor Circ GU7 150 E7
Tudor Cl
Ashford TW15 13 E4
Banstead SM7 77 E4
Cheam SM3 58 E4
Chessington KT9 56 E5
Cobham KT11 73 F6
Coulsdon CR5 80 A1
Crawley RH10 202 D5
East Grinstead RH19 205 F8
Grayshott GU26 188 D2
Hampton TW12 16 C3
Hamsey Green CR2 81 B4
Little Bookham KT23 94 A3
Smallfield RH6 162 B3
Wallington SM6 60 C3
Woking GU22 70 A2
Wokingham RG40 25 F5
Tudor Ct
Biggin Hill TN16 83 E2
16 Egham TW20 12 A3
19 Egham TW20 12 A3
Farncombe GU7 150 E5
Feltham TW13 15 C4
Haslemere GU27 208 C7
6 Knaphill GU21 68 D2
4 Purley CR8 80 A8
12 Redhill RH1 119 A2
4 Stanwell TW19 2 E1
5 Sutton SM2 59 C4
Teddington TW11 16 F2
Tudor Dr
Kingston u T KT2 17 E3
Walton-on-T KT12 35 D1
West Barnes SM4 39 E3
Tudor Gdns
6 Mortlake SW13, SW14 7 E4
Twickenham TW1 16 F7
West Wickham BR4 63 C7
Tudor Grange KT13 53 E8
Tudor Hall GU15 65 F6
Tudor Ho
Bracknell RG12 27 B4
Feltham TW13 15 C4
2 Horsham RH13 217 F3
Mitcham CR4 41 A8
Weybridge KT13 53 A4
Tudor La SL4 11 C8
Tudor Lo KT20 97 F6
Tudor Pl CR4 20 E1
Tudor Rd
Ashford TW15 14 D2
Beckenham BR3 44 C6
Croydon CR0, SE25 43 B4
Farncombe GU7 150 E7
Hampton TW12 16 A1
Isleworth TW3 5 D3
Kingston u T KT2 18 A1
Penge SE19 22 F1
Tudors The 2 BR3 44 B7
Tudor Way GU21 88 C8
Tudor Wlk
Leatherhead KT22 94 F7
Tudor Wlk continued
3 Weybridge KT13 53 B7
TUESLEY 171 C8
Tuesley Cnr GU7 150 D3
Tuesley La
Godalming GU7, GU8 150 D1
Milford GU7 171 C7
Tufton Gdns KT8 36 B7
Tugela Rd CR0 42 D3
Tugela St SE6 23 F6
Tuggles Plat RH12 216 E7
Tugswood Cl CR5 99 D6
Tulip Cl
Croydon CR0 43 D1
Hampton TW12 15 F2
Tulip Ct RH12 217 C4
Tulip Tree Ct SM2 78 A8
Tulk Ho KT16 51 B3
Tullett Rd RH10 202 B2
Tulleys Farm★ RH10 203 D4
Tull St CR4 40 F2
Tulse Cl BR3 44 C6
TULSE HILL 22 A8
Tulse Hill SW2, SE24 22 A8
Tulse Hill Sta SE27 22 B6
Tulsemere Rd SE21, SE27 22 C6
Tulyar Cl KT20 97 B7
Tumber Cl GU12 106 A2
Tumber St KT18 96 C2
Tumblewood Rd SM7 77 E3
Tumbling Bay KT12 35 A3
Tummons Gdns SE25 42 E7
Tunbridge Ct 1 SE26 23 A5
Tunley Rd SW12, SW17 21 A6
Tunnel Link Rd TW6 3 A2
Tunnel Rd GU14 84 E1
Tunnel Rd E TW6 3 B5
Tunnel Rd W TW6 3 A6
Tunnmeade 7 RH11 200 E5
Tunsgate GU1 130 D7
Tunsgate Sq GU1 130 D7
Tunstall Ct 14 TW9 6 F6
Tunstall Rd CR0 42 E1
Tunstall Wlk 10 TW8 6 E8
Tunworth Cres SW15 7 F1
Tupwood Ct CR3 101 A2
Tupwood La CR3 101 A1
Tupwood Scrubbs Rd CR3 121 A8
Turf Hill Rd GU15 65 F8
Turfhouse La GU24 49 E2
Turing Dr RG12 27 A4
Turkey Oak Cl SE19 42 E8
Turle Rd SW16 41 E7
Turnberry RG12 26 E2
Turnberry Ho SL5 30 A1
Turner Ave
Mitcham CR4 40 F8
Twickenham TW2 16 C5
Turner Cl GU1 109 F4
Turner Ct
East Grinstead RH19 186 A3
Godalming GU7 150 D4
Turner Ho
Beare Green RH5 157 C4
12 Twickenham TW1 6 D1
Turner Lo 10 SW19 19 D7
Turner Mews SM2 59 B3
Turner Pl GU47 64 D6
Turner Rd KT3 38 D2
Turners Cl TW18 13 B3
TURNERS HILL 204 A4
Turners Hill CE Sch RH10 204 A3
TURNERS HILL PARK 204 C5
Turners Hill Rd
Copthorne RH10 183 F2
Crawley Down RH10 204 A7
Crawley RH10 203 C5
Turners Hill RH10 203 F5
Turner's Hill Rd RH19 205 B6
Turners La KT12 54 B3
Turners Mead GU8 191 C3
Turners Meadow Way BR3 43 F8
Turners Way CR0, CR9 61 A8
Turner Wlk RH10 201 F3
Turney Prim & Sec Specl Sch SE21 22 C8
Turney Rd SE21 22 D8
Turnham Cl GU2 130 C5
Turnoak Ave GU22 89 E7
Turnoak La GU22 89 E8
Turnoak Rdbt GU22 89 E8
Turnpike La SM1 59 C5
Turnpike Link CR0 61 E8
Turnpike Pl RH11 201 D8
Turnpike Rd RG42 26 D7
Turnpike Way TW7 6 A6
Turnstone Cl CR0, CR2 62 E1
Turnville Cl GU18 48 A1
Turpin Rd TW14 3 F1
Turpins Rise GU20 48 B6
Turpin Way SM6 60 B3
Turret Ct RH19 185 C3
Turret Ho KT2 17 E2
Turtledove Ave RH10 204 C5
Turville Ct KT23 94 B2
Tuscam Way GU15 64 F4
Tuscany Gdns RH10 201 E8
Tushmore Ave RH10 181 E1
Tushmore Cres RH10 181 E1
Tushmore Ct RH10 201 E8

Tushmore La RH10 ...... 201 E8
Tushmore Rdbt RH11 ... 201 D8
Tussock Cl RH11 .... 201 A4
Tuxford Cl RH10 .... 202 C4
Tweed Cl GU14 .... 84 E6
Tweeddale Prim Sch
SM5 .... 40 D2
Tweeddale Rd SM5 ...... 40 D1
Tweed La
Brockham RH3 .... 137 B5
Rusper RH11 .... 180 F1
Tweed Rd SL3 ....1 B8
Tweedsmuir Cl GU14 ..... 84 D3
Tweedy Rd 6 BR1 .... 44 F8
Twelve Acre Cl KT23 ..... 93 F3
Twelve Acre Cres
GU14 .... 84 E5
Twelve Trees Ho RG45 ... 45 C4
TWICKENHAM 17 B8
Twickenham Bridge
TW9 .... 6 C2
Twickenham Cl CR0 ...... 60 F7
Twickenham Pl KT7 ...... 55 F8
Twickenham Prep Sch
TW12 .... 36 B8
Twickenham Rd
Feltham TW13 .... 15 F5
Isleworth TW1, TW7 .... 6 A4
Richmond TW1, TW9 .... 6 C3
Teddington TW11 .... 17 A4
Twickenham Rugby
Football Union Ground
TW2 ....5 E1
Twickenham Sta TW1 .... 17 A8
Twickenham Trad Ctr
TW1 ....5 F1
Twilley St SW18 .... 20 B8
Twining Ave TW2 .... 16 D5
Twinoaks KT11 .... 74 A6
Twitten La RH19 .... 184 E4
Twitten The RH11 .... 201 C6
Two Bridges Ind Est
CR2 .... 61 D3
Two Oaks KT13 .... 53 B6
Two Rivers Sh Ctr
TW18 .... 12 E4
Two Ways RH14 .... 213 A4
Twycross Rd
Farncombe GU7 .... 150 D7
Wokingham RG40 .... 25 E7
Twyford La GU10 .... 146 B6
Twyford Par KT6 .... 38 A1
Twyford Rd
Carshalton SM5 .... 40 D1
Wokingham RG40 .... 25 B8
Twyhurst Ct RH19 .... 185 D3
Twyne Cl RH11 .... 200 F4
Twyner Cl RH6 .... 161 D4
Twynersh Ave KT16 ...... 32 F3
Tybenham Rd SW19 ...... 40 A6
Tychbourne Dr GU4 ..... 110 C4
Tydcombe Rd CR6 ...... 101 D8
Tyers Ho 1 SW16 .... 21 C3
Tylden Way RH12 .... 217 F6
Tylecroft Rd SW16 .... 41 E7
Tylehost GU2 .... 109 A5
Tylehurst Dr RH1 .... 139 F8
Tyler Gdns KT15 .... 52 C6
Tyler Rd RH10 .... 201 D3
Tylers Cl RH9 .... 121 B5
Tylers Ct GU6 .... 174 D3
TYLER'S GREEN 121 C5
Tylers Path SM5 .... 59 F6
Tylney Ave SE19 .... 22 F3
Tylney Ct KT22 .... 95 C6
Tylney Wood GU10 ...... 187 F7
Tymperley Ct RH13 ..... 217 E3
Tynamara KT1 .... 37 D5
Tynan Cl TW14 .... 15 A7
Tyndalls GU26 .... 188 F4
Tyne Cl
Crawley RH10 .... 202 C5
Farnborough GU14 .... 84 E6
Tynedale Rd RH3 .... 137 B5
Tyne Ho 4 KT2 .... 37 D8
Tynemouth Rd CR4 ...... 21 A1
Tynley Gr GU4 .... 109 D7
Tynwald Ho 14 SE26 ...... 23 A5
Tyrell Ct SM5 .... 59 F6
Tyrells Pl 15 GU1 .... 130 F8
Tyrolean Ct SM7 .... 78 B4
Tyrols Rd SE23 .... 23 D7
Tyrone Ct SW16 .... 21 D3
Tyrrell Ho BR3 .... 24 B3
Tyrrell Sq 9 CR4 .... 40 E8
Tyrwhitt Ct GU2 .... 109 B5
Tyson Rd SE23 .... 23 C8
Tythebarn Cl GU4 .... 110 B6
Tythe Cl KT12 .... 35 B3
Tytherton RG12 .... 27 C7

U

Uckfield Rd CR4 .... 41 A8
Udney Park Rd TW11 ..... 17 A2
Uffington Dr RG12 .... 27 E5
Uffington Rd SE27 .... 22 A4
Ujima Ct SW16 .... 21 E4
Ujima Ho SW16 .... 21 E4
Ullathorne Rd SW16 ...... 21 C4
Ullswater RG12 .... 26 F2
Ullswater Ave GU14 ...... 84 E3
Ullswater Bsns Pk CR5 ... 79 E3
Ullswater Cl
Bromley BR1 .... 24 E1
Hale GU9 .... 125 A6
Kingston u T SW15 .... 18 D4
Lightwater GU18 .... 48 B1
Ullswater Cres
Coulsdon CR5 .... 79 E3
Kingston u T SW15 .... 18 D4
Ullswater Rd
Lightwater GU18 .... 48 B1
West Norwood SE27 ...... 22 B6
Ulstan Cl CR3 .... 102 A4
Ulster Ct KT2 .... 17 D2
Ulverstone Rd SE27 ...... 22 B6
Ulwyn Ave KT14 .... 71 E5
Umberstone GU25 .... 31 D3
Underhill Cl GU7 .... 150 E3
Underhill La GU10 ...... 146 B7
Underhill Park Rd
RH2 .... 118 A4
Underhill Rd
Dulwich SE21, SE22 ...... 23 B8
Newdigate RH5 .... 158 B1
Undershaw Rd BR1 ...... 24 F5
Underwood
Bracknell RG12 .... 26 E3
New Addington CR0 ...... 63 C5
Underwood Ave GU12 ... 105 F1
Underwood Cl RH10 .... 204 B8
Underwood Ct CR3 ..... 100 F2
Underwood Ho KT8 ...... 36 A4
Underwood Rd
Caterham CR3 .... 100 E2
Haslemere GU27 .... 207 F7
Undine St SW17 .... 20 F3
Unicorn Prim Sch BR3 ... 44 B4
Unicorn Sch TW9 ....6 F6
Unicorn Trad Est The
GU27 .... 208 B7
Union Cl GU47 .... 45 E2
Union Ct 2 TW10 ....6 E2
Union Rd
Farnham GU9 .... 125 C2
Frimley GU16 .... 86 D8
Thornton Heath CR0 ...... 42 C2
Union St
Aldershot GU11 .... 105 A2
Farnborough GU14 .... 85 B4
Kingston u T KT1 .... 37 D7
Pirbright GU24 .... 87 A6
Union Terr 7 GU11 ..... 105 A2
Unity Cl
New Addington CR0 ...... 63 B2
West Norwood SE19 ...... 22 C3
University Ct GU2 ...... 109 B1
University Rd SW19 ...... 20 D2
Univ of Surrey GU2 ..... 109 B1
Unstead La GU5 .... 151 C7
Unstead Wood GU3 ..... 130 C1
Unwin Ave TW14 .... 3 D2
Unwin Rd TW7 ....5 E4
Upavon Gdns RG12 ...... 27 F4
Upchurch Cl SE20 .... 23 B1
Updown Hill GU20 .... 48 D4
Upfield
Horley RH6 .... 161 A1
South Croydon CR0, CR9 ... 62 B7
Upfield Cl RH6 .... 161 A1
Upfold Cl GU6 .... 174 B5
Upfold La GU6 .... 174 C5
Upfolds Gn GU4 .... 110 C5
Upgrove Manor Way 12
SE24 .... 22 A8
Upland Ct SE23 .... 23 C6
Upland Rd
Camberley GU15 .... 65 D7
Croydon CR2 .... 61 D5
Dulwich SE21, SE22 ...... 23 A8
Sutton SM2 .... 59 D3
Woldingham CR3 .... 102 B7
Uplands
Ashtead KT21 .... 95 D7
Beckenham BR3 .... 44 A7
Warlingham CR6 .... 81 F1
Uplands Cl
Haslemere GU27 .... 208 D8
Mortlake SW14 .... 7 B2
Sandhurst GU47 .... 64 B8
Uplands Dr KT22 .... 74 D5
Uplands Prim Sch
GU47 .... 64 B8
Uplands Rd
Farnham GU9 .... 125 E1
Kenley CR8 .... 80 C2
Upland Way KT18 .... 77 C1
Uppark Gdns RH12 ..... 217 F6
Upper Beulah Hill
SE19 .... 42 E8
Upper Bourne La
GU10 .... 146 B5
Upper Bourne Vale
GU10 .... 146 A5
Upper Bridge Rd RH1 ... 118 F1
Upper Brighton Rd
KT6 .... 37 E2
Upper Broadmoor Rd
RG45 .... 45 D5
Upper Butts TW8 .... 6 C8
Upper Charles St GU15 ... 65 C6
Upper Chobham Rd
GU15 .... 66 B4
Upper Church La 19
GU9 .... 125 B2
Upper Cl RH18 .... 206 F2
Upper College Ride
GU15 .... 65 E8
Upper Court Rd
Epsom KT19 .... 76 C8
Upper Court Rd *continued*
Woldingham CR3 .... 102 A3
Upper Dr TN16 .... 83 C1
Upper Dunnymans 6
SM7 .... 77 F5
UPPER EASHING 150 A4
Upper Edgeborough Rd
GU1 .... 130 F8
UPPER ELMERS END 43 F4
Upper Elmers End Rd
BR3 .... 43 E4
Upper Elms Rd GU11 .... 105 A1
Upper Fairfield Rd
KT22 .... 95 B6
Upper Farm Rd KT8 ...... 35 F5
Upper Forecourt RH6 ... 182 B7
Upper Gn E CR4 .... 40 F6
Upper Gn W CR4 .... 40 F7
Upper Gordon Rd
GU15 .... 65 D5
Upper Gr SE25 .... 42 F5
Upper Grotto Rd TW1 .... 16 F6
Upper Guildown Rd
GU2 .... 130 C6
UPPER HALE 125 B6
Upper Hale Rd GU9 ..... 125 C6
UPPER HALLIFORD 34 D5
Upper Halliford Rd
TW17 .... 34 E6
Upper Halliford Sta
TW16 .... 34 E7
Upper Ham Rd KT2,
TW10 .... 17 D4
Upper Harestone CR3 ... 121 A8
Upper High St KT17 ..... 76 E6
Upper House La GU5 .... 152 F1
UPPER IFOLD 211 F8
Upper Lodge Mews
TW12 .... 16 C2
Upper Lodge Way CR5 ... 99 D5
Upper Manor Rd
Farncombe GU7 .... 150 E6
Milford GU8 .... 149 F1
Upper Mount GU27 ..... 189 F1
Upper Mulgrave Rd
SM2 .... 58 E3
UPPER NORWOOD 22 E1
Upper Nursery SL5 ...... 30 A4
Upper Old Park La
GU9 .... 125 A5
Upper Park Rd
Camberley GU15 .... 65 E6
Kingston u T KT2 .... 18 A2
Upper Pillory Down
SM5 .... 79 A7
Upper Pines SM7 .... 78 F2
Upper Pinewood Rd
GU12 .... 106 D3
Upper Queen St GU7 ... 150 E4
Upper Rd SM6 .... 60 E5
Upper Richmond Rd
SW15 ....7 F3
Upper Richmond Rd W
TW10, SW14, SW15 .... 7 C3
Upper Rose Hill RH4 .... 136 B6
Upper St Michael's Rd
GU11 .... 126 B8
Upper Sawleywood 3
SM7 .... 77 F5
Upper School Dr
GU27 .... 207 F5
Upper Selsdon Rd CR2 ... 62 A2
UPPER SHIRLEY 62 D6
Upper Shirley Rd CR0,
CR9 .... 62 D7
Upper South View
GU9 .... 125 C3
Upper Springfield
GU8 .... 148 D3
Upper Sq
Forest Row RH18 .... 206 F3
Isleworth TW7 .... 6 A4
Upper St GU5 .... 133 A4
Upper Stanford Rd
GU24 .... 87 F1
Upper Sunbury Rd
TW12 .... 36 A8
Upper Sutton La TW5 ..... 5 A6
UPPER SYDENHAM 23 B4
Upper Teddington Rd KT1,
KT8 .... 37 C8
Upper Terrace Rd
GU14 .... 105 A8
Upperton Rd GU2 .... 130 C7
UPPER TOOTING 20 F5
Upper Tooting Park Mans
1 SW17 .... 21 A6
Upper Tooting Pk
SW17 .... 20 F6
Upper Tooting Rd
SW17 .... 20 F5
Upper Tulse Hill SW2 .... 21 F8
Upper Union St 1
GU11 .... 105 A2
Upper Union Terr 5
GU11 .... 105 A2
Upper Vann La GU8 ..... 172 A1
Upper Vernon Rd SM1 ... 59 D5
Upper Verran Rd GU15 ... 65 D3
Upper Village Rd SL5 .... 29 D4
Upper Warlingham Sta
CR6 .... 81 A1
Upper Way GU9 .... 146 B8
Upper West St RH2 ..... 117 F1
Upper Weybourne La
GU9 .... 125 E7
Upper Wlk GU25 .... 31 E5
Upper Woodcote Village
CR8 .... 79 D7
Upshire Gdns RG12 ...... 27 F5
Upshot La GU22 .... 70 F2
Upton GU21 .... 69 B2
Upton Cl GU14 .... 85 D3
Upton Ct
7 Penge SE20 .... 23 C1
8 Wimbledon SW20 ...... 19 D1
Upton Dene SM2 .... 59 B3
Upton Rd
Hounslow TW3 .... 5 A4
South Norwood CR7 ...... 42 D7
Upwood Rd SW16 .... 41 E8
Urmston Dr SW19 .... 19 E7
Urquhart Ct BR3 .... 23 F1
Ursuline High Sch
SW20 .... 39 D8
Ursuline Prep Sch
SW19 .... 19 D1
Usherwood Cl KT20 ..... 116 C4
Uvedale Cl CR0 .... 82 D8
Uvedale Cres CR0 .... 82 E8
Uvedale Rd RH8 .... 122 F5
Uxbridge Rd
Feltham TW13 .... 15 D6
Hampton TW12 .... 16 B3
Kingston u T KT1, KT6 ..... 37 D4

V

Vachery La GU6 .... 194 E7
Vaillant Rd KT13 .... 53 C6
Valan Leas BR2 .... 44 E6
Vale Cl
Coulsdon CR5 .... 79 E5
Farnham GU10 .... 146 C4
Oatlands Park KT13 ...... 53 D7
Twickenham TW1 .... 17 A5
Woking GU21 .... 69 E3
Vale Cres SW15 .... 18 E4
Vale Croft KT10 .... 55 F2
Vale Ct
Ash Vale GU12 .... 106 A7
Oatlands Park KT13 ...... 53 D7
Vale Dr RH12 .... 217 B3
Vale Farm Rd GU21 ...... 69 E2
Vale Ho GU21 .... 69 E2
Vale Lo SE23 .... 23 C6
Valens Ho 1 SW2 .... 22 A7
Valentin Ct TW12 .... 16 B3
Valentine Ct SE23 .... 23 D6
Valentyne Cl CR0 .... 82 E8
Vale Prim Sch The
KT18 .... 96 E8
Vale Rd
Ash Vale GU12 .... 106 A5
Camberley GU15 .... 65 A4
Claygate KT10 .... 55 F3
Mitcham CR4 .... 41 D5
Oatlands Park KT13 ...... 53 D7
Sutton SM1 .... 59 B6
Worcester Park KT4 ...... 57 F7
Vale Rd N KT6 .... 56 E8
Vale Rd S 4 KT6 .... 56 E8
Valerie Ct SM2 .... 59 B3
Valery Pl TW12 .... 16 A1
Valeswood Rd BR1 .... 24 F3
Vale The
Ashford TW16 .... 15 A2
Coulsdon CR5, CR8 ...... 79 E5
Croydon CR0 .... 62 D8
Feltham TW14 .... 4 B1
Heston TW5 .... 4 E8
Vale Wood Dr GU10 ..... 146 D4
Vale Wood La GU26 ..... 188 C4
Valewood Rd GU27 ..... 208 C4
Valiant Way GU14 .... 104 D8
Vallance By-ways
RH6 .... 180 F6
Valley Cres RG41 .... 25 A8
Valley Ct CR3 .... 101 A5
Valley End CE Inf Sch
GU24 .... 49 A4
Valley End Rd GU24 ..... 49 B4
Valleyfield Rd SW16 ..... 21 F3
Valley Gdns SW19 .... 20 D1
Valley Gdns* TW20 ...... 30 E7
Valley La GU10 .... 146 C7
Valley Mews TW1 .... 17 A6
Valley Mushroom Farm
TN16 .... 83 D1
Valley Pl KT6 .... 37 E3
Valley Point Ind Est
CR0 .... 41 E2
Valley Prim Sch BR2 ..... 44 F7
Valley Prospect 3
SE19 .... 22 E2
Valley Rd
Beckenham BR2 .... 44 E7
Frimley GU16 .... 86 B8
Kenley CR3, CR8 .... 80 D4
Streatham SW16 .... 21 F4
Valley The GU2 .... 130 C5
Valley View
Biggin Hill TN16 .... 83 D1
Godalming GU7 .... 150 D4
Sandhurst GU47 .... 64 A7
Valley View Gdns CR8 ... 80 E4
Valley Wlk CR0 .... 62 C8
Vallis Way KT9 .... 56 D6
Valnay St SW17 .... 20 F3
Valroy Cl GU15 .... 65 D6
Vampire Way GU11,
GU14 .... 104 E8
Vanborough Ct 3 SM2 ... 59 C4
Vanbrugh Cl RH11 ...... 200 E3
Vanbrugh Dr KT12 .... 35 C3
Vanbrugh Mews KT12 .... 35 C2
Vancouver Cl KT19 .... 76 C8
Vancouver Ct RH6 ...... 162 A3
Vancouver Dr RH10,
RH11 .... 181 D1
Vancouver Rd
Forest Hill SE23 .... 23 E6
Richmond TW10 .... 17 C4
Vanderbilt Rd SW18 ...... 20 C7
Van Dyck Ave KT3 .... 38 D2
Vandyke RG12 .... 26 E3
Vandyke Cl
Putney SW15 .... 19 D8
Redhill RH1 .... 118 F3
Vanfame Ct KT3 .... 38 F6
Van Gogh Cl TW7 .... 6 A4
Vanguard Cl CR0 .... 42 B1
Vanguard Ho
7 Merton SW19 .... 20 C1
6 Stanwell TW19 .... 2 E1
Vanguard Way
Harlington TW6 .... 3 E5
Wallington SM6 .... 60 E3
Vanners RH10 .... 201 E7
Vanners Par KT14 .... 71 E6
Vann Farm Rd RH5 ...... 177 E4
Vann La
Chiddingfold GU8 .... 191 E4
Hambledon GU8 .... 171 D1
Vann Lake RH5 .... 177 F4
Vann Lake Rd RH5 ..... 178 A4
Vantage Ct
Harlington UB3 .... 3 E7
Streatham SW16 .... 21 F1
Woking GU21 .... 69 D2
Vant Rd SW17 .... 20 F3
Vapery La GU24 .... 87 D6
Varley Way CR4 .... 40 D7
Varna Rd TW12 .... 36 B8
Varney Cl GU14 .... 84 E5
Varsity Dr TW1, TW7 ....5 F1
Varsity Row SW14 .... 7 C5
Vaughan Almshouses
TW15 .... 14 B3
Vaughan Cl TW12 .... 15 E2
Vaughan Ct GU2 .... 109 B5
Vaughan Rd KT7 .... 37 B2
Vaughan Way RH4 ..... 136 A7
Vaux Cres KT12 .... 54 B4
Vauxhall Gdns CR2 ...... 61 C4
Veals Mead CR4 .... 40 E8
Vectis Gdns SW17 .... 21 B2
Vectis Rd SW17 .... 21 B2
Vegal Cres TW20 .... 11 C3
Veitch Cl TW14 .... 14 F8
Vellum Dr SM5 .... 60 A7
Venita Manor SE27 ...... 22 A3
Venner Rd SE20, SE26 .... 23 C3
Ventnor Rd SM2 .... 59 B3
Ventnor Terr GU12 ..... 105 C1
Venton Cl GU21 .... 69 B2
Venture Ho TW18 .... 13 A4
Venus Mews CR4 .... 40 E6
Verbania Way RH19 ..... 186 B1
Verdant Ct 3 SE6 .... 24 E8
Verdant La SE6 .... 24 E7
Verdayne Ave CR0, CR9 ... 62 D8
Verdayne Gdns CR6 ..... 81 C3
Vere Bank SW19 .... 19 F7
Vereker Dr TW16 .... 35 A6
Verge Wlk GU11 .... 126 A7
Vermillion Ct TW13 ...... 14 F5
Vermont Hall KT4 .... 39 B2
Vermont Rd
South Norwood SE19 ..... 22 E2
Sutton SM1 .... 59 B7
Verney Ho TW3 .... 5 C3
Vernon Ave SW20 .... 39 D7
Vernon Cl
Horsham RH12 .... 218 A4
Ottershaw KT16 .... 51 D4
Stanwell TW19 .... 13 E7
West Ewell KT19 .... 57 C4
Vernon Ct
Farnham GU9 .... 125 A2
North Ascot SL5 .... 28 D6
Vernon Dr
Caterham CR3 .... 100 C5
North Ascot SL5 .... 28 E7
Vernon Rd
Carshalton SM1 .... 59 D5
Feltham TW13 .... 14 F6
Mortlake SW14 .... 7 D4
Vernon Way GU2 .... 108 F2
Vernon Wlk KT20 .... 97 D7
Vern Pl TN16 .... 103 C6
Verona Dr KT6 .... 56 E8
Veronica Gdns CR4,
SW16 .... 41 C8
Veronica Rd SW17 .... 21 B6
Verralls GU22 .... 70 B2
Verran Rd
Balham SW12 .... 21 B8
Camberley GU15 .... 65 D3
Versailles Rd SE20 .... 23 A1
Verulam Ave CR8 .... 79 C7
Veryan GU21 .... 69 A2
Vesey Cl GU14 .... 85 A5
Vestris Rd SE23 .... 23 D6
Vevers Rd RH2 .... 139 C6
Vevey St SE23, SE6 ...... 23 F6
Vibart Gdns SW2 .... 21 F8
Vibia Cl TW19 .... 13 D8
Viburnum Ct GU24 .... 67 E6
Vicarage Ave TW20 ...... 12 B3
Vicarage Cl
Farnham GU9 .... 146 D7

Vicarage Cl continued
Kingswood KT20 . . . . **97** E3
Lingfield RH7 . . . . **164** D4
Little Bookham KT23 . . . . . . **94** A2
New Malden KT4 . . . . **38** E1
Vicarage Cres TW20 . . . . . **12** B3
Vicarage Ct
Beckenham BR3 . . . . **43** E6
East Bedfont TW14 . . . . . . **14** C8
Egham TW20 . . . . **12** B2
8 Roehampton SW15 . . . . . **19** A8
Vicarage Dr
Beckenham BR3 . . . . **44** A8
Mortlake SW14 . . . . **7** D2
Vicarage Farm Ct TW5 . . . **4** F7
Vicarage Farm Rd TW3,
TW4, TW5 . . . . **4** E6
Vicarage Fields KT12 . . . . **35** C3
Vicarage Gate GU2 . . . . . **130** A7
Vicarage Gdns
Ascot SL5 . . . . **29** A4
Grayshott GU26 . . . . **188** C3
Mitcham CR4 . . . . **40** E6
Mortlake SW14 . . . . **7** D2
Vicarage Hill
Farnham GU10, GU9 . . . . . **146** D7
Loxwood RH14 . . . . **213** A2
Vicarage Ho 2 KT1 . . . . . **37** F7
Vicarage La
Capel RH5 . . . . **178** D6
Farnham GU9 . . . . **125** B2
Farnham, Middle Bourne
GU9 . . . . **146** D7
Haslemere GU27 . . . . **207** F6
Heath End GU9 . . . . **125** C7
Horley RH6 . . . . **160** F4
Laleham TW18 . . . . **33** C6
Leatherhead KT22 . . . . **95** B5
Send GU23 . . . . **90** D1
Wraysbury TW19 . . . . **11** F7
Vicarage Rd
Ashford TW16 . . . . **14** F2
Bagshot GU19 . . . . **47** C3
Blackwater GU17 . . . . **64** E4
Crawley Down RH10 . . . . . . **204** A8
Croydon CR0, CR9 . . . . **61** A7
Egham TW20 . . . . **12** B3
Kingston u T KT1, KT2 . . . . . **37** D7
Lingfield RH7 . . . . **164** D4
Mortlake SW14 . . . . **7** D2
Staines TW18 . . . . **12** E5
Sutton SM1 . . . . **59** B7
Teddington, Hampton Wick
KT1, KT8 . . . . **37** C8
Teddington TW11 . . . . **17** A3
Twickenham, Strawberry Hill
TW2 . . . . **16** E6
Twickenham TW2 . . . . **5** C1
Woking GU22 . . . . **89** F6
Vicarage Way SL3 . . . . **1** D7
Vicars Oak Rd SE19 . . . . . **22** E2
Viceroy Ct 5 CR0 . . . . . . **42** D1
Viceroy Lo 6 KT6 . . . . . . **37** E4
Vickers Cl SM6 . . . . **60** F3
Vickers Ct 10 TW19 . . . . . . **2** E1
Vickers Dr N KT13 . . . . . . **52** E1
Vickers Dr S KT13 . . . . . . **71** E8
Vickers Rd GU12 . . . . **105** F5
Victor Ct RH10 . . . . **182** D1
Victoria Almshouses
4 Redhill RH1 . . . . **119** A4
1 Reigate RH2 . . . . **118** C1
Victoria Ave
Camberley GU15 . . . . **65** A5
East Molesey KT8 . . . . **36** B6
Hackbridge SM6 . . . . **60** A7
Hounslow TW3, TW4 . . . . . . **5** A2
Kingston u T KT6 . . . . **37** D3
South Croydon CR2 . . . . . . **61** C1
Victoria Cl
East Molesey KT8 . . . . **36** A6
Horley RH6 . . . . **161** A3
Oatlands Park KT13 . . . . . . **53** D7
Victoria Cotts 7 TW9 . . . . . **7** A6
Victoria Cres
Merton SW19 . . . . **19** F1
West Norwood SE19 . . . . . . **22** E2
Victoria Ct
Bagshot GU19 . . . . **47** E1
Guildford GU1 . . . . **130** D8
9 Horsham RH13 . . . . . . **217** D2
Penge SE26 . . . . **23** C2
Redhill RH1 . . . . **140** A6
Shalford GU4 . . . . **130** E3
Victoria Dr
Blackwater GU17 . . . . **64** C4
Putney SW15, SW19 . . . . . . **19** D7
Victoria Entertainments
Ctr The 2 GU21 . . . . **69** E2
Victoria Gdns
Biggin Hill TN16 . . . . **83** C4
Farnborough GU14 . . . . . . **84** D4
Heston TW5 . . . . **4** E6
Wokingham RG40 . . . . **25** E8
Victoria Ho 4 KT22 . . . . . **95** C6
Victoria Jun Sch TW13 . . . **15** B7
Victoria La GU3 . . . . **3** D8
Victoria Lo SW19 . . . . **19** C1
Victoria Mews
Crawley RH11 . . . . **201** D6
Englefield Green TW20 . . . . **11** C2
Wandsworth SW18 . . . . **20** C7
Weybridge KT13 . . . . **53** A6
Victoria Pl
Cobham KT11 . . . . **73** B6
Esher KT10 . . . . **55** B6
Ewell KT17 . . . . **76** E7
17 Richmond TW10 . . . . **6** D2

Victoria Pl continued
3 Woking GU21 . . . . **70** A3
Victoria Rd
Addlestone KT15 . . . . **52** D6
Aldershot GU11 . . . . **105** A2
Ascot SL5 . . . . **29** A4
Carshalton SM1 . . . . **59** D5
Coulsdon CR5 . . . . **79** D4
Cranleigh GU6 . . . . **174** D3
Crawley RH11 . . . . **201** C6
Farnborough GU14 . . . . . . **85** B4
Farnham GU9 . . . . **125** C2
Feltham TW13 . . . . **15** B7
Godalming GU7 . . . . **150** E4
Guildford GU1 . . . . **109** E1
Horley RH6 . . . . **161** B2
Kingston u T KT1 . . . . **37** F7
Kingston u T, Seething Wells
KT6 . . . . **37** D3
Knaphill GU21 . . . . **68** E1
Mitcham CR4, SW19 . . . . . . **20** F1
Mortlake SW14 . . . . **7** D4
Oatlands Park KT13 . . . . . . **53** D7
Redhill RH1 . . . . **140** A8
Sandhurst GU47 . . . . **45** E1
Staines TW18 . . . . **12** E5
Teddington TW11 . . . . **17** A2
Twickenham TW1 . . . . **17** B8
Woking GU22 . . . . **69** F2
Victoria St
Englefield Green TW20 . . . . **11** C2
Horsham RH13 . . . . **217** D2
Victoria Terr 6 RH4 . . . . . **136** A7
Victoria Tk GU11 . . . . **104** E7
Victoria Villas TW9 . . . . **6** F3
Victoria Way
East Grinstead RH19 . . . . . **205** F7
Oatlands Park KT13 . . . . . . **53** D7
Woking GU21, GU22 . . . . . . **69** E2
Victor Rd
Penge SE20 . . . . **23** D1
Teddington TW11 . . . . **16** E4
Victors Dr TW12 . . . . **15** E2
Victor Seymour Inf Sch
SM5 . . . . **59** F6
Victory Ave SM4 . . . . **40** C4
Victory Bsns Ctr The
TW7 . . . . **5** F3
Victory Cl TW19 . . . . **13** E7
Victory Cotts KT24 . . . . . **113** E7
Victory Ct KT15 . . . . **52** B6
Victory Park Rd KT15 . . . . **52** C6
Victory Pl SE19 . . . . **22** E2
Victory Rd
Chertsey KT16 . . . . **33** A1
Horsham RH12 . . . . **217** B3
Merton SW19 . . . . **20** C1
Victory Road Mews 5
SW19 . . . . **20** C1
Vidler Cl KT9 . . . . **56** C4
Vienna Ct GU14 . . . . **85** A6
View Cl TN16 . . . . **83** C3
Viewfield Rd SW18 . . . . . . **19** F8
View Terr RH7 . . . . **165** A1
Viggory La GU21 . . . . **69** C4
Vigilant Cl SE26 . . . . **23** A4
Viking RG12 . . . . **26** E4
Viking Ct TW12 . . . . **36** B8
Village Cl 3 KT13 . . . . **53** D7
Village Ct SL5 . . . . **29** C4
Village Gate TW17 . . . . . . **34** B4
Village Gdns KT17 . . . . . . **57** F1
Village Green Ave
TN16 . . . . **83** E2
Village Green Way
TN16 . . . . **83** E2
Village Mews SL5 . . . . **29** C5
Village Rd TW20 . . . . **32** C6
Village Row SM2 . . . . **59** A3
Village Sq The CR5 . . . . . . **99** D5
Village St RH5 . . . . **158** B1
Village The SL4 . . . . **10** B5
Village Way
Ashford TW15 . . . . **14** A4
Beckenham BR3 . . . . **44** A6
Sanderstead CR2 . . . . **81** A6
Villas The
Blindley Heath RH7 . . . . . . **163** E8
Woking GU21 . . . . **69** F3
Villiers Ave
Kingston u T KT5 . . . . **37** F5
Twickenham TW2 . . . . **15** F7
Villiers Cl KT5 . . . . **37** F5
Villiers Gr SM2 . . . . **58** D2
Villiers Mead RG41 . . . . . . **25** A4
Villiers Rd
Hounslow TW7 . . . . **5** E5
Kingston u T KT1 . . . . **37** F6
Penge BR3 . . . . **43** D7
Vinall Gdns RH12 . . . . . . **216** D4
Vincam Cl TW2 . . . . **16** A8
Vincent Ave
Sutton SM5 . . . . **78** D8
3 Tolworth KT5 . . . . **38** B1
Vincent Cl
Chertsey KT16 . . . . **32** E2
Esher KT10 . . . . **55** B7
Fetcham KT23 . . . . **94** B4
Harmondsworth UB7 . . . . **3** A8
Horsham RH13 . . . . **217** B3
Vincent Dr
Dorking RH4 . . . . **136** A6
Upper Halliford TW17 . . . . . **34** E6
Vincent Ho KT3 . . . . **38** F5
Vincent La RH4 . . . . **136** A7
Vincent Rd
Chertsey KT16 . . . . **32** E2
Coulsdon CR5 . . . . **79** C3

Vincent Rd continued
Croydon CR0 . . . . **42** E2
Dorking RH4 . . . . **136** A7
Hounslow, Hounslow West
TW4 . . . . **4** D4
Hounslow TW7 . . . . **5** D6
Kingston u T KT1 . . . . **38** A6
Stoke D'Abernon KT11 . . . . **73** E3
Vincent Rise RG12 . . . . . . **27** E6
Vincent Row TW12 . . . . . . **16** C3
Vincent Sq TN16 . . . . **83** C6
Vincents Cl CR5 . . . . **98** F7
Vincents Wlk 11 RH4 . . . . **136** A7
Vincent Works RH4 . . . . . **136** A7
Vine Cl
Ash Vale GU12 . . . . **85** F1
Farnborough GU11 . . . . . . **105** A6
Rowledge GU10 . . . . **146** A4
Stanwell TW19 . . . . **2** A2
Surbiton KT5 . . . . **37** F3
Sutton SM1 . . . . **59** C7
Worplesdon GU3 . . . . **88** D1
Vine Cotts GU6 . . . . **174** B3
Vine Ct KT12 . . . . **54** C4
Vine House Cl GU16 . . . . . **86** A3
Vine La GU10 . . . . **146** A5
Vine Pl TW3 . . . . **5** B3
Vine Rd
Barnes SW13, SW15 . . . . **7** F4
East Molesey KT8 . . . . **36** C5
Vineries Cl UB7 . . . . **3** A8
Viners Cl KT12 . . . . **35** C3
Vine St GU11 . . . . **105** A1
Vine Way GU10 . . . . **146** A5
Vineyard Cl
Forest Hill SE6 . . . . **24** A7
Kingston u T KT1 . . . . **37** F6
Vineyard Hill Rd SW19 . . . . **20** A4
Vineyard Path SW14 . . . . . . **7** D4
Vineyard Row KT1, KT8 . . . **37** C8
Vineyard Sch The TW10 . . . . **6** E1
Vineyards The TW13 . . . . . **15** A5
Vineyard The TW10 . . . . **6** E2
Viney Bank CR0 . . . . **62** F2
Vinter Ct TW17 . . . . **34** A4
Viola Ave
Feltham TW14 . . . . **4** C1
Stanwell TW19 . . . . **13** E7
Viola Croft RG42 . . . . **27** F8
Violet Cl
Carshalton CR4 . . . . **41** A1
Cheam SM3 . . . . **39** E1
Violet Gdns CR0 . . . . **61** B5
Violet La CR0 . . . . **61** B5
Violette Szabo Ho 4
SE27 . . . . **22** D4
Virginia Ave GU25 . . . . . . **31** C4
Virginia Beeches GU25 . . . **31** C6
Virginia Cl
Ashtead KT21 . . . . **75** D1
Kingston u T KT3 . . . . **38** C5
Laleham TW18 . . . . **33** C6
Weybridge KT13 . . . . **53** C4
Virginia Ct
Ashford TW15 . . . . **13** E4
Virginia Water GU25 . . . . . . **31** D5
Virginia Dr GU25 . . . . **31** C5
Virginia Gdns GU14 . . . . . **85** C2
Virginia Ho TW11 . . . . **17** A3
Virginia Pl KT11 . . . . **73** A5
Virginia Rd CR7 . . . . **42** B8
VIRGINIA WATER **31** C4
Virginia Water★ SL5 . . . . **30** E6
Virginia Water Sta
GU25 . . . . **31** E4
Viridian St TW13 . . . . **14** F5
Viscount Cl GU12 . . . . . . **105** F5
Viscount Ct TW15 . . . . . . **14** C1
Viscount Gdns KT14 . . . . . **71** E7
Viscount Ind Est SL3 . . . . . . **1** E4
Viscount Point 6
SW19 . . . . **20** A1
Viscount Rd TW19 . . . . . . **13** E7
Viscount Way TW6 . . . . **3** C3
Vista Ho 2 SW19 . . . . **40** D8
Vista Hts SE23 . . . . **23** E8
Vivian Ct BR3 . . . . **44** A8
Vivien Cl KT9 . . . . **56** E3
Vivien Ct CR0 . . . . **61** F8
Vivienne Cl
Crawley RH11 . . . . **181** D1
Twickenham TW1 . . . . **6** D1
Vivienne Ho TW18 . . . . . . **13** A3
Vixen Dr GU12 . . . . **105** E3
Voewood Cl KT3 . . . . **38** F3
Vogan Cl RH2 . . . . **139** B6
Voltaire 15 TW9 . . . . **6** F6
Volta Way CR0, CR9 . . . . . . **41** F1
Voss Ct SW16 . . . . **21** E2
Vowels Forest Wlk★
RH19 . . . . **204** E3
Vowels La RH19 . . . . **204** E2
Vulcan Bsns Ctr CR0 . . . . . **63** E2
Vulcan Cl
Crawley RH11 . . . . **201** C2
Sandhurst GU47 . . . . **64** A7
Vulcan Way
New Addington CR0 . . . . . . **63** E1
Sandhurst GU47 . . . . **64** B7
Wallington SM6 . . . . **60** E2
Vumba Ho 12 SM2 . . . . . . **59** C4
Vyne Ho SM5 . . . . **59** F4

W

Wadbrook St KT1 . . . . **37** D7
Waddington Ave CR5,
CR8 . . . . **100** B8
Waddington Cl
Coulsdon CR5 . . . . **100** B8
Crawley RH11 . . . . **201** A3
Waddington Way CR7,
SE19 . . . . **42** A6
WADDON **61** A6
Waddon Cl CR0, CR9 . . . . . **61** A7
Waddon Court Rd CR0,
CR9 . . . . **61** A7
Waddon Marsh Way CR0,
CR9 . . . . **41** F1
Waddon New Rd CR0,
CR9 . . . . **61** B8
Waddon Park Ave CR0,
CR9 . . . . **61** A7
Waddon Rd CR0, CR9 . . . . . **61** B7
Waddon Sta CR0 . . . . **61** A6
Waddon Way CR0, CR2,
CR9 . . . . **61** B4
Wade Ct RH18 . . . . **206** F2
Wade's La TW11 . . . . **17** A3
Wadham Cl
Crawley RH10 . . . . **182** C1
Shepperton TW17 . . . . **34** C1
Wadhurst Cl SE20 . . . . **43** B7
Wadlands Brook Rd
RH19 . . . . **185** D5
Wagbullock Rise RG12 . . . . **27** C3
Wagg Cl RH19 . . . . **186** A1
Waggon Cl GU2 . . . . **108** E2
Waggoners Hollow
GU19 . . . . **47** E2
Waggoners Way
GU26 . . . . **188** A4
Waggoners Wells Rd
GU26 . . . . **188** A2
Wagner Mews 23 KT6 . . . . **37** E4
Wagtail Cl RH12 . . . . **217** D7
Wagtail Gdns CR2 . . . . **62** E1
Wagtail Wlk BR3 . . . . **44** C4
Waights Ct 8 KT2 . . . . **37** E8
Wain End RH12 . . . . **217** D5
Wainford Cl SW19 . . . . **19** D7
Wainscot SL5 . . . . **29** F3
Wainwright Cl RG40 . . . . . . **26** A6
Wainwright Gr TW7 . . . . **5** D3
Wainwrights RH10 . . . . . . **201** D3
Waite Davies Rd SE12 . . . . **24** F8
Waitelands Ho KT3 . . . . . . **38** D5
Wake Cl GU2 . . . . **109** B6
Wakefield Cl KT14 . . . . **71** E7
Wakefield Ct
3 Horsham RH12 . . . . . . **217** B2
Penge SE26 . . . . **23** C2
Wakefield Gdns SE19 . . . . **22** E1
Wakefield Ho SE27 . . . . . . **22** B5
Wakefield Rd 21 TW10 . . . . . **6** D2
Wakefords Cl GU11 . . . . . **105** D6
Wakehams Green Dr
RH10 . . . . **182** D1
Wakehurst Dr RH10 . . . . . **201** D3
Wakehurst Mews
RH12 . . . . **216** F1
Wakehurst Path GU21 . . . . **70** C5
Wakeling Ho 8 SE27 . . . . . **22** B5
Wakelin Ho SE23 . . . . **23** E8
Wakely Cl TN16 . . . . **83** C1
Wakehams Green Dr (dup)
Walberton Rd CR8 . . . . **79** C7
Walbury RG12 . . . . **27** E5
Walcot Cl CR0 . . . . **62** A8
Waldby Ct RH11 . . . . **201** A3
Waldeck Gr SE27 . . . . **22** B5
Waldeck Rd
Brentford W4 . . . . **7** A8
Mortlake SW14 . . . . **7** C4
Waldeck Terr SW14 . . . . **7** C4
Waldegrave Ct 1
TW11 . . . . **16** F3
Waldegrave Gdns TW1 . . . . **16** F5
Waldegrave Pk TW1 . . . . . . **16** F5
Waldegrave Rd
Penge SE19 . . . . **22** F1
Teddington TW1, TW11 . . . . **16** F4
Waldegrave Sch for Girls
TW2 . . . . **16** D5
Waldegrove CR0 . . . . **61** F7
Waldemar Rd SW19 . . . . . . **20** A3
Walden Cotts GU3 . . . . . . **107** A3
Walden Gdns CR7,
SW16 . . . . **41** F5
Waldenshaw Rd SE23 . . . . **23** C7
Waldens Park Rd
GU21 . . . . **69** C3
Waldens Rd GU21 . . . . **69** D2
Waldo Pl CR4 . . . . **20** E1
Waldorf Cl CR2 . . . . **61** B2
Waldorf Hts GU17 . . . . **64** D3
Waldorf Sch of SW
London The SW16 . . . . **21** D6
Waldram Cres SE23 . . . . . . **23** C7
Waldram Park Rd
SE23 . . . . **23** D7
Waldram Pl 6 SE23 . . . . . . **23** C7
Waldron Gdns BR2 . . . . . . **44** D6
Waldron Hill RG12 . . . . . . **27** F7
Waldronhyrst CR0, CR2 . . . **61** B6
Waldron Rd SW17,
SW18 . . . . **20** C6
Waldrons The
Croydon CR0 . . . . **61** C6
Oxted RH8 . . . . **122** F4

Waldy Rise GU6 . . . . **174** E4
Wales Ave SM5 . . . . **59** E5
Walesbeech RH10 . . . . . . **202** A5
Waleton Acres SM6 . . . . . . **60** C4
Waley's La RH5 . . . . **177** C1
Walford Rd RH5 . . . . **136** C3
Walham Rise 1 SW19 . . . . . **19** E2
Walhatch Cl RH18 . . . . . . **206** F2
Walker Cl
East Bedfont TW14 . . . . . . **14** F8
Hampton TW12 . . . . **15** F2
Walker Rd RH10 . . . . **202** C4
Walkerscroft Mead
SE21 . . . . **22** C7
Walker's Ridge GU15 . . . . . **65** C5
Walkfield Dr KT18 . . . . **77** B2
Walking Bottom GU5 . . . . **154** C6
Walk The
Ashford TW16 . . . . **14** F1
Tandridge RH8 . . . . **122** A2
Wallace Cl
Fairlands GU3 . . . . **108** C4
Upper Halliford TW17 . . . . . **34** D5
Wallace Cres SM5 . . . . **59** F5
Wallace Fields KT17 . . . . . **77** A6
Wallace Fields Inf Sch
KT17 . . . . **77** A6
Wallace Fields Jun Sch
KT17 . . . . **77** A7
Wallace Sq CR5 . . . . **99** D5
Wallace Way GU11 . . . . . . **104** F3
Wallace Wlk KT15 . . . . **52** C6
Wallage La RH10 . . . . **203** D6
Wallbrook Bsns Ctr
TW4 . . . . **4** B4
Walled Garden Cl BR3 . . . . **44** B5
Walled Gdn The
Betchworth RH3 . . . . **137** D8
Loxwood RH14 . . . . **212** F7
Walled Gdn The★
TW16 . . . . **35** B6
Walled Gdn The KT20 . . . . **97** D5
Waller La CR3 . . . . **100** F4
Wall Hill Rd RH18,
RH19 . . . . **206** E5
Wallingford Cl RG12 . . . . . **27** E5
WALLINGTON **60** A4
Wallington Ct 10 SM6 . . . . **60** B4
Wallington Cty Gram Sch
SM6 . . . . **60** B6
Wallington High Sch for
Girls SM6 . . . . **60** B2
Wallington Rd GU15 . . . . . **47** A1
Wallington Sq 4 SM6 . . . . . **60** C4
Wallington Sta SM6 . . . . . . **60** B4
Wallis Ct RH10 . . . . **181** F2
Wallis Ho RH19 . . . . **185** E1
Wallis Mews KT22 . . . . **95** A5
Wallis Way RH13 . . . . **218** A4
WALLIS WOOD **176** E1
Wallner Way RG40 . . . . **25** E5
Wallorton Gdns SW14 . . . . . **7** D3
Walmer Cl
Crowthorne RG45 . . . . **45** C5
Frimley GU16 . . . . **86** A7
Walmer Ho 10 SE20 . . . . . **23** C1
Walmsley Ho 1 SW16 . . . . **21** C4
Walnut Cl
Aldershot GU11 . . . . **126** A8
Epsom KT18 . . . . **76** F4
Wallington SM5 . . . . **59** F5
Walnut Ct RH13 . . . . **217** E1
Walnut Dr KT20 . . . . **97** D5
Walnut Gr SM7 . . . . **77** D5
Walnut Ho RH2 . . . . **139** C7
Walnut La RH11 . . . . **181** B1
Walnut Mews
Bracknell RG42 . . . . **26** F8
Sutton SM2 . . . . **59** C3
Walnut Tree Ave CR4 . . . . . **40** E6
Walnut Tree Cl
Barnes SW13 . . . . **7** F6
Belmont SM7 . . . . **77** E7
Guildford GU1 . . . . **130** C8
Walnut Tree Cotts
SW19 . . . . **19** E3
Walnut Tree Gdns
GU7 . . . . **150** E7
Walnut Tree La KT14 . . . . . **71** D7
Walnut Tree Pk GU1 . . . . . **109** C1
Walnut Tree Pl GU23 . . . . . **90** D4
Walnut Tree Rd
Brentford TW8 . . . . **6** E8
Charlton TW17 . . . . **34** C7
Heston TW5 . . . . **4** F8
Walpole Ave
Chipstead CR5 . . . . **98** F8
Richmond TW9 . . . . **6** F5
Walpole Cres 12 TW11 . . . . **16** F3
Walpole Ct
Twickenham TW2 . . . . **16** E6
2 Wallington SM6 . . . . . . **60** B5
Walpole Gdns TW2 . . . . . . **16** E5
Walpole Ho
4 Aldershot GU11 . . . . . **105** B2
East Molesey KT8 . . . . **36** A4
Walpole Pl 10 TW11 . . . . . **16** F3
Walpole Rd
Croydon CR0, CR9 . . . . **61** D8
Mitcham SW19 . . . . **20** D2
Old Windsor SL4 . . . . **11** B8
Surbiton KT6 . . . . **37** E3
Teddington TW11 . . . . **16** F3
Twickenham TW2 . . . . **16** E6
Walrus Rd GU14 . . . . **104** D8

Walsham Rd TW14 15 B8
Walsh CE Jun Sch GU12 106 A1
Walsh Cres CR0 82 E7
Walsh Meml CE Inf Sch GU12 105 F1
Walsingham Gdns KT19 57 F5
Walsingham Ho TW2 16 D6
Walsingham Rd
  Mitcham CR4 40 F4
  New Addington CR0 63 C1
Walstead Ho 2 RH10 201 D5
Walter Inf Sch RG41 25 A6
Walter's Mead KT21 75 E2
Walter's Rd SE25 42 E5
Walter St 2 KT2 37 E8
Waltham Ave GU2 109 B5
Waltham Cl GU47 45 D1
Waltham Rd
  Carshalton SM5 40 E1
  Caterham CR3 101 B5
Walton Ave
  Cheam SM3 58 F7
  New Malden KT3 38 F5
Walton Bridge Rd KT12, TW17 34 E2
Walton Com Hospl KT12 54 B8
Walton Ct
  13 Croydon CR2 61 C5
  12 Richmond TW9 6 F3
  Woking GU21 70 A3
Walton Dr
  Horsham RH13 218 C4
  North Ascot SL5 28 F8
Walton Gdns TW13 14 F4
Walton Gn CR0 63 C3
Walton Heath RH10 202 D8
Walton Ho 1 KT2 17 E1
Walton La
  Lower Halliford TW17 34 D2
  Oatlands Park KT12 34 E1
  Weybridge KT12, KT13 53 C8
Walton Leigh Sch KT12 53 F6
Walton Lo KT12 34 F1
Walton Manor KT12 34 F2
Walton Oak Prim Sch KT12 35 C1
WALTON-ON-THAMES 35 C2
Walton-on-Thames Sta KT12 54 A6
WALTON ON THE HILL 97 A3
Walton on the Hill Prim Sch KT20 97 B3
Walton Park La KT12 54 D8
Walton Pk KT12 54 D8
Walton Rd
  Ashtead KT18 96 C6
  East Molesey KT8, KT12 36 B5
  Walton-on-T KT12, KT8 35 E4
  Woking GU21 70 A3
Walton St KT20 97 B3
Walton Terr GU21 70 B4
Walton Way CR4 41 C5
WANBOROUGH 128 C6
Wanborough Bsns Ctr GU3 128 E8
Wanborough Dr SW15 19 B7
Wanborough Hill GU3 128 C6
Wanborough La GU6 175 A3
Wanborough Sta GU3 107 C1
Wandle Bank
  Merton SW19 20 D1
  Wallington CR0 60 E7
Wandle Cl
  Ash GU12 106 A1
  Crawley RH10 202 C5
Wandle Court Gdns CR0 60 E7
Wandle Ct
  Wallington CR0 60 E7
  West Ewell KT19 57 C6
Wandle Ho
  Catford BR1 24 D3
  5 Redhill RH1 118 F2
  Wandsworth SW18 20 B8
Wandle Lo
  Hackbridge SM6 60 B8
  Wallington CR0 60 E7
Wandle Rd
  Croydon CR0, CR9 61 C7
  Hackbridge SM6 60 B8
  Morden CR4, SM4, SW19 40 D4
  Upper Tooting SW17 20 E6
  Wallington CR0 60 E7
Wandle Side
  Croydon CR0 60 F7
  Hackbridge SM6 60 B7
Wandle Tech Pk CR4 40 F2
Wandle Trad Est CR4 40 F2
Wandle Valley Sch SM5 40 E2
Wandle Way
  Mitcham CR4 40 F4
  Wandsworth SW18 20 B7
Wandsdyke Cl GU16 85 F8
WANDSWORTH 20 C7
Wandsworth Common Sta SW12 20 F8
Wansbeck Ho RH2 139 A6
Wansford Gn 3 GU21 68 F2
Wanstraw Gr RG12 27 E2
Wantage Cl
  Bracknell RG12 27 E4
  Crawley RH10 202 C3
Wantage Rd GU47 64 D8
Wapati Way GU14 104 D8
Waplings The KT20 97 B3
Wapshott Rd TW18 12 E3
Warbank Cl CR0 63 E1
Warbank Cres CR0 63 E1
Warbank La KT2 18 F1
Warbeck Ho KT13 53 D5
Warblers Gn KT11 73 F5
Warbleton Ho 6 RH11 200 F3
Warboys App KT2 18 B2
Warboys Rd KT2 18 B2
Warburton Cl RH19 206 A8
Warburton Rd TW2 16 B7
Warbury La GU21 68 C3
War Coppice Rd CR3 120 D7
Ward Cl
  Croydon CR0 61 E5
  Wokingham RG40 25 D8
Ward La CR6 81 D2
Wardle Cl GU19 47 E3
Wardley St SW18 20 B8
Wardrobe The 3 TW9 6 D2
Wards Cotts TW19 13 F8
Wards Pl TW20 12 C2
Wards Stone Pk RG12 27 E2
Ward St GU1 130 D8
Ware Ct SM1 58 F6
Wareham Cl TW3 5 B3
Wareham Rd RG12 27 F4
Wareland Ho 3 RH19 185 E1
Warenne Hts RH1 139 D7
Warenne Rd KT22 94 C5
Warfield Ct 1 TW12 36 B8
Warfield Pk RG42 28 A8
Warfield Rd
  Bracknell RG12 27 C8
  East Bedfont TW14 14 E8
  Hampton TW12 36 B8
Wargrove Dr GU47 64 D8
Warham Rd CR0, CR2 61 C5
Waring St SE27 22 C4
Warkworth Gdns TW7 6 A7
WARLINGHAM 81 C1
Warlingham Park Sch CR6 82 A3
Warlingham Rd CR7 42 B5
Warlingham Sch CR6 81 B3
Warltersville Way RH6 161 C1
War Meml Homes W4 7 D7
Warminster Gdns SE25 43 A7
Warminster Rd SE25 43 A7
Warminster Sq SE25 43 A7
Warminster Way CR4 41 B7
Warner Ave SM3 58 E8
Warner Cl
  Crawley RH10 202 C2
  Feltham TW12 15 F3
  Harlington UB3 3 D7
Warner Ct
  Cheam SM3 58 E8
  Sandhurst GU47 64 E7
Warner Ho BR3 24 B2
Warner Rd BR1 24 F1
Warners La GU5 132 E2
Warnford Ho SW15 7 E1
WARNHAM 216 E7
Warnham CE Prim Sch RH12 216 F8
Warnham Court Rd SM5 59 F3
Warnham Ct RH12 216 F7
Warnham Ho 9 SW2 21 F8
Warnham Manor RH12 216 C7
Warnham Nature Reserve★ RH12 217 B6
Warnham Rd
  Broadbridge Heath RH12 216 D4
  Crawley RH10 202 B4
  Horsham RH12 217 B5
Warnham Sta RH12 217 C8
Warpole Pk KT13 53 A3
Warramill Rd GU7 151 A5
Warren Ave
  Belmont SM2 58 F1
  Bromley BR1 24 E1
  Mortlake SW14, TW10 7 B3
  South Croydon CR2 62 D3
Warren Cl
  Esher KT10 55 B6
  Felbridge RH19 184 E3
  Sandhurst GU47 64 A8
  West Norwood SE21 22 C8
Warren Cnr GU10 124 C7
WARREN CORNER 124 C7
Warren Ct
  18 Beckenham BR3 24 A1
  6 Croydon CR0 42 E1
Warren Cutting KT2 18 D1
Warren Down RG42 26 E8
Warren Dr
  Crawley RH11 201 A8
  Kingswood KT20 98 A4
Warren Dr N KT5, KT6 38 B1
Warren Dr S KT5 38 C1
Warreners La KT13 53 D3
Warren Farm Cotts KT24 113 C5
Warren Farm Mobile Home Pk GU23 91 B8
Warren Hill KT18 76 D3
Warren House Rd RG40 25 D8
Warrenhyrst GU1 131 A8
Warren La
  Oxshott KT22 74 C7
  Oxted RH8 123 A1
  Woking GU22 71 B1
Warren Lo KT20 97 E3
Warren Lodge Dr KT20 97 E3
Warren Mead SM7 77 C4
Warren Mead Inf Sch SM7 77 D4
Warren Mead Jun Sch SM7 77 D4
Warrenne Rd RH3 137 C7
Warrenne Way RH2 118 A1
Warren Park Rd SM1 59 E4
Warren Pk
  Box Hill KT20 116 C4
  Kingston u T KT2 18 C2
  Warlingham CR6 81 D1
Warren Rd
  Ashford TW15 14 E1
  Banstead KT17, SM7 77 D5
  Croydon CR0 42 F1
  Farncombe GU7 150 E7
  Guildford GU1 131 A8
  Kingston u T KT2 18 C2
  Mitcham SW19 20 E2
  Purley CR8 80 B8
  Reigate RH2 118 B2
  Twickenham TW2 5 D1
  Woodham KT15 52 A1
Warren Rise
  Frimley GU16 65 F3
  Kingston u T KT3 38 D8
Warren Row SL5 28 D7
Warren The
  Aldershot GU11 104 F1
  Ashtead KT21 95 F7
  East Horsley KT24 112 F5
  Heath End GU9 125 E8
  Heston TW5 4 F7
  Kingswood KT20 97 E4
  Oxshott KT22 74 D6
  Wallington SM5 59 E2
  Weybridge KT13 53 A5
  Worcester Park KT4 57 D7
Warren Way KT13 53 C4
Warren Wood Cl BR2 63 F8
Warrington Cl RH11 200 E2
Warrington Ct
  11 Bromley BR1 24 F1
  Croydon CR0 61 B7
  13 Merton SW19 20 A1
Warrington Mews GU11 125 E8
Warrington Rd
  Croydon CR0, CR9 61 B7
  23 Richmond TW10 6 D2
Warrington Spur SL4 11 B8
Warwick RG12 27 E3
Warwick Ave
  Staines TW18 13 C2
  Thorpe Lea TW20 32 C8
Warwick Cl
  Aldershot GU11 126 C8
  Frimley GU15 66 B3
  Hampton TW12 16 C1
  South Holmwood RH5 157 B7
Warwick Ct
  1 Beckenham BR2 44 E7
  Kenley CR8 80 D5
  Merton SW19 39 F8
  Surbiton KT6 56 E8
  Weybridge KT13 53 A5
Warwick Deeping KT16 51 C5
Warwick Gdns
  Ashtead KT21 75 C2
  Thames Ditton KT7 36 F4
  Thornton Heath CR7 42 A5
Warwick Gr KT5 37 F2
Warwick Ho
  Aldershot GU11 126 C8
  6 Kingston u T KT2 37 E8
  5 Merton SW19 19 E1
  9 Redhill RH1 119 A3
Warwick La GU21 89 A8
Warwick Lo SM1 58 F6
Warwick Pl RH2 118 D1
Warwick Quadrant 22 RH1 119 A2
Warwick Rd
  Ashford TW15 13 E3
  Ash Vale GU12 106 A8
  Coulsdon CR5 79 D5
  Farnborough GU14 104 D8
  Hounslow TW4 4 B4
  Kingston u T KT3 38 C6
  Penge SE20 43 B6
  Redhill RH1 118 F2
  South Holmwood RH5 157 C7
  Sutton SM1 59 C5
  Teddington KT1 37 C8
  Thames Ditton KT7 36 F4
  Thornton Heath CR7 42 A6
  Twickenham TW2 16 E7
Warwicks Bench GU1 130 D6
Warwick's Bench Rd GU1 130 E6
Warwick Sch The RH1 119 A2
Warwick Villas TW20 32 C8
WARWICK WOLD 120 A6
Warwick Wold Rd RH1 120 A7
Wasdale Cl GU47 45 D2
Washington Cl RH2 118 A3
Washington Ct SW17 20 F2
Washington Rd
  Crawley RH11 200 E3
  Kingston u T KT1 38 A7
  North Cheam KT4 39 B1
Washpond La CR6 82 C1
WASP GREEN 162 C7
Wasp Green La RH1 162 C8
Wassand Cl RH10 202 A6
Wastdale Rd SE23 23 D7
Watchetts Dr GU15 65 C2
Watchetts Jun Sch GU15 65 B2
Watchetts Lake Cl GU15 65 D3
Watchetts Rd GU15 65 B4
Watchmoor Pk GU15 65 B4
Watchmoor Rd GU15 65 A4
Watchmoor Trade Ctr GU15 65 A3
Watcombe Cotts TW9 7 A8
Watcombe Rd SE25 43 B4
Waterbank Rd SE6 24 C4
Waterbourne Way CR8 80 D5
Watercress Pl 6 RH13 217 F3
Watercress Way GU21 69 B2
Waterden Cl GU1 130 F8
Waterden Rd GU1 130 E8
Waterer Gdns KT20 77 E1
Waterer Ho SE6 24 C4
Waterer Rise SM6 60 D4
Waterers Rise GU21 68 D2
Waterfall Cl GU25 31 A6
Waterfall Cotts SW19 20 D2
Waterfall Rd SW19 20 D2
Waterfall Terr SW17 20 E2
Waterfield KT20 97 B7
Waterfield Cl RH13 217 E3
Waterfield Dr CR6 101 C8
Waterfield Gdns
  Crawley RH11 200 E4
  South Norwood SE25 42 E4
Waterfield Gn KT20 97 B7
Waterfield Prim Sch RH11 200 E4
Waterfields KT22 95 B8
Waterford Cl KT11 73 E8
Waterford Way RG40 25 C6
Watergardens The KT2 18 C2
Watergate Sch SE6 24 B3
Waterham Rd RG12 27 B3
Waterhouse Ct 8 TW11 16 F3
Waterhouse La
  Bletchingley RH1, RH9 121 A3
  Coulsdon CR8 100 C8
  Kingswood KT20 97 E6
Waterhouse Mead GU47 64 D7
Water La
  Abinger Common RH5 155 B8
  Albury GU5 132 B5
  Bisley GU24 87 E8
  Cobham KT11 73 F5
  Enton Green GU8 171 B4
  Farnborough GU14 85 A7
  Farnham GU9 125 F4
  Kingston u T KT1 37 D8
  Limpsfield RH8 123 A8
  Lingfield TN8 165 D7
  Little Bookham KT23 93 E1
  Richmond TW10, TW9 6 D2
  South Godstone RH9 142 D5
  Twickenham TW1 17 A7
Waterlands La RH12 196 E1
Water Lane Ho 30 TW9 6 D2
Waterlea RH10 202 A5
WATERLOO 132 A4
Waterloo Cl
  Camberley GU15 66 B7
  East Bedfont TW14 14 F7
Waterloo Cotts 4 SM5 59 E7
Waterloo Cres RG40 25 E4
Waterloo Pl
  Richmond, Kew TW9 7 A8
  13 Richmond TW9 6 E3
Waterloo Rd
  Aldershot GU12 105 C1
  Carshalton SM1 59 D5
  Crowthorne RG45 45 B4
  Epsom KT17, KT19 76 D6
  Wokingham RG40 25 F5
Waterlow Rd RH2 139 D8
Watermans Bsns Pk TW18 12 D4
Watermans Ct 14 TW8 6 D8
Watermead
  East Bedfont TW14 14 E7
  Tadworth KT20 97 B6
  Woking GU21 68 F3
Water Mead CR5 78 F2
Watermead Ho 2 SM1 59 C4
Watermead La CR4 40 F2
Watermead Rd SE6 24 C4
Watermen's Sq 1 SE20 23 C1
Watermill Cl TW10 17 C5
Watermill Way SW19 40 C8
Water Mill Way TW13 16 A6
Waterperry La GU24 49 F1
Waters Dr TW18 12 F4
Watersedge KT19 57 C6
WATERSIDE 164 E7
Waterside
  9 Beckenham BR3 44 A8
  East Grinstead RH19 186 B1
  East Molesey KT8 36 E5
  Horley RH6 161 A5
Waterside Ave BR3 44 B4
Waterside Cl
  Crawley RH11 200 E4
  Godalming GU7 151 A5
  Surbiton KT6 56 E8
Waterside Ct SM6 60 A7
Waterside Dr KT12 35 B4
Waterside La GU7 150 C3
Waterside Mews GU1 109 C3
Waterside Rd GU1 109 D4
Waterside Trad Est KT15 52 E6
Waterside Way
  Wimbledon SW17 20 C3
  2 Woking GU21 69 B1
Waterslade RH1 118 E1
Watersmeet Cl GU4 110 A6
Watersplash Cl KT1 37 E6
Water Splash La SL5 29 E8
Watersplash Rd TW17 34 A5
Waters Rd
  Catford SE6 24 E5
  Kingston u T KT1 38 B7
Waters Sq KT1 38 B6
Water View RH6 161 C3
Waterway Rd KT22 95 A5
Waterworks Cl RH18 206 F3
Waterworks Cotts TW12 36 A8
Waterworks Yd 2 CR0 61 C7
Watery La SW19, SW20 39 F7
Wates Way CR4 40 F3
Watford Cl GU1 109 F1
Wathen Rd RH4 136 B8
Watlings Cl CR0 43 E3
Watlington Cotts 2 SE26 23 E3
Watlington Gr SE26 23 E3
Watney Cotts SW14 7 C4
Watney Rd SW14 7 C4
Watneys Rd CR4 41 D4
Watson Ave SM3 58 E8
Watson Cl
  Crawley RH10 202 C3
  Mitcham SW19 20 E1
Watson Ho 3 SW2 21 E8
Watson Rd RH4 135 C6
Wattenden Prim Sch The CR8 80 B3
Wattendon Rd CR8 80 B3
Wattlehurst Dr RH12 198 B7
Watts Common Rd GU11 104 E7
Watt's La
  Tadworth KT20 97 D5
  Teddington TW11 17 A3
Watts Lea GU21 69 A4
Watt's Mead KT20 97 D5
Watts Rd
  Farnborough GU14 84 F5
  Thames Ditton KT7 37 A2
Wavel Ct
  Croydon CR2 61 D5
  7 Streatham SW16 21 E5
Wavell Ct
  Aldershot GU12 105 C1
  Croydon CR0 61 F8
Wavell Sch The GU14 105 B7
Wavel Pl SE19, SE26 22 F4
Wavendene Ave TW20 12 C1
Waveney Ct BR3 44 C8
Waveney Ho 7 RH1 118 F1
Waveney Wlk RH10 202 B4
Waverleigh Rd GU6 174 E1
Waverley RG12 26 E4
Waverley Abbey★ GU9 147 B7
Waverley Abbey Jun Sch GU10 147 D5
Waverley Ave
  Kenley CR8 80 E3
  Sutton SM1 59 C8
  Tolworth KT5 38 C3
  Twickenham TW2 16 A7
Waverley Cl
  Farnham GU9 125 D2
  Frimley GU15 65 F4
Waverley Ct
  6 Horsham RH12 217 B2
  Woking GU22 69 E1
Waverley Dr
  Addlestone KT16 51 D7
  Ash Vale GU12 106 A6
  Camberley GU15 65 F5
  Virginia Water GU25 31 A5
Waverley Gdns GU12 106 A6
Waverley Ho BR3 24 B1
Waverley Hts GU9 125 E1
Waverley La
  Farnham, Compton GU9 125 E1
  Farnham GU10, GU9 147 C8
Waverley Lo TW16 35 A7
Waverley Pl KT22 95 B5
Waverley Rd
  Bagshot GU19 47 E3
  Croydon SE25 43 B6
  Farnborough GU14 85 D3
  Oxshott KT11, KT22 74 B5
  Stoneleigh KT17, KT4 58 B5
  Weybridge KT13 53 A5
Waverley Way SM5 59 E4
Waverton Rd SW18 20 C8

Wavertree Ct
Horley RH6 . . . . 160 F2
9 Streatham SW2 . . . . 21 E7
Wavertree Rd SW2 . . . . 21 F7
Waye Ave TW5 . . . . 4 A6
Wayland Cl RG12 . . . . 27 F5
Waylands Mead BR3 . . . . 44 B8
Waylett Pl SE27 . . . . 22 B5
Wayman Rd GU14 . . . . 84 E8
Wayneflete Tower Ave
KT10 . . . . 55 A7
Waynflete Ave CR0,
CR9 . . . . 61 B7
Waynflete Ho KT10 . . . . 55 B6
Waynflete La GU9 . . . . 124 F2
Waynflete St SW18 . . . . 20 C6
Ways End GU15 . . . . 65 E4
Wayside
Capel RH5 . . . . 178 D6
Crawley RH11 . . . . 200 E4
Mortlake SW14 . . . . 7 C2
New Addington CR0 . . . . 63 B4
Wayside Cotts
Churt GU10 . . . . 167 E3
Ellen's Green GU6 . . . . 195 F4
Holmbury St M RH5 . . . . 155 C6
Wayside Ct
Hounslow TW7 . . . . 5 E5
Twickenham TW1 . . . . 6 C1
Woking GU21 . . . . 68 E3
Wayswood GU15 . . . . 65 E6
Way The RH2 . . . . 118 D2
Weald CE Prim Sch The
RH5 . . . . 157 D3
Weald Cl GU4 . . . . 130 E3
Weald Day Hospl The
RH11 . . . . 201 C6
Weald Dr RH10 . . . . 202 A4
Wealden Ho GU2 . . . . 129 E8
Wealdon Ct 1 GU2 . . . . 108 F1
Wealdstone Rd SM3 . . . . 58 E8
Weald The RH19 . . . . 185 F4
Weald View Cotts
RH5 . . . . 156 D3
Weald Way
Caterham CR3 . . . . 120 E8
Reigate RH2 . . . . 139 C5
Weall Cl CR8 . . . . 79 F7
Weare St
Capel RH5 . . . . 178 B4
Ockley RH5 . . . . 177 F1
Weasdale Ct GU21 . . . . 68 F3
Weatherall Cl KT15 . . . . 52 B5
WEATHERHILL 162 A4
Weatherhill Cl RH6 . . . . 161 F3
Weatherhill Cotts
RH6 . . . . 162 A4
Weatherhill Rd RH6 . . . . 162 A3
Weatherill Ct SE25 . . . . 43 B3
Weather Way RG12 . . . . 27 C7
Weaver Cl
5 Crawley RH11 . . . . 200 E5
Croydon CR9 . . . . 61 F6
Weaver Moss GU47 . . . . 64 B7
Weavers Cl TW7 . . . . 5 E3
Weavers Gdns GU9 . . . . 145 F7
Weavers Yd 18 GU9 . . . . 125 B2
Weaver Wlk SE27 . . . . 22 B4
Webb Cl
Bagshot GU19 . . . . 47 E1
Crawley RH11 . . . . 201 B1
Webb Ct RG40 . . . . 25 E8
Webb Ho TW13 . . . . 15 E5
Webb Rd GU8 . . . . 170 C6
Webster Cl KT22 . . . . 74 B5
Webster Ct GU5 . . . . 151 F7
Websters Cl GU22 . . . . 89 B7
Weddell Rd RH10 . . . . 201 F3
Wedgewood Ct 1 BR2 . . . . 44 F5
Wedgewood Ho KT7 . . . . 36 F1
Wedgwood Pl KT11 . . . . 73 A5
Wedgwoods TN16 . . . . 103 C6
Wedgwood Way SE19 . . . . 22 C1
Weeks Ho TW10 . . . . 17 C4
Weighbridge Rd KT15 . . . . 52 B2
Weighton Rd SE20 . . . . 43 B7
Weihurst Ct SM1 . . . . 59 E5
Weihurst Gdns SM1 . . . . 59 D5
Weint The SL3 . . . . 1 C7
Weir Ave GU14 . . . . 85 A3
Weirbrook RH10 . . . . 202 A3
Weir Cl GU14 . . . . 85 A3
Weir Ho 8 SW12 . . . . 21 C8
Weir Pl TW18 . . . . 32 E8
Weir Rd
Chertsey KT16 . . . . 33 B2
Farnborough GU14,
GU51 . . . . 84 A2
Streatham SW12 . . . . 21 C8
Walton-on-T KT12 . . . . 35 A3
Wimbledon SW18, SW19 . . . . 20 B5
Weir Wood Resr Nature
Reserve* RH19 . . . . 205 D1
Welbeck RG12 . . . . 26 E4
Welbeck Cl
Ewell KT17 . . . . 58 A3
Farnborough GU14 . . . . 84 F3
New Malden KT3 . . . . 38 F4
Welbeck Rd SM1, SM5 . . . . 59 D8
Welbeck Wlk SM5 . . . . 40 D1
Welcome Cotts CR3 . . . . 102 A4
Welcomes Rd CR8 . . . . 80 C3
Welcomes Terr CR3 . . . . 80 F3
Weldon Ct
7 Carshalton SM1 . . . . 59 D5
Thornton Heath CR7 . . . . 42 B4
Weldon Dr KT8 . . . . 35 F5
Weldon Way RH1 . . . . 119 D6
Welford Pl SW19 . . . . 19 E4
Welham Rd SW16,
SW17 . . . . 21 B2
Welhouse Rd SM5 . . . . 59 E8
Welland Cl SL3 . . . . 1 B8
Welland Ct SE6 . . . . 23 F6
Wellburn Cl GU47 . . . . 64 B7
Well Cl
Camberley GU15 . . . . 65 B4
Streatham SW16 . . . . 21 F4
Woking GU21 . . . . 69 C2
Well Ct
North Cheam SM3 . . . . 58 D8
Surbiton KT6 . . . . 37 D2
Welldon Ct 1 SE21 . . . . 22 D6
Weller Cl RH10 . . . . 202 D5
Weller Dr GU15 . . . . 65 C3
Wellers Ct GU5 . . . . 133 A4
Wellesford Cl SM7 . . . . 77 F2
Wellesley Cl
Ash Vale GU12 . . . . 105 F7
Bagshot GU19 . . . . 47 C3
Wellesley Court Rd 1 CR0,
CR9 . . . . 61 D8
Wellesley Cres TW2 . . . . 16 E5
Wellesley Ct
Cheam SM3 . . . . 39 E1
Twickenham TW2 . . . . 16 E5
Wellesley Gate 3
GU12 . . . . 105 B1
Wellesley Gdn GU9 . . . . 125 C7
Wellesley Gr CR0, CR9 . . . . 61 D8
Wellesley Ho
Epsom KT19 . . . . 76 B8
12 Merton SW19 . . . . 19 E1
Wellesley Rd
Aldershot GU11 . . . . 104 E2
Croydon CR0 . . . . 42 C1
Rushmoor GU10 . . . . 168 C6
Sutton SM2 . . . . 59 C4
Twickenham TW2 . . . . 16 E5
Well Farm Rd CR3,
CR6 . . . . 101 A8
Wellfield RH19 . . . . 206 C7
Wellfield Gdns SM5 . . . . 59 E2
Wellfield Rd SW16 . . . . 21 E4
Well Ho SM7 . . . . 78 B4
Wellhouse La RH3 . . . . 137 D6
Wellhouse Rd BR3 . . . . 44 A5
Wellington Ave
Aldershot GU11 . . . . 104 F2
Hounslow TW3, TW4 . . . . 5 A2
North Cheam KT4 . . . . 58 C7
Virginia Water GU25 . . . . 31 B4
Wellington Cl
Crawley RH10 . . . . 182 E1
Sandhurst GU47 . . . . 64 C8
Walton-on-T KT12 . . . . 34 F1
Wellington Coll RG45 . . . . 45 A3
Wellington Cotts
KT24 . . . . 112 E6
Wellington Cres KT3 . . . . 38 C6
Wellington Ct
Ashford TW15 . . . . 13 E3
Stanwell TW19 . . . . 13 E8
5 Surbiton KT6 . . . . 37 E3
Teddington TW11 . . . . 16 D3
4 Upper Tooting SW17 . . . . 20 E2
Wellington Ctr The 21
GU11 . . . . 105 A2
Wellington Dr
Bracknell RG12 . . . . 27 E4
Wallington CR8 . . . . 60 F1
Wellington Gdns
Aldershot GU11 . . . . 104 F1
Teddington TW2 . . . . 16 D4
Wellingtonia Ho KT15 . . . . 52 A5
Wellingtonias RG42 . . . . 8 A1
Wellington La GU9 . . . . 125 D7
Wellington Lo SL4 . . . . 9 B6
Wellington Mews
SW16 . . . . 21 D5
Wellington Pl
Ash Vale GU12 . . . . 105 F4
Cobham KT11 . . . . 73 C7
Farncombe GU7 . . . . 150 E7
Wellington Prim Sch
TW3 . . . . 4 F5
Wellington Rd
Ashford TW15 . . . . 13 E3
Caterham CR3 . . . . 100 C5
Crowthorne RG45 . . . . 45 C4
Hatton TW14 . . . . 3 E2
Horsham RH12 . . . . 217 D2
Sandhurst GU47 . . . . 64 C8
Teddington TW12, TW2 . . . . 16 D4
Thornton Heath CR0 . . . . 42 B2
Wimbledon SW19 . . . . 20 A6
Wokingham RG40 . . . . 25 B5
Wellington Rdbt
GU11 . . . . 104 E2
Wellington Rd N TW4 . . . . 4 F4
Wellington Rd S TW4 . . . . 4 F3
Wellington St 3
GU11 . . . . 105 A2
Wellington Terr
6 Knaphill GU21 . . . . 68 E1
Sandhurst GU47 . . . . 64 C8
Wellington Town Rd
RH19 . . . . 185 D2
Wellington Way
Byfleet KT13 . . . . 52 F1
Farnborough GU11,
GU14 . . . . 104 D7
Horley RH6 . . . . 160 F5
Well La
Haslemere GU27 . . . . 208 D6
Mortlake SW14 . . . . 7 C2
Well La *continued*
Woking GU21 . . . . 69 C2
Wellmeadow Rd SE13,
SE6 . . . . 24 E7
Wellow Wlk SM5 . . . . 40 D1
Well Path GU21 . . . . 69 C2
Wells Cl
Great Bookham KT23 . . . . 94 C3
Horsham RH12 . . . . 216 F2
South Croydon CR2 . . . . 61 E5
Wells Cotts GU9 . . . . 146 A7
Wells Ct 1 CR4 . . . . 40 E8
Wellside Gdns SW14 . . . . 7 C2
Wells La
Ascot SL5 . . . . 29 B5
Normandy GU3 . . . . 107 C4
Wells Lea RH19 . . . . 185 D3
Wells Mdw RH19 . . . . 185 D3
Wells Park Ct SE26 . . . . 23 B4
Wells Park Rd SE21,
SE26 . . . . 23 B4
Wells Pl
Merstham RH1 . . . . 119 B6
Wandsworth SW18 . . . . 20 C8
Wells Rd
Crawley RH10 . . . . 201 E2
Epsom KT18 . . . . 76 B4
Guildford GU4 . . . . 110 C4
Wells The GU27 . . . . 208 C6
Well Way KT18 . . . . 76 A5
Wellwood Cl
Coulsdon CR5, CR8 . . . . 79 E5
Horsham RH13 . . . . 218 B4
Wellwynds Rd GU6 . . . . 174 E2
Welwyn Ave TW14 . . . . 3 F1
Welwyn Cl RH11 . . . . 200 E2
Wembley Rd TW12 . . . . 36 A8
Wembury Pk RH7 . . . . 163 E1
Wendela Cl GU22 . . . . 69 F1
Wenderholme CR2 . . . . 61 D5
Wendley Dr KT15 . . . . 51 F1
Wendling Rd SM1 . . . . 59 D8
Wendon Ct SM6 . . . . 60 C4
Wendover Ct
Egham TW18 . . . . 12 C3
South Croydon CR2 . . . . 61 D2
Wendover Dr
Frimley GU16 . . . . 66 C3
New Malden KT3 . . . . 38 F3
Wendover Pl TW18 . . . . 12 D3
Wendover Rd TW18,
TW20 . . . . 12 D3
Wendron Cl 2 GU21 . . . . 69 A1
Wend The CR5 . . . . 79 D5
Wendy Cres GU2 . . . . 109 A3
Wenlock Cl RH11 . . . . 201 A4
Wenlock Edge RH4 . . . . 136 C5
Wensleydale RH11 . . . . 201 C3
Wensleydale Dr GU15 . . . . 66 D5
Wensleydale Gdns
TW12 . . . . 16 B1
Wensleydale Rd TW12 . . . . 16 B1
Wentland Cl SE6 . . . . 24 D6
Wentland Rd SE6 . . . . 24 D6
WENTWORTH 30 F3
Wentworth RH6 . . . . 161 B2
Wentworth Ave SL5 . . . . 28 C7
Wentworth Cl
Ashford TW15 . . . . 14 B4
Ash Vale GU12 . . . . 106 A7
Heath End GU9 . . . . 125 F6
Long Ditton KT6 . . . . 56 D8
Morden SM4 . . . . 40 A2
Ripley GU23 . . . . 91 B6
Wentworth Cres
GU12 . . . . 106 A6
Wentworth Ct
20 Kingston u T KT6 . . . . 37 E4
6 Surbiton KT6 . . . . 56 E8
Twickenham TW2 . . . . 16 E5
Wentworth Dene KT13 . . . . 53 B5
Wentworth Dr
Crawley RH10 . . . . 202 D7
Wentworth GU25 . . . . 30 F5
Wentworth Golf Club
GU25 . . . . 31 A4
Wentworth Ho KT15 . . . . 52 B6
Wentworth Pl GU15 . . . . 65 A4
Wentworth Rd CR0 . . . . 42 A2
Wentworth Way
Hamsey Green CR2 . . . . 81 A4
North Ascot SL5 . . . . 28 C7
Werndee Rd SE25 . . . . 43 A5
Wesco Ct GU21 . . . . 70 A3
Wescott Inf Sch RG40 . . . . 25 D6
Wescott Rd RG40 . . . . 25 D6
Wesley Ave TW3 . . . . 4 F5
Wesley Cl
Crawley RH11 . . . . 200 E3
Horley RH6 . . . . 161 A5
Reigate RH2 . . . . 138 F8
Wesley Dr TW20 . . . . 12 A2
Wesley Pl SL4 . . . . 9 B6
Wessels KT20 . . . . 97 D6
Wessex Ave SW19 . . . . 40 A6
Wessex Cl
Hinchley Wood KT7 . . . . 55 F8
Kingston u T KT1, KT2 . . . . 38 B8
Wessex Ct 5 TW19 . . . . 2 E1
Wessex Pl GU9 . . . . 125 C1
Wessex Rd
Farnborough GU14 . . . . 84 E1
Harmondsworth TW19,
TW6 . . . . 2 E4
Wesson Ho 3 CR0 . . . . 43 A1
Westacres KT10 . . . . 54 F3
West Ashtead Prim Sch
KT21 . . . . 95 E7
West Ave
Crawley RH10 . . . . 202 A8
Heath End GU9 . . . . 125 D7
Redhill RH1 . . . . 140 A3
Wallington SM6 . . . . 60 E5
Whiteley Village KT12,
KT13 . . . . 53 E2
West Bank RH4 . . . . 136 A6
Westbank Rd TW12 . . . . 16 C2
WEST BARNES 39 C4
West Barnes La KT3,
SW20 . . . . 39 B5
WEST BEDFONT 13 F8
WESTBOROUGH 108 F2
Westbourne RH4 . . . . 136 C5
Westbourne Ave SM3 . . . . 58 E8
Westbourne Ct SM3 . . . . 58 E8
Westbourne Dr SE23 . . . . 23 D6
Westbourne Ho
Heston TW5 . . . . 5 A8
9 Twickenham TW1 . . . . 17 B8
Westbourne Prim Sch
SM1 . . . . 59 A7
Westbourne Rd
Croydon CR0 . . . . 42 F3
Feltham TW13 . . . . 14 F5
Penge SE26 . . . . 23 D2
Sandhurst GU47 . . . . 64 E7
Staines TW18 . . . . 13 B1
WESTBROOK 150 C5
Westbrook RH18 . . . . 206 E3
Westbrook Ave TW12 . . . . 15 F1
Westbrook Gdns RG12 . . . . 27 D8
Westbrook Hill GU8 . . . . 148 C3
Westbrook Rd
Godalming GU7 . . . . 150 C5
Heston TW5 . . . . 4 F7
South Norwood CR7 . . . . 42 D7
Staines TW18 . . . . 12 F3
Westbury Ave KT10 . . . . 55 F4
Westbury Cl
Crowthorne RG45 . . . . 45 B6
Shepperton TW17 . . . . 34 B3
Whyteleafe CR3 . . . . 80 F1
Westbury Ct BR3 . . . . 44 B8
Westbury Gdns GU9 . . . . 125 E4
Westbury House Sch
KT3 . . . . 38 D4
Westbury Pl 2 TW8 . . . . 6 D8
Westbury Rd
Beckenham BR3 . . . . 43 E6
Feltham TW13 . . . . 15 D6
New Malden KT3 . . . . 38 D4
Penge SE20 . . . . 43 D8
Thornton Heath CR0 . . . . 42 D3
Westbury Way GU12 . . . . 105 D2
WEST BYFLEET 71 B6
West Byfleet Inf Sch
KT14 . . . . 71 B7
West Byfleet Jun Sch
KT14 . . . . 71 B7
West Byfleet Sta KT14 . . . . 71 A7
Westcar La KT12 . . . . 54 B5
West Cl
Ashford TW15 . . . . 13 E4
Hampton TW12 . . . . 15 E2
Heath End GU9 . . . . 125 D7
WEST CLANDON 111 B6
West Clandon Sta
GU4 . . . . 111 B6
Westcombe Ave CR0 . . . . 41 F2
Westcombe Cl RG12 . . . . 27 E2
Westcoombe Ave
SW20 . . . . 38 F8
Westcote Rd
Epsom KT19 . . . . 57 B1
Streatham SW16 . . . . 21 C3
WESTCOTT 135 D6
Westcott CE Fst Sch
RH4 . . . . 135 D5
Westcott Cl CR0 . . . . 63 B2
Westcott Keep RH6 . . . . 161 C4
Westcott Rd RH4 . . . . 135 F7
Westcott Cotts GU26 . . . . 188 C6
Westcott St RH4 . . . . 135 B6
Westcott Way SM2 . . . . 58 C1
Westcroft SM5 . . . . 60 A6
Westcroft Gdns SM4,
SW20 . . . . 39 F5
Westcroft Ho SM5 . . . . 60 A6
Westcroft Rd SM5, SM6 . . . . 60 A6
West Cross Ctr TW8 . . . . 6 B8
West Cross Way TW8 . . . . 6 B8
West Croydon Sta CR0 . . . . 42 C1
West Ct
Guildford GU4 . . . . 110 B5
Hounslow TW7 . . . . 5 C7
Sunbury TW16 . . . . 35 B7
Wimbledon SW20 . . . . 39 B7
Westdene
Godalming GU7 . . . . 150 E3
Hersham KT12 . . . . 54 B5
Westdene Mdws GU6 . . . . 174 A3
West Dene Sch CR8 . . . . 79 F6
Westdene Way KT13 . . . . 53 E7
West Down KT23 . . . . 114 B8
Westdown Rd SE13,
SE6 . . . . 24 A8
West Dr
Belmont SM2 . . . . 58 E2
Burgh Heath KT20 . . . . 77 D1
Streatham SW16, SW17 . . . . 21 C4
Sutton SM5 . . . . 59 D1
Wentworth GU25, SL5 . . . . 30 E2
Woodham KT15 . . . . 52 B2
WEST DULWICH 22 C6
West Dulwich Sta
SE21 . . . . 22 D7
WEST END
Esher 54 F4
Woking 67 F6
West End Cotts GU23 . . . . 91 B5
Westende RG40 . . . . 25 D6
Westende Jun Sch
RG40 . . . . 25 D6
West End Gdns KT10 . . . . 54 F5
West End Gr GU9 . . . . 125 A2
West End Inf Sch
GU11 . . . . 104 F2
West End La
Chiddingfold GU27 . . . . 190 E1
Esher KT10 . . . . 54 F4
Frensham GU10 . . . . 146 A1
Harlington UB7 . . . . 3 C7
Westerdale Dr GU16 . . . . 66 B3
Westerfolds Cl GU22 . . . . 70 C2
Westerham 13 KT6 . . . . 37 E4
Westerham Cl
Belmont SM2 . . . . 59 A1
New Haw KT15 . . . . 52 C4
Westerham Lo 10 BR3 . . . . 24 A1
Westerham Rd RH8,
TN16 . . . . 123 C6
Westerley Cres SE26,
SE6 . . . . 23 F3
Westermain KT15 . . . . 52 C1
Western Ave
Brookwood GU24 . . . . 88 A6
Chertsey KT16 . . . . 33 A6
Thorpe TW20 . . . . 32 B6
Western Cl KT16 . . . . 33 A6
Western Ctr The RG12 . . . . 26 F7
Western Dr TW17 . . . . 34 D3
Western Hts SM1 . . . . 59 A5
Western Ind Area
RG12 . . . . 26 F7
Western La SW12 . . . . 21 A8
Western Par RH2 . . . . 139 B6
Western Perimeter Rd
TW19, TW6, UB7 . . . . 2 B5
Western Perimeter Road
Rdbt TW19 . . . . 2 C2
Western Rd
Aldershot GU11 . . . . 104 E1
Bracknell RG12 . . . . 26 F7
Mitcham CR4, SW19 . . . . 40 E7
Sutton SM1 . . . . 59 A5
WEST EWELL 57 E3
West Ewell Inf Sch
KT19 . . . . 57 D5
West Farm Ave KT21 . . . . 95 D8
West Farm Cl KT21 . . . . 95 C8
West Farm Dr KT21 . . . . 95 D8
WESTFIELD 89 F6
Westfield
Ashtead KT21 . . . . 75 F1
Peaslake RH5 . . . . 154 E8
Reigate RH2 . . . . 118 B4
Westfield Ave
Sanderstead CR2 . . . . 80 E6
Woking GU22 . . . . 89 E7
Westfield Cl SM1 . . . . 58 F6
Westfield Comm GU22 . . . . 89 E5
Westfield Ct
Kingston u T KT6 . . . . 37 D4
New Haw KT15 . . . . 52 D1
Westfield Dr KT23 . . . . 94 B5
Westfield Gdns 2
RH4 . . . . 136 A7
Westfield Gr GU22 . . . . 89 E7
Westfield La GU10 . . . . 145 E6
Westfield Par KT15 . . . . 52 D1
Westfield Prim Sch
GU22 . . . . 89 E6
Westfield Rd
Beckenham BR3 . . . . 43 F7
Camberley GU15 . . . . 65 B2
Cheam SM1 . . . . 58 F6
Crawley RH11 . . . . 201 B6
Guildford GU1 . . . . 109 E5
Kingston u T KT6 . . . . 37 D4
Mitcham CR4 . . . . 40 F7
Thornton Heath CR0,
CR9 . . . . 61 B8
Walton-on-T KT12 . . . . 35 E2
Woking GU22 . . . . 89 E5
Westfields
Mortlake SW13 . . . . 7 F4
Witley GU8 . . . . 170 F5
Westfields Ave SW13,
SW14 . . . . 7 E4
Westfield Way GU22 . . . . 89 F5
West Flexford La GU3 . . . . 128 E8
Westgate Est TW14 . . . . 14 B7
Westgate Ho KT18 . . . . 76 D4
Westgate Rd
Beckenham BR3 . . . . 44 C8
Croydon SE25 . . . . 43 B5
West Gdns
Ewell KT17 . . . . 57 F1
Mitcham SW19 . . . . 20 E2
Westglade GU14 . . . . 84 D4
West Gr KT12 . . . . 54 B6
WEST GREEN 201 C6
West Green Dr RH11 . . . . 201 C6
West Green Prim Sch
RH11 . . . . 201 C7
Westhall Pk CR6 . . . . 101 C8
Westhall Rd CR6 . . . . 101 B8
West Hall Rd TW9 . . . . 7 B6
West Hanger Nature
Trail* GU5 . . . . 133 A7
Westhaven SM1 . . . . 59 A5

Westhay Gdns SW14 7 B2
WEST HEATH 84 F6
West Heath GU24 87 D5
West Heath Rd GU14 84 F4
West Hill
Biggin Hill BR6 83 F7
Dormans Park RH19 185 E6
East Grinstead RH19 205 D8
Elstead GU8 148 C3
Epsom KT18, KT19 76 C6
Oxted RH8 122 D5
Putney SW15 19 D8
South Croydon CR2 61 E2
Woking GU22 89 E8
West Hill Ave KT19 76 C7
West Hill Bank RH8 122 D5
West Hill Cl
Brookwood GU24 88 B7
Elstead GU8 148 C3
West Hill Ct KT19 76 C6
West Hill Rd
Wandsworth SW18 20 A8
Woking GU22 89 E8
West Hill Sch KT22 75 A1
West Ho
Penge SE20 23 D1
9 Streatham SW12 21 C8
West Hoathly Rd
RH19 205 D4
WEST HORSLEY 112 B8
West House Cl SW19 19 E7
WESTHUMBLE 115 A4
Westhumble St RH5 115 B4
West La
East Grinstead RH19 205 D8
Wotton RH5 134 D4
Westland Cl TW19 2 E1
Westland Dr BR2, BR4 63 F8
Westlands RH13 217 E3
Westlands Ct
East Molesey KT8 36 E5
Epsom KT18 76 C4
Westlands Way RH8 122 D8
Westleas RH6 160 E5
Westlees Cl RH5 136 D4
West Leigh RH19 205 E7
Westleigh Ave CR5 79 B3
Westleigh Ct 4 CR2 61 E6
Westmacott Dr TW14 14 F7
Westmark Point 13
SW15 19 B7
Westmead
Farnborough GU14 85 B3
10 Farnham GU9 125 B2
Putney SW15 19 B8
Woking GU21 69 B2
West Mead KT19 57 E4
Westmead Cnr SM1 59 E6
Westmead Dr RH1 140 A1
Westmead Rd SM1 59 D6
Westmeads RH6 161 C3
West Meads GU2 129 F8
West Mead Sch RG40 25 E6
West Middlesex Univ Hosp
TW7 6 A5
Westminster Ave CR7 42 B7
Westminster Cl
East Bedfont TW14 15 A7
Teddington TW11 17 A3
Westminster Ct SM3 58 C6
Westminster Ct GU22 90 B6
Westminster Ct CR7 42 C7
Westminster Rd
Carshalton SM1 59 D8
Crawley RH10 202 C5
Westmoat Cl BR3 24 C1
WEST MOLESEY 36 A5
Westmont Rd KT10 55 E8
Westmoreland Dr SM2 59 B2
Westmoreland Rd
Barnes SW13 7 F6
Beckenham BR2 44 F5
Westmoreland Terr
SE20 23 B1
Westmore Rd TN16 103 C7
Westmorland Cl
Epsom KT19 57 E2
3 Twickenham TW1 6 B1
Westmorland Ct
12 Surbiton KT6 37 D2
Sutton SM1 59 C7
Westmorland Dr GU15 66 B3
Westmorland Sq CR4 41 E4
Westmorland Way CR4 41 E4
West Mount GU2 130 C7
WEST NORWOOD 22 C5
West Norwood Sta
SE27 22 C4
West Oak BR3 44 D8
Weston Ave
Addlestone KT15 52 B6
East Molesey KT8 35 F5
Thames Ditton KT10, KT7 36 E2
Weston Cl
Coulsdon CR5 99 F7
Farncombe GU7 150 E6
Weston Ct
Farncombe GU7 150 E6
3 Kingston u T KT1 37 E6
Weston Dr CR3 100 C6
Weston Farm Cotts
GU5 132 B4
Weston Farm Yd GU5 132 B4
Weston Fields GU5 132 C4
Weston Gdns
Hounslow TW7 5 E6
Pyrford GU22 70 E3
Weston Gn KT7 36 E1
Weston Gr
Bagshot GU19 47 F2
1 Bromley BR1 44 F8
WESTON GREEN 36 F1
Weston Green Prep Sch
KT7 36 E1
Weston Green Rd KT7 36 E2
Weston Lea KT24 92 D2
Weston Lo KT7 36 F1
Weston Park Cl KT7 36 E1
Weston Pk
Kingston u T KT1 37 E7
Thames Ditton KT10, KT7 36 E1
Weston Rd
Bromley BR1 24 F1
Ewell KT17 76 E8
Guildford GU2 109 A2
Thames Ditton KT7 36 E1
Westons Cl RH12 217 D7
Weston Way GU22 70 E3
Weston Yd GU5 132 C4
Westover Cl SM2 59 B2
Westover Rd SW18 20 C8
Westow Hill SE19 22 F2
Westow St SE19 22 E2
West Palace Gdns
KT13 53 B7
West Par RH12 217 C4
West Park Ave TW9 7 B6
West Park Cl TW5 4 F8
West Park Hospl KT19 75 E7
West Park Rd
Domewood RH10,
RH7 183 F5
Epsom KT19 75 F7
Horne RH7 184 B7
Richmond TW9 7 A6
West Parkside CR6 82 A3
West Pl SW19 19 C3
Westpoint BR2 44 D6
West Ramp TW6 3 A6
West Rd
Bracknell RG40 26 D2
Camberley GU15 65 D5
Chessington KT9 75 C8
East Bedfont TW14 14 D8
Farnborough GU14 85 B8
Guildford GU1 130 E8
Kingston u T KT2, KT3 38 C8
Reigate RH2 139 B8
Weybridge KT13 53 B3
West Ring GU10 126 F7
West Sheen Vale TW9 6 F3
Westside GU24 67 E6
West Side Comm
SW19 19 C3
Westside Ho RH1 140 B2
West St
Carshalton SM5 59 F6
Crawley RH11 201 D5
Croydon CR0, CR9 61 C6
Dorking RH4 136 A7
Dormansland RH7 165 A1
East Grinstead RH19 205 E8
Epsom KT18, KT19 76 C6
Ewell KT17 57 F1
Farnham GU9 125 A2
Haslemere GU27 208 C6
Horsham RH12 217 C2
Reigate RH2 117 F1
Sutton SM1 59 B5
Woking GU21 69 F2
West Street La SM5 59 F6
West Street Pl 1 CR0,
CR9 61 C6
West Surrey Est TW15 34 C8
West Sussex Ho GU2 129 E8
West Sutton Sta SM1 59 A6
West Temple Sheen
SW14 7 B2
West Thames Coll TW7 5 E6
West Thornton Prim Sch
CR0 41 F3
Westview 5 GU22 69 F1
West View TW14 14 C8
West View Ave CR3 80 F1
Westview Cl RH1 139 E6
West View Cotts RH8 122 A2
West View Gdns
RH19 205 E8
West View Rd
Headley Down GU35 187 C4
Warlingham CR6 101 B8
Westville Rd KT7 37 A2
Westward Ho GU1 109 F3
Westwates Cl RG12 27 D8
Westway
Caterham CR3 100 D5
Copthorne RH10 183 A3
Crawley RH6 182 B7
Guildford GU2 108 F3
West Barnes KT3, SW20 39 C5
West Way
Crawley RH10 202 A7
Croydon CR0 62 E7
Heston TW5 4 F6
Shepperton TW17 34 D3
Slinfold RH13 215 D3
Sutton SM2, SM5 59 D1
West Wickham BR4 44 E3
Westway Cl
West Barnes SW20 39 B6
Wormley GU8 190 F8
Westway Ct CR3 100 D4
Westway Gdns RH1 119 A4
West Way Gdns CR0 62 D8
Westways KT19 57 F6
Westwell Rd SW16 21 E2
Westwell Road App
SW16 21 E2
Westwick Gdns TW4,
TW5 4 B5
WEST WICKHAM 44 E1
West Wickham Sta
BR4 44 C2
West Wimbledon Prim Sch
SW20 39 B6
Westwood Ave
South Norwood SE19 42 C8
Woodham KT15 70 F7
Westwood Cl KT10 55 C7
Westwood Ct
3 Forest Hill SE23 23 C7
Guildford GU2 108 F2
7 Wimbledon SW19 19 F3
Westwood Gdns SW13 7 F4
Westwood Hill SE19,
SE26 23 B4
Westwood La
Normandy GU3 107 A2
Wanborough GU3 128 B7
Westwood Language Coll
for Girls SE19 22 D1
Westwood Pk SE23 23 B8
Westwood Pl SE26 23 A4
Westwood Rd
Coulsdon CR5 79 D1
Mortlake SW13, SW15 7 F4
Windlesham GU20 48 E6
Wetheral Ct SW17 20 D4
Wetherby Ct SE25 42 E7
Wetherby Gdns 2
GU14 85 C1
Wetherby Ho GU15 65 D7
Wetherby Way KT9 56 E3
Wettern Cl CR2 61 E1
Wetton Pl TW20 11 F3
Wexfenne Gdns GU22 71 B3
Wexford Rd SW12 20 F8
Wey Ave KT16 33 A6
Weybank GU23 71 E3
Weybank Cl GU9 125 C3
Wey Barton KT14 71 F6
WEYBOURNE 125 E7
Weybourne Inf Sch
GU9 125 E6
Weybourne Pl CR2 61 D1
Weybourne Rd
Aldershot GU11 126 B7
Heath End GU11, GU9 125 E6
Weybourne St SW18 20 C6
WEYBRIDGE 53 A6
Weybridge Bsns Pk
KT15 52 E6
Weybridge Ho KT13 53 D5
Weybridge Hospl KT13 53 A6
Weybridge Pk KT13 53 B5
Weybridge Rd
Addlestone KT15, KT13 52 E6
Thornton Heath CR7 42 A5
Weybridge Sta KT13 53 A4
Weybrook Dr
Guildford, Burpham
GU4 110 B6
Guildford GU4 110 B6
Wey Cl
Ash GU12 106 A1
Camberley GU15 65 B5
West Byfleet KT14 71 B6
Weycombe Rd GU27 208 C8
Wey Ct GU7 151 A6
Wey Ct 7 GU1 130 C8
Wey Ct
New Haw KT15 52 D2
West Ewell KT19 57 C6
Weydon Farm La GU9 146 B8
Weydon Hill Cl GU9 146 B8
Weydon Hill Rd GU9 146 C8
Weydon La
Farnham GU9 146 A8
Wrecclesham GU9 145 F8
Weydon Mill La GU9 125 B1
Weydon Sch GU9 145 F7
Weydown Cl
Guildford GU2 109 A6
Putney SW19 19 E7
Weydown Ct GU27 208 B7
Weydown Ind Est
GU27 208 B7
Weydown La GU2 109 A6
Weydown Rd GU27 208 B7
Weyfield Prim Sch
GU1 109 D4
Wey Gdns GU27 207 F5
Weyhill GU27 208 A6
Wey House Sch GU5 151 E8
Weylands Cl KT12 35 F1
Weylands Pk KT13 53 D4
Weylea Ave GU4 110 A4
Wey Manor Rd KT15 52 D2
Wey Mdws KT13 52 F5
Weymead Cl KT16 33 C1
Weymede KT14 71 F7
Weymouth Ct
Belmont SM2 59 A3
18 Streatham SW2 21 F8
Wey Rd
Godalming GU7 151 A5
Weybridge KT13 52 F7
Wey Ret Pk KT14 71 E7
Weyside
Farnham GU9 125 C2
Weyside continued
Weybridge KT13 53 B8
Weyside Cl KT14 71 F7
Weyside Gdns GU1 109 C3
Weyside Pk GU7 151 A5
Weyside Rd GU1 109 B3
Weysprings GU27 208 A6
Weyvern Pk GU3 130 B1
Weyview Cl GU1 109 C3
Wey View Ct GU1 130 C8
Weywood Cl GU9 125 F7
Weywood La GU9 125 E7
Whaley Rd RG40 25 D8
Wharf Bridge Rd TW7 6 B4
Wharfedale Gdns CR7,
SW16 41 F6
Wharfenden Way GU16 85 F6
Wharf La
Send GU23 90 C4
Twickenham TW1 17 A7
Wharf Rd
Ash GU12 106 A4
Frimley GU16 86 A6
Guildford GU1 109 C1
Wraysbury TW19 11 D8
Wharf St GU7 150 E4
Wharf The KT13 53 A7
Wharf Way GU16 86 A6
Wharncliffe Gdns SE25 42 E7
Wharncliffe Rd SE25 42 E7
Whateley Cl GU2 109 B6
Whateley Rd SE20 23 D1
Whatley Ave SW20 39 E6
Whatley Gn RG12 27 B3
Whatman Rd SE23 23 D8
Whatmore Cl TW19 2 A1
Wheatash Rd KT15 52 B8
Wheatcroft Ct SM1 40 B1
Wheatcroft Ho 3 KT3 38 E2
Wheatfield Way
Horley RH6 161 C4
Kingston u T KT1 37 E7
Wheathill Ho SE20 43 B7
Wheathill Rd SE20 43 B6
Wheat Ho TW19 13 E7
Wheat Knoll CR8 80 C3
Wheatlands TW5 5 A8
Wheatlands Rd SW17 21 A5
Wheatley RG12 26 E4
Wheatley Ct SW2 21 E6
Wheatley Ho 3 SW15 19 A8
Wheatley Rd
Aldershot GU11 104 F3
Isleworth TW7 5 F4
Wheatsheaf Cl
Horsham RH12 217 E5
Ottershaw KT16 51 D4
Woking GU21 69 F3
Wheatsheaf La TW18 12 F1
Wheatsheaf Par 4
BR4 44 B1
Wheatstone Cl
Crawley RH10 182 B3
Mitcham SW19 40 E8
Wheeler Ave RH8 122 D6
Wheeler La GU8 170 E6
Wheeler Rd RH10 202 B4
Wheelers La
Brockham RH3 137 C7
Epsom KT18 76 C5
Smallfield RH6 162 B3
Wheeler's St SM1 59 A7
WHEELERSTREET 170 F6
Wheelers Way RH19 184 E3
Wheelwrights La
GU26 188 A4
Wheelwrights Pl SL3 1 C7
Whelan Way SM6 60 D7
Wherwell Lo GU2 130 C7
Wherwell Rd GU2 130 C7
Whetstone Rd GU14 84 C4
Whimbrel Cl CR2, CR8 80 D8
Whinfell Cl SW16 21 D3
Whins Cl GU15 65 B4
Whins Dr GU15 65 B4
Whinshill Ct SL5 30 A1
Whipley Cl GU4 110 B6
Whistler Cl RH10 201 F3
Whistler Gr GU47 64 D6
Whistley Cl RG12 27 E6
Whitby Cl
Biggin Hill TN16 83 B1
Farnborough GU12 85 E1
Whitby Gdns SM1 59 D8
Whitby Rd SM1 59 D8
Whitchurch Cl GU11 126 D6
Whitchurch Ct SW17 20 D4
Whitchurch Ho SE6 24 C5
Whitcome Mews TW9 7 B6
White Acres Rd GU16 85 F4
Whitebeam Ct CR8 80 B8
Whitebeam Dr RH2 139 B6
Whitebeam Gdns GU14 84 C3
White Beam Way KT20 97 A6
Whiteberry Rd RH5 156 B7
Whitebines GU9 125 D2
White Bridge Ave CR4 40 D6
White Bridge Cl TW14 3 F1
WHITEBUSHES 140 B4
White Bushes RH1 140 A4
White City RG45 45 D5
White Cottage Cl
GU9 125 D6
Whitecroft RH6 161 B4
Whitecroft Cl BR3 44 D5
Whitecroft Way BR3 44 D5
White Ct GU2 109 A4
Whitefield Ave CR8 80 B3
Whitefield Ho CR8 80 B3
Whitefoot La BR1, SE6 24 D5
Whitefoot Terr BR1 24 F5
Whitegates
Old Woking GU22 89 F7
Whyteleafe CR3 101 A8
Whitegate Way KT20 97 B7
Whitehall Cres KT9 56 D5
Whitehall Ct W4 7 B8
Whitehall Dr RH11 200 E6
Whitehall Farm La
GU25 31 E6
Whitehall Gdns W4 7 B8
Whitehall La
Egham TW20 11 F1
Horton TW19 1 A1
Reigate RH2 138 F6
Whitehall Park Rd W4 7 B8
Whitehall Pl SM5 60 B6
Whitehall Rd CR7 42 A4
White Hart Ct
Horsham RH12 217 C4
Ripley GU23 91 C6
White Hart Ho TW12 36 C8
White Hart Ind Est
GU17 64 E4
White Hart La
Mortlake SW14 7 E4
Wood St V GU3 108 A2
Whitehart Lo SW19 20 C2
White Hart Mdws
GU23 91 C6
White Hart Row 2
KT16 33 A2
Whitehead Cl SW18 20 C8
White Heron Mews
TW11 16 F2
White Hill
Kingswood CR5 98 D4
South Croydon CR2 61 D1
Windlesham GU20 48 B6
Whitehill Cl GU15 65 D7
Whitehill La
Bletchingley RH1 120 D6
Martyr's Green GU23 92 C4
Whitehill Pl GU25 31 E4
White Ho 2 SW4 21 D8
White Horse Dr KT18 76 C5
Whitehorse La SE25 42 E5
White Horse La GU23 91 C6
Whitehorse Manor Inf Sch
CR7 42 D5
Whitehorse Manor Jun
Sch CR7 42 D5
Whitehorse Rd
Horsham RH12 218 B6
Thornton Heath CR0, CR7,
SE25 42 D3
White Ho The SW17 20 F3
Whitehouse Cl GU14 85 B6
White House Ct BR3 44 C8
White House Dr GU1 110 B1
White House La GU4 109 D6
White House Sch RG41 25 A3
White House Wlk
GU9 125 D7
White Knights Rd
KT13 53 C3
White Knobs Way
CR3 101 A2
White La
Guildford GU4 131 D7
Titsey RH8 103 B3
Tongham GU10, GU12 127 C7
Whitelands Coll,
Roehampton Inst
SW18 19 E8
Whitelands Cres SW18 19 E8
Whitelands Dr SL5 28 D8
White Leaf Ho 7 GU14 85 C1
Whiteley Ct 1 TW13 15 F5
Whiteley Ho 7 SW4 21 D8
Whiteley Rd SE19 22 D3
Whiteleys Ho TW13 16 A5
Whiteleys Way TW13 16 A5
WHITELEY VILLAGE 53 E1
White Lion Gate KT11 73 A5
White Lion Wlk 1
GU1 130 D7
White Lo
Ashtead KT21 95 E7
South Norwood SE19 22 B1
Whitelocke Inf Sch
RG40 25 D7
White Lodge Cl
Isleworth TW7 6 A5
Sutton SM2 59 C3
White Lodge Ct TW16 35 C8
White Lodge Gdns
RH1 140 A1
White Lodge The Royal
Ballet Sch TW10 18 D7
Whitely Hill RH10 202 F1
Whitemore Rd GU1 109 D5
White Oak Dr BR3 44 D7
Whiteoak Ho SE19 22 C1
Whiteoaks SM7 78 B6
White Pillars GU23 89 B7
WHITE POST 120 E1
Whitepost Hill RH1 118 E1
Whitepost Ho RH1 118 E1
White Post La GU10 146 A4
White Rd GU15 64 F6
White Rose La
Farnham GU9, GU10 146 B7
Old Woking GU22 90 A8
Woking GU22 69 F1
Whites Rd GU14 85 E1

Whitethorn Ave CR5 . . . . . 79 B4
Whitethorn Cl GU12. . . . . 106 B1
Whitethorn Cotts
GU6 . . . . 174 B5
Whitethorn Gdns CR0 . . . . 62 B8
White Way KT23 . . . . 94 B1
Whiteways Ct TW18. . . . . . 13 B1
Whiteways End GU10 . . . 126 D4
Whitewood Cotts
Horne RH9. . . . . 163 B7
Tatsfield TN16 . . . . 103 C7
Whitewood La RH9 . . . . . 163 B7
Whitfield Cl
Guildford GU2 . . . . 109 A4
Haslemere GU27 . . . . 189 C1
Whitfield Ct
3 Dulwich SE21 . . . . 22 E4
Merton SW20 . . . . 39 D7
Whitfield Rd GU27 . . . . . . 189 C1
Whitford Gdns CR4 . . . . . . 40 F6
Whitgift Ave CR2 . . . . 61 C5
Whitgift Ct CR2. . . . . 61 C5
Whitgift Ctr CR9. . . . . 61 C8
Whitgift Ho CR2 . . . . 61 C5
Whitgift Sch CR2 . . . . 61 C5
Whitgift St CR0, CR9. . . . . . 61 C7
Whitgift Wlk RH10 . . . . . . 201 D3
Whitland Rd SM5 . . . . 40 D1
Whitlet Cl GU9. . . . . 125 B1
Whitley Cl TW19 . . . . 2 E1
Whitley Ct 14 BR2. . . . . 44 F5
Whitlock Dr SW19 . . . . 19 E7
Whitmead Cl CR2. . . . . 61 E4
Whitmead La GU10 . . . . . 147 E4
Whitmoor La GU4. . . . . 89 D1
Whitmoor Rd GU19 . . . . . . 47 F2
Whitmore Cl GU47 . . . . 45 D1
Whitmore Gn GU9 . . . . . . 125 E6
Whitmore Hill Cotts
GU26 . . . . 188 C3
Whitmore La SL5 . . . . 30 A5
Whitmore Rd BR3. . . . . 43 F6
Whitmores Cl KT18 . . . . . . 76 C4
Whitmore Vale GU10,
GU26 . . . . 187 F7
Whitmore Vale Rd
Beacon Hill GU26. . . . . 188 A5
Grayshott GU26. . . . . 188 A4
Headley Down GU26 . . . . . 187 F7
Whitmore Way RH6 . . . . . 160 E3
Whitstable Cl BR3 . . . . 43 F8
Whitstable Pl 9 CR0. . . . . . 61 C6
Whitstone La BR3. . . . . 44 B4
Whittaker Ave TW10,
TW9. . . . . 6 D2
Whittaker Ct KT21 . . . . 75 D2
Whittaker Pl 29 TW10 . . . . . 6 D2
Whittaker Rd SM3 . . . . 58 F7
Whittam Ho SE27 . . . . 22 C3
Whittell Gdns SE26 . . . . . . 23 C5
Whittingham Ct W4. . . . . 7 E7
Whittington Coll
(Almshouses) RH19 . . . 185 A4
Whittington Ct SE20 . . . . . 43 B7
Whittington Rd RH10. . . . 201 E3
Whittlebury Cl SM5 . . . . . . 59 F3
Whittle Cl
Ash Vale GU12. . . . . 105 F5
Sandhurst GU47 . . . . 45 A1
Whittle Cres GU14 . . . . 84 F7
Whittle Rd TW5. . . . . 4 C7
Whittle Rdbt GU14 . . . . 84 C1
Whittle Way RH10 . . . . . . 182 A3
WHITTON 16 C8
Whitton Dene TW2, TW7 . . . 5 D1
Whitton Manor Rd TW7 . . . 5 C1
Whitton Rd
Bracknell RG12 . . . . 27 F6
Hounslow TW3. . . . . 5 B2
Twickenham TW1. . . . . 17 A8
Whitton Sch TW2. . . . . 16 B6
Whitton Sta TW2 . . . . 16 C8
Whitton Waye TW2, TW3. . . 5 A1
Whitwell Hatch GU27 . . . 208 D5
Whitworth Rd
Crawley RH11 . . . . 181 D2
South Norwood SE25. . . . . . 42 F5
Whopshott Ave GU21. . . . . 69 C3
Whopshott Cl GU21 . . . . . . 69 C3
Whopshott Dr GU21. . . . . . 69 C3
Whynstones Rd SL5. . . . . . 29 A4
Whyteacre CR3 . . . . 101 B7
Whyte Ave GU12 . . . . 126 D7
Whytebeam View CR3. . . . 80 F1
Whytecliffe Rd N CR8 . . . . 80 B8
Whytecliffe Rd S CR8 . . . . 80 B8
Whytecroft TW5 . . . . 4 D7
WHYTELEAFE 80 E1
Whyteleafe Bsns Village
CR3. . . . . 80 F2
Whyteleafe Hill CR3. . . . . . 80 F1
Whyteleafe Prim Sch
CR3. . . . . 80 F1
Whyteleafe Rd CR3 . . . . . 100 F6
Whyteleafe South Sta
CR3. . . . . 101 A8
Whyteleafe Sta CR3. . . . . . 80 F2
Wickers Oake SE19 . . . . . . 22 F4
Wicket Hill GU10, GU9 . . . 146 A6
Wickets The TW15 . . . . 13 E4
Wicket The CR0 . . . . 63 A5
Wick & Grove Ho
RH4 . . . . 136 A6
Wickham Ave
Cheam KT4, SM3. . . . . 58 C5
Croydon CR0 . . . . 43 E1
Wickham Chase BR4 . . . . . 44 E2
Wickham Cl
Horley RH6 . . . . 160 F4
New Malden KT3 . . . . 38 F4
Wickham Court Rd
BR4 . . . . 63 C8
Wickham Court Sch
BR4. . . . . 63 D6
Wickham Cres BR4 . . . . . . 63 C8
Wickham La TW20 . . . . 12 A1
Wickham Rd
Beckenham BR3. . . . . 44 B6
Camberley GU15 . . . . 65 E8
Croydon CR0, CR9 . . . . 62 E8
Wickham Vale RG12 . . . . . 26 E3
Wickham Way BR3. . . . . . . 44 C4
WICK HILL 27 C8
Wick Ho 1 KT1. . . . . 37 D8
Wickhurst Gdns RH12 . . . 216 E3
Wickhurst La RH12. . . . . . 216 E3
Wick La TW20 . . . . 10 F3
Wickland Ct RH10. . . . . . . 201 D3
Wicklow Ct SE26. . . . . 23 C3
Wick Rd
Englefield Green TW20 . . . . 11 B1
Teddington TW11. . . . . 17 C1
Wide Way CR4, SW16 . . . . . 41 D6
Widewing Cl TW11. . . . . . . 17 B1
Widgeon Way RH12 . . . . . 217 C5
Widmer Ct TW5. . . . . 4 E5
Wigan Rd GU14 . . . . 104 D8
Wiggie La RH1. . . . . 119 A3
Wiggins Cotts TW10 . . . . . 17 C6
Wiggins La TW10 . . . . 17 C6
Wighton Mews TW7 . . . . 5 E5
Wigley Rd TW13 . . . . 15 D7
Wigmore La RH5. . . . . 157 C1
Wigmore Rd SM5 . . . . 40 E1
Wigmore Wlk SM5. . . . . . . 59 D8
Wilberforce Ct KT18 . . . . . 76 D5
Wilberforce Way
Bracknell RG12 . . . . 27 D4
Wimbledon SW19 . . . . 19 D2
Wilbury Ave SM2 . . . . 58 F1
Wilbury Rd GU21 . . . . 69 D2
Wilcot Cl GU24 . . . . 68 A3
Wilcot Gdns GU24 . . . . 68 A3
Wilcox Gdns TW17. . . . . . . 33 F6
Wilcox Rd
Sutton SM1 . . . . 59 B6
Teddington TW11. . . . . 16 D4
Wildacre Cl RH14 . . . . 212 D3
Wild Acres KT14 . . . . 71 C8
Wildbank Ct 12 GU22. . . . . 69 F1
Wildcroft Dr
Dorking RH5 . . . . 136 D4
Wokingham RG40 . . . . 25 A1
Wildcroft Manor SW15 . . . 19 C8
Wildcroft Rd SW15. . . . . . . 19 C8
Wildcroft Wood GU8. . . . 170 D6
Wilde Pl SW18. . . . . 20 D8
Wilderness Ct GU2. . . . . . 129 F7
Wilderness Rd
Frimley GU16. . . . . 65 E2
Guildford GU2 . . . . 129 F7
Oxted RH8 . . . . 122 E5
Wilderness Rise
RH19 . . . . 186 A6
Wilderness The
East Molesey KT8 . . . . 36 C4
Hampton TW12 . . . . 16 B4
Wilders Cl
Frimley GU16. . . . . 65 E3
Woking GU21. . . . . 69 C1
Wilderwick Rd RH19 . . . . 186 A5
Wildes Cotts SM3. . . . . 58 E4
Wilde Theatre RG12. . . . . . 27 C2
Wildfell Rd SE6. . . . . 24 B8
Wildfield Cl GU3. . . . . 108 B2
Wildgoose Dr RH12 . . . . . 216 F3
WILDRIDINGS 27 A5
Wildridings Prim Sch
RG12. . . . . 27 A5
Wildridings Rd RG12 . . . . . 27 A5
Wildridings Sq RG12 . . . . . 27 A5
Wildwood Cl
Cranleigh GU6 . . . . 174 F1
East Horsley KT24. . . . . 92 F2
Lewisham SE12 . . . . 24 F8
Pyrford GU22. . . . . 70 F4
Wildwood Ct CR8 . . . . 80 D4
Wildwood La GU6. . . . . . . 194 C5
Wilford Rd CR0. . . . . 42 C2
Wilfred Owen Cl SW19 . . . 20 C2
Wilfred St GU21 . . . . 69 D1
Wilhelmina Ave CR5 . . . . . 99 C8
Wilkes Rd 3 TW8. . . . . 6 E8
Wilkins Cl CR4. . . . . 40 E8
Wilkinson Ct
4 Crawley RH11 . . . . 201 B1
Upper Tooting SW17 . . . . . . 20 D4
Wilkinson Gdns SE25. . . . . 42 E8
Wilkinson Ho
Isleworth TW7. . . . . 5 F4
Twickenham TW2. . . . . 16 D6
Wilks Gdns CR0. . . . . 43 E1
Willats Cl 5 KT16. . . . . 33 A3
Willcocks Cl KT9. . . . . 56 E7
Willems Ave GU11 . . . . . . 104 F2
Willems Rdbt GU11 . . . . . 104 F2
Willerton Lo 1 KT13. . . . . . 53 D4
Willett Pl CR7 . . . . 42 A4
Willett Rd CR7. . . . . 42 A4
Willetts RH4. . . . . 136 C4
Willetts Way RH14 . . . . . . 212 F3
Willey Broom La CR3. . . . 100 A2
Willey Farm La CR3 . . . . . 100 C1
WILLEY GREEN 107 D4
Willey La CR3. . . . . 100 D2
William Booth Rd
SE20. . . . . 43 A8
William Brown Ct SE27 . . . 22 B6
William Byrd Sch UB3. . . . . 3 D8
William Cobbett Jun Sch
GU9. . . . . 125 E6
William Ct
Cheam SM3 . . . . 58 C6
Farnborough GU14 . . . . 85 B4
9 Farnborough, South
Farnborough GU14. . . . . . 85 C1
South Norwood SE19. . . . . . 22 D1
William Dyce Mews
SW16. . . . . 21 D4
William Ellis Sch (The
Mill) RH5 . . . . 176 D8
William Evans Rd KT19. . . 76 A8
William Evelyn Ct
RH5 . . . . 134 F4
William Farthing Cl 17
GU11 . . . . 105 A2
William Harvey Ho 1
SW19. . . . . 19 E7
William Hitchcock Ho
GU14 . . . . 85 B7
William Lilly Ho KT12 . . . . 54 C5
William Marden Ho 2
SE27. . . . . 22 B4
William Morris Prim Sch
CR4. . . . . 41 D6
William Rd
Caterham CR3 . . . . 100 D5
Guildford GU1 . . . . 109 C1
Merton SW19 . . . . 19 E1
Sutton SM1 . . . . 59 C5
William Russell Ct 3
GU21 . . . . 68 E1
Williams Cl KT15. . . . . 52 B5
Williams Dr TW3. . . . . 5 A3
Williams Gr KT6 . . . . 37 C3
Williams Ho 14 SW2. . . . . . . 22 A7
William Sim Wood RG42 . . . 8 B2
Williams La
Morden SM4 . . . . 40 C4
Mortlake SW14 . . . . 7 C5
Williamson Cl GU27. . . . . 189 F1
Williams Pl GU6 . . . . 175 E5
William St SM5 . . . . 59 F7
Williams Terr CR0 . . . . 61 A4
Williams Way RH10 . . . . . 202 B5
William Swayne Ho 1
GU1 . . . . 130 E8
Williams Wlk GU2 . . . . . . 109 B5
William Wilberforce Ho 1
SE27. . . . . 22 B4
William Winter Ct
SW2. . . . . 22 A8
William Wood Ho
SE26. . . . . 23 C5
Willian Pl GU26. . . . . 188 E6
Willingham Way KT1. . . . . 38 A7
Willington Cl GU15. . . . . . . 65 B6
Willington Sch SW19. . . . . 19 F3
Willis Ave SM2 . . . . 59 E4
Willis Cl KT18. . . . . 76 B5
Willis Ct 5 CR7. . . . . 42 A3
Willis Rd CR0. . . . . 42 C2
Willows The CR0. . . . . 62 E8
Will Miles Ct 6 SW19 . . . . 20 C1
Willmore End SW19. . . . . . 40 B7
Willoughby Ave CR0 . . . . . 60 F6
Willoughby Rd
Bracknell RG12 . . . . 26 F6
Kingston u T KT2 . . . . 37 F8
Twickenham TW1. . . . . 6 D2
Willoughbys The 8
SW15. . . . . 7 E4
Willow Ave SW13 . . . . 7 F5
Willow Bank
Richmond TW10. . . . . 17 B5
Woking GU22. . . . . 89 F6
Willowbank Gdns KT20. . . 97 B5
Willowbank Pl CR8 . . . . . . 61 B2
Willow Brean RH6 . . . . . . 160 E5
Willowbrook Coury 10
TW20. . . . . 12 A3
Willowbrook Rd TW19 . . . 13 E6
Willow Cl
Addlestone KT16 . . . . 51 E8
Beare Green RH5 . . . . 157 C4
Brentford TW8. . . . . 6 C8
Catford SE6 . . . . 24 F7
Colnbrook SL3 . . . . 1 C7
Crawley RH10 . . . . 201 E8
East Grinstead RH19. . . . . 185 D3
Mytchett GU16. . . . . 85 E4
Woodham KT15 . . . . 70 F8
Willow Cnr RH6. . . . . 180 F7
Willow Cotts
Carshalton CR4 . . . . 40 F2
Dorking RH5 . . . . 136 D4
Feltham TW13 . . . . 15 E5
Richmond TW9. . . . . 7 A8
Willow Cres GU14. . . . . 85 B7
Willow Ct
2 Ashford TW16 . . . . 14 E1
Ash Vale GU12. . . . . 106 A7
5 Beckenham BR3. . . . . 44 A8
9 Chiswick W4. . . . . 7 E7
Frimley GU16. . . . . 65 D1
Guildford GU1 . . . . 109 D5
Horley RH6 . . . . 161 B6
Kingston u T KT1 . . . . 38 B6
Mitcham CR4 . . . . 40 E5
3 Streatham SW16 . . . . 21 F5
Thornton Heath CR7 . . . . . . 42 D4
Wallington SM6. . . . . 60 B3
Wokingham RG41 . . . . 25 B6
Willow Ctr The CR4 . . . . . . 40 F3
Willowdene Cl TW2. . . . . . 16 C8
Willow Dr
Bracknell RG12 . . . . 27 C8
Flexford GU3 . . . . 107 C1
Send Marsh GU23 . . . . 91 A3
Willow End KT6. . . . . 37 E1
Willowfield 4 RH11. . . . . 201 D5
Willow Fields GU12 . . . . . 106 B1
Willow Gdns TW5. . . . . 5 A6
Willow Glade RH2 . . . . . . 139 B6
Willow Gn
Dorking RH5 . . . . 136 B3
West End GU24 . . . . 68 A6
Willowhayne Ct KT12 . . . . 35 B2
Willowhayne Dr KT12 . . . . 35 B2
Willowhayne Gdns
KT4 . . . . 58 C6
Willowherb Cl RG40. . . . . . 25 E7
Willow Ho CR6 . . . . 82 B3
Willow Ho TW14. . . . . 4 B2
Willow Ho TW11. . . . . 17 C1
Willow La
Blackwater GU17. . . . . 64 D4
Guildford GU1 . . . . 110 A2
Mitcham CR4 . . . . 40 F3
Willow Lo 6 TW16. . . . . . . 14 F1
Willow Manor SM1. . . . . . . 58 F6
Willowmead TW18. . . . . . . 33 B8
Willow Mead
6 Dorking RH4. . . . . 136 A8
8 East Grinstead
RH19. . . . . 205 F8
Witley GU8. . . . . 170 E5
Willowmead Cl GU21. . . . . 69 A3
Willowmere KT10. . . . . 55 C6
Willow Mews GU8 . . . . . . 170 F5
Willow Mount CR0. . . . . . . 61 E7
Willow Pk GU12 . . . . 105 F2
Willow Rd
Farncombe GU7. . . . . 150 F8
Horsham RH12 . . . . 218 B5
Kingston u T KT3 . . . . 38 C5
Poyle SL3. . . . . 1 E5
Reigate RH1. . . . . 139 C6
Wallington SM6. . . . . 60 B3
Willow Ridge RH10 . . . . . 204 A3
Willows Ave SM4 . . . . 40 B4
Willows Ct 3 SW19. . . . . . . 20 A1
Willows End GU47 . . . . 64 B8
Willows Path KT18. . . . . . . 76 B5
Willows Pk The GU3 . . . . 107 E4
Willows The
Beckenham BR3. . . . . 44 A8
1 Bracknell RG12 . . . . 27 F5
Byfleet KT14 . . . . 71 E6
Chiddingfold GU8. . . . . 191 A4
Claygate KT10 . . . . 55 E4
Guildford, Bushy Hill
GU4. . . . . 110 D3
Guildford, Pitch Place
GU2. . . . . 108 F6
Horsham RH12 . . . . 217 D5
Lightwater GU18 . . . . 48 C1
3 Redhill RH1 . . . . 139 F8
Runfold GU10 . . . . 126 C4
Weybridge KT13 . . . . 53 A7
Willow Tree Cl SW18. . . . . 20 B7
Willowtree Way SW16. . . . 42 A8
Willow Vale KT23 . . . . 94 B4
Willow View SW19. . . . . . . 40 D8
Willow Way
Aldershot GU12. . . . . 126 E8
Forest Hill SE26. . . . . 23 C5
Godstone RH9 . . . . 121 B3
Guildford GU1 . . . . 109 B5
Heath End GU9 . . . . 125 D6
Sunbury TW16 . . . . 35 A5
Twickenham TW2. . . . . 16 B6
West Byfleet KT14. . . . . 71 C8
West Ewell KT19 . . . . 57 D4
Woking GU22. . . . . 89 E7
Willow Wlk
Box Hill KT20. . . . . 116 B5
Cheam SM3 . . . . 58 F7
Chertsey KT16. . . . . 33 B2
Englefield Green TW20 . . . . 11 C3
Redhill RH1 . . . . 140 B7
Shere GU5. . . . . 133 A4
Willow Wood Cres
SE25. . . . . 42 E3
Wills Cres TW3 . . . . 5 B1
Willson Rd TW20 . . . . 11 B3
Wilmar Gdns BR4. . . . . 44 B1
Wilmer Cl TW10 . . . . 17 F3
Wilmer Cres KT2, TW10. . . 17 F3
Wilmerhatch La KT18,
KT21 . . . . 76 B2
Wilmington Ave W4 . . . . . . 7 D7
Wilmington Cl RH11 . . . . 201 C1
Wilmington Ct SW16. . . . . 21 E1
Wilmot Ct GU14. . . . . 85 B4
Wilmot Ho 16 SM2 . . . . 59 C4
Wilmot Rd
Purley CR8. . . . . 80 A7
Wallington SM5. . . . . 59 F5
Wilmots Cl RH2. . . . . 118 C2
Wilmot's La RH1, RH6. . . . 162 E5
Wilmot Way
Banstead SM7 . . . . 78 A5
Frimley GU15. . . . . 65 F3
Wilna Rd SW18 . . . . 20 C8
Wilson Ave CR4, SW19 . . . . 40 E8
Wilson Cl
Crawley RH10 . . . . 202 D3
Croydon CR0 . . . . 61 D5
Wilson Dr KT16. . . . . 51 B5
Wilson Ho TW13 . . . . 15 A5
Wilson Rd
Aldershot GU12. . . . . 105 D1
Chessington KT9 . . . . 56 F4
Farnborough GU14 . . . . 84 F3
Wilsons KT20. . . . . 97 D6
Wilsons Rd GU35 . . . . 187 B5
Wilson's Sch SM6. . . . . 60 E4
Wilson Way GU21. . . . . 69 D3
Wilton Cl UB7 . . . . 2 D8
Wilton Cres SW19. . . . . 39 F8
Wilton Ct
Farnborough GU14 . . . . 85 D3
4 Richmond TW10. . . . . 6 E2
Wilton Gdns
East Molesey KT8 . . . . 36 A6
Walton-on-T KT12 . . . . 35 D1
Wilton Gr
Merton SW19 . . . . 39 F8
New Malden KT3. . . . . 38 F3
Wilton Hill Ct 5 RH1. . . . 139 F8
Wilton Ho CR2. . . . . 61 C5
Wilton Lo KT12 . . . . 54 C8
Wilton Par TW13. . . . . 15 B6
Wilton Pl
Beckenham BR3. . . . . 44 C6
New Haw KT15 . . . . 52 D2
Wilton Rd
Camberley GU15 . . . . 65 B3
Hounslow TW4. . . . . 4 D4
Mitcham SW19 . . . . 20 E1
Redhill RH1 . . . . 139 F8
Wiltshire Ave RG45 . . . . . . 45 B5
Wiltshire Ct CR2 . . . . 61 C5
Wiltshire Dr RG40. . . . . 25 D7
Wiltshire Gdns TW2. . . . . . 16 C7
Wiltshire Rd
Thornton Heath CR7 . . . . . . 42 A6
Wokingham RG40 . . . . 25 C7
Wilverley Cres KT3. . . . . . . 38 E3
Wilwood Rd RG42. . . . . 26 E8
Wimbart Rd SW2 . . . . 21 F8
WIMBLEDON 19 F2
Wimbledon Bridge
SW19. . . . . 19 F2
Wimbledon Central
SW19. . . . . 19 F2
Wimbledon Chase Prim
Sch SW20. . . . . 39 E8
Wimbledon Chase Sta
SW20 . . . . 39 E7
Wimbledon Cl
Camberley GU15 . . . . 46 F1
2 Wimbledon SW20. . . . . . . 19 D1
Wimbledon Coll SW19 . . . 19 D1
Wimbledon Common Prep
Sch SW19. . . . . 19 D1
Wimbledon High Sch
SW19 . . . . 19 E2
Wimbledon Hill Rd
SW19. . . . . 19 F2
Wimbledon Lawn Tennis
Mus* SW19. . . . . 19 E5
Wimbledon Park Ct
SW19. . . . . 19 F7
Wimbledon Park
Montessori Sch
SW18 . . . . 20 A6
Wimbledon Park Prim Sch
SW19 . . . . 20 B6
Wimbledon Park Rd SW18,
SW19. . . . . 19 F7
Wimbledon Park Side
SW19. . . . . 19 D7
Wimbledon Park Sta
SW19 . . . . 20 A5
Wimbledon Rd
Camberley GU15 . . . . 46 F1
Wandsworth SW17 . . . . 20 C4
Wimbledon Sch of Art
SW19 . . . . 39 E8
Wimbledon Sch of Art
Annexe SW19. . . . . 20 A1
Wimbledon Sta SW19 . . . . 19 F2
Wimbledon Stad SW17. . . 20 C4
Wimbledon Stadium Bsns
Ctr SW17. . . . . 20 B5
Wimbledon Windmill
Mus* SW19. . . . . 19 C5
Wimblehurst Ct 4
RH12 . . . . 217 C4
Wimblehurst Rd
RH12 . . . . 217 C4
Wimborne Ave RH1 . . . . . 140 A4
Wimborne Cl
Epsom KT17. . . . . 76 E6
North Cheam KT4 . . . . 39 C1
Wimborne Ho
Croydon CR0 . . . . 43 C4
Farnborough GU14 . . . . 85 D2
South Norwood SE19. . . . . . 22 D2
Upper Tooting SW12 . . . . . . 21 C5
Wimborne Way BR3. . . . . . 43 E5
Wimbourne Ct
Mitcham SW19 . . . . 20 D1
South Croydon CR2 . . . . 61 E4
Wimbourne Ho RH11. . . . 201 C6
Wimland Hill RH12. . . . . . 199 D2
Wimland Rd
Faygate RH12 . . . . 199 D1
Rusper RH12 . . . . 199 C4
Wimlands La RH12. . . . . . 199 E3
Wimpole Cl 1 KT1. . . . . . . 38 A7
Wimshurst Cl CR0 . . . . 41 E1
Wincanton Cl RH10 . . . . . 202 D6
Wincanton Rd SW18 . . . . . 19 F8

Winchcombe Rd SM5 .... 40 E1
Winchelsey Rise CR2 ..... 61 F4
Winchendon Rd TW11 .... 16 D4
Winchester Ave TW5 .... 4 F8
Winchester Cl
Beckenham BR2 .... 44 F6
Esher KT10 .... 55 A7
Kingston u T KT2 .... 18 B1
Poyle SL3 .... 1 E6
Winchester Ct TW9 .... 6 F4
Winchester Ho
Epsom KT19 .... 76 A7
Twickenham TW1 .... 17 C8
Winchester Mews KT4 ... 58 D8
Winchester Pk BR2 ...... 44 F6
Winchester Rd
Ash GU12 .... 106 A3
Beckenham BR2 .... 44 F6
Crawley RH10 .... 201 E2
Feltham TW13 .... 15 F5
Harlington UB3 .... 3 E7
Rushmoor GU10 .... 168 B7
Twickenham TW1 .... 6 B1
Walton-on-T KT12 .... 35 A1
Winchester St GU14 ..... 105 C8
Winchester Way GU17 ... 64 C6
Winchet Wlk CR0 .... 43 C3
Winchfield Ho SW15 .... 7 F1
Winchfield Rd SE26 ...... 23 E3
Winchilsea Cres KT8 ..... 36 C7
Winchstone Cl TW17 ..... 33 F5
Windborough Rd SM5 .... 60 A3
Windermere Ave SM4, SW19 .... 40 B6
Windermere Cl
East Bedfont TW14 .... 14 F7
Farnborough GU14 .... 84 E3
Stanwell TW19 .... 13 D6
1 Thorpe Lea TW20 ...... 12 B1
Windermere Ct
Barnes SW13 .... 7 F8
Purley CR8 .... 80 B4
Wallington SM5 .... 60 A7
9 Woking GU21 .... 69 A1
Windermere Ho TW1 .... 5 F2
Windermere Rd
Coulsdon CR5 .... 79 E4
Croydon CR0 .... 42 F1
Kingston u T SW15 .... 18 E3
Lightwater GU18 .... 48 B1
Mitcham SW16 .... 41 D7
West Wickham BR4 .... 63 E8
Windermere Way
Hale GU9 .... 125 A6
Redhill RH2 .... 118 E2
Windermere Wlk GU15 ... 66 D5
Windfield KT22 .... 95 B5
Windfield Cl SE26 .... 23 D4
Windgates GU4 .... 110 C4
Windham Ave CR0 .... 63 D1
Windham Rd TW9 .... 6 F4
Windings The CR2 .... 80 F8
Winding Wood Dr GU15 .... 66 B3
Windlebrook Gn 3 RG42 .... 27 A8
Windle Cl GU20 .... 48 D4
WINDLESHAM 48 C4
Windlesham Ct GU20 ..... 48 C6
Windlesham Gr SW19 .... 19 D7
Windlesham Rd
Bracknell RG42 .... 26 F8
Chobham GU24 .... 49 C3
West End GU24 .... 67 F7
Windlesham Village Inf Sch GU20 .... 48 B6
Windley Cl SE23 .... 23 C6
Windmill Ave KT17 .... 76 F8
Windmill Bridge Ho 1 CR0 .... 42 E1
Windmill Bsns Village TW16 .... 34 E8
Windmill Cl
Caterham CR3 .... 100 C6
Charlton TW16 .... 14 E1
Ewell KT17 .... 76 F7
Horley RH6 .... 161 B3
Horsham RH13 .... 218 A4
Long Ditton KT6 .... 37 C2
Windmill Ct
1 Aldershot GU12 ...... 105 C1
Crawley RH10 .... 201 D8
Windmill Dr
Headley Down GU35 ..... 187 B6
Leatherhead KT22 .... 95 C4
Redhill RH2 .... 118 E3
Windmill End KT17 .... 76 F7
Windmill Field GU20 ..... 48 D4
Windmill Gr CR0 .... 42 C3
Windmill La
Ashurst Wood RH19 ..... 206 C7
East Grinstead RH19 ..... 185 D3
Ewell KT17 .... 76 F7
Thames Ditton KT7 .... 37 B2
Windmill Lo TW16 .... 34 E8
Windmill Rd
Aldershot GU12 .... 105 C1
Bracknell RG42 .... 27 A8
Brentford TW8 .... 6 D8
Charlton TW16 .... 34 E8
Hampton TW12 .... 16 C3
Mitcham CR4 .... 41 C5
Roehampton SW19 .... 19 B5
Thornton Heath CR0 ...... 42 C2
Windmill Rd W TW16 ..... 34 E8
Windmill Rise KT2 .... 18 B1
Windmill Shott TW20 .... 11 F2
Windmill Terr TW17 ..... 34 E2
Windmill Trad Est CR4 ... 41 C5
Windmill Way RH2 ...... 118 D3
Windrush KT3 .... 38 C5
Windrush Cl
Bramley GU5 .... 151 F6
Chiswick W4 .... 7 C7
Crawley RH11 .... 200 F4
Windrushes CR3 .... 101 A2
Windrush Ho 8 RH1 .... 118 F2
Windrush Hts GU47 ...... 64 B8
Windrush La SE23 .... 23 D5
Windsor Ave
Cheam SM3 .... 58 E7
East Molesey KT8 .... 36 A6
Merton SW19 .... 40 C8
New Malden KT3 .... 38 C4
Windsor Cl
Brentford TW8 .... 6 B8
Crawley RH11 .... 201 C2
Farnborough GU14 .... 85 B4
Guildford GU2 .... 129 F7
West Norwood SE27 ...... 22 C4
Windsor Court Rd GU24 .... 49 E2
Windsor Cres GU9 ...... 125 B6
Windsor Ct
Ashford TW16 .... 15 A1
3 Horsham RH13 .... 217 F3
South Norwood SE19 ...... 42 E8
Teddington TW11 .... 16 D3
6 West Wickham BR4 .... 44 B1
Whyteleafe CR3 .... 80 F1
Windsor Dr TW15 .... 13 D4
Windsor Forest Ct SL5 ... 28 D8
Windsor Gdns
Ash GU12 .... 105 F1
Wallington CR0 .... 60 E7
Windsor Gr SE27 .... 22 C4
Windsor Great Pk★ SL4 .... 10 D4
Windsor Ho
5 Egham TW20 .... 12 A3
Reigate RH2 .... 139 B4
Windsor Lo KT3 .... 38 C4
Windsor Mews
Catford SE6 .... 24 C7
Forest Hill SE23 .... 23 E7
Windsor Park Rd UB3 ...... 3 F7
Windsor Pk SW19 .... 40 C8
Windsor Pl 2 KT16 ...... 33 A3
Windsor Pl RH10 .... 181 F2
Windsor Pl RH19 .... 206 A8
Windsor Rd
Ascot SL4, SL5 .... 9 B1
Ashford TW16 .... 15 A2
Chobham GU24 .... 49 D3
Cranford TW4, TW5 .... 4 C5
Englefield Green TW19, TW20 .... 11 E6
Farnborough, South Farnborough GU14 ...... 85 D1
Farnborough, Southwood GU14 .... 104 D8
Kingston u T KT2 .... 17 E1
North Ascot SL5 .... 29 A8
Richmond TW9 .... 6 F5
South Norwood CR7 ...... 42 B7
Teddington TW11 .... 16 D3
Worcester Park KT4 ...... 58 A8
Windsor Ride
Bracknell SL5 .... 28 C4
Sandhurst GU15 .... 65 A8
Windsor St KT16 .... 33 A3
Windsor Way
Aldershot GU11 .... 105 B2
Frimley GU16 .... 85 F8
Woking GU22 .... 70 C3
Windsor Wlk
Walton-on-T KT12 .... 35 D1
Weybridge KT13 .... 53 B5
Winds Ridge GU23 .... 90 C2
Windways GU8 .... 192 F7
Windycroft Cl CR5, CR8 ... 79 D6
Windyridge RH11 .... 201 A5
Windy Ridge Cl SW19 .... 19 D3
Windy Wood GU7 .... 150 C3
Winern Glebe KT14 ...... 71 D6
Winery La KT1 .... 37 F6
Winey Cl KT9 .... 56 C3
Winfield Ct RH5 .... 158 B1
Winfield Gr RH5 .... 158 B1
Winfrith Rd SW18 .... 20 C7
Wingate Cres CR0 .... 41 E3
Wingate Ct GU11 .... 104 F2
Wingfield Cl KT15 .... 52 B1
Wingfield Ct SM7 .... 78 A4
Wingfield Gdns GU16 .... 66 D3
Wingfield Rd KT2 .... 18 A2
Wingham Ho 3 SE26 ..... 23 B3
Wingrove Rd SE6 .... 24 E6
Wings Cl
Hale GU9 .... 125 B6
Sutton SM1 .... 59 A6
Wings Rd GU9 .... 125 B6
Winifred Rd
Coulsdon CR5 .... 79 B4
Hampton TW12 .... 16 A4
Merton SW19 .... 40 A8
WINKFIELD 8 D4
Winkfield Cl RG40, RG41 .... 25 B3
Winkfield La SL4 .... 8 D7
Winkfield Manor SL5 ...... 8 D1
Winkfield Rd
Ascot SL5 .... 29 B7
Winkfield Rd *continued*
Windsor SL4 .... 9 C8
WINKFIELD ROW 8 B2
Winkfield Row RG42 .... 8 B3
Winkfield St Mary's CE Prim Sch RG42 .... 8 B3
Winkfield St SL4 .... 8 C6
WINKFIELD STREET 8 C6
Winkworth Arboretum★ GU8 .... 172 C7
Winkworth Pl SM7 .... 78 A5
Winkworth Rd SM7 .... 78 A5
Winlaton Rd BR1, SE6 ..... 24 D4
Winner Way RH6 .... 181 D6
Winnington Way GU21 ... 69 C1
Winscombe RG12 .... 26 E4
Winsford Rd SE6 .... 23 F5
Winslade Way SE6 .... 24 B8
Winslow Way
Feltham TW13 .... 15 E5
Walton-on-T KT12 .... 54 C7
Winstanley Cl KT11 ...... 73 B5
Winstanley Wlk KT11 ..... 73 B5
Winston Churchill Sch The GU21 .... 68 F1
Winston Cl GU16 .... 85 F6
Winston Dr KT11 .... 73 E3
Winston Way GU22 .... 90 B7
Winston Wlk GU10 ...... 146 C6
Winterbourne RH12 ..... 217 F7
Winterbourne Ct RG12 ... 27 D7
Winterbourne Gr KT13 ... 53 C4
Winterbourne Inf Sch CR7 .... 42 A5
Winterbourne Jun Boys' Sch CR7 .... 42 A5
Winterbourne Jun Girls' Sch CR7 .... 42 A5
Winterbourne Mews RH8 .... 122 C5
Winterbourne Rd
Forest Hill SE23, SE6 ...... 23 F7
Thornton Heath CR7 ...... 42 A5
Winterbourne Wlk GU16 .... 85 F8
Winter Box Wlk TW10 ...... 6 F2
Winter Cl GU12 .... 106 A8
Winterdown Gdns KT10 .... 54 F4
Winterdown Rd KT10 ..... 54 F4
Winterfold RH10 .... 202 A3
Winterfold Cl SW19 ...... 19 E6
Winter Gdns RH11 ...... 201 C5
Winterhill Way GU4 ..... 110 B5
Wintersells Ind Est KT14 .... 52 D1
Wintersells Rd KT14 ..... 52 E1
Winters Rd KT7 .... 37 B2
Winterstoke Rd SE23, SE6 .... 23 F7
Winterton Ct
Horsham RH13 .... 217 D2
Teddington KT1 .... 37 D8
Winton Ct
Stoneleigh KT17 .... 58 B4
15 Surbiton KT6 .... 37 D2
Winton Rd
Aldershot GU11 .... 105 A1
Farnham GU9 .... 125 D4
Winton Way SW16 .... 22 A3
Winward Ct 15 SM2 ...... 59 C4
Wireless Rd TN16 .... 83 D4
Wire Mill La RH7 .... 184 F8
Wirrall Ho 15 SE26 ...... 23 A5
Wisbeach Rd CR0 .... 42 D4
Wisborough Ct RH11 .... 200 F3
Wisborough Rd CR2 ...... 61 F2
Wisdom Ct 6 TW7 .... 6 A4
Wiseman Ct 12 SE19 ..... 22 E3
Wiseton Rd SW17 .... 20 F7
Wishanger Farm Est GU10 .... 167 A3
Wishanger La GU10 ..... 167 B2
Wishbone Way GU21 ..... 68 F3
Wishford Ct KT21 .... 75 F1
Wishmoor Cl GU15 .... 65 E8
Wishmoor Rd GU15 ...... 65 E8
Wishmore Cross Sch GU24 .... 49 F1
WISLEY 71 E3
Wisley Court Ho RH4 .... 136 B4
Wisley Ct CR2 .... 61 D1
Wisley Gdns GU14 .... 84 D2
Wisley La GU23 .... 71 E3
Wispers Sch GU27 ...... 189 C1
Wiston Ct
Crawley RH11 .... 200 F3
1 Horsham RH12 .... 217 D5
Witham Ct SW17 .... 20 F5
Witham Rd
Hounslow TW7 .... 5 D6
Penge BR3, SE20 .... 43 C6
Witherby Cl CR0, CR2 .... 61 E6
Wither Dale RH6 .... 160 E4
Withers Cl KT9 .... 56 C4
Witherslack Cl GU35 .... 187 C4
Withey Brook RH6 ...... 160 D1
Witheygate Ave TW18 .... 13 B2
Withey Mdws RH6 ...... 160 D1
Withies La GU3 .... 129 C2
Withies The
Knaphill GU21 .... 68 E2
Leatherhead KT22 .... 95 B6
Withybed Cnr KT20 ...... 97 B4
Withy Cl GU18 .... 48 C1
Withycombe Rd SW19 .... 19 D8
WITHYPITTS 204 A3
Withypitts RH10 .... 204 A3
Withypitts E RH10 ...... 204 A3
WITLEY 170 F4
Witley CE Inf Sch GU8 .... 170 F4
Witley Centre (Visitor Ctr) The★ GU8 .... 170 C6
Witley Cres CR0 .... 63 C4
Witley Ho 5 SW2 .... 21 F8
Witley & Milford Commons Nature Reserve★ GU8 .... 170 B6
Witley Point 8 SW15 .... 19 B7
Witley Sta GU8 .... 190 F8
Witney Path SE23 .... 23 D5
Wittenham Rd RG12 ..... 27 F8
Witten Ho KT3 .... 38 D1
Wittering Cl KT2 .... 17 D3
Wittersham Rd BR1 ...... 24 F3
Wittmead Rd GU16 .... 85 F4
Wivenhoe Ct TW4 .... 4 F3
Wiverton Rd SE20, SE26 .... 23 C3
Wix Hill KT24 .... 112 B4
Woburn Ave
Farnborough GU14 .... 85 D3
Purley CR8 .... 80 A8
Woburn Cl
Frimley GU16 .... 66 A1
Merton SW19 .... 20 C2
Woburn Ct
Croydon CR0 .... 42 C1
Richmond TW9 .... 6 F4
Woburn Hill KT15 .... 52 D7
Woburn Ho SL5 .... 30 A1
Woburn Rd
Carshalton SM5 .... 40 E1
Crawley RH11 .... 201 A4
Croydon CR0 .... 42 C1
Wodehouse Pl GU1 ..... 130 E8
Wodeland Ave GU2 ..... 130 B7
Woffington Cl KT1, KT8 ... 37 C8
WOKING 69 E1
Woking Bsns Pk GU21 .... 70 B4
Woking Cl SW15 .... 7 F3
Woking Coll GU22 .... 90 A7
Woking Com Hospl GU22 .... 69 F1
WOKINGHAM 25 B5
Wokingham Hospl RG41 .... 25 A6
Wokingham Rd RG42 ..... 26 F8
Wokingham Sta RG40 .... 25 B6
Woking High Sch GU21 .... 69 D4
Woking Nuffield Hospl The GU21 .... 69 E5
Woking Rd GU1, GU4 .... 109 D5
Woking Sta GU22 .... 69 F2
Wold Cl RH11 .... 200 F4
Woldhurstlea Cl RH11 .... 201 A4
WOLDINGHAM 102 A4
WOLDINGHAM GARDEN VILLAGE 101 F6
Woldingham Rd CR3, CR6 .... 101 C6
Woldingham Sch CR3 ... 101 E2
Woldingham Sta CR3 ... 101 D5
Wold The CR3 .... 102 A5
Wolfe Rd GU12 .... 105 C1
Wolfington Rd SE27 ...... 22 B4
Wolf's Cnr RH8 .... 123 B6
Wolf's Hill RH8 .... 123 A4
Wolf's Rd RH8 .... 123 B5
Wolf's Row RH8 .... 123 B5
Wolfs Wood RH8 .... 123 A3
Wolseley Ave SW18, SW19 .... 20 A6
Wolseley Ct 3 GU21 ..... 68 C1
Wolseley Gdns W4 .... 7 B8
Wolseley Rd
4 Aldershot GU11 ...... 105 A1
Carshalton CR4 .... 41 A2
Farncombe GU7 .... 150 F6
Wolsey Ave KT7 .... 36 F4
Wolsey Cl
Isleworth TW3 .... 5 C3
Kingston u T KT2 .... 38 B8
Wimbledon SW20 .... 19 B1
Worcester Park KT4 ...... 58 A6
Wolsey Cres
New Addington CR0 ...... 63 C2
West Barnes SM4 .... 39 F2
Wolsey Ct
Bromley BR1 .... 24 F1
East Molesey KT8 .... 36 D5
Wolsey Dr
Kingston u T KT2 .... 17 E2
Walton-on-T KT12 .... 35 D1
Wolsey Gr KT10 .... 55 B6
Wolsey Ho 2 TW12 ...... 16 B2
Wolsey Inf & Jun Schs CR0 .... 63 C3
Wolsey Pl Sh Ctr 3 GU22 .... 69 E2
Wolsey Rd
Ashford, Felthamhill TW16 .... 14 F1
Ashford TW15 .... 13 F4
East Molesey KT8 .... 36 D5
Esher KT10 .... 55 B6
Hampton TW12 .... 16 C2
Wolsey Way KT9 .... 57 A5
Wolsey Wlk 7 GU21 ..... 69 F2
Wolstonbury Cl RH11 ... 201 C4
Wolvens La
Coldharbour RH5 .... 156 E5
Westcott RH4, RH5 ..... 135 B2
Wolverton Ave KT2 ...... 38 A8
Wolverton Cl RH6 ...... 160 F1
Wolverton Gdns RH6 .... 160 F2
Wolves Hill RH5 .... 178 C4
WONERSH 152 B7
Wonersh Ct GU5 .... 152 B7
Wonersh & Shamley Green CE Inf Sch GU5 .... 152 D5
Wonersh Way SM2 .... 58 D2
Wonford Cl
Kingston u T KT2, KT3 ..... 38 E8
Walton on t H KT20 .... 97 A1
Wonford Ho KT20 .... 97 A2
Wonham La RH3 .... 137 F8
Wonham Pl RH9 .... 142 E8
Wonham Way
Gomshall GU5 .... 133 D3
Peaslake GU5 .... 133 D1
Wontford Rd CR8 .... 80 B4
Wontner Rd SW12, SW17 .... 20 F6
Woodall Cl KT9 .... 56 D4
Woodall Ho TW7 .... 5 F4
Woodbank Rd BR1 .... 24 F5
Woodbarn The GU9 ..... 125 C1
Woodbastwick Rd SE26 .... 23 E3
Woodberry Cl
Ashford TW16 .... 15 A2
Chiddingfold GU8 .... 191 A5
Woodbine Cl
Sandhurst GU47 .... 64 C7
Twickenham TW2 .... 16 D6
Woodbine Cotts
Egham TW20 .... 11 F2
Shalford GU4 .... 130 E2
Woodbine Gr SE20 .... 23 B1
Woodbine La KT4 .... 58 C7
Woodbines Ave KT1 ...... 37 D6
Woodbourne GU9 ...... 125 E7
Woodbourne Ave SW16 .... 21 D5
Woodbourne Cl SW16 .... 21 E5
Woodbourne Dr KT10 .... 55 F4
Woodbourne Gdns SM6 .... 60 B3
Woodbridge Ave KT22 ... 75 A1
Woodbridge Ct RH12 ... 218 A5
Woodbridge Dr GU15 .... 65 D7
Woodbridge Gr KT22 .... 75 A1
WOODBRIDGE HILL 109 A3
Woodbridge Hill GU2 ... 109 B2
Woodbridge Hill Gdns GU2 .... 109 A2
Woodbridge Manor GU15 .... 65 D7
Woodbridge Mdws GU1 .... 109 C2
Woodbridge Park Est GU1 .... 109 C2
Woodbridge Rd
Blackwater GU17 .... 64 B5
Guildford GU1, GU2 ..... 109 C2
Woodbrook Sch BR3 ..... 43 F8
Woodbury Ave RH19 .... 186 B1
Woodbury Cl
Biggin Hill TN16 .... 83 F1
East Grinstead RH19 ..... 206 B8
South Croydon CR0 ...... 61 F8
Woodbury Dr SM2 .... 59 C1
Woodbury Ho SE26 ...... 23 B5
Woodbury St SW17 ...... 20 E3
Woodby Dr SL5 .... 29 F2
Wood Cl RH1 .... 161 A8
Woodcock Dr GU24 ...... 49 C3
Woodcock Hill RH19 .... 184 F6
Woodcock La GU24 ...... 49 B3
Woodcombe Cres SE23 .... 23 C7
WOODCOTE
Epsom 76 D3
Coulsdon 79 D8
Woodcote
Artington GU2 .... 130 B5
Cranleigh GU6 .... 174 B4
Farncombe GU7 .... 150 D6
Horley RH6 .... 161 C4
Woodcote Ave
Thornton Heath CR7 ...... 42 B5
Wallington SM6 .... 60 B2
Woodcote Cl
Epsom KT18 .... 76 D5
Kingston u T KT2 .... 17 F3
Woodcote Ct 14 SM6 ..... 60 B4
Woodcote Dr CR8 .... 60 D1
Woodcote End KT18 ..... 76 D4
Woodcote Gn SM6 .... 60 C2
WOODCOTE GREEN 60 C1
Woodcote Green Rd KT18 .... 76 C4
Woodcote Grove Rd CR5 .... 79 D5
Woodcote Hall
Epsom KT18 .... 76 D5
Wallington SM6 .... 60 B2
Woodcote High Sch CR5 .... 79 D6
Woodcote Ho KT18 ...... 76 D4
Woodcote House Ct KT18 .... 76 D4
Woodcote House Sch GU20 .... 48 B5
Woodcote Hurst KT18 .... 76 C3
Woodcote Inf Sch CR5 ... 79 D5
Woodcote Jun Sch CR5 .... 79 D5
Woodcote La CR8 .... 79 D7

Woodcote Lo KT18 76 C4
Woodcote Mews
Epsom KT18 76 D4
Wallington SM6 60 B4
Woodcote Park Ave
CR8 79 C7
Woodcote Park Rd
KT18 76 C4
Woodcote Pl
North Ascot SL5 28 F8
1 West Norwood SE27 22 B3
Woodcote Rd
Epsom KT18 76 D5
Forest Row RH18 206 F2
Wallington SM6 60 C2
Woodcote Side KT18 76 B4
Woodcote Valley Rd CR5, CR8 79 E7
Woodcote Villas SE27 22 C3
Woodcot Gdns GU14 84 D4
Woodcott Ho 1 SW15 19 A8
Woodcott Terr GU12 126 D8
Woodcourt RH11 201 C1
Wood Crest 4 SM2 59 C3
Woodcrest Rd CR8 79 E6
Woodcrest Wlk RH2 118 E3
Woodcroft 3 CR0 61 E7
Woodcroft Rd
Crawley RH11 200 D4
Thornton Heath CR0, CR7 42 B3
Wood Ct GU2 109 B2
Woodcut Rd GU10 145 F6
Woodend
Farnborough GU14 85 D3
Leatherhead KT22 95 C2
South Norwood SE19 22 C2
Sutton SM1 59 C8
Thames Ditton KT10 55 C8
Wood End RH12 218 C5
Woodend Cl
Crawley RH10 202 A8
North Ascot SL5 28 E8
Woking GU21 89 A8
Wood End Cl GU22 70 F3
Woodend Dr SL5 29 B4
Woodend Pk KT11 73 D4
Woodend Rd GU16 86 C7
Wood End The SM6 60 B2
Woodenhill RG12 26 E1
Woodenhill Prim Sch RG12 26 E2
Wooderson Cl SE25 42 E5
Wooderson Ct 10 BR3 44 A8
Woodfield
Ashtead KT21 75 D2
Thornton Heath SW16 41 F8
Woodfield Ave
Streatham SW16 21 D5
Wallington SM5 60 A3
Woodfield Cl
Ashtead KT21 75 D2
Coulsdon CR5 99 C8
Crawley RH10 201 E7
Redhill RH1 118 E3
South Norwood SE19 22 C1
Woodfield Gdns KT3 38 F4
Woodfield Gr SW16 21 D5
Woodfield Hill CR5 99 B8
Woodfield Ho
11 Forest Hill SE23 23 D5
Hinchley Wood KT7 55 F8
1 New Malden KT3 38 F4
Woodfield La
Ashtead KT21 75 E2
Streatham SW16 21 D5
Woodfield Rd
Ashtead KT21 75 D2
Cranford TW4, TW5 4 B5
Crawley RH10 201 F7
Hinchley Wood KT7 55 F8
Rudgwick RH12 214 D7
Woodfield Sch RH1 119 E6
Woodfields Ct SM1 59 C7
Woodfields The CR2 80 F8
Woodfield Way RH1 118 E3
Woodford Gn RG12 27 F5
Woodgate Ave KT9 56 D5
Woodgate Cl KT11 73 C6
Woodgate Dr SW16 21 D1
Woodgates Cl RH13 217 F3
Woodgavil SM7 77 F3
Woodger Cl GU4 110 C3
Woodglen SM4 40 E4
Woodgrange Ct 1 BR2 44 F1
Woodhall Ave SE21 22 F5
Woodhall Dr SE21 22 F5
Woodhall La SL5 48 E8
WOODHAM 52 A2
WOODHAM HALL ESTATE 70 B5
Woodham La
New Haw KT15 52 B1
Sheerwater GU21, KT15 70 D7
Woodham Park Rd
KT15 51 F1
Woodham Park Way
KT15 70 F8
Woodham Pl GU21 69 F5
Woodham Rd
Catford SE6 24 C5
Woking GU21 69 F4
Woodham Rise GU21 70 A4
Woodham Waye GU21 70 B5
WOODHATCH 139 B7
Woodhatch Rd RH1, RH2 139 E5
Woodhatch Spinney CR5 79 E3
Woodhaw TW20 12 B4
Woodhayes RH6 161 B4
Woodhayes Rd SW19 19 C2
Woodhill GU23 90 D2
Woodhill Ct GU23 90 E2
Woodhill La GU5 152 F4
Woodhouse La RH5 155 A8
Woodhouse St RG42 26 E8
Woodhurst La RH8 122 E4
Woodhurst Pk RH8 122 E5
Woodhyrst Gdns CR8 80 B4
Wooding Gr 15 RH11 201 B1
Wood La
Banstead KT20 77 F2
Bracknell RG42 26 E8
Caterham CR3 100 D3
Farnborough GU14 85 A3
Hounslow TW7 5 F7
Knaphill GU21 68 D1
Seale GU10 127 B5
Weybridge KT13 53 C2
Woodland Ave GU6 174 F3
Woodland Cl
East Horsley KT24 112 F8
Horsham RH13 218 B4
Oatlands Park KT13 53 D6
West Ewell KT19 57 E4
West Norwood SE19 22 E2
Woodland Cotts GU8 190 B8
Woodland Cres GU14 85 C6
Woodland Ct
Ewell KT17 76 F7
Oxted RH8 122 E7
Sutton SM1 59 A4
Woodland Dr
Crawley Down RH10 204 B8
East Horsley KT24 112 F8
Farnham GU10 146 B6
Ockley RH5 178 A5
Woodland Gdns
Isleworth TW7 5 E4
Selsdon CR2 81 C8
Woodland Gr KT13 53 D6
Woodland Hill SE19 22 E2
Woodland Mews SW16 21 E5
Woodland Rd
Thornton Heath CR7 42 A5
West Norwood SE19 22 F3
Woodland Rise RH8 122 E5
WOODLANDS 5 E4
Woodlands
Beckenham BR3 24 B1
Bromley BR2 44 F5
Chertsey KT15 52 E7
Crawley RH10 202 D8
Horley RH6 161 D4
Send Marsh GU23 90 F2
West Barnes SW20 39 D5
14 Woking GU22 89 E8
Woodlands Ave
Heath End GU9 125 F7
Kingston u T KT3 38 D8
Redhill RH1 139 F8
West Byfleet KT14, KT15 70 F7
Worcester Park KT4 58 A8
Woodlands Cl
Ascot SL5 28 F3
Ash GU12 106 A5
Claygate KT10 55 F3
Cranleigh GU6 174 F2
Crawley Down RH10 204 B7
Farnborough GU17 64 E1
Guildford GU1 109 E5
Ottershaw KT16 51 B1
Woodlands Copse
KT21 75 D3
Woodlands Ct
11 Bromley BR1 44 F8
Dulwich SE22 23 B8
Sandhurst GU47 45 F1
12 Woking, Mount Hermon GU22 89 E8
7 Woking, St John's GU21 69 A1
Woodlands Dr
South Godstone RH9 142 E6
Sunbury TW16 35 C7
Woodlands Gdns KT18 77 C2
Woodlands Gr
Coulsdon CR5 79 B2
Isleworth TW7 5 E5
Woodlands Ho
Sheerwater GU21 70 C5
8 West Byfleet KT14 71 A6
Woodlands La
Haslemere GU27 207 F7
Stoke D'Abernon KT11 74 B2
Windlesham GU20, GU24 48 E3
Woodlands Par TW15 14 C2
Woodlands Pk
Addlestone KT15 51 F5
2 Ash GU12 105 F1
Box Hill KT20 116 B4
Guildford GU1 110 B2
Sheerwater GU21 70 C5
Woodlands Rd
Camberley GU15 65 B5
East Grinstead RH19 186 A4
Effingham KT23 113 F6
Epsom KT18 76 A4
Farnborough GU14 84 D6
Guildford GU1 109 D5
Hambledon GU8 171 D1
Isleworth TW7 5 E5
Leatherhead KT22 74 D1
Mortlake SW13 7 F4
Woodlands Rd *continued*
Pyrford KT14 70 F5
Redhill RH1 139 F7
Surbiton KT6 37 D2
Virginia Water GU25 31 C5
Woodlands Rd E GU25 31 C5
Woodlands Rd W GU25 31 C5
Woodlands Ride SL5 29 A3
Woodlands Sch KT22 95 C5
Woodlands St SE13 24 D8
Woodlands The
Isleworth TW7 5 F5
Lewisham SE13 24 D8
Mitcham CR4 41 A6
Smallfield RH6 162 B3
South Norwood SE19 22 C1
Thames Ditton KT10 55 C8
Wallington SM6 60 B2
Woodlands Way
Ashtead KT21 76 B2
Box Hill KT20 116 C5
Woodlands Wlk GU17 64 E1
Woodland View GU7 129 E1
Woodland Way
Caterham CR3 120 E8
Croydon CR0, CR9 43 E1
Horsham RH13 218 B4
Kingswood KT20 97 E4
Merton SM4 39 F5
Mitcham CR4 21 A1
Purley CR8 80 A6
Tolworth KT5 57 B8
West Wickham BR4 63 C7
Weybridge KT13 53 D5
Woodland Wlk GU12 105 D3
Woodlark Glade GU15 65 D7
Woodlarks Camp Site GU10 146 F7
Woodlawn Cres TW2 16 B6
Woodlawn Dr TW13 15 D6
Woodlawn Gr GU21 69 F4
Wood Lea Cotts RH12 215 F7
Woodlea Dr BR2 44 E4
Woodlea Prim Sch CR3 101 F5
Woodlee Cl GU25 31 C7
Woodleigh 1 KT5 37 F4
Woodleigh Gdns SW16 21 E5
Woodley Cl SW17 20 F1
Woodley Ho GU7 150 E8
Woodley La SM5 59 E7
Woodlodge
Ashtead KT21 75 E2
4 Wimbledon SW19 19 F3
Wood Lodge La BR4 63 C7
Woodmancote Ct 5 RH12 217 D5
Woodmancote Gdns KT14 71 A6
Woodmancott Cl RG12 27 F3
Woodmancourt GU7 150 C8
Woodman Mews TW9 7 B6
Woodman Rd CR5 79 D4
Woodmans Hill RH11 201 C2
WOODMANSTERNE 78 E4
Woodmansterne La
Wallington SM5, SM6 79 A7
Woodmansterne SM7 78 D4
Woodmansterne Prim Sch
Streatham SW16 41 D8
Woodmansterne SM7 78 F5
Woodmansterne Rd
Coulsdon CR5 79 C4
Streatham SW16 41 D8
Wallington SM5 59 E2
Woodmansterne St SM7 78 E4
Woodmansterne Sta CR5 79 B3
Woodmere RG12 27 E5
Woodmere Ave CR0 43 D2
Woodmere Cl CR0 43 D2
Woodmere Gdns CR0 43 D2
Woodmere Way BR3 44 D4
Woodmill Ct SL5 28 D6
Woodnook Rd SW16 21 B3
Woodpecker Cl
Cobham KT11 73 E7
Crondall GU10 124 D8
Woodpecker La RH5 158 C2
Woodpecker Mount CR0 62 F2
Woodpeckers
Bracknell RG12 27 B5
Witley GU8 170 E7
Woodpecker Way
Turners Hill RH10 204 C5
Woking GU22 89 D3
Woodplace Cl CR5 79 C1
Woodplace La CR5 99 C7
Wood Rd
Beacon Hill GU26 188 D6
Biggin Hill TN16 83 C1
Camberley GU15 65 B1
Farncombe GU7 150 F7
Heath End GU9 125 C7
Littleton TW17 34 A5
Woodridge Cl RG12 27 C6
Wood Riding GU22 70 E4
Wood Rise GU3 108 E3
Woodrising KT13 53 C4
Woodroffe Benton Ho RH11 200 F6
Woodrough Copse GU5 152 A5
Woodrow Dr RG40 25 F6
Woodroyd Ave RH6 160 F2
Woodroyd Gdns RH6 160 F1
Woodruff Ave GU1 110 B4
Woods Hill Cl RH19 206 D6
Woods Hill La RH19 206 D6
Woodshore Cl GU25 31 B3
WOODSIDE
Ascot 9 C4
Croydon 43 A4
Woodside
Blackwater GU17 64 C3
1 Farnborough GU14 85 B7
Fetcham KT22 94 B5
Horsham RH13 218 B4
Lower Kingswood KT20 117 F7
Sandhurst GU15 64 F7
Walton-on-T KT12 35 A1
West Horsley KT24 92 C1
Weybridge KT13 53 A5
Wimbledon SW19 19 F3
Woodside Ave
Croydon SE25 43 B4
Hersham KT12 54 B6
Thames Ditton KT10 36 E2
Woodside Cl
Caterham CR3 100 E3
Chiddingfold GU8 191 B4
Knaphill GU21 68 D2
Tolworth KT5 38 C2
Woodside Cotts GU8 148 C3
Woodside Court Rd CR0, CR9 43 A2
Woodside Cres RH6 162 A3
Woodside Ct GU14 84 D5
Woodside Flats GU8 191 B4
Woodside Gn CR0, SE25 43 A3
Woodside Ho SW19 19 F2
Woodside Jun & Inf Schs CR0 43 A2
Woodside La SL4 9 C3
Woodside Park Est GU7 150 F4
Woodside Pk SE25 43 B3
Woodside Rd
Beare Green RH5 157 D3
Chiddingfold GU8 191 B5
Cobham KT11 74 A6
Cranbourne SL4 9 B3
Crawley RH10 201 F8
Croydon SE25 43 B3
Farnborough GU11 104 F7
Guildford GU2 108 F2
Heath End GU9 125 E7
Kingston u T KT2 17 E1
New Malden KT3 38 E7
Purley CR8 79 E6
Sutton SM1 59 C7
Woodside Way
Croydon CR0 43 C3
Redhill, Earlswood RH1 140 A8
Redhill, South Earlswood RH1 140 A3
Streatham CR4 41 C8
Virginia Water GU25 31 B6
Woodsome Lo KT13 53 C4
Woodspring Rd SW19 19 E6
Wood St
Ash Vale GU12 106 A6
Carshalton CR4 41 A2
East Grinstead RH19 185 D1
Kingston u T KT2 37 E8
Merstham RH1 119 C7
Woodstock
East Grinstead RH19 185 C2
West Clandon GU4 111 B7
Wokingham RG40 25 C6
Woodstock Ave
Cheam SM3 39 F2
Isleworth TW7 6 A2
Woodstock Cl
Cranleigh GU6 174 F1
Horsham RH12 217 D5
Woking GU21 69 E3
Woodstock Ct KT17 76 D7
Woodstock Gdns BR3 24 B1
Woodstock Gr GU7 150 E7
Woodstock La N KT6 56 C8
Woodstock La S KT10, KT6 56 C6
Woodstock Rd
Coulsdon CR5 79 B3
Croydon CR0, CR9 61 D7
Wallington SM5 60 A5
Woodstock Rise SM3 39 F2
Woodstocks GU14 85 D6
Woodstock Way CR4 41 C7
Woodstone Ave KT17, KT4 58 A5
Wood Street Gn GU3 108 A2
Wood Street Inf Sch GU3 108 C3
WOOD STREET VILLAGE 108 B3
Woodsway KT22 74 E5
Woodsyre SE19, SE26 22 F4
Woodthorpe Rd TW15 13 D4
Wood Vale SE22 23 B8
Woodvale Ave SE25 42 F7
Woodvale Ct SE25 42 F6
Woodvale Wlk SE27 22 C3
Woodview KT9 75 C8
Woodview Cl
Ashtead KT21 76 A3
Hamsey Green CR2 81 B5
Kingston u T SW15 18 D4
Woodview Ct KT13 53 C5
Woodville Cl
Blackwater GU17 64 B5
Woodville Cl *continued*
Teddington TW11 17 A4
Woodville Ct KT22 95 B7
Woodville Gdns KT6 37 D2
Woodville Ho SM1 59 B6
Woodville Rd
Leatherhead KT22 95 B7
Merton SM4 40 A5
Richmond TW10 17 C5
South Norwood CR7 42 D6
Woodward Cl KT10 55 F4
Woodwards RH11 201 C1
Woodway
Camberley GU15 65 B5
Guildford GU1 110 B2
Woodwicks GU6 174 F2
Woodyard La SE21 22 E8
Woodyers Cl GU5 152 B7
Woolborough Cl RH10 201 E7
Woolborough La
Crawley RH10 181 F1
Crawley, Three Bridges RH10 202 A8
Salfords RH1 161 F8
Woolborough Rd RH10 201 E7
Woolf Dr RG40 25 C7
Woolf Meml Cotts RG40 25 C7
Woolford Cl RG42 8 C1
Woolfords La GU8 169 B7
Woolhampton Way RG12 27 D4
Woolhams CR3 101 A1
Woollards Rd GU12 106 B4
Woolmead Ct GU9 125 C3
Woolmead Rd GU9 125 C3
Woolmead The GU9 125 C3
Woolmead Wlk GU9 125 C3
WOOLMER HILL 207 D7
Woolmer Hill Ho GU27 207 C6
Woolmer Hill Rd GU27 207 D7
Woolmer Hill Tech Coll GU27 207 D7
Woolmer View GU26 188 D3
Wool Rd SW20 19 B2
Woolsack Way GU7 150 E4
Woolstone Rd SE23, SE6 23 E6
Woosehill La
Wokingham RG41 25 A5
Wokingham RG41 25 A6
Wootton KT10 55 C6
Wootton Cl KT18 76 F3
Wootton Grange 3 GU22 89 E8
Worbeck Rd SE20 43 C7
Worcester Cl
Croydon CR0 63 A8
Farnborough GU14 85 B7
Mitcham CR4 41 A7
Worcester Ct
Ashford TW15 14 B3
Camberley GU15 65 B3
Redhill RH1 118 E3
9 Sutton SM2 59 B4
5 Walton-on-T KT12 35 C1
Worcester Park KT4 57 E7
Worcester Dr TW15 14 B3
Worcester Gdns KT4 57 E7
Worcester Ho 6 TW3 4 F3
WORCESTER PARK 57 E6
Worcester Park Rd KT4 57 D7
Worcester Park Sta KT4 39 A1
Worcester Rd
Belmont SM2 59 B3
Crawley RH10 201 E2
Guildford GU2 108 F3
Reigate RH2 118 A2
11 Wimbledon SW19 19 F3
Wordsworth RG12 26 F4
Wordsworth Ave CR8 80 D4
Wordsworth Cl RH10 202 B8
Wordsworth Dr KT4, SM3 58 C6
Wordsworth Mead RH1 119 B3
Wordsworth Pl RH12 217 E7
Wordsworth Rd
Addlestone KT15 52 D6
Hampton TW12 15 F4
Penge SE20 23 D1
Wallington SM6 60 D4
Wordsworth Rise 6 RH19 185 C1
Works Rd KT15 52 B2
World Bsns Ctr TW6 3 C6
World's End KT11 73 A5
Worlds End Hill RG12 27 F3
WORMLEY 170 F1
Wormley La GU8 171 B1
Worple Ave
Isleworth TW7 6 A2
Staines TW18 13 B2
Wimbledon SW19 19 D1
Worple Ct SW19 19 E2
Worple Prim Sch TW7 6 A3
Worple Rd
Epsom KT18 76 D4
Epsom KT18 76 E5

Worple Rd *continued*
Isleworth TW7 . . . . **6** A3
Leatherhead KT22 . . . . **95** B4
Staines TW18 . . . . **13** B1
Wimbledon SW19, SW20 . . **39** D8
Worple Road Mews
SW19 . . . . **19** F2
WORPLESDON **108** D8
Worplesdon Hill GU22 . . . . **88** D5
Worplesdon Hill Ho
GU22 . . . . **88** D5
Worplesdon Prim Sch
GU3 . . . . **108** D4
Worplesdon Rd GU2 . . . . **109** A4
Worplesdon Sta GU22 . . . **89** B3
Worple St SW14 . . . . **7** D4
Worple Way TW10 . . . .**6** E3
Worsfold Cl GU23 . . . . **90** B4
Worslade Rd SW17 . . . . . . **20** D4
Worsley Bridge Jun Sch
BR3 . . . . **24** A1
Worsley Bridge Rd
Beckenham BR3, SE6 . . . . **24** A2
Catford SE6 . . . . **23** F3
Worsley Ho SE23 . . . . **23** B6
Worsley Rd GU16 . . . . **85** F7
Worsted Gn RH1 . . . . **119** D6
Worsted La RH19 . . . . . . **206** B8
WORTH **202** E6
Worth Abbey★ RH10 . . . . **203** B1
Worthfield Cl KT19 . . . . . **57** D3
Worthing Rd
Heston TW5 . . . .**4** F8
Horsham RH12 . . . . **217** B1
Worthington Cl CR4 . . . . **41** B6
Worthington Ho 16
SW2 . . . . **22** A8
Worthington Rd KT6 . . . . **37** F1
Worth Park Ave RH10 . . **202** C7
Worth Rd RH10 . . . . **202** C6
Worth Way RH10 . . . . . . **202** E5
Wortley Rd CR0 . . . . **42** A2
Worton Ct TW7 . . . .**5** E3
Worton Gdns TW7 . . . . . . **5** D5
Worton Hall Est TW7 . . . . . .**5** E3
Worton Rd TW7 . . . . **5** E4
Worton Way TW3, TW7 . . **5** D5
WOTTON **134** F3
Wotton Way SM2 . . . . **58** C1
Wrabness Way TW18 . . . **33** B8
Wrangthorn Wlk CR0 . . . **61** A6
Wray Cl RH19 . . . . **206** D6
Wray Common Prim Sch
RH2 . . . . **118** D2
Wray Common Rd
RH2 . . . . **118** D2
Wrayfield Ave GU2 . . . . **118** C2
Wrayfield Rd SM3 . . . . . . **58** D7
Wray Ho 11 SW2 . . . . **21** E7
Wray La RH2 . . . . **118** A4
Wraylands Dr RH2 . . . . . **118** D3
Wraymead Pl RH2 . . . . . **118** B2
Wraymill Ct 5 RH2 . . . . **118** D1
Wray Mill Ho RH2 . . . . . . **118** E3
Wray Mill Pk RH2 . . . . . . **118** E3
Wray Park Rd RH2 . . . . . **118** C2
Wray Rd SM2 . . . . **58** F2
WRAYS **160** B5
WRAYSBURY **11** E8
Wraysbury Cl TW4 . . . .**4** E2
Wraysbury Gdns TW18 . . **12** E4
Wraysbury Rd TW18 . . . . **12** C5
Wraysbury Sta TW19 . . . . . **1** A1
WRECCLESHAM **145** E6
Wrecclesham Hill
GU10 . . . . **145** E5
Wrecclesham Rd GU10,
GU9 . . . . **145** F8

Wrekin The GU14 . . . . **85** E1
Wren Cl
Horsham RH12 . . . . **217** D7
Selsdon CR2 . . . . **62** D2
Wren Cres KT15 . . . . **52** D5
Wren Ct
Ash GU12 . . . . **106** B3
Crawley RH10 . . . . **201** E3
South Croydon CR0 . . . . . . **61** D6
Warlingham CR6 . . . . **81** C2
Wren Ho
4 Hampton TW12 . . . . **16** B2
Teddington KT1 . . . . **37** D7
Wrens Ave TW15 . . . . **14** C4
Wren's Hill KT22 . . . . **74** C4
Wren St RH10 . . . . **204** C5
Wrenthorpe Rd BR1 . . . . **24** E4
Wren Way GU14 . . . . **84** F7
Wright Cl RH10 . . . . **202** C2
Wright Gdns TW17 . . . . . **34** A4
Wrighton Ct SM1 . . . . **58** F4
Wright Rd TW5 . . . . **4** C7
Wrights Rd SE25 . . . . **42** E6
Wright's Row SM5 . . . . . . **60** B6
Wriotsley Way KT15 . . . . **52** A4
Wrotham Hill GU8 . . . . . . **192** E3
Wrotham Ho BR3 . . . . **23** F1
Wroxham RG12 . . . . **26** F4
Wroxham Wlk RH10 . . . . **202** B4
Wr Twr Hill CR0, CR2 . . . . **61** D6
Wrythe Gn SM5 . . . . **59** F7
Wrythe Green Rd SM5 . . **59** F7
Wrythe La SM5 . . . . **59** E7
Wulwyn Ct RG45 . . . . **45** A5
Wyatt Cl TW13 . . . . **15** D7
Wyatt Ct GU47 . . . . **64** D7
Wyatt Ho 11 TW1 . . . . **6** D1
Wyatt Park Mans 1
SW2 . . . . **21** E6
Wyatt Park Rd SW2 . . . . . **21** F6
Wyatt Rd TW18 . . . . **13** A3
Wyatt's Almshouses
GU7 . . . . **151** A6
Wyatt's Cl GU7 . . . . **151** A6
Wyche Gr CR2 . . . . **61** D2
Wychelm Rd GU18 . . . . . . **67** C8
Wych Elm Rise GU1 . . . . **130** E6
Wych Hill GU22 . . . . **89** D8
Wych Hill La GU22 . . . . . . **89** E8
Wych Hill Pk GU22 . . . . . **89** D8
Wych Hill Rise GU22 . . . **89** D8
Wych Hill Way GU22 . . . . **89** D8
Wychwood
Camberley GU15 . . . . **65** D7
Ifold RH14 . . . . **212** D3
Wychwood Ave
Bracknell RG12 . . . . **27** F5
South Norwood CR7 . . . . . **42** C6
Wychwood Cl
Ashford TW16 . . . . **15** A2
Ash GU12 . . . . **105** F2
Wychwood Pl GU15 . . . . . **66** B8
Wychwood Way SE19 . . . **22** D2
Wycliffe Bldgs GU2 . . . **130** C7
Wycliffe Ct RH11 . . . . . . **200** E3
Wycliffe Rd SW19 . . . . . . **20** B2
Wydell Cl SM4 . . . . **39** D3
Wydenhurst Rd CR0, CR9 . **43** B2
Wye Cl TW15 . . . . **14** B4
Wyecliffe Gdns RH1 . . . **119** C5
Wyeth's Mews KT17 . . . . **76** F6
Wyeth's Rd KT17 . . . . **76** F6
WYKE **106** E3
Wyke Ave GU12 . . . . **106** E3
Wyke Cl TW7 . . . .**5** F8
Wykeham Ho
Farnborough GU14 . . . . . **105** C8
Merton SW19 . . . . **40** A8
Wykeham Rd
Farnham GU9 . . . . **125** C3
Guildford GU1 . . . . **110** D2

Wykehurst Ho SW19 . . . . **20** D3
Wyke La GU12 . . . . **106** D2
Wyke Prim Sch GU3 . . . **106** F4
Wyke Rd SW20 . . . . **39** C7
Wylam RG12 . . . . **26** F4
Wyldewood SL5 . . . . **29** D3
Wyleu St SE23 . . . . **23** E8
Wymering Ct GU14 . . . . . **85** D3
Wynash Gdns SM5 . . . . . **59** E5
Wynbourne Ct SE20 . . . . **43** B7
Wyncliffe Ct BR2 . . . . . . **44** E5
Wyncote Way CR2 . . . . . **62** D2
Wyndham Ave KT11 . . . . **73** A6
Wyndham Cl SM2 . . . . . . **59** A3
Wyndham Cres
Cranleigh GU6 . . . . **174** A3
Twickenham TW4 . . . . **5** A1
Wyndham Ct CR7 . . . . . . **42** B3
Wyndham Lo TW7 . . . .**5** E6
Wyndham Rd
Kingston u T KT2 . . . . **17** F1
Woking GU21 . . . . **69** B1
Wyndham St GU12 . . . . **105** C1
Wyndhurst Cl CR2 . . . . . . **61** B3
Wynell Rd SE23 . . . . **23** D5
Wynfields GU16 . . . . **85** F3
Wynlea Cl RH10 . . . . **204** A8
Wynne Ct 5 TW7 . . . .**6** A4
Wynnstow Pk RH8 . . . . . **122** F4
Wynsham Way GU20 . . . . **48** B6
Wynton Gdns SE25 . . . . . **42** F4
Wynton Gr KT12 . . . . **54** A7
Wyphurst Rd GU6 . . . . . **174** E4
Wyresdale RG12 . . . . **27** F2
Wysemead RH6 . . . . **161** C4
Wythegate TW18 . . . . **12** F1
Wyvern Cl
2 Ash Vale GU12 . . . . **105** F5
Bracknell RG12 . . . . **27** A5
Wyvern Ct TW15 . . . . **13** C5
Wyvern Est The KT3 . . . . **39** A5
Wyvern Pl
Addlestone KT15 . . . . **52** B6
Warnham RH12 . . . . **216** F8
Wyvern Rd CR8 . . . . **61** B1

Y

Yaffle Rd KT13 . . . . **53** C1
Yale Cl
Hounslow TW4 . . . .**4** F2
Sandhurst GU47 . . . . **45** F2
Yarborough Rd 1
SW19 . . . . **40** D8
Yarbridge Cl SM2 . . . . . . **59** B1
Yardley RG12 . . . . **26** F4
Yardley Cl RH2 . . . . **118** B3
Yardley Ct SM3 . . . . **58** D6
Yard Mead TW20 . . . . **12** A3
Yarm Cl KT22 . . . . **95** C4
Yarm Court Rd KT22 . . . . **95** C4
Yarmouth Cl RH10 . . . . . **202** A4
Yarm Way KT22 . . . . **95** D4
Yarnold Cl RG40 . . . . **25** F7
Yarrow Cl RH12 . . . . **217** E5
YATELEY **64** A5
Yateley Ct CR8 . . . . **80** C5
Yatesbury Cl GU9 . . . . . **145** F7
Yattendon Sch RH6 . . . . . . **161**
A4 **Yaverland Dr** GU19 . . **47** D2
Yeats Cl RH1 . . . . **139** C6
Yeend Cl KT8 . . . . **36** A5
Yehudi Menuhin Sch
KT11 . . . . **94** A8
Yellowcress Dr GU24 . . . . **68** A3
Yelverton Ct 2 KT23 . . . . **94** A1
Yelverton Lo TW1 . . . . . . **17** C8
Ye Market CR0 . . . . **61** D5
Yenston Cl SM4 . . . . **40** A3
Yeoman Cl SE27 . . . . **22** B5

Yeoman Ct
Burgh Heath KT20 . . . . **97** E8
6 Carshalton SM1 . . . . . . **59** D5
Heston TW5 . . . .**4** F7
Yeoman Dr TW19 . . . . **13** E7
Yeomanry Cl KT17 . . . . . . **76** F7
Yeomans Cl
Ash GU10 . . . . **126** F8
Farnborough GU14 . . . . . . **85** A5
Yeomans Croft KT23 . . . . **94** A2
Yeomans Mews TW7 . . . . **5** D2
Yeomans Way GU15 . . . . **65** E5
Yeoveney Cl TW19 . . . . . . **12** D6
Yeovil Cl GU14 . . . . **85** D1
Yeovil Rd
Farnborough GU14 . . . . . . **85** E1
Sandhurst GU47 . . . . **45** E1
Yeovilton Pl KT2 . . . . **17** C3
Yetminster Rd GU14 . . . . **85** D1
Yewbank Cl CR8 . . . . **80** D4
Yew Cl RG42 . . . . **8** A1
Yew Cnr RG12 . . . . **27** C6
Yew Ct
Crawley RH11 . . . . **201** D5
1 East Grinstead
RH19 . . . . **185** D2
Yewdale Cl BR1 . . . . **24** E2
Yewens GU8 . . . . **191** B5
Yew La RH19 . . . . **185** B3
Yewlands Cl SM7 . . . . **78** C4
Yewlands Wlk RH11 . . . . **200** D4
Yew Pl KT13 . . . . **53** F7
Yews The
Ashford TW15 . . . . **14** B4
West Byfleet KT14 . . . . **71** E7
Yew Tree Bottom Rd KT17,
KT18 . . . . **77** C2
Yew Tree Cl
Chipstead CR5 . . . . **98** F8
Farnborough GU14 . . . . . . **84** C3
Horley RH6 . . . . **161** A4
New Malden KT4 . . . . **38** E1
Yew Tree Cotts KT10 . . . . **55** D8
Yew Tree Ct 10 SM2 . . . . **59** C3
Yew Tree Dr
Caterham CR3 . . . . **100** F2
Guildford GU1 . . . . **109** C6
Yew Tree Gdns KT18 . . . . **76** C4
Yew Tree Ho
New Malden KT4 . . . . **38** E1
5 Surbiton KT6 . . . . **37** E1
Sandhurst GU47 . . . . **64** B8
Yew Tree La RH2 . . . . . . **118** B4
Yew Tree Lo 10 SW16 . . . **21** C4
Yewtree Rd BR3 . . . . **43** F6
Yew Tree Rd
Charlwood RH6 . . . . **180** E7
Dorking RH4 . . . . **115** A1
Witley GU8 . . . . **170** D6
Yewtrees TW20 . . . . **32** C6
Yew Trees TW17 . . . . **33** F5
Yew Tree Wlk
Effingham KT24 . . . . **113** D8
Frimley GU16 . . . . **65** F1
Hounslow TW4 . . . .**4** F2
South Croydon CR8 . . . . . . **61** C1
Yockley Cl GU15 . . . . **66** D3
Yolland Cl GU9 . . . . **125** C7
York Ave
East Grinstead RH19 . . . . **206** A8
Mortlake SW14 . . . .**7** C2
York Cl
Byfleet KT14 . . . . **71** E7
Horsham RH13 . . . . **217** F3
Morden SM4 . . . . **40** B5
York Cres GU11 . . . . **104** F1
York Ct
Beckenham BR3 . . . . **44** D8
Epsom KT19 . . . . **76** A7
Kingston u T KT2 . . . . **17** D2
Wallington SM6 . . . . **60** C4
Yorke Gate CR3 . . . . **100** D5

Yorke Gdns RH2 . . . . **118** A2
Yorke Rd RH2 . . . . **118** A2
York Gdns KT12 . . . . **54** D8
York Hill SE27, SW16 . . . . **22** B5
York Ho
Bracknell RG42 . . . . **26** F8
Forest Hill SE26 . . . . **23** C3
4 Kingston u T KT2 . . . . . **17** F1
Lower Kingswood KT20 . . **117** F8
Richmond, Kew TW9 . . . . . . **7** A6
Richmond, North Sheen
TW10 . . . .**7** A2
South Norwood SE25 . . . . **42** E5
West Norwood SE27 . . . . . **22** B6
York Pl GU15 . . . . **65** D7
York Rd
Aldershot GU11 . . . . **104** F1
Ash GU12 . . . . **106** A3
Belmont SM1, SM2 . . . . . . **59** A3
Biggin Hill TN16 . . . . **103** B8
Byfleet KT14 . . . . **71** E7
Camberley GU15 . . . . **65** D7
Crawley RH10 . . . . **201** E2
Farnborough GU14 . . . . . . **84** F1
Farnborough, South
Farnborough GU14 . . . . . **85** C1
Farnham GU9 . . . . **125** C1
Guildford GU1 . . . . **130** D8
Hounslow TW3 . . . . **5** B4
Kingston u T KT2 . . . . **17** F1
4 Richmond TW10 . . . .**6** F2
Selsdon CR2 . . . . **62** D1
Teddington TW11 . . . . **16** E4
Thornton Heath CR0 . . . . . **42** A2
Weybridge KT13 . . . . **53** C6
Wimbledon SW19 . . . . **20** C2
Woking GU22 . . . . **69** E1
Yorkshire Rd CR4 . . . . . . **41** E5
York St
Carshalton CR4 . . . . **41** A2
Twickenham TW1 . . . . **17** A7
YORK TOWN **65** A4
York Town Ind Est
GU15 . . . . **65** A5
Yorktown Rd
Sandhurst, College Town
GU47 . . . . **64** E7
Sandhurst GU47 . . . . **64** C7
York Way
Chessington KT9 . . . . **56** E3
Feltham TW13 . . . . **15** F5
Sandhurst GU47 . . . . **64** B8
Youlden Cl GU15 . . . . **66** A5
Youlden Dr GU15 . . . . **66** B6
Youngman Rd RH7 . . . . . **165** B4
Youngs Dr GU12 . . . . **105** F2
Young St
Fetcham KT22 . . . . **94** F3
Leatherhead KT22 . . . . **95** A3
Youngstroat La GU24 . . . **50** E1
Yukon Rd SW12 . . . . **21** B8

Z

Zealand Ave UB7 . . . .**2** E7
Zenith Ct GU47 . . . . **45** E1
Zennor Rd SW12 . . . . **21** C7
Zermatt Rd CR7 . . . . **42** C5
Zig Zag Rd
Kenley CR8 . . . . **80** C3
Mickleham KT20, RH4,
RH5 . . . . **115** D4
Zinnia Dr GU24 . . . . **68** A3
Zion Pl CR7 . . . . **42** D5
Zion Rd CR7, SE25 . . . . . . **42** D5
Zk Pk CR0 . . . . **60** F7
Zodiac Ct CR0 . . . . **42** B1